INTERCHI '93
CONFERENCE PROCEEDINGS

Conference on Human Factors in Computing Systems
INTERACT '93 and CHI '93

BRIDGES BETWEEN WORLDS

Amsterdam
The Netherlands

24-29 April 1993

Editors
Stacey Ashlund
Kevin Mullet
Austin Henderson
Erik Hollnagel
Ted White

Sponsored by the Association for Computing Machinery/Special Interest Group on Computer and Human Interaction (ACM/SIGCHI) under the aegis of the International Federation for Information Processing (IFIP) in cooperation with the IFIP Technical Committee 13 on Human Computer Interaction (IFIP TC 13). INTERCHI '93 is hosted by the Man-Computer Interaction Group of the section on Social Aspects of Information and Automation of the Dutch Computer Society (NGI, Nederlands Genootschap voor Informatica).

The Association for Computing Machinery, Inc.
1515 Broadway
New York, NY 10036

Sample Citation Information:
...In proceedings of INTERCHI, 1993 (Amsterdam, The Netherlands, 24 April – 29 April, 1993) ACM, New York, 1993, pp. 23-35.

Ordering Information

Nonmembers
Nonmember orders placed within the U.S. should be directed to:

Addison-Wesley Publishing Company
Order Department
Jacob Way
Reading, MA 01867
Tel: +1 800 447 2226

Addison-Wesley will pay postage and handling on orders accompanied by check. Credit card orders may be placed by mail or by calling the Addison-Wesley Customer Service Department at the same number.

Please include the Addison-Wesley ISBN number with your order:

A-W ISBN 0-201-58884-6

Nonmember orders from outside the U.S. should be addressed as noted below:

Europe/Middle East:

Addison-Wesley Publishing Group
Concertgebouwplein 25
1071 LM Amsterdam
The Netherlands
Tel: +31 20 6717296
Fax: +31 20 6645334

Germany/Austria/Switzerland:

Addison-Wesley Verlag Deutschland GmbH
Wachsbleiche 7-12
W-5300 Bonn 1
Germany
Tel: +49 228 98 515 0
Fax: +49 228 98 515 99

United Kingdom/Africa:

Addison-Wesley Publishers Ltd.
Finchampstead Road
Wokingham, Berkshire RG11 2NZ
United Kingdom
Tel: +44 734 794000
Fax: +44 734 794035

Asia:

Addison-Wesley Singapore Pte. Ltd.
15 Beach Road
#05-02/09/10 Beach Centre
Singapore 0718
Tel: +65 339 7503
Fax: +65 339 9709

Japan:

Addison-Wesley Publishers Japan Ltd.
Nichibo Building
1-2-2 Sarugakucho
Chiyoda-ku, Tokyo 101
Japan
Tel: +81 33 2914581
Fax: +81 33 2914592

Australia/New Zealand:

Addison-Wesley Publishers Pty. Ltd.
6 Byfield Street
North Ryde, N.S.W. 2113
Australia
Tel: +61 2 878 5411
Fax: +61 2 878 5830

Latin America:

Addison-Wesley Iberoamericana S.A.
Boulevard de las Cataratas #3
Colonia Jardines del Pedregal
Delegacion Alvaro Obregon
01900 Mexico D. F.
Tel: +52 5 660 2695
Fax: +52 5 660 4930

Canada:

Addison-Wesley Publishing (Canada) Ltd.
26 Prince Andrew Place
Don Mills, Ontario M3C 2T8
Canada
Tel: +416 447 5101
Fax: +416 443 0948

ACM Members
A limited number of copies are available at the ACM member discount. Send order with payment in US dollars to:

ACM Order Department
P.O. Box 64145
Baltimore, MD 21264

OR

ACM European Service Center
Avenue Marcel Thiry 204
1200 Brussels
Belgium

ACM will pay postage and handling on orders accompanied by check. (Checks must be in U.S. dollars drawn on a U.S. bank.)

Credit card orders only:
+1 800 342 6626

Customer service, or credit card orders from Alaska, Maryland, and outside the U.S.: +1 410 528 4261

Credit card orders may also be placed by mail.

Please include your ACM member number and the ACM Order number with your order.

ACM Order Number: 608931
Soft Cover ACM ISBN: 0-89791-574-7
Conference Proceedings Series Hard Cover
ACM ISBN: 0-89791-575-5

From ACM/SIGCHI:

On behalf of the Executive Committee of the Association for Computing Machinery's (ACM) Special Interest Group on Computer and Human Interaction (ACM/SIGCHI), we are pleased to bring you the proceedings of INTERCHI '93. The conference provides a new opportunity to improve the tried and true, to explore the new and different, and above all to learn from the experience. This collaborative effort with IFIP TC.13 is a bold step in this direction.

SIGCHI is a worldwide group of volunteers who share an interest in the many facets of HCI. The fact that SIGCHI is the fastest-growing Special Interest Group in ACM, and has a growing number of local chapters, is evidence that this field is receiving greater and greater attention. As computers are embedded in more and more of our everyday objects, the concomitant demands for monitoring, managing, and controlling increase the need for HCI research, development and informed use.

This conference is undoubtedly the most visible activity of SIGCHI, but we do much more. We sponsor other conferences, and workshops (e.g., *Computer Supported Cooperative Work* and *User Interface Software and Technology*). We publish the quarterly *SIGCHI Bulletin*, the journal *ACM Transactions on Computer-Human Interaction*, and are currently developing *Interactions Magazine*. We support the development of HCI academic programs such as creating an HCI curriculum, financially supporting an on-line HCI bibliography, and funding research grants.

Congratulations to the conference committee and all of the volunteers on a job well done.

Austin Henderson
Peter Polson
Co-Chairs, ACM/SIGCHI

From IFIP and IFIP TC.13:

On behalf of IFIP Technical Committee 13 on Human-Computer Interaction, I welcome all participants to the Conference and all subsequent readers to this volume of Proceedings. At the initiative and invitation of the IFIP Member Society Nederlands Genootschap voor Informatica the annual ACM/SIGCHI CHI Conference and the International INTERACT series have been brought together in fruitful collaboration to create INTERCHI '93.

As an international linking organisation, the International Federation for Information Processing (IFIP) must by definition only have membership of national and regional societies and associations, and cannot have individual members. Therefore IFIP looks to its constituent Member Societies such as NGI and ACM (through FOCUS) for the dynamism and detailed work needed to increase the sharing of information and the collaborative research so essential for the worldwide growth of computer systems and applications.

Such international co-operation is especially important in Human-Computer Interaction. While the underlying chips and technology may be culture-free, the systems and applications as seen by each separate user will often need to be different and must provide appropriate utility and above all usability to suit the needs of those users; this is the key and the challenge for our field of work. The initiative of the NGI in bringing CHI to Europe and thus helping to build one of the many international bridges we need worldwide is invaluable.

Congratulations to the conference committee and all of the volunteers on a job well done.

Brian Shackel
Chairman IFIP TC.13

Welcome!

INTERCHI '93 is not just another conference. The unprecedented combination of CHI '93 and INTERACT '93 has created not a new conference, but a new partnership between the two leading professional organisations in the field of human-computer interaction. The ACM/SIGCHI (Association for Computing Machinery / Special Interest Group on Computer and Human Interaction) conference was first held in 1982. SIGCHI has evolved from its origins as a North American organisation to serve an international community, but the CHI conference has never before left the North American continent. The INTERACT conference, organised on behalf of IFIP-TC 13 (International Federation for Information Processing, Technical Committee 13 on Human Computer Interaction), has been held every 3 years since 1984. INTERACT has been an international conference from the beginning but until this year has maintained a decidedly European focus.

The theme of the conference, *Bridges Between Worlds*, offers several interpretations. The field of human-computer interaction (HCI) today spans many different cultures. Significant gaps between industry and academia, between research and application, and between users and developers can still be seen. **INTERCHI '93** brings these communities together. Increasing the focus on user interfaces and cooperation technology helps to bridge the gaps between people and their work and between people working together. The year 1993 is, indeed, a time for building bridges in the HCI community and the world at large. Amsterdam is the site for the first joint effort linking INTERACT and CHI, but the bridges being built stretch much further. Participants from every continent provide a breadth of perspective that has never been equalled in the field of human-computer interaction.

Bert Arnold
Gerrit van der Veer
Ted White

Conference Co-Chairs
INTERCHI '93

INTERCHI '93 is sponsored by the Association for Computing Machinery/ Special Interest Group on Computer and Human Interaction (ACM/SIGCHI) under the aegis of the International Federation for Information Processing (IFIP) in cooperation with the IFIP Technical Committee 13 on Human Computer Interaction (IFIP TC 13). INTERCHI '93 is hosted by the Man-Computer Interaction Group of the section on Social Aspects of Information and Automation of the Dutch Computer Society (NGI, Nederlands Genootschap voor Informatica).

Cooperating Societies

ACM Special Interest Group on Computer Graphics (SIGGRAPH)

ACM Special Interest Group on Office Information Systems (SIGOIS)

ACM Special Interest Group on the Physically Handicapped (SIGCAPH)

The Division of Applied Experimental and Engineering Psychologists of the American Psychological Association (Div. 21 of APA)

Austrian Computer Society (OCG)

British Computer Society, HCI Specialist Group

Czech Society for Cybernetics and Computer

Cognitive Science Society

Dutch Computer Society (NGI)

European Association of Cognitive Ergonomics (EACE)

Gesellschaft für Informatik, Fachgruppe Software-Ergonomie (GI)

Human Factors Society (HFS)

Human Factors Society, Europe Chapter (HFS, EC)

IEEE Computer Society Technical Committee on Computer and Display Ergonomics (IEEE-CS/CDE)

International Ergonomics Association (IEA)

International Network of the IUPsyS on Man-Computer Interaction Research (MACINTER)

Italian Association for Artificial Intelligence (AIIA)

Russian Applied Ergonomics Association

Russian Association for Artificial Intelligence (RAAI)

Schweizer Informatiker Gesellschaft, Fachgruppe Software Ergonomics (SI)

Society of Instrument and Control Engineers (SICE-HI)

Software Psychology Society

Soviet Association for Artificial Intelligence (SAAI)

Special Thanks

This conference depends heavily upon the efforts of volunteers. INTERCHI '93 would not be possible without the contribution made by the conference committee. Thanks to all of these individuals and to the corporations and institutions whose support has made the participation of the conference committee volunteers possible.

INTERCHI '93 Conference Committee members were supported by:

Apple Computer, Inc.

Bell-Northern Research

Delft University of Technology

Digital Equipment Corporation

Fraunhofer Institute

Lawrence Livermore National Laboratories

Logica Cambridge, Ltd.

Loughborough University of Technology

Microsoft Corporation

Nippon Telephone and Telegraph

Northern Telecomm Canada, Ltd.

Philips Electronics N.V.

Rutgers University

SERC

SunSoft, Inc.

University of Guelph

University of Paderborn

University of Siena

University of Twente

U S WEST

INTERCHI '93 Conference Co-Chairs

Bert Arnold
Delft University of Technology (NL)

Gerrit van der Veer
University of Twente and Vrije Universiteit (NL)

Ted White
University of Twente and University of Utrecht (NL)

Advisers

Brian Shackel
Loughborough University of Technology (UK)

Don Patterson
Lawrence Livermore National Laboratory (USA)

Piet Ploeger
Amsterdam Police (NL)

Audio-Visual

David Stubbs, Co-Chair
Portland, Oregon (USA)

Kevin Schofield, Co-Chair
Microsoft Corporation (USA)

Computing Support

Steven Guest, Chair
Loughborough University of Technology (UK)

Exhibitions

Karel Brookhuis, Chair
Traffic Research Centre (NL)

Financial Adviser

Wendy Mackay
Rank Xerox Cambridge EuroPARC (UK)

Industry Liaison

Ian McClelland
Philips Corporate Industrial Design (NL)

International Relations

Hiroshi Ishii, Co-Chair
NTT Human Interface Laboratories (J)

Don Patterson, Co-Chair
Lawrence Livermore National Laboratory (USA)

Michael Tauber, Co-Chair
University Paderborn (D)

Local Arrangements

Steven Pemberton, Chair
CWI (NL)

Astrid Kerssens, Associate Chair
Vrije Universiteit (NL)

Chantal Kerssens, Associate Chair
University of Amsterdam (NL)

Eddy Boeve
CWI (NL)

Merchandising

Tracy Roberts, Chair
Bell-Northern Research Ltd. (CDN)

Publications

Stacey Ashlund, Co-Chair
Human Interface Consultant (USA)

Kevin Mullet, Co-Chair
SunSoft, Inc. (USA)

Publicity

Beth Adelson, Co-Chair
Rutgers University (USA)

Rosemary Wick, Co-Chair
Public Relations Consultant (USA)

Victoria Bellotti
Rank Xerox Cambridge EuroPARC (UK)

Nardie Scharenborg
Gap Gemini Innovation (NL)

Registration

Steve Anderson, Chair
Lawrence Livermore National Laboratory (USA)

Student Volunteers

Geert de Haan, Co-Chair
Vrije Universiteit (NL)

Patrick Lynch, Co-Chair
Portland, Oregon (USA)

Treasurer

Paul Brennan
*Northern Telecom
Canada, Ltd. (CDN)*

Technical Programme

Austin Henderson, Co-Chair
Xerox Corporation (USA)

Erik Hollnagel, Co-Chair
CRI (DK)

Demonstrations

Dominique Scapin, Chair
INRIA (F)

Steven Feiner
Columbia University (USA)

Jean McKendree
*NYNEX Science & Technology,
Inc. (USA)*

Gale Martin
MCC (USA)

Jocelyn Nanard
LIRM (F)

Angel Puerta
Stanford University (USA)

Jon Schlossberg
Lockheed (USA)

Terry Winograd
Interval Research (USA)

Doctoral Consortium

Thomas Green, Co-Chair
MRC-APU (UK)

David Gilmore, Co-Chair
University of Nottingham (UK)

Phyllis Reisner
*Integrated Systems Solutions
Corporation, IBM (USA)*

Saul Greenberg
Calgary University (CDN)

Janni Nielsen
Copenhagen Business School (D)

Joëlle Coutaz
*Laboratoire de Génie
Informatique - IMAG (F)*

Interactive Experience

Catherine Weaver, Chair
Excelsior Writing Services (CDN)

Overviews

Allan MacLean, Chair
*Rank Xerox Cambridge
EuroPARC (UK)*

Panels

Paul Booth, Co-Chair
University of Salford (UK)

Jarrett Rosenberg, Co-Chair
SunSoft, Inc. (USA)

Russell Beale
Birmingham University (UK)

Chuck Clanton
Aratar (USA)

Francoise Decortis
CEC Joint Research Centre (I)

Janet Finlay
University of York (UK)

Rob Fish
Bellcore (USA)

Clayton Lewis
*University of Colorado,
Boulder (USA)*

Tom Ormerod
*Loughborough University of
Technology (UK)*

Angela Sasse
University College, London (UK)

Doug Young
Silicon Graphics, Inc. (USA)

Short Papers

Gilbert Cockton, Co-Chair
University of Glasgow (UK)

Teresa Roberts, Co-Chair
*U S WEST Advanced
Technologies (USA)*

Short Papers: Review Committee

Michael Atwood
*NYNEX Science & Technology,
Inc. (USA)*

Arlene Aucella
AFA Design Consultants (USA)

Elisabeth Bayle
Bayle Collaborations (USA)

Michel Beaudouin-Lafon
Faculte d'Orsay (F)

Victoria Belloti
*Rank Xerox Cambridge
EuroPARC (UK)*

David Benyon
Open University (UK)

Thomas Berlage
GMD (D)

Nigel Bevan
National Physical Laboratory (UK)

Niels Carlsen
*Technical University of
Denmark (DK)*

Alan Dix
University of York (UK)

Stephen Draper
University of Glasgow (UK)

Kate Ehrlich
SunSoft, Inc. (USA)

David England
University of Glasgow (UK)

Danielle Fafchamps
*Hewlett-Packard Laboratories
(USA)*

William W. Gaver
*Rank Xerox Cambridge
EuroPARC (UK)*

Philip Gray
University of Glasgow (UK)

Thomas Green
*MRC Applied Psychology Unit
(UK)*

Ralph Hill
Bellcore (USA)

John Hughes
Lancaster University (UK)

Thomas K. Landauer
Bellcore (USA)

J. Bryan Lewis
*IBM T.J. Watson Research
Center (USA)*

Jerry Lohse
University of Pennsylvania (USA)

Miles MacLeod
National Physical Laboratory (UK)

Andrew Monk
University of York (UK)

Michael Muller
*U S WEST Advanced
Technologies (USA)*

Dianne Murray
University of Surrey (UK)

Patrick O'Donnell
University of Glasgow (UK)

Robin Penner
Honeywell, Inc. (USA)

Tom Rodden
Lancaster University (UK)

Dominique Scapin
INRIA (F)

Mathias Schneider-Hufschmidt
*Siemens Corporate Research
and Development (D)*

Dan Shapiro
Lancaster University (UK)

Gerd Szwillus
University of Paderborn (D)

Manfred Tscheligi
Univeristy of Vienna (A)

Suzanne Watzman
*Watzman Information Design
(USA)*

Ellen White
Bellcore (USA)

Catherine Wolf
*IBM T.J. Watson Research
Center (USA)*

Special Interest Groups

Sebastiano Bagnara, Chair
University of Siena (I)

Tutorials

Tom Carey, Co-Chair
University of Guelph (CDN)

Michael Wilson, Co-Chair
*SERC Rutherford Appleton
Laboratory (UK)*

Jean Louis Binot
BIM (BLG)

Rich Helms
IBM Canada Ltd. (CDN)

Dianne Murray
University of Surrey (UK)

Neil Sandford *(UK)*

Charles van der Mast
*Delft University of Technology
(NL)*

Alan Wexelblatt
MIT Media Laboratory (USA)

Videos

Angela Lucas, Chair
Logica Cambridge Ltd. (UK)

Alison Black
IDEO (UK)

Colin Burns
IDEO (UK)

Michelle Fineblum
Coopers and Lybrand (USA)

Saul Greenberg
University of Calgary (CDN)

Brad Myers
Carnegie Mellon University (USA)

Ken Pier
Xerox PARC (USA)

Tracy Roberts
*Bell Northern Research Ltd.
(CDN)*

Workshops

Jürgen Ziegler, Chair
Fraunhofer Institute IAO (D)

John Karat
*IBM T.J. Watson Research
Center (USA)*

Michael Muller
*U S WEST Advanced
Technologies (USA)*

Yvonne Waern
University of Stockholm (S)

Papers

Guy Boy, Co-Chair
EURISCO (F)

Jakob Nielsen, Co-Chair
Bellcore (USA)

Papers: Associate Chair for Computer-Aided Review Assignment

Susan T. Dumais
Bellcore (USA)

Papers: Associate Chairs for Papers Reviews

André Bisseret
INRIA (F)

Ruven Brooks
*Schlumberger Laboratory for
Computer Science (USA)*

John M. Carroll
*IBM T.J. Watson Research
Center (USA)*

Joëlle Coutaz
*Laboratoire de Génie
Informatique-IMAG (F)*

Wolfgang Dzida
GMD - Inst. Design Techn. (D)

Steven Feiner
Columbia University (USA)

Jonathan Grudin
*University of California, Irvine
(USA)*

Jean-Michel Hoc
CNRS - Université de Paris (F)

Hiroshi Ishii
*NTT Human Interface
Laboratories (J)*

Wendy A. Kellogg
*IBM T.J. Watson Research
Center (USA)*

Thomas K. Landauer
Bellcore (USA)

Allan MacLean
*Rank Xerox Cambridge
EuroPARC (UK)*

Marilyn Mantei
University of Toronto (CDN)

Thomas P. Moran
Xerox PARC (USA)

S. Joy Mountford
Apple Computer, Inc. (USA)

Dan R. Olsen Jr.
Brigham Young University (USA)

Judith S. Olson
University of Michigan (USA)

Stephen Payne
University of Wales (UK)

Gabriele Rohr
*IBM Entwicklungslabor Böblingen
(D)*

Gitta Salomon
Apple Computer, Inc. (USA)

Chris Schmandt
MIT Media Laboratory (USA)

Norbert A. Streitz
GMD/IPSI (D)

Gerd Szwillus
Universität GH Paderborn (D)

John C. Thomas
*NYNEX Science & Technology,
Inc. (USA)*

Bruce Tognazzini
SunSoft, Inc. (USA)

Hirotada Ueda
*Hitachi Central Research
Laboratory and FRIEND21
Research Center (J)*

Floris L. van Nes
*Institute for Perception
Research/IPO - Philips Research
Laboratories (NL)*

Richard M. Young
*MRC Applied Psychology Unit
(UK)*

Jürgen Ziegler
Fraunhofer-Institute IAO (D)

Papers: Review Committee

Beth Adelson
Rutgers University (USA)

Klaus H. Ahlers
ECRC (D)

Bengt Ahlström
Royal Institute of Technology (S)

James H. Alexander
U S WEST (USA)

Nerio Allamanno
Ing C. Olivetti & C. (I)

Robert B. Allen
Bellcore (USA)

Carl Martin Allwood
Göteborgs Universitet (S)

James L. Alty
University of Loughborough (UK)

Yuichiro Anzai
Keio University (J)

Mark Apperley
Massey University (NZ)

Udo Arend
SAP AG (D)

Michael Arent
Apple Computer, Inc. (USA)

Michael E. Atwood
*NYNEX Science & Technology,
Inc. (USA)*

Philip J. Barnard
*MRC Applied Psychology Unit
(UK)*

Len Bass
*SEI / Carnegie Mellon University
(USA)*

Penny F. Bauersfeld
*Human Interface Design
Consultant (USA)*

Mathilde Bekker
*Delft University of Technology
(NL)*

Victoria Bellotti
*Rank Xerox Cambridge
EuroPARC (UK)*

Nigel Bevan
National Physical Laboratory (UK)

Randolph G. Bias
IBM Corporation (USA)

Eric A. Bier
Xerox PARC (USA)

Meera M. Blattner
*Lawrence Livermore National
Laboratory and the University of
California, Davis (USA)*

Anna-Christina B. Blomkvist
Luleå Technical University (S)

Sara A. Bly
Xerox PARC (USA)

Heinz-Dieter Böcker
GMD/IPSI (D)

Deborah Boehm-Davis
George Mason University (USA)

Richard A. Bolt
MIT Media Laboratory (USA)

Alan Borning
University of Washington (USA)

Tom Bösser
*Westfälische Wilhelms Universität
Münster (D)*

Josef Z. Bösze
Union Bank of Switzerland (CH)

Susan Bovair
*Georgia Institute of Technology
(USA)*

Douglas J. Brems
AT&T Bell Laboratories (USA)

A.C.C. Brennan
BT Laboratories (UK)

Paul M. Brennan
*Northern Telecom Canada, Ltd.
(CDN)*

John B. Brooke
*Digital Equipment Corporation,
Ltd. (UK)*

Maddy D. Brouwer-Janse
*Philips Research Laboratories -
Institute for Perception Research
(NL)*

Marc H. Brown
*Digital Equipment Corporation,
Systems Research Center (USA)*

Dermot P. Browne
*KPMG Management Consulting
(UK)*

Michael J. Burns
AT&T Bell Laboratories (USA)

Robert L. Campbell
Clemson University (USA)

Layne Cannon
WordPerfect Corporation (USA)

Stuart Card
Xerox PARC (USA)

Peter H. Carstensen
Risø National Laboratory (DK)

Richard Catrambone
*Georgia Institute of Technology
(USA)*

Stéphane Chatty
CENA (F)

Joan M. Cherry
University of Toronto (CDN)

Lesley Clarke
Logica Cambridge Limited (UK)

Ellis S. Cohen
Open Software Foundation (USA)

William Cowan
University of Waterloo (CDN)

Bill Curtis
Carnegie Mellon University (USA)

Allen Cypher
Apple Computer, Inc. (USA)

Maurizio De Cecco
Non Standard Logics, Paris (F)

Laura De Young
*Independence Technologies
Inc. (USA)*

Elisa M. del Galdo
*Digital Equipment Corporation,
Ltd. (UK)*

Françoise Détienne
INRIA (F)

Keith Dickerson
*RACE Industrial Consortium
(BLG)*

Mary Dieli
Microsoft Corporation (USA)

Alan Dix
University of York (UK)

Stephanie Doane
*University of Illinois at Urbana-
Champaign (USA)*

Miwako Doi
*Toshiba Research and
Development Center (J)*

Paul Dourish
*Rank Xerox Cambridge
EuroPARC (UK)*

Susan M. Dray
IDS Financial Services (USA)

Jonathan V. Earthy
Lloyd's Register of Shipping (UK)

Edmund Eberleh
SAP AG (D)

Dennis E. Egan
Bellcore (USA)

Kate Ehrlich
SunSoft, Inc. (USA)

Marc Eisenstadt
The Open University (UK)

Kerstin Severinson Eklundh
Royal Institute of Technology (S)

Jay Elkerton
Philips Laboratories (USA)

Kim Michael Fairchild
*National University of Singapore
(SGP)*

Steve Fickas
University of Oregon (USA)

Gerhard Fischer
*University of Colorado at Boulder
(USA)*

James D. Foley
*Georgia Institute of Technology
(USA)*

Ellen Francik
Pacific Bell (USA)

Steve Freeman
University of Cambridge (UK)

Masaki Fujihata
Keio University (J)

George W. Furnas
Bellcore (USA)

Sharon R. Garber
3M Company (USA)

William W. Gaver
*Rank Xerox Cambridge
EuroPARC (UK)*

David J. Gilmore
University of Nottingham (UK)

Rainer Gimnich
*IBM Germany, Heidelberg
Scientific Center (D)*

Robert A. Glass
SunSoft, Inc. (USA)

Robert J. Glushko
Passage Systems (USA)

Louis M. Gomez
Bellcore (USA)

Kathleen M. Gomoll
Taligent (USA)

Michael Good
*Digital Equipment Corporation
(USA)*

Peter Gorny
University of Oldenburg (D)

Charles E. Grantham
University of San Francisco (USA)

Wayne D. Gray
*Fordham University at Lincoln
Center (USA)*

Saul Greenberg
University of Calgary (CDN)

Irene Greif
*Lotus Development Corporation
(USA)*

Raymonde Guindon
Hewlett-Packard Company (USA)

Nils-Erik Gustafsson
Ellemtel Telecommunications Systems Labs (S)

Volker Haarslev
University of Hamburg (D)

Frank G. Halasz
Xerox PARC (USA)

Nick Hammond
University of York (UK)

Michael D. Harrison
University of York (UK)

H. Rex Hartson
Virginia Polytechnic Institute and State University (USA)

William E. Hefley
Carnegie Mellon University (USA)

Siegfried R. Heine
IBM Germany (D)

Rich M. Helms
IBM Canada Lab, Centre for Advanced Studies (CDN)

David R. Hill
University of Calgary (CDN)

Ralph D. Hill
Bellcore (USA)

Will Hill
Bellcore (USA)

Rumi Hiraga
IBM Tokyo Research Laboratory (J)

Deborah Hix
Virginia Polytechnic Institute and State University (USA)

Hans-Jürgen Hoffmann
University of Darmstadt (D)

James D. Hollan
Bellcore (USA)

H. Ulrich Hoppe
GMD/IPSI (D)

Stephanie Houde
Apple Computer, Inc. (USA)

Stephen Howard
Swinburne University of Technology (AUS)

Andrew Howes
MRC Applied Psychology Unit (UK)

Wolfgang J. Irler
Università di Trento (I)

Hiroo Iwata
University of Tsukuba (J)

Robert J.K. Jacob
Naval Research Laboratory (USA)

Pertti Jarvinen
University of Tampere (SF)

Robin Jeffries
Hewlett-Packard Laboratories (USA)

Bonnie E. John
Carnegie Mellon University (USA)

Peter Johnson
University of London (UK)

Sandra J. Jones
Digital Equipment Corporation (USA)

Hee-Sen Jong
National University of Singapore (SGP)

Anker Helms Jørgensen
Copenhagen University (DK)

Klaus Kansy
GMD/FIT (D)

Victor Kaptelinin
Institute of General and Educational Psychology (RUS)

Clare-Marie Karat
IBM (USA)

John Karat
IBM T.J. Watson Research Center (USA)

Solange Karsenty
Digital Equipment Corporation, Paris Research Laboratory (F)

Irvin R. Katz
Educational Testing Service (USA)

Cecilia Katzeff
SISU Swedish Institute for Systems Development (S)

Paul Kearney
Sharp Laboratories of Europe Ltd. (UK)

Rudolf K. Keller
CRIM, Montréal (CDN)

Claire Khanna
Graphic Design and American Institute of Graphic Arts (USA)

David Kieras
University of Michigan (USA)

Muneo Kitajima
Industrial Products Research Institute (J)

Alfred Kobsa
Universität Konstanz (D)

Marja-Riitta Koivunen
Helsinki University of Technology (SF)

David Kurlander
Microsoft Research (USA)

Masaaki Kurosu
Hitachi Design Center (J)

Hideaki Kuzuoka
University of Tsukuba (J)

Morten Kyng
Aarhus University (DK)

Mark Lansdale
Loughborough University of Technology (UK)

Alison Lee
NYNEX Science & Technology, Inc. (USA)

John J. Leggett
Texas A&M University (USA)

Andreas C. Lemke
ALCATEL SEL AG (D)

Gitte Lindgaard
Telecom Australia Research Laboratories (AUS)

Mark Linton
Silicon Graphics, Inc. (USA)

John Long
Ergonomics Unit, University College London (UK)

Jonas Löwgren
Linköping University (S)

Michelle A. Lund
Electronic Data Systems (USA)

Gene Lynch
Tektronix, Inc. (USA)

I. Scott MacKenzie
University of Guelph (CDN)

Jock Mackinlay
Xerox PARC (USA)

Jane T. Malin
NASA-Johnson Space Center (USA)

Gary Marchionini
University of Maryland (USA)

Hans Marmolin
Royal Institute of Technology & UI Design AB (S)

Catherine R. Marshall
Oregon Graduate Institute (USA)

Yutaka Matsushita
Keio University (J)

John C. McCarthy
University of Cork (EIR)

Jean McKendree
University of York (UK)

Cliff McKnight
HUSAT Research Institute (UK)

William W. McMillan
Eastern Michigan University (USA)

James R. Miller
Apple Computer, Inc. (USA)

Naomi Miyake
Chukyo University (J)

Thomas G. Moher
University of Illinois at Chicago (USA)

Andrew F. Monk
University of York (UK)

John "Scooter" Morris
Genentech (USA)

Michael J. Muller
U S WEST Advanced Technologies (USA)

Robert M. Mulligan
AT&T Bell Laboratories (USA)

Alice M. Mulvehill
The MITRE Corporation (USA)

Dianne Murray
University of Surrey (UK)

Brad A. Myers
Carnegie Mellon University (USA)

Manfred Nagl
Aachen University of Technology (D)

Yasushi Nakauchi
Keio University (J)

Frieder Nake
Universität Bremen (D)

Jocelyne Nanard
LIRMM, Université de Montpellier (F)

Marc Nanard
LIRMM, Université de Montpellier (F)

Bonnie A. Nardi
Hewlett-Packard Laboratories (USA)

Lisa R. Neal
EDS Center for Advanced Research (USA)

Robert Neches
USC/ISI (USA)

William Newman
Rank Xerox Cambridge EuroPARC (UK)

Kazuhisa Niki
Electrotechnical Laboratories (J)

Erik L. Nilsen
Lewis and Clark College (USA)

Shogo Nishida
Central Research Lab, Mitsubishi Electric Co. (J)

Lorraine F. Normore
Chemical Abstracts Service (USA)

Mark Notess
Hewlett-Packard Company (USA)

Else Nygren
Uppsala University (S)

Horst Oberquelle
Universität Hamburg (D)

Katsuhiko Ogawa
NTT Human Interface Laboratories (J)

Gary M. Olson
University of Michigan (USA)

Tim Oren
Apple Computer, Inc. (USA)

Ei-Ichi Osawa
Sony Computer Science Laboratory, Inc. (J)

Avi Parush
Scitex Corporation Ltd. (ISR)

Randy Pausch
University of Virginia (USA)

Annelise Mark Pejtersen
Risø National Laboratory (DK)

Gary Perlman
The Ohio State University (USA)

Richard W. Pew
BBN Inc. (USA)

Ken Pier
Xerox PARC (USA)

Peter Pirolli
Xerox PARC (USA)

Catherine Plaisant
University of Maryland (USA)

Steven E. Poltrock
Boeing Computer Services (USA)

Robin Pyburn
Independent Consultant (UK)

Paul Rankin
Philips Research, England (UK)

Phyllis Reisner
ISSC/IBM (USA)

Robert J. Remington
Lockheed Missiles & Space Company (USA)

Paul Resnick
Massachussets Institute of Technology (USA)

John Rheinfrank
Fitch RichardsonSmith (USA)

Jim Rhyne
IBM T.J. Watson Research Center (USA)

John T. Richards
IBM T.J. Watson Research Center (USA)

R. Douglas Riecken
AT&T Bell Laboratories (USA)

Robert S. Rist
University of Technology, Sydney (AUS)

George G. Robertson
Xerox PARC (USA)

Scott P. Robertson
Rutgers University (USA)

Robert W. Root
Bellcore (USA)

Mary Beth Rosson
IBM T.J. Watson Research Center (USA)

Peter L. Rowley
Ontario Institute for Studies in Education (CDN)

Richard Rubinstein
Digital Equipment Corporation (USA)

Carrie Rudman
U S WEST (USA)

Pamela Samuelson
University of Pittsburgh School of Law (USA)

Mark S. Schlager
SRI International (USA)

Franz J. Schmalhofer
German Research Center for Artificial Intelligence (D)

Kjeld Schmidt
Risø National Laboratory (DK)

Jaclyn R. Schrier
American Institutes for Research (USA)

Chris Shaw
University of Alberta (CDN)

Sylvia Sheppard
NASA Goddard Space Flight Center (USA)

Ben Shneiderman
University of Maryland (USA)

John L. Sibert
The George Washington University (USA)

Gurminder Singh
National University of Singapore (SGP)

Mark K. Singley
IBM T.J. Watson Research Center (USA)

John B. Smith
University of North Carolina (USA)

Elliot Soloway
University of Michigan (USA)

James C. Spohrer
Apple Computer, Inc. (USA)

Loretta Staples
Loretta Staples Design (USA)

Karl E. Steiner
University of Illinois at Chicago (USA)

Piyawadee "Noi" Sukaviriya
Georgia Institute of Technology (USA)

Alistair Sutcliffe
City University, London (UK)

Gen Suzuki
NTT Human Interface Laboratories (J)

Martha R. Szczur
NASA/Goddard Space Flight Center (USA)

Haruo Takemura
Artificial Intelligence Department ATR Communication Systems Research Laboratories (J)

Akikazu Takeuchi
Sony Computer Science Laboratory, Inc. (J)

John C. Tang
SunSoft, Inc. (USA)

Masayuki Tani
Hitachi, Ltd. (J)

Anne Nicol Thomas
Children Using Technology (USA)

Jo Tombaugh
Carleton University (CDN)

Roger Took
University of York (UK)

Michael Travers
MIT Media Laboratory (USA)

Randall H. Trigg
Xerox PARC (USA)

Manfred Tscheligi
University of Vienna (A)

Thomas S. Tullis
*Canon Information Systems
(USA)*

Jacob P. Ukelson
*IBM T.J. Watson Research
Center (USA)*

Claus Unger
*University of Hagen
(Fern Universität) (D)*

Igor Ushakov
The Open University (UK)

Bob Vallone
GO Corporation (USA)

Charles van der Mast
*Delft University of Technology
(NL)*

Brad T. Vander Zanden
University of Tennessee (USA)

Bill Verplank
Interval Research (USA)

Robert A. Virzi
*GTE Laboratories Incorporated
(USA)*

Yvonne Waern
Linköping University (S)

Janet H. Walker
*Digital Equipment Corporation,
Cambridge Research Laboratory
(USA)*

Paul Walsh
BNR Europe, Ltd (UK)

Colin Ware
*University of New Brunswick
(CDN)*

Clive P. Warren
*British Aerospace plc, Sowerby
Research Centre (UK)*

John A. Waterworth
*ISS, National University of
Singapore (SGP)*

David M. Weimer
AT&T Bell Laboratories (USA)

Alan Wexelblat
MIT Media Laboratory (USA)

Stephen A. Weyer
*Janssen Research Foundation
(USA)*

Steve Whittaker
*Hewlett-Packard Laboratories
(UK)*

Anna M. Wichansky
Silicon Graphics, Inc. (USA)

Russel Winder
University College London (UK)

Peter Wisskirchen
GMD/FIT (D)

Ian H. Witten
University of Waikato (NZ)

Dennis Wixon
*Digital Equipment Corporation
(USA)*

Catherine G. Wolf
*IBM T.J. Watson Research
Center (USA)*

Patricia Wright
*MRC Applied Psychology Unit
(UK)*

Peter C. Wright
University of York (UK)

Nicole Yankelovich
*Sun Microsystems Laboratories,
Inc. (USA)*

Norihiko Yoshida
Kyushu University (J)

Michael J. Zyda
Naval Postgraduate School (USA)

European Office

Elly Lammers
University of Twente (NL)

Charlotte White
University of Twente (NL)

North American Office

Carol Klyver
Foundations of Excellence (USA)

Professional Services

**Conference Management,
Executive Administrator**

Carol Klyver
Foundations of Excellence (USA)

**Conference Logistics
Management**

Iris Allebrandi
Novep (NL)

Paul Henning
CLC (USA)

Design

Wienik Everts *(NL)*

**Design Consultant,
Production**

JoAnne Maass *(USA)*

INTERCHI '93 gratefully acknowdedges the contributions of the
following Corporate Sponsors. Their generosity has helped the
conference to bring together a diverse international community in a
joint gathering unprecedented in the field of human–compruter
interaction.

 PHILIPS

RANK XEROX

vrije Universiteit

The INTERCHI '93 Technical Programme features the state-of-the-art in HCI. Presentations of work from around the world reflect both traditional views of HCI and a new perspective, in which:

- computation is present everywhere, not only via workstations,
- communication is low-cost and high-speed,
- new input and output devices go beyond keyboards, displays and pointing devices,
- applications encompass casual and critical activity, work and play, and art and science,
- isolated perspectives are integrated,
- users are recognized as part of a social, physical, and technical environment, and
- the human process of design and its supporting tools are as important as the resulting products.

The INTERCHI '93 Technical Programme features 62 technical papers, 9 panel sessions, 9 overviews, 12 formal demonstrations, and 19 formal video submissions. The materials included in the technical progamme (see descriptions at right) were selected following an exhaustive review process and represent the full range of knowledge and experience the field of HCI can offer the user interface designer, developer, manager, researcher, or interested observer.

These proceedings serve as the archival record of the INTERCHI '93 Technical Programme. The pages to follow contain the accepted technical papers, position statements from panel session organisers and participants, descriptions of each overview and formal demonstration, and abstracts for each entry in the formal video programme. Other conference activities, including tutorials, workshops, research symposium, doctoral consortium, short papers, special interest groups, and the Interactive Experience are documented in a special Adjunct Proceedings distributed at the conference to all participants.

Austin Henderson
Erik Hollnagel

Technical Programme Co-Chairs
INTERCHI '93

Papers

Technical Papers present theory, concepts, methodology, practice, and experience of interest to researchers, designers, developers, and users.

Panels

Panel sessions bring together informed speakers who present or illustrate a point of view and then conduct an open discussion of the topic area among themselves and with the audience.

Overviews

Overviews survey the current projects and activities of prominent research and development institutions with substantial involvement in HCI. The presentations cover both the content produced and the circumstances under which the work is performed. Special coverage is provided for collaborative projects and opportunities for visiting appointments are described for interested students and scientists.

Demonstrations

Formal Demonstrations of recent advances or prototype systems take place throughout the three-day conference. Demonstrations provide conference participants with a first-hand view of systems in action, along with an opportunity to discuss the systems with the people who created them.

Videos

The Formal Video Programme runs continuously in a designated video theatre area. The videos present important breakthroughs in human-computer interaction produced in academic, industrial, and governmental research and product development organisations.

Mixing oil and water? Ethnography versus Experimental Psychology in the study of computer-mediated communication.

Convenor   Andrew Monk
Department of Psychology, University of York, YO1 5DD, UK.
AM1@uk.ac.york Tel: +44-904-433148, Fax: +44-904-433181

For the ethnographers:

Bonnie Nardi
Media Technology Lab., Hewlett-Packard Laboratories, Palo Alto, CA 94304, USA,
nardi@com.hp.hpl.hplbon, +1-415-857-5121

Nigel Gilbert
Department of Sociology, University of Surrey, Guildford, GU2 5XH, U.K.,
gng@uk.ac.surrey.soc, +44-483-509292

For the psychologists

Marilyn Mantei
Department of Computer Science, University of Toronto, M5S 1A4, Canada.
mantei@edu.toronto.dgp, +1-416-978-5512

John McCarthy
Department of Psychology, University of Cork, Ireland,
mccarthyj@ie.ucc.iruccvax, +353-21-276871

KEYWORDS:

Computer-mediated communication, ethnography, ethnomethodology, experimental methods, anthropology, cognitive psychology, experimental psychology, sociology.

INTRODUCTION

The study of computer-mediated communication (CMC) has brought together investigators from very different research traditions. Investigators coming from Sociology and Anthropology have been trained in the tradition of ethnography, whereas investigators coming from Experimental Psychology and Human Factors think more in terms of the hypothetico-deductive tradition of experiment and quantitative measurement. Clearly, each of these viewpoints has something to offer in the practical quest for understanding what makes for effective CMC. There are however some potential contradictions in the concepts used and the assumptions made by investigators from these two traditions.

1) Theory and the interpretation of data:- Take ethnomethodology as an example of the ethnographic

© 1993 ACM 0-89791-575-5/93/0004/0003...$1.50

approach. The psychological and ethnomethodological traditions use very different concepts to think about "conversation". The psychological tradition in HCI is mechanistic and based around the notion of goals and intentions whereas the ethnomethodological tradition is one of descriptive phenomenology. This can lead to apparently very different interpretations of the same data. For example, an ethnomethodological study may interpret a particular extract from the transcript of a conversation in relation to "context". The same transcript might be interpreted by a cognitive experimentalist in terms of "information transfer".

2) The type of data collected:- Ethnography deals in rich contextualised data. The experimental approach prefers quantitative data that can be evaluated for their statistical significance, though qualitative data is collected. Ethnographers work in a non-causal paradigm and stress the dangers of collecting data from artificial contexts. In CMC research this means that studies should be of people communicating in their day-to-day work. The experimental approach stresses the danger of attributing causation to correlational data. This requires that participants are assigned to experimental conditions.

The position of this workshop is that these traditions can be seen as complementary rather than contradictory. Indeed it can be argued that there is already a merging of the two approaches when it comes to methods of data collection. The major differences are in the way data are interpreted. These arise from:

- differences between cognitive and social accounts of action and
- differences between positivist and interpretative approaches (loosely between causal accounts and those concerned with 'understanding' action).

Our aim is to make clearer the practical differences between these two approaches to data interpretation and to discuss how they may be blended into a smooth emulsion.

BIOGRAPHIES

Nigel Gilbert is Professor of Sociology at the University of Surrey and a member of the Social and Computer Sciences Research Group there. Previously he was involved in a large project to develop prototype systems for the UK Department of Social Security, including an expert system for use by the public to provide advice on welfare benefits. The interface for this system was informed by findings from conversation analysis. He is currently manager for the ESPRIT Sundial speech understanding project, developing a 'dialogue manager' for a telephone enquiry system and has interests in requirements analysis for CSCW and the application of distributed artificial intelligence to the simulation of social process.

Marilyn M. Mantei is currently Associate Professor of Computer Science and of Management Information Science at the University of Toronto. Prior to this Dr. Mantei was a faculty member in the Computers and Information Systems Department in the Michigan Business School where she established a doctoral program in human-computer interaction and started the Human Computer Interaction Laboratory. During her stay at Michigan she headed a collaborative work project at Electronic Data Systems Corporation's Centre for Machine Intelligence. Dr. Mantei has served the Association for Computing Machinery's Special Interest Group on Computer Human Interaction (SIGCHI) in many ways. Most recently as co-chair of the CSCW'92 Conference on Computer Supported Cooperative Work. Her current research interests include computer supported cooperative work, cognitive models of user interfaces and methodologies for incorporating HCI techniques into practical software development.

John McCarthy is a lecturer in the Department of Applied Psychology, University College Cork, Ireland where he conducts research and lectures on 'Information Technology and Organisations'. Until recently he lectured in Cognitive Ergonomics at the University of Limerick, Ireland. He previously worked on a project at the University of York, U.K. concerned with issues in electronic conferencing. His main research interests are in the organisational and social context of computer supported cooperative work, aspects of computer mediated communication, and human performance/error in complex systems.

Bonnie Nardi is an anthropologist who has worked at Hewlett-Packard Labs for four years. She received her Ph.D. from the University of California, Irvine, and has worked in both industry and academia. She is interested in theories of collaborative work, end user programming, the use of ethnographic methods in system design, and multimedia. She has done ethnographic research in Western Samoa, North Carolina, Silicon Valley and the neurosurgery department of a teaching hospital. Bonnie Nardi has conducted empirical studies of users of spreadsheets, CAD systems, presentation slide-making software, and video. She has a book on end user programming forthcoming from MIT Press, Spring 1993. Her current work involves the study of activity theory as a theoretical basis for human-computer interaction studies, and the use of multimedia in telecommuting applications.

POSITION PAPER FOR THE ETHNOGRAPHERS

Both ethnographic and experimental methods have their place in the study of human thought and behaviour. The problem is to select the right method, and then to apply it correctly.

Recent critiques have made clear why experiments are often vapid exercises:

1) the laboratory is nothing like the real world;
2) one cannot truly "control" all the variables that affect a behaviour;
3) an effort is made to wipe out context rather than to understand it;
4) subjects are given highly constrained, artificial tasks within a very short time frame;
5) little or no attention is paid to subjects' ideas, thoughts, beliefs about what is being studied.

CMC is essentially about social interaction and while experimental methods are capable of obtaining findings about individual behaviour they are ill suited to measuring or observing social action.

Applied experiments done in a naturalistic setting can be useful. For example, giving two groups of people a different system to try out for six months, and following the progress of usage can be considered an "experiment" because a specific intervention is introduced under somewhat controlled conditions (a specific time frame, perhaps a training course, etc.). Much can be learned in this way, though still there are problems of discerning people's true motivation and unfettered behaviour -- would they actually use the system if they were not being asked to by management, or paid, or otherwise prodded? Are they using the system in a way suggested by the experimenters, or in the way they would come to use it on their own? Are they typical subjects, or part of a pool (say, students or colleagues of the researchers) not representative of the actual potential user population?

We will argue that though experiments can be useful, a good ethnographer almost always finds something of value, whereas a good experimentalist often comes up dry. Thus more ethnographic studies are in order for HCI research.

In ethnographic studies, the investigator attempts to be as unobtrusive as possible, finding a group of people already engaged in some interesting behaviour. Most critically, the ethnographer adopts the position of uninformed outsider whose job it is to understand as much as possible about the "natives" from their own point of view. All else flows from this basic precept:

- the need to use a range of methods including intensive observation, in-depth interviewing, participation in cultural activities, and simply hanging about, watching and learning as events unfold;
- the holistic perspective, in which everything -- belief systems, rituals, institutions, artefacts, texts, etc. -- is grist for the analytical mill; and immersion in the field situation.

An ethnographer who follows the anthropological method as outlined above, and who takes the time to craft a good ethnography, almost always adds to the store of human knowledge, inasmuch as he or she writes about, in nuanced detail, a real human activity, events which become a part of human history. The ethnographer establishes broadly based patterns of human behaviour and thought, and provides interpretations of unfamiliar cultures. Indeed the central project of anthropology is ethnography -- literally, writing culture. The experimentalist, by contrast, often conducts a meaningless exercise of no lasting value because he or she has asked people to perform some activity in a constrained way that bears no relation to how the activity would be conducted in real life, if indeed it would ever even be conducted.

In anthropology, the main methodological error is generalising beyond one's sample. Ethnographers have become more sensitive to issues of sampling, but there is still room for improvement.

Case studies for discussion

We will argue for more ethnography in HCI, describing two studies that found surprising and significant results that would never have been found in experiments of any kind. The studies were conducted by Hewlett-Packard Labs. researchers, and concern users of spreadsheets [1,2] and users of information services [3]. Both studies have clear implications for design. For example, in [1] eleven spreadsheet users were interviewed. One important conclusion that emerges from the 335 pages of transcribed interview is the importance of having a strong visual format for structuring and presenting data. The users report how they actively engaged with the spreadsheet table as a problem solving device. The tabular structure of rows, columns and cells provides a modelling framework. It is reasonable to conclude that to be successful any end user programming system must provide an effective way of visualising the relationships between data elements.

POSITION PAPER FOR THE EXPERIMENTALISTS

"The point of applied research is to understand what matters in realistic contexts" (Landauer, 1987 [4]).

Applied research inevitably involves stretching and reshaping one's methodology to meet the demands of the problem being addressed. We will argue that best practice in applied experimental psychology already does this. Further, the demands of applied research force this reshaping to be integrative as the generation of ideas and solutions becomes more important than disciplinary purity. Of course this is not everyone's view. Some believe that experimental methodology should be abandoned altogether.

The relatively recent advent of ethnography and associated disciplines such as ethnomethodology to Human Computer Interaction (HCI) has contributed to a feeling of dissatisfaction with the older child, experimental psychology, in some quarters. Some researchers have recommended abandoning the experimental approach to HCI research altogether. Three main arguments are cited in favour of this radical position:

1) experimental method is not sensitive to the context of the behaviour observed;
2) experimental method does not pay due attention to the richness (or fine detail) of human behaviour, favouring instead the observation of a narrowly defined set of categories;
3) experimental method does not capture the subjectively defined meaning of the behaviour being observed.

These criticisms of experimental method can only be valid if addressed to 'pure experimentation', and are invalid if addressed to 'applied experimentation'. It is often further argued that ethnographic approaches, which collect data in the 'field', the minutiae of which is observed, recorded, and analysed within the frame of reference of the subject, are the ideal replacement. Such arguments understate what is possible using the experimental approach, and overstate what is possible using ethnographic approaches. To understand what is possible using experimental methods let us examine the difference between pure and applied experimentation.

Pure experimentation focuses on variables which are only of theoretical importance and admits no material difference (i.e. literally a difference that matters) between the laboratory and the real world. Pure experimentation tends to look at the effect of one variable controlled by the experimenter on one or two gross measures of performance. This indicates a very simple linear model of cause and effect, that is, the independent variable causing a unidimensional change in gross performance. Pure experimentation is either unaware of or not interested in the existence of behaviours outside of those explicitly controlled and measured. On the other hand applied research areas, such as work and engineering psychology, have produced many good examples of applied experimentation. Applied experimentation looks for variables which have theoretical and applied significance and often involves people performing their real task in their real workplace or at the very least a high fidelity simulation under reasonably realistic work conditions (see [5] for example).

With regard to the three criticisms enumerated above, we argue that best practice in applied experimental psychology is context sensitive and has a rich perspective on data. Applied experimental psychology could profit in all three areas from a careful reading of ethnography. Ethnography might also benefit from a careful reading of applied experimental psychology particularly with respect to inter- and intra-individual variation, and generalising from data. The conclusions about a very intensely studied group working in its rich environment are valid truths about that group perhaps, but they do not extrapolate as theories that apply to a larger population. The workgroup and the conditions under which they were studied may be much more bizarre and unrepresentative than the experimental study that such complaints are levied against.

Any result in experimental psychology must have demonstrable reliability and validity. Reliability and validity are well developed technical concepts with associated methodological techniques such as sampling from a specified population and using carefully constructed control groups. These methodological techniques are backed up with statistical techniques that can demonstrate generality in a way that is easily inspectable by other investigators. The mechanical nature of the procedures for summarising data in experimental psychology does limit their scope. On the other hand it also makes them much more inspectable and much less open to the biases of a particular investigator. No doubt most ethnographers take great care to avoid personal bias and to check the generality of their conclusions against a large corpus of data but is this always the case and how do you argue with someone when only a small carefully selected part of the data is presented?

A case study for discussion

Sellen [6] describes a carefully controlled laboratory study of video-mediated communication. Twelve groups of three each held 'debates' using each of three communication media: face to face and two video set ups. One of the video set ups was designed in her laboratory to facilitate turn taking in multi party communication.

A variety of detailed measures were derived from recordings of the participant's speech. These show that there is a higher proportion of simultaneous speech in the face to face condition that seems to result in faster switching times when the speaker changed. There were no significant differences between the two video conditions. Ratings of statements such as "I was able to take control of the conversation when I wanted to" and "I could selectively attend to one person at a time" tell the same story. Ratings were higher in the face to face condition but the two video conditions were not significantly different. The conclusion is that the new video set up, as currently configured, does not provide the expected gains in communication efficiency. Suggestions about how it might be made more effective are made.

REFERENCES

1. Nardi, B. & Miller, J. (1990). The spreadsheet interface: A basis for end user programming. Proceedings of Interact'90. 27-31 August, 1990. Cambridge, England. Pp. 977-983.

2. Nardi, B. & Miller, J. (1991). Twinkling lights and nested loops: Distributed problem solving and spreadsheet development. International Journal of Man-Machine Studies 34, 161-184. (Also reprinted in Computer Supported Cooperative Work and Groupware, S. Greenberg, ed. Academic Press, London, 1991; and IEEE Tutorial on CSCW, 1992).

3. O'Day, V. & Jeffries, R. Orienteering in an Information Landscape: How to Get There from Here. Submitted to INTERCHI'93.

4. Landauer, T.K. (1987) Relations between cognitive psychology and computer system design. In Carroll, J.M. (Eds.), Interfacing thought: cognitive aspects of human-computer interaction, MIT Press, pp. 1-25.

5. McCarthy, J.C., Miles, V.C. & Monk, A.F. An experimental study of common ground in text-based communication. In Robertson, S.P., Olsen, G.M. & Olsen, J.S.(Eds.), Human factors in computing systems: reaching through technology, CHI'91 conference proceedings, ACM, pp. 209-215, 1991.

6. Sellen, A. J. (1992) Speech patterns in video-mediated conversations. In Bauersfeld, P., Bennett, J. & Lynch, G. (Eds.), CHI'92 conference proceedings, New York: ACM, pp. 49-59.

Preserving Knowledge in Design Projects:
What Designers Need to Know

James D. Herbsleb
The University of Michigan
701 Tappan Street
Ann Arbor, MI 48109-1234, USA
herbsleb@csmil.umich.edu

Eiji Kuwana
NTT Corporation
1-9-1 Kohnan Minato-ku
Tokyo 108 JAPAN
kuwana@mickey.ntt.jp

ABSTRACT
In order to inform the design of technology support and new procedural methods for software design, we analyzed the content of real design meetings in three organizations, focusing in particular on the questions the designers ask of each other. We found that most questions concerned the project requirements, particularly what the software was supposed to do and, somewhat less frequently, scenarios of use. Questions about functions to be performed by software components and how these functions were to be realized were also fairly frequent. Rationales for design decisions were seldom asked about. The implications of this research for design tools and methods are discussed.

KEYWORDS: Design tools, design methods, design rationale, user scenarios.

INTRODUCTION
The difficulty, expense, and unpredictability of large software development projects are so well known and so widely discussed that the term "software crisis" has become passé. This is not because the difficulties have been overcome -- there has been no silver bullet [1] -- but rather, we suspect, because the difficulty of the task is no longer a surprise. Empirical research has a major role to play in the process of bringing about incremental improvements. As we attain a better understanding of the cognitive and organizational demands of large software development projects, we are in a better position to introduce methods and tools which are precisely tuned to the biggest problems.

One of the suggestions most often heard is to provide developers with access to more knowledge about various aspects of the development project. But the views about precisely what knowledge to provide are many and diverse. Here are a few of the major contenders:

Rationale for Design Decisions
Much attention is currently focused on methods, notations, and tools for recording rationales for design decisions.

What is represented in this approach is not primarily the application domain or the system design itself, but rather the space or history of arguments surrounding the actual decisions made as development progresses (see [17]). The most commonly advocated framework for selecting and organizing this kind of data is argument structure (e.g., gIBIS, [3], SIBYL [14], and QOC [16]). It typically includes nodes such as *issue, alternative, argument, criterion, goal,* and *claim*. These are linked up into structures by relations like *achieves, supports, denies, presupposes, subgoal-of,* and *subdecision-of*. The most expressive language to date is Decision Rationale Language (DRL)[15], which includes all of these and more. What is represented is the "rhetorical" space around decisions, and structure is created by links which have strictly rhetorical significance. If this sort of information is found to be sufficiently useful, it could be maintained independently or integrated with traditional design representations (e.g., [20]).

Knowledge of application domain
In a major study of software development projects, Curtis, Krasner, & Iscoe [4] found that one of the problems that was most salient and consistently troublesome was "the thin spread of application domain knowledge." Particularly rare and important was command of the larger view, i.e., the integration of all the various and diverse pieces of domain knowledge. This was essential for creating a good computational architecture, and for forging and communicating a common understanding of the system under development.

Recently, there has been increased attention to analysis of problem domains and representing domain knowledge (see, e.g., [5]). Methods using such notations support the representation of the problem domain in terms of nodes like *entities, objects, processes,* or *data structures*, and links such as *data flow, control flow, relations, inherits, subclass-of,* and so on. The basic idea is to represent the domain and the system, generally in terms which domain experts would understand.

Scenarios of use
Closely related to application domain knowledge is knowledge of scenarios of use. In contrast to general domain knowledge, knowledge of scenarios of use concerns the ways in which the system will need to fit into the dynamic flow of activities in its environment. As noted

by Guindon [7], scenarios of use are one of the major kinds of knowledge developers bring to bear in designing software. These scenarios are very important for understanding the requirements, and appeared to play a role in the sudden unplanned discovery of partial solutions. In a similar vein, Curtis et al. [4] also concluded from their extensive interviews with software developers that scenarios of use were very important for understanding the behavior of the application and its relation to its environment. Yet they observed that while it is common for customers to generate scenarios as they are determining their requirements, they very seldom pass them on to the developers. As a consequence, the developers had to generate their own scenarios, and could only predict the obvious ones and not ones which created unusual conditions. There is also anecdotal evidence that scenarios of use are very helpful in the user interface design process [12].

Scenarios of use could be made available to designers in several ways. At least one software engineering method, *Objectory* [10] explicitly incorporates scenarios of use ("use cases") as a central part of the method. There are also other, less formal techniques, (e.g., [11]) for making this kind of knowledge available during design. Finally, techniques that get users actively involved in the design process (e.g., [18]) may serve, among other purposes, to inject knowledge of user scenarios into the design process.

Knowledge generated by design methods
Finally, there are many software design methods, each with an associated notation, and embedded in rules-of-thumb, principles, and a development philosophy. They fall within several broad categories, including structured analysis and design, entity-relation modeling, and object-oriented design. There are many claims by advocates of these techniques, and also some empirical evidence, e.g., from research on software errors [19], that these methods can have a significant positive impact on the development process. It is unclear how much of this effect is attributable to an improvement in the ongoing design process and in the quality of the design decisions made, and how much is attributable to capturing knowledge in the system's notation so that the knowledge can be used at later stages. But it seems very plausible that capturing this sort of knowledge could significantly impact the later stages of development.

What is really needed?
Each of these ideas for capturing project knowledge and making it available for later use embodies empirical hypotheses about the knowledge needs of the software design process. Testing these claims should be given top priority, since they determine the potential of various classes of tools to make positive contributions to the design process.

Unfortunately, it is very difficult to test these hypotheses directly, i.e., by building an appropriate tool then designing a software system and assessing the results. The expense, risk, and the difficulty of interpreting the results of complex processes in the real world make this option untenable. Laboratory studies solve some of these problems by isolating the effects of selected variables, but they do not provide the opportunity to take advantage of many of the potentially most beneficial features of knowledge-preserving tools and techniques, since there is generally no realistic organizational or project history in a laboratory context. Preserving small quantities of knowledge for the duration of a typical experiment, i.e., an hour or two, is radically different from preserving potentially enormous quantities of knowledge for more realistic time periods of months to years.

This research attempts to inform this issue by taking a different approach. To begin to assess the basic knowledge needs in upstream software development, we examine the *questions* that arise in actual requirements specification and design meetings among software engineers. The central assumption is simply that the questions asked in these meetings by experienced, professional software designers are a reasonably good indicator of the kinds of knowledge that an ideal method should make available. It is certainly not a perfect indicator, since designers may be unaware of their lack of information, or they may be asking a question just to test their understanding. We assume, however, that asking a question very often indicates that the asker believes the answer contains knowledge important in the immediate context, and that the asker does not currently possess this knowledge.

In a previous paper [13], we briefly described this method, and presented basic frequency data on questions concerning software requirements. Here we provide a more detailed description of our method, present data concerning questions about all of the software development stages, and draw out the implications of our findings for design tools and methods.

METHOD
Data Profile.
We use two basic kinds of data in this study. The first is a set of minutes from 38 design meetings at Nippon Telegraph and Telephone Corporation (NTT) Software Laboratories that took place over an eight month period. The task was to specify requirements and design for version 1.5 of an existing software development environment. The meetings from which our data are drawn involved external behavior analysis and preliminary design. Individual members of the team wrote the minutes, generally a day or two after the meeting, using their notes and documents from the meeting. The chore of taking minutes rotated through the development team.

This corpus of data covers a substantial continuous period of time on a large re-design project. One potential weakness of this data stems from the fact that it is filtered through and reconstructed by the individual taking minutes. Presumably, this will not cause too much distortion, since minutes customarily capture the most important points, and the minute-takers were experts in the software design domain. But the second data source was included, in part, to compensate for these possibilities.

The second type of data we used is videotape protocol data gathered in the United States from three software requirements and preliminary design meetings. Each meeting had software requirements and/or preliminary design as its primary activity, had either four or five participants, and lasted from slightly under one hour to slightly over two hours. These particular meetings were selected, in part, to span early requirements through preliminary design phases of development.

Two of the meetings were teams at Andersen Consulting (AC). One was a preliminary design meeting concerned with specifying a client-server architecture to be used by Andersen to build systems for a variety of customers. The other AC meeting, involving a different team, was concerned with detailed requirements of "reverse engineering" software which would heuristically identify and describe structure in large, old, unstructured, assembly-language programs. In the third meeting, a team at Microelectronics and Computer Corporation (MCC) was an early discussion of the requirements for a knowledge-base editor, trying to determine its basic functionality.

As one would expect, the three organizations from which the data are taken differ with respect to development methods. NTT's development process was governed by internal NTT guidelines similar to those published by IEEE (e.g., [8, 9]. These guidelines spelled out what documents must be created and what each should contain. The development style was based on Composite Design Methods and SA/SD. The Andersen Consulting projects made use of Method/1, a proprietary method with very detailed specification of required documents and deliverables. The style tended to be process-oriented, postponing consideration of data structures. Development on the MCC project was in the context of a research-oriented artificial intelligence project, and was thought to be much less structured than in the other two settings.

These two data sets complement each other. The videotape data are unfiltered and unreconstructed, and so do not suffer from those potential sources of distortion. The chief disadvantages of the videotapes are first, that we have no real way of knowing which of the questions we identify would be considered important by the software engineers themselves; and second, these are only three brief snapshots of three different projects, a sample with many potential biases. The NTT minute data compensates for these weaknesses, since it is a continuous eight month sample of questions deemed important enough to record.

Data Analysis.

As we mentioned above, our basic assumption is that the questions software engineers ask provide a good heuristic for identifying knowledge that should be preserved and made available to designers. We extracted from our data not only explicit questions, but also implicit requests for information, including statements of ignorance that were interpreted as questions. We excluded such things as rhetorical questions, questions intended as jokes, questions that were embedded in digressions and clearly bore no relationship to the task, requests for action that were worded as questions, and questions that asked for a restatement of something that was badly worded or just not heard clearly.

Once we had identified the questions, we coded them according to the following scheme.[1] First, we identified one or more **targets** for each question. A **target** is simply the thing, happening, or task that the questioner was asking about. So, for example, if a question asked about a particular component of the design, that component is a **target**. Many questions had more than one **target**.

Second, we coded each target according to the **attribute** which the question referred to. We adopted a simple classification of target attributes into **who, what, when, why,** and **how**. This turned out to be a simple, yet meaningful and comprehensive set of categories. In brief, we used the following criteria to determine the attribute: Questions about who built a target or performed a task, or about skills needed, were coded as **who**. **What** questions concerned the external behavior or function of a target, i.e., what it was or what it did, without regard to how that function was actually carried out. **How** questions focused on the particular way that a target carried out its function or the way a task was performed. For example, a question about how a user would accomplish a user task with the functionality described in a particular software requirement, would be coded **how**. Questions about deadlines and scheduling were coded as **when**. Finally, questions asking why some decision was made, or about an evaluation that was assigned or might be assigned to some alternative, or soliciting a comparison of alternatives, or arguments about alternatives were coded as **why**. If a question referred to two or more attributes of a single target, each was coded separately and is reflected in our results.

Next, we categorized the target according to the **stage** in the traditional software life cycle in which the target was (or would be) created. We used a scheme which included **requirements specification, design, implementation, testing** and **maintenance**. We used software engineering textbooks (e.g., [6] and IEEE guidelines [8, 9] to help define these stages. In general, descriptions of what the

---

[1] Additional details are available from the authors.

software system, as a whole, is supposed to do are **requirements**. **Design**, on the other hand, concerns determining the modules into which the system will be decomposed and the interfaces of these modules (preliminary design), and the ways in which their functionality is to be realized (detailed design). **Implementation** was defined just as writing and compiling statements in a programming language, and was relatively easy to identify. **Testing** was also straightforward. The date the software was released marked the beginning of the **maintenance** phase. See Table 1 for some example questions, the targets we identified from the questions, and the attributes and target creation stages.

Example Question	Target(s) for that example	Attribute(s) asked about	Stage when target would be created
What kinds of high level interfaces do we want to support?	specifications for high-level interfaces	What	Requirements
You want the user to specify either that he wants everything or a range of the diagram, right?	specification for the way a user designates part of a diagram	How	Requirements
What is the correct behavior [of a component] in [a given situation]?	behavior of a software component	What	Design
And that's [data structure] used by context management?	use of data structure	How	Design
Why should I have two tasks running simultaneously when I want to get to local data?	simultaneous tasks	Why	Design
If I [i.e., a user] have a diagram on the screen, what do I need to do to print it?	specification for printing a diagram	What & How	Requirements

Table 1. *Typical questions from Design and Requirements stages. The last question mentions both the what and the how attributes of the target. The relation between these attributes is realize, since it is asking about the way some functionality will be accomplished, or realized.*

We also wanted to see how the knowledge needs of a software design team changed over time. As mentioned above, the videotapes were selected in order to have an example of a meeting in early requirements specification, late requirements specification, and preliminary design. The minutes were taken from 38 meetings which spanned these same stages. In order to divide the questions from these meetings (to a rough approximation) into these same three stages, we simply put the questions in temporal order and divided them into thirds. In this way, we were able to look at how distributions of target and question types changed over these early project stages.

In order to establish the reliability of our coding, we independently coded the **attributes** and **target creation stages** of three samples of questions, and obtained interrater agreement rates from 68-73%. As we discussed our differences, we discovered that they were nearly always due to a failure of the person less familiar with a dataset to understand the terms or the context of the question, or to language problems in translating between Japanese and English. Upon discussion, we agreed in virtually every case. We each then coded the dataset with which we were most familiar, so we believe the agreement rates substantially underestimate the accuracy of the coding, and are acceptable for data of this type.

As mentioned earlier, many questions had more than one target. Targets were not randomly bundled in a single question, but rather the targets were generally related in some way, and the relation was an important, often the central, aspect of the question. In order to investigate these relations, we categorized them into one of five categories: 1) **evolve** is the relation between an earlier and later version of a component, 2) **task assignment** is the relation between persons and tasks they are performing, 3) **interface** is the relation between communicating components or systems, 4) **realize** is the relation between a higher-level function or behavior and the lower-level pieces which actually carry it out, and 5) **same** is a question about whether targets are identical in some way. In order to establish reliability of this coding, we separately coded a sample of questions and achieved an agreement rate of over 90%.

RESULTS
One of the most interesting and surprising findings is the extraordinary degree of similarity in our results between the two datasets. Table 2 gives the correlations between the videotape and minute data for the basic frequencies we report. This degree of similarity was quite unexpected, given the enormous differences between the projects from which the data were drawn.

Target Creation Stage Frequencies	.98
Target Attribute Frequencies	.97
Relation Frequencies	.92

Table 2. *Correlations between the basic frequencies for the two datasets.*

Target Characteristics.

In both datasets, as one would expect, targets created in the **requirements** stage were by far the most frequently asked about. (61%), and **design** was a distant second (36%). None of the other stages exceeded 1.5%. This is not terribly surprising, since the projects themselves were in the requirements and early design stages. On the other hand, it is a little surprising that targets which would be created during the later stages were almost **never** asked about.

As the projects themselves moved from early requirements into the design phase, the percentage of **requirements** targets declined linearly from 81% to 48%, while the **design** targets rose from 19% to 52% (chi-squared = 89.48, df=8, p=.0001).. The direction of change was expected, but it is significant that even well into the design stage, nearly half the targets asked about were **requirements**.

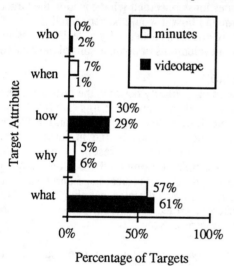

Figure 1. *Percentage of targets for which the given attributes were asked about.*

Figure 1 shows that the **what** attribute was asked about much more often than any other, with **how** also at a relatively high frequency. So the engineers asked about twice as many questions about the basic functionality or external behavior of a target as they did about the details of **how** it would work. This would certainly seem to support the notion that understanding what the software is supposed to do is a bigger problem than figuring out how to make it behave properly once "properly" is understood.

These values changed somewhat over time. **What** targets increased from 55% to 69%, while **how** declined from 39% to 25% (chi-squared = 34.96, df=8, p=.0001).. **Why** remained at a constant 6%. So **how** questions were generated most often in the requirements stage of the project, asking, for example, how a user would do X with a given set of system functions.

One of the biggest surprises here is the relatively low frequency of **why** questions. This is the sort of knowledge that design rationale notations are designed to capture, and given the very high level of interest and expected benefits from such systems, we anticipated that we might see a great many **why** questions.

Table 3 shows the most frequently occurring pairs of **attributes** and **target creation stages**. By far the most frequent is the **requirements-what** combination, with **requirements-how**, **design-what**, and **design-how** each around one-third as frequent.

	Requirements	Design
what	404 / 43%	153 / 16%
why	33 / 4%	20 / 2%
how	118 / 13%	156 / 17%

Table 3. *The frequencies / percentages of the six most frequent combinations of attributes and target creation stages (out of 940 total targets). No omitted cell contains more than 1.5% of the targets.*

Relations Between Targets.

About half (48%) of the questions in our sample had multiple targets. Nearly all of these (97%) had two targets, a few had three, and one had four. In all, nearly two-thirds (65%) of our targets appeared in multiple-target questions.

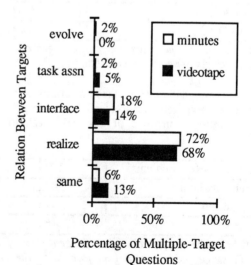

Figure 2. *Distribution of relations among targets in multiple-target questions.*

By far the most frequent relation among targets, as shown in Figure 2, was **realize**, with a significant portion of **interface** and **same**, but very few **task assignment** and **evolve** relations. Clearly, **realize** is a very broad category, including, e.g., the relation between an external behavior and software components, a module function and an algorithm, a function and OS calls, and so on. The extremely high frequency of **realize** relations is perhaps best illustrated by the fact that 30% of *all* targets in our data (278 out of 940) enter into a **realize** relation. We take this very high frequency of questions concerning the **realize** relation as an indicator of its importance, so we decided to examine the attributes of the targets that enter into this relation more closely.

In order to perform this additional analysis, we extracted only those questions which involved the **realize** relation. Disregarding the very few questions involving more than two targets, each of the two-target questions involves a pair of attributes, one for each target, e.g., what-how. Examining the frequencies of these pairings gives us an indication of the kinds of **realize** questions most often asked. It is also instructive to look at the creation stages of the targets, to see, for example, if the designers are asking most frequently about **realizing** some **requirement** in the **design**, or **realizing** a user **requirement** with given system functions.

Tables 4 and 5 show the results of these analyses. Table 4 reveals that over 90% of the questions involving the **realize** relation, targets have one of three pairs of attributes: **what-how**, **what-what**, and **how-how**. (Each of the other pairings accounts for less than 3% of the total.)

What-How	121	59%
What-What	57	28%
How-How	13	6%
All Others	13	6%

Table 4. *The frequencies and percentages of attribute pairs for targets joined by **realize** relation.*

Table 5 shows that most of these relations join targets created in the requirements stage. In particular, by far the most common occurrence of a **realize** relation is in questions

Requirements-Requirements	107	52%
Requirements-Design	47	23%
Design-Design	44	22%
All Others	6	3%

Table 5. *The frequencies and percentages of target creation stage pairs for targets joined by the **realize** relation.*

with **requirements-how** and **requirements-what** targets (33%, or 69 of 208 total questions with **realize** relations).

These questions asks about the particular ways (**how**) a user would accomplish goals using some particular function of the system under design (**what**). For example, "How would you [i.e., a user] use it [some functionality to be provided by the system]?" These data clearly show that user scenarios are a frequently asked about type of information in software design.

Summary of results.

• Different types of data from software design meetings in different corporations and even different countries showed an astonishing degree of similarity in the frequency with which different types of questions were asked.

• Most questions in our sample of software design meetings concerned the **requirements**. In particular, developers tended to ask questions about **what** the **requirements** are, and this continued to be the most frequent sort of question as the project progressed from early requirements definition through preliminary design.

• User scenarios were frequently asked about. This is shown both by the significant overall percentage of **requirements-how** targets, and by the high proportion of multi-target questions which ask how a user will make use of some particular functionality of the system.

• Most questions concerned **what** function the target was to perform and **how** it would be performed.

• Very few questions asked **why** a decision was made, or solicited evaluations or comparisons of alternatives.

DISCUSSION

This degree of similarity between the questions taken from the minutes of design meetings at NTT and from videotaped design meetings at AC and MCC is quite startling. The questions in the minutes were filtered through a scribe, and represent an extended and continuous sample of a single subgroup on a single project. The videotaped data is unfiltered and unreconstructed, and is taken from three unrelated meetings. The data come from different projects, different corporations, and even different countries.

This similarity is important for two reasons. First, it greatly strengthens the findings. Any single data set is subject to many biases, and may be atypical with regard to software design in general. But similar results with widely different kinds of data suggest that the findings have considerable generality. Second, we think it is very important to establish a baseline against which questions from meetings supported with different sorts of tools, or using different methods, can be compared. The uniformity in our results gives us considerable confidence that they will be useful for this purpose.

As we mentioned earlier, a result that was particularly unexpected is the low frequency of **why** questions. There are several possible explanations for this finding. One is that the kind of information elicited by **why** questions, i.e., the rationale behind decisions, is simply relatively unimportant.. This certainly runs counter to the intuitions of many individuals experienced in software development, but it is not ruled out by our data. A variation on this theme is that this information is simply *perceived* to be unimportant, and perhaps even actively avoided by designers wishing to escape the overhead of becoming domain experts. A second possibility is that **why** questions and the information they elicit are very important, but they are relatively unlikely to arise in meetings as compared with other settings in which design work is done. One plausible line of reasoning is that in meetings, the context, as well as the content, is generally clear to all the participants. **Why** questions may often be used to establish this context when it is unclear. A third possibility is that the information that could be directly elicited with a **why** question is often elicited with **how** or **what** questions. If one knows enough about the possible rationales behind a decision, one may be able to infer the correct rationale by using clues obtained in this indirect way. If this turns out to be the case, it suggests that there is considerable overlap between design rationale tools (focusing on **why** questions) and other design tools which focus on creating the design itself. In other words, a good representation of the **what** and **how** of the design may enable one to infer many of the **why**s Finally, it may be that **why** questions are seldom asked in meetings because the participants realize that they cannot generally be answered in current practice, with current tools. This interpretation, of course, suggests that representations of design spaces or histories would often be consulted if available.

One suggestion concerning the **why** questions that we find somewhat less plausible than the ones just discussed is that although **why** questions are low in frequency, they are more important than other kinds of questions. Our skepticism stems from the observation that the percentage of **why** questions is nearly identical in the minutes and the videotapes. If the **why** questions tended to be more important than the other types of questions, one would expect to see them represented more often in the minutes, since the questions recorded there have been filtered by a scribe and selected for their importance. The nearly identical frequencies imply that the **why** questions in our sample were not more important than the other questions, at least as importance was judged by the scribes.

In any case, it is clear that more research is needed to sort out all of these importantly different possibilities. Given the extremely high level of interest in design rationale notations and tools, it is critical to begin to look at how, when, and in what settings such representations might be most useful. Without such research, there is a grave risk of building tools that provide the answers to the wrong questions.

The fact that the **requirements** are very often asked about supports those who have suggested that particular attention

should be paid to tools, methods, and notations for this part of the software life cycle, e.g., [4, 5]. The most frequent single type of target asked about (43% of all targets) is simply **what** the system is supposed to do, i.e., **what** the **requirements** are.

The data also strongly suggest that the scenario of use is an extremely important type of information (see, e.g., [11]). What makes this finding particularly significant is that with only a few exceptions that we are aware of (e.g., [10]), software design methods and notations do not provide rich facilities for representing user scenarios. Data-flow diagrams, for a typical example, represent users as a simple node, a "terminator" (see, e.g., [22] pp. 64-73), which functions as a source and a destination for flows of data. There is typically no simple way to represent expected sets of interactions with users. We suggest that this is a relatively neglected area of potentially great importance. In the area of user interface design, there are a number of notations which can be used for expressing scenarios of use (e.g., GOMS [2] and UAN [21]). Although for questions that arise in upstream software design, these notations are often too fine-grained, but extensions or analogs might be very useful.

The high frequency of questions about **realize** relations also suggests that notations and tools for design should optimize for retrieval and display of this relation and the objects (or components or functions, etc.) that enter into **realize** relations. This property is often called *traceability*, and the high frequency of **realize** relations supports those who stress its importance.

ACKNOWLEDGMENTS
This work has been supported by the National Science Foundation (Grant No. IRI-8902930), and by the Center for Strategic Technology Research (CSTaR) at Andersen Consulting, and by a grant from the Center for Japanese Studies at the University of Michigan. We would particularly like to thank Libby Mack, Nancy Pennington, Barbara Smith, and Bill Curtis for their help in the collection and analysis of the data. We also wish to acknowledge the important contribution of the researchers at NTT Software Laboratories who made data available to us. We would also like to thank Kevin Crowston, Michael Knister, Gary M. Olson, Judith S. Olson, and Atul Prakash for their valuable comments and suggestions.

REFERENCES
1.   Brooks, F.P., *No silver bullet*. IEEE Computer, 1987. **20**: p. 10-19.

2.   Card, S.K., T.P. Moran, and A. Newell, *The psychology of human-computer interaction.* 1983, Hillsdale, NJ: Erlbaum.

3.   Conklin, E.J. and K.C.B. Yakemovic, *A process-oriented approach to design rationale*. Human-Computer Interaction, 1991. **6**: p. 357-391.

4.   Curtis, B., H. Krasner, and N. Iscoe, *A field study of the software design process for large systems.* Communications of the ACM., 1988. **31**: p. 1268-1287.

5.   Davis, A.M., *Software requirements: Analysis and specification.* 1990, Englewood Cliffs, NJ: Prentice Hall.

6.   Ghezzi, C., M. Jazayeri, and D. Mandrioli, *Fundamentals of software engineering.* 1991, Englewood Cliffs, NJ: Prentice Hall.

7.   Guindon, R., *Knowledge exploited by experts during software system design.* International Journal of Man-Machine Studies, 1990. **33**: p. 279-304.

8.   IEEE. *Guide for software requirements specifications*, 1984, Std 830-1984.

9.   IEEE *Recommended practice for software design descriptions*, 1987, Std 1016-1987.

10.   Jacobson, I., *Object-oriented software engineering.* 1992, Reading, MA: Addison-Wesley.

11.   Karat, J. and J.L. Bennett, *Using scenarios in design meetings -- a case study example*, in *Taking software design seriously*, J. Karat, Editor. 1991, Harcourt Brace Jovanovich: Boston. p. 63-94.

12.   Karat, J. and J.L. Bennett, *Working within the design process: Supporting effetive and efficient design*, in *Designing interaction: Psychology at the human-computer interface*, J.M. Carroll, Editor. 1991, Cambridge University Press: New York. p. 269-285.

13.   Kuwana, E. and J.D. Herbsleb. *Representing knowledge in requirements engineering: An empirical study of what software engineers need to know.* in *IEEE International Symposium on Requirements Engineering.* 1993.

14.   Lee, J. *SIBYL: A tool for managing group design.* in *CSCW '90.* 1990. Los Angeles:

15.   Lee, J. and K.-Y. Lai, *What's in design rationale.* Human-Computer Interaction, 1991. **6**: p. 251-280.

16.   MacLean, A., *et al.*, *Questions, options, and criteria: Elements of design space analysis.* Human-Computer Interaction, 1991. **6**: p. 201-250.

17.   Moran, T. and J. Carroll, ed. *Design Rationale.* in press.

18.   Muller, M.J. *Retrospective on a year of participatory design using the PICTIVE technique.* in *CHI '92.* 1992.

19.   Nakajo, T. and H. Kume, *A case history analysis of software error cause-effect relationships.* IEEE Transactions on Software Engineering, 1991. **17**: p. 830-837.

20.   Potts, C., *Supporting software design: Integrating design processes, design methods, and design rationale*, in *Design Rationale*, T. Moran and J. Carroll, Editor. in press,

21.   Siochi, A.C., D. Hix, and H.R. Hartson, *The UAN: A notation to support user-centered design of direct manipulation interfaces*, in *Taking software design seriously: Practical techniques for human-computer interaction design*, J. Karat, Editor. 1991, Academic Press: Boston. p. 157-194.

22.   Yourdon, E., *Modern structured analysis.* 1989, Englewood Cliffs, NJ: Yourdon Press.

From "Folklore" To "Living Design Memory"

Loren G. Terveen
600 Mountain Avenue
AT&T Bell Laboratories
Murray Hill, NJ 07974
(908) 582-2608
terveen@research.att.com

Peter G. Selfridge
600 Mountain Avenue
AT&T Bell Laboratories
Murray Hill, NJ 07974
(908) 582-6801
pgs@research.att.com

M. David Long
2000 N. Naperville Road
AT&T Bell Laboratories
Naperville, IL. 60566
(708) 979-5648
mdlong@ihlpb.att.com

ABSTRACT

We identify an important type of software design knowledge that we call *community specific folklore* and show problems with current approaches to managing it. We built a tool that serves as a *living design memory* for a large software development organization. The tool delivers knowledge to developers effectively and is embedded in organizational practice to ensure that the knowledge it contains evolves as necessary. This work illustrates important lessons in building knowledge management systems, integrating novel technology into organizational practice, and managing research-development partnerships.

KEYWORDS: organizational interfaces, organizational design, knowledge representation, software productivity

INTRODUCTION

Developing and maintaining large software systems is notoriously difficult and expensive. Several factors contribute to this situation. Software development is a new discipline; this leads to rapid change in languages, tools, and methodologies. Relatively simple software constructs and components can be composed to build large systems; this leads to systems that perform very complex tasks, are built by many people, and are beyond the understanding of any single person. Software is a highly malleable medium; this raises the possibility of change, and market pressures ensure the necessity of change.

A crucial implication of this picture is that the knowledge required for effective software development is vast, complex, heterogeneous, and evolving. Much of the knowledge required to be a successful developer in a particular organization is *community specific*, concerning the application domain, the existing software base, and local programming conventions. This knowledge typically has the status of *folklore*, in that it is informally maintained and disseminated by experienced developers. This process is (1) ineffective – not everyone gets the knowledge they need, (2) inefficient – communication of knowledge, whether in formal meetings or informal consulting, comes to take up

more and more time, and (3) fragile – loss of key personnel can mean loss of critical knowledge.

We addressed the problem of managing design knowledge in a software development organization in AT&T. The goal of our work was to construct a system for recording and effectively disseminating "folklore" design knowledge throughout the organization. We aimed to improve both the software product and the software development process. We describe this type of system as a *living design memory*. The term "living" emphasizes that the system must be embedded in the organization's normal design process, in particular, that it must evolve in response to problems detected with it or changes in the knowledge situation of the organization. We constructed a system according to these guidelines and deployed the tool in the organization.

We have learned important lessons from this work, starting with technical issues involved in developing a system for managing design knowledge (see [22] for details). Here we emphasize more general lessons that concern embedding any technical solution in organizational practice and carrying out a successful research-development partnership. The two most important lessons are:

- knowledge of *facts* is not enough; it also is necessary to know *how the knowledge is be used* – where in the process it fits, how to access only relevant knowledge, and how to allow for change;
- the members of the community in which a system is to be deployed must *own* the system – they must be able to use it effectively and modify it when necessary; this leads us to reject the metaphor of "technology transfer" in favor of "knowledge communication" as an appropriate paradigm for a research-development partnership.

The focus of this paper is to elaborate the context in which these lessons were learned. We first explore the knowledge management problem in more detail and discuss challenges to acquiring, maintaining, and disseminating design knowledge. We then describe a framework for integrating a design memory tool into an existing software development process, making it living. We next present the implemented tool that instantiates the framework. We emphasize how the tool evolved in response to the expectations of the user community and the shifting of "ownership" from the research members of the team to the developers. We conclude by comparing our work to other approaches, bringing out unique characteristics of our work through the comparison, and describing areas for future work.

THE KNOWLEDGE MANAGEMENT PROBLEM IN LARGE SCALE SOFTWARE DEVELOPMENT

The work described here was a collaboration between AT&T research (represented by the first two authors, LGT and PGS) and a large AT&T software development organization (represented by the third author, MDL). The collaboration was initiated to address problems in managing design knowledge in the development organization, which consists of several thousand people who maintain and enhance a large telecommunications software system. It is important to realize that software development in this organization never begins "from scratch"; it always involves enhancing or repairing an existing, deployed software system.

Our work has focused on the design process. This process starts with a specification document, originating from either a customer request or an internal source. The specification document describes a new feature of the software in customer (behavioral) terms. This document is used by a software developer to produce a design document, which describes how that new feature will be implemented and added to the existing software architecture. This design document then is formally reviewed by a committee of experts. If necessary, feedback is incorporated into the design and the process iterates. Once the design document is complete and approved, it is passed to a coding phase. This process is shown in figure 1.

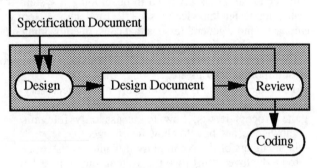

Figure 1: The Design Process

One major problem in the design process is the lack of accessible general design knowledge. This knowledge involves such things as *real-time and performance constraints* ("one real-time segment shouldn't take more than 200 milliseconds or overall performance will suffer"), *properties of the current implementation* ("the terminating Terminal process is already close to its memory limitation, so you can't add much to it"), *impact of design decisions on other aspects of the software* ("if you modify the Automatic Testing process, you'll need to update the customer documentation"), *local programming conventions* ("call the central error reporting mechanism if your function get a bad message"), and *personnel and organization* ("ask Nancy about that; she knows about local stack space"). This kind of knowledge usually is not written down, rather, it is part

of the community specific folklore that is maintained and disseminated by experienced individuals in the organization. This form of knowledge maintenance and dissemination is unsatisfactory. First, not only are experts difficult to locate when needed, but individuals must know who the expert is for their particular problems. Studies in this organization have shown that successful developers are those who have effective "expertise networks" and thus know who to ask about particular problems. Second, experts can spend more time disseminating knowledge than solving problems relevant to their jobs. Third, knowledge often is generated (e.g., in design, review, testing, fault analysis) only to be lost, thus depriving the organization of a valuable resource and leading to potential duplication of effort in the future. Finally, since key knowledge often is only known to a few individuals, loss of personnel can mean loss of knowledge. Failure to manage design knowledge effectively can result in sub-optimal designs, late and costly detection of errors, long delivery times, and personal frustration.

AT&T has been trying to improve its software development productivity for some time. A major emphasis has been to institute various quality initiatives aimed at formalizing the process to make it measurable, repeatable, and more easily managed [6]. As in the design process shown in figure 1, sequences of steps have been defined, suppliers and customers identified, and inputs and outputs specified. Any solution to the problem of managing design knowledge will be deployed in the context of the existing design process.

The organization tried to address the problem of managing design knowledge by documenting as much knowledge as possible in structured text files. Even if all relevant facts could be captured in this manner, this approach still is inadequate for three reasons:

- The documents are not *organized for efficient access* – without adequate indexing, the resulting information base is simply too large to be very useful (busy people, including software developers, will not read large documents that are not immediately relevant to their current task).
- There is no way to ensure *compliance* – that is, it is impossible to be sure that developers and reviewers have consulted all the information that is relevant for a particular design problem.
- There is no natural way to ensure *evolution* of the documents – documents will be incomplete and incorrect, and the programming constructs, requirements, constraints, and methodologies they describe all will change over time.

From our perspective, the crux of the problem is that the on-line documents are not a *living* design memory. They are not well integrated into organizational practice and do not address how knowledge is to be used and changed. For a design memory tool to be adequate, developers must use the tool consistently and at appropriate points in the development process. Then they have to incorporate knowledge from the tool into their designs (the fundamental purpose of the tool is to produce *better* software designs).

In addition, there should be an organizational method for encouraging tool use and checking whether the tool was used and the advice followed. Finally, exceptions and modifications to the advice need to be captured, both for maintenance and to assure credibility with the developers. The maintenance issue is critical: improperly maintained knowledge will, rightfully, go the way of improperly maintained documentation.

A FRAMEWORK FOR LIVING DESIGN MEMORY

We have developed a framework for integrating a design memory tool into a software development process that addresses the above requirements. The framework is based on two components. First, a *design knowledge base* records relevant information. Second, a *Designer Assistant* program provides access to the knowledge base, following the general paradigm of interactive assistance for software development [21]. Our framework assumes the Designer Assistant augments the existing development process. This process uses *informal* design artifacts, i.e., text documents. Therefore, the Designer Assistant provides textual advice to developers, and it is their responsibility to incorporate the advice into their designs or explain why the advice does not apply to their designs. Attempts to formalize design artifacts through the use of knowledge-based tools [1, 16, 19, 20] are complementary to our approach.

However, this framework is flawed; it would be adequate only if all relevant design knowledge could be captured completely, once and for all. This clearly is an unlikely and unrealistic assumption. As Clancey states particularly well [5], a knowledge base is always subject to additional refinement and re-interpretation. More important, the world changes: the software base changes (indeed, this is the goal of the design activity), the hardware and software technology changes, protocols and conventions change, customer requirements change, faults are observed in the running software, and all the other assumptions and constraints are subject to continual, if slow, evolution. This places some additional requirements on our framework, in particular, that it support (1) the elaboration and evolution of design knowledge as the tool is used and evaluated; and (2) the addition of new knowledge generated during design activities.

To support the first requirement, we record a trace of user interactions with the Designer Assistant and annotate the Design Document with this trace. This allows those aspects of the design that were influenced by the advice to be traced during design review. In addition, we modify the review process slightly to make the *advice itself an object of review*. To support the second requirement, note that the problem is not to *produce* new knowledge, but rather to ensure the new knowledge already generated during normal development activities is *captured* in the knowledge base. We do this in three ways. First, the Designer Assistant elicits comments from developers concerning revisions or additions they think should be made to the knowledge base. Second, when a fault is observed in the running software system, and analysis shows that it was due to a design error, a report detailing the problem and its solution is generated to be encoded in the knowledge base. Finally, we add a knowledge base maintenance activity to the design process. This activity takes as input information to be added to the knowledge base, in particular, fault reports and the annotated design document and reviewer comments; it produces changes or updates to the design knowledge base as necessary. Figure 2 shows the complete framework.

To summarize the framework, the design knowledge base contains information relevant to design tasks in the application domain. As developers design, the Designer Assistant program helps them to access relevant knowledge. The result of the design process includes the design document, feedback from the developer about updates to the design knowledge base, and a trace of the interactions of the developer with the Designer Assistant. At the review, reviewers examine the design and identify issues, some of which result from the advice of the design assistant. Such issues lead to (proposals for) modifications of the design knowledge base. Other issues lead to (proposals for) addition of new knowledge to the knowledge base. All pro-

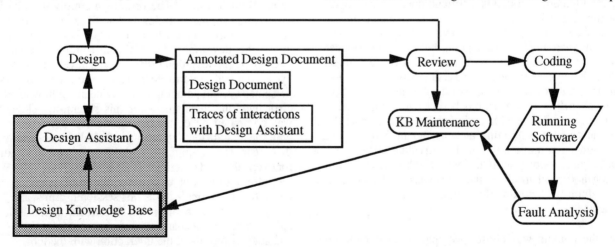

Figure 2: The Living Design Memory Framework

posals for updates to the knowledge base that are generated during design, review, or fault analysis are collected and sent to a knowledge base maintainer. The knowledge base maintainer then updates the knowledge base. The Designer Assistant is embedded in organizational practice so that it evolves in response both to shortcomings in its own knowledge and to changes in the external situation.

EVOLVING A DESIGN MEMORY TOOL

We developed a design memory tool within our framework that contains significant "folklore" knowledge in the telecommunications software domain. The knowledge has been acquired by engineering several domains and analyzing several fault reports. The tool works by leading developers through a dialogue concerning characteristics of their design, then providing advice based on the answers. The tool is integrated into the development process, and all levels of the organization, from high-level management to developers, view the tool favorably. Work continues on engineering new domains. We focus here on tracing the evolution of the tool, emphasizing that making the tool successful involved a process of *transfer of ownership* to the development organization.

Constructing a Prototype

We first identified a design knowledge sub-domain in which to construct a prototype. We selected an error handling mechanism that is critical to the system's fault-tolerance. This mechanism is used if the code being designed reaches an illegal state. The mechanism is implemented as a macro call with a number of arguments that have various effects on the system. For example, one value of one argument initializes the processor that is running the current process. Other arguments cause the dumping of different kinds of data needed to diagnose the problem or schedule a data-checking audit. Thus, when developers decide to use this error mechanism, they have to make a series of decisions about exactly how to invoke it. Some of these decisions are quite complicated and interact in various ways.

This domain, while limited, still has the following important features. First, it is a difficult domain: developers typically do not know when to use the mechanism, how to use it, or even how to find out about it. This is especially true of novices in the organization, but even experienced developers commonly misuse the construct (in fact, many of the existing uses in the code base are incorrect). Second, there are local experts who have extensive knowledge about this mechanism. However, this knowledge is managed as folklore, as we described it earlier: experts disseminate this information in a frustrating and inefficient manner, i.e., one-to-one communication with individual developers. Finally, discussions with developers showed that this domain is typical in all of these respects, and that many other domains within the organization share these problems.

Once the domain was chosen we spent dozens of hours interviewing several domain experts about the knowledge

needed to use this mechanism and studying the existing written documentation. We took a set of examples of the mechanism in the current code base and asked the experts to categorize the examples in terms of *design attributes*, the features of a design that all the uses of the mechanism in each category responded to. This was a very important abstraction step because it meant that the tool interaction could use terms that are familiar to developers, rather than refer to syntactic features of the construct. Presumably developers won't be familiar with the latter vocabulary, since it is precisely this they are getting help about.

After several iterations, the experts succeeded in generating a small number of design attributes with almost complete domain coverage. Each attribute could be expressed as a yes/no question, e.g., "Does your design update data in the Database?". Attributes could be arranged in a generalization hierarchy, with more general attributes subsuming more specific attributes. Thus, under the previous question might be the additional question "Is it possible for dynamic and static data to become de-synchronized?". Then, for each design attribute, we elicited from the domain experts advice about how to use the error handling mechanism in this situation. Some advice might apply only to very specific design situations (the leaf nodes in the attribute hierarchy), while other advice could apply to more general situations (interior nodes). The advice was distilled into small units of text that we call *advice items*. Indexing by design attribute has proved to be a very useful way of acquiring and organizing knowledge in this and other domains. (See [22] for details about the representation of design attributes and advice items.)

The next task was to construct a prototype design memory tool. To do so, we had to represent the information we had acquired and construct an interface to allow developers to access the information. We used the language CLASSIC [3,4] to represent the information. We then developed a simple dialogue-based interface. Because of the wide variety of terminals used within the target organization, the tool had to be ASCII-based, independent of any specific window or platform features. The prototype simply used basic C input and output routines. The interaction basically consisted of the tool asking a developer yes/no questions to guide the developer down the attribute hierarchy (an interactive classification task); when a developer responded "yes" to a leaf node in the attribute hierarchy, the system presented several paragraphs of advice about how to use the error handling mechanism for this situation. The advice was computed by collecting the advice items associated with the leaf attribute description and all generalizations of that attribute description (in addition, several mechanisms for overriding and ordering advice were applied [22]). When the interaction was complete, the tool asked several evaluation questions – "Was this session useful?" and "Was the level of detail about right, too much, or too little?" – and gave the user a chance to enter more detailed comments and suggestions about the interaction with the tool.

The output of the tool is a script of the interaction. The script is added to the formal design document for two reasons. First, the advice becomes part of the document and gets reviewed during the formal review process. The reviewers have a chance to verify that software developers did receive information relevant to their design situation and either followed the advice of the tool or determined that their situation was an exception to the situation anticipated by the tool – in such cases, the exception itself is worth noting, discussing and acquiring. Second, the advice itself can be reviewed, and changes and modifications can be directed to the maintenance process illustrated in figure 2.

From Prototype to Deployed Tool

We next carried out informal user tests on the prototype. We created a realistic software design problem and asked half a dozen developers to write a section of design involving the error handling mechanism. They used the tool to get advice on how to do so. Their reaction was highly favorable; in some cases, it was asserted that the 20 minutes spent using the tool saved from 4 to 8 hours of their time! The reason for this is that the only other way to find out the knowledge presented by the tool would have been to track down the local experts or search through large documents, both notoriously time-consuming activities.

Considering these results to be very positive, we deployed the Designer Assistant in the design process. That is, the formal process definition was modified to include the steps "run the Designer Assistant and append the resulting transcript to your Design Document." We sent email to all the developers in the organization announcing the availability of the tool. Within 15 days, more than 85 developers had used the DA. Their feedback was unexpectedly negative. Only 38% judged the interaction "useful" and 58% said the level of detail was "too little". These rating and detailed comments from the users indicated that the DA had two major problems. First, developers would not consider it useful until it had more knowledge – it was more trouble than it was worth to run a tool that contained information about just one small domain. Second, the interface did not match user expectations, e.g., it gave no guidance in entering legal answers, and the overall structure of the dialogue was unclear.

Thus far in the project, the research members of our team, LGT and PGS, had designed and implemented the prototype. However, responsibility for the tool now was shifting to MDL. He was faced with the two problems of improving the interface and adding more knowledge. To do so, he took a major step, re-implementing the Designer Assistant in an internal AT&T system development environment, the Data Collection System (DCS). DCS is a tool for constructing screen-based, menu-driven interfaces. DCS provided much useful functionality, including input type checking, ability to revisit and re-answer any previous question, text and cursor-based menus, automatic recording of user responses, and output of a transcript in a convenient database format, so it solved many of the user complaints. The re-implementation illustrates several interesting points:

(1) MDL now "owned" the re-implemented Designer Assistant – it was a facile tool for him. This meant that he could modify or add knowledge easily.

(2) DCS was a known resource in the repertoire of the developers but not the researchers. Once the researchers moved out of their world of workstations and X Windows, their knowledge of system development environments was limited. We learned that making a new tool meet user expectations is facilitated by exploiting the system development environments available in the target user community. More generally, this highlighted for us that a research-development partnership involves *mutual learning* [14], and that the type of learning required may be impossible to anticipate.

(3) Changing the underlying technology from CLASSIC to DCS involved some tradeoffs. Gains in ease of interaction and ownership by MDL came at the expense of great loss of representational power. However, where the CLASSIC prototype focused on elegant representation and efficient computation of advice, experience showed that it was much more important to be able to manage structured hierarchical dialogues effectively, and DCS was much better at this. This illustrates another general lesson. Any design project inevitably involves tradeoffs. Those members of the design team who actually implement the design have great influence in deciding how the tradeoffs are resolved [9]. Research and development members of a joint design team might well judge how to resolve particular tradeoffs differently. Thus, tradeoffs that have not been articulated and discussed may well become the occasion for re-design or re-implementation as ownership of a system shifts from researchers to developers.

(4) The re-implementation shed new light on what had been accomplished thus far in the project. We came to see the CLASSIC prototype as a "running specification" of the behavior for an adequate tool. In a new partnership undertaken by LGT and PGS, all parties have agreed up front that this is what the researchers will produce.

When the re-implemented Designer Assistant was deployed, complaints about the interface ended. However, user feedback was only marginally more positive. Of 67 users who provided feedback, 42% rated the interaction "useful", and 46% now said the level of detail was "about right". More knowledge still had to be added before a majority of developers would consider the tool useful.

Since then, much new knowledge has been added, including one large domain – impacts of design decisions on customer documentation – and several smaller domains. In addition, rules derived from analysis of several fault reports have been encoded. The knowledge can be divided into three categories, (1) *expert knowledge* – like the error handling mechanism, specialized areas of design knowledge that most designers are not familiar with, (2) *impact knowledge* – how characteristics of a design impact another area of the software, and (3) *fault prevention knowledge* – how characteristics of a design could lead to a fault, and how the fault can be avoided. To facilitate adding knowledge, MDL designed a simple rule language tailored for representing hierarchies of design attributes and a compiler that produces DCS code from the rules. The Designer Assistant now contains more than 250 rules. The ongoing process of knowledge acquisition has shown that one of the most useful results of the project has been the principle of organizing knowledge in terms of questions that index from characteristics of a design situation (that are familiar to developers) to advice about a particular domain (e.g., use of the error handling construct, impact on customer documentation, necessary changes to the database). This heuristic is useful for acquiring domain knowledge from experts, organizing the knowledge, and providing efficient access to the knowledge.

User satisfaction with the current version of the Designer Assistant is significantly higher. Since it has been deployed, 354 developers have used the system and 256 have provided feedback. Of those who provided feedback, 61% judged the interaction "useful" and 63% said the level of detail was "about right". Table 1 summarizes user judgements of the three versions of the Designer Assistant that have been in use.

metric	Classic	DCS 1	DCS 2
number of users	≥ 85	95	354
users giving feedback	85	67	256
% judging "useful"	38	42	61
% judging "about right"	41	46	63

Table 1: Usage statistics for the Designer Assistant

User evaluation of the current tool is positive, but not highly so. However, the development organization considers the Designer Assistant to be very successful since it does record knowledge that previously was available only as informal folklore or in inefficient documents. Developers are using the system on a daily basis and are able to access information effectively. Further, it is clear that what is required to increase user satisfaction is still more knowledge, and progress on this front is very good. Several additional domains and fault analyses are ready to be encoded. The knowledge base should grow by 50% within the next few months. Finally, there is managerial commitment to the Designer Assistant approach to managing design knowledge and to providing the resources necessary to increase its effectiveness. We discuss additional ways of evaluating the success of the Designer Assistant in the next section.

To summarize, the research members of our team constructed a prototype Designer Assistant that served the role of a "running specification." Ownership of the prototype was transferred to the development organization, with successful transfer requiring a re-implementation. A knowledge acquisition and organization heuristic (indexing by design attribute) developed in building the prototype has proved extremely useful in ongoing knowledge engineering.

DISCUSSION

We next compare our living design memory approach to other related work, bringing out important characteristics of our framework by contrast. First, AI and expert systems work also is aimed at capturing knowledge in particular domains. These systems contain a knowledge base and a reasoning component that computes the desired inferences, e.g., relating patient symptoms to disease classifications [23] or customer computer orders to a configuration diagram [18]. Expert systems typically are intended to *automate* a task, i.e., to perform *like an expert* in their domain. Expert systems work to the extent that knowledge in a domain can be completely formalized; this requires both articulating the knowledge precisely and encoding it in a format that allows the system to compute the proper inferences. This type of approach applied to software design might involve deriving a program from some (formal or informal) specification of a problem to be solved.

However, we see limits on the applicability of the formalization that expert systems require. First, various researchers have advanced strong theoretical arguments that many domains cannot be completely formalized and that AI-style knowledge bases are inherently incomplete [5, 24, 26]. Second, attempts to construct automated software design systems [2] have proved unsuccessful, leading the field to shift its emphasis to assisting people in designing software (e.g., the annual Knowledge-Based Software Engineering Conference; this trend also appears in AI approaches to design in general, e.g., the annual International Conference on AI in Design). Our work is part of this trend. Our experience has shown the effectiveness of giving software designers efficient access to relatively informal information, like "ask Nancy; she knows about local stack space." This sort of information helps to reduce the high communications overhead in large organizations by making some information available through the Designer Assistant and guiding developers directly to the relevant expert when additional communication is required. We also have addressed not just acquiring factual knowledge, but also how the knowledge is to be used – for example, at what point in the process it should be consulted, how it should be indexed for efficient access, and when and how it should evolve. Thus, our focus is on helping a software development organization manage its knowledge effectively, rather than automating parts of the software development process.

Second, there has been previous work that has called for a design memory (10, 19) and even suggested that a design memory must evolve over time. However, this work has used formal representations of design artifacts and components, e.g., code modules. Much power is gained from this formal representation, e.g., a design assistant system can help in fitting new designs into a library of existing designs, acquiring and organizing the rationale for designs, and can use rules to evaluate designs, judge trade-offs, etc.

We view this work as complementary to ours (in fact, we have done similar work in the past [25]). However, there are several differences. First, in the development organization we have worked with, design artifacts are English documents; thus, an approach that required a formal representation of design artifacts was not possible immediately. However, we see this as a promising area of future work, and our success to date increases the likelihood that this more radical innovation will be considered. Next, the "folklore" knowledge we have captured is a much broader class of knowledge than these systems have handled, and we deliver it in different ways. Finally, we go beyond these approaches to focus on how *any* design memory must be integrated into organizational processes – we view the design memory and organizational processes as mutual resources that must be co-designed to ensure a *living* design memory. In particular, while previous proposals for supporting evolution have focused on the *individual* designer, in our approach, knowledge evolution is a formal organizational process – it is neither fully automated nor is it left up to individual designers. There are a number of reasons for this, chiefly that it is been our experience that systems must have "owners" (in our case, the knowledge maintenance group), since if no one is responsible for the integrity of a system, it decays rapidly over time.

Third, work on design rationale [1, 7, 11, 12, 17, 20] also is relevant. Design rationale captures the reasons behind the design, including issues that were considered, alternative resolutions of these issues, and arguments for and against the different resolutions. Many approaches to capturing and using design rationale exist, ranging from very formal AI-type representations [12, 20] to relatively informal text or hypertext representations [7]. Work reported by Conklin and Yakemovic [7] in applying the IBIS [17] methodology to a software development project is most relevant to the concerns of this paper. They developed a simple textual form of IBIS that was suitable for use on the technology of the development organization with which they were working. The development project successfully used this method to record and consult information relevant to their evolving design. One important reason why the IBIS technology was effective was that it incrementally improved an existing task (that is, participants in a design project already kept track of relevant information with handwritten notes) instead of creating a whole new task. The new technology offered some payoff with minimal cost of adoption and disruption of existing organizational practice.

We addressed the same general issue, how to develop a system for managing design knowledge that could be integrated into existing organizational practice. However, the "folklore" knowledge we were concerned with is more general than design rationale, and it must be used and modified not primarily in one design project, but over time in many projects in the AT&T development organization. We focused not just on integrating the Designer Assistant program into existing *practice*, but also into existing organizational *processes*, modifying these processes as necessary. Specifically, we instituted knowledge review and maintenance processes to ensure the evolution of the knowledge. We also share Conklin and Yakemovic's commitment to cost-benefit analysis [15] concerning the adoption of new technology. The Designer Assistant is quick and easy for developers to use – no training is required, and the average session lasts about 10 minutes – and it offers substantial benefits, e.g., they do not have to read long documents, waiting time is reduced, review meetings can be smaller, thus scheduled more quickly, and reviewers can be satisfied more easily. Domain experts have a larger burden, since they are asked to cooperate with the knowledge maintenance group to encode their domains. However, we have found that experts are eager to do so because it reduces the amount of time they have to spend on consulting and lets them accomplish other work, and it helps to ensure that design rules they think are important are communicated throughout the development community.

Finally, our framework responds to many of the points made by Curtis, Krasner, and Iscoe [8] in their discussion of large software development projects. They state that software development must be seen as a learning and communication process. They recommend that software development tools facilitate the enterprise wide sharing of knowledge, accommodate change as a normal and expected process, and serve as mediums of communication for integrating people and information. We identified a particular type of knowledge to be managed, developed a tool for managing and a heuristic for acquiring it, and constructed a framework for integrating the tool into the software development process.

We conclude by discussing areas for future work. First, we will continue to encode new knowledge in the Designer Assistant. Thus far, indexing by design attributes has proved effective; however, we are looking for types of knowledge that cannot be coded adequately in this way. Second, we will do more evaluation of the system. We will track the metric *number of faults per line of source code due to the design process*. As the Designer Assistant contains more and more knowledge, including knowledge of past design faults, we expect this number to decrease by at least 25%. We will examine feedback from developers who have used the system and interview individual developers to identify "success stories" of the form "I would have made the following design error if not for advice from the Designer Assistant..." Third, we will improve the knowledge maintenance process by defining the process more precisely and by developing a tool to assist knowledge maintainers in updating the design knowledge base. We postponed work on such a tool until we gained experience with how the process of updating the knowledge base was working in practice. We now can begin to state requirements for this tool. Finally, several other organizations within AT&T are very interested in using the Designer Assistant tool and methodology to manage their knowledge, and we have begun working with them to enable them to do so.

REFERENCES

1. Bailin, S.C., Moore, J.M., Bentz, R., & Bewtra, M. 1990. KAPTUR: Knowledge Acquisition for Preservation of Tradeoffs and Underlying Rationale. *Proc. 5th Annual Knowledge-Based Software Assistant Conference.* (Syracuse, NY, Sept. 1990), pp. 95-104.

2. Barstow, D.R. 1979. An Experiment in Knowledge-Based Automatic Programming. *Artificial Intelligence.* 12(2): 73-119.

3. Borgida, A., Brachman, R.J., McGuinness, D.L, & Resnick, L.A. 1989. CLASSIC: A Structural Data Model for Objects. *Proc. ACM SIGMOD Int'l. Conf. on Management of Data.*

4. Brachman, R.J., McGuinness, D.L., Patel-Schneider, P.F., Resnick, L.A., & Borgida, A. 1990. Living with CLASSIC: When and How to Use a KL-ONE-Like Language, in Sowa, J., Ed. *Formal Aspects of Semantic Networks.* Morgan Kauffman.

5. Clancey, W. 1991. The Frame of Reference Problem in the Design of Intelligent Machines. In vanLehn, K., Ed. *Architectures for Intelligence: The Twenty-Second Carnegie Symposium on Cognition.* Hillsdale, NJ: Lawrence Erlbaum Associates.

6. Colson, J.S. & Prell, E.M. 1992. Total Quality Management for a Large Software Project. *AT&T Technical Journal.* 71(3): 48-56.

7. Conklin, E.J. & Burgess Yakemovic, KC. 1991. A Process-Oriented Approach to Design Rationale. *Human-Computer Interaction.* 6 (3-4): 357-391.

8. Curtis, B., Krasner, H., & Iscoe, N. 1988. A Field Study of the Software Design Process for Large Systems. *CACM.* 31(11): 1268-1287.

9. Ehn, P. & Kyng, M. 1991. Cardboard Computers: Mocking-it-up or Hands-on the Future. In [13].

10. Fischer, G., Grudin, J., Lemke, A.C., McCall, R., Ostwald, J., & Shipman, F. 1992. Supporting Indirect, Collaborative Design with Integrated Knowledge-Based Design Environments. To appear in *Human-Computer Interaction.* 7(3).

11. Fischer, G., Lemke, A.C., McCall, R., & Morch, A.I. 1991. Making Argumentation Serve Design. *Human-Computer Interaction.* 6 (3-4): 393-419.

12. Franke, D.W. 1991. Deriving and Using Descriptions of Purpose. *IEEE Expert.* April 1991.

13. Greenbaum, J. & Kyng, M. 1991. *Design at Work: Cooperative Design of Computer Systems.* Hillsdale, NJ: Lawrence Erlbaum.

14. Greenbaum, J. & Kyng, M. 1991. Introduction: Situated Design. In [13].

15. Grudin, J. 1988. Why CSCW Applications Fail: Problems in the Design and Evaluation of Organizational Interfaces. *CSCW-88.* 85-93.

16. Johnson, W.L., Feather, M.S., & Harris, D.H. 1991. The KBSA Requirements/Specification Facet: ARIES. *Proc.s 6th Knowledge-Based Software Engineering Conference* (Syracuse, NY. Sept. 1991), pp. 57-66.

17. Kunz, W., & Rittel, H. 1970. Issues as Elements of Information Systems. Working Paper 131. Center for Planning and Development Research. The University of California at Berkeley.

18. McDermott, J. 1982. R1: A Rule-Based Configurer of Computer Systems. *Artificial Intelligence.* 19: 39-88.

19. Mark, W., et al. 1992. Commitment-Based Software Development. *IEEE Transactions on Software Engineering.* October 1992.

20. Ramesh, B. & Dhar, V. 1991. Representation and Maintenance of Process Knowledge for Large Scale Systems Development. *Proc. 6th Annual Knowledge-Based Software Engineering Conference.* Syracuse, NY. Sept. 1991), pp. 223-231.

21. Rich, C.H., & Waters, R.C. 1990. *The Programmer's Apprentice.* Reading, MA: Addison-Wesley.

22. Selfridge, P.G., Terveen, L.G., & Long, M.D. 1992. Managing Design Knowledge to Provide Assistance to Large-Scale Software Development. *Proc. 7th Knowledge-Based Software Engineering Conference,* (McLean, VA, Sept 1992).

23. Shortliffe, E.H. 1976. *Computer-Based Medical Consultation: MYCIN.* New York: American Elsevier.

24. Suchman, L.A. 1987. *Plans and Situated Action.* Cambridge: Cambridge University Press.

25. Terveen, L.G. & Wroblewski, D.A. 1991. A Tool for Achieving Consensus in Knowledge Representation. *AAAI-91.*

26. Winograd, T. & Flores, F. 1986. *Understanding Computers and Cognition.* Norwood, NJ: Ablex.

Where Did You Put It?
Issues in the Design and Use of a Group Memory

Lucy M. Berlin[†], Robin Jeffries[†], Vicki L. O'Day[†], Andreas Paepcke[†], Cathleen Wharton[‡]

[†] *Hewlett-Packard Laboratories*
1501 Page Mill Rd., Palo Alto, CA 94304
E-mail: berlin@hpl.hp.com

[‡] *University of Colorado at Boulder*
Department of Computer Science and Institute of Cognitive Science
Boulder, CO 80309-0430.

ABSTRACT

Collaborating teams of knowledge workers need a common repository in which to share information gathered by individuals or developed by the team. This is difficult to achieve in practice, because individual information access strategies break down with group information — people can generally find things that are on their own messy desks and file systems, but not on other people's.

The design challenge in a *group memory* is thus to enable low-effort information sharing without reducing individuals' finding effectiveness. This paper presents the lessons from our design and initial use of a hypertext-based group memory, *TeamInfo*. We expose the serious cognitive obstacles to a shared information structure, discuss the uses and benefits we have experienced, address the effects of technology limitations, and highlight some unexpected social and work impacts of our group memory.

KEYWORDS: collaborative work, information sharing, information search and retrieval, group memory, group conventions.

INTRODUCTION

In a previous study of the information needs of technical workers in many domains, we confirmed that computers are used to save masses of ad-hoc, mostly textual information crucial to people's work [11]. In our own field of software research we exchange design ideas and alternatives, schedules and constraints. We track other projects and the names of contacts. We exchange software pointers, bugs, and tricks of use. When we need an information nugget to make progress, that item — the bug work-around, decision, phone number or procedure — becomes critical.

Currently such sharable information is individually archived and managed. People save what they expect to need, using electronic mail folders and files. However, such individual

caches have four disadvantages:

- Each individual has the overhead of deciding what to save, where, and how to manage changes, updates, and weeding.
- As team members' tasks change, they must go to others to find information they deleted when it wasn't relevant, or information they never saw.
- New members of a project do not inherit a store of project-related information.
- When any person leaves, much of their saved expertise is lost to the rest of the team.

For these reasons, organizational redesign experts, software reuse experts, and many knowledge workers have expressed a desire for a shared repository for informal, group-relevant information [12, 2, 4] However, there are two major obstacles to such a shared repository. First, ad-hoc, textual data doesn't fit traditional information models — models designed for published documents or database records. Second, individual information-management strategies do not map well onto group information.

As part of an ongoing project on shared information access, we have designed TeamInfo, a prototype *group memory*. The first four authors have been using TeamInfo for our project's information needs since the summer of 1992. As of Nov 1992 it contains some 1500 items, including an initial set of 1000 items copied from our individual e-mail folders. Our research goal for TeamInfo is to help identify the features and social issues crucial to a useful group memory, to expose conflicting individual strategies for managing information, and to serve as a basis for trying out alternate solutions.

We define a *group memory* broadly as a common repository of on-line, minimally structured information of persistent value to a group. It is a variation of Walsh and Ungson's concept of an organizational memory [15], but tailored to the needs of a collaborating work-group. A group memory is still a broad concept; a group memory must be appropriate to its context — the heterogeneity, stability, computer sophistication, goals, and social environment of its users.

Our TeamInfo prototype is designed as a shared repository for information useful to multiple people in a small, stable team of knowledge workers. We decided to initially focus on stable teams, because their shared experiences help them anticipate which information might be in the group repository. We chose knowledge workers because their tasks require problem-solving. They are a particularly appropriate group, because their problem-solving requires shared information about work-flow, tasks, and hardware and software environments[12].

We view TeamInfo as a shared library of informal information — a repository of items of long-lived value. It is explicitly not another communication channel that bombards users with time-critical information. Users may browse to see what's new, ask to be notified of acquisitions in a given category, or simply search for information relevant to a current task. Our current focus is on the types of information that engineers and computer scientists save on the computer for longer-term reference: meeting notes, design documents, software installation instructions, bug work-arounds, pointers to reports, bits of information about interesting projects and products, and personal recommendations (e.g., restaurants).

TeamInfo combines features of other systems that address aspects of the data overload faced by individuals and teams. TeamInfo provides mixed manual and automatic classification of mail-based information, hypertext links, notification, and a browser- and query-based interface with simple full text retrieval.

Systems with goals related to TeamInfo include electronic mail filters such as the Information Lens [10] and Strudel [13]. These help users organize their e-mail and facilitate the structuring of discussions. However, they do not support the sharing of such information after it has been saved. Issue management systems such as gIBIS [5] also help teams track design alternatives, supporting positions and objections, but they require a very structured representation of discussions. And, systems such as Answer Garden [1] provide a decision-tree-based structure for recording software questions and answers, but do not span as broad a range of information types as TeamInfo, nor do they provide automatic classification or full text retrieval.

Our initial prototype does not try to cover all technical issues or information types. We omit security levels beyond Unix security, which is reasonable given our focus on single teams. The TeamInfo prototype handles only textual data; we believe that gives enough value while avoiding the complex issues of indexing voice, bitmaps, schematics, or video.

We provide full-text regular-expression searching, but our research focus is not on text retrieval. We agree with Evans that real-world problems of complex text management require representations that can recognize concepts from the relations among words, "but the facilities required to solve [such] problems are very complex. In general, they are not portable, not extensible, and not easy to implement or maintain." [7]. So, even though TeamInfo's platform is extensible to multiple text retrieval platforms, we have chosen not to immediately add lexicons, thesauri, or latent semantic indexing. Instead, we are trying to avoid the complex task of automatic concept recognition by TeamInfo's mixed manual and automatic classification.

After introducing TeamInfo, this paper describes our project's experiences with developing a shared classification, the effects of TeamInfo's design and technology choices, and the emerging social and work impacts of a group memory.

TEAMINFO: A GROUP MEMORY PROTOTYPE

TeamInfo is group memory application based on the prototype Group Memory Manager, GMM, developed by Cathleen Wharton during her summer internship at HP Laboratories. [16]. Both versions are built on top of a general-purpose hypertext system, Kiosk, also developed at HP Laboratoriess [6]. Kiosk provides a flexible nodes and links model implemented using Unix text files, an InterViews-based interface [9], and inter-process communication and concurrency control using the BART *software bus* mechanism [3]. Kiosk also provides the Cost^{++} automatic linking tool, which enables us to specify declarative rules to extract patterns from files and to link messages to the appropriate classification nodes.

We chose an electronic mail-based input model to TeamInfo for four reasons. First, e-mail submission minimizes the hurdle of submitting information by enabling users to stay in the context of an e-mail reader or editor. Second, since much of our information comes via e-mail, users can easily forward the useful nuggets of information they receive — items such as software installation notes, product ordering information, bug work-arounds, and technical report abstracts. Third, the team's e-mail discussions can be trivially archived in TeamInfo by adding the repository to the messages' *cc* list. Fourth, any other on-line document types can be easily converted into e-mail messages.

TeamInfo first parses each mail message and extracts data from structured fields such as sender, date, subject, and message-id. If a message is part of a conversation thread, i.e. a set of messages and replies on one topic, TeamInfo locates the message's predecessor and links the two messages.

Next, TeamInfo classifies the message, linking it to one or more group-defined categories. Messages are classified using a combination of automatically extracted and sender-provided information. Senders assign each item to one or more of a small number of categories, such as *Literature*, *Events*, or *Miscellaneous*. Senders may also specify any number of keywords or phrases that are potentially useful to finding the message, using a free vocabulary. Cost^{++} then scans the message and pattern-matches to the expressions, terms, and phrases that we have specified as indicative of a category.

In order to alert users of potentially interesting additions without inundating them with notifications, we began sending periodic summaries of new contributions via e-mail. This is similar to a library's sending a monthly list of new acquisitions. If the sender wants a team member to see the item quickly, one uses the usual mail mechanism and adds that person to the mail's *cc:* list.

Thus, in our model, users go to TeamInfo when they have a question to answer, or when they see an interesting contribution title. TeamInfo supports both query-based and browser-based search. The query-based access uses regular expression searching over the messages' contents. Since one can sometimes more effectively recognize appropriate items than specify a good query to retrieve them, TeamInfo also supports browsing and navigation through the classification hierarchy.

FORCED COGNITIVE COHABITATION:
Reconciling Long-Lived Filing Habits

An inherent problem of a shared repository is that individual finding strategies do not work for a group. Individual filing systems have four advantages. First, there is no negotiation overhead: users do not have to discuss explicitly their classification conventions. Second, consistency is less important: users remember their own classification rules, the changes, and the exceptions. Thus, they can guess a small set of classes where they might have put the item. Third, users are less dependent on a classification. Since they had read all the items they'd saved, they are likely to remember a unique word or phrase, and be able to use use text search. Fourth, if the initial searching attempts fail they will try different strategies, since they *know* the item is there, somewhere.

A group memory does not have these benefits. Users won't know another user's idiosyncratic rules and exceptions, won't be sure an item is there, and won't necessarily be able to search for a remembered unusual word or phrase. Thus, the first challenge in a common repository is for the group to develop some classification conventions that allow individuals freedom of expression, while maintaining some constraints that will ensure a high rate of findability.

Since our goal was to have TeamInfo span all of a team's shared information needs, we didn't think that unstructured text items would include enough of the descriptors needed for findability *by someone other than the person who had submitted an item*. We adopted a two-pronged approach to facilitate findability. First, as mentioned above, we added a *keywords* field to the e-mail messages, allowing authors to specify likely search terms. Second, we hypothesized that browsing would become more important in a group repository — that searchers would want to cast a net broadly and then try to recognize the right information, rather than trying to guess at the right retrieval terms. Thus, we designed a group classification to serve as an initial clustering. The classes serve two purposes: they enable browsing and they serve as natural contexts for queries.

We decided to design a simple classification: one with no more than ten top-level classes and a maximum of two levels of hierarchy. The goal of simplicity was driven by the desire to minimize the overhead for submitting an item to TeamInfo, and the knowledge that complex controlled vocabularies require extensive training for effective indexing and retrieval. On the other hand, given the very small (<0.20) agreement in users' spontaneous word choices for objects [8], we felt that a small controlled vocabulary was necessary to give an initial clustering.

We expected to sit down, agree on a single, simple classification, and be done. Given our similar project goals, computing environment, and research interests, our only concern was that we were too homogeneous to have interesting differences in personal styles. We were wrong. Very wrong. Fortunately we

had approached this systematically – after an initial discussion we listed our personal votes for the top ten (or fewer) categories, then sat down to create a group list. We audiotaped our discussions, so as to capture the reasons for individual positions and the habits that underlie different choices.

Over a few meetings we agreed on a set of core candidates we could live with. These included our two major project foci: *DIME* and *Group Memory*; a set of secondary activities (such as our study group, *Datalunch*) which became categories under *Sidelines*; and *Project-Miscellaneous*. Beyond that, we had categories such as *Events*, *Technology Hacks* (for messages about hardware and software tools, tricks etc), *People+Projects*, *Topic Tracking* [with subcategories], *Archive* [with subcategories] and finally a global *Miscellaneous*.

It's not enough to agree on a set of categories

Beneath our surface agreement on the categories lay crucial differences, exposed when we compared how we would classify a set of test messages based on project members' activities and recent e-mail. We differed along the following five dimensions:

1. purists and proliferators
2. semanticists and syntacticists
3. scruffies and neatniks
4. savers and deleters
5. the expected *purpose* for which the item is saved

Here are descriptions and examples of the differences in each dimension:

Purists and proliferators

Many items might fit into multiple categories. The purists wanted to put things into one place as an author, and were willing to look into multiple places as a searcher. As one said, "I prefer this to proliferating [virtual] copies all over the place. As a reader, I want the buckets uncluttered and thematically clear." For the proliferators, no one choice was correct — for example, an article about project "Papyrus" clearly belonged in both *Literature* and *People+Projects*; to them it would be frustrating to not be able to find all Papyrus-related things within *People+Projects*; to have to also search *Events*, *Literature*, and perhaps even *Project-Misc*.

Semanticists and syntactists

For the syntactists, structural and episodic clues are important for retrieval, and unlike semantic classification, they are unambiguous. Thus, the syntactists wanted articles and issues discussed at Datalunch, our weekly study group, to be visible under *Datalunch*. On the other hand, he semanticists wanted to find the Datalunch discussion of Nardi's latest groupware study under *CSCW*, and the next week's discussion of ethics in video research under *Miscellaneous*. Those who use episodic cues were quite discomfited at the thought of playing detective to find the semantic category that *someone else* decided a Datalunch item belongs into. The proliferators had an easier time choosing — they would put each item into both. However they too wound up being affected by others' styles: they expected to be able to find the items under both the semantic and syntactic categories.

Scruffies and neatniks

We drastically differed in our optimal classification granularity – the scruffies had originally wanted TeamInfo to have just five top-level categories while the neatniks are used to living with up to three hundred fine-grained (and hierarchical) e-mail folders. The neatniks deplored the loss of clustering in Team-Info caused by stuffing items on a dozen software packages onto *Hacks*, and our information on all relevant projects under *People+Projects*. To each person, the effort required to adopt other's style is burdensome at exactly the wrong time: the scruffies want to minimize the up-front cognitive load of filing, and are willing to spend more effort at retrieval time; the neatniks, on the other hand, want items to be pre-organized, and browsable. They prefer to spend up-front time to reduce the retrieval cost.

When we settled on a relatively small number of categories, we really weren't settled: the neatniks asked for documents to at least be given keywords that might permit future subclassification, or personal views at smaller granularity. Only extended use may show whether the scruffies will continue to generate these keywords, and whether such informal indexing meets the needs of the neatniks.

Savers and deleters

Our individual styles also affected what we each thought belongs in TeamInfo. The savers would like TeamInfo to include individual wisdom of potential group utility, such as restaurant recommendations, or the steps and pitfalls to editing a book. The deleters wouldn't have dreamt of cluttering TeamInfo with items that don't represent project-related group activities, or with e-mail design discussions of unknown future value.

Purpose-based filing

Even after we agreed on the set of TeamInfo categories, the category that seemed appropriate depended on our roles and expected future tasks. For example, here the engineers and manager disagreed on how to file a report we had written, evaluating another HP project's CD-ROM interface:

researcher1: I think that's *Technology Tracking*
manager: No, this is ...definite[ly] ...I would put in *People+Projects*.
researcher1: I don't care about *the people* — I mean this is a technology that I am tracking, right?
manager: I save those things because at some point as a manager I am going to need to know this for something. That is, I am going to need to know: "who is the manager of it?" ..."what's going to be different in it?" ...That is exactly what *People+Projects* are [for] and it will be hard to get me to change to put that under *Technology Tracking* although I can see exactly what your argument is for it.
researcher2: And I would put it under, in my old categorization, under *Project-Miscellaneous* and under *People+Projects* because it is [both] something that we did as a minor activity and it has to do with an ongoing project that I might be tracking. ...[much of] my tech-

nology tracking is likely to be under *People+Projects* because there's a lot of technologies that I track based on who is doing [what].

Over the discussion sessions we developed models of one another's idiosyncratic styles, so that we could compensate somewhat when searching (e.g. "Ah, she might have put it under *People+Projects* or *Events*"), but our theories weren't reliable, and remain very foreign to our natural habits. Given that our predictions are unreliable even within this ideal case — a stable group — we expect that individuals in more dynamic groups would have many more problems. New group members would have to learn not only the group's categories and filing rules, but also the fact that only some people file things under multiple categories, and that some hardly ever put items under *People+Projects*.

Personal vs. Group Information Habits

The differences described above are based on long-lived filing habits and our varied goals for the information. Thus, even after we had agreed on common categories in TeamInfo, we were faced with ongoing dissonance between the group memory classification and our personal e-mail folders and our natural tendencies. This dissonance was immediately visible in meetings when we re-visited TeamInfo policy issues (such as whether items could be in *Miscellaneous* plus another category). It was hard to remember what we'd agreed to, and what each person remembered tended to drift toward the person's initial position.

DESIGN AND TECHNOLOGY CHOICES

To learn from any prototype one must ask how well the task model is supported by the fundamental data model choices, and where the prototype's usefulness is affected by technological obstacles. Here we give our observations to date of the utility of two data model decisions in TeamInfo: (1) the hypertext model and (2) the model of mail-based input. We also discuss our experiences with and technical requirements for notification and for the searching and browsing interface. These issues are also applicable to the design of other shared information systems such as electronic bulletin boards and asynchronous conferencing systems.

Is Hypertext a good model for a group memory?

We find that hypertext links add value at the implementation level, but at the user's level a group memory requires a layer above hypertext. The user model of TeamInfo is that of documents put into one or more thematic categories, not of nodes linked to classification nodes. Users should not care that, at an implementation level, documents are linked to classification or query nodes – it is more familiar to think of the classes as an indexing hierarchy.

Hypertext links provide an understandable conceptual model for threaded messages in an e-mail conversation, but the user-level link-following operations are little used. When reading an e-mail conversation we find it choppy to bring up a separate window for each conversational turn. To handle that, we've thought of presenting the messages as speech acts in a conversation, and having the system build a transcript to be read as a consistent whole, perhaps with an index showing the author, date, subject and keywords for each message. Such a linear transcript would reduce the overhead of reading, make it easier to maintain context, and could simplify skimming or searching within a vaguely-remembered conversation.

The hypertext data model provides a clean way to link information. We link messages and their replies, queries and their results, classification nodes and the items within them, and keywords and the items which refer to them. The Kiosk platform provides a powerful filtering mechanism that is link-aware – we can search for, say, all messages by person X by searching the "author" link. Again, that is useful functionality, but it can be provided by pre-computed indexes or by queries over database records (such as provided in Tapestry [14]); it does not require the "author" attribute to be represented by a link.

Mail-based information

We are quite happy with the choice of mail-based input to team memory. It is easy to *cc:* TeamInfo on e-mail discussions and to forward information we get via e-mail. Also, many useful attributes of an item (date, sender's name, ID, reply-to ID, original sender...) are automatically generated. Thus, the author needs only to fill out the class and keywords fields in the augmented mail header. Since people sometimes forget to fill in those fields, TeamInfo provides graceful failure by also running the automatic classification rules on all new items. A more sophisticated solution would be to run the classification at send-time, and ask the sender to verify whether the identified categories are correct. This would reduce the cognitive load to the sender and avoid missing categories, but it would require extensions to each different mail interface used by the team members.

However, the mail model does have an impact on our interaction style. Items within TeamInfo are editable, so there is no *technical* reason keeping us from changing a submitted item (e.g. a bug report, or a set of instructions). However, that's strongly not in the model of e-mail. For that to feel comfortable within the e-mail model would require a mechanism to mark and timestamp the revisions and authors, and to allow us to notify others that an item has been modified.

Similarly, the e-mail model doesn't support shared dynamic documents. Dynamic documents — such as a software release to-do list, a list of open questions, a bibliography file, or a file of useful commands for infrequent activities — do not just get appended to; information is added in the middle, updated, and sometimes deleted. We generally haven't put such potentially sharable documents into TeamInfo, even though Kiosk does provide concurrency control. We are beginning to analyze why that is. It may be because we're still switching our work styles to make use of TeamInfo, but we are also bothered by fundamental obstacles such as TeamInfo's lack of a browser of "commonly accessed documents"; the lack of change bars and time/namestamps for changes; and each person's desire to use a favorite editor to search and edit complex documents.

Will the real sender please stand up?

As we said, messages sent to individuals are often forwarded to TeamInfo. In the initial design we became erroneously listed as the item's author. A similar problem occurred whenever we forwarded a team-member's messages to TeamInfo if we noticed that the original author forgot to *cc* TeamInfo. Fortunately with the mail-based input we were able to fix this, since a mail message preserves info on both senders, as well as both dates, message-ID's and subject lines. Using these, TeamInfo is now able to sort messages by their original send dates, and figure out *reply-to* links appropriately, even if the original message in a discussion thread is submitted after some of the replies.

The multiple IDs, subject lines, dates, and authors in forwarded messages pose a challenge when designing the browser-based interface. Which name, date, and subject line should appear in the message header? Which is the real message-id for the item? We chose to present the most recent (and usually most informative) subject line, but the original date and author. Using the original date and author helps compensate for us forgetting to *cc* TeamInfo. It also allows anyone to resend an item (e.g. about a new software release) without appearing to become the message's author. On the other hand, we miss the low-cost *mutual awareness* we could get by knowing who forwarded a message to TeamInfo; the sender's name provides an indirect window onto team-members' expertise and interests.

Notification

In TeamInfo, new items may be added without other people being notified of the additions. This makes sense for items that are of only future relevance to others: for example, when one of us began using a laptop computer, others did not want to see the nuggets of knowledge, strategies and work-arounds he was acquiring until we began to use laptops ourselves. Thus, individuals can avoid being bombarded by items with only potential future relevance. On the other hand, there are advantages to notification. If one has even glanced at an item that's in such a repository, one may recall the title, a keyword, or an unusual phrase, and will search more creatively and persistently than if one doesn't know it's there.

We have experimented with both styles, and we believe that notification does aid findability, but it has to have low cognitive overhead. We believe that the notification messages shouldn't interrupt a train of thought or demand immediate action. The messages should be informative, directly manipulable, and come at recipient-controlled times. Notification messages need to show the item's summary line, and let recipients individually mark, acknowledge or directly view the items. We are experimenting with periodic summaries of messages recently added to TeamInfo, and are designing customizable notification based on individuals' registration of their interests.

Many external messages are sent to the whole team. In our project, the social convention is that anyone may forward these to TeamInfo. To avoid redundant copies, we've sometimes used the notifications to check whether someone else has already submitted a particular item to TeamInfo. However, it would make more sense to see this *within the e-mail reading context*; just like there is a 'deleted' flag on each message header, one could imagine an 'archived' flag. This unfortunately would require a centralized model of e-mail, one in which all recipients view the same copy of a mail message. With a central e-mail server, one person's archiving action could trigger the 'archived' flag for other readers in a team. Of course, with distributed responsibility, the more common problem may be that nobody will submit a message to Team-Info. That is a question of social conventions — notification or central e-mail with an 'archived' flag makes distributed responsibility possible, but will not alone make it work.

Searching and Browsing

The initial prototype provides full-text searching with optional case sensitivity, but without structured search of e-mail fields. Since the documents are e-mail messages, we really wanted to be able to express restrictions based on fields such as date range, author, or keywords. We also wanted to be able to express structural constraints such as "search these two categories, and their subcategories" or "search all messages in this thread". Both of these features are planned but not yet available.

We do use the query-based interface, but primarily for brute-force search when we know that an item is there somewhere, and when we remember some unique phrase that we can search for. However, the limitations on its expressiveness and its slower speed inhibit its use, even among those who expected to always use queries.

We were able to get by with the more limited search capabilities once we revised the browser view's message summary lines to show date, author, subject, and also keywords. After that, the query-results browser generally gave enough information on each message to let us quickly find the target items. However, this wasn't true for design discussions, in which a half dozen or more messages had the same title — again suggesting the need for a more task-oriented representation of conversation threads.

We had strong differences in how much we expected to use the browser interface – some of us expected to always use queries and never to use the browser based interface, while others felt they could often recognize a hit more effectively than they could describe it in a query. The final answers are not yet in; our use patterns still vary as a result of changes in the functionality, presentation information, and the performance of the query and the browsing interfaces. However, browsing seems especially useful in three situations: (1) when we have an imprecise notion of *when* the item was created, so that a time-sorted view helps in searching, (2) when we expect to recognize the item but don't quite know how to describe it, and (3) when we're not sure whether the right information is in TeamInfo but figure we know where it is likely to be. Browsing gives a better feel for what's in a category, the time sequence of its items, and the keywords that have been used to describe items.

Browsing also leads to serendipitous finds. We had seeded TeamInfo with around 1000 items from our personal folders. Since these items were often forgotten, our browsing led to unexpected "discoveries" ranging from forgotten article pointers, to text formatting tricks, to rollerblading recommendations. The browser's quick overview of its contents enables *grazing* — semi-random wandering through the space, stopping at interesting-looking messages.

Our use of the browser and the query interfaces confirm our desire for an integrated query and browser mechanism supporting incremental refinement. The mechanism should include queries over previously retrieved sets, relevance feedback on matching items, and a browser of query results — sorted by category, and with secondary sorts by time, number of hits, author, etc.

WORK AND SOCIAL IMPACT OF TEAMINFO

Use of TeamInfo is slowly becoming a habit, both for information saving and for retrieval. Its use requires one to remember that an item is worth archiving for the group or that an item is likely to be in TeamInfo. As with most repositories, the more we find TeamInfo useful, the more we remember to use it and the more willing we are to add information.

TeamInfo is changing our information management style. We are increasingly submitting items to TeamInfo without *cc*'ing team members, items such LaTeXtricks, recommendations, and sometimes older information that ought to be in TeamInfo. We used to toss away many such items once they were no longer needed. Instead, we are starting to ask each other "do you want to see such in TeamInfo," and are often getting the answer "yes." Thus more information of potential relevance is archived, rather than being discarded or disseminated to others who have no immediate need for it.

Even though we are in the early phases of evaluating the system's utility for specific tasks, many areas of social impact are already apparent: we are facing issues of trust in TeamInfo's longevity; we've evolved a *curator* role; we are beginning to see effects on our e-mail, information saving and organizing habits; we are seeing issues of privacy and ethical use; and are dealing with issues of reward and social pressure.

Dependence on the group memory

Saving items in TeamInfo rather than one's personal files requires trust in the system's longevity. This is an issue for us, as it will be for any users of a group memory. Individuals are used to taking their personal e-mail folders with them as they switch projects, sometimes even companies. With TeamInfo, each item now raises the question of whether to save it in one's individual mail folders or to save it in TeamInfo. The latter decision requires trust that TeamInfo will last for the useful lifetime of the information, or that the information will be easily exportable if the individual leaves the group. Clearly, much of the information does not only belong to the group; it is often useful to and "belongs" to individuals even independently of their role in the group. Thus, to be trustworthy in a dynamic organization, a group memory must provide export facilities that let individuals retrieve copies of relevant items which they and their team-members had entrusted to the repository.

The curator role

The Cost[++] automatic classification tool uses a set of declarative rules to match text expressions to classes. This is extremely useful for classifying a corpus of messages, but the rules require significant experience to use well. One has to become aware that terms like "report" are verbs as well as nouns, that *CHI* should be specified case-sensitive, but *LaTeX* shouldn't. Since classifications are cached in the items, incorrect automatic classifications must be repaired by a custom script. The amount of detailed knowledge required for these functions encourages specialization, and thus we have made one person be the system's *curator*.

In TeamInfo's case, the curator does not make sure the right things are archived; that is still a distributed responsibility. However, she or he is alert to and fixes classification problems, and brings up classification issues for group discussion.

Changes in e-mail use

TeamInfo subtly but definitely changes our use of e-mail. It requires some cognitive overhead to decide whether a message to a team-member or a reply is worth archiving, and if so, to give it meaningful keywords. It requires more effort to slip into the group's mindset and classify it using the group's conventions. In addition, we try to catch ourselves sending mail without cc'ing TeamInfo; and we have trained ourselves to check if team-members' messages went to TeamInfo. That too requires vigilance.

The permanence and sharability of items in the repository raises issues of trust and etiquette. People usually feel fine about saving sensitive messages in their own e-mail folders, but not necessarily in a group repository. Thus, even if thematically a message sent to an individual belongs with other items already in the memory, it may not be put there. Thus, there is a tension between the group-memory culture of sharing relevant information, and the usual e-mail etiquette that treats as private e-mail sent to an individual.

The persistence of items in the repository has other effects as well. Some of us feel a subtle pull to be more cogent, more serious, and more accurate in choosing keywords. In regular e-mail one often writes subject lines whose meaning is clear in the current context, such as "the list you asked for", or whose meaning is clear once the message is read. One sometimes writes amusing or cute titles, where the pleasure to the recipient is worth the loss of subject line information. Thus, a major software release may have the title "try it, you'll like it." – or a bug report the subject line "arghh". Such levity may work less well when the messages are archival and the titles become a major retrieval cue. This would be a pity; the informality and levity help maintain the personal relationships in a team, and more informative subject lines do take more effort to compose.

Rewards

Since we are trying to figure out the necessary features for a useful group memory, we are currently under a moral contract to use the system. Thus, it is hard to evaluate whether TeamInfo's utility outweighs the overhead of contributing, or how individuals will decide whether to forward information sent to the whole group, and when they will rely on someone else to do that. The summary of submitted messages may exert a subtle pressure, by making it visible who is contributing and

who isn't. [1] However, longer use and experiments with other groups will be needed to explore reward issues, to see whether the utility outweighs the overhead of putting material in, and what factors the utility depends on.

Evolution of categories and project direction

In individual information files, individuals choose when to begin new categories, or whether to modify their organization to reflect name changes. As individuals, we are often comfortable with inconsistencies. For example, if we have conference-based e-mail folders, we might continue to file the *INTERCHI* items under *CHI*, and not bother with an ephemeral category. However, such a simplification will only make sense to those team members who are already aware of the relationship between *INTERCHI* and *CHI*. Thus, in a group repository, people feel the need to maintain group consistency, despite the additional overhead.

Division of categories also triggers group discussion. In our individual files, we create new categories when an old one gets too big, or when a subsidiary activity takes on a life of its own. Generally, we don't take the effort to extract the relevant messages from the old combined category — we just remember the divergence time and search accordingly. However, in a group repository this is not acceptable. The old items (that belong to the new category but are hidden within the old general category) would be inaccessible to those team members who are not familiar with the repository's history. Thus, evolution of categories requires group agreement on the new structure, and then it requires work by the curator to retroactively reclassify items.

Our discussions about new categories sometimes force us to re-examine the group's goals. Because we have to agree what belongs in TeamInfo and on how to classify items, we wind up discussing whether an activity is part of a project major focus or a sideline, and how sidelines such as task forces may affect our future direction. It's not yet clear whether such discussions are premature or if they are beneficial (by making us grapple with project goals and tradeoffs earlier). In either case, the introspection and discussions are an impact we hadn't foreseen.

SUMMARY AND CONCLUSIONS

This paper explores the feasibility and implications of a *group memory*, a shared repository of minimally structured information of long-lived value to a group. Our design experiences and pilot use of TeamInfo illuminate some of the social and technological issues inherent in this groupware tool.

Even though TeamInfo is an early prototype, it has become useful to our project. Our initial observations are confirming the utility of design choices such as e-mail based input, mixed manual and automatic classification, periodic notification, and the need for integrated browser-based and query-based capabilities for information finding. Our problems with the TeamInfo prototype also confirm other (familiar) requirements for effective

---

[1] This is reduced by the fact that forwarded messages' summary lines show the original author, not the TeamInfo contributor.

information retrieval: fast query and browser response, a good query language with boolean and proximity operators, and an interface that facilitates iterative refinement of the queries.

As a system used for real tasks, the TeamInfo prototype has been invaluable in exploring the cognitive aspects of information sharing. It has helped expose the conflicts between saving information in a personal vs a group repository, the social issues of rewards and responsibility for the care and feeding of the group memory, and the subtle changes in our communication styles and our use of e-mail.

This paper has shown that information management strategies that are appropriate for individuals break down in a shared information repository. We have described how individuals' long-lived filing habits differ along a number of fundamental dimensions, complicating the design of a shared information space. Our experience shows that even after agreeing on categories for TeamInfo, our filing styles made us likely to classify the same items differently. Individual differences in the favored retrieval clues, the tendency toward filing under single or multiple categories, the expected use of information, and the willingness to expend effort at filing time versus retrieval time, affect (1) *which* classes seem appropriate for an item, (2) *how many* categories we put an item into, and (3) whether we each *choose to spend the up-front energy* to add keywords to further describe an item.

With extended use of TeamInfo, we may identify potential solutions to the forced cognitive cohabitation in a group information system. Extended use is also needed to expose long-lived social barriers to shared information. Other important issues include the scalability of the classification and information retrieval mechanisms, and the social issues related to ownership, deletion, and changing group membership.

As researchers in shared information, we believe that group memory systems have the potential of being useful. However, this will not be an easy task. As this paper has shown, many cognitive and social issues must be addressed in order to develop a successful design. We hope that our observations of use, our technological suggestions, and the research hypotheses raised by our reflective use of the TeamInfo prototype will serve as a guide to practitioners and applied researchers in CSCW and group information retrieval.

ACKNOWLEDGEMENTS

Mike Creech, Dennis Freeze and Mark Gisi made major extensions to Kiosk to address the needs of TeamInfo's task domain. Mike Creech, Mark Gisi, Bob Leichner, Bonnie Nardi, and Glenn Trewitt also gave helpful comments on earlier drafts.

References

[1] M. S. Ackerman and T. W. Malone. Answer Garden: A tool for growing organizational memory. In *Proceedings of the Conference on Office Information Systems*, 1990.

[2] V. R. Basili, G. Caldiera, and G. Cantone. A reference architecture for the component factory. *ACM Transactions on Software Engineering and Methodology*, 1(1), Jan 1992.

[3] B. Beach. Connecting software components with declarative glue. In *15th Annual International Conference on Software Enginnering*, 1992.

[4] J. S. Brown. Research that reinvents the corporation. *Harvard Business Review*, 69(1), 1991.

[5] J. Conklin and M. L. Begeman. gIBIS: A hypertext tool for team design deliberation. In *Hypertext '87 Proceedings*, Nov. 1987.

[6] M. L. Creech, D. F. Freeze, and M. L. Griss. Using hypertext in selecting reusable software components. In *Hypertext '91 Proceedings*. ACM, 1991.

[7] D. Evans. First order solutions to second-order problems in information manageement. In *Proceedings of the Bellcore Worshop on High-Performance Information Filtering*, 1991.

[8] G. W. Furnas, T. K. Landauer, L. M. Gomez, and S. T. Dumais. The vocabulary problem in human-system communication. *Communications of the ACM*, 30(11), 1987.

[9] M. A. Linton, J. M. Vlissides, and P. R. Calder. Composing user interfaces with InterViews. *IEEE Computer*, 22(2), 1989.

[10] T. W. Malone, K. R. Grant, F. A. Turbak, S. A. Borbst, and M. D. Cohen. Intelligent information-sharing systems. *Communications of the ACM*, 30, May 1987.

[11] V. L. O'Day and A. Paepcke. Understanding information needs in technical work settings. Technical Report HPL-92-123, Hewlett-Packard Laboratories, 1992.

[12] C. H. P. Pava. *Managing New Office Technology*. The Free Press, 1983.

[13] A. Shepherd, N. Mayer, and A. Kuchinsky. Strudel: An extensible electronic conversation toolkit. In *Proceedings of the Conference on Computer Supported Cooperative Work*, 1990.

[14] D. Terry, D. Goldberg, D. Nichols, and B. Oki. Continuous queries over append-only databases. In *Proceedings of the 1992 ACM SIGMOD International Conference on Management of Data*. ACM Press, 1992.

[15] J. P. Walsh and G. R. Ungson. Organizational memory. *Academy of Management Review*, 16(1), 1991.

[16] C. Wharton and R. Jeffries. Understanding the role of structure in information filtering in the context of group memories: Some application and user requirements. In *Proceedings of the Bellcore Workshop on High-Performance Information Filtering*. Bellcore, 1991.

Facile 3D Direct Manipulation

Dan Venolia

Apple Computer, Inc.

20525 Mariani Avenue

Cupertino, CA 95014 USA

(408) 974-4121

danv@apple.com

ABSTRACT

An experimental 3D interface is described, including rendering acceleration hardware, a 3D mouse, and 3D interaction techniques. A 3D cursor, controlled by the augmented mouse, allows direct manipulation of 3D objects. Objects are selected by placing the tip of the cursor inside. Objects can be moved in 3D, or simultaneously moved and rotated using a technique called "tail-dragging." A method called "snap-to" helps users align objects. The interface is designed without using explicit modes or commands. Sounds accentuate the interaction. Details of the implementation and informal user observations are described, as well as topics for future work.

KEYWORDS: Interaction, Direct Manipulation, Three Dimensional Graphics, Input Devices, Audio Output.

INTRODUCTION

With the growing speed of personal computers, tools for creating in 3D are increasingly available to designers. Unfortunately, the usefulness of the tools is restricted by their complicated, indirect interfaces that are tailored more to the drafter than the designer. This paper describes explorations into 3D interface techniques that are more casual, direct and natural than are presently available.

Creating and manipulating 3D objects is a complicated task. Autodesk's AutoCAD™ has thousands of commands, subcommands and dialogs. Some of this complexity is required by the task; much of it could be eliminated by a more facile user interaction metaphor. While this research does not come close to AutoCAD in capabilities, it does examine how designers can casually and directly interact with 3D models. This design, as much as is possible, tries to isolate the complexity within the computer, rather than in the interface or in the user's mind.

The methodology used for initial investigations has been to artificially restrict both the user's task and the interface designer's tools. Traditional interface elements, like menus, palettes, control panels, modifier keys, etc., were shunned, both to simplify the interface and to determine what could be done using only direct manipulation. As the task grows more complicated, the standard user interface elements will be re-introduced as necessary. Because of this methodology, the techniques discussed here should continue to be relevant when the task grows to supporting real designers in their daily work.

Extensive casual user observations have yielded valuable, and sometimes unexpected, insight into the strengths and weaknesses of the interface. An observation session typically starts with a demonstration of the system in action, then the subject is given control. After a period of exploration of about ten minutes, the subject is requested to perform specific tasks, such as placing one object atop another. Users' reactions to the interface are discussed in each section below.

THE TASK

The task that the interface supports is arrangement of 3D objects in a scene. In real-world terms, this could mean moving furniture in a house, plants in a landscape or machines and materials in a factory. In these experiments, it quite often means moving geometric objects in an abstract space. The task and the objects in the scene will become more realistic as system performance increases.

GRAPHICS HARDWARE

To present an interactive 3D scene, the computer must redraw the image repeatedly, fast enough to maintain a plausible

Figure 1: The small cone toward the upper-right is a 3D cursor, which enables direct manipulation of 3D objects.

Figure 2: Moving the 3D cursor inside an object highlights it, indicating that it is ready to be moved. Moving toward the center of the object changes the cursor from a cone to a jack, indicating a different mode. (See Venolia, Color Plate 1)

illusion of continuous motion and to allow eye-hand coordination. If the computer can update at thirty frames per second (FPS), slow-moving objects will appear to move continuously; fast-moving objects need a higher rate [16], up to the scan rate of the display device, typically 60-75 FPS. The illusion of motion breaks down below that rate, and eye-hand coordination appears to break down below five or ten FPS.

Rendering a 3D scene is typically done by decomposing the objects into triangles, computing where the triangles appear to a "virtual camera," then filling in each of the triangles [7]. The time to render a scene depends on its complexity (the number of triangles, for example) and the rate at which triangles can be computed and filled. The image in Figure 1 is composed of about 500 triangles. One software implementation on an Apple Macintosh Quadra™ 900 personal computer takes longer than a second to render it—not nearly fast enough to be considered interactive. To get interactive frame rates, either the scene must be simplified (it's already pretty simple) or the hardware must be made faster.

This interface investigation is coupled with a hardware development effort to accelerate 3D rendering [13]. The hardware chipset takes the task of filling the triangles from the computer. The chipset can fill about 220,000 triangles per second; an extended system will be capable of about four times that. The Quadra must do extensive processing to determine where the triangles appear to the camera, so an additional arithmetic processor is needed to drive the chipset to its peak performance. The fastest prototype to date can render Figure 1 ten FPS.

The hardware design effort has focused on 3D rendering acceleration specifically for interaction. Wireframe images are no faster than smooth-shaded solid images, so there is no artificial impetus to use that unnatural visual representation. Objects may be rendered as translucent without a performance penalty, encouraging its use in the interface. The hardware supports hard-edged shadowing, giving users a strong cue to depth relationships between objects in a scene as well as greater understanding of the shape of individual objects [15].

3D MOUSE

Users are able to perform better when the design of the controller corresponds to the demands of the task [12]. Much of the interface complexity in existing 3D design tools comes from trying to use a two degree-of-freedom device—a mouse or tablet—to do a three degree-of-freedom job. For example, Paracomp's Swivel™ application program has five palette modes

that allow objects to be moved along or rotated about any axis. In a system developed by Gleicher [10], the mouse changes between moving the a 3D cursor in a plane or perpendicular to the plane depending on the state of a modifier key.

Instead of using modes or modifier keys to make a mouse control objects in 3D, a 3D pointing device can be used. The Polhemus Isotrak™ and other similar technologies sense the absolute position and orientation of a stylus in 3D. Researchers have developed powerful 3D sculpting programs using these devices [8, 14]. Unfortunately, these technologies tend to be expensive, and are often fatiguing for users.

To address these problems, a 3D pointing device has been developed, based on the standard 2D mouse, to enable direct manipulation in 3D. The "roller mouse" (Figure 3) has the standard mouse ball encoder on the underside as well as two wheels on the front, on either side of a single mouse button. The wheels are fixed to a common axle so that they control a single degree of freedom. The device can be used equally well by left- and right-handed people.

3D CURSOR

The 3D mouse is used to control a 3D cursor, shown toward the upper-right of Figure 1. Moving the body of the roller mouse moves the cursor in the familiar plane—up, down, left and right. Moving the wheels of the roller mouse moves the cursor closer to and farther from the camera. If an object obscures the cursor,

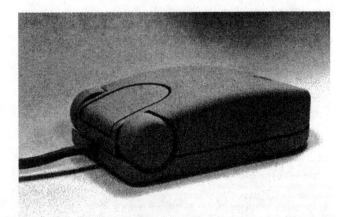

Figure 3: The "roller mouse" allows the user to move the cursor in three dimensions simultaneously.

Figure 4: An object can be moved in three axes simultaneously by click-dragging on it with the jack cursor and moving the mouse and its wheels. (See Venolia, Color Plate 2)

the object is rendered translucent so that the cursor remains visible.

The 2D cursors that we are familiar with on our personal computers have a fixed orientation—the Macintosh arrow cursor always points north-by-northwest. The 3D cone cursor changes orientation as it moves, using a technique called "tail-dragging," which is covered in depth in a later section. While the mouse controls the 3D position of the tip, the body of the cone cursor drags along behind it. Tail-dragging affects only the appearance of the cursor, not its function. Even so, it is an important asset: small movements, especially ones toward or away from the camera, are made more visually apparent by a change of both position and orientation. Tail-dragging, perspective and shadows are some of the depth cues that help the user determine the position of the cursor in the 3D scene.

Of special importance to Apple is the integration of 3D interaction with the 2D environment. While the mouse has been adapted to control a 3D cursor, it remains a good 2D pointing device. As the 3D cone cursor crosses off the edge of a 3D view, it changes to the familiar 2D arrow. When the arrow is moved over the 3D view, it changes back to the 3D cone, at the same depth as when it last exited. Because of the integration of 2D and 3D controls, the full battery of 2D interface elements remains usable—though presently unused—without changing modes or devices.

Two ways of mapping the roller mouse movements to 3D cursor positions have been implemented. The first is "camera-centered mapping"—the wheels are mapped to the "camera normal" vector, the mouse vertical axis to the "camera up" vector and the mouse horizontal axis to the vector that is perpendicular to those two vectors. The second, "screen-centered mapping," keeps the tip of the 3D cursor under the screen pixel where the 2D cursor would appear by the movements of the mouse body, and the wheels control the depth at that pixel. With the camera-centered mapping, the apparent motion of the cursor changes with depth, which may be both an inconvenience and a powerful depth cue. The relative merits of the two techniques will be better understood with further user testing.

User observations have indicated that the 3D cursor is a natural extension of the familiar 2D cursor. Users seem to be able to control the cursor with the mouse, even mastering the complex interplay between the mouse body, the button and the wheels. One unexpected observation is that people seem to have

built-in collision detection: they tend to move the cursor around objects rather than through them, and they avoid moving the cursor outside the view of the camera. After they have been shown that there is a positive effect when either "collision" occurs, they are no longer hesitant. The 3D cursor appears to help users understand the 3D space, evoking the comment, "This is great! I can finally just reach in and grab it," from one test subject.

SELECTION

Using the 3D cursor, the user can select objects and perform operations on them. When the user moves the cursor within the 3D geometry of an object, the object is "touched." The object turns translucent and crosshairs appear projecting in six directions from the tip of the cursor to the shell of the object (Figure 2, middle panel). The crosshairs are yet another cue that helps the user determine the position of the cursor, specifically how it relates to the touched object.

This differs significantly from other systems that "touch" the object that shares the pixel under the cursor. In these systems, the 2D cursor position specifies a ray or a cone that extends from the camera through the cursor to the objects. It is often ambiguous which object is the intended target. To make the ray or cone behave usefully, complex heuristics have been developed [2] that may or may not fulfill the user's intentions or expectations. A single cursor position often specifies multiple objects, requiring additional commands in the interface and burden on the user to exactly specify a single object.

The "touched" state is as close as the system presently gets to the concept of selection. There is not a sense of persistent selection, as is typically present in applications. This is not a necessary limitation, rather it is a simplification of the interface in keeping with the methodology of avoiding the traditional interface elements until needed. To add persistent selection, a visual depiction of the selected state will be developed, such as object handles or a translucent bounding box.

Presently an object is "touched" when the cursor is within the object geometry. This is not sufficient for a general system, since objects may be extremely thin, or even have no sense of inside and outside. A "touching" model based on proximity will be developed to replace the existing model.

Some users were observed initially trying to select by placing the cursor in front of, instead of inside, an object. Once they were instructed to touch the object in 3D, they had little problem with it, and never reverted to trying the other method.

Figure 5: An object can be translated and rotated simultaneously by click-dragging on it with the cone cursor. Tail-dragging is used to control the rotation while the cursor controls position directly. (See Venolia, Color Plate 3)

MOVING AN OBJECT

The system allows a user to move an object with or without rotating it at the same time. The choice depends on where the cursor is within the object when the mouse button is pressed. While touching an object, the cursor appears either as a cone when it is near the shell of the object geometry (Figure 2, middle panel), or as a six-pointed jack when it is nearer to the center (Figure 2, right panel).

The user can translate an object in three dimensions by clicking the roller mouse button when the cursor appears as the jack, and, still pressing the mouse button, moving the mouse body and wheels (Figure 4).

The center of the object is an "implicit hot-spot"—an area that behaves differently but is not distinguished visually, until the cursor changes when it is moved inside. Although implicit hot-spots are common in commercial applications, they are difficult for users because they can find it only by guessing where it should be, and moving the cursor until it is found. The implicit hot-spot at the center of objects will be eliminated in favor of an explicit, visual object handle when the interface is changed to use a persistent model of selection.

MOVING BY TAIL-DRAGGING

As mentioned above, the orientation of the cursor is determined by an algorithm called "tail-dragging." The same technique is employed to allow users to simultaneously translate and rotate objects. Tail-dragging belongs to the class of interactors called "virtual controllers" [6]—ways of controlling more degrees of freedom than are present in the device. Specifically, tail-dragging takes a stream of 3D positions as input and produces a stream of yaw and pitch orientations as output. When combined with the original 3D stream, this gives control of five different (though not independent) degrees of freedom.

Tail-dragging is loosely based on a physical model. Consider dragging a rock behind you by a rope. The rock stays a constant distance behind you, at an angle that changes depending on your path (Figure 6). Tail-dragging calls the free end of the rope the "head" and the rock the "tail." For each new head position, a new tail position is computed by stretching the rope from the old tail, then restoring the rope to its original length. More precisely, to find the tail position at time step t,

$$tail_t = head_t + \frac{tail_{t-1} - head_t}{\left\| tail_{t-1} - head_t \right\|} \left\| tail_0 - head_0 \right\|.$$

The new $tail_t$-$head_t$ vector can be compared to the original $tail_0$-$head_0$ vector to find the yaw and pitch angles to rotate between the two states. The remaining degree of freedom (rotation about the new vector, or roll) can be constrained by computing an angle to minimize its change between steps.

A user can translate and rotate an object simultaneously, using tail-dragging, by clicking the roller mouse button while touching the object with the cone cursor (Figure 5). The clicked position is considered the initial head position, and the initial tail position is computed as the point opposite the object center from the head. (Note that tail-dragging is less predictable when the tail is too close to the head, hence the object center is used as a hot-spot for translation-only dragging.) As the user drags the object by the head position, the trailing tail position causes the object's orientation to change.

Users had some difficulty controlling rotation by tail-dragging. A common unsuccessful strategy is grabbing an object by an inappropriate head point, and trying to get the desired position and orientation by fine adjustment. If the initial head point is chosen appropriately for the desired rotations, the users typically had much more success. A less common but more successful strategy involves a series of small nudges, mixing translation-only and tail-dragging moves. It is unclear at present what, besides experience, can be done to encourage the second behavior. While tail-dragging is not a decisive winner, it deserves more experimentation and evaluation.

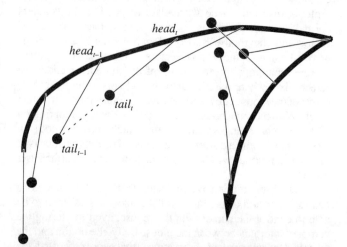

Figure 6: Tail-dragging is like pulling a rock (the circles) by a rope (the thin lines) along a path (the thick line).

Figure 7: While the user drags an object, it is attracted by other objects in the scene. As it moves closer, it is pulled away from the cursor and into alignment with the attractor, until finally the faces conjoin exactly. (See Venolia, Color Plate 4)

SNAP-TO

With the direct manipulation techniques described above, it is possible for users to position objects approximately where they want them, but exact alignment is not possible without additional mechanisms. Many commercial drawing applications (e.g. Claris MacDraw™) help users align objects by means of a ruled grid and complex alignment commands. The grid restricts the designer's expressiveness; the alignment commands complicate the interface. Another approach is to provide alignment objects, like the "guides" in Aldus PageMaker™ in 2D and Bier's "Jacks" in 3D [1]. This introduces a level of indirection in the interface: to align two objects, a third object— one that is not part of the desired result—must be introduced to mediate the alignment.

A third technique, called "gravity fields" or "snap-dragging," which uses the objects in the scene as alignment points [2, 3, 11], is making its way into commercial applications, e.g. Ashlar Vellum™ and Claris CAD™. This technique suffers from some drawbacks. When an object approaches an alignment position, it jumps to it, introducing a visual discontinuity in the motion and making it impossible for the designer to move the object close to, but not touching, the alignment point. If alignment points are clustered, small movements of the cursor can result in the object unpredictably jumping between the points. Finally, the technique has mostly been applied to align points, rather than whole objects in both position and orientation. These limitations have been overcome with a technique called "snap-to."

Snap-to uses an intuitive model of magnetic attraction to help users align objects in both position and orientation. As an object is dragged toward another (Figure 7), it is pulled away from the cursor and toward the attracting object. The pull gets stronger as the object is moved toward the attractor; the object becomes aligned exactly when it comes close enough to the attractor. The specifics of the snap-to algorithm are beyond the scope of this paper.

The snap-to effect is reinforced by visual feedback in two ways. An object that looks like a small, red spring appears between the attracting object and the object that is being dragged, at the closest points between them. The spring compresses as the objects near one another. As the dragged object is pulled away from the cursor, a thick red line stretches between the cursor and the crosshairs.

Users take advantage of snap-to with surprising ease. By exploration alone, users usually discover the existence and use

of the feature, and often spontaneously describe it as "magnetic attraction." With some coaching, users are easily taught the possibilities for alignment between combinations of faces, edges and vertices of simple objects.

Snap-to is algorithmically complex and computationally expensive. Just as graphical user interfaces take a substantial portion of the computer's processing power to increase the user's quality of life in the 2D domain, appropriate use of the increasing power of computers can make the user's experience better, not just faster, for 3D interaction.

SOUND

Sound is already an integral part of the computer experience, even though most of it does not come from the speaker. Keyboards and mice have distinctive and useful click sounds; users can get a feel for their disk activity by listening to it seek; floppy disk drives make satisfying sounds when they insert or eject a disk. Indeed, any interaction in the real world makes sound. Gaver added sounds to the Macintosh Finder™ [9] to convey both action and information, e.g. selecting a document made a sound that decreased in pitch with the size of the disk file.

The interface uses sound to accentuate the interaction. Almost every visual change in the interface and user action is accompanied by audio reinforcement: the cursor entering or leaving an object or a 3D view, switching between dragging

When	Kind	Description
Start Touching	Blip	"Tick"
While Touching	Loop	"Whirr," open and airy
Stop Touching	Blip	"Tock"
Change Drag Mode	Blip	"Snick," softly
Enter 3D View	Blip	Short "woosh," up
Exit 3D View	Blip	Short "woosh," down
Start Dragging	Blip	"Tink"
While Dragging	Blip	"Whirr"
Click w/o Touching	Blip	"Thud"
Snap-To Approach	Loop	"Humm," insistent
Snap-To Connect	Blip	"Clunk"
While Connected	Loop	"Humm" plus scrape
Snap-To Disconnect	Blip	"Rip"

Figure 8: Sound is used to enhance the interaction.

modes, grabbing an object, etc. The sounds are categorized as either short blips, typically 100 to 500 milliseconds long, or continuous loops (Figure 8).

Snap-to is enhanced greatly by audio feedback. While dragging an object close to an attractor, a loop sound plays, increasing in amplitude as the object is dragged closer, indicating the strengthening magnetic attraction. When the attraction results in full contact, a sound effect indicates the collision and the other loop sound starts. The second loop sound is a combination of the attraction loop with another sound to indicate continued, scraping contact. When the object is pulled away, a tearing sound effect plays and the attraction loop resumes. Silence returns when the objects are finally out of the range of attraction.

Buxton describes the low levels of interaction as a "body language" where individual actions (e.g. moving the mouse or clicking the button) are grouped into phrases (e.g. selecting from pull-down menu) [5]. The muscle tension caused by holding the mouse button down is a "continual active reminder that you are in an uninterruptable temporary state." In the interaction dialog, the sounds increase in urgency as the user progresses from moving the cursor, to touching an object, to grabbing it, to aligning it with another object. As the object is released, the sounds decrease to return to the original, relaxed state. The use of sound helps convey the ebb and flow of tension in the phrasing of the dialog, reducing the burden on the user's visual attentions [4]. Sounds may also help convey the "touching" and "magnetic attraction" metaphors to users.

CONCLUSION

The design of this system concentrates on facile, natural interaction at the expense of functionality and realism in the task domain. The interface relies only on direct manipulation of 3D objects in a scene, and does not yet make use of persistent modes, out-of-scene controls or explicit commands. Many basic functions, such as controlled and automatic camera motions and persistent alignment, can be added before invoking traditional interface toolkit elements. The traditional elements will yield great power as the task grows from an experiment in the lab to a tool in the design studio.

The system tries to lift the burden off the user and the interface, and puts it instead on the computer. Rather than mastering the convolutions necessary to use a 2D pointing device, a 3D mouse is provided. Instead of learning a complex set of alignment commands and their attendant selection problems, alignment is done automatically and continuously. Rather than having to understand that objects are composed of polygonal faces, edges and vertices, a simple model is promoted where objects behave more realistically, and the implementation and representation issues are hidden. Instead of manipulating wireframes or bounding boxes, objects appear more realistic, with smooth shading and shadows. Reducing the complexity and indirectness of the interface will increase the system's ease of use and the designer's quality of life.

While many of these techniques, including tail-dragging and snap-to, could be employed by traditional 2D graphic editors, the ultimate goal is to provide a set of 3D interaction tools and techniques that will support the gamut of 3D interaction, including browsing, arranging and modeling of 3D objects. The direct, facile manipulations that this interface demonstrates will lay a solid foundation for building a full 3D interface toolkit.

ACKNOWLEDGMENTS

The hardware graphics system was developed by Mike Kelley, Stephanie Winner, Kirk Gould and Alex Yen. The software rendering framework has been provided by Dave Jevans, Mike Chmilar and Jennifer Inman. The roller mouse was designed with the help of Shinpei Ichikawa. Thanks to Wolfgang Dirks and Shane Robison for supporting this ongoing research.

REFERENCES

1. Bier, E. Skitters and jacks: interactive 3D positioning tools. In *Proc. Workshop on Interactive 3D Graphics* (Chapel Hill, N. C., Oct. 1986). ACM/SIGGRAPH, 1986, 183-196.

2. Bier, E. Snap-dragging in three dimensions. In *Proc. Workshop on Interactive 3D Graphics* (Snowbird, Utah, 1990). ACM/SIGGRAPH, 1990, 193-204.

3. Bier, E., and Stone, M. Snap-dragging. In *Computer Graphics 20*, 4 (Aug. 1986), 233-240.

4. Brown, M. L., Newsome, S. L., and Glinert, E. P. An experiment into the use of auditory cues to reduce visual workload. In *Proc. CHI '89* (Austin, Apr. 1989). ACM/SIGCHI, 1991, 339-346.

5. Buxton, W. There's more to interaction than meets the eye: some issues in manual input. In Baecker and Buxton (Eds.), *Readings in Human Computer Interaction.* Morgan Kaufman, San Mateo, Calif., 1987, 366-375.

6. Chen, M., Mountford, S. J., and Sellen, A. A study in interactive 3D rotation using 2D control devices. *Computer Graphics 22*, 4 (Aug. 1988), 121-129.

7. Foley, J. D., van Dam, A., Feiner, S. K., and Hughes, J. F. *Computer Graphics Principles and Practice.* Addison-Wesley, New York, 1987.

8. Galyean, T. A., and Hughes, J. F. Sculpting: an interactive volumetric modelling technique. *Computer Graphics 25*, 4 (Jul. 1991), 267-274.

9. Gaver, W. Auditory icons: using sound in computer interfaces. *Human Computer Interaction 2*, 2, 1986, 167-177.

10. Gleicher, M., and Witkin, A. Snap together mathematics. In *Proc. 1990 Eurographics Workshop on Object Oriented Graphics*, Springer Verlag, 1991.

11. Hudson, S. E. Adaptive semantic snapping—a technique for semantic feedback at the lexical level. In *Proc. CHI '90* (Seattle, Apr. 1990). ACM/SIGCHI, 1990, 65-70.

12. Jacob, R. J. K., and Sibert, L. E. The perceptual structure of multidimensional input device selection. In *Proc. CHI '92* (Monterey, Apr. 1992). ACM/SIGCHI, 1992, 211-218.

13. Kelley, M., Winner, S., and Gould, K. A scalable hardware render accelerator using a modified scanline algorithm. *Computer Graphics 26*, 2 (Jul. 1992), 241-248.

14. Sachs, E., Roberts, A., and Stoops, D. 3-Draw: a tool for designing 3D shapes. *IEEE Computer Graphics and Applications 11*, 6 (Nov. 1991), 18-26.

15. Wanger, L. The effect of shadow quality on the perception of spatial relationships in computer generated imagery. In *Proc. Symposium on Interactive 3D Graphics* (Boston, Mar. 1992). ACM/SIGGRAPH, 1992, 39-42.

16. Watson, A. B. Temporal sensitivity. In Boff, Kaufman and Thomas (Eds.), *Handbook of Perception and Human Performance, Volume 1, Sensory Processes and Perception.* John Wiley & Sons, New York, 1986, 6·34-6·35.

FISH TANK VIRTUAL REALITY

Colin Ware
Faculty of Computer Science
P.O Box 4400
University of New Brunswick
Canada E3B 5A3
email: cware@unb.ca

Kevin Arthur and Kellogg S. Booth
Department of Computer Science
6356 Agricultural Road
University of British Columbia
Vancouver, B.C.
Canada V6T 1Z2
email: karthur@cs.ubc.ca
ksbooth@cs.ubc.ca

ABSTRACT

The defining characteristics of what we call "Fish Tank Virtual Reality" are a stereo image of a three dimensional (3D) scene viewed on a monitor using a perspective projection coupled to the head position of the observer. We discuss some of the relative merits of this mode of viewing as compared to head mounted stereo displays. In addition, we report the experimental investigation of the following variables: 1) whether or not the perspective view is coupled to the actual viewpoint of the observer, 2) whether stereopsis is employed. Experiment 1 involved the subjective comparison of pairs of viewing conditions and the results suggest that head coupling may be more important than stereo in yielding a strong impression of three dimensionality. Experiment 2 involved subjects tracing a path from a leaf of a 3D tree to the correct root (there were two trees intermeshed). The error rates ranged from 22% in the pictorial display, to 1.3% in the head coupled stereo display. The error rates for stereo alone and head coupling alone were 14.7% and 3.2% respectively. We conclude that head coupling is probably more important than stereo in 3D visualization and that head coupling and stereo combined provide an important enhancement to monitor based computer graphics.

KEYWORDS: virtual reality, scientific visualization, head coupled displays, stereopsis.

INTRODUCTION

J.J. Gibson's pioneering research showed the interrelatedness of perceptual systems. Information from a variety of systems, including the kinaesthetic feedback relating to self directed body movement coupled to image changes are crucial to our understanding of space (Gibson, 1979). Recently, Deering (1992) presented the technical components required to create a high quality 3D "virtual reality" image on a monitor by tracking the head of the user. He emphasized the importance of the accurate

coupling of the perspective image to the observer's viewpoint. We have been using the term "Fish Tank VR" to describe the same kind of display - one in which the virtual 3D scene is obtained by coupling head position with respect to a monitor to the 3D image displayed so that the correct perspective view is obtained (see also McKenna, 1992). The resulting scene can be either viewed monocularly, coupled to a single eye position, or binocularly, if suitable stereo equipment is available. Figure 1 shows the basic setup, which includes a monitor, a device for measuring head position, and stereo viewing goggles. Fish Tank VR has a number of advantages over immersion VR. We begin by describing these advantages to show why we should be interested in the properties and uses of this mode of viewing.

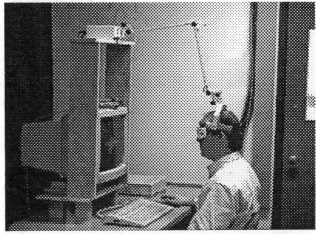

Figure 1. The head coupled display system. The subject's head position is monitored by the ADL-1. StereoGraphics glassed provide the stereo when used with a monitor (and graphics system) capable of a 120 Hz update rate, 60 Hz to each eye.

Resolution

In immersion VR with a head mounted display, the monitors are placed very close to the eyes giving a field of view which may subtend 90 deg of visual angle (Ward et al, 1992, Sutherland, 1968). Given the typical resolution of the current displays each pixel will subtend approximately 12 minutes of arc. Viewing a high resolution monitor with a 30 deg field of view yields 2 minutes of arc per pixel - close to the resolution limits of the human eye. While it is true that the resolution of head mounted displays for immersion VR will improve over time, it seems likely to be a long time before it can be expected to come close to current technology Fish Tank VR.

Depth-of-Field

Depth-of-field effects arise from the fact that we can change the focal length of our eyes and therefore things we are fixating will typically be in focus, while things we are not fixating will be out of focus. Thus if nearby objects are fixated, background objects should be out of focus. Without directly measuring the focal length of the observer's lens, it is impossible to take depth-of-field directly into account in creating images for VR. However, because of the viewing geometry in Fish Tank VR the working scene is necessarily constrained to lie within a few centimeters in front and behind the screen of the monitor, this is because things that are nearer and further away are clipped when the subject makes a head movement. It is possible to simulate depth of field effect by drawing a background that approximates an out-of-focus image.

Stability In the Presence of Eye Movements

In immersion VR the eyes are necessarily very close to the display monitors (which are mounted on a helmet) in order to get the wide field of view. This introduces an error when the eye moves off axis. As Deering (1992) has pointed out, the eye rotates about a geometric center, which is about 6.0 mm behind the optic center (first nodal point). This means that a 40 deg eye movement will result in a 3.8 mm translation of the center of the lens. Coupled with a screen placed 8 cm away from the eye this will result in a position change of nearly 3.8 cm for an object at 80 cm. This effect can only be corrected by directly measuring eye movements (which can be done but which adds considerable complication and expense). In Fish Tank VR the same effect exists, but is much smaller, only amounting to a 3.8 mm movement for objects at 80cm if they are close to the plane of the screen.

Integration of the VR Workspace with the Everyday Workspace

Immersion VR has the major advantage of a wide field-of-view which can give the feeling of existing in the graphical world. However, the cost of this is to block out the everyday world of desks, chairs and filing cabinets with the consequence that the inhabitants of VR have to have handlers to make sure that they do not hurt themselves. The Fish Tank VR workspace can be part of the office, just as the workstation can be part of the office. (We note that work is also progressing on "augmented VR", the purpose of which is to blend everyday reality and graphics using head mounted partially transparent displays with a wide viewing angle.)

DESIGN PROPERTIES OF OUR FISH TANK VR

Our first experiment was designed to investigate two of the factors leading to the subjective impression of three dimensional space, namely the relative importance of stereopsis and head coupling. We wished to examine these factors in the context of a scene that would seem as

convincingly 3D as possible, that is, it should have most of the factors that contribute to our impression of space, such as appropriate shading, shadows, and other spatial cues in addition to head coupling and stereo. This is unlike the normal study which starts with an impoverished scene and adds only a single factor, such as stereopsis. Instead, our study can be regarded as taking a scene which is rich in spatial and temporal information and subtracting either stereopsis, head coupled perspective, or both.

In the following sections we present a brief discussion of the various design decisions which went into constructing our Fish Tank VR experiments.

Figure 2. The sphere display used in the first experiment. Hardware lighting was used to achieve the specular reflection, while the fuzzy cast shadow was pre-computed.

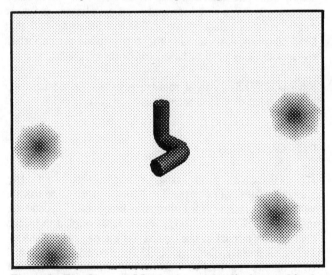

Figure 3. The Shepard-Metzler bent tube display used in the first experiment.

Objects

We constructed the two very simple scenes shown in Figures 2 and 3 for our first experiment: one consisted of a sphere with its shadow cast on a set of parallel horizontal bars below and to the left; the other consisted of a bent piece of tube based on Shepard and Metzler's (1971) mental rotation objects. Both of these scenes were given what we call our "Vection Background". This requires a little explanation.

The term "vection" is usually associated with the feeling of self movement when a large field display is moved with respect to an observer. Thus people placed in the center of a drum which rotates independent of them will, under the right circumstances, feel that it is they who are rotating, not the drum. It is often claimed that it is the wide-field-of-view peripheral stimulus that is critical for the vection experience. However, recent evidence suggests that the effect can be achieved with a small field-of-view (Howard and Heckman, 1989). Also, it is commonly observed that the vection effect can be obtained when looking out of a small airplane window across the aisle when another plane starts to move.

Howard and Heckman suggested that one of the important factors in eliciting vection is the perceived distance of a moving visual image. Images that are perceived as furthest away contributing the most. In the case of Fish Tank VR, we wish the observer to feel that the monitor is a window to an extensive space, so we reasoned that the experience of spaciousness would be enhanced with an appropriate background. Accordingly, we generated a background that consists of a random field of objects computed as though they were at infinity with respect to the observer. We call this our "vection" background.

Depth-of-Field

As mentioned in the introduction, one of the advantages of Fish Tank VR is that it constrains the field of interest to the region within the frame of the monitor, and a few centimeters in front and behind it. With this assumption, more distant objects will be out of focus. Accordingly, we made the vection background out of fuzzy discs, to give the illusion of depth-of-field. It should be understood that the vection background is not intended to be focussed on; instead it is intended to give a feeling of spaciousness when objects in the foreground are fixated.

Shading

Three types of shading information seem to be important in aiding our perception of the layout and shape of objects in space. Shading, both Lambertian and specular, tells us about the shape of surfaces, while cast shadows tell us about the positions of objects relative to each other (Wanger et al., 1992).

Spatio-Temporal Accuracy in Head Tracking

Deering (1992) presents a strong case for accuracy in both time and space being important in obtaining a strong percept of 3D space. If there are distortions in the measured position of the head - and hence the viewer's eye, then the result will be a scene that appears to be made of rubber and which flexes as the viewer moves. Performance decrements can be expected if there is temporal lag in the device that measures head position (Smith, 1962), although these may possibly be mitigated by the use of a predictive filter (Liang et al., 1991; Friedman, et al., 1992) One of the

most common devices used to track head position is the 3Space Isotrack, a six degree of freedom position sensor made by Polhemus. However, it is known that this device gives position information with a significant temporal lag, which may be as much as 80 msec behind the current position (Liang et al., 1991). We used the Shooting Star Technology ADL-1 to provide head position information without any software smoothing. This device uses mechanical linkages with potentiometers at the joints to give fast readings (see Figure 1). The lag in this device is small (2ms), much less than that induced by other factors such as the time taken to read the input buffer and to update the image on the screen. Its rated absolute positional accuracy is 0.51 cm and its resolution is 0.064 cm.

Stereo Display

To obtain a stereo view we used the StereoGraphics CristalEyes stereo system coupled with the SGI workstation's ability to display 120 frames/second (60 to each eye). Unfortunately this mode of stereo display is far from perfect and some significant ghosting can be seen from the image designated for the left eye bleeding into the right eye view, and vice versa. To minimize this effect we chose colours with only a small green component since the green phosphor has the longest decay rate on our monitor (and this is typical of most monitors - a better solution would have been to replace the monitor with one more suited for stereo display, as recommended by Deering (1992)).

High Frame Rate

Because of the desire of users of 3D stereo display equipment to display complex information, they almost always show so much information that the frame update rate drops below the maximum of 60 Hz. In fact, frame rates of only 10 Hz are more typical.

One of our design criterion was to create a scene which was reasonably rich in 3D spatial cues, but which still had a fast update rate. By carefully limiting the complexity of the scenes we were able to achieve the 60 Hz update rate with the scenes illustrated using a Silicon Graphics 4D 240 VGX.

EXPERIMENT 1: SUBJECTIVE IMPRESSIONS OF THREE DIMENSIONALITY

To compare the relative effectiveness of head coupling and stereopsis we designed an experimental protocol allowing subjects to make comparisons between pairs of presentation methods, toggling between them until they decided which contributed more to the perception of 3D space. We also questioned subjects after the experiment on their feelings about the value of the different modes of display.

The five conditions are given in Table 1. The experiment was carried out with the subjects always wearing the stereo goggles and the head tracking system. In the non-stereo conditions the same scene was presented to the two eyes. In the binocular non-stereo viewing condition the viewpoint was between the eyes. In the monocular viewing condition, the viewpoint was correct for the right eye and the subjects was asked to "Close your left eye". In the fixed viewpoint condition the perspective view was established by the subject's head position at the start of the trial. Subjects were asked to move their heads around for all conditions in order to assess the value of head coupling.

Table 1: Experimental Conditions

1	Picture
2	Stereo only
3	Head Coupled Monocular
4	Head Coupled Binocular
5	Head Coupled + Stereo

Trials

On a given trial subjects were allowed to toggle between two viewing conditions using the space bar, continuing to examine each until they had decided which gave the strongest impression of three dimensionality. When they had decided which was "best", they made the selection using the mouse. This automatically advanced them to the next pair of conditions. There were 10 pairwise comparisons of 5 conditions. A trial block was made up 20 trials consisting of the 10 pairwise comparisons for the sphere scene and the 10 pairwise comparisons for the bent tube scene. The entire block of 20 trials was repeated twice. The order of all comparisons was randomized.

Following the comparison trials, subjects were asked the following set of questions and their answers were recorded.

All of the following questions relate to the quality of the 3D spatial impression
Is head coupling as important, more important or less important than stereo?
Is the combination of head coupling and stereo better than either alone?
Is head coupling alone worthwhile? (If you had the option would you use it?)
Is stereo alone worthwhile? (If you had the option would you use it?)
Is head couplng with stereo worthwhile? (If you had the option would you use it?)
Do you have other comments on these methods of displaying 3D data?

Seven subjects were used in this experiment, four of whom were well acquainted with high performance graphics systems

RESULTS FROM EXPERIMENT 1

There were no systematic differences between the results obtained from the two scenes and so these data have been merged. The results are summarized in Table 2, which represents the combined data from all subjects. This matrix shows for each pair of conditions which condition gave the strongest 3D impression. Thus the value 89% in row 4 column 2 means that in 25 out of 28 possible responses

subjects found the Head Coupled (non-stereo) display more compelling than the Stereo only (non-head coupled) display.

Table 2

All Subjects	1	2	3	4	5	All
1 Picture		43%	1%	0%	7%	13%
2 Stereo only	57%		7%	11%	0%	19%
3HC monocular	96%	93%		29%	61%	70%
4 HC binocular	100%	89%	71%		68%	82%
5 HC + stereo	93%	100%	39%	32%		66%

What is most striking about this data is the fact that static stereo was rarely found to be more effective than head coupled viewing without stereo. The right hand column shows for each condition the overall percentage of responses for which that condition was preferred. This shows that head coupled displays without stereo were preferred somewhat more often than head coupled displays with stereo. This may possibly be attributed to the ghosting of the image which occurs due to imperfect phosphor decay, causing cross talk between the left and right eye images.

The results from the set of questions also strongly supported the usefulness of head coupled stereo viewing. All users said that they would use it for object visualization if it were available. When asked to compare the importance of head coupling with stereo, two of the seven subjects stated that they thought stereo was more important than head coupling. However, these same subjects preferred the head coupling in the direct comparison task. One subject complained about the awkwardness of the apparatus and pointed out that that would be a factor in how often it would be used.

EXPERIMENT 2: TRACING TREE PATHS

For our second experiment we chose a task that was designed by Sollenberger and Milgram (1992) to study the ability of observers to perceive arterial branching in brain scan data under different viewing conditions. The task involves the construction of two trees in 3D space, whose branches overlap considerably. A leaf of one of the trees is marked and the subject has to determine to which of the two tree roots that branch belongs. Errors are measured to assess the conditions. Sollenberger and Milgram used this task to look at trees viewed with and without stereo and with and without rotation. We used it to look at head coupled perspective viewing and stereo using the same set of conditions used in experiment 1. In addition to errors, we measured task performance time.

Tree construction: Our trees were recursively defined ternary trees. Each parent node had three child nodes connected to it by lines. The height of each child above its parent is 70% of the height of the parent above the grandparent. The lateral positions of the children were randomly placed relative to the parent. There were three levels of branches above the trunk, resulting in 27 leaves for each tree.

The following recurrence relation gives a precise specification.

HorizontalSpacing $_{root}$ = 8.0 cm.
VerticalSpacing $_{root}$ = 8.0 cm.

HorizontalSpacing$_{child}$=0.7*HorizontalSpacing$_{parent}$
VerticalSpacing$_{child}$ = 0.7*VerticalSpacing$_{parent}$

Y_{child} = Y_{parent} + VerticalSpacing(1.0 + Rand()*0.25)
X_{child} = X_{parent} + HorizontalSpacing*Rand()
Z_{child} = Z_{parent} + HorizontalSpacing*Rand()

where Rand() returns a uniform random number in the range [-1,+1]

In addition a vertical trunk of length **VerticalSpacing** is added at the base of the tree.

On each trial two trees were constructed with roots laterally separated by one cm. A yellow circle was placed on the leaf closest to the midline between the two roots, only taking the x coordinate into account. The reason for this was to eliminate trials that would be easy in all conditions because they occurred in parts of the trees where there was no overlap with the other tree. An example of a pair of trees photographed from the monitor screen is shown in Figure 4. The trees were coloured purple (monitor red plus monitor blue) on the same background as used in Experiment 1. The triangle and square at the tree roots were coloured green.

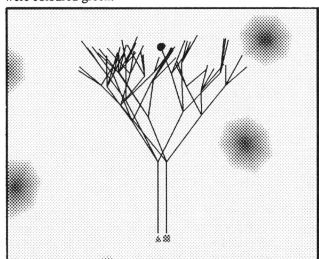

Figure 4. An example of a tree display used in Experiment 2. The purple colour was used to minimize ghosting.

The five viewing conditions listed in Table 1 were employed. Ten subjects who consisted of graduate and undergraduate students were instructed to be as accurate as they could and not to worry about how long they were taking.

Trial Blocks

A practice group of 10 trials (two in each condition) was given at the start of the experiment. Trials were given in groups of 22, with the first two trials of each group designated as additional practice trials and where all 22 trials were given in one of the five viewing conditions. A trial block consisted of all 5 groups given in a random order, and the entire experiment consisted of 3 such blocks resulting in a total of 60 trials in each of the 5 experimental conditions.

RESULTS FROM EXPERIMENT 2

The results from Experiment 2 are summarized in Tables 3 and 4. The timing data shows that the head coupled stereo condition was the fastest, but that head coupling alone was slow. There are significant differences at the 0.05 level between both conditions 3 and 4 and condition 5 (by the Wilcoxon matched pairs signed ranks test). The only other difference that is significant is between condition 4 and condition 1.

Table 3

Timing data	times (sec)
1 Picture	7.50
2 Stereo only	8.09
3 HC monocular	8.66
4 HC binocular	9.12
5 HC + stereo	6.83

Table 4

Error data	% errors
1 Picture	21.8
2 Stereo only	14.7
3 HC monocular	3.7
4 HC binocular	2.7
5 HC + stereo	1.3

The error data is more interesting, with errors ranging from 21.8% in the static, no stereo condition, to 1.3% for the head coupled stereo conditions. All of the differences are significant in pairwise comparisons except for the difference between conditions 3 and 4, the two head coupled conditions without stereo.

Overall, the error rates obtained are lower than those obtained by Sollenberger and Milgram (1991), but the pattern is strikingly similar despite the differences in the stimulus trees, the viewing condition and the experimental protocols. There are two other similarities between our findings and those reported by Sollenberger and Milgram: we found motion to be more important than stereo, even though their motion was simple rotation of the object whereas ours resulted from head coupling; and we found the combination of motion (head coupling in our case) and stereo to be more effective than either in isolation.

DISCUSSION

The strong preference expressed by most subjects for the head coupled displays over the stereo displays in Experiment 1 and the enthusiastic response of viewers to a head coupled display both suggest that people who observe 3D scenes with graphics systems capable of real-time update rates should consider investing in some method of tracking head position and in coupling the displayed image directly to the viewpoint of the observer. Once this is done the subjective results suggest that stereopsis may add only marginally to the perception of three dimensionality of objects.

Experiment 2 provides objective evidence that head coupled stereo can help users to comprehend a complex tree structured graphical object. Here the evidence shows that both head coupling and stereopsis contribute to performance. The task maps well into two domains of considerable current interest, the domain of medical imaging where doctors may wish to trace blood vessels in brain scan data, and the domain of 3D software visualization where software engineers may wish to trace object dependencies between software modules represented as networks in 3D space (Robertson, et al., 1991, Fairchild et al., 1988). In both applications error rates are critically important and our finding is that head coupled stereo can reduce error rates by a factor of sixteen over a static pictorial display.

It can be argued that it is the motion-induced depth (Wallach and O'Connell, 1953) and not the head coupling as such that produced both the improved spatial percept and the improved performance on the tracing task. Our current evidence does not counter this objection. However, it is likely the head coupled image motion (note that the object appears fixed in space, it is the image which moves) is a way of providing spatial information which is more appealing than displaying the scene rocking back and fourth about a vertical axis, as is commonly done in molecular modelling packages.

ACKNOWLEDGEMENTS
Financial support for this project was provided by the Natural Sciences and Engineering Research Council of Canada and the British Columbia Advanced Systems Institute.

REFERENCES

1. Deering, M. (1992) High Resolution Virtual Reality. Computer Graphics, 26, 2, 195-202.

2. Fairchild, K.M., Poltrock, E.E. and Furnas, G.W. (1988) SemNet: Three-Dimensional Graphic representations of large knowledge bases. In Cognitive Science and Its Applications for Human-Computer Interaction. Ed Raymond Guindon, Lawrence Erelbaum, 201-233.

3. Friedman, M., Starner, T and Pentland, A., (1992) Device Synchronization using and optimal linear filter. 1992 Symposium on Interactive 3D graphics, Special Issue of Computer Graphics, 57-62.

4. Gibson, J.J. (1979) The Ecological Approach to Visual Perception. Houghton Mifflin: Boston.

5. Howard, I.P. an Heckman, T. (1989) Circular vection as a function of the relative sizes, distances and positions of two competing visual displays. Perception, 18 (5) 657-665.

6. Liang, J., Shaw, C., and Green, M. (1991) On temporal realism in the virtual reality environment. UIST'91 19-25.

7. McKenna, M, (1992) Interactive viewpoint control and three-dimensional operations. 1992 Symposium on Interactive 3D graphics, Special Issue of Computer Graphics, 53-56.

8. Robertson, G.G. Mackinlay, J.D. and Card, S.K. (1991) Cone trees: Animated 3D visualizations of hierarchical information. Proc of CHI'91: 189-194.

9. Shepard, R.N. and Metzler, J. (1971) Mental rotation of three-dimensional objects. Science, 171, 701-703.

10. Smith, K.U. (1962) Delayed sensory feedback and behavior, W.B. Saunders, Philadelphia.

11. Sollenberger, R.L., and Milgram, P. (1991) A comparative study of rotational and stereoscopic computer graphics depth cues. Proceedings of the Human Factors Society 35th Annual Meeting, San Francisco, 1452-1456.

12. Sutherland, I. (1968) A head-mounted three dimensional display. Fall Joint Computer Conference, AFIPS Conference Proceedings, 33, 757-764.

13. Wallach, H. and O'Connell, D.H. (1953) The kinetic depth effect. Journal of Experimental Psychology, 45, 205-217.

14. Wanger, L.R. Fewerda, J.A. and Greenberg, D.P. (1992) Perceiving spatial relationships in computer generated images. IEEE Computer Graphics and Applications, 12(3) 44-59.

15. Ward, M., Azuma, R., Bennett, R., Gottschalk, S., and Fuchs, H. (1992) A demonstrated optical tracker with scalable work area for head mounted display systems. 1992 Symposium on Interactive 3D Graphics, Special Issue of Computer Graphics, 43-52.

A Space Based Model for User Interaction in Shared Synthetic Environments

Lennart E. Fahlén
Distributed Systems Laboratory
tel:+46 8 752 15 39
lef@sics.se

Charles Grant Brown
Knowledge Communication Group
tel:+46 8 752 15 15
carl@sics.se

Olov Ståhl
Distributed Systems Laboratory
tel:+46 8 752 15 67
olovs@sics.se

Christer Carlsson
Distributed Systems Laboratory
tel:+46 8 752 15 60
cc@sics.se

Swedish Institute of Computer Science
Box 1263
S-164 28 Kista
Stockholm, Sweden.

ABSTRACT

In a distributed shared synthetic environment with provisions for high quality 3D visualization and interaction, it is possible to implement a powerful variant of a rooms/space metaphor based on the concept of presence or proximity between participants in 3D space. This kind of model can be used as an interface between the user and the computer, for overview and control of applications, file systems, networks and other computer resources, as well as for communication and collaboration with other users in the networked environment. We model proximity with a geometric volume of the immediate surroundings, *the aura*, of the participant's representation in the synthetic environment. This proximity, or aura, is used to establish presence at meetings, to establish communication channels and to provide interaction.

KEYWORDS: user interaction, 3D, visualization, communication, distribution, control, resource sharing, CSCW, virtual reality

INTRODUCTION

We discuss how presence and 3D space as a perception and a physical phenomenon can be exploited by virtual reality technology, that is, the use of three dimensional visualization, awareness and interaction.

We take advantage of presence and 3D-space to provide an interface to applications and resources. This technique is also used to support collaborative work between users. Using virtual reality, VR, technology in computer supported collaborative work applications permits the user to visualize, be aware of, and interact with CSCW tools and services and with other collaborators in the distributed environment.

We suggest the following advantages of this approach: Transparency of the use of multimedia tools for communication and collaboration can be enhanced. A degree of naturalness is achieved. Enablement in the use of distributed CSCW tools and services is improved. Unconstrained use is maintained. In addition, we speculate that learnability of use is enhanced.

In a distributed virtual reality environment, where the different participants are represented as stylized 3D icons, it is possible to implement a flexible and powerful variant of proximity/presence in a room/context/space metaphor which we outline below [9].

We would like to point out that the ideas presented in this paper could be applied to any domain where a suitable metric can be defined, not only 3D environments [2, 4].

BACKGROUND

The work we report has its origins in three fields: distributed shared VR, CSCW and knowledge communication. A shared distributed virtual reality system, MultiG[1] DIVE[2] (Distributed Interactive Virtual Environment), has been developed [6, 8, 11]. Examples of other shared virtual reality systems can be found in [5, 7]. We discuss the use of the DIVE system in computer supported collaborative work ap-

---

1. MultiG is a Swedish national research effort on high speed communication networks and distributed applications
2. The MultiG DIVE system was previously called the MultiG TelePresence system

plications and how transparency of one level of a communication model is supported [6]. To support a multiplicity of distributed applications and multiple forms of selective transparency, i.e., the masking of various features of distributed applications from the users, is an important goal of some research in CSCW [3].

We take advantage of the characteristics of distributed shared simulated worlds to deal with problems encountered in CSCW applications. We enhance the simulated worlds with a model of presence. We use "presence" to establish natural communication between participants in computer supported collaborative work applications and make the use of underlying communication tools and services transparent to the participants. Using this model the communication of knowledge in group collaboration becomes flexible, natural and intuitive and principles of cooperation in human communication are observed.

In traditional video-conferencing situations and also in computer based collaborative work situations, a participant has difficulty getting an overview of what is happening at other sites and in other meetings going on simultaneously. The participants wonder where the meeting is held, how large it is, which other participants are present and what the level of activity is. The topology of the meeting and the participants is not known or visualized.

It is difficult and non-intuitive to go from one video conference work situation to another. This problem is related to the lack of correlation between the video conference and activities in the organisation involved. The user has neither visualization of the structure of the organisation nor of the topology of the work situations. We want to promote visualization of the location of an activity and the relationship of that activity to other activities in the organisation.

A common characteristic of groupwork is the tendency to sub-group and re-group [1]. In short, the situation is dynamic. Video conferencing situations are usually rigid and unnatural. It is hard to do regrouping and sub-grouping. We are proposing a way to address these problems in "virtual meetings" based on the concept of proximity between participants in virtual 3D space.

In existing distributed applications, communication channels must be explicitly opened. Documents must be explicitly created. Distribution of information must be explicitly specified. We seek to remove this burden from the user. The user's communication with other participants in the simulated world should correspond closely to real world communication. Our approach permits CSCW tools and services to enable communications transparently through the use of a natural proximity metaphor.

Our goal is to support:

- dynamic virtual meetings and collaborative work situations which allow the formation of groups, sub-groups and new groups for communication and collaboration.

- the transparent use of underlying tools and services for communication and cooperation.

- natural and intuitive use of these tools and services.

- compatibility with the goals of CSCW research.

PRESENCE, AURA AND PROXIMITY

Presence is a perception used by humans in their normal process of communication and interaction. We perceive and are aware of the presence of other persons. In order to communicate, we manoeuvre ourselves to be near others or to make them aware of our presence.

The awareness of human presence involves two perceptual factors: *proximity* and *location*. Two simple examples will illustrate. First, a person who becomes aware of the presence of someone who approaches. In this case, presence is function of proximity. At some point the proximity to the person approaching makes one aware of his presence. Second, a group of people in a room who become aware of someone who goes to the dais or speaker's stand. In this case it is the location of the person at the dais which makes all in the room aware of his presence.

Aura can be defined as the *nearfield* or immediate surroundings of a person. The aura defines the region in which a person's presence may be perceived. Thus, to be perceived, a person's aura must extend to the perceiver.

In a shared synthetic environment where users have 3D representations, we model proximity as an aura surrounding each user icon, see Figure 1. In the simplest case, the aura, being a geometric volume, can be realized as a sphere centered around the icon, but other shapes are possible[3].

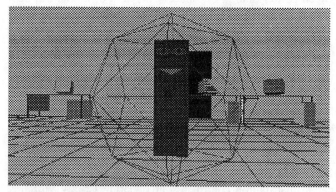

Figure 1. A 3D icon with surrounding aura

The natural concept of proximity is illustrated by one icon's aura intersecting the aura of another icon or of some tool or service in the simulated world, see Figure 2 below. We discuss tools or services in the next section.

3. All figures in this paper are snapshots from the DIVE system and that they are taken from the viewpoint of one user, present in the virtual environment. The auras seen in some of these pictures are normally not visible, but have been made so in order for the reader to get a better understanding of how auras are used.

Figure 2. Two 3D icons with intersecting auras.

When the aura of two or more icons intersect the aura of a service or tool we apply the same principle. In this case the aura of one user extends through the aura of the tool to the aura of the other user, see Figure 3. The event of auras intersecting is also used as an enabler of various services and tools.

Figure 3. Two users at conference table tool. One user not using the tool.

SERVICES AND PERCEPTUAL AURA

The tools we have implemented in DIVE include a distributed whiteboard, a conference table, a portable generalised document and a podium tool. These will be described in turn below. They provide collaborative shared tools whose operation and use is achieved through aura interaction to permit communication between users and the sharing of resources.

We extend the perception of aura to be a property of services and tools provided in the context of the virtual world. We call this the perceptual aura of a service. The perceptual aura of a service is a volume specific to the service.

The use of aura provides a consistent interface to these tools as well as transparent access to a global network of collaborators and tools.

Whiteboard

The whiteboard service [12] supports the creation and manipulation of simple geometric objects, like lines, rectangles and circles, see Figure 4. Other whiteboard functions are video, where a live video screen can be displayed on the whiteboard, and text. Participants who wish to use the whiteboard

must first move up close to it and grab a pen, which can be done by pressing a pen button. Several participants can use the service simultaneously.

Whiteboards existing at the same time can be grouped together, where whiteboards belonging to the same group are replicates of each other. This means that all operations done by participants at one whiteboard are immediately visible at the other whiteboards within the group. Groups can be formed of whiteboards placed in the same room or in different rooms.

Each whiteboard has an aura which is used both as an aura of enablement and an aura of perception. To be able to use the whiteboard, a participant has to be within its aura, and all participants are considered to be in proximity to each other. This means for instance that they can talk to each other while using the whiteboard.

Document

The document is basically just a small, portable whiteboard that a user can pick up and carry with him. The main difference between a document and a whiteboard is, apart from the appearance, that the document is a single user service. This means for example that only one user at a time can create and manipulate objects on a document. Another implication is that the document aura is only used as an aura of enablement.

Documents can be copied and distributed in several ways. A document can be placed on a whiteboard, manipulated and then taken down. Documents can be grouped, which means that a number of users can each have an active copy of the same document.

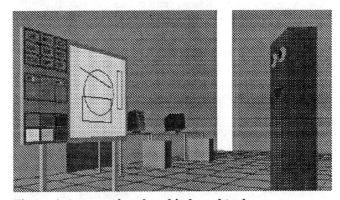

Figure 4. A user using the whiteboard tool

Conference Table

The conference table service allows a group of users to meet and have a private discussion. A user approaching the conference table will at some stage intersect the table's perceptual aura, which will make the table aware of him. This means that the user joins the conference and the table will establish communication channels between him and all other participants. This is as natural as real people joining a discussion group at a real table. Every participant at the table recognizes the presence of the newcomer and recognizes that communication extends to and from him.

The conference table service also includes a distribution tool, which is used to distribute documents among users.

When a participant places a document on the conference table, a tool is enabled to distribute the virtual document to the set of participants in the perceptual aura of the conference table service. Each participant will be given a private or active copy of the document, depending on the situation.

Each conference table has two auras, one aura of perception and one aura of distribution. The aura of perception is used to determine when a user joins or leaves the conference, while the aura of distribution is used to determine when, how and to whom a document is to be distributed.

Podium

The podium service allows one user to address a group of users, although they may not be in proximity to each other. The user standing at the podium, the speaker, is able to communicate with the group of users within the podiums aura of communication. The "listeners" are not able to communicate with the speaker (if they are not in proximity to the speaker, as defined by their individual auras).

The podium has one aura of perception that determines who is allowed to speak, and one aura of communication that defines the group of listeners.

TRANSPARENCY AND NATURALNESS OF COMMUNICATION AND INTERACTION

Natural communication can be supported in the virtual reality environment with the combination of aura and distributed services. Consider selecting an e-mail tool, selecting a mailing list, inserting a document and then initiating distribution. A realization of all these steps consists of simply placing the virtual document on a distribution service such as a conference table and the table will automatically distribute the documents to all the conference participants. Another realization is to explicitly give the document to another user. The conference table service has other tools to support natural communication. When a participant approaches the conference table his aura intersects the perceptual aura of the table. Thus he joins a conference. This means that voice (and possibly video) channels of communication are opened to all other participants at the table. A similar service is the whiteboard which offers communication possibilities to the set of participants who have approached the whiteboard. There is great flexibility in the use of these distributed services.

The use of aura merely provides a general means of extending services to participants in a natural way. Clearly different distributed services may have different communication tools. The aura approach connects participants to distributed services through the tools provided by the distributed service.

A challenge in CSCW today is to support communication, sharing and exchange of information in the most flexible possible way, without imposing control or constraints on the communication and use of services. We believe that the aura approach does not impose restrictions on the use or implementation of distributed services in a virtual environment. Rather, it provides the participant with a uniform and natural interaction both with other participants and with distributed services.

The MultiG DIVE system provides a distributed virtual reality platform upon which distributed services and tools can be built. A central feature is the inherent visualization of activities and the context of activities. This can for example be used to provide a rooms metaphor [1]. In DIVE, we have built a 3D model of our office building, consisting of a number of rooms. Users are able to manoeuvre themselves through this environment, "see" other users, represented by 3D icons, and use the "services" that the rooms provide.

Transparency in the use of distributed tools is supported through the use of the aura paradigm. Open distributed systems aim to provide the maximum possible transparency in the use of distributed services and access to information. The aura representation is used to establish a presence at meetings, establish communication channels such as video, shared whiteboards, audio etc. and to provide interaction. The DIVE environment provides the dynamic 3D visualization. Transparency is aided by using auras at several levels:

- transparency of location: Participants are unaware of the physical location of other participants. Only their stylized icons are visible.

- transparency of domain: The domain of interaction is provided by the room and distributed services.

- transparency of activity: Participants are unaware of the mechanism for running distributed services, coordination, communication and distribution.

- transparency of security: Participants are unaware of underlying tools that enforce security policies, because these tools are embedded in the distributed services. (For example, membership of group when joining a conference, access to distributed documents).

ENABLERS AND AMPLIFIERS

Aura is used for three complementary enabling mechanisms: enabling the use of services and tools, group formation/extension and enabling aura-amplification. We have outlined above the use of aura as an enabling mechanism for communication, one type of service or tool. Control or use of a service is implicitly given when a user takes an enabler-position. Enabler positions are achieved when the user's aura intersects another user's aura or the perceptual aura of a service. Examples of enabling mechanisms are:

- enable-talk: When a participant approaches another participant, voice-talk is enabled. Each participants' voice talk channel to the other is opened.

- enable-use-whiteboard: When a participant approaches a whiteboard service, the use of the whiteboard is enabled. The user is able to place information on the whiteboard and use the whiteboard tools once the whiteboard is enabled.

An important feature of collaborative work is the ability to form and reform groups and subgroups [1]. Aura is used to enable group establishment and extension. For example, when voice-talk is enabled by one participant approaching another, a group (of two) is formed. If another participant approaches the group aura, the group is extended to include the new participant and voice talk is enabled from all members of the existing group to the new member and vice-versa. This use of aura makes group formation transparent, simple and natural.

Another mechanism that makes use of aura is the enable-amplification mechanism. Here group extension is carried out through the enabling of a service or tool. We have already seen an example of this above when we discussed the use of the conference table service. We call this an amplifying service because all tools provided by the conference table (voice-talk or the distribution-tool) serve to extend or amplify the aura of communication to all participants in the aura of perception of the conference table. Examples of aura amplifiers are:

- conference-table. The aura of communication extends to all participants within the aura of perception of the table.

- white-board. The aura of communication is extends to all participants within the activity (room, or perhaps a smaller volume near the whiteboard). Aura of perception is limited to a volume near the white-board service (which limits the number of participants enabled to use the whiteboard to an arbitrary number).

- podium. The aura of communication extends to the activity (room). Voice-talk is enabled from the podium to all participants in the activity. Voice talk is not enabled from the participants to the podium. Aura of perception is limited to the one participant enabled near the podium.

A SCENARIO

The different groups of a conference or a collaborative situation can be constituted by proximity (as with our aura based approach) or possibly by other means such as touch (i.e., being pointed at by someone's 3D pointing device). Several different levels of communication ranges are possible: Being face-to-face with a person, being within the aura of a person, being within the same room or activity area as others. Aura amplifiers extend presence. A conference table with users at opposite ends allows the users to communicate even though the actual geometric distance is much greater than the individuals aura distance. That is, moving to the conference table extends ones aura to the surroundings of the table. A whiteboard can have the same functionality with the added twist of shared resource control. That may mean, for instance, that only the three (arbitrary number) users which are closest to the whiteboard can write and draw on the whiteboard, while the other participants (perhaps also arbitrarily limited in number) must wait for their turn. Variations like having a speaker use a podium (thus gaining height or "position") to address a group of listeners are possible. In the cases of the table and whiteboard, we have aura multi-casting, which in the latter case is layered. When mounting the podium there is an expansion of one's aura, i.e., aura broadcasting.

Some of the cues, then, are position, height, range, direction, pointing and even possibly gestures. Further research is needed to determine the most useful set of cues. The aim should be to establish naturalness and transparency because this makes the system easier to learn and use and perhaps more significantly lessens the cognitive load on the users.

These 3D metaphors applied in CSCW applications make possible explicit visualizations of how "real world" collaborative work extends in space and time. The participants are literally able to take a birds eye view of what is going on in the landscape of different work groups which, in some loose way, constitute the collaborative environment. For instance, the milling of participants between groups could easily be tracked, the joining together of groups into larger units and the corresponding splitting up of groups can be handled by a direct spatial, temporal, natural and visual metaphor, see Figure 5.

IMPLEMENTATION

Our goal is to provide tools for building CSCW environments. Those environments should support interaction, sequences of interaction, video and audio interaction, creation, modification and communication of documents, as well as visualization of these activities. Users should be able to move around in the environment, use the services and form groups.

Practical implementations could span the range from true virtual reality with stereoscopic immersion display helmets and gloves (and other encapsulating kinds of input/sensor devices) to a more modest evolution of 2D graphic user interfaces into 3D versions. It is important to note that virtual reality based video conferencing systems can co-exist with and communicate with more conventional and existing systems.

Our current implementation consists of a basic toolbox, which includes a whiteboard service, a conference table service, the handling and distribution of documents and support for the aura functionality. Both users and services can be assigned auras and the collision of auras can be tracked. There is, at present, no support for speech communication between users.

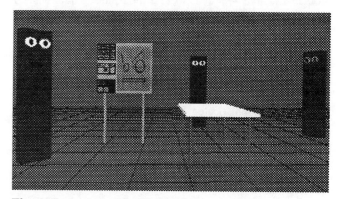

Figure 5. A group of users having a meeting.

FURTHER WORK

We plan to work in the areas of perceived and acceptable models of aura, sharing and distribution of multimedia documents, development of higher order gesture handlers and interactive, visually oriented tools together with the distributed sharing of these.

There is a need to design and run experiments that compare problem solving and collaboration in a 2D environment against a 3D environment. This should be done in collaboration with researchers from the behavioral/cognitive domain.

We hope to integrate within our environment the MultiG

CoDesk [10], a 2D window and icon based system for distributed collaboration and also the teleconferencing distribution mechanism for shared video and audio that have been developed within the MultiG program [11].

In the real world, a person can choose to ignore the presence of another person, or, as the case may be, choose to be very attentive to that person. This is one example of a social interaction issue that we want to be able to accommodate in our system. We have begun to investigate an extension to the aura model by the incorporation of attention modelled by user focus and awareness [2, 4]. This is a natural next step to take in the refinement of the model.

The important and central issue of floor control and access to services (e.g., whiteboard and other distributed resources) in a heterogeneous distributed environment will be addressed in a future paper when we have more experience with the use of the DIVE system. As we have stated above, we strive to support flexible and unconstrained use of the communication media.

DISCUSSION AND CONCLUSION

We have presented a model for human-machine-human interaction based on real world concepts of awareness and manipulation, such as presence, proximity and moving of physical objects. We propose that this is a step toward the "most natural interface", i.e., an interface where the computer becomes transparent and the components of the interface behave in a way that could be expected from similar objects in similar situations in our physical environment. An example in the present system would be the communication of documents between participants by explicitly "handing them over." A problematic area with this model is the handling of unwanted or unnatural tasks, like repetition, iteration and recursion. There is also a potential problem with what could be described as the misalignment between the real user and the user's representation in the synthetic environment. This can only partially be overcome by, for example, using real-time video inserts on the 3D icon's "face." A mechanism is needed for handling 3D sophisticated facial expressions and body language. An example of this could be the case of a conference participant rising from the conference table with an angry look in his face and then leaving the room.

REFERENCES

1. Benford, S. *Rooms Metaphor - Design of Objects*, Department of Computing Science, University of Nottingham, 1991.

2. Benford, S., and Fahlén, L. E. *Aura, Focus and Awareness*, Proceedings of the 5th MultiG Workshop, Stockholm, December 18, 1992.

3. Benford, S., Prinz, W., Mariani, J., Navarro, L., Bignoli, E., Brown, C. G. and Näslund, T. *MOCCA - A CSCW Environment*, First annual report of the MOCCA working group of COST-14 CoTech.

4. Benford, S., Bullock A., Cook N., Harvey P., Ingram R. and Lee O. *From Rooms to Cyberspace: Models of Interaction in large Virtual Computer Spaces*, The University of Nottingham, Nottingham, UK (to appear in the Butterworth-Heinmann journal Interacting With Computers in 1993).

5. Blanchard, C., Burgess, S., Harville, Y., Lanier, J., Lasko, A., Oberman, M. and Teitel, M. *Reality Built for Two: A Virtual Reality Tool*, ACM SIGGRAPH Computer Graphics 24:2, pp. 35-36.

6. Carlsson, C. and Hagsand O. *The MultiG Distributed Interactive Virtual Environment*, Proceedings of the 5th MultiG Workshop, Stockholm, December 18, 1992.

7. Codella, C., Jalili, R., Koved, L., Lewis, J. B., Ling, D. T., Lipscomb, J. S., Rabenhorst, D. A., Wang, C. P., Norton, A., Sweeney, P. and Turk, G. *Interactive Simulation in a Multi-Person Virtual World*, Proceedings of CHI'92, Monterey, May 3-7, 1992, pp. 329-334.

8. Fahlén, L. E. *The MultiG TelePresence System*, in Proceedings of 3rd MultiG Workshop, Stockholm, December 1991, pp. 33-57.

9. Fahlén, L. E. and Brown, C. G. *The use of a 3D Aura Metaphor for Computer Based Conferencing and Teleworking*, in Proceedings of 4th MultiG Workshop, Stockholm, May 1992, pp. 69-74.

10. Marmolin, H., Sundblad, Y. Tollmar K., Avatare A. and Eriksson H. *CoDesk - an Interface to The KnowledgeNet*, in Proceedings of 4th MultiG Workshop, Stockholm, May 1992, pp. 17-32.

11. Pehrson, B., Gunningberg, P. and Pink, S. *MultiG-A research Programme on Distributed MultiMedia Applications and Gigabits Networks*, IEEE Network Magazine vol 6, 1 (January 1992), pp. 26-35.

12. Ståhl, O. *Mdraw - A Tool for Cooperative Work in the MultiG TelePresence Environment*, Technical Report T92:05, SICS, 1992.

HCI in the School of Computer Science at Carnegie Mellon University

Bonnie E. John
Computer Science and Psychology
Carnegie Mellon University
Pittsburgh, PA, 15213, USA
E-mail: bej@cs.cmu.edu

James H. Morris
Head, Computer Science Department
Carnegie Mellon University
Pittsburgh, PA, 15213, USA
E-mail: jhm@cs.cmu.edu

ABSTRACT

People use *computers* to accomplish *tasks*. Consequently, understanding human capabilities and tasks is as important to the design of computer systems as understanding computer technologies. The School of Computer Science (SCS) at Carnegie Mellon University (CMU) has become home to an interdisciplinary community that performs research on HCI issues, develops systems using HCI methods of design and evaluation, and trains students in the theory and skills necessary to become HCI professionals.

THE PROBLEM

Many computer systems do not realize their full potential to enable users to accomplish tasks easily and efficiently. It seems that for every successful system, e.g. automated teller machines, there exists a score of unsuccessful systems. For instance, the average person's inability to program a VCR has become an international joke. If automated tellers are so successful, why are so many other computer systems so abysmal? We offer two answers.

First is the difficulty of "scaling up" in HCI. As tasks become more complex and less familiar, as the amount of information increases, and as decision making encompasses more variables, the best ways to facilitate interaction between humans and computers are less understood. Second, system designers need better training in the theory and practice of HCI. As long as speed, size, and cost of computers were the limiting factors in computer systems, the emphasis of computer science education was rightly placed on techniques for making faster, cheaper computers and efficient algorithms to process data. Today, however, computers are fast, powerful, and cheap, and vast amounts of information can be collected, generated, and presented to users. The limitation on completing a task has become the user's ability to sift through and interpret this information, rather than the computer's ability to store or process it.

OUR APPROACH TO HCI

The HCI community in CMU-SCS believes it is time to expand the historical scope of computer system design and education. We reaffirm the central tenet of computer science

that, ultimately, people use computers to accomplish tasks. This implies that an understanding of human capabilities and tasks is as important to the design of effective computer systems as an understanding of computer technologies (Figure 1).

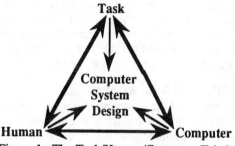

Figure 1. The Task/Human/Computer Triad.

The first fundamental element in the design of effective systems is an understanding of the tasks users need to carry out. Frequent tasks may be relatively easy to identify, but occasional tasks, or exceptional tasks for emergency conditions, are more difficult to discover. Task analysis methods, and techniques for representing tasks and mapping from tasks to system functionality are active research areas.

The second fundamental element is an understanding of the people performing the tasks. Depending on the task, this understanding may include perceptual capabilities (e.g., capacity to identify an object in context, color vision and deficiencies) cognitive characteristics (e.g., short-term and long-term memory, learning), motor capabilities (e.g., typing speed), and their social/political and organizational contexts (e.g., power relationships, organizational structure, communication protocols).

The third element, the computer, includes the technology of visual displays, manual input devices, sound and gesture recognition, gaze-tracking, interaction styles and techniques, and user interface development environments and tools. These areas are the traditional realm of CS, and continue to play an important role in any task/human/computer system.

Research and education in HCI in the SCS are not confined to a single corner of this triangle. Rather, we investigate the influences of a theory, method, or system developed in one corner on the other two corners and articulate what can be learned about designing a computer system.

RESEARCH IN HCI AT CMU-SCS

HCI research has been a hallmark of CMU-SCS for almost 20 years, producing the seminal *Psychology of Human-Computer Interaction* [2], and systems exploring new interaction techniques [4] and architectures [3].

Currently, about 30 faculty members in SCS consider HCI as their primary or secondary area of interest. Many combine backgrounds in CS or engineering with psychology, linguistics, or social science. Research projects often cross departmental lines, with joint work conducted between SCS and the Departments of Psychology, English, or Design, or various university centers (e.g., the Center for Design of Educational Computing, the Engineering Design Research Center). Current projects include understanding human information processing in the context of using computers; interactive techniques, devices, and modalities; analysis and evaluation of human-computer systems; user interface software implementation; intelligent interfaces; Computer-Supported Cooperative Work; and the study of software development and programming as a human activity (Figure 2).

EDUCATION IN HCI AT CMU-SCS

The importance of the task/human/computer triad to system design has implications for the education of all CS students. At the undergraduate level, we introduce HCI issues in many CS courses and we are developing undergraduate courses along the lines presented in the ACM SIGCHI curriculum report [1]. At the Masters level, we are developing courses for an HCI track in the Masters of Software Engineering program. At the Ph.D. level, we plan to educate all doctoral students in the importance of HCI issues and the existence of methods, techniques, and tools for designing and evaluating system design.

In addition, doctoral students wishing to concentrate in HCI should demonstrate mastery of the following skills: building a system with a UI development or prototyping tool; performing an empirical evaluation of a system; evaluating a system with an analytic method (e.g., GOMS, cognitive walkthrough). These skills will help the students to do their own research in HCI. They will increase students' understanding of the research of others. Finally, they provide a foundation for working as part of an interdisciplinary design team.

ACKNOWLEDGEMENTS

This overview is based on a report by SCS faculty interested in HCI to the CMU-SCS faculty as a whole (Tech Report CMU-CS-92-193, available from the authors). Special thanks to Duane Adams, Allen Newell, and Raj Reddy for instigating that effort.

REFERENCES

1. *ACM SIGCHI Curricula for Human-Computer Interaction*, ACM, New York, 1992.
2. Card, S. K., Moran, T. P., & Newell, A. *The Psychology of Human-Computer Interaction*, Lawrence Erlbaum Associates, Hillsdale, N.J., 1983.
3. Palay, A. J., Hansen, W. J., Sherman, M., Wadlow, M. G., Neuendorffer, T. P., Stern, Z., Bader, M., & Peters, T. "The Andrew Toolkit - An Overview." In proceedings of the USENIX Winter Conference (Dallas, TX, February 9-12) USENIX Assoc., Berkely, CA, 1988. pp. 9-21.
4. Robertson, G., McCracken, D., & Newell, A. "The ZOG approach to man-machine communication" *International Journal of Man-Machine Studies, 14,* 1980, pp. 461-488.

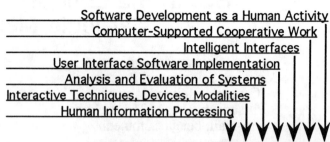
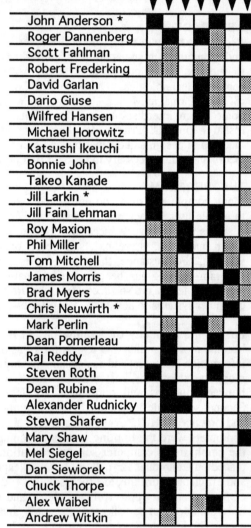

Figure 2. SCS faculty and their areas of interest (an asterisk indicates a courtesy appointment in SCS). Black indicates a primary interest; grey a secondary interest.

Human Cognition Research Laboratory
The Open University (U.K.)

Marc Eisenstadt

Human Cognition Research Laboratory
The Open University
Milton Keynes, UK, MK7 6AA
Phone: +44 908 65-3800 (Fax: -3169)
Email: M.Eisenstadt@open.ac.uk

BACKGROUND DESCRIPTION

The Open University is the UK's largest University and also its largest publisher. Our specialty is 'multimedia distance teaching' via texts, TV programmes (we have our own dedicated BBC studio/production centre on campus), radio, cassettes, videos, computers, 'home experiment kits' (e.g. chemistry labs, rock samples, etc.). Over 80,000 undergraduates are currently enrolled, as well as over 40,000 Continuing Education students (the former study for a B.A. degree, whereas the latter just take isolated courses). There are *no* entrance requirements, but strict standards are maintained by external examiners from other universities who assist with the assessment of final examinations. More than 2,000,000 people have now studied with the OU in one or other of its programmes. Approximately 20,000 students each year are involved with courses that have a 'home computing' element. A special government scheme helps to keep costs low so that computers are accessible to all students (by loan or rental, if necessary).

Although undergraduate students work from home, there are research facilities for full-time Ph.D. students on the central campus in Milton Keynes, and the Open University actively promotes a handful of research groups by means of Ph.D. research studentships, postdoctoral research fellowships, equipment and travel grants. This acts as a combination of 'pump-priming' and 'baseline' funding, which facilitates the ability of research groups to compete for external research grants. External funding is obtained in healthy measures from the usual sources: government funding councils, industry, and multinational collaborative programmes such as ESPRIT.

The Human Cognition Research Laboratory (HCRL) is one of the Open University's 'first tier' research groups, the others being Brain and Behaviour, Computer Assisted Learning (which also has a strong profile of HCI-specific research), and Petrogenesis. HCRL has two dozen members, including roughly equal numbers of full-time academic staff, research fellows, Ph.D. students, and support staff. We undertakes a combination of basic and applied research in Artificial Intelligence (AI), Cognitive Science, and Human Computer Interaction. The long-term goal of HCRL's research programme is to understand the fundamental processes of cognition, and to exploit this understanding where appropriate in the design of complex software systems. The key issues that serve to integrate several of our main research strands can be summed up as follows: 'understanding and improving the activity of computer programmers and knowledge engineers'. This

work is described in detail in [9]. HCRL results are disseminated via academic publications, software (both public domain and commercial), and a combination of Open University distance-teaching courses and industrial training packs directly influenced by up-to-date research findings. We undertake a range of entrepreneurial activities in order to bring in sufficient resources to support a productive research climate.

HIGHLIGHTS OF RESEARCH ACTIVITIES

HCRL's activities divide into five major areas: (i) Knowledge Engineering; (ii) Human Computer Interaction; (iii) Cognitive Architecture; (iv) Structure and Operation of Human Memory; (v) Problem Solving and Thinking. Representative activities involving extensive HCI work are described below.

The Transparent Prolog Machine (TPM) (Mike Brayshaw, Marc Eisenstadt, Paul Mulholland): TPM is a medium for visualizing and animating the execution of Prolog programs [3]. Conceived as a tool for use by novice and expert Prolog programmers alike, TPM provides a faithful (slow-motion) representation of the inner workings of the Prolog interpreter, yet allows a high-speed visual overview of execution for rapidly homing in on buggy code. Our current version serves as the uniform basis for textbook diagrams, video animations, and a graphics workstation implementation. Considerable effort has been put into producing a system that scales up to the demands of large applications. To complement the commercially-available Unix workstation version of TPM (from Expert Systems Ltd.), we have developed a public domain Apple Macintosh version which accompanies HCRL's *Intensive Prolog* course. This work is now entering an empirical phase: Paul Mulholland's Ph.D. research involves psychological studies of the efficacy of a range of software visualization tools, and in particular compares the behaviour of subjects using TPM and a variety of other tracers and debuggers.

Frameworks for Software Visualization (Mike Brayshaw, John Domingue, Marc Eisenstadt, Paul Mulholland, Blaine Price). Over the years, HCRL members have designed and implemented several program visualization systems, such as TPM mentioned above. In an attempt to generalize this work and extend it to encompass algorithm animation techniques, we have developed several software tools and theoretical frameworks within which a class of specific visualization systems can be implemented. Two of these frameworks are MRE [2] and Viz [5], each of which has been used to reconstruct well known visualizations as well as develop new ones. MRE is based on a cognitive psychological account of the end-user, and emphasizes the role of 'information space management', by which the user, task, and environment interact to provide the best mapping between a programming task and an appropriate way to view that task. Viz builds upon the software visualization taxonomy of Price et. al. [11], and provides an architecture for viewing arbitrary programs as a series of *history events* happening to *players*, which can be any part of a program, such as a function, a data structure, or a line of code. Players undergo state changes which are mapped onto a visual representation which is accessible to the end-user via a variety of navigation aids.

Both MRE and Viz have been used to develop novel visualization techniques: MRE has been used to implement a graphical debugger for parallel logic programming. Viz has been used to bridge the gap between program visualization (at a low level of abstraction) and algorithm animation (at a high level of abstraction). We are building a fully automatic software visualization system by combining AI program understanding techniques with Viz. By recognizing low level programming clichés and building up a hierarchy of abstraction levels, we can provide graphical mappings at each level. This prevents the system from collapsing when the code deviates from known clichés, and it allows the user (from novice programmer to professional software engineer) to choose the level of abstraction appropriate to the task at hand. This work will also be the subject of empirical evaluation in our continued studies of software environment validation.

VITAL, A methodology-based workbench for Knowledge Based Systems life cycle support (Enrico Motta, John Domingue, Stuart Watt, Marc Eisenstadt, Arthur Stutt, Zdenek Zdrahal): This is a 4.5-year ESPRIT-II project involving eight partners in Europe. It aims to produce a knowledge engineering workbench which will be an integrated project support environment for the construction, maintenance and comprehensive management of knowledge-based systems. In the context of this project, we are building upon the 'Visual Knowledge Engineering' work of Eisenstadt et. al. [8], which provided an integrated collection of tools for knowledge engineers to undertake domain analysis, sketch out conceptual models and knowledge representations, and visually monitor the behaviour of large multi-paradigm KBS implementations. The key theme of the earlier work was the smooth integration of coarse grained and fine grained views of both domain models and program execution. The VITAL project extends this work in several ways: (a) by providing navigation facilities which encompass a large part of the complete knowledge engineering life cycle; (b) by providing an infrastructure for groupware development, particularly the live editing and updating of conceptual models by teams of knowledge engineers; (c) by providing an architecture which allows the kowledge engineer to employ multiple representation paradigms yet monitor their behaviour in a consistent fashion (using Viz).

REPRESENTATIVE PUBLICATIONS, 1990-1992

(TPM for the Macintosh and our full publications list are available free by post or anonymous ftp from hcrl.open.ac.uk)

1. Brayshaw, M.. An Architecture for Visualising the Execution of Parallel Logic Programming. *Proceedings of the Twelth International Joint Conference on Artificial Intelligence (IJCAI-91).* Los Angeles: Morgan Kaufmann, 1991.

2. Brayshaw, M. Program Visualisation and Knowledge Negotiation: some proposals for visual techniques in tutorial dialog as applied to concurrent logic programming languages, In M.T. Elsom-Cook and R. Moyse (Eds.), *Knowledge Negotiation.* London: Academic Press, 1992, pp. 303-309.

3. Brayshaw, M. and Eisenstadt, M.. A Practical Graphical Tracer for Prolog. *International Journal of Man-Machine Studies,* 1991, 35 (5), pp. 597-631.

4. Domingue, J. Compressing and Comparing Metric Excecution Spaces. In D. Diaper et. al. (Eds). *Human-Computer Interaction— INTERACT '90.* Amsterdam: Elsevier (North-Holland), 1990.

5. Domingue, J., B.A. Price, and M. Eisenstadt: Viz: A Framework for Describing and Implementing Software Visualization Systems. In D. Gilmore and R. Winder, (Eds.) *User-Centred Requirements for Software Engineering Environments.* Berlin: Springer-Verlag (NATO Advanced Science Institute Series F: Computer and Systems Sciences), 1992.

6. Eisenstadt, M. and Brayshaw, M. A fine-grained account of Prolog execution for teaching and debugging. *Instructional Science.,* 19(4/5), 1990, pp.407-436.

7. Eisenstadt, M., Brayshaw, M. and Payne, J. *The Transparent Prolog Machine: Visualizing Logic Programs.* Dordrecht, The Netherlands: Kluwer, 1991.

8. Eisenstadt, M., Domingue, J., Rajan, T., and Motta, E. Visual knowledge engineering. *IEEE. Trans. Soft. Eng.,* 16 (10), 1990, pp. 1164-1177.

9. Eisenstadt, M., Keane, M., & Rajan, T. (Eds.) *Novice Programming Environments: Explorations in Human-Computer Interaction and Artificial Intelligence.* London: Lawrence Erlbaum, 1992.

10. Kiss, G., Variable Coupling of Agents to their Environment: Combining Situated and Symbolic Automata. In: E. Werner and Y. Demazeau (Eds), *Decentralized AI 3.* Amsterdam: Elsevier/North Holland, 1992.

11. Price, B.A., Small, I.S., and Baecker, R. A taxonomy of software visualization. *Proc. 25th Hawaii International Conference on System Sciences.* New York: IEEE Press, 1992, pp. 597-606.

The Integrated User-Support Environment (IN-USE) Group at USC / ISI

Robert Neches,

Peter Aberg, David Benjamin, Brian Harp, Liyi Hu, Ping Luo, Roberto Moriyón, Pedro Szekely

USC / Information Sciences Institute
4676 Admiralty Way
Marina del Rey, CA 90292 USA
Email: Neches@isi.edu

INTRODUCTION

Integrated user support environments are individual and cooperative-work systems which allow their users to perform a large quantity of their daily work on-line, and which do so by providing access to a comprehensive set of tools that interact smoothly with each other and present a uniform interface to the users. The INtegrated User-Support Environments (IN-USE) Group is developing a framework for facilitating construction of such systems. The framework is oriented toward assisting users who must timeshare between multiple, highly information-intensive data analysis and problem solving tasks. Our fundamental goals are to help developers quickly assemble support environments that offer reasonable default appearance and behavior, and to make it easy to then customize those environments as needed.

To this end, our research focuses on developing a set of principled facilities that can operate upon a shared declarative model. Application developers work by extending the model to describe their domain. This allows them to get initial versions of their system by inheriting default versions of tools, and lets them specialize the system by refinement rather than by programming "from scratch." Our current efforts to develop the framework focus on four key facilities:

- HUMANOID: a user interface development environment
- BACKBORD: a browsing and clarification aid
- Scenarios/Agendas: a multi-agent activity manager
- TINT: a tool for handling semistructured information

HUMANOID and MASTERMIND (Szekely, Luo, Moriyón, Neches)

HUMANOID's approach to interface design lets designers express abstract conceptualizations in an executable form, allowing designers to experiment with interactive behavior

even before the system model is completely stated [7]. This lets designers get an executable version of their design quickly, experiment with it in action, and then repeat the process after adding only the details needed to extend it along the particular dimension currently of interest to them.

HUMANOID is a model-based system: interfaces are specified by constructing a declarative model of how the interface should look and behave. A run-time support module allows applications to execute the model, constructing displays and interpreting input according to the information in the model. HUMANOID provides a declarative modeling language that models the functional capabilities of an application as a set of objects and operations; it further partitions the model of the style and requirements of the interface into four additional semi-independent dimensions: *Presentation, Behavior, Dialogue Sequencing, and Action Side-effects.*

In the spirit of the DARPA Knowledge Sharing Effort approach to sharing and reuse of knowledge-based systems [5], we have been collaborating with Jim Foley's group at Georgia Tech on developing a joint model of interface design. This shared model, called MASTERMIND [6], will enable integration of HUMANOID's design environment with UIDE's design critics, as well as integrating HUMANOID's run-time capability for context-sensitive presentation with UIDE's animated help facilities.

BACKBORD: A specification by reformulation shell (Aberg, Neches)

The BACKBORD system (Browsing Aid Complementing Knowledge Bases OR Databases) is our implementation of the specification by reformulation paradigm [8]. By this, we mean a paradigm of human/computer interaction in which the user develops, by successive approximations, a specification of the objects a system is to manipulate and/or the behavior it is to evince. In this style of interaction, the system provides an environment which facilitates the refinement of the specification, largely by generating feedback for the user about the specification in its current form and by providing guidance about means for modifying that specification. Our research focuses on packaging this paradigm in a library of reusable components to facilitate instantiating this paradigm in a wide range of applications.

Scenarios/Agendas(Benjamin, Szekely, Neches)

Scenarios [4] are program-like descriptions of the sub-tasks that compose extended tasks. They have been used extensively in our logistics applications, both to perform many tasks automatically and to interactively guide users through those activities not amenable to automation.

Scenarios are like very high-level procedures, in that they describe a sequence of steps to be performed. Unlike a procedure, a scenario attempts to capture the processes or sequences of tasks that are related by user-level concerns in performing an activity. Also, a scenario imposes only orderings between steps that are necessitated by dependencies between them. Scenarios operate by attaching the sub-tasks to assorted Agendas, each of which represents the completed and pending tasks of some agent that participates in the task. Scenarios and Agendas provide external memory for "unfinished business," reducing burdens on users' memories.

TINT: Aids for integrating informal and formal knowledge representations (Harp, Hu, Neches)

TINT (The Intelligent Note-Taker) acts as a user interface which allows users to enter information into the computer in the form of "semi-structured" notes that are attached to concepts in a knowledge base [2]. Both user and system can create and retrieve notes; they can use notes to exchange information and to store it for their own use. Even though the computer cannot fully understand some user-supplied notes, it can still operate with at least partial understanding, because the notes have some structure and are associated with knowledge base entries that the computer can be programmed to understand. This gives the computer a way of knowing about things it can't handle and asking for help. This reduces the brittleness of conventional expert systems, pointing the way towards a more collaborative style of human/computer interaction. TINT also lets developers do "incremental knowledge acquisition," using user notes to set targets for adding additional automation to a system.

APPLICATIONS

These tools have been put to practical use in a number of prototype application systems. These applications have ranged from logistical analysis domains (BEAMER and DRAMA) to collaborative environments for team development of knowledge bases (SHELTER), under funding from the Defense Logistics Agency, Air Force Logistics Command, and DARPA. DRAMA and SHELTER are both good examples of ISI's tradition of building useful tools and applying them to solve real problems.

DRAMA

DRAMA [1] is an intelligent data review and monitoring system for the Defense Logistics Agency. DRAMA monitors evolving databases containing weapon system design information, coordinating that design information with support requests from the services and knowledge about status of supply and procurement activities within DLA. Its function is to save DLA substantial amounts of money by ensuring that purchasing and stock management plans rapidly adapt to changes.

SHELTER

The SHELTER development environment for ontologies and knowledge bases [3] is another key application of the IN-USE framework. SHELTER provides an integrated solution to problems in managing knowledge-base size and complexity, and in managing the size and complexity of the activities required to correctly use, modify, or extend such knowledge bases. It facilitates sharing and reuse by helping developers find candidate material to reuse, and ensuring that it is used properly. There are two key ideas in SHELTER. One is an interaction paradigm that encourages reuse of specifications, embodied in a set of browsing and retrieval tools provided by BACKBORD. The other is a set of methods for helping knowledge-base system builders record design rationale metaknowledge, using structured notes from TINT which the system can interpret to assist developers in ensuring the appropriateness of later modifications.

SELECTED REFERENCES

[1] B. Harp, P. Aberg, D. Benjamin, R. Neches, P. Szekely. *DRAMA: an Application of a Logistics Shell*. In **Proceedings of the Annual Conference on AI and Logistics**, Williamsburg, VA, March, 1992.

[2] B. Harp and R. Neches, *NOTECARDS: An Everyday Tool for Aiding in Complex Tasks*. ISI Research Report RS-88-204, March, 1988.

[3] R. Neches, *Cognitive Issues in the SHELTER Knowledge Base Development Environment*. **AAAI Spring Symposium on Cognitive Issues in Knowledge Acquisition**, March, 1992.

[4] R. Neches, D. Benjamin, J. Granacki, B. Harp, and P. Szekely. *Scenarios/Agendas: A Reusable, Customizable Approach to User-System Collaboration in Complex Activities*. ISI Working Paper, 1991.

[5] R. Neches, R. Fikes, T. Finin, T. Gruber, R. Patil, T. Senator, and W.R. Swartout. *Enabling Technology for Knowledge Sharing*. **AI Magazine**, Vol. 12, No. 3, 1991, pp.36-56.

[6] R. Neches, J. Foley, P. Szekely, P. Sukaviriya, P. Luo, S. Kovacevic, and S. Hudson. *Knowledgeable Development Environments Using Shared Design Models*. In **Proceedings of the 1993 International Workshop on Intelligent User Interfaces**, Jan., 1993.

[7] P. Szekely, P. Luo, and R. Neches. *Facilitating the Exploration of Interface Design Alternatives: The HUMANOID Model of Interface Design*. In **Proceedings of CHI'92**, May 1992, pp. 507-515.

[8] J. Yen, R. Neches, M. DeBellis, P. Szekely, and P. Aberg. *BACKBORD: An Implementation of Specification by Reformulation*. In J.S. Sullivan and S.W. Tyler (Eds.), **Intelligent User Interfaces**, pp. 421-444. ACM Press, 1991.

MUSiC Video Analysis and Context Tools
for Usability Measurement

Miles Macleod and Nigel Bevan

National Physical Laboratory
Division of Information Technology and Computing
Teddington, Middlesex, TW11 0LW, UK
miles@hci.npl.co.uk
tel: +44 81 943 6097

KEYWORDS: Usability evaluation, metrics, usability engineering, observation, video analysis.

INTRODUCTION

Analysis of interaction between users and a system, based on video-assisted observation, can provide a highly informative and effective means of evaluating usability. To obtain valid and reliable results, the people observed should be representative users performing representative work tasks in appropriate circumstances, and the analysis should be methodical. The MUSiC Performance Measurement Method (PMM) – developed at NPL as part of the ESPRIT Project MUSiC: Metrics for Usability Standards in Computing – provides a validated method for making and analysing such video recordings to derive performance-based usability metrics. PMM is supported by the DRUM software tool which greatly speeds up analysis of video, and helps manage evaluations.

USABILITY AND CONTEXT

Usability can be defined in terms of the efficiency and satisfaction with which specified users can achieve specified work goals in given environments. The MUSiC Context Guidelines Handbook provides a structured method for identifying and describing key characteristics of the 'context of use' – the users, tasks and environments for which a system is designed – and key characteristics of the context of evaluation. It documents how accurately the context of evaluation matches the intended context of use.

The PMM gives measures of effectiveness and efficiency of system use, by evaluating task goal achievement and times. It also gives measures of unproductive time (e.g. problems and seeking help), plus diagnostic data about location of difficulties, helping identify where specific improvements need to be made. Efficiency and user satisfaction are not necessarily correlated – a system can be satisfying but not very efficient to use, or vice versa – so there is great advantage in measuring both. The PMM is concerned with one of the core components of usability, efficiency; another MUSiC tool (SUMI) measures user satisfaction.

SOFTWARE SUPPORT: DRUM

Video analysis has previously been very time-consuming. It can now be performed considerably faster using the Diagnostic Recorder for Usability Measurement (DRUM) which provides support for the management and analysis of usability evaluations, including the derivation of usability metrics. DRUM assists in many aspects of the evaluator's work:

- management of data through all stages of an evaluation
- task analysis to assist identification and analysis of specific events and usability problems
- video control, and creation of an interaction log of each evaluation session
- automated find and video replay of any logged event
- analysis of logged data and calculation of metrics

Iteratively developed since 1990 in collaboration with industry to meet the actual needs of usability testing, DRUM has a graphical user interface, online context-sensitive help and a comprehensive user manual. It runs on Apple Macintosh, and drives a variety of video machines.

DRUM allows evaluators to define at a suitable level of analysis the events they wish to log (hierarchically organised if desired). This overcomes difficulties of data analysis which can be encountered with capture of data at the low level of keystrokes and mouse events (Theaker et al., 1989; Hammontree et al., 1992). DRUM provides full control of the video during logging of a tape. Once any event has been logged, it can be automatically located on the video, and reviewed. There is easy access to previously created logs and other evaluation data files from its database. DRUM supports diagnostic evaluation, including the identification of evaluator-defined critical incidents, and can be used explicitly for this purpose.

ACKNOWLEDGEMENTS

This work was supported jointly by the Commission of the European Communities and the Department of Trade and Industry, UK.

REFERENCES

1. Theaker, C.J., et al. HIMS: A Tool for HCI Evaluations, in Proc. HCI'89 Conf, (Nottingham, UK, 5-8 Sept 1989) Cambridge University Press, pp 427-439.
2. Hammontree, M.L., et al. Integrated Data Capture and Analysis Tools for Research and Testing on Graphical User Interfaces, in Proc. CHI'92, ACM Press, pp 431-432.

ADEPT - Advanced Design Environment for Prototyping with Task Models

Peter Johnson, Stephanie Wilson, Panos Markopoulos and James Pycock

Department of Computer Science, Queen Mary & Westfield College,
University of London,
Mile End Road, London E1 4NS, U.K.
Phone: 44 (0)71 975 5224
Email: pete@dcs.qmw.ac.uk

ADEPT MODELS AND TOOLS

ADEPT is a novel design environment for prototyping user interfaces which allows the designer to construct an explicit model of the tasks that the user and computer will perform jointly. ADEPT incorporates task and user modelling components with a rapid prototyping user interface design tool to provide a user-task centred design environment.

ADEPT encompasses design from task analysis to the generation of a run-time system through a number of modelling stages (Figure 1). The environment provides editors, browsers, interpreters and generators that allow each of the models to be functionally employed in user interface design. The task modelling component of ADEPT provides the designer with a graphical editor which allows the designer to construct and browse models of the existing and proposed tasks described in terms of Task Knowledge Structures [1]. The output from the task modelling component feeds directly into the Abstract Interface Model (AIM) component. The AIM provides the designer with a high-level specification of the interaction, expressed in terms of the dialogue structure and abstract interaction objects. The designer can edit and elaborate the AIM using the editors and browsers of ADEPT.

The Concrete Interface Model (CIM) is a platform independent description of the interface design at a detailed level of interaction objects, their behaviour and screen layout. A generator tool creates a default CIM which the designer can edit using the CIM tools. The generator is influenced by input of user centred design characteristics from the User Model. The user model is a rule base of design principles which are tailored by the designer with facts concerning the details of the intended user group. The interaction between the CIM generator and the User Modelling components is in the form of question/answer dialogues which are carried out automatically during the generation process. The CIM may be translated into a platform dependent implementation which makes use of a standard widget set such as Open Look™. Other platforms can be accommodated by writing alternative translators.

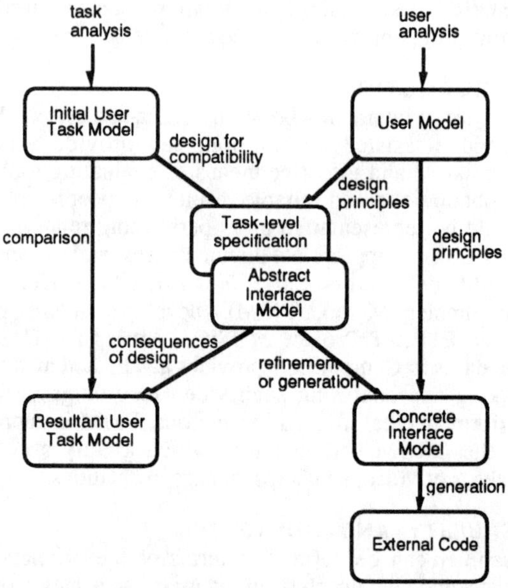

Figure 1. The models and processes of ADEPT

DEMONSTRATION OVERVIEW

The ADEPT demonstration illustrates the use of these tools and models, and provides example designs that have been constructed with the ADEPT environment. The demonstration will exemplify how the integration of task models and the models of user interfaces provide a basis for informed user interface design. It will also show how design recommendations may be generated from a user model to provide input to the design process.

ACKNOWLEDGEMENTS

We acknowledge the contribution to this demonstration from our collaborators: C. Kelly and L. Colgan, British Aerospace, J. Cunningham, BMT and S. Saunders, MJC[2] Adept is funded by the DTI/SERC (project IED/4/1/1573)

REFERENCES

1. Johnson, P., Markopoulos, P., Wilson, S., Pycock, J. (1992) Task Based Design: Mapping between user task models and user interface designs. In *Proceedings of 2nd Workshop on Mental Models in HCI*, University of Cambridge, England.

™ Open Look is a trademark of AT&T

Software for the Usability Lab:
A Sampling of Current Tools

Moderator: *Paul Weiler,* Compaq Computer Corporation
P.O.Box 692000 MC 100801, Houston, Texas 77269-2000
phone: (713) 374-4988   email: pweiler@cpqhou.se.hou.compaq.com

Panelists: *Richard Cordes,* ISSC (A subsidiary of IBM), Boulder, CO.
Monty Hammontree, SunSoft Inc., Colorado Springs, CO.
Derek Hoiem, Microsoft Corporation, Redmond, WA.
Michael Thompson, Apple Computer, Inc., Cupertino, CA.

ABSTRACT

This panel brings together usability professionals throughout the computer industry to demonstrate and discuss their usability lab software tools. These tools are specifically designed to improve the data collection and analysis process for usability labs. Their capabilities range from simple to complex and the panel will not only discuss the benefits of using the tools but also share the lessons learned during the design and development process.

INTRODUCTION

Frequently in the day-to-day battles of running a usability lab, professionals find themselves struggling to use better more efficient ways of collecting and analyzing their data to meet ever tightening product schedules. In response to these challenges, a wide array of custom software tools has been developed ranging from simple note-takers to more elaborate video capturing software.

In a current survey of Usability Professionals Association members, over 70% of those responding (n=33) currently use some form of software data collection tool. Of these, roughly 80% have created their own tool while the remaining 20% have purchased one. The custom tools are frequently designed and developed by members of the usability staff using one of the several rapid prototyping tools currently available including HyperCard and Visual Basic. Time spent on the development of these tools ranged from days to months. Of course the tools have all been developed to fill specific needs for different usability groups and therefore vary in their scope and purpose but all generally record key subject and experimenter information such as task times, errors, comments, questionnaire responses, interventions, and

observations. Some more elaborate tools incorporate capabilities such as summarizing and charting of data, performing statistical analyses, and controlling video recorders.

Richard Cordes, ISSC

Richard Cordes is a senior human factors analyst at Integrated Systems Solutions Corporation (ISSC), a wholly owned subsidiary of IBM. He is currently responsible for developing enhanced usability logging and video production tools for the company. This work is being funded by corporate IBM. His professional responsibilities are in improving software-user interfaces with research interest in usability measurement and evaluation. Rich holds a Ph.D. in Industrial Engineering and Operations Research (Human Factors option) from Virginia Polytechnic Institute and State University.

The Integrated Laboratory Controller (ILC) is a collection of programs that tie together a logger program, the participant's PC, and a VCR in order to provide an integrated system for conducting and analyzing usability evaluations. The goal for writing this program was to provide a single interface for the control and data recording requirements of the test administrator so that one person could run, log, and analyze a usability evaluation. Another objective of this program was to provide an easier to use interface than those available with current logger programs. This was accomplished by using an intelligent parser for identifying logger commands (no commands to memorize). With each word entered, the program would prompt you as to the next allowable keyword.

A big benefit of using this program is its ability to capture screen information from the application under study. The screen capturing ability frees the person logging from having to manually record the screen navigational information into the logging program. Another benefit is the ability to initiate on-line questionnaires on the participant's PC from the logger's PC and have the results sent back to the logger's PC for analysis. This saves a person from having to key-in the paper questionnaire results into a file for analysis.

The most frequently performed statistical analysis such as determining frequency counts, means, medians, confidence limits, and one-way analysis of variance can be conducted by the logger program.

The ILC program has the ability to:

Capture Screens
- Automatically capture mainframe host screen information for recording path navigation and timing
- Grab and save any host screen from the logger program

Perform Statistics
- Perform basic statistics (means, confidence intervals, medians and ANOVA) from the logger program
- Create a Statistical Analysis System (SAS) source and data file for easier analysis of advanced designs

Be a Single Point of Data and Control
- Control and issue commands to the participant's PC from the logger program
- Run on-line surveys on the participant's PC and have the results appear in the log on the logger's PC
- Control the VCR for recording user tasks either automatically or via commands

Perform Intelligent Parsing and Be Easy to Use
- Interpret English commands in a flexible manner
- Provide prompting for commands and parameters
- Allow easy editing of log lines shown in the comment window
- Constantly display participant's time-on-task (TOT)
- Automatically stop the TOT clock of an old task when starting a new one
- Sound an alarm when the TOT is equal to or exceeds a TOT criterion
- Allows easy adjustment of the VCR time stamp

The ILC programs run in DOS 3.2 or higher on all IBM XT, AT, PS/2 and true compatibles.

Currently the logging program is being enhanced to facilitate the identification of usability highlight segments and to more efficiently create a composite tape of these highlights including a method for making it available to the development team via a LAN.

Monty Hammontree, SunSoft

Monty Hammontree is a member of the Usability Engineering group at Sun Microsystems. He currently runs the usability lab at Sun's Rocky Mountain Technology Center in Colorado Springs. Prior to coming to work at Sun he worked for the Usability Sciences and Technologies Group at Texas Instruments. Monty holds a Ph.D. in Engineering and Systems Psychology from Old Dominion University.

History. Monty's dissertation work precipitated the development of a series of computerized data collection and processing tools. The original set ran under Apple's System 6.0.5. Later versions ran under Microsoft Windows 3.0 and 3.1. These initial versions were written by Billy Hensley of Texas Instruments. A new generation of usability testing tools is being developed for Sun's Solaris 2.x operating environment.

Tools. The basic tool set includes: 1) an on-line event capture program, which grabs event messages, relates them to GUI objects, and writes this data out to a log file along with time stamps and other desired outputs; 2) filter programs that translate and aggregate user-generated events into a meaningful characterization of the user's interaction with an application or system software; and 3) a video data analysis program which provides software control over lab VCRs and establishes a common time line between the various data sources. The video data analysis program is designed so that researchers can quickly view the tape segment or segments that correspond to any logged event or series of events by simple exercising a short series of point and click operations. The video data-analysis program also allows researchers to name, annotate, and save video clips for later reference or for post production purposes.

Impact of Tools. Video and computer-generated event data are very rich and complementary data sources. However, the time required to synthesize these data sources into a useful form has traditionally been too costly. In the past, it took an average of six hours or longer to process one hour of video or keystroke intensive data. With the tools described above average times have been reduced to approximately one hour of processing time per hour of raw data. As a result, event and video data have become much more viable data sources. This has translated into an improved ability to deliver findings to design teams that are both quantitatively and qualitatively strong.

Future Enhancements. Plans are to develop integrated observation logging and verbal protocol tools and to enhance the video data analyzer to include the capability to simultaneously control and synchronize multiple VCRs. Plans are also underway to develop the ability to control the event and video capture tools remotely and to be able to transmit the video and event data across a wide area network in real time. The goal is to be able to monitor, from a central lab, one or more participants working in their true native environment.

Derek Hoiem, Microsoft

Derek Hoiem is a Usability Specialist at Microsoft Corporation and a graduate of the Technical Communication department at the University of Washington. His interests include user-interface design, pen-based computing, and exploratory sequential data analysis.

History. When the Microsoft Usability Group was first established, they began collecting data by hand using paper, pencil, and pre-defined data-collection sheets like many other new usability groups. In order to have greater impact on product designs, they realized that they needed to improve the speed with which they conducted tests and analyzed the data. As a result, the group started development of data-collection and video-analysis tools.

The initial goal was to maximize the collection of relevant data during a test so that they could minimize the need for reviewing videotapes. At the time the group had no software developers, and given the urgent need for the tools Derek began work on his own tool using off-the-shelf products. He used HyperCard to build an electronic data-collection sheet. The HyperCard stack included buttons whose text corresponded to the critical events and user actions of interest. The stack also had text fields in which comments could be typed. The text of the buttons and the comments typed into the fields were time-stamped with times corresponding to the videotape and then written to a tab-delimited text file. The text file that the stack produced could later be imported into a spreadsheet or statistical software for analysis. Eventually, Derek enhanced the stack and moved it to SuperCard so he could use multiple windows and other features.

Usability Tools: Observer, Tracker, Reviewer, and Microsoft Excel. The HyperCard and SuperCard stacks evolved into the current system, which consists of three tools and Microsoft Excel. The developer for the three tools, Observer, Reviewer, and Tracker, is Jonathan Cluts, who is the support technician for the Microsoft Usability Group. Jonathan had prior programming experience with Basic, C and 6809 assembler but no experience with Microsoft Visual Basic or programming for Microsoft Windows. He developed the tools part-time over a nine-month period. Since then, more time has been invested in creating improved versions of the tools. Development costs were minimal because off-the-shelf products and the efforts of an existing employee were used. Observer and Tracker together collect data during a usability test. Reviewer and Microsoft Excel are used to analyze the data after the test.

Observer. Observer is a real-time (or post-hoc) video annotation tool which uses customizable coding schemes. Coding schemes may be saved and loaded while a test session is running. Observer also controls the VCR via a serial connection. Observer includes standard on-screen VCR controls and a "jog shuttle" for doing post-hoc data-collection. All annotations made with Observer are written to a tab-delimited text file which is synchronized

with the videotape via SMPTE timecode. Observer was created with Microsoft Visual Basic for Windows.

Tracker. Tracker collects system event data, such as menu selections, keystrokes, movement of windows on the screen, etc. Tracker resides on the subject's computer during a test session. Tracker translates system event data into more easily read descriptions and writes them to a tab-delimited text file. Tracker has no noticeable effect on the overall system speed. Tracker was created with Microsoft QuickC for Windows.

Reviewer. Reviewer enables efficient review of videotape segments using data files generated with Observer and Tracker. Reviewer integrates the data files created by Observer and Tracker and synchronizes them with each other and the videotape. Reviewer can perform searches on the Observer and Tracker data. Any section of videotape matching a search pattern can be quickly viewed and, optionally, flagged for inclusion in a highlights videotape. In addition, the coding scheme used in Observer to collect the data can be loaded into Reviewer so that corrections to the data file can be made post-hoc, ensuring coding consistency. Reviewer was created with Microsoft Visual Basic for Windows.

Microsoft Excel. For detailed analysis, the Observer and Tracker data files are imported into Microsoft Excel. Microsoft Excel's database and statistical functions are used to compile counts of interesting events and calculate statistics on the data.

Further Enhancements. In the future, the group plans to enhance data analysis capabilities. This may involve integrating Observer and Reviewer with Microsoft Excel and SPSS for Windows via Dynamic Data Exchange and Object Linking and Embedding. They may also add capabilities to do lag-sequential analysis and data visualization. The challenge in adding these new features will be to keep the tools tightly integrated and to keep the interface simple despite increased analysis power.

Impact of the Tools. The suite of tools the group developed allowed them to meet their original goal of reducing the amount of time to conduct a usability test and present results to a design team. However, the group has learned that the real value of these tools is that they allow them to collect more types of data and to be more detailed in their analyses. The searching and filtering features of the tools allow usability specialists to explore the test data quickly and to minimize "data panic" from being overwhelmed by large masses of videotape, observational, and event data.

Michael Thompson, Apple
Michael Thompson is a Human Interface Engineer at Apple Computer. Interface engineers at Apple are each

part of a multi-disciplinary team-approach to designing interfaces for both hardware and software. As a member of a design team, Michael is responsible for designing product interfaces, conducting usability testing, then working with the team to enhance or improve the interface. He has a Masters Degree in Professional Writing from Carnegie Mellon University.

Because our Human Interface Design group was moving into a new R&D building, we were lucky enough to have the chance to re-evaluate our usability lab needs without affecting our current projects. Through brainstorming sessions among those in our group who typically conduct usability tests, we ran through scenarios of typical user studies from which we created a wish list of features for a data collection tool. From these, we outlined the new tool's specifications in a document that we provided to our in-house developer. The tool is currently under development.

The scope of our data capturing tool falls into two parts: the Event logger and the Observation logger. The Event logging tool will provide for automatic data capturing of on-line user events (e.g., user selects Shutdown command). Such events will be automatically recorded in a file with a time stamp. The tool's interface will allow the observer to select from a pre-defined list which events will be recorded. For example, an observer can select "Dialog box" to ensure information about time spent on dialog box is captured. Since observers, however, will likely want to capture more data than is the focus of a particular test, they can use this same list after a study to filter a file of mostly extraneous events into something more manageable.

The Observation Logger part of the tool will allow observers to manually capture off-line user events (e.g., user connects incorrect cable to CPU). Observers will be able to key in user actions either with pre-defined hot keys (F1 = comment about preference) or by typing out a comment. The Observation logger will be tied directly to the VCR's counter. When an observer reviews the log file, an on-screen interface will control the VCR. This will facilitate the compilation of highlight videos.

Undoubtedly, the new data capturing tools will improve our group's productivity because instead of focusing on real-time event logging, we will be able to focus more on annotating the user's comments and actions (observation logging). The automatically compiled tally of events from the event logger will facilitate the analysis of user task execution strategies and task and error times. We are now investigating ways to combine the event log file with the observation log file.

A future enhancement will be creating a completely digital lab in which video output from test session will be recorded on digital tape. The lab equipment is essentially the same--the most important change will be using a digital tape recorder instead of a VCR. In such a system, all observable actions, the observation and the event log will be part of the same file. This will allow us to record and capture data from a session, compile highlight videos, and store each session in one media with one interface. We are currently building a prototype of this scenario using QuickTime, various video conversion hardware, and a digital tape recorder.

Paul Weiler, Compaq
Paul Weiler is a Human Factors Engineer at Compaq Computer Corporation working on the design, prototyping and testing of software utilities and applications. He is developing a set of human factors laboratory tools to help streamline the data collection and analysis process. Paul holds a Masters Degree in Experimental Psychology and is currently completing his Ph.D. in the same at Colorado State University.

Compaq's Human Factors' DataLogger was created to help improve the data collection process beyond the use of pencil and paper and time consuming video tape analysis. The DataLogger's initial primary function was to record testing events, experimenter comments and task times but quickly grew to include the collection of subject errors and times, the number of experimenter interventions, how and what documentation was used, and the completion of task milestones. Further enhancements included the addition of two analysis capabilities. First, a summary table including task and error times, their relative percentages and total number of interventions are computed for the subjects in a study. Second, by linking to Microsoft Excel through dynamic data exchange to produce a task time and time-in-error graph that can be included directly in the final study memo.

The core DataLogger tool was created by the author using Asymetrix ToolBook over a two week period. ToolBook was used since it was the rapid prototyping tool of choice for the group. The enhancements have been added over the course of a year as the new features were desired.

Overall, the tool has decreased the group's time spent in data analysis especially in the area of computing task and error times. DataLogger has also enabled more accurate data collection while performing field studies due to its time stamping and summary capabilities.

Future enhancements include the ability to interface with video recorders to mark key usability events and expedite the location of the segments after testing.

Do Algorithm Animations Assist Learning?
An Empirical Study and Analysis

John Stasko, Albert Badre
Graphics, Visualization and Usability Center
College of Computing
Georgia Institute of Technology
Atlanta, GA 30332

Clayton Lewis
Institute of Cognitive Science
Department of Computer Science
University of Colorado at Boulder
Boulder, CO 80309

ABSTRACT

Algorithm animations are dynamic graphical illustrations of computer algorithms, and they are used as teaching aids to help explain how the algorithms work. Although many people believe that algorithm animations are useful this way, no empirical evidence has ever been presented supporting this belief. We have conducted an empirical study of a priority queue algorithm animation, and the study's results indicate that the animation only slightly assisted student understanding. In this article, we analyze those results and hypothesize why algorithm animations may not be as helpful as was initially hoped. We also develop guidelines for making algorithm animations more useful in the future.

KEYWORDS: software visualization, algorithm animation, empirical studies

INTRODUCTION

Beginning with the premiere of the movie *Sorting Out Sorting*[1] and through the development of subsequent systems such as Balsa[5] and Tango[8], the use of dynamic graphics to illustrate the functionality and methodology of computer algorithms, so-called *algorithm animation*[4], has shown promise as an instructional aid. Algorithm animation seems particularly well-suited for use in the "Fundamental Algorithms" course in a computer science curriculum, often the second course that computer science majors take. This course usually studies sorting, searching, graph algorithms, tree algorithms, string algorithms, and so on.

Developers of algorithm animations and algorithm animation systems consistently claim that these graphical illustrations will help students more quickly and more thoroughly learn about fundamental computer science algorithms. These beliefs are understandable and appear to be the majority opinion; our intuition is that the algorithm animations provide a concrete representation of complex, abstract concepts. People clearly have a difficult time understanding abstract notions.

Unfortunately, the viability of algorithm animations as instructional aids remains rooted in intuition. No substantive empirical evidence has ever been presented to support these claims. We believe this absence results from the difficulty of conducting sound empirical testing with algorithm animations. Pragmatically, it is challenging to assemble the appropriate ingredients for an empirical study. An algorithm animation environment must be available, and most importantly, a group of subjects who are at an appropriate point in their educational careers must be available. Even this may not be enough, however, because splitting the subjects into two groups, one using animation and one not using animation, may unfairly influence student achievement and grading in the particular course in which the students are enrolled.

Although no substantive evidence exists to support or undermine the application of algorithm animation as an instructional aid, a few informal studies of algorithm animation and formal studies of closely-related matters do exist. Whitney and Urquhart used the MacBalsa system[3] and a system they built called Algorithms Lab as an instructional aid for a course on analysis of algorithms[13]. Their results were informal, but they did note that the stronger students seemed to benefit from the animations more than did the poorer students.

Palmiteer and Elkerton studied the use of animated demonstrations in performing authoring tasks on a computer system[7]. They found that subjects who were aided by animated demonstrations initially performed their tasks faster and more accurately than subjects with only textual explanations. After a 7-day break, however, the text-only group did just as well as before, but the subjects with animated demonstrations did worse.

Our goals in this study were to examine the viability of algorithm animation as a tool for learning about a particular data structure and algorithm. We wanted to discover the conditions under which algorithm animation could be most useful, and we wanted to learn more about how and when to introduce algorithm animation in an educational setting.

EXPERIMENT

In this study we used the XTango algorithm animation system[9]. XTango supports color animations and runs on top of the X Window System. XTango can be acquired via anonymous ftp (`par.cc.gatech.edu`), and a growing number of institutions are currently using XTango animations with computer science courses.

The study's focus was an animation of an algorithm involving the *pairing heap* data structure[6]. A pairing heap is a relatively new implementation for an abstract data structure called a *priority queue*. Priority queues store and manipulate nodes with key values, and they support the operations: insert a new node, delete the node with minimum key, decrease a particular node's key, and delete a particular node. They are widely used, with applications in job scheduling and many graph algorithms. We will use the term "pairing heap algorithm" to mean the actual pairing heap data structure together with the operations on the data structure to carry out the fundamental priority queue operations. Pairing heaps are an attractive implementation of priority queues because of their relatively simple structure and the nearly optimal computational complexity of their operations.

Pairing heaps are modeled as heap-ordered trees with no restrictions on the number of children a node may have. Because these multiway trees are difficult to implement in practice, pairing heaps are often implemented using the binary tree simulation of a multiway tree. The XTango animation of pairing heaps used in this study illustrates the binary tree representation of a pairing heap[10, 11]. Viewers are able to issue insert, delete min, decrease key, and delete operations and watch how the pairing heap carries out the commands. The animation supports smooth, continuous transitions between states also, to help preserve context and promote comprehension. A still frame from the XTango pairing heap animation is shown in Figure 1.

Our hypothesis prior to the study was that the animation would assist students learn about the algorithm, and in particular, would be more beneficial to procedural understanding than to declarative. Animations primarily depict how an algorithm functions, but they

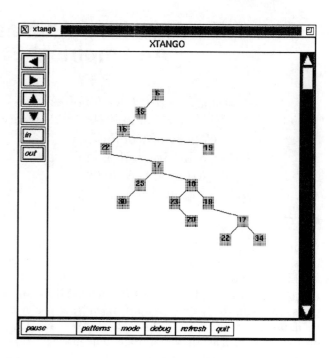

Figure 1: Frame from the XTango pairing heap animation.

do not explain the reasoning for particular actions.

The subjects of the study, all volunteers, were computer science graduate students who had taken or were taking advanced computer algorithms courses. None of the subjects had ever studied pairing heaps.

The subjects participated in the study through individual sessions. Each subject was randomly assigned to be in one of two groups, with ten persons total per group. The first group received textual descriptions of the pairing heap algorithm, and the other group received the same textual descriptions supplemented by the opportunity to interact with the pairing heap animation. The textual descriptions consisted of the first few pages of two journal articles about pairing heaps[6, 12]. These pages described the data structure, how it is implemented, and how operations on it work. By providing excerpts from articles, we sought to mimic how students often learn about algorithms and data structures in their day-to-day academic environment.

In the study, students in the text-only group were given 45 minutes to read and study the pairing heap descriptions. Students in the text-animation group were given an initial maximum of 30 minutes to read the articles, and the remaining time (to a total of 45 minutes) to interact with the animation. These students received written instructions about how to operate the animation, but they were not forced to view any particular set of operations. Rather, they were allowed to interact with the animation in any manner they desired. We chose not to present a canned animation demonstration, in fear of unfairly favoring the animation group by presenting certain important facts about the algorithm.

When the subjects had completed the 45 minute learning session, we gave them a set of questions to test their understanding of the pairing heap algorithm. Neither group was allowed to use the textual description during the examination, nor was the animation available. The subjects were given a maximum of 45 minutes to work on the exam. Three different orderings of questions were used to remove any question sequencing effects. All the questions were designed to have one correct answer, and not be open to interpretation. Unfortunately, this precludes essay-style questions that often can identify a deeper understanding of an algorithm, but this was sacrificed in this study in order to seek quantifiable data.

The exam included many different styles of questions, broadly organized around six major sections. They are grouped below:

- Eight true-false questions about manipulations on the pairing heaps. **Example:** If we run the delete operation on the heap root, this is equivalent to running the delete min operation.

- Four questions involving numerical complexity issues about how the pairing heap operations function. **Example:** What is the maximum number of comparison-link actions performed during a decrease key operation on a pairing heap which had n nodes prior to the decrease-key operation?

- Two questions involving analysis of how certain valued nodes in the heap are manipulated. **Example:** Suppose we have an existing pairing heap with root having key value x. If we insert a node with key=5, then we insert a node with key=10, and finally we perform a delete min, can the former root with key=x be the root again? If it can, for what values of x can it happen?

- Two questions about the mapping from a binary representation of a pairing heap to a multiway tree representation. **Example:** Given the following binary tree pairing heap (figure was shown), draw the corresponding multiway tree representation.

- Two questions examining the student's understanding of how pairing heaps are built up from insert operations. **Example:** Given the following sequence of operations (list was given), draw how the resulting heap would look using the multiway representation.

- Six questions presenting a picture of a pairing heap and asking the subjects how the heap would change

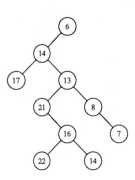

Figure 2: Figure used in one of the operation-style examination questions.

if a particular operation were to occur. Three of these questions (b, c, f) used the multiway tree representation and three (a, d, e) used the binary representation. **Example:** If we run the delete operation on the node with key=13 in the binary pairing heap representation pictured below (shown here in Figure 2), how will the resulting heap appear?

These questions tested many facets of the pairing heap algorithm. Virtually every question in some way required knowledge of a) the invariant properties of the heap, such as the key value relationship between a parent and child node and b) the methodologies of the different operations on the heap.

Certain questions in particular focused on different types of knowledge, however. For instance, the true-false questions tested more declarative or factual understanding. The computational complexity questions required analytical thinking. The six questions about performing operations on the heap tested strictly procedural knowledge.

RESULTS

Table 1 presents the results of the study. Recall that ten subjects were in each of the text-only and text-animation groups. The table lists the number of correct replies for each group. The results are listed in the same order as the description of the question categories described earlier in the article.

The animation group averaged 13.6 correct replies and the text-only group averaged 11.2 correct replies out of the 24 questions. A summary of the subjects' individual scores is presented in Table 2. We performed a two sample t-test on these scores and found a nonsignificant trend favoring the animation group (t=1.111, df=18, p<0.13).

		Text Articles	Text & Animation
True-False	a	6	6
	b	7	10
	c	8	10
	d	7	7
	e	7	8
	f	7	8
	g	7	7
	h	9	10
Complexity	a	2	5
	b	1	2
	c	6	8
	d	2	4
Analytical	a	8	9
	b	7	7
Tree rep.	a	6	6
	b	6	6
Inserts	a	2	4
	b	3	5
Operations	a	2	3
	b	4	2
	c	2	3
	d	1	4
	e	0	1
	f	2	1

Table 1: Results of the posttests. Each value lists the number of correct replies out of a total of 10 subjects.

Note that the animation group did as well as or better than the text-only group on all but two questions. Those two questions were procedural questions asking about the results of a delete min and delete operation on a multiway representation of a pairing heap. Recall that the XTango animation only displayed the binary tree representation of the pairing heap, so the animation group's deficiency here is somewhat understandable.

In general, the performance of all the subjects was poorer than we expected, and the animation's benefits over the text-only presentation was not as strong as we had expected. In particular, the animation group did not seem to benefit greatly in the procedural questions. Their performance seemed to be aided more in the declarative style questions, such as the true-false ones, and on the analytical questions.

The animation group completed their posttests slightly faster than did the text-only group. The animation group finished in an average of 37.6 of the maximum

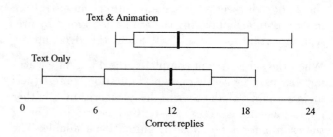

Table 2: Summary of the subjects' total scores on the posttest.

45 minutes and the text-only group averaged 41.0 minutes. Three animation subjects and four text-only subjects required the full 45 minutes.

We also included a post-experiment questionnaire for the subjects in the animation group. It included three questions: whether the subject felt that the animation aided understanding the pairing heap algorithm, what the subject liked about the animation, and what the subject didn't like about the animation.

All ten animation subjects reported that they felt the animation assisted them in understanding the algorithm. Often recognized was that the animation grabbed their interest. This fact has been noted in the other related studies discussed earlier in this article, and it appears to be one of the primary advantages of algorithm animation. A few students qualified their replies to the first question, however. One said, "The algorithm animation is good, but explanations of what is happening would help." This thought was echoed by others as well. Another student noted a loss of the animation's effectiveness as time went along, stating, "When viewing the animation it was clear what was happening, but I found it difficult to remember after finishing the animation." This comment reinforces the findings of Palmiteer and Elkerton[7] cited earlier.

In describing what they liked about the animation, the subjects most often cited its interactivity, that is, the capability for them to try out their own examples. Also noted was the relative speed control capability and the visual effect of highlighting (flashing in a different color) nodes being compared. Finally, a number of the subjects recognized the smooth movements of the heap during operations as assisting their understanding. One subject stated, "I liked how the computer slowly changed the diagram, letting me see how the change was made rather than an instantaneous change."

In citing their dislikes in the animation, the subjects noted the absence of a multiway tree view of the pairing heap and the absence of a way to step through the animation a frame at a time (XTango only includes a *pause/unpause* button). The most often cited negative was the inability to rewind or replay the animation. The subjects said that after an operation occurred, they often wanted to look at the heap as it appeared before the operation. This is an important point, and should be considered by the developers of future algorithm animation systems. Finally, a number of subjects felt that the animation should have been accompanied by textual explanations of what was occurring at that moment in the animation. One subject even asked for the addition of audio voice-over explanations.

DISCUSSION

In conducting this study we hoped to establish quantifiable evidence supporting the effectiveness of algorithm animation as a learning aid. The results were disappointing: while animation subjects outperformed text-only subjects, the difference was not large and was not statistically significant. Also, the performance of the animation group was not high in absolute terms. Why were our hopes for the animation not fulfilled?

Before results were available, one of us (CL) analyzed the experimental materials using an informal version of the programming walkthrough procedure[2]. This analysis attempted to identify the knowledge needed to answer the test questions and then to assess the likelihood that the necessary knowledge would be available to participants in the text-only and text-animation groups. The main conclusion from the analysis was that neither the text nor the animation could be expected to produce high performance. Most of the test items require the ability to accurately carry out the main procedures of the algorithm, and neither presentation seemed likely to give participants that ability. It appeared that actual experience in carrying out the procedures, or a presentation of the motivation for the steps in the procedures, which might allow participants to reconstruct the procedures at test time, would be required. Besides foreshadowing our quantitative findings this analysis finds an echo in some of the subjects comments cited above, calling for explanations and noting the difficulty of remembering what was seen.

In addition to these problems we think other factors contributed to the disappointing results. The subjects in this study, both the text-animation and text-only groups, also might have benefited by knowing what types of examination questions to expect. We simply told the subjects that they would be tested after the initial learning period. By providing sample questions, we would have allowed the subjects to tailor their learning process in a more focused manner. The animation group, in particular, could have directed their interactions with the animation in ways to clarify the most important topics and features of the pairing heap algorithm.

A second factor influencing the results of this study may in fact have a more general application to all algorithm animations and their value as learning aids. Most algorithm animations used in education are prepared by an instructor or the animation system's designer. Students, who are learning about an algorithm, view this prepared visualization. But what is an algorithm animation? It is a concrete rendering or depiction of the abstractions, entities, and operations of an algorithm. That is, it is a mapping from the abstract computational algorithm domain to the animated computer graphics domain. For a student to benefit from the animation, the student must understand both this mapping and the underlying algorithm upon which the mapping is based.

Consider the typical sorting views shown in most algorithm animations. When these animations are shown, the invariable reaction of instructors (teachers, professors, ...) is a statement much like, "Yes, this really does present the algorithm and its essence." But this reaction is coming from a person who already understands the algorithm and its details. Students just learning about an algorithm do not have a foundation of understanding upon which to construct the visualization mapping. Consequently, they do not benefit as greatly.

Therefore, we believe that algorithm animations will not benefit "novice" students just learning a new topic as much as the animations will benefit more advanced students. These "experienced" students may use the animation to refine their understanding of a particular algorithm, to clarify certain key behaviors of an algorithm, or to grasp a global, emerging methodology of an algorithm. We believe that the "novice" students would benefit more by actually constructing an algorithm animation rather than viewing a predefined one. By building an animation, a student employs an "active learning" process as opposed to the "passive learning" of watching the animation.

Conjectures

We embarked on this study seeking to gather concrete empirical evidence that algorithm animations assist learning. The evidence did not appear. Rather, the study provided insights into the use of algorithm animation as an instructional aid and the conditions under which algorithm animations may be most beneficial. In particular the study has led us to believe that

- To be most effective, algorithm animations must be accompanied by comprehensive motivational instruction. The quality of these teacher-provided explanations is perhaps even more important than the animation itself. To make algorithm animations simulate this instruction, the animation displays should be augmented by textual descriptions of the ongoing operations. An even better alternative would be a multimedia display with an audio-video window showing an instructor describing the algorithm.

- Design of instructional animations should be guided by a link between the animation and some specific instructional goals. Our walkthrough analysis suggested, after we had developed our materials, that this link was weak in the materials: there was no clear reason to think that viewing the animation would help learners perform the tasks we asked them to perform. Our results suggest that any general virtues that visual, animated presentations may possess are not powerful enough to produce good performance unless the presentations are keyed to specific learner needs.

- Before using algorithm animations in classroom settings, designers should perform user testing on each animation. The feedback from students can be invaluable in improving the instructional quality of the animation.

- Algorithm animation systems should include rewind-replay capabilities to allow users to back up and review important operations. Alternatively, some form of history showing previous states (frames) should exist.

Finally, this study's results have led us to question the value of algorithm animations used in a traditional, passive viewing sense. This methodology restricts students from actively constructing the mapping from an algorithm to its animation. Accordingly, future algorithm animation systems research must focus on ways to support students constructing their own animations. To be most effective, these systems must not require knowledge of computer graphics or advanced systems design. If such systems can be built, we are optimistic that they will be valuable for helping students learn and understand new algorithms.

ACKNOWLEDGMENTS

Chris Carothers' help in carrying out this study was indispensable. We also thank the reviewers for their helpful comments on improving this article.

REFERENCES

[1] Ronald M. Baecker and David Sherman. Sorting Out Sorting. 16mm color sound film, 1981. Shown at SIGGRAPH '81, Dallas TX.

[2] Brigham Bell, John Rieman, and Clayton Lewis. Usability testing of a graphical programming system: Things we missed in a programming walkthrough. In *Proceedings of the ACM SIGCHI '91 Conference on Human Factors in Computing Systems*, pages 7–12, New Orleans, LA, May 1991.

[3] Marc H. Brown. Exploring algorithms using Balsa-II. *Computer*, 21(5):14–36, May 1988.

[4] Marc H. Brown. Perspectives on algorithm animation. In *Proceedings of the ACM SIGCHI '88 Conference on Human Factors in Computing Systems*, pages 33–38, Washington D.C., May 1988.

[5] Marc H. Brown and Robert Sedgewick. Techniques for algorithm animation. *IEEE Software*, 2(1):28–39, January 1985.

[6] Michael L. Fredman, Robert Sedgewick, Daniel D. Sleator, and Robert E. Tarjan. The Pairing Heap: A new form of self-adjusting heap. *Algorithmica*, 1:111–129, March 1986.

[7] Susan Palmiteer and Jay Elkerton. An evaluation of animated demonstrations for learning computer-based tasks. In *Proceedings of the ACM SIGCHI '91 Conference on Human Factors in Computing Systems*, pages 257–263, New Orleans, LA, May 1991.

[8] John T. Stasko. TANGO: A framework and system for algorithm animation. *Computer*, 23(9):27–39, September 1990.

[9] John T. Stasko. Animating algorithms with XTANGO. *SIGACT News*, 23(2):67–71, Spring 1992.

[10] John T. Stasko and Carlton Reid Turner. Tidy animations of tree algorithms. In *Proceedings of the IEEE 1992 Workshop on Visual Languages*, pages 216–218, Seattle, WA, September 1992.

[11] John T. Stasko and Carlton Reid Turner. Tidy animations of tree algorithms. Technical Report GIT-GVU-92-11, Graphics, Visualization, and Usability Center, Georgia Institute of Technology, Atlanta, GA, June 1992.

[12] John T. Stasko and Jeffrey Scott Vitter. Pairing heaps: Experiments and analysis. *Communications of the ACM*, 30(3):234–249, March 1987.

[13] Roger E. Whitney and N. Scott Urquhart. Microcomputers in the mathematical sciences: Effects of courses, students, and instructors. *Academic Computing*, 4(6):14–18,49–53, March 1990.

Reducing the Variability of Programmers' Performance Through Explained Examples

David F. Redmiles

Department of Computer Science and Institute of Cognitive Science
Campus Box 430
University of Colorado, Boulder, Colorado 80309
redmiles@cs.colorado.edu

ABSTRACT

A software tool called EXPLAINER has been developed for helping programmers perform new tasks by exploring previously worked-out examples. EXPLAINER is based on cognitive principles of learning from examples and problem solving by analogy. The interface is based on the principle of making examples accessible through multiple presentation views and multiple representation perspectives. Empirical evaluation has shown that programmers using EXPLAINER exhibit less variability in their performance compared to programmers using a commercially available, searchable on-line manual. These results are related to other studies of programmers and to current methodologies in software engineering.

KEYWORDS: software engineering, user interface, knowledge representation, semantic networks, learning, analogy, programming plans.

INTRODUCTION: EXAMPLES IN PROGRAMMING

Programming requires a person to transform a general, informal understanding of a goal into a formal model using operators and components interpretable by the computer [4, 10, 13]. Program examples can aid this task by illustrating results of applying and combining specific components. When the results or goals of an example match a programmers' current goals for a task, the example provides a means of reducing the space of possible components the programmers might need, as well as illustrating how to use them. Thus, the problem-solving strategy being advocated here for programming is to use examples by analogy.

Empirical evidence of the viability of an example-based approach has come out of cognitive studies of learning and

problem solving. Lewis observed that people learning procedures can use and generalize from even a single example, relying on heuristics and some background knowledge [11]. Pirolli and Anderson observed that examples played a crucial role for students learning LISP concepts [14]. In another study, Kessler and Anderson noted variability in learners' performance and concluded that when relying on examples, learners must be able to construct correct mental models of examples [9]. Similarly, Chi and colleagues observed that students can learn well from examples, provided they are careful to explain the examples to themselves as they learn (i.e., develop good mental models) [2].

Together, these different studies imply a uniform result: learners who develop good mental models of examples can apply or transfer that knowledge to new tasks. Thus, to assist programmers, it is not always sufficient to simply provide examples; some assistance aiding the development of a mental model of the example may also be required.

This conclusion is the fundamental assumption of a programming tool called EXPLAINER. EXPLAINER combines code examples with knowledge equivalent to the programming plan [20, 19, 17] underlying the example. Through a hypermedia interface, programmers can explore the relationship between the abstract programming plan and the concrete implementation components in an example related to their programming task. An empirical evaluation has shown that providing the knowledge behind an example, namely the programming plan, greatly reduced the variability of programmers' performance.

The remaining sections of this paper provide the background for the EXPLAINER research, illustrate how the EXPLAINER interface is used, describe how knowledge is represented and input, and report specific results of the empirical evaluation. Some of the sections are necessarily brief. In-depth information is found in [15].

AN EXAMPLE-BASED DESIGN PROCESS

The EXPLAINER tool is only one component of an example-based design process (see Figure 1). Examples residing in a catalog repository must be retrieved by users. Retrieval requires users to articulate some specification of requirements for the current task (such as the task in Figure 2) in order for an appropriate example to be delivered (such as the example in Figure 3). Once an example is retrieved, users must be supported in potential modification of the example to adapt it to their new task. Working with an example can lead to additional ideas about the current task, possibly leading to refinement of the original requirements specification and retrieval of additional examples.

This model of design, the interrelationship of the different components, and current systems implementations are discussed in detail elsewhere [6]. It is presented here for context and to emphasize that the examples presented to users by EXPLAINER are selected for their applicability to a programmer or designer's current task. Knowing that an example is related to their task helps people develop the analogy from example to task, which is critical to the example-based approach [7].

The features or concepts of an example that are relevant to different tasks can vary. However, the use of analogy has been simplified in our exploratory work by restricting the domain of the tasks and examples to graphics functions. Thus, in a sense, the existence of a common perspective between example and task is guaranteed; minimally, it is found in the graphics features of an example (i.e., circles, labels, etc.). Once programmers recognize the features they want in a retrieved example, they can use the EXPLAINER interface to explore how features are mapped onto programming concepts. This decomposition is essentially the programming plan for the example [20, 17] (See also [16]).

EXPLAINER USER INTERFACE

The purpose of the EXPLAINER interface (see Figures 3 and 4) is to make apparent to the programmer the relationship between abstract programming plans and the specific implementation components [13, 19]. The interface was implemented as a hypermedia tool. This implementation allows minimal information about the example to be initially presented [5, 1]. The programmers can then decide which specific features of the example they want to explore, presumedly choosing those most relevant to their current task. Information is accessed and expanded through a command menu (see Figure 4a). Almost all items presented on the screen are mouse sensitive and are equally accessible for command actions.

The interface presents multiple presentation *views* of the information comprising an example, code listing, sample execution, component diagrams, and text. These views are initially selected for EXPLAINER due to their popularity in existing computer-aided software engineering (CASE) tools [18]. Unique to EXPLAINER is the characteristic that the same information is presentable in different views. For

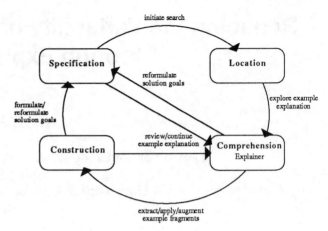

Figure 1: An Example-Based Design Process

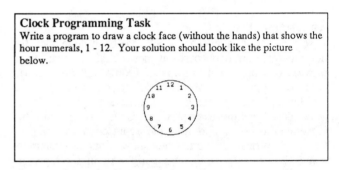

Clock Programming Task
Write a program to draw a clock face (without the hands) that shows the hour numerals, 1 - 12. Your solution should look like the picture below.

Figure 2: Clock Task as Described to Programmers

instance, in the Cyclic Group Example shown in Figure 3, the LISP concept of the call to the function that draws the circle is presented as a stylized fragment of the code listing, as a circle graphic object in the sample execution, or as node in a component diagram. The possibility to view the example information in different external forms accommodates different individual preferences. Redundant views also provide reinforcement of new concepts.

Within each view, the programmer can access information from different representation *perspectives*. Currently, the different perspectives are selected from a list (Figure 4b), appearing after a command is selected (Figure 4a). For instance, in the diagram view, the programmer has created diagrams of the example from the Plot Features and LISP perspectives (upper right of Figure 3—the LISP perspective being only partially visible). Text has been presented from LISP, Program Features, and Cyclic Operations perspectives (lower right of Figure 3).

Thus, the EXPLAINER interface allows programmers to access information about programming plans through different views and from different perspectives. Highlighting and textual descriptions allow programmers to understand the relationships between elements of programming plans and system components. Figure 3 is the actual state of the EXPLAINER interface as produced by one of the test subjects during the evaluation. The subject was exploring this example program to perform the programming task of

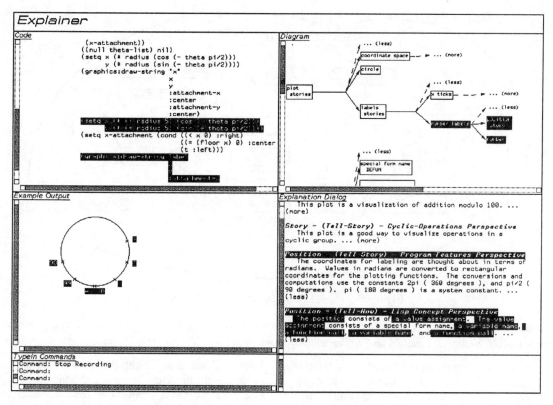

Figure 3: Exploring the "Cyclic Group" Example in EXPLAINER

The above screen shows the actual state of the EXPLAINER interface at the end of one programmer's test session. The programmer was exploring the information in this example in learning how to complete the programming task of Figure 2.

Figure 2. The screen shows that the subject had accomplished the following:

- expanded the diagram view to explore the components of labels in the Plot Features perspective (clicking on "(more)" cues);

- redrawn the initial diagram from its Plot Features perspective to a LISP perspective—only a portion is visible in the middle of the diagram pane (menu action "Diagram");

- retrieved the story, displayed in the explanation-dialog view, about the concept of labels in the Program Features perspectives (menu action "Text Story");

- generated a description of how labels are implemented in the LISP perspective (menu action "How"); and

- highlighted the concepts having to do with labels common across the several different perspectives and the four views.

This specific information enabled the test programmer to identify the LISP function called to draw the label, the assignment function that calculated the position, and what variables the position calculation depended on. The programmer could then apply the same functions in the solution of the clock task, or in this case, simply modify a copy of the example to place the labels inside the perimeter of the circle.

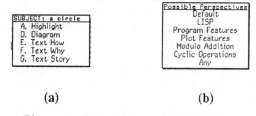

(a)   (b)

Figure 4: Pop-up Menus in EXPLAINER

KNOWLEDGE REPRESENTATION, USE, AND INPUT

The representation of plan information in EXPLAINER is accomplished using semantic networks (see Figure 5). In EXPLAINER, nodes in a semantic network correspond to *concepts* in a given *perspective*. A perspective is a theme or point of view under which the example may be described. Three perspectives appear in the scenario: a programming language perspective of LISP concepts, a Plot Features perspective, and a problem-domain perspective of Cyclic Operations in group theory. Concepts in the LISP perspective consist of function calls and arguments. Concepts in the Plot Features perspective consist of graphic concepts such as "number labels" and "x ticks." Concepts in the Cyclic Operations perspective consist of problem-domain concepts such as "operator" and "elements."

The networks connect nodes through three kinds of links: *components, roles,* and *perspectives.* The components link connects one concept to zero or more concepts that may

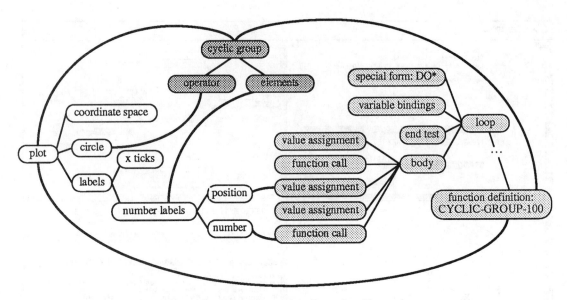

Figure 5: Partial Repesentation of an Example

Three perspectives are shown in this figure: Plot Features (unshaded ovals), LISP concept (shaded ovals), and Cyclic Operations (darkest ovals). The straight lines represent components/roles links. The arcs correspond to perspectives links.

comprise it. In the above example, the "plot" consists of a "coordinate space," a "circle," and "labels." The components link captures the "how to" or implementation knowledge in a example. The roles link is the inverse of the components link and supples one kind of "why" or goal knowledge. For example, a "circle" is drawn as part of the "plot." Concepts are identified with one specific perspective. However, they can have equivalent or analogous counterparts in other perspectives. This relationship is captured in the perspectives link and provides the information used for highlighting the correspondences between the different perspectives. For example, the "position" and "number" components of the "number labels" concept in the Plot Features perspective are equivalent to a "value assignment" and a "function call" respectively in the LISP perspective.

In sum, concepts in different perspectives are composed into semantic networks. The networks in different perspectives are interrelated through the perspectives links of individual concepts. Thus, as a whole, an example program is one semantic network that may be interpreted according to various perspectives.

Essentially all of the implementation of EXPLAINER is devoted to supporting the user interface. Since all of the commands are accessing information about an example, they are always accessing concepts in the semantic network representing that example. The minimal information presented initially on the screen provides starting points of concepts in this network. The actions on the command menu initiate searches through the network and expose additional information. Applying the "Text How" command to a concept causes that concept's components to be formated (through simple patterns) and presented in a sen-

tence. Using the "Highlight" command exposes all the perspective links from a specified concept by highlighting equivalent concepts in all the views. The search pattern is basically breadth-first, though various characteristics of the search path can be controlled to find concepts of specific perspectives, views, or distances.

The scheme for construction of new examples relies on work done with Andreas Girgensohn in conjunction with his research on systems for end-user modifiability [8]. Additional examples are found in [6]. Briefly, the input of knowledge about examples is a semiautomated process. The creator of the knowledge is currently assumed to be the original author of the example. Once an example program has been written, its code is parsed automatically into a semantic net of LISP concepts. Higher-level perspectives can be created by a concept input menu (not shown). Using a concept editing menu (see Figure 6), concepts from different perspectives can be equated. For instance, as shown in the figure, the concept "elements" of the Cyclic Operations perspective (highlighted in the diagram pane) can be equated to the LISP perspective concept "label-list" (highlighted in the code pane). The network of concepts associated with a program example is saved together with the example.

With all knowledge-based interfaces, the issue of the cost of entering knowledge arises. The techniques discussed in the preceding paragraph simplify this process. The information for the Cyclic Group Example required 2.5 hours to input after about 5 hours of planning the content of the example. The example introduces 30 new concept classes while reusing 63 existing classes. As the number of examples collected increases, the number of new classes needed is expected to decrease. The Cyclic Group Ex-

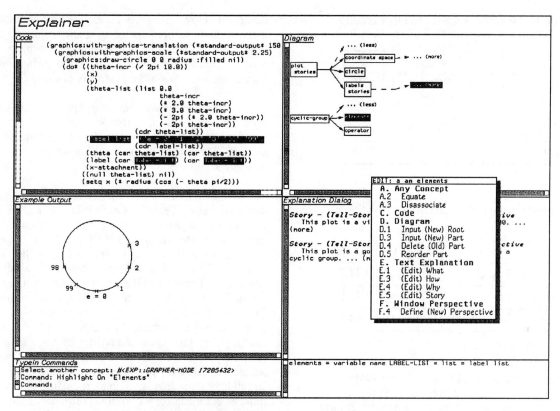

Figure 6: Authoring an Example in EXPLAINER

Two parts, "elements" and "operator" are defined and added to the new concept "cyclic group" through the concept editing menu. The "elements" part is then equated to the code concept of "label-list" through the same menu.

ample illustrates 6 of 70 components in a graphics library. While a systematic analysis of "coverage" has not be performed, the total number of examples for adequately illustrating this library is expected to be small.

EMPIRICAL EVALUATION

The empirical evaluation of EXPLAINER tested three conditions under which subjects solved the programming task of drawing a clock face (see Figure 2). In all three conditions, programmers were given the same example, a program illustrating operations in a cyclic group (see Figure 3). The conditions varied the programming tool that the three groups of subjects worked with to help them understand the example. In the first condition, subjects worked with the EXPLAINER tool as described above. In the second condition, subjects also worked with the EXPLAINER tool; however, the interactive menu was deactivated (the example information was fully expanded when subjects began the test). In the third condition, subjects worked with a commercially available, searchable on-line manual which contained descriptions of all the functions used in the example. The purpose of the intermediary second condition was to determine if only the difference in information content between EXPLAINER and the on-line manual affected the results. In Tables 1-4, the three conditions are identified as "E", "O", and "D" for EXPLAINER, menu-Off EXPLAINER, and commercial documentation.

The evaluation measured the performance of programmers with respect to variability in two senses. First, a notion of "directness" was defined as the number of different variations programmers would try in solving a task. The rationale was that the more support the programmers had from the example and tool in solving the task, the lower the number of trial and error variations would be. The observed measures are defined below and these are compared across groups. Second, within each group the variance in the observed measures is calculated and then compared across groups. The rationale with this test was that the more support the example and tool combination provided, the more uniform (smaller variance) the programmers' behavior as measured would be within a condition.

Eight subjects were tested for each condition and were randomly assigned to conditions. The subjects all had roughly the same background knowledge in LISP programming, being recruited from masters-level artificial intelligence classes in computer science. However, they were not already familiar with the graphics functions required by the task. Despite the equivalent backgrounds, one subject in the on-line documentation group (condition D) dropped out after working for 26 minutes. That subject's data are not reported in the tables because of the requirements of the calculations; if included, they would shift the results further in EXPLAINER's favor. Thus the frequencies represented in the tables are 8, 8, and 7 for conditions E, O, and D.

Table 1: Means of Session Data by Condition

	E	O	D
Points Completed	4.63	4.63	4.71
Solution Time	43.25	39.00	36.14
Changes	7.38	9.75	13.14
Runs	4.75	6.50	9.57

Table 2: Means of Ratio Data by Condition

	E	O	D
Changes/Points	1.57	2.06	3.14
Runs/Points	1.03	1.41	2.45
Solution Time/Points	9.41	8.96	8.64

Table 3: Variances of Session Data Compared by Squared-Rank Test (Explainer Against Document-Examiner)

	E	D	|Z|	$p <$
Points Completed	0.55	0.57	1.92	.1
Solution Time	175.93	445.14	1.17	—
Changes	4.55	67.14	2.91	.01
Runs	2.21	78.29	2.91	.01

Table 4: Variances of Ratio Data Compared by Squared-Rank Test (Explainer Against Document-Examiner)

	E	D	|Z|	$p <$
Changes/Points	0.08	7.86	2.72	.01
Runs/Points	0.08	9.71	2.70	.01
Solution Time/Points	6.41	56.61	1.70	.1

The means of the performance measures are summarized in Table 1. Points Completed measures how many of five subtasks were completed by subjects. The subtasks were identified by steps that would be required to solve the Clock Task. Identifying the subtasks allowed partial grading of tasks not fully completed and allowed a more realistic programming situation in which subjects would not necessarily know a priori what subtasks would have to be performed. Partial solutions are compensated for by ratios described below. Solution Time measures how long a subject worked before declaring their solution complete. Changes measures how many attempts a subject made before completing the task. Runs measures how many trial executions were made (i.e., to verify changes).

To compensate for the fact that subjects might complete different numbers of subtasks, ratios of the different measures per Points Completed were calculated for each subject. The means of the resulting ratios are summarized in Table 2.

The first evaluation of variability considered the measurements of Tables 1 and 2. On first inspection, the values of the two tables present a mixed picture. Table 1 indicates that none of the groups differed greatly in the degree of their solutions (Points Completed) nor in the time taken (Solution Time). However, the number of variations made and tried (Changes and Runs) tended to increase from condition E to O to D. This trend is borne out in the ratios in Table 2. The EXPLAINER group appeared to complete the programming task more "directly" while the documentation group proceeded according to a "trial-and-error" method. Furthermore, the Points Completed measure is actually inflated for condition D since the eliminated subject did not complete any goals. Including that observation reduces the mean for Condition D for Points Completed to 4.13. Unfortunately, the standard ANOVA test did not indicate a significant difference in means for the measures, including Changes and Runs.

The second evaluation of variability considered the variances of the measures within each condition. Tables 3 and 4 show variances for the different measures and the significance yielded by the Squared-Rank Test. Except for Solution Time, the difference in variances was statistically significant. For brevity, only the comparison between the two extreme conditions (E and D) is shown here. In general, the trend of increased variance from condition E to O to D holds with statistical significance. Detailed values and comparisons are available in [15].

As a group, then, the subjects using EXPLAINER performed the programming task more directly, and they performed it with less inter-subject variability. Subjects using the online documentation tool proceeded in a trial-and-error fashion and, not surprisingly, exhibited great inter-subject variability. It is important to note that the reduction in variance was not at the cost of performance. The "better" end-point values (high values for Points Completed, low for other measures) of the ranges of the measures were similar—good performers were about the same in all conditions. The reduction in variance resulted from "worse" end-point values coming closer to the "better" end—otherwise poor performers were helped by EXPLAINER.

CONCLUSIONS

The variability of the programmers' performance in the online documentation group is consistent with other studies of programmers (see the survey by Egan [3]). Furthermore, the provision of an example by itself was insufficient to prevent this variability, as also observed by Kessler and Anderson and noted earlier. However, the provision of an example, supplemented by information constituting a representation of a programming plan and with a means of exploring the relationship of the programming plan to a specific example solution, did stem the variability. Programmers who needed to compensate for variation in background knowledge, skill, or other predispositions, were supported by the EXPLAINER tool and approach.

The kind of support that the EXPLAINER tool provides is becoming increasingly important in the software field. Consider the widely-acclaimed methodology of software reuse [12]. The premise is that ever-growing repositories (subroutine libraries or software packages) of proven components (subroutines, functions, object classes, etc.) are made available to programmers to use as operators in new programs. Though this approach does save a programmer the effort of redevelopment, the essential cognitive problem of programming remains: programmers still must know when and how to apply which components or operators to achieve specific results [4]. This knowledge central to the examples as represented by EXPLAINER.

ACKNOWLEDGMENTS
I thank all of the students who participated in the empirical study. I thank Gerhard Fischer, Clayton Lewis, John Rieman, and Robert Rist for their comments and support. This research was funded in part through grants from the Army Research Institute (ARI MDA903-86-C0143) the National Science Foundation (IRI-9015441), and the Colorado Advanced Software Institute (TT-93-006).

REFERENCES
1. J.B. Black, J.M. Carroll, S.M. McGuigan. What Kind of Minimal Instruction Manual Is The Most Effective. *Human Factors in Computing Systems and Graphics Interface, CHI+GI'87 Conference Proceedings (Toronto, Canada)*, ACM, New York, 1987, pp. 159-162.

2. M.T.H. Chi, M. Bassok, M. Lewis, P. Reimann, R. Glaser. Self-Explanations: How Students Study and Use Examples in Learning to Solve Problems. *Cognitive Science 13*, 2 (1989), 145-182.

3. D.E. Egan. Individual Differences In Human-Computer Interaction. In M. Helander (Ed.), *Handbook of Human-Computer Interaction*, North-Holland, Amsterdam, 1991, Chap. 24, pp. 543-568.

4. G. Fischer. Cognitive View of Reuse and Redesign. *IEEE Software, Special Issue on Reusability 4*, 4 (July 1987), 60-72.

5. G. Fischer, T. Mastaglio, B.N. Reeves, J. Rieman. Minimalist Explanations in Knowledge-Based Systems. Jay F. Nunamaker, Jr (Ed.), *Proceedings of the 23rd Hawaii International Conference on System Sciences, Vol III: Decision Support and Knowledge Based Systems Track*, IEEE Computer Society, 1990, pp. 309-317.

6. G. Fischer, A. Girgensohn, K. Nakakoji, D. Redmiles. Supporting Software Designers with Integrated, Domain-Oriented Design Environments. *IEEE Transactions on Software Engineering, Special Issue on Knowledge Representation and Reasoning in Software Engineering 18*, 6 (1992), 511-522.

7. M.L. Gick, K.J. Holyoak. Analogical Problem Solving. *Cognitive Psychology 12* (1980), 306-355.

8. A. Girgensohn. *End-User Modifiability in Knowledge-Based Design Environments*. Ph.D. Thesis, Department of Computer Science, University of Colorado, Boulder, CO, 1992. Also available as TechReport CU-CS-595-92.

9. C.M. Kessler, J.R. Anderson. Learning Flow of Control: Recursive and Iterative Procedures. *Human-Computer Interaction 2* (1986), 135-166.

10. W. Kintsch, J.G. Greeno. Understanding and Solving Word Arithmetic Problems. *Psychological Review 92* (1985), 109-129.

11. C. Lewis. Why and How to Learn Why: Analysis-Based Generalization of Procedures. *Cognitive Science 12*, 2 (1988), 211-256.

12. B. Meyer. Reusability: The Case for Object-Oriented Design. *IEEE Software 4*, 2 (March 1987), 50-64.

13. N. Pennington. Stimulus Structures and Mental Representations in Expert Comprehension of Computer Programs. *Cognitive Psychology 19* (1987), 295-341.

14. P.L. Pirolli, J.R. Anderson. The Role of Learning from Examples in the Acquisition of Recursive Programming Skills. *Canadian Journal of Psychology 39*, 2 (1985), 240-272.

15. D.F. Redmiles. *From Programming Tasks to Solutions -- Bridging the Gap Through the Explanation of Examples*. Ph.D. Thesis, Department of Computer Science, University of Colorado, Boulder, CO, 1992.

16. C.H. Rich, R.C. Waters. *The Programmer's Apprentice*. Addison-Wesley Publishing Company, Reading, MA, 1990.

17. R.S. Rist. Schema Creation in Programming. *Cognitive Science 13* (1989), 389-414.

18. J. Sodhi. *Software Engineering Methods, Management, and CASE Tools*. TAB Professional and Reference Books, Blue Ridge Summit, PA, 1991.

19. E. Soloway, J. Pinto, S. Letovsky, D. Littman, R. Lampert. Designing Documentation to Compensate for Delocalized Plans. *Communications of the ACM 31*, 11 (November 1988), 1259-1267.

20. E. Soloway, K. Ehrlich. Empirical Studies of Programming Knowledge. *IEEE Transactions on Software Engineering SE-10*, 5 (September 1984), 595-609.

Mental Representations of Programs by Novices and Experts

Vikki Fix
Computer Science Department
University of South Dakota
Vermillion SD 57069, USA
phone: (605), 677-5388
email: vikkif@charlie.usd.edu

Susan Wiedenbeck
Computer Science Department
University of Nebraska
Lincoln, NE 68588, USA
phone: (402) 472-5006
email: susan@cse.unl.edu

Jean Scholtz
Computer Science Department
Portland State University
Portland, OR 97207, USA
phone: (503) 725-4103
email: jean@cs.pdx.edu

ABSTRACT

This paper presents five abstract characteristics of the mental representation of computer programs: hierarchical structure, explicit mapping of code to goals, foundation on recognition of recurring patterns, connection of knowledge, and grounding in the program text. An experiment is reported in which expert and novice programmers studied a Pascal program for comprehension and then answered a series of questions about it designed to show these characteristics if they existed in the mental representations formed. Evidence for all of the abstract characteristics was found in the mental representations of expert programmers. Novices' representations generally lacked the characteristics, but there was evidence that they had the beginnings, although poorly developed, of such characteristics.

KEYWORDS: program comprehension, mental representation of programs

INTRODUCTION

In this paper we are concerned with the characteristics of the mental representation that expert and novice programmers form while studying a program for comprehension. Knowing what kind of information understanders have at their disposal and how it is characteristically organized is crucial to understanding mental representations and predicting performance on comprehension-related programming tasks. The comparison of novices and experts is important because the differences found in a direct comparison help to define the contribution of expertise to task performance. We propose that an expert's mental representation exhibits five abstract characteristics, which are generally absent in novice representations:

1. It is hierarchical and multi-layered;
2. It contains explicit mappings between the layers;
3. It is founded on the recognition of basic patterns;
4. It is well connected internally;
5. It is well grounded in the program text.

ABSTRACT CHARACTERISTICS

Some past research on program comprehension [1, 8, 9] has focused on the classes of information that programmers extract during program comprehension. An interest in this research has been to determine whether programmers build a representation consisting mostly of concrete information about *how* the program works or of functional information about *what* the program does. A general finding has been that better comprehenders are distinguished from poorer comprehenders by their mastery of functional information. In the research reported here we do not focus on the classes of information making up the content of the representation but rather on the representation's general features. We investigated a group of features which had been suggested in the programming literature as characteristic of mature mental representations in programming: hierarchical multi-layered structure, explicit mappings, incorporation of basic recurring patterns, well connectedness, and foundation in the program text. We call these *abstract features* of a representation to distinguish them from the categories of information that form the content of the representation, as studied by Adelson and Pennington. In our view these features are manifestations of general comprehension mechanisms used in program understanding, and they help to explain at a deeper level why certain categories of information are extracted by programmers during the comprehension process. While some of these features have been studied empirically, many of them have not been studied or have not been studied specifically in the context of program comprehension tasks. Each of the features is described below with references to related work.

A **hierarchically structured** mental representation of a program is one which conceptualizes elements of a program as forming a layered network of arbitrary depth and breadth, depending on the specific program [6]. A hierarchical structure of mental representations by programmers has been suggested by some observations of programmers carrying out programming tasks. Both Jeffries [4] and Nanja and Cook [7] observed that advanced programmers, but not novices, used a strategy of reading a program in the order in which it would be executed, and they believed that this led to development of a hierarchical understanding of the program. However, Holt, Boehm-Davis, and Schultz [3], using a free recall technique, found no significant difference between novices and experts in the depth of their mental models of programs. We hypothesized that expert programmers would show more evidence of hierarchical structure in their mental representations of a program than would novices, when comprehending a well-written program with clear hierarchical relations embedded in it.

An important feature of the mental representation is not just the existence of multiple layers of representation but the existence of **explicit mappings** between the layers. Letovsky [6] has argued that the overall goals of a program are usually readily understandable to programmers from such sources as mnemonic names or documentation. Likewise, the lowest level, the implementation, which consists of the data structures and actions of the program, is also readily understandable, i.e., a programmer can understand the action of each line of code in isolation. The problem in comprehending programs is to create a mapping between high-level goals and their code representation. In empirical work, Pennington [8] found that the most skilled expert programmers tied their hypotheses about a program's function to specific information in the program code itself. This was not true of some less skilled experts who made numerous, speculative hypotheses about a program's function from triggers like variable names, without ever really verifying them by figuring out what the segments of code did. We expected a strong difference between novices and experts in their ability to link specific segments of code to program goals. However, we did not expect a correspondingly strong difference in their ability to understand overall program goals.

The use of **recurring basic patterns** as a foundation for knowledge representation has been a theme of programming research for a number of years. According to Soloway and Ehrlich [10], programming knowledge is represented as a set of frame-like structures, called plans, for handling stereotypical situations which arise frequently in programming. If basic programming knowledge is stored as plans, then one would expect to see evidence of plan recognition during program comprehension and plan-like structures in the mental representation of individual programs. Soloway and Ehrlich presented evidence that experienced programmers' comprehension was disrupted by programs that were written in an unplan-like way, thus supporting the idea that plan recognition must occur in comprehension. We hypothesized that there would be a difference between novices and experts in their ability to connect program code with plan labels for all but the very simplest plans.

A **well connected** representation is one where the programmer understands how parts of the program interact with one another. Interactions are difficult to understand, probably because they embody instances of delocalized plans, i.e., plans in which the code implementing them is scattered throughout the program, rather than localized in one place [11]. This lack of contiguity introduces difficulties in comprehension, since one cannot see the plan implementation as a single coherent unit. Jeffries, Turner, Polson, and Atwood [5] found that experienced

programmers designing a program pay special attention to parts of the code that interact, for example the design of interfaces between related modules. Given the difficulties posed by the interaction of segments of code, we expected that experienced programmers would try to extract such information in the comprehension process and it would thus be included in their mental representation of the program. Novices, on the other hand, would be unlikely to concentrate on this type of information.

Representations which are **well grounded** in the program text are also suggested in the literature as characteristic of good mental representations. Well grounded representations include specific details of where structures and operations occur physically in the program. An understanding grounded in the program text is useful because it allows programmers who have studied a program once to relocate with minimal search information which is needed to carry out programming tasks. In her protocols Jeffries [4] observed that expert programmers, but not novices, were very skillful at locating information which they had previously seen in a program when it was needed a second time. We tested experts' and novices' ability to locate information in a program text with the hypothesis that experts would surpass novices at locating most, but not all, kinds of information.

METHODOLOGY

Subjects
Twenty novice and 20 expert programmers took part in the study. All of the subjects were volunteers. The novice programmers were undergraduate students who had recently completed a first semester Pascal course. The expert subjects were professional programmers with a median of 7 years of experience.

Materials
The program used in this study was written in Pascal. It was 135 lines long and occupied 3 printed pages. The program manipulated student data. The program consisted of a main program and 9 subprograms. The deepest nesting of program blocks was 4 levels deep. The operations contained in the program had been covered in the beginning computer science courses taken by the novices: reading and writing files, interactively reading and writing to the terminal, manipulating arrays, sorting, searching, finding an average, and finding a maximum value. The use of procedures and functions, parameter passing, local variables, and the nesting of subprograms were all taught. Mnemonic identifiers were used in the program, which was also indented in a normal style to show nesting of blocks and of individual statements inside compound statements. No documentation was given.

The comprehension questions which subjects answered are described in Table 1. Comprehension questions have been used as a method of measuring understanding in past research on program cognition (see[2]). The questions focused on determining whether programmers exhibited the abstract characteristics in their representations of the program. The questions required recalling information

Question Number	Question Content	Abstract Category	Significant Difference
1	Match procedure names to the procedures they call	Hierarchical structure	p=.0043
2	List procedure names	Hierarchical structure	n.s.
3	Write description of goals of selected procedures	Explicit Mappings	p=.0001
4	Write description of principal goals of program	Explicit Mappings	n.s.
5	Label complex code segments with plan label	Recurring patterns	p=.0001
6	Label simple code segments with plan label	Recurring patterns	n.s.
7	List names used for same data objects in different program units	Well connected	p=.0013
8	List important variable names	Well connected	n.s.
9	Fill in names of program units in a skeleton outline of the program	Well grounded	p=.0007
10	Match variable names to the procedures in which they occur	Well grounded	p=.0006
11	Indicate physical location of invariant program parts	Well grounded	n.s.

Table 1: Summary of comprehension questions

about different objects or relations in the program The correspondence of the questions to the abstract characteristics is discussed below. The different questions relevant to one particular abstract characteristic were balanced to require a similar amount of information from the subject.

Questions 1 and 2 were designed to elicit whether the subjects' mental representations had a hierarchical, layered structure. The stimulus program reflected a clear hierarchical, layered structure in its use of nested procedures and functions. Question 1 asked subjects to match procedure names to the procedures which they called. A high score on this question would indicate that a subject had understood the hierarchical structure of the program and made it a part of the mental representation. Question 2 required subjects simply to list the names of the procedures used in the program, without regard to their physical order or the calling sequence. Thus, this question dealt with the same program elements, procedure names, but independent of their hierarchical context. A lack of difference between groups on this question would suggest that a difference on Question 1 was not explained merely by overall better memory of program elements.

Questions 3 and 4 were relevant to judging the ability to link code to program goals. Question 3 asked the subject to write a brief description of two procedures in the program, telling what program goals they realized. Thus, it was a measure of the subjects' ability to map between the code and the program goals. Subjects were also asked to write a sentence or two about *how* the procedure carried out its goals. This was included to gather information about whether subjects' mental representations also contained information about methods by which goals were implemented. Question 4, by contrast, asked the subject to write a brief description of what the whole program did, including the main goals. In asking about only the high level goals, Question 4 involved information which was likely to be available to programmers superficially, without a need for detailed understanding of what code implemented the various goals or how. It was expected that both novice and experienced programmers would be able to extract the overall goals asked for in this question but that there would be group differences in the ability to map between high level goals and the program code, as required by Question 3.

Questions 5 and 6 looked for evidence of the incorporation of basic plan knowledge in the understanding of the program. In each question the subject was given brief code segments from the program and was asked to give a label to each segment, consisting of a few words, to tell what it did (e.g., "initializes variable"). The patterns in Questions 5 and 6 were of different levels of complexity. Question 5 contained somewhat complex patterns, including the linear search for the largest value in the array, the segment which read input in a loop until end of file and counted the elements read, the sort routine, and the binary search routine. Question 6 also contained stereotyped patterns but ones of the most elementary kind, e.g., incrementing a counter. Being able to label any of the code segments in Questions 5 or 6 with an appropriate plan label is evidence of the use of plan knowledge in the understanding of the program. However, the different levels of complexity of the patterns in the two questions was meant to distinguish the ability of programmers at different skill levels to bring plan knowledge to bear in representing the code.

Questions 7 and 8 were relevant to judging the well connectedness of the representation. Question 7 gave subjects a list of variable names and asked them to indicate what other names, if any, those variables were known by in different program units. Thus, to answer this question subjects had to have an idea of what a data item represented, and they had to understand how it was passed through the program, possibly with different identifiers, while still representing the same object. Question 8 asked subjects to list the names the major variables in the program. Generating these would indicate knowledge of the essential objects in the program, but it would not indicate well connectedness in the representation.

Questions 9, 10, and 11 were used to judge how well grounded the representation was in the program text. Question 9 presented a list of the names of the program units and beside that a skeletal template of the program which represented the location of the program units by boxes. Nested units were shown by a box within a box. Subjects had to write the given subprogram names in the proper boxes in the template. High performance on this task would be an indication that the subject had synthesized an overview of the location of procedural units and incorporated it in the mental representation. While Question 9 had to do with the location of actions in the text, Question 10 concerned the location of objects. Question 10 required subjects to match different variable names to the program units in which they appeared (including some names which occurred in more than one unit). The ability to do this would also show well groundedness because the subject had a representation of where objects occurred in the text. The last question asked the subject to indicate the location of certain elements in the program text which are invariant in that they can be described by a relative location which is unchanging from one program to the next (e.g., Question: "Where is the end statement of the main program located?" -- Answer: last line of text; Question: "Where were the declarations

for local variables of the procedures located?" -- Answer: after the procedure heading). Correct answers on Question 11 would show some ability to handle the program as a piece of text having a particular structure, based on syntactic knowledge. However, it would not show program-specific grounding of knowledge in the program text.

Procedure

Subjects were run individually or in groups of 2 or 3. The subject was given a listing of the program to study for 15 minutes. They were told to study the program in detail in order to understand its structure and function as fully as possible. At the end of the study period the program listing was taken away. Subjects were given a question booklet with one question per page. The questions were not arranged in the numerical order shown in Table 1 but in an order chosen so that an earlier question did not give away the answer to a later question. Subjects were not allowed to return to a previous questions once they had turned the page. They were allowed to take as long as they needed to work through the question booklet. For experts the times ranged from 40 minutes to 1 1/4 hours with the average around one hour. For novices the times ranged from 45 minutes to 1 1/2 hours with the average around 1 1/4 hours.

RESULTS

First a MANOVA was run to test whether there was an overall difference in performance between experts and novices. It was found that the experts scored significantly higher than the novices (F(11, 28) = 8.9635, p = .0001). Following the significant MANOVA, individual ANOVA procedures were run on the different questions. For these ANOVAs on the individual performance variables the alpha level was set at .0045, i.e, .05 divided by 11, the number of tests performed. This was done to reduce the likelihood of Type I errors, i.e., rejecting null hypotheses that were true. The results of the individual ANOVAs are presented in the following paragraphs.

1. Hierarchical, multi-layered structure. Question 1 tested the presence of hierarchy in the subjects' representations. Experts scored significantly higher than novices (F(1,38) = 9.20, p = .0043). The expert mean score was 6.03 out of a possible score of 7 (if the subject had all the correct calls asked for and no spurious ones). The novices' mean was 3.40. Question 2 tested knowledge about the same program units as Question 1 but without requiring an understanding of the hierarchical structure. The ANOVA was not significant. The experts' mean score was 4.25 out of a possible score of 7, and the novices' mean score was 2.85.

2. Well developed mapping of code to goals. Question 3 asked for information about how two subprograms fulfilled goals of the program. The subjects' descriptions were analyzed for the presence of 7 specific information elements. Experts scored significantly higher than novices on Question 3 (F(1, 38) = 11.87, p = .0014). The expert mean out of the 7 elements was 5.2, while the novices' mean was 2.8. Although our main interest was

subjects' ability to link code to program goals, we also analyzed subjects' statements about the methods which the subprograms used to achieve their goals. For this analysis, subjects' descriptions were scored for the presence of 4 specific information elements related to method. Experts also scored significantly higher on this measure ($F(1, 38) = 34.45$, $p = .0001$). The experts' mean was 2.90 out of the 4 elements, and the novices' mean was .85. Question 4 asked only about the overall goals of the program. There was no significant difference between novices and experts on Question 4. The experts' mean was 6.15 and the novices' mean was 5.50 out of 7 elements on which the descriptions were scored.

3. Recurring patterns. Question 5 contained moderately complex recurring patterns, while Question 6 contained very simple recurring patterns. The results showed that there was a significant difference on Question 5 ($F (1, 38) = 57.58$, $p = .0001$). Out of a possible score of 4 the experts' mean was 3.7 and the novices' mean was 1.7. There was no significant difference between novices and experts on Question 6. Out of a possible score of 4 the experts' mean was 4 and the novices' mean was 3.7.

4. Well-connected representation. Question 7 probed about knowledge of data connections by asking what were the names used for the same conceptual objects in different subprograms. The experts were superior to the novices ($F(1, 38) = 11.99$, $p = .0013$). The experts' mean was 3.55 out of a possible score of 7, and the novices' mean was 1.43. Question 8 simply asked for a listing of names of data elements, independent of any connections to other data names used in the program. There was no significant difference between the two groups on the 7 principal variables. The experts' mean was 4.80 out of 7 and the novices' mean was 3.90.

5. Well grounded in the text. There was a significant difference on Question 9, the location of subprogram names on the program template ($F(1, 38) = 13.58$, $p = .0007$). The expert mean was 8.8 out of 9 names, and the novices' mean was 6.7. Question 10 involved linking variable names to the context in which they appeared. The experts performed significantly better than the novices ($F(1, 38) = 14.08$, $p = .0006$). The experts' mean was 5.63 out of a possible score of 10, while the novices' mean score was 1.65. Question 11 asked about locations of elements in the code that have a fixed absolute or relative location. There was no significant difference on this measure. The experts' mean was 9.3, and the novices' mean was 9.1 out of 10.

DISCUSSION AND CONCLUSIONS

The results of this study tend to support the existence of the five abstract characteristics in the mental representations of expert programmers. However, novice programmers do not show the same characteristics in their mental representations, or do not show them to the same degree. Experts extract many different kinds of information from a program which become a part of their mental representations. They are not distinguished from a novice along a single dimension or just a couple of

dimensions. Taken together, these differences in the mental representation may provide a partial explanation of why novice performance is poorer than expert performance on tasks which have program comprehension as a prerequisite. The results suggest that a number of skills contribute to the formation of the mental representation, for example, skill at recognizing basic recurring patterns, skill at understanding the particular structure inherent in a program text, skill at recognizing the links tying the separate program modules together, etc. When a programmer exercises these skills, a good representation which supports comprehension-related programming tasks is likely to emerge.

A limitation of this experiment is the lack of "naturalness" of the task and its possible implications. The subjects were instructed to study the program in order to comprehend in detail its structure and function. While the novices did not consider this an unusual task, apparently some of the experts did. A few of them commented that in studying a program they normally had a concrete objective in mind, such as finding a bug or determining the effects of a potential modification. In this case they were on a fishing expedition and, as a result, were not sure where to focus their efforts. This raises the question of what information experts would extract during program comprehension when given a more concrete goal. We speculate that the objects and relations recalled could change quite significantly depending on the nature of the situation posed in the instructions. For example, a modification instruction in which the subject was told the modification to be made would be likely to lead to concentration on a specific part of the program at the expense of other parts. Also, the size of the program and the familiarity of its domain would influence the information gathered during comprehension. Thus, with respect to the results reported here, we can only claim that experts are capable of creating a broad, multi-faceted representation, not that they necessarily do so every time they work with a program. However, we do expect that maintenance programmers who work with a large program over a period of time eventually develop a multi-faceted representation similar to what we found.

One may question why novices do not exhibit the same characteristics in their mental representations as experts. Clearly, some of the difference is simply the result of possessing less programming knowledge. For example, knowledge of recurring patterns may be deficient among novices and need to be built up through study and practice. On the other hand, some other characteristics of expert mental representations are based on information readily available in the program, yet novices do not extract it. Examples are the hierarchical structure inherent in the flow of control of the program and the connections between modules which are represented in the passage of data among modules. It may be that novice programmers do not pick up some information because they are using a different program comprehension strategy than experts, as suggested by Jeffries's observations [4] of a different order of program reading among novices. A different reading or study strategy may obscure some information selected by experts and at the same time may highlight other information less useful to support programming tasks. We also suggest that novices may lack basic skills necessary to developing an expert-like representation, particularly skill at performing symbolic execution. Novices inability to carry out symbolic execution or their use of it in inappropriate circumstances has been noted in the past [4, 5]. Attention to study strategy and to appropriate use of symbolic execution in instruction may aid novices in developing more expert-like representations.

REFERENCES

1. Adelson, B. When novices surpass experts: The difficulty of a task may increase with expertise. *Journal of Experimental Psychology: Learning, Memory and Cognition* 10 (1985), 483-495.

2. Boehm-Davis, D. A. Software comprehension. In *Handbook of Human-Computer Interaction*, M. Helander, Ed., NY: North-Holland, 1988, pp. 107-121.

3. Holt, R. W., Boehm-Davis, D. A., and Schultz, A. C. Mental representations of programs for student and professional programmers. In *Empirical Studies of Programmers: Second Workshop*, G. M. Olson, S. Sheppard, and E. Soloway, Eds., Norwood, NJ: Ablex, 1987, pp. 33-46.

4. Jeffries, R. A comparison of the debugging behavior of novice and expert programmers. Paper presented at the American Educational Research Association Annual meeting, 1982.

5. Jeffries, R., Turner, A. A., Polson, P. G., and Atwood, M. E. The processes involved in designing software. In *Cognitive Skills and Their Acquisition*, J. R. Anderson, Ed., Hillsdale, NJ: Erlbaum, 1981, pp. 255-283.

6. Letovsky, S. Cognitive processes in program comprehension. In *Empirical Studies of Programmers*, E. Soloway and S. Iyengar, Eds., Norwood, NJ: Ablex, 1986, pp. 58-79.

7. Nanja, M. and Cook, C. R. An analysis of the on-line debugging process. In *Empirical Studies of Programmers: Second Workshop*, G. M. Olson, S. Sheppard, and E. Soloway, Eds., Norwood, NJ: Ablex, 1987, pp. 172-184.

8. Pennington, N. Comprehension strategies in programming. In *Empirical Studies of Programmers: Second Workshop*, G. M. Olson, S. Sheppard, and E. Soloway, Eds., Norwood, NJ: Ablex, 1987, pp. 100-113.

9. Pennington, N. Stimulus structures and mental representations in expert comprehension of computer programs. *Cognitive Psychology* 19 (1987), 295-341.

10. Soloway, E. and Ehrlich, K. Empirical studies of programming knowledge. *IEEE Transactions on Software Engineering* 10 (1984), 595-609.

11. Soloway, E., Pinto, J. Letovsky, S., Littman, D., and Lampert, R. Designing documentation to compensate for delocalized plans. *Communications of the ACM* 31 (1988), 1257-1267.

Touch-Typing With a Stylus

David Goldberg and Cate Richardson

Xerox Corporation
Palo Alto Research Center
3333 Coyote Hill Rd.
Palo Alto, CA 94304
goldberg@parc.xerox.com
(415)-812-4423

ABSTRACT

One of the attractive features of keyboards is that they support novice as well as expert users. Novice users enter text using "hunt-and-peck," experts use touch-typing. Although it takes time to learn touch-typing, there is a large payoff in faster operation.

In contrast to keyboards, pen-based computers have only a novice mode for text entry in which users print text to a character recognizer. An electronic pen (or stylus) would be more attractive as an input device if it supported expert users with some analogue of touch-typing.

We present the design and preliminary analysis of an approach to stylus touch-typing using an alphabet of *unistrokes,* which are letters specially designed to be used with a stylus. Unistrokes have the following advantages over ordinary printing: they are faster to write, less prone to recognition error, and can be entered in an "eyes-free" manner that requires very little screen real estate.

KEYWORDS

Stylus, electronic pen, handwriting, printing, recognition, text entry, pen-based computing, shorthand.

INTRODUCTION

Keyboards are a vital part of today's computers. Although keyboards are somewhat bulky, they are well suited to PCs (even portable laptops) and workstations. In the future of Ubiquitous Computing [17], pocket-sized and wall-sized computers will be common. A keyboard is not very suitable for these sizes of computers. Although some manufacturers have put tiny keyboards on hand-held computers, such small keyboards are hard to operate, and impossible to use for high speed touch-typing. Similarly, keyboards do not work well for large wall-sized displays [3], because a keyboard is fixed and can't be reached from all parts of the display.

Thus many manufacturers are providing electronic pens or styli (we use the two terms interchangeably) as the primary input device for computers. A stylus is attractive because it works very well over the entire range of sizes. However, it is not very convenient for text entry. The state of the art is to print characters, with boxed entry recommended to improve accuracy [1]. This is slow and error prone [10]. Although it is true that computer interfaces use text input more than necessary (compare the Macintosh or MS-Windows with the older DOS or UNIX shell), considering how much of our daily lives involves reading and writing, it seems likely that interacting with computers will involve a significant amount of text entry for a long time to come. This suggests that a major impediment to the widespread use of styli is the problem of finding a convenient way to enter text.

Some manufacturers of pen computers suggest that the solution to this problem is to use uninterpreted handwritten text. Although this works well for scribbling a note in a personal calendar, uninterpreted text is not suitable for composing even a short memo if it needs to be filed in a form that can be later searched. Thus the problem this paper will address is: what is a convenient way to enter *interpreted* text?

There is an analogy between keyboards and styli. Keyboards can be used with no training: the letters can be tapped out one-by-one using hunt-and-peck. This is similar to what is currently done with styli. No new training is required, and letters are printed one-by-one. However, unlike styli, keyboards have a "growth path." With practice, hunt-and-peck with two fingers can become faster than handwriting. If even higher speeds are desired, then keyboard users can learn touch-typing. Touch-typing not only achieves high speeds, it also enables "eyes-free" operation, that is, the ability to type without having to look at your hands. This suggests that the solution to the problem of stylus text entry requires developing an analogue of touch-typing.

UNISTROKES AND HEADS-UP WRITING

Our approach to developing touch-typing for a stylus is based on introducing a special alphabet. Like touch-typing for keyboards, this is a system that has to be learned.

The traditional secretarial shorthand systems of Gregg and Pitman are one possible candidate for stylus touch-typing. Although these shorthand systems achieve very high speeds, they are at least as difficult to recognize as cursive handwriting, which is to say, using them for interpreted input does not appear practical at the present time [6] [8].

Shorthand systems can be classified as orthographic or phonetic. Orthographic systems use conventional spelling, and have one symbol for each letter of the ordinary Roman alphabet (this paper only considers text entry in English). Phonetic systems spell phonetically, and in the case of Gregg and Pitman, use a special phonetic alphabet. Phonetic systems are harder to learn, but can achieve very high speeds. This suggests that designing a stylus alphabet involves a trade-off between speed and ease-of-learning. Phonetic systems offer the fastest speed and are the hardest to learn, while orthographic systems are easiest to learn, but give a smaller speedup.

The system described in this paper is designed for ease of use, and thus is orthographic. Although its speed advantage over ordinary printing is modest, it has two other important advantages described in the next two sections: it is more accurate and it supports *heads-up writing*. If even higher speeds are desired, the system of this paper can be combined with techniques from existing shorthand systems that use the ordinary alphabet, such as Speedwriting [13].

Sloppiness Space

Ordinary Roman printed characters are not very robust in the face of rapid (hence sloppy) writing, since there are many pairs of letters that blur together when written quickly. For example, in the following figure, is the first letter an 'r'

or a 'v'? The second an 'a' or a 'd'? The third an 'N' or a 'W'? The fourth a 'g' or a 'q'? Although in any alphabet it is possible to draw symbols halfway between two valid letters, the ambiguities in the figure occur quite commonly in practice.

We have developed a system using *unistrokes*, which are designed somewhat like error correcting codes: they are well separated in *sloppiness* space. To explain this term, imagine that each unistroke letter is described by d features, and so can be thought of as a point in a d-dimensional space. Sloppiness space results when the features are chosen so that the changes caused by writing a letter more quickly (hence more sloppily) correspond to small changes in a letter's position in the d-dimensional space. Thus unistrokes that are well separated in sloppiness space can be robustly

distinguished even when written sloppily. Sloppiness space is a useful concept even if the precise set of features defining it is not known.

Because unistrokes are designed to be well separated in sloppiness space, they have a higher accuracy rate than ordinary printed Roman letters, and thus the net speed of producing a correct document will be higher than might be suggested by raw input speeds.

Heads-up Writing

The second advantage of unistrokes over ordinary Roman letters arises because each unistroke is a single stroke (pen-down/pen-up motion), hence the name *unistroke*. There are no symbols like 'f' or 'H' that require multiple strokes. This is very important, because it enables heads-up writing, as will now be explained.

When writing with a pen or pencil, each successive letter must be in a different spot, for the simple reason that if one letter is written on top of the next, the result is a jumble that can't be easily read. However, when writing with a stylus, the computer sees each stroke as it is written, and writing a new letter on top of a previous one does not affect the information already recorded for the earlier stroke. There is a problem implementing this using the ordinary Roman alphabet due to letters consisting of multiple strokes. For example, writing 'T' followed by 'H' gives a total of five strokes, and is not obvious that these five strokes should be grouped into two strokes for the 'T', and then three strokes for the 'H'. This is not a problem with unistrokes, where each letter is a single stroke.

Thus unistrokes lend themselves to writing each letter on top of another, which we call heads-up writing. This has several advantages:

- *Little writing area is needed.* Heads-up writing is especially convenient on very small computers. A writing space need only be as large as the space needed for one letter.

- *Eyes-free operation.* Like touch-typing, heads-up writing does not require writers to look at their hands while writing. This is useful for transcribing text, for taking notes in a lecture, for writing in dim rooms, etc.

- *Easier on the wrist.* Heads-up writing does not require wrist movement when writing and is less fatiguing than ordinary handwriting. Although this may sound a bit far-fetched at first, it can be verified with an ordinary pen or pencil on a piece of paper. Try writing a sentence without moving your wrist, printing each letter on top of another. Most people find this experiment quite convincing.

The one drawback of heads-up writing is that the space separating words must somehow be indicated. Since space is much more frequent than any letter, we use a dot (that is, a tap of the pen) to indicate a space.

Discussion

One alternative to handprint recognition for text entry is to display a picture of a keyboard, and enter text by tapping on the displayed keys with a stylus. This is not as good as a real keyboard because there is no tactile feedback. Nonetheless, for some users it is faster than printing slowly enough to be reliably recognized.

The advantages of unistrokes over a displayed keyboard are that they require much less screen real estate, and that they support eyes-free operation. Unistrokes will probably be faster for most writers, because (with heads-up writing) precise positioning is not required for the start of each new stroke.

To summarize, we propose that "power" users who frequently use a stylus for text entry will benefit from learning a new alphabet consisting of single stroke letters called unistrokes. Although these letters can be written in a conventional manner, the full benefit of unistrokes comes from writing in a touch-print fashion, in which letters are written on top of one another.

THE DESIGN OF UNISTROKES

The three major criteria for designing unistrokes are, in order of importance: easy to learn, well separated in sloppiness space, fast to write.

The last goal is the simplest to implement. Straight strokes are faster to draw than curved or bent strokes. Thus unistrokes map frequent letters (e, t, a, i, r) to straight strokes.

Properly satisfying the second goal would require precise information about the features that describe sloppiness space. Lacking this information, our approach was to pick a set of strokes that appeared to be well separated, and then observe them being written in real use to see whether they were well separated in practice. The results are reported in the section on measurements.

The first goal was achieved by making many unistroke characters the same (or similar) to ordinary Roman characters. The unistroke alphabet has seven characters that are essentially identical to Roman letters and eight characters that are natural sub-strokes of Roman letters. Heuristics exist for most other characters.

Tricks

The design of unistrokes involves two "tricks." It is clear that the fewer characters that need to be encoded, the easier it is to design a set of unistrokes that are well separated. The character space can be divided in half by not having separate symbols for upper and lower letters. Thus the first trick is to use a button as a caps shift key, and to not have separate unistrokes for each case.

The simplest button to press is one on the side barrel of the stylus itself. For our current prototype systems, we use a stylus supplied by Scriptel Corporation which has a side button

1.5 inches from the tip of the pen. Although this is too high to be convenient for most users, upper case letters occur sufficiently infrequently so that this has not been a serious problem. For future work, we have designed our own stylus with a side button that is both easy to press and unlikely to be pressed by accident. For systems without a side button, an on-screen button can be used as a case toggle-switch.

The second trick exploits a difference between ordinary pens and electronic pens. When looking at characters written with an ordinary pen, there is no simple way to distinguish a vertical stroke written from top to bottom from one written in the other direction, from bottom to top. But as seen by a computer, these strokes are totally different. Thus a vertical stroke can be used for two different unistroke characters. This is especially useful because strokes written in opposite directions are widely separated in sloppiness space.

The Unistroke Alphabet

The alphabet of unistrokes is based on these five strokes.

Each stroke comes in four different orientations.

Furthermore, each stroke can be written in two directions.

Since there are 5 basic shapes, 4 orientations, and 2 directions, this gives $5 \times 4 \times 2 = 40$ unistrokes, more than enough to encode 26 letters.

Assigning Unistrokes to Roman Letters

There are seven symbols that map directly to their ordinary representation in the Roman alphabet.

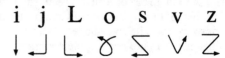

Although the unistrokes are shown with sharp corners, they can be drawn equally well with rounded corners (this is a small change in sloppiness space). Thus either of the two forms below could be written for 's'.

Next there are eight unistrokes that are subsets of the ordinary alphabetic characters. For example, the unistroke for 'b' represents the bowl of the 'b', etc. Actually, the unistroke for 'x' isn't a subset, but rather one way of writing an ordinary 'x' as a single stroke.

b   d   f   h   t   w   x   y

Then there are six letters that are best thought of as matching pairs. The letter 'v' has been seen before.

n   m   p   q   v   u

Finally, there are six "oddballs" with less natural mnemonics. For example, the unistroke for 'c' looks like the ordinary letter, but is written bottom-to-top. The unistroke for 'k' is one of the three straight line strokes of the 'k', but the one used is somewhat arbitrary.

a   c   e   g   k   r

Although the assignments of unistrokes was done primarily with an eye towards matching the ordinary alphabet as closely as possible, straight line strokes are assigned to five of the most common letters.

e   a   t   i   r

Discussion

It might seem that it would be simpler to develop an alphabet by directly stylizing each ordinary Roman printed letter. However, such a system will not be totally mnemonic. For example 'f' and 't' would have to be converted to single strokes, pairs close in sloppiness space (e.g. 'u', 'v') would have to be separated, and so on. By the time this is done, the resulting system would not be substantially easier to learn than unistrokes, and wouldn't benefit from the planning that exploited direction and mapped frequent letters to straight lines.

MEASUREMENTS

The full evaluation of a stylus text entry system should involve a preliminary design to get started, an evaluation of that design to pick out flaws, possibly several more design iterations, and then finally a head-to-head comparison with the best commercial pen user interface that uses ordinary printing. The development of unistrokes is still in the first design iteration. This section describes the results of evaluating the initial design described in the previous section.

We wanted to evaluate our system being used for a real task, rather than during some artificial experiment. Thus we built a mail sending program (Figure 1), and asked volunteers to send several messages per day using this program. The mail

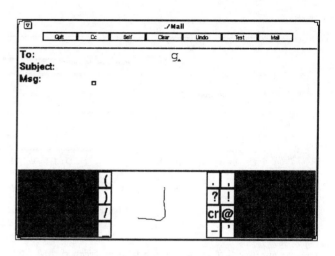

Figure 1   Stylus mail sending program

sender ran on a *scratchpad*, a unit containing a transparent tablet mounted on top of an LCD display, connected by a cable to the user's workstation [4].

Our measurements consisted of timings of strokes collected while running the mail sending program, recognition errors collected from a 'dictation' task, and informal impressions from users. The informal impressions were quite positive. About six people learned the unistroke alphabet by running a simple training program. All were able to correctly print unistrokes without looking them up on a reference sheet after about 10 minutes. Unfortunately, only three scratchpads were available, so only three users were able to use the mail sending program on a regular basis. They all seemed positive about using unistrokes as an alternative to ordinary Roman letters.

The Mail Sender and Stroke Timings

The mail sending program is written in Modula-3 [11], and is a front-end to the ordinary Unix mail program. It consists of three sections: a row of buttons at the top, a form in the middle, and a writing pad surrounded by buttons at the bottom. In the figure, the writing pad contains the unistroke for 'g' (⌐), which has been echoed in the 'To:' field. As characters are entered on the writing pad, they are echoed in the current field. The current field is changed by tapping with the stylus on the field labels. The mail is delivered by tapping on the 'Mail' button, which is the rightmost button on the top row.

The time spent during text entry has two parts, the time a stroke is actually written (from pen-down to pen-up), and the time between strokes (from pen-up to pen-down). The times spent writing strokes for one user as collected by the mail program are graphed in Figure 2. The value for each letter is the median of the collected times in milliseconds. As expected, dot (space) is fastest at 90 milliseconds, followed by straight-line unistrokes which cluster around 150 milliseconds. The fastest curved unistroke letter, 'j' (⌐), took 236 milliseconds to draw. Note that "retrograde"

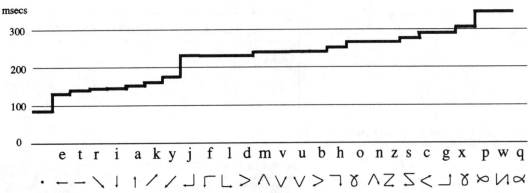

Figure 2 Median time in milliseconds spent drawing each unistroke

strokes such as 'e'(←) which are written from right-to-left do not appear to be significantly slower to write than their more usual left-to-right counterparts. In fact 'e'(←) is faster than 't'(→) and 'm'(∧) is faster than 'n'(∧). On the other hand, strokes written from bottom to top do seem to be somewhat slower (e.g. 'c' (<) and 'g'(⌐)). To get some idea of the variation in times, Table 1 gives the statistics for space and the first ten letters from Figure 2.

Writing time for different strokes varied by about a factor of two (from 150 msecs to 300 msecs). The variation in the time spent between strokes was much larger. This is not surprising. After about ten minutes, users pass from the stage of looking up unistrokes on a reference card to the stage where they are memorized. At this point, inter-stroke timings depend on the speed of cognitive recall. As users gain more experience, writing unistrokes begins to become a motor skill. The variations in inter-stroke timings reflect this mixture of cognitive and motor skills. From the pairs of unistrokes that occurred at least five times for the user in Table 1, Table 2 lists the median of the inter-stroke times of the six fastest pairs and six slowest pairs. The median over all pairs was 158 milliseconds.

char	median	average	std dev	n
space	91	91	22	244
e	135	143	44	117
t	143	146	22	95
r	149	152	28	84
i	150	152	28	84
a	155	162	36	70
k	162	165	15	9
y	180	191	50	24
j	236	230	26	4
f	237	248	32	26
l	237	245	36	51

Table 1: Data for first ten unistrokes in Figure 2

pair	time	n	pair	time	n
mi	66	7	an	237	6
fi	82	6	ec	237	5
db	87	6	so	320	8
be	94	8	on	371	5
ne	94	7	ha	378	5
st	94	8	ou	577	9

Table 2: Fastest and slowest median elapsed times between pairs of unistrokes

One surprising thing in Table 2 is that the fastest times do not belong to pairs with the smallest travel time from pen-up to pen-down. It might be expected that combinations like 'te'(→ ←), which consist of one stroke ending at the same point as the next stroke begins (assuming heads-up writing), would have the shortest inter-stroke times. There were in fact 9 'te' pairs, with a median time of 151, very near the median of all letters. On the other hand, 'mi', the fastest pair, consists of an unmatched pair, with 'm'(∧) ending low, and 'i'(↓) starting high. This suggests that very little would be gained by changing the design so that the unistroke pairs of the most frequent digraphs (such as 'th', 'in', 'er') have little travel time.

Analysis of Timings

The primary purpose of collecting timings was to discover whether a different unistroke design would enable faster input speeds. Using the durations from Table 1, an inter-stroke time of 158 milliseconds, and letter frequencies obtained from outgoing mail logs, the average writing rate is 2.8 letters/second (throughout this section we ignore errors, and consider peak error-free writing speeds). If the same unistroke symbols were used, but the most frequent letter were mapped to the unistroke fastest to draw, and so on, the time would change to 3.0 letters/second. This is a gain of less than 10% in speed. Since this reorganization would make unistrokes harder to learn, and since speed gains much greater than 10% can almost certainly be achieved using techniques from shorthand (as in [13]), assigning unistrokes

pair	it	il	en	at	in
1 day	689	1102	419	369	524
1 week	157	221	237	299	303

Table 3: Median inter-stroke timings in msecs after one day, one week

entirely based on writing times does not appear to be a good design.

Shorthand textbooks suggest that the controlling factor in writing speed is not the time to write a stroke, but rather the pauses between strokes [5]. This is consistent with our data. For one of the writers measured, writing speed was 0.5 letters/sec the first day, and 1.0 letters/sec after a week. The first day, the average (weighted by frequency) time to write a unistroke was 344 msecs. After after one week, the average was 270 msecs, a modest gain. The median between-stroke pauses went from 1606 msecs to 654 msecs. Presumably certain pairs were being committed to motor memory. The fastest pairs after one week with at least three samples are given in Table 3, together with their timings after one day. From this table, it seems plausible that with further practice the median inter-stroke timing would drop to 300 msecs. Assuming the time to write strokes would remain the same, writing speed would approach 1.8 letters/sec.

A similar analysis for the user of Tables 1 and 2, who was writing at a rate of 2.8 letters/second, suggests that with further use the inter-stroke timing will drop to 100 msecs, giving a writing speed of 3.4 letters/sec. Not surprisingly, there is quite a variation in writing speeds from user to user. For comparison, the peak typing speeds of these two writers were 4.8 and 7.0 letters/sec, suggesting that writing speeds may be correlated with typing speeds.

As mentioned above, we used timings collected from everyday use of the mail program rather than perform artificial timing experiments. However, we did measure the user from Tables 1 and 2 repeatedly writing the sentence "touch typing with a stylus." The results agreed fairly well with the predictions above: the median inter-stroke time was 104 msecs, the writing rate was 3.2 letters/sec. For comparision, Van Cott and Kinkade [16] give values of 1.0–1.3 letters/sec for ordinary printing. However, this comparison needs to be viewed very cautiously because it doesn't control for different users, error rates, and so on.

Sloppiness space
In order to test how well unistrokes were separated in sloppiness space, each user wrote several dictated sentences, using a variant of the mail program. The sentence to be written was displayed, and no echoing was done until the complete sentence was written.

The dictation test turned up three recognition problems. The first has to do with dot detection. Although the difficulty of detecting dots has been recognized as a problem before [14],

dots are used much more extensively in heads-up writing than in previous systems, since space is more common than any single character.

Dot detection is highly pen specific. For example, the program illustrated here also runs on the liveboard [3] which uses a different stylus technology from scratchpads, and requires a different dot detector. Even for a fixed stylus, we were unable to find a dot detector that worked universally well for all writers, although it was easy to find one that worked well for a given writer. Thus the first recognition problem had to be solved by introducing a writer-settable parameter for dot detection.

The second problem concerned pairs of unistrokes such as 'l' and 'i'

Some users would write strokes like the one on the right: half-way between an 'i' and 'l'. However, in practice these ambiguous symbols were always intended to be an 'l', so this second problem was solved by adjusting the recognition algorithm.

The third problem concerned pairs like 'h' and 'n'.

Some users wrote the stroke on the right, which is half way between 'h' and 'n'. One possible solution would be to change the unistroke for 'n' to be much sharper, like this:

and to interpret the ambiguous character above an 'h'. Further testing is required to validate this solution, and to check that this does not introduce new ambiguities. For example, if a stroke is drawn so narrowly that the two legs coincide, it will no longer be possible to distinguish between 'm'($\wedge$) and 'n'($\wedge$).

THE USER INTERFACE OF TEXT ENTRY
An earlier paper [4] argued that the user interface surrounding a text recognizer is at least as important as the recognizer itself. Unistrokes enable a different style of interface from current pen-based interfaces such as PenPoint.

In PenPoint, the default behavior for text entry uses a four step process. First a writing pad is created. There are two kinds of pads, popup and embedded. A popup pad has a single row of boxes, an embedded pad has several rows and takes up a substantial fraction of the screen. Then, text is entered by writing into boxes. After text entry, the next phase is entered by tapping on the 'OK' button, which causes a first attempt at recognition. During this phase, writing is interpreted immediately. The intention is that users will write corrections on top of misrecognized letters, although new text can also be entered. Finally, tapping on 'OK' a second time finishes the process, by dismissing the pad and causing the newly written text to be inserted into the document. In contrast, the user interface of the mail entry program has no modes. A small writing pad about the size of a single PenPoint letter box is always present, and at any time, text can be written on it, causing text to be inserted at the location of the caret.

Although the modeless interface of the mail sending program could be used with a conventional text recognition system such as that used in PenPoint, it is not a good match for the following reasons. First, keeping a pad permanently visible is only practical if it is small, and this implies heads-up writing, which works best with a unistroke alphabet. Second, because of the ambiguity of ordinary printing, a conventional text recognizer can do a better job if it sees a whole block of text before attempting to recognize, rather than recognizing on the fly. Third, when an error is made, a correction has to be written. With a boxed writing pad, the correction can be easily made right on top of the error. Things are not so simple in a modeless system, because the characters in the document are much more closely spaced than in the writing pad (by a factor of four in PenPoint). Once the incorrect letter has been inserted into the document, the close spacing of letters makes it difficult to write a new letter on top of the incorrectly recognized one. Thus a modeless system is not a good fit to a system when recognition errors are expected to be common.

The modeless interface of the mail program is quite similar to current keyboard interfaces, with the always visible writing pad playing the role of the always present keyboard. Heads-up writing with unistrokes is a much better match to this style of interface than ordinary printing. However, it is possible to provide a modeless interface to conventional recognizer. Casio sold a wristwatch and a palm sized "data bank" around 1984 that used a modeless heads-up writing interface. In these products, the user had to pause between each letter to enable the recognizer to group strokes into letters.

SUMMARY AND FUTURE WORK

It is our belief that the widespread use of styli would be greatly facilitated if there were an expert text entry system available, serving much the same function as touch-typing does for keyboards. This paper has explored basing such a system on a special alphabet.

A goal of our system was ease of use, so we chose an alphabet that is one-to-one with the ordinary Roman alphabet and is orthographic, that is, words are spelled in their usual fashion rather than phonetically. We call the symbols of our alphabet unistrokes, because each is a single stroke. Unistrokes are designed to be written unambiguously at high speed, and to exploit features present in a stylus but not in

an ordinary pen, such as stroke direction and existence of a button to use as a caps shift-key. Although unistrokes can be written one next to another as in ordinary printing, to get the maximum advantage they should be touch-printed, that is, written one on top of another.

Early experience with our system has suggested that the unistroke design is within 10% of the maximum achievable in terms of speed, but can be improved in terms of accuracy. In our next version, we intend to modify the family of unistrokes including 'm'(∧) and 'n'(∧) to be better separated in sloppiness space.

All the users of the system reported that they assumed it would be hard to learn a new alphabet, but instead found that it was quite easy, because most unistroke symbols are the same as or very similar to their Roman letter counterparts. This suggests that it might be better to present unistrokes to users as a constrained version of the Roman alphabet, rather than as a new alphabet.

Future work can be divided into three areas. First, the current system needs to be refined and then tested head-to-head against the best commercial hand-print recognizer. One area for refinement is the separation of unistrokes in sloppiness space: the current design is quite *ad hoc* in this regard. It would be nice to bring knowledge about motor aspects of handwriting [7], [12], [15] to bear on this problem. Another area that needs to be refined is the method for entering punctuation and digits. In the mail sending program, punctuation is entered by pressing buttons surrounding the entry pad. Since period and comma are more frequent than letters such as 'q' and 'z', these two punctuation marks (at least) should be assigned unistrokes. There are at least four ways that digits could be entered: via buttons surrounding the entry pad, via buttons on a popup pad that appears in response to a special unistroke, using ten unistrokes from the basic set of 40 shapes, or by going into a special mode and using strokes resembling Arabic numerals. A special mode would be required in this last option to avoid ambiguity between (for example) '1' and '2' with the unistrokes for 'i'(↓) and 'z'(↗).

A second area of future work is to explore other methods for stylus text entry. We have focused on printed characters. However, it may be possible to design a cursive alphabet that is easy to recognize. There are also approaches that don't use special alphabets at all. For example, the redundancy of English might be exploited as in the reactive keyboard [2].

Finally, there is the problem of developing a system that has the speed of touch typing with a keyboard. It is worth noting however, that products for speeding up typewritten input have not been commercially successful [9], so the importance of very high speed input may be overrated. We have estimated that unistrokes may be able to support a rate of as high as 3.4 characters/sec, whereas touch typists can achieve rates of 6-7 characters/sec. One way to close the gap would be to borrow ideas from shorthand. Given that shorthand systems using the Roman alphabet such as Speedwriting often perform better in practice than traditional Gregg and Pitman shorthand [18], the most promising avenue for further speedups may be to combine Speedwriting with the unistroke alphabet.

ACKNOWLEDGEMENTS

We owe a special thanks to Mark Stefik, who made the observation that writing letters on top of one another makes sense with a stylus, and to William Newman, who was an early advocate of unistrokes and not only had the idea of using a mail sending program for testing, but also wrote the first version of a mail sender. We also thank Tom Moran for his helpful comments on a draft of this paper, and Bill Buxton for informing us about the Casio data bank.

REFERENCES

1] Robert Carr and Dan Shafer. *The Power of PenPoint*, Addison-Wesley, 1991.

2] John J. Darragh, Ian H. Witten, and Mark L. James, "The reactive keyboard: A predictive typing aid" *IEEE Computer*, 41-49, Nov 1990.

3] Scott Elrod, Richard Bruce, Rich Gold, David Goldberg, *et, al.* "LiveBoard: A large interactive display supporting group meetings, presentations and remote collaborations," *Proceedings of the Conference on Computer Human Interaction (CHI)*, 599-607, May 1992.

4] David Goldberg and Aaron Goodisman. "Stylus user interfaces for manipulating text." *Proceedings of the Fourth Annual ACM Symposium on User Interface Software and Technology (UIST)* 127-135, Nov, 1991.

5] John R. Gregg, Louis A Leslie, and Charles E Zoubek, "Gregg Shorthand Dictionary", McGraw-Hill, 1972.

6] Khaled Kamel and Ibrahim Iman, "A computerized transcription system for cursive shorthand writing", *Proceedings of IEEE SouthEastcon*, Knoxville, Tennessee, 336-339, April 1988.

7] H. S. R. Kao, G. P. van Galen, R. Hoosain (eds) *Graphonomics, Contemporary Research in Handwriting*, North Holland, 1986.

8] C. G. Leedham and A. C. Downton, "On-line recognition of Pitman's handwritten shorthand—an evaluation of potential," *International Journal of Man-Machine Studies*, 375-393, 1986.

9] Bill Machrone, *PC Magazine*, pp 67-68, January 16, 1990.

10] Walter S. Mossberg, "Notepad PCs Struggle With One Small Task: Deciphering Writing.", *Wall Street Journal*, Thursday July 23, 1992.

11] Greg Nelson (ed.), *Systems Programming with Modula-3*, Prentice-Hall, 1991.

12] R. Plamonden, C. Y. Suen, and M. Simner (eds) *Computer Recognition and Human Production of Handwriting*, Word Scientific, 1988.

13] Joe M. Pullis, *Speedwriting for Notetaking & Study Skills*, Macmillan, 1990.

14] C. C. Tappert, "Speed, accuracy, flexibility trade-offs in on-line character recognition,", IBM Research Report RC13228, October 1987.

15] A. J. W. M. P. Thomassen, P. J. G. Keuss, F. P. van Galen (eds), "Motor aspects of handwriting.", *Acta Psycologica* 54 (1-3), 1983.

16] Harold P. Van Cott and Robert G Kinkade (eds), *Human Engineering Guide to Equipment Design*, U. S. Government Printing Office, 1972.

17] Mark Weiser. "The Computer for the 21st Century," *Scientific American*, 94-104, Sep 1991.

18] Patricia D. Whitman, "An Evaluation of four shorthand systems after one year of instruction", Ed.D dissertation, University of Southern California, 1984.

Half-QWERTY: A One-handed Keyboard Facilitating Skill Transfer From QWERTY

Edgar Matias[†], I. Scott MacKenzie[§], William Buxton[‡]

[†]The Matias Corporation
178 Thistledown Boulevard
Rexdale, Ontario, Canada M9V 1K1
(416) 749-3124 ematias@dgp.toronto.edu

[§]Dept. of Computing and Information Science
University of Guelph
Guelph, Ontario, Canada N1G 2W1
(519) 824-4120 mac@snowhite.cis.uoguelph.ca

[‡]University of Toronto & Xerox PARC
c/o Computer Systems Research Institute
University of Toronto
Toronto, Ontario, Canada M5S 1A4
(416) 978-1961 buxton@dgp.toronto.edu

ABSTRACT

Half-QWERTY is a new one-handed typing technique, designed to facilitate the transfer of two-handed typing skill to the one-handed condition. It is performed on a standard keyboard, or a special half keyboard (with full-sized keys). In an experiment using touch typists, hunt-and-peck typing speeds were surpassed after 3-4 hours of practice. Subjects reached 50% of their two-handed typing speed after about 8 hours. After 10 hours, all subjects typed between 41% and 73% of their two-handed speed, ranging from 23.8 to 42.8 wpm. These results are important in providing access to disabled users, and for the design of compact computers. They also bring into question previous research claiming finger actions of one hand map to the other via spatial congruence rather than mirror image.

KEYWORDS: Input devices, input tasks, human performance, one-handed keyboard, QWERTY, portable computers, disabled users, skill transfer.

INTRODUCTION

The idea of a one-handed keyboard is not new. As early as 1968, Engelbart and English [2] used a one-handed chord keyboard in conjunction with a newly developed input device — the mouse. The user entered text with one hand, while using the mouse to enter spatial information with the other. However, unlike the mouse, acceptance of one-handed keyboards has been limited to very specific

applications, such as keyboards for the disabled. There are several reasons for this, but chief among them is the need to learn a new typing technique. For most people, the benefit of touch typing with one hand is not worth the cost of learning to do it.

This paper describes a new approach to one-handed text entry which exploits the skills already developed in two-handed typing. It is called, "Half-QWERTY," because it uses only half of the QWERTY keyboard. The technique can be used on an unmodified standard QWERTY keyboard (using only half of the available keys, Figure 1), or with a special half keyboard (Figures 2 & 3). The former provides wide access to the technique. The latter provides a compact keyboard with full-sized keys supporting touch typing on portable computers, for example.

The present study examines the degree to which skill transfers from QWERTY to Half-QWERTY keyboards.

THE HALF-QWERTY CONCEPT[1]

Most one-handed keyboards are chord keyboards. Half-QWERTY is not. The design builds on two principles:

1. A user's ability to touch type on a standard QWERTY keyboard.
2. The fact that the human hands are symmetrical — one hand is a mirror image of the other.

A Half-QWERTY keyboard is comprised of all the keys typed by one hand, with the keys of the other hand unused

---

[1]Patents pending. International Application # PCT/CA90/00274 published March 21, 1991, under International Publication # WO91/03782.

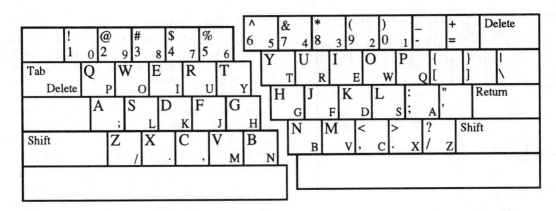

Figure 1. Left- and right-hand Half-QWERTY layouts on a standard QWERTY keyboard.

or absent. When the space bar is depressed, the missing characters are mapped onto the remaining keys in a mirror image (Figure 1), such that the typing hand makes movements homologous to those previously performed by the other hand. Thus, using the space bar as a modifier, a typist can generate the characters of either side of a full-sized keyboard using only one hand.

Depressing and releasing the space bar within a timeout generates a space character. The timeout reduces the number of erroneous spaces generated as a side-effect of using the space bar as a modifier key. It is often the case that a typist will depress the space bar with the intention of

mirroring the state of another key but then change their mind and release. Without the timeout, such actions would result in an unwanted space character. For this experiment, the timeout was 16/60 seconds, or 267 ms.

Modifier keys (such as shift and control) are supported via a "latch" mechanism, commonly known as "Sticky Keys." Depressing and releasing a modifier key once activates it for the next key pressed. Depressing it twice locks that key until it is unlocked by depressing it again. Sticky Keys allows one finger to do the work of several, when performing key sequences that would otherwise require the simultaneous depression of two or more keys.

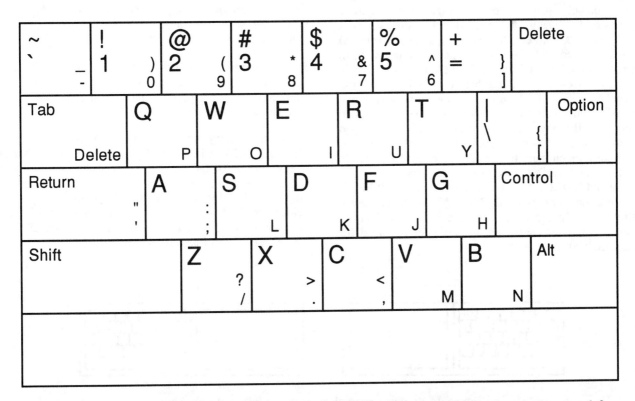

Figure 2. Left-hand portable keyboard (actual size). When a key is depressed, the character in the upper left of the key is entered. When preceded by holding down the space bar, the character in the lower right is entered.

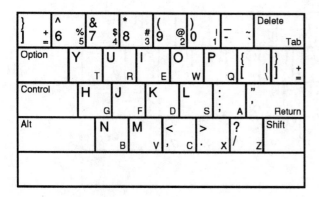

Figure 3. Right-hand portable keyboard. When a key is depressed, the character in the upper left of the key is entered. When preceded by holding down the space bar, the character in the lower right is entered.

Application and Implementation

The original objective of this design was to establish a keyboard for palmtop computers: one that was small yet permitted touch typists to use their existing skills. Prior efforts tended toward reducing the size and spacing of the keys of standard QWERTY [18]. Such attempts are problematic since they lead to keyboards that are too small to accommodate two hands. We have side-stepped this by requiring only one hand for typing. However, the idea is versatile, and has more applications.

Using a Half-QWERTY keyboard in one hand, and a pointing device, such as a mouse, in the other recaptures the two-handed flavour of Engelbart and English's system [2]. Text can be entered with one hand, and items selected and manipulated with the other. Since both hands are in "home position" for their respective task, no time is lost in moving between devices. Furthermore, by implementing the Half-QWERTY keyboard on a standard keyboard, one can easily switch between this type of input and two-handed typing. Finally, since each side of the keyboard is mapped onto the other side when the space bar is depressed, the user can choose which hand to use for one-handed typing. In effect, the user has a choice of three keyboards in one: a two-handed QWERTY keyboard, and two Half-QWERTY keyboards, one for each hand. All of this we have achieved entirely in software. This is especially beneficial to disabled computer users, since it obviates the need for specialized hardware.

Which Hand to Use?

Given the keyboard described above, we must now decide which hand is 'best' for one-handed typing. In general, we believe this is the non-dominant hand. This would free the more dexterous dominant hand to use a mouse (or other device) to enter spatial information. This arrangement would work especially well on a palmtop computer. For example, the computer could open horizontally, like a wallet (Figure 4), thus keeping the keyboard comfortably to the side (where the hand is) and the screen in the centre (where the eyes are). If equipped with a touch screen, concurrent entry of text and graphics is possible. Note also that the left-hand and right-hand versions of Half-QWERTY are physically identical (Figures 2 & 3), differing only in their key cap markings and the mappings. So, a left-hand typist can easily adapt a right-hand keyboard for left hand use, and vice versa.

Furthermore, two-handed typing can be performed using two of these half keyboards together. This has the added benefit of allowing the user to adjust each keypad independently to whichever position is most comfortable.

Wearable Computers

A computer that is worn, rather than carried, has significant advantages for data collection "in the field." By eliminating infrequently used keys (e.g., the number keys) and reducing the size of the space bar, a Half-QWERTY keyboard can be made small enough to wear on the wrist of the dominant hand. With an LCD screen worn on the other wrist, the resulting typing posture allows the user to type and view the screen, simultaneously. Note that this arrangement is consistent with the convention of wearing one's wrist watch on the non-dominant arm.

Such a computer would be extremely portable, allowing fast data entry without the need of a table or other supporting surface required by most computers today. Data could even be entered while standing or walking.

Hand Symmetry vs. Spatial Congruence

Half-QWERTY is based on the principle that the human brain controls typing movements according to the finger used, rather than the spatial position of the key. Thus, the finger used to hit a key is the critical invariant — the critical similarity that is maintained across the training and transfer tasks — in the transfer of skill from QWERTY to Half-QWERTY. Lintern [8] writes:

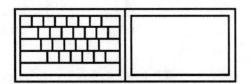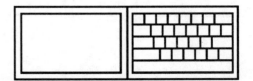

Figure 4. Various screen placements for left- and right-hand palmtop computers equipped with Half-QWERTY keyboards.

If critical invariants (specifically, those that pose a meaningful learning challenge) remain unchanged, [skill] transfer will be high even when many other features of the environment, context, or task are changed ... If an operator's perceptual sensitivity to critical invariants can be improved, that enhanced sensitivity will serve to facilitate transfer. (p. 262)

The mirror image encoding scheme (described above) follows from this. A rival encoding scheme is that of spatial congruence, which maintains that the spatial position of the key is the critical invariant. There is disagreement in the literature as to which of these schemes is 'better.' In the context of this experiment, we believe mirror image mapping is preferred.

Grudin [7], in his analysis of error patterns in transcription typing, found that homologous substitution errors are among the most common errors. These occur when the character corresponding to the mirror image position on the keyboard, is substituted for the one required. For example, substituting *D* for *K* (middle finger of either hand) is a homologous error. These findings, which were confirmed by Munhall and Ostry [10], suggest a predisposition among QWERTY typists to mirror image mapping.

During the evaluation of a one-handed chord keyboard, Rochester, Bequaert, and Sharp [17] trained one student using the right hand only. The subject was later retrained to type with the left hand only. The subject "reached close to his right-hand typing speed in less than one third the time he spent learning right-handed typing" (p. 62). Their left-hand keyboard was a mirror image of the right-hand version.

Gopher, Karis, and Koenig [5] trained subjects on a two-handed chord keyboard and then investigated whether the skill thus acquired transferred to the other hand by mirror image or spatial congruence. Their conclusions suggest that spatial congruence is the dominant mapping. They also tested a third condition, a combination of the two, using keyboards mounted vertically rather than horizontally. Hand-to-hand mapping was best in this condition.

This suggests that spatial congruence was stronger than mirror image mapping, which would seem to contradict what we have argued above. However, closer inspection reveals that the combined scheme was actually the equivalent of the mirror image keyboard, but with a vertical rather than flat posture (i.e., with the hands positioned as though playing a saxophone, as opposed to a piano).

Furthermore, despite the efforts of Gopher et al. [5] to keep error rates low, the errors that did slip through were primarily homologous errors made by subjects using the spatial congruence keyboard. This suggests a predisposition among chord keyboard typists to mirror image mapping.

In the following section, we describe an experiment intended to test the degree to which skill transfers from QWERTY to Half-QWERTY keyboards, among skilled touch typists.

METHOD

Subjects
Ten right-handed, computer literate, QWERTY typists from a local university served as paid volunteers. Subjects used their non-dominant (left) hand when typing with one hand. The Edinburgh Inventory [13] was used to determine handedness.

Equipment
Tasks were performed on Apple *Macintosh II* and *IIci* computers using a standard Apple keyboard. A cardboard shield was placed between the keyboard and the subjects' eyes in order to prevent them from looking at the keyboard.

Procedure
Each subject performed 10 sessions, with no more than one session per day. Each session contained a two-handed pretest, multiple blocks of one-handed typing, and a two-handed post-test. The first session included a few specially prepared one-handed blocks, designed to ease subjects into understanding the operation of the keyboard. All one-handed typing was performed with the left hand.

Measure	Hands	Session									
		1	2	3	4	5	6	7	8	9	10
Speed	1	13.2	18.3	21.1	24.4	27.1	29.0	30.7	31.6	33.6	34.7
(wpm)	2	58.5	59.8	62.3	61.6	63.7	63.3	64.0	64.6	66.2	64.9
Errors	1	15.96	12.13	9.93	9.70	9.21	8.98	7.55	8.23	7.54	7.44
(%)	2	3.25	3.40	2.45	3.05	3.40	3.55	3.55	3.55	3.30	4.20

Figure 5. Mean performance scores for speed and accuracy on one-handed and two-handed typing over 10 sessions.

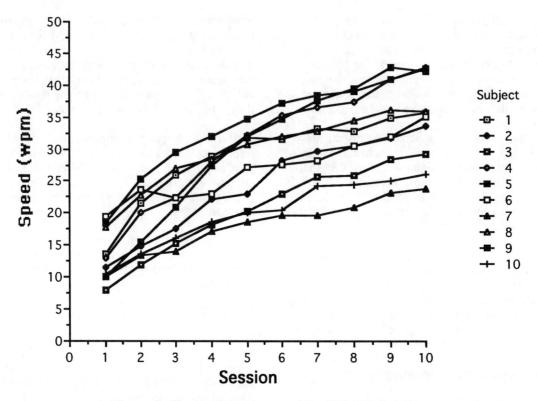

Figure 6. One-handed typing speed by subject and session.

The interface was similar to that of *Typing Tutor IV*[1] with the subject's typing displayed beneath the input text. The delete key was disabled so subjects could not correct errors. A beep was heard for every error made. Subjects were instructed to type as quickly and accurately as possible, while remaining in sync with the input text. They could rest as desired between blocks.

The text for all typing was taken from a novel about Japanese-American relations. It contained only upper and lower case letters, and simple punctuation (comma and period).

Design

This experiment is an investigation of the learning potential of the Half-QWERTY keyboard. Each 50 minute session consisted of a series a text blocks typed by the subject. The block length was set to 60 characters by 4 lines in the first session (using Courier 14 point type), and was increased to 6 lines when subjects managed to type 30 one-handed blocks in one session. Subjects completed as many blocks as were possible in a session, ranging from 7 to 35 blocks, depending on speed and the amount of rest.

The dependent measures were typing speed and error rate. Typing speeds are given in words per minute (wpm), with a word defined as 5 characters (4 letters plus a space). Error

rates are given as a percentage of total keystrokes (the lower the better). Subjects had to type the correct character in the correct position. Thus, they had to type in sync with the text on the screen. If they fell out of sync, it was considered an error (as consistent with *Typing Tutor IV*).

Complete keystroke level data were also collected which allowed for a detailed examination of interkey timings across states (space-up, space-down) and fingers, and of error patterns across letters and state sequences. Due to space limitations, these analyses are not provided in the present paper.

RESULTS

Subjects were able to adapt to Half-QWERTY typing very quickly. As shown in Figure 5, session 1 resulted in an average speed of 13.2 wpm, with over 84% accuracy. This performance is impressive, especially considering how little training was given. For instance, subjects were not required to memorize the layout before starting the one-handed typing task, and therefore had to rely entirely on skill transfer from two-handed typing.

One-handed speed improved significantly over the ten sessions ($F_{9,81} = 80.7$, $p < .0001$) to reach a tenth session average of 34.7 wpm. Improvement in one-handed error rate was also statistically significant ($F_{9,81} = 14.6$, $p < .0001$) dropping to an average of 7.44% errors in the tenth session. This is approximately double the rate of errors made in two-handed typing.

[1]Kriya Systems, Inc. Published by Simon & Schuster Software, Gulf+Western Building, One Gulf+Western Plaza, New York, NY 10023, USA.

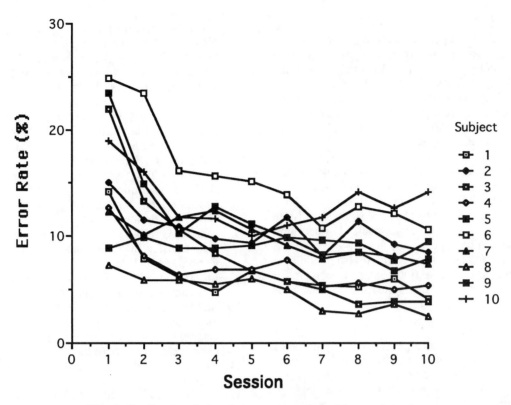

Figure 7. One-handed typing error rates by subject and session.

As Figures 6 and 7 show, one-handed performances varied a great deal among subjects. For example, subject 6 averaged 19.5 wpm in session 1. Subject 7 did not reach a comparable speed until session 6. Many factors likely contribute to this disparity among subject performances: two-handed speed and accuracy, regularity of practice, etc.

Note that none of the subjects had peaked by session 10, even though three of them were typing in the low 40 wpm range. Subjects 5, 8, and 9 have agreed to undergo further long-term testing to determine what possible peak speeds can be achieved. These tests, which are on-going, indicate a potential for touch typists to achieve 88% (or more) of their two-handed speed.

Also worthy of note is that two-handed typing speeds improved significantly over the ten sessions ($F_{9,81} = 4.43$, $p < .0001$). This is likely due to subjects getting accustomed to the software and the feel of the keyboard. One-handed typing may also have had an effect. There was no significant reduction in two-handed error rates over the ten sessions ($F_{9,81} = 1.12$, $p > .05$).

DISCUSSION
On average, subjects were able to exceed hunt-and-peck typing speeds after about 3-4 hours. Wiklund et al. [18] determined the average speed for one-handed hunt-and-peck typing on a standard keyboard to be approximately 23 wpm. Performances on the different compact keyboards tested were considerably worse. They ranged from 15-21 wpm, depending on key type, size, and spacing. Our subjects

were typing in this range in less than two hours of practice, and exceeded 50% of their two-handed speed after about 8-9 hours of use. This is comparable to Wiklund et al.'s [18] measure of average handwriting speed (33 wpm). By the tenth session, subjects were typing between 41% and 73% of their two-handed speed. These speeds ranged from 23.8 to 42.8 wpm. This is strong evidence that skill transfers hand-to-hand by mirror image and not spatial congruence.

It is instructive to compare these results to the learning curves of chord keyboards. Gopher and Raij [6] tested subjects' rate of skill acquisition on both one-handed and two-handed chord keyboards, as well as standard QWERTY. After 10 hours, the one-handed group was typing at approximately 21 wpm and the two-handed group at 22 wpm. This compares to the Half-QWERTY subjects' tenth session average of 34.7 wpm. Gopher et al.'s [6] one-handed and two-handed subjects did not reach comparable rates until the sessions 29 and 26, respectively. Therefore, from an economic standpoint, it is more cost effective for a QWERTY typist to adopt the Half-QWERTY technique than to learn to type on a one-handed chord keyboard.

Gopher et al. [6] also found that until about session 25, two-handed performance was only slightly better than one-handed performance on their chord keyboard. This begs an interesting question: What percentage of two-handed speed can be achieved with one hand? This, of course, is not yet known, but we feel it may be as high as 88%. The answer is likely different for chord and Half-QWERTY keyboards. More study is required.

CONCLUSIONS

We have shown that it is possible for QWERTY typists to achieve high one-handed typing rates (40+ wpm) in a relatively short period of time (< 10 hr) using the Half-QWERTY technique. These speeds are 2-3 times the rates achievable using compact keyboards, and exceed handwriting speeds. These high learning rates are due to the transfer of two-handed skill via Half-QWERTY's mirror image hand-to-hand mapping scheme.

These results lead to new possibilities for human-computer interfaces. By exploiting standard two-handed typing skill and the Half-QWERTY concept described above, we have demonstrated the potential to build a keyboard with full-size keys, but no larger than a paperback book. Furthermore, since the design can be implemented in software, wide and convenient access to one-handed typing is also possible on a standard keyboard. These findings are important for designers of compact computing systems and systems for disabled users.

ACKNOWLEDGEMENTS

We would like to acknowledge the contributions of Jonathan Cheng who wrote the software and the Input Research Group at the University of Toronto who provided the forum for the design and execution of this project. In addition, we gratefully acknowledge the support of the Natural Sciences and Engineering Research Council of Canada, Digital Equipment Corporation, Xerox Palo Alto Research Centre (PARC), Apple Computer's Human Interface Group, IBM Canada's Toronto Laboratory Centre for Advanced Studies, and the Arnott Design Group of Toronto.

REFERENCES

1. Buxton, W. (1990). Chord keyboards. *The pragmatics of haptic input, Tutorial 26 Notes of CHI'90*, 6.1-6.9.
2. Engelbart, D., & English, W. K. (1968). A research center for augmenting human intellect. *Proceedings of the Fall Joint Computer Conference* (pp. 395-410). Washington, DC: Thompson Book Co.
3. Gentner, D. R., Grudin, J. T., Larochelle, S., Norman, D. A., & Rumelhart, D. E. (1983). A glossary of terms including classification of typing errors. In W. E. Cooper (Ed.), *Cognitive aspects of skilled typewriting* (pp. 39-43). New York: Springer-Verlag.
4. Gentner, D. R. (1983). Keystroke timing in transcription typing. In W. E. Cooper (Ed.), *Cognitive aspects of skilled typewriting* (pp. 95-120). New York: Springer-Verlag.
5. Gopher, D., Karis, D., & Koenig, W. (1985). The representation of movement schemas in long-term memory: Lessons from the acquisition of a transcription skill. *Acta Psychologica, 60*, 105-134.
6. Gopher, D., & Raij, D. (1988). Typing with a two-handed chord keyboard: Will the QWERTY become obsolete? *IEEE Transactions on Systems, Man, and Cybernetics, 18*, 601-609.
7. Grudin, J. T. (1983). Error patterns in novice and skilled transcription typing. In W. E. Cooper (Ed.), *Cognitive aspects of skilled typewriting* (pp. 121-143). New York: Springer-Verlag.
8. Lintern, G. (1991). An informational perspective on skill transfer in human-machine systems. *Human Factors, 33*, 251-266.
9. Litterick, I. (1981, January 8). QWERTYUIOP — dinosaur in a computer age. *New Scientist*, pp. 66-68.
10. Munhall, K. G., & Ostry, D. J. (1983). Mirror-image movements in typing. In W. E. Cooper (Ed.), *Cognitive aspects of skilled typewriting* (pp. 247-257). New York: Springer-Verlag.
11. Noyes, J. (1983). Chord keyboards. *Applied Ergonomics, 14*, 55-59.
12. Noyes, J. (1983). The QWERTY keyboard: A review. *International Journal of Man-Machine Studies, 18*, 265-281.
13. Olfield, R. C. (1971). The assessment and analysis of handedness: The Edinburgh inventory. *Neuropsychologica, 9*, 97-113.
14. Ostry, D. J. (1983). Determinants of interkey times in typing. In W. E. Cooper (Ed.), *Cognitive aspects of skilled typewriting* (pp. 225-246). New York: Springer-Verlag.
15. Potosnak, K. M. (1988). Keys and keyboards. In M. Helander (Ed.), *Handbook of human-computer interaction* (pp. 475-494). Amsterdam: Elsevier.
16. Provins, K. A., & Glencross, D. J. (1968). Handwriting, typewriting and handedness. *Quarterly Journal of Experimental Psychology, 20*, 282-320.
17. Rochester, N., Bequaert, F. C., Sharp, E. M. (1978, December). The chord keyboard. *Computer*, 57-63.
18. Wiklund, M. E., Dumas, J. S., & Hoffman, L. R. (1987). Optimizing a portable terminal keyboard for combined one-handed and two-handed use. *Proceedings of the Human Factors Society — 31st Annual Meeting — 1987* (pp. 585-589). Santa Monica, CA: Human Factors Society.

Incremental Recognition in Gesture-Based and Syntax-Directed Diagram Editors

Rui Zhao

Cadlab, Cooperation University of Paderborn and
Siemens Nixdorf Informationssysteme AG
Bahnhofstr. 32, D-W-4790 Paderborn, Germany

Email: zhao@cadlab.cadlab.de

ABSTRACT

Diagram editing is an attractive application of gestural interfaces and pen-based computers which promise a new input paradigm where users communicate with computers in diagram languages by using gestures. A key problem in building gesture-based diagram editors is the recognition of handsketched diagrams. Existing approaches concentrate either on gesture recognition or on parsing visual languages, there has been a lack of integrated recognition concepts. This paper presents novel concepts and techniques based on an incremental paradigm of gesture recognition and a cooperative communication between modules for pattern recognition and for diagram parsing. These concepts and techniques have been used successfully to build several experimental gesture-based and syntax-directed diagram editors.

KEYWORDS: gestural interfaces, pen-based computers, diagram languages, incremental recognition, diagram editors

INTRODUCTION

In computer-aided design, software engineering, and many other areas, there is growing interest in visual programming. Visual languages used in these domains are mainly graphical diagrams such as Petri nets, Statecharts, Pictorial Janus, flowcharts, various types of block diagram, and many others. For supporting these diagram languages, various diagram editors have been developed. The user interfaces of these diagram editors are mainly menu and command selection based graphical user interfaces improved by direct manipulation techniques such as rubberbanding or dragging. Though the diagram output is greatly supported by many advanced computer graphics techniques, the input of diagrams is a cumbersome process with many complex modes.

The recent advances in pen-based computer technology promise that the pen-based user interface will emerge as a real alternative to the keyboard and mouse based one. Diagram editing is an attractive application of gestural interfaces and pen-based computers which allow the user to communicate with computers in diagram languages by using handsketches so that the user can draw diagrams in the same way as with paper and pen.

While gesture-based diagram editors offer significant benefits, building such editors is difficult. The key component is a gesture recognizer which allows the user to sketch diagrams with relatively few restrictions. From the user's view, a gesture-based diagram editor should be modeless and intelligent to give the user a feeling that the editor understands the diagram language. There are clearly two problems involved in such a gesture recognizer: on-line pattern recognition and diagram language parsing, and most important the two must work together in a diagram editor.

Recently, research in this domain concentrates either on pattern recognition or on parsing visual languages. There have been relatively few concepts for an integrated solution.

Kim [6] presented a gesture recognizer based on feature analysis which has been improved and redesigned by Lipscomb [8] who combines techniques of angle filtering and multi-scale recognition. Dean Rubine [12] presented a trainable statistical gesture recognizer for single-stroke gestures. Moreover, he combines gesture recognition with direct manipulation techniques to support the so-called eager recognition.

In the domain of visual languages, most of the existing approaches of parsing visual languages are grammar-based and batch-oriented. Examples are the constrained set grammars [4], the unification-based grammars [13], and the picture layout grammars [2]. A grammar-based visual language parser is designed to be generated from a grammar definition. Its user interface is similar to conventional program compiler. The input is a picture in certain format such as a picture description [2], PostScript [5], or Bitmap [13]. The output of the parser consists of a statement about the syntactical correctness of the input picture and an attributed parse structure.

In this paper, we present new concepts and techniques of incremental gesture recognition which integrates on-line handsketch recognition and diagram parsing in general graphical editors. We found that there are more relationships

© 1993 ACM 0-89791-575-5/93/0004/0095...$1.50

between these two components than simply a pipe connection in which the diagram parser takes the recognition result of the handsketch recognizer as input, such as stated in [4]. The diagram syntax can improve the performance of the handsketch recognizer similar to that of approaches which use context as an aid in character recognition [10].

Our idea is to design an integrated gesture recognizer with two cooperative components, one for recognizing hand-sketched graphical symbols, and the other for interpreting these graphical symbols as gesture commands for creating and manipulating the underlying diagram. Moreover, the handsketch recognizer is designed to be incremental as well to allow the user sketching multiple-stroke gestures stroke by stroke.

The rest of this paper describes the concepts and techniques of our incremental recognition, presents briefly a gesture-based statecharts editor based on these concepts, and discusses the performance and usability achieved by experiences with the statecharts editor and other diagram editors.

INCREMENTAL RECOGNITION

The input medium of a gesture-based diagram editor is sequence of point coordinates captured by the input devices. We call a recognizer which transforms such point coordinates into graphical symbols, a *low-level recognizer* (LLR). The LLR determines the class and the attributes of the graphical symbol drawn by the user. Further, a gesture-based diagram editor needs a *high-level recognizer* (HLR) to transform these basic symbols into editing commands which are interpreted by a diagram editor in turn to create the internal diagram structure. Figure 1 shows the design of our gesture recognizing system in a LLR and a HLR.

The essential idea of incremental gesture recognition is to allow the high-level recognizer to incrementally transform the graphical symbols recognized by the LLR into editing commands for creating and manipulating the underlying diagram. This differs from existing approaches in the following two aspects:

1. Existing visual language parsers consider usually a complete picture as input, our HLR treats each graphical symbol the user has just drawn incrementally.

2. In contrast to other incremental visual language parsers (e.g. [13]) which create directly the internal diagram representation, the output of our HLR are editing commands which are *compatible* with conventional diagram editors. This has the advantage that the gesture recognizer can be integrated into existing diagram editors which allow the user not only to draw new diagrams, but also modify existing diagrams with gestures.

Communications

As mentioned before, existing approaches merely identified a global data flow from LLR to HLR, and therefore treated gesture recognition and diagram parsing as two separate and

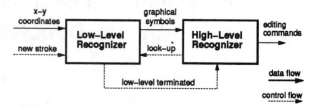

Figure 1: Relationships between the low-level and high-level recognition

independent problems. The key issue of our concept is to consider LLR and HLR as two cooperative and tightly integrated components of the recognizing system of a gesture-based diagram editor. The cooperative communication between these recognition subcomponents support our incremental gesture recognition, in which the user can sketch the desired diagram stroke by stroke, and the user immediately sees what happens after each stroke is drawn.

In order to achieve this incremental gestural dialog without any explicit command from the user such as "draw something, and click a button for parsing", control signals within the recognizing system must be considered. We identified several important control signals related to the communication besides the obvious data flow from LLR to HLR. As illustrated by dotted arrow-lines in figure 1, each pen-down event at the beginning of a new stroke produces automatically a "new stroke" signal which can be used to trigger the low-level recognition. The termination event of the LLR can be used to activate the HLR to parse the graphical symbols just drawn.

Symbol Database An important technique related to the communication between the two components is the issue of how to use the diagram syntax to control *when* the graphical symbols should be transferred from the LLR to the HLR. This is supported by a common accessible database for graphical symbols. This database acts as a buffer between the HLR and the LLR, which is crucially important for incrementally recognizing multiple-stroke gestures. Recognizing multiple-stroke gestures has to cater for the so-called *closure* problem [11], that is, to determine the end of a gestural dialogue phrase. The diagram syntax can be used to recognize the closure signals automatically. Simply speaking, the graphical symbols recognized by the LLR are buffered in the database until a valid symbol is drawn. In case such a symbol is found, and all syntactical constraints are fulfilled, this symbol will be transformed into an editing command by the HLR. After that, all graphical symbols stored in the database will be deleted to begin a new sketching phrase.

Low-Level Recognition

In addition to the global incremental recognition strategy related to the communication between the LLR and the HLR, the LLR is designed to be incremental as well. The goal is to recognize graphical symbols which are sketched with an arbitrary number of strokes without any additional action from the user such as explicit pauses between drawing two symbols. Figure 2 illustrates several examples of multiple-stroke gestures. The essential techniques for achieving this

Figure 2: Handsketched graphical symbols have usually an arbitrary number of strokes

goal can be summaried in the following two points:

1. Each stroke is recognized immediately after it has been drawn, and its ink is replaced by the recognized graphical symbol. The user sees directly how the ink is changed into a regular symbol.

2. The LLR stores each just recognized stroke in the aforementioned database, and merges every two connected symbols incrementally. The merged symbols are displayed and the original symbols are removed from the database.

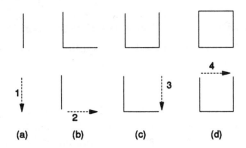

Figure 3: Incremental recognition of a multiple-stroke rectangle

The single-stroke recognition is based on hierarchical feature-analysis which is described in [14]. In this paper, we concentrated on the incremental aspects which can be shown best by an example. Figure 3 illustrates the merging effect by depicting the intermediate steps in a drawing example of a 4-stroke rectangle. In the bottom area of this figure, inkings are drawn by using dotted arrow-lines, and the already recognized single-strokes are drawn with solid lines without arrows. In the top area of the figure, the current recognition results are illustrated, these symbols are stored in the database. From (a) to (b) the two single strokes 1 and 2 are merged together to a "L"-form (top area of (b)). In the same style, this "L"-form is merged with the third stroke into a "U"-form. As a result, the user sees immediately the effect of how the stroke just drawn is composited with other strokes into a new symbol. He can then draw other necessary strokes incrementally to complete each handsketched geometrical figure.

High-Level Recognition

In contrast to the low-level recognition, the high-level recognition is syntax-directed and diagram-editor-dedicated. A significant feature of our gesture recognition concept is that the HLR generates editing commands which can be interpreted by the diagram editor in the same way as other non-gesture commands. The HLR does not manipulate the internal diagram structure directly. Therefore, the functionality of our HLR differs from a conventional visual language parser.

The key issue of the high-level recognition is how to specify the underlying diagram syntax. Our idea is similar to Arefi's approach [1] which provides a mechanism to unify the specification of the language and its manipulations. We consider a visual language as an initial object and a collection of gesture editing operations. Any object that can be obtained by applying a sequence of allowed editing operations is then defined to be in the language. A visual program is therefore a dynamic object which can be changed from one form to another by applying different editing operations. The syntactical correctness of the edited diagram is guaranteed by the correctness of each editing operation which has to be guaranteed by the editor developer.

Specification Mechanism

We specify the underlying diagram by defining a set of gesture objects, each one corresponding to an editing operation. As a matter of fact, we designed an object-oriented mechanism for specifying such gesture objects in a form of classes which understand basic recognition protocols. With this mechanism, each gesture class specifies the following three members: gesture shape, gesture constraints, and gesture semantics.

A gesture shape can be chosen from the set of graphical symbols which can be recognized by the LLR. A gesture shape builds the front-end of the high-level recognizer. Its meaning is similar to type information in a textual programming language, which is not enough to guarantee the syntactical correctness of a gesture command. Several different gestures may define the same graphical symbol for their gesture shapes. They can only be recognized with additional *gesture constraints*. Checking gesture constraints can be done by examining the spatial relationship between test symbols and the graphical representation of the part of the already recognized diagram.

One goal in designing the HLR is to permit an easy integration of a gesture recognizer within an object-oriented editor architecture. To achieve this goal, gesture semantics are defined by our HLR as the generation of "normal" editing commands which can be interpreted by the underlying diagram editor in the same way as other commands.

Structure Recognition

The HLR maintains a set of gesture objects which can be considered as a knowledge base for the underlying diagram language. Graphical symbols stored in the symbol database are transformed into editing commands incrementally by the HLR as follows: Once the LLR has recognized the stroke just drawn, the HLR tries to find a valid gesture from graphical symbols stored in the database. This is done by matching each gesture object in turn by the following three steps:

1. Matching the gesture shape with graphical symbols stored in the database.

2. Checking gesture constraints in case that the gesture shape has a match.

3. Creating a command object defined by the gesture semantics in case that all constraints are fulfilled.

Checking constraints is the most important task of recognizing structure commands, which depends on the basic structures used in the underlying diagram language. Connectivity and hierarchy are the two most frequently used structures within diagram languages. For example, connections are represented usually by lines or arrow lines. The gesture shape of a connection-gesture is therefore a line-symbol. The gesture constraints are defined that the two endpoints of the corresponding line are connected with desired diagram components. Within our incremental recognition strategy, the HLR can recognize a connection gesture only if the diagram components, which shall be connected, already exist.

APPLICATION

In order to examine how well our incremental recognition works, we built several experimental diagram editors. In this paper we briefly describe a gesture-based statecharts editor.

Statecharts have been introduced as a visual formalism for specifying the behavior of complex reactive systems [3]. They extend classical state transition diagrams by three essential elements which are hierarchy, concurrency, and communications. We choose statecharts as an example because statecharts have a well-defined and relatively complex visual syntax which is appropriate for examining the usability of our incremental recognition concept.

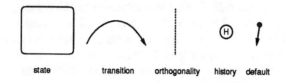

Figure 4: Graphical symbols used in statecharts

The key design issue in building a gesture-based diagram editor is to analyze the diagram syntax, and to consider how each diagram component can be created by using gestures. Figure 4 depicts the graphical symbols used in statecharts. For designing gesture shapes we follow two basic principles to achieve a so-called *What you draw is what you get* (WYDIWYG) interface:

1. We use a few "standard" language-independent gestures which are used in many other pen-based applications as well, for example, a cross-symbol for deleting objects or a circle for selecting objects.

2. We use the graphical symbols of the underlying diagram language directly as the corresponding gesture shapes for creating them. For example, a rectangle is the gesture shape for creating state objects. However, if the graphical symbol is not easy enough to draw, a simplified symbol can be used. For example, we use just a circle as the gesture shape for creating history symbols without writing the character 'H' inside the circle.

The current implementation is done in C++ by using InterViews and Unidraw [7] for its general graphical editing functionality. It is worth noting that our design goal of making the gesture recognizer compatible with a general editor framework, has greatly reduced the required implementation efforts.

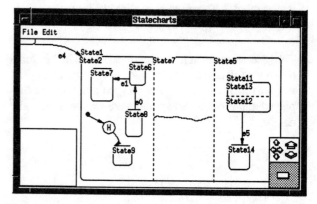

Figure 5: Gesture-based and syntax-directed statecharts editor

The gesture-based statecharts editor provides a complete gesture set for creating and manipulating a syntactically correct statechart. Figure 5 shows a screen image in which the user has just sketched a line which is a "add orthogonal state" gesture. This gesture command splits the state State7 in two additional orthogonal states.

DISCUSSION

The usability and the performance of our incremental recognition concept can be discussed from several perspectives. From the user's point of view, the recognition rate, the recognition speed, and the directness of the user interface are the most important factors which influence directly the usability and the performance of a gesture-based and syntax-directed diagram editor.

Recognition Rate

The experiences gained from working with the experimental applications show that both the low-level recognizer and the high-level recognizer produce satisfactory recognition results.

The recognition rate of a gesture recognizer is the fraction of gestures that it correctly recognizes. Although our recognition system consists of a low-level recognizer and a high-level recognizer, the recognition rate depends mainly on the low-level recognizer. This is because the correctness of a high-level recognizer should be guaranteed by the corresponding gesture constraints, that is, each error produced by the high-level recognizer is considered as a program error, and not as a recognition error.

Usually, the recognition rate of a pattern recognizer is given as a percentage. While such numbers are very meaningful for character recognizers, in particular for off-line recognizers, they reflect only one aspect of an on-line handsketch recognizer. This is because the recognition rate of an on-line recognizer depends strongly on the accuracy of the drawing and on the input device. The statistical measurements indicate that our low-level recognizer achieves a recognition rate of over 98%, if the user draws carefully.

Further, a number of recognition errors can be corrected in a very easy way due to our *incremental* recognition method. A typical situation for this is, for example, the user wants to draw a circle. Occasionally, the stop point is not close enough to the start point, and the circle is not recognized. In this case, the user can draw additional strokes which complete such circles.

Recognition Speed

The subjective impression indicates that the low-level recognizer is so fast that immediate feedback is always displayed after a stroke is finished. The user is not aware of any recognition time. In comparison to the low-level recognizer, the high-level recognizer produces tiny delays in editing large diagrams. For getting some quantitative descriptions of the recognition speed, we put several output statements into the source code of corresponding methods to report the execution times both of the low-level recognizer and the high-level recognizer.

Stroke size (No. of points)	Dot	Circle	Square
	(milliseconds)		
≈ 2	0.5	-	-
≈ 20	-	4	7
≈ 50	-	7	20
≈ 200	-	12	85

Table 1: Recognition speed of the low-level recognizer

The quantitative measurements show that the recognition speed of the low-level recognizer depends on the size (number of digitized points) of each handsketch. The number of digitized point coordinates again depends on the size of each symbol and the speed of drawing. The experiences of the author indicate that an average stroke consists of between three and forty point coordinates. Furthermore, the gesture shape determines how many features must be analyzed within the hierarchical feature-analyzer of the low-level recognizer. Table 1 shows the average recognition speed of the low-level recognition measured on a Sun 4 (SparcStation 1, SunOS 4.1.1). In the table, three representative shapes are chosen from about 30 recognizable graphical symbols. Recognizing

a `dot` is fastest, and recognizing a `square` is slowest. The time required to recognize a `circle` represents the average speed.

Context No. of obj.	State	History	Orth.	Trans.
	(milliseconds)			
≈ 10	5	4	15	15
≈ 50	22	18	80	93
≈ 200	91	60	200	380

Table 2: Recognition speed of the high-level recognizer

Table 2 presents the measurements of the recognition speed of the high-level recognition. Firstly, the recognition speed of the high-level recognizer depends on the number of existing diagram objects which the recognizer has to take into account. This is because the underlying constraints checker has to examine the spatial relationships between each gesture and all related graphical objects, which requires many time consuming calculations on graphical objects. Secondly, it depends obviously on the complexity of the constraints which are defined on each gesture. Thirdly, the recognition speed of the high-level recognizer depends on the performance of the editor framework being used and the efficiency of the implementation language. The values in table 2 are measurements for several gestures defined for the statecharts editor. One important result which becomes obvious is that the recognition of connection gestures, such as "create transition" in the statecharts editor takes much more time than gestures such as "create state" due to the the complexity of corresponding gesture constraints.

Usability

Each input technique has its own strengths and weaknesses, just as each application has its own unique demands. The essential point is to check how well it matches the requirements of the application. The gesture-based input technique is particularly appropriate for drawing diagrams because the main task in editing diagrams is drawing as well. It is obvious that a *sketch*-based interface is closely matched to a *sketch*-dominated application. Our incremental recognition concept is particularly appropriate for drawing diagrams because humans draw diagrams stroke by stroke as well.

An important advantage of this input technique is that the input is modeless, and thus the user draws in the same way as always. It is not required to know the current edit mode because only one sketching mode is available. The user can therefore concentrate on the real work, that is, the content of the diagram.

One important criterion of a direct manipulation interface is the feeling of directness. Our incremental recognition technique improves the directness in the following two ways:

- The distance between a user's thoughts and a gesture-based diagram editor is reduced because the translation from *what a user <u>wants</u> to do* to *what a user <u>has</u> to do* is simple and straightforward.

- Similar to the so-called WY**S**IWYG *output*-principle, our WY**D**IWYG *input*-principle is direct because the diagram elements can be created in exactly the same form as they are defined in the visual language, and as they will look on the screen.

Syntax-directed editors designed for textual programming languages find only limited acceptance because the difficulties in use outweigh the benefits. Neal [9] presented an analysis based on a five-dimensional user model, the computer expertise, programming expertise, programming language expertise, learning strategy, and level of risk aversion. In the following, we examined these aspects of our gesture-based and syntax-directed diagram editors.

Pen-based computers have just a pen as the single input device, thus the required computer expertise is obviously lower than that required to use keyboard and mouse with many buttons. A significant advantage of visual languages is that they are easy to use and easy to learn. Therefore the required programming expertise and programming language expertise are reduced. Compared to a textual programming language which defines usually up to a hundred keywords, most diagram languages use only between three and ten graphical symbols.

Our incremental recognition strategy strongly supports learning by doing. On the one hand, the user can draw anything at any time just like using a pen to make sketches on a piece of paper. Inking and low-level recognition provide immediate feedback independent of the underlying diagram syntax. On the other hand, the user can learn quickly to draw syntactically correct gestures, because only such gestures can be recognized and transformed into diagram components. The experiences of several colleagues of the author show that both novice and experienced users accept the user interface favorably. Furthermore, our editor provides an "any time usable" undo gesture to encourage the confidence and control of the user.

CONCLUSION

This paper presented concepts and techniques to support incremental gesture recognition in gesture-based and syntax-directed diagram editors. The essential idea of our concept is the tight integration between on-line pattern recognition and diagram parsing. The main advantage of the tight integration is that the underlying diagram syntax helps significantly in the gesture recognition. The incremental recognition strategy improves not only the recognition performance, but also the directness of gestural interfaces. Our concept for gesture-based diagram editing supports an interesting compromise between pure syntax-directed editing and general unconstrained editing. The key point here is the automatic gesture recognition of unconstrained handsketches.

ACKNOWLEDGEMENTS

The author would like to thank Franz Rammig and Gerd Szwillus for fruitful discussions and suggestions.

REFERENCES

1. Farahangiz Arefi, Charles E. Hughes, and David A. Workman. Automatically generating visual syntax-directed editors. *Communications of ACM*, 33(3):349–360, 1990.

2. Eric J. Golin. *A Method for the Specification and Parsing of Visual Languages*. PhD thesis, Brown University, 1991.

3. D. Harel. Statecharts: A visual formalism for complex systems. *Science of Computer Programming*, 8:231–274, 1987.

4. Richard Helm, Kim Marriott, and Martin Odersky. Building visual language parsers. In *Proceedings of the Conference on Human Factors in Computing Systems (CHI)*, pages 105–112, 1991.

5. Ken Kahn. Concurrent constraint programs to parse and animate pictures of concurrent constraint programs. Technical Report SSL-91-16, P91-00143, System Sciences Laboratory, Palo Alto Research Center, 1991.

6. J. Kim. Gesture recognition by feature analysis. IBM Research Report RC12472, T.J. Watson Research Center, IBM Corporation, January 1987.

7. Mark A. Linton, Paul R. Calder, John A. Interrante, Steven Tang, and John M. Vlissides. *InterViews Reference Manual, Version 3.1*. Stanford University, 1992.

8. James S. Lipscomb. A trainable gesture recognizer. *Pattern Recognition*, 24(9):895–907, 1991.

9. Lisa Rubin Neal. User modeling for syntax-directed editors. In *Human-Computer Interaction – INTERACT'87*, pages 131–134, 1987.

10. J. Pittman. Recognizing handwritten text. In *Proceedings of the Conference on Human Factors in Computing Systems (CHI)*, pages 271–275. ACM Press, 1991.

11. J.R. Rhyne. Dialogue management for gestural interfaces. IBM Research Report RC-12244, T.J. Watson Research Center, IBM Corporation, 1986.

12. Dean Rubine. Specifying gestures by example. *ACM SIGGRAPH'91, Computer Graphics*, 25(4), 1991.

13. Kent Wittenburg, Louis Weitzman, and Jim Talley. Unification-based grammars and tabular parsing for graphical languages. Technical Report ACT-OODS-208-91, MCC, June 1991.

14. Rui Zhao. On-line geometry recognition using C++, an object-oriented approach. In *Proceedings of the 7th International Conference & Exhibition of Technology of Object-Oriented Languages and Systems, TOOLS 7*, pages 371–378, April 1992.

INTEGRATING THEORETICIANS' AND PRACTITIONERS' PERSPECTIVES WITH DESIGN RATIONALE

Victoria Bellotti

Rank Xerox Cambridge EuroPARC
61 Regent Street
Cambridge CB2 1AB, U.K.
Bellotti@EuroPARC.Xerox.com

ABSTRACT

QOC design rationale represents argumentation about design alternatives and assessments. It can be used to generate design spaces which capture and integrate information from design discussions and diverse kinds of theoretical analyses. Such design spaces highlight how different theoretical approaches can work together to help solve design problems. This paper describes an example of the generation of a multi-disciplinary QOC design space which shows how designers' deliberations can be augmented with design contributions from a combination of different theoretical HCI approaches.

KEYWORDS: Design rationale, theoretical modelling, multi-disciplinary integration, design.

INTRODUCTION

System user-interface design has inspired many theoretical HCI analytic approaches from various disciplines, including cognitive science, linguistics, and computer science. Their aim is to elucidate system and user properties which contribute to the success or failure of designs (e.g., [1, 5, 7, 8, 9, 15]). However, the proliferation of such approaches has not been matched by increasing application of theory to design practice, particularly by non-HCI specialists.

Two possible reasons why current theoretical approaches are not used by designers are that they are narrow in scope and that it is unclear how they relate to one another or to design problem solving [1, 2]. There is scant evidence that the range of issues any one approach can tackle is adequate for designers' needs. So theorists need to relate their approaches to others from different disciplines as well as to demonstrate how they can support designers.

The research reported here took place within a project aimed at beginning to address these issues. I outline a design exercise in which the goal was to use a notation for design rationale, QOC [10, 11, 12], to characterise, compare and highlight relations between designers' and a number of different theoretical approaches' contributions to a design problem. Such a representation may help researchers from

different disciplines to identify how their theoretical approaches can be assimilated with one another and to demonstrate and improve their ability to tackle design problems. This work represents a move towards improving the applicability and integration of theoretical HCI approaches from different scientific disciplines.

The first two sections explain QOC and the methodology within which the design exercise took place. The remaining sections describe how designers' deliberations about a design problem from a real project were captured with the QOC notation and how QOC was used as a mediating representation for theoretical analyses of the same problem. The resulting design space illustrates how input from different approaches can be combined and used to augment the results of the designers' deliberations.

REPRESENTING DESIGN AGUMENTATION

QOC is a semi-formal notation for representing design rationale, consisting of Questions, Options and Criteria. It provides a structured representation of argumentation which explains why a designed artifact is the way it is. A QOC design space analysis captures argumentation about multiple possible solutions to design problems. The space is structured by Questions expressing design issues. Each Question is linked to multiple Options which are alternative solutions to the same problem. Options are positively or negatively assessed by each of a set of Criteria. An Option can also spawn consequent Questions which assume that Option is part of the design context of further argumentation (for details on the QOC notation see [12]).

We can think of design deliberations and theoretical analyses as argumentation about design problems. Argumentation based design representations assist in communication, comparison and synthesis of multiple design perspectives [6, 12, 13]. In QOC, which is such a representation, issues confronted and solutions proposed in design are expressed as Questions and Options. Problems and criticisms of solutions are expressed as assessment of Options by Criteria.

QOC was used to capture design information from designers' discussions and different theoretical analyses addressing the same set of issues. This design input was represented in a multi-disciplinary QOC design space to clarify the scope and nature of contributions made by different approaches. Such a representation helps us to see how theoretical analyses might be related to one another, and how their design input might be relevant to designers' deliberations.

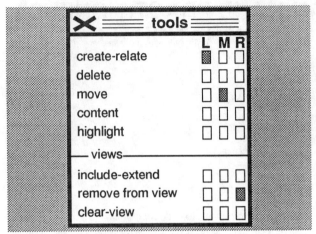

Figure 1. The scenario design solution.

THE SCENARIO METHODOLOGY

The *scenario methodology* was intended to enable bridges to be established among theoretical approaches and to design practice [14]. Instead of working within a design project where analysts and designers might have focused on different aspects of the design, a set of short *design scenarios* were used to ensure that the endeavours of all concerned were focused on the *same set of issues*.

A design scenario is a snapshot description of a real project, target users, requirements, etc., raising a particular set of problems. Scenarios were selected in a project-wide vote by modellers and commercial designers considering diversity, realism and how challenging they were for theoretical analysis [8]. Each scenario was presented separately to modeller and designer groups as a design problem. The designers' discussions were video-taped and transcribed and the modellers generated reports of their analyses. It was then possible to compare theoretical design contributions with what designers achieved without theory-based advice.

This comparison was achieved by filtering each transcript of designers' discussions and each analytic report, looking for every instance of what could be a Question, Option or a Criterion. Questions are the *issues* driving the deliberations, Options are *proposed solutions*, and Criteria are *justifications* for or *criticisms* of solutions. Repeated information was removed and the remaining Questions, Options and Criteria were then structured into a separate QOC design space for each group (for details of the process of translation into QOC see [11] and [12]). The aim was not to follow the exact rhetorical structure of their arguments, but to summarise and organise the diverse *significant design moves* they made.

AN EXAMPLE FROM A DESIGN SCENARIO EXERCISE

To illustrate how the content of design discussions and theoretical analyses might be integrated, I focus on a design issue tackled by designers and theoreticians in one scenario exercise. This scenario was taken from a design project which was ongoing at the time of the research. It describes a system called Dominie in which users manipulate an object hierarchy consisting of screens, files, procedures, etc. Dominie incorporates a commercial, hierarchical structure editor which lets users reassign eight object manipulation

functions to any of three mouse keys via a menu (see figure 1). Dominie's designers thought that reassignment might be better than menu invocation for conveying a strong direct manipulation feel in their UI. They reasoned that users would only need a small subset of the eight commands at any time. There was no provision for feedback in the design to tell users what the current assignments of mouse keys were (for details of this scenario exercise see [8]).

Designers' Argumentation

This scenario was presented to two software designers with between 3 and 6 years commercial experience. These designers volunteered to take part in this design exercise but were not involved in our research project. They were given 25 minutes to critique and consider improvements to Dominie's design. They then discussed their ideas, guided by a list of questions, such as: Did you come up with a solution? and, What knowledge did you draw on?

Part of the QOC design space based on the designers' discussion transcript is shown in figure 2. Design solutions and justifications given in the scenario description are shown as boxed Questions, Options and Criteria. The designers' new contributions to the design appear as unboxed QOC.

Some interesting aspects of the designers' deliberations were clarified by the QOC representation. They covered many different issues and design alternatives during the short time they had to consider the scenario. They disliked Dominie, saying nothing to commend it. They made four criticisms of the reassignment solution. In the part of the QOC design space shown in figure 2, these criticisms are shown as four Criteria negatively assessing the Dominie Option, *O:Reassign all functions via menu*. These Criteria trade off against the scenario justification for Dominie's design which we characterised as *C:Direct function access* which positively assesses the scenario solution.

By contrast with the four negative assessments of Dominie, there was only one negative assessment of just one of the designers' own alternatives. They thought that one of their solutions might be too complicated for users (in QOC terms it would be criticised by *C:Low complexity*). The few other Criteria generated from the designers' assessments of their solutions were all used to support their own ideas. QOC also highlighted the fact that the designers never explicitly assessed most of the solutions they themselves proposed.

Assigning Functions to Keys

I now consider one issue tackled by the designers, to show how different perspectives can be compared using QOC. The problem was that the designers disliked reassignment, but approved of the rapid invocation made possible by assigning functions to mouse keys. Only three could be fixed permanently to the keys, unless some way of disambiguating multiple functions on the same key could be found.

This issue is captured in QOC as *Q:How to assign wide range of functions to mouse keys*. This Question, shown in figure 2, compares the (boxed) Dominie Option and the designers' alternative Options. As stated above, the designers had several criticisms of function reassignment and proposed several alternatives. Some functions need not be assigned to

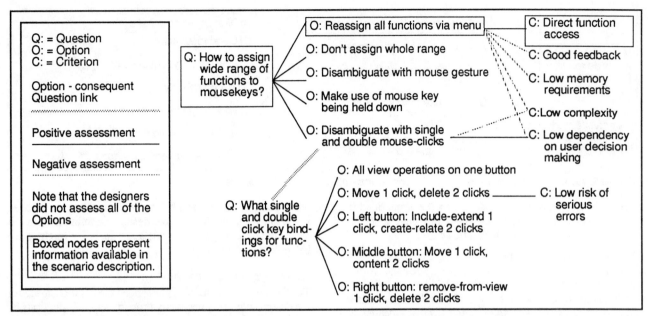

Figure 2. QOC summarising designers' discussions of graphical editor mousekey assignment

keys at all; *O:Don't assign whole range.* So clear-view, which is not object specific, could be on a menu, and highlight could be offered within the object. They also proposed three ways to disambiguate multiple functions bound to a single key; *O:Disambiguate with mouse gesture*, *O: Make use of mouse key being held down*, and *O:Disambiguate with single and double mouse-clicks.*

The designers detailed several solutions for disambiguating functions with mouse clicks. They even devised a scheme for assigning all six remaining functions to one of each of the keys. We characterise these ideas in figure 2 as Options for a consequent Question *Q:What single and double click key bindings for functions?* The designers were not committed to these particular solutions, stating that they would want more information before making specific recommendations. This is reflected in the lack of Criteria we were able to derive from their discussions to support these assignments. However when asked whether they thought they could benefit from theoreticians' advice they said they did not.

Integrating Designers' and Theorists' Argumentation

In this section I discuss theoretical contributions to the scenario design, focusing, in particular, on the issue of how to assign many functions to three mouse keys. The point of interest is how using QOC helps us see what theorists offer in relation to each other and to the designers. Three theoretical modelling groups analysed this scenario:

- Cognitive processing resource modelling [1]
- Cognitive knowledge modelling [15]
- Formal systems modelling [9]

Cognitive Modelling Analysis

Both cognitive groups modelled a number of strategies which users might adopt in using Dominie. For example, they might reassign all keys opportunistically, or restrict the number of keys which they treated as reassignable, or they might always assign each function to a particular mouse key. Through

cognitive modelling of function execution and reassignment via each of the possible user strategies, each approach identified multiple design flaws. According to their analyses, regardless of the strategy adopted, the user would forget or get confused about current assignments.

Various Criteria suggesting usability problems were found in the cognitive analyses. For example, the knowledge modelling group criticised Dominie because their analysis showed it required a good deal of mental effort to execute a function which was not currently assigned to a mouse key. We characterise this in QOC terms as a negative assessment by a Criterion, *C:Low effort for frequent invocations.* They also criticised Dominie because a cognitive simulation predicted that users would often forget to go back to an habitual assignment after a temporary key reassignment. This would cause an error next time they pressed that key expecting to execute the usual function. In QOC terms this is a negative assessment by *C:Avoid trailing sub-goal errors.*

The cognitive resource modelling group predicted user problems based on not being able to tell which functions are currently assigned to the mouse. We represent this as failure to satisfy a Criterion *C:Assigned function set is obvious.* They also pointed out a closely related problem of the user not knowing which one of the three keys a function is assigned to which we represent as a negative assessment by *C:Unambiguous function-to-key relation.*

The cognitive resource modelling group proposed extensions to the design to give feedback about current assignments. However, they predicted that users would still make many slips with Dominie. They also recommended that users be restricted to pre-set fixed combinations of assignments.

Cognitive Modelling Input to the Assignment Problem

I now consider how the cognitive modellers' analyses contributed to the problem identified by the designers of *Q:How to assign wide range of functions to mouse keys?*

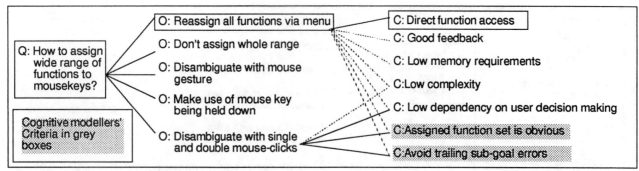

Figure 3. Adding Cognitive modellers' Criteria to the designers' design space

They did not consider alternatives to the scenario design solution of reassignable mouse keys but their models led them to predict many user difficulties with it.

Figure 2 showed that, although we were able to generate four negative assessments of the scenario design from the designers' discussions, we could only identify two further assessments of one of the designers' own Options by two of these Criteria, *C:Low complexity* and *C:Low dependency on user decision making*. They felt that the Dominie required users to make too many decisions about which function to assign to which key, whereas their suggestion of disambiguating functions with one or two mouse clicks cut out decision making. In this respect they viewed their own solution as an improvement on the scenario design.

However, though they considered Dominie to be too complicated for users, they were not sure that disambiguation of functions with mouse clicks was a low complexity alternative. So there was only *C:Low dependency on user decision making* to support the Option which inspired their detailed fixed assignment scheme. This characterisation reflects the designers' complaint that they had insufficient information to be confident about their proposals.

The cognitive modellers' Criteria are a source of information which we can use to make stronger arguments in favour the designers' solution. Figure 3 shows how two of them have been integrated into the designers' design space to support the mouse click disambiguation Option.

The Criterion *C:Assigned function set is obvious*, from the cognitive resource modellers, negatively assessed the scenario solution *O:Reassign all functions via menu*, because they showed that it would be unclear to the user which functions were currently assigned to mouse keys. However, it must support the designers' fixed assignment solution, since a fixed function set never changes.

The Criterion *C:Avoid trailing sub-goal errors* from the knowledge modellers also criticised Dominie because of the risk of users temporarily reassigning keys and forgetting to switch back to habitual assignments. This problem cannot occur with the designers' fixed assignment solution[1].

So Criteria from the cognitive analyses lent support to the designers' claim that fixed key assignments are better than

reassignable keys. Since the designers stated that they lacked sufficient information to make design recommendations, it seems that the cognitive modellers' analyses might have helped them in this respect.

Formal System Modelling Analysis
The formal system modellers expanded the solution space for the design, exploring necessary properties of the functions by producing a formal model of each one. The model for each function captured the set of attributes whose values are either changed by it, or must be known for it to be executed.

Dominie's design was found to violate a formal design principle, defined in QOC terms as *C:Predictability* [9]. This states that a given user action in a particular, visibly distinct, display context should always have the same (predictable) effect. This Criterion is clearly violated by the scenario design. The formalists' approach was able to show that the effect of clicking a mouse key would be non-deterministic.

Formal System Modelling Input to the Assignment Problem
The negative assessment by *C:Predictability* prompted the formalists to reject reassignable mouse keys, as did the designers. They then tackled the same issue of how to assign a large number of functions to just three mouse keys. They proposed two alternative schemes, using their function models as a basis for their solutions. The first scheme was that mouse key clicks could be combined in "chords" with keyboard key presses to distinguish functions bound to the same key. The second scheme used the display context to disambiguate interpretation of mouse key clicks.

As with the cognitive modellers, we summarised the output from the formal modellers' analysis in a design space. In QOC terms, the formalists proposed *O:Disambiguate with context of mouse clicks* and *O:Disambiguate with keyboard & mouse key chords*. We were able to add this information to the designers' design space as two additional Options for the Question *Q:How to assign wide range of functions to mousekeys?* as shown in figure 4.

The formal modellers, like the designers, did not generate many Criteria to support their disambiguation schemes. However, the Criteria from the cognitive modellers which favoured the designers' fixed assignment suggestion over the scenario design, also favour the formalists' two fixed assignment schemes for precisely the same reasons.

The QOC design space in figure 4 also shows how the

---

1. In figures 3 and 4 neutral assessments of the Options by the modellers' Criteria are not shown, in order to avoid clutter.

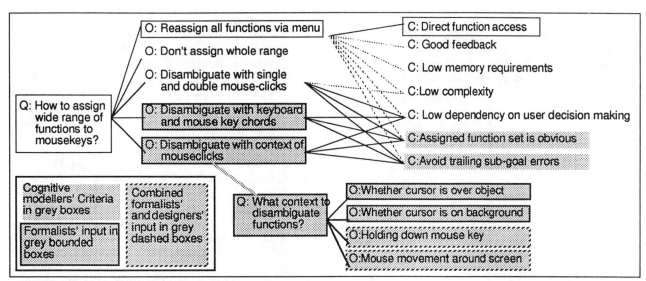

Figure 4. Adding formal modellers' input to the design space

formalists expanded on *O:Disambiguate with context of mouse clicks* with more detailed solutions. We characterised their analysis as posing a consequent Question, *Q:What context to disambiguate functions?* Each of the Options derived from their analysis represents a display or action context which can disambiguate functions.

Two of the formalists' Options in figure 2 were equivalent to, and can thus be combined with two of the designers' Options. The designers' *O: Disambiguate with mouse gesture* was equivalent to the formalists' *O:Mouse movement around screen*, and the designers' *O: Make use of mouse key being held down*, was equivalent to the formalists' *O:Holding down mouse key*. We are able to represent these Options in QOC as detailed methods for disambiguating functions, bound to the same key, using context[2].

QOC highlights the fact that the formalists did not determine whether their solutions were appropriate since they did not generate appropriate Criteria to assess them from a user-oriented perspective. Such Criteria are clearly something which cognitive modelling approaches should supply. This is therefore an example of where QOC helped us to identify a design problem where multiple theoretical approaches could be integrated in order to generate and select design solutions.

DISCUSSION

The goal of this work was to use QOC to characterise, compare and highlight relations between designers' and theoreticians' contributions to a design problem. Our experiences of using QOC as a common representation for multi-disciplinary input to a design scenario problem suggest that this may be a useful exercise for HCI researchers and developers of multi-disciplinary design methodologies.

QOC can be used to characterise the *nature* of contributions from diverse approaches, highlighting their strengths and

---

2. Restructuring design spaces in this way improves the consistency of Options for each Question in terms of level of detail. This ensures more appropriate comparison of Options which are equally well fleshed out, or at the same level of abstraction [3].

weaknesses. The design spaces described in this paper highlighted the fact that the designers exhibited an apparent confirmation bias, only negatively assessing the existing scenario design solution and positively assessing their own alternatives. QOC also underlined the fact that, in addition to evaluating the scenario design and finding flaws, some theoreticians generated alternatives. Two modelling groups reacted to their own analytic conclusions by suggesting alternatives which overcame the design flaws identified.

We found it useful to combine designers' and theoreticians' contributions to the same problems in a single design space. This helped us to compare and identify *relations between* approaches, showing how they might work together to generate and assess design solutions. Sometimes they contributed different solutions to the same Question, and sometimes contributions from different approaches were very similar. In our example the systems designers and formalists generated some different and some equivalent Options.

Sometimes Criteria identified from one approach could be related to Options supplied by another. We saw how cognitive modellers' Criteria could be used to assess the designers' and formalists' Options. The formalists modelled the properties and improved on invocation of the scenario functions but did not make recommendations as to which function should be assigned to which key. The cognitive modellers provided useful critiques of the scenario design but did not generate alternative design solutions, other than the feedback suggested by the cognitive resource modellers. So, even in the small example from the scenario exercise reported in this paper, we identified a number of places where theoretical approaches needed to be brought together to generate and assess solutions adequately.

The designers in the scenario exercise were asked if they felt they could have benefitted from theoretical insight. Although they lacked confidence in their own solutions, they said that they did not think they could. However, this QOC exercise suggested that they could have been supported by input from theorists in a number of ways.

In our example, the cognitive modellers provided explicit reasons why reassignable functions would cause users problems. These were expressed as assessments by QOC Criteria which could have backed up the designers' rejection of Dominie's design and supported their alternative solutions.

The formal system modellers provided two alternative schemes for disambiguating functions bound to the same mouse key. They were also able to generate workable schemes for multiple key bindings by providing detailed methods for disambiguating key clicks. A QOC summary of this analysis could have been useful to the designers, by summarising alternative schemes for disambiguating functions on single mouse keys.

This research begins to suggest ways in which HCI theoretical approaches, which have previously been demonstrated as isolated analytic techniques, can be brought together, and productively integrated with input from system designers, to tackle design problems.

Scenario exercises, like the one described here, represent a first step in a process of integrating theory with practice. It seems that there are potential bridges between different theoretical approaches and between theoretical analyses and the kinds of issues which designers address. However, further work still remains to be done in improving the process of bridging between design approaches. This will involve improving the process of translation of information into QOC design spaces by getting theorists and designers to take part in their creation. We also want to ensure that modellers and designers can communicate with and react to one another one another in a design context. Finally, we plan to embed such integrated analytic endeavours within design practice where they can actually inform design decisions.

CONCLUSIONS

The reassignable function scenario exercise described here, and others we have carried out, suggest that QOC may help HCI theoreticians and analysts in clarifying the nature of contributions of different theoretical approaches to a design problem. It highlights their identification of important design issues, assessment of design solutions and generation of alternative solutions.

Furthermore, QOC characterises design input from designers and HCI theoreticians in such a way that their output can be compared and integrated. The use of a single representation to mediate between different perspectives on the same design problem highlights ways in which theoretical modelling approaches can contribute and how they might work together to support generation and assessment of design solutions.

ACKNOWLEDGEMENTS

The research reported in this paper was undertaken within the AMODEUS Esprit project (BRA 3066). I wish to thank Allan MacLean for considerable input to the work and Paul Dourish, Bill Gaver, Wendy Mackay, Abi Sellen, Scott Minneman, Sara Bly, Matthew Chalmers and Rachel Hewson for their comments on drafts of this paper. Special thanks are due to the collaborators in the AMODEUS project for their part in the work the paper describes.

REFERENCES

1. Barnard, P. Cognitive resources and the learning of human-computer dialogues. In J.M. Carroll (Ed.) *Interfacing thought: Cognitive Aspects of Human-Computer Interaction*, Cambridge University Press, 1987, pp. 112-158.

2. Bellotti, V. Implications of current design practice for the use of HCI techniques. In D. M. Jones, & R. Winder. (Eds.), *People and Computers IV: Designing for Usability*, Proc. HCI'88 (Manchester, U.K., September, 5-9, 1988), Cambridge University Press, pp. 13-34.

3. Bellotti, V. MacLean, A. and Moran, T. Generating good design questions. EuroPARC Technical Report EPC-91-136.

4. Bellotti, V. and MacLean, A. Generating QOC design space analyses for design scenarios with multi-disciplinary modelling input. AMODEUS Project Deliverable D21 (1992).

5. Card, S. Moran, T. and Newell, A. *The Psychology of Human-Computer Interaction*. Lawrence Earlbaum Associates, Hillsdale, NJ, 1983.

6. Conklin, J., and Yakemovic, KC B. A process-oriented approach to design rationale. *Human Computer Interaction*, Vol 6 (3&4) 1991, pp. 357-391.

7. Coutaz, J. Architecture models for interactive software. In S. Cook (ed.) *ECOOP'89*, Proc. 3rd European Conference on Object Oriented Programming (1989), Cambridge University Press, pp. 383-399.

8. Hammond, N. and Myers, K. Integrating models of HCI into design: An empirical investigation. AMODEUS Project Deliverable D17 (1992).

9. Harrison, M., & Thimbleby, H. (Eds.). *Formal Methods in Human-Computer Interaction*. Cambridge University Press, 1990.

10. MacLean, A. Young, R. and Moran, T. Design Rationale: The argument behind the artifact. In Proc. CHI'89: Human Factors in Computing Systems (Austin, April 30 - May 4, 1989), ACM Press, pp. 247-252.

11. MacLean, A. Bellotti, V. and Young, R. What Rationale is there in design? In Proc. Human-Computer Interaction - INTERACT'90 (Cambridge, U.K., August 27-31, 1990), Elsevier, North-Holland, pp. 207-212.

12. MacLean, A. Young, R. Bellotti, V. and Moran, T. Questions, Options, and Criteria: Elements of Design Space Analysis. In *Human Computer Interaction*, Vol 6 (3&4) 1991, pp. 201-250.

13. Rittel, H.W.J. Second generation design methods. In Cross (Ed.) Developments in Design Methodology. John Wiley & Sons Ltd, Chichester, 1984, pp. 317-327.

14. Young, R. and Barnard, P. The use of scenarios in human-computer interaction research: Turbocharging the tortoise of cumulative science. In Proc. CHI+GI'87: Human Factors in Computing Systems and Graphics Interface (Toronto, April 5-9, 1987) ACM Press, pp. 291-296.

15. Young, R. Green, T. and Simon, T. Programmable user models for predictive evaluation of interface designs. In Proc. CHI'89: Human Factors in Computing Systems (Austin, April 30 - May 4, 1989), ACM Press, pp. 15-20.

MANAGEMENT OF INTERFACE DESIGN
IN HUMANOID

Ping Luo, Pedro Szekely and Robert Neches

USC/Information Sciences Institute
4676 Admiralty Way, Marina del Rey, CA 90292
E-mail: {ping, szekely, neches}@isi.edu

ABSTRACT

Today's interface design tools either force designers to handle a tremendous number of design details, or limit their control over design decisions. Neither of these approaches taps the true strengths of either human designers or computers in the design process. This paper presents a human-computer collaborative system that uses a model-based approach for interface design to help designers search the design space effectively and construct executable specifications of application user interfaces. This human-in-the-loop environment focuses human designers on decision making, and utilizes the bookkeeping capabilities of computers for regular and tedious tasks. We describe (a) the underlying modeling technique and an execution environment that allows even incompletely-specified designs to be executed for evaluation and testing purposes, and (b) a tool that decomposes high-level design goals into the necessary implementation steps, and helps designers manage the myriad of details that arise during design.

KEYWORDS: Interface-Building Tools and Techniques, Design Processes, Development Tools and Methods, Rapid Prototyping, Interface Design Representation.

INTRODUCTION

Today's interface design tools do not strike an adequate balance between giving designers control over an interface design, and providing a high level of design automation. Tools that give designers extensive control over details of a design, like interface builders [14], typically force designers to control *all* details of the design. Tools that automate significant portions of interface design, like MIKE [15] and UofA* [16], typically let designers control *few* of the details. This paper describes our efforts to combine the benefits of these two classes of tools to provide extensive human control without drowning designers in details. Our thesis is that model-driven programming plus decomposition of design goals lets us provide an environment that allows humans and computers work from their strengths in the design process. In the system described below, humans focus on setting high-level policies, while the computer focuses on bookkeeping and details that humans do not want to address.

Our approach is motivated by a view of interface design as a search in a space of design alternatives. This search space contains an unmanageable number of design alternatives. It is defined by design decisions such as determination of the operations to be supported and parameters they require, presentation of these operations and their parameters, presentation of application objects of interest, choice of input gestures, and control of sequencing among the gestures and operations. Given that there are many choices for each of these considerations, the design space explodes combinatorially. Thus, the key problem is to help designers search the design space quickly and effectively.

It is interesting to consider how interface builders and automated generation systems, the two main current approaches, fare when judged in terms of support for exploration of design alternatives.

Interface builders [13, 14] allow designers to draw the screens of an application. They are most effective for concrete tasks such as constructing the static portion of interfaces and editing screen layouts. But, working at this level, they force designers to handle far too much detail. To use the tools, designers are forced to make design commitments down to the level of individual widgets. This distracts them from design decision making at a conceptual level (e.g., committing to support selected objects in the interface without committing to how they will be presented). Furthermore, the number of steps entailed to change a high-level commitment discourages exploring many alternatives. Missing from interface builders are support for design abstraction and the ability to defer design commitments.

Automatic interface generation systems [2, 5, 7, 15, 16] generate user interfaces based on a description of application functionality. The main purpose of these systems is to hide interface design complexity by automating all design decisions made by human designers. Because of this, they provide human designers with very little control over those decisions. Unfortunately, generating good interface designs is intrinsically difficult. Thus, the resulting automatically-generated interfaces either are not good enough for real use [10], or have rather limited styles. (The best is the menu-driven style, which is limited to generating the dialogue portions of the display because the application display area is too hard to generate automatically.) The technical barriers to effective automation are hard to overcome. The design space is large and contains many bad designs. Principles of good user-interface design are not yet well specified [4], and cannot be used to automatically prune the search space. It is hard to

© 1993 ACM 0-89791-575-5/93/0004/0107...$1.50

tell an automated interface design system about application-specific considerations that affect weighting of alternatives.

Our approach strives to retain the best aspects of both approaches. We allow designers to control design decisions like interface builders do, but with the additional ability to control decisions with respect to a broader set of concerns (e.g. presentation and sequencing, not just layout). We preserve the ability of automation tools to let designers insulate themselves from some design details, but provide hooks to control those details if desired. We facilitate design exploration by supporting different levels of abstraction to maximize modularity of the design space and control of its search. We also provide aids for managing the details of implementing conceptual designs. In this environment, human designers focus on design decision making and evaluation (which is very hard to automate but can be performed quite effectively by humans). The system helps designers reduce their memory burden and mental work load by managing regular and tedious tasks, such as decomposing designs into easily achievable sub-designs.

Our approach consists of two parts: a model-based design and execution environment [18, 19], and a human-computer collaborative design exploration environment. The model-based environment provides a modeling language for many aspects of interface design, ranging from the abstract considerations that arise early in the design, to the concrete ones that define the details of the interface [12]. The model-based environment also provides the run-time system to execute the modeled interfaces, even before they are fully concretized. The collaborative design environment helps designers effectively search the design space by helping them construct the models and by helping them keep track of: (a) alternative design alternatives about which they must make decisions and (b) consequences of those decisions which require handling.

The rest of the paper is organized as follows. We first briefly describe the enabling technology, a model-based system that provides capabilities for modeling and for design model execution. Next, we present the collaborative design environment in action using a design example to show: how we decompose design goals, how we divide labor between the designer and the computer, and how the human designer interacts with computer. We then close with our current status and plans for future work.

MODEL-BASED DESIGN & EXECUTION ENVIRONMENT

HUMANOID [19], the base layer of our environment, is a model-based system. Interfaces are specified by constructing a declarative model of how the interface should look and behave. The HUMANOID model provides the enabling technology for supporting different levels of abstraction to maximize the modularity of design.

The Interface Model

HUMANOID's design model captures information about an application's functionality (objects and operations), and information about all features of the interface. HUMANOID factors the model of an application and its interface into five semi-independent dimensions: *Application semantics design*

represents the operations and objects that an application program provides; *Presentation* defines the visual appearance of the interface; *Manipulation* defines the gestures that can be applied to the objects presented, or equivalently, the set of manipulations enabled at any given moment; *Sequencing* defines the order in which manipulations are enabled; and *Action side effects* declare the actions that an interface performs automatically as side effects of the action of a manipulation. (see [19] for details).

The Run-Time System

HUMANOID provides a run-time support module, which is included in every application. The module executes the design model; that is, it constructs application displays and interprets input according to the specifications in the model.

To produce or update the display of an application data structure, the run-time system searches the presentation model hierarchy for a presentation component capable of displaying the data structure. The model returns the most specific presentation component suitable for displaying the data in the given context (e.g. taking into account data type congruence and spacing restrictions) and the run-time system uses it to produce or update the display. Note that the presentation component obtained from the model might either be a default inherited from HUMANOID's generic knowledge base, or a more specific presentation component specified by an interface's designer. The defaults enable designers to execute incompletely specified designs for testing and evaluation purposes.

This provides HUMANOID the capability to support delay of design commitments which allows designers specify only those aspects that they want to address. Also, with the run-time system, developers do not need to write code to update the display. They specify declaratively the dependencies between presentation methods and application data structures. HUMANOID uses this information to dynamically reconstruct the displays when the application data structures change.

HUMANOID's Interactive Modeling Tools

The model-based approach in HUMANOID leads to an interface design environment with a number of benefits not found in current interface building tools [20]:

- *Supports design reuse.* The system provides an easy way to access all the design models by presenting components of the models as graphical objects which can be selected, dragged and dropped into a position for reference and reuse.

- *Helps to understand design models.* The environment presents the designer both the model and sample displays of the interface specified by the model. By using explicit models, HUMANOID can reduce designers' mental effort to understand the specification in two ways. First, it helps by showing designers connections between components of the model and components of the display. Second, it helps designers understand the impact of a potential design change by identifying where the altered portion of the model would be applied. For example, designers can point at an interface display object of interest and let

HUMANOID identify and fetch the part of the model that defines that object; designers can also ask HUMANOID to highlight all the interface objects on the display that are controlled by a particular part of the model (see [20] for more details).

- *Reduces the cost of modeling.* Although a model-based approach provides the benefits above, it does so at a price of additional specification effort. The design environment reduces the cost of obtaining these benefits by assisting with the burdens of building the model. The HUMANOID model are presented in a context-sensitive, graphical working environment which allows designers to build and modify the models interactively. Any modification of the model will force recomputation of the interface defined by that model, and thus provides immediate feedback. This eases the design of dynamic aspects of the interface, including conditional display, interactive behavior, and sequencing control, yet still retains the descriptive power of language-based systems.

COLLABORATIVE DESIGN ENVIRONMENT

This section uses an example to illustrate how the environment divides labor between human and computer to utilize what each does best in design. We first argue that design is complex in nature and we cannot hide complexity from designers without losing designers' control over design decisions. We then introduce an agenda system that we use for the bookkeeping needed to manage design tasks. Following that, we illustrate how we decompose design goals and how the designer interacts with the system to implement a design policy decision.

The Nature of Design: Where Support is Needed

To use any design tool that provides extensive control over the design, designers must know (a) how to break down high-level design goals into activities that are supported by the tool and (b) how to resolve interactions between these activities. Although the HUMANOID interactive design environment combines the strength of interface builders and model-driven programming, it is not immune to this problem. Decomposing an interface design is a difficult task (if it is doable at all by non-programmers).

Since interface design is a rich domain, most high-level goals break down into multiple lower-level goals. There are often many ways in which to achieve the lower level goals, giving rise to complexity that distracts designers from current design issues by requiring effort to keep track of design steps and update agendas of activities. This is not an artifact of the model-based approach, but an intrinsic characteristic of design. One still must face decisions about exactly how to implement design policy decisions, regardless of whether one uses a model-based approach, interface builders or hand programming. All that differs between these paradigms is how explicitly those decisions are expressed, and therefore how much help the system can provide in effecting them.

The following example illustrates the complexities in what appears to be a simple interface design decision. Consider the interface for the object browser shown in Figure 1a. The main body of the object browser window shows a list of slot-value pairs. The designer would like to make the values selectable so that commands can be applied to them. Figure 1b shows the object browser having the selection capability.

Figure 1. Object Browser Example.

(a) Browser with no notion of "current selection"

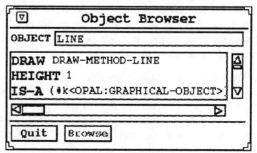

(b) Browser with support for selection

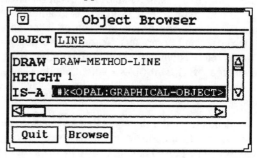

In general, to implement such a capability, one has to perform many tasks. For each task (which we label below for future reference) there can be many possible methods:

- *TASK-1. Determine whether single or multiple objects can be selected.*

- *TASK-2. Specify or create a variable to record the current selected object* (called an application input in the HUMANOID jargon). Once an object is selected, it must be stored in a variable that can be referenced by commands that use the selection.

- *TASK-3. Define the manipulation that selects the object.* This entails the following sub-tasks:

  - *TASK-3.1.* Choose the mouse button or key that invokes the selection behavior.

  - *TASK-3.2.* Determine the area of the presentation where the mouse can be clicked to select the object. It could be the complete presentation of the object, only a hot-spot within its presentation, or an area larger than the presentation (if the presentation is very small).

  - *TASK-3.3.* Specify the mapping from (a) the presentation area where the selection is triggered, to (b) the application object implied by the selection. In general, a presentation can display multiple components of an application data structure, and it is necessary to specify which one is the one to be selected.

- *TASK-4. Design the feedback used to show the selected object.* The feedback can be represented by an icon associated with the selected object (e.g. a check mark), or by highlighting the display of the selected object using different shapes, colors, and filling styles.

There are also many potential interactions between the tasks just listed and decisions that may have been made elsewhere in the design. Some examples: (a) other behavior on the objects should not use the same mouse button as is used for selection; (b) the type of the variable where the selection is stored must be consistent with the type of the value to be stored in it; and (c) if highlighting feedback is used, it should not be confused with other possible highlightings used for other purposes in the same presentation.

Notice that these complexities involve fundamental design decisions. No matter what tools we use, we cannot hide the complexity without reducing the design space, which would unduly limit designers' control over design decisions (recall our argument on automatic interface generation systems in the introduction of this paper).

Since this complexity is inevitable, the question is one of how best to cope with it. Our approach is to ameliorate the problems by introducing a new division of labor between human designers and computers. To do so, we decompose design goals into system-supported collaborative tasks. We take advantage of HUMANOID's explicit models, and add another layer of modeling to describe interface design activities.

The main idea is to model the goals that an interface design must satisfy, and to model the methods for achieving the goals. Goals can be posted automatically by the system (e.g. "all application commands should be executable by end-users"), or they can be posted by the designer (e.g. "the objects displayed should be selectable"). Complex design goals, like the example above, are decomposed into simpler goals until they bottom out in goals that can be achieved by simple editing operations on the interface design (e.g. adding a menu-item to a display).

By modeling interface design in a goal-oriented way, it is possible to use a "goal management" system to help designers keep track of what goals still need to be achieved, to offer designers different methods for achieving goals, to keep track of which methods have been tried, and to warn designers about previously achieved goals that become violated by the solutions to other goals.

Similar to Framer [8], our collaborative environment seeks to avoid the problems of automating human design responsibilities and to overcome weaknesses of human cognitive limitations (e.g. short term memory). Unlike Framer, our system supports both system and designer initiated design goals. The system-initiated goals are implementation oriented, like those generated by the critics in Framer. Our designer initiated goals are more oriented toward design intentions, but designers have the choice to post implementation oriented goals as well. Our environment goes beyond Framer in the following additional respects:

- *It is an active collaborator.* The system can react promptly by deriving necessary tasks from the current

design and updating its task agenda automatically in response to interface model changes. As a side effect, this frees designers from potential limitations that might be imposed upon designers by our modeling tools. The designer can do modeling by any other means and still get a valid agenda from the system.

- *It helps in evaluating designs by providing prompt results.* With HUMANOID, changes to the model are immediately reflected in the sample display that is generated from the current design. This provides quick design-evaluation-redesign iteration and makes the relationship between models and the interfaces generated from the models more understandable.

- *It supports interleaving design tasks.* By making all current tasks available to designers, we let designers choose to concentrate on any issue they want, and allow them to carry out design tasks in parallel. Designers can shift focus among their design tasks freely, without losing track of their other design tasks and without losing the feedback provided by the derived interface.

The rest of this section is organized as follows. First we describe our goal management mechanism, called Scenarios/Agendas. Then, we briefly describe the goal decompositions relevant to our object browser design example. Following that, we present an example of how the system assists a designer in managing the details that arise in implementing design decisions in that example. We summarize the benefits of this approach at the end.

Scenarios/Agendas

Our goal management system performs design task book-keeping, i.e., it decomposes high-level design goals, and maintains and presents a valid task agenda. It is based on Scenarios/Agendas [11], a tool for building applications where users need to manage a set of activities over an extended period of time.

Scenarios/Agendas provides two constructs for modeling activities: goals and methods. A goal represents a desired state of design (e.g. the interface provides at least one way for the user to invoke any application commands). Goals can have one or more methods for achieving them (e.g. to make all commands invocable by the user, one method is to use a menu-bar with all the commands). Scenarios/Agendas supports three kinds of methods. *System methods* automatically run a procedure that achieves the goal. This provides a way to encode default behavior that does not require user involvement. *Interactive methods* prompt the user for some information and then invoke a procedure. *Decomposition methods* replace a goal with a set of simpler goals that the user or the system can pursue individually.

Scenarios/Agendas provides a default interface for managing a large collection of activities. The interface presents an agenda of the set of goals that are to be met, and allows the user to choose among all the applicable methods for accomplishing the goal. In addition, Scenarios/Agendas provides ways for filtering the agenda to focus on different types of goals (e.g all "present-object" goals), goals that refer to particular types of objects (e.g. all goals that refer to a particular command), or goals created by a particular person or on particular dates.

Scenarios/Agendas monitors the relevant data objects in the domain. When the data structures change, the satisfying conditions of any affected goals are re-evaluated, and their status is updated appropriately on the agenda. Our collaborative environment makes use of this facility to monitor the interface design model, and keep the goal agenda up to date as the design evolves.

Decomposing Interface Design

The design goals and their decompositions, which model the interface design process, are used by our goal management system to derive the design task agenda.

We have identified a set of design goals and methods that can be used to decompose the design process for constructing a wide variety of graphical interfaces. (Appendix 1 contains a catalogue of the top-level interface design goals we have identified.) In our scheme, knowledge about these goals and their decomposition is built into the system, rather than being a concern of individual designers.

Goals can be defined in terms of sub-goals or primitive steps. All goals define queries to the design model to test the appropriate condition. Non-primitive goals are decomposable into other goals that are easier to achieve. Below, we show the decomposition of the "made an object selectable" goal that was discussed previously.

Goal *Made Object Selectable*
  Subgoals:
  Selection Manipulation Elaborated   {for TASK-3}
    Subgoals:
    Single/Multiple Selection Specified   {for TASK-1}
    Application Variable Specified   {for TASK-2}
    Start Where Specified   {for TASK-3.1}
    Event Specified   {for TASK-3.2}
    Value To Set Specified   {for TASK-3.3}
  Selection Feedback Specified   {for TASK-4}

The Design Environment In Action

In this section, we show (a) how the system leads designers to map their conceptual designs into executable interface specifications; (b) how the system reduces burdens that

designers otherwise have to bear; and (c) how the system lets designers take control without forcing them to handle details that they do not care about. As an example, we show the system helping designers add selection capabilities to the object browser shown in Figure 1. The previous section showed the subgoals entailed by this goal. Figure 2 shows the enhancements to the design model required to specify this new interface feature. The elements that need to be added are shown with a thick border; they consist of new presentation model components labeled SELECTION-AREA, SELECTION-FEEDBACK and SELECT-VALUE. The figure does not show details of the parameters of the newly added design objects. The rest of this section describes the steps that the designer follows in modeling the desired new feature.

In the collaborative environment, designers express their intentions by selecting goals from the system's design goal library and then posting instances of those goals to the agenda. The system also posts goals when it detects new design tasks. In our example of adding the select-object feature to the object browser, a designer selects the Made Objects Selectable goal from the goal library and, prompted by the system, specifies the display object to be made selectable. The latter is done by mousing on that object in the display of the sample implementation; the goal is then posted on the agenda. This collaboration lets designers keep control, because they can post goals at whatever level is appropriate; simultaneously, it lets the system help by taking responsibility for determining consequences of goals.

When the goal Made Objects Selectable is instantiated, the agenda system computes the goal decomposition and the necessary tasks from the design model in that context, and presents the agenda as shown in Figure 3. (The goals are shown in bold face with their parameters in square brackets.) Associated with each goal are all the known methods for achieving that goal. The methods will be displayed in the agenda when designers click on the icon to the left of a goal. Designers can select any method of any goal in any order, or they can edit the design directly using the HUMANOID direct-manipulation interface for editing the model. This approach lets designers choose among design alternatives without saddling them

Figure 2. The presentation and behavior model of an object browser application. The browser shows object slots and values.

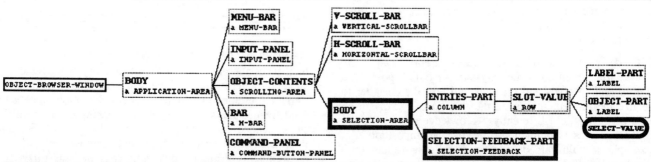

The display is defined by the OBJECT-BROWSER-WINDOW presentation method. Its body, APPLICATION-AREA, has five parts. Four of the them (MENU-BAR, INPUT-PANEL, COMMAND-PANEL, and HORIZONTAL-BAR) are generic to a wide class of application windows, and are inherited from the HUMANOID generic presentation model. The part SELECTION-AREA of OBJECT-CONTENTS is specific to our application for displaying slot-value information of a user specified object and for presenting feedback of the selected object.

with the full burden of generating those options.

Figure 3. Agenda after `Made Object Selectable` is posted, and `Made Object Selectable` and `Selection Feedback Specified` are expanded by designers. Goals are shown in bold face with their parameters in squared brackets. Methods are in italic. The indentation presents the decomposition relation.

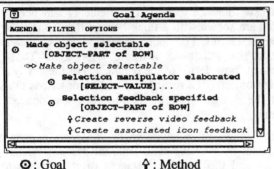

⊙ : Goal   ⇧ : Method
⊷⊙ : Satisfied Goal   ⊪⇨ : Method in Progress

In this case, as shown in Figure 3, the system provides two methods for achieving the `Selection Feedback Specified` goal. The *Create Reverse Video Feedback* modifies the design to highlight the selected object using reverse-video. The *Create Associated Icon Feedback* modifies the design to indicate the selected object using an icon (e.g. a check-mark) displayed next to the selected object.

Suppose the designer chooses the *Create Reverse Video Feedback* method. That method posts two new goals on the agenda: `Selection Area Specified` and `Feedback Presentation Elaborated` (Figure 4). Since both subgoals have default system methods, the system executes them. Accordingly, the icons next to the posted subgoals are changed to show that they have been satisfied. Notice that the environment utilizes several means to inform designers about effects of its default methods: (a) the model in Figure 2 changed to present that the default methods added a `SELECTION-AREA` and a `SELECTION-FEEDBACK` to the design; (b) the sample interface generated from the model was updated to reflect the presentations and behaviors of the new model; (c) the agenda presented the new status of the goals and methods by using different icons. At this point, the designer can still choose other methods and change the way in which the goal was satisfied by the system. This mechanism of providing defaults allows designers to off-load onto the system portions of design they do not want to be concerned about, while retaining control when they so desire.

If the designer had chosen the *Create Associated Icon Feedback* method, the system would post the corresponding goals and methods and lead the designer to realize the implementation of the `Selection Feedback Specified` goal differently. Knowledge about design inconsistencies is defined in the goal decomposition. For example, a multi-valued input needs a list of values not a single value. If the designer had chosen the single selection to realize the `Single/Multiple Selection Specified` subgoal and a multi-valued input to satisfy the

`Application Variable Specified` subgoal, the system would handle the bookkeeping tasks of posting the corresponding goals and methods to resolve the conflict.

Figure 4. Agenda after *Create Reverse Video Feedback* method is selected.

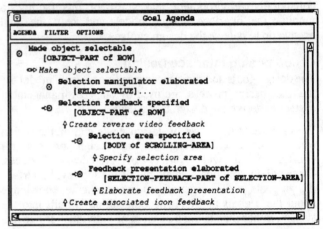

Figure 5 shows the subgoals of `Selection Manipulator Elaborated` that designers need to fill in the application-specific information. Satisfying the `Selection Manipulator Elaborated` goal adds the remaining elements to the design.

Figure 5. Agenda after `Selection Feedback Specified` is closed and `Selection Manipulator Elaborated` is expanded.

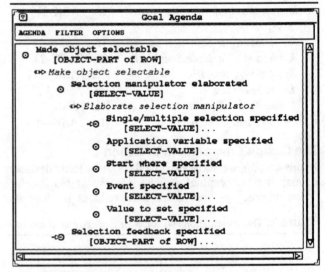

Benefits of the Collaborative Environment

In the collaborative environment, activity management is handled by the system. All the design options at each design step are presented to designers for consideration; there is no need for designers to worry about keeping track of all the steps needed to implement a top level goal. Equally important, the system does not impose any design commitments during the design process; designers have full control on design decisions. When tasks have been decomposed to the lowest level, the designer's activities are then supported by the HUMANOID modeling environment, an effective system for detailed modeling.

The collaborative environment utilizes the strength of human designers for design decision making, and the strength of the computer for bookkeeping and automating regular and tedious tasks. More specifically, it has the following benefits and novel features:

- *Designers can express their design intentions explicitly.* Designers can express high-level design goals (e.g, making an object selectable or draggable). Our collaborative environment maps them into refinements to the design model (as shown in Figure 3-5), thereby overcoming cognitive difficulties in directly expressing desired design features in the modeling language.

- *Designers have extensive control over design decisions but are freed from cumbersome design details.* In the collaborative system, designers always have the freedom to pursue design issues in any direction they choose. They keep control of the aspects they care about, while off-loading onto the system things they do not want to be concerned about (by accepting default methods, e.g. achieving the `Selection Feedback Specified` subgoal in the design example). The system manages the multitude of details that arise during interface design (e.g. the task of specifying selection feedback in the design example) by providing agendas with management and filtering mechanisms, along with built-in capabilities for keep agendas up-to-date.

- *Designers can work outside the collaborative environment.* Designers can directly edit designs using the Humanoid interactive tools, or by editing a textual representation in a text editor. The goals affected by these changes will be automatically checked. If the modifications change the state of the design so that goals become satisfied, they will be marked as such. If the modifications introduce inconsistencies, the appropriate inconsistency resolution goals will be posted. However, the system does not do plan recognition to try to infer new goals to capture the high-level intentions behind the editing operations performed outside the environment. So, the environment can provide assistance when requested, and does not hinder designers when they do not require assistance.

- *The system smooths the transition from conceptual design to implementation.* Dichotomizing design activities as conceptual design and implementation has led to disjointed interface design tools addressing different aspects of the design problem (e.g. [3, 21] and [13, 14]). This disjointedness imposed a gap between conceptual design and implementation where no tool in the middle ground supports the mapping from conceptual design into functioning interfaces. The system described in this paper bridges that gap by mapping designers' intentions into executable interface specification. Thus it supports an intertwined design and implementation working environment [17], a previously neglected need.

CURRENT STATUS AND FUTURE WORK

The HUMANOID model-based design and execution environment is implemented in Garnet [9] and CommonLisp. We have used it within our group to implement the interfaces for two large applications, a logistics analysis system (DRAMA), and a knowledge base development environment (SHELTER). In addition, the HUMANOID interactive design environment is itself implemented with HUMANOID.

We have done a theoretical study on identifying and classifying design goals, and have built the initial system described in this paper by adapting the current Scenarios/ Agenda mechanism to support the interface design environment in full scale. We plan to perform usability tests to see how well the goals are understood and used by a wider range of designers and how well they lead designers execute interface design into functioning interfaces.

We also plan to provide design critics by integrating the kinds of design critics found in UIDE [5] into our system. The critics will detect design inconsistencies and provide some design evaluation automation. In our environment, the design critic would post a goal to remove the inconsistency. For some inconsistencies, system methods would fix the problem automatically and for others sub-goaling would be used to guide the designer to a solution.

ACKNOWLEDGEMENTS

We want to thank Peter Aberg, David P. Benjamin and Brian Harp for their helpful comments throughout the preparation of this paper. The research reported in this paper was supported by DARPA through Contract Numbers NCC 2-719 and N00174-91-0015. Contents represent the opinions of the authors, and do not reflect official positions of DARPA or any other government agency.

APPENDIX

The following is a summary of the top-level interface design goals and subgoals that we have identified up to now. These goals were identified by analyzing many of the interfaces that our group has built [1, 6, 11, 22] and also by analyzing interfaces of commercial products (e.g. FrameMaker) to understand how they would be modelled in HUMANOID.

Made-Command-Executable
  Made-Command-Invocable
    Made-Command-Invocable-By-Pulldown-Menu
    Made-Command-Invocable-By-Button
    Made-Command-Invocable-By-Popup-Menu...
    Made-Command-Invocable-By-Dragging/Dropping...
    Made-Command-Invocable-By-Keyboard-Accelerator
  Had-Set-Method-For-Inputs
    Set-By-Default-Value
    Set-By-Dragging/Dropping...
    Set-By-Selection...
    Set-By-Type-In...
    Set-By-Chosen (In Case Of Alternative Values)
    Set-By-Dialogue-Box
    Set-By-Factoring

Sequencing-Control-Elaborated
  Executed-When-Read-To-Run
  Reset-Inputs-After-Execution
  Confirmed-Before-Execution

Shown-Dialogue-Box
Show-Dialogue-Box-When-Needed (Execute Otherwise)
Made-Command-Current-Selected
Made-Command-Default-Command

Has-Set-Method-For-Application-Inputs
Set-By-Default-Value
Set-By-Dragging/Dropping...
Set-By-Selection...
Set-By-Typing-In
Set-By-Chosen (In Case Of Alternative Values)

Made-Notified-When-Wrong-Value-Specified-For-Input
Beep-When-Incorrect
Revert-When-Incorrect
Message-When-Incorrect
Reset-When-Incorrect
Reinput-When-Incorrect
Error-Recover-When-Incorrect

Made-Object-Draggable
Dragging-Interactor (Behavior)-Elaborated
Start-Where-Specified
Event-Specified
Value(s)-To-Set-Specified
Command-To-Invoke-Specified
Command-Input(s)-To-Set-Specified
Feedback-Template-Elaborated

REFERENCES

1   P. Aberg and R. Neches. Clarification Dialogs: More Than Just Appearances For User Interfaces. *ISI working paper.*

2   W. Bennett, S. Boies, J. Gould, S. Greene and C. Wiecha. Transformations on a Dialog Tree: Rule-Based Mapping of Content to Style. In *Proceedings of the ACM SIGGRAPH Symposium on User Interface Software* and Technology, pp. 67-75, November 1989.

3   J. Conklin and M.L. Begeman. gIBIS: A Hypertext Tool for Exploratory Policy. In Proceedings CSCW'88. September 1988, pp. 140-152.

4   S. Draper and D.A. Norman. Software Engineering for User Interfaces. *IEEE Transactions on Software Engineering.* pages 252-258. March 1985.

5   J. D. Foley, W. C. Kim, S. Kovacevic and K. Murray. UIDE: An Intelligent User Interface Design Environment. In J. S. Sullivan and S. W. Tyler, editors, *Intelligent User Interfaces.* pp. 339-384. ACM Press, 1991.

6   B. Harp, P. Aberg, D. Benjamin, R. Neches, P. Szekely. DRAMA: An Application of a Logistic Shell. *ISI/RR-91-284.* March 1991

7   P. J. Hayes, P. Szekely and R. Lerner. Design Alternatives for User Interface Management Systems Based on Experience with COUSIN. In *Proceedings SIGCHI'85.* April 1989, pp. 169-175.

8   A. C. Lemke and G. Fischer. A Cooperative Problem Solving System for User Interface Design. *Proceedings of AAAI-90*, pp.479-484.

9   B. A. Myers, et. al. Garnet: Comprehensive Support for Graphical, Highly-Interactive User Interfaces. *IEEE Computer* 23(11), pp. 71-85, November, 1990.

10 B. A. Myers. State of the Art in User Interface Software Tools. In H. Rex Hartson and Deborah Hix. Ed., *Advances in Human-Computer Interaction, Volume 4,* Ablex Publishing, 1992.

11 R. Neches, D. Benjamin, J. Granacki, B. Harp, and P. Szekely. Scenarios/Agendas: A Reusable, Customizable Approach to User-System Collaboration in Complex Activities. *ISI working paper.*

12 R. Neches, J. Foley, P. Szekely, P. Sukaviriya, P. Luo, S. Kovacevic, and S. Hudson. Knowledgeable Development Environments Using Shared Design Models. *The 1993 International Workshop on Intelligent User Interfaces (IWIUI'93).* January 4-7, 1993.

13 Neuron Data, Inc. 1991. *Open Interface Toolkit.* 156 University Ave. Palo Alto, CA 94301.

14 NeXT, Inc. 1990. *Interface Builder,* Palo Alto, CA.

15 D. Olsen. MIKE: The Menu Interaction Kontrol Environment. *ACM Transactions on Graphics,* vol 17, no 3, pp. 43-50, 1986.

16 G. Singh and M. Green. A High-level User Interface Management System. In *Proceedings SIGCHI'89.* April 1989, pp. 133-138.

17 W. Swartout and R. Balzer. On the Inevitable Intertwining of Specification and Implementation. CACM 25, 7 (July 1982), pp. 1-9.

18 P. Szekely. Template-based mapping of application data to interactive displays. In *Proceedings UIST'90.* October 1990, pp. 1-9.

19 P. Szekely, P, Luo, and R. Neches. Facilitating the Exploration of Interface Design Alternatives: The HUMANOID Model of Interface Design. In *Proceedings SIGCHI'92.* May 1992, pp. 507-515

20 P. Szekely, P. Luo, and R. Neches. Beyond Interface Builders: Model-Based Interface Tools. In *Proceedings INTERCHI'93.* April 1993.

21 Y.Y. Wong. Rough and Ready Prototypes: Lessons from Graphic Design. In *Poster and Short Talks of CHI'92.* May 1992, pp.83-84.

22 J. Yen, R. Neches, M. Debellis, P. Szekely, and P. Aberg. BACKBORD: An Implementation of Specification by Reformulation. In J. S. Sullivan and S. W. Tyler, editors, *Intelligent User Interfaces.* pp. 421-444. ACM Press, 1991.

THE EVOLUTION OF AN INTERFACE FOR CHOREOGRAPHERS

Tom W. Calvert, Armin Bruderlin, Sang Mah, Thecla Schiphorst, Chris Welman

School of Computing Science
Simon Fraser University, Burnaby, B.C. Canada V5A 1S6
604-291-4588
e-mail address: tom@cs.sfu.ca

ABSTRACT

This paper describes the evolution of the interface to *Life Forms*, a compositional tool for the creation of dance choreography, and highlights some of the important lessons we have learned during a six year design and implementation period. The lessons learned can be grouped into two categories: 1) Process, and 2) Architecture of the Interface. Our goal in developing a tool for choreography has been to provide computer-based creative design support for the conception and development of dance. The evolution was driven by feedback from the choreographers and users who were members of the development team, combined with our knowledge of current thinking on design and composition. Although the interface evolved in a relatively unconstrained way, the resulting system has many of the features that theoretical discussion in human interface design has projected as necessary. The *Life Forms* interface has evolved incrementally with one major discontinuity where adoption of a new compositional primitive required a completely new version.

The choreography and composition of a dance is a complex synthesis task which has much in common with design. Thus, the lessons learned here are applicable to the development of interfaces to such applications as computer aided design.

KEYWORDS: Composition, design, user interface, dance, complexity, choreography, human animation.

1. INTRODUCTION

Like design, the composition and choreography of dance is a complex synthesis task. The design process contains elements that are recognized as common to all creative activity. Dance is the most technically complex form of human movement that exists in our culture, so development of a computer tool to assist in the creation of dance poses several research challenges. Choreography is a compositional design task that requires a set of skills related to creating, structuring, and forming. Building a computer interface that interacts with a choreographer's design skill set requires an understanding of the mental model of the choreographer's design process. As Herbert Simon noted, "The ability to communicate across fields--the common ground--comes from the fact that all who use computers in complex ways are using computers to design or to participate in the process of design."[13]

This area of research relates to the observation and understanding of how our creative process operates when we interact with computer systems, and how computer interface designers can help provide a more intuitive, direct, and transparent relationship with the creative idea [7,9]. In dance, where the creative idea is a movement idea, the goal is to visualize and create body movement in an immediate and responsive way, so the computer tool must become a "visual idea generator.". This paper summarizes the evolution of *Life Forms*, a computer based system to support composition and choreography, and discusses the lessons learned during the development (note that during the early stages of its development the *Life Forms* software was known as *Compose*). Many of the observations of the effectiveness of the interface came from users of the system: choreographers and dancers, as well as members of the design team. An example of a user who has had great impact on the evolution of the interface is Merce Cunningham who has been using the system for three years in New York City. *Life Forms* has been described in more detail at CHI'90 [12] and elsewhere [4].

In the years before starting this project in 1986, we had acquired considerable experience in working with dancers and choreographers and in the development of computer based systems for editing and interpreting dance notation [5,6]. Although systems for editing and interpreting notation have an important role in recording dance, archival tools are not necessarily very useful as tools for composition. In order to address the goal of supporting the compositional process we began the development a completely new system which would directly assist the working choreographer in creating movement. Merce Cunningham noted when he began working with *Life Forms*, "The thing that interested me most, from the very start was not the memory -- it wasn't simply notation --

but the fact that I could *make* new things" [LA Times May 15 1991].

The design and development was carried out by an interdisciplinary team made up of users such as choreographers, as well as systems architects and implementers. The process of designing the interface has been highly iterative - beginning from a very simple concept many, many alternatives have been suggested and evaluated while only a few have been implemented. At times the introduction of a new concept or approach has required a discontinuous design shift to occur in the otherwise incremental process.

Life Forms , which has been licensed to Kinetic Effects Inc. (Seattle, WA.), was initially developed on Silicon Graphics Iris workstations and this remains the platform for our research. However, to provide a version which would be more accessible to working dancers and choreographers we have also developed a version for the Apple Macintosh (this is now available from Macromedia).

2. DANCE COMPOSITION AND CHOREOGRAPHY

Typically, in composing a new dance, a choreographer starts from a particular stimulus. The stimulus can be as varied as a specific physical movement, a musical phrase, a visual image, or a state of mind. Even in the case of movement or an idea without particular context, what may be called "pure dance", the choreographer frequently develops thematic material through an exploratory structuring technique. Or the choreographer may develop the initial movement idea through some event or comment in the environment. If there is a specific context, such as a particular exploration of space, a striking dream image, or a piece of music or dramatic plot, the choreographer may draw out or illustrate spatial possibilities, may simply think or muse about a striking image to make further connections, or may listen to the music or observe the story and absorb its "sense", its dynamic qualities, its tempos or in the case of expressive dance its statement of emotional flow [2]. From all of these stimuli the choreographer explores or develops the generative idea, either intuitively or constructively using chance or deterministic structuring procedures, or "interprets" music, image, feeling or narrative, creating or finding movement that seems to successfully mirror its essence.

In the studio the choreographer works with the dancers to build the piece. The dancers may improvise with the choreographer's initial compositional material to provide movement. Some choreographers may work with notes, sketches, and floor plans, and some will record work in progress with a video camera to act as an objective eye, and a memory aid. This is an iterative and interactive process and proceeds over a period of weeks or months until the dance is complete. Some choreographers begin first with

the broad spatial outlines and then go back to develop the detailed movements, while others will begin with some specific movement material, then develop phrases, and then sections. Structurally, a choreographer will always need to move between the design of the overall dance and the design of the more detailed levels of section, phrase, and particular movement or gesture.

The computer based system is designed to assist, not to replace this process. Dance itself is still a kinesthetic experience and cannot be replaced by technology. But the computer based system can provide an extension, a visual idea generator that supports the iterative and interactive nature of the choreographic process. And like video, the tool also provides a record of compositional process while it has the advantage of storing movement in three dimensional space and allowing editing and modification to occur.

3. EVOLUTION OF THE INTERFACE

3.1. Concept

The first iteration of the system was conceived as a planning tool which would allow the choreographer to block out how individual dancers would move. Thus, some token for each dancer would be placed on a movable stage and when the configuration was acceptable, the configuration would be saved. The choreographer would then reconfigure the dancers for the next important scene. This would in turn be saved and the process would continue until the piece was complete. This is similar to the storyboard used by film directors and animators to help in planning a scene or action sequence. By flipping through these *keyframe* configurations, a crude animation could be produced for the composer to review.

From this early concept, the system's development has progressed through two main evolutionary stages. In the first, the tokens which served as the basic building block for a composition were static body shapes, or stances. In the second stage, the basic building block became an entire movement *sequence*. A description of the system at these stages has been given in some detail elsewhere [12, 4]. A synopsis is be provided here to summarize the system and highlight recent features before considering the lessons learned during the development process.

3.2. Composition Based on Stances

In the first useful version of the system, key scenes are constructed by placing figures in particular stances on a stylized stage at a specific point in time. The stage itself can be tilted and turned to view the scene from any vantage

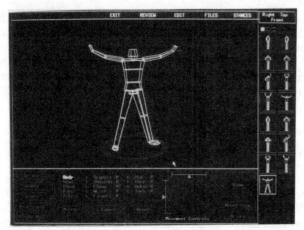

Figure 1: a) Old Stance-based Body Editor.

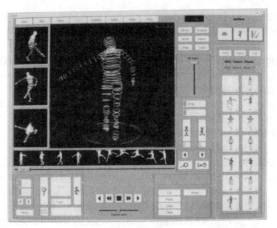

Figure 1: b) New Sequence Editor.

point. The stances are selected from a collection of menus (see right side of Figure 1a), each of which display a number of different body shapes to choose from. A typical menu, for example, might consist of ballet shapes, or perhaps different lying positions. Once several keyframe configurations have been entered, the scene can be played back. During playback the system performs simple interpolation of position, orientation and body shape for each figure, to give the composer a quick approximation of how the scene might appear in a live performance.

The Body Editor allows the choreographer to create new body shapes and add them to the menus, or to edit existing shapes. In a separate window a simplified three dimensional representation of the human body is presented for editing. A limb segment can be selected and its position interactively adjusted with a hemispherical slider conceptually similar to a virtual trackball [8]. When a posture has been fully defined in this manner, the shape can be transferred to one of the stance menus. In this way the user can refine and extend the palette of shapes available.

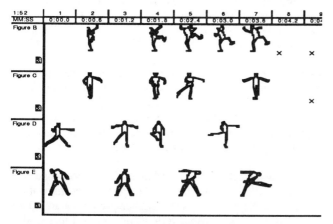

Figure 2: The stance-based Macintosh timeline window.

A third window, the Timeline, provides a summary of the body stances for each figure as they develop over time, similar to the notion of a musical score (Figure 2). The Timeline provides information about the temporal development of the composition which is lacking in the previous windows, showing both the relative timing of the key stances assigned to a figure, as well as the temporal relationship between different figures. Simple editing operations provide a mechanism by which movement over time can be copied, cut and pasted in a manner familiar to anybody who has used a word processor.

This simple stance-based system has proved to be a viable tool for choreography and human figure animation, and is the model implemented in the Macintosh version of the program.

3.3. Composition Based on Sequences

As the users gained experience with the earlier system, they came to realize that a better building block for a dance composition was a movement sequence rather than a simple stance. To meet this need, a major redevelopment was necessary. Menus of stances were replaced by menus of movement sequences, which could be as short as a single stance or as long as many hundreds of keyframes. As before, composition in space involves making a selection from a menu and placing it on the stage. However, rather than dragging and orienting a single stance, now the user works with a complete movement sequence as a primitive. Although the stage view still displays only a single shape to represent a sequence, a line indicating the path traveled by the figure during the sequence is also displayed. Multiple sequences can be strung together for a single figure, just as multiple stances were before.

To facilitate the creation and editing of sequences, most of the functionality of the earlier version was combined to form a new Sequence Editor (Figure 1b), which replaced the Body Editor. In this window a single figure can be manipulated into a series of keyframe stances, which may then be played back as an animation. A timeline strip below the figure offers the same editing capabilities as the original Timeline window (see Figure 1b centre display strip). In addition the timing of portions of the sequence can be adjusted by stretching or shrinking ranges on the timeline. A major enhancement has been the addition of direct manipulation of the figure with *inverse kinematics* [14], allowing the user to drag a chain of body parts around rather than adjusting each part individually (Figure 3). Sequences may also be imported from external sources and added to menus. Another major addition is the provision of procedural movement which is generated by algorithms rather than frame by frame specification of the choreographer. An example is the generation of customized walks[3].

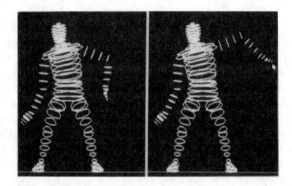

Figure 3: Selecting and dragging the arm using inverse kinematics - the cursor is on the hand.

With detailed timing within a sequence being adjusted in the Sequence Editor, the main Timeline becomes simpler (Figure 4). The sequences assigned to each dancer are simply shown as boxes which can only be edited (cut, copy or paste) as a unit. However, in this mode the choreographer can very quickly build up complex movement for each dancer by assembling sequences. Users found it helpful if the Timeline is displayed on top of a stage view so that the multiple dancers can be animated at the same time that the inter-relationships in time are being reviewed.

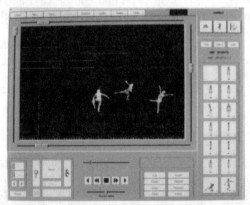

Figure 4: The new Timeline in sequence-based system.

A recent addition to the system is the ability to add digitized sound to the composition. The choreography can be synchronized with the soundtrack during playback.

This description reflects the current state of the system which runs on the Silicon Graphics family of IRIS workstations.

4. LESSONS LEARNED

The Evolution of the *Life Forms* interface came about through many iterations. Each incremental development phase was accompanied and even initiated by new understanding, based on observations and experience with using the interface. Often these lessons prompted new ideas that resonated strongly enough within the design team to affect the conception, design and implementation of the interface. These lessons can be loosely grouped into two categories. *Process* refers to the design process and choreographic process in terms of how it was experienced and affected by the interface. *Architecture* of the Interface refers to experiences and observations dealing more directly with what technical interface design issues became focal points of our work.

4.1. Process

Observation 1: An Interdisciplinary Development Team is Necessary

An interdisciplinary development team involving users, systems architects and implementers is essential. In this case the users were choreographers, most of whom had no technical background, and particular attention was given to maintaining the level of their involvement in the design process. Users who are members of the team often become involved in the technical developments and lose their detachment. Thus some limited turnover in team membership can be helpful.

Observation 2: The Role of Users

Involvement of users who are part of the development team, although very useful, is no substitute for external users who can bring a perhaps technologically naive yet creatively insightful point of view to the process. At all stages the system under development must be tested by appropriate (i.e. naive and expert) users.

There is a special role for a "Mentor User" - someone who is a true leader in the field and who can pioneer innovation. In our case New York choreographer, Merce Cunningham recipient of the MacArthur fellowship amongst many other choreographic honors and awards has served as a Mentor User for three years. Cunningham has spent almost 50 years challenging assumptions and traditional notions of what dance is and how it can be made, and continues to do so in his use of *Life Forms*. Cunningham balances the computer's precise representation with the realities of human physicality, "I look at some things and say, "well that's impossible for a dancer to do. But if I look long enough I could think of a way it could be done. Not exactly as its done on the screen, but it could prompt my eye to see something I've never thought of before." [Merce Cunningham, quoted in the LA Times, May 15, 1991]

Observation 3: Discontinuities in Development Are Sometimes Necessary

As experience was gained with the original stance-based system and as hardware capability increased, it became obvious that a higher level building block for dance composition was necessary. The implementation of a sequence as the design building block (rather than a stance) enabled choreographers to develop design "chunks". This allowed composition to occur on more than one conceptual level. A sequence can be created, manipulated, varied and placed with other sequences at a rate that enables the visual response to provide a meaningful creative feedback loop. Major design re-implementation was required to meet this need, and correspondingly a major break in the development process was necessary. Merce Cunningham noted in response to this development in *Life Forms*: "What was like photographs is now like film, and what started out as work with positions has developed into work with phrases. .. It's remarkable, they keep adding things to it ... it will enlarge it [dance]. The system now has multiple possibilities".

Sometimes a new concept requires a major re-implementation of a system. Discontinuities of this type should be minimized, but from time to time are necessary, especially when they provide a major conceptual breakthrough to occur.

Observation 4: Time from Conception to Implementation

Design is an iterative process, and for this project, at least, the process of designing the way the program functions and how that functionality is presented to the user has been no exception. The existing system is a result of many iterations, based largely on comments and suggestions from the users within the development team. Unfortunately the realities of software development mean that the turnaround time from idea to implementation is often measured in weeks (or more). In our experience, this not only inhibits the whole design process, but also may tend to make developers resistant to good suggestions that make prior work obsolete. A strict adherence to standard modular coding practices has been beneficial, limiting the scope of source code changes required to support new features. Also the adoption of a GUI toolkit and interactive interface designer has been a great help for rapid prototyping and modifications to the interface. The emergence of more comprehensive toolkits for interactive 3D applications,

such as SGI's Inventor [11], also promises to decrease the time from idea to realization.

Observation 5: Impact of *Life Forms* on the Way Choreographers Work

Often, choreographers who learned to use the system reported that it had changed the way they thought about choreography and how they went about composing. This is interesting, but indicates the difficulty in objectively evaluating a tool, which changes the user's conception of the task. At the same time it illustrates that the ideas and work of all members of the development team have a direct effect on one another, and that artists are willing to risk, to experiment and to ask questions about new ways of working. Cunningham, always willing to expand his experience of looking at and creating movement, has said, "The common thread in all these dances [made with *Life Forms*] is that they are all different. That's what interests me. I am not interested in the idea of repeating something. What's exciting is when I come across an idea that I'm unfamiliar with, or when I have a question for myself, ... if its something that interests you deeply, you will find a way." [Anchorage Daily News Feb. 23 1992]

Among comments from other choreographers who used *Life Forms* to create movement were the following: "I was able to work more directly with internal imagery. It freed me from my own personal movement bias. I was able to have dancers on the screen take on movements that I wouldn't have dreamed of attempting on my own"; or, "I was much more likely to use movement outside my comfort range and vocabulary and venture into the realm of the unknown."; and, "Working with the system inspired me in new ways simply because of the visual nature of working with it.", and "I found my choreographic process with *Life Forms* to be more intuitive, more 'out of body', not hampered by my own limitations or concerns for dancers well-being, nor even concerned with the outcome necessarily." [York University Choreographic Workshop, Summer 1992]

Much of the creative process reflected in the previous responses relate to the visual nature of the interface, and the creative process that is evoked by working with choreography in a visual way. Choreography is also very often a kinesthetic experience and it is well known that different choreographers have preferred methods of working. One choreographer in particular found that , "I discovered how little I rely on visual awareness in the studio, that I tend to work with a kinesthetic awareness of the body, and of movement coming from within the body. I initially found it quite difficult to make the transition from recognizing the computer image on the screen and seeing it on the body in the studio"

These comments reflect both the multiplicity of methods in which choreographers conceive and create dance, and also an unexpected willingness to work with what exists, even when it may be different from what has been learned before.

Again, perhaps Cunningham says it best when he stated, "My point in working with *Life Forms* is not to complain about what it can't do, but to look and see what it can do. *Life Forms* can enlarge possibilities and help the way that people look at dance." [LA Daily News, May 9 1991]

4.2. Architecture of the Interface:

Observation 6: Reduce Task Complexity with Alternate Views

Early in the development process it was realized that the original concept of letting the choreographer do all development on the Stage (as in a real studio) was limiting. The only way to review how the piece developed in time was to play it through as an animation and although the animation is useful, just as in reviewing a musical composition, it is often possible to obtain insights from the score which are not obvious in a performance. Thus, it was decided to add a display which set out a representation of the piece as it develops in time.

Another simple addition to the original system was a window in which the body stance of individual dancers could be built up, edited and customized. After considerable experimentation we developed a Body Editor similar to that shown in Figure 1a) which was later extended to the Sequence Editor shown in Figure 1b).

These observations indicate that task complexity can be reduced by providing alternative ways to view the development of the piece. This is consistent with other experience in complex problem solving [13].

Observation 7: Separating High Level Specification from Detailed Choreography

When the original stance-based system was replaced by a sequence-based system, the power of the user to create dances was greatly increased. This change allowed the user to work with a higher level primitive. Of course, it was still necessary to create these sequences on a frame by frame basis, unless a procedural method was used.

As noted, when a body editor was added to the original system, it made it possible to separate the detailed choreography of individual figures from the more general choreography of multiple interacting figures. In the same way, when the Sequence Editor was added to the sequence based version of the system, it made it possible to edit the timing of the moves of an individual figure separately from the more general timing in the Timeline of the sequences assigned to all dancers.

These observations confirm that the process is hierarchical and that the composer is empowered by separating detail from higher level actions. However, we have observed that users frequently switch back and forth between low level

detail and higher level actions, so these changes must be made as easy as possible.

Observation 8: Access to Explicit Knowledge

It is obvious that those involved in creative synthesis tasks do not start from scratch. They bring to each new composition the history of their own previous work, as well as that of others. They also have a background in the standard concepts of their field. The menus in our system are visual archives for these types of knowledge. Browsing is supported by allowing the user to click on a menu item to reveal a flip-book animation of the stored sequence.

In this class of tasks, the most powerful access to knowledge is through the memory of the artist. But this should be supplemented where possible with readily accessible files of previous work and with procedural generators.

Observation 9: Procedural Generation of Movement Sequences

While the sequence-based system empowers the user, the movement sequences still have to be generated somehow; building up sequences frame by frame in the Sequence Editor is extremely tedious. A more powerful approach involves finding a procedural method to generate a whole class of movements such as locomotion. Bruderlin [3] has developed a procedural approach to walking - this can generate a wide variety of walks which can be used in building sequences. The interface shown in Figure 5 allows the user to customize the walk by changing parameters (e.g.. velocity, bounciness, torso sway) to characterize the person being animated - an older person, a child, a tired person, etc.

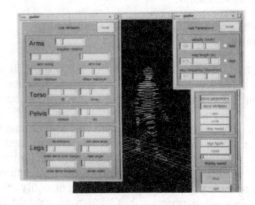

Figure 5: Interface for real-time, procedural walking module.

The knowledge of movement available through a procedural generator greatly increases the power of the user providing the procedures can be customized. This tool can replace a part of the choreographic process by automatically generating a feasible movement pattern. But it need not take anything away from the creative choreographer, since the sequence generated can be modified for specific situations.

Observation 10: Simple Abstract Models may be as Useful as more Realistic Models

As shown in Figure 6, a variety of body models have been used - they include a simple stick figure, an outline figure, a figure defined by contours and a shaded solid figure. In early implementations the simplest figures were used because they could be drawn most quickly. With faster processors it has become possible to use more complex and realistic figures. However, users often find that the simplest figures are effective for their needs - research in psychology has shown that we can perceive human movement quite accurately from only a few points on the body [10]. The shaded figures certainly add realism - but it is not clear whether users prefer this to an abstraction. Also, users are more likely to be critical of imperfections in more realistic figures while they accept abstractions for what they are.

Body models which are simple abstractions are often quite acceptable and may be preferred over more realistic shaded models.

kinematic chain. This is intuitively attractive and users like the facility, but our experiences have shown that it may be difficult to accurately duplicate specific body stances.

Users like direct manipulation, but it does not always give the best results.

5. DISCUSSION AND CONCLUSIONS

The composition and choreography of dance is a complex synthesis and design task. Many computer based tools have been developed to assist designers but very few of these systems give users sufficient freedom to experiment and be creative. Our goal in developing a tool for choreography was to use the computer to provide creative design support during the process of conceiving of and developing a dance. Design evolution was often initiated by feedback from the choreographers and users who were members of the design team, combined with our knowledge of current thinking of design and composition [1, 13]. We started with a very simple concept (blocking figures on a stage) and over a six year period have evolved a very sophisticated system.

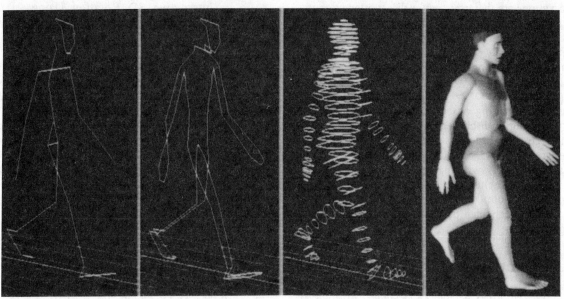

Figure 6: Four different body models: stick, outline, contour and "fleshed out" figures.

Observation 11: Users Prefer Direct Interaction

In the original Body Editor, the user had the choice of adjusting limb orientation either by directly manipulating it on the screen with the mouse or by using linear or spherical potentiometers on the screen. Direct manipulation was generally preferred, but sometimes it was difficult to see just how the 3-d body was being moved on the 2-d display. Inverse kinematics allows the user to move the endpoints of limbs without first adjusting other segments in the

The principal conclusion that can be drawn is that this model for the development process has been successful and that a very useful system has evolved. The system evolved incrementally with one major discontinuity where adoption of a new compositional primitive required a completely new version. Another conclusion is that although the interface evolution was driven in a relatively unconstrained way by the choreographers in the design team, the resulting system has many of the features that theoretical discussion has projected as necessary [12,13]. Specifically:

• The process is hierarchical and tools should support high level (more conceptual) and low level (more detailed) specification.

• The complexity of the task can be minimized by making alternate views available (e.g. Stage, Sequence Editor, Timeline).

• The composer is empowered by access to knowledge. In general, the internal knowledge of the user can be supplemented with (a) explicit knowledge in the form of stances, sequences, etc stored in libraries and displayed in menus; (b) procedural knowledge where algorithms have been developed to capture the essence of common movements (procedural walking is discussed above); and (c) declarative knowledge, where rules and constraints are stored in a knowledge base and are available to an expert system for resolution of complex interactions. The current interface provides access to explicit and procedural knowledge and users have found this to be valuable. Methods to incorporate declarative knowledge still have to be developed.

Other observations are that users prefer direct interaction in specifying body stances although they may sacrifice specificity of exact joint location in space. Users prefer interactivity to accuracy. Users also prefer abstractions in objects such as body models over realism when realism affects real-time display.

One of the more startling observations we have made in relation to working with choreographers is that not only has the interface evolved in response to user feedback, but that choreographers method of creating has evolved or enlarged as a result of working with a computer-based creative tool. Our conclusion is that the design process is symbiotic, and that both the design of the interface and the design of the task for which the interface is created effect one another deeply.

6. REFERENCES

1. Akin, O. How Do Architects Design?, In *AI and Pattern Recognition in Computer Aided Design,* ed. Latombe, IFIP, North-Holland, 1978, pp. 65-103.

2. Brightman P. Making dances with algorithms: Towards a theory of choreography, based on the use of computer programs and Laban concepts. M.A. Thesis, Columbia University, 1984.

3. Bruderlin, A. and Calvert, T.W. Goal-Directed, Dynamic Animation of Human Walking. *Computer Graphics (SIGGRAPH 89)*, vol. 23, (1989), pp. 233-242.

4. Calvert, T.W., Welman, C., Gaudet, S., Schiphorst, T. and Lee,C. Composition of Multiple Figure Sequences for Dance and Animation. The Visual Computer, vol. 7, 1991, pp. 114-121.

5. Calvert, T.W. Towards a Language for Human Movement. Computers and the Humanities, 20:2, (1986), pp. 35-43.

6. Calvert, T.W., Chapman, J., and Patla, A. Aspects of the Kinematic Simulation of Human Movement. IEEE Computer Graphics and Applications, vol. 2, (November 1982), pp. 41- 50.

7. Card, S., Moran, T., and Newell, A. The Psychology of Human-Computer Interaction. Lawrence Erlbaum Assoc., Hillsdale, N.J., 1983.

8. Chen, M., Mountford, J. and Sellen, A. "A Study in Interactive 3D Rotation Using 2D Control Devices". *Computer Graphics* 22, 4, 1988, pp. 121-129.

9. Hartson, H.R., and Hix, D. Human-Computer Interface Development: Concepts and Systems. ACM Computing Surveys 21, 1, (1989), pp. 5-92.

10. Johansson, G. *Perception and Psychology,* 14, pp. 201-211, 1973.

11. Strauss, P., and Carey, R. An Object-Oriented 3D Graphics Toolkit. Computer Graphics (SIGGRAPH 92), 26, 2, (July 1992), pp. 341-349.

12. Schiphorst, T., Calvert, T., Lee, C., Welman, C. and Gaudet, S. Tools for Interaction with the Creative Process of Composition, Proc. CHI'90, (Seattle, April 1990), pp. 167-174.

13. Simon, H.A. *The Sciences of the Artificial.* MIT Press, Cambridge, MA., 1969.

14. Welman, C. "Inverse Kinematics Through Differential Manipulation". In Proceedings of the Western Computer Graphics Symposium , (1992), pp. 123-128.

Human-Machine Perceptual Cooperation

Francis K.H. Quek and Michael C. Petro

Artificial Intelligence Laboratory

The University of Michigan
Ann Arbor, MI 48109
E-mail: quek@eecs.umich.edu

ABSTRACT

The Human-Machine Perceptual Cooperation (HMPC) paradigm combines a human operator's high level reasoning with machine perception to solve spatio-perceptual intensive problems. HMPC defines two channels of interaction: the *focus of attention* (FOA) by which the user directs the attention of machine perception, and *context*. As the user moves the FOA across a display via a pointing device, a *smart cursor* operates proactively on the data, highlighting objects which satisfy the current context. The FOA permits foveal emphasis, enabling the user to vary motor precision with image clutter. HMPC provides for contexts at four levels of abstraction. This permits the efficiency of the system to degrade gracefully as data quality worsens. We describe a document analysis application to which HMPC is applied. [1] In this project, a human operator works with a machine to convert scanned raster maps into vector format.

KEYWORDS:

Human-Computer Interaction, Shared Perception, Map Conversion, Document Image Analysis, Telerobotics.

INTRODUCTION

Interest in telerobotics and teleoperation has spurred significant interest in how humans and machines may share in the control of articulated and free-flying robots. Such efforts usually concentrate on robotics and ways in which human motion may be transduced into robot control signals. The need to perceive and model the external world is invariably placed on the human operator. The operator's perceptual system is loaded with sensor data by stereo goggles, video screens and

[1] This research is supported by the NASA CCDS's Space Automation and Robotics Center and The Center for Mapping, Subgrant number 333747SC.

tactile information to facilitate direct teleoperation. In such operation, sensing, computation and communications serve entirely as means for presenting perceptual information to the operator. This perceptual loading is unnecessary and undesirable. The purpose is to complete the robotic task – not to extend the human operator's experience. The application of virtual reality technology is inappropriate and at times undesirable [4] for such endeavours. More importantly, the capability of human operators to perform teleoperation using systems "whose sole purpose is to provide the operator with the property of 'teleexistence' or 'telepresence'" has recently been called into question. Lumelsky [10] states: "... the observed difficulties go beyond the system design and seem to relate to the ability (or, rather, inability) of the operator to process geometrical data. .... The human capability for space orientation and motion planning even in relatively simple planning tasks is quite limited."

The work described in telerobotic literature deals predominantly with the sharing of motor control. We are not aware of any work which studies how we can bring machine vision to bear on the problem by facilitating the sharing of perceptual tasks. We present an approach called *Human-Machine Perceptual Cooperation* (HMPC) which permits a human-machine interaction at different levels of abstraction and which exploits both human and machine perceptual capabilities.

HMPC is a paradigm which permits the sharing of perceptual load between a human operator and computer vision/image processing. The goal is to apply computation as a proactive aide to solve perceptio-motor intensive problems in a symbiotic fashion. While HMPC was originally conceived for telerobotics, it is a general human-machine interaction paradigm applicable to a class of problems which involves spatial and perceptual interaction. These include medical image interpretation, target acquisition, and remote sensing. Our first application, which we offer as an instance of HMPC, is in document interpretation.

Key to the development of an effective human-machine interaction strategy is an understanding of what is "intuitive" to the human user. In our quest for the appropriate channels for human- machine discourse of spatial and perceptual information, the questions we ask are: How do humans exchange such information? What are the native mechanisms of the human perceptual system which respond to such intercourse? What kinds of feedback are neccessary to assist the 'speaker' (here used loosely to represent the originator of the information)? And, how might we apply computation to approximate this interaction? In the rest of this paper, we shall define HMPC, providing some psychological/biological and linguistic motivation for it, and describe our architecture for supporting HMPC and outline the machine vision/image processing applied.

HMPC

Consider the interaction in which one map reader provides directions for another. The first person may say, "We shall pick up the highway here [*pointing roughly to a portion of a highway*], and get off this exit [*pointing again*]." This intercourse embodies the gist of HMPC. Two kinds of information are conveyed: *context* (what to look for) and *focus of attention* (FOA) (where to look). The level of abstraction employed in the discussion is that of task level objects (highways and exits). We posit that these elements of communication are necessary and sufficient for the exchange of spatial and perceptual information. HMPC adopts these two channels and provides for several levels of context abstraction.

Motivation

A large body of literature describes research on visual attention (e.g. [23, 13, 20, 11]). An in-depth review of the relevant psychological, biological and linguistic literature is beyond the scope of this paper. We shall, however, provide motivation for our approach by reviewing a representative sample of attention research in computational vision [8], experimental psychology [20], neuro-physiology [11], and linguistics [6].

Hurlbert and Poggio [8] suggest that computer vision needs mechanisms for focus of spatial attention to be able to perform recognition tasks. They cite several psychophysical experiments which indicate that human vision possesses a parallel feature-based pre-attention mechanism as well as a serial search mechanism. The former mechanism detects (but does not identify) separable features and provides direction for visual focus. The latter is a 'searchlight' based serial mechanism for feature conjunctions and recognition. The authors further suggest that the focus of attention may serve to suppress processing in irrelevant domains and enhance processing in the salient region. They further suggest that the power of attentional mechanisms is neither fully understood nor tapped in machine vision research.

Sagi and Julesz [20] report experiments in which they measured the processing time of human subjects during target detection and target discrimination as a function of the number of targets in the test. It was found that the processing time increases with number of targets for discrimination, and remains constant for detection of feature orientation. While humans perform visual detection and localization in parallel, discrimination has to be done serially. "Knowing 'what' even a single feature is requires time-consuming search by focal attention."

Moran and Desimonne [11] posit that our immediate awareness of only a small fraction of the vast quantity of stimuli indicates that most of the information is filtered out centrally. They investigated the effect of stimuli as they pass from the straite cortex (V1) through the prestriate areas into the inferior temporal cortex (IT) of rhesus monkeys. Cells along this pathway have increasingly large receptive fields (respond to larger regions of stimuli in the visual field). They performed single cell recordings in the visual cortex of the monkeys. They first located cells which respond to features in small portions of the visual field. The monkeys were trained to attend to stimuli at one location and to ignore those at another location in the visual field. Identical stimuli were presented at both locations so that any difference in readings can be attributed solely to attention. Their experiments showed that a prestriate area V4 cell's response was significantly attenuated when the animal attended to the ineffective stimuli even though the effective stimuli is in the receptive field of the cell. When the animal attended to the effective stimuli, the cell's response was strong. They concluded from this that "... attenuation of irrelevant information can be based purely on spatial location." Striate cortex cells were unaffected by attention. Furthermore, they discovered that while cells in V4 are attenuated only when their visual fields encompass both attended and unattended stimuli, none of the cells in the IT respond well to unattended stimuli – indicating that there is at least a two-stage filtering process in selective attention.

Hinrichs and Polanyi [6] examined a corpus of *Spatial Planning Protocols* to study how speakers construct plans interactively. In their experiment, subjects played a "Travelling through Europe" game. Two subjects played against a researcher on a game board showing a map of nine cities. The goal of the game was to devise an itinerary of travel to visit all the cities with the smallest number of moves along legal routes. The subjects were allowed to update and change plans at any time during the game. It was found that without considering pointing gestures made by the subjects, the interactive discourse was incomplete, but when gestures were factored in, the elliptical fragmentary discourse became intelligible plans of action.

Principles Gleaned and Applied

While the necessary understanding to develop a general attention focusing algorithm is yet beyond the scope of current knowledge, if a human operator were to direct the attention searchlight, the principles of selective attention may be applied.

That discrimination within the FOA is a serial process suggests that conventional hardware and vision algorithms may be sufficient to analyze the data in FOA regions with acceptable performance. In HMPC, the FOA takes the form of a square region centered around a cursor which tracks a pointing device (e.g. a mouse). Each time the focus region changes, the data in the FOA region is processed. We call the entity which tracks the FOA and performs the processing the *smart cursor*.

Processing within the FOA may be opportunistic. Since whatever mechanism drives selective attention also provides cues of what features/objects are salient, the computation can aggressively reject ineffective stimuli or accept effective stimuli. HMPC processing, likewise, employs an aggressive recognition/filtering strategy. Since the human operator selects the context, the system can apply very specific operators to extract the specified entity. HMPC provides immediate feedback to the user by highlighting or not highlighting objects in the FOA. This feedback serves as the system's response in the human-machine dialog. The user is free to accept the interpretation (by clicking a mouse button) or to reject the interpretation by redirecting the FOA.

HMPC applies the above principles in its machine perception component on the belief that mimicking human perceptual characteristics will provide for a more intuitive interface. If humans communicate spatial information with each other by directing their conversant's attention and providing contextual information, this would make similar communication with a machine more natural for the user. This intuition is borne out by [6]. The interactive discourse between subjects in the experiment described integrates deictic gestures (which direct attention) and speech which provides the contextual information. That it was not possible to interpret the gestures without the audible utterances suggest the importance of the contextual aspect of the intercourse.

The subjects in [6] referred to task level entities (cities, legal routes etc.) in their discourse. At times, the conversant would use demonstratives (e.g. this, that) or locatives (e.g. here, there) without specifying the particular referent objects. In these cases, the referent is one of a possible set of objects. The ambiguity is resolved because only one object in that set appears in the area specified by deixis. This suggests humans communicate at least two levels of abstraction in spatial discourse accompanied by deixis: the object and the class levels. In the former, the identity of the target object is provided, while in the latter, the context is a set of candidate objects. By extension, HMPC adds two levels to the hierarchy, specifying the *class*, *object*, *feature* and *data* levels. If the system fails to recognize an object, it requests the user to locate distinguishing features. In interpersonal discourse, this is equivalent to a cloud gazer helping a companion to see an ostrich-like form by directing her attention to a long thin cloud segment which constitutes the neck. If all else fails, the user may provide precise locations with the cursor cross hairs. In this case, the system performs no perceptual processing. This constitutes data level interaction.

HMPC MAP CONVERSION SYSTEM

We are applying HMPC conversion of paper-based maps into vector representation (lines, regions, and symbols). This is the most pressing need in data acquisition for GIS. The United States Geological Survey (USGS) alone maintains quadrangle maps which cover all of U.S. territory [1]. Each city maintains a plethora of utility, political, and road-system maps. To date, fully automated conversion of these maps to vector form is not possible [21]. In their 1979 survey paper, Nagy and Wagle [12] describe map conversion as a labor-intensive task of manually tracing maps on digitizing tables. By and large, the same situation exists today [21, 5, 18, 22]. Maps are digitized one point at a time by a human cartographer "with a hand-held 'cursor' – a mouse-like device with cross-hairs and keypad" [18]. This work requires a high degree of visual-motor coordination and is susceptible to the attendant operator fatigue and digitization error.

The impediment to fully automated digitization is that existing maps are meant for human consumption and thus "exploit the human user's heuristic reasoning and world knowledge."[9] Consequently such maps pose severe problems for computer perception systems. Often, lines representing rivers or roads are broken to accomodate text placement; political boundaries often blend into geographic entities like rivers; etc. The result is that automatic map conversion systems generally require a significant amount of human inspection and editing to remove interpretation errors.

We are implementing an HMPC system for map conversion[16]. The system performs interactive line extraction of solid lines of various thicknesses and extraction and recognition for isolated symbols. In this section, we shall describe the architecture of HMPC and detail the work done on line following and symbol handling. Figure 1 is a sample of the kind of map on which the system operates. The system is written in C++ in

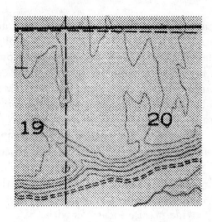

Figure 1: The 512 × 512 map image

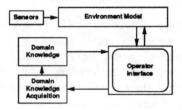

Figure 2: General HMPC system architecture

an X11/Motif environment.

Architecture

Figure 2 outlines the four major components which make up a HMPC system. The salient aspect of this architecture is that all perceptual operations are mitigated through the operator interface. It is here that machine perception algorithms are integrated with human input.

Environment Model: The *environment model*, EM, represents the data on which HMPC operates. In map conversion, this involves two databases: the original raster data and the entities extracted. Maps to be handled by the systems are typically very large (maps are normally scanned at 500 to 1000 pixels per inch). In our system, these large scanned maps are sub-divided into several raster files for handling. The EM raster database handles these raster files in such a way that the user 'sees' a virtual extended map. This involves managing the necessary coordinate transformations, caching the raster images for processing and performing the necessary scaling operations for display in the operator interface. The EM also keeps track of the interpreted vector entities. Each vector object in the database possesses attributes relating it to the raster object from which it was extracted and other relational and parametric information. The EM keeps book on which which objects are extracted from which raster file. The EM is a dynamic evolving representation of the HMPC envir-

onment, hence its name.

Domain Knowledge: The *domain knowledge* is coded as a model database of the objects which the system is required to perceive. While the EM is dynamic, the *domain knowledge* is a static representation of expected objects and features anticipated for the application. The principal component of HMPC *domain knowledge* is a *context*. The *active context* determines the *level of abstraction* at which HMPC operates and the entities which the system currently recognizes.

A **class** level context specifies a set of objects to be recognized. For example, the operator may select a railway context. Embedded in this context is a set of *models* of railway lines, railway junction symbols, railway bridge symbols, station symbols and railway crossing symbols. As the operator moves the FOA around the screens, entities which satisfy any model in this set will be highlighted for the operator's acceptance or rejection.

An **object** level context specifies a single object for recognition. As with class contexts, symbols matching an object context are highlighted for operator acceptance as the FOA passes over them. The operator may, for example, specify a road context. Notice that the particular parametric model and image processing details are hidden from the operator. In both the class and object layers, the operator interacts with HMPC in terms of the semantic entities contained in the map. When an object context is active, HMPC extracts entities in the FOA which match the model of the object. Examples of object level contexts are roads (of various line thicknesses), political boundaries (these may be broken lines of various interval patterns and thicknesses), city symbols (or any other symbol), text characters of various fonts and text strings.

Consider the situation in which the entity to be extracted is deformed by noise or occlusion such that object level interpretation is not possible. In this case, HMPC can descend to a **feature** level context. Each object model has encoded in it a local feature decomposition. In the context of map reading, features may take the form of blobs (regions) with a bounding box threshold, contour segments, line segments, circular arcs, and corners. The operator is then prompted for the location of these features (by highlighting the desired feature on a 'prompting image' of the parent object). The mechanism for the user to provide the feature locations is again by moving the FOA to the desired feature. Such component features are prompted for in turn until the entity is extracted.

The lowest level of abstraction in HMPC is the **data level** at which the operator specifies precise locations of objects. For line extraction the operator will have to align cursor cross- hairs to way-points of the desired line and the system will 'connect-the-dots' with straight line segments. For symbol extraction, the operator will specify the point where the symbol resides and provide the identity of the symbol on a keyboard. This, incidently, is the way 'heads-up' digitization is performed in the GIS industry[21].

The different levels of abstraction allows HMPC to operate along a continuum of perceptio- motor loading on the operator. This allows the performance system to degrade gracefully while maintaining support for interpretation of the data.

Domain Knowledge Acquisition: This component of the system adds new models to the domain knowledge database. The methods by which these models are built are application dependent. There are two modes in which this is done. The first, which we are currently employing, is to have libraries of contexts and models hand-coded and incorporated to the HMPC system. The second is to have the system compute its own models under operator guidance (teach-by-showing paradigm).

The hand-coding of context and model libraries is analogous to adding rule-bases to a production system shell in expert systems. To have HMPC handle a different kind of map, the user will have to either purchase a new library or have one written.

In the teach-by-showing mode, the user will be queried as to the type (linear object or isolated symbol) and constraints (whether scale and rotation variation is allowed) of the object. Based upon these specifications, the system selects the appropriate features to be applied. The user then picks out the blob or line segment which represents the entity and the system computes the feature parameters for recognition.

Operator Interface: The operator interface is the heart of an HMPC system. It is here that the operator provides the *context* and FOA for the machine, and where the machine provides feedback and prompts the operator for information. The operator interface also allows the operator to view the contents of the EM, specify the data to be viewed, perform global processing on the sensory data, and add new models to the domain knowledge database. We shall discuss these under the headings of *FOA and the Smart Cursor*, *Context Specification*, and *Map Display Management*.

FOA and the Smart Cursor: In HMPC the FOA is defined as a square region surrounding a graphic cursor. We term the active component of HMPC which performs the computation in the FOA the *smart cursor*, SC. In our system, this cursor appears as a cross hair and

a box around the FOA, and is controlled by the mouse pointing device. The SC possesses a working raster area and an active operating function (the SCO) which is determined by the active context. When the human operator moves the mouse cursor in the active map window, the FOA region under the cursor is copied into the SC working area and the SCO is activated. This operation is repeated whenever the mouse moves in the window. For map reading, the SCO begins with a histogram-based thresholding operation followed by a connected component analysis. The first primitive which the SC uses is a run length description of the regions (called RLR for run length region) in the FOA.

If an object in the FOA satisfies the active context (as computed by the SCO), it is highlighted for user acceptance or rejection. If more than one RLR in the FOA satisfies the active context, we use a weighting function to select the appropriate one. Here, we introduce the concept of *foveal significance*.

We specify a foveal weighting mask in the FOA comprising concentric squares of different weights:

$$\mathcal{M} \equiv \bigcup_{j=1}^{n} \Gamma_j \tag{1}$$

$$\Gamma_j \equiv \mathcal{A}_j \bigcap \overline{\mathcal{A}_{j-1}} \tag{2}$$

$$\mathcal{W}_{p_i} = w_j \ \forall p_i = (x_i, y_i) \in \Gamma_j \tag{3}$$

where

$\mathcal{M}$	= foveal weighting mask
$\mathcal{A}_k$	= $[(x,y) \mid (x_0 - \frac{1}{2}\ell_j < x < x_0 + \frac{1}{2}\ell_j),$ $(y_0 - \frac{1}{2}\ell_j < y < y_0 + \frac{1}{2}\ell_j)]$
j	= $1, 2, 3, \cdots, n$
w_j	= weighting factors
$\mathcal{W}_{p_i}$	= mask weight of point p_i
(x_0, y_0)	= center of the FOA
ℓ_j	= dimension of the jth foveal ring, $\ell_0 = 0$

We used $n = 3$, $\ell_1 = 4$, $\ell_2 = 8$, $\ell_3 = 32$, $w_1 = 10$, $w_2 = 2$, and $w_3 = 1$ (the operator can change ℓ_3 from the keyboard).

The *foveal significance* $\mathcal{F}$ of an RLR R in the FOA is therefore given by: $\mathcal{F}(R) = \sum_{p_i \in R} \mathcal{W}_{p_i}$

The foveal significance allows the operator to select a single object close to several similar objects by placing the center of the FOA closer to it and to select objects free of clutter with less motor precision.

Our system utilizes X11/Motif event handling for SC cursor operation. The SCO is invoked each time an X windows `PointerMotion` (the mouse has moved) or `EnterWindow` event is flagged. Running on a Sun/SPARCstation 1+, the system performs well

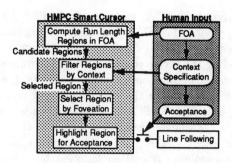

Figure 3: FOA processing for line extraction

enough for a human operator to perceive real-time performance in the FOA computation and feedback.

Context Specification: HMPC provides a level of organization above contexts called the *context environment*, CE. A CE comprises a set of contexts from which the user may select. A CE is associated with each type of map. Thus, the operator is presented with only the set of contexts needed for interpreting the map at hand.

During HMPC operation, the operator is free to select a new context at any time. A context stack is maintained so that the user may resume a previous context. This is useful, for example, when the operator digitizing a road network switches from the road context to extract a symbol missed in earlier processing. After extracting that symbol, the user only needs to pop the context stack to continue where he left off.

Map Display Management: The operator interface also keeps track of the registration of the displayed map area with the extended map representation. Scaling, scrolling, display of raster maps, zooming in/out, etc. are performed by the display manager.

Line Extraction

In HMPC, line following is broken up into two parts: seed finding and line following. Figure 3 shows the SCO for determining the seed line segment on which the line following algorithm operates. As the operator moves the FOA in the window displaying the map, the SCO computes the run length regions (RLR) under the FOA. These regions are filtered by 'line thickness' and the most foveally significant (by equation 1) of the correct thickness is highlighted on the screen. All this processing takes place in real-time as the cursor is being moved. If the highlighted region falls on the desired line, the operator clicks a mouse button to perform the line following. The line thickness filter in the SCO is essentially the same operation as the line following algorithm described hereafter.

We apply a unique line following algorithm that does not depend on line thinning or 'line walking'. Line thickness

is not computed as a post process of the line following, but is integral to the 'recognition' of the line being followed. We extract the line directly from the RLR obtained from the raw data segmentation. A fast finite-state machine based algorithm due to Quek [14] is used to extract RLR boundaries (both external and internal) as a set of positively directed (x, y) point chains. Once the boundary of a candidate line region is found, the point chain is divided into two and one of the chains is reversed. A 'walking' algorithm then pairs the closest points in both chains, producing a point chain describing the axis of the line [16].

When the user clicks the mouse button to accept a seed line region, line following outside the FOA kicks in, applying our boundary pixel pairing algorithm. The next segment is extracted by moving the SC (now under system control) such that the point where the previous line segment exits the previous FOA is centered on the new FOA boundary. This process is carried out in each direction until the line leaves the map image or until the algorithm fails owing to line intersections (in which case the twin chains diverge) or a break in the line (in which case the twin chains merge).

While a chain of points certainly describes a contour accurately, this representation does not readily provide the predictive information necessary to follow broken or intersecting lines. We use a linear and cubic spline based boundary representation to assist in tracking these more difficult contours. Such a functional form allows us to extrapolate an interrupted contour to select from among several candidates for its continuation.

We first apply a recursive curve splitting algorithm [17] to obtain a piecewise linear approximation. For each line segment, a test derived from the 'runs' test of nonparametric statistics [3] determines if it should be replaced by a cubic spline. This test detects higher order curves by examining the sign of the residual error of successive contour points. If the errors for two successive contour points are of the same sign, and of sufficient magnitude, a higher order curve is suggested. Minor fluctuations about a basically straight portion of the curve will not pass this test and these approximating segments will remain linear. The cubic spline equation for any curve segment is specified by the starting and ending breakpoints and the tangent vectors at these points [19]. We compute an ordered set of rays connecting the appropriate breakpoint with successive points along the contour. The maximal absolute error norm of each ray over all intervening points is computed. The last ray whose error norm falls within a threshold is our estimate for the unit tangent. The tangent magnitude influences the curvature of the spline and is proportional to the length of the original line segment.

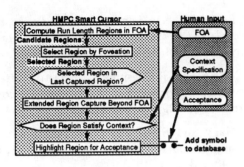

Figure 4: FOA processing for symbol extraction

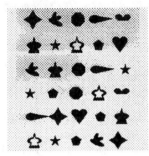

Figure 5: Sample symbol image on which the symbol extraction was tested

Symbol Extraction

Our system extracts isolated symbols with fixed scale and rotation. Symbols are rapidly retrieved by moving the FOA over any part of the desired symbol. The FOA directs the application of the symbol extraction algorithm to an *active region*, derived by foveation in the FOA window (see Figure 4). The specified *context* provides a protoypical description of the target symbol, and is used to highlight candidate symbols for user approval. Regions that do not fit the contextual model of the requested symbol are rejected by the algorithm and are not presented to the operator.

The symbol extraction algorithm comprises two modules: region capture and symbol recognition. Region capture finds the largest connected component containing the active region (extracted as an RLR) specified by the FOA. This capture is performed by a region growing algorithm [16]. Once the isolated region is obtained, symbol recognition is accomplished by a feature vector comparison of the binary-valued captured region with a context vector. Feature-vector methods reduce the dimensionality of the pattern space while maintaining discriminatory power [2]. We chose this statistical pattern recognition model because it is fast and works well on the global features which can easily be computed from the isolated symbol regions. The system utilizes some basic geometric properties of images, namely area, perimeter, aspect ratio, and the X and Y second central

moments [7] as feature-vector elements. Additional features we use are the height of the region bounding box and the ratio of dark to bright pixels within the bounding box.

To qualify as a candidate for operator acceptance the captured region features must each lie within upper and lower bounds of the corresponding feature in the vector model (as set by the context). This constraint permits rapid cut-off of computations of candidate regions should one feature be grossly out of bounds. In addition, the captured region must be "close" to the desired symbol in feature space. The captured region features are normalized against the prototype features and the square of the Euclidean length of the weighted vector is computed by $d = \sum_{i=1}^{N} w_i \left(\frac{f_i}{p_i}\right)^2$ where $\mathbf{F}_R = [f_1, \cdots, f_N]$ is the feature vector computed on the region R, $\mathbf{P} = [p_1, \cdots, p_N]$ is the feature vector computed on the prototype, and $\mathbf{W} = [w_i, \cdots, w_N]$ is the weight vector. The region is accepted as a candidate for operator approval if this distance is within a threshold. The weights w_i sum to 1 and are used to vary the relative importance of the individual features. The feature bounds, weights, and the distance threshold constitute the symbol extraction context.

CONCLUSION

While we have presented a system for map conversion, HMPC is a general paradigm. It can be readily applied to other two-dimensional vision applications such as medical image analysis (e.g. for a medical technician to extract organ boundaries), remote sensing and engineering drawing analysis. All that would be necessary is to define different sets of smart cursor operations (SCO's). We envision HMPC to be applicable to three-dimensional operation as well. In fact, the seeds of the HMPC concept were sown in the first author's earlier work in tele- robotics [15]. Consider a scenario of a pharmaceutical researcher performing experiments in a hazardous hermetically sealed laboratory cell. The operations in this cell involve the moving of chemicals, beakers, test tubes, cultures etc. Instead of having the researcher manually control a robot manipulator (an operation which requires tremendous perceptio-motor coordination and dexterity), the researcher may simply point at an object to be moved and permit the vision component of the HMPC system to determine the pose of the object and direct the end-of-tool frame of the robot. Should the system fail to extract the object (for example a beaker), the system could prompt the researcher to locate the elliptical beaker lip (i.e. descending to the feature level of operation). Hence, HMPC will permit the robotic work-cell to operate as a 'lab-technician' to the researcher.

From the viewpoint of vision application, HMPC provides an avenue to bring algorithms rapidly to bear on problems hitherto too complex for full automation. Much research, though, remains to be done. We intend to flesh out the full HMPC architecture in the course of bringing the map conversion system to full implementation. The importance of *foveal significance*, for example, only became apparent when we tried to digitize closely bundled hypsographic contour lines. We intend to pursue development of other HMPC systems which operate in two and three- dimensional domains to establish the generality of the paradigm.

References

[1] W. R. Allder and A. A. Elassal, "USGS digital cartographic data standards. digital line graphs from 1:24,000 scale maps," Circular 895-C, US Geological Survey, 1984.

[2] H. C. Andrews, *Introduction to Mathematical Techniques in Pattern Recognition*, John Wiley & Sons, Inc., New York, 1972.

[3] P. J. Besl and R. C. Jain, "Segmentation through variable-order surface fitting," *IEEE Transactions on Pattern Analysis and Machine Intelligence*, vol. 10, no. 2, pp. 167–192, Mar. 1988.

[4] C. Blais and R. Lyons, "Telepresence: Enough is enough," in *Proceedings of the International Symposium on Teleoperation and Control*, C. Mason, editor, pp. 217–226, Bristol England, July 12-15 1988.

[5] L. W. Carstensen Jr., "Developing regional land information systems: Relation databases and/or geographic information systems," *Surveying and Mapping*, vol. 46, no. 1, pp. 19–27, 1986.

[6] E. Hinrichs and L. Polanyi, "Pointing the way: A unified treatment of referential gesture in interactive discourse," *Papers from the Parasession on Pragmatics and Grammatical Theory, Chicago Linguistics Society*, vol. 22nd Meeting, pp. 71–78, 1986.

[7] B. K. P. Horn, *Robot Vision*, MIT Press, Cambridge, MA, 1986.

[8] A. Hurlbert and T. Poggio, "Visual information: Do computers need attention?," *Nature*, vol. 321, pp. 651–652, 1986.

[9] R. Kasturi, R. Fernandez, M. L. Amlani, and W.-c. Feng, "Map data processing in geographic information systems," *Computer*, vol. 22, no. 12, pp. 10–21, December 1989.

[10] V. Lumelsky, "On human performance in telerobotics," *IEEE Transactions on Systems, Man and Cybernetics*, vol. 21, no. 5, , Sep.-Oct. 1991.

[11] J. Moran and R. Desimone, "Selective attention gates visual processing in the extrastriate cortex," *Science*, vol. 229, pp. 782–784, Aug 23 1985.

[12] G. Nagy and S. Wagle, "Geographic data processing," *ACM Computing Surveys*, vol. 11, no. 2, pp. 140–181, June 1979.

[13] M. Posner, "Orienting of attention," *Quarterly Journal of Experimental Psychology*, vol. 32, pp. 3–25, 1980.

[14] F. K. Quek, *On Three-Dimensional Object Recognition and Pose-Determination: An Abstraction Based Approach*, PhD thesis, The University of Michigan, Ann Arbor, 1990.

[15] F. Quek, R. Jain, and B. Mitchell, "Teleperception," in *Proceedings of the SPIE Conference on Space Station Automation IV*, volume 1006-19, Cambridge, Massachusetts, 1988.

[16] F. Quek and M. Petro, "Interactive map conversion: Combining machine vision and human input," in *IEEE Workshop on Applications of Computer Vision*, Palm Springs, CA., Nov. 30-Dec. 2 1992.

[17] U. Ramer, "An iterative procedure for the polygonal approximation of plane curves," *Computer Graphics & Image Processing*, vol. 1, pp. 244–256, 1972.

[18] K. Robinson, "Computers make smarter maps: layers of the land," *Computerland Magazine*, pp. 12–19, Jan./Feb. 1989.

[19] D. F. Rogers and A. J. Adams, *Mathematical Elements for Computer Graphics, 2nd Ed.*, McGraw Hill, New York, 1990.

[20] D. Sagi and B. Julesz, ""Where" and "what" in vision," *Science*, vol. 228, pp. 1217–1219, 1985.

[21] J. M. Skiles, "Using scanning, automated conversion, and raster data to speed GIS implementation and lower cost," in *Proceedings of the GIS/LIS*, volume 2, pp. 476–483, Anaheim, CA, 1990.

[22] M. Stiefel, "Mapping out the differences among geographic information systems," *The S. Klein Computer Graphics Review*, pp. 73–87, Fall 1987.

[23] A. Treisman and G. Gelade, "A feature integration theory of attention," *Cognitive Psychology*, vol. 12, pp. 97–136, 1980.

VideoMAP and VideoSpaceIcon:
Tools for Anatomizing Video Content

Yoshinobu TONOMURA, Akihito AKUTSU, Kiyotaka OTSUJI, Toru SADAKATA

NTT Human Interface Laboratories

1-2356 Take, Yokosuka, Kanagawa, 235 Japan

phone:+81-468-59-3112   email: tonomura@nttvdt.ntt.jp

ABSTRACT
A new approach to interacting with stored video is proposed. The approach utilizes VideoMAP and VideoSpaceIcon. VideoMAP is the interface that shows the essential video features in an easy to perceive manner. VideoSpaceIcon represents the temporal and spatial characteristics of a video shot as an intuitive icon. A video indexing method supports both tools. These tools allow the user's creativity to directly interact with the essential features of each video by offering spatial and temporal clues. This paper introduces the basic concept and describes prototype versions of the tools as implemented in a video handling system. VideoMAP and VideoSpaceIcon are effective for video handling functions such as video content analysis, video editing, and various video applications which need an intuitive visual interface.

KEYWORDS: Video Handling, Visual Interface, Icon, Index, Image Processing, Visualization

INTRODUCTION
Since the introduction of video display boards for computers, many video applications have been attempted. In an early work, Hodges, et al. developed multimedia learning environments using one of the earliest video workstations [1]. Multimedia synchronized editing using the time line was introduced. In the last three years, thanks to advances in the standardization of video compression algorithms and digital signal processing, several multimedia platforms capable of storing, accessing, and displaying video have been developed. The first commercial versions of multimedia operating systems are now becoming available. Various application systems such as desktop video editors and electronic video libraries have been developed by many vendors.

Video Handling Issues and Previous Researches
Although computers strongly support traditional application systems, they cannot yet handle video as efficiently as text. This is because computers do not "speak" the video language. Text handling functions such as automatic full text searches, keyword generation, and structured editing, are powerful and well match the characteristics of texts. On the other hand,

© 1993 ACM 0-89791-575-5/93/0004/0131...$1.50

video content is extremely vague and difficult to specify. Therefore, most video application systems rely on humans to input the necessary data. To eliminate this dependency on humans, many research issues must be defined and resolved. The key issues are creating intuitive visual clues to help users perform their tasks efficiently, developing a structure of video data management, and utilizing image processing to automatically extract the representation of a video.

A visual interface is essential to activate the user's visual sense and stimulate the user's intuition especially when manipulating video. Brondmo and Davenport introduced Micon(moving icon) to represent the video content of hypermedia journals [2]. One of us (Tonomura) has already proposed a content oriented visual interface using video icons and other intuitive visual interfaces for video handling [3]. The video icon is based on a structured icon model that has a shadow corresponding to the video segment footage. Mills, et al. proposed a magnifier tool for video data that offers a range of views, from wide to close, of video data [4]. The tool is simple but effective in supporting video manipulation. The research to date has tried to develop effective visual interfaces but the clues they offer the user are rather limited.

Video data management is important for establishing flexible systems. The management should resolve the two main questions: what kind of information should be used to represent the video content and how the information should be handled. Davenport, et al. proposed a framework that used layered information management [5]. The important idea of "granularity of meaning" was noted:the degree of information coarseness needed for efficient multimedia handling. MacNeil developed a visual programming environment which uses a case-based reasoning approach to support multimedia designers[6]. A vertical slice of each video frame image is simply shown over time for users to see the visual rhythm of the shots in video.

The development of a system supported by image processing is important because the clues must be extracted automatically if we are dealing with a large video database. One of us (Tonomura) proposed a video handling architecture that used, as the basic clues, the video indexes created automatically by image analysis [7]. The automatic detection of video cuts, one of the video indexes, was realized by analyzing the intensity histogram data. Ueda, et al. reported an editing support system that used image analysis to achieve cut detection and image flow analysis, in which image processing was performed only by software [8]. In these more recent works, however, the number and styles of clues to video content are still limited compared to the rich information present within videos.

Our Focus

Our research focus is to establish universal clues, that would be useful enough to handle a video in many different ways. We were also interested in creating and testing promising new video tools that would lead to enhanced video applications. Our research results were realized in our prototype video handling system.

This paper:

- Discusses a video information reference model to clarify the origin of the information contained with a video.
- Describes the basic concept of our video handling system to explain how the video indexes work.
- Proposes VideoMAP which displays useful video features as a tool for video indexing.
- Describes VideoSpaceIcon which represents temporal and spatial video features as icons.

VIDEO INFORMATION REFERENCE MODEL

As shown in Fig. 1, a lot of information about a video is related to its creation and use. The information includes filming parameters, how it is stored, and how it was edited. The left hand side of Fig. 1 lists the physical information and the right hand side lists how people interact with the video through creation and editing. Our intention is to extract as much information as possible from the video itself. Furthermore, a long term goal is to estimate the intention of the people associated with the video production.

The most basic data in our video handling system are cut points and camera operations. A cut point is a seam in the video sequence generated by camera stop and start or subsequent editing. Camera operations include panning, tilting, and zooming. The director's intent is reflected either implicitly or explicitly in the cut points and camera operations. Editing effects are such as fades, wipes. Telecine conversion is to convert photographic films into videos. By analyzing the video, such information can be extracted and described in a structured manner.

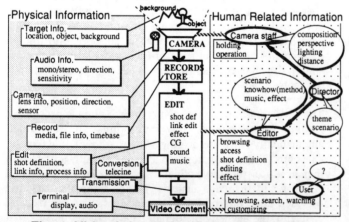

Fig. 1 Video Information Reference Model

FROM ANALYSIS TO APPLICATION: VIDEO INDEXED BASED VIDEO HANDLING

The processing structure of our video handling system is shown in Fig. 2. The attributes of the video data are located lower while applications fall in the top layer. Video data are expressed in HVC (Hue, Value, and Chroma) because this mirrors human image perception. Value means intensity.

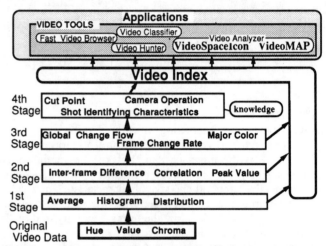

Fig. 2 Processing Structure of Video Handling

The first stage process is image processing for general feature extraction on each frame in the video sequence. For example, the average intensity, intensity distribution, and intensity histogram are calculated from individual pixel values. This stage outputs a new time-based data stream. The second stage filters the output of the first stage to extract more specific features; for example, inter-frame difference, correlation, representative peak value. As a result of the filtering, new time-based data streams are generated. The third stage processes the data streams to generate the basic information needed for characterizing the video. For example, the frame change rate is defined by the inter-frame difference of intensity, which means how rapidly the images change. The global change flows are obtained by analyzing the images of time-based data stream. The details are explained in later sections. The video indexes are viewed from the aspect of movies in the fourth stage. Cut points, camera operations, and other shot-identifying characteristics such as shot color are obtained. The typical usage of cut points is to define the unit of video access and storage. We have established an effective cut detection method using intensity data [9]. In the method, cut detection is performed by thresholding the frame change rate. Camera operation detection is realized by analyzing the global change flows. The processes in this stage can be supported by knowledge of the mechanics of video creation. For example, telecine conversion is detected observing a periodic frame change rate because we know the characteristics of the conversion. We treat the features generated in the first to fourth stages as video indexes.

The application stage offers several very effective video tools such as a fast video browser which shows a long video within a short time, a video hunter which retrieves a specific video, a video classifier, and a video analyzer which analyzes video at various levels of granularity. Real applications are being built using the tools. VideoMAP and VideoSpaceIcon, described later, are prototype video tools of the video analyzer.

Generated in Off Line, Used in Real Time
One of the advantages of using video indexes is that we don't need very fast image processing computers to use the application. Once a video is indexed, the indexes are attached to the video data and stored in a data base. The application can be run on a relatively slow computer because time consuming image processing is not needed. It is possible that an industrial index maker could generate the video indexes with a very fast task-specific computer.

Granularity of Handling
By using the video indexes generated in different stages, granular video handling is possible. The more abstract the video index is, the coarser the expression of the video content becomes. A multi-layered video index management scheme that will permit access to the video indexes of any stage is needed in order to realize the smooth management of granularity.

VIDEOMAP
External Representation of Video Index Features
VideoMAP is the interface that expresses essential video features as video indexes. It also provides direct access to specific parts of the video. In other words, VideoMAP is the visual representation of the video indexes held in the computer. The indexes are displayed on a time line. The method of feature visualization depends on the feature's characteristics. By pointing at some part of the feature pattern, the corresponding video frame appears in the video window. One of the advantages of this interface is that users quickly develop a concept of the behavior of each feature on the time line and also the correlation between features.

Example: 20 Seconds at a Glance: Six Features
A typical VideoMAP layout is shown in Fig. 3. The time line runs from left to right. In this case, there are 600 frames so the total time line represents 20 seconds. The intensity histogram, intensity average, inter-frame difference of intensity histogram, video X-ray image which is explained later, and hue histogram follow from top to bottom. Features shown in VideoMAP can be selected from the index list to match the user's requirements. The order of the feature rows can also be changed by the user. (See also Tonomura, Color Plate 1.)

The cut points are clearly shown in each feature as pattern discontinuities. In the plot of histogram intensity, the intensity values of all pixels in each frame are quantized into 16 levels. Each quantized frequency value is represented with a gray scale where white indicates high frequency. Intensity average in the second row is calculated from the intensity histogram. The plot of inter-frame difference of intensity histogram (third row) shows the big peaks which clearly indicate the cut points. The image flow patterns (fourth and fifth rows) is obtained by filtering the edge images of spatio-temporal video frames. The number of edge image pixels is summed on vertical and horizontal axes. The result of filtering is a kind of projection from the top and the side. We call this the **video X-ray**. White pixels indicate the existence of a large number of edge image pixels on that axis. The hue histogram (bottom row) has a resolution of 256 hues: from the top, purplish red -> blue -> green -> yellow green -> green -> orange -> red. Cut points are clearly discernable. One or more apparent bars are seen in several shots. The bar in the center indicates green while the upper bar indicates blue. Since the target video is a scene from a baseball game, the green corresponds to the turf and the blue the fence. The players' uniforms are white but white is not directly represented as a hue. White does, however, directly influence intensity. The images on the top are the first frame

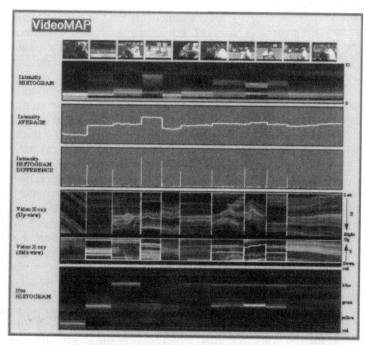

Shot Reference

Intensity Histogram
bright
↕
dark

Intensity Average

Intensity Histogram Difference

top view ⎱
side view ⎰ Video X-ray

Hue Histogram

Fig. 3 VideoMAP (600 frames, 20 seconds)

of each shot. By comparing the image with each of the cut's patterns we can readily discern pattern origin.

Video Sign: Identification Information of Shot

The intensity histogram and image flow contain interesting patterns that include important information. We call this kind of pattern **Video Sign** and use it for identification. Video Sign is equivalent to the voice print of the audio field. The exact form of Video Sign depends on the content, but it is possible to perceive general patterns. For example, patterns in the intensity histogram can indicate the presence of editing effects commonly applied at the beginning or the end of a shot. Note that the example shown in Fig. 3 does not contain such patterns. Camera operations and object motion within a scene can be discerned from the video X-ray. For example, the first shot in the top view of the video X-ray (fourth row in Fig. 3) contains slanting lines which show that camera was panned. The last shot contains lines that diverge. This is a typical zooming pattern. Detailed analysis of these patterns led us to develop the VideoSpaceIcon. With further research we could employ pattern matching to identify scenes or shots. We are still testing VideoMAP to determine the most effective features that will fully engage the power of human intuition.

VIDEOSPACEICON

VideoSpaceIcon is a tool that displays spatial and temporal video features as icons. It utilizes the camera operation parameters that can be automatically detected from the video X-ray of VideoMAP.

Video Space: Space Oriented Video Content View

An example of a VideoSpaceIcon is shown in Fig. 4. It is an extended (3-D) rectangle not the conventional square 2-D image icon. The original video shot showed a girl appearing on the left through a door, walking to the right and sitting on a chair. The camera was panned from left to right following the girl. Conventional icons or video screen can only show actual frames, but a VideoSpaceIcon can show the entire physical space. We call this the **video space**. The conventional video display process employs only a time oriented approach, but VideoSpaceIcon is space oriented; it allows us to grasp the physical space of the shot at a glance. The shape of the VideoSpaceIcon is drawn in Fig. 6. Our system is able to display views in different angles other than front. The three dimensional figure of the icon allows us to grasp how the camera was operated at a glance. The top and side view can be replaced by video X-ray images in X-ray mode. Fig. 5 shows the VideoSpaceIcon in that mode: modified video X-ray images, top and side view, are displayed with a front view. The straight lines parallel to the time line in Fig. 5 are created from the background and objects that remain stationary over a long period of time. The top and side views are useful to grasp object movement because movement is indicated by non-parallel lines which are clearly visible.

How VideoSpaceIcon is Created

The VideoSpaceIcon is created by changing the image position and size for each frame according to the camera operation parameters. Camera operation information is

Fig. 4 VideoSpaceIcon: Example 1 (front view: panning shot)

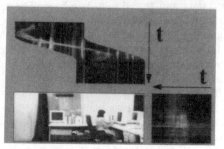

Fig. 5 VideoSpaceIcon (temporal mode of Fig. 4)

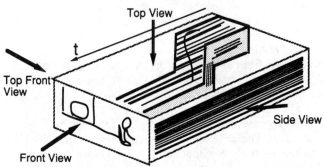

Fig. 6 Views of VideoSpaceIcon

available beforehand only in specific applications and demands the use of a special camera. However, what we are interested in is creating video spaces for video shots for which the camera operation is unknown.

What the camera captures in a frame has more or less global changes. For example, when the camera is panned to the right, background and static objects move to the left. This movement can be tracked with motion vectors. By analyzing the flow generated by the motion vectors, camera operation parameters can be determined. Our former research [10] and Ueda's IMPACT [8] are based on motion vector analysis. Unfortunately, it takes too long to compute the results and robustness is suspect in many situations. Our newly proposed method uses the video X-ray images, is rapid, and is robust enough to analyze most videos. When the camera is fixed, the video X-ray images contain many lines parallel to the time line that were generated from the background. When the camera is panned, the lines are slanted; the degree of slanting depends on the panning speed. When the camera is zoomed, the lines diverge. A moving object generates non-parallel lines. In our experiments, as long as the background contains some distinctive features, global flows are clear enough to calculate camera operation parameters.

The degree of slanting can be converted into the three major camera operation parameters: panning, tilting, and zooming. Tilting is vertical panning. Panning and tilting vary the camera's optical axis. Zooming changes the camera's focal length. Other operations include lateral camera movements such as tracking, and dollying. These basic camera operations are shown in Fig. 7. In our current system, panning, tilting, zooming, and any combination of these operations can be represented by VideoSpaceIcon. The other operations are not currently supported because reconstructing the video space would be much more complex.

Constructing a VideoSpaceIcon from camera operation parameters is shown in Fig. 8. The icon image position shifts to indicate panning and tilting, while the image size is changed to express zooming. Zooming has little effect on the video space itself, but the zoomed part has higher resolution than usual. Another example of VideoSpaceIcon is Fig. 9. Its form mirrors the camera operations: tilt down, pan to right, fix, and pan to left. (See also Tonomura, Color Plate 2.)

Structured Icon Model
An icon is a representation of one or more features of something and permits interaction with the something. By clicking on the video space, the correspoinding frame image

is accessed and displayed. While the actual creation of a VideoSpaceIcon is performed as is explained above, logical icon handling for visualization and interaction in software is achieved by using the structured icon model. We have proposed the structured video icon model and the simple video icon that has shadow [4]. VideoSpaceIcon is an extension of this technique. The structure model of the VideoSpaceIcon is shown in Fig. 10.

Moving VideoSpaceIcon:
Reproducing Object Motion in Video Space
One interesting aspect of the VideoSpaceIcon is that object movement can be reproduced in a very simple manner. By overlapping sequential image frames in the video space, a moving object actually moves. Fig. 11 shows this idea using Fig. 4. In this example, the girl's image really walks. This is a new effect that is not possible with traditional video. We can see the entire space in which the shot was actually taken. When creating a video from a cinemascope movie, the original movie is often trimmed and some of the picture is lost. Under some constraints, it is possible to reconstruct the

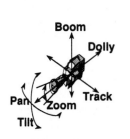

Fig. 7 Basic Camera Operations

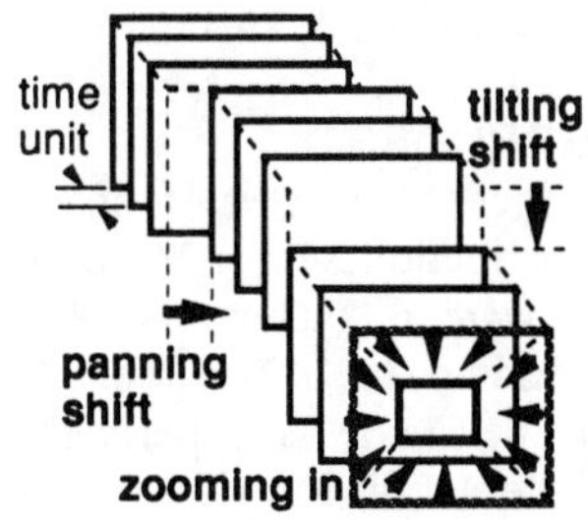

Fig. 8 Construction of VideoSpaceIcon

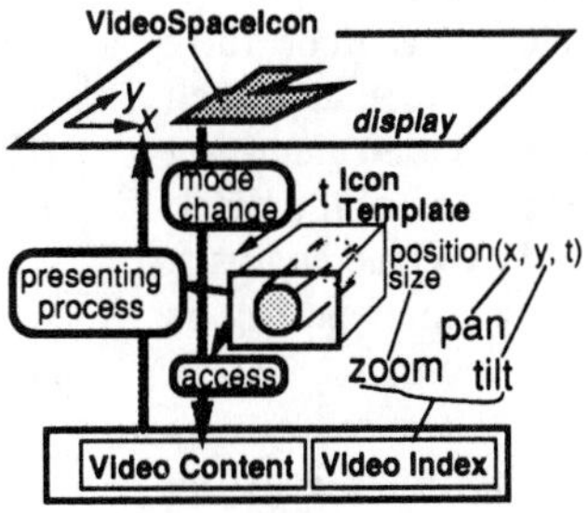

Fig. 10 Icon Structure Model

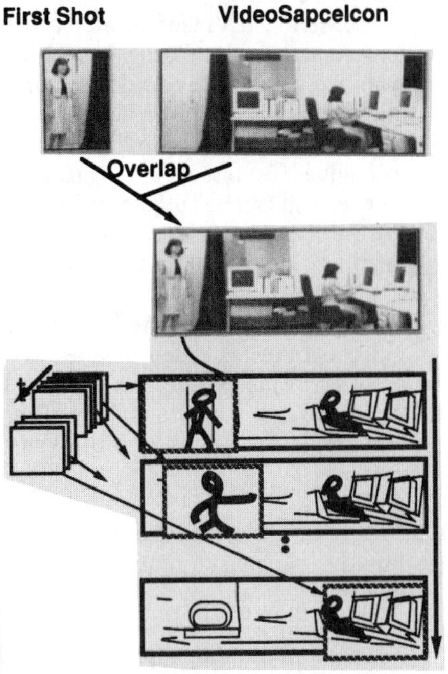

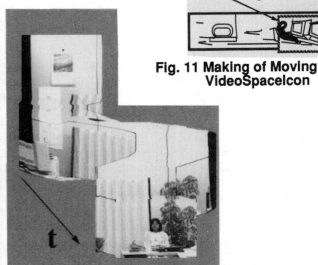

Fig. 11 Making of Moving VideoSpaceIcon

(a) X-ray mode

(b) normal mode: top front view)

Fig. 9 VideoSpaceIcon: Example2 (panning, tilting)

original image with our method. Also, by windowing the video space created, a video with a different view from the original one can be obtained.

Video Space Monitor: New Display Possible
If the size of the video space is increased, it is no longer just an icon, but it is also a display screen on which video content can be viewed. Two types of display mode are possible: space oriented and anti-vibration.

In the space oriented mode, the video space is simply enlarged. In this mode camera operations are not discerned. In the anti-vibration mode, the video space shows only those frames for which rapidly changing camera operation is detected. In this mode, normal camera operations are observed. This is what we call the video space monitor; it is different from the conventional monitor display in that its screen shape dynamically changes and does not remain square. However, this idea is not fully implemented because of the problems of lens skew. Given some reasonable constraints, however, it is possible.

CONCLUSION
VideoMAP and VideoSpaceIcon were proposed as new tools for interacting with videos. VideoMAP realizes a direct visual interface with intuitive video features. VideoSpaceIcon fully utilizes the power of the video space oriented icon approach and suggests the possibility of many new video handling techniques. Both tools are visual representations of the video indexes that can be automatically extracted by video analysis. We believe that video-indexing-based video handling is important and useful for future video applications.

We are currently testing VideoMAP to optimize existing video features as video indexes as well as to uncover new features. VideoSpaceIcon is now being used to analyze camera usage in movie making. These tools were developed and implemented as a prototype interface for research purposes.

Problems and Future Study
Finally, we must point out several issues regarding our research.

First, we need more sophisticated video features that can be used as video indexes. We currently have about a dozen features based on intensity and hue data. For future applications, we need to consider how movie and video experts deal with video to discover more features.

Second, the robustness of the algorithms used to detect the features must be increased to allow all videos to be processed. We have successfully performed cut detection and camera operation extraction on several videos, including some that were over 2 hours in length. We now know what algorithm parameters are appropriate for what conditions. More experience is needed to confirm that we have a sufficient number of parameters.

Also needed is an enhanced visualization style for the video indexes. The interface shown in this paper is a prototype system and its design and functions may not satisfy the general user. The visual interfaces of these tools should be refined considering human factors. This is our next step.

VideoMAP does not use color to enhance the features to prevent sensory overload and subsequent confusion. An argument has been made that the limited use of color is warranted and we will try to confirm this.

The VideoSpaceIcon described above is not always effective because of the problem of camera lens skew. In one sense, this is not a problem when the icon is small and used only as an icon. To use it as a video space monitor, however, this problem should be resolved. In such conditions, anti-skew transformation is needed. The parameters needed for the process could be obtained from the video X-rays.

Lastly, when the camera operation is tracking or dollying, in which the camera position changes, the above method of creating VideoSpaceIcon can not be simply applied. A three dimensional space model is needed. This is for further study.

ACKNOWLEDGEMENTS
The authors are grateful to Mr. Tomio Kishimoto, Executive Manager of Visual Media Laboratory, NTT Human Interface Laboratories, for his encouragement of this research. We would like to thank Susumu Ichinose for his helpful advice.

REFERENCES
1. Hodges, M. Sasnett, R. and Ackerman, M. A Construction Set for Multimedia Applications. IEEE Software, 6, 4, (January 1989), 37-43.
2. Brondmo, H.P. Davenport, G. Creating and Viewing the Elastic Charles-a Hypermedia Journal, in Hypertext, State of the Art. R. McAlesse and C. Greene, eds., Intellect Ltd., Oxford, England, 1990.
3. Tonomura, Y. Abe, S. Content Oriented Visual Interface using Video Icons For Visual Database Systems. JVLC, 1, 2, Academic Press, 1990, 183-198.
4. Mills, A Magnifier Tool for Video Data. in Proc. CHI'92, (Monterey May 1992), 93-98.
5. Davenport, G. Aguierre, S. Pincever, N. Cinematic Primitives for Multimedia. IEEE CG&A, 11, 4, (July 1991), 67-74.
6. MacNeil R. Generating Multimedia Presentation Automatically using TYRO, the Constraint, Case-Based Designer's Apprentice. in Proc. IEEE Workshop on Visual Languages, (Kobe Oct. 1991), 74-79.
7 Tonomura, Y. Video Handling Based on Structured Information For Hypermedia Systems. in Proc. ACM Int'l Conf. on Multimedia Information Systems, (Singapore Jan. 1991), 333-344.
8 Ueda, H. Miyatake, T. Yoshizawa, S. IMPACT:An Interactive Natural-Motion-Picture Dedicated Multimedia Authoring System. in Proc. CHI'91, 343-350.
9. Otsuji, K. Tonomura, Y. Ohba, Y. Video browsing using brightness data. in Proc. SPIE VCIP'91, 1606, (Boston Nov. 1991), 980-989.
10. Akutsu, A. Tonomura, Y. Hashimoto, H. Ohba, Y. Video Indexing using motion vectors. in Proc. SPIE VCIP'92, (Boston Nov. 1992).
11. Ripley, G.D. DVI - A Digital Multimedia Technology. CACM, 32, 7, (July 1989), 811-822.

Automatic Structure Visualization for Video Editing

Hirotada Ueda, Takafumi Miyatake, Shigeo Sumino and Akio Nagasaka

Central Research Laboratory, Hitachi, Ltd.
1-280, Higashi-koigakubo, Kokubunji-shi, Tokyo 185, Japan
Tel: +81-423-23-1111, Fax: +81-423-27-7718
E-mail: ueda@crl.hitachi.co.jp, miyatake@crl.hitachi.co.jp,
sumino@crl.hitachi.co.jp, akio-n@crl.hitachi.co.jp

ABSTRACT

We developed intelligent functions for the automatic description of video structure, and visualization methods for temporal-spatial video structures obtained by these functions as well
as for the functions. The functions offer descriptions of cut
separations, motion of the camera and filmed objects, tracks
and contour lines of objects, existence of objects, and periods
of existence. Furthermore, identical objects are automatically
linked. Thus the visualization methods supported by object-
links allow users to freely browse and directly manipulate the
structure including descriptions and raw video data.

Keywords: Multimedia, Authoring, video editing, motion
picture, video structure, visualization, image recognition

INTRODUCTION

Even with up-to-date technology, multimedia authoring (especially when it includes video, i.e., natural-motion-picture)
is still quite difficult when compared with conventional character-based media. Therefore, support is needed for these
systems from various information-processing technologies
that can help the user to edit or browse multimedia [1].
Authoring is an intelligent and creative activity, in which the
user plays the main role. However, if the user can receive
competent assistance from an intelligent authoring system, he
can devote himself to creative activities. We have been
developing a multimedia authoring system, called IMPACT,
Interactive Motion Picture Authoring system for Creative
Talent [2]. Our objective is to achieve a system that can
encourage user creativity.

In the IMPACT project we examined new approach that
makes use of image-recognition technology. In a previous
paper [2], we showed some results from our prototype which

indicated the appropriateness of this approach. Through the
development and experimental use of the system, we learned
that there were three important research topics. The first is to
analyze, in place of the user, the structure of the multimedia
information which extends in time and space. The second is
to effectively describe and store this structure in the system.
The third is to provide the user with a good visualization of the
structure.

The idea of a moving icon (micon) to handle video is shown
in [1]. A hierarchical layer structure of user annotations
attached to video is proposed in [3]. The importance of
visualization to smoothly integrate the details and overall
context of the information is emphasized in [4]. A magnifier
tool for the temporal axis of video is proposed in [5]. There
is now a strong need for the integration of these research
results in more user-centered multimedia systems.

In this paper, we introduce some video analysis functions
developed in the IMPACT project. Then we propose visualization methods, that users can easily understand and handle,
for the temporal-spatial video structures that video analysis
functions automatically extract. We also discuss the visualization of these functions because it is very important for the
users to know how they work and to understand how to apply
them in the user's environment.

BASIC CONCEPT

Figure 1 shows the hierarchical structure of video information. The scenario is an entire story composed of a number of
scenes. Each scene consists of one or more cuts (the basic
components of a motion picture). Scenes may have sub-
scenes. In this structure, the upper parts have symbolic
descriptions and the lower parts have more visual descriptions. The lowest parts of this structure (i.e., cuts) contain raw
video data. The symbolic descriptions consist of verbal and
semantic indications, such as the names of persons or places,
their actions and relations, etc. The visual descriptions consist
of geographical and temporal indications. Examples of these
descriptions are the shapes and positions of certain objects, the

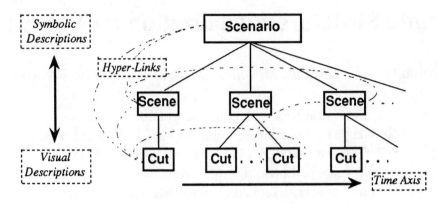

Figure 1. Structure of video information

tracks of moving objects, the times when objects appear or disappear, and the times when objects meet in the video. We have been developing a system which can analyze and visualize a structure, including hyper-links between descriptions, such as that shown in Figure 1. Image-recognition technology is used to achieve automatic descriptions and hyper-links of video structure.

IMPACT can be seen as a platform to examine how users and computers can work together in an intelligent environment. It is an environment where the user and the computer interactively analyze and edit video information to improve it's quality. To achieve this, we have to provide facilities that show the user how functions work and how to customize them. It is also important to develop a representation that can effectively show how the system recognizes the structure of the information (video) which the user is processing.

VIDEO ANALYSIS FUNCTIONS
Cut Separation
The automatic cut-separation function divides a video strip into cuts in order to visualize the basic structure of the video. As reported in [2], the cut-separation function evaluates the correlation between the color of two adjacent frames in a video. Each separated cut is assigned a miniaturized moving icon (micon) and the video equipment's time code is stored with it. Since there are a few cases in which the results do not satisfy users because of imperfections of the function or differences in the user's filming intention, we provide an undo function and a sensitivity adjustment for the cut-separation function as explained in a later section.

Motion Analysis
The motion analysis function in IMPACT looks at the motion characteristics of the filmed object or at the camera operation (zooming and panning). This is one type of optical flow estimation method [2]. When the camera is panning, small regions of video frames move in parallel. When the camera is zooming, regions move radially. When objects move, regions move locally in parallel. Therefore, the final result can be calculated using a statistical operation for those small region movements. The detected zooming, panning, and object motion information are stored as descriptions of cuts to be used in the editing stage.

Object Extraction
To extract a moving object from the motion picture, two differential images of three consecutive frames are binarized and the logical AND operation of these two is performed [2]. After the user checks the result of the first frame (if necessary, with adjustment of parameters for the above procedure), the moving object extraction function follows the same procedure for the remaining hundreds of frames of the cut. To extract a still object, we use edge detection along with color and brightness comparison. These functions provide descriptions by means of contour lines of the objects, track data of the moving objects, and time codes when the object enters and exits the screen (to define object existence periods).

Object Presence Judgment
This new function determines the presence of objects by their unique color combinations. The original algorithm of this function was reported in [6]. Figure 2 (see also Ueda, Plate 1) shows a processing example of this function. Frame (a) contains a target object (a girl in a blue tee-shirt), and the user marks the object area with a black rectangle. Frame (b) contains this object. Frame (d) does not contain the object. In Figure 2, (c) and (e) show the intermediate results of the judgment function. Here, sixteen color combinations in the object area marked in the frame (a) are used for the judgment. The sixteen reduced images (c) and (e) show the locations where these color combinations are found in (b) and (d) respectively. Fourteen color combinations out of sixteen are found in (c), thus it is judged that the object is present in frame (b). Frame (d) is judged as not having the object because only eight combinations are found in (e).

When the user specifies a certain filmed object in one frame,

Figure 2. Processing of object presence judgment

the function automatically extracts all objects in the remaining frames which have the same color combination. With the object extraction method previously described, the user has to judge the object identity between each cut. However, the object presence judgment function enables an automatic description of every cut in which a specific object appears. In other words, the function builds up hyper-links between identical objects in different cuts.

Conventionally, the node of the hyper-link is merely a key frame of a video or a button icon drawn on the key frame. In our system, the node of the link is the filmed object itself which, users normally feel, carries semantic information. This difference in node has enabled great progress in visualization and in handling of the hierarchal video structure. Therefore, we call it an "Object-Link." We discuss this further in a later section.

VISUALIZATION

Davenport, et al. [4] are investigating a system which enables the user to attach semantic and structural variables to a video (camera position, lighting, causal actions, narrative structures). The goal is to represent these user annotations in "strata," a hierarchical structure used to enhance video editing and multimedia browsing applications.

In our project, we represent descriptions which are automatically provided by video analysis functions, as well as user annotations. In designing visualization as an interface of the intelligent video authoring system, there are two important considerations: visualization of the results of automatic analysis in the video structure and visualization of how the intelligent functions work in the interactive session. In this section, we show these two kinds of experimental results and discuss what should be visualized and how.

Descriptions for Video

To offer a useful visualization, descriptions for the hierarchical structure of video are very important. The basic description in our system consists of the automatic cut separation results. Motion data of objects and the camera are obtained by motion analysis. Tracks and contour lines of the object and the object existence period are obtained by the object extraction function. The presence of objects, the object existence period, and hyper links of identical objects are obtained by the object presence judgment.

These temporal-spatial descriptions are integrated (therefore the accuracy is higher) and stored as attributes of cuts. Hyper links are extended to upper layers of the structure either automatically or manually by users. Users can correct these descriptions and add their annotations, as well as refer to them in the editing session, by using the dialog window. This change of attributes also propagates along the object-links, to automatically perform necessary adjustment for descriptions and annotations, or to advise the user to check and adjust them. Users can also use these attributes for retrieval navigated by the object links.

Visualization for Video Structures

Figure 3 (see also Ueda, Plate 2) shows the screen when the user edits a video along the time axis. A video signal is supplied from a VCR or writable laser disk to a workstation (IRIS 4D/210 GTX) with a video capturing function. The components window at the lower part of the screen shows a visual list of cuts which are automatically separated. A cut is represented by a moving icon (micon). Each micon is displayed as a box with a depth which indicates the time length of the cut. This representation compactly visualizes the temporal structure of the video obtained by the automatic cut separation function.

Figure 3. A screen of the time axis editing stage

Figure 4. A screen of the object link navigation stage

Further, some micons have color arrows superimposed on them to indicate the motion of the filmed objects and the camera which are obtained by video analysis functions (the arrows can also warn the user when motion is not smooth or too fast: red for too fast, blue for moderate, and orange for a lack of smoothness). Therefore, the user can intuitively understand at a glance the temporal-spatial structure of the entire video simply by looking at this visual list.

When the user selects object link navigation, as shown in Figure 4, the object index window (a close up is shown in Ueda, Plate 3) opens. Micons at the left of this window are indices of objects. To search where a certain object exists, the user clicks one of the index micons, then the corresponding cut icons in the components window are colored as shown in Figure 4 (a close up is shown in Ueda, Plate 4). The colored portions on the cut micons' box surfaces indicate the object existence periods in each cut. Note that, in this representation, rather than the first frame of the cut, the first frame of the period where the target object appears is shown at the proper temporal depth within the box.

The bar charts to the right of the object index window show the object existence periods in the time span of the video. Therefore, the user can easily see an overview of the existence of the object in the video. The user can even see and check whether two (or more) objects meet in a certain cut, because the thin vertical lines indicate cut separations. Furthermore, when the user clicks one of these bars, the corresponding single cut in the components window is colored in the same way as descrived above. Using these facilities, the user can intuitively grasp the structure of scenes and the context of a video that is being composed. The user can also freely browse related detailed descriptions and select any desired cut for editing.

Visualization for Functions

To ensure usable visualization of a function, the algorithm of the function should be designed so that it can be understood and used intuitively. For instance, the algorithm of cut separation is to detect a large change in the correlation between neighboring frames. The original algorithm works well for almost all cases. However, we found in experimental use that the user considers a scene to be continuous as long as the video camera or objects are moving at a constant speed, even if the correlation change is large. Thus we modified the function to calculate the rate of correlation change in order to match this human perception.

Then we offered the user a facility to observe in real-time how separation sensitivity changes by directly manipulating the line that shows the threshold for testing the correlation value. The cut-separation step in IMPACT is shown in Figure 5. The upper-left window shows a video picture supplied to a workstation. Yellow rectangles on the window show the regions where large correlation changes are detected. The upper-right window shows graphs of magnitude of the correlation and the rate of change of correlation which includes the threshold line. When the rate of change crosses the threshold, scene separation is performed. Each separated cut is reduced to a micon and put into the lower window in time order. Thus the user can easily adjust the sensitivity of the function. At the same time, the user can see where scenes vary too quickly by referring to the graph. Thus the user can avoid showing audiences unsuitable video.

In our system, all the intermediate results in the processing of functions are made visible. Therefore it is easy even for non-experts in image processing to adjust the procedural parameters of functions such motion analysis, object extraction and object presence judgment.

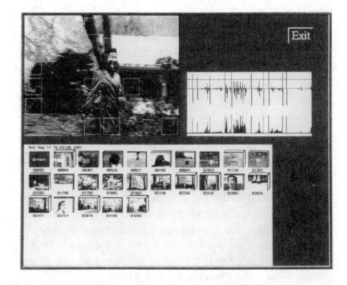

Figure 5. A screen of the cut-separation stage

DISCUSSION

Conventional video editing requires numerous repetitions of fast-forward and rewind operations until an overview of the structure, as shown in the components window of Figure 3 is firmly fixed in the user's mind; this is very time consuming. The prototype system, however, uses image recognition technology to remove this time-consuming step in video editing. Thus, the user can start from the selections of cuts (if necessary, with trimming, i.e., adjustment of the length of a cut) and arranges them in the desired order in the upper right editing window to achieve time-axis editing by direct manipulation of cut micons. The system then edits the video by controlling the video equipment based on the time codes assigned to the cuts.

The window at the upper left of the screen (see Figure 3) is a monitor. Users can play any cut or a series of selected cuts. However, it was very interesting to observe that throughout the session, especially in the time axis editing stage, users seldom used the monitor window. We believe this is because users can recognize what these cuts or series of cuts look like when played only by looking at the visualized temporal-spatial structure. For example bad combinations of panning directions, the rhythm caused by the varying lengths of successive cuts, and the time sequence of object appearances are obvious from the system visualization.

As object presence judgment in our current system is based on color combinations, this function does not work well for colorless objects or between two objects which have a similar color combination. In such cases, the user has to manually add or delete the links by direct manipulation of micons and bars (see Figure 4). However, the object links which this function offers were found to be very powerful. The basic part of the time-consuming linkage process was done by the system. Users only does corrections. Also, users can effectively use the structure and the descriptions of video information that IMPACT offers through the object links. In the next stage we are planning to add a speaker identification function to reinforce the object presence judgment.

CONCLUSION

We have developed several intelligent video analysis functions for the automatic description of video structure, in our IMPACT project. The functions offer descriptions of cut separations, motion of the camera and objects, tracks and contour lines of the object, the existence of the object, the period of existence, and most importantly, links between identical objects. These temporal-spatial descriptions are integrated and stored as attributes of cuts.

Users can correct these descriptions and add their own anno-

tations, as well as refer to them in the editing session or use them for browsing and retrieval which is navigated by the object links. One of the advantages of our system is that the node of the links is the filmed object itself.

We also discussed and proposed visualization methods which users can easily understand and operate, for the temporal-spatial video structures which the video analysis functions extract, and for showing how these functions work. The prototype system, using these functions and visualization methods, allows users to directly manipulate the structure, including descriptions and raw video data, without paying too much attention to the levels within the hierarchy of video information.

The results show the usability of our basic concept of showing the user how functions work and how the system recognizes the structure of the user's information (video). The next step is to develop more meaningful visualizations, which may include some semantic recognition in the hierarchical structure of information (including audio), in order to achieve a more friendly and cooperative environment for users of computing systems.

Acknowledgment

This work was performed partly under contract with the Institute for Personalized Information Environment as a part of the FRIEND21 project of the Ministry of International Trade and Industry.

References

[1] Mackay, E. W. and Davenport, G. "Virtual Video Editing in Interactive Multimedia Applications," Communications of the ACM, 32(7), pp. 802-810 (July 1989).

[2] Ueda, H., Miyatake, T. and Yoshizawa, S. "IMPACT: An Interactive Natural-Motion-Picture Dedicated Multimedia Authoring System," CHI'91, ACM, pp. 343-350 (1991).

[3] Davenport, G., Aguierre-Smith, T. and Pincever, N. "Cinematic primitives for multimedia," IEEE Computer Graphics and Applications, 11(4), pp. 67-75, (July 1991).

[4] Card, S. K., Robertson, G. G. and Mackinlay, J. D. "The Information Visualizer, an Information Workspace," CHI'91, ACM, pp. 181-188 (1991).

[5] Mills, M., Cohen, J. and Wong, Y. Y. "A Magnifier Tool for Video Data," CHI'92, ACM, pp. 93-98 (1992).

[6] Nagasaka, A., and Tanaka, Y. "Automatic Video Indexing and Full-Video Search for Object Appearances," Proc. IFIP WG 2.6 2nd Working Conference on Visual Database Systems, pp. 119-133 (1991).

Agentsheets: A Tool for Building Domain-Oriented Visual Programming Environments

(Demonstration)

Alex Repenning

Department of Computer Science and Institute of Cognitive Science
Campus Box 430
University of Colorado, Boulder CO 80309
(303) 492-1218, ralex@cs.colorado.edu
Fax: (303) 492-2844

ABSTRACT

Visual programming systems are supposed to simplify programming by capitalizing on innate human spatial reasoning skills. I argue that: (i) good visual programming environments should be oriented toward their application domains, and (ii) tools to build domain-oriented environments are needed because building such environments from scratch is very difficult. The demonstration illustrates how the visual programming system builder called Agentsheets addresses these issues and demonstrates several applications built using Agentsheets.

PROBLEM

Different approaches employed in visual programming systems vary in their degree of domain orientation:

- *General purpose visual programming systems* visually represent concepts found in conventional programming languages (e.g., boxes and arrows represent procedures and procedure calls). These systems have two advantages. First, they are applicable to a wide range of domains. Second, visual representations can facilitate syntactic constructions. For instance, shapes in BLOX Pascal (Figure 1) guide the programmer towards making syntactically correct constructions [3]. However, general purpose visual programming systems are difficult to use for non-programmers (e.g., BLOX Pascal still requires basic Pascal knowledge) and provide little - if any - gratification to expert programmers.

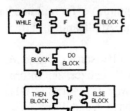

Figure 1. BLOX Pascal

- *Domain-oriented visual programming systems* represent artifacts pertinent to the end users' task at hand. A system like the pinball construction kit (Figure 2) is easy to use for non-programmers [1]. The process of programming in a construction kit-like environment consists of selecting components (e.g., pinball

components) and assembling them. However, it is difficult to reuse systems tailored to a specific domain for other domains. For instance, the pinball construction kit could not be reused for numerical applications such as tax forms. Perhaps the biggest problem with domain-oriented systems is that no high-level substrate exists facilitating their creation.

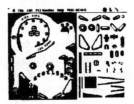

Figure 2. Pinball Construction Kit

Empirical tests suggest that despite their versatility, general purpose visual programming languages, in many situations, provide little or no advantage over conventional textual programming languages [4]. Domain-oriented visual programming systems, on the other hand, seem to be very useful for non-programmers but are hard to build from scratch [2]. The problem is, therefore, to find a new mechanism that will overcome the disadvantages of each approach without sacrificing their advantages.

THE AGENTSHEETS SYSTEM

Agentsheets facilitates the *creation* of domain-oriented visual programming systems. A spatial metaphor consisting of "communicating agents organized in grids" is used by a visual programming system designer to create a visual language specific to a problem domain.

In a typical utilization of Agentsheets, a visual programming system designer will define the look and behavior of domain-specific building blocks called agents. The behaviors of agents determine the meaning of spatial arrangements of agents (e.g., what does it mean when two agents are adjacent to each other) as well as the reaction of agents to user events (e.g., how does an agent react if it gets activated by the user). These agents constitute the elements of a high-level, domain-oriented visual programming language that can be used readily by end users.

End users arrange agents in a work area. The work area has an underlying grid structure analogous to the rows and columns in a spreadsheet. Relationships between agents can be explicitly specified by connecting agents with links or implicitly specified simply by position within the grid structure.

The Agentsheets system is object-oriented. It provides a large set of built-in agent classes supplying typical behaviors to visual programming system designers. The designer extends this set with new classes achieving the domain-oriented behavior.

EXAMPLE APPLICATIONS

The spatial organization of agents in a grid and their ability to communicate with each other can be used to simulate the semantics of flow. Individual agents representing flow conductors (e.g., pieces of wire or water pipes) are connected simply by placing them next to each other. Figure 3 shows two applications relying on flow semantics. Users can interact with more complex conductor agents like switches and valves to control the flow.

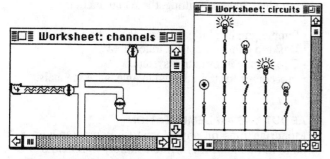

Figure 3. Flow Semantics: Channels (left), Circuits (right)

The ability to animate agents (change look, move, play sounds) can be used to realize very different Agentsheets applications. Figure 4 shows an application to simulate ecosystems. End users build environments consisting of mountains, grass tundra, etc. Then, they set out animals (wolfs, bear, etc.) in those environments.

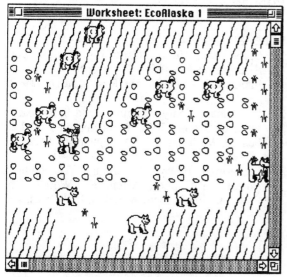

Figure 4. Ecosystem Simulation

The individual patches of the environment and the animals are agents. End users define simple behaviors for all

ecosystem agents. The objective for users is to create ecologically stable environments as well as to get an intuition for the relationships between local behavior and global behavior.

Figure 5 below depicts a more "traditional" visual programming environment based on Agentsheets used to design and run phone-based voice dialog applications [5]. This application includes two different interfaces for two types of users:

- *the customer interface* simulates the very limited touch-tone-button-input/voice-output user interface of an ordinary telephone.

- *the voice dialog designer interface* shows a voice dialog designer a trace of usage and allows the designer to modify a design, while the system is in use, based on customer's suggestions or problems.

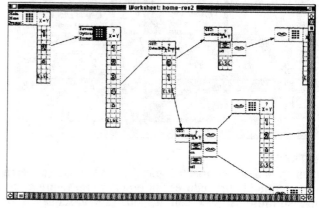

Figure 5. Phone Based Voice Dialog Environment

REFERENCES

1. G. Fischer and A. C. Lemke, "Construction Kits and Design Environments: Steps Toward Human Problem-Domain Communication," *HCI*, Vol. 3, pp. 179-222, 1988.

2. E. P. Glinert, M. M. Blattner and C. J. Freking, "Visual Tools and Languages: Directions for the '90s," 1991 IEEE Workshop on Visual Languages, Kobe, Japan, 1991, pp. 89-95.

3. E. P. Glinert, "Towards "Second Generation" Interactive, Graphical Programming Environments," *IEEE Computer Society, Workshop on Visual Languages*, Dallas, 1986, pp. 61-70.

4. T. R. G. Green, M. Petre and R. K. E. Bellamy, "Comprehensibility of Visual and Textual Programs: A Test of Superlativism Against the 'Match-Mismatch' Conjecture," *Empirical Studies of Programmers: Fourth Workshop*, New Brunswick, NJ, 1991, pp. 121-146.

5. A. Repenning and T. Sumner, "Using Agentsheets to Create a Voice Dialog Design Environment," *Proceedings of the 1992 ACM/SIGAPP Symposium on Applied Computing*, Kansas City, 1992, pp. 1199-1207.

Mondrian: A Teachable Graphical Editor

Henry Lieberman

Media Laboratory
Massachusetts Institute of Technology
Cambridge, Mass. USA
lieber@media.mit.edu

ABSTRACT

Mondrian is a object-oriented graphical editor that can learn new graphical procedures through programming by demonstration. A user can demonstrate a sequence of graphical editing commands on a concrete example to illustrate how the new procedure should work. An interface agent records the steps of the procedure in a symbolic form, using machine learning techniques, tracking relationships between graphical objects and dependencies among the interface operations. The agent generalizes a program that can then be used on "analogous" examples. The generalization heuristics set it apart from conventional "macros" that can only repeat an exact sequence of steps. The system represents user-defined operations using pictorial "storyboards" of examples. By bringing the power of procedural programming to easy-to-use graphical interfaces, we hope to break down the "Berlin Wall" that currently exists between computer users and computer programmers.

KEYWORDS

Programming by demonstration, machine learning, artificial intelligence, graphical editing, end-user programming, direct-manipulation interfaces.

ABOUT THE DEMONSTRATION

Mondrian's ability to learn new operations from interactions with the user can only be appreciated by seeing it in action live. The demonstration will show Mondrian's basic operations, and present a set of prototype application examples. Time permitting, these may include

• Simple graphical illustration construction and editing.
• Desktop publishing. (illustrated above)
• Geographic information systems.
• Procedures for training and maintenance manuals.

ABOUT THE IMPLEMENTATION

Mondrian runs on any Macintosh computer with 8 MB or more of memory. It is written entirely in Macintosh Common Lisp and makes extensive use of the Common Lisp Object System.

ACKNOWLEDGMENTS

Major support for this work comes from a research grant from Alenia Corp. The research was also sponsored in part by grants from Digital Equipment Corp., Kansa Corp., NYNEX, DARPA, and Paws, Inc.

REFERENCES

1. Lieberman, Henry, Capturing Design Expertise by Example, in East-West Conference on Human-Computer Interaction, St. Petersburg, Russia, August 1992.

2. Lieberman, Henry, Dominoes and Storyboards: Beyond Icons on Strings, IEEE Workshop on Visual Languages, Seattle, Washington, USA, September, 1992.

3. Lieberman, Henry, Mondrian: A Teachable Graphical Editor, in Cypher, Allen, ed. Watch What I Do: Programming by Demonstration, MIT Press, 1993.

USABILITY MEASUREMENT - ITS PRACTICAL VALUE TO THE COMPUTER INDUSTRY

Panel organisers: M Maguire and A Dillon

The HUSAT Research Institute
The Elms, Elms Grove
Loughborough
LEICS LE11 1RG
tel: +44 509 611088, fax: +44 509 234651, email: m.c.maguire@lut.ac.uk

PREFACE

This panel will consider the role of usability measurement in the design process. It will address the time needed to perform usability evaluations and compare this process with that of expert assessment. This topic will be discussed in the industrial context of developing computer products within strict timescales. However it will also be seen against the traditional problem of needing to set usability goals and to measure their achievement if usability is to be given the same priority as the more technical software engineering objectives.

KEYWORDS

Usability measurement, Usability metrics, Usability evaluation, Industrial practice.

INTRODUCTION

Usability is now widely recognised as an important software quality alongside technical aspects such as functionality, internal consistency, reliability etc. In the same way that software engineers are developing objective measurement techniques to assess the achievement of these technical qualities, so the Human Factors community have striven to understand what measures can be taken to assess the usability of a software product or system. A number of approaches have been followed including:

(i) the measurement of the user's performance when interacting with the system.

(ii) the measurement of the user's attitude towards the system (often based on rating scales).

(iii) the measurement of the mental effort required to use the system or stress caused in using it.

(iv) the formal analysis of the system itself to assess the operational complexity of using it.

The Esprit MUSiC project 5429 (Metrics for Usability Standards in Computing) has been developing methods for usability measurement following each of these four strands. The aim is to develop methods and metrics which can be applied to a wide range of IT products in order to assess their usability in an objective way. Although the project has achieved early success in technology transfer to industry, there is a need for greater awareness of the practices and needs of software designers and developers if such methods are to be taken up on a large scale. From a survey carried out by the HUSAT Research Institute (Sweeney, Dillon and Maguire 1992), it was found that IT companies expressed a willingness adopt usability measurement procedures only in so far as they are cost effective and fit their design and development procedures. This panel aims to discuss in more detail what industry really requires in terms of usability measurement and how such techniques can be of maximum practical value to them. The panel will be composed of industrial representatives with clear views of the requirements of IT companies, and human factors practitioners who are aware of current methods that may be used. The aim is thus to achieve some form of consensus on the effective utilisation of usability measurement techniques in an industrial context.

ISSUES TO BE DISCUSSED

The panel will consider the following issues:-

- The role and importance of usability evaluation in their companies' design processes and the industrial world in general.

- The value and feasibility of usability goal setting as opposed to simply identifying or diagnosing problems.

- The need for user testing compared with analysis by experts.

- The value of specific metrics to measure usability based on their previous experience of particular products and systems.

- The relevance of standards in software design either formal (ISO, BSI etc) or de facto standards such as MS Windows, CUA, Open Look, Apple Guidelines etc. and the European Directive on Display Screens which refers to software usability.

- The type of evaluations they would normally perform, the data captured and the analysis carried out, as well as the time and resources that can be made available for this type of work.

LIKELY ISSUES FOR DEBATE

It is expected that a number of controversial issues will be raised such as:

- The value of user-based evaluations in predicting real-world acceptability of the product.

- What are the cost/benefits of performing a formal usability study in the context of the timescales normally associated with the design process? How does this compare with 'quick and dirty' expert or user assessment?

- Can generalised usability metrics, applicable across a range of products, really measure relevant aspects of usability?

- How reliable can usability metrics be?

SESSION FORMAT

Panelists will be asked to give a short presentation of their position on usability measurement in industry. In order to generate focussed and contrasting views, each panelist will be asked to begin their presentation by briefly answering the following three questions:

• What single measure or metric would they choose to apply to the evaluation of a generic office product

• What is the most important single piece of advice they give in advising an evaluator performing usability measurement?

• What usability measurement activity can they identify as having either succeeded or failed in their own company or organisation?

They will then be asked to briefly describe their overall position on usability measurement and its value in the IT or computer industry.

After each presentation, one or two brief questions will be taken by the relevant panelist to clarify any particular aspect of the presentation. When all presentations are completed, further questions and comments will be taken from the floor, broadening out the discussion. Before the end, the chairman will spend a few minutes summarising the main views expressed during the session and describing any progress made in reaching a consensus on the future of usability measurement in the industrial context.

The order of the speakers will be such as to highlight potential differences in view on the use of more or less formal approaches to usability evaluation and to develop different themes such as standardisation, early evaluation and iteration in the design process, practical difficulties etc. The following is a likely scenario of the themes that will be developed by each speaker:

Dr Brooke will be invited to speak first and present his view that formalised, lab-based measurement is neither necessary nor of maximum value in assessing usability but that knowledge of the user population, task and (in particular) working environment is critical to establishing valid and comparable results.

Dr Gervan will follow and argue that while formal evaluation methods may be useful, companies will not be prepared to spend money on them until there is a change of attitude towards usability as a concept being of equal importance in cost/benefit terms to other system characteristics.

Dr Bevan will then give an overview of the approach of the MUSiC project in developing formalised usability methods to produce results that can be compared across systems and between system versions. The importance of emerging standards for usability will also be raised

Dr Karat will complete the presentations by highlighting the need to tailor evaluation approaches to meet the differing demands of stages in the design cycle. He will demonstrate that there are still many more practical problems to address before formal methods can be applied in the real-world.

Following a brief discussion of the points raised and major points of contention, Prof. Brian Shackel will open the discussion to the floor.

PANELISTS - BACKGROUNDS AND POSITION STATEMENTS

The panelists have provided the following position statements and background information:

Dr John Brooke - DEC

Our aim in developing computer systems should be to build systems appropriate to the needs of their users. The more generic the systems that are built, the less likely it is that we can build solutions appropriate to the needs of any specific user performing a particular task in a given environment, because what constitutes usability in any given set of circumstances varies widely. Therefore before undertaking ANY system development, it is important to define what usability means for this particular context and how one can measure it, and thus decide, whether the system being developed is usable. Only after defining this framework can one begin to take design decisions such as whether to follow particular style guides, what standards to conform to, etc.

It is my belief that the metrics defined do not need to be particularly formal. The most important part of this process is to understand the context in which usability is being considered and to be able to articulate that context, and how usability is measured in that context to other people involved in the development, use and support of a system. If there is no common understanding of the term "usability" then different people will invariably take differing positions on corrective actions to take in terms of design, use and support of a system.

Background information

John Brooke has a BSc from the University of Liverpool and a PhD from the University of Birmingham in Psychology. He is a member of the User-Centred Systems group at Digital Equipment Co Ltd, Reading, UK which focuses on the development and delivery of systems appropriate to users' needs. John has worked on various international standards bodies including ISO TC159/SC4/WG5 and TC159/SC4/WG6 and chaired the subgroup of TC159/SC4/WG5 which developed ISO

9241 Part 11, which provides a framework for usability specification and measurement.

Address
European Technology Management
Evolutionary Systems Centre
Digital Equipment Co Ltd
Gateway House
Newbury Business Park
NEWBURY RG13 2PZ
United Kingdom

Dr Johan van Gerven - IBM Nederland N.V.

The Usability/Human Factors group at IBM Nederland has 7 professionals, with broad skills in industrial design, psychology, computer science, information development, marketing and business skills. Our aim is to participate in a project right from the beginning. This means that we either want to design the user interface ourselves or assist the development groups during the design and perform a usability tests on the prototype. Most of the time we perform verification tests on the end-product and also evaluate the product when it is in production for some time.

We are interested in usability measurements but at the moment do not put too much effort in it. Most of the products we have to test today do have a user interface of which you can predict the problem areas. So we have to educate/assist our developers in producing usable products and only then apply more sophisticated tests and measurements to assess the usability. There is still a long way to go before we reach this goal.

Background information

Johan C. J. van Gerven has worked for IBM for 24 years now. He has been manager of a software test group and since then has had a variety of management jobs, e.g., technical automation, systems support, systems assurance, information development. Presently he is manager of the Usability/Human Factors group of ISNL (Information Systems Netherlands). ISNL is an international software development center that develops applications for internal use by IBM. These applications are installed in several countries around the world.

Address
IBM Nederland N.V.
ISNL Development, Usability/Human Factors
Watsonneg 2
1423 ND UITHOORN
The Netherlands

Dr Nigel Bevan - NPL.

Current specifications for computer systems rarely contain anything explicit about usability requirements. The major benefit of measuring usability is that it gives the potential for usability requirements to be specified prior to design and for usability to be controlled by repeated measurement during design. Product developers are often criticised for ignoring usability issues. However, unless usability is part of the product specification, they have little choice: their major responsibility is to deliver the product to specification, within budget and on time. It is difficult to justify the resources to go beyond the specification in improving usability if it increases the risk of taking the development costs over budget and delivering late.

In addition to developing metrics, the MUSiC project has therefore put considerable emphasis on deriving usability goals from the overall business goals for a product. Appropriate metrics and criterion values can then be used to operationalise each of the goals. Analytic measures may be used early in design, or later, measures of user performance, satisfaction or mental workload. The requirement to meet these goals justifies the use of appropriate user-centred techniques during design to improve the probability that the goals are achieved.

The project also emphasises the importance of measuring usability as the actual outcome of interaction in a realistic context of use, and has made significant contributions to the development ISO 9241-11 "Guidance on usability specification and measures" which defines usability in a similar way. Adherence to user interface guidelines, such as those found in other parts of ISO 9241, should improve the probability of a better interface, but does not alone ensure that usability, as measured by user performance and attitude, will be achieved.

Background information

Nigel Bevan is head of the Human Computer Interaction Section in the Division of Information Technology and Computing at the National Physical Laboratory, Teddington, England. He is also an active participant in several ISO standards groups which are developing user interface standards, and is editor of ISO 9241-11 on usability.

Address
National Physical Laboratory
DITC HCI Group
TEDDINGTON
Middlesex TW11 0LW
United Kingdom

Dr John Karat - TJ Watson. IBM

In the last ten years the focus on measuring usability has shifted from measurements of the quality of completed (or nearly completed products) to providing information for early design of IT products. However, while the tools that most usability experts were trained on (e.g., experimental techniques for measuring performance) were well suited for quality measurement and problem detection, they have not proved suitable for providing timely information for early design decisions. This has contributed to an increased utilization of expert opinion in product development, and a decrease in the emphasis on formal testing methods.

Is this a good situation? It depends on the skills of the experts providing advice, and the knowledge and tools they bring to bear on the problems they face. There are times when techniques such as formal analysis are called for, and times when less-formal evaluations with potential users of the IT product are appropriate. While we might long for a "better" world in which there was plenty of time and resource for usability measurement, it is more important to face the reality of IT design, and attempt to address how to best provide the information relevant to the design activity.

Background information

John Karat is a research staff member at IBM's T J Watson Research Center. Prior to his current position, John worked in hardware and software product development within IBM, and on the team which developed IBM's Common User Access (CUA) guidelines. He is chair of the ANSI/HFS Human Computer Interaction Standards Committee and chair of the user characteristics subgroup of the ISO Man-Machine dialogue standards committee (ISO TC159 SC4 WG5). He is also the United States representative to IFIP TC 13 (Human-Computer Interaction). His current research activity is focused on early collaborative design activities in the development of computer systems.

Address
TJ Watson Research Centre
IBM
30 Saw Mill River Road
HAWTHORNE NY 10532
USA

CHAIR

Professor Brian Shackel from HUSAT will chair the debate.

Brian Shackel graduated in Classics and later Psychology from Cambridge University. After research at the Medical Research Council's Applied Psychology Unit in Cambridge, he moved to establish and head the Ergonomics Department at EMI Electronics Ltd.

At Loughborough University he was Head of the Department of Human Sciences and Dean of the School of Human & Environmental Studies. He has been a member of the SERC Information Engineering Committee and consultant to a number of organisations, including the Consumers Association, the Council of Industrial Design, the Department of Employment, a range of computer manufacturers and the ISPRA Research Centre of the European Commission. He also carried out a key survey of HCI (Human-Computer Interaction) in Europe which led to the setting up of the European Community's ESPRIT programme to fund collaborative IT (Information Technology) research and development projects involving European companies and academic institutions.

In 1970 Brian Shackel founded the HUSAT Research Institute, which started as a group of 9 researchers and has grown to approximately 45 research staff in 1992. This is now recognised as one of the world's leading Human Factors research institutes.

Brian has been one of the authors of several key papers presenting a framework for usability measurement and proposing the use of operational definitions of usability.

REFERENCE

Sweeney, M., Dillon, A. and Maguire, M., A survey of current practices in usability evaluation and requirements for support within the European IT Industry. HUSAT Memo No. 585, 1992.

The Growth of Software Skill:
A Longitudinal Look at Learning & Performance

Erik Nilsen,[1]   HeeSen Jong,[2]   Judith S. Olson,[3]   Kevin Biolsi,[3]   Henry Rueter,[3]   & Sharon Mutter[4]

    1. Lewis & Clark College
    2. National University of Singapore
    3. The University of Michigan
    4. Western Kentucky University

Contact at: Lewis & Clark College
615 Palatine Hill Road
Portland, OR 97219
nilsen@lclark.edu

ABSTRACT

This research follows a group of users over time (16 months) as they progress from novice towards expert in their use of Lotus 1-2-3. Quantitative and qualitative measures of performance are compared with expert users having over three years of experience. The results indicate that the motor aspects of performance are relatively stable over time, while improvement in the cognitive components of the skill are dependent on aspects of the menu structure and how many things must be retrieved from memory, among other things. These results imply extensions to the Keystroke Level Model of skilled performance as well as suggest ways to design the user interfaces so as to speed the acquisition of expertise.

KEYWORDS: Models of the user, user-interface design issues, GOMS, menu design.

INTRODUCTION

Although today's software applications are very powerful, people rarely master all of the offered functionality. Often users learn a subset of functions, enough to get their work done, though not necessarily efficiently. People persist in using the "default" method for accomplishing a task, e.g., setting fonts for titles of sections one by one, rather than investing in the learning of a specialized method, such as styles. And yet, with time, some people do become experts. They spend enough time using the software to acquire a deeper understanding of it, allowing them to perform tasks quickly and efficiently. What is it in the process of learning the software that leads to this? How can we design software to encourage better learning, more complete use of the software for the speedy, effective use of the power offered?

The literatures of both human-computer interaction and cognitive psychology have begun to inform us about this important process. Within human-computer interaction, studies of the growth of skill in the use of software showed that people attempt to fully master the current task-related skills before moving on to more complex, advanced skills or those relevant to other tasks. Also expertise is often associated with learning specialized methods that help the work be more time-efficient (e.g., building macros, defining styles, or assigning function keys to customized uses)[4, 14]. We also know some of the processes and pitfalls during the early stages of learning, such as the tendency for novices to guess at commands that seem to match their task goal, called "label following" [5, 13]. Within the GOMS framework, we know both how quickly experienced users will perform routine tasks and that mental preparation time, **M**, drops significantly when people repeat a task one right after the other [2, 11, 12].

But, there is not much known about the details of skill progression over longer periods of time when people use software. We want to know not only how knowledge of the software's functionality grows, but also what changes occur in performance over a period of months or years?

In the psychological literature, studies of skill learning in the laboratory focus on the improvement in performance. There, tasks vary from simple perceptual motor skills to cognitively demanding problem solving skills such as generating geometry proofs [8]. Typically, in these skill learning experiments, subjects repetitively perform some tasks, with the results showing improvements in time associated with the amount of practice. While learning rates differ among tasks, a generalized power law of practice fits the data across many experiments [9].

Theories of learning account for this power law of practice with two primary mechanisms, chunking and strength of productions [1, 6]. In these theories, the knowledge is assumed to be stored in production rules consisting of condition-action pairs. When a set of such productions are frequently executed in the same temporal sequence, they are chunked together to produce a specialized production, with a complex condition attached to a series of actions. Furthermore, each time a production rule is used, the strength is increased. The time to execute a production rule is a function of its strength; the more often the rule is used, the faster the response. The primary learning mechanisms from this perspective are temporal contiguity which leads to the formation of new productions, and frequency of activation which results in increased speed of performance.

To date, however, we do not have an integrated view of both the qualitative aspects and the performance details of how learning takes place as people learn in the real world. Most of the laboratory studies track learning over at most a number of hours, and qualitative studies typically compare novices and experts [1, 3, 8, 9][1].

We undertook a longitudinal study of learning in the real-world, looking at both the qualitative aspects of skill development and the evidence from timing performance for theoretical learning mechanisms. We examined the learning of a popular piece of software, Lotus 1-2-3, over the course of a year and a half. While we tested twenty six people in the laboratory under standard conditions, the skill they were learning was acquired outside the laboratory, in training sessions, through group use, and from documentation. Since the software was used in various classes the students were enrolled in, there was motivation to learn it and occasions to use it in homework. In addition, we had seven true experts perform the same tasks as our longitudinal subjects, providing us with benchmark data for comparison purposes.

There are two purposes for this work. One is to extend our theoretical understanding of skill development, evaluating the boundary conditions of extant research through an empirical, longitudinal study. Additionally, we want to highlight aspects of the interface that designers can control which in turn can influence the users' skill development.

METHOD

General Procedure

Thirty-six entering students in the University of Michigan MBA program were taught Lotus 1-2-3 using a paper-based tutorial. Within a week, these students came individually to the laboratory to be tested in standard spreadsheet tasks on one of four (counterbalanced) sample spreadsheets.

---

[1]Doane et al [4] studied a group of UNIX users over the course of two years, but did not look at the details of timing performance.

Twenty six students returned to all four session, at the end of their first, second, and third semesters, to perform the same standard spreadsheet tasks on three other but equivalent spreadsheets.

At each session, the subjects were asked to perform a number of tasks in rough proportion to those they were performing in natural settings. For each session, we assessed the number of tasks they performed correctly, the total time per task, and the pattern of keystrokes. The patterns of keystrokes were used to reveal both time patterns and method choice, following the Keystroke Level Model (KLM) of Card, Moran, and Newell [2], and as used in spreadsheet tasks in Olson and Nilsen [11]. Each of these measures was compared within subjects as they progressed, as well as to that of experts.

Seven experts were chosen from the same general Business School population, including Business Ph.D. students, in response to a survey. The survey asked experienced Lotus users to report both how long and in what setting they used Lotus, which of a set of functions they knew how to use, and how many ways they knew how to do each. Respondents who had both used Lotus for three years or more and knew multiple methods were chosen to participate in this study, embedded in another study which focused on experts' choice of methods [10].

Training of Novices

The Novices were trained in groups in a large, open computing laboratory at the Business School. Each student was seated individually at a personal computer. Each was given an eleven-page tutorial developed by the staff of the computing center. The tutorial ran about an hour, with the instructor giving a five-minute introduction on how to access Lotus 1-2-3, and then asking students to work through he paper tutorial at their own pace. In the tutorial, students were guided through entering and changing a simple 4 column by 10 row cash-flow spreadsheet. In the session, students were explicitly taught to move around the spreadsheet with cursor keys, enter words and values, to change the text justification, column widths and value formats, to enter formulas, to copy a formula from one cell to another, and to store a file. Following this session and throughout their 2 year MBA program, students had free access to reference material available in the computing center.

Individual Testing Sessions

Each experimental session consisted of constructing a small spreadsheet (approx 100 cells) and then making a series of modifications to it. We call these two sets of tasks Construction and Modification. In an effort to avoid constraining subjects in the order in which they did the tasks, we had them work only from a printout of what the final spreadsheet should look like. Using a sheet of instructions, they wrote on the printout any notes they needed to remember, such as formatting details or the formula specifics. The instruction sheet was then taken away and the subjects performed the tasks as quickly as possible in whatever order they wished. The only criterion was that the final product match the specifications as noted on the instruction sheet and appear as shown on the printout.

During the performance of the spreadsheet task, keystroke sequences and times were recorded using an event logging program which ran in the background, transparent but known to the user.

A different spreadsheet was presented to the subjects for each of the four sessions. These spreadsheets were designed to be nearly equivalent. They required the use of the same commands and were approximately the same size. The tasks were chosen as representative of the basic functions of Lotus 1-2-3. They included navigating around the spreadsheet, entering values, entering formulas, entering text, justifying text, copying cell contents, setting column widths, deleting cells, inserting cells, and saving files. Advanced features were purposely avoided as were features that have proven difficult in previous studies (e.g., printing).

The four spreadsheets used in this experiment differed in the words used for the row and column titles, values in the cells, and formulas required. The order of the spreadsheets presented across sessions was counterbalanced across subjects. Each spreadsheet appeared an equal number of times in the four experimental sessions.

RESULTS

Comparison of Three Novice Groups

A total of 26 Novice subjects completed all four sessions (72% of the original 36). Post hoc, this group was divided into three subgroups, based on their performance in session four. Fourteen of the subjects completed all of the tasks presented in the instruction sheets. We call these subjects the *Stars*. Seven subjects performed most of the tasks correctly but ended up with some minor errors, involving incorrect formatting, omitting a task, and performing incorrect additional tasks. This group is called the *Intermediates*. The remaining five subjects committed multiple errors which displayed a basic lack of knowledge about Lotus. All of them, for example, failed to enter any formulas. Wherever a formula was required, they simply entered the value which was the product of the formula. The instruction sheets clearly specified that formulas were to be used. Without the formulas, the spreadsheet is merely a static representation, lacking the recalculation function

used in "what if" analyses, the hallmark of spreadsheet software. This failure reveals in these subjects a serious lack of understanding of the use of spreadsheet software and hence these subjects are called *Duffers*.

The three groups of subjects performed the various tasks with differing success, showing the levels of difficulty of some of the tasks. The initial numbers in Table 1 show the percent of sub-tasks completed, below which in italics is the percent of subtasks which were completed with the most *efficient* method.

	Novice Group		
		Interme-	
	Stars	diates	Duffers
Sub-Task			
Enter Formulas	100%	100%	0%
	79%	*57%*	*0%*
Set Col Width	100%	100%	80%
	86%	*71%*	*60%*
Justify Text	100%	71%	20%
	36%	*0%*	*0%*
Format Numbers	100%	71%	20%
	36%	*0%*	*0%*
Delete Cells	100%	100%	60%
	79%	*71%*	*0%*
Insert Cells	100%	86%	60%
	93%	*29%*	*60%*

Table 1. Comparison of the three Novice groups' success in completing the various subtasks and (in italics) the percentage of them that did each with the most efficient method

This table clearly shows the differences in completion rates and efficiency among the various groups of Novices. The Duffers have a lower completion rate than both other groups for all of the subtasks as well as a lower rate of completing them with the most efficient method. And, even the Stars, who completed the tasks successfully, have difficulty performing some of them with the most efficient method offered (e.g. justify text and format numbers).

The remainder of the analyses reported here focus only on the 14 Stars and 7 Experts, following the progress these Stars made toward expertise. We analyze their speed of performance at various levels of granularity. Then we turn to a comparison of the strategies they used and the efficiency of method choice between our Stars and true Experts.

Drop in Total Session Time

Not surprisingly, the Stars' performance improved markedly over the course of sixteen months. The total session time decreased monotonically and significantly over the four sessions.[2] Combining the times for the Construction and the Modification tasks shows a drop from 46 minutes and 16 seconds to 25 minutes and 24 seconds from session one to session four F(3,39)=19.91; p<.0001.

Even after sixteen months of using Lotus 1-2-3 in coursework, not even the Stars were performing at the level of proficiency of the Experts. We compared the Experts' performance with the four Novices who entered precisely the same spreadsheet for session four. The Experts took on average half the time to complete all the tasks: 12 minutes and 54 seconds compared to 23 minutes and 27 seconds for the Stars F(1,9)=10.07, p<.01.

Drop in Subtask Times

The total times were further broken down into sub-task times. The sub-tasks are listed in Table 2 in descending order of frequency in the experiment. The times reported here are the total amount of time which the Stars spent on the various subtasks during both the Construction and Modification phases of the experiment. The times include any fumbling which could clearly be identified as part of a subtask. All keystrokes which could not be associated with a subtask are combined under Errors in the table. The attained significance level from a repeated ANOVA comparing all four sessions is noted with asterisks. The degrees of freedom for each comparison is (3,39). Also shown are the times and percent drop for sessions one and four.

All of the task times decrease from session one to session four, most of them significantly. The amount of time spent making errors drop sharply from session one to four. The Stars are clearly doing a lot less fumbling around after sixteen months experience.

Session four task times for the Stars are much longer than for the Experts in many of the sub-tasks, as shown in Table 3. Since the Experts all used the XYZ spreadsheet, the cleanest comparison is with the four Novices who also used the XYZ spreadsheet in session 4. Here factorial

---

[2]All of the task time analyses are based on a repeated measure ANOVA since the spreadsheets are isomorphic in the sense that they involve the same subtasks and approximately the same number of keystrokes. The same pattern of results is obtained using a factorial design.

ANOVA's with (1,9) degrees of freedom form the basis for the attained significance levels.

TASKS	SESS. 1	SESS. 4	% DROP	SIG.
Navigating	624 sec.	402 sec.	36%	***
Entering Values	129	97	25%	*
Entering Text	684	413	40%	***
Copying	263	159	40%	
Formulas	299	115	62%	*
Saving Files	82	52	37%	**
Column Widths	87	46	47%	***
Justifying Text	97	76	22%	
Formatting numbers	97	63	35%	
Deleting Cells	49	33	33%	*
Inserting Cells	52	27	48%	
Errors	397	75	81%	***

(*=.05, **=.01, ***= .001)

Table 2 . Drop in sub-task times from sessions one to four for the Stars. (all spreadsheets)

The Experts are performing all of the subtasks in less time than the Stars in session four. This suggests that even after sixteen months of using Lotus 1-2-3, the Novices have room for improvement in performing many basic spreadsheet commands. Notice the extremely low time spent by the Experts making errors.

Drop in Keystroke Times

To gain a more detailed understanding of where the improvement in performance is located, we turn to an analysis at the level of individual keystrokes. Three of the menu commands were selected (file, column width, and copy) as being representative tasks. The **M** and **k** operators from the KLM model of Card, Moran, and Newell (1983) were assigned to all of the observed keystrokes for these three tasks. The assignment of operators for saving a file named XYZ, for example, is shown below:

Mk[f] **Mk**[s] **Mk**[X] **k**[Y] **k**[Z] **Mk**[Enter]

The average times for the 2 KLM operators (**M** & **k**) separated by task and session are shown in Figure 1.[3] The x-axis here is plotted in calendar time to show the relative experience for the Novices and the Experts at the time of performance. For the Novices, this time is determined from the time of the practice session in the experiment. For the Experts, it is the average time they reported having used Lotus 1-2-3.

TASKS	STARS SESSION 4	EXPERTS	% DROP	SIG.
Navigating	360 sec.	212 sec.	41%	**
Entering Values	66	55	17%	
Entering Text	403	242	40%	*
Copying	151	84	44%	*
Formulas	115	41	64%	**
Saving Files	55	33	40%	
Column Widths	33	17	48%	*
Justifying Text	64	21	67%	*
Formatting #'s	55	31	44%	
Deleting Cells	33	15	55%	
Inserting Cells	38	14	63%	
Errors	101	19	81%	*

(*=.05, **=.01)

Table 3 Comparison of Stars and Experts on sub-task times (XYZ spreadsheet only)

Interestingly, in the Novice data, the keystrokes containing mental operators (**Mk**) showed a significant drop over the four sessions for all three tasks, (means comparison for **Mk**'s of session 1 & 2 vs. 3 & 4 yields $F(1)=31.35$, $p<.0001$) eventually falling lower than the predicted KLM value of 1.63 sec. by session three for the copy tasks. There is no evidence of these times leveling off in this data. The value of the mental operator is quite

---

[3]We report the actual latencies for keystrokes which contain an **M** instead of subtracting out a constant value for the motor **k** time. Therefore, the figures show the time for mental operations as **Mk**. Only correct keystrokes are included in this data. All error keystrokes are removed.

different among the three tasks, with the more frequent copy task taking less time. In contrast, the physical keystroke operator (**k**) remained steady at approximately 400 msec. for all three tasks across the four sessions. A means comparison contrast of sessions 1 & 2 with sessions 3 & 4 support this $F(1)=.0012$, n.s.

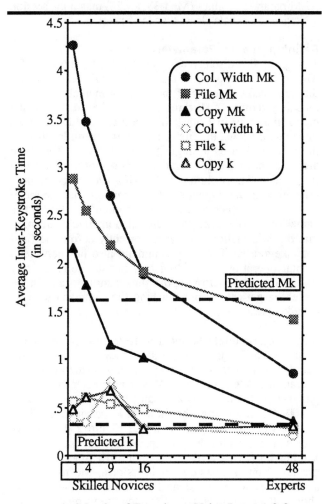

Figure 1. - Observed and Predicted Values for KLM Operators for Column Width, File and Copy Tasks .

For the Experts, the observed times are much faster than for the Novices. In particular, the **Mk** times for the Copy task are extremely fast (.36 sec.). The **Mk** times for the column width and file tasks are slower (.85 and 1.42 sec. respectively); however, both are much faster than the predicted value from the KLM (1.63 sec.). These results present two problems for the KLM in its current form.

The single **M** operator posited in KLM for all tasks does not predict the large difference in the observed mental times for these three tasks. Additionally, the KLM claims to predict the times for Expert users. For the Experts in this study, the observed times for mental operations are significantly faster than predicted. In fact the original KLM parameter values (**M**=1.35, **k**=.28) match the session 4 Novice (Star) data closer than the Experts.

Refining the M Parameter

To explore this discrepancy between KLM predictions for **Mk** times and our data, we examined the differences among the three tasks in terms of the types of mental operations that they require. All three tasks involve traversing the menu hierarchy in Lotus. The column width task uses three menu levels, the file task uses two menu levels, and the copy task uses a single menu selection. The three tasks also have mental operations that do not involve menu traversal. The column width and file tasks include remembering and typing some information after the menu traversal, a number for the column width task, and a file name for the file task. Both task also involve confirming that the information was typed correctly before the final enter keypress. The copy command also has non-menu mental operations, including locating the cells to copy from and to and confirming that the cursor is located in the correct target cell before finishing the command with an enter keypress.

Since Experts might be inclined to learn common menu sequences and retrieve them as if they were words, we decided to separate the menu and non-menu mental operations. We split the KLM **Mk** parameter into 2 new parameters, Menu and Non-menu **Mk**'s. We ran two-way ANOVA's involving the new **Mk** parameters (2) x Sessions (4) for the Novice data. Figure 2 graphically shows the results for the two separate mental operators and **k** times for saving a file. The menu **Mk** times show the greatest drop in times over the sessions. Means contrast analyses reveal that sessions 3 & 4 times are significantly shorter than sessions 1 & 2 for the menu mental times $F(1)=17.85$; $p<.0001$, whereas it is not significant for the non-menu times $F(1)=0.98$; n.s.

Looking at the Experts' values for these parameters is also revealing. Here the menu **Mk** time is identical to the **k** times while the non-menu **Mk** time is still over two seconds. This is strong evidence that mental preparation drops out completely for the menu selection in this task. Other recent work reports a similar reduction in menu selection time for expert users [7]. We show that the speed-up does not involve all mental retrievals, rather it is localized in the menu traversal.

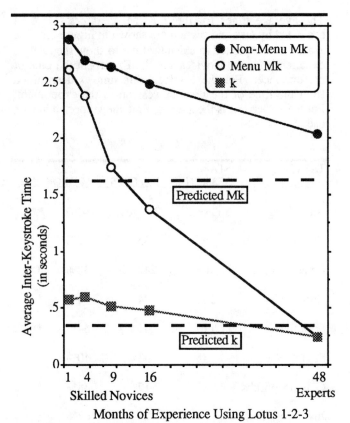

Figure 2. - Observed and Predicted Values for revised KLM Operators for File Tasks .

Comparison of Strategies and Method Choice

The Experts and Novices differed on more than speed alone. There were marked differences in strategies used to accomplish some of the spreadsheet tasks. The Experts invariably used more efficient methods than the Novices.

One example of the inefficient methods used by the Stars concerns menu selection in general. Lotus provides two methods to select menu items. The most efficient method is to type the first letter of the command which immediately selects it. The second method, much less efficient, is to use the arrow keys to move the cursor until the desired command is highlighted. Two of the Stars persisted in using this arrow method throughout the study. None of the Experts used this method. One feature of the arrow method is that when a menu item is highlighted, information is displayed which gives the user information about what that command will do and/or what the next menu level will contain. It is possible that the subjects who persisted in using this method were actively searching for help in deciding how to accomplish the tasks.

The most striking contrast in efficiency was in the specification of formulas. One type of formula that appeared on each of the spreadsheets was a summation of a column of numbers. All of the Experts used the @sum function, which is the most efficient method. It involves typing the function name and specifying the first and last cells in the range to be summed. Three of the 14 skilled Novices used a less efficient method, selecting each cell in the range and adding them up with "+"s. While this method is appropriate for adding 2 cells, it is very time consuming for a larger range of cells. Another marked difference in formula entry was the order in which the user specified the cells. The summation formulas were located below the numbers they referenced. All seven of the Experts selected the near (bottom) cell first followed by the far (top) cell. This strategy minimizes the keystrokes needed to specify the formula. Four of the Experts used a specialized navigation method involving the end+arrow keys, which reduces the keystrokes even more. In contrast, all 14 of the Novices added the cells from top to bottom, using the arrow keys exclusively.

Another notable difference in strategy concerned the setting of the column widths. The instructions called for one column to be set to one width, and all of the other columns to be set at to a second width. The optimal method involves two commands. One sets the global column width, and another sets the width for the one exception. Six out of seven Experts used this optimal strategy. Only two of the fourteen Novices did. The other subjects set each column width individually, more than doubling the number of keystrokes.

DISCUSSION

Taken as a whole, this study shows that users do not quickly and readily learn to use software packages, not even over two years of intermittent experience. In fact, experience does not guarantee that users will learn even the basic functionality of a sophisticated software package. Nearly half of the MBA's who completed the study had difficulty completing basic spreadsheet tasks after more than a year of experience using the software in their professional training. Even after sixteen months of use, skilled software users have a long way to go to become experts on both quantitative and qualitative measures. This is apparent in the comparison of total and subtask times, keystroke level analyses of performance, and in the inefficient strategies for accomplishing tasks.

Various results support the theoretical mechanisms of learning from the literature in cognitive psychology. First, there seems to be a gradual strengthening of productions: Improvement in task times is gradual, as is improvement

in sub-task times and indeed the individual M parameters. Whereas the gradual improvement in tasks might be accounted for by adoption of more efficient methods, the improvement in M itself cannot. Furthermore, the tasks that are practiced more often in everyday experience have lower Ms, further evidence for the strengthening and thus quickening of the productions. Interestingly, the ks, the motor components of the commands, do not improve with practice. Not all parts of actions speed up with repeated use.

In addition, there seems to be evidence for learning beyond strengthening. Experts use different methods than Novices. And, when using the same methods, their performance times are much faster. The details of their performance timing show that the Experts perform at the same speed for the aspects of the commands that must be retrieved on the spot, but the aspects that could be learned and chunked are much faster. We have evidence for both chunking and speed-up from strengthening, as well as the acquisition of new actions, the more efficient methods.

This has implications for software designers. It suggests that wherever possible, incorporating constant sequences of keystrokes in commands will facilitate both learning and eventual expert-level performance. Additionally, the fewer parameters which have to be remembered and entered the better. The cost of these operations remain high regardless of experience level.

ACKNOWLEDGEMENTS.

This line of work has benefitted greatly from long discussions with Peter Polson. This research was supported in part by a grant from the Army Research Institute (MDA-903-89-K-0025) to Judith S. Olson and Peter G. Polson.

REFERENCES

1. Anderson, J.R. (1982) Acquisition of cognitive skill *Psychological Review*, 89(4), 369-406.

2 Card, S. K., Moran, T. P., and Newell, A. (1983) *The Psychology of Human-Computer Interaction*. Hillsdale, NJ: Lawrence Erlbaum Assoc.

3. Ericsson, K. A. and Smith, J. E. (Eds) (1991) *Toward a general theory of expertise: Prospects and limits*. Cambridge, UK: Cambridge University Press.

4. Doane, S. M., Pelligrino, J. W., and Klatzky, R. L. (1990) Expertise in a computer operating system: Conceptualization and performance. *Human Computer Interaction, 5*, 267-304.

5. Kieras, D. E. and Polson, P. G. (1985) An approach to the formal analysis of user complexity. *International Journal of Man-Machine Studies*, 22, 365-394.

6. Laird, J.E., Newell, A. and Rosenbloom, P. S. (1987) SOAR: An architecture for general intelligence. *Artificial Intelligence*, 33,1-64.

7. Lane, D. M., Napier, H. A., Batsell, R. R., and Naman, J. L. (1991) The application of Card, Moran, and Newell's keystroke-level model to the operation of hierarchical menu systems. Unpublished manuscript under review, Rice University.

8. Neves, D.M., and Anderson, J.R. (1981) Knowledge compilation: Mechanisms for the automatization of cognitive skills. In J.R. Anderson (Ed.) *Cognitive skills and their acquisition.* Hillsdale, NJ: John Wiley and Sons, 57-84.

9. Newell, A., and Rosenbloom, P. S. (1981) Mechanisms of skill acquisition and the law of practice. In J.R. Anderson (Ed.) *Cognitive skills and their acquisition.* Hillsdale, NJ: John Wiley and Sons, 1-55.

10. Nilsen, E., Jong, H., Olson, J. S., and Polson, P. G. (1992) Method engineering: From data to model to practice. *Proceedings of CHI'92 Human Factors in Computing Systems,* NY: ACM Press, 313-320.

11. Olson, J. R. and Nilsen, E. (1987-1988) Analysis of the cognition involved in spreadsheet software interaction. *Human-Computer Interaction*, 3, 309-349.

12. Olson, J. R. and Olson, G.M. (1990) The growth of cognitive modelling in human-computer interaction since GOMS. *Human-Computer Interaction*, 5, 221-265.

13 Polson, P.G. and Lewis, C.H. (1991) Theory-based design for easily learned interfaces. *Human-Computer Interaction,* 15, 191-220.

14. Rosson, M. B. (1984) Effects of experience on learning, using, and evaluating a text editor. *Human Factors,* 26, 463-475.

EMBEDDING COMPUTER-BASED CRITICS IN THE CONTEXTS OF DESIGN

Gerhard Fischer[1], Kumiyo Nakakoji[1,2], Jonathan Ostwald[1], Gerry Stahl[1], Tamara Sumner[1]

[1]University of Colorado at Boulder
Department of Computer Science
Boulder CO USA 80309-0430
(303) 492-1592

[2]Software Research Associates
Software Engineering Laboratory
1-1-1 Hirakawa-cho, Chiyoda-ku
Tokyo 102, Japan

E-mail: {gerhard, kumiyo, ostwald, gerry, sumner}@cs.colorado.edu

ABSTRACT

Computational critiquing mechanisms provide an effective form of computer-human interaction supporting the process of design. Critics embedded in domain-oriented design environments can take advantage of additional knowledge residing in these environments to provide less intrusive, more relevant critiques. Three classes of embedded critics have been designed, implemented, and studied: *Generic critics* use domain knowledge to detect problematic situations in the design construction. *Specific critics* take advantage of additional knowledge in the partial specification to detect inconsistencies between the design construction and the design specification. *Interpretive critics* are tied to perspective mechanisms that support designers in examining their artifact from different viewpoints.

KEYWORDS: Generic critics, specific critics, interpretive critics, design environments, specification, construction, domain orientation, perspectives, critiquing systems.

INTRODUCTION

We view design as a process of successive refinement through trial, breakdown, interpretation, and reflection [15, 16, 18, 21]. Critiquing – the communication of a reasoned opinion about an artifact or a design – plays a central role in the design process. Computational critic mechanisms provide an effective form of computer-human interaction supporting this important aspect of design. We have developed a series of design environments containing critiquing mechanisms to investigate how such environments can provide timely and relevant knowledge to designers.

Our research group's early work focused on building and evaluating stand-alone critiquing mechanisms. Critical analyses of these and other systems [7, 17], combined with empirical evaluations, led us to realize that the challenge in building critiquing systems is not simply to provide design

feedback: the challenge is to say the "right" thing at the "right" time. We claim that embedding critics in domain-oriented design environments has provided an effective response to this challenge. Design environments are computer programs that support designers in concurrently specifying a problem, constructing a solution, and interpreting an emerging design from alternative perspectives. Embedded critics can provide more focused, less intrusive critiques by taking advantage of knowledge of the contexts of design: the domain, the construction situation, the partial specification, and interpretive perspectives.

While we have investigated critiquing in numerous domains such as computer network design [5] and lunar habitat design [19], the examples for this article will be based on floor plan design for kitchens [6]. This paper first describes the evaluations and theoretical motivations that led to the redesign and extensions of our critiquing mechanisms; we analyze early systems and empirical results that exposed the deficiencies of stand-alone critiquing mechanisms. Next, we present our redesign, three classes of embedded critics: generic, specific, and interpretive critics. We conclude with a discussion of the benefits of this new approach.

ANALYSIS OF EARLY CRITIQUING SYSTEMS

Our analyses identified several shortcomings in early critiquing systems that hindered their ability to say the "right" thing at the "right" time:

- lack of domain orientation;
- insufficient facility for justifying critic suggestions;
- lack of an explicit representation of the user's goals;
- no support for different individual perspectives;
- timing problems with critic intervention strategies.

Saying the "right" thing...

LISP-CRITIC [3, 8, 12] allows programmers to request suggestions on how to improve their code. The system proposes transformations that make the code more cognitively efficient (i.e., easier to read and maintain) or more machine efficient (i.e., faster or smaller). However, lack of domain orientation limits the depth of critical analysis the critiquing system can provide. Without domain knowledge, critic rules cannot be tied to higher level concepts; LISP-CRITIC can answer questions such as whether the Lisp code can be written more efficiently, but it cannot assist users in deciding whether the code can solve their problem.

FRAMER [13] enables designers to develop window-based user interfaces on Symbolics Lisp machines. FRAMER's knowledge base contains design rules for evaluating the completeness and syntactic correctness of the design as well as its consistency with interface style guidelines. Evaluations of FRAMER showed that many users did not understand the consequences of following the critic's advice or why the advice was beneficial to solving their problem. We have observed that when users do not understand why a suggestion is made, they tend to follow the critic's advice whether or not it is appropriate to their situation. FRAMER II [12] provided short explanations to address this problem. However, in design there are not always simple answers; access to argumentative discussions are necessary [15].

JANUS [6, 7] is a step towards addressing the previous shortcomings. JANUS allows designers to construct kitchen architectural floor plans. It contains two integrated subsystems: a domain-oriented kitchen construction kit and an issue-based hypermedia system containing design rationale. Critics respond to problems in the construction situation by displaying a message and providing access to appropriate issues. However, these critics often give spurious or irrelevant advice resulting from the lack of an explicit representation of the user's task. The only task goal built into JANUS is one of building a good kitchen. With an explicit model of the designer's intentions for a *particular* design, critics can be selectively enabled and provide less intrusive and more relevant advice.

It is not possible to anticipate all the knowledge necessary for a critiquing system to say the "right" thing in every design situation. Design domains are continually evolving as new knowledge is gained. JANUS-MODIFIER [10] was developed to respond to this problem by making the domain knowledge (including critics) end-user modifiable. But, being able to add new knowledge is not sufficient; different users must be able to organize and manage design knowledge and critics to reflect *their* perspectives on design. Design environments need to support interpreting a problem from many perspectives (technical, structural, functional, aesthetic, personal), and critiquing accordingly.

... at the "right" time
A number of systems [1, 8] investigated critic intervention strategies, i.e., strategies determining when and how a critic should signal a potential problem. This research focused on studying *active* versus *passive* intervention strategies. Active critics continually monitor user actions and make suggestions as soon as a problematic situation is detected. Passive critics are explicitly invoked by users to evaluate their partial design.

A protocol analysis study [12, 13] showed that passive critics were often not activated early enough in the design process to prevent designers from pursuing solutions known to be suboptimal. Often, subjects invoked the passive critiquing system only after they thought they had completed the design. By this time, the effort of repairing the situation was prohibitively expensive. In a subsequent study using the same design environment, an active critiquing strategy was shown to be more effective by detecting problematic situations early in the design process.

However, experience with our early critiquing systems showed that active critics are not a perfect solution either: they can disrupt the designer's concentration on the task at the wrong time and interfere with creative processes. Interruption becomes even more intrusive if the critics signal breakdowns at a different level of abstraction compared to the level of the task users are currently engaged in.

What is needed is a strategy that: (1) alerts designers to problematic solutions, (2) avoids unnecessary disruptions, and (3) allows users to control the critic's intervention strategy. Embedding critics in design environments allows users to *control* critic intervention through interaction with the construction, specification, and interpretation design contexts.

THEORETICAL MOTIVATION
Our evaluations of computer-based critiquing mechanisms show that while critics provide useful support for people engaged in design tasks, a number of problems arise if the critics are not adequately attuned to the task at hand. Design methodologists and proponents of situated cognition have argued that human critical reflection during designing is *situated* in various ways, suggesting that computational critics should be made similarly *context-dependent.*

Suchman [20] argues that when pursuing a task people do not necessarily follow an explicit step-by-step plan they have mentally worked out ahead of time. Rather, they respond to their changing environment based on tacit skills. Schoen [16] describes design as a process of reflection-in-action where each design move creates a new situation, which may challenge the assumptions and strategies under which the designer is operating. These situations signal the designer of a need to reflect upon the design context and possibly to formulate new strategies.

Another approach is suggested by Rittel [15], who sees design as a process of argumentation. A domain like kitchen design consists of a variety of issues to be resolved in completing a task. Within the context of a specific design project, arguments for various answers to these issues can be debated from many perspectives. Solutions are not dependent only upon the unique task, but also upon the background, interests, and commitments of the various stakeholders: i.e., the designers, their clients, and the eventual users. More generally, Winograd and Flores [21] stress the role of interpretation in design. Designers interpret the task, the consequences of possible design decisions, and competing design rationale from their shared or individual perspectives.

These theorists reject waterfall models of design according to which designers first derive an exhaustive specification of a task and then proceed to methodically implement the specification. Rather, design is viewed as an integrated process of problem framing (task specification), problem solving (design construction), and problem interpretation (interpretive perspectives).

These theoretical considerations suggest that critical reflection is most effective when seen as embedded in a number of inter-dependent contexts. Critiquing mechanisms need to be embedded in design environments in order to support critical reflection in design. Design environments represent a variety of design contexts (see Figure 1). First, there is the context of knowledge of the *domain* itself. We represent this as an issue-base capturing the accepted wisdom of the field, a catalog of illustrative past designs, and a palette of domain-oriented components. Unlike the rule-base of an expert system, the issue-base is neither complete nor consistent, but can evolve gradually, supporting design as an argumentative process by incorporating alternative and opposed viewpoints. Second, we represent the current state of *construction* in a graphical display. Third, the evolving partial *specification* is included to guide evaluation of the adequacy of design. Finally, support is provided for the definition of group and personal versions of domain knowledge that can represent critical *interpretations* [18]. By embedding critics in the contexts of the domain, construction, specification, and interpretation, we overcome the problems of stand-alone critic systems.

EMBEDDING CRITICS IN DESIGN ENVIRONMENTS

In response to our evaluation of early critiquing mechanisms and to the theoretical arguments for contextualization, we have explored three types of mechanisms for embedding critics in computational design environments: *generic*, *specific*, and *interpretive* critics. These mechanisms will be described below in a scenario involving HYDRA [4], a design environment which illustrates our multifaceted architecture.

Integrated Design Environments

Reflection on the shortcomings of JANUS [6] led us to extend it by incorporating representations of additional aspects of the design context. Like its predecessor JANUS, HYDRA contains both a construction and an argumentation component. HYDRA also supports a specification component [9] and a catalog of designs. The specification format is based on questionnaires used by professional kitchen designers to elicit their customers' requirements, such as the kitchen owner's cooking habits and family size. The catalog is a repository for past designs that are illustrative of the possible design space. Catalog entries support case-based reasoning and provide concrete design examples of issues discussed in the argumentation

component. Perspective mechanisms allow the user to switch viewpoints corresponding to different interests or concerns [18]. These software components of the HYDRA system provide design creation tools and information repositories which reflect the real-world contexts of the design process.

Embedding critiquing systems in integrated design environments has several benefits. First, they have an increased level of critical analysis because critiquing mechanisms have been tied to the partial construction and the domain knowledge. The argumentation base and catalog of designs provide rich sources of domain knowledge that the critiquing mechanism can use in its explanation process. Second, the specification component provides an explicit representation of the designer's intentions for a specific design. The critiquing mechanism can take advantage of this information to enable sets of critics to evaluate the current design construction selectively for adherence to the designer's stated goals. Third, critiquing can be done from specific viewpoints, such as construction costs, resale value, plumbing concerns, or work flow. Personal and group perspectives can also be developed to provide critiquing from different cultural, socio-economic, or idiosyncratic viewpoints.

Scenario Illustrating Generic, Specific and Interpretive Critics

Bob has been asked to design a kitchen for the Smith family. Working with the Smiths, Bob enters the partial specification shown in Figure 1.

Bob begins working on a floor plan in the HYDRA construction. He moves the dishwasher next to the cabinet. Bob's action triggers a *generic critic*, and the message, "The dishwasher is too far from the sink," is displayed. Generic critics reflect knowledge that applies to all designs, such as accepted standards, building codes, and domain knowledge based on physical principles. Often, this generic knowledge can be found in textbooks, training curricula, or by interviewing domain practitioners. Bob highlights the critic's message and elects to see its associated argumentation. The argumentation explains that plumbing guidelines require the dishwasher to be within one meter of the sink. Bob follows the critic's suggestion and moves the dishwasher next to the right side of the sink.

This action triggers a *specific critic* with the rule, "If you are left-handed, the dishwasher should be on the left side of the sink." Specific critics reflect design knowledge that is tied to situation-specific physical characteristics and domain-specific concepts that not every design will share. These critics are constructed dynamically from the partial specification to reflect current design goals. This particular critic rule was activated because Bob specified that the primary cook is left-handed (see Figure 1). Bob examines the supporting argumentation, "Having the dishwasher to the left of the sink creates an efficient work flow for a left-handed person." Bob decides this is an important concern and puts the dishwasher on the left side of the sink.

Then Bob remembers that the Smiths are remodeling mainly to increase their property value in anticipation of selling in two years. So Bob decides to examine his design from a resale-value perspective. When Bob switches to the Resale-value Perspective, an *interpretive critic* is triggered with the rule, "The dishwasher should be on the right side of the sink." Interpretive critics support design as a interpretive process by allowing designers to interpret the design situation from different perspectives according to their interests. In this perspective, the critic about the dishwasher and sink has been redefined and its associated rationale has been modified. Now the argumentation says, "Optimizing your kitchen for left-handed cooks can adversely affect the house's resale value since most kitchen

users are right-handed." Bob decides that enhancing the Smiths' resale value is the more important consideration and moves the dishwasher. As long as he remains in the Resale-value Perspective, Bob will be informed by the critics whenever they detect a feature negatively affecting resale value; access to argumentation concerning designing for resale practices will be provided.

Three Embedded Critiquing Mechanisms
Embedded critics increase the usefulness of design environments by making information structures more relevant to the task at hand [9]. The basic critiquing process consists of the following phases: (1) the set of appropriate critic rules to be enabled is identified; (2) the

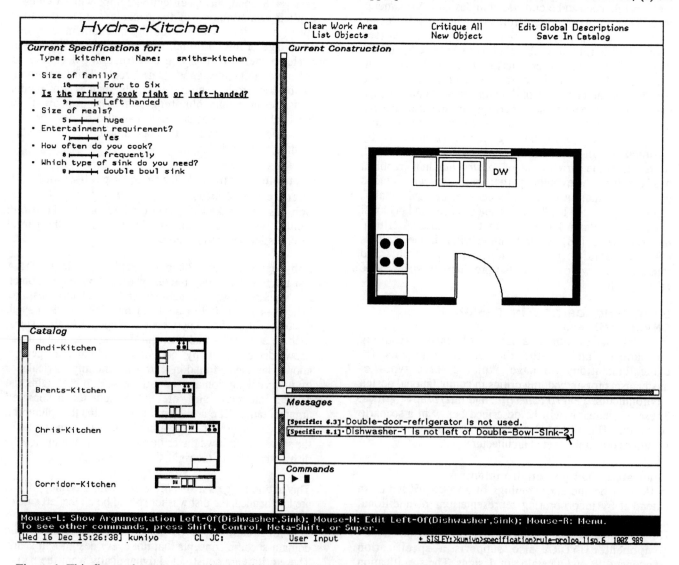

Figure 1. This figure shows a screen image of HYDRA . The "Current Specification" window shows a summary of currently selected answers using the specification component. An indicator attached to each of the selected answers allows users to assign weights of importance to the specified item in order to set priorities [9]. The "Catalog" window shows previous kitchen designs that can be examined or reused. The "Current Construction" window shows a partial construction being built using components provided in a palette of kitchen design units (not shown). The "Messages" window is used to present critic notification messages. The number attached to the critic message is a weighted measure indicating the relevance of the fired critic.

design construction is then analyzed for compliance with the currently enabled set of critic rules; (3) when a lack of compliance is detected, the critic signals a possible problem and provides entry into the exact place in the argumentative hypermedia system where the appropriate explanation is located; and (4) concrete catalog examples that illustrate the explanation given in the form of argumentation can optionally be delivered [7].

Generic critics. All three critic mechanisms – generic, specific, and interpretive – use a production system style of knowledge representation and follow the basic critiquing process described above. Critic rules consist of condition and action clauses plus links into the argumentation context. The *condition* clause checks whether a certain situation exists in the current design construction and is defined in terms of spatial relations between design units, such as near, far, next-to, etc. The *action* clause notifies the designer that a particular situation has been detected.

Each critic rule is linked to a particular issue in the argumentation base. The designer can view the critic's associated argumentation by selecting the initial notification message to display an entry-point into the hypermedia issue-base. Such argumentative explanations help designers determine why the design situation identified by the critic message may be significant or problematic. Designers can optionally explore the issue-base or select an issue and an associated answer in the argumentation and request to see a positive example or a counter-example from the catalog of designs.

The three mechanisms for embedded critics differ from one another in how they determine which set of critic rules

should be enabled. Generic critics provide the default set of enabled critics by evaluating the construction situation based on an assumption that a designer wants to design a "good" kitchen. "Good" in this sense refers to a kitchen that meets commonly accepted practices of most kitchen designers.

Specific Critics. Specific critics evaluate the construction situation for compliance with the partial specification. Specification-linking rules are used to dynamically identify the set of specific critics to be enabled [9].

A specification linking rule represents a dependency between an issue/answer pair in the specification and associated pro and con arguments in the argumentation-base. As shown in Figure 2, a specification linking rule connects the argumentation issue "Where should the dishwasher be placed?" with the specification item "Is the primary cook right or left-handed?" The shared domain distinction "left-handedness" is used to establish a dependency between this particular specification item and the argumentation issue.

Each specification item has either an associated critic condition or an associated domain distinction. Domain distinctions are a vocabulary for expressing domain concepts, like left-handedness, safety, and efficiency. Whenever the designer modifies the specification, the critiquing system recompiles the specification-linking rules to reflect the newly relevant domain distinctions. In this way, critiquing criteria are tied to a representation of the partially articulated goals of a specific design project.

Interpretive Critics. Interpretive critics [18, 19] provide

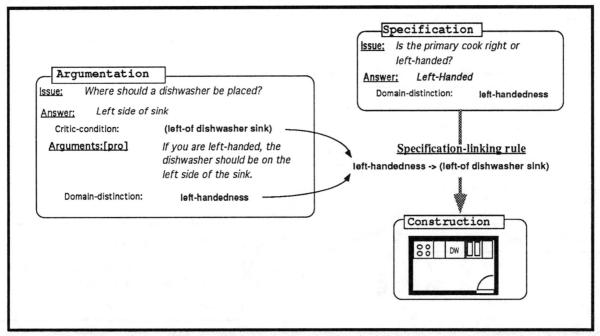

Figure 2. Illustration of a specification-linking rule that enables the "dishwasher should be on the left side of the sink" critic. The domain distinction associated with a specification item ("left-handedness") is paired with a matching pro or con argument in the argumentation (left-of dishwasher sink) to form a *specific critic rule*.

support for design as a hermeneutic (interpretive) process. They allow designers to interpret the design situation according to their interests. Interpretive critics are associated with design *perspectives* rather than with partial specifications. Perspectives are a mechanism for creating, managing, and selectively activating different sets of critics and design knowledge, such as spatial relations, domain distinctions, palette items, and argumentation.

The perspectives mechanism organizes all the design knowledge in the system. It allows items of knowledge to be bundled into personal or topical groupings or versions. For instance, a Resale Perspective might include critics and design rationale pertinent to homeowners concerned about their home's resale appeal. Another perspective could be created for the Smith's kitchen; it might include considerations specific to the design of that kitchen.

The designer always works within a particular perspective. At any time, the designer can select a different perspective by name. New perspectives can also be created by assigning a name and selecting existing perspectives to be inherited. Bob, the designer working with the Smiths in the previous scenario, would create a Smith's Kitchen Perspective and select the Resale Perspective to be inherited by it.

Perspectives are connected in an inheritance network; a perspective can modify knowledge inherited from its parents or it can add new knowledge. Designers switch perspectives to examine a design from different viewpoints. Switching perspectives changes the currently effective definitions of critics, the terms used in these definitions, and other domain knowledge (Figure 3).

The organization of knowledge by perspectives encourages users to view the knowledge in terms of structured, meaningful categories which they can create and modify. It provides a structure of contexts which can correspond to categories meaningful in the design domain. This can ease the cognitive burden of manipulating large numbers of alternative versions of critics and other design knowledge.

DISCUSSION

Embedded critics represent another iteration cycle in our continuing research into computer-based design environments and critiquing systems. Embedded critics were designed and built in response to deficiencies uncovered in our early critiquing systems (LISP-CRITIC, FRAMER, JANUS), as well as insights gained from design theorists [2, 15, 16] and situated cognition researchers [11, 20, 21].

Recently, we have built design environments in a variety of domains including lunar habitat design [19], phone-based interface design [14], computer network design [5], and user interface design [12]. These design environments go beyond conventional CAD systems by modeling domain semantics in several design contexts and not just modeling geometric relationships. Though the knowledge bases of these research prototypes are not exhaustive, they exhibit a high degree of complexity with their many design units, catalog entries, critics, and domain distinctions. Exploration of these environments has confirmed that simple browsing mechanisms are insufficient and that critiquing mechanisms capable of delivering the right information at the right time are desirable.

Design environments support designers in creating and modifying the problem framing throughout the design process, not just in the beginning. Problem framing in design environments is supported by the specification component, where designers articulate their goals and priorities for the design. The problem framing as represented in the partial specification does not serve as a

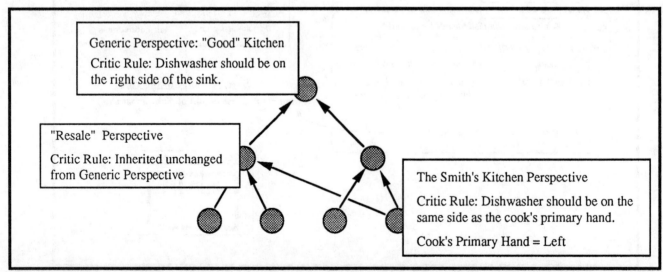

Figure 3. Design contexts are arranged in an inheritance network. Three perspectives - the generic, the resale, and the Smith's – are shown. The preferred placement of the dishwasher depends on the perspective selected.

rigid template for constructing a solution, but rather as a flexible framework in which to operate. Embedded critics support the integration of problem framing and problem solving [15] by making explicit relationships between the partial specification and the construction situation. Embedded critics evaluate the construction situation for compliance with the partial specifications, within a chosen perspective. When critics detect a conflict, the need to reflect-in-action [16] is signaled to the designer. Resolving the conflict might require a modification of (1) the specification by reframing the problem or (2) the construction by rearranging design units.

The three classes of critics we have explored correspond to three dimensions of embedding. Generic critics are embedded in the construction, because they are enabled by the placement of design units in the work area. Specific critics are embedded in the partial specification by being dynamically constructed from domain distinctions tied to specification items. Specific critics reduce the intrusiveness [13] of generic critics by narrowing the enabled critics to those that are relevant to the partially specified task at hand. Interpretive critics are embedded in the hierarchy of perspectives that supports the evolution of alternative viewpoints on designs. Using these critics, designers are able to consider their designs critically from multiple viewpoints.

Embedding critics in integrated design environments is an important step towards applying the critiquing paradigm to create more useful and usable knowledge-based computer systems. Embedded critics focus the attention of the system on the concerns of the designer in order to deliver the "right" thing at the "right" time. Future research will focus on evaluating embedded critiquing systems in naturalistic settings, i.e., observing the systems in use by professional designers in their regular design activities.

ACKNOWLEDGMENTS

We thank the HCC group at the University of Colorado, who contributed to the conceptual framework and the systems discussed in this paper. The research was supported by: the National Science Foundation under grants No. IRI-9015441 and MDR-9253425; the Colorado Advanced Software Institute under grants in 1990/91, 1991/92, 1992/93; US West Advanced Technologies; NYNEX Science and Technology Center, and by Software Research Associates, Inc. (Tokyo).

REFERENCES

1. R. Burton and J. S. Brown, "An Investigation of Computer Coaching for Informal Learning Activites," in *Intelligent Tutoring Systems*, D. Sleeman and J. S. Brown, Ed., London, Academic Press, 1982, pp. 79-98.

2. P. Ehn, *Work-Oriented Design of Computer Artifacts,* arbetslivscentrum, Stockholm, 1989.

3. G. Fischer, "A Critic for LISP," *Proceedings of the 10th International Joint Conference on Artificial Intelligence*, Milan, Italy, 1987, pp. 177-184.

4. G. Fischer, A. Girgensohn, K. Nakakoji and D. Redmiles, "Supporting Software Designers with Integrated, Domain-Oriented Design Environments," *IEEE Transactions on Software Engineering, Special Issue on Knowledge Representation and Reasoning in Software Engineering,* Vol. 18, pp. 511-522, 1992.

5. G. Fischer, J. Grudin, A. C. Lemke, R. McCall, J. Ostwald, B. N. Reeves and F. Shipman, "Supporting Indirect, Collaborative Design with Integrated Knowledge-Based Design Environments," *HCI*, Vol. 7 (Special Issue on Computer Supported Cooperative Work), 1992.

6. G. Fischer, A. Lemke, T. Mastaglio and A. Morch, "Using Critics to Empower Users," *CHI '90*, Seattle, WA, 1990, pp. 337-347.

7. G. Fischer, A. C. Lemke, T. Mastaglio and A. Morch, "The Role of Critiquing in Cooperative Problem Solving," *ACM Transactions on Information Systems,* Vol. 9, pp. 123-151, 1991.

8. G. Fischer, A. C. Lemke and T. Schwab, "Knowledge-Based Help Systems," *Human Factors in Computing Systems, CHI'85 Conference Proceedings (San Francisco, CA),* pp. 161-167, 1985.

9. G. Fischer and K. Nakakoji, "Making Design Objects Relevant to the Task at Hand," *Proceedings of AAAI-91, Ninth National Conference on Artificial Intelligence,* pp. 67-73, 1991.

10. A. Girgensohn, "End-User Modifiability in Knowledge-Based Design Environments," Technical Report CU-CS-595-92, Department of Computer Science, University of Colorado at Boulder, 1992.

11. J. Lave, *Cognition in Practice,* Cambridge University Press, Cambridge, UK, 1988.

12. A. C. Lemke, "Design Environments for High-Functionality Computer Systems," Unpublished Ph.D. Dissertation, Department of Computer Science, University of Colorado at Boulder, 1989.

13. A. C. Lemke, "Cooperative Problem Solving Systems Must Have Critics," *Proceedings of the AAAI Spring Symposium Workshop on Knowledge-Based Human Computer Communication,* pp. 73-75, 1990.

14. A. Repenning and T. Sumner, "Using Agentsheets to Create a Voice Dialog Design Environment,"

Symposium on Applied Computing (SAC '92), Kansas City, MO., 1992, pp. 1199-1207.

15. H. Rittel and M. Webber, "Planning Problems are Wicked Problems," in *Developments in Design Methodology*, N. Cross, Ed., John Wiley & Sons, New York, 1984, pp. 135-144.

16. D. A. Schoen, *The Reflective Practitioner: How Professionals Think in Action,* Basic Books, New York, 1983.

17. B. Silverman, "Survey of Expert Critiquing Systems: Practical and Theoretical Frontiers," *CACM,* Vol. 35, pp. 106-127, 1992.

18. G. Stahl, "Toward a Theory of Hermeneutic Software Design," Technical Report CU-CS-589-92, Computer Science Department, University of Colorado at Boulder, 1992.

19. G. Stahl, "Supporting Interpretation in Design," Accepted to *Journal of Architecture and Planning Research, Special Issue on Computational Representations of Knowledge,* Forthcoming in Summer 1993.

20. L. Suchman, *Plans and Situated Actions: The Problem of Human-Machine Communication,* Cambridge University press, Cambridge, 1987.

21. T. Winograd and F. Flores, *Understanding Computers and Cognition: A New Foundation for Design,* Addison-Wesley, Menlo Park, CA, 1986.

How To Aid Non-Experts

Mark Neerincx and Paul de Greef

Department of Social Science Informatics, University of Amsterdam
Roetersstraat 15, 1018 WB Amsterdam, The Netherlands
(31)20-5256792
mark@swi.psy.uva.nl

ABSTRACT

Aiding functions may be added to a computer system, so that users with insufficient knowledge can perform their tasks. The aiding should be integrated into the task execution of such users. Empirical knowledge is lacking about the conditions for successful aiding. We evaluated the on-line help system of the statistical software package SPSS/PC. It appears that the addition of help facilities to the system worsens the task performance and learning of novices substantially. In our view, the addition of help is harmful, because communication with the system is more complex as a result, whereas the help hardly provides the task support that novices need.

De Greef *et al.* [5] provide two design principles that result in consistent communication and aiding in correspondence with users' needs: (i) the design of aiding functions is an integrated part of interface design and (ii) aiding is based upon an expert model of the users' task. We evaluated an interface for the statistical program HOMALS, which was designed according to these principles. As a consequence of the addition of aiding functions, non-expert users perform their tasks better and learn more.

KEYWORDS: intelligent interfaces, help, task analysis, design, summative evaluation, usability testing.

INTRODUCTION

Powerful software tools are available for many specialist expert tasks such as statistical analyses. Much of this software will be used by non-experts. They will try to perform tasks with the system almost immediately, even if they do not know how to do the task: this is known as the production paradox [2].

Often, systems have help facilities that resemble manuals. To use the facilities, users have to retrieve the information needed at a certain moment and, after that, they have to use this information for their task execution (cf. [10]). These activities are troublesome; moreover, non-experts will hardly use "screen-manuals" according to the production paradox. It would be better to integrate the help into the task execution of the user. The system should take the initiative to present knowledge the user is lacking. The knowledge presentation should come at the right moment and only refer to information that is relevant in the current context. Most readers will probably agree with the last statement, but actually there is hardly any empirical evidence available concerning conditions for effective aiding [9].

Karat [17] distinguishes several methodologies for the evaluation of software. The most complete usability test is an analysis of the task performance of prospective users [6],[16]. In our view, help systems should be evaluated in an experiment in which the performance of users working with an *aiding interface* is compared with the performance of users working with a *minimal interface*, i.e. the same interface without aiding. This kind of comparison could even be performed during the design of a system by using prototypes or mock-ups (Wizard of Oz, [4]).

We have used this experimental methodology to investigate whether, or, under which conditions a help system is effective. This paper presents two experiments. The first evaluates a commercially available system, and the

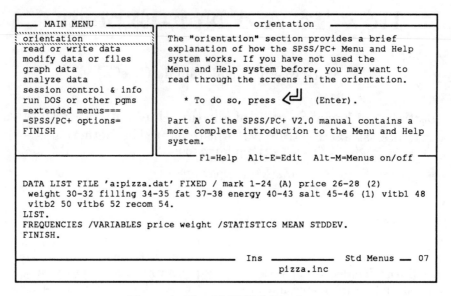

Figure 1: The SPSS/PC-interface.

second evaluates a system developed with a method for designing aiding systems. We have identified two crucial conditions: (i) the system should provide the knowledge the user is lacking, which, as a consequence, means that the help should be based on an expert model of the users' task, and (ii) the costs of communication with the help facilities should be minimal.

AIDING WITH STATISTICAL ANALYSES

Many users of statistical software are occasional users who are not experts in statistical analyses. These users would probably be pleased with effective aiding. SPSS is a well-known software package for various statistical analyses. To aid the users with their analyses, a help system has been added to the PC-version of SPSS (see figure 1).

SPSS may be viewed as a command language, with which users specify a statistical analysis. SPSS/PC has aiding facilities for the construction of such a specification or program. The SPSS-program is presented in the command-editor window (the middle section of figure 1). The user searches for an appropriate SPSS-command in the hierarchical help menu (the left top of figure 1), places it in the editor window, and, finally, executes it. The window in the right top presents information about the menu item that is activated.

Experiment

In a SPSS-course[1], we compared the SPSS/PC-interface, the aiding interface, with a version of the same software of which the help system was stripped of: the minimal interface. The minimal interface only consists

[1]for an extensive description of the experiment see [20]

of the command-editor window (the menu and help window do not appear on the screen). Fifty-nine students participated in the SPSS-course; they had basic knowledge of statistics, but had not previously used SPSS. The students used one of the two interfaces during the course. They had to construct SPSS-programs for several statistical analyses in four two-hour sessions, one session a week. After the course, students got a recall test; they had to construct a short SPSS-program on paper (no help was available).

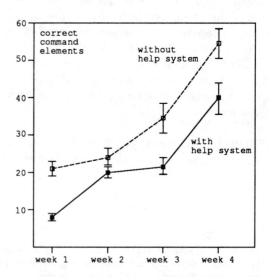

Figure 2: The SPSS-task performance of the students in the four successive weeks. Vertical bars indicate the standard error of the mean.

Figure 2 shows the mean performance of the students in four successive weeks. Performance is the number of command elements the students executed correctly per session. The students who used the aiding interface completed 35.5% less commands correctly ($F(1,57)=13.54$, $p<0.01$). The number of correct command elements increased with each successive session ($F(3,119)=118.54$, $p<0.001$). The interaction between interface type and week number is not significant, i.e., the rate of increase of performance level is equal for the two user groups. In the recall test, students who did not use the help system in the course produced 8 correct command elements on average, whereas the other students produced 3.16 correct elements (separate variance estimate: $t=-3.77$, $df=30.76$, $p<0.01$). The recall of the students with the minimal interface was 1.5 times better than the recall of those who had to use the help system; they appeared to learn more about the functions of SPSS (i.e. the operations SPSS can execute) and more about the syntax of SPSS.

Discussion

The conclusion of the experiment is that the help system of SPSS/PC decreases learnability and usability for novices. This result is surprising, especially because the help seems to be integrated into the task of the user. In our view, the help system is harmful because it corresponds insufficiently with the user's task to specify a statistical analysis. We distinguish two levels in the user's task: the communication level and the functional level [19], [11], [14]. An analysis of the help system of SPSS shows mismatches at both levels.

The interaction-language of the help system differs completely from the SPSS-language. The users have to learn and use the complex SPSS-command language *and* the different language of the help system. The communication would be much easier if only one communication style was used.

At the functional level, the information in the help system has a logical structuring, but this structure disagrees with the structure of subtasks the user must perform [13]. Therefore, the user does not get the right information at the right moment. Moreover, the information is incomplete: it does not tell the user completely how to do a statistical analysis (cf. [8]).

Following this line of reasoning, the effect of aiding should be better if (i) it does not complicate the communication, and (ii) it provides sufficient knowledge to the users about what to do next. The next section presents two design-principles for such aiding, a system designed according to these principles, and a summative evaluation of this system.

AIDING BASED ON AN EXPERT MODEL
Design principles
De Greef *et al.* [5] provide two principles for the design

of aiding functions. The first is that the design of aiding should be integrated into the design of the rest of the system. Their article describes the profits of such an approach. Here, one effect is important: the design of a consistent communication.

The second principle is that the aiding functions should be based on an expert model of the users' task; this ensures completeness and allows system initiative for presentation of task knowledge. The two principles are made operational in the design method of de Greef *et al.* [5],[4]. This method consists of three steps.

The first step of the design method centres on modelling a *minimal interface* that provides sufficient functionality for expert users. It starts with a decomposition of the task (cf. [22],[7]) and is based on current software engineering techniques, such as functional modelling using hierarchical data flow diagrams and data modelling using entity relationship diagrams [24],[21]. These techniques are extended to specify the allocation of subtasks to user or system, the data flows that have to cross the user-system partition (the user views), and the allocation of the initiative for the information exchanges. The result is a cooperation model, i.e., an abstract specification of the minimal interface that provides just sufficient functionality given the allocation of subtasks. Transformation of this specification to a WIMP-interface is straightforward (Windows, Icons, Mouse and Pull-down/pop-up menus [23],[3]).

In the second step of the design method, a sample of users performs tasks using a mock-up of the minimal interface. The purpose of this analysis is to test whether the users have sufficient knowledge to do their share of the work, if not, the third step of the method is entered.

The third step of the design method centres on modelling an aiding function. It starts with an analysis of the users' task to construct an expert model. This hierarchical task model describes the events or conditions for which subtasks should be executed. It may be viewed as a recursive GOMS-model (Goals, Operators, Methods and Selection rules [1],[14]), but de Greef *et al.* advocate to construct an executable expert model using techniques from software engineering and artificial intelligence. Whereas a GOMS-model is generally based on existing documentation of the software ([18],[10]), they use thinking-aloud problem-solving protocols from, and interviews with experts. The *aiding interface* then is the minimal interface plus a generic function that uses the expert model to provide context-specific help.

HOMALS-design
To learn more about its effectiveness, the above-mentioned method has been applied for the design of an interface for HOMALS, a statistical program for the

analysis of nominal data. For a data-set, HOMALS computes five statistics. In the first phase of the analysis, the user has to check whether the data-set meets several requirements. The data-set must be modified and the statistics must be recomputed until all requirements are met. In the second phase, the user may draw conclusions from the statistics about the data.

We have started from an existing program to compute the statistics and we have developed new interfaces. First, the minimal interface was specified (see [5]), and transformed to an implementation of the minimal interface. It has windows for presenting the statistics, a menu to select a statistic, and a menu to activate data modification tasks (remove variable, recode variable, remove outlier, add dimension and remove dimension).

This interface was then tested with several HOMALS-users. According to experts in this particular method, task performance left much to be desired. Therefore, design of an aiding function was warranted.

The modelling of this function started with the acquisition of knowledge about the HOMALS-task by consulting documentation, interviewing HOMALS-experts, and observing experts who - thinking aloud - performed tasks. The knowledge was compiled in a procedural expert model for HOMALS, which prescribes an efficient sequence of task executions and selection rules for tasks (see figure 3).

The expert model was transformed to an aiding function. The addition of the aiding function to the minimal interface resulted in an aiding interface. Figure 4 shows what the aiding interface looks like during the task "inspect object-scores" (see figure 3). The window "objectscores" and the menu "statistics" are inherited from the minimal interface. The window "interpret objectscores" comprises the aiding function; it shows the data modifications that can be done with respect to the object-scores (buttons right), the conditions for which the modifications must be done (buttons left), and a button to continue the analysis. A click on a left button causes the presentation of a text window that clarifies the condition.

The interfaces were implemented as mock-ups (VAX-VMS, TeleUse), i.e., clicking on the task buttons in the action window does not result in the actual execution of the task. The user is asked to continue the Homals analysis as if the system has executed this task. After a justified removal of an object (an "outlier"), the mock-up presents adjusted statistical data.

Experiments

We compared the aiding interface with the minimal interface in two experiments. Twenty students participated in each experiment, 10 in the minimal interface condition and 10 in the aiding interface condition. They had to interpret five data-sets in a session of 1.5 hour. During the analysis, the students had a questionnaire asking for conclusions about the data-set. The performance measures were (i) the number of data modifications performed correctly, and (ii) the number of correct conclusions in the questionnaire.

In the first experiment, users participated without knowledge of HOMALS. There was no difference between the performance of students working with the minimal interface and students working with the aiding interface: performance levels were very low in both conditions. This might be due to the fact that the data-sets required few data modifications and warranted few conclusions. It might also be that the aiding simply is not effective for users without any task knowledge. Another reason could be that this type of aiding in general has no positive effect. To rule out this last possibility, we conducted a second experiment.

In the second experiment, we used data-sets requiring more data modifications and warranting more conclusions, as to obtain a finer grained performance measure. We also added a recall test to the experiment: at the end of the session, the students had to describe on paper when data modifications are required and what kind of conclusions can be drawn. The subjects had some knowledge of HOMALS, but were no experts; they had just finished an introductory HOMALS course. The results are shown in the following table.

Interface	#Correct data modifications	#Correct conclusions	Recall
minimal	5.6	11.4	6.5
aiding	9.5	15.7	11.6
p-value	0.10	0.03	0.02

With the aiding interface, students performed more correct data modifications (not significant; $F(1,18)= 2.95$, $p=0.10$), formulated more correct conclusions ($F(1,18)= 5.36$, $p<0.05$), and recalled more task knowledge ($F(1,18)= 7.07$, $p<0.05$). Further, it appeared that users of the aiding interface did less often need to look back at statistics already seen.

The conclusion of the experiments is that the application of the design method results in an interface that provides effective support to users with a basic knowledge of the analysis task.

CONCLUSION
Design principles for aiding interfaces
The SPSS-experiment shows that a help system may

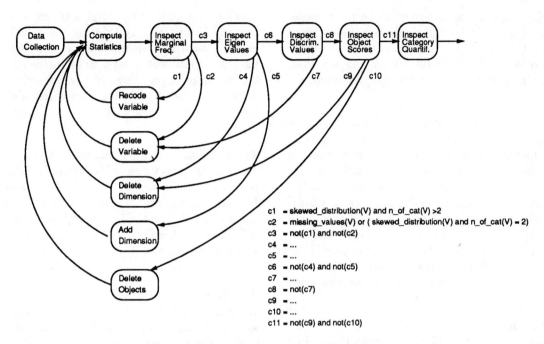

c_1 = skewed_distribution(V) and n_of_cat(V) >2
c_2 = missing_values(V) or (skewed_distribution(V) and n_of_cat(V) = 2)
c_3 = not(c_1) and not(c_2)
c_4 = ...
c_5 = ...
c_6 = not(c_4) and not(c_5)
c_7 = ...
c_8 = not(c_7)
c_9 = ...
c_{10} = ...
c_{11} = not(c_9) and not(c_{10})

Figure 3: Expert model of the HOMALS-task.

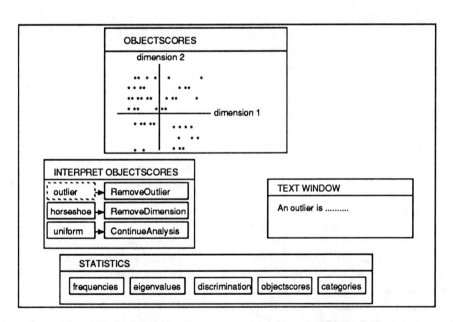

Figure 4: Outline of the aiding interface of HOMALS.

be harmful. Two conditions seemed to be the cause of this. At the functional level, the help is not structured in correspondence with the users' task, and the help information is incomplete. At the communication level, the SPSS help system causes a more complex communication.

After that, we turned to aiding designed according to two principles: (i) integrate the design of aiding functions into interface design, so that communication is consistent and not complicated by the addition of aiding, and (ii) construct a complete expert model of the users' task, and transform this model to an aiding function that takes initiative to provide users with complete context-specific task knowledge. This type of aiding is beneficial for users with rudimentary knowledge of HOMALS. The conclusion is that the application of the two design principles results in easier to use and learn interfaces in the statistical domain.

Empirical evaluation

Often, controlled experiments are thought to be time consuming and expensive. Karat [17] even maintains that they are held in a higher regard than their results would support. In contrast with this statement, our results show that experiments are valuable for the evaluation of (parts of) existing systems and for the evaluation of human-computer interaction theory.

Teachers, users, and -apparently- designers assumed that the help system of SPSS/PC was beneficial. The experiment proved that the help system was harmful for novices. To test the usability of software, one should analyse users performing tasks with the interface (cf. [6],[16]). Summative evaluation proves to be a good method to assess the utility of help; it identifies beneficial *and* harmful effects. Compared to the total effort of system design, it is not expensive, especially when you use prototypes or mock-ups as in the HOMALS-experiment.

DISCUSSION

In recent years, empirical research has sought to model complex user tasks in a hierarchical, goal-oriented manner for system design [10], [14], [12], [15]. Such a model seems to capture real user characteristics. In the study of Gugerty *et al.* (1991), subjects recalled medical procedures in a GOMS-like structure and remembered more in one condition if the procedures were presented in such a structure. The recall tests in our study are in line with this finding: learning from the 'unstructured' SPSS-information proved to be hard, whereas learning from the 'structured' HOMALS information seemed to be relatively easy.

Substantial improvements of the usability of systems

may be accomplished by bridging the gaps between practice and theory, and by bridging the gaps between disciplines, such as human-computer interaction, human factors, experimental psychology, artificial intelligence and software engineering. In our research, such an approach resulted in a design method for aiding systems [5], and an evaluation of the method in the statistical domain.

The question is whether this method is suitable for the design of systems for complex, dynamic tasks with interruptions of tasks and parallelism, e.g. process control. For such tasks, we may need different modelling languages and different aiding functions. Future research will centre on the design of an aiding interface for railway traffic control.

ACKNOWLEDGEMENTS
We thank Katrinus de Vries, Bernhard Slaap, Marjolein van Hooff, and Klaas van Aarsen for their contribution to the research. Our thanks are also due to the Homals-experts for their provision of knowledge about HOMALS, and the anonymous reviewers for their helpful comments.

REFERENCES

[1] S. Card, T. Norman, and A. Newell. *The psychology of Human-Computer Interaction*. Lawrence Erlbaum, 1983.

[2] J.M. Carroll and M.B. Rosson. Paradox of the active user. In J.M. Carroll, editor, *Interfacing thought: cognitive aspects of human-computer interaction*, pages 80–111. MIT, Cambridge Mas., 1987.

[3] R.B. Coats and I. Vlaeminke. *Man-computer interfaces: an introduction to software design and implementation*. Blackwell Scientific Publ., Oxford, London, etc., 1987.

[4] H.P. de Greef and J.A. Breuker. Analysing system-user cooperation in KADS. *Knowledge Acquisition*, 4:89–108, 1992.

[5] H.P. de Greef, M.A. Neerincx, and C.M.M. Hurts. Integrating human-computer interaction with software engineering. In G. van der Veer, editor, *Human-Computer Interaction: preparing for the nineties*, 1992.

[6] H.W. Desurvire, J.M. Kondziela, and M.E. Atwood. What is gained and lost when using evaluation methods other than empirical testing. In

A. Monk, D. Diaper, and M.D. Harrison, editors, *People and Computers VII: Proceedings of the HCI'92 Conference*. Cambridge University Press, 1992.

[7] D. Diaper. Task analysis for knowledge descriptions (TAKD): the method and an example. In D. Diaper, editor, *Task analysis for human-computer interaction*, pages 108–159. Ellis Horwood, Chichester, 1989.

[8] S.M. Doane, D.S. McNamara, W. Kintsch, P.G. Polson, and D.M. Clawson. Prompt comprehension in UNIX command production. *Memory & Cognition*, 20:327–343, 1992.

[9] J. Elkerton. Online aiding for human-computer interfaces. In M. Helander, editor, *Handbook of Human-Computer Interaction*, pages 345–364. Elsevier, North-Holland, 1988.

[10] J. Elkerton and S.L. Palmiter. Designing help using a GOMS model: an information retrieval evaluation. *Human Factors*, 33:185–204, 1991.

[11] D.M. Frohlich and P. Luff. Some lessons from an exercise in specification. *Human-Computer Interaction*, 4:101–123, 1989.

[12] W.D. Gray, B.E. John, and M.E. Atwood. The precis of project Ernestine or an overview of a validation of GOMS. In P. Bauersfeld, J. Bennett, and G. Lynch, editors, *CHI'92 Conference Proceedings*, pages 307–312. Addison Wesley, 1992.

[13] L. Gugerty, S. Halgren, J. Gosbee, and M. Rudisill. Using GOMS models and hypertext to create representations of medical procedures for online display. In *Proceedings of the Human Factors Society 35th annual meeting*, pages 713–717. Human Factors Society, Santa Monica, CA, 1991.

[14] B.E. John and A.H. Vera. A GOMS analysis of a graphic, machine-paced, highly interactive task. In P. Bauersfeld, J. Bennett, and G. Lynch, editors, *CHI'92 Conference Proceedings*, pages 397–404. Addison Wesley, 1992.

[15] P. Johnson. *Human-computer interaction: Psychology, task analysis and software engineering*. McGraw-Hill, London, etc., 1992.

[16] C.M. Karat, R. Campbell, and T. Fiegel. Comparison of empirical testing and walkthrough methods in user interface evaluation. In P. Bauersfeld, J. Bennett, and G. Lynch, editors, *CHI'92 Conference Proceedings*, pages 397–404. Addison Wesley, 1992.

[17] J. Karat. Software evaluation methodologies. In M. Helander, editor, *Handbook of Human-Computer Interaction*, pages 891–903. Elsevier, North-Holland, 1988.

[18] D.E. Kieras. Towards a practical GOMS model methodology for user interface design. In M. Helander, editor, *Handbook of Human-Computer Interaction*, pages 135–157. Elsevier, North-Holland, 1988.

[19] T.P. Moran. The command language grammar: a representation for the user interface of interactive computer systems. *International Journal of Man-Machine Studies*, 15:3–50, 1981.

[20] M.A. Neerincx and H.P. de Greef. When the help system does not help: an evaluation of two SPSS-interfaces used by novices. In F.J. Maarse, A.E. Akkerman, A.N. Brand, L.J.M. Mulder, and M.J. Van der Stelt, editors, *Computers in Psychology: Tools for experimental and applied psychology*, volume 4. Swets and Zeitlinger, Lisse, 1992.

[21] J. Rumbaugh, M. Blaha, W. Premerlani, F. Eddy, and W. Lorensen. *Object-oriented modeling and design*. Prentice Hall, Englewood Cliffs, New Jersey, 1991.

[22] S. Sebilotte. Hierarchical planning as method for task analysis: the example of office task analysis. *Behaviour and Information Technology*, 7:275–293, 1988.

[23] B. Shneiderman. *Designing the user interface: strategies for effective human-computer interaction*. Addison-Wesley, Reading, Massachusetts, etc., 1987.

[24] E. Yourdon. *Modern Structured Analysis*. Prentice Hall, Englewood Cliffs, N.J., 1989.

A Design Space For Multimodal Systems:
Concurrent Processing and Data Fusion

Laurence Nigay, Joëlle Coutaz

Laboratoire de Génie Informatique (IMAG)
BP 53 X, 38041 Grenoble Cedex, France
Tel: +33 76 51 44 40
E-mail: nigay@imag.imag.fr, joelle@imag.imag.fr

ABSTRACT

Multimodal interaction enables the user to employ different modalities such as voice, gesture and typing for communicating with a computer. This paper presents an analysis of the integration of multiple communication modalities within an interactive system. To do so, a software engineering perspective is adopted. First, the notion of "multimodal system" is clarified. We aim at proving that two main features of a multimodal system are the concurrency of processing and the fusion of input/output data. On the basis of these two features, we then propose a design space and a method for classifying multimodal systems. In the last section, we present a software architecture model of multimodal systems which supports these two salient properties: concurrency of processing and data fusion. Two multimodal systems developed in our team, VoicePaint and NoteBook, are used to illustrate the discussion.

KEYWORDS: Modality, multimodal interaction, taxonomy, design space, software architecture, data fusion, concurrency.

INTRODUCTION

In parallel with the development of graphical user interfaces (GUI), significant progress has been made in natural language processing, computer vision and gesture analysis. Systems integrating these techniques as multiple modalities open a complete new world of experience [1]. But as pointed out in [2], differences of opinion still exist as to the meaning of the term "multimodal".

This paper presents our analysis of the integration of multiple communication modalities between a user and an interactive system. To do so, a software engineering perspective is adopted. First, the notion of "multimodal system" is clarified. Based on a precise definition of multimodality, we then propose a design space and a method for classifying multimodal systems. In the last

section, we present a software architecture model that supports the most salient properties of such systems: concurrent processing and data fusion.

MULTIMODAL SYSTEM: A DEFINITION

In the general sense, a multimodal system supports communication with the user through different modalities such as voice, gesture, and typing [3]. Literally, "multi" refers to "more than one" and the term "modal" may cover the notion of "modality" as well as that of "mode".

- Modality refers to the type of communication channel used to convey or acquire information. It also covers the way an idea is expressed or perceived, or the manner an action is performed [4].
- Mode refers to a state that determines the way information is interpreted to extract or convey meaning.

In a communication act, whether it be between humans or between a computer system and a user, both the modality and the mode come into play. The modality defines the type of data exchanged whereas the mode determines the context in which the data is interpreted. Thus, if we take a system-centered view, multimodality is the capacity of the system to communicate with a user along different types of communication channels and to extract and convey meaning automatically. We observe that both multimedia and multimodal systems use multiple communication channels. But in addition, a multimodal system is able to automatically model the content of the information at a high level of abstraction. A multimodal system strives for meaning.

Our definition of multimodality is system-oriented. A user-centered perspective may lead to a different definition. For instance, according to our system-centered view, the NeXT voice electronic mail [5] is not multimodal. It is multimedia only. Indeed, it allows the user to send mail that may contain graphics, text and voice messages. It does not however extract meaning from the information it carries. In particular, voice messages are recorded but not interpreted. On the other hand, from the user's point of view, this system is perceived as being multimodal: the user employs different modalities (referring to the human senses) to interpret mail messages.

Our system-centered definition of multimodality conveys two salient features that are relevant to the software design of multimodal systems:

- the fusion of different types of data from/to different I/O devices, and
- the temporal constraints imposed on information processing from/to I/O devices.

Data fusion and temporal constraints provide the basis for the design space presented in the next section.

MULTIFEATURE SYSTEMS: A DESIGN SPACE

Previous attempts to systematize the description of interfaces have already been made. However, these approaches focused primarily on input devices. In this paper, we are concerned with both the input and output attributes of an interface. At the lower level of abstraction, classifications of input devices such as those proposed by Buxton [7] and by Card et al. [8], are based on physical properties (such as motion and pressure), the data that a device returns (discrete or continuous) and the dimensions of input a device provides.

At a higher level of abstraction, Foley et al. focus on graphics sub-tasks and propose a taxonomy according to the sub-tasks a device is capable of performing [9]. Our design space is located at this higher level of abstraction; it deals with tasks at the granularity of commands. We address the issues of how a command is specified using the different available modalities and how a command is built from raw data.

Recently, D. Frohlich proposed a framework for describing the design space of interfaces. This framework includes both input and output design spaces [6]. It embeds the different types of modalities and takes into account the human senses. Our design space also includes both input and output attributes of an interface, but our goal is different. Our design space is intended for classifying systems within a framework, and for helping software designers to identify the software implications and constraints for the development of a system.

Our design space is defined along three dimensions: Levels of Abstraction, Use of modalities and Fusion. Figure 1 illustrates some possible values along each dimension and the corresponding classes of systems.

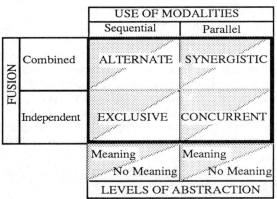

Figure 1: The multi-feature system design space.

Levels of Abstraction

As far as inputs are concerned, data received from a particular device may be processed at multiple levels of abstraction. For example, speech input may be recorded as a signal, or described as a sequence of phonemes, or interpreted as a meaningful parsed sentence. Each representation corresponds to a particular level of abstraction. For outputs, the process is similar: data may be produced from symbolic abstract data or from a lower level of abstraction without any computational detection of meaning. For example, a vocal message may be synthesized from an abstract representation of meaning, from pre-stored text or may simply be replayed from a previous recording.

The important point is that data is represented and processed at multiple levels of abstraction. This transformation process makes possible the extraction of meaning from raw data and conversely the production of data from symbolic abstract representations. To simplify the presentation, we consider only two values along the axis "Levels of Abstraction": "Meaning" and "No Meaning". As discussed in the previous section, a multimodal system falls in the "Meaning" category of Figure 1.

Use of Modalities

"Use of modalities" expresses the temporal availability of multiple modalities. This dimension primarily covers the absence or presence of parallelism at the user interface. The granularity for concurrency ranges from the physical actions at the I/O device level to the task-command level. Absence of parallelism is referred to as "Sequential use" whereas presence is called "Parallel use".

A system that supports "Parallel use" allows the user to employ multiple modalities simultaneously. Conversely, a system characterized by the sequential use of modalities, forces the user to use the modalities one after another.

Fusion

Fusion covers the possible combination of different types of data. As discussed above, a data type is associated with a particular modality. The absence of fusion is called "Independent" whereas the presence is referred to as "Combined".

According to the design space, fusion may be performed with or without knowledge about the meaning of the data exchanged. For example, synchronization of audio and video data as supported in the ACME platform [10], is a temporal fusion which does not involve any knowledge of meaning. The ACME platform (Abstractions for Continuous MEdia) is based on the concepts of strands which correspond to streams of audio or video data, of ropes which are combinations of strands, and a logical time system that allows several strands and ropes to be played synchronously. This example of fusion is distinct from the fusion that involves meaning as in the "put that there" paradigm. Fusion based on meaning mixes modalities to build an input or output expression which results in an interpretation at a high level of abstraction in the task domain.

The design space as a whole

The three orthogonal dimensions of our design space (Levels of abstraction, Use of modalities, and Fusion) define eight distinct classes for multi-feature systems. According to our definition, a multimodal system takes the value "Meaning" along the "Level of abstraction" axis.

Having selected the value "Meaning" for "Levels of abstraction", let us considerer the four classes of systems resulting from the combination of the axis "Fusion" and "Use of modalities". We get the following categories: "Exclusive", "Alternate", "Concurrent", and "Synergistic". These classes are discussed in a following section and illustrated with our own multimodal systems: VoicePaint and NoteBook [11].

VOICEPAINT AND NOTEBOOK

VoicePaint is a graphics editor implemented on the Macintosh using Voice Navigator, a word-based speech recognizer board. As a picture is drawn with the mouse, the user can talk and ask the system to change the attributes of the graphics context (e.g., the foreground or background colors, the thickness of the pen, the brightness, the filling pattern, etc.). This system is similar in spirit to the graphics editor used by Ralph Hill to demonstrate how Sassafras is able to support concurrency for direct manipulation user interfaces [19].

NoteBook is a personnal electronic book implemented on the NeXT machine using Sphinx, a continuous multi-locutor speech recognition system [21]. It allows a user to create, edit, browse, and delete textual notes. In particular, to insert a note between two notes, the user can say "Insert a note" while simultaneously selecting the location of insertion with the mouse. To edit the content of a note, one modality only is available: typing. Browsing through the set of notes is performed by clicking dedicated buttons such as "Next" and "Previous" or by using spoken commands such as "Next note". To empty the note book, a "Clear notebook" command may be specified using voice or clicking the mouse on the "Clear" button.

Next section shows how the design space can be used to classify a particular multimodal system.

CLASSIFYING MULTIMODAL SYSTEMS

Any classification is based on a set of relevant features f_i. In our case, an interesting set of features is the commands that the system supports. Each feature f_i is weighted according to an estimated importance and has a position p_i within the design space shown in figure 2. For example, the weight w_i can be defined as the frequency of use. As shown in Figure 3, four weighting values have been defined but other rules may be applied. Position p_i can take one of the four discrete values:

Exclusive, Alternate, Concurrent and Synergistic. Thus a feature, f_i is formally defined as the couple:

$$f_i = (p_i, w_i)$$

The position, C, of a system corresponds to the center of gravity of its features as expressed by the following equation:

$$C = \frac{1}{\Sigma_w} \times \sum_i p_i \times w_i \qquad \Sigma_w = \sum_i w_i$$

(1)

To illustrate the method, we consider the NoteBook commands presented above.

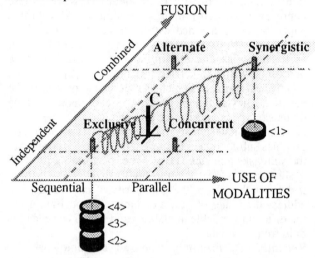

Figure 2: A method to classify multimodal systems: the NoteBook example.

"Insert a note", denoted as Feature <1> in Figure 2, is a synergistic command: it is specified using speech and mouse clicks simultaneously and it requires the fusion of data from multiple input devices. In addition, it is used frequently. Thus <1> is defined as the couple (synergistic, frequent use). The second command "edit the content of a note", denoted as Feature <2> in Figure 2, is characterized by the couple (exclusive, very frequent use): while editing the content of a note only one modality is available (typing) and no other command can be invoked in parallel. For example, it is not possible to turn the pages of the note book while writing the content of a note. Although exclusive, this task is performed very often. Similarly, commands about browsing, denoted as Feature <4>, are used very frequently but are exclusive: the user has the choice between multiple modalities to express the command (speech or mouse clicks) but only one modality is used to specify the command. In addition, no other command can be issued in parallel. The last command to be considered, "clear the note book", is exclusive for the same reason as <3> but is rarely used. Location C of NoteBook in the design space is obtained by applying the formula (1) (see Figure 2). We observe that NoteBook is close to the exclusive class of multimodal systems.

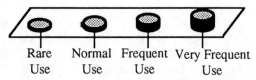

Figure 3: For example four weights which can be associated with a command according to its frequency of use.

A similar process has been applied to VoicePaint and showed that this system is mostly synergistic. Indeed, all of the very frequent commands, which are concerned with drawing, allow the combined and parallel use of speech and mouse gesture.

NoteBook and VoicePaint provide examples for exclusive and synergistic commands only. As an example of concurrency at the command level, one may consider VoiceFinder, a system that adds voice input to the Macintosh Finder. Within VoiceFinder, the user can issue a voice command like "empty the trash" while simultaneously invoking another command such as opening a document with the mouse. "Alternate" requires the fusion of data from/to multiple devices to build up a command but these devices must be used in a sequential manner. For example, the MMI2 [20] system is primarily alternate. In this system, the interaction is driven by natural written language. Deictic references that may occur in a sentence such as "this", are solved by looking for mouse selections in the next following act of interaction: modalities are combined but acquired in a sequential manner.

In summary, the contribution of our design space and classification scheme is three-fold:
- the design space makes it explicit the way different modalities are supported by a particular system,
- the classification scheme makes it precise the location of a system within the design space,
- the design space can be used in conjunction with the classification scheme to study the effect of shifting commands within the design space with regard to the user's expertise or to the task to be performed [12]. Using this methodology, the usability of an interface can be measured.

Usability is the extent to which a user can exploit the potential utility of a system [13]. Usability can be evaluated from the command language itself as illustrated in [13]. Given that the command language barrier is surpassed, usability can be further tested by establishing whether particular modalities are adequate for expressing a given command. For instance, if a command has a small weight in the synergistic position and a large weight in the exclusive position, the choice of modalities for the synergistic command may be inadequate and/or the chosen modalities may be incompatible.

Having identified two salient features for multimodal systems, concurrency and data fusion, we need now to address their implications on software design. Next section describes a model that describes the software organization of synergistic multimodal systems.

SOFTWARE ARCHITECTURE FOR SYNERGISTIC SYSTEMS

Technically, synergistic systems subsume the other three classes of multimodal systems. Although synergistic systems provide a powerful style of interaction [14], they are functionaly more demanding and therefore more complex to build than, for example, exclusive systems. The following architectural model, based on PAC-Amodeus [16], is concerned with the most sophisticated case.

PAC-Amodeus

As shown in Figure 4, the PAC-Amodeus model reuses the components of Arch [15] but refines the dialogue controller in terms of PAC agents [22]. This refinement has multiple advantages including an explicit support for concurrency.

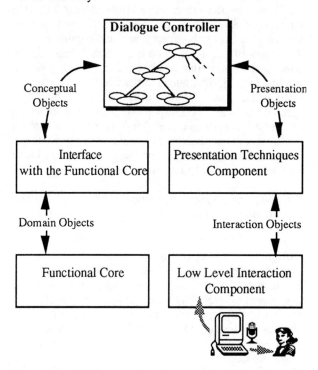

Figure 4: The software components of the PAC-Amodeus model and the interfaces between them.

The Functional Core (FC) implements domain specific concepts in a presentation independent way. The Interface with the Functional Core (IFC) maps Domain objects from the Functional Core onto Conceptual objects from the Dialogue Controller and vice versa.

The Dialogue Controller (DC) is the keystone of the model. It has the responsibility for task-level sequencing. Each task of the user corresponds to a dialogue thread. This observation suggests a multi-agent decomposition where an agent, or a collection of agents, can be associated with each thread. A set of rules that identify the agents necessary for a particular system is presented in [16].

The Presentation Techniques Component (PTC) defines two multi-valued mapping functions that link Presentation and Interaction objects. The PTC describes the presentation (i.e., input and output interfaces). It implements the perceivable behavior of the application for output and input commands. It is only at this level of abstraction that the modality of interaction is taken into account.

The Low Level Interaction Component (LLIC) denotes the underlying software and hardware platform. It supports the physical interaction with the user. It manages user's events from different media (time-stamps and queues) and has the responsibility for their lexical analysis. Some of the low-level events are not transmitted to the Presentation Technique Component. Indeed, lexical tasks such as window resize, are locally performed by the Low Level Interaction Component. In addition, in the case of spoken-utterances, this component can include mechanisms for confirmation allowing the user to intercept a wrong recognition.

The roles of the PAC-Amodeus components can be compared to a similar architecture devised for virtual worlds. In [17], dialogue is structured by a set of three level rules. The Specific Level rule set is linked to specific hardware. It corresponds to the LLIC component of the PAC-Amodeus model. The Generic Level rule set transforms events into more general interaction. It can be mapped onto the PTC. Finally, the Executive Level rule set manages tasks and thus corresponds to the DC.

We need now to show how concurrent processing and data fusion are performed within our architectural framework.

Concurrent processing of data

Concurrent processing of data is achieved at different levels of abstraction. Raw data is captured in the LLIC component by event handlers. There is one event handler per input device. Event handlers correspond to the strands in the ACME system [10]. They process in parallel.

Concurrency is also supported in the PTC which receives low level events (Interaction objects) from the LLIC and transforms them into more abstract interaction techniques. For example, a mouse click is transformed into the Select interaction technique. There is one abstracting process per supported modality. A modality, for instance a gestural language, may be supported by different physical devices (and so different events handlers), such as a mouse and a data glove combined with computer vision.

Finally, the multi-agent architecture of the Dialogue Controller offers an interesting conceptual framework to support concurrency. Agents can process data (i.e., Presentation objects) received from the PTC in parallel.

Data fusion

Non-multimodal systems transform data from Interaction objects to Presentation objects, then from Presentation objects to Conceptual objects, up to Domain objects and vice versa. These transformations must also be performed in a synergistic system, but in this case, the task may be more complex. The synergistic use of modalities implies fusion of data from different modeling techniques. Each technique is associated with a modality.

We have identified three levels of fusion: lexical, syntactic and semantic that can be mapped to the three conceptual levels defined by Foley et al. [18]. Lexical fusion corresponds to the Binding level which establishes the interface with the hardware primitives. Therefore lexical fusion is performed in the LLIC component. The syntactic and semantic fusions correspond respectively to the Sequencing and Functional levels. These fusions are thus handled by the component responsible for task-level sequencing: the dialogue controller.

Lexical fusion. Lexical fusion is performed in the LLIC. A typical example of lexical fusion may be found in the Macintosh where the shift key combined with a mouse click allows multiple selections. Lexical fusion involves only temporal issues such as data synchronization.

Syntactic and semantic fusion. The Dialogue Controller is responsible for syntactic and semantic fusions. Syntactic fusion involves the combination of data to obtain a complete command such as the "Insert a note" in the NoteBook system. Semantic fusion combines results of commands to derive new results. For instance, in VoicePaint, the combination of the command "Draw line" with the command "Modify color" results in a two color line. (These two commands can be specified simultaneously.)

Syntactic and semantic fusion requires a uniform representation: the melting pot object. As shown in Figure 5, a melting pot object is a 2-D structure. The structural parts correspond to the structure of the commands that the Dialogue Controller is able to interpret. Events generated by user's actions are abstracted within the PTC and mapped onto the structural parts inside the Dialogue Controller. These events may have different time-stamps. A command is complete when all of its structural parts are filled up by at least one piece of data. Multiple data for the same structural part may denote redundancy or reveal inconsistencies.

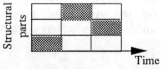

Figure 5: The melting pot object as a common representation for data fusion within the DC.

The non-sequential, hierarchical and distributed features of the multi-agent architecture adopted for the Dialogue Controller make it particularly well suited to perform fusion. Data is combined in parallel and incrementally along the levels of the hierarchy. The fusion mechanism is composed of a set of micro-fusions performed within each agent. The fusion process is based on two criteria: the time (e.g., data belonging to the same temporal window) and the structure of the objects to be combined. Furthermore, an agent may add new data from its own state, to the fusion process.

An example of fusion. Figure 6 illustrates a two-level fusion process for a graphics editor that supports speech and mouse gesture. In this example, the user says "put that there" and at the same time, uses the mouse to select the object to be moved and to indicate the destination in a distinct workspace. A workspace is a drawing area. As in most graphics editors, each workspace has a companion window, a palette that displays the graphics tools. By applying the heuristics rules described in [16], one obtains the architecture shown in Figure 6.

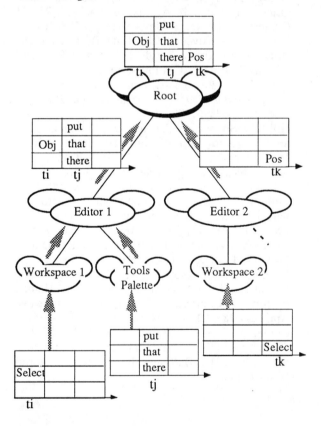

Figure 6: An example of different levels of fusion inside the hierarchy of PAC agents.

At the bottom of the hierarchy, agents Workspace1 and Workspace2 interpret the events that occurred in the drawing areas. Similarly, ToolPalette agent is in charge of the events issued in the palette. Editor agents, such as Editor1 and Editor2, combine information from lower

levels into higher abstractions. For the particular example, the three agents Workspace1, ToolPalette, and Workspace2 each receive a melting pot object from the PTC. Each melting pot object corresponds to a user's actions. The agent Workspace1 translates the Select action into the selected graphical object Obj while in parallel, the agent Workspace2 translates the Select action into a position Pos. The cement agent, Editor1, then performs a first level of fusion by combining the "put that there" with the selected object. A second level of fusion is then performed by the Root agent to obtain the complete command to be sent to the functional core.

Abiding with the requirements for building synergistic systems, our model supports concurrent processing of data and offers a framework to perform data fusion. Furthermore our model supports immediate feedback and satisfies the flexibility criterion. Immediate feedback can be performed by each agent, even before full fusion is accomplished. Specific feedback can be generated at each level of fusion. A high degree of flexibility is achieved by this model for the following reasons:
- a physical hardware device may be changed by modifying the Low Level Interaction Component,
- a modality may be changed by modifying the Presentation Techniques Component,
- the Dialogue Controller is modality-independent. It depends only on the structural composition of the commands that the system supports.

SUMMARY AND CONCLUSIONS
We have presented a classification space that describes the properties of both input and output interfaces of multimodal systems. From the software perspective, this classification space highlights two main characteristics of such systems:
- concurrency of data processing, and
- data fusion.

The contribution of our classification space is two-fold:
- four salient classes of systems can be used as the extrema of a reference space,
- the reference space provides a way to characterize and reason about the I/O properties of interactive systems. In particular, it may be useful to compare the location of a command or the whole system devised at the design stage with the effective location measured through usability testing.

As a complement to the classification space, a software architecture model that supports concurrency and data fusion is proposed. Three levels of fusion have been identified with the appropriate method to implement them. In addition, the model satisfies three crucial quality criteria: code re-usability, support for immediate feedback and flexibility. In the near future, we will continue to test and verify our results through the design of systems supporting multiple output modalities. We will also need to study how to enhance the robustness of the interaction with pragmatics and with an embedded user model.

ACKNOWLEDGMENTS
This work has been supported by project ESPRIT BR 7040 AMODEUS as well as by PRC Communication Homme-Machine, France. This paper was influenced by stimulating discussions with J. Caelen (ICP, Grenoble) and A. Gourdol and D. Salber (LGI). We wish to thank Alex Rudnicky, of CMU, for providing the facilities (and the enthusiasm) to make possible the implementation of the Notebook example. Many thanks to G. Serghiou for reviewing the paper, and to James L. Crowley for help with style and English Grammar.

REFERENCES

1. Kjelldahl L., Introduction. In Proc. 1st Eurographics Workshop, Stockholm, Sweden (April 18/19,1991), Springer Verlag, pp. 3-5.

2. Blattner M.M. and R.G. Dannenberg R.G. CHI'90 Workshop on multimedia and multimodal interface design. SIGCHI Bulletin 22, 2 (Oct. 1990), pp. 54-58.

3. Byte, Special Issue on Computing without Keyboard, (July 1990), pp. 202-251.

4. Coutaz J. Multimedia and Multimodal User Interfaces: A Taxonomy for Software Engineering Research Issues. In Proc. Second East-Weat HCI conference (St Petersburg, Aug. 1992), pp.229-240.

5. Webster B.F. *The NeXT Book*. Addison Wesley, New York, 1989.

6. Frohlich D.M. The Design Space of Interfaces. Multimedia Systems, Interaction and Applications. In Proc. 1st Eurographics Workshop, Stockholm, Sweden (April 18/19,1991), Springer Verlag, pp. 53-69.

7. Buxton W.A.S. Lexical and pragmatic considerations of input structures. ACM SIGGRAPH Computer Graphics 17 (Jan. 1983), pp. 31-37.

8. Card S.K., Mackinlay J.D. and Robertson G.G. A Morphological Analysis of the Design Space of Input Devices. ACM Transactions on Information Systems 9, 2 (April 1991), pp. 99-122.

9. Foley J.D., Wallace V.L. and Chan P. The Human factors of computer graphics interaction techniques. IEEE Computer Graphics and Applications 4,11 (Nov. 1984), pp. 13-48.

10. Anderson D.P., Govindan R. and Homsy G. Abstractions for Continuous MEdia in a network window system. Technical report UCB/CSD 90/596, Computer Science Division (EECS), University of California, Berkeley (Sept. 1990).

11. Gourdol A., Nigay L., Salber D. and Coutaz J. Two Case Studies of Software Architecture for Multimodal Interactive Systems: VoicePaint and Voice-enabled Graphical NoteBook. In Proc. IFIP Working WG2.7 Working Conference, Engineering for Human-Computer Interaction (Ellivuori, Aug. 1992).

12. Chalfonte B.L., Fish R.S. and Kraut R.E. Expressive richness: a comparison of speech and text as media for revision. In Proc. CHI'91 (April 27-May 2 1991), ACM Press, pp. 21-26.

13. Vainio-Larsson A. Evaluating the usability of user interfaces: research in practice. In Proc. INTERACT'90 (Amsterdam, 27-30 August 1990), Elsevier Science, pp. 323-328.

14. Hauptmann A.G. Speech and Gestures for Graphic Image Manipulation. In Proc CHI'89 Human Factors on Computing Systems (April 1989), ACM Press, pp. 241-245.

15. The UIMS Workshop Tool Developers A Metamodel for the Runtime Architecture of an Interactive System. SIGCHI Bulletin, 24, 1 (Jan. 1992), pp. 32-37.

16. Nigay L. and Coutaz J. Building User Interfaces: Organizing Software Agents. In Proc. ESPRIT'91 Conference (Bruxelles, Nov. 1991), pp. 707-719.

17. Lewis J. B., Koved L. and Ling D. T. Dialogue structures for virtual worlds. In Proc CHI'91 (April 27-May 2 1991), ACM Press, pp. 131-136.

18. Foley J.D., van Dam A., Feiner S.K. and Hughes J.F. *Computer Graphics, Principles and Practice*. Addison-Wesley, 1990.

19. Hill R.D. Supporting Concurrency, Communication and Synchronization dans Human-Computer Interaction-The Sassafras UIMS. ACM Transactions on Graphics 5, 2 (April 1986), pp. 179-210.

20. Wilson M. The first MMI2 Demonstrator, A Multimodal Interface for Man Machine Interaction with Knowledge Based Systems. Deliverable D7, ESPRIT project 2474 MMI2, Tech. report Rutherford Appleton Laboratory, Chilton Didcot Oxon OX11 0QX, RAL-91-093, 1991.

21. Lunati J.M. and Rudnicky A.I. Spoken Language Interfaces: The OM system. In Proc. CHI'91 Human Factors on Computing Systems (News Orleans, April 27-May 2 1991), ACM Press, pp. 453-454.

22. Coutaz J. PAC: an Implementation Model for Dialog Design. In Proc. Interact'87, (Stuttgart, Sept. 1987), H-J. Bullinger, B. Shackel ed., North Holland, pp. 431-436.

VoiceNotes: A Speech Interface for a Hand-Held Voice Notetaker

Lisa J. Stifelman*†, Barry Arons*, Chris Schmandt*, Eric A. Hulteen†

*Speech Research Group
MIT Media Lab
20 Ames Street, Cambridge, MA 02139
617-253-8026, lisa@media-lab.mit.edu

†Human Interface Group/ATG
Apple Computer, Inc.
20525 Mariani Ave., MS 301-3H
Cupertino, CA 95014

ABSTRACT

VoiceNotes is an application for a voice-controlled hand-held computer that allows the creation, management, and retrieval of user-authored *voice notes*—small segments of digitized speech containing thoughts, ideas, reminders, or things to do. Iterative design and user testing helped to refine the initial user interface design. VoiceNotes explores the problem of capturing and retrieving spontaneous ideas, the use of speech as data, and the use of speech input and output in the user interface for a hand-held computer without a visual display. In addition, VoiceNotes serves as a step toward new uses of voice technology and interfaces for future portable devices.

KEYWORDS

Speech interfaces, speech recognition, non-speech audio, hand-held computers, speech as data.

INTRODUCTION

How can you capture spontaneous ideas that come to you in the middle of the night, when you are walking down the street, or driving in your car? Pen and paper are often used to record this information, but it is difficult to read and write while driving, and scraps of paper with notes can become scattered or lost. A portable computer can provide better organization, but it is impossible to carry a computer, type, and look at the display while walking down the street. Some people use microcassette™ recorders since voice is a particularly fast and easy way to record such information. However, one is left with a long linear stream of audio and cannot randomly access individual thoughts. In a study of microcassette recorder users, this lack of random access was found to be the user's worst frustration [5].

This paper presents a speech interface for a hand-held[1] computer that allows users to capture and randomly access

voice notes—segments of digitized speech containing thoughts and ideas. The development of the VoiceNotes application explores: (1) the problem of capturing and retrieving spontaneous ideas; (2) the use of speech as data; and (3) the use of speech input and output in the user interface for a hand-held computer.

WHY VOICE?

With advances in microelectronics, computers are rapidly shrinking in size. Laptop computers are portable versions of desktop PCs, but the user interface has remained essentially unchanged. There are also a host of small specialized electronic organizers, travel keepers, and even pocket-sized PCs that present the user with a tiny display and a bewildering array of keys. As computers decrease in size, so does the utility of traditional input and output modalities (keyboards, mice, and high resolution displays). Functionality and ease-of-use are limited on these small devices in which designers have tried to 'squeeze' more and more features into an ever decreasing product size. Rather than simply shrinking the size of traditional interface elements, new I/O modalities must be explored.[2]

The work presented in this paper explores the concept of a hand-held computer that has no keyboard or visual display, but uses a speech interface instead. Information is stored in an audio format, as opposed to text, and accessed by issuing spoken commands instead of typing. Feedback is also provided aurally instead of visually.

Voice technology has been explored for use in desktop computers and telephone information systems, yet the role of voice in the interface for a hand-held device has received little attention. There are two important research challenges for this work: (1) taking advantage of the utility of stored voice as a data type for a hand-held computer while overcoming its liabilities (speech is slow, serial, and difficult to manage); (2) determining the role of voice in the user interface for a hand-held computer given the limitations in current speech recognition technology.

Research and experience using voice in user interfaces has revealed its many advantages as well as its liabilities.

---

[1] The term 'hand-held' is used to refer to the size of the device. The device may actually be something worn on a belt.

[2] Small pen-based computers are an effort in this direction, but the interface is primarily suited for visual tasks.

Voice allows the interface to be scaled down in size. In the extreme case, the physical interface may be negligible, requiring only a speaker and microphone. Speech provides a direct and natural means of input for capturing spontaneous thoughts and ideas. In comparison to writing, speech can provide faster output rates, and allows momentary thoughts to be recorded before they are forgotten [8]. In addition, voice can be more 'expressive' than text, placing less cognitive demands on the communicator and allowing more attention to be devoted to the content of the message [3]. Voice as an access mechanism is also direct (the user thinks of an action and speaks it), and allows additional tasks to be performed while the hands or eyes are busy [11].

Speech is a natural means of interaction, yet recording, retrieving, and navigating among spoken information is a challenging problem. Speech is fast for the author but slow and tedious for the listener [8]. When reviewing written information, the eye can quickly scan a page of text, using visual cues such as highlighting and spatial layout to move from one idea to the next. Navigating among spoken segments of information is more difficult, due to the slow, sequential, and transient nature of speech [1][12]. The research presented in this paper addresses the issue of how voice input can be used to record, retrieve, and navigate among segments of speech data using a hand-held device that has no visual display.

RELATED WORK

The work detailed in this section highlights key issues considered in the development of VoiceNotes including: the use of voice in hand-held environments, navigating in speech-only interfaces, and notetaking.

Degen added two buttons to a conventional tape recorder that allow users to 'mark' segments of audio while recording [5]. The audio data is then digitized and stored on a Macintosh® computer for review. In an evaluation of this prototype, users expressed the desire to customize the meanings of the marks, for more buttons to uniquely tag audio segments, and the ability to play back the marked segments directly from the device. VoiceNotes addresses these issues by using speech recognition and storage technology to allow users to create and name personal categories, and a user interface for direct entry, retrieval, and organization of audio data from a hand-held device.

Hyperspeech, a speech-only hypermedia system, addresses important design considerations for speech-only interfaces [1]. Hyperspeech provides the ability to navigate through a network of recorded speech segments using isolated word recognition. The Hyperspeech database was created and organized by the author of the system. In contrast, VoiceNotes is composed of information created and organized by the user. Additionally, voice notes are automatically segmented by the application, while the

Hyperspeech audio data was manually segmented by the author.

Notepad, a visual notetaking program, is a tool for "thought-dumping—the process of quickly jotting down a flood of fleeting ideas" ([4], p. 260). Cypher emphasizes the importance of allowing users to quickly record an idea with a minimum amount of interference. VoiceNotes, like Notepad, is intended to allow 'thought-dumping' so the interactions must be efficient—the 'tool' should not impede the user's thought process. However, the considerations for designing a voice interface are very different from those for a visual interface. While a visual interface can present information simultaneously in a multitude of windows, VoiceNotes must be more efficient in its presentation of speech data.

VOICENOTES

VoiceNotes is an application for a hand-held computer (Figure 1) that allows the creation, management, and retrieval of user-authored voice notes [15]. For example, "call mom to wish her happy birthday" can be recorded as a voice note. Voice notes can be categorized according to their content. For example, the note "call mom..." could be put into a category of notes named "phone calls."

Figure 1: Photograph of hand-held prototype.

Usage Scenarios

A demonstration of the VoiceNotes application in the context of how it might be used during the course of a user's day is provided in Figures 2 and 3.

Description of VoiceNotes

VoiceNotes provides a simple digital audio file system for organizing recorded segments of speech. The user can create lists of voice notes. Each list has a category name and a collection of associated notes. For example, the user might create a "things to do" list with associated notes such as "pay the rent," and "pick up the cleaning" (Figure 4). VoiceNotes allows the user to create multiple lists of notes.

Figure 4 shows additional examples of categories such as "calls" to make, "movies" to rent, and "groceries" to buy. These are just examples—the names of the categories are defined by the user.

The user selects the "Things to do" category:
User: "THINGS TO DO"
Hand-held: "Moving into *Things to do*"[3]
                 "*Pay the rent*"
                 "*Pick up clothes from cleaners*"

The user interrupts to add a note to the category:
User interrupts: "RECORD"
Hand-held: "Recording note"
User: "*Stop at the grocery store*"
Hand-held: "New note added"

Figure 2: Waking up in the morning, checking and updating the day's activities.

The user plays the list of categories:
User: "CATEGORIES"
Hand-held: "Moving into *Categories*"
                 "*Things to do*," "*Calls*"

The user adds a new category called "Groceries":
User interrupts: "RECORD"
Hand-held: "Recording category"
                 "*Groceries*"
                 "New category added"

The user selects the "Groceries" category:
User: "GROCERIES"
Hand-held: "Moving into *Groceries*,
                 list is empty"

The user adds notes to the "Groceries" category:
User: "RECORD"
Hand-held: "Recording note"
User: "*Milk*"
Hand-held: "New note added"
User: "RECORD"
Hand-held: "Recording note"
User: "*Orange juice*"
Hand-held: "New note added"

Figure 3: In the kitchen making breakfast, creating a grocery list.

The category name provides a method for organizing a collection of notes as well as a handle for accessing them. When the user speaks a category name[4], it is simulta-

neously recorded for playback and trained for speech recognition. Category names allow random access across lists; to select and play back a list of voice notes, the user simply speaks the category name. Since training the recognizer only requires a single utterance, the user's spoken category name becomes a voice command without a separate training process.

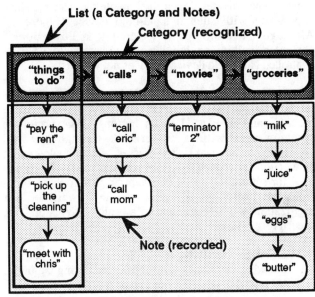

Figure 4: Sample VoiceNotes speech database.

The VoiceNotes user interface provides a simple set of voice commands for recording, navigating, and managing voice notes. Figure 5 lists some of the basic voice commands and their associated actions.

Command	Action
Play	Plays each item in a list
Record	Records an item at the end of a list
Stop	Interrupts the current activity
Next, Previous	Plays the next/previous item
Categories	Plays all of the categories
<Category name>	Selects a category and plays notes
Delete	Deletes the current item in the list
Undelete	Retrieves the last item deleted
Scan	Plays a portion of each item in a list
First, Last	Plays the first/last item in a list
Stop-listening	Turns recognition off
Pay-attention	Turns recognition on
Where-am-i	Plays the current category name
Move	Moves a note to another list

Figure 5: Basic voice commands.

In this design the "record", "next", "previous", and "delete" commands can apply to either voice notes or categories of notes depending upon the user's current position in the speech database.

---

[3]Note that "moving into" is replaced by a 'list opening' sound effect if non-speech audio feedback is selected by the user. For the purposes of this demonstration, speech rather than non-speech feedback is used.
[4]A category name consists of a single short utterance.

In the first hand-held prototype, there were equivalent button controls for most of the voice commands. While the goal of this research has been to explore voice interfaces and applications in hand-held computers, there are cases in which button input provides a better, or more appropriate, interface.

Hand-Held Prototype

A prototype was developed to simulate the user interface experience with such a hand-held device (Figure 1). Although the prototype is tethered to a PowerBook™ computer, it allows exploration of the interface for a voice-controlled hand-held device that does not yet exist.

In the prototype, a Motorola® 68HC11 microcontroller was placed inside the shell of an Olympus® S912 microcassette recorder and interfaced to its buttons. The prototype communicates with a PowerBook through a serial connection to indicate button presses, and an analog audio connection for speech I/O. The original volume control is used for setting the speed of playback. Microphone input from the prototype is routed to the PowerBook for digitization and storage, and to a Voice Navigator™ for speech recognition.[5]

INTERFACE DESIGN ISSUES

The following key issues were considered during the initial phase of interface design, prior to user testing.

User-Definable Category Names

The most important use of speech input in the VoiceNotes application is for naming new categories and randomly accessing them. The user's ability to personalize the application by creating their own category names is essential. Since a category might contain the name of a friend, company, or an acronym, category names cannot come from a fixed recognition vocabulary. Users must be able to create these categories in real-time to support the spontaneous capture of information. Speaker dependent isolated word recognizers typically allow new words to be added to the recognition vocabulary in real-time based on acoustic data alone, whereas, some speaker independent recognition systems require a phonetic spelling of the word. Requiring users to spell or type in new words would defeat the premise underlying the use of voice (e.g., spontaneity, speed of entry). In addition, since the hand-held is a personal device, speaker independent recognition is not necessary.

Navigation

Since there is no visual display, users must be able to maintain a mental model of the VoiceNotes speech database. Voice notes are organized into a two-dimensional matrix (Figure 4), allowing the user to navigate within a particular list of notes, or between categories of notes. It was anticipated that users would have difficulty keeping track of their position in the speech database if the

organization of notes was too complex. Therefore, the database was limited to a one-level hierarchy (a category of notes cannot contain a sub-category).

While graphical hypermedia systems can show the user's navigational path visually, speech is transient and leaves no trace of its existence. Navigating between lists of notes and keeping track of one's position is simplified if there is always an active list. The current list position does not change unless the user explicitly issues a navigational command. It is important that the user feel 'in control' of the navigation, so automatic actions are avoided and commands are provided to give users complete control over their movement.

Voice and Button Input

The user interface for VoiceNotes combines multiple complementary input and output modalities. Combining voice and button input takes advantage of the different capabilities provided by each modality while allowing the limitations of one type of input to be overcome by the other. VoiceNotes can be operated using voice alone, buttons alone, or any combination of voice and button input. This flexibility is important, since the user's selection of how to interact with the application at any given time will be dependent on several factors.

The task. List selection by voice is direct, fast, and intuitive and gives the user control over the number of lists and the category names. Given a flexible number of lists, voice can provide a one-to-one correspondence between each list and the command for accessing it, while buttons cannot due to space limitations. However, buttons are better for tasks requiring fine control such as speed and volume adjustment since voice commands such as "faster, faster..." are awkward.

The context. The acoustic environment, social situation, and current user activity affect the choice of using voice or button input. Button input allows the hand-held to be operated when speech recognition accuracy is degraded due to background noise. Furthermore, button input supports the use of VoiceNotes in social contexts when it is inappropriate or awkward to speak aloud to one's hand-held computer. Alternatively, when the user's hands and eyes are busy (e.g., while driving), or vision is degraded (e.g., in darkness), voice input allows users to operate the application without requiring them to switch their visual attention in order to press a button.

Individual user preference. Some users may prefer to use buttons rather than speak to the computer while others may prefer to use speech input all the time.

---

[5]The Voice Navigator is a speaker dependent isolated word recognizer.

Speech and Non-Speech Audio Output

Speech and non-speech audio[6] [7] output are the primary means of giving feedback to the user—they indicate the current state of the interface whenever the user issues a voice command or presses a button. Just as the combination of speech and button input provides the user with a richer set of interactions, the combination of speech and non-speech audio output is also powerful.

The type of feedback presented depends on the action being performed, the type of input used (voice or button), and the user's experience level and preference. Speech output is used, for example, to play back the contents of a voice note when it is deleted, while a page-flipping sound[7] indicates movement between notes. Speech feedback is used more often in response to voice input rather than button input, since speech recognition is error prone and requires the system to provide evidence that the correct command was recognized [9]. However, too much speech output becomes laborious and slows down the interactions. For example, spoken feedback both before and after recording a note ("recording note". . . "new note added") is tedious when recording several notes in a row. Non-speech audio (i.e., a single beep before recording and a double beep after) is faster and less intrusive on the user's task.

Streamlining the Speech Interaction

In graphical interfaces screen real estate is the most limited resource, yet for speech interfaces, time is the most valuable commodity [14]. Feedback must be brief, yet informative, to conserve time and to reduce the amount of information that the user must retain in working memory [17]. Audio output must be interruptible at all times—VoiceNotes provides the ability to jump between notes on a particular list, between different lists, or to stop playback at any instant. According to Waterworth, "If he can stop the flow, obtain repeats, and move forwards and backwards in the dialogue at will, he can effectively receive information at a rate that suits his own needs and capabilities" ([17], p. 167).

In addition, it is valuable to provide users with interactive control of the rate of playback. There are a range of techniques for time-compressing speech without changing the pitch (summarized in [2]). VoiceNotes allows the speed of playback to be increased up to several times the speed of the original recording. Research suggests that a speed up of more than two times the original rate presents too little of the signal in too little time to be accurately perceived [10]. However, comprehension of time-compressed speech increases with practice and users tend to adapt quickly [16]. VoiceNotes allows users to dynamically adjust the speed of playback in order to browse a list, speeding up during some portions and slowing down when reaching a note of interest. In addition, users can select a fixed rate of playback that they find comfortable for normal listening.

ITERATIVE DESIGN

The initial design of the VoiceNotes interface described above was developed through an iterative design process. Each aspect of the interface, especially navigation and feedback, went through many changes prior to user testing.

Moded vs. Modeless Navigation

The first VoiceNotes interface was moded—only a subset of the voice commands was valid at each point in the interaction. For example, when the last note on a list was played, the system would return to a 'top level' mode, causing users to lose their position in the speech database. The user was essentially 'dropped off the end of the list' and commands like "next" and "previous" were no longer valid.

The interface was redesigned in an attempt to create a modeless interface and to simplify navigation. In this design, all commands are always valid. When the last note is reached, if the user says "next" the system responds "end of list," and retains the user's position on the last item. Now, the user can issue commands like "next" and "previous" without fear of 'falling off the end of the list'. In this way, the beginning and end of a list act as 'anchors' for navigational control instead of drop off points.

Distinct Feedback

There were several problems with the initial design of the feedback provided by VoiceNotes. One problem was that feedback for different voice commands was not distinct, making it ambiguous as to whether or not a command was correctly recognized. For example, when selecting a category (e.g., "things to do") or saying "where-am-i", the system played the category name in response to both commands. Another problem with the feedback for selecting a list was that merely echoing the category name did not indicate any movement from one list to another.

In order to address these problems, the response to each command was made distinct and the feedback for selecting a category was changed to indicate movement ("moving into *things to do*"). Once this change was made, however, the feedback became too wordy. Therefore, an option was added to allow "moving into" to be replaced by a shorter duration sound effect (auditory icon).

USER TESTING

An informal user test (of the type described in [13]) was performed to help further refine the initial design of the VoiceNotes interface. The goal was to observe users to determine those aspects of the interface with which they had the most difficulty; particularly, how well users could navigate the speech database, given the structure shown in Figure 4. In addition, we solicited their initial reactions to the application.

---

[6]VoiceNotes uses mostly *auditory icons*, everyday sounds used to convey information about computer events [7].
[7]This is an example of an *auditory icon*.

Method

Six participants, three male and three female, used VoiceNotes to perform an inventory task and were subsequently interviewed. Each subject used VoiceNotes for a one hour period. The tests were video taped for later analysis. One of the participants used a microcassette recorder extensively at home and in the car for recording things to buy, videos to rent, books to read, etc. Another participant was considering buying a microcassette recorder to help keep track of personal information. None of the participants had ever used a speech recognizer before. Participants were told to 'think out loud' as they performed the different tasks [6].

First, each user trained the speech recognizer[8] on the voice commands (Figure 5). Next, the user was briefly instructed on VoiceNotes operations. Following training, the user walked around an office[9], performing an inventory task of several cubicles. The user created a category for the name of the person occupying the office and a note for each piece of equipment contained in the office. While taking inventory, users were interrupted occasionally and asked to create and add items to a grocery and a to-do list. The user was free to use either voice or buttons for any task.

Observations

Performance varied widely across the users tested. Some users learned the application very quickly and had few problems performing any of the tasks, while others struggled throughout the test. Several problems with the interface design were consistently observed during the testing.

Navigation. Users sometimes lost track of their position in the VoiceNotes speech database. This often occurred when selecting a category of notes, after which, the notes in the category would automatically begin to play. This automatic playback was unexpected and made the user feel out of control of the interaction. While some used the "where-am-i" command to determine their location, most wanted some kind of visual indication on the device of the current list and note.

Despite our efforts to create a 'modeless' interface, users still perceived the interface as moded (users referred to 'category' and 'notes' modes). Since the record, delete, previous, and next commands were overloaded (used for both categories and notes), users were often confused as to whether they were operating on categories or notes. When playing back the list of categories, some users stopped when they heard the category they wanted and attempted to record a note. Since they didn't first move into the list, their 'note' was actually interpreted as a new category. When asked to add a new category, users would often say "new list" instead of "record". These 'modes' also negated

the benefit of list selection by voice, since most of the users thought they had to be in 'category' mode in order to select a new category.

Interruption. A related problem was that users were unable to determine how to interrupt the speech output. During the user test, interruption by voice input was not enabled, although the ability to interrupt was available using the stop button. Users had a bias towards using voice to interrupt—when attempting to interrupt the user said "stop" rather than using the button. One user said, "I interrupt people that way [with voice], so why shouldn't I be able to interrupt this machine the same way."

Voice Input. VoiceNotes always listens for voice input, under the assumption that this allows more spontaneous use of the application. However, this makes it difficult to determine when the user is speaking a command (the system must differentiate between background noise and voice commands). Therefore, VoiceNotes remains silent unless a word is correctly recognized. During testing, if the user spoke a command and VoiceNotes did not respond, rather than repeat the command, users waited for a response, thinking that the system was still processing the input or busy performing the task. This caused the user to become confused and frustrated. Furthermore, background conversation often falsely triggered playback, making the user feel out of control because the device appeared to be operating spontaneously. Users expressed concern over the embarrassment that would be caused if this happened during a meeting or when talking to one's supervisor.

Interviews

At the end of the test, participants were interviewed about their difficulties with the user interface, their preference for voice or buttons, and their potential use of the application.

Feedback. Users perceived the interface as overly talkative or wordy—partly due to problems with interrupting the output, and due to the feedback initiated by falsely triggered recognitions. One user wanted the ability to turn the speech feedback off or select an alternative method of response.[10]

Voice vs. Buttons. When performing tasks, users employed both voice and button input. Users who obtained poor recognition results simply used buttons instead. Furthermore, during the test there was often background noise (e.g., a printer) that interfered with recognition, and users similarly compensated for this. When asked which input modality was preferred, some users said they would prefer voice if it was reliable enough, but all the users tested said they wanted both voice and buttons for communicating with the device.

Potential Use. All but one user said that they would like to use a hand-held device for creating personal voice notes. In

---

[8]Users were prompted to speak each word in the VoiceNotes vocabulary one time.
[9]The device was used under realistic ambient noise conditions.

[10]Non-speech feedback was not available during testing.

addition, some wanted to use the device to listen to voice mail and electronic mail messages while driving.

Implications for Redesign

The information gathered during user testing uncovered aspects of the VoiceNotes interface requiring further design development.

Navigation. One solution for addressing the user's confusion between operating on categories versus notes, is to provide separate commands for each (e.g., "new category", "new note"). Another solution is a one-to-one mapping between categories and buttons on the device. A visual indicator for each category could also help users keep track of their position.

Interruption and Voice Input. Although the ultimate goal is to allow users to pick up the device and speak a command immediately, an alternate approach must be taken due to problems with speech recognition in noise. One solution is to provide a 'push-to-talk' button. This approach also provides a consistent mechanism for interrupting the VoiceNotes speech output.

Feedback. The type of feedback (i.e., primarily speech or primarily non-speech) and amount (i.e., verbose or terse) used by VoiceNotes should be user definable. The perception of VoiceNotes as 'wordy' indicates the need to make these customization capabilities easily accessible to the user.

Voice vs. Buttons. When asked whether they would use the device if only one input modality was provided, the users consistently responded that they wanted both voice and buttons. This reinforces our original assumption about the value of offering both of these input modalities.

CONCLUSIONS

In developing VoiceNotes, many lessons were learned that are applicable to other speech and small computer interfaces:

- The use of multiple input and output modalities (in this case voice and button input, speech and non-speech output) combines the capabilities of each, while allowing limitations of a particular modality to be overcome.

- In speech interfaces like VoiceNotes, time is a valuable commodity. Feedback must be as brief and responsive as possible, audio output must be interruptible at all times, and dynamic control over the rate of playback should be provided. Furthermore, despite the best attempts to design informative, unambiguous, and brief feedback, it is important to allow users to customize both the amount and type of system feedback.

- Voice input was found to be especially valuable for categorizing and randomly accessing information (in this case, small segments of digitized speech).

- Navigation in speech-only interfaces remains a challenging design problem. Audio feedback must provide a sense of movement when navigating. Navigational 'anchors' must represent the limits of the information space, helping users to keep track of their position and maintain control over their movement.

This work has explored the use of voice, both as the data and the access mechanism in the user interface for a hand-held computer. In addition to addressing the problems of capturing and retrieving spontaneous ideas, VoiceNotes serves as a step toward new uses of voice technology and interfaces for future portable devices.

ACKNOWLEDGMENTS

We would like to thank several people for their contributions. The user testing was done in collaboration with Richard Mander, Jesse Ellenbogen, Eric Gould, and Jonathan Cohen; Andrew Kass and Nicholas Chan contributed to the software development; Derek Atkins and Lewis Knapp developed the hand-held prototypes.

This work was sponsored by Apple® Computer, Inc.*

REFERENCES

1. Arons, B. Hyperspeech: Navigating in speech-only hypermedia. *In Proceedings of* Hypertext '91, pp. 133-146. ACM, 1991.

2. Arons, B. Techniques, perception, and applications of time-compressed speech. *In Proceedings of* AVIOS '92, pp. 169-177. American Voice I/O Society, 1992.

3. Chalfonte, B.L., Fish, R.S. and Kraut, R.E. Expressive richness: A comparison of speech and text as media for revision. *In Proceedings of* CHI '92, pp. 21-26. ACM, 1991.

4. Cypher, A. The structure of users' activities. In Norman, D.A. and Draper, S.W., editors, *User Centered System Design*, chapter 12, pp. 243-263. Lawrence Erlbaum Associates, 1986.

5. Degen, L., Mander, R. and Salomon, G. Working with audio: Integrating personal tape recorders and desktop computers. *In Proceedings of* CHI '92, pp. 413-418. ACM, 1992.

6. Ericsson, K.A. and Simon, H.A. Protocol Analysis. The MIT Press, 1984.

7. Gaver, W.W. The SonicFinder: An interface that uses auditory icons. *Human-Computer Interaction*, 4(1):67-94, 1989.

8. Gould, J.D. An experimental study of writing, dictating, and speaking. In Requin, J., editor, *Attention & Performance VII*, pp. 299-319. Lawrence Erlbaum, 1978.

9. Hayes, P.J. and Reddy, D.R. Steps toward graceful interaction in spoken and written man-machine communication. *International Journal of Man-Machine Studies*, 19:231-284, 1983.

10. Heiman, G.W., Leo, R.J., Leighbody, G. and Bowler, K. Word intelligibility decrements and the comprehension of time-compressed speech. *Perception and Psychophysics*, 40(6):407-411, 1986.

11. Martin, G.L. The utility of speech input in user-computer interfaces. *International Journal of Man-Machine Studies*, 30:355-375, 1989.

12. Muller, M.J. and Daniel, J.E. Toward a definition of voice documents. *In Proceedings of* COIS '90, pp. 174-182. ACM, 1990.

13. Nielsen, J. Usability engineering at a discount. In Salvendy, G. and Smith, M.J., editors, *Designing and Using Human-Computer Interfaces and Knowledge Based Systems*, pp. 394-401. Elsevier, 1989.

14. Rudnicky, A.I. and Hauptmann, A.G. Models for evaluating interaction protocols in speech recognition. *In Proceedings of* CHI '91, pp. 285-291. ACM, 1991.

15. Stifelman, L.J. VoiceNotes: An application for a voice-controlled hand-held computer. Master's Thesis. Massachusetts Institute of Technology, 1992.

16. Voor, J.B. and Miller, J.M. The effect of practice upon the comprehension of time-compressed speech. *Speech Monographs*, 32:452-455, 1965.

17. Waterworth, J.A. Interaction with machines by voice: A telecommunications perspective. *Behaviour and Information Technology*, 3(2):163-177, 1984.

Communicative Facial Displays
as a New Conversational Modality

Akikazu Takeuchi and Katashi Nagao
Sony Computer Science Laboratory, Inc.
3-14-13 Higashi-Gotanda
Shinagawa-ku, Tokyo 141, Japan
TEL: +81-3-3448-4380
{takeuchi,nagao}@csl.sony.co.jp

ABSTRACT

The human face is an independent communication channel that conveys emotional and conversational signals encoded as facial displays. Facial displays can be viewed as communicative signals that help coordinate conversation. We are attempting to introduce facial displays into computer-human interaction as a new modality. This will make the interaction tighter and more efficient while lessening the cognitive load. As the first step, a speech dialogue system was selected to investigate the power of communicative facial displays. We analyzed the conversations between users and the speech dialogue system, to which facial displays had been added. We found that conversation with the system featuring facial displays was more successful than that with a system without facial displays.

KEYWORDS: User interface design, multimodal interfaces, facial expression, conversational interfaces, anthropomorphism.

INTRODUCTION AND MOTIVATIONS

In designing computer-human interaction, human face-to-face conversation has provided an ideal model. One of the major features of face-to-face communication is the multiplicity of communication channels. A channel is a communication medium associated with a particular encoding method. Examples are the auditory channel that carries speech, and the visual channel that carries facial expressions. A modality is the sense used to perceive signals from the outside world. One channel may be perceived by more than one sense. The senses of sight, hearing, and touch are all examples of modalities.

Multimodal user interfaces are interfaces with multiple channels that act on multiple modalities. To realize a true multimedia/modal user interface, it is necessary to study how humans perceive information and to which information humans are sensitive.

In usual face-to-face communication, many channels are used and different modalities are activated. Conversation is

supported by multiple coordinated activities of various cognitive levels. For instance, syntactic and semantic processing are coupled, and object-level processing (relevant to the communication goal) and meta-level processing (relevant to communication regulations) are executed in parallel as part of these coordinated activities. As a result, communication becomes highly flexible and robust, so that failure of one channel is recovered by another channel, and a message in one channel can be explained by the other channel.

In fact, face-to-face communication is the primary communication style, evolved over aeons, from primates to human beings. Our brain has adapted to this style of communication. As the terms "face-to-face" and "interface" indicate, faces play an essential role in communication. In the field of neurophysiology, it is well-known that a particular region of primates' brains is dedicated to facial information processing [14]. This implies that the ability to process facial information is a major factor in surviving natural selection.

The study of facial expressions has attracted the interest of a number of different disciplines, including psychology, ethology, and interpersonal communication. Facial expressions are viewed in either of two ways. One regards facial expressions as expressions of emotional states [8]. The other views facial expressions in a social context, and regards them as communicative signals [9]. The term "facial displays" is equivalent to "facial expressions", but does not have the connotation of emotion. In this paper, we use the term "facial displays."

The present paper assumes the second view. A face is an independent communication channel that conveys emotional and conversational signals encoded as facial displays. A facial display can be also seen as a modality because the human brain has a special circuit dedicated to the necessary processing. Taking this as a starting point, we are attempting to bring facial displays into computer human interaction as a new modality that makes the interaction tighter and more efficient, while lessening the cognitive load.

Another reason for placing attention on faces is that faces provide a human with social interfaces. As J. S. Brown indicated in the closing talk at CHI'92, future CHI technologies should help people establish and strengthen their social relationships. Humans are social animals. Facial displays are usually directed not at oneself, but at others. They have been evolved to help us develop better social relations with others. Facial displays are primarily communicative and thus are subject to social factors that regulate their occurrence [2]. Therefore, the study of facial displays is expected to reveal important characteristics of social interfaces.

RELATED WORK

Our approach is classified into the so-called "multimodal interfaces." Blattner surveyed a range of models to design a multimodal interfaces [1]. Among them, the conversational model and the anthropomorphic models are closely related to our approach.

The conversational model places greater emphasis on conversation structure [10]. In communication, different communication channels are used and several modalities will be activated. A conversation structure exists throughout all of these and helps to coordinate the conversation. To clarify and abstract the (possibly linguistic) structure of conversation is the goal of the conversational model. Our approach focuses on a specific communication channel and modality, namely, human faces. Through evolution, humans developed sophisticated communication using faces. Knowing about the roles of communicative displays leads us to an understanding of how people coordinate conversation by sending signals through multimodal channels, that is, understanding the dynamics of conversation. By applying that knowledge, we will be able to realize a new user interface that can exchange even subtle information using sophisticated communicative displays.

The anthropomorphic model has been a controversial topic in recent CHI conferences [4]. While there are some ad hoc anthropomorphic interfaces, carefully designed interfaces such as GUIDES illustrate the possibilities of new user interfaces [5]. This research is an attempt to computationally capture the communicative power of human faces and to apply it to user interfaces. The resulting interface will, of course, be anthropomorphic. However, we use faces as an additional communication channel connected to an unexplored modality, rather than as a humanity option for the interfaces.

STUDIES OF FACIAL DISPLAYS

Facial displays have been the subject of scientific study for a long time. Darwin identified two aspects of facial expression; that related to emotion, and that related to communication [3]. We will give a brief introduction to the theory of communicative facial displays below.

Theory of Communicative Facial Displays

Fridlund and Gilbert [9] proposed that the primary role of facial displays is to provide information that augments the verbal component of communication, rather than to provide emotional information. The theory makes two major assumptions.

The first is that facial displays are primarily communicative. They are used to convey information to other people. The information that is conveyed may be emotional information, or other kinds of information, for example, syntactical information, indications that the speaker is being understood, relationship definition, listener responses, etc. [2]. Facial displays can function in an interaction as communication on their own. That is, they can send a message independently of other communicative behavior. Facial emblems such as winks, facial shrugs, and listener's comments (agreement or disagreement, disbelief or surprise) are typical examples. Facial displays can also work in conjunction with other communicative behavior (both verbal and nonverbal) to provide information. For example, facial displays in social interaction may function to reduce ambiguity in spoken language, as stress patterns, voice tone, and kinetic behavior also act in the same way. This is done by illustrating or adding information, or by meta communication, that is, communication about how a message should be taken. (e.g., smiling when joking).

The second assumption is that facial displays are primarily social. They occur for the purpose of communicating information to others. Their occurrence is regulated more by the social situation than by any underlying emotion processes.

Facial Displays in Conversation

There have been several attempts to categorize facial displays according to their communicative roles [2,6,15]. In a similar vein, the categorization of emotional facial displays by Ekman and Friesen [8] is well known. Emotional facial displays are basically independent of the situation, that is, their meanings are the same wherever and whenever they appear. Unlike the emotional categorization, in communicative categorization almost all displays, except for those displays known as facial emblems, are situation dependent. Namely, the interpretation of a communicative facial display depends upon the situation in which it appears. Conversational context and chronological relations (e.g., synchronization or delay) with other communication channels have a significant impact in their interpretations.

Table 1 is assembled from previous work on categorizing communicative facial displays [2,6,15]. The table lists three major categories:

Syntactic Displays. These are defined as facial displays that (1) mark stress on particular words or clauses, (2) are connected with the syntactic aspects of an utterance or (3) are connected with the organization of the talk.

Speaker Displays. Speaker displays are defined as being facial displays that (1) illustrate the idea being verbally conveyed, or (2) add additional information to the ongoing verbal content.

Listener Comment Displays. These are facial displays made by the person who is not currently speaking and which are made in response to the utterances of the other person.

SPEECH DIALOGUE WITH FACIAL DISPLAYS

As a first step, a speech dialogue system was selected to investigate the power of communicative facial displays.

Prototype Architecture

The system consists of two subsystems, a facial animation subsystem that generates a three-dimensional face capable of facial display, and a speech dialogue subsystem that recognizes and interprets speech, and generates voice output. Currently, the animation subsystem is running on an SGI 320VGX, and the speech dialogue subsystem on a Sony NEWS workstation. These two subsystems communicate with each other via an Ethernet network. Figure 1 illustrates the system architecture.

Facial Animation Subsystem

The face is modeled three-dimensionally. The face is composed of approximately 500 polygons. The face may

Table 1: Communicative Categorization of Facial Displays

SYNTACTIC DISPLAYS	
1. Exclamation marks	Eyebrow raising
2. Question marks	Eyebrow raising or lowering
3. Emphasizers	Eyebrow raising or lowering
4. Underliners	Longer eyebrow raising
5. Punctuations	Eyebrow movements
6. End of an utterance	Eyebrow raising
7. Beginning of a story	Eyebrow raising
8. Story continuation	Avoid eye contact
9. End of a story	Eye contact
SPEAKER DISPLAYS	
10. Thinking/Remembering	Eyebrow raising or lowering, Closing the eyes, Pulling back one mouth side
11. Facial shrug/ "I don't know"	Eyebrow flashes, Mouth corners pulled down, Mouth corners pulled back
12. Interactive/ "You know?"	Eyebrow raising
13. Metacommunicative/ Indication of sarcasm or joke	Eyebrow raising and looking up and off
14. "Yes"	Eyebrow actions
15. "No"	Eyebrow actions
15. "Not"	Eyebrow actions
17. "But"	Eyebrow actions
LISTENER COMMENT DISPLAYS	
18. Backchannel/ Indication of attendance	Eyebrow raising, Mouth corners turned down
19. Indication of loudness	Eyebrows drawn to center
Understanding levels	
20. Confident	Eyebrow raising, Head nod
21. Moderately confident	Eyebrow raising
22. Not confident	Eyebrow lowering
23. "Yes"	Eyebrow raising
Evaluation of utterance	
24. Agreement	Eyebrow raising
25. Request for more Info	Eyebrow raising
26. Incredulity	Longer eyebrow raising

be rendered using a skin-like surface material with Gouraud shading or by applying a texture map taken from a video frame or a picture.

In 3D computer graphics, a facial display is realized by local deformation of the polygons representing the face. Waters showed that deformation that simulates an action of the muscles underlying the face looks more natural [18]. Therefore, we used the numerical equations simulating muscle actions as defined by Waters. Currently, the system incorporates 16 muscles and 10 parameters controlling mouth opening, jaw rotation, eye movement, eyelid opening, and head orientation. Waters determined these 16 muscles by considering the correspondence with the action units in Facial Action Coding System (FACS) [7]. For details of the facial modeling and animation system, see [16].

Takeuchi, Nagao, Color Plate 1 shows 26 synthesized facial displays corresponding to those listed in Table 1, as well as two additional displays. All facial displays are generated by the method described above, and rendered with a texture map of a young boy. The additional displays are "smile" and "neutral." The neutral display features no muscle contraction, and is used when no conversational signal is needed.

At run-time, the animation subsystem awaits a request from the speech subsystem. When the animation subsystem receives a request that specifies values for the 26 parameters, it starts to deform the face using the received values. The deformation process is controlled by the following differential equation:

$$\dot{f} = a - f$$

where f is a parameter value at time t and $\dot{f}$ is its time derivative at time t. a is the target value specified in the request. Using this equation, deformation is fast in the early phase, slowing in the later phase to mimic the real dynamics of facial displays. Currently, the base performance of the animation subsystem ranges from 20-25 frames per second on an SGI Power Series. This is satisfactory for real-time animation.

Speech Dialogue Subsystem

Our speech dialogue subsystem works as follows: First, a voice input is acoustically analyzed by a built-in sound processing board. Then, a speech recognition module is invoked and outputs word sequences that are assigned higher scores by a probabilistic phone model. These word sequences are syntactically and semantically analyzed and disambiguated by using a relatively loose grammar and a restricted domain knowledge. From the semantic representation of the input utterance, a plan recognition module extracts the speaker's intention. For example, from the utterance "I am interested in Sony's workstation," the module interprets the speaker's intention as "he wants to get precise information about Sony workstation." Once the system determines the speaker's intention, the response generation module is invoked. It generates a system response that satisfies the speaker's intention. Finally, the system's response is output as voice by a voice synthesis module.

Each module, except the voice synthesis module, can send messages to the facial animation subsystem about which facial display should be generated. The correspondence between the situation of speech dialogue and facial displays are listed in Table 2.

The task of the system is to provide information about Sony's computer-related products. For example, the system can answer questions about price, size, weight, and the specifications of Sony's workstations and PCs.

Next, we will present a more detailed description of modules in the speech dialogue subsystem.

Speech recognition. This module was developed in cooperation with Tokyo Institute of Technology. Speaker-independent continuous speech input is accepted without special hardware. To obtain a high degree of accuracy, the context-dependent phone Hidden Markov Models are used to construct phone-level hypotheses [11]. This module can generate N-best word-level hypotheses.

Syntactic and semantic analysis. This module consists of a parsing mechanism, a semantic analyzer, a relatively

loose grammar that contains 24 rules, a lexicon that includes 34 nouns, 8 verbs, 4 adjectives and 22 particles, and a frame-based knowledge base with 61 conceptual frames. Our parsing mechanism is based on Tomita's generalized LR parsing method [17]. Our semantic analyzer can disambiguate ambiguous syntactic structures and generate a semantic representation of the speaker's utterance [12].

Plan recognition. This module determines the speaker's intention by constructing his belief model and dynamically adjusting and expanding the model as the dialogue progresses [13]. The module also maintains the topic of the current dialogue and resolve anaphora (reference of pronouns) and ellipsis (omission of subjects).

Response generation. This module generates a response by using domain knowledge (database) and text templates (typical patterns of utterances). It selects appropriate templates and combines them to construct a response that satisfies the speaker's intention.

Correspondence between conversational situations and facial displays. The speech dialogue subsystem recognizes a number of typical conversational situations that are important in dialogue. We associate these situations with facial displays. For example, in situations where speech inputs are not recognized or where they are syntactically

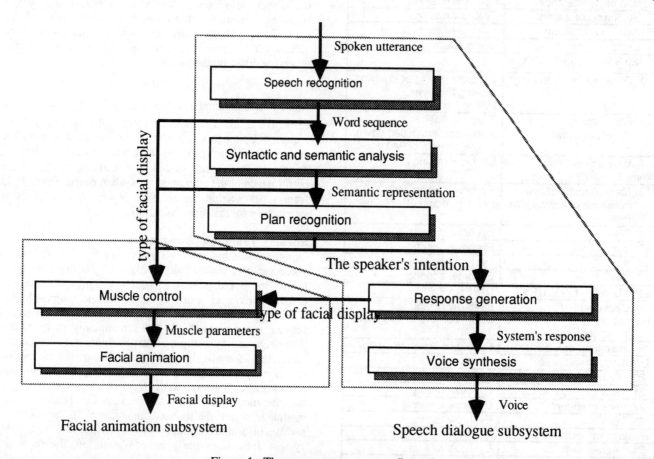

Figure 1. The prototype system configuration

invalid, the listener comment display #22 "not-confident" is displayed. If the speaker's request is out of the system's domain knowledge, then the system displays a facial shrug and replies with "I cannot answer such a question." The relationships between conversational situations and facial displays are listed in Table 2.

EXPERIMENT WITH THE PROTOTYPE SYSTEM

Method
To examine the effect of facial displays in computer-human conversation, experiments were performed using the prototype system.

Subjects. The prototype system was tested on 32 volunteer subjects. Half were from the engineering staff of the computer product development division of Sony, while the remainder were university-level computer science students. The average age of the subjects was 26. All had experience of using computers, with an average career length of 7 years.

Experiments. Two experiments were prepared. In one experiment, called F, the subjects held a conversation with a system having facial displays. In the other experiment, called N, the subjects held a conversation with a system that displays short phrases instead of facial displays. The short phrases are four- or five-word sentences describing the corresponding facial displays. For example, instead of displaying #22 display "Not confident", "I am not confident" appears on the screen. The subjects were divided into two groups, FN and NF. As the names indicate, the subjects in the FN group first took experiment F then N, while those in the NF group first took N and then F.

In both experiments, the subjects were given the same conversation goal of enquiring about the functions and prices of Sony computer products. In each experiment, the subjects were requested to complete the conversation within 10 minutes.

Measurements. During the experiments, the number of occurrences of each facial display was counted. The conversation content was also evaluated based on the number of topics a subject visited. The results were scored using the following equation:

$$s = (3 + 2 * n + m) / t$$

where *s*, *n*, *m*, and *t* are scores for conversation, number of topic shifts, number of successful answers, and the duration of the conversation. The subject's face and the system's face were videotaped during the experiments for later review. After completing both experiments, the subjects were asked to answer an inquiry sheet that asked the subjects to rate the qualities of speech recognition, facial displays, etc.

Results
The results are shown in Takeuchi, Nagao, Color Plate 2, which plots the relative frequencies of facial displays (displays with no occurrence are omitted) and conversation scores (ACHIEVEMENT). Note that the conversation scores has a different scale from the others. Each experiment can be classified into one of two types, according to the characteristics of its result. The first type is "successful conversation" in which the conversation score is relatively high, and the displays "moderately confident", "beginning of story" appear more often. The second type is "not successful conversation" in the which conversation score is lower, and the displays "neutral" and "not confident" appear more often.

In Figure 2, the first experiments of the two groups are compared. It is clear that conversation with facial displays is more successful than conversation with short phrases. We can conclude that upon first contact facial displays clearly help conversation.

Table 2. Relation between conversational situations and facial displays

Conversational situations	Facial displays
recognition failure	listener comment display #22 "not-confident"
syntactically invalid utterance	listener comment display #22 "not-confident"
many recognition candidates with close scores	listener comment display #21 "moderately-confident"
beginning of dialogue	listener comment display #18 "indication-of-attendance"
introduction to a topic	syntactic display #7 "beginning-of-story"
shift to another topic	syntactic displays #7 "end-of-story" and #9 "beginning-of-story"
answer "yes"	speaker display #14 "yes"
answer "no"	speaker display #15 "no"
out of the domain	speaker display #11 "facial shrug"
answer "yes" with emphasis	listener comment display #23 "yes" and syntactic display #3 "emphasizer"
violation of pragmatic constraints	listener comment display # 26 "incredulity"
reply to "thanks"	listener comment display #23 "yes"
…	…

Figure 3 compares the overall results of both groups. The graph shows that the FN group is more successful than the NF group. Because the only difference between the two groups is the order in which experiments were conducted, we can conclude that early interaction with the system with facial displays improves later interaction.

Figure 4 compares the experiments with facial displays (1st of FN and 2nd of NF) and the experiments with short phrases (2nd of FN and 1st of NF). Contrary to our expectations, the results show relatively little influence by facial displays. This implies that the learning effect occurring over the first and second experiments is equal to the effect gained with facial displays. However, we believe that the effect gained with facial displays will be able to better the learning effect if the qualities of speech recognition and facial animation are improved.

DISCUSSION AND FUTURE DIRECTION

The experiments show that facial displays are helpful especially upon first contact with the system. It is also shown that early interaction with facial displays improves successive interaction, even when there is no facial display. These results prove quantitatively that interfaces with facial displays reduce the mental barrier between the users and the computing systems.

Several premature facets of the prototype system fail to realize the potential advantages of a system with communicative facial displays. The system currently lacks lip synchronization and has a limited vocabulary. If these aspects are improved, the results would be much better. All subjects were relatively familiar with using computers. Experiments with non computer-literate users should also be done.

As a new research direction, the integration of more communication channels and modalities offers great promise. Among them, prosody information processing in speech recognition and speech synthesis are of special interest, as well as the recognition of a user's gestures and facial displays.

So far, conversation with computer systems has been over-regulated. This is because communication is done through limited channels. It is necessary to avoid information collision in these narrow channels. Multiple channels reduce the necessity of conversation regulation, so that new styles of conversation will appear, which have smaller granularity and high interruptibility, and which can invoke more spontaneous utterances. Such conversation is closer to our daily conversation with family and friends, and this

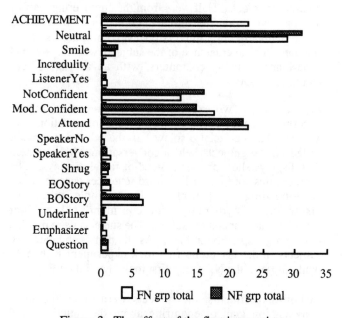

Figure 3. The effect of the first interaction

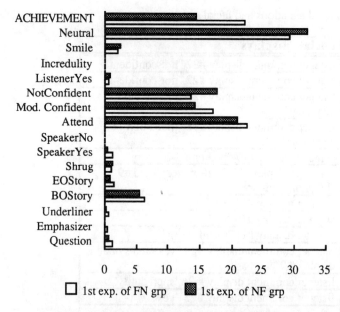

Figure 2. Comparison of the first experiments

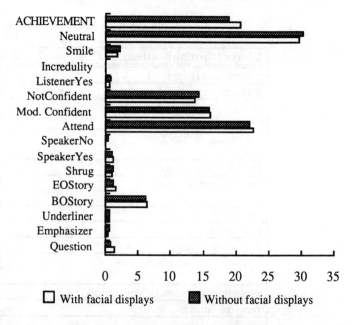

Figure 4. With or without facial displays

will further increase the user-friendliness of computers.

ACKNOWLEDGMENTS

We would like to thank Alan Bond and Leslie Brothers for their suggestions and guidance in the early stage of the research. We also thank Steve Franks and Katunobu Itou for their contributions to implementing the prototype system. Special thanks to Keith Waters for permission to access his original animation system. Finally we thank Mario Tokoro and our colleagues at Sony CSL for their encouragement and discussion.

REFERENCES

1. Blattner, M. *Multimedia and Multimodal User Interface Design: CHI'92 Tutorial Course Note 4*. ACM Press, 1992.
2. Chovil, N. *Communicative Functions of Facial Displays in Conversation*. Ph.D. Thesis, University of Victoria, 1989.
3. Darwin, C. The Expression of Emotion in Man and Animals. University of Chicago Press, Chicago, 1965.
4. Don, A. and Brennan, S. and Laurel, B. and Shneiderman, B. Anthropomorphism: from Eliza to Terminator 2, In Proc. CHI'92 Human Factors in Computing Systems (Monterey, May 3-7, 1992), ACM Press, pp. 67-70.
5. Don, A. and Oren, T. and Laurel, B. GUIDES 3.0, in Proc. CHI'91 Human Factors in Computing Systems (New Orleans, April 27-May 2, 1991), ACM Press, pp. 447-448.
6. Ekman, P. and Friesen, W. V. The repertoire of nonverbal behavior - categories, origins, usage, and coding, Semiotica 1 (1969), pp. 49-98.
7. Ekman, P. and Friesen, W. V. *Facial Action Coding System*. Consulting Psychologists Press, Palo Alto, California, 1978.
8. Ekman, P. and Friesen, W. V. *Unmasking the Face*. Consulting Psychologists Press, Inc., Palo Alto, California, 1984.
9. Fridlund, A. J. and Gilbert, A. N. Emotions and facial expression, Science, 230 (1985), pp. 607-608.
10. Hindus, D. and Brennan, S. *Conversational Paradigms in User Interfaces: CHI'92 Tutorial Course Note 11*. ACM Press, 1992.
11. Itou, K. and Hayamizu, S. and Tanaka, H. Continuous speech recognition by context-dependent phonetic HMM and an efficient algorithm for finding N-best sentence hypotheses, in Proc. ICASSP'92, IEEE Press, pp. I 21-I 24.
12. Nagao, K. A preferential constraint satisfaction technique for natural language analysis, in Proc. ECAI-92, (1992), pp. 523-527.
13. Nagao, K. and Osawa, E. *A Logic-Based Approach to Plan Recognition and Belief Revision*. Tech. Report. SCSL-TR-92-007, Sony Computer Science Laboratory, Inc., Tokyo, 1992.
14. Perret, D. I. et al. Neurones responsive to faces in the temporal cortex: studies of functional organization sensitivity and relation to perception. Human Neurobiology, 3 (1984) 197-208.
15. Sherer, K. R. The functions of nonverbal signs in conversation, in *The Social and Psychological Contexts of Language*, St. Clair, R. N. and Giles, H. (Eds.), Lawrence Erlbaum, Hillsdale, NJ, 1980, pp. 225-244.
16. Takeuchi, A. and Franks, S. *A Rapid Face Construction Lab*. Tech. Report. SCSL-TR-92-010, Sony Computer Science Laboratory, Inc., Tokyo, 1992.
17. Tomita, M. An efficient augmented-context-free parsing algorithm, Computational Linguistics, 13 (1987), pp. 31-46.
18. Waters, K. A muscle model for animating three-dimensional facial expression, in Computer Graphics 21, 4 (July 1987), 17-24.

Sign Language Interfaces

Nancy Frishberg (moderator), P.O. Box 282022, San Francisco, California 94128-2022, USA, +1 415 592 8559 (voice & TTY) *nancyf@seiden.com*

Serena Corazza, Istituto di Psicologia, Consiglio Nazionale delle Ricerche, c/o Istituto Statale Sordomuti, Via Nomenatana 56, 0061 Roma, Italia +39 6 440 36 85 (fax)

Linda Day, Centre for Deaf Studies, School of Education, University of Bristol, 22 Berkeley Square, Bristol BS8 1HP, England +44 272 257875 (fax)

Sherman Wilcox, Department of Linguistics, University of New Mexico, Albuquerque, New Mexico 87131, USA.+1 505 277 6720 (voice) *wilcox@carina.unm.edu*

Rolf Schulmeister, Zentrum fur Deutsche Gebardensprache und Kommunikation Gehorloser, Universitat Hamburg, Rothenbaumchaussee 45, 2000 Hamburg,13, Germany +49 40 23 240 (voice),+49 4041 23 6587 (fax) *ger.xuu0001@applelink.apple.com*

ABSTRACT

This panel will start to build the bridge between behavioral scientists who know deaf communities worldwide, their languages and cultures, and experts in technical disciplines relating to computers and human interfaces.

KEYWORDS: Sign languages, natural language processing, computer assisted language learning, multimedia, intercultural issues in interface design, gestural representation; deaf.

INTRODUCTION

Sign languages of deaf people are fully formed natural languages linked to cultural values and social behaviors of deaf communities [1]. Sign languages differ from spoken languages of the majority, hearing communities in obvious ways: their modality of production (gestural vs. oral) and perception (visual vs. aural) [5]. This panel (by demonstration) will show the capacity of several sign languages to support the discourse of scientific inquiry, and will indicate how elements of deaf culture must necessarily be considered whenever deaf and hearing people engage in shared tasks.

By *sign language interfaces* we mean ways of representing deaf sign languages for computer storage and display in order to permit input, retrieval, and manipulation by people. Computer technology offers the opportunity to create tools that enable literacy and learning in ways accessible to signing users. Technology also gives us the opportunity to make sign language traditions accessible to wider audiences of

non-signers. Successful sign language interfaces will come from collaborations between those knowledgeable about technology and those knowledgeable about the cultures and languages of deaf people. This panel combines expertise in theory and practice of sign language learning and teaching, research on linguistic processing, and in software development.

Introduction of technology to new user communities proceeds more successfully, we believe, when members of the target community are involved in the development of their interfaces. Of the dozen or more projects worldwide which are building sign language interfaces, four are represented on this panel. The panelists are two hearing and two deaf researchers. They represent four countries, each with a distinct sign language tradition. Three panelists are native or fluent in the sign language of their respective countries, one is a novice. Three are part of teams of deaf and hearing people working together, making decisions about sign language interfaces; one has been working independently with local technical assistance.

Each project has emphasized a different user population or technology to access stored or coded language data. Two panelists describe projects for language learning, one involving deaf children's acquisition of literacy in the majority (spoken/written) language, and the other aimed at hearing (or deaf) adults learning sign language. The two other panelists describe dictionary making; in one case redesigning a successful print dictionary for multimedia treatment and the other designing a bilingual dictionary directly for the computer

Language Learning

Who is the audience for a language learning task? Young children cannot be assumed to read text at all. Young deaf children cannot make use of digitally stored or synthesized speech signals provided for computer

© 1993 ACM 0-89791-575-5/93/0004/0194...$1.50

applications aimed at preschool or primary school-aged hearing children. Deaf children may be less familiar with the alphabet and other pre-reading activities than their hearing age-mates. Even a sign language interface (whether "synthesized" or drawn from stored video) will not serve the estimated 90% of deaf children from hearing families who enter a formal school setting with no familiarity in the sign language of the country's deaf community [2]. These children will be acquiring their first and second languages, and perhaps their first computer exposure at the same time.

Hearing adults undertaking the study of a second language already know at least one (spoken/written) language. In this respect they differ from deaf children using a computer for language learning tasks. Adults need to acquire the habits of the new language and become familiar with the culture of the people who use the language regularly. Hearing adults, even today, cannot be assumed to be familiar with the computer and its interface elements.

Lexicography
Good dictionaries of sign languages predate personal computers. The use of a computer, however, offers new and different ways to organize monolingual and bilingual dictionaries. How should well-conceived materials available in print be reworked into computer-based, multimedia documents? What new forms can sign language dictionaries take (and for what audiences) when designed for computer delivery?

Transcription and Full Text Search
What is a sufficient inventory of "phonetic" symbols to capture the distinctions in a single deaf sign language? In all known deaf sign languages, none of which have a traditional written form? Once a symbol set is chosen, what new difficulties arise in providing a text searching or text analysis tool? Shall the symbols be available to or usable only by the research/developer community?

Non-text Representations and Displays
Consider three possible forms of representation:
• analog (e.g. signs on videodisk),
• digital (e.g. video signals on a compact disc or as QuickTime movies), or
• parametric (e.g. generated at runtime from stored features).
Will the technology (or the funding agency) dictate the choice or will the application determine what technology is chosen? What compromises are we making today which we anticipate will be mooted in the future (e.g. because of advancements in performance)? When is digital storage of actual signed utterances appropriate? When is analog storage desirable? When is some other representation sufficient or preferred? How can a user access such material with a non-text interface?

Nancy Frishberg (*moderator*) *is a linguist, sign language interpreter and teacher, who has made the transition to usability specialist and multimedia application designer. Author of* Interpreting: An Introduction, *she serves on an advisory board to a study investigating the uses of groupware with deaf and hearing people in educational and workplace settings. She enjoys finding new ways for hearing people to have eye-opening experiences in sign language.*

PANELIST STATEMENTS
Serena Corazza *has been a key member of the CNR research group studying the structure and acquisition of Italian Sign Language (LIS) for the past dozen years. A native of Trieste, she is a presenter and participant in numerous international conferences, and spent a year as a visiting scholar at Gallaudet University in Washington, DC.*

"Animals of the Savannah" is an interactive multimedia videodisk program intended to introduce new information to deaf children through the use of Italian Sign Language (LIS), as used nowadays in Rome, and written Italian texts, graphics and motion video (cf.[3]). The Olivetti 386/25 PC was equipped with a Videologic DVA 4000 card and attached to a Sony LDP-3600D laserdisk player. Specialized software for this application was developed using Asymetrix Toolbook, Olivetti IM-AGE Authoring Toolset, and Olivetti Media Control Library (MCL).

A team from Istituto di Psicologia CNR and Olivetti Ricerca has investigated the experiences of 20 deaf children (ranging in age from 6 to 15 years) using the videodisk program once a week over a period of nine months. For each subject, data collected concerned
• how the child navigated the program, to analyze the role played by each source of information
• what spontaneous writing each child produced within the notebook provided by the program, and
• how each child answered questions posed in signs, speech, and writing after the entire educational experience.

Some of the children chose to watch the video and the sign language descriptions; another group of children watched the film and read the Italian written text. Only a few of the children studied did not have sufficient linguistic competence in either LIS or written Italian to acquire new information from the multimedia environment.

The general problem concerns the affordances for acquisition of new information provided by linguistic and media competencies. Can a general didactic model be found for the transmission of knowledge to both deaf and hearing children? What lessons about structuring information for the new technologies can be learned from the timing and techniques of presenting visual information in sign language?

Linda Day *has been a research associate at the School of Education in Bristol for the past seven years, investigating social and cultural aspects of the British deaf community. She has taken a leading role in developing the curriculum for the computer-based language application described here, including constructing and analyzing the survey of deaf club members that would lead to the dialog and cultural material underlying the lessons. She is currently completing her post-graduate studies.*

Students undertaking the course in British Sign Language (BSL) have been impeded in their learning by having to rely on a live model (i.e., the teacher in class) to improve their production skills by correcting errors the students make. Practice with video recordings alone does not provide students with feedback on whether their attempts at signing match those of the model.

The current project at Bristol aims to provide students of BSL (generally hearing people, but also deaf students in bilingual programs [6]) with full language laboratory materials: viewing dialogues on culturally appropriate topics which the students can view repeatedly (with or without translations), recording themselves signing along with the model presented in the computer, and instantly comparing their own performance with the signer in the lesson. The system also functions as a BSL-English, English-BSL dictionary. The associated linguistic database enables students and teachers to look up examples of grammatical features of BSL and construct lessons based on these features.

DV-I has been chosen for storage and replay of the lessons, because of its capacity for mixing pre-recorded material on CD with camera signals.

Sherman Wilcox *is on the faculty of the Linguistics Department at the University of New Mexico. He holds certificates in interpretation and sign language instruction. His research interests include educational aspects of language use, physiological studies of sign language; he is an advocate for academic credit for sign language study. With Phyllis Wilcox, he is author of the book for language teachers* Learning to See, *a discussion of second language acquisition of American Sign Language.*

The *Dictionary of American Sign Language* (DASL) was the first truly bilingual dictionary for a sign language [4]. In DASL, signs are written using a specialized symbol set and are ordered by their formational properties (handshapes, locations, and movements), rather than by an alphabetic ordering of their English translations. "Multimedia Dictionary of American Sign Language" (MM-DASL) is turning the DASL into a multimedia document. The (re-)design of the dictionary will be affected by answers made to questions, such as the following:

- Who are the intended users of the MM-DASL: monolingual deaf users? deaf students of English? hearing English speakers learning ASL?
- Where will the users find the MM-DASL: in the public library? at home? on their notebook computers?
- What are the consequences for the interface and the contents of the MM-DASL of these different choices of audience and context of use? How will users get access to the signs, definitions, usage notes and example phrases or sentences? Will all of these elements be provided in ASL? Current plans have signs stored digitally (as QuickTime movies).
- What are the limits (e.g., number of entries and other elements) that might impact the MM-DASL as a commercially viable product?
- What parts of its production might be reusable modules that could speed up the preparation of similar dictionaries of other sign languages?

Rolf Schulmeister *has been associated with the Zentrum fur Deutsche Gebardensprache und Kommunikation Gehorlose since its founding. He also directs academic computing at Hamburg Universitat and has a special interest in multimedia technology. He was the first Macintosh Developer in Germany.*

The CD-ROM of terms for computer technology marks the initial volume in a series of dictionary projects intended as learning materials for vocational education of deaf people. The intended audiences include teachers of the deaf and sign language interpreters who need to find appropriate signs for technical terms from German or English, and deaf individuals who are interested in learning more about computers.

A team of 14 deaf people, all experts in computing or experienced computer users, collected sign equivalents for the 1500 target terms from German and their English translations.

The resultant electronic dictionary allows users to browse terms, definitions, explanations, and examples as they would in leafing through a printed book. But, the user of the electronic dictionary also can look up the corresponding signs of Deutsche Gebardensprache (DGS) in the form of movies. The electronic dictionary also is hierarchically structured, and permits easy retrieval of related terminology. A user can switch views from a list of terms to a list of categories to a text view presenting definitions and sample sentences. All occurrences of terms in the explanatory material are treated as hypertext words, allowing the user to find other entries mentioning the same term. The dictionary also contains figures, diagrams, graphical representations of objects, QuickTime movies of objects, and animations of relations and processes.

DGS signs are represented both as transcriptions and as QuickTime movies. Transcriptions use the Hamburg Notation System (HamNoSys) with symbols for each specification of formational properties of handshape, finger direction, palm orientation, hand location and movements. HamNoSys symbols are represented by a custom font and can be entered via the keyboard or using a special editor where pictures cue selection of components of a sign. Digitized and compressed QuickTime movies of 1600 signs in the dictionary (lasting between 7 and 20 frames) have been reduced in scale by 50% and playback in 24 bit or 8 bit color or a 256-greyscale, running at 30 frames/sec (on a Macintosh Quadra) or 15 frames/sec (on a Macintosh IIcx). Supplementing each movie are enlarged images of key handshapes which are too small to recognize in the movie.

REFERENCES

1. Padden, C. & Humphries, T. *Deaf in America: Voices from a Culture.* Harvard University Press, Cambridge, Massachusetts, 1989.

2. Volterra, V. Sign Language Acquisition and Bilingualism. In S. Prillwitz and T. Vollhaber (eds.), *Sign Language Research and Application.* Signum Press, Hamburg, 1990.

3. Hanson, V. & Padden C. The use of interactive videodisk for bilingual education of deaf children. *Golem* 1, 12, (1989) p. 5-6.

4. Stokoe, W., Casterline, C. & Croneberg, D. *A Dictionary of American Sign Language on Linguistic Principles.* Gallaudet University Press, Washington, D.C., 1965. (reprinted by Linstok Press, Silver Spring, Maryland, 1976.)

5. Klima, E. and Bellugi, U. *The Signs of Language.* Harvard University Press, Cambridge, Massachusetts, 1979.

6. Kyle, J. (ed.) Sign and School: *Using Signs in Deaf Children's Development.* Clevedon; Multilingual Matters, 1987.

INTERCHI '93

ITERATIVE METHODOLOGY AND DESIGNER TRAINING IN HUMAN-COMPUTER INTERFACE DESIGN

Gregg (Skip) Bailey, Ph.D.

Manager of Human Factors
The Church of Jesus Christ of Latter-day Saints
50 E. North Temple, Salt Lake City, Utah 84150 (801) 240-3105

ABSTRACT

One of the most promising methods for user interface design is the iterative design methodology. To this point only case study support for this method has been given. There are still many unanswered questions about the effectiveness of this method.

One difficulty encountered in user interface design is knowing what set of knowledge and skill the designer must possess to ensure good user interface design. Many different people have designed user interfaces for computer systems. These people came from a variety of backgrounds and viewpoints. Two of the most common groups involved in user interface design are human factors specialists and programmers.

This study investigates these two issues. One factor in this study is the iterative design methodology. An empirical evaluation of this method was conducted. The strengths and weaknesses of this method are discussed. A second factor in this study is a comparison of human factors specialists and programmers in an actual user interface design task.

The results of this study indicate that iterative design methodology can improve the usability of a product. The amount of the improvement may be constrained by the original design. This study also supports the use of human factors specialists in user interface design. A significant difference between designs produced by human factors specialists and programmers was found.

KEYWORDS: Iterative design methodology, user interface specialists, programmers.

INTRODUCTION

The quality of the user interface partially determines how useful, efficient, and satisfying a computer system is [1]. Although interest in, and demand for good user interface design is great, it is not clear what constitutes a good user interface design. Even the "experts" on user interface design may not agree on what constitutes good design. Many espouse a fairly common set of principles, but there is still disagreement about what is most important in user interface design [1,2,3,5,6,20,26].

Not only is it difficult to agree on the quality of a user interface, it is not clear how to produce a good user interface. Many journals, courses, and seminars provide information for improving the user interface design. These sources of information report many theories and methodologies [7,9,11,12,14,15,17,21,24,25,27,28]. Although there are reports of successful systems that have been constructed using some of these theories or methods [10,13,22,23], little quality research has shed light on the important factors that produce good user interface designs.

Not only is there disagreement about how to arrive at a good user interface design, it is not even clear who, on the development team, should be responsible for this task. In short, we don't know who or what kind of knowledge is most advantageous in producing good interface design. The responsibility for the user interface has been relegated to a variety of people with a variety of backgrounds.

Methodological Approach

There are at least two general approaches that have been utilized in user interface design. First, some have argued that good user interface design results from the use of good tools or methods. The second approach relies on the training and knowledge of the designers themselves. Methods, such as iterative design techniques, have been widely discussed. The use of prototyping tools and usability labs are increasing in popularity [4,10,19]. Perhaps testing and prototyping are so popular because of our limited ability to produce quality user interfaces based solely on principles and guidelines.

There are few head-to-head studies to compare the effectiveness of the various methods. Case studies have shown that some methods work but we do not know why they work. In addition, there has been little work to show which design team members are in a better position to use these methods.

One important study compared four of the methods that are most commonly used to make user interface improvements [16]. This study compared heuristic evaluation, usability testing, guidelines, and cognitive walkthroughs.

The results show the heuristic evaluation group found the most problems (105), while the usability testing group found the fewest (31). However, when the problems were weighted for severity, the usability testing group found a reliably higher average of severe problems ($p < .01$). This group also found a higher proportion of severe errors (90%) compared to a low by the heuristic evaluation group where only 35% of the errors they discovered were considered severe.

In their case study, Gould et al. [10] demonstrated how the iterative design methodology resulted in a successfully built system. The Gould et al. [10] paper raised two issues that this study begins to address. The people involved in the case study were all experienced user interface designers. The initial design that they started with was good and the iterative process improved it. The case study merely showed that the design went from good to better. Also, because they were experienced user interface designers, they could maximize improvement on each iteration. They knew what to look for. Could an inexperienced designer produce the same quality system? If so, would it take more iterations?

If a design is weak, then iterative design methodology may not be able to optimize the software. The initial design requires skill and expertise. A poor initial design may not ever be as good as a design that starts off good, even with a lot of iterations.

The present study will only examine a "bare bones" version of iterative design methodology. The user interface designers in this study will only have access to users via video tape. No formal analysis technique will be taught to the designers to enhance their observations. Most of the designers in this study have no formal training in observation nor usability. None of the programmer designers have been involved in a formal iterative design process. None of the programmer designers in this study have had extensive experience in observing human performance. Therefore, the iterative design methodology being tested in this study will consist of designers making observations (via video tape) of users using their systems. Then the designers will make changes based on these informal observations (see the Method section of this paper for more details).

Training Approach

A second approach that has been employed in user interface design relies on the training and knowledge that the designer possesses. Some have argued that special knowledge or expertise leads to good design. Just what subset of knowledge is important is not generally agreed upon. A case can be made for several types of knowledge that contribute to a good interface design.

There is some evidence that training and experience do make a difference in the mental models that designers have [8]. Gillan and Breedin [8] used hierarchical cluster analysis and Pathfinder Networks to show differences in the mental models used by software developers, human factors experts, and software users.

The Gillan and Breedin [8] study suggests that the training and experience of the human factors specialist somehow resulted in their thinking about the user interface in a different way than system developers and users. This different way of thinking about the user interface does not necessarily mean that they will produce better user interfaces.

The present study will examine actual user interface design differences between programmers and human factors specialists. This examination is intended to serve as a beginning in defining what set of skills are needed by user interface designers. These two groups (human factors specialist and programmers) were selected as representative of the majority of user interface designers in industry.

METHOD

Subjects

The designers consisted of four human factors analysts and four computer programmers. These designers participated as part of their work responsibilities.

The human factors analysts all had at least four years of user interface design experience (mean = 6.25). One of them had eight years of full-time experience designing user interfaces. A typical educational background for user interface designers does not yet exist. The field itself is influenced by many disciplines. These human factors analysts all had master's or doctoral degrees in either Educational Psychology or Instructional Design. Each of the human factors analysts had attended several conferences and seminars on human-computer interface design. They had all used at least two different prototyping tools. Their experience with the tool used in this study was limited to one exercise they participated in at least nine months before this study.

The programmers all had at least five years of experience in designing computer systems. Some of the programmers had as much as thirteen years of full time programming experience (mean = 9). All had some formal education in computer science and two had a B.S. in computer science or a related field. The programmer's experience ranged from main frame programming to PC programming. They represented a wide range of programming language skills. The programmers were all application programmers. The programmer's formal training in user interface design ranged from zero to four courses. None of the programmers expressed expertise in user interface design. All of the programmers had some experience in building user interfaces in real systems.

The systems were tested on 96 retired volunteers that were on service missions for The Church of Jesus Christ of Latter-day Saints. The elderly volunteers were used as test subjects for three reasons. First, most have limited or no experience with computers. Second, this is a difficult group to design for; they tend to be less flexible and experience more computer-phobia than younger participants. Finally, there was a large group of these subjects available. Three different volunteers were tested on each iteration for each of the eight designs.

Apparatus

The prototype systems were developed using Protoscreens. This software operates on IBM PC and compatible machines. The testing of the prototypes took place in a usability laboratory where the entire interaction was videotaped.

Procedure

This experiment employed a hierarchical, between-subject design with four main independent variables. These variables include the type (T) of designer (programmer or human factors), the individual designers (D) (nested in type of designer), the iterations (I) that each designer went through, and the users (U) that were tested on the designs. Because each user only participated once, users are nested within the other factors in this study. Thus, this study could be described with the following symbolism U/ID/T. The user factor and the designer factor were treated as random variables.

The eight designers were given an introduction to Protoscreens, a rapid prototyping tool. During this introduction the designers learned the features of Protoscreens. The programmers were also given a practice exercise (a check book balancing program) that required them to use all of the features that were needed for the actual experiment. Three of the human factors analysts had completed a similar practice exercise at least nine months before this study as part of a seminar in which had they participated. One of the Human Factors Analysts had not participated in the seminar where the practice exercise was used. She completed the practice exercise in the same way the programmers did.

Once the designers completed the practice exercise, they were given the design problem. The designers built a prototype that allowed users to input recipes into a database. The prototype also allowed the users to search for recipes and make an automated shopping list from the recipes. The designers were told which recipes the user would add, search for, etc.

During development, the experimenter was available to answer questions about the prototyping tool. However, the experimenter did not assist with the design of the systems. The designers contacted the experimenter by phone when they had questions.

Three users were tested on each of the eight prototype designs. Each user was given seven tasks to complete using one of the prototype recipe programs. The users were not given any instruction about how to use the prototype recipe programs. Any help or instructions had to be provided by the designers in an online fashion. The users completed as many tasks as they could in 45 minutes. They had to complete the tasks in a specified order. The users were stopped when they had completed the seven tasks or when 45 minutes was up, whichever came first.

The experimenter was available to help the users if they needed help. Help was only given (a) if the users requested help by calling the experimenter on the phone, (b) if the recipe program went down, and (c) if the users began to complete tasks out of order. At that point the experimenter entered the room and asked them what they where trying to do and what they where expecting the system to do. After these questions were asked, the experimenter helped the users with the task they were trying to accomplish. This interaction was videotaped and the number of helps and type of helps was analyzed.

The eight designers then took the observations from the first test of their systems and made improvements. These observations were made by viewing the videotape of the first test of their prototype. The re-designs were then tested with three additional volunteers. This test led to another redesign and so on until the designer felt they could not improve the design. In other words, the designers continued to iterate until they felt the system would be adequate to send into production. All designers stopped after three to five iterations.

Time to complete the tasks and number of errors were the main dependent measures. Design time was also recorded. Each designer worked in two-hour design sessions. The number of sessions was not limited. The design process stopped when the designers indicated that they were ready for a test.

The users were selected by their work supervisors based on criteria set by the experimenter. These criteria included some ability to type and little or no experience with computers. The users were made available when a designer indicated that they were ready for a test.

RESULTS

Six main dependent measures were evaluated in this study. The first was the number of tasks that users completed in the allotted time (45 min.). Seven tasks were assigned to the users. This measure will be referred to as "tasks completed." For example, the first task in this study was to enter a recipe. This task required the users to navigate to the appropriate data entry screen and enter the complete recipe.

The second dependent measure is the number of times that the experimenter had to intervene, divided by the number of tasks. A ratio is used to reflect the fact that the potential number of interventions goes up with each task completed by the user. This measure will be referred to as "interventions." An intervention occurred under any of the three situations described in the method section of this paper.

The third measure is the number of design features that led to user errors. This measure will be referred to as "design errors." A design error is defined as a condition in the user interface that caused the user to make an error. The design errors observed and recorded only include design features that actually caused a user to make an error. For example, if the design required users to press the Enter key at the end of each line of text input (did not allow for word wrap) and a user continued to type when he reached the end of the line, then a design error would be counted. This would only count as one design error, even if that particular error occurred many times. Thus, design errors are the number of different types of errors, not the total number of errors occurring. As with interventions, design errors are divided by the number of tasks completed.

The fourth dependent measure is the average time to complete each task by the users. This variable will be referred to as time.

The fifth dependent measure is the number of design errors with which more than one user per iteration had trouble. This dependent measure reflects errors that more than one user struggled with (serious errors). For example, if two or three users using the same design in the same iteration had trouble typing the title of a recipe in the proper place, a serious error would be counted for that iteration.

The sixth dependent variable compared the number of serious errors on the first iteration to the number of errors that were still present in the last iteration (repeated serious errors). For example, a repeated serious error would be counted if two users could not select the correct recipes for the shopping list in the first iteration, and two other users had the same problem in the last iteration. This dependent measure is used to show the effort across iterations to reduce the errors that were apparent in the first iteration.

The first analysis utilized a full model in the ANOVA. The variables included the type of designer, the individual designers, the iterations (first and last), and the users. The designers and users were treated as random variables. All six dependent measures where used in the analysis.

The following tables show the means from the analysis that was conducted on these data. The difference between the levels of the independent variables as well as the probability that the null hypothesis is true are also displayed.

Table 1
Means for Iterations

Dependant Variable	First Iter.	Last Iter.	Diff.	p<
Tasks Completed	5.33	6.29	-.96	.0186
Interventions	0.85	0.58	.27	.0810
Design Errors	2.75	2.09	.66	.0690
Time (seconds)	510	378	123	.0537
Serious Errors	7.63	7.63	0.0	
Repeated Serious Errors	7.63	2.75	4.88	.0017

A significant difference (p<.0186, F (1,6) = 10.239, MSE = 1.076) was found on the tasks completed variable when comparing the first iteration to the last. Users completed more tasks on last iteration than they did on the first iteration. The human factors designers created designs which allowed users to complete an average of 6.5 tasks completed, while the programmer's designs allowed users to complete an average of 5.13 tasks (p<.0181, F (1,6) = 10.371, MSE = 2.1875). The designer variable was not significant nor were any of the interactions.

The number of interventions required for the programmers' designs was reliably higher than the number required for the human factors analysts' designs (p<.0252, F (1,6) = 8.774, MSE = 0.409). Neither the designer main effect nor any of the interactions were significant. The iteration variable approached significance (p<.081, F (1,6) = 4.380, MSE = .189) for the intervention dependent variable. The number of interventions decreased from the first to the last iterations.

The programmers' systems produced more design errors than the human factors systems (p<.0131, F (1,6) = 12.115, MSE = 3.225). The first iteration had more

design errors than the last iteration but the difference was not reliable (p<.069, F (1,6) = 4.911, MSE = 1.078,). The designer main effect and all the interactions for **design errors** were not significant.

The **time** users spent on tasks was greater for the programmers' designs than it was for the human factors' designs (p<.0456, F = 6.322, MSE = 91567.19). The last iteration approached being faster per task than the first (p<.0537, F = 5.731, MSE = 31830.85). The interactions and designer main effect for the **time** factor were not significant. The number of **serious errors** was greater for the programmers' designs than it was for the human factors' designs (p<.0042, F (1,6) = 20.00, MSE = 5.0). The other main effects and interactions were not reliably different.

Table 2
Means for Designer Type

Dependant Variable	Human Factors	Pro-grammers	Diff.	p<
Tasks Completed	6.50	5.13	1.37	.0181
Interventions	0.44	0.99	-.55	.0252
Design Errors	1.52	3.32	-1.80	.0131
Time (seconds)	339	559	-220	.0456
Serious Errors	5.00	10.00	-5	.0042
Repeated Serious Errors	3.25	7.13	-3.88	.0036

Finally, the number of **repeated serious errors** in the programmers' designs was significantly higher than in the human factors' designs (p<.0036, F (1,6) = 21.356, MSE = 2.813). The number of **repeated serious errors** in the first iteration was reliably greater than in the last iteration (p<.0017, F (1,6) = 28.698, MSE 3.313). The designer main effect and interactions were not significant.

A series of planned comparisons (one tailed t-tests) was used to determine if the differences between the programmers last iteration were reliably different from the first iteration for human factors designers. Table 3 shows the means for these two groups.

These results show that for the **design error** measure

this difference is significant (p<.02815). The human factor's first iteration designs (mean = 1.782) had fewer **design errors** than the programmer's last iterations (mean = 2.922). The programmer's last iterations (mean = 10.25) produced reliably more **serious errors** than the human factor's first iterations (mean = 5.5, p<.0183).

Table 3
Means for Human Factors First Iteration and Programmer Last Iteration

Dependant Variable	Human Factors First Iter.	Pro-grammers Last Iter.	Diff.	p<
Tasks Completed	6.33	5.91	0.41	.2476
Interventions	.471	.756	-.285	.0968
Design Errors	1.78	2.92	-1.14	.0282
Time (seconds)	347.5	443.8	-96.33	.1632
Serious Errors	5.50	10.25	-4.75	.0183
Repeated Serious Errors	5.50	4.50	1.0	.1779

The iteration and designer type main effects were not significant for the second and third task times. However, for the third task time, the designer (individuals) main effect was significant (p<.0444, F (6,32) = 2.47, MSE = 35708.49).

The programmer designers and human factors designers also differed in the amount of time they took to produce and change the prototypes. For example, the programmers took an average of 12.28 hours to complete their first design, while the human factors designers took an average of 18.75 hours. The total time for all iterations for the programmers was an average of 22.09 hours, while the total design time for human factors designers was an average of 28.36 hours. These differences were not reliable.

However, one of the programmers was slower than any of the human factors designers. If the slowest programmer is removed from the analysis, the results are statistically significant (first iteration p<.0242, F (1,5) = 10.19, MSE = 2.28; last iteration p<.0124, F (1,5) = 14.56,

MSE = 1.55). It should be noted that only eight designers were used in this study. This lack of power may explain why some of these dependent measures were not reliable.

DISCUSSION

The introduction raised two main questions that this study addressed. First, does an iterative design methodology help improve user interface design? Second, does training and experience in human-computer interface design produce better human-computer interface designers?

Effectiveness of Iterative Design

When using iterative design methodology to improve user interface design, there are at least three major difficulties one must deal with. The first is to recognize usability problems based on feedback. In this case, the feedback came through watching users (via videotape) use the systems. The designer must be able to separate actual usability problems from quirks due to individual differences. Second, when a problem is identified, the designer must figure out a way to fix the problem with a design change. The third difficulty stems from trying to take a weak design and attempt to attain a "quality" design through iteration. To some extent, the designers in this study struggled with all three of these difficulties

The difficulty of identifying real usability problems is illustrated by the **repeated serious error** measure. Although the designers reliably reduced some of their original design errors from the first iteration to the last, an average of about 3 **repeated serious errors** were still found in the last iteration. The reduction in **repeated serious errors** was from an average of 7.63 to an average of 2.75. When comparing groups on this dimension, the programmers reduced their **repeated serious error** rate from 9.75 to 4.5, and the human factors analysts reduced their **repeated serious error** rate from 5.5 to 1.0. Both reductions are statistically reliable. Further reduction in these errors may have occurred if the designers had been allowed to interview the users.

Once a problem is identified, the designer must make changes that will correct the problem. Based on some of the comments by the designers and the data that were collected, this may be the most difficult part of iterative design. Some of the programmer designers made comments such as: "I know what is wrong, I just don't know how to fix it." "People are reading, they are just not listening to what they read." These comments reflect the fact that some design errors are recognized, but the designers are not sure how to fix them. There were some design decisions made by the designers that did not correct the problems they were intended to fix.

Another difficulty introduced when design problems are "fixed" is the potential for introducing new problems or uncovering old problems that were not previously apparent. A good variable to study this phenomenon is the number of **design errors** that more than one user had difficulty with. These are the **serious error** and **repeated serious error** variables. In this study, the number of **serious errors** did not reliably improve from the first iteration to the last (7.63 to 7.38). At the same time, the number of **repeated serious errors** was reduced. These data supports the idea that changes made to improve one usability problem may introduce other usability problems.

It is not entirely clear which problems were introduced as a result of fixes to old problems and which problems just appeared because users were able to complete more tasks. It is clear that simply iterating three to five times does not ensure that all usability problems will be resolved.

There is some evidence that iterative design methodology can only improve designs within a limited range. There are two ways to look at this issue. First, does iterative design methodology identify and fix all usability problems? The answer to this question is clearly no. All of the dependent variables used in this study indicated there were still usability problems after the last iteration. In fact, there were usability problems in all eight of the designs after the last iteration. It should be pointed out that this study tested a simplified or "bare bones" version of iterative design methodology. A more comprehensive design effort may have eliminated some of the problems that remained after this iterative process.

A second way to look at this issue is to see if iterations improve poor designs to the point that they are equal to good designs. In the first iteration, the human factors designers were reliably better than the programmer designers on all dependent measures except **serious errors**. The **design errors**, **serious errors**, and **repeated serious errors** are reliably different in the last iteration. In this case, the iterative design process did not improve the poorer design to match the better designs in all dimensions. It should be noted that the iterative process may be confounded by the person making changes to the system. In many real situations, programmers produce the first design and human factors specialists iterate on the design produced by programmers. It may be true that a trained professional could improve any design until it is optimized. If this is true, would the iterative process result in a completely new design? Would this be any different than starting over? These question need to be answered with further research.

It is probably safe to conclude that the better the design to start with, the better the results after iterations. This particular finding is very important for interpreting results of case studies supporting iterative design methodology [10]. Great successes reported for iterative design may be due at least in part to good initial design.

Effect of Training on User Interface Design

The strongest finding of this study is that the training and background of designers can have a large effect on user interface design. In the first analysis reported in this study, there is evidence that training and background do contribute to good user interface design. For the main six dependent variables, the human factors analysts produced better designs than the programmer group. The interesting thing about these results is the size of this difference between the two groups. For example, the human factors designs allowed users to complete tasks in 60% of the time that the programmer designs allowed users to complete tasks.

This difference is even more dramatic with the **serious errors** variable. In this case the programmers **serious error** rate went up over iterations (from 9.75 to 10.25) while the human factors **serious error** rate went down (from 5.5 to 4.5). The programmers **design errors** decreased over iterations (from 3.7 to 2.9), but the design problems that were left caused difficulty for more of the users.

As stated above, the human factors first iteration **design error** means were better than the programmer last iteration designs. Clearly the human factors designers produced better designs than the programmer designers.

Future Directions

If one looked only at the statistically significant results from this study, one could conclude that the best approach to user interface design is to get a human factors specialist to design the user interface and not to bother with iterative design. However, such a radical position is not warranted. The data do suggest that gains are made through iterative design, and it is very dangerous to draw sweeping conclusions from just one study.

A number of techniques and methods can be used to ensure good user interface design. There is a growing body of evidence to suggest that successful design is the result of a combination of many techniques [16,18]. The trick is to know the strength and limitations of these techniques and to apply them at the appropriate time.

Clearly, usability can be improved. The methods for bringing about better usability must be improved. Better techniques for identifying real problems that cause real difficulties for users must be found. There is a need to improve techniques and methods so designers don't spend time trying to improve things that are not real problems for users.

Once real problems are identified, there is a need to learn how to fix problems without introducing new problems. In some cases this may require us to do more throw-away prototyping. Many of the designers commented that they learned a lot from the iterative process but felt that they could not improve their designs without starting

over. In some cases radical changes between iterations have the effect of starting the process over. We do not know enough about when to stop, change, or start over.

New tools and methods that allow designers to easily and quickly design and test ideas will promote more of this throw-away concept. With most current tools and methods, the investment in the prototype is too great to throw it away and start over.

The real challenge for user interface professionals in the future is to improve these methods and techniques to the point that they are practical within a normal development cycle. This is becoming increasingly more challenging as industry moves to rapid application development methodologies.

References

1. Bailey, R. W. (1989). **Human Performance Engineering, Using Human Factors Ergonomics to Achieve Computer System Usability** Second Edition, Englewood Cliffs, New Jersey, Prentice-Hall.

2. Card, S.K., Moran, T.P., and Newell, A. (1983). **The Psychology of Human-Computer Interaction**, Hillsdale, New Jersey, Lawrence Erlbaum Associates.

3. Carroll, J. M. (Ed.) (1987). **Interfacing Thought: Cognitive Aspects of Human-Computer Interaction**, Cambridge, Massachusetts, MIT Press.

4. Dumas, J. S. (1989). Stimulating change through usability testing. **SIGCHI Bulletin**, 21 (1), 37-44.

5. Galitz, W. O. (1989). **Handbook of Screen Format Design** Third Edition, Welleslye, Massachusetts, QED information Sciences, Inc.

6. Gardiner, M. M., & Christie, B. (Eds.)(1987). **Applying Cognitive Psychology to User-interface Design**, Chichester, John Wiley & Sons.

7. Gilbert, T.F., & Gilbert, M. B. (1989). Performance engineering: Making human productivity a science. **Performance & Instruction**, 3-9.

8. Gillan, D.J., & Breedin, S.D. (1990). Designers' models of the human-computer interface. **CHI'90 Conference Proceedings**, 391-398.

9. Gould, J. D., & Lewis, C. (1985). Designing for usability: Key principles and what designers think. **Communications of the ACM**, 28 (3), 300-311.

10. Gould, J. D., Boies, S. J., Levy, S., Richards, J. T., & Schoonard, J. (1987). The 1984 Olympic message system: A test of behavioral principles of system design. **Communications of the ACM**, 30 (9), 758-769.

11. Grudin, J., Ehrlich, S. F., & Shriner, R. (1987). Positioning human factors in the user interface development chain. **Proceedings of CHI + GI**, 125-131.

12. Gutierrez, O. (1989). Prototyping techniques for different problem contexts, **CHI'89 Proceedings**, 259-264.

13. Hewett, T. T., & Meadow, C. T. (1986). On designing for usability: An application of four key principles. **CHI'86 Proceedings**, 247-252.

14. Ives, B., & Olson, M. H. (1984). User involvement and MIS success: A review of research. **Management Science**, 30 (5), 586-603.

15. Janosky, B., Smith, P. J., & Hildreth, C. (1986). Online library catalog systems: An analysis of user errors. **International Journal of Man-Machine Studies**, 25, 573-592.

16. Jeffries, R., Miller, J. R., Wharton, C., & Uydea, K. M. (1991). User interface evalutation in the real world: A comparison of four techniques, **CHI'91 Conference Proceedings**, 119-124.

17. Kammersgaard, J. (1988). Four different perspectives on human-computer interaction. **International Journal of Man-Machine Studies**, 28, 343-362.

18. Karat, C., Campbell, R., & Fiegel, T. (1992). Comparison of empirical testing and walkthrough methods in user interface evaluation. **Proceedings of CHI 92**, 397-404.

19. Nielsen, J., & Molich, R. (1989). Teaching user interface design based on usability engineering. **SIGCHI Bulletin**, 21 (1), 45-48.

20. Norman, D. A., & Draper, S. W. (Eds) (1986). **User Centered System Design**, Hillsdale, New Jersey, Lawrence Erlbaum Associates.

21. Perlman, G. (1989). The checklist method for applying guidelines to design and evaluation. **Proceedings of INTERFACE 89**, 271-276.

22. Polson, P. G. (1988). A quantitative theory of human-computer interaction. In J. M. Carroll (Ed.), **Interfaceing Thought: Cognitive Aspects of Human-Computer Interaction**, Cambridge Massachusetts, Bradford Book the MIT Press.

23. Rivard, S., & Huff, S. L. (1988). Factors of success for end-user computing. **Communications of the ACM**, 31 (5), 552-560.

24. Rubini, D., & Thompson, C. (1989). The box continuum: A model for design evaluation. **Proceedings of INTERFACE 89**, 101-104.

25. Schneider, E., & Wilcox, S. B. (1989). Getting designers involved with research: The case for early participation. **Proceedings of INTERFACE 89**, 29-32.

26. Shneiderman, B. (1987). **Designing the User Interface: Strategies for Effective Human-Computer Interaction**, Reading, Massachusetts, Addison-Wesley Publishing Company.

27. Shneiderman, B. (1988). We can design better user interfaces: A review of human-computer interaction styles. **Ergonomics**, 31 (5), 699-710.

28. Yadav, S. B., Bravoco, R. R., Chatfield, A. T., & Rajkumar, T. M. (1988). Comparison of analysis techniques for information requirement determination, **Communications of the ACM**(9), 1090-1097.

A Mathematical Model of the Finding of Usability Problems

Jakob Nielsen and Thomas K. Landauer

Bellcore

445 South Street

Morristown, NJ 07962-1910

USA

nielsen@bellcore.com and tkl@bellcore.com

Electronic business card for Nielsen can be retrieved by sending any email message to the server at nielsen-info@bellcore.com

ABSTRACT

For 11 studies, we find that the detection of usability problems as a function of number of users tested or heuristic evaluators employed is well modeled as a Poisson process. The model can be used to plan the amount of evaluation required to achieve desired levels of thoroughness or benefits. Results of early tests can provide estimates of the number of problems left to be found and the number of additional evaluations needed to find a given fraction. With quantitative evaluation costs and detection values, the model can estimate the numbers of evaluations at which optimal cost/benefit ratios are obtained and at which marginal utility vanishes. For a "medium" example, we estimate that 16 evaluations would be worth their cost, with maximum benefit/cost ratio at four.

Keywords: Usability problems, Usability engineering, Poisson models, User testing, Heuristic evaluation, Cost-benefit analysis, Iterative design.

INTRODUCTION

Both user testing [6][8][18][14][22] and heuristic evaluation [15][21] can be considered as interface debugging tests with respect to their positioning in the usability engineering lifecycle [16]. Their goal is to find and document as many usability problems in a user interface design as possible so that the problems can be corrected in future versions.

The two methods are quite different since user testing is based on bringing real users in and observing them as they interact with the system in order to perform a given set of tasks, whereas heuristic evaluation is based on having usability specialists judge a user interface on the basis of established usability principles. The mechanics of conducting these two kinds of evaluations are very different, and both methods have advantages and disadvantages. For example, user testing provides insights into the mindset and working methods of real users. Heuristic evaluation is easier to set up as there is no need to bring in users or to analyze interaction protocols, and exploits expert scientific and experiential knowledge of general problems and solutions.

From a general usability engineering perspective, however, user testing and heuristic evaluation have two important similarities. First, they are both debugging methods. Second, both involve aggregating results from multiple smaller evaluation studies. Even though one can in principle conduct user testing with a single test user and heuristic evaluation with a single evaluator, good practice calls for the use of several test users and evaluators. Typically, each test user or each evaluator identifies a certain list of usability problems, and these lists are then aggregated for however many test users or evaluators are employed for a given study.

Most current usability engineering work (e.g., [5][7][14][15][20][21][22]) in effect has a *post hoc* view of the actual evaluation process, analyzing the complete results of finished studies as a whole. In practical development environments, one will often be interested in looking at partial analyses of usability studies as they are performed with a view towards deciding when enough information has been gained. Especially when resources are tight and a discount usability engineering approach [12][13] is applied with an emphasis on using as few test users or heuristic evaluators as possible, one might be interested in a predictive model that can provide some estimate of the total number of usability problems in an interface, *during* the evaluation process even if all the problems have not been found yet.

DATASETS

The following analysis contains data from case studies of the empirical user testing of five user interfaces and the heuristic evaluation of six user interfaces. Table 1 lists all eleven studies and summarizes some of their pertinent char-

© 1993 ACM 0-89791-575-5/93/0004/0206...$1.50

System Tested [with publication reference]	Evaluation Method	Type of Interface	Number Subjs./ Evals.	Observed Usability Problems	Problems found by one evaluatn.	Model λ fit	N fit	R^2
Office System (integrated spreadsheet etc.) [9]	User test	Personal computer, GUI	15	145	16%	.12	166	.996
Calendar program [22]	User test	Personal computer, GUI	20	40	36%	.32	39	.986
Word processor [17]	User test	Personal computer, GUI	24	9	30%	.30	9	1.00
Outliner (manipulate hierarchical structures) [17]	User test	Personal computer, GUI	30	14	28%	.26	14	.998
Bibliography database [24]	User test	Personal computer, CUI	13	29	31%	.29	24	.969
Teledata (info on airline departures) [21]	Heuristic evaluation	Videotex, CUI	37	52	51%	.48	50	.971
Mantel (hypothetical white pages system) [11]	Heuristic evaluation	Mainframe, CUI	77	30	38%	.34	26	.937
Banking system (transfer money between accounts) [15]	Heuristic evaluation	Voice response	31 19 14	16	22% 41% 60%	.21 .38 .58	12 16 16	.965 .991 .992
Savings (info on account balances and currency exchange) [21]	Heuristic evaluation	Voice response	34	48	26%	.26	40	.988
Transport (information to public on bus routes) [21]	Heuristic evaluation	Voice response	34	34	19%	.22	27	.995
Integrating system (internal telephone company application) [20]	Heuristic evaluation	Workstation, GUI	11	40	29%	.26	40	.995
Mean values				42	33%	.31	41	

Table 1 *List of the user interface evaluations analyzed in this paper.*
Notes: GUI = Graphical User Interface, CUI = Character-based User Interface. The Banking interface was evaluated by three different groups of evaluators: 31 non-specialists, 19 usability specialists, and 14 double specialists with expertise in both usability and the kind of interface being evaluated. The mean value of N-fit was calculated using the result from only one of these groups (N-fit=16).

acteristics, as well as the results of fitting the Poisson model discussed in the next section to the data. Since the Banking System was evaluated by three independent groups of evaluators, it generated three datasets, so the total number of datasets is thirteen. The Office System was a collection of applications that together provided integrated support for standard professional work tasks, including a spreadsheet, a word processor, a file system, etc., but it was tested as a single system.

A POISSON MODEL OF THE FINDING OF USABILITY PROBLEMS

To develop the mathematical model, we make some basic assumptions about the finding of usability problems. In using the simple and well-understood probabilistic model of

Poisson processes, we assume that the probability of finding any given usability problem in any given test is independent of the outcome of previous tests. Not only is the Poisson model well-behaved, but it has also been found to describe the finding of traditional programming errors ("bugs") [1][2] in software development projects under some conditions. This problem is similar to the "debugging" of user interface designs implied by usability engineering.

For some kinds of usability evaluation, the Poisson assumption seems quite reasonable. For example, heuristic evaluations are often conducted by having evaluators inspect the interface independently of each other. With this procedure it would seem obvious that the probability of having any given evaluator find any one specific problem would be independent of whether the other evaluators had found that problem.

For user testing, the finding of a usability problem depends of two factors: First, the subject has to experience the problem, and second, the experimenter has to realize that the user experienced the problem. To the extent that user tests are run according to classic experimental methodology, subjects can probably be considered independent of each other. Regarding the experimenter's role, however, the independence assumption may not hold in all cases. Some usability problems may not be easy to recognize, and the probability of having the experimenter find the problem in a test session where a user encounters the problem may therefore be dependent on whether the experimenter had seen (but not recognized) the problem before in previous test sessions. In spite of this potential difficulty, it would still seem likely that most aspects of the experimenter's finding of usability problems can be approximated by a Poisson model.

The discussion so far has concentrated on the finding of individual usability problems. In real projects, there are of course many usability problems in any given user interface, and we would like to have a model that accounts for the finding of several usability problems. As argued above, the finding of each individual usability problem probably follows a Poisson model. However, the parameters of the Poisson model will most likely be different for each usability problem. Nielsen found that severe problems were more likely to be found than less severe problems in heuristic evaluation, though not much more so [15], and Virzi found that severe problems were much more likely to be found than less severe problems by user testing [23].

For any given interface, some problems will be easy to find, being glaring design catastrophes and/or being encountered by almost all test users, whereas others will be more difficult to find, being more subtle and/or only encountered under special circumstances. However, adding two independent Poisson processes with respective rates A and B yields a Poisson process with rate A+B [3], so we can still model the finding of the set of usability problems with a single Poisson model, even though the different problems have different probabilities of being found. This additive property of the Poisson model assumes that detection of various usability problems are independent of each other. This assumption is a simplification, since some user difficulties do tend to co-occur.

Given the assumptions discussed above (that the finding of usability problems are independent of whether they have been found before and independent of each other), we can expect a Poisson model to describe the finding of usability problems. The number of usability problems that have been found at least once by i evaluators or subjects is

$$\text{Found}(i) = N(1 - (1-\lambda)^i) \qquad \text{(EQ 1)}$$

where N is the total number of problems in the interface, and the parameter λ is the probability of finding the average usability problem when running a single, average subject, or using a single, average heuristic evaluator.[*] Table 1 shows the results of fitting this model to the data from the studies for 1 through 15 evaluators or subjects, using a least squares method. For the Integrating System, the fitted model was based on data for 1 through 11 evaluators, and for the Bibliography database, the fitted model was based on data for 1 through 13 test users. The fits are mostly very good as indicated by the high values of R^2 in Table 1, and as also seen in Figure 1, which shows the fitted model curves and the datapoints from the original datasets.

$1-\lambda$ is the probability of a usability problem remaining unfound for one more test given that it has not been found already. λ thus indicates the probability of finding a usability problem with one more person given that it has not been found yet. As can be seen from Table 1, this value corresponds fairly closely to the proportion of usability problems actually found by single heuristic evaluators or when running single subjects. The single-person values from the studies are larger than the fitted values, however. Such a discrepancy would be accounted for by a small positive correlation between the problems found by different people.

Similarly, Table 1 indicates that the model slightly underestimates the total number of usability problems N for most interfaces. The main exception is the Office System, where the model predicts 166 problems, 21 more than were found by running 15 subjects. Closer examination of the underlying data indicates that it is reasonable to assume that the Office System actually contains more usability problems than were found by the test with the 15 subjects. Out of the 145 problems that were found, as many as 76 were observed for only a single subject, thus providing some indication that there might be more remaining problems that would have been found by running additional subjects. The Office System actually comprised several different applications, so 15 subjects may simply not have been enough for an exhaustive test of this type of major integrated system. Overall, the model seems to slightly underestimate N, so applications of the model should preferably rely on estimates of the number of *remaining* problems to be found rather than the total number of problems in the interface.

---

[*] The model as presented is simplified by assuming that all evaluations (subjects or heuristic evaluators) find exactly the mean number of usability problems. (That is, if one finds 10 and another 20, we act as if both found 15, though the overlap is greater between two sets of 15 than between a set of 10 and a set of 20.) This has the effect of somewhat underestimating the probability of finding a problem, λ, and consequently also somewhat overestimating the total number of usability problems, N. The model also ignores the likely positive correlation between some problems. This has an opposing effect. (Overall, we seem to be underestimating N). Relaxing these two assumptions would lead to a more complex model with more parameters, which would, therefore, require more data before predictions could be made. From our results, it appears that the simpler model is sufficiently accurate for practical purposes.

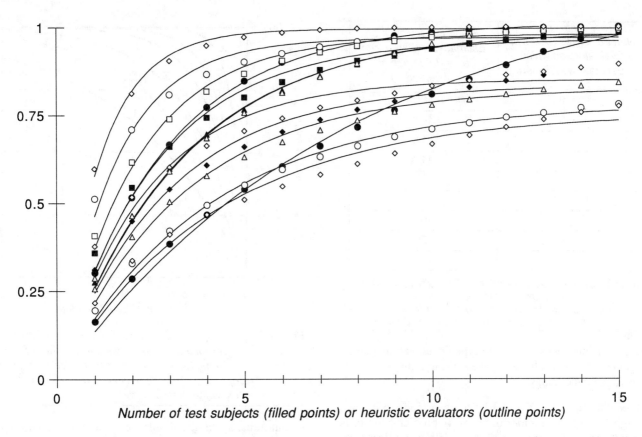

Figure 1 *Proportion of usability problems found with increasing numbers of subjects or evaluators for the interfaces in Table 1. The markers indicate the actual values from the studies and the lines indicate the fitted curves according to (EQ 1). The values from the various studies have been normalized to proportions rather than absolute number of problems to allow comparisons in a single figure.*

As can be seen from Table 1, λ varies substantially between studies. The exact value of λ in any given usability study will depend on

- The properties of the system and its interface.

- The stage of the usability lifecycle. For example, it might well be the case that usability problems are easier to find in an initial rough design with plenty of obvious problems than in a polished n'th iteration. Also, it might matter whether the interface has been fully implemented or only exists as a prototype or a paper design. For example, Nielsen [15] found that usability problems relating to missing features in a user interface were much harder to find by heuristic evaluation of paper mockups than of running prototypes.

- The evaluation method used. For example, an evaluation based on an analysis of logs of user interactions might require data from more users than a thinking aloud study would.

- The skills of the heuristic evaluators and the experimenters running a user test. For example, Nielsen [15] found that evaluators with usability expertise found many more problems in a heuristic evaluation than evaluators without such expertise and that evaluators with "double expertise" (both usability and the kind of interface being

evaluated) found even more problems. Nielsen and Molich [11] found a positive correlation of .57 between the number of usability problems found by the same evaluators in two case studies of heuristic evaluation, indicating that some people tend to be better than others even within a given expertise category. As another example, Nielsen [14] found that the number of usability problems found in user testing using the thinking aloud technique had a positive correlation of .76 with the methodological quality of the test procedures used.

- Other factors, such as whether test users are representative of the actual user population.

ESTIMATING THE NUMBER OF PROBLEMS REMAINING TO BE FOUND

One use for this model would be as an aid to deciding when to stop testing. After two or more evaluations, one can easily estimate λ and N. It is impossible to derive estimates based only on the first subject or evaluator, as (EQ 1) has two unknowns, and therefore needs at least two datapoints to be estimated. Of course, one could still get a rough estimate of N if λ was assumed to be equal to some value that had previously been found to describe usability studies in a given organization. It is unknown, however, whether the variability in λ would in fact be smaller if one only consid-

Number of Test Users or Evaluators on which Estimate was Based	Standard Deviation of Estimated N (Expressed as a Proportion of Observed N)
2	42%
3	44%
4	21%
5	11%
6	9%
7	8%
8	6%
9	5%
10	5%

Table 2 *The spread of estimates of N made on the basis of various number of test users or evaluators, expressed as the standard deviation of the estimates. Values are given across the datasets.*

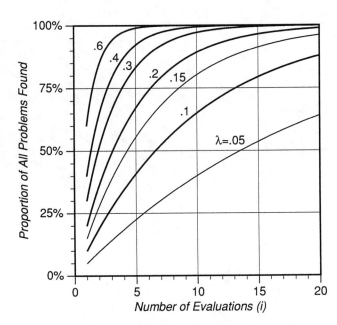

Figure 2 *Nomograph showing the proportion of usability problems found for various number of evaluations. Each curve represents a certain value of λ, as noted on the curves, from .05 (bottom curve) to .6 (top curve).*

ered user interfaces of a given type developed in a single organization and evaluated by the same usability staff using the same methodology.

Once estimates for N and λ have been made, one has a rough idea of the number of usability problems yet to be found in the user interface. The model also indicates the likely number of these problems that will be found by the next test subject or heuristic evaluator. If a usability manager knows the approximate value of finding additional problems, it is then a simple matter to decide whether it would be worth the additional cost to continue the test.

The accuracy of these estimates of N and λ will improve as more data becomes available. As shown in Table 2, the estimates are highly variable as long as they are based on data from two or three test users or heuristic evaluators, and they are reasonably tight when data is available from about six or more people. For i greater than two, the parameters can be estimated by least-squares curve-fitting, for which programs are available in many graphics and statistics packages. For $i=2$, the parameters can be estimated as follows (derived from (EQ 1) by simple algebraic manipulation):

$$\lambda = 2 - (\text{Found}(2) / \text{Found}(1)) \qquad \text{(EQ 2)}$$

$$N = \text{Found}(1) / \lambda \qquad \text{(EQ 3)}$$

where Found(i) indicates the number of different usability problems found after i evaluations. Both for curve fitting and for use of (EQ 2) and (EQ 3) it is recommended to calculate values for Found(i) that are independent of the particular sequence in which the evaluations were performed. For example, Found(1) should be the average number of usability problems found in a single evaluation and not just the number found by whatever evaluator or test subject happened to be the first. Similarly, Found(2) should be calculated as the mean number of problems found by all pairs of

evaluations, Found(3) should be calculated based on all triplets, and so on. In practice, it is not necessary to consider all permutations of evaluations, but one should sample a reasonably large number of combinations.

Estimates of N are useful for development projects as they give an indication of how many usability problems might remain in an interface and how much additional work would be required to find them. Estimates of λ can help plan a testing program based on the expected shape of the curve of found usability problems. The nomograph in Figure 2 shows such curves over a common range of λ-values.

A PRIORI ESTIMATES OF THE OPTIMUM NUMBER OF EVALUATORS AND TEST USERS

The decision of when to stop trying to find usability problems will obviously depend on the characteristics of the individual development project, including especially the specific costs of each test user or heuristic evaluator as well as the probable savings to be realized from improved usability in the released software. Given this information, as well as information about the values of N and λ that are normally found in an organization's projects, one can also calculate rough a priori estimates of the amount of usability work that will be necessary. These estimates are obviously much less reliable than estimates made by fitting the model to measured data as it is accumulated from actual usability activities, but they can still be of some value for early planning.

This section provides examples of how a priori cost-benefit estimations can be made, using sample data estimated from

Project Size	Heuristic Evaluation	User Testing
Small	9	7
Medium-large	16	15
Very large	21	20

Table 3   *Estimates of the optimal number of heuristic evaluators and test users for our examples.*

Project Size	Cost	Benefits	Benefit/ Cost Ratio
Small	$9,400	$39,500	4.2
Medium-large	$13,600	$613,000	45
Very large	$33,200	$8,200,000	247

Table 4   *Cost–benefit analysis for using the optimal number of evaluators in a heuristic evaluation.*

Project Size	Cost	Benefits	Benefit/ Cost Ratio
Small	$10,000	$37,900	3.8
Medium-large	$18,000	$613,000	34
Very large	$46,000	$8,200,000	178

Table 5   *Cost–benefit analysis for using the optimal number of test users in user testing.*

our experience and the published literature. We will consider three sample projects, called small, medium-large, and very large. In reality, the magnitude of usability projects is not a simple, one-dimensional property. Several parameters influence the scope of usability activities, including the size of the interface (whether measured in lines of code or in number of screens, dialog boxes, or other interface elements), the number of expected users, and the duration, intensity, and possible mission-critical nature of their usage.

Costs seem to be the easiest to estimate. In one analysis [20], heuristic evaluation was estimated as having fixed costs of between $3,700 and $4,800, with the variable cost of each evaluator being between $420 and $520. User testing using an extreme "discount usability engineering" approach with very little preparation or data analysis was estimated as having fixed costs of $2,600, with the variable cost of each test user being $410. Another analysis [10] did not consider heuristic evaluation, but estimated the fixed costs of user testing at $8,000 and the variable costs per test user at $2,000 (when updated to 1993 dollars).

Other studies have been less explicit in calculating the costs of usability engineering techniques, but one can convert information in one study [7] into the following estimates: The fixed cost of preparing to use heuristic evaluation was about $4,400, and the fixed cost of preparing to use user testing was about $3,400. The variable cost was about $900 per evaluator for heuristic evaluation and about $1,900 per test user for user testing. Another study [5] did not provide information about fixed versus variable costs, but estimated about $500 in total costs per heuristic evaluator and $3,000 in total costs per test user.

These estimates vary strikingly, which is understandable given the differences in user interfaces being evaluated and the methodologies being applied. For example, one would expect a test of a large system to take longer and thus be more expensive than a test of a small, walk-up-and-use system. For illustration, we will use fixed costs of $4,000 for heuristic evaluation and $3,000 for user testing and variable costs of $600 per evaluator for heuristic evaluation and $1,000 per test user for user testing, except for the "very large" project, where all costs will be assumed to be twice as large.

Benefits are harder to calculate. One analysis [20] conservatively estimated the mean benefit from having found a usability problem as $13,500, not including the software engineering savings from not having to change the interface in a maintenance release of the product. Another analysis [10] estimated the mean benefit from having found a usability problem as $19,300 (when updated to 1993 dollars). Both these estimates considered systems that were going to see fairly extensive use, and for the sake of simplicity, we will use $15,000 as the benefit estimate per usability problem found for such systems. For smaller systems that are going to be used less frequently or by fewer users (for example, much in-house software in medium-sized companies), we will use $1,000 as the benefit estimate per usability problem found.

For systems that are going to see extremely intensive use by very large numbers of users, the benefit of finding a usability problem can be considerably higher and reach into the millions of dollars [4]. Such large systems probably warrant individual analyses taking their special circumstances into account, but again for simplicity, we will use $200,000 as the benefit estimate per usability problem found.

For all systems, we will use the prediction formula in (EQ 1) with the mean values of N and λ from Table 1, $N=41$, and $\lambda=.31$. Of course, the actual values of N and λ will vary for any given development project, so the following results should be seen only as very approximate "rules of thumb" that can be used to arrive at rough estimates before the start of a project. It is recommended that project managers acquire estimates of the cost and benefit values from their own organizations and that they also refine the estimates of N and λ for their specific project as data becomes available

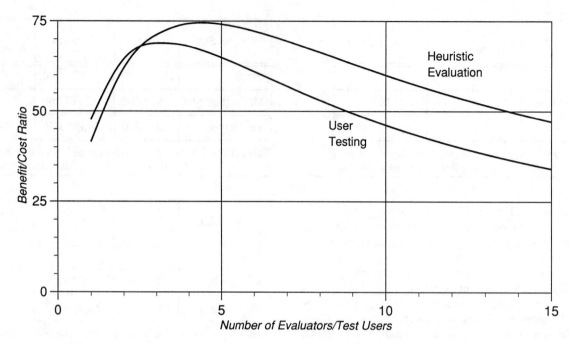

Figure 3   *Ratio between benefits and costs for using various numbers of heuristic evaluators and test users to find usability problems in a medium-large software project, as calculated using the various assumptions listed in the text.*

from their own usability activities. Of course, estimates for any specific project should also be refined as soon as a few evaluations have been performed for that project.

Given estimates for both costs and benefits as well as our prediction formula for the finding of usability problems, one can easily calculate the optimum number of heuristic evaluators or test users. The optimum number of evaluators or test users is the number for which the marginal value of the last evaluator or test user was higher than the marginal cost of that evaluator or user, but where the marginal value of one additional evaluator or user would be smaller than the marginal cost of that evaluator or user. Table 3 shows these optimal numbers. Table 4 then shows a cost–benefit analysis for using the optimum number of heuristic evaluators, and Table 5 shows a cost–benefit analysis for using the optimum number of test users.

These optimum numbers of evaluators/test users are much larger than obtained for our earlier "discount usability engineering" recommendation of using about five heuristic evaluators or test users [12]. One reason for the discrepancy is that discount usability engineering has as one of its goals to let people apply usability engineering methods on projects where budget or time constraints prevent them from using optimal methods. A second, and more fundamentally important, reason is that one would rarely evaluate a single user interface design to the bitter end without applying iterative design to fix usability problems found with the first few evaluators or test users. The estimates of the benefits of finding a usability problem assume that reasonable fixes will be introduced to the design, but by changing the design, one often introduces new usability problems. It is therefore

likely to be a better strategy to evaluate initial iterations of a design less thoroughly.

Figure 3 shows the cost-benefit model for medium-large projects under our assumptions. It can be seen that the benefits are much larger than the costs both for user testing and for heuristic evaluation. The highest ratio of benefits to costs is achieved for 3.2 test users and for 4.4 heuristic evaluators. These numbers can be taken as one rough estimate of the effort to be expended for usability evaluation for each version of a user interface subjected to iterative design.

It seems reasonable to use our model also for iterative design [19], even though we have only tested it with data from single usability studies. Presumably, the usability problems found in each iteration of an iterative design process is a combination of previously unfound problems left over from earlier iterations and new problems introduced in the revised design. Given the Poisson assumption in our model, the probability of finding the previously unfound problems in the new iteration does not depend on how much testing has been conducted on previous iterations, so the model can be applied without modifications to the finding of all the problems, no matter whether they are new or old.

A model of iterative design should also account for the cost of producing the additional iterations. Unfortunately, such software development costs are extremely difficult to estimate. For the sake of argument, we will perform the calculations for a medium-large project, assuming that a new iteration can be produced for $20,000. This cost estimate might apply to a project that was still in an early stage and was being developed with a prototyping tool making changes reasonably easy to make. Taking $20,000 as an additional fixed cost for each usability study changes the model to have the highest ratio of benefits to costs at 6.7 test users and 7.9 heuristic evaluators. If iterations can be produced more cheaply, fewer users or evaluators should be used, and if iterations are more costly, more elaborate usability evaluations should be performed for each iteration.

CONCLUSIONS

We have established that a Poisson model describes quite well the finding of usability problems in user testing and heuristic evaluation. Such a model can therefore be used to predict the eventual number of problems that will be found by a usability study even as the study is in progress. Further work remains to be done to assess the preciseness of these predictions, but similar models have been successfully applied to the related problem of determining when to stop testing software for programming bugs [1][2].

Acknowledgments

The authors would like to thank James Lewis of the IBM Design Center/Human Factors, Robert Virzi of GTE Laboratories, and Peter Wright and Andrew Monk of the University of York for providing us with the detailed raw data underlying their published studies. We also thank Clare-Marie Karat of IBM U.S. Marketing and Strategy for clarifying details regarding fixed costs in her published study. The analyses of this data in this paper are solely the responsibility of the authors of the present paper and should not be taken as necessarily corresponding to the positions of these other authors or their organizations. The authors would also like to thank the anonymous *INTERCHI'93* referees for helpful comments on a previous version of this manuscript.

References

1. Dalal, S.R., and Mallows, C.L. (1988). When should one stop testing software? *J. American Statistical Association* **83**, 403 (September), 872–879.

2. Dalal, S.R., and Mallows, C.L. (1990). Some graphical aids for deciding when to stop testing software. *IEEE J. Selected Areas in Communication* **8**, 2 (February), 169–175.

3. Erhan, S. (1975). *Introduction to Stochastic Processes*. Prentice Hall, Englewood Cliffs, NJ. p. 87.

4. Gray, W.D., John, B.E., and Atwood, M.E. (1992). The precis of project Ernestine, or, an overview of a validation of GOMS. *Proc. ACM CHI'92* (Monterey, CA, 3–7 May), 307–312.

5. Jeffries, R., Miller, J.R., Wharton, C., and Uyeda, K.M. (1991). User interface evaluation in the real world: A comparison of four techniques. *Proc. ACM CHI'91* (New Orleans, LA, 27 April–2 May), 119–124.

6. Jørgensen, A.H. (1989). Using the thinking-aloud method in system development. In Salvendy, G., and Smith, M.J. (Eds.), *Designing and Using Human–Computer Interfaces*

and Knowledge Based Systems. Amsterdam: Elsevier Science Publishers, 743–750.

7. Karat, C., Campbell, R., Fiegel, T. (1992). Comparisons of empirical testing and walkthrough methods in user interface evaluation. *Proc. ACM CHI'92* (Monterey, CA, 3–7 May), 397–404.

8. Lewis, C. (1982). Using the 'thinking-aloud' method in cognitive interface design. *Research Report* **RC-9265**, IBM T.J. Watson Research Center, Yorktown Heights, NY.

9. Lewis, J.R., Henry, S.C., and Mack, R.L. (1990). Integrated office software benchmarks: A case study. *Proc. INTERACT'90 3rd IFIP Conf. Human–Computer Interaction* (Cambridge, U.K., 27–31 August 1990), 337–343.

10. Mantei, M.M., and Teorey, T.J. (1988). Cost/benefit analysis for incorporating human factors in the software lifecycle. *Communications of the ACM* **31**, 4 (April), 428–439.

11. Molich, R., and Nielsen, J. (1990). Improving a human-computer dialogue. *Communications of the ACM* **33**, 3 (March), 338–348.

12. Nielsen, J. (1989). Usability engineering at a discount. In Salvendy, G., and Smith, M.J. (Eds.), *Designing and Using Human–Computer Interfaces and Knowledge Based Systems*, Elsevier Science Publishers, Amsterdam. 394–401.

13. Nielsen, J. (1990). Big paybacks from 'discount' usability engineering. *IEEE Software* **7**, 3 (May), 107–108.

14. Nielsen, J. (1992). Evaluating the thinking aloud technique for use by computer scientists. In Hartson, H.R., and Hix, D. (Eds.), *Advances in Human–Computer Interaction Vol. 3*, Ablex. 69–82.

15. Nielsen, J. (1992). Finding usability problems through heuristic evaluation. *Proc. ACM CHI'92* (Monterey, CA, 3–7 May), 373–380.

16. Nielsen, J. (1992). The usability engineering lifecycle. *IEEE Computer* **25**, 3 (March), 12–22.

17. Nielsen, J. (1993). Estimating the number of subjects needed for a thinking aloud test. *Intl. J. Man–Machine Studies* **in press**.

18. Nielsen, J. (1993). *Usability Engineering*, Academic Press, San Diego, CA.

19. Nielsen, J. (1993). Iterative design of user interfaces. *IEEE Computer* **26** (to appear, probably in the July issue).

20. Nielsen, J. (1993). Heuristic evaluation. In Nielsen, J., and Mack, R.L. (Eds.), *Usability Inspection Methods. Book in preparation*.

21. Nielsen, J., and Molich, R. (1990). Heuristic evaluation of user interfaces. *Proc. ACM CHI'90* (Seattle, WA, 1–5 April), 249–256.

22. Virzi, R.A. (1990). Streamlining the design process: Running fewer subjects. *Proceedings of the Human Factors Society 34th Annual Meeting* (Orlando, FL, 8–12 October), 291–294.

23. Virzi, R.A. (1992). Refining the test phase of usability evaluation: How many subjects are enough? *Human Factors* **34**, 4 (August), 457–468.

24. Wright, P.C., and Monk, A.F. (1991). A cost-effective evaluation method for use by designers. *Intl. J. Man–Machine Studies* **35**, 6 (December), 891–912.

Estimating the Relative Usability of Two Interfaces: Heuristic, Formal, and Empirical Methods Compared

Jakob Nielsen and Victoria L. Phillips[*]

Bellcore
445 South Street
Morristown, NJ 07962-1910
USA

nielsen@bellcore.com and vp0o+@andrew.cmu.edu

Electronic business card for first author can be retrieved by sending any message to the server at nielsen-info@bellcore.com

*) Current address: Carnegie Mellon University, Pittsburgh, PA 15213, USA

ABSTRACT

Two alternative user interface designs were subjected to user testing to measure user performance in a database query task. User performance was also estimated heuristically in three different ways and by use of formal GOMS modelling. The estimated values for absolute user performance had very high variability, but estimates of the relative advantage of the fastest interface were less variable. Choosing the fastest of the two designs would have a net present value more than 1,000 times the cost of getting the estimates. A software manager would make the correct choice every time in our case study if decisions were based on at least three independent estimates. User testing was 4.9 times as expensive as the cheapest heuristic method but provided better performance estimates.

Keywords: Heuristic evaluation, heuristic estimation, GOMS, User testing, Usability, User performance, Absolute performance, Relative performance, Cost-benefit estimates.

INTRODUCTION

One often needs to assess the relative usability of two or more user interfaces, designed to solve the same problem. Sometimes it will be sufficient to find which of the two is the most usable and then pick the best. In other cases, one will need to know *how much* better the preferred interface is before one can decide to use it. A typical situation, and the one that prompted the current study, is the case where one interface design already is implemented. Since there are obviously significant development costs associated with changing such an interface, one would like an estimate of the amount of money to be saved from the supposed increased usability of the alternative design.

Other examples where relative assessments of usability are needed include design teams considering alternative designs where one is expected to be more expensive than the other to implement, or cases where two alternative software packages are available for purchase, but at different prices. Common for all these cases is the basic phenomenon that the available choices have different costs associated with them, meaning that it is not possible to simply choose the best user interface. One needs to estimate whether the best interface will lead to savings that are sufficiently large to justify its higher cost. Of course, if the cheapest interface was also the best, there would be no need for any further analysis.

From a research perspective, we have a general interest in estimating the benefits of usability engineering in monetary terms [7]. Cost/benefit analyses are important assessment tools for proposed new usability engineering methods [4]. The *costs* of various usability methods are easy to measure, since they involve mostly adding up staff and subject hours and multiplying with the relevant loaded salary rates. The *benefits* of usability methods are much harder to assess, since one rarely fields two complete versions of the same product in order to measure real-world performance with the two versions (but see [3] for an example of a study doing just that and saving $2.4 million).

The study described in this paper takes a slightly simplified approach to the estimation of usability benefits. We have studied the estimation of the task time needed for expert users to perform a certain task with two alternative user interface designs. Given a task analysis of the work of the real users, one can convert such task time estimates into person-hours per year, by simply multiplying the time saved per transaction with the number of times per day each user is expected to perform the task as well as by the number of users doing the job. These person-hour estimates can then be converted into monetary terms as shown below.

A full cost/benefit analysis would include additional elements, such as estimates of learning times, error rates, and subjective user satisfaction (and its probable impact on employee turnover etc.). One would also need to consider potential differences between usability as measured in the laboratory and usability as observed in real-world usage. Furthermore, of course, much software is produced for sale on the open market rather than for use in-house or by contractual clients, and the relation between customer savings and increased market share for the vendor is not well understood.

The relative importance of the different usability variables will differ depending on the system. For many applications, initial learnability is paramount as users will not be expected to use the system more than a few times. For other applications, such as the one giving rise to the current study, users keep using the same interface repeatedly, and their performance as expert users is the dominating factor in overall usability. For example, for our full system (with more interface elements than the one discussed here), the savings from improving the interface according to the results of a heuristic evaluation were estimated at about $40,000 from reduced training costs and about $500,000 from increased expert user performance in the first year alone [12].

The study described in this paper has therefore focused on expert user performance. We have studied two alternative interface designs for a single, quite specific task: That of looking up information in one out of several databases.

We were interested in comparing various methods for estimating user performance. We collected data for the two interfaces from heuristic estimates by usability specialists, from formal GOMS analyses of the interfaces, and from user testing. Some usability specialists may argue that user testing is the only true way of getting data about user performance, but alternative methods such as formal analysis or heuristic estimates have the advantage that they can be used even when the interfaces in questions have not yet been implemented, and thus cannot be tested. Also, heuristic evaluation has mostly been used for the finding of usability problems [12], so it is interesting to assess whether it can also be used to estimate user performance.

THE TASK AND THE INTERFACES

The users' task in this study is that of issuing a query to one out of several databases on one or more data items such as telephone numbers, customer names, addresses, etc. For the purpose of the current study, we looked at queries on telephone numbers. Furthermore, we only studied queries on one or two telephone numbers, even though the actual application sometimes involves queries for more than two telephone numbers. The users will be working in a window system, and the information that is to be looked up in the databases can be assumed to be visible on the screen (possibly as the result of previous queries).

Two possible interface designs were considered. Design A was fairly simple to implement and had indeed been imple-

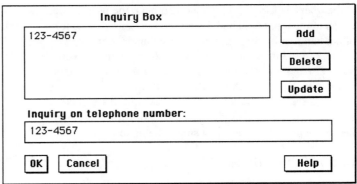

Figure 1 *Dialog box used in Design A: The Dialog Box interface. In the state depicted here, the user has just input the telephone number "123-4567" and has clicked on the "Add" button. Figure shown at 60% of screen size.*

mented in a prototype version of the full system. Design B was a potential alternative design that was arrived at in a debriefing session following a heuristic evaluation of Design A. Design B is harder to implement than Design A, since it requires the computer to parse the result of database queries performed on a remote host system and to understand the meaning of the text displayed on the screen. Also, Design A had the obvious advantage of already being implemented in the prototype.

We should emphasize that the issue of interest here is not whether these two interfaces were optimally designed. It is very likely that they could be improved by iterative design using various usability engineering methods [11]. The question of interest for our study was how to assess expected expert user performance on two given designs.

Design A: Dialog Box

To use this interface, the user first pulls down a menu from the menubar at the top of the screen. This menu contains the names of the databases and the user positions the mouse cursor over the name of the relevant database in this list. The user pushes down the mouse button and drags the mouse to the right to get a hierarchical submenu with the legal queries for the chosen database. This submenu contains an average of four alternatives, and the user moves the mouse until it highlights the option "query on telephone number." The user then releases the mouse button.

This causes a standard sized dialog box to appear in the middle of the screen as shown in Figure 1. The large field at the top is initially empty. This field will eventually list the telephone numbers to be submitted to the database as a query. The dialog box does not overlap the window with the list of telephone numbers. The user clicks in the input field (the one-line field below the prompt "Inquiry on telephone number") and types the telephone number. The user clicks on the "Add" button to add the number to the query. The figure shows the state of the dialog box after the user's click on "Add." If the query is for a single telephone number, the user then clicks on the "OK" button to submit the query.

If the query is for two telephone numbers, the user instead clicks in the input field and selects the previously typed telephone number by dragging the mouse cursor over the existing text in the input field. The user then types in the second number (thus replacing the previous selection in the input field) and clicks on the "Add" button. Finally, the user clicks on the "OK" button to submit both queries at once. In a similar manner, the user can issue queries for larger number of telephone numbers in a single dialogue.

Design B: Pop-Up Menu

As previously mentioned, it can be assumed that the telephone number(s) in question is/are already on the screen.

To query for one number, the user moves the mouse cursor to the telephone number on the screen and presses down the mouse button. This causes a pop-up menu to appear over the number with one element for each database for which queries can be performed with telephone numbers as keys.

The user moves the mouse until the desired database is highlighted in the pop-up menu. The user then lets go of the mouse button. (The system knows which number to search on because the user pointed to it when calling up the menu).

To query for two numbers, the user repeats this entire interaction sequence for the second number. The second number was normally about five lines below the first number in the window. It is possible to submit the second query before seeing the result of the first one, and the result of the first query can be assumed to appear such that it does not overlap the telephone number needed for the second query.

HEURISTIC ESTIMATES

Heuristic evaluation [9][13] is a usability inspection method [6] whereby a set of evaluators produces lists of usability problems in a user interface by going through it and noting deviations from accepted usability principles. As originally conceived, the heuristic evaluation method only involved the finding the usability problems and did not address other phases of the usability engineering lifecycle [8][11]. Subsequent work has shown how it can be extended to have the evaluators provide severity estimates for the usability problems after the lists of problems found by the individual evaluators have been aggregated [10][12].

Even severity estimates are still focused on usability problems (that is, characteristics of the interface) rather than overall user performance, even though they aim at assessing the impact of each usability problem on eventual user performance. We were therefore interested in assessing the extent to which heuristic evaluators could provide estimates of actual user performance.

Heuristic estimates were collected in three different conditions (cold, warm, and hot), varying in the extent to which the evaluators had access to actual running implementations of the interfaces. In all three conditions, evaluators were asked to estimate the time needed for expert users to issue queries on one as well as two telephone numbers with each of the two alternative interface designs. The evaluators were told to focus on expert user performance and disregard novice user performance as well as any learnability problems.

Common for all three conditions was that the evaluators had to estimate expert user performance based on their personal intuition and best guesses without having a chance to observe a real user or to perform any measurements. Of course, evaluators who had tried using one or both of the interfaces themselves could estimate their own performance and use it as a baseline for their projections of expert user performance, and several of them did so.

Cold Estimates

"Cold" estimates were collected by sending each of 12 evaluators a written specification of the two interface designs, essentially corresponding to the descriptions above. The evaluators had not seen any running implementations of the designs. This condition corresponds to the case where a design team is considering two possible solutions, none of which has been implemented.

The mean time spent by the cold evaluators was 9.9 minutes. The total cost of collecting the cold estimates also includes the time needed to write up the specification, which took about two hours. Of course, there was a further cost associated with designing the two interfaces in the first place, but that cost should probably not be charged to the comparative evaluation study.

Warm Estimates

The 10 evaluators in the "warm" condition were the same as those used for the original heuristic evaluation of the full system. They had spent about one hour each using a running prototype system implementing the Dialog Box interface as well as several other dialogue elements. After the heuristic evaluation, they were provided with a list of all the usability problems in the interface (both the ones they had identified themselves and the ones found by other evaluators) and were asked to rate the severity of each problem. Furthermore, they were provided with a written description of the Pop-Up Menu design as an alternative interface. This condition corresponds to the case where one design has been implemented and evaluated, and another is being considered based on the results of the evaluation.

There is no simple way to estimate the cost of collecting the warm estimates. Not only did the evaluators spend an hour each using the full system with the Dialog Box interface, but they also attended a one-hour briefing session explaining the full, complicated application and spent a further half hour estimating severities for the usability problems. Most of these activities were not strictly necessary for the purpose of estimating expert user performance, but they probably did provide the evaluators with additional insights into the issues surrounding the kind of dialogues they were later asked to assess. We would guess that it would be possible to collect warm estimates in about 12.1 minutes per evaluator (the mean of the cold and hot times), if their only task was to estimate expert user performance and not to find usability problems in the interface. Furthermore, it would be necessary to have a research assistant available throughout the study to help the evaluators use the software.

Hot Estimates

The 15 evaluators in the "hot" condition had used running versions of both interfaces before giving their estimates. In fact, they were given access to the same versions as those used for the user testing (described further below). For each interface, the evaluators were first given a demo of how to perform single and double number queries, and were then given a chance to use the interface themselves as long as they wished. An experimenter was present to help the evaluators in case they had problems using the interfaces. This condition corresponds to the case where two alternative applications are available for purchase, or where two alternative design solutions have both been prototyped.

The mean time spent by the hot evaluators was 14.2 minutes. This time included a few minutes to recover from system crashes in a few cases. It seems reasonable to include this time given that hot estimates require the use of running software and given that this software will often be in the early stages of development. Given the way we conducted the hot estimates, a research assistant was present during each session to help the estimators use the software, so there is a need for an additional 14.2 minutes of staff time per estimator. The time needed to develop the software implementing the two interfaces for the hot estimation was about 6 days. The same software was used for both the hot estimates and the user testing, but from a cost perspective, the development costs should be charged fully to both methods, since one would presumably use only one method for any given development project. It was also necessary to have a usability specialist spend one hour designing the study and the questionnaire given to the estimators.

The Evaluators

For all three heuristic estimation conditions, the evaluators were usability specialists with an average of nine years of usability experience. Different evaluators were used in each condition. Previous studies have shown that usability specialists are better than non-usability specialists at finding usability problems through heuristic evaluation [9]. We would therefore expect non-usability specialists (e.g., developers) to provide somewhat worse estimates of user performance than those found in this study, but we do not have any data to support this conjecture.

It is important to note that the evaluators provided their user performance estimates independently of each other. In general, we recommend collecting data from heuristic evaluation without letting the evaluators talk together before they

have provided their lists of usability problems and severity or performance estimates, in order to prevent any bias in the evaluations. It is obviously also possible to have heuristic evaluation performed by small teams working together [5].

GOMS ANALYSIS

GOMS (Goals, Operators, Methods, and Selection rules) [2] is a method for the formal analysis of user interactions with computers. The method was explicitly designed for the purpose of estimating expert user performance disregarding learnability problems and user errors, so it seemed reasonable to use it for our study. Also, GOMS has proven quite popular in recent years in the formal modelling community [15], as evidenced by the large number of papers published about GOMS, extensions of GOMS, and applications of GOMS, again indicating that it would be a reasonable method for our study.

The GOMS analysis were performed by 19 upper-division undergraduate students in a human–computer interaction class as their second assignment using GOMS. The students were given the same specification of the two user interfaces as that used for the "cold" heuristic evaluators. They were asked to build GOMS models of the two interfaces based on the specification and to estimate the time needed for expert users to perform single and double telephone number queries. Just as for the heuristic estimates, each GOMS analysis was performed by an individual student working alone.

We should note that the quality of the GOMS models built by the students in this study was probably not as good as the quality of models that might be built by true GOMS experts with more extensive experience in the use of the method. On the other hand, even though better performance could probably be achieved by using GOMS experts, highly experienced GOMS experts are not readily available in most development organizations. If formal usability analysis becomes a successful approach in industry, it may be not be unrealistic to expect GOMS analyses to be performed by people with a medium level of expertise.

The mean time spent by each student to perform the GOMS analysis of the two interfaces was 108 minutes. The total cost of using the GOMS method would also include the time to produce the written specification (about two hours).

USER TESTING

User testing was conducted with 20 test users who were students recruited from a local college or summer students involved in non-usability projects at Bellcore. All test users were required to be experienced mouse users, since previous experience shows that problems with mouse usage will otherwise dominate a user's performance.

The study design was a within-subjects experiment where all test users tried both interfaces such that half of the users (randomly assigned) used the Dialog Box interface first and the other half used the Pop-Up Menu interface first. The

	N	Dialog Box 1 Query	Dialog Box 2 Queries	Pop-Up Menu 1 Query	Pop-Up Menu 2 Queries	St.Deviations as % of Means
Cold heuristic estimates	12	20.3 (26.1)	29.4 (30.4)	8.0 (7.4)	14.0 (15.1)	108%
Warm heuristic estimates	10	12.9 (10.7)	21.4 (21.6)	4.7 (2.7)	9.1 (5.3)	75%
Hot heuristic estimates	15	13.8 (6.1)	20.0 (9.5)	6.1 (3.5)	9.4 (5.5)	52%
GOMS analyses	19	16.6 (3.7)	22.6 (5.4)	5.8 (0.8)	11.2 (1.9)	19%
User testing	20	15.4 (3.0)	25.5 (4.7)	4.3 (0.6)	6.5 (0.9)	17%

Table 1   *Mean time estimates in seconds arrived at by different methods. Numbers in parentheses indicate the standard deviation of the estimates. The last column is averaged across the four data columns and indicates variability.*

within-subjects design was chosen since learning and transfer of learning was irrelevant for the study, whereas controlling for individual variability was important. Since learnability was not a concern in this study, the test users were instructed in the use of the interfaces and were given help as needed during their initial use. For each interface, the test users were first allowed to practice until they had reached a steady plateau of expert user performance, after which the measurement part of the experiment began. Users were presented with a sequence of randomly chosen tasks, randomly alternating one-, two-, and three-number queries (the latter were not used in the analysis). They were instructed to work as quickly as possible while avoiding errors. Users were given error messages whenever they made errors, and they were also shown a feedback curve tracking their transaction rate throughout the experiment. After their use of each interface, the users were given a two-question subjective satisfaction questionnaire to assess how well they liked the interface.

Erroneous transactions constituted 6.5% of the expert user mode transactions for the Dialog Box interface and 3.8% for the Pop-Up Menu interface. These errors were eliminated from the data before it was analyzed.

Each user test session (with two interfaces) took about two hours, involving both the test subject and an experimenter. The time needed to develop the software implementing the two interfaces for the user testing was about 6 days. There was also the need to have a usability specialist spend two hours designing the experiment as well as having a research assistant and a test user spend two hours on a pilot test.

Subjective Satisfaction. On a 1–5 scale, with 1 being best, users gave the dialog box interface a mean evaluation of 4.0 for pleasantness and 3.9 for efficiency. The pop-up menu interface was evaluated as 3.2 for pleasantness and 2.3 for efficiency. In other words, users strongly preferred the pop-up menu interface (the differences are statistically significant at $p < .01$ for both variables according to paired t-tests).

COMPARING THE ESTIMATES

Table 1 shows the mean estimates for the four task-by-interface combinations for each of the five studies. A striking result is the extent to which all the estimation methods overestimate the time needed for a two-number query in the pop-up menu interface. Given the way the interface is defined, a two-number query is exactly identical to two single-number queries, so it may be natural for the estimators to more or less double their estimate from the one-number query. In actual use, however, repeating exactly the same sequence of actions a second time is faster than doing it the first time since some mental steps are eliminated[*] the second time around, so the ratio between two and one queries was measured as 1.5. Even though this phenomenon is known in the GOMS literature [14], the students doing the GOMS analyses were not familiar with this refinement of the model, and they arrived at a ratio of 1.9 between two- and one-number queries. The fact that extensive knowledge of modifications like this is needed for a complete GOMS analysis is one reason it is seen as intimidating by some developers [1]. The heuristic estimators apparently did not consider the faster execution of the repeated operations either, except for the ones in the hot condition who had tried the interface themselves and estimated a ratio of 1.6 between two- and one-number queries. The cold estimators' ratio was 1.8, and the warm estimators' was 1.9.

The user test results in Table 1 may be slightly misleading with respect to true user performance in the field. Expect field users may be faster at using the dialog box interface because they typically develop extremely fast keyboarding skills. Even though we trained our users to expert performance on the interface as such, we could obviously not train their keyboarding skills to the level of an experienced operator. However, reducing the user test times for the dialog box interface by one second per telephone number to be entered only reduces the relative advantage of pop-up menus from 74% to 72%. Reducing the time to type in each telephone number by two seconds still only reduces the rel-

---

* Potentially, a redesigned pop-up interface might be faster for repeated queries if some of the physical operators were eliminated: Making the database from the previous query the default menu choice would allow repeated queries simply by clicking the mouse on the telephone number, thus avoiding the need to select a menu option. We were not interested in iterative design for the purpose of the current study, however.

	Absolute Advantage of Pop-Up Interface				Relative Advantage of Pop-Up Interface			
	Estimate of absolute number of seconds saved	$\frac{Max}{Min}$ ratio	$\frac{Q_3}{Q_1}$ ratio	**N** to get standard error of 10% and 20%	Estimate of relative proportion of time saved	$\frac{Max}{Min}$ ratio	$\frac{Q_3}{Q_1}$ ratio	**N** to get standard error of 10% and 20%
Cold heuristic estimates	27.6 (126%)	18.6	2.9	159; 40	52% (26%)	4.3	2.9	7; 2
Warm heuristic estimates	20.6 (146%)	21.0	3.5	213; 53	51% (34%)	2.7	1.7	12; 3
Hot heuristic estimates	18.1 (57%)	7.8	3.0	32; 8	53% (27%)	3.4	1.4	7; 2
GOMS analyses	11.1 (41%)	5.3	1.9	17; 4	55% (21%)	2.6	1.4	4; 1
User testing	15.0 (22%)	2.5	1.3	4; 1	74% (4%)	1.1	1.1	1; 1

Table 2   Mean estimates of the advantage of pop-up menus in absolute terms (seconds saved per transaction) and relative terms (how large a proportion of the time that could be saved by going from the dialog box interface to the pop-up menu interface). Both estimates assume an even mix of one- and two-number queries. Numbers in parentheses after the value estimates indicate the standard deviation of the estimates as a proportion of the mean value.

ative advantage of pop-up menus to 69%, thus confirming the general result of the user test. We will therefore use the user test results as the best indicator of "true" user performance, keeping in mind that field studies would probably show a slightly smaller advantage for the pop-up menus.

Table 2 shows the estimates of the absolute and relative advantage of the pop-up menu interface, assuming an even mix of one- and two-number queries. The table also shows three ways of assessing the spread of the estimates: standard deviation (in parentheses after the means), ratio between the largest and smallest estimate, and ratio between the third and first quartile (top 25% vs. bottom 25%). Estimates of relative performance are much tighter than are estimates of absolute performance, indicating a higher degree of agreement on the relative estimates. Thus, even though the estimators and analysts may disagree on exactly how fast users would be on the two interfaces, they agree somewhat on the proportional difference between the interfaces. Similarly, the standard deviation for the user test data is much smaller for the relative comparison than for the absolute comparison between the interfaces, basically taking advantage of the fact that individual differences are smoothed over by the within-subjects design of the experiment.

Since relative usability estimates have a smaller spread than absolute usability estimates, we would recommend relying on relative estimates whenever possible. If absolute estimates are needed, a larger number of estimates must be gathered to achieve a sufficiently small measurement error. The standard error can normally be estimated as the standard deviation divided by the square root of the number of observations. Using this estimator, Table 2 also shows the number of estimators/analysts/test users needed to achieve a standard error of 10% as well as 20% of the mean value for absolute and relative estimates of usability. It may not always be necessary to aim for a standard error of 10% of the mean estimate. The values listed for a standard error of

20% of the mean estimate thus provide a reasonable indication of the minimum number of estimates to acquire.

Experienced usability specialists might have been expected to provide better estimates than less experienced usability specialists. This is not the case, however, given two simplistic measures of usability expertise. The heuristic estimators were asked to state their usability experience in number of years (ranging from 1 to 30 years, mean=9, SD=6). They were also asked to state their experience with graphical user interfaces on a 1–3 scale (little, some, or extensive), with nobody giving their GUI experience as "little." Regressions between the experience measures and measures of estimation accuracy were all statistically insignificant, having very low correlation coefficients (typically R=.1). This is not to say that one might not be able to get better at performance estimates with some forms of experience, but just that other factors might be at play than simply the person's number of years of experience in the usability field in general. It is an interesting issue how to improve the estimation abilities of usability specialists as well as of regular developers. We believe that an important element in the acquisition of such skills is the observation of multiple user tests where real users use a variety of interface designs for a variety of tasks. We only have anecdotal evidence to support this conjecture, however. One supporting observation is the fact that our best heuristic estimate was provided by a usability specialist from a major computer vendor who had recently completed a set of empirical studies of input techniques.

COST-BENEFIT ANALYSIS

A cost-benefit analysis is very difficult to perform for the problem discussed in this paper as there is no way to quantify the value of having estimates of a certain accuracy.

Assuming that the estimates were to be used as the basis for making a decision on what interface to implement in a development project, the benefit would be the increased probability of making the correct decision. To get a rough idea of the benefits, let us assume that the time to implement the dialog box interface in the full system would be 200 hours and that the time to implement the pop-up menu interface in the full system would be 800 hours. Assuming the loaded cost of a software professional to be $100 per hour, the cost of the dialog box interface is $20,000 and the cost of the pop-up menu interface is $80,000. Let us furthermore assume that the system will have 3,000 users when it is released and that they will spend 2% of their working days performing queries, evenly divided among one- and two-element queries. These assumptions are reasonable given the underlying application that gave rise to this study.

Based on the above assumptions, a total of 3000 (users) × 236 (working days per year) × 0.02 (time doing queries) = 14,160 person-days per year would be spent issuing queries with the dialog box interface. Then the user test data indicates that the users would save 74% of this time, or about 10,480 person-days per year by using the pop-up menu interface, corresponding to $1,048,000 if a user costs $100 per day. Further assuming that the system release is slightly more than a year in the future, that the system is to be used for two years before an update can potentially be made to correct any design errors, and that the savings are to be discounted by 10% per year, gives a value of $870,000 for the first year's savings and $790,000 for the second year's saving. Thus, the present value of choosing the pop-up menu interface is $1,660,000. Deducting the additional implementation costs result in a final benefit of making the correct choice (the pop-up menu interface) of $1,600,000.

Assume for the sake of argument that a software development manager is only willing to approve a more expensive user interface element if its expected benefits are at least ten times larger than the expected incremental cost of implementing it. Event though the exact factor can be discussed, it would certainly be reasonable of the project manager to insist on a large number, since the implementation costs are certain (except for the ever-present risk of a cost overrun) and are to be spent here and now out of the manager's budget, whereas the reduced user costs are projected and will be accrued by the user organization over time. This assumption means that the software manager will make the correct decision whenever the pop-up menu design is estimated to save at least $600,000 (corresponding to a relative advantage of 30% for the pop-up menus).

Under these assumptions, the software manager would make the correct decision every time when relying on estimates from user testing of even a single test user, as well as when relying on any single warm heuristic estimate or any single GOMS analysis. For the cold heuristic estimates, the software manager would make the correct decision 92% of the time when relying on a single estimate, 98% of the time when relying on the mean of two estimates, and 100% of the time when relying on the mean of three estimates. For

	Cost formula (U.S. dollars)	Cost of a good relative estimate
Cold heuristic estimates	200 + 17N	$319
Warm heuristic estimates	800 + 38N	$1,256
Hot heuristic estimates	1300 + 42N	$1,594
GOMS analyses	200 + 90N	$560
User testing	1470 + 83N	$1,553

Table 3   Cost estimates for the five methods. The last column indicates the cost to achieve a relative estimate with a standard error of 10% by setting N (the number of estimators/analysis/subjects) equal to the numbers listed in Table 2.

the hot heuristic estimates, the manager would make the correct decision 93% of the time when relying on a single estimate, and 100% of the time when using the mean of two.

The cost estimates in Table 3 have been arrived at under the following estimates for the loaded hourly cost of various types of staff: Usability specialist: $100. Research assistant: $25. Test user (student): $10. The cost estimates include fixed costs to set up the studies as indicated in the description of the procedure earlier in this paper as well as variable costs for each estimator/analyst/subject. Furthermore, the cost formulas for warm and hot heuristic estimates as well as user testing include half an hour of research assistant time per person for the scheduling of appointments. Cold heuristic estimates and GOMS analyses can be handled simply by mailing out the written interface specification to people who can deal with it at their own convenience. The GOMS analysis cost formula reflects only half of the time actually spent in the study, since we would assume that experienced analysts would be faster than the students used by us. We see that cold heuristic estimation is the cheapest method (but as indicated by Table 1 and Table 2 also the worst), and that hot heuristic estimation is the most expensive, being 5.0 times as expensive. User testing is almost as expensive as hot heuristic evaluation, being 4.9 times as expensive as cold heuristic evaluation.

Combining our estimates of the costs and the benefits, we find that the benefits are between 1,000 and 5,000 times greater than the costs, confirming the value of usability engineering, no matter what method is used.

CONCLUSIONS

We have compared various ways of arriving at estimates of user performance with interface alternatives. User testing still seems to be the best method for arriving at such estimates, but one should remember that laboratory testing is not always a perfect predictor of field performance. User testing was also much more expensive than "cold" heuristic estimates and somewhat more expensive than GOMS analyses, both based on interface specification. The main reason for the added expense of user testing was the implementation cost needed to get a running prototype of sufficient stability to allow for user testing.

Heuristic estimates were better in the hot condition where estimators had access to running versions of the two interfaces, than in the cold condition based on specifications only. Since hot heuristic estimation was slightly more expensive than user testing, one might as well perform user testing if running interfaces are available. Heuristic estimation may have advantages in cases where the running software is too unstable for use in a user test or in cases where only one of the interface alternatives has been implemented.

In general, estimates of the relative advantage of one interface over the other were much better than estimates of the absolute time needed by users to perform various tasks. GOMS analyses and heuristic estimation were about equal for relative estimates, so heuristic estimation might be recommended based on its lower costs. GOMS analyses were superior for absolute estimates, however.

As a final conclusion, the results from this study show that performance estimates from both heuristic estimation and GOMS analyses are highly variable, with the absolute estimates from heuristic estimators being extremely variable. It is therefore highly recommended not to rely on estimates from a single usability specialist. Instead, one should gather estimates from several specialists, use the mean value, and keep in mind that the true value is likely to be somewhat different. Even so, performance estimates provide reasonable ball-park values that can be used as the basis for cost-benefit decision-making in a usability engineering process, and they would have led to the correct decision 100% of the time in the case study presented here, assuming that at least three independent estimates were collected.

It would be interesting to consider semi-formal estimation methods that might combine the best of the GOMS and heuristic approaches for some kind of "back of the envelope" type estimation procedures. It is likely that one of the reasons for the lower variability of the GOMS estimates was the use of a single, specified procedure for arriving at the estimates, and a less formal procedure might still be of some help at getting better estimates.

This study has focused on expert user performance, even though other usability parameters such as learnability are more important for the success of many user interfaces. In principle, one can use most of the same methods (except GOMS) to estimate system learnability. Unfortunately, there is no way of extrapolating the relative accuracy of the methods for this purpose from the current study.

Acknowledgments

The authors would like to thank Erik Nilsen of Lewis and Clark College for collecting data from his students on their GOMS analyses of the two interfaces. We also thank Professor Nilsen's students for participating in the study. The analyses and conclusions based on this data in this paper is solely the responsibility of the authors of the present paper, and does not necessarily correspond to the positions of study participants. The authors would like to thank Rob Fish, Erik Nilsen, and the anonymous referees for helpful comments on previous versions of the manuscript.

References

1. Bellotti, V. (1988). Implications of current design practice for the use of HCI techniques. In Jones, D.M., and Winder, R. (Eds.), *People and Computers IV,* Cambridge University Press, Cambridge, U.K., 13–34.

2. Card, S.K., Moran, T.P., and Newell, A. (1983). *The Psychology of Human–Computer Interaction.* Erlbaum Associates, Hillsdale, NJ.

3. Gray, W.D., John, B.E., and Atwood, M.E. (1992). The precis of project Ernestine, or, an overview of a validation of GOMS. *Proc. ACM CHI'92* (Monterey, CA, 3–7 May), 307–312.

4. Jeffries, R., Miller, J.R., Wharton, C., and Uyeda, K.M. (1991). User interface evaluation in the real world: A comparison of four techniques. *Proc. ACM CHI'91* (New Orleans, LA, 27 April–2 May), 119–124.

5. Karat, C., Campbell, R., and Fiegel, T. (1992). Comparisons of empirical testing and walkthrough methods in user interface evaluation. *Proc. ACM CHI'92* (Monterey, CA, 3–7 May), 397–404.

6. Mack, R.L., and Nielsen, J. (1993). Usability inspection methods. *ACM SIGCHI Bulletin* **25**, 1 (January).

7. Mantei, M.M., and Teorey, T.J. (1988). Cost/benefit analysis for incorporating human factors in the software lifecycle. *Communications of the ACM* **31**, 4 (April), 428–439.

8. Nielsen, J. (1992a). The usability engineering life cycle. *IEEE Computer* **25**, 3 (March), 12–22.

9. Nielsen, J. (1992b). Finding usability problems through heuristic evaluation. *Proc. ACM CHI'92* (Monterey, CA, 3–7 May), 373–380.

10. Nielsen, J. (1992c). Reliability of severity estimates for usability problems found by heuristic evaluation. In *Digest of Posters and Short Talks, ACM CHI'92 Conference* (Monterey, CA, 3–7 May), 129–130.

11. Nielsen, J. (1993a). *Usability Engineering,* Academic Press, San Diego, CA.

12. Nielsen, J. (1993b). Heuristic evaluation. In Nielsen. J., and Mack, R.L. (Eds.), *Usability Inspection Methods,* book under preparation.

13. Nielsen, J., and Molich, R. (1990). Heuristic evaluation of user interfaces. *Proc. ACM CHI'90* (Seattle, WA, 1–5 April), 249–256.

14. Olson, J.R., and Nilsen, E. (1988). Analysis of the cognition involved in spreadsheet software interaction. *Human–Computer Interaction* **3**, 4, 309–349.

15. Olson, J.R., and Olson, G.M. (1990). The growth of cognitive modeling in human–computer interaction since GOMS. *Human–Computer Interaction* **5**, 2&3, 221–265.

An Evaluation of Earcons for Use in Auditory Human-Computer Interfaces

Stephen A. Brewster, Peter C. Wright and Alistair D. N. Edwards

Department of Computer Science
University of York
Heslington
York, Y01 5DD, UK.
Tel.: 0904 432762
sab@minster.york.ac.uk

ABSTRACT

An evaluation of earcons was carried out to see whether they are an effective means of communicating information in sound. An initial experiment showed that earcons were better than unstructured bursts of sound and that musical timbres were more effective than simple tones. A second experiment was then carried out which improved upon some of the weaknesses shown up in Experiment 1 to give a significant improvement in recognition. From the results of these experiments some guidelines were drawn up for use in the creation of earcons. Earcons have been shown to be an effective method for communicating information in a human-computer interface.

KEYWORDS

Auditory interfaces, earcons, sonification

INTRODUCTION

The use of non-speech audio at the user-interface is becoming increasingly popular due to the potential benefits it offers. It can be used to present information otherwise unavailable on a visual display for example mode information [9] or information that is hard to discern visually, such as multi-dimensional numerical data [4]. It is a useful complement to visual output because it can increase the amount of information communicated to the user or reduce the amount the user has to receive through the visual channel. It makes use of the auditory system which is powerful but under-utilised in most current interfaces. There is also psychological evidence to suggest that sharing information across different sensory modalities can actually improve task performance (see [2] section 3.1). Having redundant information gives the user two chances of identifying the data; if they cannot remember what an icon looks like they may be able to remember what it sounds like. The foveal area of the retina (the part of greatest acuity) subtends an angle of only two degrees around the point of fixation [12]. Sound, on the other hand, can be heard from 360 degrees without the need to concentrate on an output device, thus providing greater flexibility. Sound is also good at capturing a user's attention whilst they are performing another task. Finally, the graphical interfaces used on many modern computers make them inaccessible to visually disabled users.

Providing information in an auditory form could generally help solve this problem and allow visually disabled users the same facilities as the sighted.

This evaluation is part of a research project looking at the best ways to integrate audio and graphical interfaces. The research aims to find the areas in an interface where the use of sound will be most beneficial and also what types of sounds are the most effective for communicating information.

One major question that must be answered when creating an auditory interface is: What sounds should be used? Brewster [2] outlines some of the different systems available. Gaver's *auditory icons* have been used in several systems, such as the SonicFinder [5], SharedARK [6] and ARKola [7]. These use environmental sounds that have a semantic link with object they represent. They have been shown to be an effective form of presenting information in sound. One other important, and as yet untested, method of presenting auditory information is the system of *earcons* [1, 13, 14,]. Earcons are abstract, synthetic tones that can be used in structured combinations to create sound messages to represent parts of an interface. Blattner *et al.* define earcons as "non-verbal audio messages that are used in the computer/user interface to provide information to the user about some computer object, operation or interaction". Earcons are composed of motives, which are short, rhythmic sequences of pitches with variable intensity, timbre and register.

One of the most powerful features of earcons is that they can be combined to produce complex audio messages. Earcons for a set of simple operations, such as 'open', 'close', 'file' and 'program', could be created. These could then be combined to produce, for example, earcons for 'open file' or 'close program'.

As yet, no formal experiments have been conducted to see if earcons are an effective means of communicating information using sound. Jones & Furner [8] carried out a comparison between earcons, auditory icons and synthetic speech. Their results showed that subjects preferred earcons but were better able to associate auditory icons to commands. Their results were neither extensive nor detailed enough to give a full idea of whether earcons are useful or not. This paper seeks to discover how well earcons can be recalled and recognized. It does not try to suggest uses for earcons in the interface. The first experiment described attempts to discover if earcons are better than unstructured bursts of sound and tries to identify the best types of timbres to use to convey information. Blattner *et al.* suggest the use of simple timbres such as sine or square waves but psychoacoustics (the study of the perception of sound) suggests that complex musical instrument timbres may be more effective [10]. The second experiment uses the results of the first to create new earcons to overcome some of the difficulties that came to light. Some guidelines are then put forward for use in the creation of earcons.

EXPERIMENT 1

Figure 1: Rhythms and pitch structures for Folder, File and Open used in Experiment 1

Sounds Used

An experiment was designed to find out if structured sounds such as earcons were better than unstructured sounds for communicating information. Simple tones were compared with complex musical timbres. Rhythm and pitch were also tested as ways of differentiating earcons. According to Deutsch [3] rhythm is one of the most powerful methods for differentiating sound sources. Figure 1 gives some examples of the rhythms and pitch structures used for the different types of objects in the experiment. The experiment also attempted to find out how well subjects could identify earcons individually and when played together in sequence.

Three sets of sounds were created:

    1. The first set were synthesised musical timbres: piano, brass, marimba and pan pipes. These were produced by a Roland D110 synthesiser. This set had rhythm information.

    2. The second set were simple timbres: sine wave, square wave, sawtooth and a 'complex' wave (this was composed of a fundamental plus the first three harmonics.

Each harmonic had one third of the intensity of the previous one). These sounds were created by SoundEdit. This set also had rhythm information.

    3. The third set had no rhythm information; these were just one second bursts of sound similar to normal system beeps. This set had timbres made up from the previous two groups.

The sounds for all sets were all played through a Yamaha DMP 11 mixer controlled by an Apple Macintosh and presented using external loudspeakers.

Experimental Design

Three groups of twelve subjects were used. Half of the subjects in each group were musically trained. Each of the three groups heard different sound stimuli. The musical group heard set 1 described in the previous section. The simple group heard set 2 and the control group heard set 3. There were four phases to the experiment. In the first phase subjects heard sounds for icons. In the second they heard sounds for menus. In the third phase they were tested on the icon sounds from phase I again. Finally, the subjects were required to listen to two earcons played in sequence and give information about both sounds that were heard.

Phase I

The subjects were presented with the screen shown in Figure 2. Each of the objects on the display had a sound attached to it. The sounds were structured as follows. Each *family* of related items shared the same timbre. For example, the paint application, the paint folder and paint files all had the same instrument. Items of the same *type* shared the same rhythm. For example, all the applications had the same rhythm. Items in the *same* family and type were differentiated by pitch. For example, the first Write file was C below middle C and the second Write file was G below that. In the control group no rhythm was information was given so types were differentiated by pitch also. The icons were played one-at-a-time in sequence to the subjects for them to learn. The whole set of icons was played three times.

When testing the subjects the screen was cleared and some of the earcons were played back. The subject had to supply what information they could about type, family and number of the file of the earcon they heard. When scoring, a mark was given for each correct piece of information supplied.

Phase II

This time earcons were created for menus. Each *menu* had its own timbre and the *items* on each menu were differentiated by rhythm, pitch or intensity. The screen shown to the users to learn the earcons is given in Figure 3. The subjects were tested in the same way as before but this time had to supply information about menu and item.

Phase III

This was a re-test of phase I but no further training time was given and the earcons

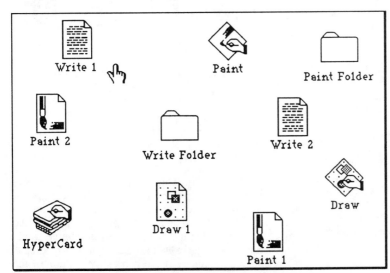

Figure 2: The Phase I icon screen

were presented in a different order. This was to test the subjects to see if they could remember the original set of earcons after having learned another set.

Phase IV

This was a combination of phases I and II. Again, no chance was given for the subjects to re-learn the earcons. The subjects were played two earcons, one followed by another, and asked to give what information they could about each sound they heard. The sounds they heard were from the previous phases and could be played in any order

MENU 1	MENU 2	MENU 3
OPEN	SAVE	UNDO
CLOSE	COPY	EDIT
DELETE	PRINT	
CREATE		

Figure 3: The Phase II menu screen

(i.e. it could be menu then icon, icon then menu, menu then menu or icon then icon). This would test to see what happened to the recognition of the earcons when played in sequence. A mark was given for any correct piece of information supplied.

Results and Discussion

From Figure 4 it can be seen that overall the musical earcons came out best in each phase. Unfortunately this difference was not statistically significant.

Phase I: A between-groups ANOVA was carried out on the family scores (family was differentiated by timbre) and showed a significant effect (F(2,33)= 9.788, p<0.0005). A Sheffe F-test showed that the family score in the musical group was significantly better than the simple group (F(2,33) =6.613, p<0.05). This indicates that the musical instrument timbres were more easily recognised than the simple tones proposed by Blattner *et al*. There were no significant differences between the groups in terms of type (differentiated by rhythm). Therefore, the rhythms used did not give any better performance over a straight burst of sound for telling the types apart.

Phase II: The overall scores were significantly better than those for phase I. An ANOVA on the overall scores showed a significant effect (F(2,33)=5.182, p<.011). This suggests that the new rhythms were much more effective (as the timbres were similar). The simple and musical groups performed similarly which was to be expected as both used the same rhythms. Sheffe F-test showed both were significantly better than the control group (musical vs. control F(2,33)=6.278, p<0.05, simple vs. control F(2,33)= 8.089, p<0.05). Again, this was to be expected as the control group had only pitch to differentiate items. This shows that if rhythms are used correctly then they can be very important in aiding recognition. It also shows that pitch alone is very difficult to use.

A Sheffe F-test showed that overall in phase II the musical group was significantly better than the control group (F(2,33)=4.5, p<0.05). This would indicate that the musical earcons used in this group were better than unstructured bursts of sound.

An ANOVA on the menu scores between the simple and musical groups showed an effect (F(1,22)=3.684, p<0.68). A Sheffe F-test showed that the musical instrument timbres just failed to reach significance over the simple tones (F(1,22)=3.684, p<0.10). A within-groups t-test showed that in the musical group the menu score (differentiated by timbre) was still significantly better than the item score (T(11)=2.69, p<0.05). This seems to indicate, once more, that timbre is a very important factor in the recognition of earcons.

Phase III: The scores were not significantly different to those in phase I indicating that subjects managed to remember the earcons even after doing another very similar task. This implies that, after only a short period of learning time, subjects could remember the earcons. This has important implications as it seems that subjects will remember earcons, perhaps even as well as icons. Tests could be carried out to see if subjects can remember the earcons after longer periods of time.

Phase IV: A within groups t-test showed that, in the musical group, the menu/item combination was significantly better than the family/type/file combination

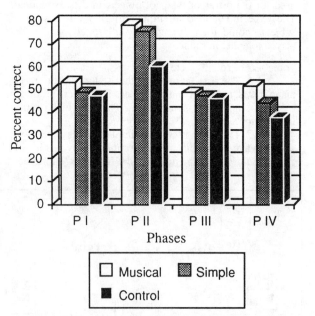

Figure 4: Breakdown of overall scores per phase for Experiment 1

(T(11)=2.58, p<0.05). This mimics the results for the musical group from phases I and II. When comparing phase IV with the other phases performance was worse in all groups with the exception of type recognition by the musical group and family recognition by the simple group. This indicates that there is a problem when two earcons are combined together. If the general perception of the icon sounds could be improved then this might raise the scores in phase IV

Summary of Experiment 1:   Some general conclusions can be drawn from this first experiment. It seems that earcons are better than unstructured bursts of sound at communicating information under certain circumstances. The issue of how this advantage can be increased needs further examination. Similarly, the musical timbres come out better than the simple tones but often by only small amounts. Further work is needed to make them more effective. The results also indicate that rhythm must be looked at more closely. In phase I the rhythms were ineffective but in phase II they produced significantly better results. The reason for this needs to be ascertained. Finally, the difficulties in recognising combined earcons must be reduced so that higher scores can be achieved.

EXPERIMENT 2

From the results of the first experiment it was clear that the recognition of the icon sounds was low when compared to the menu sounds and this could be affecting the score in phase IV. The icon sounds needed to be improved along the lines of the menu sounds which achieved much higher recognition rates.

Sounds Used

The sounds were redesigned so that there were more gross

Figure 5: New rhythms for Folder and File in Experiment 2 (cf. Figure 1)

differences between each earcon. This involved creating new rhythms for files, folders and applications each of which had a different number of notes. Each earcon was also given a more complex within-earcon pitch structure. Figure 5 shows the new rhythms and pitch structures for folder and file.

The use of timbre was also extended so that each family was given two timbres which would play simultaneously. The idea behind multi-timbral earcons was to allow greater differences between families; when changing from one family to another two timbres would change not just one. This created some problems in the design of the new earcons as great care had to be taken when selecting two timbres to go together so that they did not mask one-another.

Findings from research into the perception of sound were included into the experiment. In order to create sounds which a listener is able to hear and differentiate, the range of human auditory perception must not be exceeded. Frysinger [4] says "The characterisation of human hearing is essential to auditory data representation because it defines the limits within which auditory display designs must operate if they are to be effective". Moore [10] gives a detailed overview of the field of psychoacoustics and Patterson [11] includes some limits for pitch and intensity

ranges. This lead to a change in the use of register. In Experiment 1 all the icon sounds were based around middle C (261Hz). All the sounds were now in put into a higher register for example, the folder sounds were now made two octaves above middle C. The first files were an octave below middle C (130Hz) and the second files a G below that (98Hz). These frequencies were below the range suggested by Patterson and were very difficult to tell apart. In Experiment 2 the register of the first files were three octaves above middle C (1046Hz) and the second files at middle C. These were now well within Patterson's ranges.

In response to informal user comments from Experiment 1 a delay was put between the two earcons. Subjects had complained that they could not tell where one earcon stopped and the other started. A 0.1 second delay was used.

Method

The experiment was the same as the previous one in all phases but with the new sounds. A single group of a further twelve subjects was used. Subjects were chosen from the same population as before so that comparisons could be made with the previous results.

Results and Discussion

As can be seen from Figure 6, the new sounds performed much better than the previous ones. An ANOVA on the

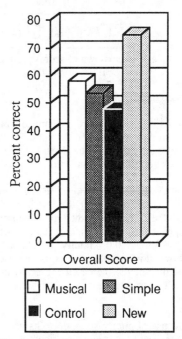

Figure 6: Percentage of overall scores with Experiment 2

overall scores indicated a significant effect ($F(3,44)=$ 6.169, $p<0.0014$). A Sheffe F-test showed that the new group was significantly better than the control group ($F(3,44)=5.426$, $p<0.05$) and the simple group ($F(3,44)=$ 3.613, $p<0.05$). This implies that the new earcons were more effective than the ones used in the first experiment. Comparing the musical group (which was the best in all phases of Experiment 1) with the new group we can see that the level of recognition in phases I and III has been raised to that of phase II (see Figure 7). However, t-tests revealed that phase IV was still slightly lower than the other phases. The overall phase I score of the new group was significantly better than the score in phase IV (T(11)=3.02, p<0.05). The overall recognition rate in phase I was increased because of a very significantly better type score (differentiated by rhythm etc.) in the new group (F(1,22)= 26.677, p<0.05). The scores increased from 49.1% in the musical group to 86.6%. This seems to indicate that the new rhythms were effective and very

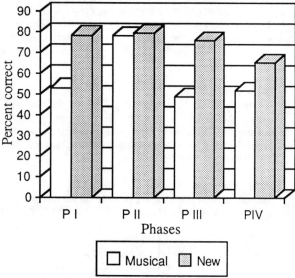

Figure 7: Breakdown of scores per phase with Experiment 2

easily recognised.

The scores in phase II were unchanged from the previous experiment as was expected. In phase III the scores were not significantly different to phase I, again indicating that the sounds are easily remembered.

In phase IV the overall score of the new group just failed to reach significance over the musical group (F(1,22)= 3.672, P<0.10). However, the type and family scores were both significantly better than in the musical group (type: F(1,22)=9.135, p<0.05, family: F(1,22)= 4.989, p<0.05). This shows that bringing the icon sound scores up to the level of the menus increased the score in phase IV but there still seems to be a problem when combining two earcons.

The new use of pitch also seems to have been effective. In phase I the new group got significantly better recognition of the file earcons than the musical group (F(1,22)=4.829, p<0.05). This indicates that using the higher pitches and greater difference in register made it easier for subjects to differentiate one from another.

The multi-timbral earcons made no difference in phase I. The family score for the new group was not significantly different to the score in the musical group. There were also no differences in phases II or III. However, in phase IV the

recognition of icon family was significantly better than in the musical group (F(1,22)=4.989, p<0.05). A further analysis of the data showed that there was no significant difference between the phase I and phase IV scores in the new group. However, the phase IV score for the musical group was worse than phase I (T(11)=4.983, p<0.05). This indicates that there was a problem in the musical group that was overcome by the new sounds. It may have been that in phases I, II and III only one timbre was heard and so it was clear to which group of earcons it belong (icons sounds or menu sounds). When two earcons were played together it was no longer so clear as the timbre could be that of a menu sound or an icon sound. The greater differences between each of the families when using multi-timbral earcons may have overcome this.

MUSICIANS AND NON-MUSICIANS

One important factor to consider is that of musical ability. Are earcons only usable by trained musicians or can non-musicians use them equally as effectively ? The earcons in the musical group from Experiment 1 were, on the whole, no better recognised by the musicians than the non-musicians. This means that non-musical user of a system involving earcons would have no more difficulties than a musician. Problems occurred in the other two groups of Experiment 1. Musicians were better at types and families in the simple group and families, menus and items in the control group. The results also show that there is no significant difference in performance between the musicians and non-musicians with the new sounds in Experiment 2. This seems to indicate that musical earcons are the most effective way of communicating information for general users.

GUIDELINES

From the results of the two experiments and studies of literature on psychoacoustics some guidelines have been drawn up for use in the creation of earcons. These should be used along with the more general guidelines given in [13, 14]. One overall result which came out of the work is that much larger differences than those suggested by Blattner *et al* must be used to ensure recognition. If there are only small, subtle changes between earcons then they are unlikely to be noticed by anyone but skilled musicians.

• *Timbre*: Use synthesised musical instrument timbres. Where possible use timbres with multiple harmonics. This helps perception and avoids masking. Timbres should be used that are subjectively easy to tell apart e.g. use 'brass' and 'organ' rather than 'brass1' and 'brass2'.
• *Pitch*: Do not use pitch on its own unless there are very big differences between those used (see *register* below). Complex intra-earcon pitch structures are effective in differentiating earcons if used along with rhythm. Some suggested ranges for pitch are: Max.: 5kHz (four octaves above middle C) and Min.: 125Hz - 150Hz (an octave below middle C).
• *Register:* If this alone is to be used to differentiate earcons which are otherwise the same, then large differences should be used. Three or more octaves difference give good rates of recognition.
• *Rhythm*: Make them as different as possible. Putting different numbers of notes in each rhythm was very

effective. Patterson (1982) says that sounds are likely to be confused if the rhythms are similar even if there are large spectral differences. Small note lengths might not be noticed so do not use notes less than eighth notes or quavers. In the experiments described here these lasted 0.125 sec.

• *Intensity*: Although intensity was not examined in this test some suggested ranges (from [11]) are: Max.: 20dB above threshold and Min.: 10dB above threshold. Care must be taken in the use of intensity. The overall sound level will be under the control of the user of the system. Earcons should all be kept within a close range so that if the user changes the volume of the system no sound will be lost. If any sound is too loud it may become annoying to the user and dominate the others. If any sound is too quiet then it may be lost.

• *Combinations*: When playing earcons one after another use a gap between them so that users can tell where one finishes and the other starts. A delay of 0.1 seconds is adequate. If the above guidelines are followed for each of the earcons to be combined then recognition rates should be sufficient.

FUTURE WORK
No research has been done to test the speed of presentation of earcons. The earcons took between 1 and 1.5 seconds to play. In a real application of earcons they would need to be presented so that they could keep up with activity in the interface. A further experiment would be needed to test the maximum rate of presentation obtainable at which the earcons would maintain their high rates of recognition.

CONCLUSIONS
The results indicate that earcons are an effective means of communication. The work shown has demonstrated that earcons are better for presenting information than unstructured bursts of sound. Musical timbres for earcons proved to be more effective than the simple tones proposed by Blattner *et al.*. The subtle transformations suggested by Blattner have been shown to be too small to be recognised by subjects and that gross differences must be used if differentiation is to occur. The results of Experiment 1 indicated that earcons were effective but needed refinements. The results from Experiment 2 show that high levels of recognition can be achieved by careful use of pitch, rhythm and timbre. Multi-timbral earcons were put forward and shown to help recognition under some circumstances. A set of guidelines has been suggested, based on the results of the experiments, to help a designer of earcons make sure that they will be easily recognisable by listeners. This research now means that there is a strong experimental basis to prove that earcons are effective. Developers can create interfaces that use them safe in the knowledge that they are a good means of communication.

ACKNOWLEDGEMENTS
We would like to thank all the subjects for participating in the experiment. Thanks also go to Andrew Monk for helping with the statistical analysis of the data.

This work is supported by SERC studentship 90310837.

REFERENCES
1. Blattner, M. Sumikawa, D. & Greenberg, R. (1989). Earcons and icons: Their structure and common design principles. *Human Computer Interaction*, 4(1), pp 11-44.

2. Brewster, S.A. (1992). *Providing a model for the use of sound in user interfaces*. University of York Technical Report YCS 169, York, UK.

3. Deutsch, D. (1980). The processing of structured and unstructured tonal sequences. *Perception and Psychophysics*, 28(5), pp 381-389.

4. Frysinger, S.P. (1990). Applied research in auditory data representation. In D. Farrell (Ed.) *Extracting meaning from complex data: processing, display, interaction*, Proceeding of the SPIE, 1259, pp 130-139.

5. Gaver, W. (1989). The SonicFinder: An interface that uses auditory icons. *Human Computer Interaction*, 4(1), pp 67-94.

6. Gaver, W. & Smith, R. (1990). Auditory icons in large-scale collaborative environments. In D. Diaper *et al.* (Eds.) *Human Computer Interaction - INTERACT '90*, Elsevier Science Publishers B.V. (North Holland), pp 735-740.

7. Gaver, W., Smith, R. & O'Shea, T. (1991). Effective sounds in complex systems: the ARKola simulation. *CHI'91 Conference proceedings, Human Factors in Computing Systems, "Reaching through technology"* New Orleans, pp 85-90, ACM Press: Addison-Wesley.

8. Jones, S.D. & Furner, S.M. (1989). The construction of audio icons and information cues for human-computer dialogues. *Contemporary Ergonomics, Proceedings of the Ergonomics Society's 1989 Annual Conference*, T. Megaw (Ed.)

9. Monk, A. (1986). Mode Errors: A user-centered analysis and some preventative measures using keying-contingent sound. *IJMMS*, 24, pp 313-327.

10. Moore, B.C.J. (1989). *An Introduction to the Psychology of Hearing*, pp 1-10. London: Academic Press.

11. Patterson, R.D. (1982). *Guidelines for auditory warning systems on civil aircraft*, C.A.A. Paper 82017, Civil Aviation Authority, London.

12. Rayner, K. & Pollatsek, A. (1989). *The Psychology of Reading*, pp 9-10. Englewood Cliffs, New Jersey: Prentice-Hall International, Inc.

13. Sumikawa, D. (1985). *Guidelines for the integration of audio cues into computer user interfaces*, Lawrence Livermore National Laboratory Technical Report, UCRL 53656.

14. Sumikawa, D., Blattner, M., Joy, K. & Greenberg, R. (1986). *Guidelines for the syntactic design of audio cues in computer interfaces*, Lawrence Livermore National Laboratory Technical Report, UCRL 92925.

SYNTHESIZING AUDITORY ICONS

William W. Gaver

Rank Xerox Cambridge EuroPARC
61 Regent Street, Cambridge CB2 1AB, U.K.
gaver@europarc.xerox.com

ABSTRACT

Auditory icons add valuable functionality to computer interfaces, particularly when they are parameterized to convey dimensional information. They are difficult to create and manipulate, however, because they usually rely on digital sampling techniques. This paper suggests that new synthesis algorithms, controlled along dimensions of events rather than those of the sounds themselves, may solve this problem. Several algorithms, developed from research on auditory event perception, are described in enough detail here to permit their implementation. They produce a variety of impact, bouncing, breaking, scraping, and machine sounds. By controlling them with attributes of relevant computer events, a wide range of parameterized auditory icons may be created.

KEYWORDS

interface techniques, multimedia, auditory interfaces, sound

INTRODUCTION

Over the last several years, I have been developing a strategy for creating *auditory icons*, everyday sounds mapped to computer events by analogy with everyday sound-producing events [6, 8]. Auditory icons are like sound-effects for computers: Objects make sounds as they are selected, dragged, bumped against one another, opened, activated, and thrown away. But they are not designed merely to provide entertainment; rather they convey information about events in computer systems, allowing us to listen to computers as we do to the everyday world.

A number of systems have been created which illustrate the potential for auditory icons to convey useful information about computer events. In particular, these systems suggest that sound is well suited for providing information:

- about previous and possible interactions,
- indicating ongoing processes and modes,
- useful for navigation, and
- to support collaboration.

For instance, the SonicFinder used sound to supplement a single-threaded, single-user graphical interface [7].

Although most of the sounds indicated simple user-initiated actions, the system demonstrated that sound could be incorporated in the interface in natural and useful ways.

More powerful functions for sound were demonstrated in the ARKola system [9]. This used the SharedARK environment [12] to create a simulation of a manufacturing plant which participants ran with or without auditory icons. Our observations suggested that sounds changed both the way participants perceived the plant and the way they worked together. These two examples, along with several others, indicate that auditory icons can both complement and supplement more traditional graphical cues in interface design.

PARAMETERIZED ICONS

Auditory icons not only reflect categories of events and objects as visual icons do, but are *parameterized* to reflect their relevant dimensions as well. That is, if a file is large, it sounds large. If it is dragged over a new surface, we hear that new surface. And if an ongoing process starts running more quickly, it sounds quicker.

The possibility of parameterizing icons, whether auditory or visual, has largely been neglected in interface design [though see 4]. But parameterized icons can serve as more than mere labels for their referents, providing rich sources of information about relevant dimensions such as size, age, or speed as well. Parameterization allows single objects or events to be assessed along a number of dimensions. In addition, it creates families of icons that retain perceptual similarity while allowing comparison among members [c.f. 1]. In general, parameterized icons allow a great deal of information to be conveyed perceptually rather than symbolically.

Creating Parameterized Auditory Icons

Unfortunately, it is difficult to parameterize auditory icons because it is difficult to control a virtual source of a sound along relevant dimensions. Standard synthesis techniques have been developed for creating music, and thus afford changes of a sound's pitch, loudness, duration and so forth. But they do not make it easy to change a sound from indicating a large wooden object, for instance, to one specifying a small metal one. It is easy to create a wide variety of beeps and hums using standard synthesis techniques, but difficult to create and manipulate sounds along dimensions that specify events in the world.

Because of the limitations of standard synthesis techniques, interfaces using auditory icons have relied on digital sampling in their implementations. Desired sounds are captured by recording them on a computer, shaped by a designer, then played back and manipulated under the control of the interface (see Appendix A for a brief introduction to sampling and synthesis). This enables the use of much more complex and realistic sounds than can be created by readily available synthesis algorithms. However, there are several drawbacks of sampling that limit its utility as a technique for creating and using auditory icons:

- It is difficult to capture an actual event that sounds like what is desired, because sounds are invariably coloured by the technologies used to record them.

- Shaping recorded sounds along dimensions relevant for auditory icons is difficult because available software is designed for making music.

- Real-time modification of sounds on playback is even more limited.

- The amount of memory needed for complex auditory interfaces is often prohibitive (on the order of 10K bytes per second of sound).

These factors constrain the possibilities for designing auditory icons, and make their creation difficult and time-consuming.

In this paper, I suggest an alternative in the form of a new type of synthesis algorithm developed as a result of basic research on auditory event perception [6, 8], and describe several examples in sufficient detail to allow readers to implement and explore them. These algorithms allow sounds to be specified in terms of their sources rather than their acoustic attributes. They promise to overcome both the limitations of traditional synthesis algorithms and of sampling by allowing parameterized auditory icons to be specified along dimensions of virtual source events.

ACOUSTIC INFORMATION FOR EVENTS

Creating algorithms that allow synthesis of virtual events implies an understanding of the acoustic information for event attributes – how sounds indicate the material or size of an object, for instance. Such attributes often have very complex effects on sounds, effects that must be described as functions of frequencies and amplitudes over time that describe the *partials*, or frequency components, that make up a sound. If these functions are understood, source attributes can be specified directly, instead of via separate controls over partial frequencies, amplitudes, and durations. But how can we determine what these functions are?

Analysis and Synthesis of Events

One approach to this problem is suggested by the analysis and synthesis methods [11] used by computer musicians to capture the relevant properties of traditional instrument sounds (Figure 1). This approach involves recording sounds that vary along dimensions of interest and analyzing their acoustic structure using Fourier analysis or similar techniques. Hypotheses about acoustic information suggested by the analysis can be tested by synthesizing

sounds based on simplified versions of the data. For instance, if one supposes that the temporal features of a sound indicates the event that caused it, but that its frequency makeup is irrelevant, one might use the amplitude contour from the original sound to modify a noise burst. The hypothesis can then be assessed simply by listening to the result.

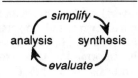

Figure 1: Traditional analysis and synthesis.

In practice, however, it is often difficult to identify the acoustic information for events in the mass of data produced by acoustic analyses. Thus it is useful to supplement them with analyses of the mechanical physics of the event itself (see Figure 2). Studying the physics of sound-producing events is useful both in suggesting perceptible source attributes and in indicating the acoustic information for these attributes. Acoustic analyses help both in checking the adequacy of physical models and in evaluating particular parameters. Finally, the resulting models can provide the basis for synthesis algorithms that allow sounds to be specified in terms of sources attributes.

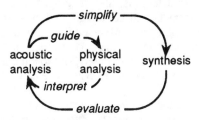

Figure 2. Analyzing and synthesizing events requires physical as well as acoustic analyses.

In the following sections, I discuss several case studies of events that have been studied in this manner and describe the synthesis algorithms that have resulted. The algorithms have been chosen for their utility in creating auditory icons, and are described in order of their complexity. I start with the sounds made by mechanical impacts, which involve a simple interaction of objects. Next I describe how more complex bouncing, breaking, and spilling sounds can be produced by specifying the temporal patterning of a series of impacts. A third algorithm distinguishes objects from the interactions that cause them to make sound, allowing the same virtual object to be hit and then scraped. Finally, I describe an algorithm for producing machine-like sounds, showing that high-level attributes of complex events may be synthesized directly.

IMPACT SOUNDS

Many of the sounds we hear in the everyday world involve one solid impacting against another. Tapping on an object, placing it against another, letting it fall – all involve impact sounds. In the interface, impact sounds are useful in the design of a variety of auditory icons that indicate events such as selecting a file, moving it over another, or attaching one object to another.

Several studies have explored the perceptible attributes of impact events and the acoustic information about them. In this section, I briefly review these studies, then show how the information they provide can be used to create a synthesis algorithm that allows impact sounds to be specified along dimensions of the virtual source.

Mallet Hardness, Material, and Size

Freed [5] studied people's perception of the hardness of mallets used to strike objects. He recorded the sounds made by hitting cooking pans with mallets of various hardnesses, asked people to judge hardness from the sounds, and used a model of the peripheral auditory system to analyze the acoustic correlates of their judgements. He found that the ratio of high to low frequency energy in the sounds and its change over time served as the most powerful predictors of subjects' hardness judgements. To a good approximation, then, mallet hardness is conveyed by the relative presence of high and low frequency energy.

I studied the acoustic information available for the length and material of struck wood and metal bars and people's abilities to perceive these attributes [6]. I recorded and analyzed the sounds made by wood and metal bars of several different lengths, and developed a model of the physics of impacts that combined analytical solutions to the wave equation for transverse vibrations in a bar [e.g., 10] with empirical measurements of damping and resonance amplitudes. This model was used both to aid interpretation of the acoustic analyses and to synthesize new tokens.

The material of the bars made several effects on the sounds they made. Perhaps most important, materials have characteristic frequency-dependent damping functions: the sounds made by vibrating wood decay quickly, with low-frequency partials lasting longer than high ones, while the sounds made by vibrating metal decay slowly, with high-frequency partials lasting longer than low ones. In addition, metal sounds have partials with well-defined frequency peaks, while wooden sound partials are smeared over frequency space. These results accord with Wildes and Richards' [14] physical analyses of the audible effects of the internal friction characterizing different materials, which show that internal friction determines both the damping and definition of frequency peaks.

Changing the length of a bar, on the other hand, simply changes the frequencies of the sound it produces when struck, so that short bars make high-pitched sounds and long bars make low ones. However, the effects of length may interact with the effects of material. For instance, frequencies change monotonically with length, but the frequency of the partial with the highest amplitude depends on material and thus may change nonlinearly with length [6]. These nonlinearities – and the perceptual confusion they cause – may be avoided by simplifying the model so that partial amplitudes do not depend on material.

A Synthesis Algorithm for Impact Sounds

These results may be captured in a synthesis model that uses frequency and amplitude functions to constrain a formula for describing exponentially decaying sounds. This formula describes a complex wave created by adding together a number of sine waves with independent initial amplitudes and exponential decay rates:

$$G(t) = \Sigma_n \, \Phi_n \; e^{-\delta_n t} \; \cos\omega_n t \qquad (1)$$

where $G(t)$ describes the waveform over time, Φ_n is the initial amplitude, δ_n the damping constant, and ω_n the frequency of partial n.

This formula has two properties that make it a useful foundation for synthesizing auditory icons. First, its components map well to event attributes. Second, it can be made computationally efficient using trigonometric identities.

Mapping Synthesis Parameters to Source Attributes
By constraining the values used in this formula, useful parameters can be defined which correspond well to the attributes of impact sounds discussed above. The formula involves three basic components: the initial amplitudes of the partials Φ_n, their damping $e^{-\delta_n t}$, and their frequencies $\cos\omega_n t$. These can be set separately for each partial. However, these three components also correspond to information for mallet hardness and impact force, material, and size and shape respectively (see Table 1). Thus it is more useful to define patterns of behaviour over the partials for each component.

Table 1: Mapping Parameters to Events

Term	Effect	Event Attribute
Φ_n	initial amplitudes	mallet hardness; force or proximity
$e^{-\delta_n t}$	damping	material
$\cos\omega_n t$	partial frequencies	size; configuration

For example, the partial frequencies ω_n can be constrained to patterns typical of various object configurations. The sounds made by struck or plucked strings, for example, are harmonic, so that $\omega_n = n\omega_1$. The sounds made by solid plates, in contrast, are inharmonic and can be approximated by random frequency shifts made to a harmonic pattern. The sounds made by solid bars can be approximated by the formula $\omega_n = (2n + 1)^2/9$. Finally, the sounds made by rectangular resonators are given by the formula $\omega_{(p,q,r)} = c/2 \, \sqrt{(p^2/l^2 + q^2/w^2 + r^2/h^2)}$, where c is the velocity of sound, l, w, and h are the length, width and height of the box respectively, and p, q, and r are indexed from 0 [14]. An algorithm based on Formula 1, then, can be constrained so that one of these patterns is used to control the partial frequencies ω_n. In addition, ω_1 can be specified such that $\omega_1 \propto 1/size$ to reflect the size of the object (this affects all the other partial frequencies).

The initial amplitude of the partials, Φ_n, can be controlled by a single parameter corresponding to mallet hardness. Recalling that Freed's [5] results identified the ratio of high to low-frequency energy as a predictor of perceived mallet hardness, we might maintain a linear relationship among the partial's initial amplitudes, and use the slope from Φ_1 to control perceived hardness. Thus $\Phi_n = \Phi_1 + h(\omega_n - \omega_1)$, where h is the slope – note that h should often be negative, so that higher partials have less amplitude than low ones; thus a useful range of amplitude slopes might range from about -0.001 to 0.001. Φ_1 (and thus all the amplitudes) may also be changed to indicate impact force or proximity.

Finally, the damping constants for each partial (δ_n) can be controlled by a parameter corresponding to material. A useful heuristic is to set $\delta_n = \omega_n\delta_0$, with δ_0 ranging between about .001 for metal and about .5 for a highly-damped material like plastic. This means that high harmonics will die out relatively quickly for highly damped materials and last longer for less damped materials (e.g., metal, which has low damping, tends to ring; wood, which is highly damped, tends to thunk). This strategy is suggested both by Wildes and Richards [14], and by my own research [6].

In sum, Formula 1 can be controlled by parameters that make effects corresponding to attributes of impact events. Controlling overall frequency corresponds to the object's size, while the pattern of partial frequencies corresponds to its configuration. The overall initial amplitude corresponds to the force or proximity of the impact, while the pattern of partial amplitudes corresponds to mallet hardness. Finally, the degree of damping corresponds well to the virtual object's material. By controlling these five parameters, then, a wide range of sounds can be created which vary over several useful dimensions.

An Efficient Algorithm for Synthesis

Formula 1 is useful in allowing parameters to be defined in terms of source events. It is also attractive because it can be implemented in a computationally efficient way.

An efficient implementation of this formula relies on Euler's relationship $e^{i\omega t} = \cos\omega t + i\sin\omega t$ to rewrite Formula 1 as:

$$S_n = \text{Re}[(a_n + ib_n)(p + iq)]$$
$$= \text{Re}[(a_np - b_nq) + i(b_np + a_nq)] \qquad (2)$$

where S_n is the nth sample, a_0 is the initial amplitude, $b_0 = 0$, $i = \sqrt{-1}$, $p = e^{-\delta t}\cos\omega t$ and $q = e^{-\delta t}\sin\omega t$. (A full derivation is available upon request.)

Samples can thus be generated by calculating p and q, setting a and b to the initial amplitude and 0, and applying equation 2. The output sample is the real part of the result, and a and b are updated to the real and imaginary parts respectively (see pseudocode in Figure 3). Computationally expensive sine and cosines need only be calculated once, and only four multiplications, one addition and one subtraction are needed for each partial for a given

sample. The efficiency of this implementation allows fairly complex impact sounds to be generated in realtime on many computers.

```
p = cos(freq * 1/samplerate) * power(e, -1 * damping.rate
        * 1/samplerate);
q = sin(freq * 1/samplerate) * power(e, -1 * damping.rate
        * 1/samplerate);
a = initial.amplitude;
b = 0;

repeat for duration.in.secs / samplerate:
    real.part = a * p - b * q;
    imaginary.part = b * p + a * q;
    a = real.part;
    b = imaginary.part;
    output = real.part;
end repeat;
```

Figure 3. Pseudocode for efficient generation of a exponentially-decaying cosine wave (equation 5).

BREAKING, BOUNCING, AND SPILLING

The impact algorithm can serve as a fundamental element in algorithms used to synthesize more complex sounds. For instance, an early example of analysis and synthesis of sound-producing events is Warren and Verbrugge's [13] study of breaking and bouncing sounds. In this study, they used acoustic analyses and a qualitative physical analysis to examine the auditory patterns that characterize these events, and verified their results by testing subjects on synthetic sounds.

Consider the mechanics of a bottle bouncing on a surface (Figure 4A). Each time the bottle hits the surface, it makes an impact sound that depends on its shape, size, and material (as discussed above). Energy is dissipated with each bounce so that, in general, the time between bounces and the force of each impact becomes less. Thus bouncing sounds should be characterized by a repetitive series of impact sounds with decreasing period and amplitude.

When a bottle breaks, on the other hand, it separates into several pieces of various sizes and shapes (Figure 4B). Thus a breaking sound should be characterized by an initial impact sound followed by several different, overlapping bouncing sounds, each with its own spectrum and period.

Acoustic analyses of bouncing and breaking sounds confirm this informal physical analysis. In addition,

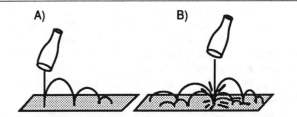

Figure 4. Bouncing (A) and breaking (B) sounds are characterized by the temporal patterning of a series of impacts [After Warren and Verbrugge, 13].

Warren and Verbrugge [13] found that people were able to distinguish tokens of bouncing and breaking sounds that were constructed by using these rules to splice tapes of impact sounds together.

Synthesized Breaking, Bouncing and Spilling

To create bouncing sounds, then, we need simply imbed the impact algorithm in another that calls it at exponentially decaying intervals. To create breaking sounds, the bouncing algorithm is imbedded in another algorithm that calls it with parameters specifying sources of different sizes at times corresponding to several exponentially decaying time series.

Several new event parameters become relevant for these algorithms: The initial height of the virtual object is indicated by the time between the first and second bounce, its elasticity by the percentage difference of delays between bounces, and the severity of breaking by the number of pieces produced. In addition, the asymmetry of the perceived object can be varied by adding randomness to the overall temporal pattern.

It becomes clear upon listening to sounds synthesized using this algorithm that although Warren and Verbrugge [13] claimed that information for breaking and bouncing depends only on temporal patterning, the perceived event depends on the virtual materials involved as well. For instance, if impacts specifying wooden objects are produced in a temporal pattern typical of breaking, we are liable to hear spilling rather than breaking. Similarly, if each of several virtual objects has different material properties, we again hear several spilling objects rather than breaking.

In sum, the impact algorithm described above can be used not only to generate the sounds made by mallets of different hardness striking virtual objects of a wide variety of shapes, sizes, and materials, but can also serve as the basis for more complex bouncing, breaking, and spilling sounds. As such, it serves as a research tool that allows the space of such sounds to be explored. Moreover, it provides an efficient method for generating families of related auditory icons. For instance, parameterized impact, bouncing, breaking and spilling sounds might be used to differentiate and provide details about the results of actions involving icons, windows, containers, and so forth.

FROM IMPACTS TO SCRAPING

The sounds made by impacts and patterns of impacts are generally useful for creating auditory icons, but it is desirable to have access to sounds made by a wider range of events. In particular, it would be useful to generate the sounds made by the same object being interacted with in different ways. Using such algorithms, auditory interface designers might map a particular file to a virtual object, and then hit, bounce, or scrape it depending on the relevant computer interaction.

In order to create such algorithms, it is necessary to separate the specification of a virtual object from that of the interaction that causes it to produce sound. This turns out to be possible because objects tend to vibrate only at certain invariant resonant frequencies. For example, the spectrogram in Figure 5 shows the sound made by a piece of glass being hit and then scraped across a rough surface. Note that despite the different temporal patterns of the sounds, the resonant modes of each are the same. These modes specify the object, then, interaction determines the temporal pattern and amount of energy introduced to each.

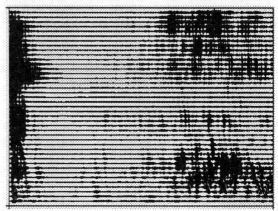

Figure 5. Spectrogram of a piece of glass being hit and then scraped: The resonant frequencies remain invariant over different interactions.

Because the effects of interactions and objects are distinct, each can be modelled separately. The resonant modes of a virtual object may be modelled as a bank of filters that allow energy to pass at particular frequencies. Interactions, then, can be specified by the pattern of energy passed through the filter bank.

Modelling Objects as Filter Banks

A simple formula for a bank of one-pole filters is:

$$y_n = \sum_m \Phi_m(c1_m x_n + c2_m y_{n-1} - c3_m y_{n-2}) \qquad (3)$$

where Φ_m is an amplitude scalar for partial m, y_n is the nth output, x_n is the nth input, and:

$$c1_m = (1 - c3_m) [(1 - c2_m{}^2)/4c3_m]^{.5}$$

$$c2_m = (4c3_m \cos 2\pi f_m)/(c3_m + 1)$$

$$c3_m = e^{-2\pi b}m;$$

where f_m is the frequency and b_m the bandwidth of partial m.

The parameters used to control the impact algorithm can also be used to control this sort of filter bank. However, manipulating filter bandwidths to control damping actually provides more information for material than do simple manipulations of sine wave damping. Bandwidth b is proportional to damping: the narrower the resonance peak of the filter the longer the resonant response to excitation. This correlation between damping and the smearing of partials in frequency space corresponds well to the characteristics of sounds made by materials such as wood or metal [6, 14].

Simulating Interactions with Input Waveforms

A virtual object can be defined by the characteristics of the filter bank described above. The waveform passed through the filter bank, then, models the interaction that causes the object to sound. In this section, I describe two sorts of input waveforms that I have explored. The first models impact forces, the second scraping.

When objects are struck, the input forces are characterized by short impulses such as those shown in Figure 6. The energy of such impulses is spread out over many frequencies: the pulse width reflects low frequency energy, while its angularity reflects high frequency components. This corresponds to Freed's characterization of mallet hardness [5]. Hard mallets introduce force suddenly to an object, deforming it quickly, and thus introduce a relatively high proportion of high frequency energy to the resonant object. Soft mallets, in contrast, deform as they hit the object, introducing energy relatively slowly, and thus the corresponding impulses are characterized by a high proportion of low frequency energy. Shaping the impulses used to excite a filter bank, then, is a physically realistic way to control perceived mallet hardness.

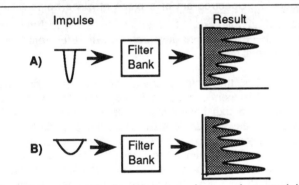

Figure 6. Sample impulse waveforms characterizing different impacts (see text).

When an object is scraped, force is applied more continuously. Scraping has been relatively unexplored in terms of its physical or perceptual attributes. However, an informal physical analysis suggests that the pattern of force on an object generated as it is scraped across a surface can be approximated by band-limited noise, where the center frequency of the noise corresponds to dragging speed, and the bandwidth to the roughness of the texture (see Figure 7). Although these parameters are only approximate, being less well motivated physically or psychologically than those used to model impacts, experience shows that a wide variety of realistic scraping noises can be produced using these heuristics.

In sum, the filter-based algorithm described in this section is based on a physically plausible model of sound producing events. By separating the parts of the model that specify the object from those specifying the interaction, a wide range of virtual sound-producing events can be simulated. The model can create any of the impact sounds that the algorithm described in the last section can.

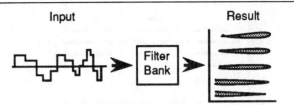

Figure 7. A sample force waveform characterizing a scrape with increasing speed.

In addition, it can also be used to create a variety of scraping sounds (and, potentially, any other sound involving solid objects).

The ability to generate the sounds of the same object being caused to sound by different interactions offered by this algorithm has great potential for the creation of auditory interfaces. It allows the design of parameterized auditory icons in which the same interface object (e.g., a file) might make sounds indicating a variety of events (e.g., selecting, dragging, opening).

MACHINE SOUNDS

Just as complex interactions such as scraping can be modelled by a few summarizing parameters, so might still more complex events be captured succinctly by high-level descriptions. For instance, another class of sounds useful for auditory icons are those made by small machines. Sampled machine sounds were used effectively in the ARKola simulation [9], indicating ongoing processes that were not visible on the screen. More generally, they might be used to indicate background processes such as printing or compiling in more traditional multiprocessing systems.

A detailed account of the mechanical physics of machinery seems prohibitively difficult. But just as the scraping waveforms described above model the overall parameters of a complex force rather than each of the contributing details, so an approximate model of machines might capture some of the high-level characteristics of the sounds they produce. In particular, three aspects of machine sounds seem relevant for modelling: First, the overall size of the machine is likely to be reflected in the frequencies of sounds it produces; second, most machines involve a number of rotating parts that can be expected to produce repetitive contributions to the overall sound; and third, the work done by the machine can be expected to affect the complexity of the sound.

FM Synthesis of Machine Sounds

I have been exploring an efficient algorithm for creating a variety of machine-like sounds that capture these properties. The basic strategy is to synthesize a sound using complex tones that vary in a repetitive way, indicating cyclical motion. The rate at which the virtual machine is working, then, can be indicated by repetition speed, the size of the virtual machine by the base frequency, and the amount of work by the bandwidth of the sounds (see Figure 8).

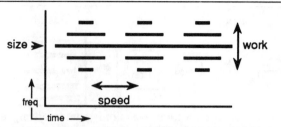

Figure 8.   Machine sounds can be characterized by a complex wave that varies repetitively over time.

This class of sound may be synthesized efficiently using Frequency Modulation (FM) synthesis [2]. FM synthesis involves modulating the frequency of a carrier wave with the output of a modulating wave. This produces a complex tone with a number of frequency components spaced equally around the carrier wave and separated from one another by the modulating frequency. The number of components (and thus the bandwidth of the sound) depends on the amplitude of the modulating wave (see Figure 9). Thus machine sounds can be created simply by associating the carrier frequency with the size of the virtual machine, setting the maximum amplitude of the modulating wave to the amount of work done by the virtual machine, and modulating the amplitude of the modulator according to the speed of the virtual machine (see pseudocode in Figure 10).

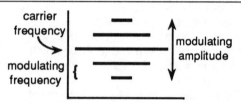

Figure 9.   FM synthesis, which allows simple control over complex sounds, is useful for generating machine sounds.

The resulting sounds are pitched humming noises that pulse at the speed of the virtual machine. When "work" is low, the throbbing is subtle; when it is high, it becomes quite pronounced. Moreover, the quality of the sounds can be varied by changing the ratio of modulating to carrier frequency: when the two are an integral multiple of one another, the resulting sound is harmonic, when they are not, the sound is inharmonic or noisy. Because the physical and acoustic analyses underlying this algorithm are far more approximate than those used for the various impact and scraping algorithms described above, the sounds it

```
mod.wave.amp = work * sin(speed * time/samprate);
mod.wave.sample = mod.wave.amp * sin(mod.freq *
    time/samprate);

output = amp * sin((size + mod.wave.sample) *
    time/samprate);
```

Figure 10: Pseudocode for generating machine-like sounds characterized by speed, size, and work.

produces are far less realistic. Nonetheless, they seem to capture some of the features of machine sounds well enough to use as indicators of ongoing processes in multiprocessing systems.

CONCLUSIONS

The algorithms described here allow the synthesis of a variety of everyday sounds specified in terms of attributes and dimensions of the events that cause them. Because they are based on a combination of acoustic and physical analyses and use relatively sophisticated synthesis techniques, they capture a great degree of the richness and complexity of their naturally produced counterparts. Because they are specialized for the classes of event they are to simulate, they are easy to implement, efficient, and can generate sounds in realtime on many computers. Finally, because they have been designed with potential applications in mind, the events they simulate are those useful for auditory icons.

These algorithms vary in their physical accuracy. Some are based on quantitative physical analyses, while others are based on more qualitative, informal descriptions of events. Moreover, even the quantitative analyses are only approximate. For instance, the physics of a struck bar of wood is much more complex than implied by the simple account given here. Insofar as these algorithms are approximate, the sounds they produce will differ from those made by real events.

Nonetheless, these algorithms do produce quite realistic sounds. Listeners comment that they have the impression of hearing an actual event rather than a synthesized sound. Insofar as the sounds do differ from those made by real events, they may be considered as "cartoon-sounds," sounds which capture the relevant features of their sources just as visual caricatures (or graphical computer icons) capture those of theirs. For the purposes of simulating sound-producing events, then, these algorithms are adequate. For the purpose of creating auditory icons, they show great potential, combining flexibility, intuitive controls, efficiency, and relevance.

I have specified these algorithms here in sufficient detail that readers may implement and explore them, in the hope that they will spur further research on parameterized auditory icons. These algorithms open many possibilities for the design of rich auditory interfaces. Impact and scraping sounds can be used to increase the tangibility of graphical objects in direct manipulation interfaces. Bouncing, breaking, and spilling sounds can be used to indicate events in virtual reality systems. Machine sounds might allow us to hear a remote printer as our job reaches the queue, and characteristics of the sound might tell us how fast the job is printing or how much time it will take. In sum, using these algorithms we can design interfaces that we can listen to the way we do to the everyday world.

ACKNOWLEDGEMENTS

I am grateful to Dave Woodhouse and Roy Patterson for help with the physical and acoustical analyses presented here, and to Don Norman, Anne Schlottmann, William Mace, Allan Maclean, Wendy Mackay, and Michael Turvey for valuable discussions about this research.

REFERENCES

1. Blattner, M., Sumikawa, D., & Greenberg, R. Earcons and icons: Their structure and common design principles. *Human-Computer Interaction*, 4 (1989).

2. Chowning, J. The synthesis of complex audio spectra by means of frequency modulation. *Journal of the Audio Engineering Society*, 21 (1973): 526-534.

3. Dodge, C., & Jerse, T. *Computer music: Synthesis, composition, and performance*. New York: Schirmer Books, 1985.

4. Draper, S., Waite, K., & Gray, P. Alternative bases for comprehensibility and competition for expression in an icon generation tool. *Proceedings of Interact'90* (Cambridge, UK. 27 - 31 August, 1990). Amsterdam: North Holland..

5. Freed, D. Auditory correlates of perceived mallet hardness for a set of recorded percussive sound events. *Journal of the Acoustical Society of America*, 87 (1990): 311-322.

6. Gaver, W. Everyday listening and auditory icons. Unpublished doctoral Dissertation, University of California, San Diego, 1988.

7. Gaver, W. The SonicFinder: An interface that uses auditory icons. *Human-Computer Interaction*, 4 (1989): 67-94.

8. Gaver, W. What in the world do we hear? An ecological approach to auditory source perception. *Ecological Psychology*, 5 (1993): 1-29.

9. Gaver, W., Smith, R. B., & O'Shea, T. Effective sounds in complex systems: The ARKola simulation. *Proceedings of CHI 1991* (New Orleans, April 28 - May 2, 1991) ACM, New York.

10. Lamb, H. *The dynamical theory of sound*. 2nd ed. New York, Dover, 1960.

11. Risset, J., & Wessel, D. Exploration of timbre by analysis and synthesis. In D. Deutsch (Ed.), *The psychology of music*. New York: Academic Press, 1982.

12. Smith, R. A prototype futuristic technology for distance education. *Proceedings of the NATO Advanced Workshop on New Directions in Educational Technology*. (Nov. 10 - 13, 1988, Cranfield, UK.)

13. Warren, W. & Verbrugge, R. Auditory perception of breaking and bouncing events: A case study in ecological acoustics. *Journal of Experimental Psychology: Human Perception and Performance*, 10 (1984): 704 - 712.

14. Wildes, R., & Richards, W. Recovering material properties from sound. Richards, W. (ed.), *Natural computation*. Cambridge, MA: MIT Press, 1988.

APPENDIX A: DIGITAL SAMPLING AND SYNTHESIS

Digital sampling and synthesis both rely on the fact that analog sound waves may be described by a stream of numbers (or *samples)* that represent the amplitude of the wave over time (see Figure 11). These samples, in turn, can be used to control a loudspeaker, recreating the sound.

As Figure 11 suggests, the accuracy with which a waveform may be represented depends on the sampling rate: waves at frequencies over 1/2 the sampling rate (the *Nyquist frequency*) cannot be specified unambiguously. Similarly, the number of bits per sample determines the different levels of amplitude that may be captured.

Digital sampling involves recording a sound, digitizing the waveform, and then recreating the waveform using the (possibly manipulated) samples.

Synthesis, in contrast, involves generating sample values algorithmically. Many synthesis algorithms rely on Fourier's theorem that complex waves may be analyzed – and thus synthesized – as the sum of many (possibly varying) sine waves. In any case, synthesis algorithms are merely methods for creating streams of numbers that describe sounds.

There are several software packages that facilitate synthesis (e.g., the Csound software from the MIT Media Lab, or Cmusic from UCSD, both of which can be obtained without charge for educational and research purposes). The algorithms described in this paper may be explored using such packages. However, for use in interfaces, these algorithms should be implemented as functions to be called by other software; the samples they produce can simply be sent to the onboard digital-to-analog converter just as sampled sounds are.

Clearly this is only a brief introduction to the basic concepts of digital sampling and synthesis. More detailed introductions to these topics may be found in several textbooks [e.g., 3].

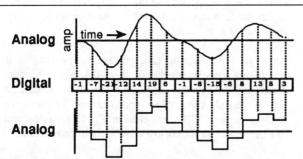

Figure 11. Analog waveforms can be represented as samples indicating the wave's amplitude over time.

Computer Aided Conversation for Severely Physically Impaired Non-speaking People

Norman Alm
MicroCentre
University of Dundee
Dundee, Scotland, U.K.
Tel: +44 382 23181
nalm@uk.ac.dund.mcs

John Todman
Psychology Department
University of Dundee,
Dundee, Scotland U.K.
Tel: +44 382 23181

Leona Elder
Business Studies
Department
Dundee Institute of
Technology
Dundee, Scotland, UK
Tel: +44 382 308000

A. F. Newell
MicroCentre
University of Dundee
Dundee, Scotland, U.K.
Tel: +44 382 23181
afn@uk.ac.dund.mcs

ABSTRACT This paper reports the development of a computer-aided conversation prosthesis which is designed for severely physically impaired non-speaking people. The research methodology was to model aspects of conversational structure derived from the field of conversation analysis within a prototype conversational prosthesis. The prototype was evaluated in empirical investigations which also suggested successful strategies for carrying out satisfying conversation using such a system. Two versions have been built and tested, one using an able-bodied operator to test the feasibility of creating conversation from prestored material, the second being used by a physically impaired non-speaking operator. The prototype demonstrated the advantages of this interface design in helping the user to carry out natural sounding and satisfying conversations.

KEYWORDS: human-computer interaction, user study, interface design, user observation, dialogue design, discourse analysis, user interfaces, retrieval models, search process, selection process, disability, speech synthesis

INTRODUCTION

People can be so severely physically impaired, either through paralysis or lack of muscle control, that they are unable to speak. Many such individuals can communicate via a keyboard (or special switches) connected to a speech synthesiser. However, the general lack of muscle control which usually accompanies loss of speech means that they are very slow in controlling any sort of input device. The result is that, even with currently available technical help, users typically only achieve 2-10 words per minute [7]. Unimpeded conversation, by contrast, usually proceeds at 120-200 words per minute [5], and slowness of communication and long silences tend to be interpreted negatively

by listeners [12,16]. Non-speaking users of current communication systems also have great difficulty in taking the initiative in conversations, and retaining conversational control [9].

The fact that most people whose physical impairments keep them from speaking are cognitively intact, and can understand what is communicated to them, makes their situation even more frustrating. The development of high quality speech synthesis and the widespread availability of portable computers would seem to offer a potential solution to this problem, but the progress thus far has been modest. Current systems either allow the user to build utterances word by word, giving the typical communication rate already cited of 2-10 words per minute, or allow the storage and retrieval of phrases and sentences. Although this could offer much higher communication rates, in practice users found it impractical to remember all but a small part of what they had stored, and how to access it [1].

TOWARDS A MORE INTELLIGENT COMMUNICATION AID

A more promising approach to this problem, however, is to have the communication system itself keep track of the user's conversation, and offer help in selecting the next thing to say. Rather than just passively storing material, such a system might use information about conversational structure and the pragmatics of dialogue to retrieve conversational items depending on what is currently happening in the conversation, and what would be likely candidates for the next thing to say.

Although, of course, conversation can be unpredictable, it is a highly rule-governed activity [3,17], and, 'an enormous amount of natural language is formulaic, automatic, and rehearsed, rather than propositional, creative, or freely generated' [Fillmore, cited in 6]. Thus the content of many conversations is to a certain extent predictable.

With Fillmore's observation as a starting point, a reasonable focus is to consider ways of aiding a user to store and retrieve reusable conversational material. Following the development of a predictive system which helps a user to open and close conversations and give feedback to the other speaker [2], work has been proceeding on developing ways to incorporate predictive and conversation modelling techniques into a system which would help a user to take part in topic discussion, drawing on a store of reusable conversational material.

The way that an interface is designed between the user and this store of reusable material should reflect the pragmatics of the conversation. The pragmatics of a language concerns how the language is used to accomplish interactional purposes. It is on the top of the hierarchy of language analysis which has the usual stages: lexical, syntactic, semantic, and pragmatic. To give an example, the utterance 'Could you pass me the salt?', stripped of its pragmatic component, is simply a request for information. More than semantics is needed to interpret this phrase as a polite request for action.

Pragmatic analysis is important both in interpersonal communication, and in human-computer interaction. [11,18]. In the application described here pragmatic considerations are important, both at the user-computer and user-listener interface. The interface with the system needs to be sensitive to what the user is wanting to accomplish in the dialogue with the other person, rather than operating at the low level of individual words which are being used. Such sensitivity would increase the speed of the communication and give a transparency to the computer operations which would allow the user to concentrate on the interaction. Interpreting the interaction with the other person in terms of pragmatics suggests a communication system which helps the user to accomplish certain interactional goals, rather than simply to send messages.

An aspect of designing for people with disabilities is that the requirement that a system be as easy to use as possible is not an optional, but an essential feature of a system where most users will need to exert a great deal of effort to make any sort of directed movement. In fact, we are all disabled in a number of ways from the point of view of a computer, particularly in the bandwidth by which we are able to communicate with it - it is just that some of us are more disabled than others [10].

Given the extreme slowness with which a severely impaired person would be able to input text for speaking, the assumption made in this research was that the items to be spoken would be entered in advance, in their own time, by the user.

The interface design began with a simulation using text written on index cards. In this simulation, a researcher took the role of a non-speaker, and prepared on file cards plausible contributions to a conversation on 'job inter-

views'. Conversations were then conducted with volunteers by means of the researcher pointing at a card whenever she wished to communicate what was on that card. The content of the card was then read out by another volunteer. Repeated runs of this system lead to the addition, deletion, and alteration of cards as problems became apparent through breakdowns in the conversation. The participants reported that they found the conversations reasonably natural, and control passed satisfactorily between the card user and the conversation partner.

LESSONS FROM CONVERSATION ANALYSIS

In addition to lessons learned from the above simulation, the interface design was also based on a number of aspects of conversational structure which have been established by conversation analysis research. The aspects which were incorporated were the predictability of opening and closing sequences, the alteration of speaking turns and perspectives, the orderly movement through topics in a conversation. and the importance of rapid and continuous feedback to the other speaker.

Opening and closing sequences

Opening and closing sequences are an important and frequently performed conversational feature. People do not just start talking about something with each other. They work at getting started, and they work at finishing the conversation gracefully [8,15]. If steps are left out of these sequences, the impression is created of rudeness, or lack of social training. A common opening sequence is GREETING & SMALLTALK. A common closing sequence is WRAPUP REMARKS & FAREWELL. For this prototype, the opening sequence was GREETING & INTRODUCTION, and the closing sequence was WRAPUP REMARKS & FAREWELL. Because the system was to be tested in a laboratory experimental situation, it was thought that introductory remarks were more appropriate than smalltalk.

Alternating perspectives

Conversation tends to consist of alternating turns, with alternating perspectives on the topic being expressed [4]. For the conversational content of the system it was decided to enable the user to have a dialogue on the subject of 'holidays'. The prototype allows the user to change perspectives and select an appropriate new set of texts by choosing three aspects of the topic of holidays: person, time, and orientation. The person aspect is either ME or YOU. The time aspects are PAST, PRESENT, FUTURE. The orientation aspects are WHERE, WHAT, HOW, WHEN, WHO, WHY. For instance, selecting ME-WHO-PAST would produce a set of candidate texts all on the subject of people who, in the past, accompanied the user on holiday, or who they met on past holidays (see Figure 1).

Topic shifts

The way speakers tend to move through topics in a conversation is governed by rules of relevance. It is usual to change topic in a 'step-wise' fashion, by small incremental moves [14]. The system presents the user with a set of candidate texts for speaking, which have been selected on the basis of the perspective chosen. The user may speak the texts in sequence, which produces a coherent narrative, or select and speak any text or any sequence of texts within the chosen set. If the user wishes to change topic, the selection of a new choice for one of the aspects will bring up a new set of texts, which share the other two aspects with the previous set. The user is free to reset two, or all three aspects if they wish.

Feedback remarks

Rapid and continuous feedback from listener to speaker is important in a conversation. The model of an active speaker and a passive listener is a simplification. Conversation is a simultaneous creation of all the participants. The speaker relies on a continuous stream of feedback from the listeners, and will tend to modify what they are saying and how they say it accordingly [20]. This is a particularly difficult problem for physically impaired non-speakers, who find it very difficult, or impossible, to give appropriate feedback to another speaker. (As a consequence they can be wrongly thought of as deaf, unintelligent, or not paying attention.) The importance of timing

of feedback remarks suggests that it is better to say something which is more or less appropriate than to take too long to say a precise remark. The system thus incorporates a feature developed in an earlier experimental prototype, which gives immediate output of randomly selected exemplars of a selected speech act [2]. For instance, selecting AGREE would result in phrases such as "I"m with you on that.', and 'Yes, I agree with you there.' Trials of the earlier prototype suggested that, with speech acts such as feedback remarks, users might accept a trade-off between speed and specificity [2]. This is not surprising, since, for many non-speaking people, the communication rate problem simply precludes them from using these speech acts effectively.

IMPLEMENTATION

The system was developed in Hypercard on a Macintosh computer with an external speech synthesiser. The intention was to have as simple a control procedure as possible, thus leaving the user free to concentrate on the interaction and not spend a great deal of time looking at the computer screen. Two types of user actions were envisaged : to speak, and to request more choices. The user employs a mouse to point and click over the relevant areas of the screen. An example of the interface in use is shown in Figure 1. When the user clicks on any of the text windows in the centre of screen the displayed text is spoken through the speech synthesiser. The displayed texts are replaced when the user selects a new perspective from the left part of the screen. On the right are a set of feedback

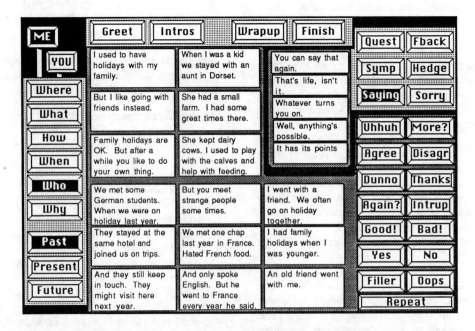

Figure 1 : Example of control screen in use

remarks. When one of these is selected, a suitable speech act of that category is spoken immediately through the speech synthesiser. Opening and closing sequences are selected from the top area of the screen. Also available are comments, which are intermediate between very general feedback remarks and fully specific content remarks. Thus, comments are phrases which are more effective if selected depending on the immediate context. A quick feedback remark might be to THANKS (e.g. 'Thanks very much.'). A comment might be a SAYING (e.g. 'Well, anything's possible, I suppose').

EVALUATION WITH AN ABLE-BODIED USER

The purpose of the initial evaluation was to determine the feasibility and observe the process of using such a system in conversation. Evaluations were done in the first instance with one able-bodied user and one physically impaired non-speaking user.

The system was first tested by a researcher loading it with conversational material about holidays. In all 1600 conversational items were put into the system. The items were stored in structure which mapped the categories of utterance described above, i.e. they were stored as openers/closers, comments, quick feedback remarks, and substantive contributions grouped by perspective.

Conversations were held with eight student volunteers on the subject of holidays. No time limit was put on the conversations. They varied from 5 to 15 minutes in length. For comparison purposes three conversations were held between two student volunteers talking about the same subject. All conversations were audio recorded and transcribed.

Below is an extract from one of the computer-aided conversations :

Computer-aided speaker :
    I went to France last year, to Marseilles.
Natural speaker :
    I've never visited Marseilles. I've sort of driven round the outskirts, but never actually gone into Marseilles.
Computer-aided speaker :
    Surprisingly, it's really beautiful.
Natural speaker :
    Really? I just imagine it as sort of a port, and just like any other large city, with nothing particularly interesting.
Computer-aided speaker :
    You expect a major port to be fairly grotty, don't you ?
Natural speaker :
    [LAUGH] That's right [LAUGH].

Computer-aided speaker :
    We also visited other places on the coast, but we decided to give St. Tropez a miss.
Natural speaker :
    That's one place I'd like to go.
Computer-aided speaker :
    I've heard it's pretty grotty now, and crowded.
Natural speaker :
    Really ? Oh, well, maybe give it a miss then. Of course, there's always the chance to see Brigitte Bardot there.
Computer-aided speaker :
    Whatever turns you on.

In the person-person conversations, the mean rate of speech was 144.4 words per minute (standard deviation = 4.9). The mean rate in the computer-aided dialogues was 88.2 words per minute (standard deviation = 20.6), with the individual rates for the computer user and her partners being 67.4 words per minute (standard deviation = 14.7) and 132.9 words per minute (standard deviation = 22.2) respectively. For the computer-aided dialogues, the mean length of utterance by the computer user (mean = 6.1 words) and that of her speaking partners (mean = 6.7 words) did not differ significantly in a one-tailed related t test (t (df=7) = 0.74; p > 0.05). In order to ensure that the speaking partner was not accommodating to the computer-aided speaker, a comparison was made between the normal speakers' mean utterance length in the dialogues with a computer-aided speaker (6.7 words) and in the person-person dialogues (6.0 words). An unrelated t test showed no significant difference between these means (t (df=12) = 0.85; p > 0.05).

The interface was designed so that the number of mouse clicks needed to output an utterance varied from 1 to 4. The minimum number occurred when the desired utterance was on the screen and merely had to be clicked on to be spoken. The maximum number occurred when the user made changes to all three aspects of the perspective and then clicked on a displayed text. The usage statistics showed that selections involving more than two mouse clicks were rare (2 out of 422 total selections).

In debriefing interviews, the volunteer conversationalists evaluated the communication system and the competence of the user positively and several expressed surprise at how normal and satisfactory the conversation had seemed, apart from the use of an artificial voice and the longer pause times preceding computer-user turns at speech (median value = 3.4 seconds). Preliminary analysis of ratings of the content of the conversations, obtained in a follow-up experimental study, suggests that the content of the computer-aided conversations was viewed at least as favourably as that of the person-person conversations. Further support for the 'normality' of the computer-aided conversations comes from sequential dependency analyses showing considerable similarity between the 'speech act structures' of the aided and unaided conversations (Chi-square (df=1) = 122; p < 0.0001) [19].

EVALUATION WITH A PHYSICALLY IMPAIRED NON-SPEAKING USER

Having established that holding a satisfying conversation with prestored material was possible, a version of the system was tested by a non-speaking physically impaired volunteer. The volunteer was a 20-year old young man with cerebral palsy, who had been non-speaking from birth. This person had a number of communication methods which he employed to try to convey his meaning. His primary means of communication was a word board with 400 words which he pointed to. He augmented this with some gestures and a few vocalisations for simple responses like 'Yes' and 'No'. He also had a portable speech output word and phrase storage device, which he used primarily for names of people and places and specialised words which were not on his board.

He was able to operate a mouse and to make single clicks with it. (For physically-impaired people who have more difficulty operating a mouse, a number of adaptations and emulators are available). In common with many people who have had no expressive language abilities, however, he had problems with reading. This meant that the interface needed to be simplified somewhat for ease and speed of use. A smaller number of text windows was used, and the perspective switching feature was changed to a simpler range of buttons to change to another topic.

The system was tested with this person not as a replacement, but in addition to his other devices and methods. The intention was to measure its effectiveness as a means to include longer narratives and conversational contributions than were possible with his existing methods, while leaving him free to use these as much as necessary. A series of conversations were held on the subject of a trip abroad for a disabled swimming competition which the person had done in the previous year. He held six conversations using his normal communication methods, and six with the addition of the system. Of his conversation partners, half were known to him, and the other half were strangers, who had never communicated with a non-speaker before. They were distributed equally between the system in use and system not in use conditions. A single-case study design was employed with an ABAB sequence, to allow for any learning effects. The conversations each lasted 15 minutes. They were all video-recorded and transcribed. Video recording was necessary in order to capture the non-speaker's gestural communication. All utterances in the transcriptions were coded using a classification system derived from Prutting and Kirchner [13]. Of particular interest were 'Initiators' - utterances which indicated a control over the interaction, which is normally difficult for non-speakers, and 'Responders' - responses to the other speaker's utterances.

The results were encouraging. It seemed subjectively clear that the non-speaker was making good use of the system during the times it was available, and that this had the effect of helping him to take a fuller part in the conversations. The objective measures, from the coded transcripts bore this out. The results are shown in Table 1. The mean number of words spoken by the speaking partners in the conversations is about the same, whether the system is in use or not. Using the system increases the non-speaker's mean number of words nearly 3½ times. Conversational control, as measured by the balance between 'Initiators' and 'Responders', also improved when the system was being used. The improvements in number of total words used and number of Initiators used were statistically significant

One unexpected outcome of the research was that the non-speaking volunteer has used the prototype system as a lecturing giving aid (Giving a talk, followed by answering questions from the audience). Using the system, he has given lectures in Scotland, the U.S. and Canada on the subject of his experiences as a non-speaking person. He has also been interviewed on local radio using the system.

	Non-speaker without system	Non-speaker with system
Mean number of words		
Natural speaker	917	999
Non-speaker	143	534
Mean number of initiators		
Natural speaker	48	50
Non-speaker	10	27
Mean number of responders		
Natural speaker	19	36
Non-speaker	87	71

Table 1 : Performance with and without the computer-aided conversation system

CONCLUSIONS

This work has indicated that it is possible to hold reasonably satisfying conversations using a computer-based communication system with prestored material, if appropriate material is available to the user in a suitable form. By applying principles derived from conversation analysis, a prototype system has been developed which helps a user to take part in a conversation in a way which is a marked improvement over existing systems, both in terms of amount of participation, and degree of conversational control exerted. The next step in this research will be to expand the conversational range of the system to cover multiple topics. In order to help the user cope with what will become a very large store of material, predictive techniques will be explored which will offer the user the continual opportunity to move out of the current topic area into other parts of the conversational database.

ACKNOWLEDGEMENTS

This research was supported by a grant from the research Initiatives Committee of Dundee University, and by a charitable donation from the Digital Equipment Corporation.

REFERENCES

1. Alm, N. Towards a conversation aid for severely physically disabled non-speaking people. Ph.D. Thesis, Dept. of Mathematics and Computer Science, University of Dundee, Dundee, Scotland, U.K., 1988.

2. Alm, N., Arnott, J. L., Newell, A. F. Prediction and conversational momentum in an augmentative communication system. *Communications of the ACM*. 35,5 (May 1992), pp 46-57.

3. Beattie, G. *Talk -- An Analysis of Speech and Nonverbal Behaviour*. Open University Press, Milton Keynes, 1983.

4. Duncan, S. Some signals and rules for taking speech turns in conversations. *Journal of Personality and Social Psychology*. 23, 2 (1972), pp 283-292.

5. Foulds, R. Communication rates for non-speech expression as a function of manual tasks and linguistic constraints. In *Proceedings of the International Conference on Rehabilitation Engineering*, (Toronto, Canada, 16-20 June). Rehabilitation Engineers Society of North America, Toronto, 1980, pp 83-87.

6. Gumperz, J. *Discourse Strategies*. Cambridge University Press, London, 1982, p 137.

7. Kraat, A. *Communication Interaction Between Aided and Natural Speakers: A State of the Art Report*. Canadian Rehabilitation Council for the Disabled, Toronto, 1985, p 82.

8. Laver, J. Communicative functions of phatic communion. In Laver, J. *Semiotic Aspects of Spoken Communication*. Edward Arnold, London, 1974.

9. Light, J. Interaction involving individuals using augmentative and alternative communication systems: state of the art and future directions. *Augmentative and Alternative Communication*. 4, 2 (June 1988), pp 66-82.

10. Macmillan, W. Computing for users with special needs and models of computer-human interaction. Proceedings CHI, 1992, (Monterey, California, May 3 - May 7, 1992) ACM, New York, 1992, pp 143-148.

11. Marcus, A. and van Dam, A. User-Interface Developments for the Nineties. *Computer*. 24,9 (1991), pp 49-57.

12. Newman, H. The sounds of silence in communicative encounters. *Communication Quarterly*. 30, 2 (Spring 1982), pp 142-149.

13. Prutting, C. and Kirchner, D. Applied pragmatics. In Gallacher, T. and Prutting, C., (eds.) *Pragmatic Assessment and Intervention Issues in Language*. College Hill Press, San Diego, 1983.

14. Sacks, H. Lecture 5, Spring 1972. University of California at Riverside, pp 15-16. Cited in Atkinson, J. and Heritage, J., (eds.) *Structures of Social Action - Studies in Conversation Analysis*. Cambridge University Press, London, 1985, p 198.

15. Schegloff, E. and Sacks, H. Opening up closings. *Semiotica*. 8 (1973), pp 289-327.

16. Scherer, K. Personality markers in speech, in Scherer, K., ed. *Social Markers in Speech*. Cambridge University Press, London, 1979.

17. Stubbs, M. *Discourse Analysis -- The Sociolinguistic Analysis of Natural Language*. Basil Blackwell, Oxford, 1983.

18. Suchman, L. *Plans and Situated Actions*. Cambridge University Press, London, 1986.

19. Todman, J., Elder, L., Alm, N., File, P. Sequential dependencies in computer-aided conversation. *Journal of Pragmatics*. Under review.

20. Yngve, V. On getting a word in edgeways. *Papers from the Sixth Regional Meeting of the Chicago Linguistic Society*, Chicago Linguistic Society, Chicago, 1970.

MicroCentre, Dundee:
Ordinary and Extra-ordinary HCI research

Professor Alan F. Newell, Director, MicroCentre,
Department of Mathematics and Computer Science
University of Dundee, Scotland, DD1 4HN

Tel. #44 382 23181, Fax. #44 382 23435, e-mail afn@uk.ac.dund.mcs

BACKGROUND

The main feature of the MicroCentre research group is a concern for users with a very wide range of characteristics. In addition to main-stream HCI research, it contains the largest academic group in the world investigating the application of computer systems for disabled people, and has a particular interest in systems for people with communication impairment.

The MicroCentre was instituted in 1980, and, since the mid 1980s, part of its work has been concerned with researching into, and promoting the relationship between "ordinary" and "extra-ordinary" HCI research: that is, the similarities between users with ordinary and extra-ordinary capabilities (e.g. disability) in ordinary and extra-ordinary situations (e.g. high work load).

The unit has an annual research income of approximately £350,000, and a staff of over twenty researchers led by computer and human factors engineers. The group contains a unique and stimulating blend of disciplines including computer scientists and engineers as well as psychologists, therapists, school teachers, a linguist, a philosopher and researchers with social work training. It collaborates closely with the University Medical School and Social Work Department as well as the local Education and Therapy Services. User evaluation and trials are conducted in the laboratory, and in local schools, clinics, and residential and private homes.

A number of software systems which have been developed by MicroCentre staff have been licenced to the commercial sector. Funding for research is from government grants, charitable bodies and project support and sponsorship from industry.

The group has formal links with a number of organisations including Digital, N.C.R., G.E.C. Avionics, C.R.I.(Denmark), Bertin(France), The University of Delaware (USA) and the Rehabilitation Institute at Hoensbroek (The Netherlands).

METHODOLOGY

The focus of the work is research into and development of software systems for HCI in real applications for both able bodied and disabled users, with the long term aim of producing commercially exploitable systems.

The research projects in the Centre are integrated within an overall strategy addressing major research issues with a number of parallel and complementary projects. The interdisciplinary team approach follows the philosophy of having a clear understanding of the application areas, and a detailed knowledge of the characteristics of potential users. The research methodology includes close collaboration with users and other professionals in the field, and an awareness and, where necessary, close study of literature and methodologies of a range of disciplines (e.g. speech therapy, discourse and conversation analysis, interpersonal communication).

Prototypes systems are implemented (usually in software), and are evaluated with users in real situations. The evaluation results, and users' and professionals' perceptions of the effectiveness of the systems, are fed back into the design cycle. An underlying modular structure ensures that successful techniques are shared between individual projects, and a closely coupled mangement team, together with informal contacts between researchers, encourages a creative approach.

The knowledge of the problems presented by disabled people and the utility of particular solutions, has led the group to have an unusual perspective on HCI problems. The needs and requirements of disabled and able-bodied people are closer than is sometimes realised by designers. A study of the extremes has proved to be a very effective research technique in this field as it has in many others.

A particularly important problem of HCI for disabled people is that of information transfer rate: a physically disabled non-speaking person, for example, may only be able to input data into a communication prosthesis at between two and ten words per minute. This means that interactions are very slow, and two way communication with other people is frustratingly un-natural. A major research strand, involving a number of projects, is the investigation of techniques to improve the effectiveness of information transfer between a user and their communication system.

MicroCentre, University of Dundee, Scotland

SPECIFIC PROJECTS:

Computers for Children and Adults with Special Needs

The MicroCentre's predictive writing system, PAL, increases effective information rate, and has been found to provide significant advantages as a writing aid for people with a wide range of special educational needs. Facilities such as the provision of phonetic and syntactic information have been particularly valuable for people with severe spelling and language dysfunction. An industrial project is examining the use of such predictive techniques in other application domains.

Extra-ordinary human computer operation

The ECHO (Extra-ordinary human computer operation) project is examining the needs of disabled people with the aim of providing new insights and interfaces which will be valuable for all users of computers, particularly those in out-of-the-ordinary situations, such as extreme environments and high work loads. A high quality, multi-modal workstation for disabled users has been developed. This includes speech, eye-gaze and gesture recognition, and incorporates attention monitoring and intention inferencing to improve the efficiency of the system.

In collaboration with a number of European industrial partners, this research has been extended to the development of a generic and integrated multi-modal workstation, designed specifically for high work load and safety critical situations. A number of specific applications will be implemented on the workstation by the partners. Research within European projects also includes the development of a workstation which provides access to broad-band telecommunication networks for disabled people, and includes the development of computer-supported collaborative work, and other special services for this user group.

Communication Systems for Non-Speaking People

A number highly efficient interfaces are being developed to facilitate the use of synthetic speech output systems for inter-personal communication by non-speaking people. The long term aim is to provide an integrated prosthesis which will facilitate all types of interpersonal communication. Developments include the CHAT, PROSE, TalksBack and MOSCO systems. These are designed to encourage social interaction, and are based on conversation analysis and the use of speech acts, and knowledge based and artificial intelligence techniques to improve their efficiency and efficacy. These systems are being developed for and evaluated with a wide range of clients including those with severe expressive and receptive language dysfunction

Within the HAMLET project, algorithms are being developed to add emotional characteristics (e.g. happiness, sadness, grief) to synthetic speech. A further project is investigating the use of animation to assist the understanding of simple iconic languages by users with severe language impairment.

Listening Typewriter Simulations

Research using a full-speed speech recognition simulation, in collaboration with a software natural language understanding system, has examined user acceptability of a listening typewriter. The human factors and dialogue design issues of using speech in this situations of this nature were also studied using this simulation.

The speech transcription system used was a machine shorthand developed by staff of the MicroCentre, and now used in Law Courts, for other reporting applications, and as a translation aid for deaf people.

Applications of Computers in Social Work

InterView, a computerised interviewing system, based on an analysis of interviewing and counselling methodologies, has been developed which is designed especially to elicit sensitive information. This is being evaluated and extended in collaboration with the Social Work Department, and a secure mental hospital.

Awards

Awards include a U.K. National Training Award, The British Computer Society Award (Socially Beneficial Application of Computers), Finalist in the Toshiba Year of Invention Competition, '89, and the I.E.E. Prize for Helping Disabled People (Cert. Of Commendation)

Key Products and Results

Systems developed by MicroCentre staff have been licenced to the commercial sector for exploitation. These include, the Palantype Shorthand Transcription System, the PAL/PALSTAR predictive word processor, SPELLER, a spelling corrector system for extreme spelling dysfunction, and a communication system for non-speaking people.

Results from experimental work, and descriptions of software developments, have been reported widely in the academic literature, and at speech, HCI and the North American RESNA conferences. Book chapters can be found in:

Ainsworth, W.A. (ed.) *Advances in Speech Hearing and Language Processing*. J.A.I. Press, London, England, 1992.

Edwards, A.D.N. (ed.) *Extra-Ordinary Human Computer Operation*. Cambridge University Press, England. 1993

Human-Computer Interaction Research
at Massey University, New Zealand

Mark Apperley and Chris Phillips
Department of Computer Science
Massey University
Palmerston North, NEW ZEALAND
Phone: ++64 6 356 9099   E-mail: m.apperley@massey.ac.nz

This overview describes the activities of the human-computer interaction research group in the School of Mathematical and Information Sciences at Massey University, Palmerston North, New Zealand.

CONTEXT
Massey University is a campus with some 8000 internal students, and 14000 distance or extramural students. Although historically it has a strong agricultural bias, and is best known for this and its extramural programme, it covers a broad range of disciplines. The human-computer interaction group, based in the School of Mathematical and Information Sciences, is the major focus of HCI activity in New Zealand.

FOCUS, THEMES AND HISTORY
One of the authors (Apperley) has been involved in HCI research for the past 20 years. This spans work at Imperial College (UK) on the MINNIE computer-aided circuit design system in the early 1970s, then at the University of Waikato (New Zealand) where a commercial version of this software was developed, and now at Massey University, where the HCI research group has been prospering since 1989.

The activities of the group cover a broad range of HCI topics. However, the underlying philosophy is the development of methodologies, processes and tools for the successful design, implementation and evaluation of highly interactive graphical user interfaces, from the simplest embedded systems, to interfaces to the most complex of worlds. In addition to the consequential focus on notations, methodologies, prototyping and implementation environments, there are a number of projects to develop interfaces in specific application areas, aimed at providing not just solutions in these areas, but also test-beds for more general techniques, exemplars of interface styles and innovations, and results which can be generalised for wider application.

Other projects involve visual languages, hypertext navigation, and data display and interaction techniques. All of this work tends to be research based, rather than directed

at commercial products, but there is some consultation in interface design, and increasingly in interface evaluation.

An important feature of HCI at Massey is the close relationship that exists between research and teaching. HCI is taught as a distinct topic at both undergraduate and graduate levels. Practical work is carried out in both Apple Macintosh and Unix workstation environments.

PEOPLE
The majority of those involved in the research group are staff and students from within the Department of Computer Science, but there is active participation from staff in both the Information Systems and Management Systems departments. Currently the group numbers 14 members, with 4 PhD students, and a further 3 involved in masters-level research.

SPECIFIC PROJECTS
A principle thread of the work of the group stems from the development of *Lean Cuisine*, a tree-structured visual notation originally proposed for describing menu-based systems [3]. Lean Cuisine is now being extended into an object-based multi-layered executable notation providing for the specification of the full range of constraints and dependencies which exist between selectable dialogue primitives in a direct manipulation environment [10]. This work is aimed at producing a comprehensive tool and associated methodology to support the high-level design of interfaces at an early stage of the interface life-cycle.

A Lean Cuisine implementation which translated a description into an equivalent event-response system [1] has now progressed to a more general model based on the notion of dialogue activation. In a hierarchy of dialogue groups, a user is able to directly interact only with an active dialogue. A dialogue becomes active only if its parent is active, and if it receives one of a set of possible activating events. A *Dialogue Activation Language* (DAL) has been developed based on this model, together with a prototyping environment which translates DAL into a process based event-response system [2].

As a part of the overall design and implementation process, one project is aimed purely at evaluation techniques. Earlier work [5] concentrated on evaluation of components of the interface; currently attention is focused on the development of an integrated multi-dimensional approach to the evaluation of the whole interface, drawing on critical (expert), quantitative, and qualitative (user) techniques to provide an overall assessment [4].

Two application-oriented projects have led the group to work on visual languages. The first of these projects set out to develop a highly interactive environment for image processing, with the aim of providing an insight into the design process involved in the interface. This work has produced a visual language with a large set of iconic primitives which can be cascaded to form an iconic sentence representing the data flow of image information between operations. Each image operation has its own control panel for parameter settings; the effect of adjusting a parameter can be seen immediately [8]. A related project has involved the development of a system for the high-level design of integrated circuits, to be used as input to a silicon compiler. This too has resulted in a visual language based on dataflow principles, in which the complete behaviour of the required circuit can be specified [9].

A further application area which is receiving the attention of the group is that of expert systems. Of particular interest here is the provision of explanation. This has been seen by many as a separate component of the system, but work here suggests that it is an integral part which needs to be seamlessly incorporated into the interface [6].

Hypermedia systems pose a range of problems which are of interest to the group and are the focus of some attention. From a long-standing interest in navigation issues, the problems of finding one's way through a complex hypermedia environment have led to the development of a tool for providing dynamic and predefined paths. Effort has also been directed at the problem of the effective conversion of conventional linear text (for example, a novel) into hypertext form, so that the full benefits and potential of the medium are realised. A third project is examining the use of a visual notation for describing the structure of a hypermedia system both from the point of view of design, and also as documentation.

General techniques for the display of information, and for interacting with this information, pervade a number of the applications being explored. Of particular interest at the present time is the use of distortion-based display techniques in the representation of topological networks [7]. This work is currently focused on the development of an overall taxonomy of available techniques, and a relationship between this taxonomy and the strengths of the techniques in particular application areas. A number of implementations are also underway.

FUTURE DIRECTIONS
Increasing recognition of the interface as a key component of any computer system, or computer based technology, guarantees the continued relevance of the work of the group. Focus will continue to be on high-level descriptions, as an aid to design and understanding of human interface issues, and leading to a total design environment. Associated work with hypermedia and visual languages will also continue to develop.

KEY PUBLICATIONS

1. Anderson, P.S. and Apperley, M.D. An Interface Prototyping Systems Based on Lean Cuisine, *Interacting with Computers*, 2(2), 1990, 217-226.

2. Anderson, P.S. and Apperley, M.D. Dialogue Activation: A Design Approach for Direct Manipulation Interfaces, *Massey Computer Science Report 91/2*, 1991.

3. Apperley, M.D. and Spence, R. Lean Cuisine: a low-fat notation for menus, *Interacting with Computers*, 1(1), 1989, 43-68.

4. Burger, S.V. and Apperley, M.D. A Multi-dimensional Approach to Interface Evaluation, *Proc. IFIPS Conf. on Human Jobs & Computer Interfaces*, Tampere, Finland, 1991, 205-222.

5. Field, G.E. and Apperley, M.D. Context and Selective Retreat in Hierarchical Menu Structures, *Behaviour and Information Technology*, 9(2), 1990, 133-146.

6. Kemp, E.A. Communicating with a knowledge-based system, *Proc. ECAI-92 Workshop W15 'Improving the Use of Knowledge-Based Systems with Explanations'*, Report No. 92/21, ed. P. Brezillan, Institut Blaise Pascal, August 1992.

7. Leung, Y.K. Human-computer interaction techniques for map-based diagrams, *Advances in Human Factors/Ergonomics 12B*, Elsevier, Amsterdam, 1989, 361-368.

8. Ngan, P.M. OpShop: an iconic programming system for image processing, *Proc. Australian Apple Universities Consortium Conference*, ANU, Canberra, Australia, July, 1991.

9. Pearson, M.W., Apperley, M.D. and Lyons, P.J. Data Flow Diagrams as Input to a Silicon Compiler, *Proc 9th Australian Microelectronics Conference*, Adelaide, Australia, 1990, 221-226.

10. Phillips, C.H.E. Towards a Notation for Describing the Behaviour of Direct Manipulation Interfaces, *New Zealand Journal of Computing*, 3(1), 1991, 11-25.

The MultiG Research Programme –
Distributed Multimedia Applications on Gigabit Networks

Björn Pehrson
Distributed Systems Laboratory
Swedish Institute for Computer Science
S-164 28 STOCKHOLM-KISTA, Sweden
Phone: +46-8-7521510
Email: bjorn@sics.se

Yngve Sundblad
Interaction and Presentation Laboratory
Numerical Analysis and Computing Science
KTH (Royal Institute of Technology)
S-100 44 STOCKHOLM, Sweden
Phone: +46-8-7907147
Email: yngve@nada.kth.se

CONTEXT

The MultiG research programme is an effort conducted in broad cooperation between academia and industry with public support. The main goals are to strengthen the academic infrastructure and industrial competitiveness, to integrate the major research sites in Sweden, and to demonstrate operating prototypes of novel applications and Gigabit networking concepts. The spirit of the program is similar to the spirit of the Gigabit research part of the US NREN effort.

MultiG started formally in July 1990 and is currently funded until June 1993. SiREN, a plan for a six-year extension to a national programme 1993-1999 is being discussed and will be put forward to the Swedish parliament early 1993.

THEMES

Significant issues addressed are:
• A CSCW-environment, the KnowledgeNet, and its user interface, the CollaborativeDesktop - integrating videophone conferencing, group management and shared workspaces.
• DIVE - a distributed interactive virtual environment for nvestigation of virtual worlds as computer-human interfaces and as means for human communication and collaboration
• A Walkstation with MINT, a mobile Internet router
• Language-oriented application generators for distributed applications
• Distributed multimedia interface builders, presentation servers and workstations
• High-level protocols and run-time environments for distributed applications integrating isochronous media streams and asynchronous event sequences
• New transport layer functionality, supporting multimedia and broadband services, and new internetworking problems between high-speed, medium-speed and wireless networks
• Host interfaces to high-speed networks
• DTM, Dynamic synchronous transfer mode, a high-speed networking concept that goes beyond ATM

© 1993 ACM 0-89791-575-5/93/0004/0246...$1.50

FOCUS ON CSCW

On the application side, MultiG focuses on CSCW - Computer Supported Cooperative Work. General issues relevant to collaboration are investigated as well as issues relevant to a specific work task: design and standardization of new communication protocols.

A common abstract model of these distributed environments adopted in MultiG is *TheKnowledgenet*, an information network supporting cooperation in teams where the team members have access to a common base of information about who-knows-what, [6].

Computer-human interfaces to the Knowledgenet are explored in two directions:
- *TheCollaborativeDesktop*, a distributed desktop in the conventional 2D workstation environment. The prototype, Codesk, includes teleconferencing and messaging and other groupware support as well as tools for information retrieval.
- *DIVE*, a 3D environment based on distributed virtual worlds visualized in Goggle, a head-mounted stereoscopic display. The DIVE prototypeincludes 3D audio and a robot control system helping disabled people manipulate their physical environment.

Besides these end-user applications, tools for supporting design of new applications are developed, e.g. a distributed multimedia interface builder, DMIB, [2].

Behavioural and social studies of practical use of CoDesk are carried out at one of our industrial partners, Ellemtel.

PARTICIPANTS

The MultiG programme is conducted in broad cooperation between academia and industry with substantial support from public sources. On the research side, the main actors currently are the Royal Institute of Technology in Stockholm (KTH) and the Swedish Institute of Computer Science (SICS). The main industrial participants are companies in the Ericsson and Swedish Telecom groups.

About 10 senior researchers are involved, not only from computer and telecommunication sciences but also from psychology and sociology. About 15 research students are active in MultiG.

TESTBED: STOCKHOLM GIGABIT NETWORK

A first testbed is being built between the campus of the Royal Institute of Technology in downtown Stockholm and Electrum, a center for research and education in the information technology area, where the Swedish Institute of Computer Science is situated. The direct distance is 11 km and fiberwise the distance is 22 km. Swedish Telecom has provided 4 parallel fiber buses between three sites. The testbed is under extension to SGN, the Stockholm Gigabit Network, with several other sites in the Greater Stockholm area, including Ericsson and Swedish Telecom research laboratories.

SGN will be used in CSCW applications in regular working situations as well as for networked education.

COLLABORATIVE DESKTOP - CoDesk

CoDesk is the user interface to the KnowledgeNet, consisting of a browser and a set of tools supporting cooperation and the communication infrastructure. CoDesk could be regarded as a generic shell for CSCW.

The set of tools includes:
- shared workspaces, folders, whiteboards, spreadsheets, editors, etc.
- a multicast packet-video teleconferencing facility with separately controllable audio and video channels.
- bulletin boards and message services for asynchronous communication
- the team map, a browser showing the availability of other team members
- the meeting process: any shared process can be identified as a meeting which will cause video phone connections to be established between concurrent users of the process This could be used to organize formal meetings, but also to support informal interaction between users waiting for a busy common resource, such as a printer.

Basic principles in the CoDesk interface are direct manipulation, a box room metaphor and generic communication. In the current CoDesk prototype, the knowledge base is organized as an X.500 directory.

The CoDesk environment is in 1993 integrated with the normal working environment of a team of engineers at Ellemtel, where we will conduct behavioural and social studies of its impact on the work and communication environment.

DIVE

In the DIVE project, 3D-interaction is explored as a computer-human interface and as a means for communication between humans. The main issues are visualization, interaction and distribution.

The conventional desktop metaphor is extended to a 3D rooms metaphor, [3]. The 2D-restricted mouse is exchanged for 3D interaction tools, such as a track-ball, wand, data-glove or even data-suit. The conventional screen can still be used to visualize 3D but the full benefit from this extension can be gained only with some sort of 3D-display, e.g. a light head-mounted display providing a stereoscopic presentation, and a head-tracker, or body-tracker, to give the user a sense of being present in the virtual world presented in the display. In the MultiG-project Goggles, [1], a high-resolution color display

based on a 1" CRT is being developed. If the head-mounted display is transparent, the virtual world can be superimposed on the real world to allow the user to participate both in the virtual and the real world.

3D-sound adds extra substance to the feeling of presence, [9]. Real-time registration of real objects (3D camera technology) is not available in the MultiG environment which means that 3D videophones are still fiction although technologies like 3D-scanners and displays, including holography are surveyed. This means that real 3D-objects, like participants in human communication must be represented by icons which are controlled by the interaction tools available for each particpant. Communication in Telepresence is accomplished by sharing the virtual world between participants by making the database defining the world distributed.

When moving to 3D environments, there will be many new challenges in the interface builder area. To build virtual worlds, a coupling between 3D CAD-tools and the Telepresence run-time environment is investigated in the DMIB work mentioned above.

DMIB is itself intended to be a distributed multi-user application supporting collaborative user-interface design.

KEY PUBLICATIONS

1. Jan Bogdanski: A Color Helmet Mounted Display, in *Proceedings 4th MultiG Workshop*, Stockholm, May 1992

2. Björn Eiderbäck, Per Hägglund, Yngve Sundblad: A Distributed Multimedia Interface Builder: User Interface, Constraints, Events and Applications, in *Proceedings 2nd MultiG Workshop*, Stockholm, June 1991

3. Lennart E. Fahlén, Olov Ståhl, Christer Carlsson, Carl Brown: A Space Based Model for User Interaction in Shared Synthetic Environments, in *These Proceedings*

4. Gerald Q. Maguire, Björn Pehrson, Jens Zander, Walkstation-The Swedish Electronic Notebook/Walkstation Extension Program, in *Proceedings 4th MultiG Workshop*, Stockholm, May 1992

5. Hans Marmolin, Yngve Sundblad and Björn Pehrson: An Analysis of Design and Collaboration in a Distributed Environment, in *Proceedings ECSCW'91*, Amsterdam, Sept 1991

6. Hans Marmolin: The KnowledgeNet - An Environment for Distributed Design, in *Proc.eedings 2nd MultiG Workshop*, Stockholm, June 1991

7. Proceedings from MultiG Workshops 1-5, Stockholm, Nov 1990, June 1991, Dec 1991, May 1992 and Dec 1992

8. Björn Pehrson, Per Gunningberg, Stephen Pink: Distributed Multimedia Applications on Gigabit Networks, *IEEE Network*, Vol.6 No.1, Jan 1992

9. Stephen Travis Pope, Lennart Fahlén: An Aural Perspective Engine for a Distributed Interactive Virtual Environment, SICS Research Report, Sept 1992

Flexible, Active Support for Collaboration with ConversationBuilder

Simon M. Kaplan, William J. Tolone, Douglas P. Bogia and Theodore Phelps

Human-Computer Interaction Laboratory
Department of Computer Science
University of Illinois at Urbana-Champaign
Urbana, IL 61801, USA
+1 217 244 0392 {kaplan,tolone,bogia,phelps}@cs.uiuc.edu

ABSTRACT
We overview the ConversationBuilder system and its demonstration at INTERCHI 93.

KEYWORDS
Collaboration Environment

ABOUT THIS DEMONSTRATION
ConversationBuilder [1] (CB) is an *open architecture for collaborative work* which builds on earlier efforts [2] [3]. Our goal has been to create an environment that provides active support to its user community in an open and flexible way. Open support means the tools can be tailored to different domains and cultures of collaborative activity. Active support means that users are provided context-sensitive help by the system, enabling them to find out how they got into a situation, what can be done now, what others are doing, and what obligations they have. Active support is provided through our ability to define protocols to the system, which in turn utilize the mechanisms provided by the CB kernel.

Flexible support means that the system can dynamically alter to reflect changed situations. For example, if a user is waiting on approval of a project from a manager, who goes on vacation, the task dependency structure in the system can be modified to remove the approval, pass it to another, and so forth. Further, as one works on a task one tends to find problems that should be fixed by others, and so forth. The ability to work on multiple tasks simultaneously, context switching among them, and evolve arbitrary webs of obligations, allows us to model this kind of behavior on the fly.

CB also has a notion of shared hypertext, with hyperlinks. Hypertext nodes can be used to hold the shared information manipulated by users, such as program text, documents, IBIS issues, positions and argu- ments, and so forth. The types of nodes and links in the system are defined as part of protocol specifications.

CB supports a notion of user awareness: the system has WYSIWIS features, and this is used to keep users aware of each others actions.

As part of the development of CB we've developed a set of interesting new tools, including a message bus for tool interconnection, a widget server for dynamic tool interface construction and sharing, graph browsers and shared drawing tools. We are investigating tech- niques and mechanisms for the dynamic, collaborative construction of dynamic user interfaces by multiple ap- plications; the demonstration will show off the entire CB system through use of these facilities.

We have deployed CB in several different application domains by writing appropriate protocols. CB has been used to support synchronous collaboration in situation such as semi-structured design activities of the IBIS or Design Rationale type, and code walkthrough/review meetings. Examples of asynchronous support include the modeling of a software quality assurance process, and the modeling of a shared versioning and configu- ration management system, which is used to maintain complex documents such as the source code and docu- mentation of the CB system itelf.

ACKNOWLEDGEMENTS
This work is supported in part by the National Science Foundation/DARPA under grant CCR-9007195, by the US Army Corps of Engineers, and by Intel, Bull, Open Systems Solutions Inc., Sun Microsystems and Hewlett- Packard.

REFERENCES
[1] Simon M. Kaplan *et al.* Flexible, active support for collaborative work with conversationbuilder. In *Proc CSCW 92*, November 1992.

[2] Fernando Flores *et al* Computer Systems and the Design of Organizational Interaction. *ACM TOIS*, 6(2), April 1988.

[3] Allan Shepherd *et al.* Strudel: an extensible elec- tronic conversation toolkit. In *Proc CSCW 90*, Oc- tober 1990.

A Groupware Engine Using UIMS Methodologies

Lever Wang

U.I.M.S., Inc.
1590 La Pradera Dr. Suite 12
Campbell, CA, 95008 USA
Tel: +1 408 866 4600
E-mail: lever@tdd.sj.nec.com

Keywords:
groupware, computer supported cooperative work, user interface management system

Abstract

This paper presents a groupware engine running under Microsoft's Windows developed using a User Interface Management System (UIMS). This groupware engine will demonstrate some of the important groupware features such as concurrency control, security, view control, and how these features are best implemented using a UIMS. By demonstrating these features in a groupware engine the advantages of applying the UIMS methodology will become self evident, as well as, the need for such a methodology.

The main purpose of a UIMS is to separate the user interface code from the application code. This idea suits the groupware concept very well, since most of the groupware applications are built around a central host with UI clients distributed across a local area network, or worse yet, accessible only via a low-bandwidth modem line. With this in mind, we have developed a strategy for utilizing the following UIMS models to build the groupware:

* Presentation Model - In this product this model is built around a SQL-based predicate engine which is used for view control, as well as, spontaneous user feedback from different UI clients in a work group. This model is based on classes defined in the Microsoft Foundation Class (MFC) library, but the actual application and semantic feedback from the user interface is handled by derived classes from the MFC library developed by us.

* Dialog Model - The dialog language is C++ which is the same programming language as the UIMS applications, Microsoft C++ Version 7.0. Additional classes were added to describe sequential, multiple-threaded dialogs, and the state machine for other dialog models. We believe UIMS/Groupware application programmers do not want to learn another programming language, and that object-oriented paradigm should be the foundation for all dialog models in UIMS world.

* Application Model - In this product the key component of this model is the SQL-predicate engine. All applications communicate with the user interface modules through this simple database management system. This groupware engine utilizes the predicate engine for security and concurrency control when multiple users in a work group are all controlled from a single database management system.

The groupware engine is implemented using a client/server architecture to minimize CPU latency. The server in this groupware engine is the database engine. There are two types of clients in this engine. One type is the UI client which serves the presentation and dialog models, and resides on the local UI machine (vs. the host machine for the database server), the other is the application client. An example of an application client would be a schedule manager.

This architecture allows us to operate using very low bandwidth communication between clients and the server, since there is no need for the clients to communicate with the server except for database updates and queries. Also, and more importantly, most of the user interface dialogs are executed locally on the UI client's machine. We are actually going to demonstrate this product running on two personal computers linked with a 9600-baud serial line.

STORYBOARD

The first demonstration shows two graphics editors modifying a space shuttle drawing simultaneously, but each with a different view, one normal and one zoomed. The second demonstration shows a game of tic-tac-toe being played by two players and watched by an audience. This game demonstrates the use of a database to control a sequence plays in a groupware environment.

We also would like to show other groupware applications we have developed which demonstrate the flexibility and completeness of the UIMS methodology and this engine.

RELEVANCE to HCI

We strongly believe this groupware engine based on the UIMS models presents a unique and powerful combination of this often misunderstood technology. Many vendors today propagate the idea that e-mail is a groupware product, but we believe that there is much more to groupware, and the foundation for it is UIMS technology which is slowly accepted in both the academic and commercial worlds.

User Involvement In The Design Process:
Why, When & How?

C. Dennis Allen, Word Perfect Corporation, 1555 North Technology Way, Orem, UT 84057, (801) 222-7427

Don Ballman, Mead Data Central, P.O. Box 933, Dayton, OH 45401, (513) 865-1446

Vivienne Begg, SunSoft, Inc., Boston Devel. Center, 2 Elizabeth Dr., Chelmsford, MA 01824, (508) 442-0574, vbegg@east.sun.com

Harold H. Miller-Jacobs, TASC, 55 Walkers Brook Dr., Reading, MA 01867, (617) 942-2000, hhmiller-jacobs@tasc.com

Michael Muller, US West Advanced Technologies, 4001 Discovery Dr., Suite 280, Boulder, CO 80303, (303) 541-6564, michael@advtech.uswest.com

Jakob Nielsen, Bellcore, MRE-2P370, 445 South St., Morristown, NJ 07962-1910, (201) 829-4731, nielsen@bellcore.com

Jared Spool, Moderator, User Interface Engineering, 40 Dascomb Rd., Andover, MA 01810 (508) 470-1213, spool@northeastern.edu

ABSTRACT

For years the CHI community has championed the importance of the user in system development. As many of us develop systems, we find that the concept of user involvement is not so easy to implement. Does one always strive to involve the user in the design process? Are there situations when the users should not be involved? What if the user is reluctant to change? How is user involvement handled when the user claims to know all the answers and wants to design the entire interface his or her way? What if the users, or even potential users are not available? How can user involvement be accomplished under these developmental restrictions?

User Involvement, therefore, may be a goal - not a given, and how to effect user involvement is not as straight forward as the text books convey!

To assist the process of user interface development, many techniques have been developed such as Heuristic Evaluation, Participatory Design, Cognitive Walk Throughs, Task Analysis and Rapid Prototyping. These techniques vary considerably in the extent of user involvement that they require. This panel will attempt to match the technique with the degree of user involvement that the developer is faced with or can achieve.

The issues discussed in this session are important to the entire user interface community. Developers will be happy to hear that they are not alone; others have similar problems with users. They will learn which of the techniques are best suited

for each development situation. Methodologists will gain greater insight into the breadth and depth of working with, and attempting to satisfy various types of users. They may be able to better refine the technologies we now have available to meet the needs of user interface developers.

Members of the audience will be invited to participate as developers and methodologists.

KEYWORDS: Heuristic Evaluation, Human Factors, Participatory Design, Rapid Prototyping, User Interface Evaluation/Methodology, User Involvement

PARTICIPANTS

C. Dennis Allen spearheaded and now manages the User Interface Development Group at WordPerfect Corporation. One of his critical tasks is to get to know the eleven million registered users of WordPerfect in over twenty countries.

Don Ballman is the Manager of Mead Data Central Usability Testing Laboratory. He has 14 years experience in various facets of product development and product testing, including training development, user interface design and usability testing.

Vivienne Begg has worked in various experimental forms of software engineering, encompassing network monitoring, knowledge acquisition, and work flow management at Bolt, Beranek and Newman, NCR, Prime Computer and Xerox. She is currently employed in the Human Interface Engineering group at Sun Microsystems, where she is experiencing total job satisfaction.

Harold H. Miller-Jacobs of TASC, Reading, MA has been using and advocating the use of rapid prototyping as one of the most effective tools for requirements analysis and user interface development. At last year's CHI conference he participated in the panel "In Search of the Ideal Prototype". For the previous three conferences, he chaired Special Interest Groups on rapid prototyping tools. When he's not prototyping, he's teaching at Tufts University.

Michael Muller is a member of the technical staff at US West Advanced Technologies, where he works on the design and assessment of systems, and on the development and assessment of methods for design and assessment. Michael Muller and Sarah Kuhn were co-chairs of PDC '92, the Participatory Design Conference (6-7 November 111992, MIT, Cambridge, MA US).

Jakob Nielsen is a member of the Computer Sciences Department in Bellcore Us Applied Research Area. He has a Ph.D in computer science and user interface design. His main interests are usability engineering, with a special emphasis on developing cost-effective methods for the improvement of usability in practical development environments, hypertext, and next-generation user interfaces. Nielsen coined the term Rdiscount usability engineeringS to indicate low-cost usability work with a high payoff. His books include Hypertext and Hypermedia which was recently published in a Japanese translation, and the new Usability Engineering.

Jared Spool is a founding principal at User Interface Engineering, a product design firm in Andover, MA. Jared works closely with users, developers and methodologists - as he is one of each. In addition to consulting, he teaches and is very active in the Greater Boston Special Interest Group in CHI. He organized the successful panel at CHI '92, "In Search of the Ideal Prototype".

POSITION STATEMENTS - DEVELOPERS
C. Dennis Allen - WordPerfect Corp.

Everybody has a UI opinion these days: programmers, marketing managers, sales reps, customer support operators, enhancement coordinators, testers, usability specialists and platform coordinators, not to mention trade journals and magazines. With so many user advocates out there a software developer might ask, "Who needs real users?"

The answer is: we do. Users are central to everything and frighteningly distant. In developing retail software, we must satisfy the needs of all potential users, meaning *everyone*.

As I try to meet the demands of users and buyers, I like to consider every user as the keeper of the solution. Unfortunately, users are often unaware of being insiders with secret knowledge. They tend to trivialize their expertise or make up stories about what they do.

To get the "secret knowledge" I need to meet market expectations I must have:

- methodologies to compile meaningful, useful, and usable user profiles for commercial software products with millions of users
- better ways to do task, system, and process analysis not only for individual users but organizations of users
- fast and easy methodologies to get, evaluate and validate user data from secondary sources such as customer support operators
- techniques to rapidly turn data from user inquiries into UI solutions
- simpler methods to design and validate software functionality
- more reliable ways to organize features into menus and dialog boxes based on user data
- approaches that enable me to know and understand the user's lexicon so we can communicate using the same language

So, methodologists, what solutions or assistance can you offer?

Don Ballman - Mead Data Central

Let's start with the whole premise of including users in software UI evaluation. It's a good one; build what users say they want, in the manner they wish, and you'll have a successful product. At least, that's the theory. In practice, these lofty goals are much more elusive.

Why? It's not just enough to include users in the product development process; they should be the *right* users. Too often, though, testers have to extrapolate from "problem" users who bring a set of "hidden agendas" with them to the test session. The usability techniques we have now simply do not sufficiently accommodate this reality of "real world" testing.

When I test a new on-line product, I a interested in assessing its value to potential customers, its usability by those who will actually use the product to perform work tasks, and its potential for actually being purchased. Unfortunately, the great majority of customers of on-line systems are infrequent and unsophisticated users.

These users are unaware of technological advances, are afraid of disrupting established routines, or only evaluate products in terms of the cost of required hardware and software upgrades. Their usability data is often confounded by risk averse behavior or intentionally conservative product ratings. This is particularly true of on-line system products, where (unlike standalone applications) users do not have the option of choosing the previous version of your product or accepting the new.

And, "problem users" may be only mildly familiar with competitors' products, reducing the ability to gather comparative usability data.

Because product value is often measured during usability testing, the narrow focus of such test subjects can skew test results and doom promising designs to the ash can prematurely or (worse) send design teams down the wrong paths entirely.

Moreover, those who decide to purchase a new product are often not those who actually will use it. Using system purchasers as test subjects does not validate a product's design and usability in the same way as using system users. Yet, products as delivered must first satisfy the purchasers. This cycle is especially troublesome in professions, such as the law and financial research, where purchasing decisions can be made by personnel who are many years removed from the actual job supported by the product being tested.

In my experience, virtually all participants in usability tests are self-selected, with all the hazards that entails. Typically, test participants are recruited from an existing client base, suggesting they may be excessively positive about your product or have deeply held complaints to air. They may be those who match the target test pool exactly, or those who "come close" and can spare 2-3 hours from their business day to participants. They may be a junior staff member "volunteered" by a client one does not wish to offend. A carefully constructed test cadre can be skewed by last minute cancellations, or inaccurately answered screening questions. None of these situations is especially heartwarming to the usability specialist charged with bringing back accurate and complete design data.

All these "problem users" substantively (or substantially) affect the quality, robustness and completeness of the data obtained during usability testing -- and the design decisions based on them. The techniques we presently employ for conducting usability assessments assume much more classical control over user characteristics than the above usability conditions permit.

I do not concede that these weaknesses negate the value of usability evaluations entirely. But, we can do better. It's not just enough to say, "Find better test subjects". They *do* exist; but they often don't have the time or the inclination to assist your carefully planned testing. Given the alternative (no data at all), the usability specialist's only recourse is to make do with the data that can be gathered.

What methodologies can we employ to get data from "problem users" that helps rather than hinders product design?

Vivienne Begg - SunSoft

There are three kinds of people that have proved difficult to work with in my experience of developing human interfaces. The first are experts who find it difficult to express what it is they do when they work. We could call them "Witch Doctors". They are in part engaged in a legitimate attempt to preserve their professional integrity (the mystery of their craft), and, in part, unable to express cognitive activity which is both complex and intuitive.

The second are developers (or more usually the managers of development groups) who know a little about a new technology and are eager to apply the latest gizmo to their current problem whether it is appropriate or not. We could call them "Eager Beavers".

Then there are the engineers who are constitutionally incapable of seeing the point in paying attention to the human interface. We could call them "Techno-Nerds". We would all appreciate guidance on how to deal with each of these types, and in particular, how to persuade the Techno-Nerd that even though he (and it is almost always "he") finds an interface "intuitively satisfying", other human beings with average IQ's and not enough time find that it lacks affordance, consistency, and coherence.

POSITION STATEMENTS - METHODOLOGISTS
Harold H. Miller-Jacobs - Rapid Prototyping

Rapid prototyping is a comparatively fast and effective technique for allowing both users and developers to gain insight into the proposed functionality of a system. After an initial examination of a system's requirements, a simulation is generated that looks at the system from the perspective of the ultimate system user. In practice, a representation of the user interface is developed, preferably on a computer screen, that simulates what the user would see. In the ideal case, it would be interactive, that is, enable some of the system functionality to operate. It is not just simply 'a pretty picture', but a graphical representation of the functions that the system would perform - from the viewpoint of the ultimate user.

The technique is very effective for involving the user in the development process. When used by developers to explain their understanding of the requirements and their thinking of the proposed functionality of a system, such as during a design review, they obtain immediate and understandable feedback from users. It essentially facilitates users involvement in the process. Rather than a document several inches thick (that few ever read), all users and system stakeholders can relate to a rapid prototype. Reluctant users can get involved; belligerent users can focus their energies on specifics; and harried users can spend a few minutes and get the essence. In practice, the communications bandwidth between developers and users becomes greatly increased!

Michael Muller - Participatory Design

Participatory design is a body of practice and theory that emphasizes direct, empowered, collaborative action by users, in concert with software professionals. This action ideally takes place during both design activities and decision-making activities regarding computer systems (and other social systems). Through participatory design, users move out of roles such as observer, approver, "knowledge repository," or "component of the system," and into roles such as peer co-designer, design co-owner, expertise contributor, and self-advocate.

Participatory design is not, of course, The Answer to every design or assessment problem. However, there are a variety of techniques available within the domain of participatory design, including structured conferences, ethnographic methods, theatrical approaches, low-tech simulations, high-tech prototyping, semi-structured games, and sophisticated post-implementation customization environments. These can be used selectively to meet a number of different situational challenges. They can help transform our view of users (and the users' view of us!) from "other person as problem" into "other person as partner." The goal, then, becomes: to select or develop techniques and practices to achieve excellent designs or product evaluations through group processes that recognize (a) the individual members' differences in perspective; (b) the diversity of the impacts of the system upon their work-lives; (c) the different stakes that each stakeholder brings to the shared work; (d) the varied strengths and competencies that they bring to their collaboration; and (e) the opportunities that they jointly possess for mutual education and validation.

Jakob Nielsen - Heuristic Evaluation

Heuristic evaluation is a usability engineering method for finding the usability problems in a user interface design so that they can be attended to as part of an iterative design process [Nielsen and Molich 1990; Nielsen 1993]. Heuristic evaluation involves having a small set of evaluators (typically, 3-5) examine the interface and judge its compliance with recognized usability principles (the "heuristics"). Heuristic evaluation thus falls in the category of usability inspection methods rather than the category of empirical user testing.Furthermore, heuristic evaluation is one of the most informal usability inspection methods and is explicitly designed as a "discount usability engineering" method that is easy and cheap to use in practice.

Heuristic evaluation is especially valuable in situations where other methods are difficult to use because of extreme time or resource constraints or because representative users are hard to bring in for user testing. In cases where users are available, but only in very small numbers, heuristic evaluation can be used to avoid "wasting users" on the finding of trivial usability problems. Instead, the interface can be debugged to a large degree by heuristic evaluation, leaving the precious users to find more complex and task-related usability problems.

Finally, with respect to the recent debate on whether heuristic evaluation should completely replace user testing [Jeffries and Desurvire 1992], I want to go on the record as a firm believer in user testing. Heuristic evaluation has always been intended as one of several elements of the discount usability engineering approach, with other essential elements being visits to customer sites, scenario-building, and user testing. These methods supplement each other and should be used in combination. Indeed, one way in which evaluators can build up the usability expertise needed for optimal performance as heuristic evaluators [Nielsen 1992] is likely to be observation of test users.

REFERENCES

Jeffries, R., and Desurvire, H. Usability testing vs. heuristic evaluation: Was there a contest? ACM SIGCHI Bulletin 24, 4 (October 1992), 39-41.

Nielsen, J. Finding usability problems through heuristic evaluation. Proc. ACM CHI'92 (Monterey, CA, 3-7 May 1992), 3373-380.

Nielsen, J. Usability Engineering, Academic Press, San Diego, CA, 1993.

Nielsen, J., and Molich, R. Heuristic evaluation of user interfaces. Proc. ACM CHI'90 (Seattle, WA, 1-5 April 1990), 249-256.

Exploding the Interface:
Experiences of a CSCW Network

John Bowers
Dept of Psychology
Manchester University
Manchester
U.K
E-mail: bowers@psy.man.ac.uk

Tom Rodden
Computing Department
Lancaster University
Lancaster LA1 4YR.
U.K.
E-mail: tom@comp.lancs.ac.uk

ABSTRACT

The development of human computer interaction has been dominated by the interface both as a design concept and as an artefact of computer systems. However, recently researchers have been re-examining the role of the interface in the user's interaction with the computer. This paper further examines the notion of the interface in light of the experiences of the authors in establishing a network to support cooperative work. The authors argue that the concept of the single interface which provides a focus for interaction with a computer system is no longer tenable and that richer conceptions of the inter-relationships between users and computer systems are needed.

KEYWORDS

Cooperative Systems, User Interface Models, Observational Studies, Organisational Effects, CSCW.

INTRODUCTION

This paper considers the inter-relationship of users and computer systems within a cooperative setting. The paper examines this relationship in terms of the traditional concept of the user interface. It is our belief that the strength of the interface as a simple abstract model of the real world is problematic. Computer systems within real world organisations are set within a complex environment of cooperating users, complex and inter-related tasks and organisational prejudices and practices. The vagaries of the organisation are an essential part of actual cooperative systems and current conceptions of the interface fail to fully incorporate the issues involved.

We will begin by examining the development of traditional views of the interface from a technical perspective and the challenges to them presented by some researchers within Human Computer Interaction (HCI). In addition, we argue that recent sociological studies of computer use in organisational settings can be taken as indicating how restricted some accepted notions of the interface in HCI are. We then develop this view through a presentation of some of our own field work concerning the installation and maintenance of a computer network in a central government

setting. We document the many conceptions of the interface which arose within the network. Accordingly, we conclude by arguing that a richer conceptualisation of the inter-relationship between users and the systems which support their work is required. This reconsideration of the interface will be important to the kinds of technical and social scientific work emerging in Computer Supported Cooperative Work (CSCW) and to HCI more generally.

EXPLORING THE INTERFACE

The notion of the interface predominates research and development within HCI. It provides the focus for much of the research and thinking within the subject. As we shall analyse in more depth below, the term 'interface' traditionally evokes the image of two distinct domains. Typically in HCI, one domain is taken to be inhabited by human users working on a range of different tasks, while the second domain consists of constituent parts of the computer system. The accepted role of HCI on this view has been to bridge between these two domains to allow the concerns and tasks of users to be successfully manifested within the computer.

However, other understandings of 'interface' are possible. For example, the concept has been used for a considerable time within computer science to define the relationship between identified system components. The ambiguity and complexity surrounding how the concept of interface should be applied presents challenges for theoretical and practical work in HCI. In the next two subsections, we will first examine the technical development of user interface systems as this is discussed in computer science and then consider the general concept of the interface as a theoretical notion within HCI.

User Interface Systems

The user interface manifests itself in most computer systems as a identifiable component devoted to serving the needs of user interaction. As the concept of the user interface has altered so have the demands placed on user interface systems and these have changed to meet these needs. Obviously, for work in CSCW, the most significant feature of this development has been the extension of the user interface to incorporate the needs of more than one user. However, it is important to place the extension of the user interface within some context. This section briefly reviews the various shifts in perspective which have influenced the user interface component of interactive systems.

The Sequential View: Single User and Single Application. Initial interface systems focused on connecting a single user to a single application and concentrated on the interaction between the user undertaking a task and the application which supported this task. This focus allowed developers to consider the functionality of the interface in terms of a dialogue between users and applications. Developers and researchers often adopted a linguistic approach to the design and construction of interface software [6]. This approach was most evident in the initial development of sequential dialogue based systems using formalisms based on grammar descriptions (e.g., SYNGRAPH [21]) or state transition diagrams evocative of syntactic structures (e.g., RAPID/USE [29]).

The Asynchronous View: Single User and Multiple Applications. As computer systems grew in power it became commonplace for a user to exploit multi-tasking environments to allow a range of applications to be used in combination. This altered the approach adopted by developers of interface software and functionality grew to allow a single user to interact with a range of different applications. This new generation of user interface management systems bore little relationship to their predecessors and focus was on the support of a range of applications. Designers and developers increasingly adopted models which supported multi-threaded dialogue to describe the interface. The majority of these exploited event based models of the interface [8]. The development of network based window systems such as NeWS [28] and X Windows [23] extended these models of the user interface to include applications existing on more than one machine.

Multiple Users Interfaces. The emergence of CSCW as a research area has also seen the development of a wide range of cooperative applications with multi-user interfaces. Lauwers [18] outlines two approaches for the development of multi-user interfaces. The development of special purpose applications which are *collaboration aware*, and the adapting of existing single user applications to provide *collaboration transparent* shared applications. Collaboration transparency is often achieved by merely replicating the display portion of existing single user interfaces [12] without altering the interface.

In contrast to the transparent approach to multi-user interfaces, collaboration aware solutions provide facilities to explicitly manage the interface between different users. This approach has been adopted by a range of applications including Cognoter [26] and rIBIS [22]. Each of these systems incorporate many aspects of the management of user interfaces within the application and have adopted a centralised architecture. Recently researchers have started to examine how this arrangement can be generalised to provide supporting interface architectures for collaboration aware applications. These architectures [2, 9, 16] have adopted an increasingly distributed view of the user interface and some have started to consider how the user interface can be 'deconstructed' to meet the needs of distribution [3].

The user interface as a component of applications has altered dramatically over the last two decades. We have moved from a blinkered world where the user interface was focused on a singe user interacting with a single application to undertake a particular task. This has generalised to the situation where modern windowing systems allow users to simultaneously interact with a number of different applications (potentially executing on a range of machines) to undertake a wide variety of tasks. It becomes less obvious exactly what technical component constitutes the user interface in this scenario. The development of cooperative systems has further confused the situation where a variety of users are undertaking a range of tasks, exploiting different machines and potentially different interfaces to many applications.

The Concept of the User Interface

In HCI there have been a number of critical discussions of the concept of the interface. For example, Grudin [11] criticises the interface for been overly focused on a software controlled dialogue to the exclusion of the other organisational features (e.g., documentation and training, organisational procedures, colleagues, consultants etc.) which collectively constitute the interface. As Grudin states:

> These artefacts, processes, and people are so significant in shaping our interaction with the computer that it is myopic not to see them as part of a user's interface to the computer (p271)

If the interface is to extend to incorporate this heterogeneous collection of features the question arises as to what actually constitutes the interface and where the focus of the interface should lie? In a related paper, Grudin [10] examines the shifting focus of the user interface and suggests that we are experiencing a process where the computer has "reached out" over the last forty years to include progressively more and more facets of the organisation.

Similarly, Bannon and Bødker [1] have criticised the field of HCI for its dependence on a narrow cognitivism in its psychological theory and in having a restricted view of it own remit:

> The HCI label appears to be self-explanatory, i.e. anything to do with *people interacting with computers*, yet it has been interpreted more narrowly as simply the study of user interfaces, which seems an extremely limited view. (p5)

Bannon and Bødker go on to note that separating off user interface design issues from a knowledge of the domain in which the system being developed is to be used is bound to lead to inappropriate and potentially unusable systems. The upshot of their argument is a scepticism about the very concept of the interface and even of the field of HCI itself:

> There is a lot of talk about the user interface, but what exactly *is* the interface? Where do we draw the boundary? ... Being provocative, perhaps the very concept of HCI as a distinct topic or discipline concerned with user interfaces needs to be re-thought, and emphasis moved from surface similarities of systems, in terms of interaction style, to understanding their use! (p.9)

Ultimately, for these authors, understanding use means appreciating computer artefacts within workplace activities rather than in terms of the more 'abstract' properties an analysis in cognitive psychological terms may offer.

We are sympathetic with many of these points but rather than go on to directly endorse any alternative theoretical framework for HCI (as Bannon and Bødker do with 'activity theory' or Winograd and Flores [30] do with 'hermeneutics' or Carroll and Campbell [5] do with 'artefact analysis'), we would like to stay with the concept of the interface a little longer and unpack it conceptually in the light of the writers we have discussed and the technical review presented in the previous subsection. In so doing, we want to reflect a little on what has to be assumed before research questions can be entertained as related to 'the interface' (rather than some other notion).

The concept of interface, we would suggest, is intimately tied to the following four conceptual operations:

Separation. A separation or division is made between two kinds of entity. For example, in much talk about user interfaces, a separation is made between the user (conceived of typically as an *individual* human being) and the machine. Similarly, within computer science the interface is used to define relations between separated system sub-components. However, exactly what kinds of entities are separated has varied historically as we and Grudin argue.

Attribution. Having been separated, the entities on either side have certain kinds of properties attributed to them. As many authors have observed, in orthodox HCI, the properties attributed to individual humans are typically gleaned from cognitive or information processing psychology. However, other properties can be imagined, sociological ones for example (as in [27]).

Problematisation. Having separated out two entities and furnished them with properties, problems become apparent or are identified. These often have to do with the *relation* between the two sets of properties, which may be seen as 'incompatible', 'disjoint' or 'mismatched'. Again in orthodox HCI, we hear much of the mismatch between the user's model of the system and that embodied in the system leading to unacceptable or unusable systems (e.g. [20]).

Localisation. Finally, some place or site is identified at which the problems need to be solved or where solutions can be found. This place - *the interface* - is then the focus of our research endeavours. When human individuals are separated from machines, and when the problem is conceived as how to match the presentation of the system with human cognition, the interface often becomes the dialogue between the user and the machine or approximates the screen-plus-keyboard-plus-mouse arrangement of many contemporary workstations. However, these 'interfaces' are historically contingent ones and the *outcome* of the conceptual acts of separation, attribution, problematisation and localisation. (Our identification of these 'conceptual acts' has been influenced by a number of contributions to the sociology of science. Indeed, much of this literature suggests that acts analogous to what we've called separation, and so on are very general features of scientific work. See Latour [17], Callon [4], Star [24] inter alia.)

REWORKING THE INTERFACE

Identifying what is at issue in the concept of interface is also of use for organising different views of what HCI is. We suggest that different views of the field can be distinguished in terms of the responses which would be given to abstract questions such as: what do you see as separate from what? what are the properties of those entities? what are the problems which arise from how to inter-relate those sets of properties? where are solutions to be found? As long as answers can be given to these questions, a coherent concept of interface might be achieved. That is, organising the field of HCI around 'interface issues' will continue to be workable. However, if researchers become unhappy with their usual answers or with these very questions themselves, the interface may seem a less tenable concept and HCI may require an abrupt shift of focus.

The Interface Yields

Let us illustrate these points by reference to some recent sociological studies of technology in the workplace. Heath and Luff [14, 15] have extensively studied the activity of control room operators in the London Underground. The working environment of the operators includes a number of different artefacts - notebooks, schedules, timetables, computer screens, headsets, microphones. In addition, along the length of one of the walls of the control room is a representation of the underground line - called 'the fixed line diagram' - using a strip of lights. The location of trains is shown by illuminating the lights corresponding to the section of track where the train is. In this way, the goal of a regular, uninterrupted service can be seen at a glance as a series of equally spaced illuminations. Heath and Luff document in some detail how two control operators coordinate their activities while maintaining their different responsibilities. This is principally achieved by overhearing and other forms of surreptitious monitoring of the other's conduct which establish coordination without interruption. A number of points can be made about this example. First, the workers have available to them a heterogeneous assembly of representational technologies. There are several artefacts in play and juxtaposing the properties of one with the properties of another is an important aspect of the work which amongst other things encourages fault tolerance under time-critical conditions. When we consider a 'working practice' as our unit of activity, it seems that we should no longer speak of an interface but of interface*s*. Furthermore, consider the fixed line diagram. That it is publicly available matters greatly to the working activity of the controllers. Both can see it and both can see that the other can see it. If we wish for a notion of the interface as the 'material surface' of the system, its significance changes. The interface is no longer a private affair between a single user and a single piece of technology as is classically studied in HCI. The interface is publicly available as a resource for social action and interaction.

Greatbatch et al. [7] continue this theme of interface issues as being of social-interactional significance in their study of the usage of a computerised medical records system in primary health care. They analyse a series of examples where doctors interact with the records system during a consultation with the patient. These indicate that, while the doctor is typing in to the system, the patient will tend to speak only at (or shortly after) those junctures which are signalled by the press of the return key. That is, patients seem to time very precisely how they interact with the doctor if the doctor is interacting with the system. It turns out that, with this records system, hitting return is the way in which the doctor is able to move the insertion point from one field to the next and that this is a consistent feature of the system's interface. Thus, as hitting return corresponds to what might be considered as a boundary between two segments of activity on the doctor's part, the patient's timing behaviour serves to locate the moments when the doctor is more readily interruptible. Greatbatch et al. now make an important point. User interface consistency is often emphasised in the HCI literature because of the cognitive advantages of consistency with respect to learnability and so on. However, consistency has aspects which go beyond just the advantages which might accrue to an individual user, for it is interface consistency which, in this case, enables the patient to 'project' when the doctor might be interruptible and hence when it is appropriate for the patient to initiate interaction.

Given this complex pattern of interaction that surrounds and involves the records system: what now is its interface? And how do we accommodate the different parties involved? Do we give each a point of view onto the system and imagine that each involves a different interface? What is the interface from the patient's point of view and how does it differ from the doctor's? The designer's? The machine's? While it may seem fanciful to ask for the machine's point of view (but see [31,11]), these questions emphasise the difficulty of adhering to certain familiar notions of user interface while appreciating the sociality of working activities.

Ethnographies of Technology
Our argument so far has been that several recent studies of interaction with computers in actual workplace settings suggest that familiar notions of the user interface as a boundary between an individual user and a machine are beginning to yield to a more socialised concept. That is, once we appreciate computer use in organisational settings, we need to change our commitments as to what is separated from what, and what properties get attributed etc. In Harper, Hughes and Shapiro's [13] ethnographic study of a failed attempt at computerisation in air traffic control (ATC) what was problematic for the controllers was the relation between their socially organised working practices and a computer system deficient in properties such as "robustness" and "trustworthiness". This is not to say that properties such as user interface consistency or issues such as menu and icon design might not also be important to the success of an ATC system. Rather, we are arguing that, *from the point of view of the controllers*, the salient issues lie elsewhere and concern properties of the system relevant to the coordination of their working activity, rather than individual cognition.

Ethnographic studies of technology like Harper et al.'s are increasingly popular in HCI and CSCW. One of the main benefits proponents of ethnography identify is that such studies uncover the organisation of working activity at a level of detail which other methods trivialise or cannot access. However, ethnographies have another feature worth noting. They encourage a scepticism on the part of the analyst for all 'received' wisdom and taken for granted theoretical categories which we might feel tempted to impose on what is observed 'in the field'. Thus, the ethnographer tends not to be tempted into assuming that the most important aspects of human computer interaction *must* lie at the user interface or in any other single, fixed location for that matter (cf. [31]). Rather, the task of the ethnographer is to *find out* what happens to be problematic in the specific field site in question and to see how participants produce and work with *their own* received wisdom and taken for granted categories. In terms of our analysis of what is at stake in formulating a concept of interface (separation, attribution, problematisation, localisation), ethnographic studies of computing technology enable us to pose the questions: where do *participants* (organisation members) see the interface as residing? what do *they* treat it as being? between what separated entities? with what properties? raising what problems? This ethnographic orientation and these questions have framed the field study we report in the next section.

THE FIELD STUDY: A 'CSCW NETWORK' IN A U.K. CENTRAL GOVERNMENT ORGANISATION
The setting for our fieldwork has been an organisation within the United Kingdom's central government. This organisation, which we shall call 'CGO', is responsible for developing the standards, procurement policies and specifications of good practice which central government organisations should observe with respect to government computing. Amongst CGO's various branches, the Future Technology Branch (FTB) is most concerned with exploring new computing developments and research in computer science and allied trades. Anticipating that it may be of relevance to central government computing, FTB has conducted a number of studies of CSCW, employing a series of consultants over the last four years who have between them written a review monograph on the subject and explored how CSCW may impact upon more established methods of systems analysis and design. Over the last 18 months, FTB have themselves installed a network of computers which runs a variety of applications of the sort discussed in CSCW. It is this network, the issues involved in its construction and maintenance and in the use of the applications present and how all of these matters are experienced in CGO which is the subject of the rest of this section.

Our account of the network and of CGO is based on a three year study of this organisation and its interest in CSCW. One of us (JB) has conducted numerous interviews (mostly open ended and tape-recorded) with organisation members throughout this period as well as tape-recording meetings, and being present as a participant-observer while work was being done. The other (TR) has been closely involved with the technical issues surrounding the initial set up and configuration of the network. What follows is based on both the experiences of establishing a CSCW network and analyses of the varied and large corpus of materials we have accumulated related to its use (transcriptions, field notes, documents, memos, correspondence).

The Architecture of the Network

The principle focus for investigating the applicability of CSCW at the FTB was the procurement and installation of the CSCW network. Initially the network consisted on an Ethernet connecting 10 Macintoshes spread across 4 floors of the central building. However, as the organisation was spread over two different sites a number of Macintosh™ Powerbooks™ were acquired to allow remote access to the network. These machines quickly became considered part of the CSCW network by the members of FTB. Each machine connected to the network had a number of groupware systems installed including:

Inforum™	A computer conferencing system
Timbuktu™	A screen sharing application
MeetingMaker™	A group diary system
Quickmail™	An advanced electronic mail facility
Aspects™	A group editing application
Markup™	A group commenting and annotation system

Rather than evaluate these individual applications in an isolated and experimental manner the intent of the network was to allow users to utilise these applications to support the work of FTB in as naturalistic a manner as possible.

A major impact on the use of the network by the group was the model of distribution used to construct groupware applications. Almost without exception all of the groupware applications exploited some variant of the client server model. This architecture is interesting in its impact on the various interfaces presented to the group by the network. In particular, this architecture provides us with a simple framework for examining the various concepts of interface to emerge within the network.

The client server model divides distributed applications into two distinct components each with particular functionality. The server acts as the central hub of the application and provides a set of services for surrounding client processes. In groupware systems the client process normally presents an interface to the user and manages user interaction with the distributed application. In fact three distinct classes of interface proved to be significant for most groupware systems on the network.

The User Interface Provided by the Server. In general groupware systems required a particular server component on the network, this was realised as a separate application which ran on a dedicated machine. In addition to acting as a server for distributed clients these applications provided a specialised configuration interface which allowed some

notional 'privileged user' to configure the groupware system. In our case where a separate systems administrator was not available this configuration became a burdensome overhead for the particular group members involved in setting up the groupware systems.

Additionally, the use of a separate application to simultaneously work as a groupware system server and a means of configuring the system often yielded major inconsistencies. Simultaneously the same user would be called, "Tom Rodden", "T Rodden", "Tom", and, in particularly bizarre cases involving licence restrictions applied to a server, " BigMac210" and "Jon in Ipswich".

The User Interface Provided by the Client. The client component of groupware systems provided the 'normal' user interface for individual group members. In groupware systems these clients were realised as distinct applications running on machines connected to the network. These applications existed within the personal domains of users individual machines. Subsequently users felt free to adapt and tailor client applications in line with the accepted practice of modern interface thinking. However, rather than being individual applications these clients were linked via the servers to clients applications of other users. Users often customised either their individual operating system (through the Macintosh interface) or altered particular settings within the application which effected the overall groupware system.

This independence of the client application led to particular problems with the CSCW network. These included:

- The alterations of menu settings causing confusion when screens were been shared by users.

- Inadvertently changing the properties of shared folders to prevent access by members of the group.

- The use of incompatible style settings within shared editing applications.

- The alteration of Macintosh system settings to alter the name of the either the machine or the user.

Users within the network had distinct problems accepting that applications on their 'personal' machine played an important role in groupware systems and that the consequences of amending certain attributes of these applications impacted others. In fact, some people on the network were resistant to the intrusion of others on their machine and went to some lengths to maintain the individual identity of their machine. In some cases network users insisted on using incompatible versions of system software.

The Client Server Interface. In addition to the different interfaces provided to users by both client and server programs a further interface was crucial to the effectiveness of the network. Supporting the interface between the client and server programs was crucial to the distributed groupware systems installed on the network. Administration within the CSCW network was neither allocated to a specialised system administrator nor added to the normal working practice of the group using the network. As a result it became the responsibility of a small number of individuals to ensure the network was behaving "normally". As one network user stated: "The problem is people assume that these applications are easy to install but they don't realise that I seem to spend all my time fixing the network". Fixing the network consisted of ensuring availability of servers on the network. Problems emerged which often highlighted a number interfaces of significance to the network. These interfaces included:

The Personal-Public Interface. Within the network users often altered their personal machine and in the process would halt a server application providing a service to a number of other network users. This personal action of a user altering their own machine often had public consequences with a direct and negative effect on group relationships.

The Departmental Interface. The CSCW network was non-standard within CGO. However the network was connected to the standard corporate network and interference between the protocols used within the CSCW network and the corporate network occasionally occurred. This interference and the subsequent accounts of responsibility highlighted the distinctions between different departments within the organisation.

The Organisational Interface. Users within the CGO worked within the bounds of policy outlined by the organisation. This policy often proved problematic in maintaining network services. For example, accepted policy within the organisation was that all machines should be turned off when users were not present. If a machine running a server application were turned off then the work of connected users would be severely disrupted!

This subsection has examined some of the various concepts of the interface which emerged within a cooperative network. It is not particularly surprising that a number of different perceptions of the interface are relevant within a complex system such as a cooperative network. However, it should be stressed that the network as a whole depended on the combined effects of these different interfaces and the relationships between these were a significant feature in determining the behaviour of the network. Perhaps, then, if we are to retain a unitary concept of *the* interface, it is best applied to how the group view and interact with the network *as a whole*. However, any adoption of a network-as-the-interface concept would be far from simple as the following subsection illustrates.

The Network as a Heterogeneous Object

Throughout our study of the CSCW network, we have noted a wide variation in the ways organisation members talk about and treat their work, the network and the organisation itself. For example, the network is often discussed in a technical discourse in terms, say, of the processing and storage capacities of the machines and how their communication protocols relate to those observed in other networks in the organisation. However, we also hear the network formulated as an economic object ("CGO have

invested a lot of money in this network; we have to demonstrate a return"), a political entity ("CSCW and a lot of networking hype are all about greater workplace democracy but this organisation isn't really like that"), a source of individual empowerment ("using the network I should be able to communicate much more effectively with other people; I could deal with problems immediately and not have to wait for someone's next free slot in their diary"), an object with potential organisational implications ("if this network were to be successful, lateral communication across the whole of CGO would improve; the left hand would know what the right was doing!"), a personal matter connected with the project manager's own individual interests and ambitions ("it is after all Dan's baby"), etc. etc.

Depending on whether the network is conceived technically, economically, politically, organisationally, or in personal terms, different problems identified (e.g. inter-operability, costs, working conditions agreements, project management issues, Des' lengthy working hours and high motivation) and different entities are named (e.g. operating systems, budgets, trade unions, project teams, Des). The network has raised a whole set of radically *heterogeneous* concerns. Indeed, especially in the early stages of the CSCW network project at CGO, it was unclear which, if any, of these concerns was paramount. It would certainly be misleading to assume a priori that, say, individual empowerment or economic efficiency is *the* issue which frames all the others, misleading both for us theoretically and as a description of the CGO workers in their own orientation to the network. Anyway, this presumption would defeat our 'sceptical' ethnographic orientation. Rather, a more appropriate stance is to study how the organisation members *themselves* orient towards and manage this heterogeneity (cf. [19]).

As an example of this, we can cite how one of the senior managers participating in the network project, Jon, came to regard this heterogeneity - the mass of different ways different organisation members had for dealing with and talking about the network - as indicating a confusion about the aims of the CSCW networking project. That is, Jon problematised the heterogeneity itself. To address this, Jon suggested a distinction should be observed between "the operational" and "the experimental". The former category is explicated by Jon as referring to the technical aspects of the CSCW network, how the network relates to others in the organisation and how it should be managed so as to ensure consistency between software version numbers and such like. According to Jon, it is this alone that Dan, the project manager, should concern himself with (assisted by one of us - TR). In contrast, the experimental aspects of the network are formulated by Jon as concerned with "the impacts of the network on teamwork". Indeed, the non-existence (according to Jon) of teamwork in FTB and in CGO more generally is often taken by him as one of the major problems that the organisation faces, especially in the light of the recent organisational changes mentioned above. For Jon, the experimental aspects of the network are closely tied to quantitative evaluation: the impacts of the network on teamwork are to be assessed by comparing "performance indicators". Furthermore, it should be the main task of one of us (JB) to refine appropriate performance indicators and make the measurements. In this way, Jon is offering a strategy for sorting out the heterogeneity, distinguishing between the important and the unimportant, while defining roles for Dan, TR and JB which they are invited to fill. Much of Jon's activity in the more recent phases of the project involves attempts to rally the team members around this distinction so that they can see themselves and their duties in this common picture of what the project is all about. (These strategies can be compared with others which have been noted in studies of scientific and technical work: e.g. 'enrolment' as documented by Callon [4] and Latour [17], the creation of 'boundary objects' [25].)

These aspects of our experience working with the CSCW network project in CGO underline the difficulty of sustaining an accepted concept of interface to aid understanding what's going on. First, the multiplicity of different ways the users (network group members) have for orienting towards the network (economic, organisational and the rest) make it hard to pick out just one boundary between entities and call that *the* interface. One can just as readily talk about the interface between the networking-system and budgetary and accounting practices as that between it and the individual users. If a single site for the interface does emerge, it is because strategies to simplify this multiplicity (like Jon's described above) have been successful. But this is a contingent feature of a particular work setting, something which may or may not work out (Jon's attempts to identify where the problems lie may not be successful). Whether a single site for the interface emerges certainly cannot be predicted in advance and hence should not be assumed at the outset of analysis. Furthermore, when more traditional notions of interface *are* oriented towards by participants, the *organisational significance* of interface design is typically also in attendance. For example, the layout of the Macintosh screen has been variously described as "not a CGO-style interface", "not in accordance with our standards" and such like. Even when a recognisable (from the point of view of much work in HCI) concept of interface is encountered, it swiftly leads to other concerns and from there to yet others and so on.

CONCLUSION
In this paper we have examined the different views of the interface which have emerged from HCI and their relevance to CSCW. We have examined the interface both as a technical component and as a theoretical concept to support an understanding of human computer interaction. The notion of the interface appears to be under considerable pressure when considered from either of these perspectives. Rather than suggest an alternative concept to replace the interface we have attempted to discover the applicability and usefulness of the interface as a theoretical framework within actual work settings. This has been undertaken by direct reference to a field study of the development and installation of a CSCW network within a government organisation.

When we examine the use of the network containing a range of groupware systems we discover a plethora of interfaces of importance to the users. These interfaces are technical, organisational, procedural, social, political and even emotional. No single interface appears to be always dominant and at various times during the life of the network different interfaces have particular prominence for different users.

Grudin [10] claims that the computer is reaching out. We would like to compliment this view by suggesting that the organisation is also *reaching in*. As are workplace politics, emotions and the rest. *Interfaces are the provisional and temporary sites where these trajectories collide and problems get articulated*

The strength of the concept of the interface as an abstraction and reification of the real world proves especially problematic within cooperative settings of the sort studied in CSCW. Rather than the properties of any single interface what appears to be most significant are the various interactions and dependencies between these interfaces. Computer systems within work settings are complex artefacts existing within a social setting. Understanding and discovering the different relationships between users, the computer systems and the actual work will be of fundamental importance in developing systems to support this work. If this means 'exploding' the interface into many fragmentary sites where 'interfacing' goes on, then so be it.

ACKNOWLEDGEMENTS
The authors acknowledge support from both CCTA, Department of the Treasury, HM Government and the Commission of the European Community (ESPRIT Basic Research Project 6225 - COMIC). We also thank the support provided by Rank Xerox EuroPARC and comments on earlier versions from colleagues and anonymous reviewers.

REFERENCES
1. Bannon, L., Bødker, S. 'Beyond the Interface: Encountering Artefacts in Use', in *Designing Interaction: Psychological Theory at the Human-Computer Interface*, Carroll, J. (ed), Erlbaum, 1989.

2. Bentley R, Rodden T, Sawyer P, Sommerville I, ' An architecture to support tailorable multi-user displays', *Proceeding of CSCW'92*, Toronto, November 1992, ACM press.

3. Bier E., Freeman S 'Deconstructing the Workstation' in Arnold, D.B., Day, R.A., Duce, D.A., Gallop, J.R, Sutcliffe, D.C., Distributed Systems, Theory and Practice:, Eurographics Technical Report Series, ISSN 1017-4656, Eurographics Association. Springer-Verlag.

4. Callon, M. 'Some Elements of a Sociology of Translation: Domestication of the Scallops and the Fishermen of St. Brieuc Bay', in *Power, Action and Belief: A New Sociology of Knowledge?* Law, J. (ed), Sociological Review Monograph 32, Routledge and Kegan Paul, 1986.

5. Carroll, J., Campbell, R. *Artefacts as Psychological Theories: The Case of Human Computer Interaction*, IBM RC 13454 (#60225), 1989.

6. Foley J.D. ' The structure of interactive command languages', In proceedings of the IFIP workshop on the Methodology of interaction. North Holland, Amsterdam, pp 227-234.

7. Greatbatch D., Luff P., Heath C., Campion P. 'Interpersonal Communication and Human-Computer Interaction: an examination of the use of computers in medical consultations', Interacting with Computers, in press.

8. Green M, ' A survey of three Dialogue models', ACM transactions on Graphics, 5 (3) , July 1986, pp 244-275.

9. Greenberg, S., Bohnet, R., 'GroupSketch: A multi-user sketchpad for geographically-distributed small groups.', in *Proceedings of Graphics Interface*, June 5-7, Calgary, Alberta, 1991.

10. Grudin, J. 'The Computer Reaches Out: The Historical Continuity of Interface Design.' Proceedings of ACM CHI'90 Conference on Human Factors in Computing Systems. Evolution and Practice in User Interface Engineering. pp261-268.

11. Grudin, J. 'interface.' Proceedings of ACM CSCW'90 Conference on Computer-Supported Cooperative Work. User Interfaces in the CSCW Context. Pages: 269-278.

12. Gust, P., 'Shared X: X in a distributed group work environment', *presented at the 2nd Annual X conference*, MIT, Boston, January 1988.

13. Harper, R. R., Hughes, J. A., Shapiro, D. Z., 'Working in harmony: An examination of computer technology in air traffic control.', in *Proceedings of the 1st European Conference on Computer Supported Cooperative Work* (EC-CSCW '89), September 13-15, Computer Sciences House, Gatwick, Slough, UK, 1989.

14. Heath, C., Luff, P. 'Collaborative Activity and Technological Design: Task Coordination in London Underground Control Rooms', in *Proceedings of ECSCW'91*, Bannon, L., Robinson, M., Schmidt, K. (eds), Sept 25-27, Kluwer, 1991, pp 65-80.

15. Heath, C., Luff, P. 'Collaboration and Control: Crisis Management and Multimedia Technology in London Underground Line Control Rooms', Computer Supported Cooperative Work, in press.

16. Hill, R.D. 'The Abstraction-Link-View Paradigm: Using Constraints to Connect User Interfaces to Applications.' Proceedings of ACM CHI'92 Conference on Human Factors in Computing Systems. Pages: 335-342.

17. Latour, B. *Science in Action*, Open University Press, 1987.

18. Lauwers, J. C., Lantz, K. A., 'Collaboration awareness in support of collaboration transparency: Requirements for the next generation of shared window systems', in *Proceedings of CHI '90*, April 1-5, Seattle, Washington, ACM, 1990, pp 303-311.

19. Law, J., 'Technology and Heterogeneous Engineering: The Case of Portugese Expansion', in *The Social Construction of Technological Systems: New Directions in the Sociology and History of Technology*, MIT Press, 1987.

20. Norman, D., 'Cognitive Engineering', in *User Centered System Design*, Norman, D., Draper, S. (eds), Erlbaum, 1986.

21. Olsen, D., 'Automatic Generation of interactive systems'. Comput. Graph 17,1, January 1983, pp53-57.

22. Rein, G. L., Ellis, C. A., 'rIBIS: A real-time group hypertext system', *International Journal of Man Machine Studies*, 34(3), March 1991, pp 349-368

23. Scheifler, R. W., Gettys, J., 'The X Window System', ACM Transactions of Graphics, 5(2), April 1986.

24. Star, S. L. *Regions of the Mind: Brain Research and the Quest for Scientific Certainty*, Stanford University Press, 1989.

25. Star, S. L., Griesemer, J., 'Institutional Ecology, "Translations", and Coherence: Amateurs and Professionals in Berkeley's Museum of Vertebrate Zoology, 1907-1939', Social Studies of Science, 19, 387-420, 1989.

26. Stefik, M., Foster, G., Bobrow, D. G., Kahn, K., Lanning, S., Suchman, L., 'Beyond the chalkboard: computer support for collaboration and problem solving in Meetings', *Communications of the ACM*, 30(1), January 1987, pp 32-47.

27. Suchman, L. *Plans and Situated Actions: The Problem of Human Machine Communication*, Cambridge University Press, 1987.

28. Sun Microsystems, 'NeWS Manual', 800-1632-10, Revision A, March 1987.

29. Wasserman, A. I., Shewmake, D.T. ' Rapid prototyping of interactive information systems'. ACM SIGSOFT Software Engineering Notes, Dec 1982. pp 1-18

30. Winograd, T., Flores, F. *Understanding Computers and Cognition: A New Foundation for Design*, Ablex, 1986.

31. Woolgar, S. 'Configuring the User: The Case of Usability Trials', in *A Sociology of Monsters: Essays on Power, Technology and Domination*, Law, J. (ed), Sociological Review Monograph 38, Routledge and Kegan Paul, 1991.

SEARCHING FOR UNITY AMONG DIVERSITY: EXPLORING THE "INTERFACE" CONCEPT

Kari Kuutti
University of Oulu
Dept. of Information Processing Science
Linnanmaa, SF-90570 Oulu FINLAND
E-mail: kuutti@rieska.oulu.fi

Liam J. Bannon
University of Limerick
Dept. of Computer Science and Inf. Systems
Limerick, Ireland.
E-mail: bannonl@ul.ie

ABSTRACT

Despite widespread interest in the human-computer interaction (HCI) field, there remains much debate as to appropriate conceptual frameworks for the field, and even confusion surrounding the meaning of basic terms in the field. HCI is seen by many as focusing on the design of interfaces to computer systems, yet exactly what is implied by this focus on "interfaces" is unclear. In this paper we show how a better understanding of what is meant by the interface is possible via the concept of abstraction levels. We show how this levels approach can clarify some ambiguities, and also how it can be related to different phases in the evolution of the human-computer interaction field itself. In this context, we are able to account for the recent interest in activity theory as a possible alternative framework for HCI work, while stressing the need for HCI research and design to consider each of the separate, but related, levels.

KEYWORDS: interface, user interface management systems, abstraction levels, activity theory

INTRODUCTION

The field of human-computer interaction (HCI) is characterised by a healthy heterogeneity of distinct disciplinary frameworks, - cognitive psychology, software engineering, human engineering, etc., focusing on a wide variety of issues surrounding the human use of computer systems. Likewise, a wide range of orientations can be found, from a focus on more practical concerns of system design and use to quite fundamental discussions concerning human information processing strategies in interacting with computers. This eclecticism of disciplinary backgrounds, and mix of academic and commercial concerns lends colour and vitality to the HCI community, as witnessed by the variety of topics covered, and approaches described, at the annual ACM SIGCHI Conferences. However, attempting to establish some coherence concerning fundamental concepts or issues in such a melting pot of ideas and orientations is no easy task.

It would be helpful if we could formulate an overarching "theory" of HCI as a research and design field, taking into account its multifaceted, yet holistic, nature. The theory would need to provide some coherence and links between

© 1993 ACM 0-89791-575-5/93/0004/0263...$1.50

the existing subdomains, despite their different and incommensurate conceptualisations, models and explanations. The need for such a theoretical framework has been raised by several researchers. For example, Barnard [3] comments:

"This chapter has considered bridging between specifically cognitive theory and behavior in human-computer interaction. This form of bridging is but one among many that need to be pursued. For example, there is a need to develop bridging representations that will enable us to interrelate models of user cognition with the formed models being developed to support design by software engineers. Similarly there is a need to bridge between cognitive models and aspects of the application and the situation of use. Truly interdisciplinary research formed a large part of the promise, but little of the reality of early HCI research. Like the issue of tackling nonideal user behavior, interdisciplinary bridging is now very much on the agenda for the next phase of research" (Barnard [3], pp. 122-123).

On the other hand, some researchers are deeply sceptical if such overarching theories can ever exist:

"For the most part, useful theory is impossible, because the behavior of human-computer systems is chaotic or worse, highly complex, dependent on many unpredictable variables or just too hard to understand. Where it is possible, the use of theory will be constrained or modest, because theories will be so imprecise, will cover only limited aspects of the behavior, will be applicable only to some parts or some systems, and will not necessarily generalize; as a result, they will yield little advantage over empirical methods" (Landauer [18], p. 60).

Despite this scepticism, we suggest in this short paper that the quest for such theories may not be totally Utopian. The "integrative perspectives" approach put forward here argues that HCI as an object of research and design — an integrated, systemic whole — can consist of a system of mutually irreducible subdomains, each having their own unique conceptualisations and explanations, and thus each requiring their own "perspective". The integrity of the systemic whole is maintained by "integrating" the perspectives ("bridging" in the vocabulary of Barnard in the previous quotation). This idea of "integrative perspectives", while not new, has recently re-surfaced in several disciplines struggling with similar kinds of problems[*].

In order to show the implications of such an argument, we take the reader on a journey through the terminological

---

[*] For example, Tobach [32] and Tolman [33] explicitly discuss such a programme for psychology.

minefield we have uncovered surrounding a very fundamental concept within HCI, namely "the interface". We first uncover a number of different usage's of the term, and note some of the distinctions people have made in this area. We next attempt to provide a more coherent conceptual framework for discussing the interface concept, arguing that the term is used in a variety of different ways, which can be accounted for if we take an "integrated perspectives" approach, discussing the different meanings of the term from each perspective. In the remaining sections of the paper, we broaden our horizon, and show how the development of the whole field of HCI can be viewed in terms of shifting perspectives on the basic unit of analysis for the field. We believe that such an approach helps in understanding the current debate within the field concerning an appropriate theoretical framework for HCI.

CHARACTERISING THE INTERFACE

Much of the discipline of human-computer interaction necessarily revolves around the design and use of the human-computer interface. By this is usually meant all aspects of the interaction between the computer system and the person, and not only that part of the computer system that deals with input and output. Indeed, for many people, the whole field of human-computer interaction (HCI) is synonymous with the design and use of interfaces to computing systems. However, discussions of the "interface" involving, for example designers and users, or even different members of an interdisciplinary design team, can become rather confusing if the differences in use of the term [see, e.g. Grudin, 10] are not made clear at the outset. There have been a number of calls from interdisciplinary design groups for clarifying confusions surrounding the use of "interface" and other terms in HCI, through the development of a common dictionary of concepts, so as to alleviate problems of miscommunication between people from different disciplinary backgrounds. Apart from problems surrounding practical enforcement procedures for such a grand unifying plan, the very idea is, we believe problematic. The problems cannot be resolved simply by making more exact definitions. This is because the use of the terms is spread across a variety of disciplines, and it is impossible to enforce a single meaning of a term already in use across these quite distinct, even if overlapping communities. The meanings of terms that are shared in a community of practice are not easily changed by stipulative definitions from some legalistic body, as these meanings are embodied in use in the different communities and quite resistant to such attempts at changing definition and usage. The least that we could do would be try to make the contexts of use of the term clearer for all the parties involved, so that they can recognise that use of the same term at different times, by different groups, does *not* imply similar meanings.

Interface separability

While the HCI area is acknowledged to be an interdisciplinary one, the loudest voice has usually belonged to psychologists. A line of demarcation between programmers and psychologists in software design is sometimes drawn by focusing on the separation of the "interface" from the underlying "functionality" of the system. As Robinson [28] notes: "The interface stands as the boundary between what is the work of HCI and what is the work of the software engineer. The "true" nature of the system - what it does - is defined by the state of the software 'behind' the interface...the neutral and objective functionality of the 'internal' state (of the machine) may be realised by alternative interface designs". Such an approach has had the unfortunate effect of reifying the interface concept for much of the HCI community as the prime object of study. This reification has also tended to result in an undue emphasis on rather "surface" aspects of interface design, within many of the different interpretations of the interface that are commonly used. Thus studies on how to redesign menus, or make more meaningful command abbreviations become seen as prototypical. Yet, paradoxically, this reification of the interface as the domain of HCI has actually marginalized its impact. For example, Seymour Papert [26] recently commented: "...if only the interface (is changed), and what lies behind it and what you can do with the system isn't changed, you're only scratching the surface. The interface is only the surface.."; and Mike Hammer [13] put it bluntly: "In reality, user interface is a second-order factor...".

Over the past few years, a number of people have pointed to the neglect of the task context in which human-computer interaction is taking place, and an undue emphasis on lower level interface issues [2, 5, 8, 12, 24, 31]. They argue that much of the HCI world pays too little attention to the underlying functionality of the computer applications and their usability in everyday work contexts. The idea that we can separate out the design of the interface from the design of the functionality of the system, and perhaps also the coding of the interface from the coding of the rest of the application has generated a lot of discussion over the last several years. As we have seen, it can be seen as a possible territorial division of responsibility between software engineers and HCI people, as well as having implications for the software development process, and the modularization of code. The popularity of User Interface Management Systems (UIMS's) significantly contributed to the impression of this separability, despite some warnings about the limitations of such systems, even by their proponents [e.g. see Tanner & Buxton, 30]. In designing a program or system, we obviously must pay attention to the needs of the user and the use situation, and to how the design will meet these needs. The idea that in such situations a neat separation between interface and functionality can be accomplished is open to question.

So far we have discussed some problems with the meaning of the "interface" term as well as the choice of the "interface" as the object of study for HCI. The simple interface-functionality separation begs many questions. What we need is some kind of a general framework that provides a more grounded and conceptually coherent set of concepts within which to discuss the design of computer systems which people can use in their daily work. In the next section we introduce one such framework, which has been used in the information systems design community, and which we believe can provide a useful starting point for developing such a framework.

THE INTERFACE IS NOT A UNITARY CONCEPT

One reason for the evolving meaning of important terms in the field is linked to the shifting focus of interface research and development. For example Grudin [11] has argued for a five-phase shift, starting from 'the interface at the hardware' and ending with 'the interface at the work setting', each phase having a different viewpoint and emphasis. It is thus not surprising that the idea of clarifying meanings through discussing the interface from several perspectives, or levels, has appealed to a number of researchers [4, 7, 9, 16, 27, 29, 34]. There are some problems with these attempts, however. Although the use of different perspectives may help in clarifying different approaches to the interface, it does not necessarily help in relating them to each other because of the lack of any unifying background. Even in those cases where a hierarchical, layered model has been proposed [7, 29], the result is more *ad hoc*. Perhaps the most useful is the Rasmussen [27] five-level abstraction hierarchy, which is based on the general functional properties of a technical system.

There is, however, yet another tradition concerning use of different perspectives, namely, that of the information systems (IS) community. It has a closer relationship to interface issues than the "technical systems" discussed by Rasmussen and we suggest that it might be beneficial to use the experience collected there in clarifying some of the confusions noted above. It can also serve as an example of a practically -oriented, long-term, project to develop what we mean by "integrative perspectives" in a related field.

Integrative perspectives in information systems

There has been a long history in the IS field relating to the development of a set of interrelated models which together could be capable of grasping the multifaceted nature of information systems - in design and use. The nature of these model-sets corresponds closely to our idea of "integrative perspectives". Different researchers call these perspectives with different names such as "abstraction levels" [Iivari, 15], or "object system contexts" [Lyytinen, 21]. Because the following discussion of IS views is based primarily on Iivari's work, we use his terminology, although we do not fully subscribe to his notion of "levels"[*].

What are "abstraction levels"? The term refers to a widely accepted principle that in order to handle the complexity of IS design it must be divided into several levels or subdomains, which can each be treated relatively independently, each having their own models, concepts, methods and background theories (See Iivari, 1989 for an explication). The three levels of abstraction commonly discussed in the IS community are: *organisational, conceptual, and technical*. The organisational level contains a description or model of organisational practice to be

supported by the IS, and a description of IS functions. Sometimes the definition of this domain is called the *requirements* of the system. Traditionally, this has been developed by the system analyst, but during recent years more participatory forms of development have surfaced. The conceptual level is the most central in most development methodologies, containing abstract, conceptual models of both the object domain ('universe of discourse') and the system itself. Sometimes the definition of the domain has been called the *specification* of the system. Finally, the technical level contains practical, concrete objects and processes: databases, programs, machine and communication architectures, input and output devices etc. The links between the domains consist of different transformation procedures, formal and informal [For more on these subdomains and relations between them, see e. g. 25]. It does not matter if it is impossible to discuss topics at the organisational level using the concepts and vocabulary of the technological level and vice versa, as long as we can establish the transformational procedures needed in order to cross the borders. In the next section we will briefly note how such a structure could be utilised within HCI to clarify some of the interface issues which we have been discussing.

The interface in terms of integrative perspectives

Following the IS example above, we suggest that it might also be beneficial to have several different definitions of interface - one for each level. Note that this layering is fundamentally different from attempts to make a separation between the 'interface' and the 'application'. In our suggestion the demarcation line is not drawn between the interface and application, but between the different design domains of an application, each containing also an interface as an integral part. The nature of the relationship between what is assumed to belong to the 'interface' and the 'application' parts need not remain the same from level to level.

What, then, are the appropriate definitions of the interface for each level? First, the 'uppermost' level must be redefined. In our opinion, the term 'organisation' is too broad, yet we wish to go beyond individual work support, so we discuss the interface at the *work process or use situation* level. At this level we are quite happy with a definition put forward by Andersen [1]: "Instead of seeing it (i.e. the interface) as a part of the program I propose that we view it as a relation between program and use context....It does not make sense to say that a system in isolation has an interface; interfaces "emerge" when the system is used...". Thus, from the user's viewpoint in the use situation, the interface *is* the system. There is no possibility to separate interface from functionality, for the interface is the way a user's work is supported by the system. At the *conceptual* level, the interface is that part of a system or application which must be understood and mastered in order to utilise the system meaningfully for some purpose in some definite use situation. An implication is that the role of the interface can vary in different applications. In fact, we have a whole spectrum of applications: At one end we have applications which have no human interface whatsoever, e.g. EDI (electronic data interchange) programs. At the other end of the spectrum we

---

[*] There is a danger of interpreting the different "levels" simply in terms of level of detail. The relationships between the subdomains (despite terms such as 'hierarchical' and 'level') have nothing to do with levels of detail or hierarchical decomposition. The relationship is more like a means-ends relation: the 'lower' levels describe the means used to realise the ends of the next-upper level which again contains the means to realise the next level and so on. So there is a certain top-down determinacy, but not vice versa: the same ends can be achieved using different means. Of course, the 'lower' levels form the potential resources for realisation and may enable or restrict the achievement of certain 'upper'-level goals.

have programs which can be claimed to contain nothing but the interface, e.g. scientific visualisation, where it can be argued that the whole application belongs to the interface (Kuutti & Bannon, 1991). Finally we have the interface at the *technological level*. Newman and Sproull's (1979) definition of the interface in their classic text comes close to what we mean here: "(the interface is) that part of the program that determines how the user and the computer communicate".

We can now see how the relationship between 'interface' and 'application' can have different and even seemingly contradictory interpretations within different design domains. At the work process level they are unified, at the conceptual level probably partially overlapping, and at the technological level they may be fully separated. The relative independence of the different domains can be maintained only when we can establish 'links' - practical transformation procedures - between the domains. Such links are not yet in existence in most cases, though we can interpret the work on UIMS's as an attempt to develop automatic transformation procedures between the conceptual and technological level, so that the design and manipulation of (some aspects of) interfaces can happen at a conceptual level and the result is automatically transformed to the technological level (e.g. window managing, menu building etc.). We simply must be careful that the UIMS does not restrict the attainment of the design goals stated at the work process or conceptual levels. Because many UIMS's are grown 'bottom-up' - the main emphasis being the management of code - this may be a potential source of problems.

Having discussed issues surrounding the use of the term interface in HCI and hopefully clarified some of the confusions, we now turn briefly to discuss how we could re-conceptualise the very field of HCI in what we believe to be an interesting way, one that points out the links between existing HCI research traditions.

THE LINK BETWEEN INTEGRATIVE PERSPECTIVES AND HCI RESEARCH TRADITIONS

In this Section we show the relationship between the integrative perspectives outlined above and on-going HCI research. Firstly, the conceptual level in our perspective is obviously the domain where the bulk of HCI research based on the cognitive psychology of information processing - mental models and their correspondence with the real world etc. has been concentrated. Secondly, our physical/technical implementation level corresponds well with the concerns of early "low-level" human factors studies, vestiges of which remain in specific areas of current HCI work. Finally, the recent discussion about the need for "better social contextualization" of HCI work [6] is clearly an attempt to extend HCI in the direction of our work process level. We can characterise the situation as in Figure 1.

What is the relationship between different levels? It must be noted that the connections between the research done at "technical interaction level" and that at "conceptual interaction level" are weak indeed despite the great need to organize and contextualize all the bits and pieces of knowledge already collected in psychophysiologically oriented HCI research. The research done at conceptual interaction level has clearly failed to provide any "hooks" for them. Neither has that research been very successful in

its ability to inform practical design in other areas as well. This has caused lots of criticism (like that expressed in [6]) and fuelled recent attempts to enlarge both domain and background theories towards the "third" level.

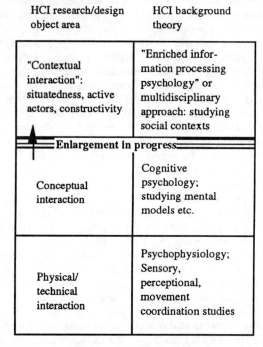

HCI research/design object area	HCI background theory
"Contextual interaction": situatedness, active actors, constructivity	"Enriched information processing psychology" or multidisciplinary approach: studying social contexts
Enlargement in progress	
Conceptual interaction	Cognitive psychology; studying mental models etc.
Physical/ technical interaction	Psychophysiology; Sensory, perceptional, movement coordination studies

Figure 1. A proposed 3-phase model of the enlargement of the HCI research domain (adapted from Kuutti, 1992)

While we see this progress towards better contextualization as necessary and healthy, we have not yet become convinced that "conceptual interaction" as a research domain could and should be totally subsumed under some other frame of reference. We believe that the unfruitfulness of the research this far is more due to the limited and mechanistic conception of the mainstream approach - information processing psychology - over the nature of the domain than the importance of the domain itself. Thus we think that independently of the efforts to enlarge the frame of reference it is necessary to search other alternatives for the research within that domain. And it would be absolutely necessary to have a better connection between that domain and the technical interaction one.

Having demonstrated the relationship between these perspectives and different aspects of HCI, we now face the question of its utility. Given that currently HCI suffers from a lack of any firm theoretically informed design methodology, from a practical viewpoint all we can say of our approach is that at least in the field of IS practice, it has been possible to integrate and use these three levels in the design process, and so there is some hope that they might prove useful in HCI also. From a theoretical viewpoint, we wish to outline briefly an argument that there exists a general theoretical framework that can subsume the different integrative levels we have identified.

Integrating perspectives through activity theory
Having seen some benefit to taking a levels approach to understanding apparently confusing concepts in HCI, we

still require a coherent theoretical framework within which each of these levels can be adequately elaborated. The framework must also provide means for linking these different perspectives into a more general conceptual structure. While there may be several candidate frameworks, here we concentrate on showing how the general psychological theory known as Activity Theory, or the cultural-historical approach, might be useful. This Soviet-inspired tradition has recently received some attention in HCI circles [2, 5, 17, 18, 22] as it appears to provide some coherent framework for integrating across the different HCI research traditions that we have outlined.

One of the fundamental conceptualisations in Activity Theory is that activities - the basic units of social life - have a hierarchical inner structure. Activities consist of single actions or chains of actions, which in turn consist of operations. When we participate in an activity, what we are actually doing is just performing conscious actions. The actions cannot really be understood, however, without a frame of reference created by the corresponding activity. An activity may be realised using different actions, depending on the situation, while one and the same action can belong to different activities. Before an action is performed in the real world, it is consciously planned - using a model. The better the model, the more successful the action. This phase is called orientation. Actions are realised as chains of operations, which are well-defined routines used by the subject subconsciously as answers to the conditions faced during the performance of the action. All operations start out as actions initially, but when the corresponding model is good enough and the action has been practised long enough, the orientation phase will fade and the action will be collapsed into an operation, which is much more fluent. At the same time a new action is created which will have broader scope and will contain the recently formed new operation as a subpart of itself. On the other hand, when conditions change, an operation can again "unfold" and return to the level of conscious action (i.e. it is not simply a conditioned reflex).

Thus we can say that Activity Theory forms a coherent theoretical system which contains the three levels or perspectives described earlier: activities as contexts of interactions, conscious actions where conceptual interaction is taking place, and finally operations, which are dependent on the pertinent conditions, at the physical interaction level. What makes the Activity Theory approach of special interest is that it explicitly attempts to manage the relationships between the different levels, rather than simply labelling them. Since there are few such general conceptual frameworks available to our knowledge, further work on developing this approach in the specific context of HCI concerns seems worthwhile. Whether this will lead to more practical advice for designers is still an open question.

CONCLUSIONS

This paper has discussed certain problems within the field of HCI which we believe are caused by confusion over basic concepts and terms. In an effort to alleviate some of this confusion and clarify the important underlying arguments, we propose a three-level framework within which to discuss the field. This "integrative levels" approach has been used successfully in other fields. We apply this idea in HCI to the interface concept, showing how it can help alleviate some of the current disputes concerning its meaning. We then apply it at a more general level, to the whole of the HCI field, and show how it can structure some of the on-going shifts in the focus of research over the years. In this context, we can explain the recent interest in the use of activity theory in HCI. Our perspective points to the importance of considering all three levels in HCI research and development work, both separately and combined.

ACKNOWLEDGMENT
Liam Bannon has done the research for this paper while working for Computer Science Department, Copenhagen University (DIKU).

REFERENCES
1. Andersen, P.B. (1991) A Semiotic Approach to Construction and Assessment of Computer Systems. In H.-E. Nissen, H.K. Klein & R. Hirschheim (eds.) *Proceedings of ISRA-90 Conference*. Elsevier/North-Holland, Amsterdam, pp. 465-514.

2. Bannon, L. J. & Bødker, S. (1991) Beyond the Interface: Encountering Artifacts in Use. In J. Carroll (Ed.) *Designing Interaction: Psychology at the Human-Computer Interface*. Cambridge University Press, Cambridge, pp. 227-253.

3. Barnard, P. (1991) Bridging between Basic Theories and the Artifacts of Human-Computer Interaction. In Carroll, J. M. (Ed.) *Designing Interaction: Psychology at the Human-Computer Interface*. Cambridge University Press, Cambridge, pp. 103-127.

4. Booth, P. (1989) *An Introduction to Human-Computer Interaction*. Lawrence Erlbaum, Hove and London.

5. Bødker, S. (1990). *Through the Interface – a Human Activity Approach to User Interface Design*. Lawrence Erlbaum, New Jersey.

6. Carroll, J. (Ed.) (1991) *Designing Interaction: Psychology at the Human-Computer Interface*. Cambridge University Press, Cambridge.

7. Clarke, A.A. (1986) A three-level human-computer interface model. *Int. J. Man-Machine Studies*, vol. 24, pp. 503-517.

8. de Montmollin, M. (1991) Analysis and models of operators' activities in complex natural life environments. In *J. Rasmussen & H. B. Andersen (Eds.) Human-Computer Interaction: Research directions in cognitive science*. Lawrence Erlbaum, Hillsdale, pp. 95- 112.

9. Gaines, B. R. & Shaw, M. L. (1986) Foundations of dialog engineering: the development of human-computer interaction. *Int. J. Man-Machine Studies*, vol. 24, pp. 101-123.

10. Grudin, J. (1990a) interface. In *CSCW'90, Proceedings of Conference on Computer Supported Cooperative Work*, (Los Angeles, October 1990) ACM Press, New York, pp. 269-278.

11. Grudin, J. (1990b) The Computer Reaches Out: The historical continuity of user interface design. In *Proceedings of CHI '90, ACM SIGCHI Conference*, (Seattle, April 1990), ACM Press, New York, pp.. 261-268.

12. Göransson, B. & Lindt, M. & Pettersson, E. & Sandblad, B. & Schwalbe, P. (1987) The Interface is often not the problem. In J. Carroll & B. Tanner (eds.) *Human Factors in Computer Systems IV*, North-Holland, New York, pp. 133-136.

13. Hammer, M. (1984) The OA Mirage. *Datamation*, Feb. 1984, pp. 36-46.

14. Hollnagel, E. (1991) The influence of artificial intelligence on human-computer interaction: Much ado about nothing? In J. Rasmussen & H. B. Andersen (Eds.) *Human-Computer Interaction: Research directions in cognitive science*. Lawrence Erlbaum, Hillsdale, pp. 153-202.

15. Iivari, J. (1989) Levels of Abstraction as a Conceptual Framework for an Information System. In D. Falkenberg & P. Lindgreen (eds.) *Information System Concepts: An In-depth Analysis*, Elsevier/ North-Holland, Amsterdam pp. 323-352.

16. Kammersgaard, J. (1988) Four different perspectives on human-computer interaction. *Int. J. Man-Machine Studies*, vol. 28, pp. 343-362.

17. Kaptelinin, V. (1992) Human Computer Interaction in Context: The Activity Theory Perspective. In Gornostaev, J. (Ed.) *Proceedings of the 2nd EWHCI-conference*, ICSTI, Moscow, pp. 7-13.

18. Kuutti, K. (1992) HCI research debate and Activity Theory Position. In Gornostaev, J. (Ed.) *Proceedings of the 2nd EWHCI-conference*, ICSTI, Moscow, pp. 13-22.

19. Kuutti, K. & Bannon, L. (1991) Some Confusions at the Interface: Re-conceptualising the "interface" problem. In Nurminen, M.I. & Weir, G.R.S. (Eds.) *Human Jobs and Computer Interfaces*. Elsevier/North-Holland, Amsterdam, pp. 3-19.

20. Landauer, T.K. (1991) Let's Get Real: A Position Paper on the Role of Cognitive Psychology in the Design of Humanly Useful and Usable Systems. In Carroll, J. M. (Ed.) *Designing Interaction: Psychology at the Human-Computer Interface*. Cambridge University Press, Cambridge, pp. 60-73.

21. Lyytinen, K. (1987) A taxonomic perspective of information systems development: theoretical constructs and recommendations. In Boland, R. &

Hirschheim, R. (eds.): *Critical issues in information systems research*. John Wiley & Sons, Chichester, pp. 3-41.

22. Nardi, B.A. (1992) Studying Context: A Comparison of Activity Theory, Situated Action Models, and Distributed Cognition. In Gornostaev, J. (Ed.) *Proceedings of the 2nd EWHCI-conference*, ICSTI, Moscow, pp. 352-359.

23. Newman, W.M. & Sproull, R.F. (1979) *Principles of Interactive Computer Graphics*. McGraw-Hill, New York.

24. Norman, D.A. (1990) "An interview with Don Norman" by H. Rheingold. In Laurel (1990), pp. 5-10.

25. Olle, T.W. & Sol, H.G. & Verrijn-Stuart, A.A. (eds.) (1982) *Information System Design Methodologies: a comparative review*. North-Holland, Amsterdam.

26. Papert, S. (1990) Interview in "Byte´s 15th Anniversary Summit", *Byte* September 1990, p. 230.

27. Rasmussen, J. (1986) *Information Processing and Human-Machine Interaction. An Approach to Cognitive Engineering*. North-Holland/Elsevier, New York.

28. Robinson, H. (1990) Towards a Sociology of Human-Computer Interaction. In P. Luff & N. Gilbert & D. Frohlich (eds.) *Computers and Conversation*, Academic Press, London, pp. 39-50.

29. Stary, C. (1990) A Knowledge Representation Scheme for Conceptual Interface Design. In A. Finkelstein, M. J. Tauber & R Traunmuller (Eds.) *Human Factors in Information Systems Analysis and Design*. North-Holland, Amsterdam, pp. 157-171.

30. Tanner, P. & Buxton, W. (1985) Some Issues in Future User Interface Management Systems (UIMS) Development. In G. Pfaff (ed.) *User Interface Management Systems*, Springer, Berlin, pp. 67-80.

31. Thomas, J., & Kellogg, W. (1989). Minimizing Ecological Gaps in User Interface Design, *IEEE Software*, January 1989, pp. 78-86.

32. Tobach, E. (1991) Activity Theory and the concept of integrated levels. *Multidisciplinary Newsletter for Activity Theory*. No. 7/8 1991, pp. 17-24.

33. Tolman, C. W. (1991) Theoretical Indeterminacy, Pluralism and the Conceptual Concrete. *Theory & Psychology*, Vol. 1 No. 2 pp. 147-162.

34. Weir, G. R. S. (1988) *HCI Perspectives on Man-Machine Systems*. Scottish HCI Centre, Strathclyde University, Report No. AMU3588/01S.

The Cost Structure of Sensemaking

Daniel M. Russell, Mark J. Stefik, Peter Pirolli, Stuart K. Card
User Interface Research Area, Xerox Palo Alto Research Center
3333 Coyote Hill Rd., Palo Alto, California 94304
Phone: 415-812-4308   Email: DMRussell.parc@Xerox.com

ABSTRACT

Making sense of a body of data is a common activity in any kind of analysis. *Sensemaking* is the process of searching for a representation and encoding data in that representation to answer task-specific questions. Different operations during sensemaking require different cognitive and external resources. Representations are chosen and changed to reduce the cost of operations in an information processing task. The power of these representational shifts is generally under-appreciated as is the relation between sensemaking and information retrieval.

We analyze sensemaking tasks and develop a model of the cost structure of sensemaking. We discuss implications for the integrated design of user interfaces, representational tools, and information retrieval systems.

KEYWORDS: sensemaking, cost structure, representation search, representation shift, learning loop, information access.

INTRODUCTION

When confronted with problems that have large amounts of information, an often proposed solution is to improve information retrieval (IR). However, even in tasks that require much retrieval of information, speeding retrieval by itself may help very little. IR subtasks are best understood in their embedding in a larger overall task structure. The larger task often involves sensemaking, the process of encoding retrieved information to answer task-specific questions.

A person performing an information-rich task has an array of resources -- both internal cognitive resources and external resources for information storage and computation. Methods for carrying out a task can be described in terms of operations, where each operation requires particular resources. The benefit of each approach depends on how it changes the relative costs and utilities of various operations, and thereby, the time versus quality tradeoffs in the method. Collectively, these factors and tradeoffs form a cost structure guiding choices made during sensemaking. In this paper we consider the cost structures of sensemaking tasks, quantifying some of the effects of external representations and automation.

CASE STUDY: Making sense of laser printers

We present a case study to lay the groundwork both for our description of sensemaking tasks and our approach to determining their cost structures. For these purposes, this example case is representative of many others we have studied the last year.

In the summer of 1989, a team from the Xerox education division designed a new generic training course on laser printing for Xerox technicians. Prior versions of the laser printer course were pedagogical tours of kinds of printers organized around market categories such as high, low and medium copy volumes. A major goal of the new course was to decrease overall training time by unifying terminology and shifting common material from courses on specific printers to the general introductory course. The course needed to cover a wide range of laser printers including new ones manufactured by Xerox and other companies. The group decided to use IDE (the Instructional Design Environment) [6] a hypermedia knowledge-structuring tool to capture and organize information for the course. To use IDE for analysis, users create and link hypermedia nodes that are instances of a larger representation schema, as shown in Figure 1.

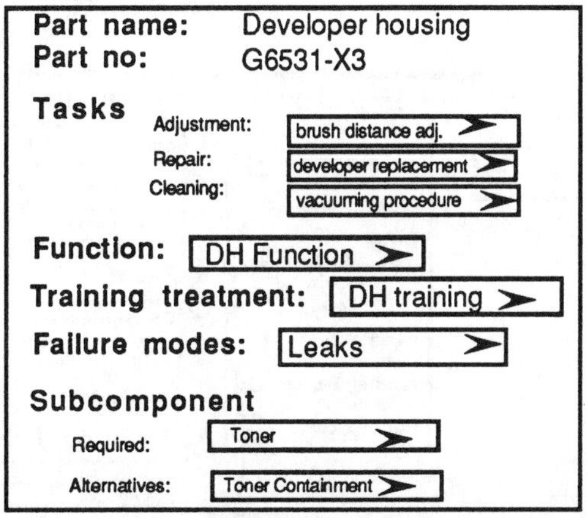

Figure 1. An instantiated IDE schema describing a printer (an encodon). Boxed values indicate links to other encodons.

In the first part of the process, the lead group identified 21 different kinds of laser printers and several different kinds of scanners to be used as source material for the course.

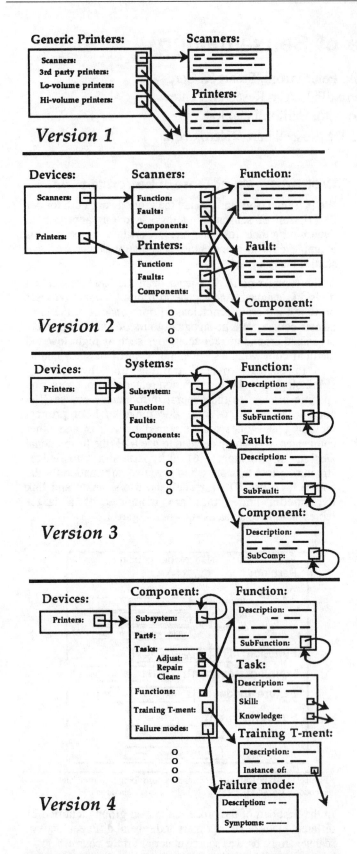

Figure 2. Representations and their associated use procedures evolve as new requirements are uncovered and properties of a representation are understood. In this case, the representation went through 3 major shifts, each time improving usability or decreasing cost-of-use. Note that each box stands for an IDE node type with a set of specified slots.

They quickly discovered that the schemas for their old course did not adequately characterize the information needed for the new one and modified their domain analyses for the new course. Ultimately, this led to a decomposition of printer descriptions in terms of subcomponents, functions, failure modes, and even techniques for training. The evolution of the IDE schemas they developed is charted in Figure 2. Figure 3 shows the process they used to produce the schemas in Figure 2 and ultimately their course design.

The final version of the schemas set the stage for the two main subtasks: understanding the similarities and differences between the various printers or their subsystems, and developing a course outline of the identified concepts. The work was divided among three work groups. During the next five months, the groups collected and entered information about their assigned printers, using the schemas from the lead group.

The next phase used computers to compare the different printers and to identify recurring concepts. An automatic clustering program took as input the schema descriptions, synonym dictionaries, and clustering parameters. It created as output clusters of closely related elements, such as clusters of related subsystems, clusters of related functions, and so on. The clustering algorithm selected an element in the database and measured a "distance" between it and other objects. The distance metric used information from the schemas such as slot names, type information, and relations, and from the text descriptions in the slots. These clusters were the basis of the concepts for the training course.

The last phase was to create an outline by organizing the concepts found in the analysis. An outline was represented by education concepts sequenced by relational links.

Learning Loops in Sensemaking

Figure 3 reveals that the team's attempt to make sense of information about laser printers consisted of cyclic processes of searching for representations and then encoding information in them to reduce the cost of operations. We call this recurring pattern in sensemaking a "learning loop complex" as illustrated in Figure 4.

The learning loop complex has three main processes:

1. Search for representations. The sensemaker creates representations to capture salient features of the data in a way that supports the use of the instantiated representation. This search cycle is the *generation* loop. Both representations and procedures for using them are created.

2. Instantiate representations. The sensemaker repeatedly identifies information of interest and encodes it in a representation that emerged from the generation loop. Instantiated schemas are called *encodons* and are created in the *data coverage* loop.

3. Shift representations. Representation shifts during sensemaking are intended to reduce the cost of task operations. Forcing a change to the representation in this way is a bottom-up or data-driven process. *Residue* is ill-fitting or missing data and unused representations. The *representational shift* loop is guided by the discovery of residue. When there are relevant data without a place in the representation, the schemas can be expanded. When data do not fit the established categories, the original schema categories may need to be merged, split, or new categories may be added. Thus, sensemaking iterates between the top-down representation instantiation and bottom-up representation search processes.

4. *Consume encodons.* The sensemaker then uses the encodons in some task-specific information processing step. In sensemaking, schemas provide top-down or goal-directed guidance. They prescribe what to look for in the data, what questions to ask, and how the answers are to be organized.

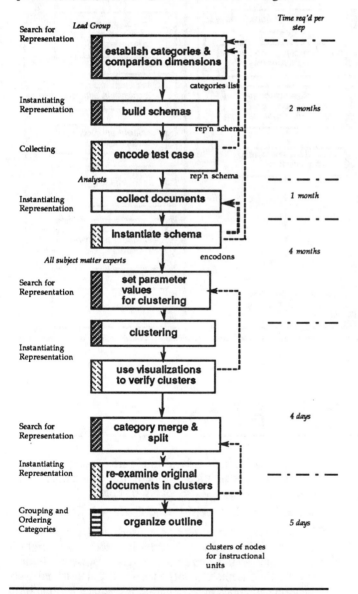

Figure 3. This diagram shows the steps the analysts went through to make sense of laser printers They collected and organized information, then found clusters of common terms, ideas, subsystems and functions in data describing twenty-one different laser printers.

But representation search is not simply top-down. If there were no surprises in creating encodons, sensemaking would be trivial; merely define the schemas and then instantiate them. Sensemaking seldom works this way. Schemas

must be revised when there are surprises creating encodons, or as new task requirements come to light.

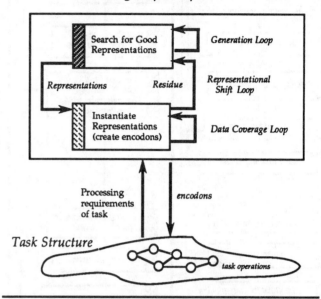

Figure 4. Sensemaking is finding a representation that organizes information to reduce the cost of an operation in an information task. The product of the learning loop is the representation and encodon set

Ubiquity of Learning Loops

Is this learning loop pattern peculiar to the case at hand or is it widespread in information-rich tasks? Over the past year we have carried out several studies including four retrospective studies of information systems for sensemaking [6] and several field studies of information workers at Xerox and other companies in the Bay Area.

Figure 5 shows process sensemaking process flow diagrams for four of these studies. The first of these is the laser printer case from Figure 3. The second flow diagram maps the activities of a study group over a ten week period creating a report about the research potential for a new technology. The third diagram maps the activity of a group of students over eight weeks in an instructional design class developing detailed plans for teaching high school algebra. And the fourth flow diagram describes the activity of a business analyst who writes monthly newsletters analyzing high technology areas.

In each case, the same basic operations and cyclic processes describe the activities used to make sense of the information. For these four cases (and for all other studies we have made) we find that each is an expansion of the learning loop complex. Despite differences in domain, approaches or individual styles, making sense of a complex body of information always appears to follow a common pattern.

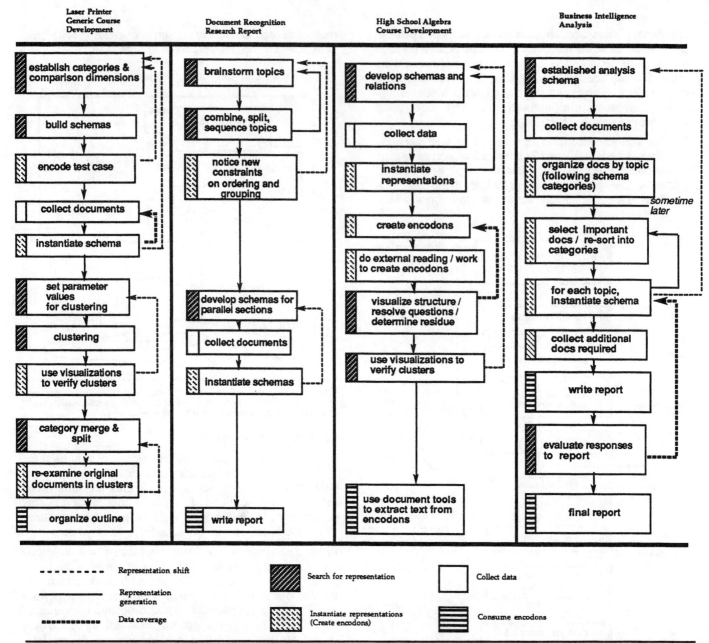

Figure 5. Sensemaking in four different information-rich tasks..

ANALYZING PRINTER SENSEMAKING

Even when different representations are equivalent from an information-content point of view, they can differ radically in the cost of carrying out particular operations. It is well known that the form of a representation profoundly affects the effectiveness of search during problem-solving. [4, 9]

It is not surprising then, that in a sensemaking task of any significant complexity, external representations are used to support the cognitive demands made on the user. However, creating a representation is a significant problem. The first representation created is rarely the best or correct one. In the following analysis, we show that sensemakers change representations either to reduce the time of the overall task, or to improve a cost versus quality tradeoff. In this analysis of the cost-effects of different representations, we consider two subtasks from our printer case -- (1) finding the central course concepts through cluster analysis (the

middle boxes labeled "4 days" in Figure 3) and (2) ordering them under pedagogical sequencing constraints (the organize outline box at the bottom of Figure 3).

Example 1: Lowering the Cost of Clustering

The analysts in the printer case used an IDE operator to cluster data about printers in order to discover a central set of key concepts in a large body of data. However, finding the central concepts in a large corpus is a non-trivial task. Clustering methods always define a distance computation like the following:

$$d_{ij} = \sum_{k=1}^{n} w_k \Delta_{ijk}$$

In other words, for each kind of object being compared, there is a set of properties, P_i. Each property has a value. (For example, the properties for document handlers would include the set of acceptable paper sizes, the capacity, a category such as "recirculating," and a description of the mechanism.) Given two objects we assume that it is possible to compare their property values. This distance equation indicates that the overall distance between two objects is a weighted sum of the differences between their property values, where the weights reflect the relative importances of the considered properties. To account for interactions among properties, more sophisticated distance metrics are often employed. However, the phenomena of interest to sensemaking arise even in the use of this simple distance metric.

There are different ways to compute clusters, but most methods include the following steps: (1) assign values to the weights, (2) compute distances between the objects and the cluster centers, extracting property data from the documents as needed, (3) add objects to a cluster if they are near enough and form new clusters otherwise, and (4) evaluate the cluster pattern. If the cluster pattern is unsatisfactory, such as if most of the objects fall in one cluster, then the weights are adjusted and the process repeats. In typical educational analyses, this process is informally carried out, primarily because the cost of careful computation (and re-computation!) is exorbitant.

The Main Cost: Data Extraction

Extracting data from documents is a key subtask in clustering and encoding. Extraction requires finding the relevant documents containing the information, selecting the document parts containing the information, and then transforming the information into a canonical form. The document parts may be particular paragraphs, table entries, or graphical elements from figures. In the cases we have examined, data extraction is often the most time-consuming task in sensemaking.

In this case study, the analysts extracted data to perform their encodings from a variety of source documents including training manuals, service documentation, engineering documents and customer support manuals. Each printer was documented by 10 - 20 documents, ranging in size from 30 - 300 pages. Virtually none of them were indexed for such access. Thus, each printer was documented with 300 - 6,000 pages. The lead group spent two months designing the IDE schemas, instantiating them to evaluate their usefulness. Then the three analyst groups spent five months extracting data and encoding it using the schemas. They created 21 computer databases, one per printer, each containing between 300-1000 entries each. In approximate numbers, each group processed about 190 pages per day, encoding on the average of 30 individual schemas each working day.

For this task, data extraction and encoding required over 75% of the total time from beginning the project to final course outline.

The Main Gain:　Automated Clustering

When sensemakers make an investment of this magnitude, they are betting that there will be a payoff either as a reduction in the overall task time or in the improved quality of their results.

Consider the sequence of representation shifts of Figure 2 in light of this representational investment. These shifts took place in the representation shift loop labeled 1 in Figure 3. In version 1 of the representation in Figure 2, differences in principles of operation did not show up as discrete differences in properties. Since the schemas had no substructure and no specification of domain concepts such as components, mechanisms or failure modes, it was not likely that the properties would be encoded uniformly even if they were encoded at all. For this version the extraction processes for each property would require sophistication beyond the reach of automation. Version 2 made more of the relevant properties explicit, but still lacked a recursive mechanism for representing component substructure. Version 3 had provisions for recursive structure, but permitted representational ambiguities between subsystems and components. Two different encoders could reasonably choose quite different representations for a printer -- thus complicating the canonicalization phase of property extraction. Version 4 remedied this problem and provided a robust and computationally tractable representation for both human use during encoding and algorithmic clustering.

In summary, this illustrates how shifts in representation made large changes in the cost structure of the clustering task.

Anytime Algorithms

An important observation about many sensemaking methods is that they are *anytime* algorithms. Anytime methods provide the best solution that they can find in given limited time. Given more resources, they continue to search for better solutions. We call the common use of such tradeoffs in information processing tasks the *anytime principle*.

A key parameter governing the complexity of clustering is the number of iterations for altering property weights and searching for appropriate cluster patterns. In this case study, automating the clustering process drastically reduced the cost per iteration, enabling the course designers to fine tune the parameters over many iterations and to search more thoroughly and systematically for the printer concepts to be included in the general course.

Another key parameter is the number of properties considered per object. The more properties considered, the more costly the encoding and comparison processes, but also, the more accurate the characterization of concepts. For the new course, the designers were able to consider many more (2 - 3 times) properties than before, using time gains from automation to extend the comprehensiveness of search.

Example 2: Lowering the Cost of Ordering

Another important task in course design is organizing the concepts into a teachable sequence -- the last box in Figure 3. This task is governed by pedagogical rules. For example, presentation of the prerequisites for a topic should precede presentation of the topic and the structure of the course should help students identify the main points through progressive disclosure.

Figure 6 shows a boxes-and-arrows representation of a partial ordering of topics for a course. This is a variation on the representation observed in similar cases. A box around a set of topics (shown simply as letters in the figure) indicates a set, and an arrow starting from a topic or set to another represents an order constraint. In the figure, topics a and d are candidate starting nodes. Since topic a comes before the set t, it comes before the elements of that set: topics c, r, and u. By transitivity, it also comes before the elements of the v set and the y set.

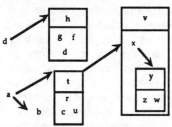

Figure 6. A graph showing partial ordering of constraints for presentation. In this example, 5 explicit ordering constraints and 4 grouping constraints suffice to order 16 nodes.

A direct manipulation interface provides an active representation for rapidly exploring alternative outlines. With computational support for the constraint reasoning, many alternative orderings of topics can be explored in a few minutes [7]. In the final phase of course development, a sequence exploration tool of this type was used, allowing a much larger space of possible sequences to be explored. The analysts estimated that they explored approximately 10 times more topic sequences than in earlier courses without such a tool, and a perceptible gain in the quality of the final course design. Again, a shift in external representation of the information resulted in a shift in the cost structure of the task.

THE COST STRUCTURE OF SENSEMAKING

From the standpoint of systems designed for sensemaking, we are concerned with evaluating different approaches to sensemaking, particularly when the introduction of alternative technologies can dramatically change the efficiency or effectiveness of the overall process. That is, we are concerned with an analysis of the steps as defined in the learning loop complex. As a way to analyze these costs, we begin by defining the following cost terms:

- *FR*:   finding a representation schema to support the required operators in the target task,
- *IE*:   instantiating the encodons,
- *FD*:   finding data to create the encodons, including both finding the documents and selecting the information,
- *TT*:   the target task.

The costs of sensemaking are the combined costs of the steps in the learning loop complex. The total cost, C_T, is the cost of sense making, C_{SM}, plus the cost of the target task, C_{TT},

$$C_T = C_{SM} + C_{TT} \qquad (1)$$

where

$$C_{SM} = C_{FR} + C_{IE} + C_{FD} \qquad (2)$$

In the following, we define **gain** as the increase in quality or quantity of work performed by using a particular method. Optimizing a sensemaking system is searching through the space of combinations of methods to maximize the expected gain to cost ratio.

The task of sensemaking or its corresponding target task may be either recurring or happen once-only (one-off tasks). The laser printer case is one-off sense-making with a one-off target task of producing a course outline. The business intelligence example has one-off sensemaking (the production of schemas) with the continuous target task of encoding new intelligence items and writing newsletters. Each type of sensemaking task has different optimization characteristics.

One-off Tasks

In one-off tasks the sensemaker chooses methods to maximize the expected gain within a cost or time limit.

Typically, the one-off optimization problem can be greatly simplified. In the laser printer case, the gain is the number of common instructional elements placed into the general course. We compare two methods by associating a gain function g_m with the manual method of producing the course and g_c with the computer-based method for finding concept clusters and ordering concepts. For small investments in sensemaking (especially t_{FR}, t_{IE} and t_{FD}) the manual method is more cost-effective than the computer-based one, but for large investments in sensemaking the computer-based method is more profitable. Figure 7 shows that the computer-based strategy should only be chosen if the deadline is after t_c, the crossover point.

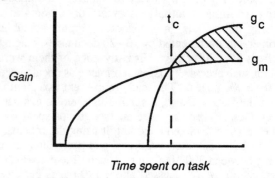

Figure 7. Tradeoffs in the gain achieved by a manual method (gm) or computer-based method (gc). The best solution is determined by maximizing gain while minimizing total cost within the deadline time.

Recurring Tasks

For recurring sensemaking subtasks the optimization problem is to maximize long-term rate of gain over many task cycles. This occurs in the jobs of business and financial analysts who scan, select, and integrate information from new reports to produce their own highly standardized periodic newsletters.

We can think of knowledge workers as organisms in an information ecology, roaming among information sources. Their problem is to choose their information sources to obtain the best gain for time spent. This metaphor leads to modeling recurring sensemaking with concepts from foraging theory. The following assumptions are often used in such analyses:

- The sensemaking subtasks are encountered and processed exclusive of one another. For instance, tasks are often structured such that one cannot search for data at the same time one is instantiating encodons, and one usually cannot create multiple encodons simultaneously.

- The subtasks come in k subtypes. Such task typing can often be performed on the basis of the kinds of data being processed. For instance, a business intelligence analyst may find certain periodicals or sections of periodicals (e.g., research news) more profitable than others. Often it is assumed that each subtype is encountered over a given unit of time as a Poisson process with parameter $l_i, 0 < i \leq k$. That is, different types of periodicals arrive at the sensemaker's desk at varying rates. As the periodicals arrive, they demand different subtasks for processing.

- Associated with each subtype i of the sensemaking subtasks is a gain function $g_i(t_i)$, which indicates the expected gain as a function of the time t_i spent on that subtask. The gain function eventually show diminishing returns over time.

When these conditions hold, then can we maximize the long-term rate of gain, R, by determining the amount of time t_i to spend in each subtask. To do this, one ranks the subtask types by their expected profitabilities. The rate of gain for subtask i is:

$$\frac{g_i(t_i^*)}{t_i^*} = \max_{t_i} \left[\frac{g_i(t_i)}{t_i} \right] \tag{3}$$

The sensemaker keeps a list of the subtasks in order of descending profitability by computing each subtask's long-term rate of gain.

$$R = \frac{\sum_{i=1}^{j} \lambda_i g_i(\hat{t}_{ij})}{1 + \sum_{i=i}^{j} \lambda_i \hat{t}_{ij}} > \frac{g_{j+i}(t_{j+1}^*)}{t_{j+1}^*} \tag{4}$$

The $\hat{t}_{ij}$ are the rate-maximizing times for the i_{th} task when the subtasks to perform (pursuit list) includes items through rank j. Choosing which subtasks to discard from this list can be calculated according to a marginal value theorem formulated by Charnov [3]. Stephens and Krebs [8] discuss the implications of Equations 3 and 4, which model an agent foraging through an open ecology, and discuss on the underlying constraints and assumptions.

If variations the model of Equations 3 and 4 hold, then uniform improvements in access costs to the types of data on the pursuit list mean that selection should become even more restrictive (assuming no additional constraints on which data to process). For instance, suppose that a new information access technology increases the rate of delivery of both high- and low-quality periodicals arriving at an analyst's desktop. The optimal strategy in the face of uniform increases in the rate of encounter with data is to exclude more low-quality periodicals, rather than processing all newly available periodicals.

The assumptions of the foraging model do not hold for all cases we have considered. For example, the first assumption that only one task can be processed at a time breaks down when there is more than one sensemaker. This is especially important in the case where some of the sensemaking agents are computational and therefore operate on a different cost basis.

In addition, there are interaction effects in sensemaking not covered by this model. For example, in sensemaking tasks requiring several kinds of data, the evaluation of gain for different subtasks can vary as some data requirements become satisfied. This is a simple example of a more general phenomena in which part of the job of sensemaking is to establish the goals of the task.

TECHNOLOGY AND SENSEMAKING

There are many possible ways that technology can affect sensemaking, and we can only consider a few here. By the anytime principle, a reduction of cost (or increase in gain) associated with a step frees time to invest in other steps. For instance, if a representation is supplied at the beginning of a task, then C_{FR} is zero, and more effort may be placed into other areas (e.g., increasing the amount of information).

In the laser printer case and several others that we have observed, most of the time in sensemaking is in data extraction. This focuses attention on reducing costs of the three steps of data extraction -- finding the relevant documents, selecting the information, and transforming the information into canonical form. In one of our case studies, the sensemaker looks up data about laptop computers in a collection of magazines and product sheets. His goal is to make a purchasing recommendation meeting given constraints. The data representation created by sensemakers carrying out this task invariably includes tables giving properties of competing laptops. Representation shifts are changes to the table structure as the sensemaker decides which properties are most relevant and retrievable and ultimately are able to help solve the problem of determining the best choice.

The laptop case lends itself both to proposing technology for the sensemaker and to estimating the benefits of using it. Consider the moment when the sensemaker has filled in the name of the laptop for which he is seeking information, and needs data for the memory size column. It is clear that the next data sought is the memory size of that laptop and that the sensemaker's next activity will be to extract that from the document.

For online documents, automatic specialized methods could use encodons to generate queries for retrieving document fragments likely to contain the needed information, displaying the relevant parts, and canonicalizing the data to the form needed. For paper documents, a handheld scanner might be coupled with specialized extraction methods to reduce encoding time. In both cases, the savings make time for other activities, such as using visualization tools to survey the effects of different choice criteria.

CONCLUSIONS

This paper presents preliminary steps in understanding the cost structure of sensemaking and the role of sensemaking in various information processing tasks. The goal is to provide widely applicable predictive models of task performance and prescriptive models for recommending system features.

The ideas that information retrieval is part of a larger process of information use, that computer systems should amplify information-based work processes, and that information has costs associated with search and access have been reported earlier [e.g., 1,2]. What is new in our current analysis is the emphasis on representation use and shifts in analyzing task performance, the identification of the learning loop, the anytime principle and the characterization of sensemaking.

Representation design is central to the sensemaking enterprise. The learning loop complex crystallizes the pattern of activity in which representations are changed to reduce the cost of task operations, changing the sensemaking cost and gain structures.

By characterizing sensemaking as an interlocking set of different types of subtasks, we show how tradeoffs can be made in one place for gains in another (the anytime principle). The relative sensitivity of different parameters in the sensemaking process suggests places where changing methods or representations can produce payoffs. Our studies in information visualization methods indicate the extreme effects -- both positive and negative -- that different visualizations can have on users. In order to design information systems, we need to understand the most important factors that determine a user's ability to interact-with and perceive information. The studies presented here show that focussing on a single aspect of the problem while ignoring the entire process may be shortsighted.

This picture is still incomplete with many interaction effects still unaccounted. Nevertheless, this model provides a beginning of a comprehensive approach to the integrated design of user interfaces, information retrieval and representation using systems.

REFERENCES

1. Card, S.K., Robertson, G.G., Mackinlay, J.D., The Information Visualizer (1991), *CHI '91 Conference Proceedings*, New Orleans, 181-188.

2. Card, S.K. (1989) Information Workspaces, *Friend21 International Symposium on Next Generation Human Interface Technologies*, Tokyo, 5-A:1-9.

3. Charnov, E. L. (1976). Optimal foraging: The marginal value theorem. *Theoretical Population Biology, 9*, 129-136.

4. Larkin, J., Simon, H. A. (1987) "Why a picture is (sometimes) worth ten thousand words" *Cognitive Science*, 11, 65-99.

5. Hancock, C., Kaput, J.J. (1990) Computerized tools and the process of data modeling. 14th International Conference on the Psychology of Mathematics Education.

6. Russell, D. M., Stefik, M. J. (1992) "Beyond information retrieval: Sensemaking:" Xerox PARC ISTL Technical Report.

7. Stefik, M., Foster, G., Bobrow, D.G., Kahn, K., Lanning, S., & Suchman, L. (1987) Beyond the Chalkboard: Computer Support for Collaboration and Problem Solving in Meetings, *Communications of the ACM*, 30:1, 32-47,.

8. Stephens, D. W., & Krebs, J. R. (1986). *Foraging theory* Princeton University Press, Princeton, NJ.

9. van Baalen, J. (1992) Automated design of specialized representations, *Artificial Intelligence*, 54, 121-198.

Prototyping an Intelligent Agent
through Wizard of Oz

David Maulsby *   Saul Greenberg *   Richard Mander ⬥

* Department of Computer Science
University of Calgary
Calgary Alberta T2N 1N4 Canada

maulsby or saul@cpsc.ucalgary.ca
+01 403-220-6087

⬥ Human Interface Group, Apple Computer Inc.
20525 Mariani Ave.
Cupertino CA 90514 USA

mander@appleLink.apple.com
+01 408-974-8136

ABSTRACT

Turvy is a simulated prototype of an instructible agent. The user teaches it by demonstrating actions and pointing at or talking about relevant data. We formalized our assumptions about what could be implemented, then used the Wizard of Oz to flesh out a design and observe users' reactions as they taught several editing tasks. We found: a) all users invent a similar set of commands to teach the agent; b) users learn the agent's language by copying its speech; c) users teach simple tasks with ease and complex ones with reasonable effort; and d) agents cannot expect users to point to or identify critical features without prompting.

In conducting this rather complex simulation, we learned some lessons about using the Wizard of Oz to prototype intelligent agents: a) design of the simulation benefits greatly from prior implementation experience; b) the agent's behavior and dialog capabilities must be based on formal models; c) studies of verbal discourse lead directly to an implementable system; d) the designer benefits greatly by becoming the Wizard; and e) qualitative data is more valuable for answering global concerns, while quantitative data validates accounts and answers fine-grained questions.

KEYWORDS: Intelligent agent, instructible system, programming by demonstration, Wizard of Oz, prototyping

INTRODUCTION

We used the Wizard of Oz method to test a new design for an instructible agent. In this paper we describe how end users learned to teach a simulated agent called Turvy, in particular the set of instructions and commands they adopted. These findings will be valuable to implementors of programming by demonstration systems. We also explore the lessons we learned using the method, which experimenters can apply in their own studies of intelligent interfaces. These lessons differ from other Wizard of Oz experiences in being oriented towards prototyping an implementable system, rather than a proof of concept.

The paper begins with a brief discussion of intelligent

© 1993 ACM 0-89791-575-5/93/0004/0277...$1.50

agents and the Wizard of Oz method. It then describes the Turvy experiment and results, and ends with a retrospective on our use of Wizard of Oz.

Intelligent agents

When given a goal, [an intelligent agent] could carry out the details of the appropriate computer operations and could ask for and receive advice, offered in human terms, when it was stuck. –Alan Kay (1984)

Intelligent interface agents have been touted as a significant new direction in user interface design. Videos from Apple and Hewlett-Packard show futuristic interfaces in which agents play a dominant role, serving as computerized office clerks, database guides and writing advisors. Reality is a bit behind, but prototype intelligent agents have been implemented by researchers. For example, Eager (Cypher, 1991) detects and automates a user's repetitive actions in HyperCard; it matches examples by parsing text strings and by testing numerical relationships. Metamouse (Maulsby, 1989) learns drawing tasks from demonstrations; it applies rules to find significant graphical constraints.

Yet today's agents are "intelligent" in the narrowest sense of the word. They understand only specialized or highly structured task domains, and lack flexibility in conversing with users. Kay (1984) suggests that agents should be illusions that mirror the user's intelligence while restricting the user's agenda. Unfortunately, because most work on agents stems from the field of Artificial Intelligence, users' needs are second to algorithm development. While the systems prove that particular approaches can be codified in algorithms, they rarely pay more than lip service to the usability tradition of Human Computer Interaction. As a result, they tend to fail as interfaces.

Agents must be designed around our understanding of what people require and expect of them. However, the traditional approach of system building is an expensive and unlikely way to gain this understanding. The underlying discourse models and algorithms for agents are usually so complex and entrenched with assumptions that changes—even minor ones—may require radical redesign. Moreover, because agents act as intermediaries between people and their applications, the designer must craft and debug the agent/application interface as well. A viable alternative to system building is Wizard of Oz.

Wizard of Oz

Wizard of Oz is a rapid-prototyping method for systems costly to build or requiring new technology (Wilson and Rosenberg, 1988; Landauer, 1987). A human "Wizard" simulates the system's intelligence and interacts with the user through a real or mock computer interface.

Most Wizard of Oz experiments establish the viability of some futuristic (but currently unimplementable) approach to interface design. An example is the use of complex user input like speech. Gould et. al., (1982), who pioneered the method, simulated an imperfect listening typewriter to find out whether it would satisfy people used to giving dictation. Similarly, Hauptmann (1989) tested users' preferences for manipulating graphic images through gesture and speech, by simulating the recognition devices.

Other Wizard of Oz experiments concentrated more on human behavior than futuristic systems. Hill and Miller (1988), for example, investigated the complexities of intelligent on-line help by observing interaction between users of a statistical package and a human playing the role of help system. Likewise, Dahlbäck, Jönsson and Ahrenberg (1993) studied differences between human-human and human-computer discourse through a variety of feigned natural language interfaces. In another experiment, Leiser (1989) showed that people can be led to use a language understood by the computer through *convergence*, a phenomenon of human dialog in which participants unconsciously adopt one other's speech pattern. When users typed a natural language database query, the Wizard, using only certain terms and syntactic forms, would verify it by paraphrasing. Convergence occurred when users adopted those same terms in their queries. We will return to this theme in our discussion of "TurvyTalk".

THE TURVY EXPERIMENT

Our research concerns both the technical and usability aspects of programming by demonstration. Previously implemented systems have had problems with competence or usability; we had in mind a more general purpose, easily instructed system that would be nonetheless practical to implement in the near future. The system we envisioned starts with easily coded, primitive knowledge of datatypes and relations, and more specialized knowledge defined by application authors. It then learns higher-level constructs and procedures specific to the individual user's work. For practicality, it must learn under the user's guidance, so it needs an intuitive and flexible teaching interface. We decided that an agent metaphor would help us explore the design issues; the agent is Turvy.

We wanted to see how end users would teach an agent with perfect memory and primitive knowledge. We wanted to see how they structured lessons and whether they could focus its attention correctly. Would they be able to translate cultural concepts (like *surname*) into syntactic search patterns (like *capitalized word after Mr. or Ms.*), and how could Turvy minimize the annoyance of doing so? What kinds of instructions and commands would they use, and what wording? Could verbal input, based on pseudo-natural language or even keyword-spotting, work in conjunction with pointing? We decided to use a Wizard of Oz simulation to investigate these issues, involving end users up front, before making too many commitments in our design.

Using the Wizard of Oz to prototype programming by demonstration makes unusual demands on the Wizard, and we had some special concerns. We wanted to simulate a "buildable" Turvy, so we designed a formal model of the learning system and required the Wizard to obey it. We wanted to separate the agent's behavior (what it can understand and how it can react) from the illusion it presents in the interface, so we let users explore Turvy's abilities through discovery, finding its limits as it responded to their own commands and teaching methods. Finally, we wanted detailed qualitative and quantitative results, so we designed a set of tasks to reveal interaction problems, videotaped sessions, and interviewed the users.

Motivation: previous implementation experience

We had completed a user study of Metamouse, a fully implemented programming by demonstration system personified by an agent named Basil. Basil learns repetitive graphical edits, such as aligning or sorting by height, *provided* the user makes all relevant spatial relations visible by drawing construction lines. In that study we gave users six tasks, all of which Basil could learn in principle. But in practice, Basil frustrated users' attempts to teach it. First, though they discerned the need for constructions, users did not grasp Basil's strict procedural interpretation, and they sometimes used a line to suggest a relation rather than define it. Second, users didn't think it possible to construct some features, like height; they would have preferred to say it in English. Third, they were confused by aspects of the agent metaphor concerning how it searched for sets of objects and created branching procedures. Finally, limitations on Basil's inferencing ability, and occasional crashes due to bugs, compounded their problems and made our observations harder to assess.

We wanted to overcome these deficiencies. We wanted people to converse with the agent through a multi-modal dialog, using demonstrations, English, or property sheets. We wanted people to learn through conversation (verbal or graphical) what the agent could understand. We wanted a metaphor that would present the right illusion. We also knew that a reincarnated Metamouse was not the vehicle for this study, because we would be shackling ourselves to ideas embedded in a big system. We turned to Turvy.

Turvy as agent

We made four key assumptions about the sort of agent we would build, each with consequences for usability. • First, Turvy learns from a user's demonstrations, pointing, and verbal hints. It does not have human-level abilities or knowledge; like Metamouse, it forms search and result patterns from low-level features, and users must refer to them during demonstrations. • Second, unlike Metamouse, Turvy does not equate the user's demonstration with a procedure; actions may be interpreted as focusing attention or extending a pattern, and Turvy can revise an interpretation as more examples are seen. This enables a dialog where users can

Class	From User	From Turvy
Command	√ Watch and learn what I do	√ Show me what to do
	√ End of lesson	√ All done
	Do the next step	√ May I take over?
	√ Do the rest of this example (iteration)	√ May I continue?
	√ Do the next example (iteration)	√ [May I] do the next one?
	√ Do all remaining examples (iterations)	√ [May I] do the rest?
	√ Stop (you've made a mistake)	
	~ Undo [one step] [to the start of this iteration]	~ Undo [last step?] [this iteration?]
	√ Ignore my actions (I'm fixing something)	
	1 Let me take over	You take over
	1 Always let me do these steps	Do you want to do this manually?
Focus attention	1 I'm repeating what I did before	√ I've seen you do this before
	This is similar to [indicates previous example]	√ Treat this like [describes similar item]?
	This case is different	? What is different about this case?
	R Look here (this is important)	? Is this [describes item] important?
	√ Look for [describes item]	√ I should look for [describes item]
	R I did this [conditional branch] because [points at something and/or lists features]	√ Is this [describes feature] what distinguishes the two cases [or new special case]?
	1 I'm changing the way I do this task	You've changed the method here, why?
Response	R OK / yes	√ OK / yes
	R No	√ No
	R I don't know / I don't want to discuss that	√ I don't know, show me what to do

Legend: √ – used without difficulty; 1 – given by only 1 user; R – given only in response to a prompt from Turvy; ~ – not differentiated in usage; ? – questions asked by Turvy that caused user confusion; blank – not used.

Table 1. Messages used in the Turvy study.

teach new concepts on the fly. • Third, an implementable Turvy would not have true natural language capabilities, and our system only recognizes spoken or typed keywords and phrases, using an application-specific lexicon. This poses problems for a user of Turvy's language, for they must learn this lexicon. Verbal inputs are either commands (like *Stop!*) or hints about features (like *look for a word before a colon*), where keywords (*word, colon*) are compared with actual data at the locus of action to determine their meaning. This implies that users must accompany verbal descriptions with editing or pointing actions. • Fourth, Turvy predicts actions as soon as possible, verbalizing them on the first run through. Eager prediction gives users efficient control over learning. Speech output signals the features Turvy has deemed important, without obscuring text or graphic data. As a side effect, the users also learn Turvy's language.

Turvy as system

This section supplies a brief description of Turvy's built-in knowledge, inference mechanism, and interaction model. Maulsby (1993) provides more detail. Turvy learns procedures and data descriptions — specialized types, structures, orderings (cf. Halbert, 1984). Turvy's learning strategy is to make a plausible generalization from one example, then revise it as more are seen or when the user gives descriptive hints. Turvy's tactic is to elicit hints by predicting.

We designed a formal model of the learning system in terms of a grammar for tasks it could learn, then chose an application (text editing), and made a detailed model of Turvy's background knowledge, in the form of an attribute grammar for textual search patterns. The knowledge is more primitive than that in Myers' (1991) demonstrational text formatter. Untutored Turvy recognizes characters, words,

paragraphs, brackets, punctuation, and properties like case and font. Turvy learns to search for sequences of tokens with specified properties.

We designed a model of interaction—an incomplete model, formulated as a list of 32 kinds of instructions implied by the learning model. If a person gives all the instructions, the system can learn without inferencing, but we predicted that people would use only the subset listed in Table 1. We believe the user will give incomplete or ambiguous instructions, which the system will complete by making inferences and eliciting further details. Note that we told Turvy's users only that it could understand "some English"; they did not receive a list of instructions or wordings. In turn, the Wizard as Turvy responded only to instructions whose intention corresponded to some message in the interaction model.

Tasks and an example user/Turvy dialog

We made up six tasks and a data set, on the theme of formatting a bibliography:

a. italicize journal titles
b. quote the titles of conference and journal papers
c. create a citation heading with the primary author's surname and year of publication (illustrated in Figure 1)
d. put authors' given names and initials after surnames
e. put book titles in Times-Roman font
f. strip out colons that separate bibliographic fields

Tasks involved domain concepts like "title," "journal vs. book," and "list of authors," concepts Turvy does not understand. Users were shown before and after snapshots of example data for each task; no mention was made of the syntactic features Turvy would learn. This tested Turvy's ability to elicit effective demonstrations and verbal hints.

Philip E. Agre: *The dunamic structure of everyday life.* PhD thesis: MIT Artificial Intelligence Lab: 1988.

John H. Andreae, Bruce A. MacDonald: "Expert control for a robot body." *J. IEEE SMC:* July 1990.

Michalski R. S., J. G. Carbonell, T. M. Mitchell (eds): **Machine Learning II.** Tioga: Palo Alto CA: 1986

Kurt van Lehn: "Discovering problem solving strategies." Proc. Machine Learning Workshop, pp. 215-217: 1989.

[Agre 88]
Philip E. Agre: *The dunamic structure of everyday life.* PhD thesis: MIT Artificial Intelligence Lab: 1988.

[Andreae 90]
John H. Andreae, Bruce A. MacDonald: "Expert control for a robot body." *J. IEEE SMC:* July 1990.

[Michalski 86]
Michalski R. S., J. G. Carbonell, T. M. Mitchell (eds): **Machine Learning II.** Tioga: Palo Alto CA: 1986

[van Lehn 89]
Kurt van Lehn: "Discovering problem solving strategies." Proc. Machine Learning Workshop, pp. 215-217: 1989.

a. before editing

b. after putting first author and date into heading

Given the document on the left, users were asked to place the first author's name and the date of publication in square brackets with bold styling prior to each reference. When correctly reformatted the bibliography would appear as on the right.

Figure 1. Sample data from Task c, "make citation headings".

Similar concepts were repeated in later tasks, to see whether users adopted Turvy's description.

Figure 1 shows a sample of the data for Task c. The user is supposed to make citation headings for each entry, using the primary author's surname and part of the date. From Turvy's point of view, these items are the word before the first colon or comma in the paragraph, and the two digits before the period at the paragraph's end. Exceptional cases to be learned include a baronial prefix (eg. "van Lehn") and initials after surname (eg. "Michalski R. S.").

```
TaskC:  repeat (FindSurname  FindDate)
FindSurname:  if find pattern (Loc := BeginParagraph
    SomeText Surname := ({0 or more LowerCaseWord}
    Word) [Colon or Comma])
    then do MakeHeading  else TurvyAllDone
MakeHeading:  select Surname; copy Surname;
    put cursor before Loc;  type "[";  paste Surname;
    type (DateLoc := Blank "]");  type Return;
    select styleMenu;  select "citation"
FindDate:  if find pattern (Date := (Digit Digit)
    Period  EndParagraph)
    then do CopyDate  else TurvyAskUserForDemo
CopyDate:  select Date;  copy Date;
    put cursor after DateLoc; paste Date
```

Figure 2. Pseudo-code derived by analyzing Task c
(from Figure 1) with Turvy's inference model.

Prior to the experiment, we analyzed this task using the inference model and got code similar to that in Figure 2 (we've omitted the code for handling initials after a surname). Coding helps the Wizard act consistently, even if users teach somewhat different procedures. The code loops over all entries in the bibliography. Each step involves finding a pattern in the text (to instantiate data descriptions) and then executing a macro; if not found, a default action is done. Macros are straight-line procedures that refer only to instantiated variables. Mnemonic variable and macro names are shown in italics.

Below is the trace of a dialog between Turvy and "Kate", a composite of two users in our study (the first paragraph was spoken by the one, the rest by the other). Kate is working through Task c: the first example is "Agre" in Figure 1.

Kate: *Take the last name, it will be in some cases before a colon. [Kate copies "Agre", pastes it into a new paragraph, types the brackets and sets the style.] This is a list of publications. Now we're going to add the last two digits of the date [types "88"].*

Kate gives hints about the syntax ("before a colon", "last two digits") and the subject matter ("name", "a list of publications"). Turvy interprets only the hints about syntax, and then only in relation to actions demonstrated (so "last two digits" is taken to mean the digits typed, not those at the end of the paragraph).

Kate then signals the end of the lesson and gives Turvy a chance to take over or get another example. Turvy edits the next entry (not shown in Figure 1).

Kate: *Do you want another demo?*
Turvy: I can try if you want. — *Kate: OK.*
Turvy: Looking for word before first colon in next paragraph [picks surname], OK? — *Kate: OK.*
Turvy: [while doing actions] Copy, go to start of paragraph, type return, paste, type brackets, change style to "citation", OK? — Kate: *OK.*

Now Turvy makes a mistake. Kate shows the right action and Turvy echoes back a new hypothesis reflecting her hint from earlier on.

Turvy: Type in blank space "88", OK?
Kate: *No, the last two digits at the end.*
Turvy: Show me please. — [Kate picks digits.]
Turvy: Two digits before period at end of paragraph?
Kate: *Yes.*
Turvy: Continue? — *Kate: OK.*

The next example introduces a new case, multiple authors (see the second entry in Figure 1). Turvy's search pattern selects the last one. Kate tries to correct Turvy by giving a hint, but Turvy insists on a demonstration to go with it.

Turvy: [picks "MacDonald"] — *Kate: No – stop.*
Turvy: Show me please.
Kate: I want the last name of the first author.
Turvy   I don't understand – show me please.
Kate: When you have a number of authors, choose the first [picks "Andreae"]. *It's before the comma.*
Turvy: Word before first comma or colon? — *Kate: Yes.*

A little later on, Turvy comes to an entry in which the surname happens to precede the initials ("Michalski in Figure 1). Turvy's search pattern picks the last initial.

Turvy: [picks "S."] — *Kate: No.*
Turvy: Show me please.
Kate: I want you to take in this case the very first word [picks surname], *then continue as before.*
Turvy: You skipped back over words ending in period?
Kate: Yes.
Turvy: Continue? — *Kate: OK.*

Finally, Kate teaches Turvy how to parse names with baronial prefixes ("van Lehn" in Figure 1).

Turvy: [picks "Lehn"]
Kate: Ok, um, stop [hesitant]. *In this case I want you to select the last two words.*
Turvy: Show me please. [Kate picks "van Lehn".]
Turvy: What's different about this case?
Kate: Hmm [confused].
Turvy: You selected these two words, why?
Kate: Because these two words make up his last name.
Turvy: Is there some feature of that word [hilites "van"] I should look for? That word exactly?
Kate: In this case, yes [hesitant].

As in previous lessons, Kate gives an explanation with her demo, but it fails to distinguish this case. When she is stymied, Turvy suggests a plausible (though wrong) hypothesis, which she accepts for now.

To summarize the dialog: Kate's goal is to get Turvy to do the task (until a new case requires further teaching), and Turvy's goal is to get more specific instructions from Kate. Typically, Kate does an example, then Turvy does the next one. Turvy describes actions when predicting them the first time. When Turvy errs, Kate demonstrates the right steps and gives a verbal hint; Turvy echoes back an interpretation. If it cannot make use of Kate's hint, Turvy proposes a guess, to elicit further explanation.

We realized from the outset that it would be all too easy for the Wizard to slip out of character, despite our formal models. In order to sustain the simulation of algorithmic intelligence, we decided to minimize the amount of new information the Wizard has to cope with. Hence we had users do standard tasks on data the Wizard had prepared. Moreover, all tasks were designed to limit the user's options: there were no "inputs" (data was merely cut, copied, pasted) and few points at which the order of steps could be varied. As mentioned above, each task was analyzed beforehand, so that inferences made from examples (given in a standard sequence) were in effect pre-scripted. Thus the Wizard was able to focus on the user's speech and gestures, and respond consistently. We also made Turvy a little extra stupid (for instance, guessing "van" rather than lowercase), to get more experimental data.

Hypotheses

Formalizing the inference and interaction models revealed the complexity of various kinds of instructions and the information needed to interpret them. This helped us form hypotheses about the way people would construct lessons and the instructions they would use. We had four main working hypotheses.

1 All users would employ the same small set of commands, those given in Table 1, with only minor variations in wording.

2 Users would learn "TurvyTalk" (Turvy's low-level terminology for describing search patterns), but only as a result of hearing Turvy describe things. Moreover, if Turvy uttered (perhaps in the form of a question) some instruction the user had previously given but with different wording, users would thereafter adopt Turvy's wording. This hypothesis is based on verbal convergence (Leiser, 1989), as mentioned in the introduction.

3 Users would teach simple tasks with ease and complex ones with reasonable effort. In other words, the complexity of instruction would depend on the task, not on peculiarities of Turvy's learning method.

4 Users would point to focus Turvy's attention on parts of a search pattern. Pointing avoids the problem of how to name something, but has the disadvantage of being ambiguous; the teacher must rely on the learner to infer the correct granularity and property.

Experimental setup

In our experiment users sat at a Macintosh computer and worked on bibliographic entries using the Microsoft Word text editor. A facilitator sat next to the user. Nearby (but out of eye contact) sat Turvy, played by the system designer, who had a second keyboard and mouse also connected to the Macintosh. The video signal from the computer was split-routed to both the user's and Turvy's screens. This setup allowed them to view the document simultaneously, yet restricted their physical interaction to pointing on screen with the cursor. They competed for control of the cursor, but this caused no problems in practice. For each task, the facilitator opened an on-screen document containing the references, then showed an annotated picture of the reformatted result. The user would practice on several entries until able to reformat them correctly. At this point the facilitator would ask the user to teach Turvy, and the Wizard became active, speaking and acting as if Turvy were present in the software. To reinforce the fantasy, the Wizard spoke in clipped sentences, with rather mechanical intonation. While we did not deceive users, they quickly bought into the illusion. They spoke more curtly to Turvy than to the facilitator, and referred to Turvy and the Wizard as two separate entities.

In this study, we did a pre-pilot, a pilot and a final run. Originally, we planned a Wizard of Oz without speech. The

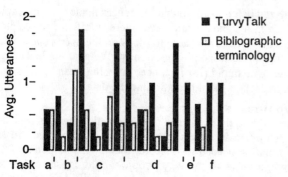

Figure 3. The language spoken by users.

pre-pilot used a menu, with the facilitator-to-be acting as user. When it became clear that our user misunderstood the menu commands, we realized we ought not to predetermine the user's language. In the pilot, four users tested a speech input version of Turvy; they could compose their own commands, but initially Turvy spoke only to ask very general questions like "What's important here?" Generality confused them, but was rectified when questions were made context specific, and when Turvy described its actions and proposed guesses. In the main experiment, eight subjects (five with some programming experience) tested the revised version, whose behavior was held constant.

OBSERVATIONS AND RESULTS

Our data consists of video tapes, transcripts, and the experimenters' subjective observations. We studied comments made by users while working with Turvy and during interviews. We also did content analyses, counting the number of bibliographic terms vs. TurvyTalk in users' instructions, and measuring indicators of confidence, hesitation and confusion at various points of interest during the session.

Command set (Hypothesis 1)

Users gave a close-fitting subset of the instructions we had predicted. From Table 1 we see that nearly all commands were used and caused no difficulty. The actual wordings subjects used were quite consistent, especially after they heard Turvy ask the corresponding question: they would turn it into a command, such as "Do the rest." (See TurvyTalk, Hypothesis 2).

Instructions for focusing attention were problematic. Users almost never volunteered vague hints like "I'm repeating actions," "this is similar," and even "look here." On the other hand, users would give hints in answer to Turvy's questions. The wording of focus instructions was more variable than for commands or responses.

TurvyTalk (Hypothesis 2)

We found that users did learn to describe things like titles and surnames in terms of their syntax. In post-session interviews, all users said that Turvy does not know about bibliographies; few could describe the sort of terminology it does understand, but they could list examples. We did a content analysis of users' speech to confirm these findings. Dividing the entire session into 16 events for different phases of tasks (first example, points where Turvy would err, etc.), we counted the number of user utterances referring

to features in terms Turvy understood (TurvyTalk) versus those involving bibliographic terminology (eg. "paste after the author's name"). The analysis confirmed our qualitative findings. In particular, as shown in Figure 3, use of bibliographic terminology tapers off and TurvyTalk increases. We conclude that Turvy's speech quickly trained users to mirror its language—verbal convergence occurs. Even more interesting is users' tendency to juxtapose both languages in one instruction, as if trying to relate their concepts to Turvy's.

Teaching difficulty (Hypothesis 3)

One of our chief aims is to make simple tasks easy to teach, and complex tasks teachable with reasonable effort. In our study, easy tasks (like changing underlined text to italics) were trivially taught by giving a demonstration. The hard tasks (like reversing author's surnames and initials) involved more verbal description of special cases.

All but one user reported that Turvy was easy to teach, once they had realized it learns incrementally and continuously so they needn't anticipate all special cases. However, one user told us at the outset that no computer could be taught without anticipating all cases, and therefore refused to try. No one complained about having to speak TurvyTalk.

We sought to objectify users' impressions of teaching effort in a content analysis of speech characteristics, with ratings measuring high confidence through to confusion. We found that users had a fairly neutral feeling of control; however, dealing with unexpected cases caused anxiety.

Speech versus pointing (Hypothesis 4)

One instructional technique we hoped to find was pointing to focus attention, but we observed almost none (apart from explicit selections required by tasks). When Turvy asked users to explain a new case by "pointing to something in the text," they were confused, if the distinguishing feature was a property rather than a string. We concluded that this query is ineffective; instead, Turvy should propose a guess.

Dialog

We found two distinct styles of interaction, not anticipated in our hypotheses. One type of user is highly interactive, talkative; the other is quiet, non-inviting. A talkative user describes a task before starting it, then does one example and gets Turvy to try the next. Some feel duty-bound to explain expected special cases in advance, but find this hard to do. Soon they learned to wait for special cases to arise.

In contrast, a quiet user works silently through the first example and goes on to the next one without inviting Turvy to try, nor even signaling that the first is done. When Turvy detects repetition, it butts in "I've seen you do this before, may I try?" The user consents, and the rest of the dialog proceeds much as for talkative users, though a quiet one is more likely to tell Turvy to skip a troublesome case than try explaining it.

Talkative users say less as they grow more adept at using Turvy; quiet ones stay quiet. A content analysis showed that talkative users gradually grow more confident, with lapses at special cases, while quiet ones, initially very confident, lose their edge as tasks get harder.

In the post-session interviews (see the Appendix for sample questions), we found that both types of user formed similar models of Turvy's inference and interaction. They recognized that it learns primarily by watching actions, but also understands verbal hints. All users liked the way Turvy is eager to predict after one example, because they believed this gave them more control over learning. All users were concerned about completeness, correctness and autonomy, believing it would be foolhardy to leave Turvy unsupervised until all cases had been covered. Some of the programmers thought that seeing a printout of the procedures Turvy learned would be helpful; the other users disagreed.

All users (apart from the one who refused to teach) said they would use Turvy in their daily work, if only it were real. Most wished that Turvy would learn their language.

To generalize the experiment, we also tried Turvy on drawing and file management with four different subjects. The results were the same, except that we saw some use of pointing (at fields in file listings).

LESSONS LEARNED USING WIZARD OF OZ

Turvy is the most complex Wizard of Oz simulation done to date. The lessons we learned will be of value to those who want to use the Wizard of Oz in their own studies of intelligent interfaces. These lessons differ from other Wizard of Oz experiences, being oriented towards implementable systems, rather than proof of concepts.

Ironically, prior implementation experience is invaluable. The chief danger in using a Wizard of Oz is ascribing to the Wizard powers which no real system could have. This casts doubt on the validity of hypotheses and yields inappropriate, optimistic results. We wanted Turvy to help us design a system of the near future, so the danger is magnified. A prior implementation (like Metamouse) suggests limitations to be put on the Wizard's intelligence, as well as interesting research questions.

The Agent's behavior should be based upon an algorithm. Another way to keep the simulation honest is to base it on an algorithm or at least a fairly detailed formal model. This ensures consistent behavior and experimental repeatability. When the algorithm is too complex for the Wizard to run in real time, it can be used to analyze tasks in order to script the Wizard's behavior. We did this in Turvy by designing a formal learning model, and by "scripting" the Wizard's responses by running the tasks through the model and codifying the results.

The Agent's dialog capabilities should be based upon a constrained interaction model. Similarly, true natural language understanding by computers is far in the future. A realistic dialog must be constrained by an interaction model that explicitly lists the kinds of instructions the system can understand and the feedback it can formulate.

You can build real systems derived from studies of verbal Wizard-human discourse. Even given an interaction model, some would argue that discourse rules derived from studies of verbal dialog cannot be incorporated in today's technology. We offer a glimpse into our current work as an existence proof that this is indeed possible. Moctec (Maulsby, 1992) is a working prototype, limited to simple search and replace tasks, and using a subset of the Turvy instructions without an agent metaphor. Users direct it by menus, voice buttons, and text-based pseudo-natural language hints. Cima (in progress) is a full implementation of Turvy's inferencing and interaction techniques.

The Designer benefits by becoming the Wizard. Perhaps the most important aspect of Turvy was the "training" the designer received by playing the role of agent. Being personally responsible for a user's discomfort and confusion motivates revisions! And simulating an incomplete design reveals its ill-defined aspects.

Qualitative results are the most valuable. By acting as Wizard, facilitator, and interviewer, the experimenters become immersed in the experiment and many important results become obvious. The most interesting experimental questions cannot be answered by statistics, at least in small, cheap studies. Still, measurements are useful: they validate the opinions of experimenters and users, and allow a detailed (if myopic) exploration of particular activities.

Interviews are essential, and video records are useful. We want to know what works, what doesn't, and why. Moreover, we want to know what concepts the users are constructing to explain the system to themselves. Accounts based on running commentaries and interviews are the most efficient means of finding out. Video records permit content analyses of speech and gesture in the users' visual context.

CONCLUSIONS

We prototyped an instructible computer agent using a Wizard of Oz simulation. The agent, Turvy, learns procedures and data descriptions from one or more examples done by the user, combined with verbal and pointing hints. The Wizard of Oz allowed us to test ideas without implementing a system, and thereby involve end-users in several iterations of Turvy's design. The simulation was constrained by formal models of inference and interaction, so that Turvy would have realistic limitations. As a result, we found a natural teaching protocol that we believe we can implement in a real system; in fact, we have implemented parts of it in a second prototype.

In some ways, the Turvy we tested was more stupid than one we would implement. It had no special purpose task knowledge and no ability to apply what it learned in one task to another one later on. Moreover, it learned concepts, but not the user's terminology. Nonetheless, users accept Turvy because it learns new cases on the fly, and makes good use of both demonstrations and verbal hints.

We learned valuable lessons about the Wizard of Oz, in particular the benefits of formal models, detailed task analysis, and direct feedback from users to the designer.

ACKNOWLEDGMENTS

Apple Computer Inc. and the Natural Sciences and Engineering Research Council of Canada provided the funding. Allen Cypher and Shifteh Karimi advised us (Thanks!).

REFERENCES

A. Cypher (1991) "EAGER: Programming repetitive tasks by example." *Proc. ACM CHI'91*, pp. 33-40.

N. Dahlbäck, A. Jönsson, L. Ahrenberg (1993) "Wizard of Oz studies—Why and how." *Proc. ACM International Workshop on Intelligent User Interfaces.*

J.D. Gould, J. Conti, T. Hovanyecz (1982) "Composing letters with a simulated listening typewriter." *Proc. ACM CHI'82*, pp. 367-370.

D.C. Halbert (1984) "Programming by example." Xerox PARC Research report OSD-T8402. Palo Alto CA.

A.G. Hauptmann (1989) "Speech and gestures for graphic image manipulation." *Proc. ACM CHI'89*, pp. 241-245.

W.C. Hill, J.R. Miller (1988) "Justified advice: a semi-naturalistic study of advisory strategies." *Proc. ACM CHI'88*, pp. 185-190.

A. Kay (1984) "Computer software." *Scientific American*, 251(3), pp. 53-59, September.

T.K. Landauer (1987) "Psychology as a mother of invention." *Proc. ACM CHI+GI'87*, pp. 333-335.

R.G. Leiser (1989) "Exploiting convergence to improve natural language understanding." *Interacting with Computers*, 1(3), pp. 284-298.

D. Maulsby, K.A. Kittlitz, I.H. Witten (1989) "Metamouse: specifying graphical procedures by example." *Proc. SIGGRAPH '89*, pp. 127-136.

D. Maulsby (1993) "Simulating an instructible interface: the Turvy experience," in *Watch What I Do: Programming by Demonstration*, A. Cypher et al eds (in press).

D. Maulsby (1992) "Prototyping an instructible interface: Moctec." *Proc. ACM CHI'92*, pp. 52-53.

B.A. Myers (1991) "Text formatting by demonstration." *Proc. ACM CHI '91*, pp. 251–256.

J. Wilson, D. Rosenberg (1988) "Rapid prototyping for user interface design." In *Handbook of Human-Computer Interaction*, pp. 859-875, M. Helander ed., New York, North-Holland.

APPENDIX — INTERVIEW QUESTIONS

Questions asked of users during post-session interviews are listed below. The questions are intended to focus the user's thoughts on key aspects of working with Turvy: translating cultural concepts into syntactic proxies, speech input and output, eager prediction and supervision. We also asked users how they felt about our experimental method. We often reworded questions to refer to specific things that happened during a session. For lack of time, we did not ask all questions of all users.

Did you find some tasks hard to do yourself? Which ones?

How much English do you think Turvy understands? Does he understand whole sentences?

Were you surprised at what Turvy understood? What had you expected?

You gave Turvy some instructions like "select the author's last name." Do you think Turvy understood those?

Do you think Turvy can learn a concept like "name"? Do you think Turvy understands instructions like "look for the word before the italic text"?

What kinds of bibliography features do you think Turvy can recognize? What did Turvy know before you taught him?

Turvy described what he was doing. Did this help you? Did you find the details distracting?

Can you recall one or two descriptions Turvy read out?

Do you think Turvy can learn from verbal instructions alone — can you simply tell him what to do and then get him to do it?

Could you list some commands Turvy recognizes?

Did you want Turvy to start predicting actions as soon as he did? How many examples do you think Turvy should wait for before he starts predicting?

Sometimes Turvy would change the order of the steps you had demonstrated when he did them. Did this bother you?

Do you think it's best to tell Turvy in advance about all the special cases, or wait for them to arise?

Sometimes Turvy would say "What's different here, can you point to something in the text?" Did you understand this question? What did Turvy want you to do?

Do you think Turvy remembers what he learned in one task when you teach another one? For instance, you did two tasks that involved searching for surnames. Did you expect Turvy to remember?

Did you feel comfortable with the fact that Turvy made a number of mistakes while learning? Would you run out of patience if using Turvy for real?

At some point in every task you would let Turvy "do the rest". Did you watch him closely while he zipped through them? Would you rather watch step by step or review his work afterwards?

Would you trust Turvy to ask you about questionable items, or do you suppose he would just do them, stupidly?

Would you like to be able to see a printed program or script of the task as Turvy learns it? Would this help you?

What did you like about Turvy? What did you dislike?

Would you like to be able to see Turvy (as an icon)?

Would you use Turvy in your day-to-day work?

What additional kinds of knowledge (if any) do you think Turvy should come bundled with?

During the experiment, did you get the impression that Turvy was real, or were you constantly aware that you were talking to a person?

Did the experiment cause you any problems? Were the tasks too difficult? Did it go on too long? Did you feel pressured, or that you were being tested?

A Synergistic Approach to Specifying Simple Number Independent Layouts by Example

Scott E. Hudson
Chen-Ning Hsi

Graphics Visualization and Usability Center
College of Computing
Georgia Institute of Technology
Atlanta, GA 30332-0280
E-mail: scott.hudson@cc.gatech.edu, hsic@cc.gatech.edu

ABSTRACT

A grid-based technique to specify simple number independent layouts by example is described. This technique was originally developed to support layout specification for a parallel program visualization system but can be applied to aid other simple graphical layout tasks as well. The technique works by allowing the user to construct an example layout using a grid-based interaction technique. This example can then be generalized into a layout algorithm which can be applied to create layouts of any size. However, rather than simply choosing the "best" generalization, the system described here takes a synergistic approach. New examples from a set of alternative generalizations are presented to the user so that they can guide and control the generalization process. This provides more understanding and control of the generalization process and typically allows a correct generalization to be constructed from only one small example.

Keywords: layout specification, programming by example, grid-based layout, generalization, end-user customization.

1 INTRODUCTION

In a number of application domains, it is important to be able to create customized layouts of graphical objects with a minimum of effort. For example,

when using program visualization systems in a debugging context, very little time can be devoted to specifying a display layout. On the other hand, displays must be flexible enough to accommodate varying numbers and sizes of display elements. This paper describes a new technique for specifying simple layouts of this type by example and its implementation in a small prototype system.

This system provides an easy to use grid-based interaction technique for creating an example layout in a constrained fashion. Based on an example created with the grid, the system guides the user in quickly exploring alternative generalizations that can be used to turn the single example layout into a more general layout algorithm.

A central feature of the technique presented here is its synergistic approach which combines automated generalization with specific user choice and control. The technique allows users to quickly consider alternative inferences rather than trying to find the "best" generalization in a fully automatic fashion. This provides more control and understandability than typical by-example approaches, but still provides the ease of use advantages of pure by-example systems that require no explicit specification or programming.

2. AN EXAMPLE

To illustrate the techniques to be described here, this section will provide a small but complete example. Here, the system is used to specify the layout of a visualization in our parallel program visualization application. This particular visualization is designed to show the communication patterns among a group of

This work was supported in part by the National Science Foundation under grant IRI-9015407.

processes at some stage in a parallel algorithm. As illustrated in Figure 1, layouts generated by the system have a hierarchical structure. In this case, the layout consists of a static component containing a pair of buttons along with a sequence of process visualizations. Each process visualization in turn contains within it a sequence of sub-visualizations representing the buffers and communication channels of the process object. The number of processes and buffer displays within each process is determined at run-time. This hierarchy results in a simple boxes-within-boxes visualization (as shown later in Figure 5).

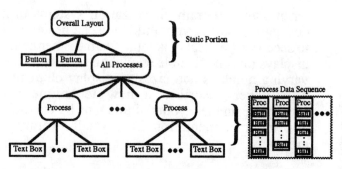

Figure 1. The Structure of an Example Layout

Parts of the hierarchy where the number of items is known in advance can be constructed in a direct manipulation fashion by simply snapping items to a grid as shown in Figure 2. In this case we know the size and type of the two button items in the first row in advance and can use a direct representation of those items. In the case of the process visualization sub-grid (in the third row), a variable sized placeholder item is used to represent a range of potential sizes. As described in Section 4, the grid provides a simple mechanism for adapting to varying sized objects.

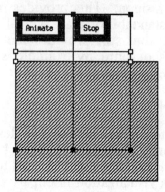

Figure 2. Using the Grid for a Static Layout

For layouts where items come from a varying length sequence, a graphical representation of the sequence is used to construct a single example. As with the static portions, this example is constructed by snapping numbered elements from the sequence to a grid. Two such example layouts (one for the layout of buffers within each process and one for the overall display of processes) are shown in Figure 3

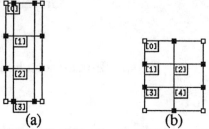

(a)   (b)

Figure 3. Two Example Layouts

After snapping together an example and manipulating the grid spacing, the user can ask the system to generalize the example into a layout procedure which can handle any number of examples. The system does this by generating a series of viable generalizations (using the mechanism described in Section 5). Each of these generalizations represents a layout procedure. These procedures are then employed to generate additional examples based on longer sequences. Figure 4 shows this process for the example from Figure 3b. Here the user is presented with a set of new examples and allowed to choose among them in order to select the final generalization. Alternately, the user can request additional generalizations.

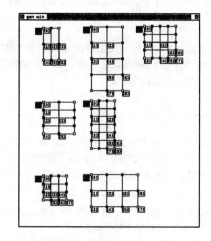

Figure 4. New Examples Illustrating Generalizations of Figure 3b

The generalizations presented in Figure 4 are generated using a fixed set of generalization strategies (as described in Section 5). Note that many of the generalizations illustrated in Figure 4 are clearly not what the user intended. In fact, this is to be expected of essentially any generalization method since only one very small example has been given and there is very little basis for making a correct choice. By providing more examples (as well as perhaps a set of negative or counter-examples) a generalization system might be able to perform much better. However, this would be dramatically more work for the user and much more cumbersome. Instead, by getting the user involved in the selection process, the correct generalization can normally be selected with minimal effort (e.g. from only one small example).

To finish our example, Figure 5 shows a complete display of real data from our application constructed from generalizations of the examples shown in Figures 2 and 3. (Note that the horizontal, vertical, and diagonal lines in this example represent messages and are not laid out by the system itself, but are simply drawn between buffer visualizations as part of the final animated display).

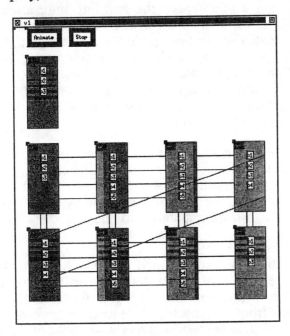

Figure 5. A Completed Visualization

In the next section techniques from related work will be discussed. Then, Section 4 will briefly describe the operation of the grid layout technique and Section 5 will describe the generalization strategies employed by the system. Finally,

Section 6 will consider limitations of the system, describe future work, and provide conclusions.

3. RELATED WORK

A number of systems have provided direct manipulation interfaces to layout specification (see for example [Hend86]). These system essentially allow layouts to be specified by drawing them. In addition to its inherent speed and interactivity, this approach has a number of advantages over more traditional programmatic specifications. In particular, layout specifications are expressed as concrete entities, the objects of interest are visible and can be directly manipulated, and the effects of changes can be made immediately apparent. In addition, these systems have the advantage of using primarily visual means to describe visual entities.

Unfortunately, many direct manipulation layout or presentation editors are limited to fixed displays containing static elements. Although techniques such as constraints have allowed some interactive layout specification systems to support size independent layouts (see for example [Card88, Huds90]), few if any support layouts where the *number* of items is not fixed in advance. Although tolerable for many user interface applications, this limitation makes it difficult to employ these systems in data-rich environments (such as visualization). In these environments the nature of the display needs to be influenced more by the actual data encountered than by the fixed structure of the application. The system presented here produces layouts which are both object size and number independent.

The work presented here builds on previous work in specification or programming *by example* or *by demonstration* (see for example [Mau89, Cyph91]). These systems attempt to infer a general procedure for carrying out some task based on one or more examples. For example, the Peridot system and its successors [Myer86, Myer87, Myer89] have been very successful in inferring the specification of interaction techniques and simple constraints by demonstration. In addition, these systems take some steps toward user involvement in the inference process by allowing users to reject inferences. However, alternatives are not presented to the user directly, and examples are not generated to aid with selection. The work presented here goes further by using examples both for specification and for evaluation of the results or exploration of alternative results.

By-example systems maintain many of the advantages of direct manipulation approaches. However, they go further by eliminating any explicit or implicit programming step all together. However, by-example systems also have drawbacks. In particular, if the system fails to infer what the user intends by an example — chooses the wrong generalization(s) from the example to a full procedure — difficulties can arise. In some cases, the user can simply specify more examples or provide counter examples. However, generalization techniques are currently limited and tend to be very domain specific. As a result, the user often must try to "reverse engineer" the inferences being made in order to coerce the system into choosing the correct generalization(s).

The system presented here attempts to overcome this difficulty by allowing the user to play a stronger role in the generalization process. In particular, the system plays the role of creating or suggesting generalizations, but the user (who has more explicit knowledge of the intended result) controls the process by evaluating and choosing between generalizations.

This synergistic approach proposed here is related to the one taken in the FLATS system [Koch90a, Koch90b, Koch90c] which allows a design space of computer generated floor plans to be interactively explored by the user. Unlike the FLATS system, the work presented here seeks both to create and express the action of a procedure by means of examples (rather than aiding in the choice of a single design instance from a set of automatically created designs).

4. USING THE GRID LAYOUT TECHNIQUE

As illustrated in the example of Section 2, the first step in creating a layout is to use a grid to construct an example layout based on a small number of elements. This section describes the grid interaction technique and how it may be used to construct constrained layouts suitable for the generalizations described in the next section.

Requiring all layout elements to lie on grid points restricts the nature of the layouts. This can be constraining and limits the form of layouts that can be produced — in fact, this limitation can be seen as a central drawback of the work presented here. However, grids provide structure to the layout process, are very easy and natural to use, and are suitable for reuse in new design contexts. These properties, particularly the provision of structure to the layout, allow a more powerful generalization technique to be applied. In addition, although grids can be restrictive, because they establish a common framework for designs they have been used successfully (and in fact advocated) for general graphic design [Hurl78, Mull81, Fein88] as well as tasks such as text or table layout [Beac85].

In the prototype described here, the grid is implemented as an interactor object (sometimes called a *widget*) in the Artkit user interface toolkit [Henr90]. This same interactor (with different default appearance and action) is used both for creation or editing of the initial layout and to manage the display of the layout in the final interface. As a result, the system requires no extra code or special provisions to allow the end-user to modify or customize the layout (when this is desirable).

As one would expect, the grid interactor allows objects to be snapped to the intersection of its horizontal and vertical guide lines. In addition, the grid provides operations to reposition rows and columns, flip, rotate, and exchange a selected area, and interactively modify the point of attachment (e.g. to the top, bottom, left, right, middle, etc. of each object).

By default, items are simply attached to grid points and the position of adjacent row and column grid lines is independent of the size of these items. Optionally, the size of items can be taken into account when computing grid line positions for the final layout. When this option is invoked (on a selected set of rows or columns), grid line positions are constrained to be relative to the nearest edge of the largest item in the row or column. For example, if a grid line is 5 pixels away from the largest sample items in an adjacent row, then in the resulting final layout, the grid line will be placed at a distance of 5 pixels from the widest item in that row. This strategy is similar to the stretching behavior described in [Card88] and can be used to create layouts which automatically adjust to the size of the objects within them.

A final operation provided by the grid is a special clean up or *normalization* operation. This operation can be used to adjust both distances between adjacent grid lines and object size scale factors so that they form ratios of small integral multiples. This technique allows approximate placements to be "cleaned up" by the system. For example, a set of 5 grid lines could be initially placed with the first 4 at nearly uniform distances and the last with close to double this spacing. After normalization, the resulting rows would have exactly 1:1:1:2 spacing.

Figure 6 shows the algorithm used for normalization. This algorithm accepts a set of N input distances (or sizes), and computes scale factor plus the closest integral ratio such that all elements of the ratio are less than a small fixed limit M (e.g. each element of the ratio may range from 0 to M). For our systems we have used M = 9 successfully. The final distances (or sizes) are computed as the product of the scale and ratio number.

```
/*   Input:        int in[i], i = 1, N
     output:       int ratio[i], i = 1, N
                   int scale;
*/
     int scale, error, minerror, temp;

     minidx = find_minidx(&in[0]);

     minerror = MAXERROR;
     for (i = 1; i <= M; i ++)
     {
         scale = in[minidx]/i;
         error = 0;
         for (j = 1; j <= N; j++)
         {
             temp = in[j] / scale;
             error += abs(temp * scale - in[j]);
         }
         if (error < minerror)
         {
             min_ratio = i;
             minerror = error;
             if (error == 0) break;
         }
     }

     scale = in[minidx] / min_ratio;
     for (i = 1; i <= N; i++)
     {
         ratio[i] = in[i]/scale;
     }
```

Figure 6. Normalization Algorithm

5. GENERALIZING FROM EXAMPLES

A layout instance defines the positions and sizes for a fixed number of objects in a specific layout. A generalization process is employed to convert this example into a complete procedure that can work with any number of elements. The generalizations used by the system are based on the assumption that the objects in the layout come from an ordered sequence (more complex structures are currently being explored as a part of future work). Following that order, a list of vectors traveling from the first object to the last object can be calculated. The path produced by these vectors forms the basis of our generalization strategies. For example, Figure 7 shows the path resulting from the placement of three objects. Note that each vector of a path is recorded in units of grid position not in absolute coordinate values.

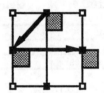

Figure 7. An Example Path

In each of the generalization strategies, the path formed by the traveling vectors is deemed as a pattern. Each generalization strategy represents one method of enumerating new instances from that pattern. The two overall strategies currently employed are interpolation and repetition. Interpolation takes the viewpoint that the original pattern is the desired overall shape of the layout and that a larger or smaller layout with the same shape is the desired result. As illustrated in Figure 8, this generalization strategy works by inserting points into line segments of the path and uses those extra points to layout the objects.

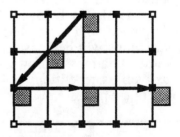

Figure 8. An Interpolation of Figure 7

Repetition takes the viewpoint that the example path forms a primitive shape and the desired result is some repetition of this shape. Figure 9, illustrates one form of repetition.

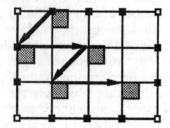

Figure 9. An Example Repetition of Figure 7

Each of the two overall generalization strategies has several variations. For the interpolation approach, interpolation can be done horizontally, vertically, or both. This results in three different specific generalizations as listed below.

Line Segments of Interpolation	Generalization Strategy No.
horizontal	(1)
vertical	(2)
horizontal and vertical	(3)

The repetition generalization strategy has three orthogonal ways in which it can be varied. Different scale factors can be applied to repeated sub-patterns, different rotations can be applied to the repeated sub-patterns, and the repeated sub-patterns can be related to their parent patterns at different points. In our initial prototype we have limited the choices for these variations. Only small number of scale factors (1 and 1/2) and rotation factors (0° and 90°) are considered, and three variations are used for selecting repetition positions. They are repetition only at end points, repetition at each *child point*, and repetition at each point in the pattern. Here, the set of child points includes every point in the initial pattern except the first point and all the points generated by the sub-pattern repetition. This results in 12 specific generalizations as shown below. After more experience is gained with these generalizations, additional variations will be considered. These include several variations on row and column expansion as well as repetitions at identifiable extreme points of the pattern.

Generalization Strategy No.	Repetition Positions		
	end point	child points	all points
(Scale, Rotation) (1,0)	(4)	(5)	(6)
(1/2, 0)	(7)	(8)	(9)
(1,90)	(10)	(11)	(12)
(1/2, 90)	(13)	(14)	(15)

Figure 10 shows examples of a number of these generalization strategies. Note that in Figure 10, only 10 alternatives are present. The others are not shown because position collisions occur among objects during application of those generalization strategies to large examples. This criteria is used to cull potential generalizations before presentation to the user (the size of examples considered in this test is set by the user).

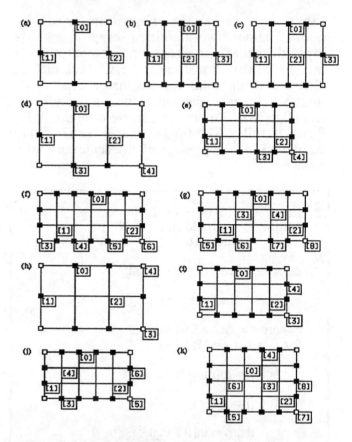

Figure 10. Examples of using generalization strategies: (a) original layout, (b) — (k) after applying generalization strategies (1), (3), (4), (7), (8), (9), (10), (13), (14), and (15).

New strategies can also be created by composing the above fifteen basic generalization strategies. This composition can be done by applying the generalization strategies repeatedly. If none of the first-time generalization is desired, users can pick a partially correct generalization and request additional generalization. This process can continue until the desired layout is generated. When a layout generated using multiple strategies is chosen, a composite generalization strategy is formed.

In addition to the sequence of basic strategies applied to create a composite generalization, the system also records one parameter for each strategy. This parameter records the number of points inserted by an interpolation strategy or the number of replications done by a repetition strategy. Based on the ratio formed by these numbers, the composite strategy generalizes layouts by proportionally applying the respective basic strategies. For instance, a composite strategy composed of a two-point horizontal interpolation and one end-point repetition will generalize a layout by inserting 2N points horizontally and repeating the resulting pattern N times at the end points (i.e. in a 2:1 ratio).

Using composed layouts provided by the mechanism described above allows the system to produce a wider range of more interesting layouts than can be generated from a simple example. Additional variations on the composition mechanism are also under study. Including exploration of different kinds of composition and an automatic mechanism for promoting "interesting" composite strategies to basic ("one-step") strategies.

Although the use of rectangular grids and only a few generalizations strategies would seem to severely limit the class of layouts that can be produced, in practice many simple layout strategies can be effectively specified in a very simple fashion. To illustrate the flexibility of this method, the generalizations needed to produce a complete breadth-first binary tree layout are presented below.

To specify this layout, the user initially places three objects in the grid as shown in Figure 11(a). The user then stretches the grid to adjust the distances among those objects. When the distances look right as shown in Figure 11(b), the user sets the grid edge distances to "dependent on the object size", and then applies the normalization operation to clean up the example. In this instance, both the horizontal distance ratio and vertical distance ratio are normalized to "1:1:1". The object size normalization operation produces horizontal and vertical scale ratios of "1:1" and "3:2". Next, the user asks the system to generalize. From the generated layouts presented the user picks the example resulting from generalization strategy 8 (shown in Figure 10(f)). The binary tree layout can then be saved and used to layout different

number of objects with different sizes. Figure 11(c) and 11(d) shows the use of the algorithm to lay out different numbers of objects and objects with different sizes, respectively.

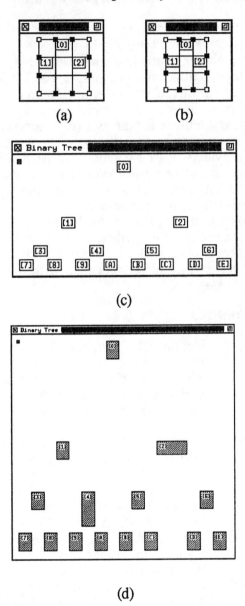

Figure 11. Laying out a binary tree by example.

6. CONCLUSIONS AND FUTURE WORK

The specific prototype system presented here has a number of limitations. Central amongst these is the use of a fairly limited set of generalizations. We are currently exploring extensions in this area. However, the intent of this system has been to serve not as a final solution for by-example layout, but instead to serve as a testbed for exploring synergistic by-example techniques. Further, despite its limitations, the system has performed very well for our parallel visualization application. In particular, most common layout patterns in the domain can be specified, common layouts can be reused, and the system is very easy to use.

We believe the synergistic techniques presented here have potential for many by-example systems. By involving the knowledge and capabilities of the user in the inference process, a good balance between automatic inference and "manual" user action is achieved. Tasks which are easy for the system and tedious for the user (e.g., generating a range of candidate generalizations) are performed by the system. Tasks which are hard for the system but can be performed quickly by the user (e.g., evaluation and selection of the proper generalization) are performed by the user. By employing examples at each stage. Little additional work is needed on the part of the user, and correct results can be obtained with fewer examples and more reliably than with pure by-example systems.

REFERENCES

[Beac85] Beach, R., *Setting Tables and Illustrations with Style.*, Ph.D. Thesis, Dept. of Computer Science, University of Waterloo, Ontario, 1985. (Xerox PARC Report CS-85-3, May 1985).

[Card88] Cardelli, L., "Building User Interfaces by Direct Manipulation", *Proceedings of the ACM SIGGRAPH Symposium on User Interface Software*, Banff, Alberta, Canada, October 1988, pp. 152-166.

[Cyph91] Cypher, A., "Eager: Programming Repetitive Tasks by Example", Proceedings of CHI '91, May 1991.

[Fein88] Feiner, S., "A Grid-Based Approach To Automating Display Layout.", *Proc. Graphics Interface '88*, 1988, pp. 192-197.

[Hend86] Henderson, D.A., "The Trillium User Interface Design Environment", Proceedings of CHI '86, April 1986, pp. 221-227.

[Henr90] Henry, T.R., Hudson, S.E., Newell G.L., "Integrating Gesture and Snapping into a User Interface Toolkit", Proceedings of the *ACM/SIGGRAPH Symposium on User Interface Software and*

Technology, October 1990, pp. 112-121.

[Huds90] Hudson, S. Mohamed, S., "Interactive Specification of Flexible User Interface Displays", *ACM Transactions on Information Systems*, v 8, n 3, July 1990, pp. 269-288.

[Hurl78] Hurlburt, A., *The Grid.*, NY: Van Nostrand Reinhold Co., 1978.

[Koch90a] Kochar, S., *Cooperative Computer-Aided Design*, Ph.D. Dissertation, Harvard University, 1990.

[Koch90b] Kochar, S., "A Prototype System for Design Automation via the Browsing Paradigm", Proceedings of Graphics Interface '90, Halifax, Canada, May 1990, pp. 156-166.

[Koch90c] Kochar, S, and Friedell, M., "User Control in Cooperative Computer-Aided Design", Proceedings of the ACM Symposium on User Interface Software and Technology, October, 1990, pp. 143-151.

[Mau89] Maulsby, D.L., Kittlitz, K.A., and Witten, I.H., Metamouse: Specifying Graphical Procedures by Example, Proceedings of SIGGRAPH '89, Boston, July 1989, pp. 127-136.

[Mull81] Muller-Brockmann, J., *Grid Systems in graphic design.*, Niederteufen, Switzerland: Verlag Arthur Niggli, 1981.

[Myer86] Myers, B. and Buxton, B., "Creating Highly-Interactive and Graphical User Interfaces by Demonstration.", *Computer Graphics*, 20:4, August 1986, pp. 249-258.

[Myer87] Myers, B., "Creating User Interfaces By Demonstration", University of Toronto Technical Report, CSRI-196 (Ph.D. Thesis), May 1987.

[Myer89] Myers, B., Vander Zanden, B., Dannenberg, R., "Creating Graphical Interactive Application Objects by Demonstration", Proceedings of the ACM Symposium on User Interface Software and Technology, November 1989, pp. 95-104.

Marquise: Creating Complete User Interfaces by Demonstration

Brad A. Myers   *Richard G. McDaniel*   *David S. Kosbie*

School of Computer Science
Carnegie Mellon University
5000 Forbes Avenue
Pittsburgh, PA 15213
{bam, richm, koz}@cs.cmu.edu

ABSTRACT

Marquise is a new interactive tool that allows virtually all of the user interfaces of graphical editors to be created by demonstration without programming. A "graphical editor" allows the user to create and manipulate graphical objects with a mouse. This is a very large class of programs and includes drawing programs like MacDraw, graph layout editors like MacProject, visual language editors, and many CAD/CAM programs. The primary innovation in Marquise is to allow the designer to demonstrate the overall behavior of the interface. To implement this, the Marquise framework contains knowledge about palettes for creating and specifying properties of objects, and about operations such as selecting, moving, and deleting objects. The interactive tool uses the framework to allow the designer to demonstrate most of the end user's actions without programming, which means that Marquise can be used by non-programmers.

KEYWORDS: User Interface Software, User Interface Management Systems, Interface Builders, Demonstrational Interfaces, Garnet.

INTRODUCTION

One important goal of the Garnet project [6] is to allow user interface designers who are not programmers to design and implement the *look and feel* of user interfaces. The Marquise tool is the newest addition to the Garnet environment, and it ties together all the previous tools, while supporting, for the first time, interactive specification of the entire user interface.

In particular, Marquise allows the overall graphical appearance of the interface to be drawn, and the behaviors for object creation, selection and manipulation to be demonstrated.

Unlike many previous tools which concentrate on widgets, Marquise is aimed mostly at the main drawing window of graphical editors where the user creates and manipulates graphical objects with a mouse. For example, with Marquise you can demonstrate how the rubber banding will appear as you move the mouse, rather than having this as a hard-wired, unchangeable component. Another important capability in Marquise is demonstrating the modes of the interface. Although "mode-free" interfaces are often touted, all modern graphical interfaces are in fact highly moded. For example, in most drawing tools such as Macintosh MacDraw, a palette controls whether the next mouse click will select an object, insert a text string, or draw a rectangle, circle, polygon, etc. Other modes include the current colors, line styles, and arrowhead styles for the objects that will be created. Marquise provides an intuitive, demonstrational method for specifying the modes that control and are affected by an operation.

With Marquise, we have concentrated on providing complete control of when and how the behaviors are initiated. The primary innovations in Marquise are: (1) the use of special icons to represent the mouse positions while demonstrating the behavior, so the designer can then demonstrate what happens at those locations, (2) sophisticated control over the locations where those events should take place to begin and end behaviors, (3) a "mode window" to make explicit the modes of the interface that control the behaviors and values, (4) the formalization of "palettes" to control modes and object properties, and (5) the ability to interactively specify the attributes for built-in layout operations and objects.

Marquise stands for <u>M</u>ostly <u>A</u>utomated, <u>R</u>emarkably <u>Q</u>uick <u>U</u>ser <u>I</u>nterface <u>S</u>oftware <u>E</u>nvironment. (A "marquise" is a gem having the shape of a short, pointed oval with many facets.) Marquise is part of the Garnet system, which is a comprehensive user interface development environment written in Lisp for the X window system.[1]

---

[1]The Garnet system is available by anonymous FTP. Although Marquise is not yet ready for distribution as this paper is being written, you can get the toolkit, the Gilt interface builder, and Lapidary. Send mail to `Garnet@cs.cmu.edu` for information.

RELATED WORK

Previous design tools have shown that it is possible to interactively specify the graphical appearance and behavior of limited parts of an application's user interface. For example, many interface builders, such as the NeXT Interface Builder, UIMX for Motif, Druid [8], and Gilt [7], allow the designer to interactively specify the placement of widgets. Peridot [3] allows new widgets to be created interactively without programming, and Lapidary [4] allows application-specific graphical objects to be demonstrated. Marquise goes beyond these tools since it supports creating, editing, and deleting of objects at run time, and allows the overall behavior to be defined. DEMO [10] used the idea of demonstrating the end-user's actions that start a behavior (called the ''stimulus'') and then demonstrating the response to that stimulus. DEMO II [1] added sophisticated techniques for inferring constraints to control how objects are placed or moved. Marquise uses the stimulus-response idea, here called ''train'' and ''show,'' but concentrates on which high-level actions are appropriate and the context of the stimulus.

Some previous systems have provided frameworks to help code graphical editors. Unidraw [9] and many graph editors (e.g., [2]) provide a standard set of built-in operations as methods, and the designer writes code to override these methods for the specific application. However, none of these other systems allow new behaviors to be defined by demonstration.

USER INTERFACE

The basic windows for Marquise are shown in Figure 1. There is a palette of objects that can be drawn, some palettes for controlling the properties of those objects, and a set of commands in a menubar. In all conventional interface builders there are two modes: *Build* and *Run*, where in Build mode the designer constructs the interface, and in Run mode it is tested. Marquise adds two additional modes to demonstrate behaviors: *Train* and *Show*. Train mode is used to demonstrate what the end user will do, and Show mode is used to demonstrate the system's response to that action. A different mouse cursor for each mode insures that the designer always knows what the current mode is.

In Build mode, the static parts of the interface are drawn. For example, the designer might add to the window some widgets that should always be visible. Lines could be added as decorations. Many applications contain palettes that show which objects can be created, or that show various values for a property (like color, line-style, etc.). These palettes are drawn with Marquise in Build mode. In Run mode, the interface can be exercised to see how it will operate for the end user.

In Train mode, the designer operates the mouse and keyboard in the same way the end user would, and then goes into Show mode to demonstrate what the system's response should be. While in Train mode, the end-user behaviors are operational, but in addition, the keystrokes and mouse movements are saved. In Show mode, the designer can create and edit objects exactly the same as in

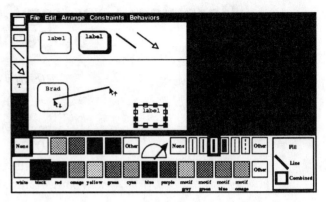

Figure 1:
The main Marquise windows: the basic object palette on the left, the main work area, and the palette for controlling the color and halftones for filling-styles and line-styles at the bottom. The designer is creating an interface with a ''create palette'' at the top containing two types of nodes and two types of links. The node at the lower right of the work window is selected. The Marquise commands are in the menubar at the top. The ''Constraints'' menu allows graphical constraints to be specified. The ''Behaviors'' menu allows objects to be declared as palettes, and displays the mode and feedback windows.

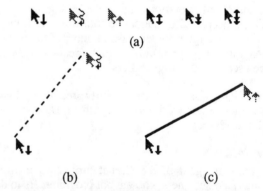

Figure 2:
(a) The icons that show where the mouse was pressed, moved to, released, clicked (pressed and released in the same place), double-clicked, and double clicked and released. (b) In Train mode, the designer pressed the mouse down and moved, and then in Show mode, drew a dotted line as the interim feedback. (c) Going back to Train mode, the designer released the mouse button, and in Show mode, deleted the dotted line and drew a solid line.

Build mode, except that the operations are remembered so they can be attached to the events demonstrated in Train mode.

As an example, here is how the designer would demonstrate that when the mouse button goes down, a feedback dotted line should be drawn which follows the mouse, and then when the button is released, the dotted line should be erased and a real line drawn. First, the designer would go into Train mode, press down the mouse button,

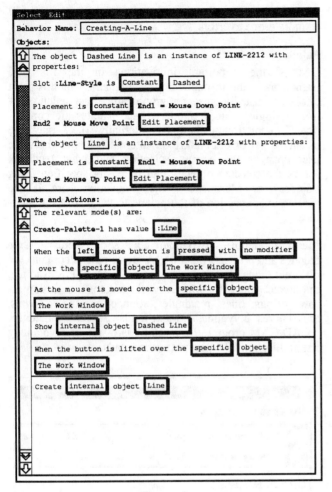

Figure 3:
The feedback window for behaviors. At the top is a pull-down menu of commands, then the name of the behavior, then the objects that participate in the behavior, and finally the events and actions. Pushing on the buttons displays a popup window of the other possible choices. Changing the option at the beginning of a "sentence" will change the options available for the rest of the sentence. An entire section of the window can be selected and cut, copied, etc.

and move away from the initial press. Without releasing the mouse button, the designer would change to Show mode. The window will now contain two icons which show where the mouse was pressed and to where it was moved. Now in Show mode, the designer draws a dotted line between the icons (Figure 2-b). Marquise infers that a dotted line should be created on the down press and one end should follow the mouse as it moves. Then the designer presses the mouse button somewhere on the background and switches to Train mode with the mouse button still down, so the mouse *release* can be demonstrated. Because this second demonstration does not include a downpress, the original down-press icon is retained. Next, in Show mode, the designer deletes the dotted line and draws a solid line from the initial down press icon to the final button release icon (Figure 2-c). This entire behavior takes less than 30 seconds to demonstrate, and very few new

concepts or commands are necessary, since the designer already knows how to draw and delete objects in the editor.

If the mouse had been pressed and released in the same place, then a click icon would be displayed instead of the down, move and up icons. Double-clicking or double-clicking followed by a move are also supported. To allow modes to be changed while mouse buttons are being held down and while the mouse is at a particular place, keyboard accelerator keys are used to change modes.

Marquise generalizes from the designer's example actions to create the user interface. Any system that tries to generalize will sometimes guess wrong. Various mechanisms have been explored in other systems to show the user what has been guessed, so that users can verify and correct the inferences. Older systems, such as Peridot [3] and Druid [8], required the user to confirm each inference, which can be disrupting and annoying. In Marquise, a feedback window (Figure 3) shows the inferred operation. The labels and buttons can be read as a sentence, and the buttons can be pressed to pop up a list of other alternatives and change the values. Since Marquise appears to guess correctly most of the time, Marquise applies the inferred property immediately, and allows the designer to verify or change it afterwards in the feedback window.

ENVIRONMENT

Marquise makes heavy use of many features of Garnet. Garnet uses a retained object model and a prototype-instance object system. This means that there is an object in memory for every object on the screen, and that any object can be used as the prototype to make a copy or instance. Since all Garnet objects are represented the same way, there is a single mechanism for copying and creating objects, whether they are simple rectangles or aggregates containing many components. Therefore, Marquise can always generate appropriate code to create items for run time, without having to know the types of the objects the designer has drawn.

Implementing the behaviors that are demonstrated is quite straightforward once they have been determined because Marquise can create instances of "interactor" objects [5] and fill in the appropriate attributes. Each interactor implements a particular kind of behavior, such as selection, creation, moving, etc., and contains attributes to support most of the popular interaction styles.

The object system supports *constraints*, which are relationships that are declared once and maintained by the system. Constraints are used to maintain the relationships among the graphical objects in Marquise. Constraints can also be used to connect application data to Marquise-generated interfaces, or else application-specific call-back procedures can be invoked when a behavior is completed.

Garnet contains a number of other high-level interactive tools, such as the Lapidary tool for creating individual widgets or objects, the Gilt tool for editing dialog boxes, the Jade tool for automatically creating dialog boxes, and the C32 spreadsheet system for specifying complex constraints. Because all the tools use the same data structures and file format for describing objects, Marquise does not have to re-implement the functionality already provided by those tools—it can concentrate on the global behavior. The designer can have more than one tool operating at the same time, and use whichever is appropriate for the current part of the task.

FRAMEWORK

Marquise is able to construct the interface from the demonstrations because it has built-in knowledge of the kinds of operations that are common in graphical editors. This knowledge is part of the underlying Marquise framework that supports the interactive front end. The operations include: creating an object of the type in a palette, selecting objects, directly manipulating the size and shape with the mouse, specifying properties of objects (color, font, etc.) with a palette or property sheet, miscellaneous editing operations (deleting, duplicating, etc.), and application-specific commands.

Modes

It is very common in user interfaces for different behaviors to result from the same action, determined either by the location of the initiating event or by the value of a global mode variable. As an example of the first case, in MacProject II for the Macintosh, pressing the mouse button down will start text editing (if inside a box), select a box (if at its edge), create a new box (if in the background), draw a link between two boxes (if pressed in one box and released in another), grow a box (if pressed on a selection handle), or draw a link and create a box (if pressed in one box and released outside). Designers specify these differences in Marquise by demonstrating the different operations. Marquise notices what objects are underneath the demonstrated events (including the mouse release), so it can distinguish the correct times to use the different behaviors. The object being used is shown in the feedback window, and the buttons there can be used to edit the choice.

In other cases, the selection of the behavior is determined by the value of a global mode variable, which is set by a palette or an external application program. To make these modes explicit and visible, Marquise provides a *mode window*, shown in Figure 4, which lists each mode variable and its current value. The values displayed will change as the interface is operated, and the designer can directly edit the values for user modes. When the value has a fixed list of choices, these are available in a pull-down menu. To make an interaction dependent on whether a mode has the current value, it is only necessary to click on the check box next to the mode name before demonstrating the behavior. When a user action causes a mode to change, this can be demonstrated by simply editing the value in the mode window while in Show mode.

The combination of the icons and mode window make the control of the behaviors explicit and direct. In contrast, DEMO II [1] uses multiple examples to determine in which

situations the operations should occur, which we feel will be more prone to errors.

Palettes

One of the important innovations in the Marquise framework is the formalization of a *palette*, which is a list of options, usually presented graphically. Each palette controls a single value or mode. Since palettes are conventional interaction techniques internally (i.e., they are usually a list of buttons), their internal behavior (how the user changes the current selection and what feedback shows the selected objects) can be easily specified using Lapidary or Marquise. The innovation here is the automatic connection of the palette to the rest of the interface.

Marquise identifies two main classes of palettes: *create* palettes and *property* palettes. A create palette contains the different kinds of objects that can be created. For example, the create palette for MacDraw II contains a selection arrow, strings, lines, rectangles, rounded-rectangles, ovals, arcs, curves, polygons, and text fields. A create palette for a CAD/CAM program for circuit boards might have a long list of different IC types, plus wires, pads, etc.

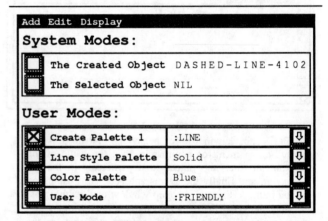

Figure 4:
The mode window showing the defined modes and their current values. The designer can click on the check box at the left of a row to indicate that the next action depends on the mode having the specified value. Modes based on palettes change as the palette is operated. Applications can also directly set a mode, and one of the actions resulting from a behavior might be a mode change.

A property palette contains the different values for a single property. MacDraw II has a property palette for the filling style at the top of the window, and property palettes for the line style, font size, font style, etc. in pull-down menus. Marquise supports palettes which are not always visible, and a palette can even be a subset of the items in a different widget (e.g., a section of a pull-down menu). In addition, the list of choices can be dynamically changing, for example, if the application has commands to read new libraries or to edit the palette itself.

There are two important distinctions between the two types of palettes. First, the create palette usually enables different interaction techniques. For example, the selection arrow enables selection, the rectangle enables dragging out new rectangles, and the text string enables clicking to start entering text. A property palette is assumed to only set values of properties and not to control interaction techniques.[2] Note that a create palette can enable various kinds of behaviors, such as selecting and deleting, and not just creating. The second difference between the two types of palettes is that Marquise assumes that objects cannot change type, so that selections in the create palette cannot affect the selected objects. However, clicking in property palettes usually changes the value of that property for the selected objects.

Create Palettes. To make a create palette, the designer only needs to draw the set of objects using Marquise or Lapidary, select them, and declare them to be a create palette using a menu command. Marquise will then add a row to the mode window (Figure 4) showing the palette and its current value. The designer would select the new row in the mode window, click on each item in the palette to put the system into the appropriate mode, and demonstrate the desired behavior.

The create palette has some additional attributes which control common features found in graphical editors. Some of these can be demonstrated, and the rest are specified in dialog boxes.

- In some palettes, when the user clicks on an item, that sets up a mode so that the next operation will create the kind of object represented by that item. This was shown in the example above, and is the way that MacDraw works. In other cases, clicking in the palette causes the object to be created immediately (e.g., at the current mouse position for a popup menu of choices, or at a computed place if the objects are laid out automatically by the system). Other times, objects are dragged off the palette.
- After an object is created, some applications select the newly-created object, some leave the selection unchanged, others add the new object to the selection set (if objects were selected before the create), and yet others clear the selection.
- Sometimes, after the object is created, the mode of the create palette will change. For example, in MacDraw II, after creating a rectangle, the mode changes back to selection (the arrow). However, if you double-click on the palette, the mode does not change after creation. In the original MacDraw, all object creation modes changed back to selection except for text strings.

Property Palettes. Property palettes allow the user to control the value of properties of objects. Typically, the same palette is used for specifying the global default value used

for newly-created objects, and for changing the property of selected objects. The same palette might also be used to *show* the value for the selected object.

To create a property palette, the designer only needs to draw a set of objects representing the different values (for example, the line-style items of Figure 5), and declare them to be a property palette. Marquise then checks whether a single property seems to change in each element (as it does in Figure 5 and in most graphical property palettes), and if so, proposes this as the property to use. Alternatively, the user can specify the name of the property and the value for each item of the palette.

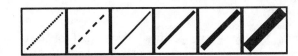

Figure 5:
After drawing this picture, the designer would select the lines, and declare them to be a property palette. Marquise would notice that the line-style changes, and would create an appropriate palette description.

Each primitive Garnet object describes which properties are relevant to it, and the designer can add additional properties for application-specific objects. Therefore, Marquise can automatically guess which properties are probably relevant to each type of object that is created. These guesses are reflected in the feedback and mode windows (Figures 3 and 4), and if Marquise guesses wrong, then the designer can adjust the values.

Some attributes for property palettes provided by Marquise are:

- Whether setting the property of a particular (selected) object also changes the global default used when a new object is created.
- If an object is selected that does not have the property represented by the palette (e.g., if the palette is for the font property and a line is selected), whether the palette goes inactive (greyed out) or not. When there are multiple objects selected, whether the palette is valid if at least one of the objects has this property, or only when all of the objects have this property.
- When an object is selected, whether the palette shows the value of that object. If more than one object is selected, then the palette might show the value only if all objects have the same value, pick the value of one of the objects to show, show the global default value, or just be cleared to show no value.
- If the palette does not echo the value of the property when the selection changes, then the newly selected object might get the current value of the property (as opposed to requiring another click in the palette after changing the selection).

Positions of new objects

Once Marquise knows which object to create, there is then

[2]This restriction could be lifted in the future if it becomes onerous, but it is consistent with the behavior of all editors we have studied.

the question of where and how to create it. There are two possibilities: the position is computed automatically, or is specified by the user with the mouse.

Automatic Layout. Garnet has built-in routines for list, table, tree, and graph layout. These automatically place the nodes, rather than requiring the user to specify a location. Each type of layout has a set of methods for creating and deleting nodes, and Marquise allows the designer to demonstrate how these methods are invoked and how their attributes are specified. Many previous systems have allowed a designer to build custom graph layout applications by writing code, but Marquise is the first to allow the look of the nodes to be drawn and the editing behaviors (creating, deleting, editing labels, etc.) to be demonstrated interactively.

First, the designer specifies which kind of layout is desired.[3] Next, the designer draws pictures to show the graphics for the nodes (and the graphics for the arcs for trees and graphs). If these have complex internal structure, then the Lapidary tool will be useful for drawing them. The built-in layout algorithms have many attributes that control the display, and some of these can be demonstrated (e.g., the spacing and direction). The rest are specified in a dialog box.

Next, the designer demonstrates the creation behavior. Using knowledge of the type of layout in use, Marquise tries to determine if the new object should be placed in some relation to a selected object, or globally with respect to all objects. For example, in a directed-graph editor, there might be commands for "Add new child" and "Add new parent." Marquise does not try to understand the words in the command names. Instead, the designer would go into Run mode and select a node, and then in Train mode the designer would select the command. Finally, in Show mode, the new object would be created with the correct relationship to the selected node.

In some cases, the new object's position will not depend on the selection, but rather on global properties. For example, the new object might always go at the end of a list. In this case, the designer would make sure that no objects are selected before demonstrating the position of the new object, and Marquise would try to determine the appropriate place for the object. Alternatively, the position might depend on some global mode, so the appropriate row of the mode window would be selected before the demonstration. Usually, the position will be obvious (e.g., first or last), but if Marquise cannot guess it, then currently the designer will have to write a Lisp function to compute the position, possibly based on values in the mode window.

User Layout. Most graphical editors, however, require the user to explicitly specify the position of new objects. The

example of Figure 2 shows how the simple case of a new line can be demonstrated in Marquise.

It is very common for the objects to be constrained in their placement. Marquise has built-in knowledge about gridding, so this can be easily used in an application. A more interesting problem is attachment. For example, an arrow connecting the boxes in Figure 6 might always be attached to the centers of the boxes. In an earlier article [4], we discussed how Lapidary allows the arrow prototype to be defined interactively with parameters that refer to the objects to which it should be attached. Lapidary creates constraints that keep the arrows attached as the objects move. Marquise allows the designer to interactively show how those parameters are filled in based on the designer's actions. For example, look back at Figure 1 where a creation palette is being drawn. To demonstrate the arrow creation mode, the designer would select the arrow in the create palette while in Run mode. This will change the value shown in the mode window for the create palette mode (Figure 4). The designer would then click on the check box next to this mode, which tells Marquise that the mode is significant for the next operation.

Assume that the arrow was defined so that setting the *from* and *to* parameters with objects would cause the line to be attached to those objects. In Train mode, the designer would press down inside a rounded-rectangle, and drag outside. Then, in Show mode, the designer would create an instance of the arrow with the shaft end inside the rounded-rectangle and the arrow end at the ⌖ icon. Then, the designer specifies that the rounded-rectangle corresponds to the *from* parameter, and Marquise infers that it should determine the parameter value based on where the mouse is first depressed, and that the other end should follow the mouse. Next, the designer demonstrates the mouse button-up response by deleting the feedback line and creating a new arrow between the two nodes. These nodes are declared as the *from* and *to* parameters. In the future, we will provide facilities for *gravity* so the designer could specify that while the mouse is moving, the feedback should jump to the attachment points of objects if they are close enough.

Selection

One of the most important operations in a graphical editor is selecting objects. Typically, the selected object will be shown by changing its appearance (e.g., to reverse video) or by showing "selection handles" around it (Figure 6). Marquise supports virtually any graphical response to show the selection. The designer simply draws an example of the selection graphics (or if the object itself changes, the designer draws the object first in its normal and then in its selected state). If the standard Garnet selection widget is desired, then it is only necessary to go into Show mode and select an object. A special line of the mode window shows which objects are selected, and this value can be edited to show whether the interaction being demonstrated adds to the selection set, removes from it, clears it, etc. This provides a uniform, intuitive mechanism for specifying almost any selection behavior. The designer can also specify

---

[3]Marquise cannot infer a new layout algorithm. For example, if a new kind of graph layout is required, the designer has to program it in Lisp, but it can then be used by Marquise-generated programs.

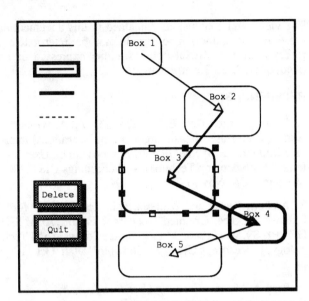

Figure 6:
The arrows are constrained to be in the centers of the boxes. Box 3 has "selection handles" around it, which show that it is selected, and the user can click on white handles to move it or black handles to grow it. The formula that computes the labels was hand-coded using C32.

whether a different form of feedback is used when there are multiple selections (as in Macintosh PowerPoint and MacProject II).

Moving and Growing Objects

Demonstrating what commands cause objects to be moved and grown works similarly to demonstrating how they are created: first, the designer demonstrates in Train mode what user action causes the interaction to start, and then in Show mode, moves or grows the appropriate object. Since the standard editing actions work in Show mode, the designer would just use the Marquise move-grow selection handles to demonstrate the behavior. Of course, if other objects are attached to the moved object with constraints, they will also move.

One complication is that often the object that the mouse is over is not the object that should be modified. For example, with selection handles, the user clicks on a handle, but wants to grow the object *underneath*. Marquise knows about this special case, and if the object the designer moves is attached by a constraint to the object clicked on, then this is reflected in the generated behavior.

Other Properties of Objects

Many properties of objects are controlled by palettes, but some are not. In some graphical editors, a menu command or double-clicking on an object opens a property sheet or dialog box with other properties. Marquise provides hooks to pop up a property sheet or a dialog box created automatically by Jade or interactively using Gilt. Of course, the designer can specify which fields are presented.

Miscellaneous Editing Commands

Because Garnet uses a retained object model, there is a standard format for all Garnet objects. Therefore, common editing commands such as bringing objects to the top (uncovered), sending to the bottom, cutting, copying, pasting, deleting (clear), duplicating, and printing in PostScript, are all provided. The designer simply demonstrates what action causes it to occur, and then which operation is desired. Note that unlike other frameworks that provide messages that must be overridden by each application, the code provided by Marquise for these operations can often be used without change.

Semantic Actions

Naturally, many of the commands in a graphical editor will invoke application-specific functions (sometimes called "semantic actions"). Since these may involve arbitrary computation, it is impossible for Marquise to infer these from a demonstration. However, techniques like those previously reported for Gilt [7] are used to allow the application procedures to be independent of the way they are invoked (from a button, menu, double-click, etc.) and somewhat independent of the graphics. However, most functions will want to walk through the graphical objects computing values, so they will clearly have to look at the graphical objects in the window.

If the result of the function is a change to the graphic appearance of nodes, then this can be specified demonstrationally. For example, a "critical-path" command in a graph editor might want all the nodes on the critical path to turn red. The designer can bring up a property sheet on the nodes, add an `on-critical-path` property,[4] and demonstrate that the nodes are black when it is NIL and red when it is T. Then, the critical-path function would only be responsible for setting the `on-critical-path` value in each node. This makes the application function more independent of the graphical response to its actions.

Semantic feedback can often be provided in the same way. For example, Marquise supports highlighting of only those objects that an object is being dragged can legally be dropped into, as in the Macintosh Finder. Here, a function could be called to set a particular property of each object to T or NIL. Then, the designer would demonstrate the appropriate color change when the node is over an object which has the value T for that property.

Similarly, if the application wants to control which mode is in effect, it can simply change the value of one of the mode variables, and the designer can demonstrate interactively what this controls.

EDITING

An important aspect of an interactive builder is how to edit the interfaces after they have been created. It is easy to edit

---

[4]The Garnet object system allows properties to be added to objects at any time.

the graphics, since they can be directly manipulated in Build mode. For the behaviors, the feedback window of Figure 3 shows the properties. When in Train mode, the feedback window continually shows the name and properties of the behaviors being executed, so the designer can determine which behaviors are associated with which events. There are also commands to list all the behaviors, or all those affecting a particular object.

CONCLUSION

One of the important questions for an interactive tool is what is the range of interfaces that it can create. Unfortunately, this is very difficult to quantify, except by example. Using the Lapidary, Gilt and Marquise tools in Garnet, it is possible without programming to create complete user interfaces like those in Macintosh MacDraw, MacDraw II, PowerPoint, and MacProject II (which are surprisingly different), as well as applications with various kinds of automatic layout for nodes. Later, we hope to expand the range of Marquise to handle gestural interfaces (the Garnet toolkit already supports gesture recognition), and those with 3-D graphics. We also plan to add support for animations, which will probably make possible the demonstration of various visualizations and video games. Another addition will be to support defining constraints among objects directly in Marquise, probably using demonstrational techniques similar to Peridot [3] or Druid [8].

Marquise is still under development. When it is more robust, we will perform user-testing to see if the demonstrations and feedback are understandable to both non-programmers and programmers. After that, we will release it for general use as part of the Garnet system. All this will help show what kinds of behaviors it can capture, and we will continually work to expand the range.

We believe that interactive, demonstrational creation of user interfaces is easier, faster, and more fun than programming. Many interactive builders have already shown that dialog boxes and forms can be created interactively. Marquise shows that direct manipulation techniques can be used to generate the user interfaces of a much wider class of graphical applications as well.

ACKNOWLEDGEMENTS

For help with this paper, we would like to thank Dario Giuse, Brad Vander Zanden, Andrew Werth, and Bernita Myers.

This research was sponsored by the Avionics Laboratory, Wright Research and Development Center, Aeronautical Systems Division (AFSC), U. S. Air Force, Wright-Patterson AFB, OH 45433-6543 under Contract F33615-90-C-1465, ARPA Order No. 7597.

REFERENCES

1. Gene L. Fisher, Dale E. Busse, and David A. Wolber. Adding Rule-Based Reasoning to a Demonstrational Interface Builder. ACM SIGGRAPH Symposium on User Interface Software and Technology, Proceedings UIST'92, Monterey, CA, Nov., 1992, pp. 89-97.

2. Anthony Karrer and Walt Scacchi. Requirements for an Extensible Object-Oriented Tree/Graph Editor. ACM SIGGRAPH Symposium on User Interface Software and Technology, Proceedings UIST'90, Snowbird, Utah, Oct., 1990, pp. 84-91.

3. Brad A. Myers. *Creating User Interfaces by Demonstration.* Academic Press, Boston, 1988.

4. Brad A. Myers, Brad Vander Zanden, and Roger B. Dannenberg. Creating Graphical Interactive Application Objects by Demonstration. ACM SIGGRAPH Symposium on User Interface Software and Technology, Proceedings UIST'89, Williamsburg, VA, Nov., 1989, pp. 95-104.

5. Brad A. Myers. Encapsulating Interactive Behaviors. Human Factors in Computing Systems, Proceedings SIGCHI'89, Austin, TX, April, 1989, pp. 319-324.

6. Brad A. Myers, Dario A. Giuse, Roger B. Dannenberg, Brad Vander Zanden, David S. Kosbie, Edward Pervin, Andrew Mickish, and Philippe Marchal. "Garnet: Comprehensive Support for Graphical, Highly-Interactive User Interfaces". *IEEE Computer 23*, 11 (Nov. 1990), 71-85.

7. Brad A. Myers. Separating Application Code from Toolkits: Eliminating the Spaghetti of Call-Backs. ACM SIGGRAPH Symposium on User Interface Software and Technology, Proceedings UIST'91, Hilton Head, SC, Nov., 1991, pp. 211-220.

8. Gurminder Singh, Chun Hong Kok, and Teng Ye Ngan. Druid: A System for Demonstrational Rapid User Interface Development. ACM SIGGRAPH Symposium on User Interface Software and Technology, Proceedings UIST'90, Snowbird, Utah, Oct., 1990, pp. 167-177.

9. John M. Vlissides and Mark A. Linton. Unidraw: A Framework for Building Domain-Specific Editors. ACM SIGGRAPH Symposium on User Interface Software and Technology, Proceedings UIST'89, Williamsburg, VA, Nov., 1989, pp. 158-167.

10. David Wolber and Gene Fisher. A Demonstrational Technique for Developing Interfaces with Dynamically Created Objects. ACM SIGGRAPH Symposium on User Interface Software and Technology, Proceedings UIST'91, Hilton Head, SC, Nov., 1991, pp. 221-230.

LogoMedia: A Sound-Enhanced Programming Environment for Monitoring Program Behavior

(Demonstration)

Christopher J. DiGiano[1]
Ronald M. Baecker
Russell N. Owen

Dynamic Graphics Project
Department of Computer Science
University of Toronto
Toronto, Ontario, Canada M5S 1A4

ABSTRACT

Even for the programmer, computer software can be a mysterious black box. But what if the programmer were able to give the box a good shake and listen to things rattle inside? Are there tools like the doctor's stethoscope that can help programmers listen to the heartbeat of their software? These are the kinds of questions we decided to explore by building LogoMedia, a sound-enhanced programming environment. LogoMedia supports the ability to associate non-speech audio with program events while the code is being developed. These associations cause subsequent test runs of the program to generate and manipulate sounds which can aid in the comprehension and analysis of the program's behavior.

KEYWORDS: Program Auralization, Non-Speech Audio, Software Visualization, Programming Environments

PROGRAMMING WITH SOUND

Just what does it mean to for a programming environment to feature sound enhancements? Some researchers describe the use of sound in programming as *program auralization*. We prefer to define programming with sound somewhat more broadly as a category of *software visualization* (SV). Software visualization through sound is the process of forming mental images of the behavior, structure and function of computer programs by listening to acoustical representations of their execution or specification. In contrast to traditional SV systems using text or graphics, sound-enhanced programming environments employ musical tones, voice, and prerecorded and synthesized sounds to help elucidate a program.

[1]Author's current address: Department of Computer Science, C.B. 430, University of Colorado, Boulder Colorado, 80309-0430. telephone: (303) 492-1218. email: digi@cs.colorado.edu.

Researchers in the field of SV have begun to assigning sound important and sometimes essential roles in visualizations. In their taxonomy of SV systems, Price, Baecker, and Small [4] are careful to include a category for audio information. Brown and Hershberger [2] incorporate an impressive computer-generated audio track along with their graphical animations of algorithms. Sounds are generated corresponding in pitch to elements being inserted into a hash table, items being sorted, and to the number of active threads. Francioni, Jackson, and Albright [3] use audio to improve the programmer's awareness of the behavior of parallel programs by playing sounds based on trace data recorded during execution. Program events being monitored caused a unique note or melody to be played using a particular timbre mapped to each of 16 processors.

MONITORING PROGRAMS WITH LOGOMEDIA

The LogoMedia programming environment supports the ability to associate non-speech audio with program events while the code is being developed. LogoMedia is based on an earlier prototype, LogoMotion [1], which provided extensions to the Logo language for associating animation procedures with programs. Programmers specify auralizations by annotating their code with software *probes*. Probes have an *action* which is the collection of external commands to execute, and a *trigger* which determines just when during execution the action takes place.

LogoMedia supports two types of probes: control probes for monitoring control flow and data probes for data flow. LogoMedia programmers associate control probes with statements in their Logo program which trigger sound commands just prior to their execution. As special cases of this we can trigger actions upon procedure entry or exit. Data probes are associated with arbitrary Logo expressions, such that changes to the expressions trigger sound commands as well. Sound commands can turn on synthesized musical instruments, play back sound samples, or make adjustments to a sound's pitch or volume. Such audio probes cause subsequent runs of a program to generate and manipulate sounds which can aid in the comprehension and analysis of the program's behavior.

SPECIFYING SOUNDS GRAPHICALLY

In order to facilitate the beginning LogoMedia programmer, encourage the spontaneous use of sound, and provide easy access to common probing paradigms, LogoMedia features a graphical interface for specifying both control and data probes. Both types of probes can be created using a similar series of interactions with the computer's mouse and keyboard. Control probe interface items occupy the left most column in LogoMedia's document window as shown in Figure 1. As depicted in Figure 2, a special window called the *Probe Sheet* is used for interacting with graphical representations of data probes.

To associate a probe with a line of code or a Logo expression, the programmer chooses from one of the popup menus which appear as floating icons at the top of a LogoMedia document or the Probe Sheet. The four different icons correspond to the different types of probes available using the graphics interface: *audio probes*, *graphics probes*, *text probes*, and *generic probes*. Audio probes are for making sounds based on program events. Graphics probes are for assisting in animation and text probes for printing tracing messages. The generic probe is for specifying arbitrary visualization code not necessarily related to sound.

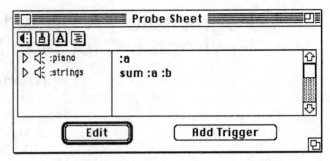

```
                    fibonacci.logo
  ┌─────────────────────────────────────┐
                  to fibonacci :num
  ▷ ◁ :guitar       if equalp :num 0 [
  ▷ ◁ :tomhi           output 0
                     ]
                     if equalp :num 0 [
  ▷ ◁ :crash           output 1
                     ]
                     make "a fibonacci difference :num 1
                     make "b fibonacci difference :num 2
                     output sum :a :b
                  end
```

Figure 1: A LogoMedia document window with the probe pop-up menu icons at the top. Three audio control probes are shown associated with lines in the buggy `fibonacci` procedure.

Control probes can be associated with a particular line of code by selecting that line with the mouse and then choosing a probe from one of the pop-up menus. A labeled icon appears to the left of the line. Figure 1 illustrates the use of an audio control probe to auralize a buggy program for generating Fibonacci numbers using a recursive algorithm. Here the programmer has connected three audio control probes to three key lines in the program in order to assess its flow of control. A guitar note is used to mark the start of each call to the `fibonacci` procedure. Percussion sounds are used to distinguish the two possible base cases for terminating the procedure. Now when `fibonacci` is run, the programmer hears a rapid series of guitar sounds, a tom-tom drum, then a never ending sequence of guitar notes. The absence of a crashing sound points to a problem with the second base case.

Figure 2: The LogoMedia Probe Sheet window for manipulating data probes

Data probes are associated with program variables through the Probe Sheet window. The programmer first adds a Logo expression containing the desired variables to Probe Sheet and then connects a data probe to that expression in the same way control probes are linked to a line of code. Figure 2 illustrates two audio data probes established using the graphical interface to monitor data items in the `fibonacci` procedure. The first causes a piano tone to be played when the Logo variable `a` is modified. The second demonstrates how data probes can monitor Logo expressions containing more than one variable. Here a strings sound is played if the sum of `a` and `b` changes.

THE DEMONSTRATION

At the conference we will demonstrate more complex applications of LogoMedia and discuss our experiences in its testing and use.

REFERENCES

1. Baecker, R. M., and Buchanan, J. W. (1990). A Programmer's Interface: A Visually Enhanced and Animated Programming Environment. *Proceedings of Twenty-Third Annual Hawaii International Conference on Systems Sciences*, Hawaii. IEEE Computer Society, 531-540.

2. Brown, M. H., and Hershberger, J. (1992). Color and Sound in Algorithm Animation. *IEEE Computer* 25 (12): 52-63.

3. Francioni, J. M., Jackson, J. A., and Albright, L. (1991). The Sounds of Parallel Programs. *Proceedings of the 6th Distributed Memory Computing Conference*, 570-577.

4. Price, B. A., Baecker, R. M., and Small, I. S. (1992). A Principled Taxonomy of Software Visualization. *Submitted for review.*

A Telewriting System on a LAN
Using a Pen-based Computer as the Terminal

HIGAKI Seiichi   TANINAKA Hiroshi   MORIYA Shinji

Department of Electrical Communication Engineering, Tokyo Denki University

2-2 Kanda-Nishiki-cho, Chiyoda-ku, Tokyo 101, Japan

E-mail : moriya@cck.dendai.ac.jp   TEL&FAX : +81 3 5280 3335

The system we developed is software for implementing a "telewriting" terminal. Here, we propose a method for implementing this telewriting terminal as an application program running on pen-based computers.

"Telewriting" is a technology in which the ink data (written with a pen on one terminal) is transmitted in real time to other terminals and displayed on their monitors. When this process is carried out between two terminals in both directions, two users using telewriting terminals can mutually and simultaneously transmit and view visual information. If two users can use a combination of this telewriting and telephone, they can send to and receive from each other audio-visual information in real time. Consequently, two users can communicate smoothly without having to interrupt their flow of conversation.

Already, there are some systems which can be used to conduct telewriting and others called shared drawing tools. Examples are Displayphone (Bell Telephone Laboratory, U.S.A.), Scribophone (Philips, Holland), Sketchphone (NTT, Japan), MERMAID (NEC, Japan), Commune station (Xerox Palo Alto Research Center, U.S.A.), etc. These systems are only used for conducting telewriting, or as multi-media communication systems in which telewriting is just a minor function, or as systems for studying cooperative work in distributed environment. At present, none of these systems is being widely used.

We presume that the two reasons why these systems have not enjoyed widespread are, these terminals are expensive and also because of the minimal opportunities for using them. We think that, in order to make telewriting more widespread, it (i.e. telewriting) should be developed and implemented as one of the application programs for pen-based computers. We believe that our research is significant because it proposes a method for implementing a telewriting system and also shows how a pen-based computer can be used as a tool towards the realization of such a system.

The telewriting system we developed can be used by connecting the terminal (pen-based computer) to LAN (Ethernet). At present, we are testing our system on the LAN in Tokyo Denki University. Also, we are using the telephone (within our university) in combination with

telewriting. Our system has other features also. In our telewriting system, during telewriting, (i) Users can simultaneously write and delete ink data on shared document, and (ii) Users can edit shared document seeing different portion of the document on their respective screen. (iii) Also, two user-interfaces are provided corresponding to the two situations when telephones are not used and when they are. (iv) Users can also load already-created ink-files and can also save such files.

Also, separately, we conducted other experiments using our telewriting system and observed that, (i) for a telewriting system to work efficiently, two users at distant terminals should be able to perform all of their operations (writing, deleting, scrolling, etc.) in real-time, and, (ii) both users should be able to view the whole document on their screens.

Regarding future telewriting, future telewriting systems will run not only on the LAN, but will be implemented using wireless communication such that any person can communicate with any other person in any part of the world. We are doing research towards the realization of such a system.

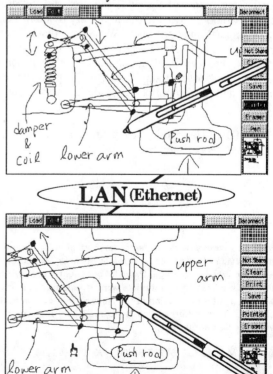

Figure 1. An instance of telewriting being conducted between two terminals. (Pen was pasted on figures.)

Heuristics in Real User Interfaces
INTERCHI'93 Panel

Brad A. Myers
School of Computer Science
Carnegie Mellon University
Pittsburgh, PA 15213
bam@a.gp.cs.cmu.edu

Richard Wolf
Lotus Development Corporation
One Rogers Street
Cambridge, Mass. 02141
Richard_Wolf@crd.lotus.com

Kathy Potosnak
Aldus Corporation
411 First Ave. South
Seattle, WA 98104
kathy_potosnak@aldus.com

Chris Graham
Microsoft Corporation
One Microsoft Way
Redmond, Washington 98052
chrisgr@microsoft.com

ABSTRACT

It is the conventional wisdom in user interface design that direct manipulation is best and that interfaces should be predictable. This tends to argue against having a system "guess" or use heuristics or other AI approaches. However, an increasing number of today's successful software products *do* use heuristics in their interfaces. The heuristics are used to help guide the user and to perform tasks that would be too difficult to specify by conventional direct manipulation approaches. We believe that user interface designers will increasingly need to consider using heuristic techniques in their interfaces. This panel discusses a number of today's successful products using heuristics and the important HCI design issues such as feedback.

KEYWORDS: Heuristics, Demonstrational Interfaces, Artificial Intelligence, Agents.

DEFINITION

"Heuristics" are a problem solving technique in which the most appropriate solution is chosen using rules. Interfaces using heuristics may perform different actions on different data given the same command. A simple example is that the Macintosh *moves* a file if dragged from one folder to another, unless the folders are on different devices, in which case the file is *copied* instead. The designers naturally try to make sure that the system will choose the correct solution, but sometimes the system may do the incorrect action. Thus, these systems can be said to *guess* what the user wants to do in this situation. However, since these are deterministic algorithms, many people object to the term "guess" applied to the computer. However, it may not appear deterministic to users if they cannot tell why the command now operates differently than it did the last time it was invoked.

Virtually all Artificial Intelligence (AI) systems use heuristics of one form or another: they try to make an intelligent choice about what the operation should be. Whereas applications that are clearly labeled as "AI" are not particularly popular in today's marketplace, heuristics are being used in small ways in a large number of programs, and their use is increasing. The range of "intelligence" of these interfaces is enormous, from a single easy-to-understand rule to a complete rule-based system. This panel will survey a number of real products that use heuristics and discuss the significant design issues that they have in common. (Intelligent user interfaces in general is the topic of a series of workshops [4], the most recent of which was held in Orlando, Florida in January, 1993.)

USE OF HEURISTICS TODAY

Many of the computer programs that millions of people use every day are now using heuristics in small ways. Interfaces of the near future will be using heuristics in large ways.

For example, Microsoft Word version 4.0 for the Macintosh has a renumber command that looks at the selected text and tries to determine how the paragraphs are numbered. Current versions of the Lotus 1-2-3 and Microsoft Excel spreadsheets have a feature called auto-sum or smart-sum that tries to guess the extent of what should be added when you point to a single cell. These spreadsheets also use heuristics to try to generate an appropriate chart when you select a range of cells and request a business graph. Aldus has a new product called IntelliDraw for PCs and Macintoshes that tries to infer constraints among graphical objects. Microsoft has introduced ''wizards'' in some of their products that in some cases use heuristics to guide users to more efficient ways to execute commands.

The next generation of user interfaces will involve gesture and character recognition, speech and natural language recognition, and intelligent agents. All of these involve using heuristic techniques that will sometimes interpret the user's actions incorrectly. Whereas this panel does not address these new input techniques directly, many of the same issues arise, including feedback, dealing with errors, and allowing the user to feel in control.

ISSUES

There are important issues that are shared by all interfaces that use heuristics. The panelists discuss how these have been addressed in existing systems.

- What are the general advantages of heuristic methods?
  - They can save the user time since the user does not have to specify all the low-level details.
  - They can be easier to learn since the system does part of the work.
- What are the general disadvantages of heuristic methods?
  - They can perform an incorrect action which might not be noticed by the user.
  - The user might not understand why the system did a different action or how to get the desired action to occur.
  - The users might have the feeling that the system was unpredictable and that they no longer are in control.
- What can be done to overcome these problems?
- How can you let the user control the heuristics? For example, can the users control which heuristics are applied? Can they set parameters of the heuristics? Can they enter entirely new heuristics? Does providing this control alleviate the problem of not feeling in control of the system?
- What are some examples of systems where heuristic methods been successful and unsuccessful?

- What characterizes a situation in which a heuristic method is appropriate for a user interface?
- How should the system provide feedback so the user knows what the system is planning to do?
- What is the tradeoff between too much feedback (slowing the user down) and the user not knowing what is happening? For example, the smart-sum command in Excel requires the user to click to confirm the range of cells to be summed, but 1-2-3 just executes the command without confirmation.
- What is the tradeoff between using conventional direct manipulation and heuristic methods? Any heuristic system can be turned into a direct manipulation system where all of the choices the system chooses from are directly provided to the user. When are there too many choices so that this is inappropriate? If there are only a few choices, is it sometimes still better to let the system guess?
- Are there any basic principles that can guide the design of future heuristic interfaces, or do they all need to be ad-hoc and refined through user testing?

POSITION STATEMENTS

Brad A. Myers

I believe that the number of systems using heuristics in user interfaces is about to explode. Each new version of consumer software adds new features and new commands, and therefore becomes increasingly complex. The result is that, even in the best direct manipulation interfaces, users are sometimes not able to find the commands they need to perform their tasks. The use of intelligent interfaces to help guide the user and automate parts of the tasks is increasingly necessary. Even if some aspects of what the computer does are not exactly what the user would want, it is usually good enough, and far better than if the user had not been able to perform the task at all because the conventional interface was too hard to learn or use!

One particular style of heuristic interfaces that I believe will be increasingly important is *demonstrational interfaces* [3]. In these, the user gives examples of the desired operations, and the system generalizes from the examples to create a program. For instance, when designing a new kind of graphical menu, the user will give examples of the strings to be displayed, but the resulting menu will work for any list of strings. Significant research has shown that demonstrational interfaces can be successful, and the benefit substantially outweighs the problems. As always with heuristic techniques, the key user interface issue is feedback to the user. Demonstrational interfaces are surveyed in a recent book [1] and were discussed at a CHI'91 panel [2].

Richard Wolf

I believe that heuristics have played an important role in improving user interface design in a number of present day commercial products and I believe the use of heuristics will increase in the near future.

In my opinion, heuristic techniques can actually *increase* the overall predictability of a user interface. If one examines predictability from a vantage point a bit removed from the immediate mechanics of the user interface, it is apparent that for the majority of users, many higher level tasks are not predictable even though the low level mechanics of the user interface are extremely predictable.

For example, modern spreadsheet products allow the user to format a spreadsheet by setting the typeface, point size, cell borders, color, and shading. However, most users do not know how to harness the variety of commands required to produce spreadsheets that are aesthetically pleasing and effective at communicating numerical data. When shown an example of an attractive spreadsheet, many users do not even know how to reproduce it. If they are not shown an example but must begin from scratch, even experienced spreadsheet users typically do not know how to structure their spreadsheets to produce attractive results. The net effect is extremely frustrating for users, who know that they possess a tool that can deliver the results they desire, but do not know how to make it happen.

An effective solution to this problem employs heuristics to parse spreadsheet data, determining which rows and columns are labels, partial aggregates (e.g., sub-totals), and final aggregates. This heuristic approach then applies font and cell border attributes to the constituent parts of the spreadsheet according to a set of predetermined formats designed by graphic artists. A similar approach has been applied to graphing spreadsheet data, where many users do not understand how to form the correspondence between their spreadsheet data and the relevant portions of a data chart, such as legend labels, x and y axis labels, and data series.

The above examples employ heuristics to accomplish high level tasks that users might not know how to do. Heuristics are also useful as short-cuts for actions that users are capable of accomplishing. Examples include automatic summing of spreadsheet columns and automatic filling of spreadsheet ranges.

The obvious downside of employing heuristics is the risk of decreased predictability, but there are other less obvious detrimental side effects. Heuristics introduce additional user testing costs to determine whether the heuristics are sufficiently predictable to users and to tune the heuristic or its presentation. In addition, heuristics also introduce additional documentation and quality assurance costs. Although heuristic techniques do not require that typical users understand the details of the algorithms employed, they must nonetheless be specified in sufficient detail to allow testing and adequate user documentation.

Kathy Potosnak

When employing heuristics in software applications, the most important consideration is user control. Users should be able to control when the program makes inferences. They should be able to display the effects of the heuristics (e.g., via visual feedback). They should be able to undo the

effects of the heuristics. In many cases users should be given control over programmatic inferencing by setting parameters within which the heuristics operate. In particular cases it is also desirable for users to be able to query the inference mechanism or knowledge base to get an explanation of the system's behavior.

One drawback to the use of heuristics is that when the software "guesses" incorrectly users can be frustrated. Making the guesses visible to the user, allowing actions to be undone, and letting users set the parameters of the automatic inference can reduce this disadvantage. In some cases, it is necessary to show the user what the effect will be in advance of the rules being applied.

User control was a primary consideration in the design of Aldus IntelliDraw, a constraint-based drawing product for PCs and Macintoshes. IntelliDraw uses heuristics in many ways to give users greater precision and flexibility in aligning, distributing, constraining, and connecting objects. An auto-align feature allows the user to visually see the alignments that the system guesses while dragging an object in the proximity of other objects. Another command, "Keep Aligned," can be used to make an alignment choice permanent. Users can "Match" the width, height, size (both height and width), and angle of objects to constrain the attributes of the selected objects. The "Suggest Alignment" command lets the user choose from among the potential alignments that the software detects for the selected objects. Distributing objects is done in a dialog box with proxy objects showing the results of various distribution choices before the command is applied to the objects the user has drawn.

Since IntelliDraw has multiple levels of Undo as well as multiple levels of Redo, the negative effects of wrong guesses on the part of the software are minimized. Other features of the product that allow the user to maintain control while the software assists with heuristics include the ability to make suggested alignments temporary or permanent, visual examples of the effects of the alignment and distribution choices, and control over the proximity variable that activates the rulebase. The most complex functions are accessible via a "Show Links" window. From here the user can change the directionality of constraints, the effects of copying and deleting an object on its associated links, and many other attributes.

The value of heuristics in this drawing product is that they streamline some of the processes that users normally create workarounds to achieve. For example, many designers learn to use a surrogate object (e.g., a line segment) as a guideline for aligning a set of objects and afterwards they delete the guideline object. IntelliDraw allows a user to align objects with each other without an intervening step of creating a guideline. Such alignment is faster since it operates on all of the selected objects at once, whereas without heuristics, the user must align each object to the guideline separately. Another benefit is that users are no longer constrained by the precision of the display device, since the constraints are based on attributes of the objects rather than locations on the screen display. Finally, the use of heuristics in IntelliDraw extends the functionality of guides. For example, almost any object, including a single point, can be used for alignment of other objects.

Other Aldus products that employ heuristics are TrapWise, an automated trapping product, and FreeHand, an illustration package. Trapping is a technique used to ensure that colors which should abut in a multi-color print job do not have gaps between them due to misalignment on the printing press or paper distortion during the printing process. Trapwise allows users to set the trapping parameters of various zones on the page and automatically creates the traps based on heuristics. Automatic trapping allows users to produce much more complex artwork that can be printed with higher quality than was possible with more traditional trapping methods. FreeHand uses heuristics in its AutoSpread function, which is a partial trapping solution. During the design of both products, the ability of users to control the application of the heuristics was a primary consideration. In the case of TrapWise, the user control issue guided a good deal of the user interface design. With FreeHand, customer input was used to determine the default setting (i.e., activated or deactivated) of the AutoSpread function.

Chris Graham

Microsoft Excel includes features based on heuristics including AutoSum, AutoFill and AutoFormat. AutoSum is implemented as a toolbar button. When pressed with a range selected it automatically determines what numbers in the range the user would want summed and inserts sum formulas. AutoFill automatically fills a single or multi-cell selection into an extension of the selection as a series based on a complex set of rules. The rules handle single or multiple cell selections that contain a wide range of data types such as numbers, dates, strings and mixtures of these data types. AutoFormat automatically applies a user-chosen table style to a selected worksheet range by heuristically determining and formatting components such as titles, subtotals and totals based on an analysis of the table.

These features were introduced as part of the ongoing effort to enhance the usability of Microsoft Excel. This might seem to contradict the common wisdom that heuristics in user interface design detract from usability because they make the interface less predictable. However, extensive usability testing prior to release confirmed that users per-

formed well with these features, and liked them. Furthermore, after these features were released, they were acclaimed by users and reviewers as major additions to worksheet usability.

When used correctly, heuristics can greatly simplify and yet increase the power of the user interface by interpreting the current context to allow a single user action to cause a result that would otherwise have required more effort to perform using more elementary actions.

Successful use of a heuristic requires that:

1. A majority of users would predict the same result of an action performed in a given context.

2. An algorithm can be developed which interprets the context and produces the result most users expect.

3. In cases where the algorithm does not do what a user requires, it should still give a result that is interpreted as reasonable, and the result must not be harmful.

4. It should be undoable.

5. The user can discover ways to override the default behavior when necessary.

Usability testing shows the heuristics in Excel to be predictable, i.e., they do what users expect them to do. Therefore heuristics aren't bad. But they are a very powerful user interface tool that takes a lot of skill to design well.

REFERENCES

1. Allen Cypher, et. al. (Ed.) *Watch What I Do: Programming by Demonstration.* MIT Press, Cambridge, MA, 1993.

2. Brad A. Myers, Allen Cypher, David Maulsby, David C. Smith, and Ben Shneiderman. Demonstrational Interfaces: Coming Soon? Human Factors in Computing Systems, Proceedings SIGCHI'91, New Orleans, LA, April, 1991, pp. 393-396.

3. Brad A. Myers. "Demonstrational Interfaces: A Step Beyond Direct Manipulation". *IEEE Computer 25*, 8 (August 1992), 61-73.

4. Joseph W. Sullivan and Sherman W. Tyler (Ed.) *Intelligent User Interfaces.* ACM Press, New York, 1991.

Exploring the Applications of User-Expertise Assessment for Intelligent Interfaces

Michel C. Desmarais   *Jiming Liu*

Centre de recherche informatique de Montréal

1801 ave. McGill College, bureau 800

Montréal, Québec, Canada H3A 2N4

Tel: 514-398-1234   Fax: 514-398-1244

e-mail: desmarais@crim.ca   jiming@crim.ca

ABSTRACT

An adaptive user interface relies, to a large extent, upon an adequate user model (e.g., a representation of user-expertise). However, building a user model may be a tedious and time consuming task that will render such an interface unattractive to developers. We thus need an effective means of inferring the user model at low cost. In this paper, we describe a technique for automatically inferring a fine-grain model of a user's knowledge state based on a small number of observations. With this approach, the domain of knowledge to be evaluated is represented as a network of nodes (knowledge units—KU) and links (implications) induced from empirical user profiles. The user knowledge state is specified as a set of weights attached to the knowledge units that indicate the likelihood of mastery. These weights are updated every time a knowledge unit is reassigned a new weight (e.g., by a question-and-answer process). The updating scheme is based on the Dempster-Shafer algorithm. A User Knowledge Assessment Tool (UKAT) that employs this technique has been implemented. By way of simulations, we explore an entropy-based method of choosing questions, and compare the results with a random sampling method. The experimental results show that the proposed knowledge assessment and questioning methods are useful and efficient in inferring detailed models of user-expertise, but the entropy-based method can induce a bias in some circumstances.

KEYWORDS

User-expertise assessment, probabilistic reasoning, evidence aggregation, entropy, intelligent interfaces, adaptive training systems, knowledge spaces.

INTRODUCTION

Knowledge assessment is a fundamental component of user modeling. It has been used to adapt the level of technical details of on-line documentation and error messages; it is also an essential ingredient found in practically every intelligent tutoring systems, coaches, and consultants (see for e.g., [12, 15]). Its widespread use in commercial applications, however, remains very limited, or non-existent. We suspect that, among other things, one reason for this is the unavailability of simple and efficient knowledge assessment modeling techniques that non-specialists of AI/cognitive-modeling can use while developing their applications. There exist a number of approaches, from simple and not-that-useful, to sophisticated and costly, but the tradeoff between complexity, development-cost, and usefulness rarely allows the application of expertise modeling techniques outside the experimental laboratory.

The most simple approach to this problem consists of categorizing the user onto a novice-expert scale. Although this approach is feasible with moderate development cost, it provides only very coarse information. Another technique is based on the idea that a knowledge domain can be defined as a set of knowledge units (KU). An individual's knowledge state is defined as a subset of it. This model thus constitutes a *fine grain* assessment to the extent that it provides information about each individual KU. Moreover, the set of KUs can be structured with various types of relations [8]. One such relation is the *precedence* relation, which indicates the order in which KUs are learned. A number of researchers have used this type of relation to infer user knowledge state (e.g., [1, 10, 14]). The main problem lies in building this structure of relations among KUs, which can be a very tedious task when the number of KUs is more than a few tens, unless the task can be automated.

This paper presents a technique for automatically constructing a structure of precedence relations among KUs from a small number of subject's knowledge states. The structure is thereafter used in conjunction with the Dempster-Shafer evidential reasoning method [9, 13] for assessing someone's knowledge state. This provides an entirely algorithmic approach to knowledge assessment, relieving the developer from the burden of building such tools.

In the remainder of the paper, we provide an overview of the knowledge structure induction and user knowledge inference techniques, and describe a series of empirical tests on an implemented module with two approaches to knowledge inference: a first approach in which KUs are chosen at random (a situation similar to that of a non-obstructive user-modeling facility, where KUs are observed but not chosen) and a second one in which KUs are subject to explicit choices based on entropy-minimization.

OVERVIEW

In the current modeling approach, the domain knowledge is represented as a *knowledge structure* [7], whose nodes are the fine-grain knowledge units (KU). An individual's knowledge about the domain, i.e., a knowledge state, is modeled by a collection of numerical attribute values attached to the nodes. Each value indicates the likelihood (i.e., probability) of a user's knowing a specific KU. In the network, KUs are connected by implication (precedence) relations. An implication relation is in fact a gradation constraint which expresses whether a certain concept has to be understood before another difficult one, or whether a certain skill is acquired prior to an advanced one.

Empirical Construction of Knowledge Structures

In contrast to other work that also adopted similar approaches (see in particular [1]), the knowledge structure in the current study is induced entirely from empirical data composed of samples of knowledge states. Because the knowledge structure induction process is automatic, it allows a much larger number of KUs to be included than other approaches.

The basic idea behind the empirical construction is that if there is an implication relation $A \Rightarrow B$, then ideally we would never expect to find an individual who knows A but not B. This translates into two conditions: $P(B|A) \approx 1$ and $P(\neg A|\neg B) \approx 1$. These conditions are verified by computing the lower bound of a $[1 - \alpha_{\text{error}}]$ confidence interval around the measured conditional probabilities. If the confidence intervals are above a predefined threshold, an implication relation between the two KUs is asserted. Two weights are associated with the relation (according to the two directions of the inference, i.e. *modus tollens* vs. *modus ponens*). They correspond to the relation's conditional probabilities $P(B|A)$ and $P(\neg A|\neg B)$. The weights express the degree of certainty in that relation. This method is inspired by previous work [3, 4]. A more detailed treatment of the knowledge structure construction method is given in [11].

Aggregation of Evidence

Once a knowledge structure is obtained, it can be used as a basis for knowledge assessment. The knowledge state of a user is built and updated as soon as some observations are made (e.g., questions are answered). Each observation can be viewed as a piece of evidence. This new information may be propagated to other nodes in compliance with the gradation constraints (inference structure).

In the present work, we applied the Dempster-Shafer (DS) evidential reasoning to recursively propagate evidential supports (whether confirming or disconfirming) throughout the knowledge structure. Different degrees of support, gathered from different sources of evidence, are combined to yield a new weight using the Dempster's rule of combination [9].

Selecting Questions

Observations about a user's knowledge state can be driven by a user monitoring module that reports evidence of known KUs[1], or they can be made through a sequence of question-and-answer sessions. In the first approach, evidence of known and unknown KUs is not under control and can thus be considered a random process. However, in the question-and-answer sessions, the evidence gathering process can be controlled during the knowledge assessment through an entropy-driven selection method. This approach, advocated in a number of previous studies (e.g., [6, 7]), applies the rule of minimum entropy and chooses the most *informative* questions. In the entropy-driven method, the expected information yield of each individual question over all the possible answers/outcomes (i.e., the entropy before and after the question is answered) is computed and weighted by the likelihood of each outcome. The information yield of a single question is thus given by the sum of differences between initial and updated entropy:

$$\Delta H = \sum \left[H(KU_i) - \left(p_k H_k'(KU_i) + p_{\neg k} H_{\neg k}'(KU_i) \right) \right]$$

(1)

where $p_k H_k'(KU_i)$ is the entropy of the updated knowledge structure given the user knows KU_i (weighted by the likelyhood factor p_k that KU_i is known), and where $p_{\neg k} H_{\neg k}'(KU_i)$ is the converse.

The question that has the maximum expected information yield is chosen as the most informative one. Both the random and entropy-driven methods of selecting a question are tested in this study.

IMPLEMENTATION

We have implemented the knowledge-structure induction procedure and the evidential reasoning scheme described in the previous section. The resulting knowledge assessment engine, UKAT (User Knowledge Assessment Tool), is composed of a set of C library routines. The observation gathering module of UKAT allows the questions to be selected either randomly or non-randomly. The algorithmic details of the modules can be found in [11]. The UKAT interface was developed in X-windows using the Motif widget package. In addition to presenting questions, acquiring answers (either text or choices), and building fine-grain models, it also permits users to browse and select the previously (un)answered questions and to look up scores (see Figure 1).

---

[1] In [2] for instance, observation of text-editing methods by a plan recognition module indicated which commands were mastered by the user.

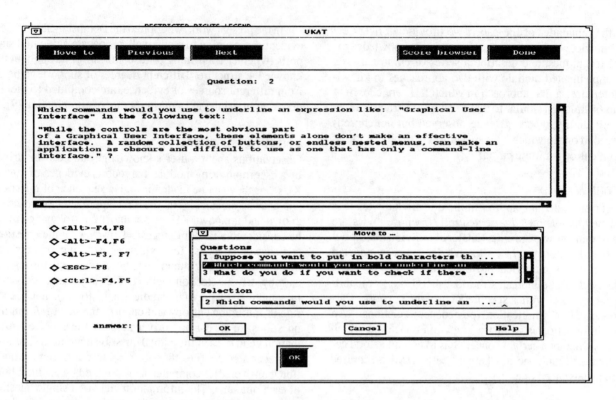

Figure 1: The interface of UKAT — A User Knowledge Assessment Tool

Hence, the interface can easily be extended into a drill-and-practice training system.

EXPERIMENTAL RESULTS

In order to validate our modeling technique, we have chosen the WordPerfect[TM2] text editor as a domain of which users' knowledge states are to be evaluated. This domain knowledge is composed of 192 identified KUs (knowledge units) that correspond the mastery of WordPerfect commands (see [5] for details).

Empirical Data

The implication relations (i.e., gradation constraints) among the KUs are generated with the knowledge structure construction method, applied to a number of empirically obtained subjects' knowledge states. We used 47 sample knowledge states; each of them is the result of a test covering all 192 KUs. All 192×192 pairs of KUs were tested for implication relations, using the statistical criterion mentioned earlier (where $P(B \mid A) > 0.5$ and $P(\neg A \mid \neg B) > 0.5$ with $\alpha < 0.05$). As a result, 2,368 implications were included in the knowledge structure.

In order to test the derived knowledge structure, we performed a series of user modeling simulations. Each simulation run consisted of selecting (in either a random or an

---

[2] WordPerfect is a trademark for WordPerfect Inc.

entropy-driven fashion) a proportion of a subject's knowledge state and propagating evidence to update the probability that a certain KU was mastered by the subject. Prior to the inferencing, all the nodes of the knowledge structure were assigned initial beliefs (i.e., initial probabilities). The results of simulations, based on 26-subject test data, are described below.

Building Fine-Grain User Models: The Knowledge Unit Level Assessment

The first level of testing corresponds to the residual errors in individual KUs assessment. Each KU is associated a weight that indicates the probability of knowledge and which is updated after each new observation (evidence). The difference between those weights and the actual knowledge state represents the residual errors.

The basic measure of performance is the global standard error of estimate:

$$\sigma_{node} = \sqrt{\frac{\sum_{i=1}^{26} \sum_{j=1}^{192} \left(x_{\text{obs}_{ij}} - x_{\text{est}_{ij}}\right)^2}{N_s \times N_k}} \quad (2)$$

where N_k is the number of knowledge units (192). N_s is the number of subjects used for the test (26). $x_{\text{obs}_{ij}}$ is 1 if the corresponding KU_j is *known* and 0 otherwise, and $x_{\text{est}_{ij}}$ is the estimated probability of mastery.

In addition to the standard error of estimate which is an indicator of the dispersion around the estimate based on the

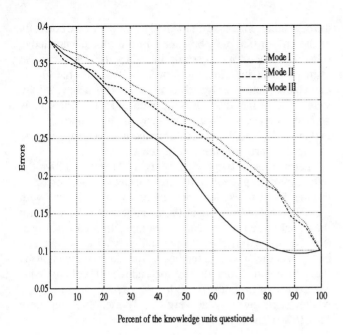

Figure 2: The residual errors in estimating probability of knowledge of individual KUs as measured by the *standard errors of estimate*. It shows the uncertainty convergence in three diffferent operating modes. The solid line, the dashed line, and the dotted line correspond to mode I (entropy-driven evidence gathering), II (random evidence gathering), and III (no inference condition), respectively.

second moment, we also investigated the bias around the estimate, which is given by the first moment:

$$\frac{\sum_{i=1}^{26} \sum_{j=1}^{192} \left(x_{\text{obs}_{ij}} - x_{\text{est}_{ij}} \right)}{N_s \times N_k} \quad (3)$$

The results of the system's performance in three different simulation modes are displayed in Figures 2 and 3. These show, respectively, the standard error scores and the bias over 192 KUs and 26 subjects. The three simulation modes are:

(I) *inferences based on the entropy-driven question selection*: nodes were given their initial probabilities and, when the chosen question is asked (based on entropy minimization), they are assigned 0.9 for a successful answer and 0.1 otherwise, and inference propagation is performed around the node according to the Dempster-Shafer algorithm;

(II) *inferences based on random sampling of the questions*: same as (I) but questions are chosen at random; and,

(III) *no inference condition*: same as (II) but no inference propagation is performed.

Note that we have assigned 0.9 and 0.1 weights for successful and unsuccessful answers respectively to reflect the

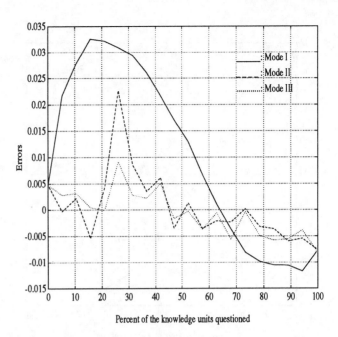

Figure 3: Absolute errors in estimating probability of knowledge of individual KUs, as measured by the *sum of the differences* between the observed KU mastery and its estimated probability. The results show a clear bias for the entropy-driven method (mode I).

residual uncertainties associated with such a process (e.g. good answers by chance and bad errors by mistake). Consequently, the expected score at 100% observation is below the perfect score since the nodes' weights are matched against 1 and 0 and not against 0.9 and 0.1.

The results from Figure 2 clearly indicate that the entropy-driven approach (mode I) is more efficient in reducing the standard error of estimate. However, Figure 3 shows that below 60%, it has a tendency to underestimate the probability of knowledge. This tendency is slightly reversed above 70%. A plausible explanation for this behavior is that the system asks questions that are likely to be failed at the beginning, leaving more successful questions for the end. Although this order does not introduce any error in the standard error score, it does introduce a bias when we simply sum up the differences between observed and estimated values. This phenomenon is further discussed later.

As far as mode II is concerned, Figure 2 indicates that it is consistently better than mode III, but less efficient in reducing the errors than mode I, especially when the amount of observation is greater than 20%. It is not subject to a bias as mode I is, however.

Estimating User Overall Scores: The Knowledge State Level Assessment

We have studied the performance of the system at estimating whether or not each individual KU is known by a subject. Another useful application of our technique is to guess an

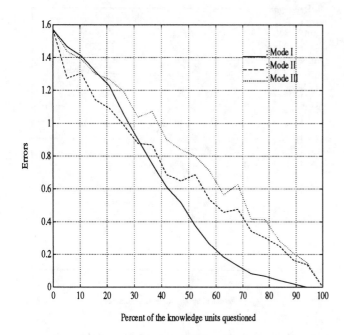

Figure 4: The residual errors in estimating global knowledge states as measured by the *standard error* scores of the three operating modes.

individual's *overall score*, as it is often required in adaptive training systems.

The performance scores are given by a similar measure as KU level assessment, namely the standard error of estimate: $\sqrt{\frac{\sum (x_{obs} - x_{est})^2}{N_s}}$. However, x_{obs} and x_{est} represent, respectively, $\sum_{i=1}^{192} x_{obs_i}$ and $\sum_{i=1}^{192} x_{est_i}$, where x_{est_i} is 0 if $KU_i < 0.5$ and 1 otherwise.

Figure 4 show the residual errors of the performance. A bias similar to the one in Figure 3 was also found in this experiment, although those results are not shown here for brevity. Figure 4 indicates that both modes I and II are consistently better than mode III in guessing the scores (except mode I with less than 16% observation). However, the advantage of mode I over mode II is only manifest after 40% sampling.

Discussion and Further Results

As conjectured by previous researchers [7], the above results have provided an empirical demonstration that the minimum entropy inference is effective in reducing the inferences' standard error, or uncertainty about a knowledge state. However, an interesting finding of this investigation is that the minimum-entropy approach induces a bias at the knowledge state level score and thus may not be appropriate for the purpose of inferring users' *global* scores, where this bias would manifest itself.

The explanation we have given for this bias lies in the fact that if the system asks the questions that will likely be failed at

the beginning, and those that will likely be answered correctly at the end, a bias will be found in the global knowledge state. This does not necessarily introduce more errors in the estimations of individual KU probabilities, i.e., the global knowledge state entropy. The cause for this behavior may stem from the fact that given the average knowledge state is 46% of all KUs, it is likely that there are more nodes closer to 0 than to 1, and thus a greater reduction in entropy will be achieved by bringing these nodes closer to 0.

Let us look at two typical individual cases in which the minimum-entropy *searching* behavior can best be illustrated. Figures 5 and 6 display scores of two subjects — one with the actual score lower than the average and the other with the actual score higher than the average. In Figure 5 (lower than average score), the entropy method is shown to do much better than the other two methods, since lowering weights is the right direction for reducing uncertainties of the knowledge state, whereas in Figure 6 (higher than average), the entropy method starts lowering the weights only after observing more than 16% of the total KUs.

CONCLUSION

The results presented in this paper indicate that in general, the approach to knowledge assessment is efficient in inferring new information and deriving the knowledge states of users, given either random or non-random observations. Two important applications of this technique in the context of adaptive user interfaces have been addressed. One involves building fine-grain user models; the other is guessing users' overall scores or levels of expertise. While both random and minimum-entropy-based observations are useful and effective, the latter appears to affect the order of questions asked and consequently the average knowledge state scores. In other words, the entropy method is the best for reducing uncertainties, but may generate a bias in assessing global user knowledge at the beginning. This result has rejected the previously held, rather intuitive, belief that the entropy minimization technique is a monotonically informative solution to the assessment/diagnostic problems.

ACKNOWLEDGEMENTS

We are grateful to Leslie Daigle and Jeanne-Estelle Thebault for their helpful comments on previous drafts of this paper. Jean-François D'Arcy is the author of the interface to the UKAT software.

REFERENCES

[1] F. de Rosis, S. Pizzutilo, A. Russo, D. C. Berry, and F. J. Nicolau Molina. Modeling the user knowledge by belief networks. *User Modeling and User-Adapted Interaction*, 2(4), 1992.

[2] Michel C. Desmarais. *Architecture et fondements empiriques d'un système d'aide assistée par ordinateur*

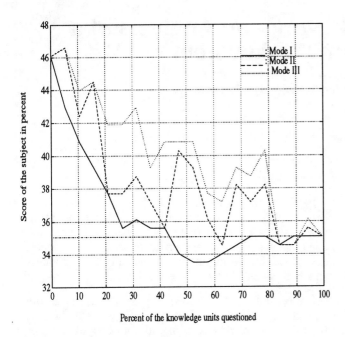

Figure 5: The estimated *scores of knowledge state* for subject 1. The true subject's score is 35% (shown at 100% of KUs asked) and the average of all subjects is 46% (shown at 0%).

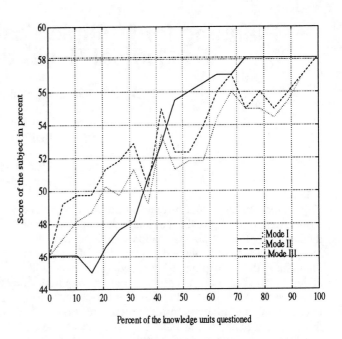

Figure 6: The estimated *scores of knowledge state* for subject 15. The true subject's score is 58% (shown at 100% of KUs asked) and the average of all subjects is 46% (shown at 0%).

pour l'édition de texte. PhD thesis, Université de Montéal, Département de psychologie, 1990.

[3] Michel C. Desmarais, Luc Giroux, and Serge Larochelle. Fondements méthodologiques et empiriques d'un système consultant actif pour l'édition de texte : le projet EdCoach. *Technologies de l'information et société*, 4(1):61–74, 1992.

[4] Michel C. Desmarais, Luc Giroux, Serge Larochelle, and Serge Leclerc. Assessing the structure of knowledge in a procedural domain. In *Proceedings of the Cognitive Science Society*, pages 475–481, 14–17 August, Montréal 1988.

[5] Michel C. Desmarais and Jimming Liu. Experimental results on user knowledge assessment with an evidential reasoning methodology. In *International Workshop on intelligent user Interfaces*, 1993. To appear.

[6] Jean-Claude Falmagne and Jean-Paul Doignon. A class of stochastic procedures for the assessment of knowledge. *British Journal of Mathematical and Statistical Psychology*, 41:1–23, 1988.

[7] Jean-Claude Falmagne, Jean-Paul Doignon, Mathieu Koppen, Michael Villano, and Leila Johannesen. Introduction to knowledge spaces: how to build, test and search them. *Psychological Review*, 97(2):201–224, 1990.

[8] I.P. Goldstein. The genetic graph: a representation for the evolution of procedural knowledge. In Sleeman and Brown [15], pages 51–77.

[9] J. Gordon and E. H. Shortliffe. The dempster-shafer theory of evidence. In B. G. Buchanan and E. H. Shortliffe, editors, *Rule-Based Expert Systems*. Addison-Wesley, Reading, M. A., 1984.

[10] A. Kobsa. Modeling the user's conceptual knowledge in BGP-MS, a user modeling shell system. *International Journal of Man-Machine Studies*, 6:193–208, 1990.

[11] Jiming Liu and Michel C. Desmarais. Knowledge assessment based on the dempster-shafer belief propagation theory. Technical Report CRIM–92/09–06, Centre de recherche informatique de Montréal, 1992.

[12] J. Self. Student models: what use are they? In P. Ercoli and R. Lewis, editors, *Artificial intelligence tools in education*. North-Holland, Amsterdam, 1988.

[13] G. Shafer. *A Mathematical Theory of Evidence*. Princeton University Press, Princeton, N. J., 1976.

[14] D. Sleeman. UMFE, a user modeling front end subsystem. *International Journal of Man-Machine Studies*, 23:71–88, 1985.

[15] D. Sleeman and J.S. Brown, editors. *Intelligent Tutoring Systems*. Academic Press, London, 1982.

Planning for Multiple Task Work - an Analysis of a Medical Reception Worksystem

Becky Hill, John Long, Walter Smith and Andy Whitefield

Ergonomics Unit, University College London
26 Bedford Way, London
WC1H 0AP
Tel: +44 71 387 7050
E-mail: ucjtebh@ucl.ac.uk

ABSTRACT

This paper presents an investigation of interactive worksystem planning in the multiple task work domain of medical reception. In an observational study of a medical reception worksystem, three different types of plan were identified: the task plan, the procedure plan and the activity plan. These three types of plan were required for effective working in the domain of medical reception, because of the many similar concurrent tasks, the frequency of behaviour switching between tasks and the need for consistency within the worksystem. It is proposed, therefore, that to design effective interactive human-computer worksystems for the domain of medical reception (and possibly for other work domains of a similar nature), the designer must specify the three different types of plan and the relationships between them. The three types of plan in medical reception are discussed in the context of design issues such as the allocation of planning structures.

KEYWORDS

medical reception; planning and control; multiple tasks.

1 INTRODUCTION

This paper presents an observational study of the plans and planning behaviour of a medical reception worksystem. The study was carried out to develop further an existing design-oriented framework of the planning and control of multiple task work (PCMT) (Smith, Hill, Long and Whitefield, 1993 [5]). Section 1 provides some background information about medical reception (MR), and identifies it as a 'PCMT design problem'. Section 2 describes the particular medical reception worksystem studied and how the observational data were collected and analysed. Section 3 contains the resulting model of PCMT in medical reception, while Section 4 presents more detailed accounts of the three different types of plan used by the medical reception worksystem. The model is intended to have appropriate content to aid in reasoning about design, but is not yet in a suitable form for use within an existing design methodology. Section 5 identifies design issues addressed by the model.

1.1 Medical Reception (in the UK)

Informally, we can identify medical reception worksystems as those interactive systems, comprising combinations of people and office devices, which support the effective interaction between medical practitioners and their patients in medical general practices.

Jeffreys and Sachs (1983) [1] have described the emergence of medical reception worksystems in the UK. In 1966, there was a boost to the employment of receptionists and secretaries, because the Family Doctors Charter was implemented, which gave provision for GPs to reclaim 70% of the salaries paid to their staff. Closely related to the increasing employment of receptionists was the growth in the use of appointment systems in general practice, as an appointment system could not be implemented without the employment of receptionist staff. General practices have begun in the last few years to be computerised, however the number has been small. The British government has more recently introduced a scheme of partial reimbursement of computer costs to increase computerisation.

Medical reception, therefore, presents an example of what might be described as an emerging Human Computer Interaction (HCI) design problem. Following the approach of Dowell and Long (1989) [2], the medical reception HCI design problem might be stated as: to specify the structures and behaviours of a human-computer interactive medical reception worksystem which will carry out work in the domain of medical reception to a desired level of performance.

1.2 Medical Reception as an Instance of the Planning and Control of Multiple Task Work

There are many different issues to be addressed in the design of medical reception worksystems. The set of issues addressed in this paper are those concerning PCMT. The general aim of the present research is to construct an appropriate model to aid designers reasoning about alternative solutions to this medical reception-PCMT design problem. The aim of the observational study reported here was to investigate the types of planning and plans used by medical reception worksystems to carry out work effectively.

The computerisation of worksystems typically increases the speed with which simple routine activities can be accomplished, e.g. searching for data, compiling revised/updated tables of information and their communication. The changing nature of routine activities has consequences for the management and supervision of work. Some of the most challenging human factors design issues for computerised systems, therefore, concern these higher-level behaviours which are here referred to as planning and control. The design of planning and control behaviours is particularly important where the worksystem carries out several ongoing tasks concurrently.

1.3 A Design-Oriented Framework of PCMT-MR

The notions of multiple task work and planning and control used in this paper are based on a previously constructed PCMT framework (Smith, Hill, Long and Whitefield, 1992a [3]; 1993 [5]). This section briefly outlines a PCMT-MR framework, the application of the PCMT framework to medical reception, in sufficient detail to understand the resulting model presented in Section 3.

The 'PCMT-MR' framework is based on Dowell and Long's (1989) conception for an engineering discipline of HCI which expresses the HCI general design problem. The conception makes a fundamental distinction between an *interactive worksystem*, comprising one or more users and computers, and its *domain of application*, comprising the transformations carried out by the worksystem which constitute its work. The effectiveness with which work is carried out is expressed by the concept of *performance* which can be defined as a function of two factors: the *quality* of the product (i.e. how well the desired state of the domain is achieved compared with the state specified in the goal); and the incurred *resource costs* (i.e. the resources required by the worksystem in accomplishing the work).

The interactive worksystem, its domain of application and performance. In medical reception, the worksystem is the receptionist plus devices such as an appointment book, telephone and prescription filing system, a wider notion of worksystem used in order to analyse to-be-computerised systems. The medical reception domain is conceptualised as the provision of support for medical cases, i.e. patients consulting with medical practitioners. Medical reception performance concerns the effectiveness with which support is provided for the medical cases.

Multiple task work. The medical reception domain is an instance of multiple task work since support is given concurrently for multiple ongoing and temporally overlapping medical cases. A single medical reception task is the transformation of a single medical case object, comprising a patient object, medical practitioner object(s), diagnosis object(s) and treatment object(s). This task might require a diverse range of behaviours spread over a long period of time, for example: arranging a suitable appointment for patient P, notifying patient P of test results.

Planning and control behaviour. It has been argued elsewhere (Smith et al, 1992b, [4]) that for an adequate characterisation of the planning and control structures of worksystems which carry out work in complex and dynamic domains, it is necessary to make explicit the relationship between planning, control, perception and execution behaviours. Planning, in medical reception, entails specifying how medical case objects are to be supported by specifying either required transformations of medical case objects and/or required behaviours. Control entails deciding which behaviour to carry out next, such as arranging an appointment for patient P1 or preparing notes for P2. Perception and execution behaviours are, respectively, those whereby the medical reception worksystem acquires information about the medical case objects and those whereby it provides the required support.

Cognitive structures and allocation of function. The PCMT-MR framework expresses the worksystem at two levels of description. Firstly, the framework describes the cognitive structures of the worksystem, expressed as four processes - *perceiving, planning, controlling* and *executing* - and two representations - *knowledge-of-the-tasks* and *plans*. This relationship is illustrated in more detail in the description of the PCMT-MR model (Section 3). Secondly, the framework describes the distribution of these cognitive structures across the physically separate user and devices of particular worksystems. The framework therefore allows the construction of alternative models of the distribution of cognitive structures across the user and devices, and thus, it supports reasoning about allocation of function.

2 AN OBSERVATIONAL STUDY OF MEDICAL RECEPTION

This Section describes an observational study of a medical reception worksystem. The aim of the observational study was to investigate the types of planning and plans used by medical reception worksystems to carry out work effectively.

2.1 The Medical Reception Worksystem

The medical reception worksystem chosen for the study supported the provision of medical care in a general practice with four doctors and two nurses. This worksystem was physically divided into two different workstations, with two receptionists working from a 'front desk' and a 'back desk'. The front desk workstation comprised a receptionist and devices, such as a telephone, and an appointments book. The back desk workstation comprised a second receptionist and devices, such as a prescription book, telephone and a computerised database. The front desk was positioned in front of a hatch through which the receptionist interacted with patients arriving at the surgery Under guidance of the receptionist, patients passed from the hatch to a waiting room before seeing a medical practitioner.

2.2 The Nature of the Medical Reception Domain

As described in Section 1.3, the medical reception domain involves multiple task work. These tasks are characterised by:

(i)   **well-defined, routine sub-tasks;**

(ii)   **variable durations,** of between one day and several weeks

Figure 1 The Model of PCMT-MR

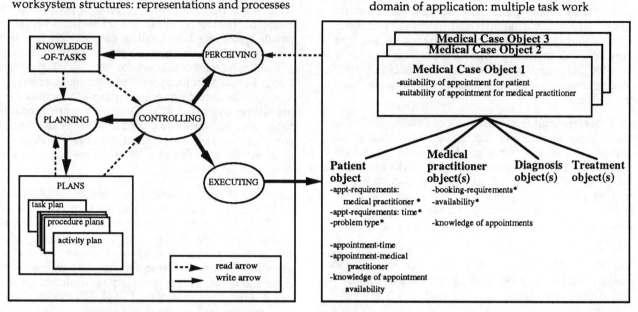

worksystem structures: representations and processes   domain of application: multiple task work

(iii)   a high frequency of **autonomous events**; that is, task-relevant events which occur independently of any worksystem behaviour, for example: the arrival of a patient at the hatch or an incoming telephone call.

2.3 Data Collection

Video-recordings were taken of the two workstations. Two video cameras were used simultaneously, one camera focused on the appointment-booking system of the front desk, while the other camera recorded the interactions within the whole reception area including both desks. Video-recordings were taken, both during and outside surgery hours, for one morning and afternoon in which time one pair of receptionists was relieved by another. At a later date, after initial analysis, an interview was carried out with one receptionist, to obtain clarification of selected details concerning the work. Only the analysis of video-recordings is reported here, although this analysis was assisted by the interview.

2.4 Data Analysis

Only the two videos recorded in the morning were analysed, because sufficient data were gathered from these two videos. The following analysis was carried out on both videos. From the 240 minutes of video-recording a sequence of between 30 - 90 minutes was selected for analysis. This selection was based mainly on the criteria that (i) the observed behaviours were interpretable, and (ii) the analysed period appeared to be busy in support of medical cases (and so was presumed to include behaviours of interest).

The first stage of the analysis was the documentation of behaviours and task-related events to a level of description considered to be at, or below, that necessary for the identification of planning and control behaviours. This first description allowed the identification of: (i) a low-level description of the physical domain objects (e.g., prescription); (ii) a low-level description of the

physical worksystem devices (e.g., phone1, prescription box). Behaviours and events were documented in chronological sequence in a manner illustrated as follows:

telephone1	BUZZ
receptionist1	PICK UP pencil
receptionist1	PICK UP receiver-phone1
receptionist1	SELECT-LINE phone1
receptionist1 (over telephone):	Hello can I help

event: P PUT prescription in prescription-box

receptionist1 (over telephone):	Dr S?

From this first analysis, it was possible to identify sequences of behaviours which were generic to particular activities carried out by the receptionist worksystem, for example appointment-booking.

3 A MODEL OF PCMT-MR

Section 1.3 described the conceptual framework of PCMT-MR constructed prior to carrying out the observational study outlined in Section 2. Sections 3 and 4 now describe the model of PCMT-MR constructed by using the observations of medical reception tasks and behaviours to instantiate the concepts of the framework.

The modelling of the observations of medical reception can be divided into two parts. First, a description of the medical reception worksystem and domain was generated, which is presented in this section. Second, a detailed description of the observed plans was constructed, presented in Section 4. Figure 1 provides a selective overview of the model of PCMT-MR which is now described

Table 1: Medical case object

Attribute	Initial value	transform	Final value
suitability of appointment for patient	not known	--------->	suitable
suitability of appointment for doctor	not known	--------->	suitable

Table 2: Patient Object

Attribute		Initial value	transform	Final value
appointment-requirements: who	(*)	Dr Y		Dr Y
appointment-requirements: when	(*)	Wednesday		Wednesday
problem type	(*)	No emergency		No emergency
appointment-time		none	--------->	Wednesday
appointment-medical practitioner		none	--------->	Dr Y
knowledge of appointment availability		not informed	--------->	informed

Table 3: Medical practitioner object

Attribute		Initial value	transform	Final value
booking requirements	(*)	squiggles open		squiggles open
availability	(*)	all appointments		all appointments
knowledge of appointment		not informed	--------->	informed

(For an explanation of a squiggle please see Section 4.1)

3.1 The Medical Reception Worksystem

The expression of the medical reception worksystem in Figure 1 shows cognitive structures taken from the PCMT-MR framework (described in Section 1.3). These cognitive structures are expressed at a generic level; that is, they depict the cognition of the medical reception worksystem prior to any allocation of function between the receptionist and devices. The relationships between the cognitive structures in Figure 1 embody the definitions of the planning and control behaviours described in Section 1.3. (For more detail see Smith et al, 1992b [4]). The *plan* representation structure in Figure 1 has been 'opened-up' to show the different types of plan identified in the study which are described in detail in Section 4.

3.2 The Medical Reception Domain

Following the PCMT-MR framework, the medical reception domain is expressed as those objects whose transformation constitutes the work of medical reception. Thus, the domain contains multiple medical case objects, each medical case object comprising a patient object, medical practitioner object(s), diagnosis object(s) and treatment object(s). Each task constitutes the transformation of a single medical case object with respect to the values of a number of attributes. In order to transform the medical case object attributes, the attributes of the medical case sub-objects (which are in a part-whole relationship with the medical case object), must be transformed. Tables 1-3 describe the transformation of the objects associated with the sub-task of appointment-booking. One of the attributes of a medical case object which must be transformed is appointment suitability for the patient. To transform the value of this attribute, the values of some of the attributes of the patient sub-object must be transformed.

The study revealed that the required transformation of each medical case object could be divided into a number of sub-transformations concerning particular sets of attributes. The division of the tasks into sub-transformations was consistent across all the tasks, and therefore the sub-transformations could be labelled **generic sub-tasks**. The generic sub-tasks identified in this study of medical reception were: appointment-booking, preparation of repeat prescriptions, registration of new patients, preparation (and updating) of medical notes for medical practitioners, and notification of patients test results.

Associated with the set of identified generic sub-tasks there were a corresponding set of **activities**. An activity is that set of behaviours which carry out a generic sub-task.

The activities identified in medical reception were: booking of appointments, preparing repeat prescriptions, registering new patients, preparing (and updating) medical notes for medical practitioners, and notifying patients of test results. Due to limitation of space, only appointment-booking will be described in detail.

Figure 1 shows only those attributes which apply to the generic sub-task of appointment-booking. Attributes may be affordant or dispositional. Affordant attributes are transformed by the worksystem; their transformation constitutes the work done. Dispositional attributes are relevant to the work but their transformation does not itself constitute work (often dispositional attributes do not change their values). The attributes marked with an asterisk (*) in Figure 1 and Tables 1-3 are dispositional, for appointment-booking.

4 PLANS AND PLANNING IN THE MEDICAL RECEPTION WORKSYSTEM

Following the PCMT-MR framework, plans are representations of how tasks are to be accomplished, specified to some level of completeness, some level of detail and in some format. In the study of medical reception, it was possible to identify three different plans employed by the worksystem. This section describes these three plans in turn and shows how they were interpreted as instances of three general types of plan: a task plan, an activity plan and a procedure plan.

4.1 The Task Plan

The receptionists used two appointment books (one for doctors and one for nurses) to represent and record details of patient appointments with the medical practitioners. Figure 2 schematically depicts the information represented in the appointment book for doctors: names of patients occupying particular appointment slots; whether or not the patient had entered the waiting room; slots which were still available; slots which the medical practitioners wanted to be left open; slots which could be used in emergencies. The receptionists also used what can be called 'mental markers'; that is, they made mental notes of temporarily significant appointment slots, such as the next available appointment of a particular medical practitioner or a slot which was in the process of being offered to a patient but not yet accepted.

Figure 2 The Appointment Book for the Doctors - a Partial Task Plan

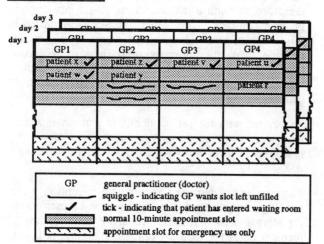

From other perspectives, the appointment books might be regarded as plans for the whole practice. In the present analysis, the appointment books plus the associated mental markers were regarded as plans of the medical reception worksystem because they guided its behaviour; for example, they represented the patients whose medical notes needed to be prepared for the doctor, and the patients who should be let into the waiting-room. In terms of the PCMT-MR framework, the appointment books were plans which represented information about domain object attribute values. Specifically, they represented information about the patient object attributes of *appointment-time* and *appointment-practitioner*, and medical practitioner object attributes of *availability* (see Figure 1).

The information represented in the appointment books was specific to particular objects, i.e. patients and medical practitioners, in the medical reception domain and was therefore specific to particular tasks, i.e. transformations of medical cases. The appointment books, with associated mental markers, were therefore identified as instances of a generic type of plan - the **task**

plan. In general, task plans are specifications of either behaviours or domain object transformations relating to specific task instances. The appointment books were therefore partial task plans.

4.2 The Activity Plan

As described in Section 3.2, the medical reception worksystem carried out a number of different activities, e.g. appointment-booking, preparing medical notes. From the video-recording and interview, it was possible to identify that the receptionists had a shared daily schedule of activities, mentally represented, to be carried out by the front and back desk receptionists. Figure 3 shows the activity schedule of the observed medical reception worksystem on the day of recording. This schedule was not rigidly adhered to as many activities, such as notifying of test results, were carried out in direct response to autonomous events such as patients telephoning the surgery.

Figure 3 The Activity Plan

BACK DESK	FRONT DESK
morning	**morning**
dealing with mail	booking of appointments
updating medical record	preparing repeat pr escriptions
envelopes	(requests, >10.00am)
preparing repeat prescriptions	
afternoon	**afternoon**
dealing with mail	booking of appointments
updating medical record	
envelopes	
preparing repeat prescriptions	

The information represented in the activity schedule was specific to the carrying out of particular activities, as opposed to particular tasks. The activity schedule was therefore identified as an instance of a generic type of plan - the **activity plan.** In general, activity plans are specifications of sequences of activities to be carried out; where each activity is a set of behaviours relating to a particular generic sub-task of the domain (see Section 3.2).

4.3 The Procedure Plan

Through analysis of the video-recordings, supported by interviews, it was possible to identify that the receptionist went through well-established sequences of behaviours when carrying out a particular activity. Thus the receptionists had mental routines, with in-built conditionals, for carrying out each activity, such as preparing medical notes, booking of appointments, preparing repeat prescriptions, etc.

These mental routines, which represented information about behaviours and their contingencies for particular activities, were identified as instances of a generic type of plan - the **procedure plan**. In general, a procedure plan specifies an effective sequence of behaviours, and their contingencies, for carrying out a particular activity which relates to a generic sub-task of the domain (see Section 3.2).

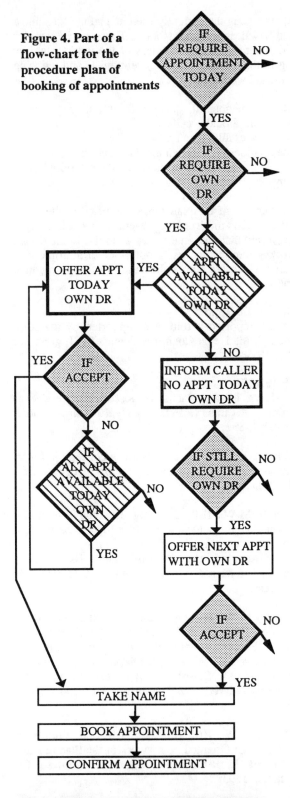

Figure 4. Part of a flow-chart for the procedure plan of booking of appointments

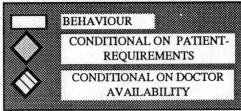

As an illustration, the procedure plan for booking of appointments is now described in detail. Figure 4 shows a flow diagram of behaviours, with associated conditionals, carried out in the activity of booking of appointments. The conditionals imply other behaviours; for example, the first conditional in Figure 4 implies that the controlling process must initiate the behaviour of reading the contents of *Knowledge of tasks* and, if necessary, to perceive the patient's requirement for appointment time (see Figure 1). Thus this procedure plan for booking of appointments describes the behaviours of the worksystem in terms of both the planning, control, perception and execution behaviours and the transformation of the medical case objects that constitute the generic sub-task of appointment-booking (see Section 4.4).

4.4 The Relationship between the Different Plans

The following scenario of an appointment being booked illustrates the relationship between the three plans shown in Figure 1, and shows how they operated in combination to guide the worksystem's behaviour.

At the beginning of the day, the controlling process reads the **activity plan** - which specifies that receptionist R should carry out booking of appointments from the front-desk during the morning (Figure 3) - and sets the parameters of the perceiving, executing and planning processes appropriately.

Later, an autonomous event occurs associated with the domain: patient P telephones the surgery requiring an appointment. The controlling process then reads from the **procedure plan** for booking of appointments (Figure 4) which guides control decisions to activate the following sequence of behaviours:
• <u>perception</u>: perceiving the values of patient P's attributes and updating *knowledge-of-tasks*: with the following attribute values:
appointment-requirements-who: own Dr (Dr X)
appointment-requirements-when: today
problem type: not emergency
• <u>planning</u>: selecting and (mentally) marking a possible appointment slot in the **task plan** (i.e. the appointment book): Dr X, time t
• <u>execution</u>: offering the selected appointment to patient P, i.e., attempt to transform P's attribute values to:
appointment-practitioner: Dr X
appointment-time: time t
• <u>perception</u>: updating *knowledge-of-tasks* to register the acceptance of the appointment and patient P's name.
• <u>planning</u>: adding a representation of the agreed appointment to the **task plan**
• <u>perception</u>: confirming the appointment details with patient P.

5 THE ROLE OF THE MODEL IN SUPPORTING THE DESIGN OF MEDICAL RECEPTION WORKSYSTEMS

The study of medical reception showed how the worksystem used three types of plan to carry out its work effectively. The relationship between the use of these different plan types and performance, i.e. the effectiveness with which the multiple task work was carried out will now be described along with their implications for the design of interactive worksystems.

• The task plan, observed in the form of patient appointment books, supported the effective carrying out of the many ongoing tasks by:
1) giving guidance for the carrying out of behaviours relating to specific tasks, e.g. whether to admit patient P1 to the waiting room, preparing medical notes for P2;
2) co-ordinating different tasks e.g. ensuring that appointments were unique for each task.

• The activity plan, observed in the form of a (mentally represented) daily schedule of activities, supported the effective carrying out of tasks by:
1) supporting large-scale sharing of effort across separate tasks; e.g., when carrying out the activity of preparing repeat prescriptions, all of the medical notes for the patients requiring repeat prescriptions would be collected together at one time, thus reducing the behavioural costs to the worksystem;
2) co-ordinating the activities with the task-relevant changes in the domain; e.g., the activity of preparing repeat prescriptions was carried out during surgery hours, so that the prescriptions were ready for the doctors to verify and sign when the surgeries finished.

• Procedure plans, observed in the form of mental routines, supported the effective carrying out of repetitive sub-tasks which were generic across tasks (such as booking of appointments) by:
1) providing quick responses in a domain where there was a very high frequency of autonomous events (patients arriving, incoming telephone calls);
2) maintaining consistency which supported the rotation of the four receptionists around the two medical reception workstations;
3) supporting shared user behaviour, such that if one workstation was left unattended because a receptionist was busy the other receptionist on that shift could take over at the unattended workstation.

In computerising, and therefore redesigning, the medical reception worksystem described in this paper, a designer should specify how the identified plans will be supported in the new design. For example it may be advisable to re-allocate some of the mental plans to computerised devices, by:
i) having a partial procedure plan for booking of appointments device-based

ii) incorporating the currently used mental markers into a device-based appointment book. These two examples would enhance the effectiveness of the worksystem by aiding in the training of new receptionists and reducing their mental workload.

Therefore, in general, designs for medical reception worksystems should specify:
(i) instances of all 3 plan types
(ii) the relationship between the different plans
(iii) the allocation of the plans across the receptionist and the physically separate devices of the worksystem.

The generality of the plan types identified in the study reported here is uncertain at present. However, it might be suggested that the same issues will arise in the design of worksystems which carry out work in multiple task domains which are similar in nature to that of medical reception.

ACKNOWLEDGEMENT
The work reported herein was supported by the Joint Councils Initiative in Cognitive Science/HCI, grant no: SPG 8825634.

REFERENCES
[1] Jefferys, M. and Sachs, H. **Rethinking General Practice: Dilemmas in Primary Health Care**. London Tavistock,1983.

[2] Dowell, J. and Long, J. Towards a conception for an engineering discipline of human factors. **Ergonomics**, **32**, (1989), 1513-1536.

[3] Smith, M.W., Hill, B., Long, J.B. and Whitefield, A.D. The Planning and Control of Multiple Task Work: a Study of Secretarial Office Administration. In **Proceedings of the Second Interdisciplinary Workshop on Mental Models**, Cambridge, (1992a), 74-83, in press.

[4] Smith, M.W., Hill, B., Long, J.B. and Whitefield, A.D. Modelling the Relationship Between Planning, Control, Perception and Execution Behaviours in Interactive Worksystems. In D.Diaper, M.Harrison and A.Monk (Eds) **People and Computers VII; Proceedings of HCI '92**. Cambridge University Press, 1992b.

[5] Smith, M.W., Hill, B., Long, J.B. and Whitefield, A.D. A Design-Oriented Framework of the Planning and Control of Multiple Task Work. Submitted for publication, 1993.

The Diary Study: A Workplace-Oriented Research Tool to Guide Laboratory Efforts

John Rieman

Department of Computer Science and Institute of Cognitive Science
University of Colorado
Boulder, CO 80309-0430
(303) 786-0447
rieman@cs.colorado.edu

ABSTRACT

Methods for studying user behavior in HCI can be informally divided into two approaches: experimental psychology in the laboratory and observations in the workplace. The first approach has been faulted for providing results that have little effect on system usability, while the second can often be accused of yielding primarily anecdotal data that do not support general conclusions. This paper describes two similar approaches in another field, the study of animal behavior, and shows how they produce complementary results. To support similar complementary interactions between research approaches in the HCI field, the paper describes the diary study technique, a tool for research in the workplace that achieves a relatively high standard of objectivity. A diary study is reported that focuses on exploratory learning.

KEYWORDS: Diary studies, methodologies, participatory design, situated cognition, exploratory learning

METHODS FOR STUDYING USER BEHAVIOR

In the field of human-computer interaction (HCI), methods for studying user behavior can be informally divided into two approaches: experimental psychology in the laboratory and observations of users in the workplace.

The laboratory-based approach of experimental psychology grows out of a long history of work in the human factors field. In this style of research, investigators bring users into a laboratory situation and make quantitative observations of their behavior. The users are chosen from a single population, and the laboratory situation is carefully designed to vary only a few independent variables. The situation may have little in common with real computer usage. In the conservative version of this approach, a large number of subjects are tested, yielding data that can be interpreted with statistical methods and projected to a larger population [10]. A related method uses protocols taken from a few subjects and analyzed in depth, as in thinking-aloud studies or individual user modelling efforts [11,13].

The second dominant approach is to collect data in the workplace, with the researcher often interacting closely with users in an informal way. The most radical version of this approach is participatory design, often identified with the European and particularly the Scandinavian HCI community [5]. In participatory design, users and designers work together to identify system goals and to iteratively produce systems that meet the users' evolving needs. Some other workplace-oriented methodologies include user surveys, monitoring the use of prototypes, and contextual design [18]. Although it is not always the case, investigations in the workplace are generally less controlled than laboratory efforts, involving fewer subjects and relying more heavily on subjective judgments and personal interactions. These efforts are most often described as design methodologies, not research tools, and the data they yield tend to be less predictive, more anecdotal, more limited to the individual situation under investigation.

Most HCI researchers are aware of this distinction, and many design projects use a mixture of the two approaches [6]. Nonetheless, the polarity is informative. On the one hand, the laboratory approach typically yields objective data that can be interpreted statistically to predict the behavior of a population, but the data concern the behavior of subjects in a contrived situation. Critics of this work, including proponents of the situated cognition view, argue that it has little impact on the usability of real systems [14,18]. By contrast, information gathered in the workplace as part of a design project reflects the real, day-to-day work of the participants, but extracting objective, general data from these reports may be difficult.

This paper offers some insights into the interaction between these two general approaches, based on the interaction of similar approaches in another research field, animal behavior. The paper then describes a method, the diary study, which is intended for use in the workplace, but which yields data that are more objective and more generalizable than many workplace-oriented methods. As an example, a diary study of exploratory learning is described.

LESSONS FROM THE STUDY OF ANIMAL BEHAVIOR

The study of animal behavior is much older than HCI, with the roots of its modern theories going back at least as far as Pavlov and Darwin in the nineteenth century. But as with HCI, there are fundamentally two research approaches. The first of these is to study animals in the laboratory, an approach usually associated with experimental psychology. The second is to study animals in natural field situations, an approach taken by ethologists.

Like experimental psychology in HCI, experimental psychology with animals often involves contrived situations that are far from natural: rats are encouraged to visit the arms of radial mazes where cheese appears and disappears as if by magic; pigeons learn to dance from microswitch to microswitch in response to colored lights or photographs; cats are forced to escape from boxes with trick latching devices. Subject animals are carefully chosen from an artificially bred population, and groups for a given experimental condition may be surgically disabled, drugged, or raised in exceptional environments. But the data produced are clearly objective.

By contrast, ethological investigations are typically performed in the field, with randomly selected members of the naturally occurring population. Much of the work is simple visual observation of natural behavior. Other research relies on artificial devices, such as radio collars to track animal movement patterns, and some projects involve experimental manipulations, such as substitution of differently colored eggs in field sites. Ethologists strive to be objective, but the research is unavoidably influenced by behavioral coding decisions, and reported data are often based on small samples of a population. As with workplace HCI, some of this research may involve participation and highly subjective judgments: Konrad Lorenz with geese, Diane Fossey with gorillas. Interestingly, this approach, like workplace HCI, also has a history that is more closely associated with the European than the American research community.

Reconciling the Two Approaches

As with the two polar approaches to HCI research, there is clearly a tension between the two approaches to the study of animal behavior. However, several researchers have recently suggested that the two approaches can be complementary, in both a theoretical and a practical sense [1,4,12].

In a theoretical sense, the approaches can be seen to ask different, but complementary, questions. Ethological research in the field asks *functional* questions: how is the survivability of a species enhanced by a given behavioral characteristic, and why did that characteristic evolve? [7] To provide convincing answers to these questions necessarily requires that as much as possible of the organism's natural environment be considered in the analysis. On the other hand, experimental psychology in the laboratory asks *causal* (proximate) questions: what combination of cues does an organism perceive that causes it to behave in a certain way, and what cognitive algorithms does it use to define its behavior? The theoretical interplay is made especially interesting by the requirement that behavior which might be functionally optimal must be approximated by algorithms that an organism can process with its available memory and cognitive power [4].

It is this interaction between theoretical questions that also sets up the practical interaction between the two research approaches. The data and theories of ethologists suggest functionally optimal behavior; experimental psychologists can then design experiments to uncover mechanisms that implement or approximate this behavior.

Clark's Nutcracker: A Suite of Studies

As an example of the interaction between field and laboratory research in animal behavior, consider a series of studies investigating the behavior of Clark's Nutcracker, a bird found in the conifer forests in the western part of North America. Observations of naturalists have revealed that the seeds of pine trees form a major part of this species' diet. During the seed harvesting season, which lasts about one month, nutcrackers remove the seeds from pine cones and bury them in shallow holes, called caches, for retrieval during the rest of the year [15].

The relationship between the nutcracker and the pine trees is a close one. The beak of the nutcracker is specialized for removing seeds from cones and carrying them to cache sites or the nest, and the nutcracker's range closely parallels the range of the pine trees that provide its food. The range of the forest, in turn, is influenced by the nutcracker's activities: not all cached seeds are recovered, and unrecovered seeds may germinate and grow into new trees.

Field studies in the ethological style investigated this relationship between bird and forest, with particular attention to the nutcracker's effectiveness in caching and recovery [15,17]. Using a combination of energy calculations, field examinations of recovered caches, and direct observation, these researchers concluded that an individual bird must store on the order of 32,000 seeds each year, in roughly 8,000 caches. Although some of these caches are stolen by rodents, and others are unrecovered and left to germinate, an estimated 60 to 86 percent of the caches are located and recovered by nutcrackers.

These results of this investigation into functional issues raised causal questions that field research alone could not easily answer. Specifically, what were the mechanisms that nutcrackers used to achieve this high recovery rate? Was there some common pattern of storage and search to which all nutcrackers were privy, making the caches a communal resource? Or, did the birds actually possess the spatial memory needed to recall and recover their own caches? If so, did they rely on local, visual cues, such as the shape of a rocks and trees near the cache, or did they navigate using some more sophisticated system?

To answer these questions, researchers transferred the investigation from the field to the laboratory [16,9]. A large outdoor flight cage was constructed, with a dirt floor and various objects, such as logs and rocks, to simulate a forest setting. In this setting, a series of controlled experiments eliminated olfactory and other possible cues that could not be controlled in the field. The results confirmed that a nutcracker's primary means of cache relocation was, indeed, spatial memory of the locations in which it had stored its own seeds, cued by large objects near to each cache.

Applying Similar Principles to HCI Research

The time-course of the nutcracker investigations illustrates an effective research paradigm. First, informal observations of naturalists identified the basic relationship between the nutcracker and the pine forest. Second, formal fieldwork investigated the functional relationships, raising questions as to the causal mechanisms involved. Third, laboratory experiments, designed to mimic important features of the natural environment, probed those mechanisms.

A similar complementary research approach can be effective in HCI research. Anecdotal evidence and insights acquired during participatory activities with users can suggest questions for more objective field studies in the workplace. These studies, in turn, can point to questions for investigation in the laboratory. They can also be used to suggest laboratory situations that reflect the critical constraints of the user's real environment.

An essential component of this approach is a set of objective tools for workplace investigations during the second phase of the research, along with guidelines for interpreting the data they yield. While these tools should reflect participatory design's fundamental concern with the rights and interests of the user, they should be structured primarily for objective data collection. One such tool is the diary study.

THE DIARY STUDY TECHNIQUE

The diary study, as described here, is based on a technique used by Ericsson and his colleagues to investigate expert behavior of concert musicians [3]. In a diary study, participants are asked to record their daily activities on a preprinted log form. The log breaks the day into brief intervals, typically 15 or 30 minutes. The activities are initially recorded using the participant's own description, i.e., "had dinner with Kelly," or, "dentist — ouch!" Later, all activities are assigned to predefined categories, such as "meals" or "physical exercise." Diaries are typically kept for one or two weeks; any longer would be a burden for many participants. The diary record itself is usually supplemented with a post-study interview of the participant, addressing behavior over a longer term than the diary covers.

The activity categories in the daily log can be based on established categories for time-budgeting activities [8]. However, the log can be tailored to the questions of interest in the study by adding to or specializing these categories. The size of the time intervals and the hours of each day covered by the log can also be adjusted.

Data Provided by the Diary Study

The diary study provides several kinds of data. Most powerfully, the record of time spent in each activity category is quantitative data, amenable to statistical analysis. Ericsson and his colleagues used this data to correlate practice times with levels of expertise in concert pianists and violinists [3]. Because the diary participant is forced to record *all* activities for the period covered, the data reported in the diary are arguably more reliable than reports of time spent, if any, on one specific activity each day.

The second kind of data provided by the study are the statements collected in the interview. Although interview data standing alone are a relatively soft and unreliable, the participant's statements are "hardened" by relating them to the diary record. For example, if an interviewee says, "No, I hardly ever use my spreadsheet program," and a two-week diary confirms this, the evidence is much stronger than an interview statement without further support. The diary record can also suggest questions for the interview.

Finally, the diary study provides an opportunity for the researcher to interact with a number of users in their workplaces. The informal insights gained through this interaction are similar in kind to those achieved in less formal approaches, such as participatory design. This information is useful in suggesting appropriate tasks for controlled investigation in the laboratory.

EXAMPLE: A DIARY STUDY OF EXPLORATORY LEARNING

An ongoing project of our research group is the study of how users learn the functionality of computer systems during their daily work, outside a formal training situation. We refer to this activity as "exploratory learning" [2]. A subsidiary question is how users explore a system in the absence of a given task, simply out of curiosity. In preparation for laboratory studies of this behavior, we performed a diary study to find out how prevalent task-free exploration is and where it occurs.

The diary study involved four data-collection activities: (1) a daily log, (2) "Eureka Reports" of learning incidents, (3) daily debriefing interviews, and (4) a longer interview following the one-week diary period. These activities were all designed to focus on computer-related learning, while avoiding a bias in favor of any one learning technique.

The time during which the daily log was kept was limited to the participant's working hours. We had no interest in what a participant did during his or her time away from the job, and minimizing invasion of privacy helped the researcher achieve a good working relationship with the participants. As shown in Figure 1, the log was focussed on the area of interest by including categories for several computer-related activities, rather than a single one for "computing." The log did not include a category for "learning," an activity orthogonal to the categories listed. Learning episodes were identified during the daily debriefing and through the Eureka Reports (Figure 2). A Eureka Report was to be filled out whenever a participant realized he or she had learned something, or solved a problem, or attempted unsuccessfully to learn or problem-solve.

The daily debriefing interview was a critical part of the study. During the day, the participant filled in the activities column of the log, describing activities in half-hour intervals. At the end of each day, or early the next day, the researcher met with the participant and assigned the activities to categories. The discussion accompanying this interaction gave the researcher an opportunity to discover any learning episodes that had taken place and to ensure that they had been recorded on Eureka Reports.

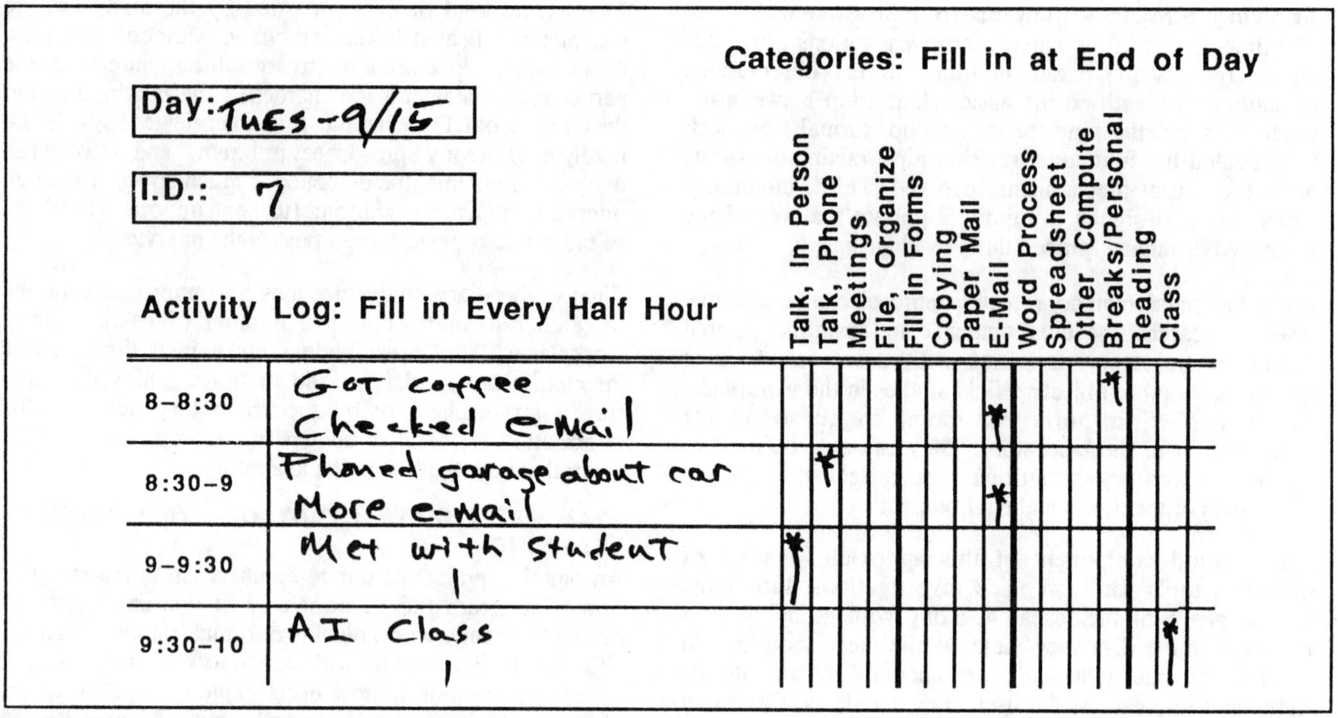

Categories: Fill in at End of Day

Day: Tues – 9/15

I.D.: 7

Activity Log: Fill in Every Half Hour

Time	Activity	Talk, In Person	Talk, Phone	Meetings	File, Organize	Fill in Forms	Copying	Paper Mail	E-Mail	Word Process	Spreadsheet	Other Compute	Breaks/Personal	Reading	Class
8–8:30	Got coffee Checked e-mail								*				*		
8:30–9	Phoned garage about car More e-mail		*						*						
9–9:30	Met with student	*													
9:30–10	AI Class														*

Figure 1. The beginning of a diary log sheet for one day. The participant records activities on the left as the day proceeds. The researcher assigns categories during the end-of-day debriefing.

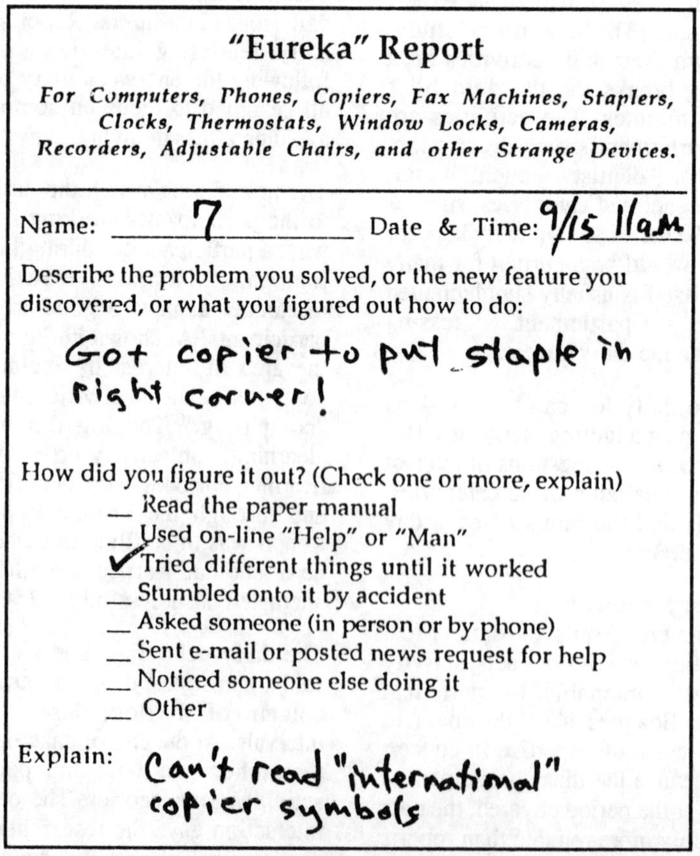

"Eureka" Report

For Computers, Phones, Copiers, Fax Machines, Staplers, Clocks, Thermostats, Window Locks, Cameras, Recorders, Adjustable Chairs, and other Strange Devices.

Name: 7 Date & Time: 9/15 11am

Describe the problem you solved, or the new feature you discovered, or what you figured out how to do:

Got copier to put staple in right corner!

How did you figure it out? (Check one or more, explain)

__ Read the paper manual
__ Used on-line "Help" or "Man"
✓ Tried different things until it worked
__ Stumbled onto it by accident
__ Asked someone (in person or by phone)
__ Sent e-mail or posted news request for help
__ Noticed someone else doing it
__ Other

Explain: Can't read "international" copier symbols

Figure 2. A "Eureka Report," for noting episodes in which new information is sought or acquired.

The one-week diary study of each participant was concluded with a one-hour structured interview, covering the participant's experiences in learning about computers and other devices outside the time span of the diary. After a week of daily debriefings, the researcher and participant had established a rapport and common vocabulary that significantly enhanced the final interview.

The study provided converging evidence of varying quality. We did not simply ask the participants, "Tell us when and how you learn something." Rather, we asked for a complete report of their days, and we discussed each day with them to discover learning episodes. The Eureka Reports served to further focus on this issue, and interview questions allowed us to identify behavior that the subject considered uncharacteristic, as well as to gain an understanding of reasons for the activity patterns reported. This approach yielded evidence that was stronger than isolated anecdotal reports, while avoiding the biasing influence of researchers who actually participate in the users' work.

Results of the Study and Their Significance for Future Investigations

Ten participants completed five-day diaries (one work week) for the exploratory learning study. Participants were selected from a variety of backgrounds to get an overview of how and when computer learning activities occurred. Two of the subjects were secretarial personnel, two were undergraduates with part-time clerical assistant jobs, two were university faculty members (one in computer science), and four were full-time researchers in computer science. The last group was where we expected to find the most frequent occurrence of task-free exploratory learning.

As described, the sampling was too small and inhomogeneous to support strong projections to a larger population. However, the Eureka Reports, supported by the daily logs and the follow-up interviews, revealed several points that will guide the next phase of our research.

Based on the number of Eureka Reports generated, the participants could clearly be divided into two groups: explorers and non-explorers. The explorers included only two of the participants, one in the field of computer science and one outside that field. These users actively sought new information about their computer systems almost every day. Each of the explorers generated 18 Eurekas during the five-day diary study. The remaining eight participants, the non-explorers, generated an average of 4 Eurekas over the five days, with a minimum of 2 and a maximum of 8. Two of the four subjects with the lowest Eureka counts (2 or 3) were computer scientists.

The explorer who was not a computer scientist was the only participant to engage in a significant amount of learning that was not directly demanded by work-related tasks. As we had hypothesized, these activities were structured around tasks created primarily for the purpose of investigating the computer system.

The categories on Eureka Reports describe how participants made their discoveries. For the total of 69 Eurekas reported by all participants, the three most common ways of learning were: trying things until something worked (42 times); reading the manual or using on-line help (41 times); and asking for help, either in person or occasionally by e-mail (18 times). There was often more than one method noted for a single Eureka, and a common combination was reading the manual along with trying things. Further insight is yielded by the distribution of these methods among the explorers and the non-explorers. Explorers were about twice as likely to use the manual (30 times in 36 Eurekas) as non-explorers (11 times in 33 Eurekas). They were also more likely to try things (26 times for explorers, 16 times for non-explorers), but slightly less likely to ask for help (6 times for explorers, 10 times for non-explorers).

These results provide guidance for our continuing research into exploratory learning. We can be alert to potentially large differences in behavior, perhaps bimodally distributed, and not tied to any obvious characteristics. And contrary to our original hypothesis, we have evidence that task-free exploration is not limited to computer scientists.

We can also design laboratory situations to investigate exploratory learning under real-world task conditions. Our diary participants showed a strong reliance on written documentation, often as the first step in investigating a system feature. Asking subjects to begin exploration in the laboratory without access to documentation would not reflect a natural situation. Further, the diaries and the follow-up interviews both revealed the frequency with which users ask for help. Again, the natural lab situation should somehow support this fall-back action, instead of forcing subjects into extended trial-and-error behavior.

Methodological Lessons From the Study

Experience in setting up and running this study has taught us several lessons about the diary technique. First, personal interactions are a key part of a successful study. Participants must be convinced to make a considerable effort over a week's time to record their activities. Several participants agreed to maintain a diary but initially failed to record sufficient detail. One participant filled in the log sheet for the first day with a single word: "programming." Another subject waited until the end of the day, then wrote down the entire day's activities, noting that this was the way he had kept log sheets in a previous job. After some discussion, the researcher convinced both participants to maintain their logs with greater detail, on an ongoing basis.

A second lesson was that participants inevitably tried to focus their logs, and even adjust their activities, to emphasize areas that they thought would interest the researcher. The participant who had written "programming" for the day's activities explained, "I didn't do anything you were interested in." More than one participant apologized to the researcher at the end of the day for not having learned anything new, and participants sometimes made comments such as, "I guess I should spend some time learning about this new program so I can fill out a Eureka Report."

Avoiding this bias is difficult. Our participants had several clues as to the study's purpose: the Eureka and log forms, the legal release, the end-of-day debriefings, and sometimes prior knowledge. As noted, the current study broadened the focus by addressing learning in general, rather than highlighting task-free exploratory learning. In addition, the researcher made a conscious effort to impress upon participants the need to record their normal activities, not activities that they thought would be interesting.

A third lesson is that the process is quite effortful. Even though the debriefings only take about 15 minutes each day, those periods must be scheduled at the participant's convenience, and the researcher must arrive at the participant's workplace on time, prepared to wait until the participant finishes his or her current task. Logging the activities of more than two participants in a week is usually impossible for a single researcher.

Finally, because it takes a day or two for the participant to become comfortable with the process, it is a good idea to start participants on different days of the week. Otherwise, the diaries may all have questionable data for the weekday, typically Monday, on which all logs are started. Starting midweek also allows activities performed during the weekend to be captured as an integral part of the study.

SUMMARY
The two fundamental methods of HCI research, observations in the workplace and controlled laboratory studies, can complement each other in an effective research program. The diary study is a tool that can help bridge the gap between these methodologies, providing objective data about the workplace to guide further study in the laboratory.

ACKNOWLEDGEMENTS
Discussions with Anders Ericsson were instrumental in defining the diary study methodology and in clarifying the larger methodological issues. Thanks is extended to Evelyn Ferstl, Marita Franzke, Alcinda Lewis, Clayton Lewis, Peter Polson, and the CHI'92 Doctoral Consortium for their comments. Support for this research has been provided by the National Science Foundation, grants IRI 8722792 and 9116640, and by US West Advanced Technologies.

REFERENCES
1. Brain, P.F. Ethology and experimental psychology: from confrontation to partnership. In *Ethoexperimental Approaches to the Study of Behavior*, R.J. Blanchard, P.F. Brain, D.C. Blanchard, and S. Parmigiani, Eds., Kluwer, Dordrecht, The Netherlands, 1989, pp. 19-27.

2. Carroll, J.M., Mack, R.L., Lewis, C.H., Grischkowsky, N.L., and Robertson, S.P. Exploring a word processor. *Human Computer Interaction 1* (1985), 283-307.

3. Ericsson, K. Anders, Tesch-Römer, C., and Krampe, R.T. The role of practice and motivation in the acquisition of expert-level performance in real life: An empirical evaluation of a theoretical framework. In *Encouraging the Development of Exceptional Skills and Talents*, M.J.A. Howe, Ed., The British Psychological Society, Leicester, 1990, pp. 109-130.

4. Fantino, E., and Abarca, N. Choice, optimal foraging, and the delay-reduction hypothesis. *Behavioral and Brain Sciences 8* (1985), 315-330.

5. Floyd, C., Wolf-Michael, M, Reisin, F.-M., Schmidt, G., and Wolf, G. Out of Scandinavia: Alternative approaches to software design and system development. *Human-Computer Interaction 4* (1989), 253-350.

6. Gould, J.D., Boies, S., and Lewis, C. Making usable, useful, productivity-enhancing computer applications. *Communications of the ACM 34* (1991), 74-89.

7. Houston, A., Kacelnik, A., and McNamara, J. Some learning rules for acquiring information. In *Functional Ontogony*, David McFarland, Ed., Pitman, London, 1982, pp. 140-190.

8. Juster, F.T., and Stafford, F.P. (Eds.) *Time, Goods and Well-being*. Institute for Social Research, The University of Michigan, Ann Arbor, Mich., 1985.

9. Kamil, A.C., and Balda, R.P. Cache recovery and spatial memory in Clark's Nutcrackers. *J. Exp. Psych., Animal Behavior Processes 11* (1985), 95-111.

10. Landauer, T.K., Research methods in human computer interaction. In *Handbook of Human-Computer Interaction*, M. Helander, Ed., Elsevier Science, Amsterdam, 1988, pp. 905-928.

11. Lewis, C. Using thinking aloud protocols to study the "cognitive interface." Research Report RC 9265, IBM Thomas J. Watson Research Center, Yorktown Heights, N.Y., 1982.

12. Miller, D. B. Methodological issues in the ecological study of learning. In *Issues in the Ecological Study of Learning*, T.D. Johnston and A.T. Pietrewicz, Eds., Lawrence Erlbaum, Hillsdale, N.J., 1985, pp. 73-95.

13. Shrager, J., and Klahr, D. Instructionless learning about a complex device: The paradigm and observations. *International Journal of Man-Machine Studies 25* (1986), 153-189.

14. Suchman, L. A. *Plans and Situated Actions*. Cambridge, England: Cambridge University Press, 1987.

15. Tomback, D.F. Foraging strategies of Clark's Nutcracker. *Living Bird 16* (1978), 123-161.

16. Vander Wall, S.B. An experimental analysis of cache recovery in Clark's Nutcracker. *Animal Behavior 30* (1982), 84-94.

17. Vander Wall, S.B., and Balda, R.P. Coadaptations of the Clark's Nutcracker and the piñon pine for efficient seed harvest and dispersal. *Ecological Monographs 47* (1977), 89-111.

18. Wixon, D., Holtzblatt, K., and Knox, S. Contextual design: An emergent view of system design. In *Proceedings of the Conference on Human Factors in Computing Systems* (Seattle, Wash., April 1-5, 1990). ACM, New York, 1990, pp. 331-336.

Turning Away from Talking Heads: The Use of Video-as-Data in Neurosurgery

Bonnie A. Nardi, Heinrich Schwarz, Allan Kuchinsky, Robert Leichner

Hewlett-Packard Laboratories
1501 Page Mill Road, Palo Alto, CA 94304 U.S.A
Internet: nardi@hpl.hp.com

Steve Whittaker

Hewlett-Packard Laboratories
Stoke Gifford, Bristol BS12 6QZ United Kingdom

Robert Sclabassi

Department of Neurosurgery
University of Pittsburgh, Pittsburgh, PA 15213, U.S.A

Abstract

Studies of video as a support for collaborative work have provided little hard evidence of its utility for either task performance or fostering telepresence, i.e. the conveyance of a face-to-face like social presence for remotely located participants. To date, most research on the value of video has concentrated on "talking heads" video in which the video images are of remote participants conferring or performing some task together. In contrast to talking heads video, we studied *video-as-data* in which video images of the *workspace* and work objects are the focus of interest, and convey critical information about the work. The use of video-as-data is intended to enhance task performance, rather than to provide telepresence. We studied the use of video during neurosurgery within the operating room and at remote locations away from the operating room. The workspace shown in the video is the surgical field (brain or spine) that the surgeon is operating on. We discuss our findings on the use of live and recorded video, and suggest extensions to video-as-data including its integration with computerized time-based information sources to educate and co-ordinate complex actions among distributed workgroups.

Keywords: Multimedia, video, collaborative work, task coordination, computers and medicine.

Introduction

The integration of video into groupware systems seems a logical next step in the quest for more effective computer support for collaborative work. Many such systems are currently under development, such as Portholes [3], Cruiser [6], ClearBoard [9], SharedView [10], CAVECAT [11], and Hydra [14]. (See [1] for an overview.) Videoconferencing systems in which participants gather in specially equipped conference rooms have been in existence for over 30 years [4]. The Picturephone from Bell Laboratories was introduced at the 1964 World's Fair.

Talking heads video presents images of remote participants conferring or performing some task together. A large body of research has shown, however, that it does not enhance performance for a variety of tasks such as information transmission and collaborative problem solving [2, 4, 5, 15]. Alternatively, investigators have been hopeful that talking heads video will foster *telepresence*, that is, give users a rich physical and psychological sense of the other people with whom they are remotely interacting via cues obtained from gaze, gesture, facial expressions, body language [5, 15].[1] But this has been difficult to achieve [7] and thus far little in the way of concrete value has been demonstrated for telepresence video [2, 4, 5, 15]. For example, Egido [4] reported on the history of videoconferencing and Picturephone, noting that videoconferencing remains "a small conglomeration of 'niche' markets." Only about 75 companies in the U.S. have videoconferencing systems, and those include telephone and videoconferencing vendors. The Picturephone is a well-known failure, and while there are many possible reasons for this, Egido observed that trial use of Picturephone was met with "disturbing reports of phenomena such as users' feelings of instant dislike toward parties they had never seen before, self-consciousness about 'being on TV' ... and resulting low acceptance" [4].

What about "desktop video" systems such as Portholes [3], Cruiser [6], CAVECAT [11], and Hydra [14]? Will they prove a more successful application of video than videoconferencing and Picturephone? Possibly they will, but to date there is little research to rely on for objective evaluation. Reports of the actual use of the desktop systems are often anecdotal and may involve both use and evaluation of the system by its developers and colleagues of the developers – a highly biased situation (e.g. [3, 11]). A few systems have been tested in short trials on

[1] The term "telepresence" does not yet have a firm definition, and people use it in different ways. There is a need for a word to precisely denote remote *human* presence, as opposed to virtual reality or remote shared task space. It is in the sense of human presence that we use telepresence. Used in this way, telepresence resonates with terms in common usage such as "social presence," "stage presence" and simply "presence." Webster's defines the latter as "a quality of poise and effectiveness that enables a performer to achieve a close relationship with his audience," which is very much like what we are trying to achieve via technology for remotely located participants.

students or paid research subjects (e.g. [6, 14]), but the results have not been convincingly positive.

None of the current research systems as they are now configured provides strong evidence that video is an important support for collaborative work. For example, in a four-week trial of Cruiser it was found that Cruiser did not supply value added beyond telephone or email; Fish et al. [6] reported that, "For the most part, people perceived and used [Cruiser] like a telephone or an electronic mail system . . . " Fish et al. [6] suggest extensions to Cruiser which may improve its utility in the future, but it would be difficult to convince a disinterested observer of the value of video based on the implementations and related empirical findings of the current talking heads systems, as they are reported in the literature.

While available evidence on the utility of video for collaborative work promotes skepticism more than enthusiasm, does this mean that video is an unimportant technology for collaborative work? We believe that the answer is no for two reasons.

First, current systems that attempt to facilitate telepresence have many problems such as lack of support for eye gaze, or requiring a move to a special (expensively outfitted) room to utilize the technology. These problems will be overcome in time. Systems such as Hydra [14] which support natural eye gaze and leave a small footprint on the desktop seem promising for remote meetings and informal conversations among four or fewer remotely located people. ClearBoard [9] also allows for gaze awareness, and provides an innovative shared drawing space for two users. Once the technical challenges of the telepresence systems are met, and the systems are more specialized to support specific tasks (just as ClearBoard supports intensive interaction between two people working closely together on a shared task), a more objective assessment of their worth will be possible. A large question will be the cost-effectiveness of telepresence video. Cost-effectiveness will have to be monitored as the technology and its price structure evolve over time.

Second, we think that video is a valuable support for collaborative work because a different aspect of video usage – video-as-data – has been in use for many years in medical and industrial settings, and has become indispensable in many applications. Video-as-data stands in contrast to talking heads video: it is not used to support telepresence, but rather provides images of the workspace – the "data" – to convey critical information about the work. People can see the work objects, and how they are changing and being manipulated within the work context. These images are used by teams of workers to coordinate demanding, highly technical tasks in real-time situations, and to support research and technical training. For example, in power plants, live video of remote locations is used to monitor plant operations [16]. Video is used in telerobotics and remote surveillance [12].

The possibilities for extensions and enhancements to basic video capabilities are many. Milgram et al. [12] have a system that combines stereoscopic video and stereoscopic computer graphics so that users can point to, measure and annotate objects within the video. Tani et al. [16] have proposed "object-oriented video" in which the real-world objects in the video become computer-based objects that can be manipulated so that users will be able to reference, overlay, highlight, and annotate them, as well as use the objects for control and information browsing. In Tani et al.'s prototype system for power plants, users can, for example, point to a burner on a boiler in the live video and bring up a document that explains how the ignition system of the boiler works. Users can get a more detailed video or related video of an object by pointing to the object, obviating the need to directly control remote cameras. Users can control remote devices through direct manipulation techniques such as clicking and dragging; for example, "pushing" a button on the video image engages a real button on the remote device [16]. Such uses of video are quite distinctive from talking heads video, and open up a whole new realm of video-based applications.

In this paper we report on an ethnographic study of the use of video-as-data in a medical setting, where live color video is used to coordinate team activity during neurosurgery, and both live and recorded video are used for training in neurosurgery. During the critical parts of neurosurgery, such as the removal of a brain tumor, the neurosurgeon looks through a stereoscopic microscope to view the brain as he[2] works. A video camera co-mounted with the optics of the microscope displays a video image of what the surgeon sees on a monitor on a cable TV link. Thus everyone in the operating room (hereinafter abbreviated "OR," the term used in the hospital) can see what the surgeon sees, though the video image is 2D and is a somewhat smaller view of the surgical field than what the surgeon sees. This technology has been in existence (though not universally available) for over twenty years, and is now an indispensable part of OR activity in many hospitals. A microphone mounted on the microscope provides audio capability for remote broadcast.

In this paper we examine the ways in which the live video image of the brain or spine coordinates the demanding work of neurosurgery among the many neurosurgical team members. The technical complexity of neurosurgery is remarkable, and in the teaching hospital setting that we studied, the neurosurgical team includes an attending neurosurgeon, resident or fellow neurosurgeon(s), surgical technician, scrub nurse, circulating nurse, nurse-anesthetist, anesthesiologist, neurophysiologist, neurotechnician and sometimes an anethesiology resident. We also examine how the live video in the OR promotes education: student nurses, medical students, residents, fellows, and visiting neurophysiologists and physicians[3] are often present in the OR during an operation. In addition, we studied the use of remote video and audio facilities to enable remote collaboration during neurosurgery.

Our main argument is that video-as-data is an important application of video technology in computer-based systems, and that we should not lose sight of its potential by over-focusing on talking heads video, and in particular, by placing too much

---

[2] Our use of the pronoun "he" is strictly for convenience' sake; any other construction would make it very awkward to describe individual roles in the operating room. We alternate he and she as generics.

[3] Neurophysiologists usually have Ph.D.'s not M.D.'s, though some have an M.D. degree.

emphasis on the lack of demonstrated utility of talking heads systems to date. We will describe how live video coordinates tasks within the OR, provides critical educational opportunities, and is used for remote monitoring by neurophysiologists. We discuss the extensions to both live and recorded video which will be useful for research, training, diagnostic, legal, and archival purposes across a broad range of applications that potentially go far beyond the medical domain. In particular, the need to integrate and synchronize video images with other time-based data sources will be critical.

Methodology

We conducted an ethnographic study comprised of observations in the OR; audio-taped, semi-structured interviews; informal interaction (such as going to lunch with informants[4] and casual conversation in hallways, offices, etc.); and "shadowing." The shadowing technique involved following around a single individual for several days to track and record his or her activity in as much detail as possible. We used this technique with the neurophysiologists to study their use of the remote video. We had originally hoped to quantify this information in terms of times-per-task, but because of the complexities of hospital life we would have needed at least 3-6 months of shadowing to iron out anomalies and make statistically valid statements. The shadowing was nevertheless very informative as we learned a great deal about the daily activities of neurophysiologists, and had many opportunities for informal conversation.

The fieldwork team included six investigators – three psychologists, two anthropologists, and one computer scientist. A total of 14 person-weeks of fieldwork was conducted. One investigator was in the field for five weeks and one for three weeks (the anthropologists). During these weeks the observations and some shadowing were done, as well as many of the interviews. The other investigators contributed interviews and shadowing. Over 500 pages of transcripts resulted from interviews with about 35 informants.

The operating room

It is necessary to provide some background on work flow and work roles in the operating room to be able to make sense of the discussion of the use of the video in the next section of the paper. Our observations were conducted in the operating room during a series of brain and spine surgeries. In some cases we observed complete surgeries, and in others we spent a period of hours in the OR (neurosurgeries can last from about 5 to 24 hours).

At the beginning of an operation the patient is tranquilized, anesthetized and connected to a variety of monitors and drips. The attending anesthesiologist plans the general course of the

anesthesia to be used for the operation, and is usually present during the "prep" period. The attending anesthesiologist works with the nurse-anesthetist and/or resident anesthesiologist to administer the anesthesia and insert the appropriate intravenous lines for blood, and a catheter for urine. After the initial set-up, the attending anesthesiologist generally leaves the OR to attend to another operation or to take care of other tasks. The resident and/or nurse-anesthetist then monitor the patient's basic physiological functions: heart rate, blood gases, blood pressure, breathing, urine concentration, etc. The attending anesthesiologist returns to the OR when necessary. He can be reached by phone via his pager, and he makes "check-in" visits to see how things are going.

The beginning of the operation is also the time when the patient, after being anesthetized, is connected to the electrodes that will be used to monitor muscle and nerve activity. Neurophysiological monitoring is a relatively recent innovation in neurosurgery which reduces morbidity by constantly tracking and providing feedback on central nervous system activity to see that it is maintained within acceptable parameters. During neurosurgery, there is a high risk of damage due to the surgery itself; for example, cutting, stretching or compressing a nerve, or cutting off the blood supply to parts of the brain. Neurophysiological monitoring helps prevent such untoward events.

The neurophysiologist and neurotechnician apply the electrodes which provide "evoked potential" data. Throughout the course of the operation the patient is given electrical stimulation (electrical potential for activity is actually evoked by stimulation) to make sure that muscles and nerves are responding appropriately, and are not being damaged by the surgery. The neurophysiologist supervises the neurotechnician and all on-going cases, and is ultimately responsible for the interpretation of the neurophysiological data. The neurotechnician does the more routine monitoring. She sits in front of a computer screen viewing data from a networked computer system that processes the neurophysiological data, showing it as plotted line graphs.[5]

The neurophysiological data can also be viewed in other locations outside the OR because the graphs can be displayed on remote nodes on the networked computer system. The system allows neurophysiologists to monitor operations remotely from many nodes: their offices, other operating rooms, or conference rooms where the system is installed. The system can display all of the neurophysiological data for any operating room where the system is connected. A neurophysiologist, when on call, thus usually spends a part of the day in the various ORs and a part of the day in his office, monitoring the evoked potentials via the computer displays. Neurophysiologists typically monitor as many as six operations concurrently (they have a back up person assigned to help in case of overload). When not in the OR, they communicate with the neurotechnician in the OR via telephone.

After the prepping of the patient, the neurophysiologist, like the attending anesthesiologist, may leave the OR to go to other operations that he is monitoring. Or he may go back to his office

---

[4]In ethnographic studies, participants are called "informants" in the sense that they are to *inform* the investigator, rather than that the investigator is to *subject* participants to an experiment (as in psychology), in which case they are subjects. (The American Psychological Association has very recently recommended the use of the word "participant" in lieu of subject.) The essential notion is that the investigator is ignorant of the understandings possessed by the informant, but wishes to learn as much as possible through interaction and observation.

[5]For more information on this system, please contact the first author.

to monitor the operation remotely. If during the course of the operation, the neurotechnician suspects a problem, she reports it to the surgeon, and she may also telephone the neurophysiologist if he is not in the OR at the time. The neurophysiologist then returns to the OR to evaluate the data and possibly communicate with other members of the surgical team such as the attending neurosurgeon or anesthesiologist.

After the prep, the patient is "opened" – that is, the incision made – by the resident or neurosurgical fellow. The resident or fellow then continues to cut and drill until he is down to the point in the brain or spine where the most delicate surgery is required; for example, the brain tissue that must be "picked through" to reach a tumor, aneurysm or blood vessel compressing a nerve. At this point the attending neurosurgeon arrives in the OR to take over. Often the procedures used by the neurosurgeon are "micro-procedures," i.e. those requiring the use of the microscope. The resident or fellow neurosurgeon watches the operation through a second (2D) lens on the microscope, while the attending neurosurgeon views the surgical field through the main stereoscopic lens. When the microscope is being used, the video is on as well, so those in the OR can watch the surgery on the TV monitor. The audio portion of the system is on as soon as the microscope is turned on, typically at the beginning of the operation, long before the microscope is needed. A recent innovation is that some neurophysiologists have a cable TV link in their offices so that they can access video and audio broadcast from the OR. This enables them to see the microscope video and hear much of what is said and done in the OR. The operation may or may not be recorded, according to the discretion of the attending neurosurgeon.

Throughout the surgery the scrub nurse hands the surgeon the instruments and supplies that he requests. The circulating nurse makes sure that the scrub nurse has everything she needs; the circulating nurse is a bridge between the sterile operating area and non-sterile areas of the OR. At the hospital we studied, scrub nurses and circulating nurses are cross-trained, so each can do the other's job.

When the attending neurosurgeon has finished his work, the patient is "closed" – that is, the incision is repaired – by the resident or fellow. The patient is revived from the anesthesia in the OR, and asked to wiggle his toes and say something. He is then wheeled to recovery.

In addition to the visual displays used to monitor physiology and neurophysiology function, some of the equipment provides (intentionally or not) auditory cues to the progress of the operation or the patient's state. For example, the suction device tells everyone in the OR how much blood is being suctioned; a lot of blood might indicate a problem. The audio broadcast to remote locations clearly transmits the sounds of much of the OR equipment.

Findings

Video is used in the neurosurgical setting to *coordinate* and *educate*. In this section we examine how the live video supports task coordination and education within the OR. We also report preliminary findings on the use of remote video and audio in the offices of neurophysiologists.

Task coordination in the operating room

"Coordination" is distinct from communication and from collaboration. By coordination we mean the smooth enactment of actions requiring more than one person, or requiring information from another's actions. Collaboration, by contrast, is at a higher level of abstraction than an action, and involves shared goals and the enactment of a web of actions that allows goals to be fulfilled. Communication refers to the transmission of information. We do not have space here to fully explore these concepts, but they are delimited in activity theory (see [13] for an overview of activity theory and a bibliography).

The live video is used in the OR to coordinate activity during the most critical part of the surgery when the neurosurgeon is working deep in the brain or spine on very small structures that he sees only by looking through the microscope. In a sense, even though OR personnel are co-located, the video provides "remote" access; the surgical field is invisible, without an intervening technology, to all but the surgeons. The video is used by the scrub nurse, anesthesiologist, nurse-anesthetist, circulating nurse, neurophysiologist, and neurotechnician.

The most important function of the live video in the OR is to allow the scrub nurse to anticipate which instruments and supplies the surgeon will need. As one scrub nurse said, the video is "the only indication we have of what's going on in the head." The circulating nurse positions the monitor so that the scrub nurse has an unimpeded view.

During the critical parts of the surgery, events move very quickly, and the surgeon must be able to work steadily and without interruption. He changes instruments as often as every few seconds, and he needs to work in tight coordination with the scrub nurse who is selecting an instrument from over one hundred instruments arrayed on the sterile table near the operating table. The scrub nurse may also need to hand the surgeon one of hundreds of types of supplies (sutures, sponges, teflon pads, etc.) brought to her by the circulating nurse. The work of a neurosurgical operation is extremely detailed and fast-paced, and the better idea the scrub nurse has of the surgeon's needs, the more smoothly the operation proceeds. Even with the video, the surgeon calls out the instrument or supply he needs next, but the ability of the nurse to anticipate what the neurosurgeon will want is considered very important by OR personnel. One neurosurgeon used a sports metaphor to explain how the video supports neurosurgeon-scrub nurse coordination:

Neurosurgeon: ... an operation is like team work, [for example], ice hockey – the center brings the puck around, and the forward goes to the appropriate position, and the puck is coming in and he hits it. ...Surgeon and scrub nurse ... – it's mutual team work ...So a good scrub nurse looks at the video and knows what's coming next – instrument in and out, instrument giving and taking. It's all team work, [like] sports activity. So if you don't have the video, there's no way to do so [i.e. coordinate activity quickly]. ...So it's uniform, harmonious work.

As she watches the video, the scrub nurse is tracking the course of the operation and looking for unusual events to which she must respond with the correct instrument or supply. For example, she may know that the surgeon is approaching a time in the operation when a clip will be needed. Or she may see the surgeon nick some tissue, in which case a cautery device will likely be called for to repair the nick.

The scrub nurse's effective use of the video depends on her own knowledge and understanding of what she is seeing; the presence of the video image is not a guarantee that she will be able to anticipate the surgeon's needs and respond quickly. There is an interaction between her level of expertise and understanding, and the presence of the video in the environment. As one neurosurgeon explained:

Neurosurgeon: . . . Some scrub nurses are excellent when they look at the video, they know what's next and they are very good. But other scrub nurses are not at that level yet, so [I] have to tell her what I need and even if she's looking, [she] is not at level yet, so it is more time consuming.

Because the scrub nurse is listening to the surgeon, selecting instruments and supplies and handing them to the surgeon, her use of the video involves very quick glances at the monitor to see what is happening. All the more reason she must instantly understand what she is seeing.

In contrast to the scrub nurse's quick glances at the monitor, the others in the OR who watch the video may watch it intently for long stretches of time. Their use of the video helps them keep track of the progress of the surgery, but generally they do not rely on the video for split-second reactions as does the scrub nurse. Anesthesiologists, nurse-anesthetists, circulating nurses, and neurotechnicians watch the video in part to remain attentive to the surgery, to maintain interest and concentration at times when they may have very little to do. For example:

Interviewer: . . . What does [the video] tell you about what you have to do?
Anesthesiologist: In the neurosurgical procedure, the microscopic part actually is quite long and boring usually for us because once we get to that part of it, . . . the patient usually is very stable. . . . It's nice to see where they are, how much longer are they going to be. Is he [the surgeon] still dissecting or is he [finishing] up? I don't have to ask the surgeon that.

Many anesthesiologists, nurse-anesthetists, circulating nurses, and neurotechnicians commented that watching the video was "interesting" and that it was much better than just sitting there with nothing to do. The video thus alleviates boredom and provides a focal point of attention that helps maintain shared awareness of the work being done by the surgeon.

This is critical because events can change very quickly during an operation. Suddenly what is seen on the video monitor can dictate that someone take action or that a new interpretation of an event applies. OR personnel look for a variety of events such as the placement of a retractor or clip, where the surgeon is drilling, if there is bleeding, how close to a tumor the surgeon is. For example, a nurse-anesthetist explained that anesthetic

requirements vary depending on the surgeon's actions:

Nurse-anesthetist: . . . The anesthetic requirements [for] drilling through bone are different from the anesthetic requirements when they are working inside the head, where there are not pain fibers.

In this example, the actions of anesthesia personnel must be coordinated with those of the surgeon, and depend critically on what he is doing at a given moment in the surgical field. The video provides this information to anesthesia personnel.

Neurophysiologists and neurotechnicians interpret the graphs they watch on the computer display in concert with events shown on the video. One neurotechnician explained that they can "decipher the responses better" when they know what the surgeon is doing; for example, when a retractor is placed, a delayed response may result which should not necessarily be attributed to nerve damage, but may have been caused by the retractor itself. Interpreting the neurophysiological data is difficult because its meaning can be affected by signal noise, the type and amount of anesthesia used, surgical events, and random variation. The video provides an important source of information for making better inferences in a highly interpretive task. Again, the use of the video allows tasks to be coordinated appropriately by supplying neurophysiologists and neurotechnicians with critical information about the neurosurgeon's actions.

Education in the operating room

At a teaching hospital, education is of critical importance. Anesthesiology and neurosurgical residents and fellows, student nurses, and neurophysiologists- and neurotechnicians-in-training observe and/or take part in operations as a critical part of their education. While the neurosurgical resident or fellow uses the second 2D lens on the microscope to view the operation when the attending neurosurgeon is operating, others in the room watch the video. We observed students, residents and fellows training at the hospital watching the video, and also visiting students, residents and fellows from other hospitals. On several occasions they entered the OR, parked themselves in front of the video monitor and watched for the duration of the micro-procedures (which may go on for several hours).

Because many of the operations performed at the hospital we studied are in the neurosurgical vanguard, the OR accommodates neurosurgeons, anesthesiologists and neurophysiologists, many of them eminent in their own specialties, from other institutions around the world who come to learn about the new procedures. One of their main activities in the OR is to watch the video.

The use of remote video and audio to monitor operations

Much of the time the physical presence of the attending neurosurgeon or neurophysiologist is not needed in the OR, and an extension to the networked computer system being tested is the use of multimedia (audio and video) to enhance the remote monitoring of operations (now supported by the plotted line graphs). Only a few such multimedia links are functional in the current system (for neurophysiologists), so our findings about their use are preliminary at this time. The idea behind the remote audio and video is that neurophysiologists and neurosurgeons can make better use of their time in their offices monitoring multiple operations, or working on other tasks such as research, taking calls from patients, or attending meetings. They will also be able to remotely monitor operations in other ORs from the OR they happen to be in at a given time. Using the remote monitoring, neurophysiologists and neurosurgeons should be able to simultaneously monitor a larger number of operations, spreading scarce expertise over a greater area and making more efficient use of their time.

What kinds of information do the video and audio provide to neurophysiologists? The remote video provides the kind of information provided by the video within the OR, as described above. Neurophysiologists can interpret the graphic data more easily with the addition of the video information, anticipate what will happen next in the surgery, and generally keep track of what is going on in the surgery at a particular moment. For example, one neurophysiologist explained:

Neurophysiologist: [One time I was watching the remote video and] I could see that the surgeon was in trouble, that he was having a problem, like there was a big bleed, for instance. Then I would go to the operating room.

The remote audio provides additional information from two sources: (1) what is being said in the OR, (2) the overall atmosphere in the OR. Together, the audio and video provide a much more complete picture of OR activity than the plotted line graphs alone:

Neurophysiologist: When you look at the computer data by itself [from a remote location], it seems to be one dimensional. When you add the rest of it [audio and video], you get a very rich picture of what's going on [in the OR].

The audio information is very important in the remote situation. The neurosurgeon often explains what he is doing or discusses his anticipated actions with the other neurosurgeon(s). Anesthesia personnel discuss the patient's physiological function. This information is useful to the neurophysiologist: the progress of and plans for the operation revealed by the comments of the neurosurgeons, and physiological data revealed by the comments of the anesthesia team, help him to interpret the neurophysiological data he is looking at, and to anticipate what will happen next.

In many cases, the neurophysiologist actually has better access to what is being said when he is in a remote location than when he is in the OR. Within the OR, it is sometimes difficult to hear clearly some of what is being said because of the noise of equipment and random conversations. There may even be a radio playing. Listening to the audio in a remote location, by contrast, one gets a clear transmission of what the neurosurgeons and the anesthesia personnel are saying, as they are positioned closest to the microscope (on which the microphone is mounted). One neurophysiologist explained:

Neurophysiologist: In fact, the audio is better over the network than it is in the operating room because you can't hear what the surgeons

are saying in the operating room so . . . if you don't know the case, you kind of guess what they're doing. With the audio, you know exactly what they are doing. . . . Because they talk to each other about the steps they are going to take. So you can really anticipate what potentially might happen.

This is an example of "beyond being there" [8] where at least one aspect of being remote is preferable to being co-located.

The audio also allows the remotely located neurophysiologist to hear what the neurotechnician is telling the surgeon, and how the surgeon responds to that information. The neurophysiologist can see for himself what the neurotechnician sees on the graphs, but the response of the neurosurgeon is very important – does he reply that he's not doing anything that might be causing a problem, that he doesn't understand the response, that he will change an action he is taking, or say nothing? Or, the neurophysiologist may not agree with what he hears the neurotechnician tell the surgeon:

Neurophysiologist: In that case, I heard the technician say something to the surgeon that I didn't agree with . . . [He] said there was a change in the response. There wasn't.
Interviewer: . . . So what did you do, you called?
Neurophysiologist: Called right away . . . Told the surgeon there was no change.

Here the audio information directly influences the neurophysiologist's behavior: he telephones the OR to provide a different interpretation of the neurophysiological data than that given by the neurotechnician.

Other audio information provides an overall impression of the atmosphere in the OR. The surgeon's voice may sound nervous, or there may be a dead silence indicating a tense moment in the operation. As one neurophysiologist said:

Neurophysiologist: The microphone is very close to the surgeon so I can really get a good feeling for whether he feels like the case is going well or not. . . . you can hear it from his voice. You can hear how much activity is in the room, whether the people are scrambling.

Again, this information influences the neurophysiologist's behavior, in this case his decision as to whether to go to the OR from his office:

Neurophysiologist: Well, if people are agitating, there's a lot going on. I probably would have a much lower threshold for going to the room because I'm alerted then that there's something going on in the room, and that's maybe an opportunity for me to make a significant contribution.

Our preliminary findings indicate that the information from the remote multimedia sources concerning the course of the surgery, the surgeon's observed and anticipated actions, the content of key comments made by personnel such as the neurotechnician, and the overall atmosphere in the OR allow the remotely located neurophysiologist to perform his job more efficiently and effectively. He can better plan and coordinate his visits to the OR because he has richer information with which to decide when he needs to visit a particular OR, or whether he wants to place a telephone call. If he does need to go to the OR, he arrives with better information about the status of the operation. If the neurophysiologist is communicating with the neurotechnician via the telephone, again he has a better idea of what is happening in the operation if he has the video and audio data in addition to the graphs of neurophysiological function.

The use of remote multimedia facilities does not eliminate the need for neurophysiologists to be physically present in the OR for at least part of the operation. Rather, it re-distributes their allocation of time across ORs, their offices and other locations in the hospital such as conference rooms. The use of multimedia appears to give neurophysiologists more flexibility to move about the hospital on an as-needed basis, rather than to stay tied exclusively to a small number of ORs.

Discussion

We were struck by the extent to which the use of video-as-data in the operating room and in remote locations serves a number of highly varied functions. The overall goal of the video is to provide a window into the unseeable world of the surgical field, but the uses to which the surgical information is put, and the way the information is gathered, vary greatly depending on the specific tasks associated with the differing roles within the operating room or remote offices. As we have seen, the video image can coordinate fast-paced exchanges of instruments and supplies between neurosurgeon and scrub nurse; it can serve as a means of maintaining attention and focus over long stretches of time during which some OR personnel are relatively inactive; it helps OR personnel to choose the correct action or interpretation depending on the event portrayed in the video; it educates a variety of medical personnel; and the video plus audio may allow neurophysiologists and neurosurgeons to decide when their presence is needed in the OR from a remote location. The use of video in neurosurgery shows the utility of one well-chosen artifact, and the many activities it permits and coordinates. It demonstrates the utility of video-as-data, in contrast to telepresence video.

Looking more closely, we see that the use of video in the neurosurgical context is quite different than some of our standard notions of what it means to support collaborative work; rather than facilitating direct interpersonal communication (as many CSCW systems are intended to do), in many crucial instances, the video permits individuals to work *independently*, actually obviating or reducing the need for interpersonal communication. The video supplies enough information so that the need for interpersonal communication is reduced or eliminated, and individuals can figure out what they need to know based on the video itself, circumventing the need to talk to or gesture at someone. Thus we may find that in settings where video is data, the provision of visual information at key moments provides a different channel of communication than that which would be provided through verbal, gestural or written communication. Rather than facilitating collaboration through interpersonal interaction, the video itself informs OR personnel of the collaboration – in the sense of tasks that need to be performed to advance the work – that is needed. Collaboration and coordination are enabled as each member of the neurosurgery team interprets the visual information, and proceeds to do his

or her job based upon an interpretation of that information. The video data, plus individual knowledge and understanding, combine to produce an interpretation that leads to the desired collaboration, with little or no interpersonal interaction.

In other cases, the content of the video image becomes the basis for discussion and interaction, another aspect of its use as a shared workspace. For example, we observed a nurse-anesthetist in the OR watching the video with a student nurse-anesthetist and describing to her the progress of the operation. Indeed, we ourselves profited from explanations in which the video was a key point of reference as OR personnel educated us about many aspects of neurosurgery. Visitors, residents, fellows, etc. also discuss what is being shown on the video monitor.

Our findings about the importance of the on-going use of video-as-data in a real work setting with demanding requirements (as opposed to brief experiments or testing within research labs) should encourage us to pursue our understanding of how video-as-data can be extended and used in other work settings. Within medicine, video is used in many kinds of surgery including orthopedic surgery and general surgery that employs micro-procedures. Non-medical applications of video-as-data could include monitoring and diagnostic tasks in complex mechanical or electrical systems such as the Space Station, power plants, or automated factories; and training for many aspects of using, designing, monitoring and repairing such systems. Wang, a computer and instrument manufacturer, uses video to train people in the use of their equipment [4], and it is easy to imagine many training applications for video-as-data. Real estate agents might show properties remotely, and attorneys are making increasing use of video data in courtroom presentations. There is a large number of potential applications for video-as-data.

Video-as-data may change our sense of what it means to be "remote" or "co-located." In the OR, even though people are co-located, the surgical field is remote, because it is invisible to anyone not looking directly through the microscope. The surgical field is accessible only through the video to most OR personnel. Thus it is not necessarily the location of *people* that is important in the video-as-data situation, but rather of the *workspace*. Aural information in the OR, on the other hand, is not remote, so we have a situation in which the aural and visual do not share the same valence on the dimension of co-location. One can imagine other such situations; for example the repair of a delicate piece of machinery with many small parts might be a situation in which a view of the workspace is remote, while aural information is not. For neurosurgery, we also have a "beyond being there" situation in which the aural information may be richer in the remote location, via broadcast audio, as we described for the remote audio used by the neurophysiologists.

Future Directions

In this paper, we have concentrated on the use of live video, but many important extensions to video-as-data lie in recorded video.

In the medical application that we studied, recorded video is already used for classroom teaching and to review events in past operations. Integration of video with other computerized time-based data is the next step. Uniform storage, access, and presentation methods for data will be needed. Means of visualizing complex relationships between datasets of varying types will provided added value. Informants in the study who have research interests underscored the need for future tools that will allow for the synchronization of video with other data sources, in particular the instrument data relevant to a particular specialty. Anesthesiologists, for example, would want to see the video synchronized with the physiological data they monitor such as blood pressure, blood gases, heart rate, pulse, temperature. They might want to do this during an operation, with video and instrument data they had just recorded. Neurophysiologists want to see video synchronized with the many measures of nerve and muscle response that they monitor. In general, users want to be able to "scroll through" a video/instrument dataset, finding a particular video or instrument event or time, so that they can view all related data for the event or time.

Integration of video-as-data with other data sources would also be useful in many applications for training, legal and archival purposes. Potential users of such video technology will want to be able to edit, browse, search, annotate, overlay, highlight, and display video data.

Whether such extensions to video-as-data will be cost-effective remains to be seen; video is an expensive technology. Current applications of video-as-data such as the present study, the power plant applications described by Tani et al. [16], and Kuzuoka's work [10] suggest that there is tremendous potential for video to enhance collaborative work. Future research should go beyond talking heads to recognize the value of video-as-data, and should be concerned with offering good video utility in a cost-effective manner.

Acknowledgments: We would like to thank Erik Geelhoed and Bob Simon for their help with data collection. Steve Gale's previous work on the project was of great value. Within HP, for support and encouragement, we acknowledge Dan Fishman, Mark Halloran, Nancy Kendzierski, John Limb, Jim Miller, Ian Page, Frank Prince, Dick Schulze and Bill Sharpe. Robin Jeffries, Jim Miller, Vicki O'Day, Andreas Paepcke and Bill Williams gave insightful comments on earlier drafts. At the hospital we thank the secretaries who helped us to track down and schedule interviews with peripatetic medical personnel. Our many informants in the hospital generously allowed us to follow them around, ask endless questions, and watch them for hours on end at their jobs. For their good cheer and thoughtful answers to our questions, we offer grateful thanks.

References

[1] Buxton, W. Telepresence: Integrating shared task and shared person spaces. *Proceedings of Graphics Interface'92* (Vancouver, 11-15 May, 1992), 123-129.

[2] Chapanis, A. Interactive human communication. *Scientific American*, 232 (1975), 36-42.

[3] Dourish, P., and Bly, S. Portholes: Supporting awareness in a distributed work group. *Proceedings CHI'92.* (Monterey, 3-7 May, 1992), 541-547.

[4] Egido, C. Teleconferencing as a technology to support cooperative work. In *Intellectual Teamwork.* J. Galegher, R. Kraut, C. Egido, Eds. Lawrence Erlbaum, Hillsdale, NJ, 1990, 351-371.

[5] Gale, S. Adding audio and video to an office environment. *Studies in Computer Supported Cooperative Work*: Theory, Practice and Design. J. Bowers and S. Benford, Eds. North-Holland: Amsterdam, 1991, 49-62.

[6] Fish, R., Kraut, R., Root, R., and Rice, R. Evaluating video as technology for informal communication. *Proceedings CHI'92.* (Monterey, 3-7 May, 1992), 37-48.

[7] Heath, C., and Luff, P. Disembodied conduct: Communication through video in a multi-media office environment. *Proceedings CHI'91.* (New Orleans, 27 April-2 May, 1991), 99-103.

[8] Hollan, J., and Stornetta, S. Beyond being there. *Proceedings CHI'92.* (Monterey, 3-7 May, 1992), 119-125.

[9] Ishii, H., and Kobayashi, M. ClearBoard: A seamless medium for shared drawing and conversation with eye contact. *Proceedings CHI'92.* (Monterey, 3-7 May, 1992), 525-532.

[10] Kuzuoka, H. Spatial workspace collaboration: A Shared-View video support system for a remote collaboration capability. *Proceedings CHI'92.* (Monterey, 3-7 May, 1992), 533-540.

[11] Mantei, M., Baecker, R., Sellen, A. Buxton, W., Milligan, T., and Wellman, B. Experiences in the use of a media space. *Proceedings CHI'91.* (New Orleans, 27 April-2 May, 1991), 203-215.

[12] Milgram, P., Drascic, D., and Grodski, J. A virtual stereoscopic pointer for a real three dimensional video world. *Proceedings Interact'90.* (Cambridge, UK, 27-31 August, 1990), 695-700.

[13] Nardi, B. Studying context: A comparison of activity theory, situated action models, and distributed cognition. In *Proceedings, St. Petersburg Human Computer Interaction Workshop.* (St. Petersburg, Russia. 4-8 August, 1992), 352-359.

[14] Sellen, A. Speech patterns in video-mediated conversations. *Proceedings CHI'92.* (Monterey, 3-7 May, 1992), 49-59.

[15] Short, J., Williams, E., and Christie, B. *The Social Psychology of Telecommunications.* John Wiley & Sons: London, 1976.

[16] Tani, M., Yamaashi, K., Tanikoshi, K. Futakawa, M., and Tanifuji, S. Object-oriented video: Interaction with real-world objects through live video. *Proceedings CHI'92.* (Monterey, 3-7 May, 1992), 593-598.

ONE IS NOT ENOUGH:
MULTIPLE VIEWS IN A MEDIA SPACE

William Gaver [1,4], *Abigail Sellen* [1,2], *Christian Heath* [1,3], *Paul Luff* [1,3]

[1] Rank Xerox Cambridge EuroPARC
61 Regent Street, Cambridge CB2 1AB, UK
<surname>@europarc.xerox.com

[3] Department of Sociology
University of Surrey, Guildford GU2 5XH, UK

[2] MRC Applied Psychology Unit
15 Chaucer Road, Cambridge CB2 2EF, UK

[4] Industrieel Ontwerpen
Technische Universiteit Delft
Jaffalaan 9, 2628 BX Delft, Nederland

ABSTRACT

Media spaces support collaboration, but the limited access they provide to remote colleagues' activities can undermine their utility. To address this limitation, we built an experimental system in which four switchable cameras were deployed in each of two remote offices, and observed participants using the system to collaborate on two tasks. The new views allowed increased access to task-related artifacts; indeed, users preferred these views to more typical "face-to-face" ones. However, problems of establishing a joint frame of reference were exacerbated by the additional complexity, leading us to speculate about more effective ways to expand access to remote sites.

KEYWORDS

cscw, social interaction, media spaces, video

INTRODUCTION

Over the last few years, several laboratories have built experimental *media spaces*, computer-controlled networks of audio and video equipment, in order to explore issues concerning the support of collaboration among distributed colleagues [4, 6, 12, 18]. Media spaces provide more than basic video conferencing and picture-phones, creating a "space" for interaction that exists alongside the everyday physical environment. They are intended to support a wide range of shared work activities, from focused collaboration to a more general awareness of events in the workplace [6].

Despite the promise of these systems, our experience suggests that their main value is in providing casual awareness of remote colleagues or as a prelude to more focused, co-present communication [see also 4]. Current systems *can* support focused collaboration, but it seems that even experienced users prefer to be physically co-present for a variety of focused collaborative tasks.

Experimental studies, on the other hand, tend to suggest that allowing people to see one another does not add significantly to the process of collaboration. Comparisons among co-present, video plus audio, and audio only interactions suggest that access to visual information has no significant effect on the dynamics of conversation [14, 15]. Visual access also tends not to affect the outcome of intellectual, decision-making, and creative tasks. Tasks that rely on social cues, in contrast, such as situations of conflict, bargaining and negotiation do tend to be affected by the presence or absence of the visual communication channel [1, 13, 16].

Does this mean that media spaces might support general awareness, but are no better than telephones for focused collaboration? In this paper, we suggest that the problem is not inherent to the medium, but rather to the beliefs about collaboration that guide the design of current media spaces. In particular, we challenge the assumption that a face-to-face, head and shoulders view is most important for collaboration – an assumption made both in most media spaces and in most experiments assessing the effects of video [though see, e.g., 19]. We describe a study in which we evaluated the possibility of overcoming the limitations of media spaces by providing multiple views on a collaborative task. Using these data, we discuss the strengths and weaknesses of the multiple camera strategy and speculate about more effective ways to offer increased access to remote sites.

FACE TO FACE VIEWS ARE NOT ENOUGH

Face-to-face interaction is only one of many shared activities undertaken by co-present collaborators, yet most media spaces are configured to support little else. For instance, Figure 1 shows a typical media space node: a video monitor sits on the desk, with a camera on top of it and a microphone and speakers somewhere nearby. This sort of arrangement allows local users to see their colleagues, but prevents access to many other aspects of the remote environment, such as their documents, their workstations, and other nearby objects. Although cameras may be moved, in practice they seldom are, because of the inconvenience of repositioning cables, the jerky images such movement produces, and the difficulty of aiming the camera at the desired location.

Figure 1: A typical media space node

Observational studies of naturally-occurring collaboration suggest that many of the subtle interactions involved in successful shared work are disrupted by the limitations of these kinds of views. Workers in control rooms and architectural practices, for instance, perform much of their work without explicit face-to-face communication [11]. Instead they modify their speech and gestures to provide and acknowledge information, revealing considerable peripheral sensitivity to their colleagues' activities. The limited views provided by typical media spaces disrupt these ways of working [9]. Collaborators in media spaces are often frustrated by their inability to show each other artifacts such as paper or screen-based documents [see also 4]. Moreover, many of the actions performed via nonverbal behaviour seem to lose their interactional significance when conducted through a media space. In sum, current media spaces fail to support peripheral monitoring and involvement in collaborative tasks.

These observations are complemented by an analysis of the affordances of media spaces – the properties of the environment that have implications for perception and interaction [5, 7]. Perhaps the most important limitation of the audio-video medium, according to this analysis, is that cameras are stationary or only moved locally in most media spaces. This restricts the possibility of visually exploring remote spaces, and implies that information must be actively presented to remote colleagues. It also seems to worsen problems associated with the asymmetry of information flow typical of media spaces. For instance, seeing a colleague in a media space does not imply that one can be seen. Prediction is difficult, and people cannot move to compensate for their partners' inaccuracies.

Taken together, experimental, sociological, and ecological studies converge in suggesting significant constraints due to the limited field of view offered by a single fixed camera configured for face-to-face interaction. These constraints go beyond the inability to share access to a relevant artifact. Rather, collaboration depends on the ability to explore perceptually the relevant task environment, maintaining a sensitivity towards one's colleagues in the context of their current activities. This does not imply that face-to-face

views are useless, but it does stress the need to provide more, and more flexible, access to remote sites.

THE MULTIPLE TARGET VIDEO STUDY

As a first attempt to provide more flexible access to remote working environments, we designed an experimental system called Multiple Target Video (MTV) which allowed users to switch among multiple cameras in a remote site. We then observed pairs of collaborators using the system to work on two shared tasks.

The MTV System

Two offices at EuroPARC were equipped with four cameras each as well as two monitors, a microphone, and speakers, and connected with audio and video links (see Figure 2). In each office, the view of the remote office was shown on a colour monitor and selected using a video switch with a rotary control. In addition, whatever the person in the remote office was viewing was shown on a smaller, monochrome "feedback monitor".

We arranged the cameras to provide views based on our understanding of the visual information that co-present individuals use during shared work. One camera in each office was mounted over the main monitor, as it is in typical media spaces, to provide a *face-to-face view*. A second camera was mounted above and to the side of the main work area to give an *in-context view* of people in relation to their workspace and the objects within it (including the two video monitors). The third view was provided using a high-resolution, monochrome camera, giving a *desk view* allowing documentation to be shared.

These views were roughly the same for each office; however, the fourth camera was arranged differently depending on the office. In the *Design Office*, the camera was arranged to support one of the tasks that we gave participants. This task, which will be described below, involved the manipulation of a physically embodied architectural representation (i.e., a dollhouse) located in the office. Thus the fourth camera in the Design Office provided a *dollhouse* view for the remote participant. In the *Remote Office*, a camera was mounted in a corner of the room and a wide-angle lens was used to provide a *birds-eye view* showing most of the room.

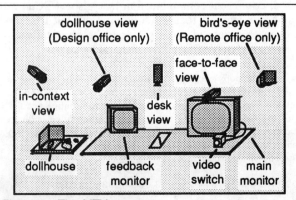

Figure 2. The MTV set-up.

Data Collection

Further connections were made to a third office between the two, allowing the study to be monitored and data to be collected. We used a picture-in-a-picture device to record four video streams simultaneously. The in-context view from each office was recorded to provide an overall impression of the participants' activities and the views that participants were currently using were recorded to observe their switches and the information they had available.

The Study

Six pairs of participants took part in the study: two from EuroPARC, and four from the MRC Applied Psychology Unit subject pool. Members of most pairs had known each other for at least a few months, but one of the pairs had not met before the study. The two pairs recruited from EuroPARC had some experience with media spaces, while the other four had not.

The Room Task

The first task was designed to familiarise the participants with the equipment and with each other. Each participant was asked to draw the layout of their partner's office, including major pieces of furniture and equipment. We explicitly suggested that they help one another, because neither of the offices was entirely visible from the combination of views they had available. Subjects were told that it should take about 10 or 15 minutes to complete the task, and that they would be observed and recorded from the third office.

The Design Task

In the second task, we asked participants to select and arrange furniture in a dollhouse located in the Design Office, to draw the final layout, and to write a list of reasons for their decisions. This task was designed to encourage collaborative work that focused on and around relevant artifacts. One member of each pair was assigned to the Design Office containing the dollhouse and thus could move the dollhouse furniture directly. The other member of the pair was in the Remote Office, and had to rely on their partner to rearrange the furniture.

Participants were given conflicting hidden agendas for the task. One was assigned the role of a designer from the Cheep 'n' Tasteless Vacation Rental Co., and told to imagine that he or she would receive a substantial bribe if all the furniture were used. The second participant, in contrast, was given the role of a designer from the award-winning Integrity Design Company and told to arrive at a tasteful solution that did not necessarily use all the furniture. In addition, Cheep 'n' Tasteless designers were told to finish the design quickly because they were paid for the job, while Integrity designers were told not to hurry, both to make sure that the design was optimal and because they were paid by the hour. Participants were not explicitly told that they would be rivals, but most seemed aware that some sort of conflict had been arranged. They usually took about 45 minutes to complete the task, but we stopped them if they seemed unable to reach a solution.

The aim of these tasks was two-fold. First, previous studies have largely neglected video-mediated collaboration centered around objects [though see 8]. We wanted to evaluate the MTV system's ability to support such collaboration, particularly when the objects were physically available to only one partner. Second, previous empirical results [1, 13, 16] have suggested that face-to-face interaction is important for negotiating conflict. We expected the focus on objects to reduce face-to-face interaction, but wanted to see if people would use face-to-face connections more in the competitive Design Task than in the cooperative Room Task.

RESULTS AND DISCUSSION

All the participants were able to work together successfully on the tasks, and the multiple cameras clearly supported them in doing so. Both tasks were designed to be highly visual in nature, so it is difficult to imagine that participants could have pursued them using face-to-face or audio connections alone. MTV was more complex than typical face-to-face media spaces, but we found that participants quickly developed a range of strategies for using the views to pursue the tasks.

Viewing patterns are captured by strip charts such as the one shown in Figure 3, which shows the switching behaviour of a representative pair of participants over an entire session. The charts show the five possible views that participants might have (face-to-face, in context, desk, birds-eye, and doll house) vertically, and record the time each participant spent in a view along the horizontal axis. This representation provides a general impression of participants' switching behaviour. For instance, this pair tended to switch more in the Room Task than they did in the Design Task, a pattern we found for all participants. In addition, relatively long periods using one view were punctuated by short bursts of switching among the others.

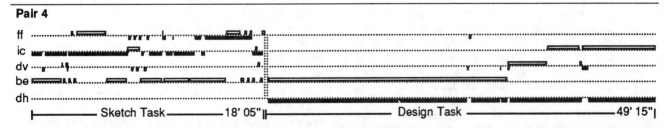

Figure 3. Switching data from an entire session. Hollow strips show the view from the Design Office; solid strips that from the Remote Office. Only the Design Office had the birds-eye view; the Remote office had the dollhouse view.

Table 1: Percentage of Time in Each View

task	office	face/face	con-text	desk view	birds eye	doll-house
room	design	6	12	32	50	–
	remote	14	58	27	–	1
design	design	12	24	36	28	–
	remote	10	12	7	–	71
TOTAL		11	23	24	17	25

As can be seen from Figure 3, all the cameras were used by the participants. Table 1 shows the percentage of times spent in each view averaged over all participants. Random viewing would yield percentages of about 25%. Instead, clear patterns of use become evident from these data.

Face-to-Face Views Were Rarely Used

One of the most striking results is that participants rarely used the face-to-face views (only 11% of the total time). Even more rarely were they truly "face-to-face," with both members simultaneously using the face-to-face views (about 2%). Instead, the switching times and video data suggest that participants preferred to maintain views which showed objects more directly relevant for the tasks.

The only substantial period of shared face-to-face viewing came about when one pair of participants engaged in lengthy negotiations near the end of the Design Task. Most participants maintained a shared focus on relevant artifacts (i.e., the dollhouse or drawing) even while engaged in intense discussions. In fact, several stated that they avoided using the face-to-face views, particularly when they were trying to convince their partner of some action.

These data suggest that, given the choice between face-to-face views and views that give access to shared work objects, people will choose the latter. This is not due merely to the conflict we introduced in the Design Task; the face-to-face views were seldom used in either task. It also did not appear to be affected by the familiarity of partners; people who had never met before behaved in much the same way as those who knew each other well. Instead, it seems to be because both tasks were designed to require access to the remote environment and objects within it, as suggested by observations of real-world collaboration [11].

The assumption inherent in the design of many current media spaces that face-to-face views are the most valuable is seriously challenged by these data. This is not to suggest that face-to-face views are useless. We saw numerous occasions in which participants would make very short connections to their partners' face-to-face view, seemingly to assess their engagement and mood. The numerical data here may well under-emphasize the importance of such "glances," but it also highlights the utility of other views.

Use of Views

The video data suggest a variety of ways that participants used the views. For instance, the face-to-face view was used as much to see the office behind the remote partner as to engage in conversation. The in-context and birds-eye views were used to gain access to the remote office for the Room Task, to determine the remote partner's current orientation, and to observe pointing at video images or at the room itself. The desk view was used to offer information to partners about one's local office, to check sketches of the remote one, and to provide detailed views of artifacts such as the dollhouse furniture. Finally, the ability to switch between views provided flexible access to the remote office. For instance, it allowed one participant to track her partner moving around the office pointing out features of interest. In general, each view was not used merely for one predictable purpose; rather, the views were appropriated as resources for pursuing the tasks.

Limitations of MTV

While there were clear benefits of the increased access to remote environments offered by multiple cameras, difficulties with the approach became evident upon analysis of the video data. Understanding the problems of using multiple cameras to extend access to remote sites is valuable in suggesting alternative possibilities for design.

Lost in Space

In the following sections, we describe a representative episode in some detail to illustrate the difficulties participants had while working with the MTV system. This episode occurred as a pair of participants were working on the Room Task. Mary, attempting to draw Sue's office, asks about a detail she cannot see. Sue starts to sketch her own office to show Mary, but has problems making clear which part of the room she is sketching:

Sue: ... No, none of the monitors are going to show you any of it. I tell you what, I'll sketch it for you...

Mary: Oh brilliant. Yeah, great.

Sue: Now behind me, right...

(Mary switches to desk view to see Sue's sketch.)

Sue: If that's the corner of the room... (pointing to part of her sketch) where you're getting the view of me...

(Sue reaches towards her video switch, pauses.)

Sue: Let me just see what... Just switch to the view of me... (Mary switches to birds-eye view.) Right. (Sue points to feedback monitor, which shows Mary's view of her.) Can you see that, the corner where... there's a sort of... (stops pointing at monitor, points up to corner of the room) ...I'm pointing up to the corner now.

Mary: Yeah.

Sue: Right... uh going back along that wall... (reaches for her video switch, withdraws) Now go back to my drawing.

(Mary switches through several views to the desk view)

Mary: Hang on... there you are.

Sue: There we are, right... (drawing on page) There's that... and then the doorway is like this...

Consider how easy it would have been to establish the correspondence between the drawing and the room if the two partners had been co-present. A mere gesture over the document followed by one towards the relevant part of the room would have served. The participants in this episode, in contrast, used a variety of methods to achieve the same goal, facing continual errors and breakdowns of reference. While they managed to recover from these problems, the greater access provided by the MTV system was clearly balanced by its limitations.

Each of the problems that these participants encountered is representative of those facing all the users of this system. In the following sections, we describe each of these difficulties in turn.

The Configuration is Never Right

Sue: No, none of the monitors are going to show you any of it. I tell you what, I'll sketch it for you...

Despite the use of four cameras per office, each adjusted to provide what we felt was a maximally effective view, it became clear on observing participants that the views provided were still not optimal for the tasks we gave them.

Evidence for the inadequacy of views can be found not only in participants' remarks, but in their use of the views as shown in Figure 3 and Table 1. For each task, participants spent a clear majority of time using only one of the four views. In the Room Task, participants tended to use the views that gave them the most access to the remote site – the in-context view for those in the Design Office, and the birds-eye view for those in the Remote Office. In the Design Task, inhabitants of the Remote Office were completely dependent on the views for access to the dollhouse. Not surprisingly, most used the dollhouse view. This view allowed them to monitor the current arrangement of furniture, but it did not allow them to keep track of their remote partner. In fact, one remote participant used the in-context view most during the Design Task, claiming afterwards that she took this strategy so that she could keep track of both her partner and the dollhouse. Inhabitants of the Design Office, in contrast, usually seemed to ignore the video connections, concentrating instead on the dollhouse itself. Some even made use of the limited access their partner had: one participant argued that her partner couldn't judge the arrangement because of the poor view provided by video, while another hid a piece of furniture simply by moving it off camera.

Observations such as these suggest that no configuration of stationary cameras will provide adequate access for all tasks. In the Room Task, participants often compensated for the limited access they had by drawing their own offices for their partners, as Sue does in the example above. This raised further difficulties, however, in establishing the relations between the drawing and the room itself.

Difficulties in Establishing Reference

Sue: Now behind me, right...
(Mary switches to desk view to see Sue's sketch.)
Sue: If that's the corner of the room... (pointing to sketch) ...where you're getting the view of me...

The different views provided by the cameras caused problems in relating different scenes to one another – for instance, in pointing out a feature of the sketched layout and then indicating which part of the room it represented. There were problems in mapping one view to another, and in establishing the correspondence between a representation (e.g., a drawing) and its referent.

Difficulties in establishing reference have been noted before in descriptions of traditional point-to-point media space connections [9]. By increasing the number of cameras, however, we seem to have seriously increased these problems. Not only did participants have to cope with the differences between their view of a remote colleague and their colleague's view of them, but with discontinuities in the views they had of the remote office, differences in their view of a local artifact and that of their partner, and so forth. Strategies for dealing with these problems were further constrained by difficulties in establishing mutual orientation, as discussed below.

Unequal Control Of Orientation

(Sue reaches towards her video switch, pauses.)
Sue: Let me just see what... Just switch to the view of me... (Mary switches to birds-eye view.) Right.

The system also hindered the ability to direct the attention of remote partners, interfering with the establishment of a mutual orientation to relevant objects. In co-present situations, people use gestures, pointing, and so forth to direct their colleagues' attention and negotiate a mutual orientation towards a task. The ability to do this might have helped in establishing the relations among various views, but these tactics were ineffective using the MTV system. Indeed, one-sided control over the views meant that even less subtle tactics failed: participants seemed to want control over their partners' views, with aborted gestures towards their own switches often preceding a verbal request that their partners change views.

Problems involving control over orientation and action arose in other situations as well. For instance, co-present partners can gesture to indicate where marks should go on a document if they don't have a marker. The MTV system made this difficult. We observed several participants try to direct their partners by pointing at a document on their monitor while their partner watched using the in-context view, but this appeared to have limited success. More often participants would resort to verbal directions. For instance, one pair of subjects working on the Room Task had difficulty in establishing shared reference to a drawing:

John: Now this is hard... how do I point at your document? Ann: I know, I also had trouble – I was pointing to the TV screen... which is pretty stupid, because you can't see it.... How about if I move my finger around and then you can tell me when to stop? (Ann moves finger over drawing.) John: Ok, up and to the left... (Ann moves finger accordingly)...

In both of these situations, participants' inability to direct attention flexibly to things both in the local and remote environments meant that they had to resort to explicit verbal control. Though a number of strategies were developed to deal with these problems, all were relatively troublesome.

Video Images as Shared Artifacts

Sue: (points to feedback monitor, which shows Mary's view of her) Can you see that, the corner where... there's a sort of... (stops pointing at monitor, points up to corner of the room) ...I'm pointing up to the corner now.

Because people had unequal access to objects themselves, video images sometimes seemed to serve as shared artifacts to a greater degree even than the local scenes they displayed. In the Room Task, for instance, we observed many occasions in which local participants, trying to describe their own offices to their participants, would point to features on the feedback monitor (which showed the view seen by their remote partner) rather than to the room itself. Similarly, inhabitants of the Design Office frequently checked their feedback monitor to assess the current appearance of the dollhouse while arguing for some arrangement. In these instances, participants appeared to act towards images as objects having greater mutual accessibility than the things they represented.

Treating video images as shared artifacts caused problems, however, when participants assumed that they had access not only to the image, but also to the space around it. Co-present collaborators communicate using gestures and movements within the space around a shared artifact [2], but this was impossible using the MTV system. We repeatedly witnessed participants gesturing and pointing at the screen image of the document as if the space around that document was mutually accessible. These gestures, of course, largely went unnoticed by their partners; even when they were seen using the in-context or birds-eye views their gestures did not move in the space around the artifact, but had to be related to the artifact by their partners. This inequality of access to artifacts compounded the problems of control and reference discussed above.

Switching is Problematic

Sue: ...Now go back to my drawing.
(Mary switches through several views to the desk view.)
Mary: Hang on... there you are.
Sue: There we are, right...

The necessity of switching among views increased the difficulty of establishing the relations among them and negotiating a mutual orientation towards the task. The arbitrary mapping between the rotary switch and the views it provided was difficult to learn, making the results of a given switch effectively unpredictable. Participants seemed to avoid the need to remember this mapping – or indeed the existence of various views – by quickly switching through the views looking for one that was adequate. Though this was usually satisfactory, views sometimes seemed to be forgotten when a scan did not reveal them. Additional experience with the system might alleviate this problem, but only if a stable set of views and settings were used.

More seriously, the restriction to seeing only one view at a time prevented a smooth transition of awareness to objects in different parts of the remote office – participants could not shift easily between the drawing and the remote office, for instance. The limited access participants had to their partners' activities disrupted the ability to negotiate mutual orientation fluidly; instead changes of orientation were often signalled only by a change on the feedback monitor. In general, the constraint implied by switched views contributed to many of the problems that participants faced. For this reason, we plan to replicate this study in the future, replacing the video switch with separate, continuously available monitors for each view.

CONCLUSIONS

In sum, providing multiple cameras allowed participants to collaborate successfully on two tasks involving remote artifacts. Moreover, our data clearly indicated that participants preferred task-centred over face-to-face views. While face-to-face views are undoubtedly useful for some tasks, these results suggest that other views provide a wide range of resources for remote collaborators.

However, our observations of the MTV system in use suggest a number of difficulties in using multiple cameras to provide access to remote sites:

- Configuring cameras to give complete access to a complex space is difficult or impossible.
- Multiple views interfere with establishing a shared frame of reference.
- One-sided control over views and artifacts inhibits negotiations of mutual orientation.
- Unequal access to the space around shared artifacts poses problems of coordination.
- Switching among multiple views accentuates their discontinuities.

Understanding these difficulties is helpful in suggesting new possibilities for extending media spaces. For instance, access to video images could be supported by providing telepointers to users, similar to those found in many shared drawing systems [see 3] but using video overlay technology [e.g., 10]. Participants could be given equal control over views by allowing them to switch views on their own office as well as remote ones. Finally, the incorporation of shared drawing tools might overcome the problems in establishing a shared frame of reference for, and mutual orientation to artifacts. However, we suspect similar difficulties would remain, given that the need to share physically embodied artifacts is likely to remain a feature of shared work.

Many of the difficulties that participants experienced using the MTV system seem to come from the need to switch between multiple, discontinuous views of remote spaces. As an analysis of the affordances of media spaces [5] suggests, the ability to move continuously in remote spaces might help with these problems. Movement allows us to change our focus of attention smoothly from place to place, either on our own initiative or in response to a colleague. This enables us to interactively establish a mutual frame of reference towards objects of interest.

From this perspective, many of the problems in using the MTV system may be ascribed to the fact that it did not allow true movement in remote sites. Techniques that allow continuous camera movement in remote spaces might overcome the limitations we observed in this study. Tracking cameras, for instance, which automatically follow a subject as he or she moves around an area, would allow participants to follow their partners' actions, but at the expense of self-guided exploration. Pan-tilt-zoom units, already used in some video-conferencing systems, would allow self-guided movement – but such systems are often slow and awkward to use. Perhaps most promising are systems that allow intuitive control over remote movement, such as the Delft depth television system [17]. The incorporation of technologies such as these into future versions of media spaces is a promising possibility.

Despite its drawbacks, however, the MTV system clearly represents a first step towards extending the capabilities of media space systems. This is an important goal: If media spaces are to serve as a true alternative space for interaction, we must question basic assumptions about how they are designed and used.

ACKNOWLEDGEMENTS

We thank Wendy Mackay for useful discussions about the design of the system and study reported here. Anne Schlottmann suggested using the dollhouse, and she, Steve Harrison, and Allan MacLean made helpful comments on this paper. Finally, Mike Molloy helped design the MTV system and set it up single-handed. For any errors in this paper, each author cheerfully blames the others.

REFERENCES

1. Argyle, M. and Cook, M. *Gaze and mutual gaze.* London: Cambridge University Press, 1976.

2. Bly, S., and Minneman, S. Commune: A shared drawing surface. *Proceedings of COIS'90*, ACM, New York, 1990, pp. 184 - 192.

3. Dourish, P., and Bellotti, V. Awareness and coordination in shared work spaces. *Proceedings of CSCW'92* (Toronto, 1 - 4 November, 1992).

4. Fish, R., Kraut, R., Root, R., and Rice, R. Evaluating video as a technology for informal communication. *Proceedings of CHI'92* (Monterey, 3 - 7 May, 1992). ACM, New York, pp. 37 - 48.

5. Gaver, W. The affordances of media spaces for collaboration. *Proceedings of CSCW'92* (Toronto, 1 - 4 November, 1992).

6. Gaver, W., Moran, T., MacLean, A., Lövstrand, L., Dourish, P., Carter, K., and Buxton, W. Realizing a video environment: EuroPARC's RAVE system. *Proceedings of CHI'92* (Monterey, California, 3 - 7 May, 1992). ACM, New York, pp. 27 - 35.

7. Gibson, J. J. *The ecological approach to visual perception.* Houghton Mifflin, New York, 1979.

8. Harrison, S., Minneman, S., and Irwin, S. Graspable implication: A study of 3-D objects in remote collaboration. Xerox PARC technical report, 1992.

9. Heath, C., and Luff, P. Media space and communicative asymmetries: Preliminary observations of video mediated interaction. *Human-Computer Interaction*, 7 (1992), pp. 99 - 103.

10. Ishii, H., and Kobayashi, M. ClearBoard: A seamless medium for shared drawing and conversation with eye contact. *Proceedings of CHI'92* (Monterey, California, 3 - 7 May, 1992). ACM, New York, pp. 525 - 540.

11. Luff, P., Heath, C., and Greatbatch, D. Tasks-in-interaction: Paper and screen based documentation in collaborative activity. *Proceedings of CSCW'92* (Toronto, 1 - 4 November, 1992).

12. Mantei, M., Baecker, R., Sellen, A., Buxton, W., Milligan, T., and Wellman, B. Experiences in the use of a media space. *Proceedings of CHI'91* (New Orleans, April 28 - May 2, 1991) ACM, New York, pp. 203 - 208.

13. McGrath, J. *Groups: Interaction and performance*, Englewood Cliffs, NJ: Prentice-Hall, 1984.

14. Sellen, A.. Speech patterns in video-mediated conversations. *Proceedings of CHI'92* (Monterey, California, 3 - 7 May, 1992). ACM, New York, pp. 49 - 59.

15. Sellen, A. Statistical measures of speech in technology-mediated conversations. Technical Report No. EPC-92-125, Rank Xerox EuroPARC, 1992.

16. Short, J., Williams, E., and Christie, B. *The social psychology of telecommunications.* London: Wiley & Sons, 1976,

17. Smets, G. Designing for telepresence: The interdependence of movement and visual perception implemented. *Proceedings of the IFAC Man-Machine Symposium*, 1992.

18. Stults, R. Media space. Xerox PARC technical report, 1986.

19. Weber, K., and Minneman, S. The Office Design Project. *SIGCHI Video Review*, 1988.

How Fluent is Your Interface?
Designing for International Users

Patricia Russo
Human Interface Engineering
SunSoft
Two Elizabeth Drive
Chelmsford, MA 01824, USA
508-442-0212
prusso@east.sun.com

Stephen Boor
Analytical Services
The Boston Company
One Cabot Road
Medford, MA 02155, USA
617-382-9242

ABSTRACT

To successfully build bridges between worlds, user interface designers must increase their awareness of cross-cultural differences, and make changes to the traditional software development process. Creating fluent interfaces for international markets goes beyond translating text and date, time, and number formats. This paper presents and explains a cross-cultural checklist of issues including text, local formats, images, symbols, colors, flow, and product functionality. Suggestions for an effective international product development cycle are provided. The suggested development cycle incorporates international design feedback and usability testing before the initial product is released.

KEYWORDS: User Interface Design, Internationalization, Localization, Cross-Cultural Differences

INTRODUCTION

As computer markets become more international, the CHI community must think about user interfaces in more global terms that include cultural awareness. Today, an increasing number of computer products are being developed for international use. In 1991, five of the six biggest U.S. computer companies derived over 50% of their income from international sales [16] (see Figure 1). We can expect these trends to continue as political and economic changes continue to open new markets in Europe, Asia and around the globe.

Within the CHI community we regularly explore multiple factors affecting the user's interaction with the computer. We consider how the user works when we do a task analysis. We consider the social dynamics of interaction when we design software for collaboration, and we consider the unique perspectives an interdisciplinary team can provide

when we engage in participatory design. However, as a community we have not always extended our view to include *cultural* awareness as an aspect of *user* awareness.

Research on the topic of designing for international users is sparse. In the past, Nielsen has provided the CHI community with the most relevant work [9, 10, 11]. However the majority of his work focuses on issues related to usability testing and problems specific to translating text. Since his work in 1990, there has been a preponderance of graphical interfaces which have introduced additional cross cultural translation issues related to images, symbols and color. This paper will highlight these additional considerations and suggest how to address them when designing for other cultures.

Internationalization and Localization

The current method of preparing a product for another culture involves two steps: first *internationalization*, then *localization*.

Internationalization refers to the process of isolating the culturally specific elements from a product; for example the isolation of French text from a program developed in France. Internationalization occurs in the country where the product is originally developed. It is not uncommon for development groups to focus only on elements related to text, numbers and dates. Sun Microsystems' Software Internationalization Guide [13], for example, contains guidelines limited to text, numbers, dates, time and collation.

Localization refers to the process of infusing a specific cultural context into a previously internationalized product [14]; for instance, translating French text and message files into Spanish for Spanish users. Like internationalization, localization is usually limited to translating the text, date and number formats. But creating a product that speaks fluently in another culture involves more than this. According to Taylor, "properly localized software applications, just like properly localized automobiles, toasters, beverages, and magazines, reflect the values, ethics, morals and language (or languages) of the nation in question" [14].

Figure 1: International Revenues as a Percentage of Total Revenues

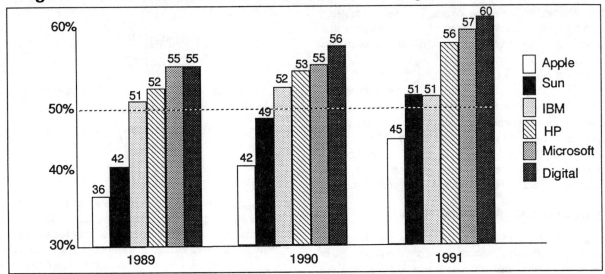

INTERNATIONAL ISSUES

A Cross-Cultural Checklist

The range of cross-cultural elements that need to be considered during internationalization and localization is wide. The interface designer must be aware of:

- Text
- Number, Date and Time Formats
- Images
- Symbols
- Colors
- Flow
- Functionality

The first two items, text and formats, are the elements that designers commonly think of when internationalizing and localizing a product. The remaining items, however, are generally overlooked.

TEXT

Translation

The first step in preparing a product for international use is to translate the text into the language of the local market. Translating the text in an interface is more complicated than translating the text in a book. An interface introduces many additional subtleties such as computer-human interaction, which can complicate a translation.

Translation problems are magnified when the translator is unfamiliar with the application content or human factors principles. For instance, when a U.S. company hired an exchange student from Indonesia to do some translation work, the student did not understand "software" and translated it as "underwear." When Sun Microsystems translated

their OpenWindows Developer's Guide product into Cantonese, the word "menu" was translated as "list of food items." To avoid such problems, translators must be familiar with the application domain and ideally, would be aware of general human factors principles such as screen layout and the design of interactive behavior. If not, they must work closely with domain experts and human interface professionals.

Jargon. Jargon is universally confusing and should be eliminated from the product during the internationalization step. For example, an American product must first be "translated" into proper American English before it can be translated into another language. Taylor [14] provides an example of German users at the Tandy computer company who encountered the error "Cannot grok rewund" when mistyping the word "rewind." Apparently the users at Tandy spent many hours trying to understand the error message. It was only when they called the technical assistance desk that they discovered "grok" was American slang for "to understand completely." When internationalizing software it is necessary to eliminate all instances of jargon.

Words that don't exist. Some terms, computer-related and otherwise, do not exist in other languages. Sukaviriya and Moran [12] report that English terms such as 'Diskette,' 'Disk Drive,' 'Zooming,' and 'Panning' have no direct translation in the Thai language. When translators encounter such words they often invent phrases to explain their meaning, only to find that after users come to understand the original term, they prefer it to the translator's explanation [12]. Translators should consider keeping the original terms for words that do not translate during localization.

Character Sets. Different languages require different character sets. Many European languages contain a variety of characters with diacritics, e.g., ĕ, â, ã. When designing applications, designers must allow for the display and input of all characters in the languages of the target markets.

Product Names. A common oversight when translating products for another market is choosing product names that do not translate well in other cultures. Illustrative examples abound in the automotive industry. For example, Fiat, the Italian auto manufacturer, had to rename their "Uno" when selling it in Finland, because "Uno" in Finnish means garbage. Similarly, Rolls Royce planned to name one of their new cars "Silver Mist" until someone pointed out that mist in German means manure [14]. At a low level this information is correct, i.e., the translation is accurate. However, at a higher level it fails because the language idioms and the cultural contexts of target cultures are not being considered.

NUMBER, DATE AND TIME FORMATS

Although most countries in the world use the Arabic number system, i.e., 0-9, number *formats* vary between countries. In Europe, a comma separates the whole part of a number from the decimal part (6,5) and periods separate large numbers (6.000.000). In the U.S., however, the reverse is true. A period separates the whole part of a number from the decimal part (6.5) and commas separate large numbers (6,000,000).

Date representations also vary. In Europe, day-month-year (07-10-92) is the standard. However, in the U.S., month-day-year is common, and within that there are a number of possible ways of displaying the information including: Oct 7, 1992, 10/07/92, Oct 7 '92. To account for the variety of forms, del Galdo [4] recommends allowing for 3 sequences of date: month-day-year, day-month-year, year-month-day. It gets more confusing in countries using non-western calendars such as Japan, China, and Israel. In Israel, years might be referred to as the 5700 decade, or the year 1990.

Like date and numbers, time conventions are equally varied. Some cultures use a 12 hour clock and include seconds: 10:45:15; other cultures use 24-hour military time: 22:45. Additionally, some cultures use the colon as a delimiter, while others use the period. del Galdo [4] recommends that "applications allow both 12 and 24 hour clock notation. Furthermore, hour, minutes and seconds components must always appear in that format."

After addressing the above elements of internationalization your interface will speak the basic language of the target population, but it may still have a heavy accent. In order for the interface to be truly fluent in another language additional elements must be considered.

IMAGES

Image Recognition

Images are the visual language of a culture. Like words, images don't always translate. What we recognize in our culture may have little or no meaning in another. Graphical interfaces are especially susceptible to this problem. For

example, because a trash can in Thailand may look like this,

(a wicker basket with flies) a Thai user is likely to be confused by this image popular in Apple interfaces [12]:

This U.S. trash can also confused British users who indicated it looked much more like a postal box than a British trash can. Similarly, Sun Microsystems found that the icon chosen for their SunView electronic mail product was problematic. This image is even confusing to some American urban dwellers who are unfamiliar with rural mail boxes.

A number of studies [1, 5] have concluded that many images do not convey the same meaning in all cultures. Some users will recognize an image, but they will not associate it with the originally intended concept. For example, business cards hold a particular meaning in the American culture: they are used to convey information about a business or its representative. In Japan, however, business cards are exchanged at the start of a business encounter, and are used to establish seniority so an interaction can proceed appropriately. If a business card icon is used to represent users on a network it may be universally recognized, but the meaning will vary between cultures.

To succeed in an international market, images must be carefully selected and designed. Designers must be sufficiently aware of differences among cultures to recognize images that are culturally specific and isolate them during the internationalization process. To do this, designers must work with international experts to determine whether images in a product are universally recognized and understood [4]. If images are not universally recognized, they must be isolated during the internationalization process.

Image Acceptability

There is a difference between what is *comprehensible* to a culture and what is *acceptable*. Because social norms vary greatly between cultures, what is acceptable in one culture can be objectionable in another. In particular, we need to be careful when designing images that contain religious symbols (e.g., crosses and stars), the human body, women and hand gestures. For example, the American "OK" hand gesture is considered vulgar in Brazil and Germany.

An inappropriate use of a simple graphic can result in a customer being offended or insulted. For instance, the following picture was developed in the U.S. for an Egyptian hygiene program [7]. When Egyptian women were shown this picture of a woman being fitted for a contraceptive diaphragm, they found it unacceptable. They commented, "We don't

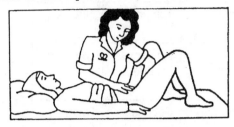

look like Western women!" and "Why is she revealing so much of her legs?" A series of design modifications resulted in the following acceptable design:

Designers need to avoid or eliminate images containing potentially controversial elements.

SYMBOLS

Commonly used symbols may also be subject to misinterpretation across cultures. For example, in the Christian world, the archetypal cross has come to be associated with prohibition, as well as with Christianity. However, in Egypt the cross is not seen as prohibitive [6]. Similarly signs of acceptance and disapproval such as crosses or checks that are

 Italic   **Bold**

common in Western cultures and appear in many graphical interfaces may not have universal meaning. Designers must allow for translation of different symbols during localization.

Symbols are often used in advertising because they work at a subtle level. Inappropriate use of symbols can destroy an advertising campaign [2]. Using a picture of a stork, for example, in Singapore is risky because it symbolizes maternal death. In Japan, the number 4 is like the unlucky number 13 in America, and 7 is unlucky in Ghana, Kenya and Singapore.

COLORS

The interpretation of color varies significantly across cultures [15] (see Table 1). For instance, while red in the U.S. means danger, in China it means happiness. Similarly, yellow in the U.S. means cowardice but in Egypt it means prosperity. Garland [6] found that using a red "X" as a prohibitive symbol in Egyptian pictures was not effective because the color red is not associated with forbiddance, and the "X" is not understood as prohibitive. Similarly, Courtney [3] found that while Americans have "virtually perfect association" for red as stop and green as go, Chinese do not. If we chose to use colors to convey information to users (e.g., *red* error messages or *yellow* warning messages) we have to allow for the appropriate translation of the colors during the internationalization process.

FLOW

Often the text and graphical components of an interface will be arranged on the screen in a way that depicts the logical flow of information. For instance, in America a series of icons or windows will be arranged from left to right and top to bottom. Such an arrangement would be counter-intuitive to an Arabic user who reads from right to left. This would be even more confusing to a Chinese user who reads top to bottom and right to left. Designers must allow for these cultural differences by providing modifiable arrangement of information.

FUNCTIONALITY

Like images, colors, and symbols, product features chosen for one culture may not be appropriate for all cultures. The developers of LYRE, a French hypertext product, discovered this when trying to market their product in Scandinavia [11]. LYRE allowed students to analyze a poem from various viewpoints. When the features were being defined in France, the team decided that students would not be able to add their own viewpoints to the system; they could only use the viewpoints the teacher had previously added. This was socially acceptable in France. However, when LYRE was considered by potential Scandinavian users, it was not well received. In the Scandinavian countries, independent discovery is greatly valued, and the idea that students could not add their own viewpoints to the application was unacceptable.

INTERNATIONAL PRODUCT DEVELOPMENT

A Translated Product becomes a New Product

When a product is translated into a new culture it becomes a *new* product. Not only is the language new, but so are the users and their requirements of the products. Nielsen talks about translated products becoming new products in his work [11], but focuses primarily on the need to re-test the product with native users after translation. We believe the implications go far beyond usability testing and extend throughout the product's development cycle. As the CHI community has discovered, usability testing alone will not guarantee a successful product.

A development team needs to think about each culture the product will be sold in from the *beginning* of the product development cycle. Are the product requirements different?

Table 1: Some Cultural Associations of Color

Culture	Red	Blue	Green	Yellow	White
United States	Danger	Masculinity	Safety	Cowardice	Purity
France	Aristocracy	Freedom Peace	Criminality	Temporary	Neutrality
Egypt	Death	Virtue Faith Truth	Fertility Strength	Happiness Prosperity	Joy
India	Life Creativity		Prosperity Fertility	Success	Death Purity
Japan	Anger Danger	Villainy	Future Youth Energy	Grace Nobility	Death
China	Happiness	Heavens Clouds	Ming Dynasty Heavens Clouds	Birth Wealth Power	Death Purity

Do the features need to be modified? How are the users different? The team needs to identify the differences, understand the design implications and design for them before the original product is released.

Establish a Relationship within the Target Market

In order to identify culturally specific requirements, development teams need to establish a close working relationship or partnership with *natives* from the target cultures. During the various stages of the product's development cycle, information must be reviewed and feedback must be provided by representatives from the target cultures. Early in the development cycle when features are being defined, they must be reviewed for errors of omission and commission by each target culture. If the target culture identifies additional features, the original development team can make the appropriate adjustments to the product's architecture to allow for the changes during the localization process. Without such a working relationship, the architecture may become fixed with serious implications for localization.

We saw such implications in the French product LYRE described above. Its developers did not work with international users and had to deal with the consequences after the fact. If the French development team had established a relationship with the Scandinavian target culture, the feature omissions would have been identified and addressed. Instead, they were uncovered only after the product had been fully implemented, and little could be done to correct the situation.

Lotus Corporation, one of the more successful U.S. players in foreign markets, worked very closely with Japanese-based consultants when they decided to adapt 1-2-3 to the Japanese market [8]. Throughout the process, the Japanese consultants educated the Lotus team on some crucial aspects of the Japanese culture. For instance, because the Japanese keep dates in years of the Emperor, Lotus thought it would be helpful to provide a feature that would allow users to change the Emperor's name, when needed. When Lotus talked to the consultants about this they quickly learned that "they should not even dream about marketing a program that appeared, in any respect whatsoever, to question the Emperor's immortality"[8]. This is a subtle issue the U.S. development could not have anticipated without the help of the Japanese experts.

International Usability Testing. International partners need to review more than the feature sets. The domestic product team must seek input from each target market at every stage of the development process, including usability testing. Today, usability testing with *international* users is performed long after the product is released in the domestic market. By this time the product architecture can not be modified. Any significant changes identified during the international usability test are difficult, if not impossible, to address.

Usability testing with international users should be performed at the same time as the domestic usability tests: before the product is released. Native users can help identify the subtle elements of an interface that may be confusing or offensive. By testing early, the results from all target markets, domestic and international, can be consolidated and incorporated into the product architecture prior to its release.

REMAINING ISSUES

In this paper we have considered ways of improving the current process of designing for international users. We presented a checklist of issues to consider when designing a product for more than one culture, and proposed ideas for an international development process. This is only the beginning: we recognize that there are numerous challenges in implementing both.

One issue is how to work out the logistics of establishing the relationship with the target cultures. Who should the contacts be? What skills, computer or otherwise, do they need to have? How do we train the contacts? How should they interact with the design team?

A second issue is how to justify the time and cost of such a process. For instance, simultaneous usability testing requires localization before the domestic version is shipped. This is bound to be costly in terms of time and money. Finally, we must develop strategies for applying and integrating the checklist into the actual design and programming processes. Changes to the traditional software development process do not happen easily. We need to work within the existing process and modify it to meet the complex needs of international markets.

ACKNOWLEDGEMENTS

We would like to acknowledge Kate Ehrlich and Hagan Heller for their help with the organization of this document, and for their comments on early drafts. We would also like to thank Matt Belge, Eric Bergman, Joann Brooks, Harry Hersh, Amy O'Connor, Laurie Anna Kaplan, Grace Myhill, Mike Seif, Hal Shubin, Nigel Simpson and Nicole Yankelovich for their feedback and support throughout the process of writing this paper.

REFERENCES

1. Cook, B.L. *Picture communication in Papua New Guinea.* Educational Broadcasting International. 13(2), 1980.

2. Copeland, L. and Griggs, L. *Going International. How to Make Friends and Deal Effectively in the Global Marketplace.* Plume, New York, 1985.

3. Courtney, A.J. *Chinese Population Stereotypes: Color Association.* Human Factors, 28(1), 1986.

4. del Galdo, E. *Internationalization and Translation: Some Guidelines for the Design of Human-Computer Interfaces.* In Jakob Nielsen (Ed.) Designing User Interfaces for International Use. Elsevier, New York, 1990.

5. Fussell, D. and Haaland, A. *Communication with pictures in Nepal: results of practical study used in visual education.* Educational Broadcasting International. 11(1), 1978.

6. Garland, K. *The use of short term feedback in the preparation of technical and instructional illustration.* In, Research in Illustration: Conference Proceedings Part II. 1982.

7. Goldsmith E. *Research into Illustration: an approach and a review.* Cambridge University Press, New York, 1984.

8. Hapgood, F. *A Journey East - The Making of 1-2-3 Release 2J.* Lotus: Computing for Managers and Professionals. 1987.

9. Nielsen, J. *Designing for International Use.* CHI'90 Human Factors in Computing Systems (Seattle, April 1-5), ACM Press, pp. 291-294) CHI 1990 Proceedings.

10. Nielsen, J. (Ed.) Designing User Interfaces for International Use. Elsevier, New York, 1990.

11. Nielsen, J. *Usability Testing of International Interfaces.* In Jakob Nielsen (Ed.) Designing User Interfaces for International Use. Elsevier, New York, 1990.

12. Sukaviriya, P. and Moran, L. *User Interfaces for Asia.* In Jakob Nielsen (Ed.) Designing User Interfaces for International Use. Elsevier, New York, 1990.

13. Sun Microsystems, *Software Internationalization Guide.* Internal Document, Mountain View, CA, April 1991.

14. Taylor, D. *Global Software.* Springer-Verlag, New York, 1992.

15. Thorell, L.G. and Smith, W.J. *Using Computer Color Effectively: An Illustrated Reference.* Prentice Hall, New Jersey, 1990.

16. 1991 Annual Reports, Apple Computer, Digital Equipment Corporation, Hewlett-Packard, IBM, Microsoft Corporation and Sun Microsystems.

Representation in Virtual Space:
Visual Convention in the Graphical User Interface

Loretta Staples

Loretta Staples Design
37 San Gabriel Ave.
San Francisco, CA 94112, USA
(415) 585-0300
staples@well.sf.ca.us

ABSTRACT

The graphical user interface (GUI) typically provides a multi-windowed environment within a flat workspace or "desktop." Simultaneously, however, controls for executing commands within this interface are increasingly being rendered three-dimensionally. This paper explores ways in which the space of the GUI desktop might be literally and figuratively deepened through the incorporation of visual devices that have emerged during the history of art—specifically, perspective and light effects. By enriching the visual vocabulary of the GUI, greater semantic complexity becomes sustainable.

KEYWORDS

User interfaces, representation, design, three-dimensional graphics, methodology, art, art history.

INTRODUCTION

The relatively brief history of the GUI has already been marked by an increasing tendency toward "realism" in the representation of interface objects. This tendency is currently reflected in the three-dimensional rendering of objects such as buttons and window frames within several popular GUIs (Fig 1). It is seen as well in the very literal rendering of devices such as CD-ROM controllers, which seek to copy their analog counterparts as closely as possible, in size, layout, and color (Fig. 2). While "the reduction of cognitive overload" is usually posited as the rationale behind this brand of "realism," this explanation ignores the extent to which realism is one of the more popular conventions within the history of visual representation in Western culture.

This history has been marked by periodic instances of hyper-realism, exemplified in the recent past by an effort to reconcile photographic and painted representations. That is, images

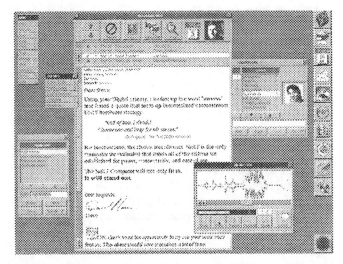

Fig. 1. NeXT interface showing three-dimensional rendering of interface elements.

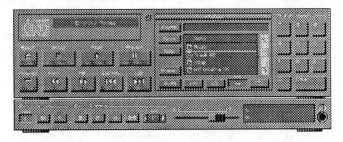

Fig. 2 Audioshop virtual CD-ROM drive.

afforded by a new technology which sought to "capture" the real versus those conjured by the imagination and made manifest through a necessary medium. The desire to render objects in the interface with such photographic realism is analogous to this very tendency within Western art, and is likely to be an extension of this very convention. As paint tried to fulfill a photographic vision, so too, pixels within the computer interface now seek to fulfill a parallel realism, derived from a photographic ideal.[1]

Undoubtedly, such literalism in the interface has its place. Why bother to invent an entirely new representation of a remote control device for a CD-ROM player when a replica of its analog will do? Nevertheless, the extent to which realism is limited in the interface to objects like buttons and "hand-held" devices illustrates the predominant vision that the GUI and its keepers espouse. This vision is limited to applications of realism to only the most obvious candidates.

The continued evolution of the GUI demands an investigation into the full range of ways in which an object might be represented in the virtual realm. It demands a highly moderated pictorial environment in which realism and abstraction exist with complementarity. If realism were taken too far within the virtual environment of the computer, we might find ourselves traversing information spaces as unwieldy, inaccessible, and time-consuming as their real world analogs. Conversely, if every interface object were stripped of its analogous cues, meaning and significance would have to be needlessly and repeatedly reinvented by the user and system designer alike.

I'd like to propose a more systematic investigation and application of the literal and the abstract within the interface and present some drawings which serve as examples of such investigation, at a very elementary level. I will focus on space as the most significant attribute of the interface. My examples will seek to illuminate existing limitations in the visual conventions currently used to depict objects within the environment of the GUI "desktop" space. I propose enriching this visual language to include conventions that have evolved during the history of art. I will focus specifically on the representation of spatial depth in the interface, presenting the visual devices whereby depth may be articulated. By considering the interface within the continuum of visual history, we can begin to recognize the extent to which problems of representation posed by the interface are similar to those posed and solved within the history of art.[2] My drawings will refer to current conventions within the Macintosh "desktop."

Keep in mind that my perspective is that of an art historian and visual designer. My purpose is not to discuss the technicalities of imaging, or the feasability of certain types of images, but rather their appearance and potential meaning.

THE SPACE OF THE MACINTOSH DESKTOP

While the Macintosh GUI supports the representation of different types of objects, these objects are represented in a space that is shallow. Windows can overlap to provide a sense of layering, but without enough differentiation to denote a truly dimensional space (Fig. 3).

Objects differ in size, but these differences are absolute in respect to classes of objects. View commands, for instance, modify all objects within a window similarly. Light is used to denote selection, but this light is never ambient. It is sustained within the parameters of an object's edges, but never extends beyond it.

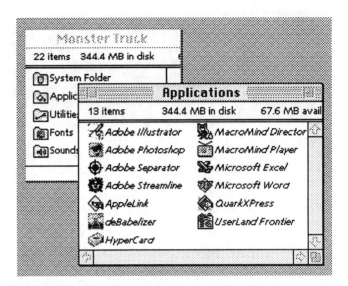

Fig. 3 Overlapping Macintosh windows.

CONVENTIONS OF SPATIAL REPRESENTATION

What visual devices could better support this sense of spatial depth?

- Perspective
- Light and Shadow
- Transparency and Opacity

Fig. 4 16th century engraving by Jan Vredeman de Vries showing perspective lines. From Jan Vredeman de Vries, *Perspective*, Dover Publications, New York, 1968, pg. 28.

Perspective, a supposed invention of the Italian Renaissance[3] (Fig. 4) articulates a space that is deep. One in which near objects are differentiated visually from those afar, and in which those objects' relativity to one another is emphasized. Perspective is achieved by projecting the lines which define an object against an imaginary plane located between the object

Fig. 5 16th century woodcut by Albrecht Dürer showing an artist and model, separated by a gridded window representing the picture plane. The artist produces his drawing on a similarly apportioned paper, transferring outlines viewed through the grid one square at a time. From Fred Dubery and John Willats, *Drawing Systems*, Studio Vista/ Van Nostrand Reinhold, London and New York, 1972, pg. 58.

and the "eye" that observes them[4] (Fig. 5). Perspective can augment the visual semantics of a pictorial scheme by increasing the number of cues available to serve as signifiers of additional meanings. For instance, nearness and farness can be used to cue the user to distance in time as well as space.

While many drawing systems exist that are capable of representing spatial depth and showing multiple views of an object simultaneously, Western perspective drawing utilizes specific devices to achieve the illusion of depth (Fig. 6). *Vanishing points* denote the convergence of parallel lines which describe an object's receding edges in regard to the *picture plane*. This convergence typically occurs at the *horizon*, a line representing the meeting of the earth and sky. Lines projected onto the picture plane that are not parallel to it are *foreshortened* to effect a receding distance. Objects appear relatively smaller when far as opposed to near to maintain a consistency of *scale*.

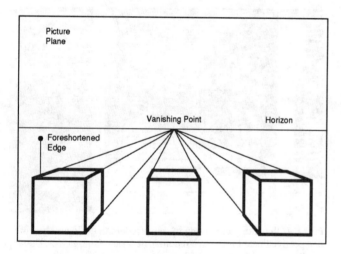

Fig. 6 The basic devices of perspective.

Light reinforces spatial depth by accentuating or diminishing the illuminated object's visible detail. Because the shadows cast by an such an object can vary in physical depth and in the extent to which they obscure underlying objects, shadows are capable of further modulating a pictorial space. Within a picture utilizing perspective, accurately rendered shadows obey specific rules in regard to the light source and the object from which the shadow is cast.

Transparency and opacity, while not specific to the illusion of perspective, contribute to an object's definition as does light. Transparency provides the opportunity for the simultaneous viewing of objects that might otherwise be obscured—stacked or layered objects, for instance.

THE APPLICATION OF SPATIAL DEVICES WITHIN THE GUI

How might the visual devices just described be applied to the desktop? How might they augment meaning?

Perspective

Attempts at perspective have already been applied to the GUI. A novel alternative to the Macintosh Finder is currently available in Ark's *Workspace* software (Fig. 7). And a kind of "false" perspective,[5] is used in Motif and New Wave icons (Fig. 8). But its application has not been to define space *per se*, but rather, to lend novelty to the drawing style. The pictorial result is still flat because these objects allude to a dimensional space

Fig. 7 Ark's roomlike Finder alternative for the Macintosh.

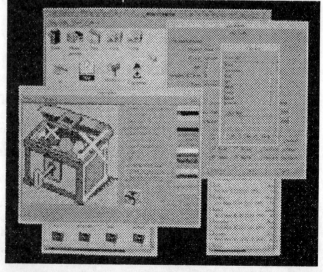

Fig. 8 Motif's dimensional icon style. From Jon Peddie, *Graphical User Interfaces and Graphic Standards*, McGraw-Hill, Inc., New York, 1992.

without depicting it. The sameness in the size of the objects also defeats any semblance of spatial depth, as does the consistent illumination of the objects. Representing these objects with greater dimensionality would entail the use of additional visual devices such as those described earlier.

The introduction of one point perspective (Fig. 9) allows many objects to be represented simultaneously, varying in relative size and "layered" in sequential planes. While the variation of sizes begins to articulate a spatial depth, the objects represented, here windows, are still relatively flat, suggesting that this device alone may be insufficient to fully support the perception of depth.

Additional cues can serve to enhance the illusion of spatial depth and augment the meaning of the symbols represented. In the next example, windows are varied in size and arranged to overlap (Fig. 10).

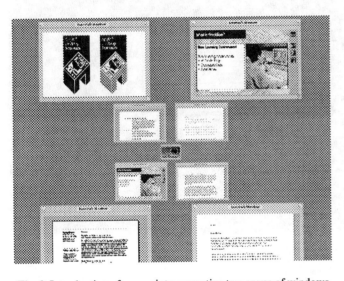

Fig. 9 Introduction of one-point perspective to a group of windows.

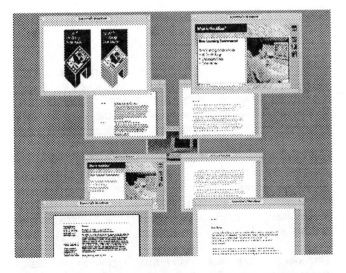

Fig. 10 Addition of overlapping to enhance the illusion of depth.

While overlapping and variation in size begin to suggest spatial depth in the previous example, the windows themselves are nonetheless flatly represented. In the next example, variation of window depth indicates, for instance, the quantity or type of items contained therein—window "boxes" secure dimensional objects whose identities do not reside in paper-based metaphors (see Staples, Color Plate 1). Alternatively, they might house arrays of documents.

The introduction of a richer set of spatial cues begins to define a space which can be traversed through a third dimension, superceding the horizontal and vertical limitations typically associated with scrolling.

Light and Shadow

The use of light effects can begin to introduce a level of naturalism that corresponds directly to the real world. Within a luminous interface, variation in the position of the light source can simulate natural light's activity in the real world. Imagine an interface whose appearance subtly differed from dawn to dusk—the absense of cast shadows might then connote noon! And since rendered shadows obey a set of perspective rules corresponding to those which apply to the objects from which they are cast, shadows reinforce pictorial realism.

Concentrated light amidst darkness can emphasize individual objects by spotlighting them (Fig. 11). Amidst uniformly lit objects, a spotlight may effect a halo (see Staples, Color Plate 2). This "unreal" instance of light, with its corresponding absence of shadow typically suggests, within the history of art, an object whose status is holy or sacred. Whether or not sacred objects find themselves represented in the computer environment, however, is not the issue here. The example simply serves to illustrate an abstract representation of light within a pictorial space.

Fig. 11 Spotlighted item within a window.

When emanating from within a closed shape amidst darkness, light can give the impression of staged activity within a confined space, corresponding to our experience of theatre, film, and television viewing (Fig. 12).

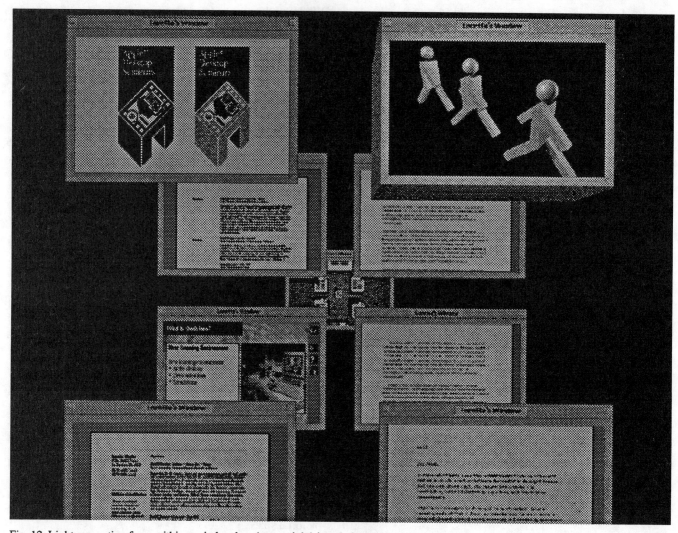

Fig. 12 Light emanating from within a window box (upper right) in a darkened environment.

Transparency and Opacity

Within the real world, only certain objects made of certain materials are transparent. As a consequence, transparency within the history of representation at times signifies yet another special status. Just as the surreal qualities of a halo suggest a spiritual entity, so too, transparency suggests a ghostly realm of supernaturalism. Because transparency within the interface could be afforded any object, this device provides a unique opportunity and challenge in the merging of real and abstract qualities.

As stated earlier, transparency allows objects which might otherwise be obscured be seen. Since a natural consequence of transparency is a greater number of visible objects at any given moment, it is obvious that transparency might not be desirable as a ubiquitous feature. However, transparency might be a desirable attribute to confer upon an object at will, allowing a user to see an object beneath another without repositioning the frontmost object (see Staples, Color Plate 3). The graduated application of transparency permits a range of visibility to be applied to objects.

With the introduction of transparency, opacity is given new significance. Within the context of the transparent, opaque objects are accentuated.

Combining the Effects

How might a collection of these effects appear within a single environment? Figure 13 (see also Staples, Color Plate 4) shows a desktop "landscape" divided by a horizon line denoting two separate areas: an active foreground space and a more passive remote space. Within the foreground area, windows and window boxes assume varying sizes as they are positioned nearer to or farther from the picture plane. They house different object types. Here, documents reside within windows while dimensional objects or arrays of objects reside within window boxes. In the remote space above the horizon line, icons and miniature windows passively await activation. To the right, disk and trash icons hover. Figure 14 shows this environment with an applied light effect: a transparent window reveals an illuminated landscape beneath.

Undoubtedly, this more differentiated environment introduces greater complexity in the behavior of objects and user

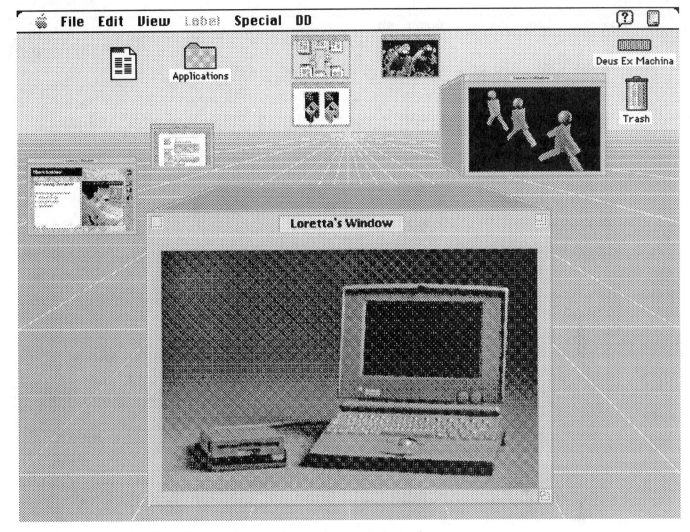

Fig. 13 Desktop "landscape" showing active foreground area and passive background area.

interaction with them. (And it remains to be seen whether this complexity is technically feasable and in the best interest of the user!) This complexity suggests a new metaphor for navigating this space, and perhaps an analogous new input device to afford this navigation.

SUMMARY

Many unexplored visual opportunities exist which have the potential to expand the realm of the graphical user interface, affording greater possibilities of form and meaning through an enriched landscape. While this paper has focused on form, only minimally suggesting meanings that might be ascribed these forms, it is obvious that a richer vocabulary of forms potentially affords a richer set of meanings. Problems of representation within the computer interface are not unlike problems of representation within any number of pictorial spaces that have emerged in art. By reviewing the history of art, we can begin to find "new" solutions to the problems of the computer interface. And concurrently, by considering the interface as an instance within a single continuum of visual history, we can begin to integrate the virtual environment more elegantly into whole of our visual experience of the world.

ACKNOWLEDGEMENTS

Many thanks to Peter Vanags for his comments on an early draft of this paper, his bringing to my attention the Ark *Workspace* interface, and his technical assistance in implementing the light effects in Figs. 11, 12 and Color Plate 2. Thanks also to Dale Horstman for allowing me to reproduce his 3-D stick figure in Figs. 12-14, and Color Plates 1 and 4. And finally, thanks to my colleagues in visual interface design at Apple Computer, where I worked when I wrote this paper, especially the Eyetalk group.

This paper is dedicated to George Kubler, Professor Emeritus in the History of Art at Yale University, who, years ago, inspired my initial studies in morphology.

REFERENCES

1. Richard Gregory describes a correspondence between photographic and retinal images that is distinct from that which the artist actually sees. Those images correspond to the "geometric perspective" typically presented in "realistic" art. Apparently, geometric perspective was to become a conven-

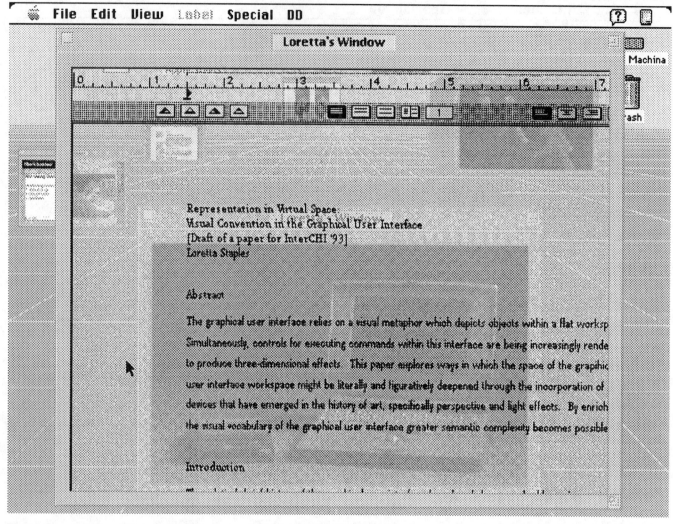

Fig. 14 Large window with transparent document overlaying desktop "landscape."

tionalized ideal. Richard L. Gregory, "Art and Reality" in *Eye and Brain: The Psychology of Seeing*, Princeton University Press, 1990, pgs. 171-195 .

2. Joe Ballay presented historic examples of visual organization within painting at CHI 92's Visual Design SIG meeting, illustrating conventions between layout and meaning transferrable to the GUI.

3. While this paper will focus on perspective as developed during the European Rennaissance, the term is also used to describe other types of drawing systems which serve to represent spatial depth. See "Perspective in Art," *Encyclopaedia Brittanica*, 15th Edition, 1990, Vol. 9, pg. 313.

4. Leonardo da Vinci described perspective as "nothing else than the seeing of a plane behind a sheet of glass, smooth and quite transparent, on the surface of which all the things approach the point of the eye in pyramids, and these pyramids are intersected on the glass plane." From Leonardo da Vinci, *Notebooks*, Dover Publications, 1970.

5. Axonometric and isometric projection are used in drawing to depict objects dimensionally, but without regard to true perspective. Isometric projection places the face of an object parallel to the picture plane, utilizes no vanishing points, and typically ignores foreshortening. Axonometric projection places the face of an object at an angle to the picture plane and displays the top of the object as if in plan (bird's eye) view. New Wave utilizes axonometric projection in its icon drawing style.

Principles, Techniques, and Ethics of Stage Magic and Their Application to Human Interface Design

Bruce Tognazzini

Sunsoft, A Sun Microsystems Business
2550 Garcia Ave. M/S MTV21-225
Mountain View, CA 94043
415-336-6725
tog@eng.sun.com

ABSTRACT

Magicians have been designing and presenting illusions for 5000 years. They have developed principles, techniques and ethical positions for their craft that this paper argues are applicable to the design of human/computer interfaces. The author presents a number of specific examples from magic and discusses their counterparts in human interface design, in hopes that human interface practitioners and researchers will, having recognized the applicability of magic, go further on their own to explore its domain.

KEYWORDS: HCI Design, Illusion, Design, Misdirection, Simulation, Dissimulation, Time, Response Time, Magic, Magician, Principle, Technique, Ethics, Anthropomorphism, Characters, Theater

INTRODUCTION

Human interface designers are struggling to generate more effective illusions for purposes of communicating to their users the design model of their applications [9, 13, 18-22]. At the same time, they are confronting serious issues of ethics: when does an attempt to create an empowering illusion become trickery, when does an attempt at anthropomorphism become cheap fraud [13, 23-24]?

Our profession has primarily drawn its lessons from psychology, computer science, and graphic design. While these have supplied much valuable material, we are still busily re-creating organized knowledge in our field that Laurel [13] points out has been well understood for thousands of years.

Perhaps no field other than magic is tied so closely to the field of graphical interface design: The people working at

Xerox PARC in the 1960's and early 1970's were aware of the principles of theatrical magic when creating the first graphical interfaces, to the extent that David Smith named the interface itself the "user illusion" [12]. We are designing interfaces for an interface system based on magic, yet there is almost nothing written about it in our literature. (An exception is a single page by Heckel [9].) Magicians have been struggling with the principles, techniques, and ethics of illusion for at least 5000 years [2]. There is much we can learn from them.

This paper is not exhaustive. On the contrary, it barely scratches the surface. My goals are to introduce other HCI professionals to the teachings of this parallel profession of magic and to excite interest in what I believe to be a powerful set of tools for interface designers. I have been an amateur magician for as long as I've been a professional interface designer and have applied the principles, techniques and ethics of magic routinely in my design work. I have found them to be applicable and valuable.

EERIE CORRESPONDENCE

It's hard to read through a book on the principles of magic without glancing at the cover periodically to make sure it isn't a book on human interface design. These books clearly delineate the basic principles and techniques that support graphical user interfaces:

- Consistency: Much of these books on magic technique dwell on the various aspects of consistency: "Consistency is the key to conviction.... No matter how effective an inconsistent part may be, the damage that it does to the routine as a whole more than offsets whatever advantages it may have in itself."— Nelms [15]. "Irregularities destroy naturalness and conviction. When naturalness disappears, and when something unnatural is evident, the spectator's attention immediately becomes vigilant and alert. In the normal course of events, this is disastrous to deception."— Fitzkee [6].

- Unity: "No first-class success in any type of entertainment, whether it be in the form of a motion picture, a stage attraction, a novel, a short story or any other type of diversion, can be achieved without endowing the undertaking with some degree of unity, no matter how fragile the connecting thread may be."—Fitzkee [4]

- Keep it Simple: "The Japanese define an artist as 'one who has the ability to do more and the will to refrain.'"—Nelms [15].

- Use of Real World Metaphors: The magician's tools should be disguised to look like objects in the real world. "If these things are common things, objects with which the spectator is familiar, this spectator will accept them in terms *as he knows them.* He will assume the device to be the same as the common article with which he is acquainted."—Fitzkee [6].

- Technique of User Testing: Nelms [15] gives a complete précis on user-testing, including the importance of choosing spectators from the target population: "If you try to dramatize a routine for a brother conjurer, you will merely bore him—unless he sees something in your routine that he can use in his own act.... When you work out a routine for laymen, test it on a friend who knows nothing about conjuring. Ask for his detailed criticism. Then try your routine on another friend and get his opinion. If several laymen find fault with the same spot in your routine, it is bad." He goes on to detail the pitfalls of taking the spectator's diagnosis too literally: "A layman's diagnosis of what is wrong will usually be false and will often be absurd, but he almost always puts his finger on the point where the problem lies."

Sound familiar?

VIRTUAL REALITIES

Both human interface designers and magicians create virtual realities. We bring ours alive on computer displays; magicians bring theirs alive on the stage. We capture our "performances" in code so they can continue to occur long after their writing; magicians traditionally appear live during their performances. We depend on our knowledge of the "mechanics" of computer technology, the aesthetics of graphic design, and the science of psychology. Magicians depend on their knowledge of the "mechanics" of their tricks, the aesthetics of showmanship, and the science of psychology.

Mechanics

Competent magicians can work fluidly with apparatus, so that the spectators are unaware that the card seemingly dealt from the top of the deck came from the bottom, or that the rabbit that seemingly arrived from out of nowhere had been residing in the magician's pocket, munching peacefully on carrots. Magicians must be competent at the mechanics of their craft, yet such competency does not

make someone a magician, any more than knowledge of a rapid-prototyping system makes someone a software designer. It sets the stage. It makes everything else possible.

Showmanship

Showmanship seems like an unimportant aspect of human interface design, but an exploration of how it applies to magic reveals some unexpected results.

What is this thing we call a human interface? Lawyers will tell you it's the "look and feel" of the software, but when you press them they will be at a loss to explain what that means. (They will also bill you $250 dollars for their failure.) Don Norman calls it the "System Image," the physical embodiment of the designer's "Design Model" [18-20]. Rubinstein and Hersh call it an "external myth" [21]. Ted Nelson calls it "virtuality" [16]. As mentioned earlier, Alan Kay and his cohorts at Xerox PARC, in deliberate reference to magic, called it the "user-illusion" [12]. All of these words are descriptive, yet all are abstract and, therefore, somewhat elusive.

Magicians work to produce illusions, but they don't call their stage presentation an illusion, they call it an act. That's a good, down-to-earth term you can get your hands around. It comes equipped with expectations: we know that an act should inform, excite, and entertain us. If it doesn't, we know what to do about it, which might or might not involve computing trajectories for rotten fruit, depending on the poverty of the performance.

Look at the most famous contemporary magicians—Doug Henning, Paul Daniels, Penn & Teller, Siegfried & Roy, David Copperfield—all are consummate showmen. Indeed, an examination of David Copperfield's tricks shows them all to be rather old and prosaic, but he performs them in such a theatrical style and on such a grand scale, that we are enthralled. Most magicians, with a suitable trap door, can perform Servais Le Roy's turn-of-the-century "Asrah" illusion, making a comely young person disappear in thin air, but David Copperfield has made a 100 ton steam locomotive disappear into thin air. Most impressive.

Many principles of magic showmanship are directly applicable to human interface design. Here are just a few from Fitzkee [4]:

- Character: "No chef would prepare a dish without seasoning. Character is the seasoning which makes your entertainment dish palatable. Everything has character, even though the character be weak and uninteresting. Your job is to develop a quality of character in your routine that makes it tasty to the spectator. Otherwise you have a mere assembly of ingredients—tasteless, unsavory, unappetizing, lacking zest."

- Smoothness: "Perfect smoothness is necessary to any routine. In no other way will your act seem finished to the spectators. Smoothness, which is a word meaning you have planned thoroughly and well, gives confidence both to the performer and to his audience."

- "Get to the point. Be Brief. Keep interesting them. Quit before they've had enough."

I submit that showmanship has an important place in computer software. It certainly was a conscious component of the Lisa and the Macintosh. As one example, we didn't adopt the trash can for file elimination just because it fulfilled the requirement of a "real-world" metaphor. We chose it because it seemed "neat," and we kept it because, when other people saw it, they loved it.

Showmanship does not mean, to use Ted Nelson's term, "adding ketchup" [17]. It implies the application of a deep understanding of human nature to the task of making software seem vital, involving, and fun. Magicians learn showmanship the hard way, by standing on a stage, receiving instant and often painful feedback from a live and lively audience. One way people can learn how to inject showmanship into software designs is through a similar, if less painful mechanism: by dragging prototypes to customer sites, computer stores, club meetings—anywhere one can find an audience.

When setting out to design Apple Presents... Apple, the first in-box microcomputer tutorial back in 1979, Dave Eisenberg and I forwent the goal of teaching everything about the computer in favor of the more attainable goal of teaching a few fundamentals in such a way that new users would become interested and confident enough to want to learn more on their own.

The application started with an "attract mode" that gently cajoled the reluctant user to "just press the Return key." It continued with a building set of "success experiences," until after approximately five minutes, even the most fearful users were usually zipping away inside the application, feeling fully in command. During its design, we tried the application on more than 300 people, making it more lively and interactive with every pass. Within six months of its release, the Apple independent dealers identified it as their most valuable sales tool: they reported it made prospective owners love the computer and that the sale was then easy.

Not everyone will immediately agree that showmanship in spreadsheets is as important as showmanship on a Los Vegas stage, but consider this reality: software must be bought before it can be used. Showmanship does not imply the injection of irrelevant frills and fancies. Showmanship is the gentle seduction of the users, leading them to accept, believe in, and feel in control of the illusory world we have built for them.

Psychology and Dichotomy

"The art of illusion is at least 95% applied psychology.... When [modern conjurers] use more than one part of trickery to nine parts psychology, they cannot hope to create the maximum impression."— Nelms [15].

The act *is* the entity in magic. The mechanical devices and techniques are there solely to support the act, showmanship is there to enliven the act, but psychology makes the act "work."

Actually, there are two simultaneous acts performed in magic: the one the magician actually does—the magician's reality—and the one the spectators perceive— the spectators' reality: The magician's reality consists of all the sleights of hand and manipulation of gimmicked devices that make up the prosaic reality of magic. The spectators' reality, given a sufficiently competent magician, is entirely different: an alternate reality in which the normal laws of nature are repeatedly defied, a reality where the magician, as well as his or her tricks, appear supernatural.

On the surface, this defiance would seem in direct contradiction to human interface design, where we more often engage in making our "supernatural" machines appear natural. However, at a deeper level, both camps spend their time doing the same thing: making people believe one thing is going on when quite another is really taking place: the Macintosh has no actual, physical trash can, and no amount of rummaging around inside with a screwdriver and a pair of wire-cutters will reveal one.

Magicians' spectators, with the exception of young children, are adversaries, there for the specific purpose of finding the magician out. Magicians often reflect their adversarial relationship in their vocabulary: "The deception the magician seeks to accomplish is an attack upon the spectator's mind. Specifically, it is an attack upon his understanding."—Fitzkee [6].

Because of the natural suspicion of their spectators, magicians have had to develop the psychology of the illusion to a high level. If we apply their techniques with our users, who are not suspicious (unless we insist on "burning" them a few times), we surely will achieve a believable result. Let's look at a few key techniques magicians use to generate their simultaneous, but alternate, reality:

Misdirection

"[Misdirection is] the psychology of deception and the application of craft and artifice for accomplishing the magician's objectives"—Fitzkee [6].

Fitzkee identifies six techniques for causing misdirection: simulation, dissimulation, ruse, disguise, monotony, and maneuver. For purposes of this paper, let us examine just the first two:

- Simulation: "Simulation is a bewildering way of saying that something is made to look like what it is not."—Fitzkee [6]. Simulation is our most powerful misdirection tool in human interface design. It is the underlying principle of Norman's System Image, Rubinstein and Hersh's "external myth," Nelson's "virtuality," Smith's user-illusion. It is used by professional designers for the express purpose of creating a dichotomy with the programmer's reality.

- Dissimulation: "Dissimulation means the act of concealing the real fact by pretense."—Fitzkee [6]. A trash can instead of a dialog requesting track and sector identification for zero-overwrite is simulation. A nicely laid-out dialog box for requesting "file name" identification for file "removal" is dissimulation: the essential reality is fully present; it is just being covered up.

Simulation and dissimulation are both important magic techniques: the magician who wishes to simulate a coin disappearing into thin air from his or her right hand had better be proficient enough at dissimulation that spectators don't notice the coin actually sliding into a pocket from the magician's left hand. However, dissimulation is there to cover-up, not to startle and amuse. For example, in the "Asrah" illusion, the assistant slides through a trap door, but appears to still be lying on the platform. Dissimulation. Dull. It is when we as spectators believe we see the assistant, shrouded in silk, slowly rising into the air with no visible means of support, following the beckoning of the magician's wand, that we become interested. Then, when the magician suddenly whips the shroud away, to reveal nothing but empty space, we are left dumbfounded and amazed. Simulation.

Amateur designers are far more likely to cover up a reality than alter it, but so are professionals who are deprived of sufficient resources to "do the right thing." In the early days of Lisa and Macintosh, we at Apple were given all the resources we needed, and we used simulation widely and effectively. Now our entire industry seems bent on power at the expense of everything else, and programs and interface systems are showing the symptoms of dissimulation. For example, Apple's confusing System 7 feature, Publish and Subscribe, is essentially raw technology, with just the lightest sugar coating (dissimulation).

In contrast, human interface and graphic designers designed Apple's QuickTime video animation tool from the ground up as a simulation responsive to the needs of its users. They repeatedly tried out the software on real users under real conditions, to see whether the design illusion was realistic, productive, and responsive. It ended up being all three.

Attention to Detail

Magicians continually stress that illusions don't work without attention to detail. Fitzkee [6]:

> When a magician simulates placing something into a container—any kind of a container, a hat, a tube, a can, a box—he goes through the exact motions he would make if the object were actually placed in the container. His attention is upon the hand apparently containing the object. It follows along as the object is placed in the container. The opposite hand, holding the container, adjusts itself to accommodate the additional weight. The performer's attention then follows the apparent presence of the object. Meanwhile, as he would if the object actually were placed in the container, he ignores the hand which formerly seemed to, or actually did, contain the object.

> ....No matter what type of simulation is used, no matter what the simulation is for, the magician is acting out a role. He must do this well or the simulation will not be effective. He must do it convincingly or he will not convey the impression he is trying to accomplish. He must do it naturally or it will seem artificial and will arouse suspicions.

Magicians talk about the "delicacy" of the illusion: a bit of light escaping from what is supposed to be a dark box or the errant corner of the assistant's dress protruding from the trap door destroys forever all hopes of maintaining the illusion. Fitzkee [6]: "The performer should be particularly careful that his handling of all of his properties, *in every respect,* is in keeping with what they are purported to be, *at all times.* If they are handled as if they are what they seem to be, this contributes to convincingness and conviction.... Naturalness is the most powerful weapon at the disposal of the magician when he seeks to deceive."

The spectator doesn't have to know details of the deception to know deception occurred, thereby destroying the illusion. In fact, the spectator can be dead wrong in his "explanation," and still the illusion evaporates: Fitzkee tells the story of a time when he was filming Howard Thurston performing "The Levitation of the Princess Karnac," in which the woman playing the Princess is actually levitated, without benefit of shroud. Fitzkee, meanwhile, was up in the balcony of the auditorium, filming the procedure, when, "several spectators heard the camera operating. They immediately connected the camera with the levitation. I could see them nudge their companions, call their attention to the camera, then point to the activity on the stage. From the way they relaxed and settled back into their seats, I am positive they felt they had solved the mystery" [6].

Most of us have seen—or even been involved in—software projects where attention to detail was slight or nonexistent, resulting in software with unclear System Images, flashing redraws, unresponsive feedback, or, even worse, a dangerous lack of forgiveness. Such breeches result in software that is confusing, awkward to use, and even frightening—not exactly our normal design goals.

Overcoming Objections Before They Arise

Once an objection, or even a suspicion, arises in the mind of the spectator, the trick is finished. Magicians put great effort into making sure their illusions develop in such a way that the spectator is not even given to questioning why a certain action is taking place. They do this by providing a motive within the spectators' reality for every action taken within the magician's reality. For example, in the "Asrah Levitation," the assistant will not actually be present during much of the performance, having slipped through the trap door. The device that takes the place of the assistant, the device that floats up into the air, is made of metal, rather than flesh and blood. It is therefore given to a certain unnatural stillness. If the spectators slowly became aware of that stillness, they might become suspicious, so to avoid their potential objection, the assistant is first seen to be hypnotized or forced to drink some poisonous elixir, thus seemingly rendering her as still as the apparatus that will replace her. The magician has overcome the objection before it arises.

Hormuz was an early program written in the PILOT language. It featured a character that would "speak" with children through the screen and keyboard. The character introduced himself as an ancient Arabian, then urged the child to "come close to the fire, for the light is weak." He then went on, after asking for the child's name, to request the child's gender: "My eyes grow dim with age: are you a little boy or a little girl" (words approximate). Having established the character as old, having established that it was dark out, the designer is then able to ask what would otherwise be an insulting question of a child. The designer has overcome the objection before it arises.

Believing in the Illusion

Magicians live in both the world of their mechanical tricks and the illusory world they are creating for their spectators, but they "believe" in the spectator's world: "All of the most successful showman-conjurers agree that you must believe in your own magic; you cannot hope to convince an audience unless you first convince yourself."—Nelms [15].

In my experience, programmers face an ongoing struggle to believe in their own illusions. They continually want to slip back into the comfort of their mechanical world down below. In the early days of software, the System Image directly reflected every convolution and limitation of the structure of the program, the programming language, and the operating system. Today's best visual interface systems are designed before the underlying systems are built, so that, while we continue to design for

the expected *capabilities* of our systems, we need no longer design to a pre-determined *structure*. Instead, we design our System Images to reflect the structure of the Design Model [19, 20, 24]. Later, when the programmers lay out the software, they tend toward a structure in general conformance with that of our System Image, neatly reversing the historical sequence.

Programmers who have not made the transition to the design model's illusion are easy to spot: they meet any attempt on the designer's part to create a new and interesting design model with, "Yes, but that's not the way it really works." The last thing a magician wants is for his spectator's model of the act to bear any relationship to "the way it really works."

While we don't share the magician's pressing need to hide this "reality," we often gain advantage by offering the user a well-constructed illusion. For example, ISDN, the new all-digital telephone system in the US, can complete a call connection in a few milliseconds, instead of today's 5 to 10 seconds, exchange data in brief, high-speed bursts, then log-off, terminating billing charges, after an additional few milliseconds. By being faithful to the realities of ISDN, we could offer our users a much faster log-on procedure, but consider how much more we can accomplish by separating the illusion of the interface from the realities of the hardware: With "instant" log-on, high-speed communication, and short-duration transmission, we can create the illusion that the user is always connected. Any time the system sees the user perform a task that requires transmission, such as dropping an addressed document in an out-basket, the system can sign on, send the document, and sign off, all without the user's conscious awareness. As far as the system is concerned, it is saving every precious penny of the user's money. As far as the user is concerned, he or she is "connected" 24 hours a day, seven days a week.

Manipulation of Time

Magicians manipulate time, as well as space. Here are two of their ways:

• Offsetting Time of Reality from Time of Illusion

Magicians use two techniques to offset the actual time a trick (the essential working of the apparatus) takes place from the time of the spectators think it takes place: Anticipation, where the magician does the trick early, before spectators begin looking for it, and Premature Consumption, where the magician does the trick late, after spectators assume it has already occurred.

I once saw a magician on television, seated before a small, 1 inch thick table, performing one of the oldest magic tricks known: Cups and Balls, described by the Roman philosopher, Seneca, in the first century AD. The spectators attempt to guess under which of three cups (or, in this magician's case, stainless steel pans) the ball lies, while the magician makes sure they cannot. The magician began with the usual sponge ball, about the size of a golf ball, which, when squeezed into the palm, becomes the size of a pea and is rather easily inserted beneath any pan desired. After the people around the table had, predictably, failed to identify the correct pan on a couple of occasions, the ball began to grow. And grow. And grow. By the end of the trick, the man tilted the pan forward, then lifted it away to reveal a bowling ball beneath. (The bowling ball, while no wider than the pan, was a great deal taller than the pan was deep.)

The table was not gimmicked in any way. The man had, from all appearances, not lifted any heavy objects. Rather, he had been very busy talking with his spectators when the bowling ball suddenly appeared.

By chance, I had videotaped the performance and was able to study it in detail. The magician had used a technique I call counterpoint: for the entire course of the act, his trickery had preceded its revelation by around 5 seconds: as he would engage in a vociferous explanation of why the spectators had failed on the last round, gesticulating with his hands for emphasis, he was actually placing the load for the next round. The choreography was superlative: like the rich counterpoint of Bach or Händel, the notes of his own reality blended perfectly with the reality he was presenting his spectators. All of that man existed in the reality of his spectators—his intellect, his emotion, his gestures, his words, his apparent actions—except some tiny part of his mind, like some little demon, which went quietly about the task of preparing the next trick. It was a beauty to behold, and, try as I might, even examining the tape frame-by-frame, I could not catch him loading that bowling ball behind the pan.

"Pipelining"—drawing screens, gathering data before needed—is a form of anticipation. Printer buffering is a form of premature consumption. These techniques illustrate that the timing of the user's illusion need not track the reality of the operating system or hardware.

One caveat: illusion is sometimes shattered on our computers when something goes wrong: telling the user that "the document has been successfully sent to the printer" when the document has in fact only been spooled to the computer's internal print buffer would seem like a good idea, but not when a difficulty arises with the print buffer software and the user ends up dragging a properly-functioning 100 pound laser printer into the shop for repair. We need to consider the entirety of the user's reality, and that consists of both the expected and unexpected.

• Stretching Time to Create the Illusion of Difficulty.

Houdini, the great escape artist, was famous for his Milk-Can Escape in which he was squeezed, half-naked and hand-cuffed, into a three-foot tall vessel brimming with water. The top of the can was securely fastened from the outside with six padlocks, and then the apparatus was curtained off from the spectators. They grew increasingly nervous as they watched the minutes tick by as he attempted to make his escape. By the time some ten minutes had passed, the tension would build to an explosive level, not at all relieved by the mounting panic seen in the faces of Houdini's helpers. Finally, the helpers would be able to stand it no longer and would tear aside the curtain to smash open the milk can. But there beside the can would sit Houdini, nattily dressed in a suit and tie, calmly reading a newspaper [10].

Houdini's fondness for reading extended to magazines, too: after his famous escape from inside a locked safe behind a screen, which took mere seconds, he spent the next fifteen minutes back stage, idly reading a magazine, after which he dotted himself with water and burst forth, looking properly sweaty and exhausted [3].

Houdini understood the importance of not making a task look too easy; the designers at Fairchild did not: Fairchild produced one of the first home video game machines called Channel F, back in the mid 1970's. It featured a first-rate tic-tac-toe game with a tragic flaw: regardless of how long the player took to plot his or her next move, the computer would respond within one-half second with its next move. Combined with the machine's skill at choosing the best possible move, this fast reaction left the user feeling puny and inadequate.

Researchers from Robert B. Miller on have been studying the psychological effects of response time on the user [1,8,10,14,22]. What the study of magic offers us is a different perspective on the subject: we are looking beyond efficiency and accuracy; we are looking at the effectiveness of the "act" and its "big picture" impact on the user.

The throwing of the I Ching is an ancient ritual involving the repeated casting of yarrow-stalks in a meditative atmosphere. The process of a single prediction can easily be stretched to the better part of an hour, and no prediction is to be repeated on the same day. I will offer no speculation on the accuracy of the prediction (although the system was designed with enough ambiguity that the diviner can "tailor" the results to the question and circumstances at hand). What I will call attention to is the immediate beneficial effect on the subject, who is being honored with a great deal of the diviner's time and attention in a warm, spiritually-comforting atmosphere. It is the epitome of "quality time."

One of the earliest programs on the Apple II was an automated I Ching caster. It could electronically "cast the stalks" in less than 1 second. You could ask one question and get 60 completely different answers in less than 1 minute! It is probably safe to say the designer was unstudied in the ways of the Tao.

By applying the magic technique of time-stretching, along with a healthy dash of showmanship, we could write a quite different I Ching program. It would ask the user many pertinent and perhaps not-so pertinent questions, "cast the stalks" in a way that was both visually interesting and very time-consuming, deliver results in a quiet, dignified, poetic way, and refuse to answer the same question again on the same day. It would likely be no more accurate in its predictions than its faster cousin; it would surely be less productive, taking hundreds of times longer to use; but it would be far more responsive to the real (if imagined) needs of the person using it.

Illusion and the Threshold of Believability

I propose that there is a "threshold of believability," a point at which careful design and meticulous attention to detail have been sufficient to arouse in the spectator or user a belief that the illusion is real. The exact point will vary by person and even by mood, so we must exceed it sufficiently to ensure believability. Disneyland and Disneyworld are above the threshold of believability; county fairs are not. Lucas's *Star Wars* was above the threshold; *Attack of the Killer Tomatoes* was not. Penn and Teller cutting a live snake in two, then restoring it, on Saturday Night Live was above the threshold; Uncle Charlie's tired, old card tricks at Christmas were not.

The original Star, Lisa, and the early Macintosh all exceeded the threshold. Some of the graphical user interfaces appearing now, with their underlying dependency on dissimulation and their lack of consistency, are falling short. If users cannot trust the system, if they are occasionally but violently thrust into the programmer's reality, they can not, will not, and should not believe in the world we are making for them.

One need sacrifice no power in building a believable illusion. For years, Macintosh programmers have been able to recover from a crashed application by typing arcane incantations in their debugger, while regular users were left with no method of recovery at all. Now, in System 7, anyone can press Command-Option-Escape to achieve the same result. Recovery is not only achievable by every end-user, but is easier for the programmers.

THE ETHICS OF IMPERSONATION

"...magicians, if they are strictly ethical, are morally under obligation to insist that their methods are purely natural" (Fitzkee [5]).

Stage magicians have been impersonating "real" magicians (such as Merlin) for a long, long time. They've had plenty of time to experiment with the ethics of stage magic and have come up with workable solutions. I present these solutions because I find them applicable to the ongoing discussion of impersonation of people by computers (anthropomorphism).

Shneiderman [23] argues strongly against having the computer personify a human, although he does suggest that young children might be exposed to a cartoon character for the sake of visual appeal. Laurel [13] agrees in part, but has expanded his horizon: "...I have argued, not for the personification of the computer, but for its invisibility.... The representation of agents or characters is a different idea altogether than the notion of 'personified' computers." She goes on to argue the benefits of visible characters in the interface.

The mainstream of magic is in essential agreement with Brenda Laurel's view: "A magician is an actor playing the part of a magician."—Fitzkee [6]. Mainstream magicians find it important that spectators do not leave the theater under the impression that the magic performed or that the magician who performed it is supernatural. This is such an important issue to them that when people claim supernatural powers, magicians flock to expose them: Houdini spent much of the latter part of his life both seeking out a true spiritualist and utterly destroying all the fakes that lay in his path [7]. Uri Geller, who claims to bend spoons and start broken watches through spiritual intervention, has had his own personal exposer, in the person of James (The Amazing) Randi, who has taken great pains over the past 15 or 20 years, to duplicate any "spiritual" trick Geller attempts with plain old-fashioned magic techniques, much to Geller's discomfort.

Applying the "super-anthropomorphism" ethics of magic to software, I see it calling for Laurel's split between the invisible computer, on one hand, and the robust, visible character on the other. This fulfills the same requirement of honesty: the magician is not supernatural; the character he plays is. The computer is not capable of human intelligence and warmth; the character we create is. People will not end up feeling deceived and used when they discover, as they must ultimately, that the computer is nothing but a very fast idiot.

CONCLUSION

If, having finished reading this paper, you feel strangely unsatisfied, I have accomplished my aim: 5000 years of magic cannot be compressed into eight pages. We have much to learn from the best of the master magicians, and several important resources for doing so. First, Fitzkee's trilogy and Nelms single volume (all currently in print), when taken together, lay out the organized knowledge of illusion-making clearly and precisely. Reading just these four books will give you a firm foundation. Second, while perhaps you were not left so strangely unsatisfied by the paper that you are ready to apprentice to Penn & Teller, you may at least want to become a more active spectator by studying the performances of master magicians, many mentioned in this paper. Finally, there is no substitute for direct experience: learning to perform just one or two tricks well will instill many of the techniques and principles I have discussed at the level not achievable by either reading or watching.

REFERENCES

1. Bergman, Hans, Brinkman, Albert, and Koelega, Harry S., "System Response time and Problem Solving Behavior," *Proceedings of the Human Factors Society,* 25th Annual Meeting, (Rochester, NY, October 12-16, 1981), 749-753

2. Burger, Eugene. *Strange Ceremonies, Bizarre Magick for the Modern Conjuror,* published by Richard Kaufman and Alan Greenberg, 1991.

3. Dawes, Edwin A. and Setterington, Arthur, *The Encyclopedia of Magic,* W. H. Smith Publishers, Inc., New York, NY, 1986.

4. Fitzkee, Dariel. *Showmanship for Magicians,* © Copyright 1943, 1945 Dariel Fitzroy. Used by permission of the publisher: Lee Jacobs Productions, P. O. Box 362, Pomeroy, Ohio, 45769-0362, 1943, 1945

5. Fitzkee, Dariel. *The Trick Brain,* © Copyright 1944, 1976 Dariel Fitzroy. Used by permission of the publisher: Lee Jacobs Productions, P. O. Box 362, Pomeroy, Ohio, 45769-0362, 1944, 1976.

6. Fitzkee, Dariel. *Magic by Misdirection,* © Copyright 1945, 1975 Dariel Fitzroy. Used by permission of the publisher: Lee Jacobs Productions, P. O. Box 362, Pomeroy, Ohio, 45769-0362, 1945, 1975.

7. Gibson, Walter B. & Young, Morris N., *Houdini on Magic,* Dover Publications, Inc., NY, NY, 1953.

8. Grossberg, Mitchell, Weisen, Raymond A., and Yntema, Douwe B., "An Experiment on Problem Solving with Delayed Computer Responses," *IEEE Transactions on Systems, Man, and Cybernetics,* (March 1976), 219-222

9. Heckel, Paul. *The Elements of Friendly Software Design.* Sybex, Alameda, CA, 1991.

10. Henning, Doug, "Houdini," The Congress Video Group, NY, NY, Video, 1986.

11. Jillette, Penn, and Teller. *Cruel Tricks for Dear Friends,* Villard Books, New York, NY, 1989.

12. Kay, Alan. "User Interface: A Personal View," In Brenda Laurel (ed.), *The Art of Human-Computer Interface Design,* Addison-Wesley, Reading, Mass., 1991.

13. Laurel, Brenda. *Computers as Theater,* Addison-Wesley, Reading, Mass., 1991.

14. Miller, Robert B., "Response Time in Man-Computer Conversational Transactions," *Proceedings Sprint Joint Computer Conference,* 33, AFIPS Press, Montvale, NJ, 1968, 267-277

15. Nelms, Henning. Magic and Showmanship, *A Handbook for Conjurers,* Dover Publications, Inc., New York, NY, 1969.

16. Nelson, Theodor Holm. "Interactive Systems and the Design of Virtuality," *Creative Computing,* Vol 6, Nos. 11 & 12, (November and December, 1980).

17. Nelson, Theodor Holm. "The Right Way to Think About Software Design," In Brenda Laurel (ed.), *The Art of Human-Computer Interface Design,* Addison-Wesley, Reading, Mass., 1991.

18. Norman, Donald, "Some Observations of Mental Models," In Gentner, Dedre & Stevens, Albert L. (Eds.), *Mental Models,* Hillsdale, N.J.: Lawrence Erlbaum Associates, 1983

19. Norman, Donald, Cognitive Engineering. In D. A. Norman & S. W. Draper (Eds.), *User Centered System Design,* Hillsdale, N.J.: Lawrence Erlbaum Associates, 1986

20. Norman, Donald, *Psychology of Everyday Things* (Now *Design of Everyday Things).* Basic Books, 1988.

21. Rubinstein, Richard and Hersh, Harry M. "Design Philosophy." Chapter 2 in *The Human Factor: Designing Computer Systems for People,* Digital Press, Burlington, MA, 1984.

22. Shneiderman, Ben. *Designing the user interface: Strategies for effective human-computer interaction.* Addison-Wesley, Reading, Mass., 1987, 1992

23. Shneiderman, Ben. "A Nonanthropomorphic Style Guide: Overcoming the Humpty Dumpty Syndrome." *The Computing Teacher* (October, 1988) 9-10.

24. Tognazzini, Bruce "Tog." *Tog on Interface.* Addison-Wesley, Reading, Mass., 1992

Perceptual vs. Hardware Performance in Advanced Acoustic Interface Design

Moderator: Elizabeth M. Wenzel
NASA-Ames Research Center
Mail Stop 262-2
Moffett Field, CA 94035-1000
(415) 604-6290
beth@eos.arc.nasa.gov

Panelists: William W. Gaver, RANK Xerox Cambridge EuroPARC
Scott H. Foster, Crystal River Engineering, Groveland, CA
Haim Levkowitz, University of Massachusetts at Lowell
Roger Powell, Silicon Graphics, Mountain View, CA

ABSTRACT
This panel brings together experts in the field of non-speech auditory displays with points of view ranging from long-term basic research in human perception to the timely production of useable tools in commercial systems. The panel will examine issues of perceptual validity and engineering performance from several different perspectives representative of current work in the field, and discuss how such issues can or should impact decisions made during technology development. Panelists' perspectives include: levels of analysis in designing and using auditory interfaces (Gaver), an example of what can be learned about implementation requirements from low-level psychophysical studies (Wenzel), designing integrated systems to encompass sonification in a three-dimensional environment (Foster), issues in the study of information transfer in representational acoustic signals (Levkowitz), and the design of a generalized technology platform for acoustic signal presentation (Powell).

KEYWORDS: Acoustic displays, multimedia, auditory perception, user-interface design issues, human performance issues

INTRODUCTION
While non-speech audio is gaining increased recognition as an important interface medium [1, 3, 4], work in the area often consists of rather speculative discussions of its potential characteristics and capabilities. In part, this has been due to the relative newness of the field but perhaps more realistically it has been due to limitations in the technology of sound generation. Such technology is starting to become both mature and inexpensive enough to be considered a viable component of relatively near-term developments in human-computer interfaces. Thus, now is

© 1993 ACM 0-89791-575-5/93/0004/0363...$1.50

a critical time for both researchers and designers to carefully assess the perceptual and human performance requirements of advanced acoustic displays and the degree to which these requirements should have a direct impact on hardware and software implementations. In order to avoid the development of perhaps flashy, but essentially irrelevant, audio interface capabilities part of this assessment should include consideration of how such interfaces can be validated in a human perception and performance sense, both during the development stages and after implementation of a particular technology platform. Conversely, constraints in building real systems may mean that "ideal" perceptual and performance requirements may not be currently realizable. The panel will examine issues of perceptual and performance validation from several different perspectives representative of current work in the field, and discuss whether such issues can or should impact decisions in technology design.

PANELISTS' POSITION STATEMENTS

Bill Gaver *received his Ph.D. in psychology and cognitive science from the University of California, San Diego in 1988. He has developed several systems which use non-speech audio cues: Apple Computer's SonicFinder, SoundShark and ARKola (with Randall Smith and Tim O'Shea), and a system of environmental audio reminders called EAR. Currently he works at Rank Xerox Cambridge EuroPARC, developing synthesis techniques that allow everyday sounds to be generated along source dimensions, extending work on auditory icons, and exploring a more general ecological approach to HCI.*

Levels of Analysis in Auditory Interface Design. The design of auditory interfaces must be addressed at a number of different levels. The first level deals with psychoacoustical issues which concern the relations between physical and perceptual dimensions of sounds as well as the interaction of multiple sounds. Understanding psychoacoustics is particularly important for the design of interfaces that use dimensions of sounds to represent dimensions of data, as well as for interfaces which use multiple simultaneous sounds.

The second level concerns the semantics of sound, what individual sounds mean. This is the concern of a study of everyday listening, which characterizes sounds in terms of perception of their events. Similar questions might be addressed in terms of music theory, aimed at discovering, for instance, the affective character of various motives.

Understanding the semantics of sounds leads to a consideration of the third level, which concerns the mapping between a particular auditory message and the data or event it is to represent. Some mappings seem more intuitive and easily-learned than others: this can be exploited in building auditory interfaces. But mappings need not be obviously representational or metaphorical. As several recent examples have shown, interfaces can be built in which individual sounds map to their referents in arbitrary ways. Although learning the meaning of any given sound may be difficult, patterns in the data are revealed naturally.

Finally, the fourth level has to do with issues relating to the affective impact of auditory interfaces. Will they be annoying, obtrusive, distracting? Or can auditory interfaces be built that merge naturally with the pre-existing auditory ambience? Several guidelines for the design of unobtrusive audio cues can be drawn from the psychological literature.

These issues are all important for the design of non-speech audio cues. Fortunately, each level of issue has been and can be studied from an empirical point of view. But I believe that, although empirical studies are useful, the real proof is in the pudding: the best way to evaluate an approach is through extended experience with a working system.

Beth Wenzel *received a Ph.D. in cognitive psychology with an emphasis in psychoacoustics from the University of California, Berkeley in 1984. From 1985-1986 she was a National Research Council post-doctoral research associate at NASA-Ames Research Center working on the auditory display of information for aviation systems. Since 1986 she has been Director of the Spatial Auditory Displays Lab in the Aerospace Human Factors Research Division at NASA-Ames, directing development of real-time display technology and conducting basic and applied research in auditory perception and localization in three-dimensional virtual acoustic displays.*

Using Psychophysical Data to Design Virtual Acoustic Displays. Since 1986, our group at NASA Ames has been working on the simulation techniques and digital technology required for the real-time generation of externalized, three-dimensional sound cues over headphones [2, 5]. The synthesis technique involves the real-time filtering of sounds with filters derived from Head-Related Transfer Functions (HRTFs) measured in the ear-canals of individual subjects for a large number of different source locations. These HRTFs act as a map of "location filters"

used in the real-time spatial sound system, the Convolvotron.

In formal psychophysical studies, we have learned several things about the strengths and weaknesses of our approach which both improve the utilization of current technology and point to areas where we need to do further development. In general, our data suggest that most listeners can obtain useful directional information from an auditory display without requiring the use of individually-tailored HRTFs. However, perceptual errors like front-back confusions, distortions in elevation, and failures to externalize do tend to be exacerbated with virtual sources, especially when the sounds are synthesized from someone else's HRTFs. Other research suggests that such errors can be minimized by the addition of dynamic cues due to head-motion, correlated visual cues, and more realistic environmental cues based on real-time models of room acoustics.

Such data indicate that display capabilities, such as dynamic, interactive head-tracking, and real-time synthesis of reverberant environments, are important requirements for accurate spatial cueing. Thus, while design compromises obviously need to be made to achieve practical technologies, the admittedly rather expensive and computationally-intensive specifications of systems like the Convolvotron have been driven by critical human sensory and performance requirements. As acoustic signal-processing technology becomes cheaper and more wide-spread, compromises based on engineering constraints will become less of an issue. In the meantime, the more expensive and elaborate systems can provide the means to study critical performance characteristics and guide the optimal distribution of processing power in future hardware designs. Particularly relevant to generalized non-speech interfaces will be the consideration of how spatial cueing interacts with signal content in multiple sound streams, since not all sounds are localized equally well. Much of this research, in turn, must await the development and integration of the more advanced sound-generation systems discussed by the other panelists.

Scott Foster *founded Crystal River Engineering in 1987 to develop digital signal processing equipment for spatial audio and navigation systems. One of his first clients was NASA-Ames, for which he developed the Convolvotron 3-D sound system for applications including audio research, communications, navigation, virtual reality and telepresence. Before establishing Crystal River, Scott was an engineer at Hewlett-Packard Laboratories working on digital signal processing for audio and instrumentation, a research scientist at Atari, Inc. where he designed a Very Large Scale Integrated (VLSI) audio synthesis chip, and a project leader at Systems Control, Inc. where he worked with Stanford's Center for Research in Music and Acoustics on a study of automatic music analysis and transcription. Mr. Foster received a B.S. in mathematics from the Massachusetts Institute of Technology in 1976.*

Integrating Sonification Systems with Three-Dimensional Environments. Recent advances in VLSI hardware have made possible the construction of real-time systems that can render environmental acoustics by tracking the position and orientation of a listener and generating synthetic binaural sound for that listener using headphones. The most sophisticated of these systems utilize supercomputing performance to render complex acoustic scenarios including transmission loss effects, reflection, nonuniform radiation, Doppler effects, and more, resulting in a compelling and natural presentation. While initially designed for virtual reality and research in psychoacoustics, such systems can be extremely useful enhancements to applications involving data sonification. For example, virtual audio could provide a three-dimensional, navigable data environment which is part of a workstation/desktop environment that may otherwise be two-dimensional.

A virtual audio system can be divided roughly into three parts: source generation, environmental effects, and modeling listener characteristics like HRTFs. While there is still plenty of work to be done, we feel that modeling listener characteristics is a largely understood problem and the issues involved in modeling environmental effects are at least fairly clearcut. Source generation, on the other hand, is a much more problematic area. How can we build a real-time system which is general enough to produce the quasi-musical sounds usually used for auditory icons as well as purely enviromental sounds like doors opening or glass breaking? The most general system would be based on synthesis via structural or acoustical models of sound source characteristics. A simpler but less versatile approach would use playback of sampled sounds and/or conventional MIDI (Musical Instrument Digital Interface) devices as in most current systems. Since very general structural models are both difficult to develop and computationally-intensive, a more practical and immediately achievable system is a hybrid approach that uses techniques like real-time interpolation and manipulation of simple parameters of sampled sounds.

With the advances in algorithms and hardware to produce such simulations, there is also a need to develop an extensible protocol for virtual audio. Such a protocol will need to encompass all the acoustic models in use today and those expected to be developed in the near future. This protocol should allow both virtual reality developers and designers of sonification systems to utilize virtual reality technology, even as that technology makes dramatic improvements in its capabilities.

Halm Levkowitz *is an assistant professor in the Department of Computer Science at the University of Massachusetts/Lowell. He is a founding member of the Institute for Visualization and Perception Research and co-Principal Investigator in the Institute's NSF-sponsored data sonification project. His recent research efforts have concentrated on the development of interactive methods for representing multi-parametric information via color, geometric, and sound encodings. He has developed new color methods for computer graphics representation of parameter distributions, and has also developed and*

implemented tools for automated psychometric evaluation of these new display methods.

Perceptual Issues in the Sonification of Multidimensional Data. Data "sonification," the representation of data in sound for analysis and exploration, is the auditory counterpart of data visualization. The fundamental technique for presenting multidimensional data in sound is the establishment of a mapping between the dimensions of a data sample and the properties of a discrete sonic event, such as pitch, loudness, and duration. Subjects have shown modestly improved performance in the few sonification experiments that have been reported; however, there has been little formal research either to measure the effectiveness of sonification techniques in real-world applications or to increase our understanding of how they work and how to improve them.

Sonification research is severely hampered by the lack of real scientific instrumentation. The sound generation and processing hardware actually available for sonification research consists mostly of MIDI devices that provide only limited control over the sound generation process. Even if money were no object, however, it is doubtful that sonification workers would be able to create the "dream" sonification system now. The reason is that our current knowledge of human auditory perception provides little guidance for the design of sonification systems in which several sound attributes are varied simultaneously. Most of the classical psychological studies have focused on the perception of single sound attributes or interactions between two attributes. Investigations of the perception of musical timbre have attempted to overcome these limitations, but there is no satisfying comprehensive theory of timbre perception nor even a generally accepted taxonomy for classifying timbres. Not surprisingly, the treatment of timbre in the available sound synthesis hardware is a hodgepodge of synthesis algorithms, pre-programmed "patches", and canned sound samples. By way of contrast, consider the situation in computer graphics: the techniques for producing realistic imagery are standard virtually across the entire industry, and the key differences among competing manufacturers' equipment often come down to how much of the standard functionality you can buy for a given price. Obviously, the situation in computer sound facilities is far from this.

In sum, it is premature to announce that we have the technology to allow us to simply add a meaningful, low-cost sonification facility (or other powerful audio interface) to computer systems. Much work needs to be done to determine what sounds we need to produce and how best to produce them.

Roger Powell *has been active in the field of electronic and computer music since the early 1970's. He has worked as a recording engineer, composer, synthesizer performer with Todd Rundgren's UTOPIA and David Bowie, and as the software designer of TEXTURE(tm), a MIDI sequencing program for the IBM PC. From 1987 to 1991, he was employed by WaveFrame Corp. to write user-interface* *software for the AudioFrame Digital Audio Workstation. In April 1991, Roger joined Silicon Graphics Computer Systems as Manager of Audio Applications for the IRIS Indigo, a 3D graphics workstation with built-in digital audio hardware. In late 1991 Roge moved to the technical staff of Digital Media Engineering within SGI.*

A Generalized Hardware/Software Platform for Acoustic Signal Presentation. Acoustic interfaces for computers require hardware and software support for generating audio. IRIS Indigo represents a computer manufacturer's integrated solution for standard audio capability. With 16-bit stereo analog and digital I/O and high-performance signal processing hardware, Indigo supports high-resolution audio as an indigenous part of the computing environment. Software interface designers at Silicon Graphics work with the practical aspects of providing sound capability as a standard feature of the operating system.

In order to more fully integrate and exploit the use of sound in the computer/human interface, a sonification server called SoundSpace is being implemented for the Indigo family of workstations. SoundSpace will become a key part of SGI's next-generation desktop user interface.

The SoundSpace project is intended to provide both an applications programming interface for developers wishing to add audio cues to applications, and a means for user-customization of sounds in the computer interface. SoundSpace utilizes the high-performance sound generation capabilities of the Indigo workstation to create discrete and evolutionary sounds in realtime.

Based on a client/server architecture, SoundSpace consists of a multi-timbral sound synthesizer server controlled via an internal MIDI port, an interactive event scheduler and a remote procedure call interface for sending client messages across a network. Developers or end users may create sonic tasks by building sound generation and event specifications using a small language designed for the purpose. The language supports the creation of complex sonic events whose behavior may be controlled by the client application.

Customization is handled through resource files in a manner similar to the way visual properties of the windowing interface may be manipulated. Sounds may be organized into categorized groups called 'sound schemes'. A standard sound scheme is provided for common system events.

Custom schemes may be developed for applications requiring specific sound vocabularies. Users can choose alternate schemes to change the 'personality' of the audio feedback.

In designing SoundSpace, both current and future flexibility has been maximized by choosing to implement real time synthesis and control using a high-level software interface rather than special-purpose hardware that is necessarily less generalizable. Instead of requiring specialized external devices or being limited to simple playback of low-resolution sounds as in many workstation environments, SoundSpace fully exploits the Indigo's fast RISC CPU and signal processing hardware while also providing a foundation for sound generation and control that can be readily expanded as digital technology becomes faster, cheaper and more powerful. For example, in the future it should be possible to create fully three-dimensional sound environments by simply expanding, not redesigning, SoundSpace's capabilities.

REFERENCES

1. Buxton, W., Gaver, W., & Bly, S. *The Use of Non-Speech Audio at the Interface.* (Tutorial No. 10). Presented at *CHI'89 Human Factors in Computing Systems* (Austen, April 30-May 4, 1989), ACM Press.

2. Foster, S.H., Wenzel, E.M., and Taylor, R.M. Real-time synthesis of complex acoustic environments. *ASSP (IEEE) Workshop on Applications of Signal Processing to Audio & Acoustics,* (New Paltz, NY, October 2- 23, 1991).

3. Gaver, W. W., Smith, R. B., & O'Shea, T. Effective sounds in complex systems: The ARKola simulation, in *Proceedings of CHI'91 Human Factors in Computing Systems* (New Orleans, April 27-May 2, 1991), ACM Press, pp. 85-90.

4. Smith, S., Bergeron. R. D., & Grinstein, G. G. Stereophonic and surface sound generation for exploratory data analysis, in *Proceedings of CHI'90 Human Factors in Computing Systems* (Seattle, April 1-5, 1990), ACM Press, pp. 125-132.

5. Wenzel, E. M. Localization in virtual acoustic displays. *Presence: Teleoperators and Virtual Environments,* 1, 1 (Winter 1992), 80-107.

Separations of Concerns in the Chiron-1 User Interface Development and Management System

Richard N. Taylor
Department of Computer Science
University of California, Irvine[1]
92717-3425
E-mail: taylor@ics.uci.edu
+1.714-856-6429

Gregory F. Johnson
Northrop Corporation
1 Research Park
Palos Verdes, CA 90274
E-mail: johnson@nrtc.northrop.com
+1.310-544-5487

ABSTRACT

The development of user interfaces for large applications is subject to a series of well-known problems including cost, maintainability, and sensitivity to changes in the operating environment. The Chiron user interface development system has been built to address these software engineering concerns. Chiron introduces a series of layers that insulate components of an application from other components that may experience change. To separate application code from user interface code, user interface agents called *artists* are attached to application abstract data types. Operations on abstract data types within the application implicitly trigger user interface activities. Chiron also provides insulation between the user interface layer and the underlying system; artist code is written in terms of abstract depiction libraries that insulate the code from the specifics of particular windowing systems and toolkits. Concurrency is pervasive in the Chiron architecture. Inside an application there can be multiple execution threads; there is no requirement for a user interface listening/dispatching routine to have exclusive control. Multiple artists can be attached to a single application abstract data type, providing alternative forms of access by a single user or coordinated access and manipulation by multiple users.

KEYWORDS: user interface management systems (UIMS), modularization of UIMS, concurrency, event-based integration, artists, GUI construction, design

[1]This material is based upon work sponsored by the Defense Advanced Research Projects Agency under Grant Number MDA972-91-J-1010. The content of the information does not necessarily reflect the position or the policy of the Government and no official endorsement should be inferred.

OVERVIEW

In this section we discuss the objectives for the Chiron project and briefly indicate key constituents of the Chiron system. The domain of discourse is user interface management systems (UIMSs) and how they relate to application software architectures. Our perspective is that of researchers and developers of UIMSs; our intended audience is other researchers and developers, as well as system architects.

The development of large systems (such as software engineering environments) poses a group of well-known software engineering problems, including maintainability, resilience to changes in the operating environment, and development cost. The objective of the Chiron project is to address these concerns by creating a user interface technology with the following properties:

- architectural flexibility and extensibility
- robustness in the presence of change
- facilitation of software reuse

The following paragraphs elaborate each of these items. We also provide a very brief description of how Chiron achieves these goals. We will explain further how Chiron achieves these goals later in the paper.

We begin with a few definitions. An *application* is the software for which Chiron is being used to provide its interface to the user. A *user interface* consists of presentations plus dialog decisions (association of behavior with events or actions). For our purposes specification of a user interface does *not* determine look-and-feel. *Processes* in the ensuing discussion refers to operating system processes. We also use the term *agent* to refer to software components that have their own thread of control. Multiple agents may reside in a single process.

Architectural extensibility and flexibility. Current user interface technologies often impose a fairly rigid set of constraints on how the application must be structured. In a large application, however, there are typically many architectural desiderata, so it is undesirable for the user interface to enforce a particular architecture.

Chiron provides architectural flexibility at two levels: within application processes, and across process and machine boundaries. Inside an application process, the Chiron dispatcher mechanism provides an unobtrusive interface between the application and the user interface layer. In Chiron, the only constraint is that the application must have data types with defined operations that manipulate them. Across process boundaries, Chiron's client/server architecture provides flexibility in terms of application languages, windowing systems and toolkits, and process inter-connection topology.

Robustness in the presence of change. In a system that has distinct groups of concerns intermingled, it becomes difficult or impossible to track changes in the environment, since changes to one part of such a system inevitably mandate changes in other, unrelated parts of the system. In the worst case one is required to do an amount of work proportional to the size of the entire system whenever a change is necessary.

Chiron provides separation of concerns at two levels: between the application and the user interface software, and between the user interface software and the underlying windowing system and toolkit.

Reusable software artifacts. A key to software reuse is to structure systems so that they use modular components with small, well-defined interfaces.

The Chiron notion of artists adheres to this principle. Each *artist*[2] is a stand-alone, reusable software agent that implements a particular user interface and has a small, well-defined interface to the application and to the server. The artist notion facilitates reuse of application software by factoring out user interface code from the application code. The design of the abstract depiction library also addresses the reuse issue. A programmer can make use of the standard class hierarchy of user interface objects, or can create new, tailored subclasses.

Specific Objectives of the Chiron Design

Turning from the general software engineering goals above to more specific design and implementation issues, Chiron was designed with the following goals:

- Support for multiple graphical and textual views, with coordinated update. Multiple coordinated views can be used either by a single user or by groups of users.

---

[2] The term originated with the Incense system [6]. We use the term to apply to a concept which is similar in purpose, but more general, powerful, and complex.

- Support for clients written in multiple languages. Even within a single application, different subsystems may be written in different languages.

- Support for concurrency, both within processes and across machine and network boundaries; the application and the user interface have independent control threads, so neither the user interface nor the application is in absolute control.

- Performance comparable to standard user interface development systems and *ad hoc*, hand-crafted systems.

- Ability to leverage work done by implementors of various toolkits, but without dependence on the details of particular toolkits.

- Limited support for groupware applications, in which multiple users see coordinated views of the system, each tailored to the particular user's needs and organizational roles.

- Support for dynamic changes to the set of active views, clients, and servers as the application executes.

The balance of the paper will indicate how the first five of these goals were achieved. Space limitations do not permit consideration of all of them. A beta version of Chiron is available for distribution. A detailed user manual is available for use in building applications [1].

Organization of the Paper

The remaining sections of this paper are as follows. We first consider some relationships between Chiron and other work in the UIMS area. The architecture of Chiron is then explored. The next section describes how a Chiron-based user interface is created. Performance figures are given, followed by a brief description of some example uses. A summary and conclusion section closes.

COMPARISON TO OTHER WORK

Ongoing research projects in the user interface area offer approaches that contrast in various ways with that of Chiron. Rather than comparing all systems on the basis of the same criteria (which is desirable but which would consume far too much space) we instead comment only on the most relevant features of these other systems.

In assessing Chiron it is important to remember that our goal has been to simultaneously achieve all the objectives listed above, not just excel in one area only.

A general architectural comparison can be made with two well-known systems, Interviews and Garnet. Inter-Views [4] uses C++, and is tightly coupled to that language. Application and user interface code are closely tied together, and a user interface listener/dispatcher is in control of the single control thread. The application is dormant until InterViews invokes application code. Application code takes the form of virtual functions in user-defined sub-classes of the InterViews class hierarchy. This is in contrast with Chiron's focus on clear separation of the user interface from the application, as well as Chiron's concurrent control model.

Garnet [8] is written in Lisp, and applications must be coded in Lisp. Garnet makes use of a combined constraint manager and object manager called KR. For the application to respond to user events, a Garnet listener is given control, and application code is again dormant until invoked by the user interface layer in response to user interactions. While architecturally this is again in contrast to Chiron, we are in the process of incorporating constraint mechanisms into Chiron to achieve many of the benefits exhibited in Garnet (and Gilt [7]).

In the Dynamic Windows/Common Lisp Interface Manager [5], presentation types are built through inheritance from application objects. This is similar in concept to the way Chiron artists are built, since they obtain much of their interface from the package specifications of the object they display. Chiron, in its Ada implementation, cannot use inheritance for this purpose.

The Suite system [2] implements a distributed architecture that supports groupware. The distributed architecture of Suite is similar to Chiron's client/server orientation, but is more fully exploited in Suite. In Suite, however, editing is the main metaphor for user interaction and graphics are not supported.

The Picasso toolkit [10] uses a programming language metaphor. User interface objects are created and destroyed on scope entry and exit, and new parameter passing modes have been devised to support user interface programming idioms. Chiron's Lo-Cal has some similarities, though it is much simpler in objective. Chiron has avoided any toolkit development, in contrast to Picasso. Picasso's triggering (based on its constraint mechanism) is similar in purpose to Chiron's dispatcher, but Chiron uses multiple, strongly-typed, concurrent mechanisms.

Serpent [11] uses a client/server relational database trigger model with restricted data types. This is similar to Chiron's dispatcher, but Chiron places no restriction on the set of types that may be displayed and does not demand that the application relinquish, to the user interface system, storage control of the objects to be displayed.

Three papers at CHI'92 are especially deserving of comment. The Rendezvous project [3] focuses on the use of the abstraction-link-view paradigm for the structuring of applications and user interfaces. Rendezvous' abstractions are akin to Chiron's application's ADTs; its links are related to Chiron's dispatchers, and its views are similar to Chiron's artists. In terms of capabilities the two systems have much in common, though Rendezvous uses constraint technology where Chiron uses a simpler event-based architecture. A key difference, however, is that to use Rendezvous the application developer must write the application in Rendezvous, "an extended object-oriented Lisp".

The AT&T Display Construction Set UIMS [9] separates applications from the UIMS via Unix pipes. The UIMS can thus receive data events from multiple processes. The data messages are not richly typed, however, restricting applications to situations where simple database records suffice to capture the object to be displayed.

NASA's TAE Plus system [12] is focused on making the generation of applications with GUI's easier than by using toolkits directly. TAE insulates the application from changes in the toolkit. TAE Plus is like many commercial systems, however, which generate an application code *template* into which the remainder of the application code must be inserted. The UIMS thus strongly determines the architecture of the application.

THE CHIRON ARCHITECTURE

The key components of Chiron are (a) the Chiron client, which consists of the application plus all artists, (b) the Chiron server, which is responsible for maintaining and rendering the logical depictions created by the artists, and (c) the tools which are used to build artists and clients. Figure 1 shows one possible configuration of the client and server components.

The process of creating the user interface software (i.e. the activities that occur before run-time) begins with identification of instances of abstract data types (ADTs) in the application that will be used as the basis for communication with the user.

For each of these ADTs an agent called an artist is written. The artists are coded to make use of Chiron's extensible library of abstract depiction classes (its "drawing elements"). The artists are associated with the selected abstract data types by means of *dispatchers* which are transparently (to the application) wrapped around the ADTs by a pre-processor.

At run-time, the dispatcher wrapped around an abstract data type intercepts all operation calls on the ADT and

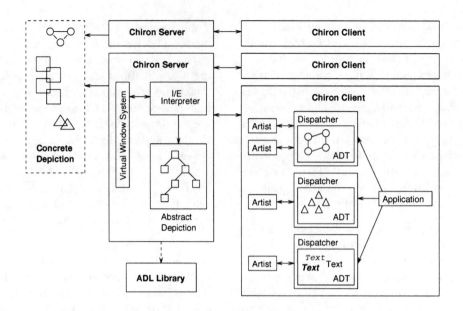

Figure 1: The Chiron runtime architecture

notifies each of the artists associated with that ADT of the operation.

Ensuing calls by the artists to create/update depictions are transmitted over an inter-process communication link to a Chiron server. The server implements the inheritance hierarchy of abstract depiction classes. Calls from artists thus create and manipulate instances of these classes; the server maintains an 'abstract depiction' of each artist's user interface. This is a complete internal representation of the user interface, so that the server can handle expose events and similar user interactions independently, without having to interact with the client. The server also oversees rendering of the abstract depiction to a concrete depiction, using a windowing system and toolkit.

In the remainder of this section we concentrate on the architecture of the client and the server, elaborating on the brief description above. The section following considers the process of creating artists and describes the tools available to aid in that activity.

Client Architecture

A Chiron client consists of an application program, a set of artists, and a set of supervisory mechanisms. Applications must be written in terms of operations on abstract data types. (This "object orientation" indicates the kinds of application domains for which the use of Chiron is appropriate: those in which there are clearly identifiable abstract data types with which user interfaces can be associated.) A dispatcher generator takes the application's source code and a list of designated abstract data types, and outputs a modified program in which the designated ADT's have had dispatchers "wrapped" around them. The operation names of the ADT are made to refer to dispatcher routines. When a call is made from within the application code to an ADT operation, the dispatcher receives control. The dispatcher typically invokes the actual ADT operation, and then notifies each of the artists attached to the ADT about the operation invoked. (A prompting-style interface can be created by having the artists perform their functions before the ADT operation is invoked.) The notice is strongly typed (in the type system of the ADT), and includes the parameters to the ADT operation that was invoked plus the ADT's return value, if any. (Artists and dispatchers must share the same address space to avoid type linearization and reconstruction.) In this scheme the application source code that an application programmer sees does not have any user interface modifications at all, yielding separation of concerns between the application and the user interface code. (Recompilation of the source is required, however, to force the application to invoke the ADT operations through the dispatcher interface.)

Artists An artist is an agent that translates application ADT manipulations into user interface depictions and behaviors. The translation is bi-directional; if the application invokes an ADT operation, the artist is notified and modifies its user interface accordingly. Conversely, if the user manipulates the user interface, the artist translates the manipulation into appropriate operation calls on the ADT.

Figure 2 shows the skeleton of a typical artist. When it starts up the artist creates its graphical user interface,

```
package body Artist is
   task body Artist is
   -- type declarations
   -- callback procedures
   begin
      -- create initial graphical objects
      -- set behavior of objects (callbacks)
      -- start processing
      loop
         select
            accept ...
         or
            accept ...
         or
            terminate;
         end select;
      end loop;
   end Artist;
end Artist;
```

Figure 2: The skeleton of a Chiron artist

and establishes behaviors in response to various user-generated events. The artist then enters a select-loop in which it waits for an event. Events are operation invocations on the associated ADT or user actions.

User events are *move*, *menu*, *select*, *key*, and *adjust* user actions detected by X. (User events not otherwise processed by the server are associated by the server with the graphical object wherein they occurred and are then routed to the appropriate client. Within that client they are further routed to the appropriate artist.)

Server Architecture

The server maintains an internal representation, or abstract depiction, of the graphical contents of each window managed by Chiron and a mapping of those windows to the clients, and artists within those clients, responsible for them. The server has an instruction/event interpreter that responds to artist requests from the client to change the abstract depiction. The instruction/event interpreter also responds to user events by invoking update methods resident in the server. Thus the server encapsulates the specific methods used to render a specified depiction and indeed all user interface aspects that are common to all clients.

UI DEVELOPMENT UNDER CHIRON

A collection of tools have been implemented to assist in various facets of user interface development. These include a dispatcher generator that inserts user interface code around designated application abstract data types, an artist template generator, a Lo-Cal pre-processor, and a pair of tools that enable use of Sun Microsystem's

GUIDE interface builder as a front-end to Chiron.

The Dispatcher Generator And Artist-template Generator

The purpose of dispatchers was described above and we noted the existence of a dispatcher generator. For clients written in Ada we provide a dispatcher generator which takes an Ada package specification (Ada's mechanism for providing the interface to an ADT) and does a source-to-source translation to produce an Ada package with, effectively, the same external interface, but which performs dispatching as well as the package's operations.

The artist-template generator operates similarly, taking the Ada package specification of an ADT and creating a separate package with an internal task (independent thread of control). This task's interface and (partial) body are set to synchronize with the dispatcher generated off the same ADT. Figure 2 shows some of the code generated by the artist-template generator.

Lo-Cal, An Artist Language

The specifics of the user interface provided by an artist are coded in a language called Lo-Cal, the purpose of which is to facilitate use of the library of abstract depiction classes (details of which are provided further below) when the language of the client is Ada. For purposes of describing the *use* of this library it is important to note that the abstract depiction library is structured as an inheritance tree of classes of user interface components. (An inheritance tree is natural for graphics applications and supports the use of widely available and popular graphics toolkits.) Since the language of the client process is likely determined by the application code, artists must (eventually) be written in that language, yet interface to the abstract depiction class library.

For Ada-based clients this presents a problem, as Ada does not support these kinds of types. Accordingly the Lo-Cal artist language was designed as an extension to Ada; the extensions enable effective access and use of the object-oriented library. The extensions are treated as macros, and a pre-processor translates the Lo-Cal code into Ada source code. The Lo-Cal features added to the language are shown in Figure 3.

The first form of Apply creates an instance of the indicated class, using the designated constructor method. The second form of Apply invokes the designated method of the specified object. The Set_Behavior function establishes the artist's callbacks that should be called in response to specified user manipulations of the given ADL object.

```
function ~Apply (
   class : class_name;
   method : method_name;
   [<parameters to class method>] )
   return object_type;

procedure ~Apply (
   class : class_name;
   instance : object_type;
   method : method_name;
   [<parameters to class method>] );

procedure ~Set_Behavior (
   object : ADL_object;
   behaviors : Behavior_Array_Type );
```

Figure 3: Lo-Cal extensions to the application language

In order for Chiron to support clients in other languages, bindings must be established between the ADL and the application language. For object-oriented application languages this binding is easy to achieve; for languages like Ada-83 it is much more work, but interoperability is seldom easy.

The Abstract Depiction Library

The abstract depiction library is a class hierarchy of user interface objects. Instances of these objects are built into visible user interfaces that are presented to the user. The class hierarchy is fairly rich and complete, and most user interfaces can be constructed directly using it. However, if necessary a sub-class of one of the standard abstract depiction library classes can be defined and used by an artist writer. In that case a customized abstract depiction library is created and saved for subsequent use.

The ADL is a superset of the intersection of the XView class hierarchy and the Motif class hierarchy. The extensions include a range of graphical objects, among them polylines, polygons, splines, and gifs. A single interface is presented that is fully independent of the two substrates. Since artists are coded in terms of the abstract depiction library, they are fully independent of the choice of toolkits; the same artist can be used with either XView or Motif. Choice of look-and-feel simply becomes a choice of server with which the client is registered — a decision that is made at run-time.

Front-end Builders

The tools described above comprise the basic infrastructure for creating Chiron artists. Much work is still required of the user, however, to write the bodies of artists. This burden can be substantially reduced through use of a graphical interface builder. Many of these are on the market, and perform roughly the same services. Rather than adding another interface builder to the market we examined how we could leverage the investment in existing tools. We discovered that the internal form generated by Sun Microsystem's GUIDE tool (GIL) was suitable for translation to Lo-Cal. Accordingly we developed two tools, gil2local and gab, which enable the use of GUIDE in creating Chiron artists.

gil2local translates the output of GUIDE to Lo-Cal, and gab allows users to update an artist template given the declarations, apply, and behaviors files generated by gil2local. The artist writer thus has a very substantial basis for creating an artist quickly, using the set of tools provided with Chiron. Manual effort is still required, however, to create and manipulate ADL application objects (like circles and polylines) which are not supported by GUIDE, and to set behaviors for objects.

An interesting side-effect of gil2local and gab is that, though GUIDE was created to support development of applications that employ the OpenLook look-and-feel, since Lo-Cal is independent of that choice GUIDE can now be used to create applications exhibiting Motif's look-and-feel.

PERFORMANCE

In the current version of Chiron, an interface with buttons, menus, a canvas, and several graphical objects on the canvas[3] takes about three seconds to come up.

An end-to-end user interaction takes approximately 16 milliseconds. This time reflects the processing of an event generated from the concrete depiction of a graphical object. The event traverses the following route through the Chiron architecture: the X11 event is transferred (C to Ada) to Chiron, scheduled and interpreted in the Chiron server, sent to the Client (process to process), mapped to the artist to which the event is relevant, executed inside of the particular artist callback, and possibly routed to the (null) ADT with which the Artist is associated. The time was measured over 1000 events and then averaged. Measurements were made on Sun Sparc-2s, with the client on one machine and the server on another. Time for dispatching is essentially the time to do a round-trip Ada rendezvous.

In terms of space, a trivial Chiron client takes about 622K, of which 320K can be attributed to the Ada run-

---

[3] 1 base frame, 1 panel, 4 buttons, 1 text editor, 1 canvas, 9 graphical objects, and 2 scrollbars.

time system. The Motif Chiron server is 4.5M, while the XView Chiron server is 6.4M. The flight simulator client described below is 1.07M. With simple clients, our experience has shown that a single Chiron server can service 10 clients, though performance typically declines substantially when more than 4 or 5 clients are served.

In terms of lines of code, the union of all Chiron generator tools and run-time code consists of 51KSLOC (thousand-Source-Lines-Of-Code) of hand-written code (22K Ada and 29K of C++). 33KSLOC were generated, for a total of 84K.

EXAMPLE USES OF CHIRON

Figure 4 shows a simple flight simulator built with Chiron. Each of the windows is associated with a separate artist. The application manages a simple set of flight laws, and continually updates the six degrees of freedom of the simulated vehicle. Artists giving various presentations of the vehicle's state are attached to the ADT's that contain the six degrees of freedom of the simulated vehicle.

Two points are of interest in this example. First, this is a simple illustration that multiple artists can attach to the same ADT and provide alternate views. Second, there is a symmetry between the application and the user: the application is active, in that it continually recomputes the flight laws and updates the state vector, and at the same time the user can manipulate the controls. With conventional user interface technologies, at any given point in time either the application is dormant and a user interface listen/dispatch routine is in control, or the application is active and the system does not respond to user interactions. The advantages of the concurrent-control model are apparent here.

Other example applications Here are a selection of other artists that have been implemented in Chiron:

- A task interaction graph viewer built on top of a general Chiron graph layout artist
- A menu-based interface to Arcadia's measurement and evaluation system (Amadeus)
- An artist generator for PGraphite artists
- An interface to the debugger component of the Anna language system
- An interface for manipulating and visualizing the infrared signatures of the tailpipe of Northrop's B-2 aircraft

The first two of these were developed by individuals not a part of the Chiron team, though both were developed at UCI. The PGraphite artist generator was developed at UCI for researchers at the University of Massachusetts, Amherst and their user community. The Anna debugger interface was developed by Chiron users at Stanford University.

SUMMARY AND CONCLUSION

Several principles guided the design of Chiron. Primary impacts of three of them on Chiron are described below.

Separation of concerns. The two areas in which the notion of separation of concerns were considered important were the separation of the application and the user interface code, and the separation of the user interface code and the underlying toolkit and windowing system. The artist concept provides separation between the application and the user interface code. The notion of abstract depiction libraries, coupled with the client/server architecture, provides separation between the user interface code and the underlying toolkit and windowing system.

Concurrency. Concurrency was achieved along a couple of dimensions. The application code can be concurrent, since multiple Ada tasks can be active in an application process. Artists run concurrently with the application. Concurrency also arises because of the client/server split. One large application could consist of several clients and servers, each running on a different machine[4].

Language and platform independence. The client-server architecture of Chiron makes it possible to have application components written in different languages work together. Artists in the clients communicate via interprocess communication links to the server, and it does not matter what language they are written in. The abstract depiction library hides the details of the particular underlying toolkit (though we recognize engineering limitations of this).

The Chiron user interface system provides separation of concerns to enhance reusability and robustness to change, architectural extensibility and flexibility in developing applications, and support for multiple-user and networked applications. At the same time, Chiron realizes a level of performance necessary for applications typical to software development environments, the original context for Chiron. We believe therefore that the principles and architectural schemes we have explored are both workable and desirable; we encourage other

---

[4] Since concurrency typically presents many new opportunities for creating buggy programs, we applied a concurrency analysis system, CATS, to Chiron. CATS performs a type of reachability analysis and checks (exhaustively) for deadlocks. The analysis found two race conditions and a deadlock, which we subsequently fixed.

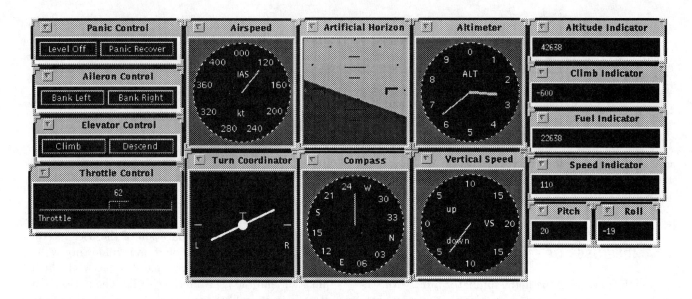

Figure 4: Flight simulator example

UIMS researchers to benefit from our efforts.

Directions. Current activities in Chiron are focused on incorporation of a constraint architecture, support for hypermedia hosted on a heterogeneous object store, and evolution based on feedback from users. Development of better artist and dispatcher composition methods is underway. This will enable, among other things, convenient support of dialog and presentation consistency through effective reuse of artist fragments that support a desired policy. We are also interested in performing an empirical study to evaluate the long-term engineering payoffs from maintaining the separations that Chiron supports.

ACKNOWLEDGEMENTS

The original architecture of the Chiron-1 system is primarily the work of Greg Bolcer, Mary Cameron, Ruedi Keller, and Dennis Troup. Recently Kari Forester and Craig MacFarlane have made many major contributions. Other important contributions have come from Ken Anderson, John Self, David Levine, Craig Snider, and Robert Zucker.

References

[1] M. Cameron, K. Forester, and C. MacFarlane. Chiron user manual. Arcadia Document UCI-91-04 (revised March 1992), University of California, Irvine, 1992. 225 pages.

[2] P. Dewan. A tour of the suite user interface software. In *Proceedings of the Third Annual Symposium on User Interface Software and Technology*, pages 57–65, Snowbird, UT, October 1990. Association for Computing Machinery.

[3] R. D. Hill. The abstraction-line-view paradigm: Using constraints to connect user interfaces to applications. In *Proceedings of CHI 92*, pages 335–342, May 1992.

[4] M. A. Linton, J. M. Vlissides, and P. R. Calder. Composing user interfaces with InterViews. *IEEE Computer*, 22(2):8–22, February 1989.

[5] S. McKay. CLIM: The Common Lisp Interface Manager. *Communications of the ACM*, 34(9):58–59, September 1991.

[6] B. A. Myers. Incense: A system for displaying data structures. *Computer Graphics*, 17(3):115–125, July 1983.

[7] B. A. Myers. Separating application code from toolkits: Eliminating the spaghetti of call-backs. In *Proceedings of the ACM Symposium on User Interface Software Technology*, pages 95–105, Hilton Head, South Carolina, November 1991.

[8] B. A. Myers, D. A. Guise, R. B. Dannenberg, B. V. Zanden, D. S. Kosbie, E. Pervin, A. Mickish, and P. Marchal. Garnet: Comprehensive support for graphical, highly interactive user interfaces. *IEEE Computer*, pages 71–85, November 1990.

[9] J. P. Rotella, A. L. Bowman, and C. A. Wittman. The AT&T display construction set user interface management system (UIMS). In *Proceedings of CHI 92*, pages 73–74, May 1992.

[10] L. A. Rowe, J. A. Konstan, B. C. Smith, S. Seitz, and C. Liu. The PICASSO application framework. In *Proceedings of the ACM Symposium on User Interface Software Technology*, pages 95–105, Hilton Head, South Carolina, November 1991.

[11] SEI. Serpent overview. SEI Technical Report CMU/SEI-89-UG-2, ESD-TR-89-08, Carnegie-Mellon University Software Enginnering Institute, August 1989.

[12] M. R. Szczur. Transportable applications environment (TAE) plus user interface designer workbench. In *Proceedings of CHI 92*, pages 231–232, May 1992.

A Second Generation User Interface Design Environment: The Model and The Runtime Architecture

Piyawadee "Noi" Sukaviriya
James D. Foley
Todd Griffith

Graphics, Visualization, and Usability Center
Georgia Institute of Technology
E-mail: {noi, foley, griffith}@cc.gatech.edu

ABSTRACT

Several obstacles exist in the user interface design process which distract a developer from designing a good user interface. One of the problems is the lack of an application model to keep the designer in perspective with the application. The other problem is having to deal with massive user interface programming to achieve a desired interface and to provide users with correct help information on the interface. In this paper, we discuss an application model which captures information about an application at a high level, and maintains mappings from the application to specifications of a desired interface. The application model is then used to control the dialogues at runtime and can be used by a help component to automatically generate animated and textual help. Specification changes in the application model will automatically result in behavioral changes in the interface.

KEYWORDS: Application Model, User Interface Model, User Interface Generation, User Interface Design Environment, Automatic Help Generation

1. INTRODUCTION

It is desirable to have user interface system which allows application programmers and interface designers to create interfaces without programming and without having to painfully learn tedious details of underlying toolkits. In 1988, we reported on UIDE, the User Interface Design Environment, which utilizes a model of an application to automatically create an interface [4]. Our vision however goes far beyond removing the programming burden from the user interface design process. We envision an environment which utilizes the model of an application to assist designers in the design process. We also see an environment where, not only are interfaces generated automatically, but also generated is procedural help on the interface utilizing the same model of the application in question.

UIDE emphasizes a model-based approach where the

existence of an application model enables several benefits [14]. An application model enables an interface to be designed and analyzed based on application tasks. The runtime environment can, in the case of UIDE, use the application model to sequence user dialogues based on task descriptions. The application model also enables the runtime environment, which knows about application tasks, to help the user in a more task-oriented fashion. We are currently using the model to automatically construct individual user models for user performance analysis [23], the results of which will be used to support adaptive interfaces and adaptive help.

We realized that the first generation model as reported in [4, 5] was just a start, and as yet is far from being sufficient to provide sophisticated interface features. Since then, we have invested our efforts in revising the model and strengthening both design-time and runtime support capabilities. In 1992, UIDE consists of a much more refined model describing not only the application, but also detailed interface features for the application interface. Its implementation platform evolved, from the Automatic Reasoning Tool [8], to Smalltalk-80, and now to C++. In this paper, we will only focus the description of UIDE's application model and will give an overview of the UIDE C++ runtime architecture.

2. BACKGROUND ON UIDE

UIDE is designed to allow interface designers to easily create, modify, and generate an interface to an application through high-level specifications. The purpose of the environment is to support the interface design process through its life cycle – from its inception to its execution. This support is made possible using a model which describes various details of an application interface including partial application semantics. In the past, our emphasis has been on the design support. Within the past few years, we have expanded our research to strengthen the quality of runtime support which can be automatically provided using the model. Design assistance includes automatic layout of menus and dialogue boxes [3,9], and transformations on interface styles using a compositional model of the user interface [10]. Runtime support includes using pre- and post-conditions to control interface objects [6], automatic generation of animated help [20], and automatic generation of textual help [22]. Should the specifications in the knowledge base change, the generated interface and help at run-time will change accordingly.

Through UIDE, a designer creates an interface for an application by first describing objects and operations in the application. The designer then chooses various interface functional components which best fit the application by linking them to application operations. Interface functional components include interface actions, interface objects, presentation objects representing application objects, and interaction techniques to be used with presentation and interface objects. These components will be described in more detail in Section 4.

Though the model has descriptions of both application tasks, and interface tasks and objects, we often refer to it as "application model." The terms "model" and "application model" will be used interchangeably throughout this paper.

Once the application model is mapped to interface functional components, the UIDE runtime environment uses the specifications in the model to generate a desired interface. The specifications are also used to control user interactions and status of interface objects at run time. While the interface is running, context-sensitive animated help on "how" to perform actions can be constructed from the specifications upon user request [20]. Help on "why" a certain widget is disabled can also be generated using pre-condition information associated with actions and interaction techniques related to the disabled widget [6].

3. RELATED WORK
Direct manipulation user interface builders such as DevGuide [24] and Prototyper [2] make designing an interface one step easier. Some direct manipulation tools such as DialogEditor [1] and Peridot [12] are intelligent and they make the interface design process less tedious and less repetitive. These tools facilitate a bottom-up approach of interface design while UIDE emphasizes a top-down approach. That is, designing a conceptual design of an application before designing its interface. Also, these tools mainly assist with layouts and do not incorporate application aspects in their assistance.

Cousin [7], MIKE [16], MICKEY [17], UofA* UIMS [19], and HUMANOID [26] use descriptions of commands and parameters to automatically generate interfaces. The same approach is used in UIDE. It is used, however, with a more sophisticated representation structure. Except for HUMANOID and UIDE, the systems above parse textual descriptions of commands and parameters, either embedded in a program structure or stored in a file, and use them as inputs to interface generators in their systems. UIDE and HUMANOID store descriptions of application actions and parameters as objects in their application model.

All these systems except UIDE do not explicitly model detailed descriptions of interface tasks beyond application commands and parameters. We explicitly model interface actions and interaction techniques, which are intended to be used by designers as ways to specify interaction styles for an application. UIDE's application model allows the mapping of application actions to interfaces to be changed without changing application actions. The model also allows an application action to be mapped to multiple interface actions; this results in multiple access to a single application command, for example.

Both HUMANOID and UIDE have explicit descriptions of application objects. They also have pre-conditions for actions which are used to determine when an action is enabled and can be performed by the user. Only UIDE uses post-conditions of actions as a way to capture application action semantics, and uses them to reason in the design process and to provide help at runtime.

4. APPLICATION MODEL
We view the application model as consisting of three layers which describe interface functionality at different levels of abstraction. At the highest level, the model captures semantics of application actions. The mid-level captures actions which exist in various interface paradigms but are independent of any specific application. The lowest level describes mouse and keyboard interactions and is designed to capture lexical groupings which define related lexical input and output. Through these layers, designers have different granularity of control over interface features which they can choose for an application. Ideally, changing an interface style is a matter of manipulating connections between these layers.

UIDE provides generic classes of various entities in the application model. These classes will be introduced in the next 5 subsections – Application Objects, Application Actions, Interface Actions, Interaction Techniques, and Interface Objects. The application model consists of instances of these classes; each instance contains information specific to an application aspect it represents or the particular interface features chosen for the application. The power of the model comes from the specific contents of these instances and also the semantic connections among these instances.

Application Objects

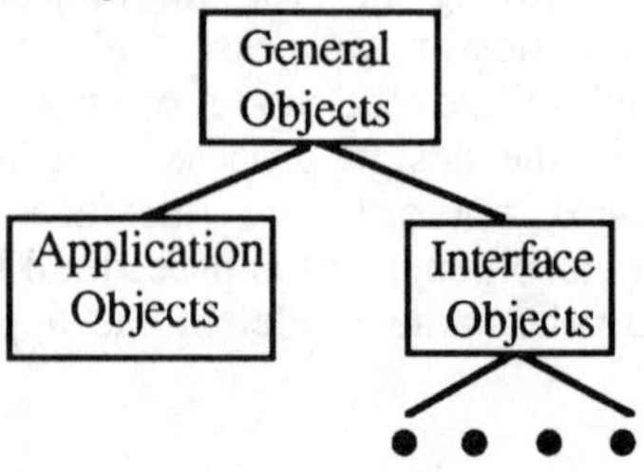

Figure 1 UIDE Object Class Hierarchy

Figure 1 shows a predefined object class-subclass hierarchy in UIDE. *Application objects* are specific entities in an application; they are entities on which application actions operate. *Interface objects* are entities which users perceive and sometimes interact with, such as a window, an icon of a NAND gate, or an audio output, etc. We will discuss more details on interface objects later in this section.

The application designer defines object classes in an application by subclassing from the UIDE application object class. Attributes of these classes are added by the designer. Figure 2 shows an example of an extended class hierarchy for a digital circuit design application. In this application, end-users create different kinds of gates and connect them to form a functional digital circuit. This application will be used throughout this paper.

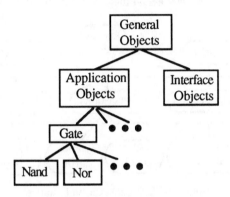

Figure 2 Object Class Hierarchy for a Digital Circuit
Layout Application

The extended class hierarchy for application objects is often referred to as the data model. We consider the data model to be part of the application model. In an application such as the circuit design program where objects are instantiated at runtime by end-users, the designer only designs class definitions of objects. Operations to create instances of these objects should be provided in the interface. In different applications where there are a fixed number of objects pre-created for end-users to interact with, the class definitions of these objects must be defined and instances created during the design process.

Application Actions

To complete the application model, the designer describes the functionality of an application which will be available to the user as a set of actions. UIDE provides *action*, *parameter*, *parameter constraint*, *pre-condition*, and *post-condition* classes to capture application actions and their semantics.

An action is a unit of activity which is meaningful to an application. Executing an action may affect objects, attribute values of objects, or object classes. An action may require parameters, hence the *parameter* class is defined to describe a parameter of an action. Constraints on parameter types and parameter values are defined as instances of the *parameter constraint* class. More detailed information about parameter constraint classes can be found in [21]. The *pre-condition* class is defined to capture what needs to be true before an action can be executed and the *post-condition* class is defined to capture what will be true after an action is executed. Both pre- and post-conditions

use first order predicate logic (but do not yet handle universal and existential qualifiers), and their class definitions capture such a representation. An action which requires parameters has pointers to its parameter instances. Each parameter points to the constraint instances associated with it. An action also points to pre- and post-condition instances associated with it. Figure 3 depicts a graphical view of an action with links to its parameters, its pre-conditions, and its post-conditions. Each parameter is also linked to its constraints.

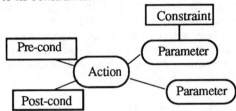

Figure 3 A View of an Action and its Associated
Components.

Examples of application actions and their parameters in the digital circuit design application are:

create-NAND-gate	(location)
create-NOR-gate	(location)
delete-gate	(gate)
move-gate	(gate, new-location)
rotate-gate	(gate, angle-of-rotation)
connect	(gate-1, gate-2)

Figure 4 shows the "connect" action instance with its related entities.

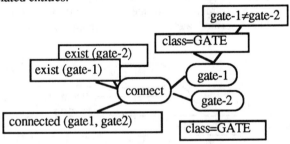

Figure 4   The *connect* Action from a Digital Circuit
Design Application.

Interface Actions

Mapping from application components – actions and their parameters – to an interface is specified as links from these components to *interface actions*. The designer does not really define interface actions. There are instances of different interface actions already defined in UIDE from which the designer can clone. Multiple interface actions can be linked to application components of one action. For example, the "rotate" action may be linked to a "select-action" interface action. Its parameters, object and angle-of-rotation, may be linked to "select-object" and "enter-integer-in-dialogue-box" interface actions respectively. On the current C++ platform, linking is done through C++ code. We do not yet have a friendly interface to the model acquisition process.

Interface actions may have pre- and post-conditions. Some pre-conditions are concerned with the status of an interface prior to performing interface actions. For example, the dialogue box, which contains the numeric input widget for entering an angle of rotation, must be visible before a number can be entered. Some pre- and post-conditions are concerned with sequencing of interface actions. For instance, an angle of rotation cannot be entered unless an object has been selected, and an object cannot be selected unless the rotate action has been selected. Sequencing pre- and post-conditions can be automatically derived by UIDE from the application semantics [10].

Interaction Techniques

Interaction techniques specify how interface actions are to be carried out by the user. Interaction technique instances are linked to interface actions. For example, if the "select-object" action is to be performed by using the mouse to click on an object, a "mouse-click-object" technique must be linked to the action. More than one interaction technique can be linked to an interface action to designate possible alternative interactions. For instance, an object can also be selected by typing in the object name. In this case, a "type-string" technique is attached to the "select-object" action.

UIDE's interaction techniques are similar in function to Myers' interactors [13]. We, however, do not model feedback as objects in UIDE. We treat feedback as different behaviors of presentation objects. Also, we do not treat an object as a parameter of an interaction technique. Rather, as will be described later, interaction techniques are attached to objects.

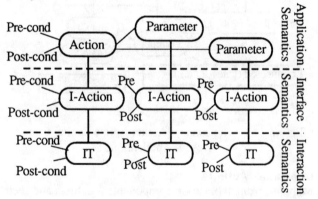

Figure 5 Specifications Layers in the Application Model

Interaction techniques may also have pre- and post-conditions. Their pre- and post-conditions tie closely to the screen context, for example, the numeric input widget must be enabled for a type-in-number technique, and will be disabled after a number is entered. Interface objects such as dialogue boxes, menus, buttons, etc., must be created

beforehand so their references can be used in the specifications in the application model.

Figure 5 depicts the overall layers in the application model for each action and figure 6 shows a graphical view of the semantic links of the "rotate" action. We omit pre- and post-condition details, and parameter information to keep the figures clear. The application semantics level serves as a starting point in the design process and is independent of the end-user interface. The application model consists of several application actions described in this structure. The same application can be mapped to multiple sets of interface actions and techniques for different environments.

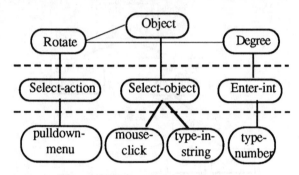

Figure 6 A *Rotate* Action Instance

Interface Objects

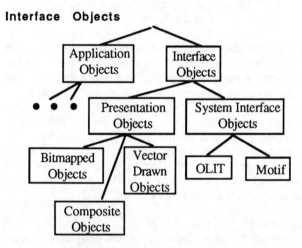

Figure 7 Interface Object Subclasses

Figure 7 illustrates the UIDE class-subclass hierarchy down from the interface object class. The 2 major subclasses of interface objects are: *presentation objects*, which represent application objects and are presented to the user through various forms or media; and *system interface objects*, which are standard objects in interface toolkits such as OLIT [25] or Motif [18]. Currently we are only working on the OLIT widget set.

The system interface object allows common interface objects to be referred to as buttons, scrollbars, etc., regardless of the underlying toolkits. Many of our interface object classes are similar to interactor classes in InterViews [11] and we maintain a part-whole structure for composite objects such as dialogue boxes in a similar fashion.

However, unlike InterViews, we allow interactive behaviors to be programmed on interface objects by attaching interaction techniques to interface object classes or instances. This is used more in the case of presentation objects where different behaviors may be desired for different forms of presentation. We have not yet supported adding behaviors to standard widgets, though this can be done using our current underlying mechanisms.

To make this point clear, let's assume that the designer wishes to make all gates movable by dragging, but only double clicking on a NAND gate would allow the user to change the time delay in nanoseconds of that gate. To achieve such a design, the designer first creates a subclass of the Bitmapped object class called GATE, then attaches a "mouse-drag" interaction technique to the class. Notice that this "mouse-drag" technique is the same instance which is linked to the "move-gate" application action. The designer then creates a NAND subclass of the GATE presentation class and attaches a "double-clicking" technique to the class. This "double-clicking" technique would be one which is linked to a "change-NAND-time-delay" action.

Creating the Model

The designer furnishes an application model for UIDE by first defining application actions, application and interface objects, then choosing interface actions and interaction techniques as she sees appropriate. This process creates the declarative model which serves as specifications for UIDE to sequence dialogues for the application. Currently, defining the model in the C++ version of UIDE is still done through the standard C++ declaration and instantiation syntax. A visual tool to create an application model has been planned.

There are constraints on which interface actions and techniques are appropriate for which types of interface objects. There are also constraints on which interface actions are appropriate for which parameter types with which they are associated. These constraints vary from rigid rules, such as a radio button bank cannot be used for entering a floating point numeric value, to style guide-like rules such as a long list of choices should be presented in a scrolling list. Declaring the model using the C++ syntax does not prevent the designer from using interface actions and interaction techniques inappropriately. It is important to incorporate this kind of constraints to assist designers in a tool for creating the model.

In addition to the model, the designer also provides, for each application action, an application routine which will be invoked at runtime when all parameter values for the action have been entered or selected. Application routines are responsible for handling necessary computations and manipulations in an application. Occasionally, application routines may need to address contextual changes in the interface. Currently, once an application object is created and registered, its corresponding presentation object will be displayed. This works well for the circuit design application we are using. More sophisticated dependencies

between application data and its interface need to be modeled.

With application routines in place, UIDE is ready to support the runtime execution of an application interface.

5. RUNTIME ARCHITECTURE

Controlling the Interface Through the Model

Most components in the application model are instances of a C++ class. In addition to members and member functions which are used to maintain specific information contents and semantic relationships in the model, these instances are designed to support runtime execution of the interface. Some examples are: 1) each system interface object has the actual calls to corresponding OLIT widgets to create or modify themselves; 2) parameter instances maintain current parameter values; and 3) parameter constraints are used to validate parameter values, etc. The UIDE runtime architecture is designed such that application action semantics are used to guide the dialogue sequencing. This means that UIDE does not hard-wire the dialogue sequence and bindings to interaction techniques in the runtime code. When the application specification in the model changes, the interface sequencing and behaviors change accordingly. In addition to instance behaviors in the model, UIDE has a "dialogue manager" which maintains the current interface context, sequences the dialogues, and updates the context when appropriate.

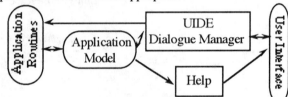

Figure 8 UIDE's Runtime Architecture

Figure 8 shows information flow among various components in UIDE's runtime architecture. The dialogue manager updates the screen context appropriately after the user finishes an interface action – an interface action could be the user has just selected an action or an object. The dialogue manager maintains the user interface context to keep track of which action the user is performing. Each application action has a pointer to its corresponding application routine. Once all parameter values of an action have been entered by the user, it invokes the application routine for that action. The application routine may update data in the data model which resides in the application model. For an application which resides on the same C++ platform such as the circuit application we use, the data model can be directly used as the data structure of the application.

A general theme for controlling the interface is as follows. First, the dialogue manager checks to see whether each application action has all its pre-conditions satisfied. A combination of: 1) traditional unification and resolution mechanisms for the predicate language [15], and 2) treating pre-condition as functions for checking conditions on

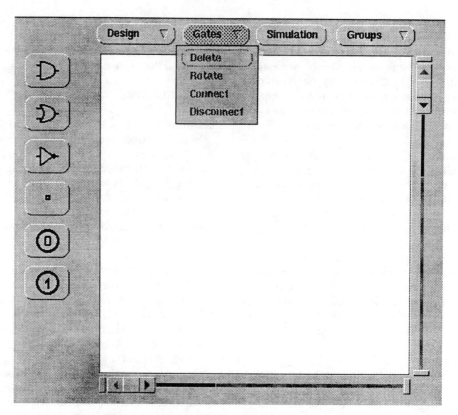

Figure 9 Interface to the Circuit Design Application

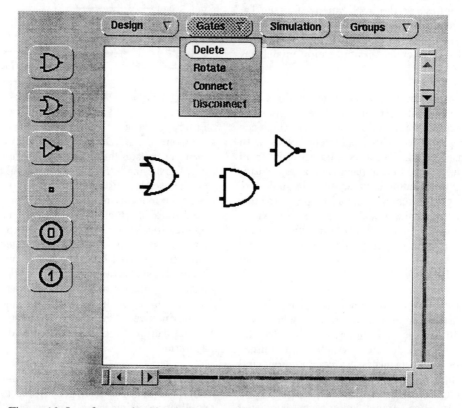

Figure 10 Interface to the Circuit Design Application with some Gates in the Design.

objects, are used for handling pre- and post-conditions. An action with all its pre-conditions satisfied is enabled, and an action with at least one pre-condition unsatisfied is disabled. This situation is reflected in the interface through links in the model. That is, the interface actions and interaction techniques associated with enabled actions are enabled. Interface objects associated with enabled interaction techniques are also enabled and their statuses are changed (i.e, from invisible to visible). Interface objects associated with disabled interaction techniques are disabled and their statuses are also changed (i.e, from solid to greyed-out) Figure 9 and 10 illustrate examples of these conditions.

Notice from the interface to the circuit design application in figure 9 that the gate icons on the left are for invoking application actions which instantiate the corresponding gate types. When one of these icons is selected, UIDE waits for a location input in the current design space. Once a location is given by the user, a gate is instantiated and its graphical view is placed at the given location. In figure 9, since there are no gates in the system, all actions in the "Gates" menu are disabled because all of them require that some gates exist in the design. This interface assumes a prefix interface paradigm – an action is selected first before objects and/or parameter values for the action are selected. Figure 10 shows the menu changed as some gates have been created.

This design can be changed so that an object must be selected before some actions on gates, "delete" and "rotate" for example, are enabled. This is done by making "select-object" interface action an action by itself (as opposed to linking to an application action), which results in a post-condition that an object exists as the current selected object (CSO as referred to in [4]). The resulting interface would be one that, though gates exist, "delete" and "rotate" menu items are not enabled unless one of the gates is selected.

Automatic Generation of How and Why Help
Two kinds of help can be automatically generated from the application model: **how** to perform an action and **why** an interface object is disabled. We use 2 types of help presentation modes, textual and animated help.

It should be obvious now that procedural steps for completing an application action can be inferred from the application model. For example, rotating an object can be done by first selecting the *rotate* action, selecting an *object* to be rotated, and then entering the *degree* of rotation. To animate this action, UIDE chooses an object of type GATE from the current context using the constraint for the "object" parameter which state that the object must be of type GATE. An integer number between 0 to 360 is chosen for the "angle of rotation" parameter according to its constraints. UIDE then illustrates the procedure by showing a mouse icon on the screen, the left mouse button being pressed while pulling down the menu where the "rotate" item is located, releasing the mouse button at the "rotate" item, clicking on the chosen object, and typing the

number chosen for the "angle-of-rotation" in the dialogue box designed for this action.

Pre- and post-conditions are used to evaluate whether a context is ready for animating an action. For example, to rotate a gate, a gate must exist. If there is no gate in the current context, a planner is invoked to search for an action in the application model which will create a gate. The animation will show creating a gate first, and then rotating the gate.

A interface object is disabled if the interaction technique associated with it is disabled. An explanation of why an interface object is disabled can be generated using pre-conditions [22]. The explanation also includes which actions must be performed the make the object enabled.

6. IMPLEMENTATION
The 1992 UIDE is written in C++ using the OLIT widget set. It runs on Sun's X Server. Though we use OLIT, UIDE does not generate conventional code with callbacks for application programmers to add their application code. All application routines must be written separately and are connected to UIDE through application actions.

A subset of the OLIT widget set has been incorporated in UIDE's interface object structure. Our major efforts have been placed on connections from the application model to the actual execution of the interface. The animated help was developed earlier in Smalltalk-80 and is now being ported to C++. Generation of WHY explanations has been developed separately in C++ but has not yet been integrated into UIDE.

7. CONCLUSIONS
The application model in UIDE consists of entities which describe an application through actions, action semantics, objects, and interface details of its interface. We have explained the structure of a model which captures the semantic relationships among these entities. We also described the runtime architecture which 1) controls the dialogue sequencing, and 2) automatically generates how and why help using the model.

Taking away the burden of having to program an interface is already a major relief to most of us who need to create an interface and who have no interest in unnecessary details which distract us from the design process. However, a greater contribution of UIDE lies in the fact that it allows application designers to focus on modeling the application even before being hassled by interface design issues. The designer can later link the high-level model of the application to interface details, and can therefore focus on tasks and communication means provided to users through the interface. This contribution is one of many benefits enabled by the model-based user interface design approach.

ACKNOWLEDGEMENTS
This work has been supported by the Siemens Corporate R&D System Ergonomics and Interaction group of Siemens Central Research Laboratory, Munich, Germany,

and the Human Interface Technology Group of Sun Microsystems through their Collaborative Research Program. The work builds on earlier UIDE research supported by the National Science Foundation grants IRI-88-131-79 and DMC-84-205-29, and by the Software Productivity Consortium. We thank the members of the Graphics, Visualization, and Usability Center for their contributions to various aspects of the UIDE project: J.J. "Hans" de Graaff, Martin Frank, Mark Gray, Srdjan Kovacevic, Ray Johnson, and Krishna Bharat. We also thank colleagues and former students at the George Washington University who contributed to UIDE: Hikmet Senay, Christina Gibbs, Won Chul Kim, Lucy Moran, and Kevin Murray. We also thank Thomas Kuehme, John Stasko, John Shilling, and the reviewers for their comments.

REFERENCES

1. Cardelli, L. Building User Interfaces by Direct Manipulation. In *Proceedings of the ACM SIGGRAPH Symposium on User Interface Software and Technology.* Banff, Alberta, Canada. October, 1988, 152-166.

2. Cossey, G. *Prototyper.* SmetherBarnes, Portland, Oregon, 1989.

3. de Baar, D.; J.D. Foley; and K.E. Mullet. Coupling Application Design and User Interface Design. In *Proceedings of Human Factors in Computing Systems, CHI'92.* May 1992, 259-266.

4. Foley, J.D.; C. Gibbs; W.C. Kim; and S. Kovacevic. A Knowledge-based User Interface Management System. In *Proceedings of Human Factors in Computing Systems, CHI'88.* May 1988, 67-72.

5. Foley, J.D.; W.C. Kim; S. Kovacevic; and K. Murray. UIDE–An Intelligent User Interface Design Environment. In *Architectures for Intelligent Interfaces: Elements and Prototypes.* Eds. J. Sullivan and S. Tyler, Reading, MA: Addison-Wesley, 1991.

6. Gieskens, D. and J.D. Foley. Controlling User Interface Objects Through Pre- and Post-conditions. In *Proceedings of Human Factors in Computing Systems, CHI'92.* May 1992, 189-194.

7. Hayes, P.J.; P. A. Szekeley; and R.A. Lerner. Design Alternatives for User Interface Management Systems Based on Experience with COUSIN. In *Proceedings of Human Factors in Computing Systems, CHI'85.* April 1985, 169-175.

8. Inference Corporation. *ART Reference Manual.* Inference Corporation, Los Angeles, CA, 1987.

9. Kim, W.C., and J.D. Foley. DON: User Interface Presentation Design Assistant. In *Proceedings of the ACM SIGGRAPH Symposium on User Interface Software and Technology.* October 1990,. 10-20.

10. Kovacevic, S. A Compositional Model of Human-Computer Dialogues. In *Multimedia Interface Design.* Eds. M.M. Blattner and R.B. Dannenberg, New York, New York: ACM Press, 1992.

11. Linton, M.; J.M. Vlissides; and P.R. Calder. Composing User Interfaces with InterViews. *IEEE Computer* 22(2): 8-22, February, 1990.

12. Myers, B. Creating Interaction Techniques by Demonstrations. *IEEE Transactions on Computer Graphics and Applications* 7 (September 1987):51-60.

13. Myers, B.; D.A. Giuse; R.B. Dannenberg; B.V. Zanden; D.S. Kosbie; E. Pervin; A. Mickish; and P. Marchal. Garnet: Comprehensive Support for Graphical, Highly-Interactive User Interfaces. *IEEE Computer* 23(11): 71-85, November, 1990.

14. Neches, R.; J.D. Foley; P. Szekeley; P. Sukaviriya; P. Luo; S. Kovacevic; and S. Hudson. Knowledgeable Development Environments Using Shared Design Models. To appear in *Proceedings of Intelligent Interfaces Workshop*, Orlando, Florida, January 4-7, 1993.

15. Nilsson, N.J. Principles of Artificial Intelligence. Los Angeles, CA: Morgan Kaufmann Publishers, Inc, 1980.

16. Olsen, D. MIKE: The Menu Interaction Kontrol Environment. *ACM Transactions on Graphics* 5,4 (1986): 318-344.

17. Olsen, D. A Programming Language Basis for User Interface Management. In *Proceedings of Human Factors in Computing Systems, CHI'89.* May 1989, 171-176.

18. Open Software Foundation. OSF/Motif Style Guide. Revision 1.0. Englewood Cliffs, New Jersey: Prentice Hall, Inc., 1990.

19. Singh, G. and Green, M. A High-Level User Interface Management System. In *Proceedings of Human Factors in Computing Systems, CHI'89.* May 1989, 133-138.

20. Sukaviriya, P., and J.D. Foley. Coupling a UI Framework with Automatic Generation of Context-Sensitive Animated Help. In *Proceedings of the ACM SIGGRAPH Symposium on User Interface Software and Technology.* October 1990,. 152-166.

21. Sukaviriya, P. *Automatic Generation of Context-sensitive Animated Help.* A Ds.C. Dissertation, George Washington University, 1991.

22. Sukaviriya, P. and de Graaff, J. Automatic Generation of Context-sensitive "Show & Tell" Help. *Technical Report GIT-GVU-92-18.* Atlanta, Georgia: Graphics, Visualization, and Usability Center, Georgia Institute of Technology, 1992.

23. Sukaviriya, P. and J.D. Foley. Supporting Adaptive Interfaces in a Knowledge-Based User Interface Environments. To appear in *Proceedings of Intelligent Interfaces Workshop*, Orlando, Florida, January 4-7, 1993.

24. SunSoft. *OpenWindows™ Developer's Guide 3.0 User's Guide.* Sun Microsystems, Inc. Part No:800-6585-10, Revision A, November 1991.

25. SunSoft. *OLIT 3.0.1 Reference Manual.* Sun Microsystems, Inc. Part-No: 800-6391-10, Revision A, june 1992.

26. Szekeley, P.; P. Luo; and R. Neches. Facilitating the Exploration of Interface Design Alternatives: the HUMANOID Model of Interface Design. In *Proceedings of Human Factors in Computing Systems, CHI'92.* May 1992, 507-515.

BEYOND INTERFACE BUILDERS: MODEL-BASED INTERFACE TOOLS

Pedro Szekely, Ping Luo and Robert Neches

USC/Information Sciences Institute
4676 Admiralty Way
Marina del Rey, CA 90292
(310) 822-1511
E-mail: szekely@isi.edu, ping@isi.edu, neches@isi.edu

ABSTRACT

Interface builders only support the construction of the menus and dialogue boxes of an application. They do not support the construction of interfaces of many application classes (visualization, simulation, command and control, domain-specific editors) because of the dynamic and complex information that these applications process. HUMANOID is a model-based interface design and construction tool where interfaces are specified by building a declarative description (model) of their presentation and behavior. HUMANOID's modeling language provides simple abstraction, iteration and conditional constructs to model the interface features of these application classes. HUMANOID provides an easy-to-use designer's interface that lets designers build complex interfaces without programming.

KEYWORDS: UIMS, Design Process, Interface Builders, Model-Based Interface Tools.

INTRODUCTION

Most tools for interface construction support the construction of the menus and dialogue boxes of an application, but provide little or no support for constructing the main application displays that show application-specific objects and let end-users manipulate those objects. Most applications have interface requirements that go far beyond the menus and dialogue boxes that can be constructed using interface builders:

1. *Data with complex structure.* Most visualization applications (e.g., TreeViz [3]) visualize complex data structures with arbitrary levels of nesting.
2. *Heterogeneous data.* Applications typically process several kinds of data (different types of notes in a music editor, different kinds of shapes in a drawing editor), which require different presentations, and which require different input behaviors for convenient manipulation.
3. *Variable amounts of data.* Applications typically process variable amounts of data that could come from data bases or other programs (visualization, command and control, simulation) or data constructed interactively

by the user (specialized editors).

4. *Time varying data.* Applications often process data that changes at run-time (command and control, simulation), or allow users to change the data (specialized editors). These applications typically show several views of the data, which must be kept coordinated and up-to-date.

Figure 1. TreeViz, a visualization tool for hierarchical information (left), and the portions of that interface that can be constructed using interface builders (right).

Figure 1. illustrates the main shortcoming of most interface building tools. The left hand side of the figure shows the display of TreeViz [3], a simple visualization application for visualizing hierarchical data. In this example, TreeViz is visualizing the cost to maintain the computers in an organization. The shapes represent different classes of members of the organization, the shading represents different kinds of computer, and the size of the areas represents the cost to maintain the computer. The right hand side of the figure shows the portions of this interface that can be specified using an interface builder. If interface builders do not support the construction of the interface for even a simple application such as TreeViz, much less do they support the interface for the application classes mentioned above. The TreeViz display cannot be specified with an interface builder because the number of objects shown varies at run-time, the shape and shading of the objects depend on attributes of the data, and the layout is recursively defined.

The challenge for interface construction tools is to embody them with a richer and more expressive model of interfaces, while making them intuitive and easy to use for designers. Interface builders do not meet this challenge. They are intuitive and easy to use, but are not expressive enough.

This paper describes a tool called HUMANOID that meets

this challenge. The HUMANOID modeling language supports the specification of most aspects of an interface (presentation, behavior and dialogue). The main contribution of HUMANOID lies in the nature of the modeling language and the way in which it is delivered to designers in an intuitive and easy-to-use interface.

HUMANOID's modeling language has abstraction, composition, iteration and conditional constructs designed to support the modeling of interfaces with the characteristics mentioned above (numbered 1-4). The abstraction mechanism allows the specification of *presentation templates* to present all the instances of a class of objects, and *behavior templates* to specify how the presented objects can be manipulated. The composition construct allows presentation templates to be composed in order to define the presentation of data with complex structure (1). The conditional constructs support the presentation of heterogeneous data (2). Coupled with the iteration construct, the abstraction and composition constructs allow the specification of presentations of variable amounts of heterogeneous data (3). Finally, the modeling language uses a data-dependency mechanism similar to spreadsheet formulas to specify the dependencies between data and presentations in order to support automatic presentation update of time varying data (4).

This paper is organized as follows. The next section presents an overview of HUMANOID's modeling language and the desiderata for the designer's interface, followed by a related work section. The body of the paper discusses the main constructs of the modeling language, the designer's interface facilities for using the modeling constructs, and shows how to construct the TreeViz interface from scratch. The paper closes with current status and conclusions.

HUMANOID OVERVIEW

HUMANOID is a model-based system. Interfaces are specified by constructing a declarative model of how the interface should look and behave. A standard run-time support module is included in every application to execute the model, that is, to construct the application displays and interpret input according to the information in the model.

The Humanoid Modeling Language

HUMANOID provides a declarative modeling language that factors the design of interfaces into five semi-independent dimensions [12]: *1. Application semantics:* represents the objects and operations of an application. The application semantics defines the domain of discourse of the interface, and is referenced by the dimensions of the model that define the presentation, behavior and dialogue sequencing of the interface. *2. Presentation:* defines the visual appearance of the interface. *3. Behavior:* defines the input gestures (e.g. mouse clicks) that can be applied to presented objects, and their effects on the state of the application and the interface. *4. Dialogue sequencing:* defines the ordering constraints for executing commands and supplying inputs to commands. *5. Action side-effects:* defines actions executed automatically when commands or command inputs change state (e.g., making a newly created object the current selection).

Only the first three dimensions will be discussed in detail in this paper. Details on the last two appear elsewhere [12].

The Designer's Interface to Humanoid

The designer's interface to HUMANOID supports a very tight design/evaluate/redesign cycle. The typical screen of a designer's workstation (Figure 2.) contains windows showing different views of the design model (windows labeled Part Editor, Presentation Template

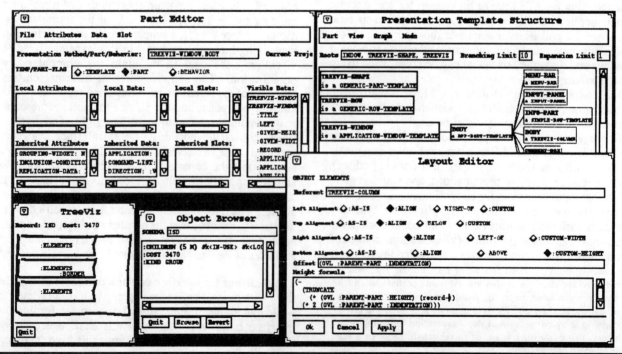

Figure 2. Snapshot of a screen showing a typical configuration of windows during a design session with Humanoid.

Structure and Layout Editor), windows showing the application data structures (Object Browser), and windows showing the interfaces that HUMANOID generates from the model (TreeViz). These windows are explained in more detail later in the paper.

The designer's interface was designed according to the following desiderata:

All features of the design should be visible and changeable by designers so that designers can control all aspects of an interface design.

Example interfaces are editable views of the model. HUMANOID capitalizes on the idea that people understand problems better when they can interact both with a symbolic representation and with illustrative examples of it [15]. So, HUMANOID shows designers views of the model (symbolic representation) and interfaces generated from the model (examples). Designers can refine the model by editing the example interfaces produced from the model.

All views of the design are linked together to help designers understand and edit the model. This requirement manifests itself in several features of HUMANOID.

- HUMANOID provides facilities to map from example features to model elements and vice-versa. Designers can point to an element of the design, and ask HUMANOID to highlight the portions of the example displays that it controls. Conversely, designers can point to a feature of an example display and ask to see the portions of the model that generated it.
- All example interfaces are kept up-to-date after every modification to the design model (even if the design is not fully specified), helping designers to immediately see the consequences of their modeling decisions. Conversely, when designers perform a refinement by demonstration they can immediately see HUMANOID's interpretation of the example in one of the design views.

RELATED WORK

Interface design and construction tools can be compared along expressivity and usability dimensions. The expressivity dimension defines the class of interfaces that can be specified, where as the usability dimension captures the level of expertise that designers need to use the tool.

At the low end of the expressivity spectrum are interface builders [9], with essentially a single modeling construct: instantiation. Designers can create instances of a predefined set of classes of interface building blocks, and set the values of their parameters. Interface builders can only be used to specify the menus and dialogue boxes of an application, but not the main application displays.

At the high end of the expressivity spectrum are programming languages, which allow programmers to create arbitrarily sophisticated interfaces by writing programs (procedural models of interfaces). Close to the programming end of the spectrum are object-oriented systems like Unidraw [13] which provide classes for building specific kinds interfaces. Even though Unidraw

greatly facilitates the programming of graphical editors, the task still requires extensive programming skills.

The usability dimension generally goes in the opposite direction. Low expressivity tools like interface builders are easy to use, and high expressivity tools like programming languages or object-oriented frameworks are hard to use.

Demonstrational Tools

Demonstrational tools such as Lapidary [5] and Druid [10] are an attempt to move up the expressivity spectrum while remaining in the high end of the usability spectrum. Lapidary, for instance, lets designers demonstrate examples of a boxes and arrows application where the arrows should remain attached to the boxes, and constructs "box" and "arrow" classes with the appropriate constraints so that instances remain connected. The generalizations that demonstrational tools make are typically not shown to designers. In the cases where designers can view the generalizations (e.g. Lapidary), there are no tools to help designers understand the relationship between features of the examples and features of the generalizations. Hence, designers find it hard to understand the generalizations.

HUMANOID differs from these tools in that the model (generalizations) plays a primary role. The demonstrational capabilities of HUMANOID are weak compared to Lapidary and Druid, but HUMANOID derives its strength from its modeling power, and the combination of explicit model and example views to construct the models.

Other Model-Based Approaches

Most model-based systems score high in expressivity, but low in usability.

UIDE [2] is a model-based interface tool whose application and dialogue sequencing models are similar to HUMANOID's, but whose presentation model is relatively impoverished compared to HUMANOID's. UIDE does not have a sophisticated designer's interface so its usability is low. UIDE's approach to usability is automation. The richness of UIDE's model enables the construction of tools like Cartoonist [11] that generates animated help, and DON that generates dialogue boxes [4]. UIDE emphasizes model analysis tools such as consistency checkers [1] and keystroke analysis [2]. Since HUMANOID's and UIDE's models are similar, the complementary advantages of both systems could be integrated in a single tool.

ITS [14] can also be characterized as a model-based system. ITS has a presentation model similar to HUMANOID's, but its dialogue and application models are less expressive. ITS does not score high in usability due to its textual specification language, but it is a production quality system.

Having reviewed related work, we now focus on how HUMANOID's modeling language and designer's interface are used to build interfaces.

APPLICATION MODEL

The first step in designing an interface is to model the application functionality, i.e., the objects and the commands that the application provides. In HUMANOID, these are formally modeled in an object-oriented way, by specifying the types and slots of each object. Commands are modeled by specifying their inputs, preconditions, and a call-back procedure. Other more advanced features of the application model are discussed elsewhere [12].

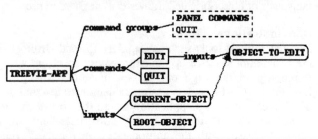

Figure 3. The application model of TreeViz.

Figure 3. shows the TreeViz application model. To start off the design we decided that there should be a QUIT command, and an EDIT command to edit the information contained in any record in the hierarchy. There is an input ROOT-OBJECT to store the root record of the hierarchy to be shown. We made the dialogue sequencing decision that there should be a notion of current selection, and that the EDIT command edits the current selection. Accordingly, we defined another global input called CURRENT-OBJECT, and tied the OBJECT-TO-EDIT input of the EDIT command to CURRENT-OBJECT. We also made a presentation decision by stating that QUIT belongs to the PANEL COMMANDS group, which tells HUMANOID which commands to present as a panel of command buttons.

If we were using an interface builder we would have started the design of the interface differently. We would have drawn a QUIT button at the bottom of the screen, and tied it to a callback procedure. We would have drawn the RECORD and COST labels at the top of the screen, but would not have been able to tie them to anything (Figure 1, right).

This is all that we could have done using an interface builder. As mentioned above, the main display of TreeViz cannot be specified using interface builders. We would not have been able to specify the EDIT command because we want a "double click" over the display area showing a record, rather than a screen button to invoke it. Interface builders have no provisions for such invisible behaviors.

The application model has several advantages over the interface builder approach:
- *HUMANOID generates a default interface for an application from the application model.* This default interface is very similar to the one constructed with an interface builder. It contains a menu-bar, an input panel, a blank area for the main application area, and a command panel at the bottom. In addition, HUMANOID provides facilities to customize the layout and other aspects of the interface to make it look as desired.
- *The application model makes all aspects of the design visible*, where as interface builders only allow designers to talk about elements that have an explicit representation on the end-user's interface. The application model allows

designers to express "hidden" notions, such as the EDIT command and the dialogue sequencing constraints.
- *The application model can also be used by automated design critics and automatic help generation tools* as illustrated by the UIDE system [1,2,4,11].

After having defined an initial version of the application model, the designer can proceed to refine the default interface to specify the presentation and behavior of the main application area or to fine-tune the default interface.

The next sections describe the refinement process that HUMANOID supports. If we were using an interface builder, we would proceed to drop into a programming language, because the interface builder support ends when the construction of the main application areas starts.

PRESENTATION TEMPLATES
In HUMANOID, designers model the presentation of an application incrementally. They first identify the major elements of the display and define presentation templates for them, which initially are just names for the display elements. Designers then proceed to define the characteristics of each display element, such as the data it presents, its parts, and its layout. For example, in TreeViz we see that the display is composed of three major elements: shapes (rectangles, ovals, etc.), columns and rows (Figure 1), so we proceed to define presentation templates for them called TreeViz-Shape, TreeViz-Column and TreeViz-Row (Figure 4).

A *presentation template* is an abstraction to model the characteristics of display elements. At run-time presentation templates are used as rubber-stamps to create as many instances of a display element as needed. Presentation templates represent the following information:
- *Is-A*: a presentation template can be defined as a refinement of an existing template, by modifying any of the attributes listed below.
- *Input data*: the type of information that can be displayed using a presentation template.
- *Widget*: the graphical object produced by a presentation template. It can be a primitive graphical object (line, icon, text, etc.) a toolkit primitive (menu, button, etc.), or a layout management widget (column, row, table, graph, etc.)
- *Applicability conditions*: predicates identifying the contexts where the template is appropriate.
- *Parts*: the decomposition of a complex display into simpler displays. Each part is modeled in terms of the input data it ought to present, and a default template for presenting the data. HUMANOID uses that default template as a starting point for a search for the most appropriate template to display the part, based on the applicability conditions of other templates in the model.
- *Behaviors*: the input behaviors that can be invoked from the display elements specified by the presentation template.

HUMANOID provides specialized editors to construct presentation templates and to specify all their attributes. The window in Figure 2. labeled Presentation

`Template Structure` shows the part decomposition of templates. The boxes represent templates and the links represent parts. The window labeled `Part Editor` shows all the attributes of a selected part in the `Presentation Template Structure` window.

```
TREEVIZ-SHAPE
is a GENERIC-PART-TEMPLATE

TREEVIZ-COLUMN
is a GENERIC-COLUMN-TEMPLATE

TREEVIZ-ROW
is a GENERIC-ROW-TEMPLATE
```

Figure 4. Initial definitions of the templates to construct the main application area of the TreeViz interface.

Figure 4. shows the initial template definitions to construct the main application area of TreeViz. We defined these templates as specializations of library templates that best approximate their desired effect (e.g. `TreeViz-Column` specializes `Generic-Column-Template`). We did not specify a particular shape for the `TreeViz-Shape` because we do not know yet what shape to use, and we want the shape to depend on the attributes of the record displayed in it. We will later need to use the conditional construct to specify this aspect of the interface. The ability to defer commitments on this issue is an example of the flexibility afforded by HUMANOID's model-based approach.

Adding Parts To Templates

In the case of TreeViz our next concern is to define the hierarchical decomposition of the display. In HUMANOID, we do this by adding parts to templates.

HUMANOID provides two ways to add parts to a template, by editing the model, or by editing an example generated from the model. To add a part by editing the model, the designer selects a template in the Presentation Template Structure window, and obtains a dialogue box to specify the name and the default presentation template for the part. To add a part by editing an example, the designer first specifies the template either by selecting it in the presentation model view, or by selecting a portion of the display in the example. Then, the designer selects the default presentation template for the part from a palette of library templates (like in an interface builder), and draws the part in the example window. When a part is specified by example, information about its size and location is incorporated into the model.

The facilities for adding parts illustrate the power of the coordinated model and example view approach. It is more convenient to select the part's parent in the model view because it shows all features of the model. The examples typically do not show the internal geometry management nodes of the display hierarchy. Also, small elements of the display which overlap each other are difficult to select. On the other hand, specifying the size and location of a new part is more conveniently done in the example window.

Our design of TreeViz proceeds by adding parts to the `TreeViz-Column` template. We need to add a BORDER part to show some kind of border around the column, and an

ELEMENTS part to specify the contents of the column.

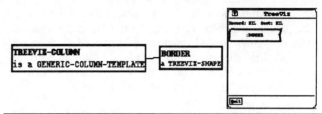

Figure 5. Once the BORDER part is added to `TreeViz-Column`, the generated example shows it.

Figure 5. shows the effects of adding the BORDER. We chose `TreeViz-Shape` as the default presentation template for the BORDER part so that the border shows the record associated with `TreeViz-Column`. HUMANOID shows the BORDER part as a sketch because the `TreeViz-Shape` template is not fully defined (it does not define a widget). The border's size is incorrect because we have not specified it yet (it should be the same size as the column).

The example illustrates how HUMANOID lets designers work in small incremental steps, without requiring them to fully define an aspect of the interface in order to get something on the screen. After adding the border we can work on any of the missing aspects of the interface. We can fix the border layout, define the conditions for choosing the appropriate shape, add the ELEMENTS part, or define the input behavior.

Suppose we add the ELEMENTS part. To fully specify it we need to specify what data it presents, what presentation template it uses for presenting its data, and how to get the part replicated as required by the data to be presented.

Specifying Part Input Data

Once a part is added to a template, it is necessary to specify the data that it should present. In general, the data presented in a part is a function of the data presented in its parent or ancestors further up the display hierarchy. These functions are typically defined by snippets of code that perform simple computations (e.g., accessing a slot value of an object, applying application-specific functions, concatenating strings, performing arithmetic). For example, in TreeViz, the ELEMENTS part presents the children of the record presented in its parent.

HUMANOID's interface for defining the values of input data of parts resembles the interface for entering formulas in a spreadsheet [7]. HUMANOID gives the designer a menu of commonly used functions and a type-in area for entering a *formula*, as these snippets of code are called in HUMANOID. Designers construct the formulas via a combination of type-in, menu-selection and pointing to enter references to other model elements (such as the input data of a template or an input of a command).

In the TreeViz example we use the spreadsheet interface to specify the value of the RECORD input data of the ELEMENTS part. We first choose the "get slot value" function from the menu, and then we point to relevant model elements to specify the object and the slot: we point to the RECORD input data of TreeViz-Column to specify that we want to access a slot of the record stored in the parent, and then we point to the CHILDREN slot in a window showing and example of a record (e.g. window labeled Object Browser in Figure 2.). From these pointing operations, HUMANOID constructs the snippet of code (g-value* (w+ :record) :children).

The spreadsheet paradigm for constructing the formulas that define the values of input data has two important benefits:

- Many computer users without programming expertise are familiar with spreadsheets, and can use them effectively.
- The recording of dependencies via references enables HUMANOID's automatic redisplay facility. When data referenced in a formula changes, HUMANOID can identify and update the affected portions of the display.

If we were using a conventional toolkit to build TreeViz, we would need to program both the propagation of data down the display hierarchy, and worry about bookkeeping for display update, say, in case a child of a record is deleted. Using HUMANOID we specified data propagation in a simple way, and we did not worry about display update at all.

Specifying Layout

Interface builders provide easy to use facilities to specify the layout of dialogue boxes. Designers simply drag and stretch the objects in the work area as needed, aided by alignment features (grids, gravity, dialogue-boxes) to neatly align the objects. Interface builders cannot be used to specify the layout of most application main displays because the objects to be laid out are computed by the application at run-time. It is necessary to specify *methods* for laying out objects rather than specifying the coordinates of concrete objects, as interface builders let designers do.

HUMANOID has a library of templates of commonly used layout methods such as rows, columns, tables and graphs. Designers use these templates by defining their templates as specializations of them (e.g., TreeViz-Column as a specialization of Generic-Column-Template). However, in many graphical interfaces, layouts different from the default ones are needed. In that case, the designer can use the layout specification facilities of HUMANOID.

Figure 2. showed a HUMANOID dialogue box for defining custom layouts. It is similar to the dialogue boxes provided in drawing editors and interface builders to define the alignment of parts, except that it is used to define the layout between two parts of a template (part and parent, or siblings), rather than two concrete objects. The dialogue box provides options for common cases (e.g., making the left side of object A be the left side of object B), and provides a custom option to allow designers to enter arbitrary formulas, should they need to. When entering arbitrary formulas, the spreadsheet paradigm is available to make it easy to enter references to other model elements.

In our TreeViz application we need to define the layout of the BORDER and ELEMENTS parts of TreeViz-Column. The BORDER part should be the same size as its parent, and we specify this by choosing the four "align" options in the

Figure 6. TreeViz examples before and after the layout of BORDER is defined.

Layout Editor dialogue box. Figure 6. shows the TreeViz example after the layout of the border is defined. We will postpone defining the layout of the ELEMENTS until we specify how to get the ELEMENTS part replicated.

The main benefits of HUMANOID's layout mechanism are:

- HUMANOID's library contains commonly used layout managers (row, column, table and graph).
- Custom layouts can be defined using dialogue boxes similar to the alignment facilities of interface builders.

If we were writing the TreeViz interface with a conventional toolkit, we would need to write some kind of recursive function to compute the layout. In HUMANOID, because it uses a constraint system [8], we specified the layout using simple formulas, entered with the spreadsheet interface. The constraint system solves the formulas to produce the correct layout, even when the window is resized.

BEHAVIOR TEMPLATES

TreeViz provides a good example of the kinds of input behavior required for manipulating the presentations of the main displays of an application. When the user moves the mouse over the visualization area, TreeViz shows, at the top of the window, a summary of the record that the mouse is pointing at. As the mouse moves, crossing the boundaries between regions, the information at the top of the window changes. When an interface is constructed using conventional toolkits, such input behaviors need to be programmed. Using HUMANOID, such behaviors can be specified by merely filling in options in a dialogue box.

HUMANOID's behavior model is based on Myers' Interactor model [6]. Myers identified seven classes of parameterized interactors that can be used to model the input behavior of a very large class of mouse and keyboard-based direct manipulation interfaces: *menu-interactor, move-grow-interactor, new-point-interactor, angle-interactor, text-interactor, trace-interactor* and *gesture-interactor*. Each interactor has between 10 and 20 parameters to specify the operation of the interactor.

We model the TreeViz behavior using a *menu-interactor*, whose menu elements are the leafs of the display tree (Myers' notion of an menu interaction is very general). Each time the mouse moves to a new leaf element, the menu interactor calls a standard action. Using the spreadsheet interface, we specify this action to set the application global input called CURRENT-OBJECT (Figure 3.) to the value of the RECORD input data of the leaf element pointed at with the mouse. The automatic update mechanism ensures that the screen is updated appropriately.

HUMANOID's behavior model has several benefits:

- Designers without programming experience can model application-specific behaviors of the kind that would require extensive programming if implemented in a traditional interface toolkit.
- The behavior model is separate from presentation, allowing designers to explore presentation and behavior features semi-independently. For example, in TreeViz the behavior works correctly even though the presentation model is not fully defined (neither the layout or the graphics of the visualization are defined). Once the presentation model is refined the behavior will still work, without modification.

ITERATION

A common concern in the design of many interfaces is to specify the presentation of variable amounts of data. HUMANOID provides an iteration construct, called *part replication*, to support this. It works by designating one of the input data of a part to be the index of the iteration construct. The run-time value of the index input data is expected to be a list. HUMANOID will instantiate (replicate) the part once for each element of the index input data. Each replication will be displayed using the default presentation template of the part. However, the conditional constructs (see next section) allow the specification of conditions to choose a different template for each replication depending on the attributes of the value of its index input data.

HUMANOID's iteration construct is very easy to use. The designer just needs to select one of the input data of a part, and designate it as the replication index.

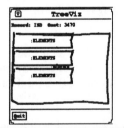 

Figure 7. Left: TreeViz example showing the effects of replication (before the size of the ELEMENTS is specified). Right: TreeViz after the sizes are specified.

In TreeViz we use the iteration construct to specify that the ELEMENTS part of TreeViz-Column should be replicated for each of the children of the record stored in the parent. In section "Specifying Part Input Data" we specified that the record input data of ELEMENTS gets all the children of the parent's record. The only thing we need to do now is to designate RECORD as the replication index. Figure 7. shows the effect of specifying the replication. The ELEMENTS part got replicated 3 times because the parent's record has 3 children. Since TreeViz-Column is a kind of column template, the elements appear in a column.

We now need to fix the size of the ELEMENTS part. The width of each element is equal to the width of its parent, and

we specify this by selecting the "align" options for "Left Alignment" and "Right Alignment" in the Layout Editor dialogue box (Figure 2). The height of each element is the height of its parent multiplied by the ratio of the COST slot of the element's record and the COST slot of the parent's record. We specify this formula using the "custom height" option for "Bottom Alignment" and use the spreadsheet facilities to enter references to the COST slot of the objects involved.

The notable aspect of HUMANOID's iteration construct is that it is simple, yet powerful. In addition, should the input data used as replication index change value a run-time, HUMANOID will automatically reconstruct the display.

Our TreeViz interface is almost finished. We now need to specify the actual shapes to be used to display each record. We do that using the conditional constructs.

CONDITIONALITY

One problem designers often face is to make presentations sensitive to the attributes of the data to be displayed. HUMANOID provides two conditional constructs to support this. The conditional constructs are designed to make it convenient to specify two common cases: hiding and showing display elements, and choosing different presentations based on the attributes of an object.

The *inclusion condition* of a part is a formula to determine whether the part appears in the display. The part is instantiated and included in the display if and only if the formula's value is true.

The *substitutions* of a template are a list of condition and template pairs that specify alternative templates to display the template's data. Substitutions can themselves have substitutions, so they form a hierarchy. When asked to display a part, HUMANOID searches the substitution hierarchy of the default template of the part to find the deepest substitution whose condition is true.

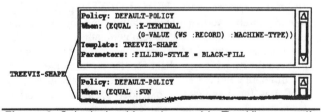

Figure 8. Substitution hierarchy used in TreeViz to specify different presentations based on the attributes of a record.

Figure 8. shows a portion of the substitution hierarchy we used in TreeViz to specify different presentations for records depending on the MACHINE-TYPE slot of the record. If the MACHINE-TYPE of a record is X-TERMINAL, then the shape should be black. Similar substitutions for other machine types and substitutions for person classes yields the finished TreeViz display shown in Figure 1.

HUMANOID provides an interactive interface to visualize and edit substitution hierarchies such as the one shown in Figure 8. Designers can add and delete nodes from the graph, and obtain dialogue boxes to edit all the attributes.

The conditional constructs of HUMANOID have several benefits. Conditionals can be added in a modular and incremental way (by adding part inclusion conditions, or adding nodes to the substitution hierarchy). Also, the use of spreadsheet paradigm to specify the conditions makes it easy for designers to define the conditions, and allows HUMANOID to automatically update displays, even if the update involves searching a substitution hierarchy again because the values of conditions changed. Once again, interface builders do not support conditional presentations, and achieving the same results through programming is much more work.

CURRENT STATUS

HUMANOID is implemented using CommonLisp, X windows and Garnet[8]. It has been used to implement the interfaces for three large applications: a logistics analysis system, a knowledge base development environment, and the HUMANOID designer's interface, which continues to be under active development.

CONCLUSIONS

HUMANOID integrates the traditional model-based approach of systems like UIDE, with the easy to use approach of interface builders and demonstrational tools. This yields a tool with the following benefits:

- *Expressivity.* Designers can specify the main windows of applications, not just menus and dialogue- boxes.
- *Ease of use.* Many aspects of HUMANOID increase ease of use: simple abstractions, all aspects of models are visible and changeable, model and example views are coordinated, spreadsheet paradigm for specifying snippets of code.
- *Support for the design process.* HUMANOID supports the design process by allowing designers to work top-down, to delay design commitments and to work on separate aspects of the interface semi-independently
- *Framework for the incorporation of more design-time and run-time support tools.* HUMANOID's explicit design model contains knowledge that can be used by automated design critics and automated help generation system. For example, a system like Cartoonist that generates animated help could be added to HUMANOID because the model contains the necessary information. In addition, the modeling language can be extended to incorporate other support tools (e.g. tools for task analysis).

ACKNOWLEDGMENTS

The research reported in this paper was supported by DARPA through Contract Numbers NCC 2-719 and N00174-91-0014. We wish to thank David Benjamin and Brian Harp for useful comments on drafts of this paper.

REFERENCES

[1] R. Braudes, A Framework for Conceptual Consistency Verification, D.Sc. Dissertation, Dept. of EE&CS, The George Washington University, Washington, DC 20052, 1990.

[2] J. Foley, W. Kim, S. Kovacevic and K. Murray, UIDE - An Intelligent User Interface Design Environment, in J. Sullivan and S. Tyler (eds.) Architectures for Intelligent User Interfaces: Elements and Prototypes, Addison-Wesley, Reading MA, 1991, pp. 339-384.

[3] B. Johnson, TreeViz: Treemap Visualization of Hierarchically Structured Information. In Proceedings CHI'92. May, 1992, pp. 369-370.

[4] W. Kim and J. Foley, DON: User Interface Presentation Design Assistant, In Proceedings UIST'90. October, 1990, pp. 10-20.

[5] B. A. Myers, B. Vander Zanden and R. B. Dannenberg. Creating Graphical Interactive Application Objects by Demonstration. In Proceedings UIST'89. November 1989, pp.95-104.

[6] B. A. Myers. A New Model for Handling Input. ACM Transactions on Informations Systems, 8(2). July 1990, pp. 289-320.

[7] B. A. Myers. Graphical Techniques In A Spreadsheet For Specifying User Interfaces. In Proceedings CHI'91. April, 1991, pp. 243-256.

[8] B. A. Myers, et. al. The Garnet Reference Manuals. Technical Report CMU-CS-90-117-R2, School of Computer Science, Carnegie Mellon University, Pittsburgh, PA 14212. May 1992.

[9] Neuron Data, Inc. 1991. Open Interface Toolkit. 146 University Ave. Palo Alto, CA 94301.

[10] G. Singh, C. H. Kok and T. Y. Ngan. Druid: A System for Demonstrational Rapid User Interface Development. In Proceedings UIST'90. October 1990, pp. 157-177.

[11] P. Sukaviriya and J. Foley, Coupling a UI Framework with Automatic Generation of Context-Sensitive Animated Help. In Proceedings of UIST '90. October 1990, pp. 142-146.

[12] P. Szekely, P. Luo, and R. Neches. Facilitating the Exploration of Interface Design Alternatives: The HUMANOID Model of Interface Design. In Proceedings CHI'92. May, 1992, pp. 507-514.

[13] M. Vlissides and M. A. Linton. Unidraw: A Framework For Building Domain-Specific Graphical Editors. ACM Transactions on Information Systems 8(3), July 1990. pp. 237-268.

[14] C. Wiecha, W. Bennett, S. Boies, J. Gould and S. Greene. ITS: A Tool For Rapidly Developing Interactive Applications. ACM Transactions on Information Systems 8(3), July 1990. pp. 204-236.

[15] M. D. Williams. What Makes RABBIT Run? Int. J. Man-Machine Studies, 21, 1984, pp. 333-352.

Tivoli: An Electronic Whiteboard
for Informal Workgroup Meetings

Elin Rønby Pedersen*, Kim McCall, Thomas P. Moran, Frank G. Halasz

Xerox Palo Alto Research Center

3333 Coyote Hill Road

Palo Alto, CA 94304, U.S.A.

Email: elin@dat.ruc.dk, {mccall,moran,halasz}@parc.xerox.com

ABSTRACT

This paper describes Tivoli, an electronic whiteboard application designed to support informal workgroup meetings and targeted to run on the Xerox Liveboard, a large screen, pen-based interactive display. Tivoli strives to provide its users with the simplicity, facile use, and easily understood functionality of conventional whiteboards, while at the same time taking advantage of the computational power of the Liveboard to support and augment its users' informal meeting practices. The paper presents the motivations for the design of Tivoli and briefly describes the current version in operation. It then reflects on several issues encountered in designing Tivoli, including the need to reconsider the basic assumptions behind the standard desktop GUI, the use of strokes as the fundamental object in the system, the generalized wipe interface technique, and the use of meta-strokes as gestural commands.

INTRODUCTION

Most of the early attempts to build computer support for meeting rooms, such as the Colab project [11], included whiteboard-sized displays to provide a shared focus of attention for the meeting participants. However, these displays were controlled at a distance by keyboard and mouse (just like a workstation). Meeting participants did not interact directly with the display surfaces as they would with ordinary whiteboards. Empirical studies of collaborative work at shared drawing surfaces [2,12] show that the physical actions around the surface itself are as important as the actual marks made on the surface to support the collaboration. Thus, the *Liveboard* system [7] was created at PARC to provide a "directly interactive, stylus-based, large-area display."[1] The Tivoli project was started to develop software for the Liveboard technology addressing two goals: (1) to discover and

---

1. Other large-surface displays are also becoming available, such as the Smart Technologies 2000 and the WACOM Meeting Staff.

explore the user interface techniques appropriate to this new kind of technology and (2) to discover and implement the functionality needed to actually support small working meetings at the Liveboard.

Nature of the User Interface

The basic direction was influenced by our early Liveboard experiences. After a dozen Liveboards had been deployed throughout PARC in meeting rooms and common areas, the most widely-used application was *Whiteboard* [7], a simple multipage pen-based image editor. It simulated a whiteboard by allowing freehand drawing and erasing. This system provided for the kind of unselfconscious, freeform scribbling that is prevalent in small group interactions, and it confronted us with the issues of the appropriate interaction techniques for and the basic nature of this genre of user interface.

The basic function of the board is to support interaction between people (and in this we agree with [4] that it is a "conversation board"). As such, the most important criteria for the user interaction with the board are to be *unselfconscious* — so as not to draw the attention of the participants from their interaction with each other — and to be *fluid* — to allow unhindered expression of ideas. While it is true that the user's "text-graphic performance" [9] involves the creation of various kinds of text-graphic objects, it does not follow that users should be required to declare these as they would be by a structured drawing program like MacDraw. In this sense we disagree with [4]. Further, we deliberately do not provide for handwriting recognition, for it would be disruptive in this context.

The Liveboard, as one component of a vision of ubiquitous computing [13], "blends into the woodwork" and appears to be just a familiar whiteboard. To follow through on this, the board should also behave as a simple whiteboard, at least initially. This not only allows first-time users immediate use of the board, but also allows users to build from their current work practices involving whiteboards.

Pen-based computing is still in its infancy. Operating system support, such as PenPoint [6] and Microsoft Windows for Pen

*Elin R. Pedersen's current address is: Department of Computer Science, Roskilde University, DK-4000 Roskilde, Denmark.

Figure 1: Photograph of Tivoli running on a Xerox Liveboard being used in an informal meeting.

Computing, is just now being provided. We want to discover appropriate ways to utilize the pen as an input device. The motions that are natural for a pen are quite different from those for a mouse. Because we are operating on a large surface, we want to keep as much facility "at hand" as possible. Gesturing (i.e. creating marks to be interpreted as commands) is an obvious extension beyond drawing and erasing. Other pen-based systems are oriented to using marks as annotations and gestures as commands over structured material, such as form-filling applications. Our situation is somewhat different in that all our material consists of informal handmade marks, and we want to preserve this look and feel. This raises new user interface issues that we are beginning to address.

Functionality for Small Working Meetings

Tivoli is targeted at supporting small working meetings, because this kind of meeting activity is prevalent at PARC and is well suited to the Liveboard. By "working" meetings (as opposed to, say, presentations) we mean meetings where the participants work closely together on a problem or an idea. For these a scribbling surface is useful for generating, communicating, and clarifying ideas and for keeping track of in-

formation. Such a working group usually needs to be small: up to about 8 people (also, the physical size of the Liveboard image, 46" x 32", precludes more people being able to gather around it effectively). Because meetings are small and informal, there is no official facilitator or scribe; all participants can have access to the board.

Our goal with Tivoli was to extend the functionality of a simple whiteboard program while preserving its basic features, spirit, and style. The early ideas for new functionality were numerous and diverse — much more than we could possibly implement. As a design strategy to sort these out, we developed a series of 14 scenarios of various kinds of meetings — varied both in content (design, review, brainstorming, administrative meetings) and in style (small to medium, informal to structured, co-located and distributed meetings). Each scenario was a 2-9 page narrative description of a meeting and its use of available wall displays, including whiteboards, flipcharts, copyboards, and Liveboards. Half the scenarios were *documentaries* of actual meetings, and half were *envisionments* of possible meetings. Writing these scenarios served to

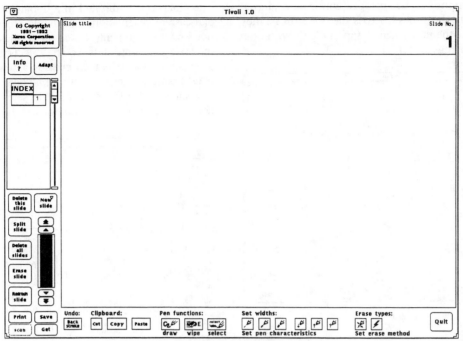

Figure 2: Tivoli window with blank slide.

integrate and concretize inputs from a variety of people, including both designers and potential users.

Analysis of these scenarios resulted in the identification of a coherent *core* of functionality needed across all meeting types and the classification of the remaining functionality into different research *thrusts*. The core functionality included simple pen and gesture scribbling and editing, multiple pages, saving and retrieving, printing, and importing images. The thrusts involved remote collaboration (shared drawing), meeting management tools, and integration with other "ubiquitous" devices. Tivoli was designed to implement the core functionality on an architecture that anticipated the explorations into the extended functionality. In this paper, we describe and discuss Tivoli 1.0, the first release that implements the core functionality.

A SCENARIO OF TIVOLI USE

The following scenario illustrates the main features of Tivoli 1.0 and motivates many of the design issues discussed in the next section. Elin, Kim, Tom, and Frank are starting a design meeting in which they intend to discuss the Tivoli object hierarchy and the possibility of implementing the "decorations" that appear on the Tivoli drawing surface as objects within that hierarchy. Elin goes to the Liveboard, which is displaying the Tivoli window shown in Figure 2. The window at this point consists of a blank *slide* for drawing in and control panels along the bottom and left edges.

In a long box at the top of the slide Elin writes "Objects in the Tivoli World." She does this as naturally and directly as if she were writing with a marker on a whiteboard. Then she lists the main classes of user-generated objects, "Stroke," "Character," and "Image." Kim points out that "Images" are now called "Pictures," so Elin taps the **wipe** button at the bottom of the window. The pen's cursor turns into an eraser. As she sweeps the pen over the word "Images," each stroke

she'd drawn is erased as a unit as soon as she touches it. She taps the **draw** button, sees her usual drawing cursor again, and writes "Picture."

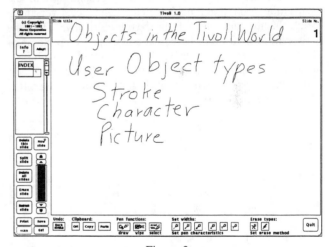

Figure 3

Elin wants a heading for these terms, but needs to create room above them to write it. She taps on the **select** button and draws a circle around the three terms, which then become selected. Then, she draws a line to show how far she wants to have the selected objects moved, which they do when she lifts up the pen. Above them she writes "User Object types." The result is shown in Figure 3.

Tom complains that Elin has been writing with too fine a pen. So she circles her list again and taps on the button for a thicker pen width. All the selected strokes get thicker as can be seen in Figure 4. But she failed to completely include the first 'U', which she deals with separately. But she has still left out the title at the top. She again taps the **wipe** button. But rather than just sweeping across the title (which would erase it), she first "dips" the pen into the button representing the preferred pen width. Now as she wipes it across the title strokes, they are all repainted at the new width. A tap of the **draw** button gives her back her regular pen.

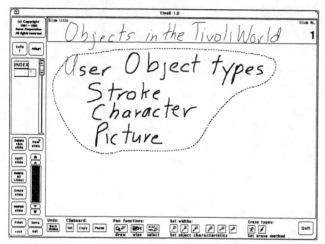

Figure 4

Elin starts a list of system-generated objects or slide "decorations." The list reaches the bottom of the slide, but Frank mentions a couple of items that were left out and really belong near the top of the list. Elin draws a horizontal line across the slide (what we call a "tear" gesture) where she wants more room and quickly taps the pen twice. Everything below the line gets selected, and she moves it down. Then she writes the desired items in the space just opened up. Some of the list is no longer visible, so she taps a small arrow button to scroll the slide. A scroll indicator near the arrow reflects where the current viewport is on the entire slide. The scrolled slide is show in Figure 5.

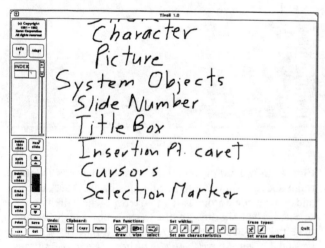

Figure 5

Now it's time to list issues concerning the objects, and Elin decides to start listing them on a separate slide; so she taps the **New Slide** button and gets a blank slide. At the top she writes "Issues" and then lists several issues as people mention them. A *slide list* to the left of the slide area contains a numbered list of all of the slides she has created. She taps on the numbers to switch between the two slides.

The group gets embroiled in a debate on the virtues of special-case representations and display routines. Elin is taking notes on the arguments, but soon decides this discussion belongs on a separate slide; so she selects it all and cuts it with a pigtail gesture. She then creates a new slide and taps the **Paste** button. The strokes that had been cut show up on the new slide. They remain selected, as seen in Figure 6, inviting her to move them, which she does.

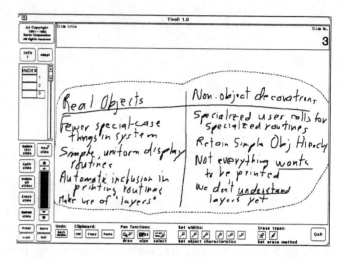

Figure 6

As the discussion starts to get very technical, Frank begins to worry about its implications for the display and object management aspects of the implementation. Kim remembers that he once prepared a slide for a formal talk illustrating the implementation modules. He goes to the Liveboard, taps the **Get** button, and selects from a dialog window the file containing his slides for that talk. Those slides are all added into the current folder of slides, which now number eight.

Unsure of which of the five new slides was the desired one, Kim taps the **INDEX** entry at the top of the slide list. This produces a system-created slide which consists of the title areas from the other slides, as shown in Figure 7. He sees that the desired Architecture slide is number seven. He thinks about just going to that slide, but decides instead to clean things up by deleting the unwanted slides. He uses the slide index to go to each slide in turn and delete it by tapping the **Delete this slide** button.

Then he goes to the Architecture slide and starts annotating it with circles and arrows. The resulting slide is shown in Figure 8. Occasionally he erases some of these, toggling back and forth between drawing and erasing by a rapid tap-tap of the pen. Because the illustration is in the *background* it is indelible. Only the annotations get erased. At one point he erases too much, deleting one arrow too many. He taps on the **Back stroke** button until he has recovered the lost arrow.

Elin wants to propose a new twist, but Kim is monopolizing the group's attention, so Elin draws a picture on a piece of paper before the idea escapes her. When the opportunity presents itself she sticks the paper into the Liveboard's attached scanner, taps the **Scan** button, and waits a minute. Then she

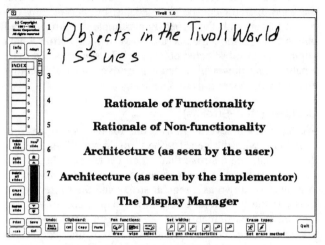

Figure 7

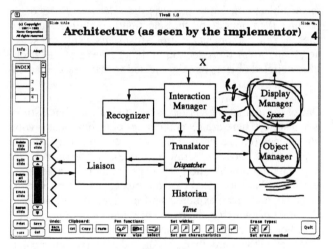

Figure 8

presses a button that imports the scanned image as the background of the current slide. Then she explains it and further annotates it.

Before anything is decided, the meeting's time has expired. Frank wants a hardcopy of the slides, so he taps the **Print** button, selects the **4 slides per page** option so that they'll all show up on one sheet, and sends it off to the printer. Tom is nominated to see whether he can condense the discussion to anything actionable. Frank finally taps the **Save** button. A dialog window comes up that suggests a default file name under which to save it. But Frank thinks up a better one, and *for the first time in the entire meeting* he uses the Liveboard's attached keyboard to specify the desired file name.

A few hours later, Tom runs Tivoli on his office workstation and reads in the folder in order to review the meeting. Imagining that this folder will form the basis for the next meeting, he decides to create another slide summarizing outstanding issues. But since his workstation has no stylus for drawing, he decides to do most of his writing with the keyboard.

The group's next meeting starts by reading in and reviewing Tom's revised version of the folder.

DESIGN FEATURES AND ISSUES

We now discuss some of the more interesting design features of Tivoli and the user interface design issues that they raise.

Assumptions Reconsidered

User interface design has converged onto a broad set of principles defining the generic graphical user interface (GUI). However, the GUI is tied to a set of assumptions about the technology (such as the mouse and the keyboard) and the usage situation (a single user at a workstation on a desk). Both our technology and our usage situation are different for Tivoli, and we found ourselves reconsidering many tacit assumptions. We give three examples:

Pen vs. mouse

A mouse is designed for pointing, whereas a pen is also for writing and drawing. Thus gestural techniques are much more natural for a pen than a mouse. A mouse is indirect in the sense that computation mediates the relationship of the physical movement of the mouse to the movement of the cursor on the display. On the other hand, the Liveboard pen is pointed directly at the surface of the display. There does not necessarily need to be a cursor; it should be where the pen is pointing (within the limits imposed by calibration error). This directness provides for a more direct interaction with objects on the display. However, the system needs to respect this physical directness. For example, we use an OpenLook scroll bar to implement the slide list. When the user points to a scroll arrow, the scroll arrows ride up and down the scrollbar like an elevator. With the mouse this is fine, because the cursor is adjusted to ride the elevator. But with the pen the elevator slides out from underneath the stationary pen, throwing the user off the scroll arrow.

Very Large Interactive Surface

Even with a large workstation display, the user can have a reasonable overview of the display from the normal viewing distance. A user standing at a Liveboard, however, is too close to have such an overview. Thus, we have had to adjust the size and placement of pop-up messages to make sure the user will always notice them. Also, tools such as buttons and menus can be physically out of the user's reach on the Liveboard. (This becomes apparent when running off-the-shelf workstation software on the Liveboard.) This implies some obvious design constraints, such as not requiring users to reach the top of the display to press a button. More generally, it places greater emphasis on keeping user control at the pen, especially for frequent actions and for actions that occur within the flow of scribbling. This is another motivation for utilizing gestural commands, which are issued from the pen *at* the place of application. The problem with gestures is that novice users may not remember them, and so we provide redundant screen buttons where possible. For example, the user can toggle between drawing and erasing either by a double tap of the pen or by reaching down and tapping the **draw** and **erase** buttons at the bottom of the display.

Multiple Users and Pens

A Liveboard is large enough to have more than one person working at it at a time — a natural working situation [11, 12]. The Liveboard is designed to have three pens to accommodate multiple users, and Tivoli was designed to operate with multiple pens. One consequence is that tools on the display are shared. For example, we cannot highlight an icon to show the current pen line thickness, since it can be different for different pens. This is yet another argument for gestural actions, which are localized to specific pens and do not have to rely on shared on-screen tools. In general, in our implementation we have had to distinguish *pen state* from *system state* (see also [3]). This distinction is not always clear-cut. For example, we consider a selection of objects to be part of a pen's state, and thus a second user cannot operate on the first user's selection (without taking the first pen). Another example is that we mark all actions with the ID of the pen that produced them, and we restrict the undoing of actions to be by the same pen (i.e, pen_2 cannot undo the relocation of strokes performed by pen_1, although pen_2 can erase those strokes).

Atomic Objects

Tivoli has an informal look and feel that is much like that of paint programs. But a major feature of the Tivoli design that distinguishes it from paint programs is that drawings are represented as *stroke objects*, not as pixel map images. A stroke is simply a series of line segments describing the path of the pen from the time it touches down on the display surface until it is lifted. A stroke is created over time, and the system cannot wait until it is completed before displaying it (as it does with keystrokes). Therefore, we provide an "inner loop" of feedback that instantly inks the display surface as the pen is moved over it. Only after the pen is lifted does the system create a stroke object.

The stroke-level granularity of this representation manifests itself when operating on the drawing. For example, erasing is done by wiping over the surface with the pen in erase mode. As the eraser goes over each stroke, that whole stroke disappears (i.e., the stroke object is deleted from the representation). This has proved to give a very nice "power boost" when erasing small to medium size strokes, such as handwriting (sweeping across a word gets rid of it without having to fuss with every little pixel). But this sometimes causes surprises when a long stroke (e.g., a large box or a long arrow) disappears when only a small portion of it has been touched by the eraser. The general issue is that objects are not homogeneous, and operations need to be designed to have a desirable effect. This issue needs much further exploration.

Another advantage of strokes as atomic units is that they provide objects for holding properties (e.g., color and thickness). Stroke properties can be changed, e.g., the color of a whole stroke can be changed, no matter how entangled it is with other strokes. And because they are geometrically defined, strokes are transformable.

Generalized Wiping

Tivoli expands the notion of object-based erasing to generalized *wiping*. Wiping is a user's back-and-forth motion across the display surface with a pen, which in wipe mode is called a *wiper*. The wiping motion *dynamically* selects objects as the wiper passes over them. A wiper has an associated operator, which it applies to objects as it selects them. Erasing is accomplished when the wipe operator is DELETE. When the user enters wipe mode, the default operator is DELETE; and

thus a novice user can simply think of this as an eraser. But the wipe operator can be changed just by tapping any on-screen button with the wiper. For example, tapping the red button changes the wipe operator to MAKE-RED, after which wiping makes all selected objects red. This has proved to be a natural and powerful technique for dynamically selecting and applying operations to objects.

Gestures (Meta-Strokes)

We have noted several motivations for the use of gestural techniques with the pen. By the term "gesture" we mean a *meta-stroke*, i.e., a stroke that is not just taken to be an element of the drawing, but is to be *interpreted as a command*. A gesture is drawn as a regular stroke and then interpreted. This has the beneficial effect in a group situation that the non-drawing participants can see the gesture before the action takes place and thus not be surprised by unexpected behavior. The most common gesture is the selection gesture, which is drawn as a closed loop of arbitrary shape around a set of objects, defining them as the *selection*. Subsequent gestures then operate on the selection: a pigtail gesture deletes the selected objects; a stroke that starts inside the selection loop moves the selection to the other end of the stroke (the encircled objects remain selected so that they can be operated on again).

One of the main design issues is how to indicate that a stroke is a gesture. There are several classes of techniques, involving devices (e.g., a gesture pen vs. a drawing pen), modes (e.g., gesture mode vs. drawing mode), "tense modes" [5] (e.g., holding down button on the pen to indicate a gesture), and so on. We attempted to avoid modes in the first version of Tivoli, and so we explored a different technique: the *postfix indicator*, which converts the preceding stroke into a gesture. For example, to select and delete a word, first draw a loop around the word, then give the indicator (which repaints the loop in the distinguished gesture color), then draw a pigtail.[2] The postfix technique allows gestures to be embedded in the drawing process. For example, a loop can be drawn (which at this point is just a regular stroke) and, if it isn't correct, erased and redrawn before indicating that it is to be interpreted as a gesture.

We explored a *double tap* of the pen as the postfix indicator (by analogy to a double-click on a mouse button). There is an inherent ambiguity with a double tap during drawing: how to distinguish it from two intentionally small drawing strokes, such as a colon or a quote mark. Thus a user writing "To:" might find that the system attempts to interpret the "o" as a gesture (unsuccessfully because the "o" is an empty loop) and all that is left is a "T".[3]

Faced with this difficulty in distinguishing double taps, especially for users with a "choppy" style of handwriting, we have moved to using a pen button as the gesture indicator in the more recent versions of Tivoli.

---

2. The pigtail does not require an indicator since it is indicated implicitly by context: When a selection is made, the system expects the user to next operate on it; and thus any stroke starting within the selection loop is taken to be a gesture.

STATUS AND FUTURE DIRECTIONS

Tivoli was first released in December 1991 and since then has been installed as the primary application on the Liveboards at PARC. It runs on Sun Sparcstations and utilizes the X Window System. It is implemented in C++ and currently uses the XView toolkit to implement control panels and buttons.

Tivoli 1.0 is only the first step in our attempt to build a collaborative meeting tool for the Liveboards. Among the many improvements and extensions we hope to eventually explore, we are currently focusing our effort on three issues: (1) a multi-site, shared version of Tivoli; (2) making the interface more accessible, or perspicuous, for casual users; and (3) exploring how Tivoli can be used to support specific meeting practices.

Multi-Site Tivoli

Our vision is to make Tivoli a true collaborative tool, supporting both multiple users standing shoulder-to-shoulder around a single Liveboard and multiple users utilizing two or more geographically-separated Liveboards (This draws inspiration from other work on shared drawing systems. such as [2, 8]. The version of Tivoli described in this paper is implemented to support only the single Liveboard case. We have implemented a multi-site version of Tivoli (Tivoli 2.0) that preserves all of the functionality in the current version [10].

Although the current version supports multiple users around a single Liveboard, the majority of our experience to date has been with situations where only a single user operates Tivoli at any given time. It remains an open question whether our current design will provide appropriate support for the multiple user (single Liveboard) case. In particular, the current Tivoli includes little mechanism for coordinating the actions among multiple users (e.g., preventing one user from changing slides while another is drawing), with the idea that such coordination can be accomplished using social rather than technological means. As we gain experience with the multiple user situation, we will be able to assess if this is in fact the case.

Another usage scenario for Tivoli involves a single meeting room containing a single Liveboard communicating with a (pen-based) laptop for each meeting participant. We hope to explore how the principles we are using to design a multi-site Tivoli will apply this co-located, multi-host case.

The Casual User

The design of Tivoli represents a deliberate balance between two often conflicting goals: interface simplicity and functionality. On the one hand, our goal was to design a Live-

board interface that maintains the natural, facile, immediately obvious feel of a conventional whiteboard. In particular, we were interested in maintaining the whiteboard's ease-of-use to casual (or never-before) users. Liveboards were designed to be placed into public meeting spaces. We wanted to make it easy for a person who has never used a Liveboard to walk up and figure out how to accomplish what they could on an ordinary whiteboard (draw in multiple colors, erase) plus a few obvious extensions (change slides, print) with little or no training. Meeting this requirement tended to push the Tivoli user interface towards simplicity, with the control panel displaying only a few straightforward buttons.

On the other hand, the Liveboard is a computational device. Another of our goals in designing Tivoli was to use this computational power to the user's advantage in supporting and augmenting the capture and organization of ideas in meetings. Accomplishing this goal tended to introduce sophisticated features and functionality into Tivoli (e.g., the generalized wipe operations) whose interface was either complex or non-intuitive or both. Moreover, the more such features we added to the program, the more widgets and buttons needed to be added to the interface.

It's clear from the feedback we've received from our user community that our current user interface design has erred in favor of increased functionality over intuitiveness, or perhaps 'interface perspicuity'. The never-before user who walks up to a Liveboard tends to find the interface so complex that she has some difficulty figuring out how to do the basics. We consider this a major problem and are exploring a revised user interface design which improves the walk-up-ability of Tivoli without decreasing the level of functionality.

Support for Specific Meeting Practices

A very explicit goal of the Tivoli project is to develop research prototypes with sufficient functionality and robustness that they can be put into widespread use in real meeting situations. Tivoli 1.0 is the first step in achieving this goal. Tivoli is currently in use on the 10 Liveboards throughout PARC, and we are beginning to accumulate feedback from users engaged in a variety of tasks and meeting types. At minimum, this feedback will guide us in making incremental improvements to Tivoli. More importantly, we are interested in examining in some detail how Tivoli is utilized for specific meeting practices. Our goal is to better understand what functionality could be added to Tivoli in order to support or augment these meeting practices. For example, Tivoli is frequently used to support brainstorming meetings. We are currently exploring how Tivoli could be expanded to support typical brainstorming activities such as list-making, categorization, and voting without altering its fundamental whiteboard-like nature.

In some sense, our search to expand Tivoli to provide support for more specific meeting practices reflects the other side of the tension between a simple, facile, whiteboard-like interface and an application that takes maximum advantage of the computational power behind the Liveboard to support its users' work practices. Clearly, the design challenge for this kind of system is to satisfy both of these goals.

---

3. Actually, the situation was much worse. The double tap was also loaded with a second function: to indicate a switch between drawing and wiping mode. A double tap would first cause the previous stroke to be interpreted as a gesture; if the gesture recognizer did not recognize it, then it caused a mode jump. Thus, an inadvertent double tap usually threw the user into wipe mode without warning, a dangerous move to say the least! This mode toggling functionality was removed from double tap in subsequent versions.

REFERENCES

1   Sara A. Bly. A Use of Drawing Surfaces in Different Collaborative Settings. *Proceedings of CSCW 88 Conference on Computer Supported Cooperative Work.* Portland, 1988, pp. 250-256.

2   Sara A. Bly and Scott L. Minneman. Commune: A Shared Drawing Surface. In *SIGOIS Bulletin*, Massachusetts, 1990, pp. 184-192.

3   Eric A. Bier, Steve Freeman. MMM: A User Interface Architecture for Shared Editors on a Single Screen. *Proceedings of the ACM Symposium on User Interface Software and Technology*, UIST'91, 1991.

4   Tom Brinck, Louis M. Gomez. A Collaborative Medium for the Support of Conversational Props. To appear in *Proceedings of CSCW 92 Conference on Computer Supported Cooperative Work.* Toronto, 1992.

5   William Buxton. Chunking and phrasing and the design of human-computer dialogues, *Proceedings of the IFIP World Computer Congress*, Dublin, Ireland, 1986, pp. 475-480.

6   Robert Carr, Dan Shafer. *The Power of the PenPoint.* Addison-Wesley, 1991.

7   Scott Elrod, Richard Bruce, David Goldberg, Frank Halasz, William Janssen, David Lee, Kim McCall, Elin R. Pedersen, Ken Pier, John Tang and Brent Welch. Liveboard: A large interactive display supporting group meetings, presentations and remote collaboration. *Proceedings of CHI '92 Conference on Human Factors in Computing Systems*, Monterey, CA, 1992.

8   Hiroshi Ishii, Minoru Kobayashi, Jonathan Grudin. Integration of Inter-personal space and shared workspace: ClearBoard design and experiments. *Proceedings of CSCW 92 Conference on Computer-Supported Cooperative Work*, Toronto, 1992, pp. 33-42

9   Fred Lakin, John Wambaugh, Larry Leifer, Dave Cannon, Cecelia Sivard. The Electronic Design Notebook: Performing Medium and Processing Medium. *Visual Computer: International Journal of Computer Graphics*, 214-226, August 1989.

10 Kim McCall, Thomas Moran, Bill van Melle, Elin Pedersen, Frank Halasz. Design principles for sharing in Tivoli, a whiteboard meeting-support tool. *Position paper for the Workshop on Real Time Group Drawing and Writing Tools, CSCW 92 Conference on Computer-Supported Cooperative Work*, Toronto, 1992.

11 Mark Stefik, Greg Foster, Danny Bobrow, Ken Kahn, Stan Lanning, Lucy Suchman. Beyond the Chalkboard: Computer support for collaboration and problem solving in meetings. *Communications of the ACM, 30(1)*, 1987. Also in Irene Greif, editor, *Computer Supported Work: A Book of Readings*, Morgan Kaufmann Publishers, 1988, pp. 335-366.

12 John Tang. *Listing, Drawing, and Gesturing in Design: A Study of the Use of Shared Workspaces by Design Teams.* Ph.D. Thesis. Stanford University, Department of Mechanical Engineering, 1989.

13 Mark Weiser. The Computer for the 21st Century. *Scientific American, Sept. 1991.*

The User-centred Iterative Design
Of Collaborative Writing Software

Ronald M. Baecker, Dimitrios Nastos, Ilona R. Posner, and Kelly L. Mawby

Dynamic Graphics Project, Computer Systems Research Institute
University of Toronto
Toronto, Ontario, CANADA M5S 1A4
Phone: (416)978-6983   E-mail: baecker@dgp.utoronto.ca

ABSTRACT

This paper presents the user-centred iterative design of software that supports collaborative writing. The design grew out of a study of how people write together that included a survey of writers and a laboratory study of writing teams linked by a variety of communications media. The resulting taxonomy of collaborative writing is summarized in the paper, followed by a list of design requirements for collaborative writing software suggested by the work. The paper describes two designs of the software. The first prototype supports synchronous writing and editing from workstations linked over local area and wide area networks. The second prototype also supports brainstorming, outlining, and document review, as well as asynchronous work. Lessons learned from the user testing and actual usage of the two systems are also presented.

KEYWORDS: Computer-supported cooperative work, groupware, user-centred design, iterative design, behavioural research, collaborative writing, writing software, synchronous and asynchronous writing.

INTRODUCTION

Most authors of documents work collaboratively from time to time; many write together with others most of the time. Yet very little is understood about how people write together, and very few systems are available to support this activity. This paper summarizes the results of our research on the process of collaborative writing, lists design requirements for collaborative writing software, and presents the user-centred iterative design of such software.

Our research on process consists of interviews with writers who have worked together collaboratively and a laboratory study of writing teams linked by different communications media. The taxonomy of collaborative writing that grew out of this work is summarized in the paper.

Our software design is user-centred in that it is based on this behavioural research. It is iterative, consisting of cycles of design, implementation of prototypes, and testing and evaluation. The first prototype, SASE, supports synchronous writing and editing in both focused and peripherally aware collaborative modes from workstations

linked over local area and wide are networks. The second prototype, SASSE (Synchronous Asynchronous Structured Shared Editor), also supports brainstorming, outlining, and document review, provides a rich set of views of document structure, content, and revision process, and allows asynchronous work on a document.

TAXONOMY OF COLLABORATIVE WRITING

Previous Research

Although research has been conducted on individual writing [4, 10], only recently has attention been turned to collaborative writing. Surveys have shown that the majority of all written work is performed collaboratively [1, 7]. Physical proximity of collaborators was found to be key to successful scientific writing [16]. Computer technology affects the communication between participants as well as the final product of the collaboration [9, 12, 23].

A Survey of Writers

In order to understand the process of collaborative writing, we conducted 10 interviews with individuals who had participated in a number of collaborative writing projects. The backgrounds of the individuals surveyed included medicine, computer science, psychology, journalism, and freelance writing. The 22 projects discussed included journal articles, course assignments, a TV script, and a best-selling book. These projects lasted from several days to several years. The collaborating groups were formed either voluntarily or were organized in work settings. Participants varied in status from peers to student supervisor teams. Further details on the interviews may be found in [24, 25].

We encountered a wide range of attitudes towards collaborative writing. People had different expectations about the effects of collaboration, yet most felt that having several co-writers would improve the final product.

The relative status of group members, either similar or different, can lead to problems in working groups. Equal status groups may experience struggles for leadership and the problem of confronting members who are not contributing their expected share of work. In groups of unequal status participants may feel pressured to conform not on the basis of the alternative arguments but on the basis of the status of the individual proposing the alternative.

Different individual working styles can also cause problems. Some individuals like to leave the work till the last minute, while others prefer to complete the task in advance of the deadline. Individual preferences often need to be suppressed for the benefit of group harmony.

Writing technology can also cause problems for groups. Use of different machines by collaborators introduced difficulties when the document segments had to be merged into a single format. Participants complained of problems keeping track of different versions of the document. For example, one interviewee complained, "I would get email saying change page 4 line 2, but in my version page 4 is completely different." Communication bandwidth was a problem for groups working at a distance. For these groups physical proximity was often a solution. One interviewee said, "I was tempted to just fly there, instead of trying to cope with it over a distance."

Laboratory Study

A controlled laboratory study was conducted in order to see if we would observe in that context the same collaborative writing processes that our interviewees had reported. We also wanted to observe the effects of the communication medium on the writing process.

Pairs of subjects were asked to write instructions for the assembly of two simple toys. We informed the subjects that the resulting two chapters of assembly instructions were to become part of a single book; thus there needed to be similarity in writing style, terminology, and format between the two chapters.

Groups had two computers available and were free to choose any writing approach. Subjects worked in one of five scenarios: in the same room communicating face-to-face, in different rooms communicating with a speaker-phone, in different rooms communicating with an audio-video connection, in different rooms with the audio-video connection plus an image of the partner's remote screen, and in different rooms with the audio-video connection and the SASSE shared editor. In addition, subjects had available electronic mail, facsimile, and courier services.

Results of this study are discussed in [26]. Here we'll briefly list the highlights. We ran 4 groups in each condition, 20 groups in total. Given the small number of groups we did not necessarily expect to obtain statistically significant results, but we wanted to observe trends.

Individual differences in group behaviour dominated the results. Personalities of the participants had significant effects of the writing approach chosen by the group. Autocratic individuals who actively took control of the group insisted on joint work to monitor the progress and control the final document. Groups composed of two dominant individuals often faced interpersonal conflicts. Cooperative groups often divided the work between participants each one trusting the other to complete the required task.

As in previous research [12], document quality, i.e., the useability of the instructions, did not vary significantly with medium of communication ($F[4, 15]=1.237$, $p<.337$).

The type of communication between participants varied with the scenario. The discussions of subjects who could see each other's work focused more on higher-level issues such as writing style, tone, and audience of their documents.

Subjects that could not easily see the other document frequently discussed lower-level details such as format and wording of their chapters.

The time to complete the task did not vary significantly with the communication medium ($F[4,15]=1.774$, $p<.187$). The medium did affect the amount of time spent working together compared to the total working time. Face-to-face subjects spent the most time working together (76%) while the speaker-phone groups spent the least (40%). The time spent working together was negatively correlated with total writing time ($r=-.418$, $p<.067$), but this may be as a result of the given task, which stressed consistency between documents.

Taxonomy of Collaborative Writing

The taxonomy of collaborative writing evolved out of attempts to categorize different components of the collaborative writing process that we observed in the interviews and again in the lab study (see Table 1). Each of the four categories of the taxonomy provides a different perspective for examining the writing process. *Roles* looks at process from the individual's point of view, at the part played by each individual on the writing team. *Activities* categorizes the actions performed while working on the project. *Document control methods* describes how the writing process is managed and coordinated. Finally, *writing strategies* focuses on the text creation process.

The choice of roles can depend on several factors including organizational structure, time constraints of the participants, relative status of the group members, and skills and expertise of the contributors:

- *writer*: converts ideas into text, records the text, freely makes changes to the text
- *consultant*: actively participates in different stages of the project but does not write the text
- *editor*: corrects text written by someone else
- *reviewer*: provides comments on the document.

Activities performed on a project can be affected by time constraints, task knowledge possessed by the group members, established organizational procedures, and participants' work styles:

- *brainstorming*: generating ideas
- *researching*: gathering information from sources external to the group
- *planning*: creating an outline for the document, and often dividing the work among group members
- *writing*: transforming ideas into text
- *editing*: making changes to the written text
- *reviewing*: generating comments about the text.

Document control methods describe how the document is managed and changes to it are made and coordinated.

- *centralized*: one person maintains the document while others make suggestions to the writer
- *relay*: one person controls the document at a time, but control passes between multiple authors
- *independent*: several people support segments of the document, while each one maintains control over an individual segment

	Interview	Lab. Study
Roles		
Writer	67%	95%
Consultant	43	75
Editor	57	80
Reviewer	85	88
Activities		
Brainstorm	82	100
Research	80	0
Plan	85	95
Write	82	95
Edit	78	80
Review	93	88
Document Control Methods		
Centralized	56	10
Relay	36	45
Independent	64	85
Shared	27	20
Writing Strategies		
Single Writer	59	15
Scribe	23	15
Separate Writers	86	90
Joint Writing	41	55

Table 1: Summary of writing approaches observed in interviews and the laboratory study. [1]

- *shared*: several people jointly control the document, having equal access and write privileges.

Writing strategies describe the document creation process, demonstrating how each segment of the text is created:
- *single writer:* text of document reflects thoughts and style of one individual with minimal assistance from others
- *scribe*: most often used in group meetings when one individual records the group's discussions with minimal guidance from the group
- *separate writers*: team members take different parts of the document and write them individually; later the parts are combined to form a whole
- *joint writing*: several team members compose the text together, where each word choice and sentence structure is decided through a group effort.

DESIGN REQUIREMENTS
The taxonomy presented in the previous section provides us with a vocabulary to describe systematically the processes of group writing. This work [24, 25], insights from our other research [19, 20], and an analysis of previous research results [16, 22, 25], have enabled us to formulate in six categories a set of design requirements for collaborative writing technology (see Table 2):

General Requirements for Individual Writing
Basic word-processing. A collaborative writing system must provide basic word-processing mechanisms.

---

[1] In roles, percentages are computed out of 60 individuals participating in projects discussed in the interviews and 40 subjects in the laboratory study. In the other categories, percentages describe how many groups employed certain activities, document control methods, or writing strategies.

Seamlessness with other work media. Users must be able to move smoothly between new groupware technology and existing single-user software [3]. Minimally, there must be a way to exchange documents with single-user applications.

General Requirements for Collaborative Writing
Preservation of identities. Collaborative writing depends upon contributions from several individuals. A collaborative writing system should record and display the identities of the contributors.

Enhanced communication. Essential to collaboration is communication among individuals who work together. They communicate about the object of their collaboration (*substantive communication*), exchange questions, revisions, and acceptances (*annotative communication*), and discuss courses of action and process plans to achieve their goal (*procedural communication*) [28].

Enhanced collaborator awareness. We define *collaborator awareness* as the knowledge of the state or actions of one's collaborators. Two dimensions that characterize levels of awareness are the degree of engagement and the amount of planning [14]. Depending on how focused and planned shared work is, collaboration may vary from focused collaboration (where people work together closely) to general awareness (where people know roughly what others are doing). We prefer the term *peripheral awareness*.

Annotations. Contributors such as reviewers of a document often record their suggestions as annotations. Ideally, a system should support several kinds of annotations — text, voice, or hand-drawn markings.

Undo. All interactive systems such as writing and drawing tools must provide the ability to undo changes made by a user. Undoing however becomes difficult when there are interleaved changes originating from multiple sources [27].

Session control. A collaborative writing system should allow users to create, join, or leave editing sessions at arbitrary times. It must also ensure that all users access the same version of the shared document.

Requirements re Roles
Explicit roles. A shared writing environment should support the different roles individuals may play in the process of document creation.

Requirements re Activities
Variety of activities. A document is created through a number of different activities including brainstorming, planning (including both outline and process plans), writing, editing, and reviewing. Each activity requires different support and functionality from a writing system. A shared writing system should be flexible enough to allow different writers to perform different activities at the same time.

Transitions between activities. A writing system should allow seamless transitions between activities, since they do not always occur in a sequential manner.

Requirements re Document Control Methods
Several document access methods. It may be appropriate to have different types, such as read-only, write, and comment.

Requirements	Aspects	GROVE	PREP	Quilt	ShrEdit	SASE	SASSE
Individual Writing							
Basic word-processing	++	–	++	–	++	+	++
Seamlessness with other media	++	–	++	++	+	+	++
Collaborative Writing							
Preserve identities	–	++	+	++	++	++	++
Enhance communication	+	–	–	–	+	–	++
Enhance collaborator awareness							
Focused collaboration	++	++	–	–	+	++	++
Peripheral awareness	–	+	–	–	–	+	++
Annotations	–	++	++	++	–	–	+
Undo	–		+	+	–	–	–
Session control	+	++	–	++	+	–	++
Roles							
Explicit roles	–	+	++	++	–	–	–
Activities							
Variety of activities							
Brainstorming	–	++	++	+	++	+	++
Researching	–	–	–	++	–	–	–
Planning (outline)	–	++	+	+	–	–	++
Planning (process)	–	–	+	–	–	–	–
Writing	++	–	++	+	++	++	++
Editing	++	–	++	+	++	++	++
Reviewing	–	–	++	+	–	–	++
Transitions between activities	+	–	++	++	+		++
Document Control Methods							
Several access methods	–	++	++	++	–	–	–
Separate document segments	++		+	++	–	–	–
Version and change control	–	–	+	–	–	–	++
Writing Strategies							
One or several writers	++	++	++	++	++	++	++
Synchronous writing	++	++	–		++	++	++
Asynchronous writing	+	+	++	++	++	–	++

Notation:　　++ system provides good support　　+ system can handle　　– system does not support

Table 2: Design requirements and comparison of collaborative writing tools.

Separate document segments. Individuals working collaboratively often subdivide the document and work on the pieces independently. Systems should provide support for multiple document segments yet maintain connections and access into the entire document.

Version control. Knowing who wrote or changed a certain part, what changes were made, and when they were made is essential.

Requirements re Writing Strategies
One or several writers. Although designed for multiple writers, a shared writing system should also support a single writer, so that one need not use a different systems for this.

Synchronous and asynchronous writing. Participants on a project may want to access the document concurrently or sequentially. Support for synchronous writing is essential especially during the stages of brainstorming and outlining. Support for asynchronous work is particularly important in the stages of writing, editing, and reviewing.

System Comparison
These requirements are summarized in Table 2, where existing shared writing systems are also evaluated. Aspects [2] is a collaborative conferencing system that runs on networked computers and provides writing, drawing, and painting tools. GROVE [8] is an outlining tool designed for users at remote sites working on networked computers. PREP [22] is a writing tool that provides asynchronous access to documents and can be thought of as a "spreadsheet for documents," because it provides a column based interface where text is presented in columns of visually linked chunks. Quilt [17] is a multi-user hypermedia communications and coordination tool which combines computer conferencing with multi-media email. ShrEdit [5] is intended for simultaneous writing by several users working on networked computers in a conference room.

THE FIRST PROTOTYPE
Our first prototype system for collaborative writing [19] was called SASE (pronounced "sassie"). This prototype was designed to support highly interactive synchronous collaborative writing.

SASE Design Requirements
Support for focused collaboration and independent work. Groups sometimes work together in focused collaboration, yet individuals or subgroups often break off from the main group to do independent work [8, 24, 25]. We felt that SASE should support both these approaches.

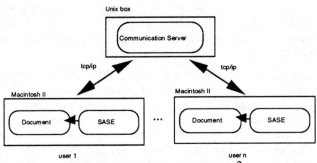

Figure 1: SASE's architecture.[2]

Support for collaborator awareness. In a synchronous writing environment, collaborators can simultaneously modify and add text to the document. Because there are multiple concurrent activities, collaborators may find it difficult to understand the changes that have been made and are currently being made to the shared document by others [6]. So SASE had to provide information to increase the individual's awareness and understanding of collaborators' actions.

Support conflict resolution. When multiple people edit the same document, it is conceivable that two or more people may attempt to modify a particular segment of text at the same time. Thus we felt SASE should provide mechanisms to help prevent users from making conflicting changes.

User Interface and Architecture

SASE allows two or more people to edit a document synchronously while working at their own Macintosh workstations. It is assumed that they will communicate via telephone or an audio/video connection.

So that collaborators can see and discuss each others' contributions as they happen, text modifications made by users immediately appear on their text windows and on the text windows of all other collaborators. Users can point to text using a hand-like pointing device called a *telepointer*. To help maintain collaborator awareness, users are provided continuous feedback of other collaborators' working locations in the document with colour coded text selections and scroll bars.

There is always one vertical scroll bar for each person currently collaborating in SASE. The rightmost scroll bar on a user's text window always belongs to that user and functions as a normal scroll bar. Additional colour-coded scroll bars indicate the current locations of collaborators, but are "read-only" and cannot be manipulated.

Users can work independently on a document in SASE, since actions such as scrolling and window sizing affect only the window of the user who initiated the action. They can also work together in a highly focused mode by locking together and synchronizing their views, thus achieving WYSIWIS (What You See Is What I See).

To avoid conflicting changes, SASE locks text at the user text selection level. This means that it is possible for collaborators to work within the same line of text. With this fine grain locking mechanism, we leave it to the

collaborating group to decide how closely they will work within the shared document.

We chose a replicated architecture (Figure 1) in which a copy of the application and the shared document reside on each collaborators' workstation. This architecture is combined with a centralized communication server which resides on a Unix box. The application copies communicate via the TCP/IP communication protocol. All message traffic is routed through the central communication server which ensures that all copies of the application receive messages in the same order. This architecture supports simultaneous text editing, usually provides reasonable response, and supports conflict resolution.

User Testing

A usability study [19] was conducted with three two-person teams using SASE to perform a series of text editing tasks required to prepare collaboratively a newspaper article for publication. Subjects communicated via a CAVECAT audio/video connection [18]. All subjects were able to use SASE effectively after a brief introduction to the system.

The multiple scroll bars improved collaborator awareness. Subjects used these to match their view of the document with their partner's view, to determine how far away their partner was in the document, and to reduce the time needed to find text in the document.

When groups were asked to do a shared task such as scanning the document for typographical errors, they first negotiated how to divide the work in order to save time. When asked to collaboratively compose text, all groups used the scribe writing strategy.

Subjects liked the fact that they could work separately or together in the document. This allowed them to save time by dividing the task. They also liked that they could ask their partner for help when necessary. They suggested that the system should provide a way of seeing what changes have been made, and a way to change the text back to the original form if necessary.

THE SECOND PROTOTYPE

The second prototype, called SASSE [20], is an extension of the first, and is based on the requirements presented earlier in this paper. Our goal was to satisfy most of them, while leaving some (e.g., providing support for explicit roles) to be handled by social protocols.

Design Requirements

Support for a variety of activities. In designing the second prototype we felt that the system should support the writing activities presented previously. SASSE supports

---

2 SASE's text editing functionality was implemented using the Word Solution Engine (WSE) [29] by DataPak Software, Inc. The WSE supports the text editing functionality of the Macintosh TextEdit Toolbox and also provides hooks into text editing procedures for purposes of customization, such as for maintaining multiple colour coded text selections .

brainstorming, outlining, and reviewing, in addition to writing and editing.

Enhanced communication and collaborator awareness. We designed views that provide information about who the collaborators are, where in the document they are working, and what they are doing.

Support for asynchronous writing. The first prototype was a synchronous shared editor. In order to support asynchronous writing, we added an annotation mechanism that allows authors to exchange notes and comments, a simple version control mechanism that shows which parts of the document were changed and by whom, as well as a centralized document storage mechanism that allows users to access shared documents easily.

SASSE User Interface and Implementation

Support for a variety of activities. SASSE's outline editor has been designed to allow writers to work with hierarchically structured shared documents. The outline editor allows users to see document structure, to display or hide parts of it, and to edit its structure as well as its contents. Baecker, et al., Colour Plate 1 shows SASSE in outlining mode. Baecker, et al., Colour Plate 2 shows the normal text display of SASSE.

During the reviewing phase writers solicit comments on versions of their document. Sometimes this results in a dialogue between the commenters and the writers, especially when the comments are unclear. SASSE's annotation mechanism allows users to write text comments that can be selectively displayed, hidden, or deleted.

Enhanced communication and collaborator awareness. SASSE's collaborator awareness mechanisms provide information about the co-authors of a document, their positions in the document, and their actions. As in SASE, colour is used to differentiate between users. Each collaborator is assigned a unique colour. This assignment is stored with the document so that the same author has the same colour each time a particular document is edited.

Collaborator awareness is further aided by views that provide information about the state or actions of collaborators. The collaborator list gives information about the authors of a document, as well as their colour assignment, and whether they are present or not present in the editing session. The shared scroll bars introduced in the first prototype were redesigned. Instead of having several scroll bars, which take up screen space, only two scroll bars are displayed: the normal scroll bar of the local user and one with multiple colour-coded indicators which correspond to the collaborators participating in an editing session. SASSE's shared scroll bars are shown in the colour plates.

Information about what user activities can range from the very abstract and global to the very concrete and local. SASSE provides two views at extremes of the spectrum. The *gestalt view* (Colour Plate 2) presents a condensed image of the entire document as well all collaborators' positions and text selections. The *observation view* (Colour Plate 1) allows users to "look over the shoulder" of a collaborator and see exactly what they are seeing and doing. Additionally, non-speech audio cues [13] provide information about collaborators' actions such as scrolling and deleting.

Support for asynchronous writing. In order to support asynchronous writing we added an annotation mechanism. Users can selectively display or hide comments written by a specific author. The comments are colour-coded for easy identification. A simple version control mechanism (implemented but not yet installed) allows users to see which parts of the documents have been changed and what the changes are. A document server is used to store shared documents in a central storage space. Collaborators are thus able to access with ease the latest version of a document.

User Testing and Results

We conducted a usability study [20] with SASSE, again using CAVECAT to provide a voice and video link. Four two-person groups used the system to carry out a set of collaborative writing and editing tasks after a brief introduction to its functionality and user interface. The tasks were designed to test the outlining and collaborator awareness mechanisms of the system. During the first part of the study the subjects were asked to edit the outline of a travel guide. During the second part they had to do both shared and independent editing tasks on an article. Subjects were asked to use the system's awareness mechanism to obtain information about their collaborators.

Three methods were used to collect information from the usability study: observation during the study, recording it on video for later analysis with our VANNA video annotation and analysis system [15], and administration of a questionnaire and an interview with subjects after the study.

Subjects used the audio link continuously but made relatively little use of the video link. Most subjects were able to use SASSE's outlining and collaborator awareness mechanisms successfully. Yet, the character-level locking produced unacceptable delays during deletions. Some subjects could not understand why some operations were failing because they would not notice the padlock indicating that they were locked out. Finally, network delays resulting in slow system response made some subjects feel uneasy and in a few cases retry an operation.

Real Use

SASSE is becoming robust enough to be used for real work. We have done so over local area networks in our lab and over a wide area network between Toronto and California. This paper was written in part with SASSE. Observations are implied in the suggestions for future work listed below.

SUMMARY AND CONCLUSIONS

We have presented the user-centred iterative design of collaborative writing technology. The work is deeply rooted in behavioural research consisting of interviews, usability tests, and studies of the technology in actual use. This has enabled us to improve the design in successive iterations, a process which continues to this day.

Our user tests and usage suggest that a coarser locking scheme, for example, at the sentence or paragraph level, would suffice. Alternatively, locking may not be needed at all because conflicts can be negotiated through use of the voice link. This would allow us to improve performance significantly. Further work is also required to achieve true "seamlessness" with other writing technology. We are currently designing and implementing an "undo" command [27] and mechanisms for automatically collecting usage data. Finally, much more work remains to be done on the design of effective visual and auditory views to enhance collaborator awareness, and on the design of better methods for the display of document changes [21].

ACKNOWLEDGEMENTS

We gratefully acknowledge the support to our laboratory from the Natural Sciences and Engineering Research Council of Canada, the Information Technology Research Centre of Ontario, the Institute for Robotics and Intelligent Systems of Canada, Apple Computer's Human Interface Group and Advanced Technology Group, Xerox PARC and EuroPARC, Digital Equipment Corporation, and the IBM Canada Lab Centre for Advanced Studies. We are also indebted to Beverly Harrison, Marilyn Mantei, Alex Mitchell, and Abigail Sellen for assistance with this work.

REFERENCES

1. Allen, N.J., Atkinson, D., Morgan, M., Moore, T., and Snow, C., What Experienced Collaborators Say about Collaborative Writing. *Iowa State Journal of Business and Technical Communication* Sept. 1987, 70-90.

2. Aspects: The First Simultaneous Conference Software for the Macintosh, Group Technologies, Inc., 1990.

3. Baecker, R., *Readings in Groupware and Computer-supported Cooperative Work: Facilitating Human-human Collaboration,* Morgan Kaufmann, 1993.

4. Bereiter, C. and Scardamalia, M., From Conversation to Composition, in *Advances in Instructional Psychology,* R. Glaser, Editor, Erlbaum, 1982.

5. Cognitive Science and Machine Intelligence Laboratory. ShrEdit, a Multi-user Shared Text Editor: User's Manual, The University of Michigan, 1989.

6. Dourish, P. and Bellotti, V., Awareness and Coordination in Shared Workspaces, *Proceedings of CSCW'92,* 107-114.

7. Ede, L. and Lunsford, A., *Singular Texts/Plural Authors: Perspectives on Collaborative Writing.* Southern Illinois University Press, 1990.

8. Ellis, C.A., Gibbs, S.J., and Rein, G.L., Groupware: Some Issues and Experiences. *CACM* 34(1), 1991, 38-58. Reprinted in [3].

9. Eveland, J.D. and Bikson, T.K., Work Group Structures and Computer Support: A Field Experiment. *Proc of CSCW'88,* 324-343.

10. Flower, L., Schriver, K.A., Carey, L., Haas, C., and Hayes, J.R., Planning in Writing: The Cognition of a Constructive Process. Center for the Study of Writing, Carnegie Mellon University, 1989.

11. Galegher, J., Kraut, R.E., and Egido, C., Editors, *Intellectual Teamwork: Social and Technological Foundations of Cooperative Work,* Erlbaum, 1990.

12. Galegher, J., Kraut, R.E., and Egido, C.., Technology for Intellectual Teamwork: Perspectives on Research and Design, in [11], 1-20.

13. Gaver, W., Sound Support for Collaboration, *Proceedings of ECSCW '91,* 293-308. Reprinted in [3].

14. Gaver, W., Moran, T., MacLean, A., Lövstrand, L., Dourish, P., Carter, K., and Buxton, W., Realizing a Video Environment: EuroPARC's RAVE System, *Proceedings of CHI '92,* 27-35.

15. Harrison, B.L. and Baecker, R.M., Designing Video Annotation and Analysis Systems, *Proceedings of Graphics Interface '92,* 157-166.

16. Kraut, R., Egido, C., and Galegher, J., Patterns of Contact and Communication in Scientific Research Collaborations. In [11], 149-171.

17. Leland, M.D.P., Fish, R.S., and Kraut, R.E., Collaborative Document Production Using Quilt, *Proceedings of CSCW 88,* 206-215.

18. Mantei, M.M., Baecker, R.M., Sellen, A.J., Buxton, W.A.S., Milligan, T., and Wellman, B., Experiences in the Use of a Media Space, *Proceedings of CHI '91,* 203-208. Reprinted in [3].

19. Mawby, K.L., Designing Collaborative Writing Tools. 1991, Unpublished M.Sc. Thesis, Department of Computer Science, University of Toronto.

20. Nastos, D., A Structured Environment for Collaborative Writing. 1992, Unpublished M.Sc. Thesis, Department of Computer Science, University of Toronto.

21. Neuwirth, C.M., Chandhok, R., Kaufer, D.S., Erion, P., Morris, J., and Miller, D., Flexible DIFF-ing in a Collaborative Writing System, *Proceedings of CSCW'92,* 147-154.

22. Neuwirth, C.M., Kaufer, D.S., Chandhok, R., and Morris, J.H., Issues in the Design of Computer Support for Co-authoring and Commenting, *Proceedings of CSCW 90,* 183-195. Reprinted in [3].

23. Olson, J.S., Olson, G.M., Storrøsten, M., and Carter, M., How a Group-Editor Changes the Character of a Design Meeting as well as its Outcome, *Proceedings of CSCW'92,* 91-98.

24. Posner, I.R., A Study of Collaborative Writing. 1991, Unpublished M.Sc. Thesis, Department of Computer Science, University of Toronto.

25. Posner, I.R. and Baecker, R.M., How People Write Together, in *Proceedings of the Twenty-fifth Annual Hawaii International Conference on System Sciences,* 1992, 127-138. Reprinted in [3].

26. Posner, I.R. and Baecker, R.M., A Study of Collaborative Writing, journal article submittted for review, 1992.

27. Prakash, A. and Knister, M.J., Undoing Actions in Collaborative Work, *Proceedings of CSCW'92,* 273-280.

28. Suchman, L.A. and Trigg, R.H., A Framework for Studying Research Collaboration, *Proceedings of CSCW 86,* 221-228.

29. Word Solution Engine Programmer's Guide, DataPak Software, Inc., Vancouver, WA, 1990.

Take CoVer:
Exploiting Version Support in
Cooperative Systems

Anja Haake, Jörg M. Haake

Integrated Publication and Information Systems Institute (IPSI)
Gesellschaft für Mathematik und Datenverarbeitung (GMD)
Dolivostr. 15, D-6100 Darmstadt, F.R.Germany
Tel.: ++49 / 6151 / 869 - 929
e-mail: {ahaake, haake}@darmstadt.gmd.de

ABSTRACT

Current CSCW applications support one or more modes of
cooperative work. The selection of and transition between
these modes is usually placed on the users. At IPSI we built
the SEPIA cooperative hypermedia authoring environment
supporting a whole range of situations arising during collaborative work and the smooth transitions between them.
While early use of the system shows the benefits of supporting smooth transitions between different collaborative
modes, it also reveals some deficits regarding parallel work,
management of alternative documents, or reuse of document
parts. We propose to integrate version support to overcome
these limitations. This leads to a versioned data management
and an extended user interface enabling concurrent users to
select a certain state of their work, to be aware of related
changes, and to cooperate with others either asynchronously
or synchronously.

KEYWORDS: CSCW, versioning, cooperation modes,
alternative object states, group awareness, hypertext

INTRODUCTION

Current Computer Supported Cooperative Work (CSCW)
applications (see [3], [9] for an overview of CSCW systems)
support a group of co-workers performing a task on a shared
information base. Usually, these systems support a specific
collaboration model, e.g., asynchronous collaboration
through draft passing, or synchronous collaboration through
joint editing. At any point in time, exactly one state of the
overall information base exists.

However, collaboration in not computer-supported environments often includes a lot of parallel work resulting in alternative or conflicting drafts. Each co-worker produces a different state of the information base which must be merged

with the other states later. In addition, co-workers use different collaboration models according to the needs of a specific
task.

Current CSCW systems do not support different collaboration models at the same time, nor do they allow for parallel
work on a shared information base or alternative states of a
shared information base.

A first step towards a solution is to support different modes
of collaboration allowing co-workers to work either asynchronously or synchronously on the same (part of the) information base. Specific support for different kinds of synchronous
collaboration is required, and the smooth transition between
the different modes must be supported. This is the approach
taken by the SEPIA cooperative hypermedia authoring environment (see [6], [12]) which allows more parallelism for
working on the same state of a hyperdocument.

To support different states of an information base we propose
to integrate version support into CSCW systems. This still
allows synchronous work on the same state of the information base but enables concurrent co-workers to select a certain state of the information base, to be aware of related
changes, and to cooperate either asynchronously or synchronously. In such a system not only an extended data management is needed, but also extended user interfaces reflecting
group awareness as well as the existence of alternative versions are required. This approach led to the development of
the versioned cooperative SEPIA system described in this
paper.

We will first explain our approach to support different modes
of collaboration taking cooperative SEPIA as an example.
After identifying a list of deficits of cooperative SEPIA we
introduce basic version support. Next, we introduce our approach of integrating version support into cooperative SE-
PIA. Using an example of collaborative authoring we illustrate how the extended system overcomes the deficiencies of
the original system. Finally, we discuss the differences to related work and the general applicability of our approach.

THE COOPERATIVE SEPIA SYSTEM

SEPIA is a cooperative hypermedia authoring environment. Its purpose is to support groups of authors who collaboratively create hyperdocuments [6]. A hyperdocument consists of three kinds of hypermedia objects: atomic nodes, composite nodes and links. Atomic nodes contain data (e.g., text, graphics, images, sound). Composite nodes contain a set of references to other hypermedia objects. Thus they allow the clustering of objects into subgraphs of the overall hyperdocument. Links represent relationships between the hypermedia objects.

Authoring Support in SEPIA

To support the general authoring activity SEPIA provides the notion of a project. A project contains all material needed for the production of a publication including the final hyperdocument. Working on a project includes different activities which are supported by four dedicated workspaces, the so-called activity spaces [11]. They comprise the Planning, Content, Argumentation and Rhetorical Space. The Rhetorical Space serves the final hyperdocument production while the others are used for preproduction activities. Associated with each activity space is a dedicated browser which offers a certain set of functions on the objects it presents. To display the subgraph contained in a composite node a new browser can be opened on the composite. In SEPIA all hypermedia objects are typed carrying certain attributes and each activity space provides activity-specific types for nodes and links [13].

Cooperation Support in SEPIA

To support the cooperation among co-authors cooperative SEPIA provides access to a shared information base by using the cooperative hypermedia server CHS [12]. SEPIA ensures a common view of the information base among all concurrent users relying on the CHS update notification service. The consistent state of the information base is maintained through the use of transactions. Access to the database is synchronized via activity markers signalling a specific status of an object (e.g., "about to be modified") which must be interpreted by the browsers before accessing or modifying the object.

Specific support is provided for the three modes of collaborative work:

♦ **Individual work** can be performed by opening a browser on a composite node which is currently not used by other authors.

♦ **Loosely-coupled work** allows several co-workers to concurrently access some part of the information base but still permits rather independent work. This work mode is supported by providing group awareness when several co-authors work simultaneously in the same composite node. Every co-author is able to work independently but sees the effects of other co-authors' activities immediately as they appear in the currently visible part of the subgraph. Activity markers are used to avoid collisions between authors accessing the same objects. This approach can be considered as the integration of general awareness – as proposed in the Portholes systems [2] for distributed office rooms – into CSCW tools themselves.

♦ **Tightly-coupled work** allows to cooperate and coordinate group work in synchronous conference-like "meetings". This work mode supports shared views among the concurrent browsers (the WYSIWIS principle: "What You See Is What I See" [10]), a telepointer for each co-author, and additional communication channels (e.g., audio and video conferences, and a shared drawing tool have been added to SEPIA. For details, see [6], [12]).

Actual collaboration proceeds by shifting between these three collaboration modes. The transitions are often prompted by needs for coordination which arise from individual work or through observing activities of co-workers in loosely-coupled work. Therefore, smooth transitions between the modes must be supported, i.e. natural and easy-to-use transitions in a non-disruptive manner have to be provided.

The smooth transitions between the modes are supported by binding these transitions to changes of the set of current users of a composite node: While working on a composite without concurrent users, an author works in individual work mode. When co-authors open a composite node already used by another author, all concurrent browsers shift into loosely-coupled mode. If some co-author in a loosely-coupled session feels the need for a synchronous conference, the co-author can initiate a tightly-coupled session between a set of specified loosely-coupled collaborators. Those who confirmed the conference request then shift into tightly-coupled mode while the others remain in loosely-coupled mode. At any time, co-authors can close their browsers, thus leaving the corresponding loosely- or tightly-coupled sessions. This way, transitions between the modes are triggered by the authors' navigational actions (open and close browsers) or by explicit conference requests.

Deficiencies

Early use of the system indicated a number deficiencies. First of all, the individual work mode, as defined above, includes two different cases which should be supported explicitly:

♦ **Isolated work**, where just one author should be allowed to work on and see the content of a specific document part (i.e., composite node).

♦ **Separate work**, where several co-authors may concurrently work on separate drafts of the same document part, but without interfering with each other.

The first case could be implemented in SEPIA using "lock activity marker" on composite nodes thus preventing others from entering the document part. The second case requires the management of alternative drafts created from one original document part, which is possible in SEPIA (through copy functions and creating links among original and copied objects) but which is not explicitly supported.

Next, copying objects for use in other composites causes problems because of **loosing the object identity**. When the copy is edited this is not visible within loosely-coupled sessions viewing the original object. This may result in conflicting changes which cannot be easily detected by co-authors.

In addition, during conference-like tightly-coupled sessions aiming at the integration of several drafts or document parts it is necessary to be able to review each of the parts and to modify them to create an integrated result. But the **integrity of the individual contributions** (drafts) must still be maintained (at least for documentation purposes). In SEPIA this requires explicit copying of objects which put additional load on the co-authors.

Moreover, **history tracking** is completely missing. Thus co-authors rejoining work e.g. after holidays found it difficult to find out what happened in the meantime. Another situation requiring history tracking arises when a bug is identified and all places have to be found where the wrong information has been used or has been contributed to.

At least three of the above deficiencies are key issues of version management (i.e., isolated workspaces, management of alternatives for separated work, and history tracking). In the next chapter we explain our approach to versioning of hyperdocuments. After that we discuss the integration of versioning into cooperative SEPIA to overcome the mentioned shortcomings.

COVER: A CONTEXTUAL VERSION SERVER

CoVer is a hypermedia version server [5]. To provide for adaptable version management CoVer has been designed as an extension of the cooperative hypermedia server CHS [12]. Thus, the versioning concepts offered by CoVer can be used by hypertext applications to define application-dependent version support. CoVer maintains context information with the versions. Context information guides version creation and in particular helps in version identification. After introducing the basic versioning mechanisms, we explain the context-based versioning mechanisms derivation history and task.

Basic version management

CHS offers persistent nodes, links, and composites but does not preserve previous states of objects. The task of basic version management is, above all to define the notion of a versioned object.

CoVer represents versioned objects by so-called **multi-state objects** (mobs). A mob represents a versioned object by gathering all states of the versioned object in its version set.

The states of a versioned object are called versions and are represented by individual nodes, links, and composites. A mob is realized on top of CHS as a composite holding references to all states of the versioned object it represents. CoVer maintains the creation time and author of each object. In order to preserve the states of versioned objects, versions of nodes, links, and composites can be **frozen** [5].

It is a key characteristic of CoVer that is does not impose a fixed structure on the versions of a versioned object. Version selection is based on viewing and browsing versions with respect to values of their attributes or relationships to other objects. Consequently, our notion of alternatives does not depend on the notion of revision (cf. below 'Derivation history') defined by a certain version graph, as found in many other approaches (see [1], [8] for an overview). Any two or more versions of a version set that match an equivalence predicate given by a query exploiting the versions' attributes are considered alternatives with respect to the equality characteristic expressed by the query.

Derivation history

CoVer's notion of revisions is subsumed by the **derivation history**. The derivation history induces a (possibly) unconnected graph structure over all versions, independently of their structuring into mobs. The derivation history is implemented using a specific link (derivation link) connecting the ascendant and the descendant version. Derivation links can be created explicitly by the application. Moreover, CoVer offers two derive operations creating either a new version as a copy of a version or a new object and installing a corresponding derivation link. Versions of the same mob connected by a derivation link may be considered revisions of a versioned object. But in addition, the derivation history records the reuse of material across document boundaries and can be navigated during version selection.

Tasks

A key concept for version creation is task tracking [14]: Users change their hypertext network to perform a task. For example, writing a document by a group of authors includes tasks such as proposing an outline, creating alternative proposals, or merging several contributions. These tasks can guide meaningful, automatic version creation. Stored persistently as contextual version information they serve version identification.

While mobs maintain the history of a single versioned object, tasks maintain the (versions of) various objects used and created in the context of performing a job. Eventually, a task maintains a state of the hyperdocument that fulfills the requirements of the respective jobs. To create such a new version of a specific object, tasks may profit from all available versions of all available objects in the overall system. Therefore any object may be included into a task by an include operation provided by CoVer. Changes to included objects will be recorded automatically in derived versions, i.e. CoVer freezes the included objects, derives new versions of these objects and executes the changes on these derived versions.

Apart from a system maintained identifier, a task is described by a short name supplied by the application, start and completion date and time - i.e. if the completion date is undefined the task is still alive, otherwise terminated - , author information, and optional application defined attributes providing detailed task information. In particular, a task holds references to all objects constituting its current state. A task may have several subtasks. Tasks may be executed sequentially or in parallel. Thus, tasks form a task hierarchy providing a framework for managing the recursive decomposition of application processes. Keeping a log of all subtasks of a task, CoVer monitors the concrete work flow. A task is implemented on top of CHS as a composite holding references to the objects determining its current state. Moreover, special types of links are used to represent the various task relationships. An initial top level task maintained by CoVer records all tasks created by the applications.

If a task is completed by the application, its current state is frozen by CoVer and delivered as a result to the supertask. These versions are the only versions visible in the supertask, i.e. all intermediate versions of the subtask are hidden. If a task is aborted by the application, CoVer also aborts all direct open subtasks and connects the completed subtasks to the parent task of the aborted task. Versions belonging to incomplete tasks are only visible to their subtasks. But versions maintained as the result of a completed subtask are accessible for everybody since they represent a state of work consistent from the point of view of the task being performed by the completed subtask. Thus, CoVer provides an **encapsulated work area** for ongoing tasks and hides inconsistent system versions from other tasks. CoVer supports set-oriented access to tasks by querying their attributes as well as browsing the task history. Thus, it offers application access to versions of both whole hypertext networks and single objects via task-related information.

INTEGRATING VERSION SUPPORT INTO COOPERATIVE SYSTEMS

This section discusses how cooperative systems can be extended by version support to alleviate the deficiencies discovered. We call such systems versioned cooperative systems. First, we focus on extensions to the implementation of SEPIA on top of the CoVer version server. Next, we show how these extensions are reflected by the user interface of the versioned cooperative SEPIA.

The System's View

Hypertext applications exploit CoVer via CoVer's application interface. As described in the previous section, CoVer naturally extends the notion of hypertext objects to the notion of versioned hypertext objects. However, the applications have to decide how those objects should be versioned, i.e. the applications have to implement their specific versioning behavior (versioning style). For each type of operation the application has to define how it affects the versioned objects by declaring the respective operation as a task.

For cooperative systems, the behavior of the cooperation modes is of particular importance. This is why, after we have described the exploitation of the versioned data model to alleviate the detected deficiencies, we will discuss how the extended cooperation modes of SEPIA are implemented using tasks. To assure the smooth transition between different cooperation modes we designed extensions to SEPIA that can be generally applied to realize group awareness in versioned cooperative systems.

Exploiting the versioned data model. A prerequisite to overcome the main deficiencies is the application of mobs to the basic object representation. A mob represents a versioned object by gathering all states of the versioned object in its version set. This representation guarantees the **object identity** of the versioned object and simultaneously represents the versions as identifiable units. The former enables the detection of conflicting changes whereas the latter is the basis to manage alternative drafts, for example for **separate work**, and to maintain the **integrity of individual contributions** when creating integrated results in tightly-coupled sessions. In addition, CoVer offers several options for **history tracking**. The application can explore the historical development according to the creation date of versions, restrict the view to versions to those created by a specific author, or use any other attribute that suggests a sensible view over the version set. Exploring the derivation history, bugs propagated by cut and paste operations may even be detected across document boundaries. In particular, tasks monitor the work flow at different levels of detail and abstraction and ease the access to historical information.

Extending the cooperation modes. We propose to support the extended set of cooperation modes by applying tasks. **Separate work** corresponds directly to parallel tasks. If several co-authors want to work concurrently on separate drafts of the same document, each author should create a successor task of that task that created the original document. CoVer's task concept automatically preserves the original and keeps the changes in separate versions not interfering with each other.

Supporting the restricted mode of **isolated work** requires a combination of CoVer's task concept with the CHS activity marker concept. If just one author should be allowed to work on and see the content of a specific document part, the original version should be totally protected, as well as all new versions created in the context of the author's task. Since the original is protected, no parallel task may be started on the original. Since new versions are protected, nobody may join the author's task (cf. below for joining tasks). Thus, unintended creation of alternatives that may lead to serious merge problems can be avoided.

Since authors may also want to modify the same version of a document, the loosely-coupled and tightly-coupled mode should also be supported in a versioned system. To enable authors to work independently in a loosely-coupled session on the same version of a document, we allow to **join tasks**. If an author is working on a task, anybody else may join this task thus shifting into loosely-coupled mode.

To monitor changes to objects performed by different authors involved in the session, the cooperative versioned SEPIA records each update to a version, which has not been performed by the version creator, in a new, derived version. Thus, revisions of objects by collaborating authors – which led to a loss of the original state if the original had not been saved in a backup copy in the cooperative SEPIA system – are automatically maintained by the versioned cooperative SEPIA. The same versioning style has been implemented for tightly-coupled sessions.

At any point in time, authors may initiate a tightly-coupled session. The versioned cooperative SEPIA records each tightly-coupled session in a task that is considered a subtask of all current tasks of users participating in this session. Beside using the backup copies saved by the system if different authors attempted to subsequently modify the same object version, authors engaged in a tightly-coupled session profit in particular from the **extended object identity** maintained by CoVer's mobs. Tightly-coupled sessions are used when several contributions developed during isolated or separated work should be merged into one group work result. During a tightly-coupled session, the authors may include their individual contributions into the task. Alternatives, i.e. versions of the same object, are identified by the system-maintained extended object identity. Since a task keeps changes to included versions automatically in derived versions, a new version covering the final result will be created automatically and the **integrity of individual contributions** is preserved.

Extending group awareness. The support of smooth transitions between the different cooperation modes is based on the notion of object identity: If users work on the same composite, they move into loosely-coupled mode. While working in loosely-coupled mode every co-author sees the effects of other co-authors' activities and activity markers are used to avoid collisions between authors accessing the same objects. These mutual observations of activities may create the need to initiate an unforeseen tightly-coupled session.

Exploiting version support enables the users to keep individual changes in alternative versions. Actually, these changes affect the same object but constitute different states of the object. Unintended generation of alternative versions may

result in unforeseen merge problems or overall consistency problems that should have been prevented.

One way to prevent these problems, is to work in isolated mode. In many situations, this approach is too restrictive. If users want to create alternative versions of the same object for different purposes, or if users want to work in parallel assuming that a later merge can be performed without major problems, they may work separately. Nevertheless, unexpected alternative updates of the same object may be problematic. Therefore, users working on separate tasks should be informed about alternative versions created by other users. If required, concurrent users working at the same time may then initiate a tightly-coupled session to solve the conflict immediately, or concurrent users working at different times may schedule an early tightly-coupled session to fix the unforeseen conflict. This is true not only for individual separate work, but also for loosely- or tightly-coupled sessions occurring in parallel. To support this behavior, CoVer's notion of an encapsulated work area (cf. subsection about tasks) has been relaxed and the implementation of CoVer on top of CHS exploits the extended object identity provided by mobs to inform applications of alternative versions.

The User's View

The cooperative SEPIA user interface looks as follows: The SEPIA main control panel allows users to create, select, and open projects. After opening a project a SEPIA Project Launcher pops up and offers access to the four activity spaces. One scrollable browser window for each activity space and for each composite node is used to display and manipulate the composites' content. In general, the state of an object is signalled using colors.

To discuss the introduction of version support into cooperative systems at the user interface, we look at the cooperative writing of a hyperdocument by a group of four authors using the versioned cooperative SEPIA authoring environment. Following well-known patterns of cooperatively writing documents, we will pick up four different situations that illustrate the four cooperation modes supported by a versioned cooperative system.

Isolated work. At one point of time, one author may enter the SEPIA system to produce a new draft proposal from the individual contributions, alternative proposals, and annotations of the co-authors. After selecting the right project, the author has to select an appropriate task determining the state of work to be initially confronted with. To do so, the author investigates the Task Browser (cf. Figure 1) maintained for each project that shows the development of the project up to the current point of time. For example, Figure 1 shows the situation after each team member has revised and extended the annotated outline of the hyperdocument. Since producing a draft proposal is a new task, the author creates a new task succeeding the four previous tasks by selecting all predecessor task icons and using the corresponding menu. Then, the author opens a new task in isolated mode to avoid changes made by others during the merge phase, i.e. a task in isolated mode assures an exclusive workspace and inhibits the creation of new versions by others.

Since the new task is a successor task of all four preceding tasks, the opened project prompts with four SEPIA Project Launchers named by a combination of project and task name representing the four different states of work. The author investigates each individual contribution and merges them into a new draft proposal.

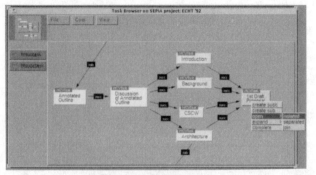

Figure 1 Task Browser

showing the development of work. One author has proposed an Annotated Outline. The group has discussed this outline and decided to split up in four groups. Now, one author merges the group works' results into a 1st Draft Proposal to be discussed eventually in a joint meeting.

While investigating a single contribution, the author may request the visualization of alternatives proposed by other contributions which will be piled beneath the selected contribution. Figure 2 shows the Rhetorical Space of the contribution provided by the task "Introduction" (cf. Figure 1 for names of tasks). Only two of the other three co-workers have also proposed a new version of the node named "Challenge of HM Authoring". To investigate these alternative proposals the author may open a Mob Browser (cf. Figure 2) on a versioned object that shows the relationships and attributes (of a specified subset) of the versions of the version set. Selecting two versions in the Mob Browser triggers the comparison of the versions' content (cf. Figure 2).

Based on the differences between the selected versions shown in the Mob Browser, the author decides to copy some sentences of the version of the node created by task "Background" into the version of the node created by task "Introduction". This update automatically leads to the creation of a new version belonging to the actual task. This new version is immediately prompted in the Mob Browser. Switching back to the Rhetorical Space, the system shows the new version of the node as an additional alternative. The author may explicitly exclude those alternatives that should not contribute to the draft proposal. Further investigation and merge may proceed in the same way leading to a new version of the hyperdocument.

Tightly-coupled work. Having finished the draft proposal, the author may schedule a synchronized session (per e-mail or any other suitable communication means) to discuss the draft proposal and eventually create a new common draft of the hyperdocument. All authors join the new task which has been initiated by the main author as a successor task of the merge task and enter the tightly-coupled session. During the meeting, the author of the draft proposal introduces the proposal. The tightly-coupled mode allows co-authors to interrupt the presentation if required (e.g., verbally using the audio channels provided by the cooperative SEPIA) and to bring up parts of their previous proposals to support the discussion of decisions made by the author of the proposal. To indicate which browsers show versions belonging to the current state of work and which browsers are visualizing previous versions, the former are presented in normal colors whereas the latter are presented in pale colors. During the discussion, the authors may jointly use the comparison facilities or edit the new proposal simultaneously. All updates will automatically be kept in new versions documenting the result of the meeting.

After finishing the draft, the team has decided to split up into three groups for further work. Two authors will work independently on different aspects of the article whereas two authors should elaborate another aspect together.

Loosely-coupled work. The group of two authors may decide to further separate the work (i.e. create separate subtasks for each author, then later merge their results in a tightly-coupled session) or to manipulate the same state of work synchronously. In the latter case, one author may join the task if the other author is already working in separate mode. Then, both move into loosely-coupled mode. Working in loosely-coupled mode, one author may unconcerned revise the changes made by the partner since alternating updates are maintained by the system, propose changes in an alternative version that will be visualized by the system, or initiate a tightly-coupled session to discuss the proposals immediately.

Separate work. Although the three different groups are working separately on different aspects of the hyperdocument, it may happen that some of them have modified the same object which led to the maintenance of alternative versions with respect to the different tasks. To check for the unintended generation of alternative versions, a user may request the system to show all alternative versions created by concurrent tasks. Icons representing these versions are presented in pale color to distinguish them from alternatives belonging to the actual state. If some alternatives seem to constitute conflicts, the involved users may initiate a tightly-coupled session to resolve the problem in a common subtask. The result of this task will be kept automatically in a new version of the object and may be used in the concurrent tasks during future work. In any case, the result of these three concurrent tasks are three new states of the hyperdocument that are kept as alternative versions that may be merged later.

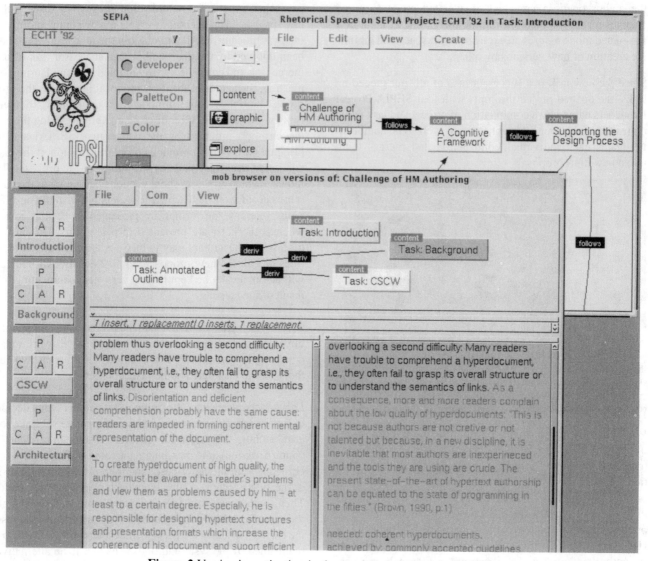

Figure 2 Version investigation in the versioned cooperative SEPIA.

RELATED WORK

Related work either focuses on cooperative work or on version support. This work has been discussed in [6] and [5], respectively. Related work on cooperative work either supports subsequent draft passing or synchronous work on a single system state only. Related work on version support allows to maintain different subsequent or parallel states of objects providing different degrees of history tracking to support the mutually intelligibility between cooperating users. In general, versioning approaches provide check-in / check-out mechanisms that may be used for enhanced draft passing as an extended means of collaboration. These mechanisms are introduced as single concepts and the integration of the concepts in a cooperative environment and user interface is not discussed.

We are aware of only two attempts to exploit version support directly to enhance cooperative work. Quilt [4] is a tool for collaborative writing of linear text. Whereas SEPIA's coop-

eration support also attempts to support unforeseen interaction and communication needs, a prerequisite to use Quilt is to define a cooperation style naming the participants and describing their social roles that define their rights and responsibilities in a certain collaboration task. Quilt allows to annotate work-in-progress (which is inherent in hypertext and thus in our approach), exchange messages, and track the status of work. It does not support synchronous work. Quilt maintains only one valid state of the linear document at a time. It is up to the users to determine when to save a version of the document. Moreover, Quilt records a complete activity log of the users' interactions that may be extended by more abstract descriptions of activities provided by the users. In our approach also basic operations may be declared as tasks and then are maintained as subtasks of more complex operations or user-defined tasks (cf. [5]). Thus, hierarchical tasks record the user interaction at different levels of detail and abstraction and automatically determine versions to be kept. In Quilt, at any time users may send messages to other users, for example to inform others about the state of their work. A notion of extended group awareness that is inherent to the system is not supported. Moreover, alternative versions in a single system state, parallel versions of the system, or joint editing of a single system state are not supported.

At the database level, Käfer [7] made a proposal to version-based cooperation control. The approach is to relax the atomicity and isolation properties of database transactions to support long duration teamwork in design environments. To do so, transactions work on object versions and additional attributes, called features, are attached to the object types. During a transaction, feature values are assigned by the applications. The actual feature value set determines the degree of consistency of the versions and triggers the sending of predefined notifications to other transactions. At a certain degree of consistency, versions may also be exchanged between transactions. Our notion of extended object identity providing the extended group awareness may be implemented on top of this database approach. Of course, Käfer does not discuss user interface issues and questions of asynchronous and synchronous work.

CONCLUSION

We have shown how the functionality and cooperation modes of cooperative systems can be enhanced by version support and how mechanisms to support the smooth transition between these modes allow a flexible use of a versioned cooperative system. We illustrated how the users of a versioned cooperative system may choose freely between various combinations of different modes of asynchronous and synchronous cooperation that best supports their actual job. In doing so, extended group awareness enables the users to decide to change their cooperation modes dynamically.

The approach presented in this paper is not limited to hypertext. Any application domain that can be modelled by interrelated objects can be mapped to hypertext. Vice versa, the version support mechanisms provided by CoVer can be applied to these data models. In addition, many application domains show similar patterns of individual and cooperative work we have identified for hypermedia authoring. In general, the transition between these cooperation modes depends on the operations and activities to be performed on the data. Having identified these transitions, CoVer may also be used to integrate the cooperation modes discussed in this paper into systems of these application domains.

The versioned cooperative SEPIA is now in its early use. The experience will guide further improvements for cooperative systems. Our next plan is to elaborate concepts to integrate pre-planned and scheduled tasks with project management tools. To make application programming easier, we investigate a notation to descriptively define the version behavior of application-defined tasks.

REFERENCES

1. Dart S. Concepts in Configuration Management. In *Proc. of the 3rd International Workshop on Software Configuration Management* (Trondheim, Norway, June 12-14, 1991), pp. 1-18.

2. Dourish P., Bly S. Portholes: Supporting Awareness in a distributed work group. In *Proc. of the CHI'92* (Monterey, California, May 3-7), pp. 541-547.

3. Ellis C.A., Gibbs S.A., Rein G.L. Groupware: Some issues and experiences. In *Communications of the ACM* 34, 1 (Jan. 1991), pp. 38-58.

4. Fish R.S., Kraut R.E., Leland M.D.P. Quilt: a collaborative tool for cooperative writing. In *Conference on Office Automation Systems* (Palo Alto, 1988), SIGOIS Bulletin, 9, 2&3, (April & July 1988).

5. Haake A. CoVer: A Contextual Version Server for Hypertext Applications. In *Proc. of the 4th ACM Conference on Hypertext* (Milano, Italy, Nov. 30 - Dec. 4, 1992), pp. 43-52.

6. Haake J.M., Wilson B. Supporting Collaborative Writing of Hyperdocuments in SEPIA. In *Proc. of the ACM 1992 Conference on Computer Supported Cooperative Work* (Toronto, Ontario, Nov. 1-4., 1992), pp. 138-146.

7. Käfer W.A. Framework for Version-based Cooperation Control. In *Proc. of the 2nd Int. Symposium on Database Systems for Advanced Applications (DASFAA)* (Tokyo, Japan, April 1991).

8. Katz R. Towards a Unified Framework for Version Modelling in Engineering Databases. *acm computing surveys* 22, 4 (Dec. 1990), pp. 375-408.

9. Rodden T.A. Survey of CSCW systems. *Interacting with Computers* 3, 3 (Dec. 1991), pp. 319-353.

10. Stefik M., Foster G., Bobrow D.G., Kahn K., Lanning S., Suchman L. Beyond the Chalkboard: Computer Support for Collaboration and Problem Solving in Meetings. In *Communications of the ACM* 30, 1 (Jan. 1987), pp. 32-47.

11. Streitz N.A., Hannemann J., Thüring M. From ideas and arguments to hyperdocuments: Travelling through activity spaces. In *Proc. of the ACM Conference on Hypertext* (Pittsburgh,USA, Nov. 5-8, 1989), pp. 343-364.

12. Streitz N.A., Haake J.M., Hannemann J., Lemke A., Schütt H., Schuler W., Thüring M. SEPIA: A Cooperative Hypermedia Authoring Environment. In *Proc. of the 4th ACM Conference on Hypertext*, (Milano, Italy, Nov. 30-Dec. 4, 1992), pp. 11-22.

13. Thüring M., Haake J. M., Hannemann J. What's ELIZA doing in the Chinese Room — Incoherent Hyperdocuments and how to Avoid them. In *Proc. of the 3rd ACM Conference on Hypertext* (San Antonio, Texas, Dec. 15-18, 1991), pp. 161-177.

14. Weber A. Publishing Tools Need Both: State-Oriented and Task-Oriented Version Support. In *Proc. of the 15th Annual International Computer Software and Applications Conference (COMPSAC '91)* (Tokyo, Japan, Sept. 11-13, 1991), pp. 633-639.

Comparative Design Review:
An Exercise in Parallel Design

Organizers: Jakob Nielsen, Bellcore, and Heather Desurvire, NYNEX

Moderator: Jakob Nielsen, Bellcore

Designers: Randy Kerr, Microsoft
             Dan Rosenberg, Borland Intl.
             Gitta Salomon, Apple Computer

Evaluators: Heather Desurvire, NYNEX
             Rolf Molich, Baltica Insurance
             Tom Stewart, System Concepts Ltd.

Abstract

Three user interface designers were asked to design interfaces for a given problem. These designs were made available to a group of usability specialists for heuristic evaluation. The reviewers will lead off the panel with specific questions to the designers regarding the usability aspects of their designs. The panel will feature a lively discussion of the designers' various approaches and solutions.

Parallel Design
Jakob Nielsen

The goal of parallel design is to explore different design alternatives before one settles on a single approach that can then be developed in further detail and subjected to more detailed usability activities, including iterative design [1].

Typically, one might have about three designers involved in parallel design. For critical products, large computer companies have been known to devote entire teams to developing multiple alternative designs almost to the finial product stage, before upper management decided on which version to release. In general, though, it may not be necessary for the designers to spend more than a few hours or at the most one or two days on developing their initial designs. Also, it is probably better to have designers work individually rather than in larger teams, since parallel design only aims at rough drafts of basic design ideas, in order to explore various parts of the design space.

Heuristic evaluation is a usability inspection method which is aimed at evaluating user interfaces in a fast, inexpensive, and effective manner [1]. The panel will illustrate this evaluation technique, and will highlight its use as an informative technique for evaluating interfaces at an early stage.

Reference: [1]. Nielsen, J. *Usability Engineering*, Academic Press, San Diego, CA, 1993.

Design Problem Given to the Designers
Heather Desurvire and Jakob Nielsen

The designers' task was to design the screen-based graphical user interface for a potential future system that allows users to play music transmitted from a central database through a broad-bandwidth network. To our knowledge, nobody is currently contemplating such a system, so the following description is purely hypothetical.

This interface can be assumed to be available due to an envisioned fiber link to home residential areas as well as businesses. The interface is a personal computer, that allows the users to select any music they want to listen to. Pricing for listening is per hour of listening, and has been calculated to be about what it would cost to purchase 200 CDs and a CD player over 10 years. The fiber link is connected to a set of stereo speakers, that can be purchased with a built in fiber link connection, or can be connected to a typical set of speakers with an adapter. The interface is via a personal computer, which is screen-based, having a graphical user interface and a mouse.

Assume that the database of music is based on the contents of at least ten thousand compact discs.

Design the user interface so that the user can select:
• one song with various artists
• one artist with various songs
• multiple selections for a certain time interval (e.g., 45 minutes of music)
• random songs in a selected genre (by singer, musician, style of music (e.g. rock, motown, classical guitar, south american))

While listening to the music, the user should also be able to manipulate the selections to:
• Pause
• Fast Forward
• Skip to the next song
• Rewind

Simplifying assumptions: Only consider music that is structured as "songs." Thus, the interface does not need to accommodate classical music or other music with a more complex structure.

Assume that the user already knows how to use the home computer and its graphical user interface.

Serenade: The Desktop Juke-Box
Randy Kerr

Serenade is a music desktop accessory that operates very similar to a juke-box. The interface factors the user's activity of listening to music primarily as *selecting* and *playing* songs. The main window controls the currently playing song and organizes the upcoming songs. A *Add Songs* sub-dialog is used to filter and select new songs from the database to be added to the play list. This dialog allows very flexible and uniform searching for a specific or random set of songs in a given category. *Serenade* is designed assuming a music service billing rate of $1.00 per hour of listening, and that the music database holds the associated CD cover images.

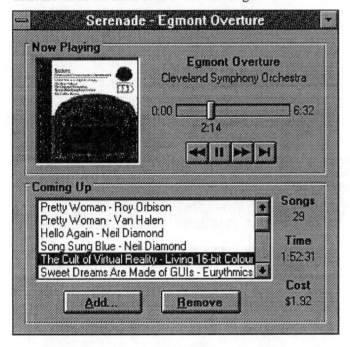

Playing Songs

The main window of *Serenade* posts the current song's name in its title bar and is divided into two cooperating panes labeled *Now Playing* and *Coming Up*. *Now Playing* displays the currently playing song's CD cover (as a memorable visual cue), title, artist and the familiar compact disc controls for rewind, pause/play toggle, fast forward, and skip to next selection. Above these buttons is a slider control which moves from left to right displaying the updating time counter as the song plays. The user may drag the slider to get to a position in the song directly. When the song is finished, the song at the top of the *Coming Up* list assumes the *Now Playing* position and begins to play from its beginning. Songs play without interruption from the rest of the interface: adding new songs or minimizing the *Serenade* window does not interrupt the playing of the song.

The *Coming Up* portion of the window displays the ordered list of songs which will be played next. The user

may re-order these songs as (s)he pleases by dragging and dropping songs in different positions in the list with the mouse. The user may remove any song from the list by selecting it and pressing the *Remove* button (disabled when there is no selection) or by hitting the Delete key. The number of songs, the total time, and the cost of the pending music is posted to the right of the *Coming Up* list and are updated dynamically as each song is played.

Selecting Songs

To add songs to the play list, the user presses the *Add...* button which invokes the dialog pictured below.

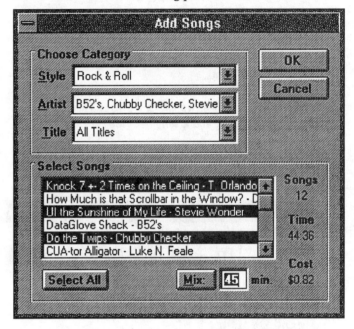

This dialog allows the user to select songs from as broad or narrow a category as (s)he wishes. Within the *Choose Category* pane the user may type a partial string or select any number of the given items in the drop-down combo boxes labeled *Style*, *Artist*, and *Title*. (The user may also leave the field unspecified by choosing "All".) Songs which match the category specified by these field values appear in the *Select Songs* pane. For instance, the above dialog filters for all rock & roll song titles sung by either the B52's, Chubby Checker, Stevie Wonder, ... (the multiple selection of artists in the drop down list). If the user is unsure of a song's full title, (s)he may type any fragment in the title field and all songs which include that fragment will appear below. To add to the *Coming Up* play list, the user selects (single-clicks) all the desired songs in the *Select Songs* pane and presses the *OK* button. *Select All* will select all songs in the list and *Mix: n min.* will select random songs in the list which amount to the user-specified *n* minutes of time, after which the user may add or remove specific songs from the selection. The total number, duration, and cost of the selected songs appear to the right assisting the time/cost tradeoffs in deciding what to hear.

Interactive Fiber Optic CD System User Interface
Designed by: Daniel Rosenberg

This UI design for a fiber optic home CD music system is characterized by the following architectural features:

1) A traditional desktop UI model is used to blend into the existing windowing environment.

2) Two object types exist, a personal CD object and a Catalog object.

3) Music can be played from either type of object.

4) Their can be as many or as few of each object type open as the user wants.

5) Each object type has two views, a **player view** (that mimics a CD player) and a **song list view**.

6) The catalog object supports query and history lists in its song list view.

7) Data relationships between author, song and disk title are supported with a built in outliner model. Expand and collapse are supported.

8) A traditional pull down menu structure is provided for editing the disks.

9) Drag-drop semantics are provided between open objects and desktop icons as well. Double-clicking on a song title in either object or view plays the song.

10) The desktop provides a context storage feature so the user can always return to a named desktop state.

The underlying rational for choosing the desktop model was that it can be expanded to other media types. For example video technology could be added to the same interface without overloading the user model. It is also possible to extend this UI with full featured editing capabilities as will be demonstrated paper presentation.

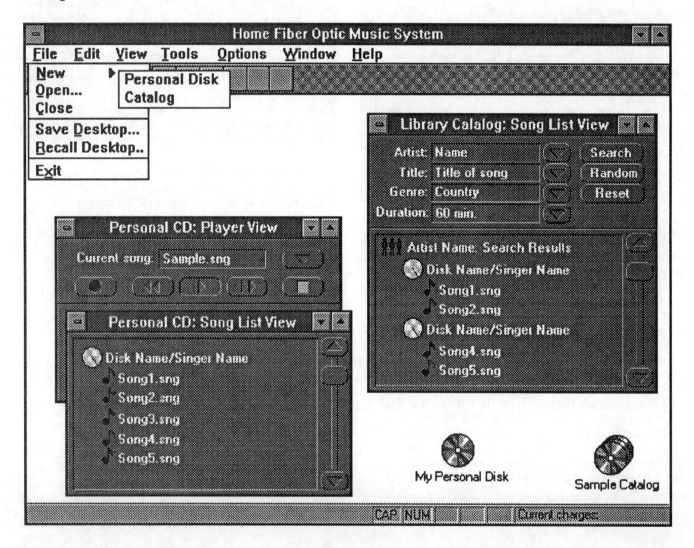

Design of the Personal Jukebox™ Interface
Gitta Salomon

The design shown below (see captions for details) provides users with access to the required functionality in a flexible way. The user can search for songs using several criteria, in both a goal-directed and browsing fashion. Although not shown below, when the user clicks in one of the "look for" fields, a scrolling list of possibilities appears. As the user enters text, this list scrolls to the appropriate place. In this way, the user can enter either an explicit or partial request, or just browse through the possibilities and select one. The interface also provides the user with a number of ways to assemble a playlist. Furthermore, because the search and playlist panels are distinct, the user can look for new material while simultaneously playing audio.

On the role of interface designers. The design problem, as presented to the panelists, already included a specification of the system's functionality. It is my belief that interface designers should be involved much earlier in the product definition process, when the functionality requirements themselves are being determined. Our job should encompass much more than only representing the functionality to users. In my work, we initially conduct informal interviews with potential end users to determine their problems, needs and expectations in a particular domain. Through this user-centered approach, we lead the way in defining what technology should be built. This often produces more desirable and usable technology.

To better make this point, I conducted a few brief interviews concerning the song delivery system and uncovered several interesting ideas for additional functionality. First, I spoke with people about how they search for songs in record stores and how they'd optimally like to find music. Some users want to be able to find songs based on their lyrics when they can't recall the artist's or song's name. If possible, this search criteria should be supported. Another user suggested a 'time machine,' whereby she could queue up an hour of music 'just like the local hit radio station played during February, 1963' (this is not so farfetched – radio stations often maintain playlists, some make them publically available). This is a compelling alternative to the "Song Search" method shown below, and is surely only one of many alternative methods for finding music. I also interviewed a few radio DJs about how listeners request songs and how they decide what to play when they receive incomplete information. DJs often rely on their colleagues' annotations or markers indicating the best, or most requested, songs on an album. If the Personal Jukebox incorporated a community's previous request data, it would allow users to select an artist's most popular songs, even if they couldn't remember or recognize a specific title. Although limited, these interviews serve to point out the role that interface designers can play at early stages in the design process.

*The **Song Search Panel** allows users to look for songs using 3 criteria: the style of music, the artist's name (here, "Sonic Youth") and the song's title. In this session the system returned 21 matches in the scrolling results list. The user has several options for choosing songs from this list: individual songs can be picked by clicking on them ("Tunic" is currently chosen); alternatively, the pulldown menu can be used to choose several songs at once. As shown, the user can click on the "Choose:" button to randomly pick 5 songs. Another menu option allows the user to choose a specific number of minutes of music from the list. Note that the user can reorder the results by clicking on the heading words (The current ordering is alphabetical by title, as indicated by the bold, underlined appearance of the word 'Title'). Users can move their choices to the playlist at any time by clicking on the "Add Choices To Playlist" button. This button either transfers the songs in the order they are shown, or in a random order, depending on the radio button modifier selected.*

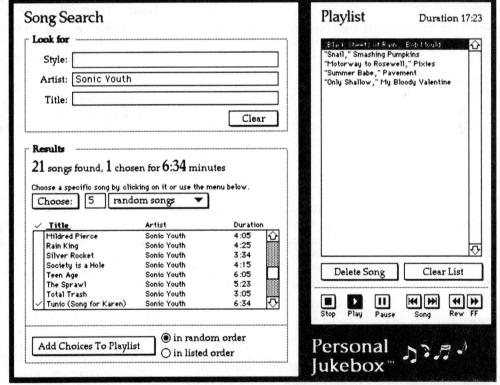

*The **Playlist Panel** contains a scrolling list of the songs the user has chosen to play. The list can be altered in several ways: it can be cleared with "Clear List" button; individual songs can be deleted by selecting them and choosing the "Delete Song" button; the order of songs can be changed by clicking on an entry and dragging it to a new position. There is a visual representation for the 'current' song – it is highlighted with inverse video – that cues the user as to which song will be acted on by requests such as 'play', 'pause', 'scan forward (ff),' etc. Buttons that visually resemble those found on standard compact disk players are provided at the bottom of the panel to allow for intuitive control of the various playing states. The current state is shown in inverse video.*

Generating User Interfaces from Data Models and Dialogue Net Specifications

Christian Janssen, Anette Weisbecker, Jürgen Ziegler

Fraunhofer-Institut für Arbeitswirtschaft und Organisation
Nobelstr. 12, D-7000 Stuttgart 80, Germany
email: janssen@iao.fhg.de, weisbeck@iao.fhg.de, ziegler@iao.fhg.de

ABSTRACT

A method and a set of supporting tools have been developed for an improved integration of user interface design with software engineering methods and tools. Animated user interfaces for database-oriented applications are generated from an extended data model and a new graphical technique for specifying dialogues. Based on views defined for the data model, an expert system uses explicit design rules derived from existing guidelines for producing the static layout of the user interface. A petri net based technique called dialogue nets is used for specifying the dynamic behaviour. Output is generated for an existing user interface management system. The approach supports rapid prototyping while using the advantages of standard software engineering methods.

KEYWORDS: Automatic User Interface Design, Dialogue Specification, Dialogue Nets, User Interface Management Systems.

INTRODUCTION

In the last years, significant advances have been made with respect to user interface development tools like user interface builders and user interface management systems (UIMS). Compared to programming with user interface toolkits, these systems help a lot in designing and implementing graphical user interfaces [10].

The development of graphical user interfaces, however, is still a time-consuming activity. With the tools commercially available today, every user interface object has to be created and layed out explicitly. Dialogue control specifications have to be added by programming (using user interface builders) or via a specialized language (using user interface management systems), which may require a large effort and needs specific knowledge.

With currently available tools, it is difficult to follow existing user interface design guidelines and style guides like [16, 4, 12, 17] and to maintain consistency across the user interface as well as consistency with other applications. Particularly, little or no support is provided for selecting

appropriate interaction objects for a specific task.

Regarding the specification of the non-interactive part of an application which is typically done in the early phases of the design cycle, user interface tools cannot make use of the models developed with general software engineering methods and tools. This leads to extra effort and potential inconsistencies when moving from the requirements analysis to user interface design. It is therefore important to use analysis results like the data model as input for user interface development tools.

The work described in this paper addresses the problems mentioned above. A method and supporting tools—the GENIUS tool environment (GENerator for user Interfaces Using Software ergonomic rules)—have been developed for the automatic generation of user interfaces from extended data models and petri net based dialogue descriptions. Our approach is suitable for the generation of animated prototypes of database-oriented applications based on notations that are commonly used in general software engineering methods. After a discussion of related work, we will introduce the overall structure of the GENIUS environment, and describe the generation of the static and dynamic parts of the user interface.

RELATED WORK
Automatic User Interface Generation

A number of research systems are documented in literature that automatically generate the user interface from higher level specifications. Jade [23] and ITS [20] are generating presentational designs from frame-like dialogue specifications. UofA* [15] and Mickey [11] are generating presentation and dialogue from a specification of the application commands. Within UIDE [5] combined with DON [9] a specification consisting of objects, attributes, attribute types, actions, parameters, preconditions, and postconditions is used. Each of these systems introduces its own notation for the higher level user interface specification. (Mickey bases on Pascal code, but introduces a new notation within comments.) However, the use of widely known notations is important for the acceptance of tools by system developers.

One of the first UIMSs which incorporates data models is HIGGENS [7]. In this system it is specified how to derive views from data models. The views, including data and methods for interacting with them, represent an abstract form of the display shown to the user. For each view the actual presentation on the physical device has to be explicitly defined. HIGGENS uses the data model for interface definition but in contrast to our approach and most of the systems mentioned above, doesn't incorporate rules for the generation of the physical user interface. So, it offers less flexibility and power with respect to the selection and layout of interaction techniques.

The system described by de Baar, Foley and Mullet [1] generates dialogue boxes and menus from enhanced data models. By this approach, descriptions from data modeling can be reused for the user interface specification, and double effort and consistency problems are avoided. On the other hand, the approach described by de Baar et al. does not include a graphical dialogue specification technique.

In the approach of Petoud and Pigneur [13] Entity Relationship models (in textual form) are used for user interface generation. The dynamics are textually specified and can be visualized by a precedence graph. The graph, however cannot be modified nor substructured, so that the system is not likely to be suitable for bigger applications.

Overall, existing systems automatically generating user interfaces either lack a proper integration into general software engineering methods, or an adequate way of defining the dynamics of the dialogue, or both.

Graphical Dialogue Specification

There are many approaches for graphical dialogue specification. Some of them (e.g. USE diagrams, [18]) are based on state-transition diagrams and therefore not suited for graphical user interfaces with concurrent input dialogues. Jacob [8] extends state transition diagrams so that multiple parallel diagrams are used. However, the global relations of the concurrent dialogues cannot be visualized by this approach. Similarly, in statecharts [19] parallelism can be handeled, but there are no transitions between parallel dia-

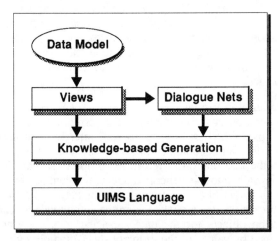

Figure 1: Overview of the GENIUS environment. Views are defined based on the data model. Transitions between views are specified in dialogue nets. A knowledge-based component generates the static user interfaces from the view definitions. As a target system, an existing UIMS is used. The dialogue nets as well are transformed into code for the UIMS.

grams which are combined in and groups. Unlike in dialogue nets, in statecharts one cannot open a state without leaving the current state. SUPERMAN diagrams [22] contain fork and join constructs, so that they can handle parallelism in principle, but lack a clear semantic concept in comparison to petri nets.

Petri nets have already been used in the context of dialogue specification and user interface management systems. Event graphs [14] can be used to describe the dynamic visibility of objects within a graphical-interactive application. Petri net objects [2] are more powerful since general object flow and object manipulation can be described. However, they are more complex than event graphs and less suited for the earlier design phases.

The technique used in our approach, dialogue nets, is similar to event graphs in modeling the dynamic visibility of objects needed for the coarse-grain dialogue specification. Compared with event graphs, they offer essential features like hierarchical dialogue structuring, and the declaration of modal dialogue windows.

GENERATING USER INTERFACES IN THE GENIUS APPROACH

In the GENIUS approach (figure 1), Entity Relationship data models are used as the starting point for the specification of the user interface. The Entity Relationship (ER) model [3] is a well established conceptual data model and is used in most of todays software-engineering methods [21] and computer-aided software engineering (CASE) tools.

In the following sections we will describe the different components of the environment.

Definition of Views

The application data model does not describe the data needed by the user for specific tasks and no partitioning of the data is shown with respect to single dialogue steps. In order to structure the information contained in the data model with respect to tasks of the user, views are defined. The generation of windows showing application data cannot be done directly from the ER model as the user may not want to see all attributes of an entity in a certain situation. Also, attributes of several entities and relationships may be needed in the same window. A *view* consists of a subset of entities, relationships, and attributes of the overall data model. Furthermore, views may be substructured, i.e. contain other views.

In order to enable an easy and powerful view definition, a number of extensions have been made to the ER data model. For specifying logical groups of attributes, complex attributes are introduced. The grouping information is used in the user interface generation process for visualizing groups of related data. For reducing the complexity of the graphical representation of ER diagrams, a set of entities and relationships can be replaced by a single symbol and edited separately.

Furthermore, functions of two different types can be associated to views. Data manipulation functions are distinguished from navigation functions. Navigation functions call other views, i.e. define the dialogue structure which can also be represented by dialogue nets (see below). The functions and their properties are used in the generation process to create appropriate controls (e.g. menu items or pushbuttons).

Because the entire information needed for the generation of application windows from views cannot be expressed in a graphical representation, it is necessary to supply additional textual descriptions. These are provided in so-called *property sheets*. Property sheets consist of two types of information:

- Descriptive properties include a name, and a short description. For attributes, properties like type, range of values, type of selection, and defaults are stored.

- Task oriented properties include frequency and type of access, and priority for the task. Functions associated to the views can also be described as properties.

In the tool environment supporting our methodology, the definition of views is done with a direct manipulation editor for ER models (figure 2). The application developer selects elements from the ER diagram. Property sheets can be popped up and edited directly. Thus, no programming skills are required for the definition of the views, and it is easy to involve non-programmers e.g. application experts and interface designers in this process.

The Knowledge Base for User Interface Generation

The views form a logical description of the application windows. This description is used as input for an expert system controlling the generation process. The knowledge base includes

- abstract interaction object types, and

- rules for selection and layout of interaction objects.

The *abstract interaction object* types contain attributes to be filled with application specific data like name and range of a data field as well as layout attributes like alignment, colour, and size. Depending on the target user interfaces and the available devices, different interaction objects may be defined. The standard interaction objects defined are windows, dialogue boxes, menus, entry fields, constant fields, exclusive choices, nonexclusive choices, operation choices, lists, and scrollbars. They are called abstract because they are independent of their physical implementation, e.g. as OSF/Motif or Open Look widgets.

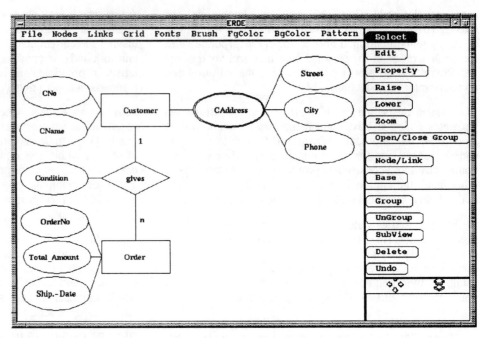

Figure 2: View definition in the ER Diagram Editor (ERDE). The view is a subset of the overall data model and contains the related entities *Customer* and *Order* with their attributes. The attribute *CAddress* is complex .

The *design rules* for the generation of the user interface are derived from existing guidelines and style guides. Most of the rules concerning formats and arrangement of data fields and field prompts are derived from Smith and Mosier [16]. Rules for the interaction object selection and layout have been extracted from the CUA [4], OSF/Motif [12] and Open Look [17] style guides.

Some attribute values of the abstract interaction objects are defined by *defaults*. The defaults give the designer the opportunity to influence the generation process and provide application or organizational preferences. They are stored outside the knowledge base in order to enable easier changes by the designer without needing to access the expert system shell.

The Generation Process

The generation of the user interface description is done in three steps. In the first step, appropriate interaction objects for the information contained in a view are selected according to the information stored in the property sheets. For each view a window is generated. General layout attributes of the windows like substructuring in status, application and information area are taken from the default values. The interaction objects for the data specified in a view are determined by values of the property sheets, mainly by the data type, range, and condition values. For example, a data field *Condition* (figure 2) with enumerated values where only one selection is permitted is represented as an exclusive choice like set of radio buttons (figure 3). If a large number of values is available for exclusive selection radio buttons are not appropriate and a list is used. For a function, its type, scope and frequency of use determine its presen-

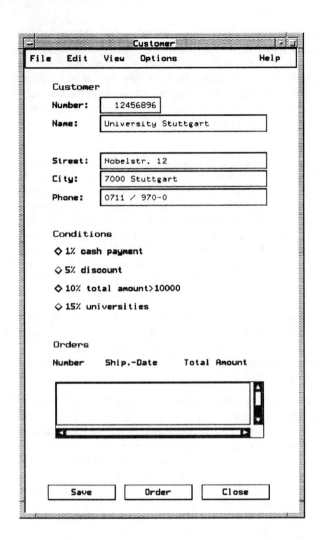

Figure 3: Sample generated window from the view definition in Figure 2.

tation as a menu item or as an operation choice such as a push button.

In the second step the attribute values for the selected interaction objects are determined. Attributes which only depend on the contents of the application (like text labels, field length, format and default values) are copied from the property sheets. A second type of attributes are obtained by the default values which exist for each interaction object type. The third type of attributes, mainly the layout information, depend on other interaction objects.

The layout is determined in the third and last step of the generation. Here, the arrangement inside complex elements like groups is determined first. Afterwards the remaining elements are arranged on the available screen space according to their priority or the given sequence.

The expert system delivers a user interface description which is then transformed in a specification interpreted by the underlying UIMS (figure 3).

The process of the automated user interface generation can be influenced in a number of ways. The simplest is modifying the default values of the interaction objects. In addition, the interaction objects and the rules stored in the knowledge base can be changed. It is also possible to have various knowledge bases for the generation of different types of user interfaces, e.g. alphanumeric and graphical.

SPECIFYING THE COARSE GRAIN DIALOGUE WITH DIALOGUE NETS

For the construction of working prototypes which are to be evaluated with users, the rapid generation of static application windows described in the previous section is necessary but not sufficient. Dialogue control information has to be passed to the generation system so that the user interface can be animated.

Two levels of dialogue control are distinguished. The *coarse grain dialogue* defines the sequencing of views (mapped to application windows) and the call of application functions as the result of user input. The *fine grain dialogue* defines state changes on the level of single user interface objects. This includes the alteration of text values and changes in the sensitivity of menu items, for example.

For the construction of the first working prototype showing the broad look-and-feel of an application, mainly the coarse grain dialogue is needed. Implementing the fine grain dialogue leads to a complete user interface for the application system and is usually not specified graphically. Textual specifications like those described in [6] are more suitable for the fine grain dialogue.

In order to integrate the dialogue specifications in the methodology described so far, it is important that the technique uses the concepts of the view definition phase, and offers a graphical representaion. Based on these requirements, a technique called *dialogue nets* has been developed.

Basic Concepts of Dialogue Nets

Like all petri nets, dialogue nets consist of places, transitions, and flow relations. In their current form, dialogue nets are elementary nets, i.e. they show the flow of undistinguishable tokens and places can only be marked with one token at a time.

Views are associated to places in the net so that the marking of a place with a token models the dynamic visibility of the view. Dialogue steps are modeled by transitions. There are basically two types of transitions:

- *Unspecified transitions* only have a meaningful label.

- *Fully specified transitions* contain a condition and an action. The condition typically contains an input event, but can also include other events and additional conditions. The actions are mainly calls to application functions, but can also contain actions related to the user interface.

A transition can only be fired if the input places (linked with the transition by an incoming flow relation) are marked and the output places (outgoing flow relation) are

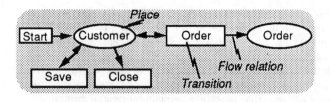

Figure 4a: Dialogue net with unspecified transitions for the specification of the order dialogue.

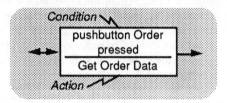

Figure 4b: Fully specified Order transition showing a condition and action.

unmarked. Tokens are removed from the input places and the output places are marked. Side places (two-direction flow relation) must contain a token before a transition fires but are not changed. Additionally, a fully specified transition can only fire if the conditions are satisfied, and the actions are executed when firing. A special transition, the *start transition* (labeled *Start*) is fired at the beginning of each dialogue.

Figure 4a shows a dialogue net with unspecified transitions. The *Customer* view is opened at the beginning. Via the *Order* transition, the *Order* view can be opened showing details of the selected order. *Save* can be executed at any time. The *Close* transition ends up the *Customer* dialogue. A fully specified *Order* transition (figure 4b) shows the condition and action for the transition.

Hierarchical Structuring of Dialogue Nets

Real dialogues may contain numerous views which cannot be shown in a single net. Therefore, a partitioning of the dialogue net is required. As a structuring mechanism, *complex places* are introduced (places with double border). A complex place is associated with a subdialogue shown in a

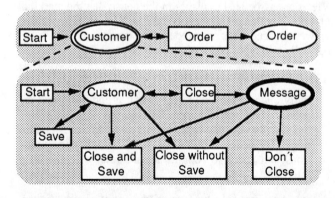

Figure 5: Hierarchical refinement of the *Customer* dialogue by a complex place and a subdialogue net.

separate dialogue net. Consequently, complex places are not directly associated with views or windows. Subdialogue nets are started when the associated complex place is marked and can be ended by removing the token from the complex place, or by removing all tokens from the subdialogue nets. In the example (figure 5) an extended *Customer* dialogue is shown in a separate dialouge net.

Modal Views

As petri nets are able to model parallelism, several views in a dialogue can be open at a time. In the examples in figures 4 and 5, the *Customer* view remains open when the *Order* transition opens the *Order* view. Even in parallel graphical user interfaces, however, modal views are needed. Modal views are modeled by *modal places* (graphically marked with a bold border) in dialogue nets. If a modal place is marked, no transition in the entire dialogue can fire except for those having that modal place as input place. The *Message* view in figure 5 is an example of a modal view.

There are some other features of dialogue nets like optional flow relations for reducing the net complexity, multiple ways of entering or exiting a subdialogue, and assigning subdialogues to transitions, that cannot be shown in the scope of this paper.

Generating Executable Dialogues from Dialogue Nets

For the animation of views in our method, it is mostly sufficient to use unspecified transitions. For each view, a place in a dialogue net is generated. For each function, a transition is inserted into the net. So, the transitions in the dialogue net correspond to functions specified in the property sheets of the views. The effect of the navigation functions, however, are more easily specified graphically through the creation of flow relations in dialogue nets, which is supported in a graphical dialogue net editor in the GENIUS environment.

From the dialogue net specification, executable rules are generated for the underlying user interface management system in two steps. First, the unspecified transitions are converted to fully specified ones. For this purpose, information from the generation process of the static user interface is used, because the controls generated may support specific event types, which determine the conditions in the fully specified transitions. In the second step, the dialogue net specification with fully specified transitions are converted to rules of the underlying UIMS.

CONCLUSIONS

Our approach facilitates the generation of executable user interfaces for database-oriented applications from a level of specification which is higher than the ones in use with today's user interface development tools. Also, the graphical notations are more familiar to software developers. The GENIUS approach offers a much better integration of the user interface development with general software-engineering methods. Double specification is avoided by using the data model as a basis for the definition of the user interface. The specification of the dynamics is much easier with the graphical dialogue net representation than with a textual language. Dialogue nets are suitable for describing the coarse-grain level of parallel dialogues in graphical user interfaces.

The support of guidelines concerning the selection and layout of interaction objects and the use of global default values for relevant parameters of the presentation considerably facilitate the development of consistent user interfaces and conformance with general, company-wide or application specific style guides.

In future work the support for maintaining consistency between view and dialogue definition will be enhanced, so that changes on either side are immediately reflected on the other. Specifications for the fine grain dialogue will be integrated in order to complete the look-and-feel definition of the generated prototypes. A further extension will be linking the view and dialogue definition to methods and tools for modeling tasks and functions.

In the current system, refinements of the generated dialogues are done by means of the underlying user interface management system. However, the first automatically generated versions are extremely valuable for an early design evaluation with the user. This evaluation can provide essential feedback for the specification of the entire software system, and can contribute to avoid major design flaws.

REFERENCES

1. de Baar, D.J.M.J., Foley, J., Mullet, K.E. (1992). Coupling Application Design and User Interface Design. CHI´92 Conference Proceedings. Reading, Addison Wesley, 259-266.

2. Bastide, R., Palanque, P. (1991). Petri Net Objects for the Design, Validation and Prototyping of User-Driven Interfaces. In: Diaper et al. (Eds.) Human-Computer Interaction - INTERACT´90. Amsterdam, North-Holland, 625-631.

3. Chen, P. (1976). The Entity-Relationship Model - Toward a Unified View of Data. ACM Transactions on Database Systems, Vol. 1, No. 1, 1976, 9-36.

4. CUA (1991). Systems Application Architecture: Common User Access – Guide to User Interface Design – Advanced Interface Design Reference. IBM.

5. Foley, J., Gibbs, C., Kim, W. C., Kovacevic, S. (1988). A Knowledge-Based User Interface Management System. CHI´88 Conference Proceedings. New York, ACM, 67-72.

6. Gieskens, D.F., Foley, J.D. (1992). Controlling User Interface Objects Through Pre- and Postconditions. CHI´92 Conference Proceedings. Reading, Addison Wesley, 189-194.

7. Hudson, S. E., King, R. (1986). A Generator of Direct Manipulation Office Systems. ACM Transactions on Office Information Systems 4 (2) April 1986, 132-163.

8. Jacob, R.J.K. (1986). A Specification Language for Direct-Manipulation User Interfaces. ACM Transactions on Graphics 5 (4), 283-317.

9. Kim and Foley (1990). DON: User Interface Presentation Design Assistant. UIST´90. Proceedings of the ACM SIGGRAPH Symposium on User Interface Software and Technology. New York, ACM Press, 10-20.

10. Myers, B.A., Rosson, M.B. (1992). Survey on User Interface Programming. CHI´92 Conference Proceedings. Reading, Addison Wesley, 195-202.

11. Olsen, D. R. (1989). A Programming Language Basis for User Interface Management. CHI'89 Conference Proceedings. ACM, New York, 171-176.

12. OSF (1991). OSF/Motif Style Guide Release 1.1. Open Software Foundation.

13. Petoud, I., Pigneur, Y. (1990). An Automatic and Visual Approach for User Interface Design. In: Cockton, G. (Ed.). Proceedings of the IFIP TC 2/WG 2.7 Working Conference on Engineering for Human-Computer Interaction. Amsterdam, North-Holland.

14. Roudaud, B., Lavigne, V., Lagneau, O., Minor, E. (1990). SCENARIOO: A New Generation UIMS. In: Diaper et al. (Eds.). Human-Computer Interaction - INTERACT´90. Amsterdam, North-Holland, 607-612.

15. Singh, G., Green, M. (1991). Automating the Lexical and Syntactic Design of Graphical User Interfaces: The UofA* UIMS. ACM Transactions on Graphics 10 (3), July 1991, 213-254.

16. Smith, S. L.; Mosier, J. N. (1986). Guidelines for Designing User Interface Software. Mitre Corporation.

17. Sun Microsystems Inc. (1990). Open Look – Graphical User Interface Application Style Guidelines – Graphical User Interface Functional Specification. Addison-Wesley, Reading, MA.

18. Wasserman, A.I. (1985). Extending Transition Diagrams for the Specification of Human-Computer Interaction. IEEE Trans. Software Engineering 11, 8, 699-713.

19. Wellner, P.D. (1989). Statemaster: A UIMS based on Statecharts for Prototyping and Target Implementation. CHI´89 Conference Proceedings. New York, ACM, 177-182.

20. Wiecha, C., Bennett, W., Boises, S., Gould, J., Green, S. (1990). ITS: A Tool for Rapidly Developing Interactive Applications. ACM Transactions on Information Systems, Vol. 8, No. 3, July 1990, 204-236.

21. Yourdon, E. (1989). Modern Structured Analysis. Prentice Hall, Englewood Cliffs, N. J., 1989.

22. Yunten, T. und Hartson, H.R. (1985). A Supervisory Methodology and Notation (SUPERMAN) for Human-Computer System Development. In: Hartson, H.R. (ed.). Advances in Human-Computer Interaction. Norwood (NJ), Ablex Publishing, 243-281.

23. vander Zanden, B., Myers, B. (1990). Automatic, Look-and-Feel Independent Dialog Creation for Graphical User Interfaces. CHI´90 Conference Proceedings. New York, ACM, 27-34.

Encapsulating Knowledge For Intelligent Automatic Interaction Objects Selection

Jean M. Vanderdonckt, François Bodart

Facultés Universitaires Notre-Dame de la Paix, Institut d'Informatique
Rue Grandgagnage, 21, B-5000 NAMUR (Belgium)
Tel. : +32 (0)81-72.49.75 - Fax. : +32 (0)81-72.49.67 - Telex : 59.222 FacNamB
eMail : JVANDERDONCKT@INFO.FUNDP.AC.BE, FBODART@INFO.FUNDP.AC.BE

ABSTRACT
TRIDENT is a set of interactive tools that automatically generates a user interface for highly-interactive business-oriented applications. It includes an intelligent interaction objects selection based on three differents concepts. First, an object oriented typology classifies abstract interaction objects to allow a presentation independent selection. Second, guidelines are translated into automatic rules to select abstract interaction objects from both an application data model and a dialog model. Third, these guidelines are encapsulated in a decision tree technique to make the reasoning obvious to the user. This approach guarantees a target environment independent user interface. Once this specified, abstract interaction objects are mapped into concrete interaction objects to produce the observable interface.

KEYWORDS: Automatic User Interface Generation, Decision Tree, Intelligent User Interface, Interaction Objects, Rule-Based System.

INTRODUCTION
Specifying the semantic of the application with a high-level language in order to automatically generate the user interface is a widespread approach [2,12,17,18] which implies two activities: (i) select adequate interaction objects from the semantic, and, (ii) lay out these objects into a more comprehensive one with a logical arrangement. Different authors have identified the following requirements for an intelligent automatic selection technique:

- *rule-based automatic generation* [18]: this can assess whether a user interface meets consistent selection rules;
- *explicit rules* [12]: built-in, code-imbedded rules are implicit in the system and, therefore, invisible and un-modifiable by the designer (textually or graphically);
- *application semantic involvement* [8]: interaction objects should vary according to the application data structure, not according to the presentation;

- *dialog model support* [1]: interaction objects should reflect the nature, the structure, the modality and the complexity of the dialog;
- *user model support* [1,9]: interaction objects have to be selected by taking into account the user experience level, the user skill to manipulate interaction media;
- *related interaction objects grouping* [2,9]: important functional groups have to be identified and formed;
- *screen space consideration* [2]: the selection should not generate overcrowded or cumbersome screens;
- *environment independence* [9,17]: the selection should work in any target environment.

Having only a presentation-independent selection [17] is not sufficient: the selection must be independent of presentation tools (e.g. OSF/Motif, Open Look,...) but also independent of the graphical window managers, UIMSs, toolkits (e.g. X-Windows, Ms-Windows,...). Why not concentrate all the knowledge about interaction objects selection into a such module? This paper describes an intelligent interaction object selection based on a decision tree technique that addresses these problems.

AUTOMATIC USER INTERFACE GENERATION
TRIDENT project [5] extends the computer-aided design methodology IDA (Interactive Design Approach) [3,4] in order to generate highly-interactive business-oriented applications along two dialog dimensions: the conversation from the architecture and specifications [13], the presentation from specifications (this is the subject of this paper). The dialog can be either asynchronous or multi-threaded. It is assumed that the semantic of the application is specified within different conceptual models and that interaction styles and modes are already given. Two conceptual models are used for the selection :

1. an information structure model provides specifications of the data structure of the application following an entity-relationship-attribute (ERA) way;
2. a dialog dynamic model provides a function chaining graph (FCG) specifying the data flow during the task performance.

The models are specified with Dynamic Specification Language, a high-level declarative specification language, and are then stored into local ERA and FCG data bases (fig. 1).

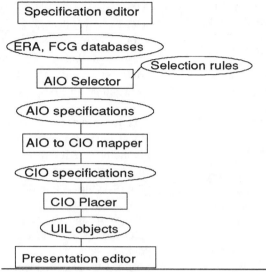

Figure 1. The TRIDENT approach.

By using rules, the AIO selector automatically selects abstract interaction objects (AIO) from the specifications and creates AIO specifications. Because these specifications are target independent, the mapper transforms AIO into concrete interaction objects (CIO) which become target environment dependent. The CIO Placer places them with three techniques inspired from [9]: physical object localisation, appropriate and aesthetic sizing and ergonomical arrangement. The complete resulting interface is translated into UIL objects which can be fully edited by a direct manipulation presentation editor.

ABSTRACT AND CONCRETE INTERACTION OBJECTS

Concrete interaction objects are graphical objects for inputting and displaying data related to the user interactive task; CIO are sometimes called widgets (window gadgets), controls or physical interactors (according to IFIP terminology). CIO specifications cover two major aspects :

1. the graphical appearance univocally determined by both presentation tool (e.g. OSF/Motif) and graphical tool (e.g. X-Windows);
2. the behaviour and constraints to be respected when the user manipulates the object.

When selecting an object, the designer have to pay more attention on the behaviour aspect because user interface communication power and ease of use are vital. Defining the presentation is an annex task to be left to a graphical artist. This observation invites to define interaction objects independently of the presentation, but not independently of their behaviour. The abstract interaction object, or logical

interactor (according to IFIP terminology), brings an abstracted view of the CIO where physical characteristics are target environment independent.

AIO sets	AIO elements (some)
action objects	menu, menu item, menu bar, drop-down menu, cascade menu, submenu,...
scrolling objects	scroll arrow, scroll cursor, scroll bar, frame
static objects	label, separator, group box, prompt, icon
control objects	edit box, scale, dial, check box, switch, radio box, spin button, push button, list box, drop-down list box, combination box, table,...
dialog objects	window, help window, dialog box, expandable dialog box, radio dialog box, panel,...
feedback objects	message, progression indicator, contextual cursor

Table 1. Table of abstract interaction objects.

Examining different target environments allows to establish a comprehensive object-oriented AIO typology divided in 6 sets by interactive capabilities (table 1). Each AIO is identified by an unique generic name (e.g. *check box*), general and particular abstract attributes (e.g. *height, width, color, states*), abstract events (e.g. *value selection, mouse click*), primitive functions (e.g. *Pr-EditBoxContent*). By definition, each AIO have no graphical appearance, but each AIO is connected to 0, 1 or many CIO in different environments with different names, presentations (fig. 2).

Figure 2. The AIO check box in different environments : Check box in Ms-Windows, XmToggleButton in OSF/Motif, BoxArray in Garnet.

Every AIO can be either *simple* (described in the typology) or *composite* (refinable as containing two or more simple AIO). Scrolling, feedback, control AIO are by nature simple whereas dialog AIO are typically composite: users may input, modify, select the values which may be buffered within the composite objects before transmission to the application.

AUTOMATIC AIO SELECTION

The first idea behind the AIO selection rests on selection rules mapping AIO from the detailed specifications of the semantic [1]. This approach has already been proved successfull with CIO selection rather than AIO selection.

MacIDA [12] selects CIO from database design: a window is mapped as for each entity type and for each relationship, an edit box is mapped for each attribute, a push button is mapped for each function. NIKL [2] includes straightforward selection rules mapping graphical CIO from the application domain model in three phases: realization, selection and redescription. Jade [27] also promotes simple and direct selection rules mapping a CIO from the data behaviour and from information contained in a look-and-feel file. UIDE [3] uses more sophisticated rules by following guidelines provided by different style guides. UIDE's selection rules map a CIO from attributes of the data object and from metadata depending of the attribute type (boolean, integer, real, enumerated and string). Observing that semantic considerations play a crucial role in the CIO selection, Selectors [8] invokes selection rules mapping a CIO from complete task-domain variables. Humanoïd [15] interprets selection rules as a template library mapping CIO from application objects, command and input objects.

Although being more and more rich and complex, we claim that selection rules still suffer from five drawbacks :

1. the selection rules do not take plenty advantage of the full power of guidelines and ergonomical rules: selecting one type of CIO may not be appropriate in another specific context;
2. the selection rules do not rely on dialog, user and screen models as suggested in [1]: complex interactive tasks, unexperienced or expert users, visual density have no influence on CIO selection;
3. the selection rules always work on CIO because they are all environment dependent: one selection rule may not work with others environments;
4. the selection rules are not observable by the designer: though some design tools allow the modifiability of the rules, all of them do not offer any mean to the designer to see the CIO selection process working;
5. the organization of selection rules is mostly formal (*if...then* rules): no graphical representation is provided.

To improve points 1-3, we restarted a full study of selection rules. Guidelines were merged from multiple style guides: the Apple Human Interface Guidelines, the Hewlett-Packard Interface Guide, the IBM Common User Access Style Guide, the OSF/Motif™ Style Guide [11] and the Sun Open Look™ Guide. They were fully rewritten in terms of AIO in a consistent and non-redundant format. Others environment dependent guidelines, namely for Apple // by Toggnazzini [16] and for OSF/Motif™ by Kobara [10], have been transformed in the same way. Precise others selection rules were added from expert ergonomical rules: Arens [1], Brown [6], Card *et al.* [7], Shneiderman [14].

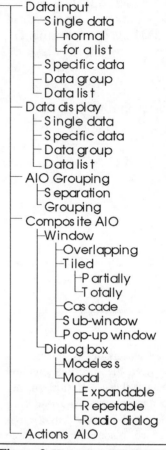

Figure 3. Hierarchy of TRIDENT selection rules

Five sets of rules select simple, composite AIO (fig. 3): rules for selecting simple AIO for data input, simple AIO for data display, static AIO to separate or group (un)related data, composite AIO depending on ERA, FCG and actions AIO.

Sets 1,2 transform a hierarchical data structure into a hierarchy of AIO with (not yet) undetermined root. The data structure supports not only simple attributes, but also group and list of attributes; arrays, trees or others complex data structures are assumed to be equivalent to organizations of groups and lists, like list of groups or group of groups. Sets 1,2 have been splitted for input and display because more suited AIO can be selected for only displaying the same data than for just inputting them on the screen. UIDE [2] also separates editing content (input) and read-only content (display). Set 3 is responsible for introducing separators, group boxes, prompts,... to concretize logical semantic proximity of AIO by surrounding, delimiting and/or separating to improve user guidance.

Set 4 selects the root object which is a composite AIO and/or any sub-composite AIO used in the hierarchy. For example, tiled windows are preferred for simultaned tasks and overlapping windows, for concurrent tasks, pop-up windows for minimal sub-tasks. Radio-dialog boxes simulate exclusive tasks in the FCG, expandable dialog boxes support tasks with frequent and rare sub-tasks, repetitive dialog boxes simulate reiterative tasks with same data. Set 5 introduces dedicated push buttons from the structure of the FCG. For example, "Ok" and "Cancel" buttons, "Help" button for complex task, "More..." button for expandable dialog, "Default" or "Reset" for specific data input or with default values.

INTELLIGENT AUTOMATIC AIO SELECTION

Selection rules generally contain four information sources: data from the application model (all), information on these data (e.g. *metadata* in UIDE [2]), others parameters (as in

Selectors [8]), user preferences (as in DON [9]). TRIDENT employs four information sources contained in ERA and CFG databases (fig. 1).

First, every application data is specified as a quadruplet

$$d = (V, dt, nvc, dv)$$

where V is the set of all possible values of d (if known); dt belongs to one of the implemented data types (hour, date, logical, integer, numeric, real, alphabetic, alphanumeric); nvc is the number of values to choose (1 for simple choice, N for multiple choice); $dv \in V$ is the default value of d (if known). V is partitioned as $V = PV \cup SV$ where PV is the sub-set of principal values and SV, the sub-set of secondary values. This characterization allows a future presentation of most frequently used values first, minimizing input and scrolling. The number of principal values and secondary values are given by $npv = \# PV$ and $nsv = \# SV$. Maximum data length is given by $l = max(length\,(v_i))\ \forall\ v_i \in V$.

Second, five metadata refine each data when relevant: *granularity-* whether the data precision is low, moderate or high; *known values-* whether V is well defined; *ordered list-* whether the values of V are sorted according a particular order (numerical, alphabetical, logical, temporal, physical, by frequence); *expandable list-* whether the user can add new vales to V and/or modify V; *continous range-* whether the values are contained in a continous range or interval. If there is some order in the values of V, then an appropriate AIO is selected (e.g. a spin button for chronological data, a scale for a bounded integer, a list box for logically ordered alphabetical data).

Third, one parameter specifies *constrained display space-* whether the selection must consider screen density to avoid too large AIO. The more constrained is the screen space, the less large AIO is selected (e.g. a drowp-down list box in place of a complete list box).

Level	User experience
3	beginner
4	novice
5	intermediate
6	expert
7	master

Table 2. User experience level

Fourth, a common user model is clarified by a *user experience level* provided by Card *et al.* [7] (table 2) and by a *user selection preference* (low or high)- whether the use is more skilled to select one value among a list of values or to enter it with the keyboard. The less is the user experience level, the more sophisticated is the guidance provided by

the object (e.g. a profiled edit box for an expert, a list box for an intermediate user, a sequence of spin buttons for a beginner).

AIO SELECTION BY DECISION TREE

To solve points 4-5 above and to really produce intelligent AIO selection, rules must be organized in a proper way which is modifiable and observable. UIDE's [2] and DON [9] selection rules are organized as *if...then* rules contained in a file editable by the designer. Drawing a flowchart benefits to the designer: this organization seems obvious (assimilating rules is easy), concise (the organization is intrinsically kept short and non-redundant) and rapid (following a path is fast). Nevertheless, the flowchart fails to show the entire space of possible values covered by each metadata.

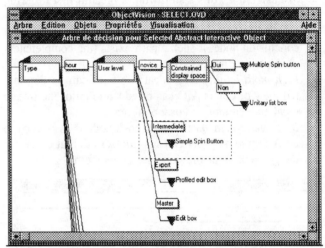

Figure 4. TRIDENT's AIO Selection tree (partial view).

TRIDENT so adopted a decision tree technique showing at each node the possible values space as a partition. A *decision tree* graphically depicts a decision logic with arcs and nodes. Each node consists of a current AIO selected and a set of nodes. Each node states a simple logical condition (e.g. is Level=5?); all arcs starting from a node cover the space of possible values (e.g. Level<5, Level=5, Level>5 in fig. 4; $nvc=1$ for a simple choice, $nvc>1$ for a multiple choice). The first arcs concern the different data types (hour, date, boolean,...). The *selection tree* represents the AIO selection logic where two kinds of nodes are reached :

1. *branching nodes*: node evaluating only one parameter to determine the path to follow at lower level and providing the AIO of the current level;
2. *conclusion nodes*: leaf node furnishing final AIO after evaluating the whole decision logic.

AIO on conclusion nodes are supposed to be the most appropriate interaction objects, if all involved parameters are known.

ADVANTAGES AND INCONVENIENCES

Practical experience showed that decision tree has benefits:

- *visibility* : the designer is able to clearly visualize why a particular AIO was choosen progressivly and to understand the result of each selection rule; the tree representation has a great influence on the effort needed to implement selection rules and to follow them;

- *easy backtracking* : applying an inappropriate rule may delay successful user interface generation; because the user interface development is iterative, the user can try a rule and, if it later discovers that this rule was inappropriate, can go back and try another instead by using other selection rules;

- *easy reasoning explanation* : trees are useful for keeping track of the intermediate application of rules;

- *fast selection* : this results from a breadth-first ordering because expansion of nodes is similar at each level; this search is guaranteed to find a shortest-length path to a conclusion node, if such a path exists (the completeness of selection rules is to be verified);

- *high modifiability* : identical sub-trees can be duplicated, new or others AIO can be added to tailor the tree to local conventions and user preferences;

- *iterative refinement* : because each node is associated to an AIO, the designer can stop the selection at every node, go back to the previous, select another rule.

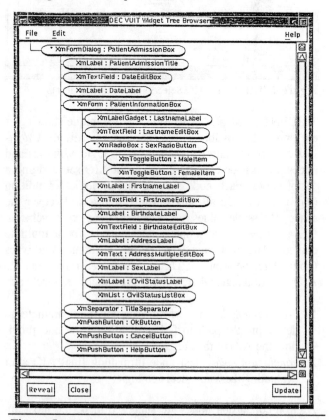

Figure 5. CIO hierarchy the presentation editor.

On the other hand, some disadvantages have been observed:

- *rule redundancy* : some identical rules are duplicated at different places in the tree because their application is relevant at different states;

- *excessive size* : the designer prefers trees with small values spaces at each node so that it is vital to reduce the conditions; an explicit tree representation can become impractical for very large selection trees.

MAPPING AIO TO CIO

Once matching AIO hierarchy has been mapped from all data structures, this AIO hierarchy is transformed to CIO hierarchy which is target environment dependant (fig. 5). Different AIO to CIO matching tables are defined. After transformation, CIO hierarchy can be captured as entry of a direct manipulation presentation editor.

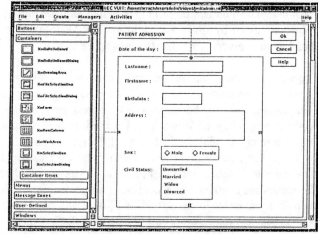

Figure 6. Resulting interface in the presentation editor.

The resulting interface can then be modified by the designer, the human factors specialist using DECVuit™ (*Visual User Interface Tool*) editor in the case of OSF/Motif™ (fig. 6). During this phase, the designer can replace behaviour-equivalent CIO (semantic integrity must be preserved), move or shift CIO whithin the tool to improve presentation, decoration and to respect physiological human limits. This modification is no longer made according to selection rules.

CONCLUSIONS

A decision tree-based AIO selection technique has been introduced to solve several problems and to induce new features which are greatly appreciated by the designers. In order to improve the range of selection rules, many *metadata* were defined and used so that this number becomes the major inconvenience to implement reasonably scaled trees. It seems that is the price to pay when enriching selection rules.

Selection rules are AIO-based rules for data management and business-oriented applications as in insurance and banking companies for instance. Graphical application may draw attention to the AIO typology, but their scope is actually not covered by this work (it was not the intended purpose). The eight supported data types with their metadata is the only investigation of the semantic for the selection rules. This not claims that all important aspects of business applications that affect the interface can be characterized by these informations. In fact, others parts of the semantic are passed to the interface generator in the CIO Placer: functional dependencies, integrity constraints, domain constraints,...

The current selection tree only requires forward chaining, but a future work concerns its extension to fully backward chaining: having a given AIO, which are the selection rules we need to apply, and from which type of data? This question occurs when the final user imperative requires to use a particular AIO which is different from the AIO selected by the tree.

On the other hand, DEC*Vuit* is now under extension for opening actual UIL object hierarchy to home-maded object classes: some interesting CIO are separately implemented and imported (e.g. group box, profiled edit box, option box, simple and extended tables,...)

ACKNOWLEDGMENTS

The auhors would like to thank all members of the TRIDENT project Anne-Marie Hennebert, Jean-Marie Leheureux, Isabelle Provot, Benoît Sacré (especially) and Louis Simon for their collaborative and participative research work. This work was supported by the FIRST (Formation et Impulsion à la Recherche Scientifique et Technologique) research program of "Direction Générale des Technologies et de la Recherche du Ministère de la Région Wallonne", Ref. RASE/SCHL319/Conv. 1487 and by the "Informatique du Futur" project of "Service de la Politique et de la Programmation Scientifique" under contract N°IT/IF/1.

REFERENCES

[1] Arens, Y., Miller, L. and Sondheimer, N., "Presentation design Using an Integrated Knowledge Base", in Sullivan, J. and Tyler, S. (eds.), *Intelligent User Interfaces,* Reading, MA: Addison-Wesley, 1991, pp. 241-258.

[2] de Baar, D., Foley, J.D. and Mullet, K.E., "Coupling Application Design and User Interface Design", *CHI'92 Conference Proceedings*, Monterey, May 1992, pp. 259-266.

[3] Bodart, F., Hennebert, A.-M., Leheureux, J.-M. and Pigneur, Y., "Computer-aided specification, evaluation and monitoring of information systems", *Sixth International Conference on Information Systems Proceedings,* Indianapolis, 1985.

[4] Bodart, F. and Pigneur, Y., *Conception Assistée des Systèmes d'Information*, Paris: Masson, 1989.

[5] Bodart, F., Hennebert, A.-M., Leheureux, J.-M., Provot, I., Sacré, B. and Vanderdonckt, J., "The TRIDENT project (Tools foR an Interactive Development ENvironmenT)", Working Conference IFIP WG 2.7, Namur, September 1990.

[6] Brown, C.H., *Human-Computer Interface Design Guidelines*, Berkeley, Ablex Publishing Corp., 1988.

[7] Card, S.K., Moran, T.P. and NEWELL, A., *The Psychology of Human-Computer Interaction*, Hillsdale, NJ: Lawrence Erlbaum Assoc., 1985.

[8] Johnson, J., "Selectors: Going Beyond User-Interface Widgets", *CHI'92 Conference Proceedings*, Monterey, May 1992, pp. 273-279.

[9] Kim, W. and Foley, J., "DON: User Interface Presentation Design Assistant", *UIST'90 Conference Proceedings*, Snowbird, October 1990, pp. 10-20.

[10] Kobara, S., *Visual Design with OSF/Motif*, Hewlett-Packard Press Series, Reading, MA: Addison-Wesley, 1991.

[11] Open Software Foundation, *OSF/Motif™ Style Guide*, revision 1.0, Englewood Cliffs, NJ: Prentice Hall, 1990.

[12] Petoud, I. and Pigneur, Y., "An Automatic and visual approach for user interface design", in *Enginnering for Human-Computer Interaction*, Amsterdam: North-Holland, 1990, pp. 403-420.

[13] Provot, I. and Sacré, B., "Proposition d'un langage de spécification de l'interface homme-machine d'une application de gestion hautement interactive", research report, Fac. Univ. N.-D. de la Paix, Namur, December 1991.

[14] Shneiderman, B., *Designing the user interface: strategies for effective human-computer interaction*, Reading, MA: Addison-Wesley, 1987.

[15] Szekely, P., Luo, P. and Neches, R., "Facilitating the Exploration of Interface Design Alternatives: The HUMANOID Model of Interface Design", *CHI'92 Conference Proceedings*, Monterey, May 1992, pp. 507-515.

[16] Tognazzini, B., *The Apple // Human interface guidelines*, Cupertino, CA: Apple Computer, 1985.

[17] Vander Zanden, B. and Myers, B.A., "Automatic, Look-and-Feel Independent Dialog Creation for Graphical User Interfaces", *CHI'90 Conference Proceedings*, Seattle, April 1990, pp. 27-34.

[18] Wiecha, C., Bennett, W., Boies, S. and Gould, J., "Generating Highly Interactive User Interfaces", *CHI'89 Conference Proceedings*, Austin, May 1989, pp. 277-282.

Providing High-level Control and Expert Assistance in the User Interface Presentation Design

Won Chul Kim

Department of Electrical Engineering and
Computer Science
The George Washington University
Washington, DC 20052
kim@seas.gwu.edu

James D. Foley

Graphics, Visualization, and Usability Center
College of Computing
Georgia Institute of Technology
Atlanta, GA 30332
foley@cc.gatech.edu

ABSTRACT

Current user interface builders provide only low-level assistance, because they have knowledge of neither the application, nor the principles by which interface elements are combined effectively. We have developed a framework that unites the knowledge components essential for effective user interface presentation design. The framework consists of an application model (both a data model and a control model), a design process model that supports top-down iterative development, and graphic design knowledge that is used both to place dialog box elements such that their application dependent logical relationships are visually reinforced and to control design symmetry and balance. To demonstrate the framework's viability, we have constructed a tool based on encapsulated design knowledge that establishes high-level style preferences and provides expert assistance for the dialog box presentation design and menu structuring.

KEYWORDS: Automatic layout, knowledge-based tool, UI design process

1. THE DESIGN PROCESS

Every interactive computer application must have a user interface (UI) to mediate between users and application functions. UI builders [3, 5, 15, 22, 23] help designers by providing components, such as menus, dialog boxes, radio buttons and scroll bars, to put together user interfaces quickly and easily. However, they do not provide intelligent assistance for generating a presentation design. They facilitate the presentation design activities at too low a level; a designer still must follow written guidelines [1, 18, 21] and graphics principles [4, 9, 10, 16] to create a good design. Interpreting the guidelines unambiguously and applying generic principles to a particular design problem is itself a major challenge. Thus, such tools may simply allow a designer to assemble a poor UI quickly.

Our objective is to integrate expert assistance into the UI design process. The essential ingredient of expert assistance is knowledge. We have thus extended the knowledge base model of User Interface Design Environment (UIDE) [7, 8, 20] to encapsulate elements, relationships, and principles of design knowledge related to the organization and presentation of menus and dialog boxes. This extended knowledge base model [12, 13, 14] consists of (1) a *conceptual design representation* which is a high-level description of an application; (2) *style knowledge*, which provides default style attributes of interface widgets; (3) *organization structures*, which define the logical groupings of application commands and parameters; and (4) a *presentation design representation*, which represents the interface object type (what interface object to use), the style selection (how the object looks), and the layout decisions (where objects are placed). The integrated knowledge base model provides a framework in which a set of reusable design rules automates various steps of the UI design process.

Based on this knowledge base framework, we have developed a UI presentation design tool called DON [12, 13]. The tool has two stages. An *organization manager* uses a top-down design methodology to assist designers in organizing the information, and selecting appropriate interface objects and their associated attributes. A *presentation manager* lays out selected interface objects in a dialog box or selected menu items, in a meaningful, logical, and consistent manner.

A difficult challenge is to accommodate user preferences and design goals in the design process. Because it is unrealistic to automate completely the UI design process, we have modeled the process and have broken it down into stages corresponding to the logical steps a designer takes. With DON, a designer specifies high-level preferences, such as acceptable range of dialog sizes or consistent margins and spacing, and each design stage automatically accommodates the preferences. The designer can view the intermediate results of each design stage and can modify them interactively, or can repeat a stage with modified preferences.

Support of Organization

The design process starts with the conceptual design

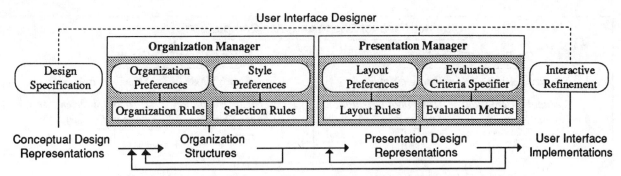

Figure 1   An overview of the design tool environment.

specification of an application. This representation of application entities and semantic relationships is used to aid the designer in determining the classifications and logical groupings of the application information to be presented to end users.

The organization manager (OM), shown in Figure 1, implements the first step of the design process and embodies two main sets of rules: (1) *organization rules* that analyze the high-level conceptual design representation and design *organization preferences* to allocate commands to menus, and attributes and command parameters to dialog boxes; (2) *selection rules* that select the appropriate interface object types and their attributes. Various existing systems [2, 6, 26] demonstrate the feasibility of rule-based, automatic mapping of application descriptions to interface object representations. The logical relationships of application commands and parameters are represented explicitly in the organization structure, which provides the basis for feedback at the organization level and for interactive modification of automated decisions. The OM allows the designer to specify high-level preferences and to modify interactively interface object type mappings stored in the organization structure. The designer can iterate through the organization process until the content organization and interaction object mappings are complete and satisfactory.

Support of Presentation Design
The OM paves the way for the presentation manager (PM), also shown in Figure 1, to complete the presentation design. Four aspects of the PM are important: (1) it automates the actual layout of menus and dialog boxes; (2) graphic design principles are embedded in the *layout rules*, which automate the layout process; (3) designer-specified *layout preferences* provide effective means to control the presentation design details; and (4) the *evaluation metrics* provide the comparative criteria that the designer can use as a guideline to evaluate and constrain design alternatives. The PM supports iterative menu structuring. For dialog box design, a combination of iterative and generate-and-evaluate methods is supported.

In the following sections, we discuss the strategies for providing high-level design control and expert assistance for dialog box presentation design.

2. AUTOMATIC DIALOG BOX LAYOUT
Success in design of forms, including dialog boxes, involves analyzing the conceptual content, designing the graphic appearance, and evaluating the form. The major goals of dialog box layout is to reinforce visually the logical relationships among items, to use space efficiently, and to generate aesthetically pleasing designs.

The layout algorithm assumes a *dialog box tree*. This tree is generated automatically by the organization rules. A dialog box tree defines the logical organization structure of the widgets that have been assigned to each dialog box. *Leaf* nodes of a dialog box tree represent the contents and labels of selected interaction objects. Initially, the bound (extent) of all leaf nodes of a dialog box is obtained. The logical *group* nodes' bounds are unknown until the layout process is complete.

The layout algorithm works with the tree of bounds, as shown in Figure 2. The strategy is to organize the bounds (extents of selected interaction objects) recursively from the leaf nodes (shown in white) up to the *root* of the dialog box tree. The bottom-up layout strategy systematically reduces the complex layout problem into many smaller layout problems for each unknown group node in similar fashion to hierarchical composition of graph [17] and tree layout algorithms [25]. Figure 2 illustrates a possible solution based on the bottom-up layout strategy, where unknown subgroup node bounds and

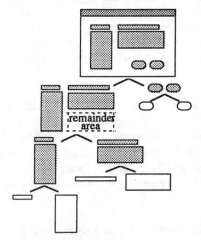

Figure 2   Illustration of the layout process, working with a tree structure of bounds.

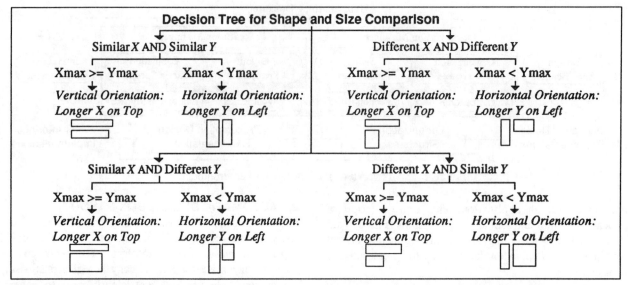

Figure 3   The *layout rule* decision tree for analyzing two rectangular items based on the comparison of shape and size.

locations are determined recursively until the shape and size of the root node are determined.

All the known bounds of a subgroup node are put into a *pool of bounds* to be laid out. Two bounds are selected, their arrangement is determined by a shape and size analysis (discussed in the following section), and the resulting group node consisting of two laid out bounds is thrown back into the pool as a single bound, with a remainder area that is maintained for possible use. This process is repeated for each unknown group node until all the bounds in the pool are exhausted. An important advantage of laying out two items at a time is that it ensures consistent alignments and gaps between items. Since the bottom-up layout is based on a logical tree structure, logically related items are arranged in close proximity, which partly ensures visual reinforcement of the logical structure.

Analysis of Shape and Size

Shape and size analysis is the central component of the layout algorithm that determines the alignment, orientation, and placement of selected pairs of bounds. The shape and size analysis is used to analyze the placement of a label with respect to its content. It is also used to categorize shapes of bounds and to formulate visual groupings based on similar shapes.

The decision tree for shape and size comparison for the two rectangular bounds is shown in Figure 3. The top level of the decision tree compares the similarity of the widths and heights of two bounds. The lower level of the decision tree compares the maximum widths and heights as the criteria to determine the orientation, alignment, and placement of the two selected bounds.

A designer can modify the similarity size ratio that is used by criteria for the shape and size comparison to determine similarity of items' lengths and widths. The default is set at 0.618, a value is derived from the golden proportion [4, 10, 16]. This option gives the designer additional fine control of the layout algorithm.

High-Level Analysis

To increase the efficiency of the algorithm and to handle special cases appropriately, DON incorporates a high-level analysis that examines many bounds at once, in contrast to the basic pair-wise comparison. The layout algorithm uses the high-level analysis to identify overflow situations, simple cases where the number of items is small, visual groupings based on similar shapes and sizes, and to assess appropriateness of a column-based design. DON handles these cases before applying the full layout algorithm.

When the area required for all the widgets exceeds the specified dialog box size, *overflow solutions* [12] are employed. For example, (1) the sizes of certain interaction objects can be reduced to the acceptable minimum, (2) the interaction object type can be changed to one that requires less space, and (3) margins and spacing can be tightened.

When the area required for all the widgets is less than the minimum dialog box size, DON suggests an increase in that minimum size, which results in a design with extra white space. The range of heights and widths for dialog boxes, as well as of limits on the size ratios, can be specified as style preferences.

With DON, the designer can explicitly specify and explore various alternative column-based styles, as shown in Figure 4. This feature allows the designer at all times to constrain layout structures to column-based arrangements of labels and dialog box contents, as suggested in the OPEN LOOK Application Style Guidelines [21]. The bottom two designs in Figure 4 are of the same dialog box representation. When a particular design is chosen—the lower-right design in this case—its

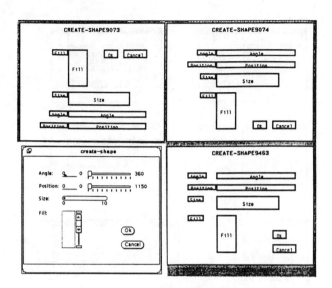

Figure 4   Alternative column-based designs for a
dialog box with four items.

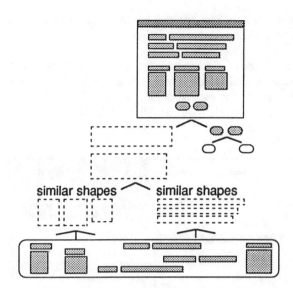

Figure 5   Groupings of bounds based on shape
and size analysis.

design representation is mapped into the OPEN LOOK GUI
components shown on the lower left.

DON also may recommend a column-based layout based on
analysis (using rules such as the following) of the number of
horizontally and vertically shaped contents, even if a designer
has not explicitly requested such consideration:

If the number of *horizontal shapes* are greater than
the sum of *none-horizontal shapes*,
then suggest column-based layout.

At each group node of a dialog box tree, the bounds are
analyzed for possible grouping based on similar shapes and
sizes. Figure 5 illustrates how the visual groupings are formed
based on similar shapes. The row or column arrangements for
a similar shape group are determined based on the shapes.
When the majority of similar bounds is horizontally shaped,
then a vertical column arrangement is recommended. When
the majority is vertically shaped, then a horizontal row
arrangement is recommended. In the interactive design mode,
these automated decisions and recommendations can be
overridden.

DON allows the designer to influence the overall organizational
constraints on items by specifying:
• That the organization be column-based
• That a label location be used consistently (usually
  accompanies column-based design)
• That a specified visual balance tendency be used
  (top-heavy, bottom-heavy, left-heavy, or right-heavy)
These organizational preferences provide higher level
constraints on the layout of all the items within a dialog box.

Iterative Design Method

An iterative design method, where alternative designs can be
prototyped, implemented, refined rapidly and easily is
advocated for developing good user interfaces. The iterative

design cycle comprises these steps: (1) a designer specifies
the layout constraints, (2) the system generates automatically
a single design based on layout constraints, and (3) the system
displays an outline of the layout structure and evaluation
results. This cycle is short because only the outline (bordering
bounds) of the layout structure is generated, and evaluation is
based on this outline.

The high-level style customization capability combined with
an iterative design strategy provides an easy to use tool that
allows a designer to explore alternative designs quickly,
without worrying about fine details. The functional user UI
code is generated only when a designer is satisfied with the
layout structure.

3. CUSTOMIZATION OF USER INTERFACE STYLE

DON provides an explicit method for specifying the layout
constraints for each dialog box design instance. The layout
rules achieve automatically the detail layout constraints
specified. Consistency is realized when same layout constraints
are applied for all dialog boxes; the framework makes it
possible to set certain specifications global to all the dialog
box instances. If the designer needs to specify exceptions,
specific constraints for each dialog box instance can be
overridden.

It is important that a design tool allow the designer to specify
the fine detail layout constraints. The designer must have
explicit control sufficient to generate a layout that fits the
design goals particular to the current application. These layout
constraints become input to the layout rules that automatically
generate the dialog box designs.

Control of Margins and Spacing

Specification of consistent margins and spacing is tedious and
difficult, even with an interactive layout tool. A simpler
approach is to allow the designer to provide a high level

specification of margins and spacing that can be applied consistently throughout the design.

Effective use of white space is the key to achieving attractive layouts. Various kinds of white space—such as inner, outer, top, foot margins, gaps separating items, and offsets between contents and labels—are controlled by the layout algorithm. Figure 6 shows the various spacings that a designer can specify.

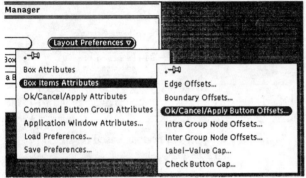

Figure 6   Margins and spacing specifications.

Control of Location and Orientation of OK and Cancel Buttons

Consistency in screen design is an important design factor that affects the usability of an interface, and thus of the application. A designer may want to force a consistent location of the OK and Cancel buttons in all dialog boxes. The Confirm (OK and Cancel) button group is considered separately based on either *specified* or *analyzed* location, alignment, and orientation.

> Alignment:
>   (left, center, right, equal-size, none)
> Orientation:
>   (above-below, left-right, none)
> Placement:
>   (top-left, center-left, bottom-left,
>   top-right, center-right, bottom-right,
>   top-center, bottom-center,
>   distribute-top, distribute-bottom,
>   distribute-left, distribute-right, none)

Figure 7 Possible alignment, orientation, and location specifications for the OK and Cancel button group.

Possible options that a designer can specify explicitly to generate consistent Confirm button group location are shown in Figure 7. If preferences are not specified, then the layout rules analyze the overall content size, shape, and remaining space available to determine the location and orientation. The Confirm button group is considered after all content item bounds are laid out. Two general cases are considered: (1) the Confirm button group as a whole in any orientation does not fit in the remainder area (examples shown in Figure 8); (2) the remainder area is large enough to hold the Confirm button group (examples shown in Figure 9).

Figure 8 shows a set of few alternative Confirm button group

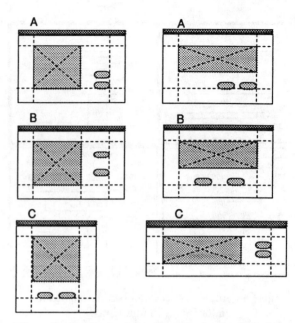

Figure 8   Determination of location and orientation for the OK and Cancel button group.

locations and orientations based on (1) vertically shaped content bound (left column) and (2) horizontally shaped content bound (right column). There are many other possible designs, not shown, with different combinations of location and orientation. Some combinations are rejected by the system because they result in awkward layout, as judged by the built-in evaluation criteria discussed in Section 4. The system defaults to a design A for both shapes considered in the example. The Confirm button group is the last logical item with which user interacts. Thus, the bottom-right location is an appropriate default location [4].

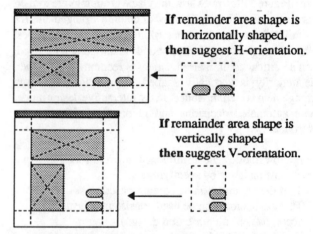

If remainder area shape is horizontally shaped, **then** suggest H-orientation.

If remainder area shape is vertically shaped **then** suggest V-orientation.

Figure 9   Determination of orientation for the OK and Cancel button group based on the shape of the remainder area.

The two examples in Figure 9 show the system default based on the shape of the remainder area. The horizontal orientation is preferred for the horizontally shaped remainder area; the vertical orientation is preferred for the vertically shaped remainder area.

Encapsulation of Style Knowledge

DON assists a designer in establishing a default style for interface object classes; this default persists, and is reusable for different design instances. This idea is similar to that used in Interaction Transaction Systems [26], which incorporates reusable style knowledge by allowing style experts to write style rules that represent both graphic arts and human factors decisions. The style knowledge consists of hierarchically structured classes of interface objects that take advantage of inheritance of attribute values. The advantages of modeling the style knowledge in this fashion are the following abilities:

- To provide default and ranges of acceptable attribute values to all interaction objects
- To allow a designer to modify defaults to generate customized styles
- To allow a designer to specialize style objects for special purposes
- To allow a designer to package a set of style attribute values

The style knowledge facilitates a designer's control of the presentation style for individual interface objects. For example, during the layout process, the layout rules use the minimum acceptable sizes to reduce the size of the interaction objects when there are too many items to fit into the specified dialog box size.

The designer can bundle together these high-level style preferences and the layout constraints to develop a customized style guide that satisfies the written style guides [1, 18, 21] yet is suited to a particular application using a particular toolkit.

4. THE GENERATE AND EVALUATE STRATEGY

The generate-and-evaluate method of design facilitates exploration by allowing a designer to view many automatically generated dialog box layouts. The designer can not only view multiple layout structures simultaneously, but also obtain various evaluation metrics on specific criteria. The designer can use the metrics to compare many alternative designs. DON further enhances exploration of the design space by combining the advantages of both the iterative design strategy and the generate-and-evaluate strategy. After selecting the generated layout structure from multiple design alternatives, the designer can use an iterative strategy to fine tune the detailed visual attributes.

Evaluation Criteria

A design tool needs quantitative measures to analyze the spatial properties of the dialog box layout. Streveler and Wasserman developed quantitative metrics [19] for analyzing digital screen layouts, and Tullis developed metrics [24] for evaluating the visual layout or design of alphanumeric displays. DON incorporates several evaluation criteria, such as symmetry, balance, dialog box size ratio, dialog box size range, and negative space percentage calculations to help a designer apply graphic design principles in dialog box layout. The algorithms for the evaluation metrics have been developed based on graphic design principles [4, 10, 11, 16].

A design achieves *balance* by placing elements of similar weight, but not necessarily precisely the same size, in relationship to one another such that there is weight at the bottom of layout as well as the top, and to the left and right to balance the whole [4]. A significant concept that contributes to balance is that an object located a greater distance away from the center will have a higher visual weight than will a more central item. A similar idea holds for two items placed at opposite ends of a fulcrum: a smaller item placed farther away from the middle is balanced by a bigger item placed closer to the middle.

To simplify the evaluation score calculation, we convert the actual extent of items laid out in a dialog box to 1s, and we convert the white space to 0s. This step is common to several evaluation calculations. The bitmap resolution can be increased for higher accuracy at the cost of computation time, by setting the parameter to the bitmap conversion function.

The formula for left-right balance calculation is as follows (top-bottom balance is computed similarly):

$$\text{Total weight for each side} = \sum 1s * f(\text{distance away from the center})$$

$$\frac{\text{Left-right}}{\text{balance}} = \frac{\text{total weight of less heavy side}}{\text{total weight of more heavy side}}$$

The method of calculating the *symmetry* of layout is straightforward. We can think of symmetry as folding a layout in half and checking all the matched areas covered by the elements on each side.

Proper use of white space is critical to an attractive layout. Nevertheless, when screen space is constrained, a designer may need to minimize *negative space* (unused white space). We compute the negative space by calculating the percentage of the white space against the total space available.

The evaluation metrics for a selected dialog box design are shown in Figure 10. From right to left, (1) a designer-specified acceptable range in each evaluation criteria is shown by brackets; (2) a designer-specified weight, which can range from 1 to 9, for each evaluation criteria is shown by the numbers surrounded by asterisks; (3) computed evaluation scores for each criterion are shown in percentages (the higher the number, the greater the balance and symmetry); each score is marked by "X" that satisfies the specified range. The left-right balance score for the example in Figure 10 is 80 percent (the left side is heavier) and the top-bottom balance score is 88 percent (the top is heavier).

DON uses evaluation metrics to constrain the design space and the layout style, and to compare and evaluate alternative designs. The high-level constraints—such as margins, spacing, and the preferred location and orientation of OK and Cancel buttons—are reflected in the generation scheme to enhance designer control in constraining the resulting design.

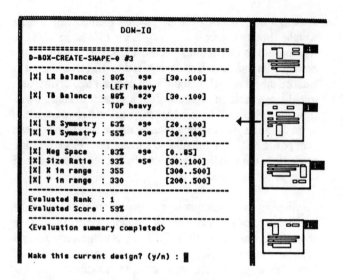

Figure 10   Evaluation results of a selected dialog box.

Design Browser

The design browser displays alternative designs that are generated automatically, and allows the designer to interact directly with these visual representations. The design browser maintains the design variants, internally, by instantiating instances of a dialog box design schema that stores left-right, top-bottom relations of bounds, exact locations of bounds, and evaluation scores of a design.

Four important aspects of the design browser are shown in Figure 11: (1) multiple layout structures can be viewed and compared, (2) designs that satisfy all the specified evaluation criteria are indicated by a bold boundary, (3) a numerical ranking based on the total evaluation score is displayed next to each visual representation of a dialog box, (4) the designer can select alternative choices to refine a selected design iteratively. DON reports detailed evaluation scores corresponding to a dialog box design when the designer clicks directly on the visual representation.

DON ranks multiple designs based on the total evaluation score, which DON calculated using specified weights for each evaluation criterion. A designer can request a certain number of designs that satisfy the specified criteria. A designer can also modify the weights, and request recalculation of the total score and reranking of multiple designs. This functionality provides an additional method to compare and evaluate multiple designs, complementing the visual feedback of the display of multiple designs.

5. IMPLEMENTATION

DON is implemented with the Automated Reasoning Tool (Inference Corp.) [11] on workstations (Sun Microsystems). The final designs from DON can be read into the Devguide [22], an interactive UI design tool, for further refinement. The presentation design representation is generic in that additional implementation models [14] can be developed that will translate it into different toolkits.

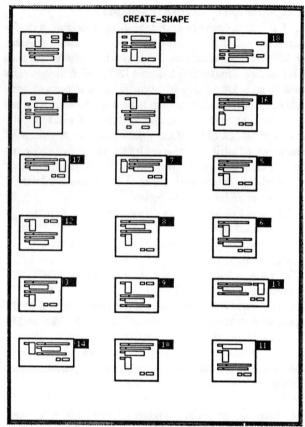

Figure 11   Automatically generated multiple designs, shown by the design browser.

6. SUMMARY

DON represents a step forward in UI development tools. It shows how we can provide high-level control and expert assistance in the UI presentation design process. These capabilities assist a designer in generating UI designs and provide easy ways for a designer to specify constraints. DON applies graphic design principles in the dialog box layout process, and uses evaluation metrics to improve visual clarity, consistency, and aesthetic appearance.

Work can be done to refine the layout rules to use more semantic information. We are exploring combining shape and size analysis with more extensive analysis of parameter relationships, such as parameter sequencing and dependencies. Visual attribute analysis can be combined with interaction object type analysis to place similar types next to each other when there are no substantial differences in the shape and size.

To enhance DON's usability, we can develop more visual tools based on the framework, such as a graphical tool that allows a designer to view the layout in progress, and to interact directly with the dialog box tree nodes to specify constraints.

The knowledge-based framework developed can be used as the basis for integrating top-down and bottom-up approaches to UI design. By sharing representation of various stages of UI design, rules can facilitate mapping from either direction. To build a true link from DON, which is a top-down iterative design tool, to the interactive UI builders, we must capture the reasons for modifications made by the designer and incorporate them back into a set of the layout rules for use during future designs.

ACKNOWLEDGEMENTS

The Graphics and User Interface Research Group at George Washington University provided intellectual environment supporting this work. Thanks to Shelly Heller, Jon Mckeeby, Lucy Moran, and Lyn Dupre whose comments helped to improve the clarity of the paper. Special thanks to Samuel Molina for his contribution in formulating evaluation metrics. Financial support was provided by NSF Grant IRI-88-13179 and DMC-84-205-29, Siemens Corporation, and Sun Microsystems.

REFERENCES

1   Apple Computer, Inc. *Human Interface Guidelines: The Apple Desktop Interface*, Addison-Wesley, Reading, MA 1990.

2   Arens, Y., L. Miller, S. Shapiro, and N. Sondheimer. Automatic Construction of User-Interface Displays, *AAAI-8 Proceedings*, St. Paul, MN, August 1988.

3   Cardelli, L. Building User Interfaces by Direct Manipulation, in *Proceedings of the ACM SIGGRAPH Symposium on User Interface Software*, ACM, New York, 1988, pp. 152-166.

4   Conover, T.E. *Graphic Communications Today*, West Publishing Company, St. Paul, MN 1985.

5   Cossey, G. *Prototyper*, SmetherBarnes, Portland, OR, 1989.

6   de Baar, D., J. Foley, and K. Mullet. Coupling Application Design and User Interface Design, in *Proceedings of CHI'92-SIGCHI Computer-Human Interaction Conference*, ACM, New York, 1992, pp. 259-266.

7   Foley, J., W. Kim, K. Murray, and S. Kovacevic. UIDE-An Intelligent User Interface Design Environment, in Sullivan, J and S. Tyler (eds.), *Intelligent User Interfaces*, Addison-Wesley, Reading, MA, 1991, pp. 339-384.

8   Foley, J., W. Kim, S. Kovacevic, and K. Murray. Defining Interfaces at a High Level of Abstraction, *IEEE Software*, 6(1), January, 1989, pp. 25-32.

9   Galitz, W. *Handbook of Screen Format Design*, Q.E.D. Information Sciences, Inc., Wellesley, MA, 1981.

10 Hurlburt, Allen. *Layout: the design of the printed page*, Watson-Guptill Publications, New York, 1977.

11 Inference Corp. *ART Reference Manual*, Inference Corporation, Los Angeles, CA, 1987.

12 Kim, W. Knowledge-Based Framework for an Automated User Interface Presentation Design Tool, *Ph.D. Thesis*, Department of Electrical Engineering and Computer Science, George Washington University, Washington, D.C., 1993.

13 Kim, W., and J. Foley. DON: User Interface Presentation Design Assistant, in *Proceedings of the ACM SIGGRAPH Symposium on User Interface Software and Technology*, ACM, New York, 1990, pp. 10-20.

14 Kim, W., and J. Rhyne. Knowledge Base Model for Automated User Interface Design, *Report GWU-IIST-89-29*, Department of Electrical Engineering and Computer Science, George Washington University, Washington, D.C., 1989.

15 Linton, M., J. Vlissides, and P. Calder. Composing User Interfaces with InterViews, *IEEE Computer*, Feb.. 1989.

16 Marcus, A. *Graphic Design for Electronic Documents and User Interfaces*, Addison-Wesley, Reading, MA, 1992.

17 Messinger, E., L. Rowe, and R. Henry. A Divide-and-Conquer Algorithm for the Automatic Layout of Large Directed Graphs, *IEEE Transactions of Systems, Man, and Cybernetics*, Vol. SMC-21, No. 1, 1991, pp. 1-12.

18 Open Software Foundation. *OSF/Motif Style Guide*, Revision 1.0, Prentice-Hall, Inc., Englewood Cliffs, NJ, 1990.

19 Streveler, D., and A. Wasserman. Quantitative Measures of the Spatial Properties of Screen Designs, in *Proceedings INTERACT'87, 2nd IFIP Conference on Human-Computer Interaction*, Vol. 1, Elsivier Science Publishers, Amsterdam, 1987, pp. 125-133.

20 Sukaviriya, P., J. Foley, T. Griffith. A Second Generation User Interface Design Environment: The Model and The Runtime Architecture, *INTERCHI'93, Conference on Human Factors in Computing Systems*, ACM, New York, 1993.

21 Sun Microsystems, Inc. and AT&T. *OPEN LOOK GUI Application Style Guidelines*, Addison-Wesley, Reading, MA, 1990.

22 Sun Microsystems, Inc. *Open Windows Developer's Guide 1.1, Reference Manual*, Part No. 800-5380-10, Revision A, Mountain View, CA, June 1990.

23 Szczur, M., and P. Miller. Transportable Applications Environment (TAE) PLUS, in *Proceedings of OOPSLA'88, Object-Oriented Programming Systems, Languages and Applications Conference*, ACM, New York, 1988.

24 Tullis, T. A Computer-Based Tool for Evaluating Alphanumeric Displays, in *Proceedings INTERACT'87, 2nd IFIP Conference on Human-Computer Interaction*, Vol. 2, Elsivier Science Publishers, Amsterdam, 1987, pp. 123-127.

25 Walker II, John. A Node-positioning Algorithms for General Trees, *Software-Practice and Experience*, Vol. 20(7), 1990, pp. 685-705.

26 Wiecha, C, W. Bennett, S. Boies, and J. Gould. Generating Highly Interactive User Interfaces, in *Proceedings of CHI'89-SIGCHI Computer-Human Interaction Conference*, ACM, New York, 1989, pp. 277-282.

Orienteering[1] in an Information Landscape:
How Information Seekers Get From Here to There

Vicki L. O'Day

Robin Jeffries

Hewlett-Packard Laboratories
1501 Page Mill Road, Palo Alto, CA 94304 U.S.A
(415) 967-8714
Internet: oday@hpl.hp.com

ABSTRACT

We studied the uses of information search results by regular clients of professional intermediaries. The clients in our study engaged in three different types of searches: (1) monitoring a well-known topic or set of variables over time, (2) following an information-gathering plan suggested by a typical approach to the task at hand, and (3) exploring a topic in an undirected fashion. In most cases, a single search evolved into a series of interconnected searches, usually beginning with a high-level overview. We identified a set of common triggers and stop conditions for further search steps. We also observed a set of common operations that clients used to analyze search results. In some settings, the number of search iterations was reduced by restructuring the work done by intermediaries. We discuss the implications of the interconnected search pattern, triggers and stop conditions, common analysis techniques, and intermediary roles for the design of information access systems.

KEYWORDS: Information search, information use, intermediaries, collaborative work.

INTRODUCTION

An important way of looking at the effectiveness of information retrieval is to see how well the resulting material and the manner of retrieval and delivery match the user's problem situation. As research directions have shifted to include the study of users of information systems, rather than concentrating solely on system characteristics [4, 7], most efforts have centered on understanding how users can express their information needs effectively to the system (e.g., [2, 3, 5]). In contrast, our work focuses on information delivery, rather than search performance – how the results of an information search are digested and used to solve the problem that prompted the search. To understand information delivery requirements, we conducted a study of how library clients deal with the information they get back from human intermediaries.

Our hypothesis, based on an examination of search examples in several domains, was that a single, static view of search

results, however appropriately designed, would often not be enough to satisfy real user needs; instead, users would use the results as a basis for exploration, perhaps examining them from different perspectives. We learned from our study that people did do exploration, often conducting a series of interconnected but diverse searches on a single, problem-based theme, rather than one extended search session per task. Like practitioners of the sport of orienteering, our searchers used data from their present situation to determine where to go next. We identified a set of common triggers and stop conditions for further search steps within an extended search. We also learned that people used a set of common analysis techniques on their data, which often involved constructing new artifacts.

The motivation for this study was in our work on information retrieval mediators [9]. We are currently building a toolkit called DIME that will allow people to create, share, and use mediators [8]. A retrieval mediator is a small, special-purpose packaging of the retrieval expertise necessary to handle a prototypical information question in a particular domain. It includes a search strategy, iterative steps if necessary to complete the search task, postprocessing of retrieved data, and default choices for information presentation. A user-level information-seeking task would typically involve several mediators. Private mediators will be used to provide a level of individual customization and extensibility in searching. Mediators will be identifiable entities in the system; high-level, task-oriented descriptions of mediators will be searchable by mediator-builders or end users.

In this paper, we describe the results of our study and the implications for the design of the mediator toolkit and other information access systems.

METHODOLOGY

We conducted an ethnographic study of fifteen clients of professional intermediaries. About half of our informants worked for the same large computer manufacturer and half worked for a variety of other companies. All of our informants regularly

---

[1] Orienteering is a sport in which individuals or teams try to complete a course leading from a common starting point through fixed intermediate points to a common destination. Orienteering events are typically held in semi-wilderness areas or large parks. Participants navigate with a map and compass, using landmarks in the environment to get their bearings and plot a route to the next point in the course. Beginners may be satisfied just to find their way to the end, but getting there faster is considered better.

conducted mediated searches on financial and business-related topics. We chose this focus in the hope that information use patterns might be clearer if there were some commonality in the language and domain expertise of the informants, but the informants were by no means a homogeneous group.

A variety of professions was represented, including financial analyst, venture capitalist, product marketing engineer, demographer, management consultant, logistics specialist, research assistant, statistician, merger and acquisition specialist, college finance officer, and sales/planning staff. The job levels of the informants ranged from entry-level to senior management. Their work settings were diverse, including engineering, education, finance, and consulting organizations. Some informants worked for companies with fewer than twenty-five employees; some worked for companies with tens of thousands of employees. Some were sophisticated users of technology, while others only used a small handful of tools such as spreadsheet programs. The backgrounds of the informants were in business, technical, and social science disciplines.

Semi-structured interviews were conducted in the offices of the participants. We audiotaped all of the interviews for which we were given permission, resulting in over 150 pages of transcripts. The length of interviews ranged from forty-five minutes to two hours; the average interview lasted about an hour.

The interview questions were designed to expose the work contexts and specific tasks that triggered search requests and to explore example search requests in detail. Informants were asked how they expressed requests to the intermediary, which formats were used for delivery of results, and what they did to understand and use the information when it arrived. When possible, the researcher and the informant examined together past search results that the informant had saved in a printed form, along with any resulting summaries, graphs, tables, and newsletters that had been produced using these search results.

It must be noted that the data gathered are based on the informants' memories of their searches, augmented by artifacts they had saved, and thus reflect whatever aspects of the searches the informants found memorable. No observations were made of actual interactions with intermediaries or "live" analyses of search results. Our informants were generous in sharing real examples of their past searches, but their current analyses would have contained material too sensitive to share.

In almost all of the work settings, the intermediaries were professional librarians. A few of the intermediaries were trained searchers without library science degrees. Throughout the rest of the paper, we will usually refer to the intermediaries as librarians.

We did two levels of analysis of the interview transcripts. At the first level, we looked for themes or patterns that appeared consistently throughout our informants' search experiences. Two patterns did become apparent. One of these, a pattern of interconnected searches, will be described in this paper. The other pattern, that virtually all of the library clients in our study turned out to be intermediaries themselves of one sort or another, will not be discussed here due to space limitations.

In the second level of analysis, we extracted from the transcripts all of the search scenarios described by the participants in the study. These search scenarios were characterized by three basic "search modes", which we will describe below. To explore the theme of interconnected searches mentioned above, we paid particular attention during our analysis to the transition steps between individual searches in a progressive search. We extracted from the transcripts the triggers and stop conditions that influenced people's decisions of whether to do further search steps. In some settings, we noted that these triggers and stop conditions were modified by an unusual work breakdown between librarian and client. Since we are interested in how people use information returned by a search, we also extracted from the transcripts the set of operations that were used by our informants to analyze their search results.

During this second phase of the analysis, two coders analyzed one-third of the transcripts and reconciled their differences in each of the three coding areas: the search scenarios found and assignment of each to one of the three search modes, triggers and stop conditions found, and analysis operations found. The differences between coders were few; the reconciliation mainly consisted of adding missed examples to the lists of triggers and analysis operations. The remaining two-thirds of the transcripts were analyzed by one coder.

In the following section, we will describe the overall pattern of interconnected searches and three different search modes, the connections between steps in a progressive search, the impact of changing the role of the librarian, and frequently-used analysis operations.

FINDINGS

Search Modes and Interconnected Searches

Our informants described 66 different search scenarios. Some of these scenarios were clearly one-time, ad hoc searches, while others represented repeated searches done either at regular intervals or whenever the informant worked on a particular task. Thus a single scenario often represented many executions of a search. In our coding of search scenarios, we distinguished between scenarios that were described very specifically, with reference to particular search parameters, and scenarios that were described generically by our informants.

These search scenarios fell into three basic "search modes": *monitoring*, *planned*, and *exploratory*. We give examples of the three modes below. A small number of scenarios (six) fell into two categories rather than one; we have folded these scenarios into the frequency counts given below by assigning one-half point to each of the two categories involved. Five of the scenarios could not be categorized due to insufficient data.

The three search modes were:

1. *Monitoring* a well-known topic or set of variables over time. (4 generic, 10.5 specific)

   Katherine[2], a financial analyst, calls the librarian every

---

[2]We have anonymized examples when necessary, and we have not used the informants' real names in this paper.

quarter to request a search on four competitor companies. She asks for their public earnings announcements, which she uses to track revenue and order growth, and she also asks for any references to the companies in the business literature so she can see if there is "anything unusual about this company." She creates a quarterly report with tables comparing her company's performance to the competitors, with explanatory notes at the bottom.

2. *Following a plan* for information-gathering suggested by a typical approach to the task at hand. (9 generic, 12.5 specific)

Larry, a process benchmarking specialist, helps groups inside his company improve their business processes in areas such as order fulfillment. When handling a particular assignment, he follows a typical plan in his library searches. First, he looks for the companies that do an outstanding job with the particular process he's investigating. To do this, he has the librarian search for any references to that process, giving her a list of synonyms that might be used to describe the process. Once he has identified the companies with the best processes, he follows up by having the librarian retrieve information about the financial performance of each of the companies, since if a company isn't doing well there may be something wrong with the process. When he's ready to visit one of the top companies, he has the librarian run a search to find any recent news on the company, so he will feel completely up-to-date before the visit.

3. *Exploring* a topic in an undirected fashion. (8 generic, 17 specific)

Bob, a management consultant, received a request from a client to give advice on certain retail distribution issues. Before getting started with the client's problem, Bob decided to look into the "basic current facts on the industry." He felt that he needed to know "whether what we are talking about is smaller than a bread box, bigger than a house - just size it." He requested general information on the industry from his librarian.

There were about twice as many specific as generic search scenarios, with a stronger bias towards specific scenarios in monitoring searches, where the library clients performed the same search on a weekly, monthly, quarterly, or annual basis and were usually able to describe very precisely what they did. The generic search scenarios may represent more actual searches than specific (non-monitoring) scenarios and may therefore be more fruitful for understanding the search process, but it is helpful to have the data anchored by a plentiful set of specific examples. There were roughly the same number of planned and exploratory searches overall, with fewer monitoring searches. However, each monitoring search scenario, whether generic or specific, represents many actual searches.

We also looked at the distribution of the use of different search modes across individual library clients, and we found that every client did more than one type of search. All but two clients did exploratory searches; planned searches and monitoring searches were done by about two-thirds of the clients.

A pattern of behavior that almost all the library clients followed was to conduct over time a series of interconnected but diverse searches on a single, problem-based theme, rather than one extended search session per task. This orienteering-style approach occurred in each of the three search modes. Some, but not all, monitoring searches led to further investigations, primarily when something new or unexpected turned up regarding the companies or other variables that were being monitored. Virtually all planned and exploration searches were done in several steps. Each stage in the search was typically followed by careful reading, assimilation, and analysis of all of the resulting material, which then triggered new directions to explore. The winding paths taken in these searches could sometimes be partially predicted by the task that motivated the search, but even in apparently routine searches there were often unexpected turns in the journey.

Here is a high-level description of a progressive search given by John, a merger and acquisition expert:

John: What you want is a thorough and efficient way that will cover first of all the leading sources and then second of all more localized sources ... So there is a kind of a general quick and dirty wanting to find out what's out there and then once you do that then you want to go in more specifically and that is where you get into more detailed searches. There is like a 30,000-foot view and then you go into specific areas.

The pattern of looking for an overview first was common to both planned and exploration searches, followed by detailed searches suggested either by the plan or by results of the initial search. This high-level view was an orienting view, often serving as an index into points of interest. Monitoring searches tended to focus on details from the beginning, since the context of the competitor companies or other monitored variables was already well-understood.

We would like to emphasize that this kind of progressive search is different from the refinement of a query within a search session, which is intended to gradually bring the result set closer to a "perfect" match to the user's information need. Systems such as those described by Williams [10] and Fischer and Nieper-Lemke [6] allow the user to provide feedback on the relevance of terms appearing in the result set, after which the query is redefined to focus on items with these terms. Such reformulation strategies assume that the user's information need is fixed throughout the search session, and a dialogue of sorts is taking place between the system and the user to help the system match the user's fixed need.

In the interconnected searches conducted by our informants, the information need shifted between search requests. Within a session, the information need was of necessity fixed, since librarians conducted the actual searches and there was rarely any interaction between a librarian and a client during a search. But between sessions, analysis of results took place and triggers for further investigation were found.

Though different information needs were reflected in different search steps, each successive search carried with it the context of the problem that prompted the searches and of the previous searches done to attack the problem. For example, there was a continued focus on the content areas that bounded the problem, such as an industry, market segment, or geographic region. Also, when a particular result suggested a follow-up search, the new search was often framed to include the context of the earlier result. For example, a search for information about the past mergers involving a particular company might trigger a search for information about the partners in those mergers. But the search on each of the partners is not comprehensive; instead, it focuses on data that relate to the partner's deal-making capacity and history. Thus there was a thread of continuity through interconnected searches, even when they wandered among different topics.

It was the accumulation of search results, not the final search result set, that had value for most of our library clients. When people finished searching, they often created summaries of the material they had found, including both overviews and detailed views and analyses. In many cases, they also presented results to the interested parties in their work settings.

This pattern of interconnected searches has also been observed by Bates [1], who described the process as "berrypicking," analogous to finding berries scattered in bunches, rather than all in one spot. She too points out that information needs change throughout a series of searches and that searchers need an accumulation of results rather than a single target result. But Bates' emphasis is on how these observations affect search techniques, assuming no intermediaries. For example, people may shift information sources as they move from one set of results to another, or they may browse in a source to find a promising new area to explore. Our library clients used librarians throughout, and our current interest is in information usage patterns and interfaces for effective information delivery rather than search techniques. To continue the berry analogy, our library clients seemed to be making a berry dessert (sometimes with surprise ingredients), rather than simply picking and eating berries. How did they decide which ingredient to hunt for next and how did they know when they were finished?

Triggers

To learn more about the pattern of interconnected searches, we examined the different types of transitions between one step and the next. The data do not allow us to provide accurate frequency counts for these triggers and stop conditions, since people did not consistently reveal the triggers that occurred in their search scenarios. However, we did collect all the triggers they mentioned, and the following four categories characterize almost all of these triggers:

1. The next step fit with the overall *plan*.
2. Something *interesting* arose and prompted exploration.
3. There was some *change* to be explained.
4. There was something *missing* from the data.

Pursuing a plan

Planned search steps do not need much elaboration. The example of the benchmarking specialist given above can serve as a prototype. Planned searches were predictable in their overall structure from the beginning, and the type of results desired was also anticipated (e.g., a list of top companies). In spite of

their predictability, planned searches were still carried out in a step-wise fashion, since analysis of one step was needed to produce parameters for the next step. Though the outline of a planned search was clear from the beginning, sometimes one or more of the other triggers occurred and expanded its scope.

Encountering something interesting

People were alert to any search results they considered interesting or unusual, and they typically wanted to follow up on these results. The library clients usually could not define precisely what "interesting" meant to them, but they felt confident that they would know it when they saw it. John, the merger expert, described his exploratory searching this way:

John: Well, 90% of what you get isn't useful. I mean, you are crawling through the sand to find the nuggets ... you have to read through the one hundred and fifty citations to find the five articles that you are really interested in. This is especially true when you don't know exactly what you are interested in ...

Sometimes the search results gave the client a new perspective on material that was already known. For example, the college finance officer examined a report of various financial data on colleges and found a number representing a college's total allocation for student living. This was a way of packaging data that he had not thought of before, and it caused him to generate the same number for his own and other institutions.

The search results often provided a new angle or twist to the overall investigation, which was considered desirable by the library client. For example, the research assistant was given an assignment to investigate and write a short piece on environmental regulation. She described her search this way:

Linda: Trying to build a story, you have to have the foundation and then the body and try to find an angle that makes sense and is interesting. As you go along you see where pieces are missing and fill those in until you feel that you are close enough ... I knew those fundamental questions and could find those answers easy enough. Interesting angles ... There were some unexpected twists of the regulation ... it had something to do with logging and Germany and sort of international trade friction based on these things.

Explaining change

Learning about a change in the environment can, of course, be seen as a version of encountering something interesting. But the situations in which the library clients did follow-up searches based on a perception of change had a different feel than the above examples of following an interesting new direction. The motivation for the follow-up searches was to solve a problem, rather than to track down an interesting new idea. Also, the data involved in change situations were much more likely to be quantitative, rather than qualitative, perhaps because changes in quantitative data are easier to detect. This does not imply, of course, that the needed explanations for the changes were quantitative in nature; the contrary was usually true.

The library clients who were in marketing or who consulted to marketing provided many of the examples in this category. The marketing engineer regularly followed revenue increases and decreases and searched for information that would help explain them. The statistician monitored certain variables related to product sales and performance, and had to find an explanation when she found that three variables she tracked had begun to correlate, instead of the two that had correlated in the past. In an example involving qualitative information, the planning staff member who did weekly searches on competitors found a reference to a new investor in the industry segment he followed, so he did a search to find out everything he could about this investor and the possible implications of his interest.

Finding missing pieces

Some of the triggers for further search and analysis were due to missing information. For example, a client was trying to find trends in the data returned by a search and discovered that certain numeric data were reported inconsistently over time. Usually there had been changes in the way the numbers were packaged. This explanation was typically found by a phone call to the information provider, rather than through an online search.

Search results sometimes stimulated new connections for the library client when they were combined with other information that was already known, leading to a need for more information to support deeper analysis. The management consultant encountered this when he related search results to his own client-provided information and his general knowledge of the industry involved: "When I fit this with what I already know, it begs a question."

Missing information also triggered further analysis or search when the library clients had clients of their own to whom search results or summaries and analyses were delivered. Sometimes these second-level clients asked for new perspectives on the information that had been delivered, perhaps a regrouping or a different slice through the data. Depending on the structure and granularity of the original information gathered by our library client, such a request might trigger new searches. Sometimes second-level clients asked for an analogous result on a related topic, such as another competitor company. This always required follow-up searches.

Stop conditions

The stop conditions for interconnected searches did not fall into clear, distinct categories in the same way that triggers did. Instead, we gathered some general impressions of the circumstances under which searches were wound down. People usually stopped searching when there were no more compelling triggers for further search or when they felt that they had done an appropriate amount of searching for the task. In a few cases, there was a specific inhibiting factor to further exploration (e.g., learning that a particular market was too small to be worth examining further).

Though our pool of informants had many different professions, they shared some common values and practices through their training and experience in business affairs. Their searches were usually prompted by decisions that had to be made by themselves or others. There was no expectation that a complete collection of relevant information to support a particular decision could be defined, much less retrieved. Alan, a planning staff member, related a lesson from business school:

Alan: And you know the rule of thumb that you can get 80% of the information fairly quickly and the last 10% will kill you. So the point that they were trying to tell was, is it really necessary to get that last 10% of information? ... And the overwhelming answer is, "no way".

Our library clients were very comfortable with making inferences; missing information is a fact of life in a world with closely-held business secrets. These clients were very satisfied with the work done by their librarians; they had faith that if not much was returned by a search, it was because not much was out there. Timeliness and brevity were strongly-held values, referred to again and again by our library clients, and these attributes were considered more important than trying to cover every angle. While it was important to achieve closure in the cumulative search results, this closure had a very pragmatic interpretation. For example, some searches stopped when the client was finally able to make sense out of numbers of interest. Others ended when a particularly evocative visualization emerged from an analysis of the latest data.

This characterization of a successful search interaction is strikingly different from the precision and recall measures that have often been used to measure a system's success in performing an information search. We found no such exactness in determining whether a match between an information need and a set of results had been achieved. Nor do task performance measures seem to apply easily in this domain; the problems are loosely-defined and often non-routine, and the outcomes have many contributing factors other than information search performance. Thus the clearest measure of system success seems to be client satisfaction with both the search process and the information delivery process.

Librarians with domain expertise

In two of the work settings of our informants, a restructuring of work had occurred that changed the nature of the interconnected search patterns experienced by clients in these settings. Librarians acquired domain expertise, either through formal training (at the management consulting firm) or experience (at the demographer's independent research organization). The librarians were then expected to do some or all of the first-level analysis of the search results and to produce an overview or other high-level output describing the search results.

The motivation for this approach was clearly given at the management consultant firm. The consultants had recognized the pattern of their interconnected searches, and they felt pressured by the time involved in communicating back and forth with the librarian to bring about the next step. Here is how the management consultant described the change in work responsibilities:

Bob: What we found happen is when they went to go through it they would go, "But there are two missing pieces here. Go back and dig deeper to find those." ... What we found is when we put the information specialist in the position of having to do that first level synthesis, that loop gets closed quicker. They also generate less raw material in the search, because they become more efficient searchers because they understand at least the first level intermediate product.

Professional searchers at this firm are given a short course in basic finance, and they are also expected to learn about particular industries and types of business analysis from the searches they do. When they get a search request, the basic goal of the search is explained. The librarians then do the search and analyze their results. They produce a package with an overview page, a set of slides and graphs with bulleted main points and views of quantitative data, and an annotated bibliography of the source material. As background for meeting preparation or an initial view of a topic, this may be enough. If a more complex synthesis is needed, a member of the management consulting staff does it based on these first-level results.

While this is considered a successful work methodology at the consulting firm, further improvements are being implemented on an area by area basis. When an information need comes up, an associate of the firm and an information specialist are teamed together to solve the need. This has begun to produce good results in the areas where it has been tried.

Bob: Because we don't think we can get the full set of business analytical skills and the full set of information search skills in the same person. We just don't think that that's realistic. But the thought is that if you create a team that has both sets of skills and the request goes to the team, not the individual, so there is not a sense of a hand-off from the information researcher to the analyst but they are in this together ... the sense of ownership is probably a critical thing that changes. Plus our sense is that there are two other things that will happen ... they will progressively disclose work in progress which will be shaped by feedback from the analyst who says, "This is helpful, this wasn't. More of this, less of that" in a much shorter interval. And the second thing is our guess that there will be a learning cycle that will take place and that the analyst will learn more about the mechanics of the search and be able to direct the search more precisely and the information specialist will learn more about the mechanics of analysis and begin to develop a better sense of what is useful and what's not ... We have learned some lessons about training, supervision, structure, etc. So, we are going to implement those and try it in [another work area].

Even when work was not restructured as dramatically as it was in the management consultant firm, some librarians and clients felt that their shared understanding improved the effectiveness of their interactions. Clients tended to latch on to a favorite librarian and return to her, even when any member of the library staff was capable of conducting a particular search. Trust was built; one client said that when he first started doing searches he sat at the librarian's elbow to watch her work and check her results, but later he just left a phone message outlining what he needed. Clients felt that their regular librarians understood their technical terms better than the librarians they used less frequently. In some cases, the librarian had developed a good understanding of the kind of work the client did (such as in the case of the process benchmarking specialist), and both the client and librarian felt that this helped to target the searches.

When librarians are involved in analysis, a higher-level information product is delivered to the client. This can affect the course of the progressive search path. In the case of planned searches, at least some steps of the plan will have already been carried out. There should be no obviously missing pieces from the result set; if there are, there is a quality problem with the information, according to the management consultant. Some unexpected angles will have been followed up, but others will not have been recognized, since these are often based on a thorough understanding of the problem or domain. The stop conditions will not change in their basic nature, but they will often be encountered sooner. The overall effect is to shorten the path to the goal.

Analysis techniques

We have described the different types of searches done by our library clients, the basic pattern of interconnected searches that most of them followed, and the triggers and stop conditions that led from one search step to the next. Now we will describe how clients went about assimilating and manipulating the data from a single result set in order to make progress in their tasks. As with triggers, we extracted the analysis examples from the transcripts and categorized them, but there was some ambiguity in attaching analyses to search scenarios and in determining which analyses were generic and which were specific. We did find a larger set of analysis examples and a larger number of analysis categories than we had found for triggers.

Initially, library clients read through the pile of material returned from the search. In most cases, they read paper copies, even when the material had been delivered electronically. A few clients scanned the information, but most said they read it cover to cover so as not to miss a valuable nugget. Most clients annotated the results while they read, to indicate what was interesting or questionable in the result set and to identify likely articles to be retrieved in full or topics to be targeted in follow-up searches.

In addition to reading and annotating, our library clients primarily did six types of analysis:

1. Looking for *trends* or *correlations*.
2. Making *comparisons* of different pieces of the data set.
3. Experimenting with different *aggregates* and/or *scaling*.
4. *Identifying a critical subset* of relevant or unique items.
5. *Making assessments*.
6. *Interpreting* data to find meaning in terms of domain or problem concepts.

Though what exactly counts as an analysis example is open to interpretation, roughly 80% of the approximately 80 analysis examples we found fell into one of these six categories. The remaining analysis techniques included cross-referencing, summarizing (a constructive technique related to several of those listed above), finding evocative visualizations, and a half-dozen others which were only encountered once each.

Trends are a very basic way of thinking about the business environment, and they provide fundamental support for decision-making. They offer a means of both tracking and predicting changes in the environment, a way of viewing the landscape of both qualitative and quantitative data. The need to find trends influenced both the data that were sought (numbers, time series) and the manipulations that resulted. Clients frequently put numeric data into spreadsheets, computed interesting numbers, and then generated a variety of graphs, tables, and other visualizations. As they looked through the visualizations, they tried to find patterns. Clients who did monitoring-type searches usually mapped trends over the long time periods of their searches. Forecasting was a common activity similar to finding trends.

Comparisons were also pervasive. A competitive environment leads to comparisons among companies, deals, processes, and more. The clients' descriptions of their high-level tasks often included comparisons. The data to be compared were often qualitative in nature, so creating the right table or graph was not enough. The data had to be summarized and salient points highlighted. The comparisons usually appeared in new artifacts created by the client, rather than in marked-up copies of the result set.

Aggregation and *scaling* were often done in conjunction with comparisons or trends. For example, a trend might only become apparent when certain industry segments were lumped together or scaled to a particular level of detail. Different buying behaviors might make sense only when customers were clustered by certain characteristics. Aggregation is a means of realizing abstractions, and we believe that along with comparison, this analysis technique is often used beyond the business domain. Again, the library clients experimented with aggregates in the artifacts they created using their search results, such as spreadsheets, graphs, and structured textual summaries.

Identifying a critical subset involved selecting from the result set those elements that met some domain criteria. Sometimes the subset simply represented a collection of interesting data points, as in the example of the sales/planning staff member choosing which paragraphs from his search results should go into the weekly newsletter he produced. Sometimes the subset became the starting point for a new search; for example, the merger and acquisition specialist chose from a set of material on potentially comparable mergers those mergers that were the *most* comparable, and then did further search and analysis on this smaller set. Sometimes a library client formed different subsets in an exploratory manner, to see which provided the most meaningful basis for a comparison operation.

Assessing was a common operation that required clients to dive into the data and use their domain knowledge to come up with meaningful conclusions. Some example questions that the library clients tried to answer as they analyzed their search results were: Is this market declining? Will this company be around in a few years? Is this product a match to this customer? What is contradictory in this information? People sometimes used domain-based analysis techniques such as financial ratio analysis to answer questions like these, but mostly they seemed to use their general experience to come up with reasonable judgements.

Interpreting is similar to making assessments, but it seems to be a more subjective type of analysis. As library clients interpreted their data, they assigned new meaning to raw in-

formation. For example, the merger and acquisition specialist looked at search results on previous deals to determine the "psychology" of the company in question: What were their problems and how did they usually go about solving them? While assessing and interpreting, library clients needed to take both broad and detailed looks at their search results.

DISCUSSION

We have described how each of the different types of searches conducted by our library clients tended to take place in separate search steps over a period of days, weeks, or months. What are the system design implications of this pattern?

The DIME retrieval mediator toolkit and runtime environment that we are building must take into account the context provided by interconnected searches. There are clear interconnections between successive mediator invocations, ad hoc queries, and requests to intermediaries. Mediators might be particularly useful for representing monitoring and planned searches, since these are repeated over time. However, even monitoring searches can lead to exploratory forays, and planned searches often require analysis operations before the next step in the plan can be undertaken. Thus a mediator must allow different kinds of intervention by the user rather than simply run from beginning to end without interruption.

DIME should provide assistance to users in finding and invoking related mediators when the relationship can be anticipated, as it can in the planned search cases. In a series of mediator invocations or ad hoc queries, we would expect to see some common information sources and common terminology used to express the boundaries of the problem area, so carrying these parameters over from one search to the next should be made easy for users. If query reformulation techniques ([6, 10]) could be extended beyond individual items and terms to include some of the surrounding context of the entire previous search, this would provide significant support to interconnected searching. This might be as simple as applying a filter with context-specific terms (e.g., industry segments or geographical areas) to a similarity-based retrieval set.

A record of an entire interconnected search thread, comprised of both requests and results, should be saved by the system in such a way that it can be deactivated (stored persistently) and activated as the search dies down and then picks up again. When a search thread is reactivated, the user should be able to browse and build on the requests, results, and planned steps of the search thus far. Many library clients had more than one search thread in progress at once, so each thread should have an independent existence. Such a record could also be used as a template to create a new mediator or set of mediators, if the search pattern should turn out to be one that recurs over time.

There are also clear interconnections within the picture that grows from successive search results. The search context and the direction of the search are closely tied to the particular triggers a user finds for further analysis and search. One way of linking search results together would be to allow users to annotate a result set with notes indicating triggers, patterns, and conclusions that are suggested by the data. This would offer the user a kind of interactive search-planning tool, which might evolve into an overview description of the search results. Similarly, as new descriptive artifacts are created using the search results as raw material, coarse-grained links back to the raw material could provide either a bibliography or a form of rationale. For example, an outlining tool with the ability to link back to segments of the search results would be useful.

The analysis techniques used by the library clients could not be automated; their use was based on the clients' understanding of the domain and the applicability of the information to the problem at hand. In some cases, analyses depended on application tools such as spreadsheets and graphics packages. However, we believe that certain generic operations to manipulate information would be useful to customers of intermediaries and mediators. The ability to perform these generic operations on application data such as spreadsheets would be valuable, but the operations should at least work on the raw search results.

To support aggregation and comparisons, users should be able to extract information chunks, label them, move them around, and create arbitrary groupings out of of them. Careful juxtaposition of information is often needed to allow side-by-side examination, expose relationships, and prepare for deeper looks at the data. As with the annotation capability suggested above, these editing operations might also help the user create descriptive artifacts along the way. The processes of identifying a critical subset, making an assessment, and making an evaluation are not well understood by ourselves or others, and more research is needed into the processes themselves before we can predict the kind of interfaces that would best support them. However, the ability to manipulate chunks of information, as suggested above, would probably make the extraction of a subset easier. The ability to create different overlays of thematically-linked user annotations would support all three of these processes.

Though there are many search situations in which automated support for querying is practical and appropriate, we do not mean to suggest that expert librarians or other intermediaries can be replaced. Retrieval mediators can be seen as an extreme example of automated support; the user does not express a query at all, but instead invokes a mediator with suitable parameters. We believe that this is a promising direction in information access research, and in this study we saw examples of searches for which mediators could be created. But mediators are only suitable for repeated queries with a predictable pattern and manageable scope. They would not make sense for unusual queries or browsing situations, for instance.

For the situations in which librarians are the best solution, our findings suggest an alternative working style for clients and librarians that involves a closer partnership than the traditional service-oriented model. With shared goals and frequent communication, partners in some settings can accomplish search tasks faster and more effectively than when each has a completely separate role. The success of this approach depends on the librarian acquiring some domain expertise, which is easier in domains such as business than in highly technical areas. But even in technical domains, librarians have shown an aptitude for picking up terminology, research themes, names of

relevant companies and individuals, and the like. We suggest that developing partnerships that use the strengths of both the user (deep domain expertise) and the librarian (deep search expertise) makes sense as a complementary approach to the current trend of empowering end users to conduct their own information searches. These partnerships would benefit from certain collaboration technologies, such as sharable document annotations and remote communication support.

In summary, we have seen that information searches have structure and continuity, even when they are very exploratory in nature. As designers of search systems, we must consider how a user's interaction with the system can be guided by this structure, without losing the flexibility to perform expert analyses of search results and to follow interesting new search directions.

ACKNOWLEDGEMENTS

We are grateful to the library clients and librarians who spent time with us describing their jobs and their library searches. We also thank Lucy Berlin, Bonnie Nardi, and Andreas Paepcke for useful comments on earlier drafts of this paper.

References

[1] Bates, M., The design of browsing and berrypicking techniques for the online search interface. *Online Review 13(5)* (1989).

[2] Belkin, N., ASK for information retrieval: Part 1. Background and theory. *Journal of Documentation 38(2)* (1982).

[3] Belkin, N., ASK for information retrieval: Part 2. Results of a design study. *Journal of Documentation 38(3)* (1982).

[4] Dervin, B. and Nilan, M., Information needs and uses. In: Williams, M., ed. *Annual Review of Information Science and Technology: Volume 21.* (Knowledge Industry Publications, Inc., 1986).

[5] Ellis, D., A behavioural approach to information retrieval system design. *Journal of Documentation 45(3)* (1989).

[6] Fischer, G. and Nieper-Lemke, H., HELGON: Extending the retrieval by reformulation paradigm. *Proceedings CHI '89* (Austin, 30 April-4 May, 1989).

[7] Hewins, E., Information need and use studies. In: Williams, M., ed. *Annual Review of Information Science and Technology: Volume 25.* (Elsevier Science Publishers, 1990).

[8] Paepcke, A., An object-oriented view onto public, heterogeneous text databases. *Hewlett-Packard Laboratories Technical Report HPL-92-84* (1992).

[9] Wiederhold, G., Mediators in the architecture of future information systems. *IEEE Computer* (March 1992).

[10] Williams, M., What makes RABBIT run? *International Journal of Man-Machine Studies 21* (1984).

Using Icons to Find Documents:
Simplicity Is Critical

Michael D. Byrne

School of Psychology and
Graphics, Visualization, and Usability Center
Georgia Institute of Technology
Atlanta, GA 30332-0170
byrne@cc.gatech.edu

ABSTRACT

A common task at almost any computer interface is that of searching for documents, which GUIs typically represent with icons. Oddly, little research has been done on the processes underlying icon search. This paper outlines the factors involved in icon search and proposes a model of the process. An experiment was conducted which suggests that the proposed model is sound, and that the most important factor in searching for files is the type of icons used. In general, simple icons (those discriminable based on a few features) seem to help users, while complex icons are no better than simple rectangles.

KEYWORDS: screen design: icons, empirical evaluation, formal models of the user

INTRODUCTION

Despite the prevalence of icons in graphical user interfaces (GUIs), the basic processes underlying the interaction of humans and icons are not well understood. Icons are used in a wide variety of ways in GUIs, one of the more common of which is the representation of objects recognized by the operating system, such as files and directories. Searching for documents which are represented by icons will henceforth be referred to as "icon search." Presumably, icons are used because it is believed that they make it easier to locate such items.

Unfortunately, there is little empirical data that either supports or refutes this claim. By and large, the assumption that has

driven the use of icons in the GUI is that icons seem to work better than having to recall and type file names, as is typical with a command-line interface. While this is likely to be the case, it not an adequate description of what processes the user may actually bring to bear, nor does it provide clear guidelines for the use of icons.

This research attempts to address many of the questions surrounding icon search.

TASK ANALYSIS

Icon search is a complex task involving a number of factors. Several factors have been identified, which are divided into three classes: general factors, visual search factors, and semantic search factors.

General factors

Mixed search. Icon search involves two kinds of search which may or may not be related to each other. This is because icons (or, at least, document icons) have two parts: the icon picture and a label, in this case a file name. Thus, search is both over the icon pictures (referred to as "visual search") and over the strings attached to the icons, termed "semantic search."

Task mapping. Icon search is a "variably-mapped" [10, 11] task; that is, targets and distractors switch roles between trials (the same file might be the target on one occasion and a distractor on another). Thus, icon search should be a relatively slow, controlled process that improves only minimally with practice [10, 11].

Target knowledge. Not only is there variable mapping between the target and the distractors, but knowledge about the target may be incomplete. Often, people do not know either the exact name of the file or what icon it will have before they begin to search for it.

Multiple matches and semantic necessity. Often in a search, the target document will share its icon picture with other documents present on the display. This makes it necessary to read the label attached to the document most or all of the time in order to compensate for the fact that the icon picture alone is ambiguous in that it may or may not represent the target document.

Motor task. In realistic measurement of icon search, there will also be a motor component—that of mouse movement to the target. This should be affected primarily by physical properties of the system, such as icon size (often a function of screen resolution), the distance to be moved, and the characteristics of the input device.

Visual factors

Size. Generally, all of the icons on a display are the same size. So while size may be a useful way to discriminate between icons, it is typically not employed in current displays.

Color. This is an interesting dimension, because many GUI displays do not support color. Thus, even if using color as a discriminating feature is effective, reliance on color differences may not be appropriate for icon designers.

Form. This is the primary dimension on which icons vary and includes a number of sub-dimensions, such as the level of detail in the form and the meaningfulness of the form.

Spatial organization. Some interfaces impose a grid-like organization on icons, others a "staggered grid" organization, and still others no organization at all—icons can be anywhere. This may or may not have an effect on search.

Number of objects. Both the size of the search set and the number of icons with pictures matching the target can vary widely from trial to trial. Probably the best-studied factor in visual search is that of set size, while the effect of multiple visual matches has been relatively ignored.

Semantic factors

Words/non-words/near-words. Since the labels on icons can typically be assigned almost any string up to a certain size, the labels may be made up of actual words, things that are not words at all (numbers, dates, etc.), and near-words (such as abbreviations). A given display may contain a mixture of all of these things.

Sorting. Often, the user has the option of sorting the display based on some features of the labels, the most common example being alphabetical sorting. Other forms of sorting are possible and available on some systems, such as sorting by time of modification or document type, which are also semantic variables.

While this description may not be entirely complete, it gives an indication of the number of issues that must be explored before one can fully understand what appears to be a fairly simple operation of pointing and clicking. Designing the "best" icons and icon-based GUI file system interface will require knowledge about all of these factors, and likely many of their interactions.

MECHANISMS
Research on Icons

By and large, the preceding factors have not been systematically investigated. Jones and Dumais [8] have done research demonstrating that it is difficult for people to find documents based on "spatial filing." In the spatial filing task studied, subjects were given documents to file according to whatever spatial scheme they wanted, and then later asked to retrieve the documents. Performance was generally poor, and clearly inferior to simple alphabetic filing. This begins to suggest that semantic information (names) are more important than visual information, but the support for this conclusion is not strong.

Byrne [2] suggests that pictures on icons do have an effect on people's ability to find documents: they slow people down. In this study, it was found that for a set size of twelve, simple empty rectangles work as well or better than icons with pictures. This work, however, was not very comprehensive and its claims are based on a relatively small sample with few trials. More critically, only one set size was examined, making it difficult to get a clear understanding of the processes involved.

Other work on icons (e.g. [1, 4, 6]) has addressed issues relating to the form of icons such as subjective user preference [6] and meaningfulness [1, 4], but generally says little about how that form will affect performance in a task such as icon search.

A Model of Mixed Search

Since the literature has largely not covered the icon search question, one approach is to develop a model of the process. There is some evidence (the verbal reports of subjects in [2], see also [4, 5]) that mixed search is actually a two-stage process: the user uses a visual search to narrow down the semantic search. For example, the user first finds all the icons on the display with pictures that match the application he or she was using and then reads the names only on those icons. Then, search time should be $f_m(n) = f_v(n) + f_s(t)$, where $f_m(n)$ is the total time for the mixed search. This is the simple sum of $f_v(n)$, the visual search time as a function of set size, and $f_s(t)$, the semantic search time as a function of the average number of icons with pictures matching the target icon (t).

A reasonable assumption to make about the semantic search is that it is a standard self-terminating serial search. Since there is no visual guidance for the search, one can reasonably expect that the user will read each file name and decide if it matches the target. If that is the case, search time should be a function of the average number of items necessary to search, which is n/2. That is, $f_s(n)$ for set size n, should be a linear function of the form $f_s(n) = m_s*(n/2) + b_s$. Additionally, if the user knows the exact file name, the decision process should be faster, and therefore the slope m_s shallower.

Times for $f_m(n)$ can be empirically estimated, and then it should be possible to estimate $f_v(n)$ by simply subtracting $f_s(t)$. Since t will be at most n (and usually less), the effectiveness of using the visual search is dependent on the nature of $f_v(n)$. If $f_v(n)$ is a linear function ($m_v n + b_v$) and its slope is large, then $f_m(n)$ can be expected to be a linear function such that $f_m(n) > f_s(n)$; that is, mixed search would always be slower than semantic search for any n. However, if $f_v(n)$ has a shallow or even zero slope, $f_m(n)$ should be more efficient than $f_s(n)$.

The visual characteristics of the icon pictures should determine $f_v(n)$ [3, 6, 12, 13]. If it is possible to discriminate icons based on one simple feature, it should be possible to conduct the visual search in parallel [12], and thus m_v should be close to zero. However, restriction to a single feature would severely limit the number of different icons possible, and most icons currently found in GUIs contain numerous features.

If it is possible to distinguish icons on the basis of a few features or a simple conjunction of features, m_v should be relatively shallow [6], perhaps even near zero [3, 13]. In this case, icons would act as a legitimate aid in searching for files. However, if icons largely contain all the same features or the same combinations of features, m_v should be steep [6, 3/13] and probably no advantage over m_s.

Empirical Investigation

The experiment described in the remainder of this paper was intended to do two things: estimate the effects of several of the factors described in the task analysis and evaluate the mixed search model. Since the model predicts that set size should have an effect on the speed of icon search regardless of the type of search conducted, set size was an important variable in the study. Since the mixed search model includes a semantic search over the set of icons with pictures that match the picture on the target icon (the "match set," which includes the target icon) was also an important variable, primarily used in the estimation of the visual search function.

Since the nature of the visual search function should itself be a function of the visual characteristics of the icon pictures, this was also varied. Color and size were not varied, since color is not possible on all displays and size is typically constant. What was varied was the complexity of the visual form of the icons, using three types of icons (see Figure 1).

Another factor that is likely to vary widely in a naturalistic setting is the knowledge that the user has about the target before the search. There are two important classes of knowledge: file name knowledge and picture knowledge. Users may know the exact name of the file and they may not. Picture knowledge varies similarly; users may not know the

picture they are searching for, they may have a guess as to the picture, or they may know exactly what picture they seek.

Since it is not realistically possible to vary the task mapping, semantic necessity, or the motor task, these factors were not investigated. Other factors were generally held constant: the same spatial organization (grid-aligned) was used, all file names were common English words of two or more syllables from 6-13 characters in length, and there was no systematic sorting of any kind.

Figure 1. Icon types (actual size)

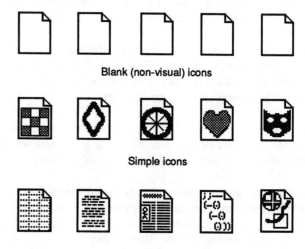

Blank (non-visual) icons

Simple icons

Complex icons

METHOD
Subjects
The subjects were 45 undergraduates from the Georgia Institute of Technology who were participating for extra credit in a psychology course. Subjects in this population are typically familiar and comfortable with computers, though actual amount of experience with GUIs varied from "almost none" to "very extensive."

Apparatus/Materials
All instructions and stimuli were presented to subjects on an Apple Macintosh IIfx personal computer running Claris HyperCard version 2.1.

Design
The design of this experiment is relatively complex. There were five factors evaluated, one of which was between subjects and the rest within. The between-subjects factor was icon type, and subjects were randomly assigned to one of three levels. The three levels correspond to the levels used in the 1991 Byrne study [2]: blank (non-visual), simple, and complex. (See Figure 1.)

The second factor, a within-subjects factor, was set size. Four set sizes were used: 6, 12, 18 , and 24. The size of the match set was also varied, which was a factor termed match level. The match level (1, 2, or 3) had a different meaning in each set size. With a set size of 6, the size of the match set was 1, 2, or 3, corresponding to the match levels of 1, 2, and 3. With a set size of 12, the match levels 1, 2, and 3 corresponded to 1, 4, and 6 matching pictures. Set sizes of 18 and 24 yielded match sets of 1, 6, 9 and 1, 6, 12, respectively. Note that in each set size, a match level of 1 corresponded to a unique (to that display) target icon.

The remaining factors, also within-subjects, were the amount of knowledge the subject had about the target before the search, both picture knowledge and file name knowledge. There were three levels of icon knowledge provided. The first level, "none," meant that no special information was provided to help the subject infer the target icon before the trial. The second level, "some," meant the subject was provided with the name of the application used to create the target document, which subjects could then use to infer the correct icon. The third level, "icon," meant that the subject was explicitly given the icon to be found.

The file name knowledge factor was varied with two levels: "yes," meaning the subject was explicitly given the name of the target, and "no," meaning the name of the target could have been any word found in the document description.

Thus, a fully-crossed design yielded 72 cells (4 x 3 x 3 x 2) for each subject, and a total of 216 cells overall. Each subject performed one trial in each cell. The factors were not counterbalanced but were randomly selected from a list prior to each trial to control for systematic interaction with practice and/or subjects' anticipation of what kind of trial would come next.

There were 15 subjects used per icon type (45 subjects total) for a grand total of 3240 observations.

Procedures and Stimuli

Subjects first received initial instructions about how to perform the task, and were given a preview of the icons that would be used in the experiment. Subjects were given three practice trials and then 72 experimental trials.

Each trial consisted of three stages: an encoding stage, a decay stage, and a search stage. In the first stage (the encoding stage), subjects were shown a screen containing a portion of the target document, a brief description of that document (which always contained the target file name), and possibly some "hints," depending on the trial. "Hints" consisted of the target icon or explicit indication of the file name, according to the manipulations described above.

The next stage (the decay stage) consisted of a blank screen with a dialog box into which the subject was instructed to type a string of 15 random lowercase characters. If the string was typed incorrectly, the subject was given a new string to type. This continued until the subject typed in a full string correctly. This was included to prevent rehearsal and avoid floor effects, which were observed in a pilot study conducted as part of [2].

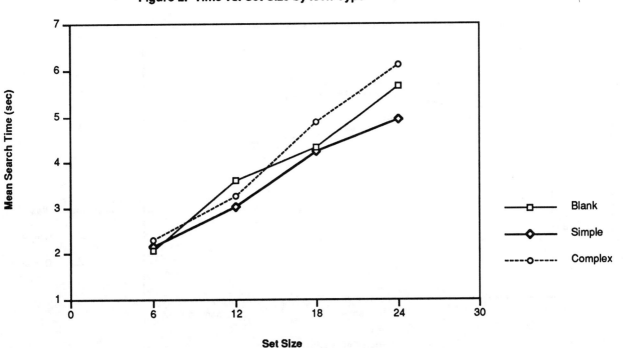

Figure 2. Time vs. Set Size by Icon Type

The final stage (the search stage) consisted of a screen resembling the Macintosh Finder. However, the main window in which the subject searched was initially blank. When he subject clicked on a button labeled "Ready," the icon display appeared and the subject attempted to click on the correct icon as quickly as possible.

The location of the target icon was randomly selected for each trial, as were the names on all the distractors. Distractor names were randomly selected without replacement from a list of 525 names until the list was exhausted, and then the list was recycled for the second half of the experiment.

RESULTS

Overall, the grand mean of the data was 4.36 seconds with a standard deviation of 6.61 seconds. Trials outside of three standard deviations from the grand mean were considered outliers and were discarded for the computation of means and regressions, but replaced by the grand mean for the ANOVA analysis (this is necessary to maintain a balanced design). 36 of the 3240 trials were outliers, which is 1.1% of the data.

Effects Involving Icon Type

While there was no overall effect for icon type, it was involved in several interesting interactions. The icon type by set size interaction was significant, $F(6, 126) = 3.13$, $p = .007$; Figure 2 presents a graph of the means. The divergence of the means between groups at large set sizes suggests that different processes are operating according to what type of icon pictures are used.

Icon type also interacted with picture knowledge, $F(4,84) = 3.51$, $p = .011$; Figure 3 shows the means. Icon knowledge affected the three types of icons differently, with simple icons apparently benefiting the most. Apparently, subjects were only able to make use of icon knowledge when the icons were simple.

Icon type interacted with file name knowledge, $F(2,42) = 4.34$, $p = .019$ (see Table 1 for means). In this case, knowledge of the file name had an effect in all three conditions, and clearly the greatest effect in the blank icon condition. However, the detrimental effect of not receiving the file name was less in the simple icon condition than it was in the complex icon condition, again suggesting that a different process is operating when searching through simple icons.

Table 1. Icon Type by File Name Knowledge means (in seconds)

	Received Filename	
Icon Type	yes	no
Blank	3.36	4.44
Simple	3.40	3.72
Complex	3.78	4.49

Figure 3. Time vs. Picture Knowledge by Icon Type

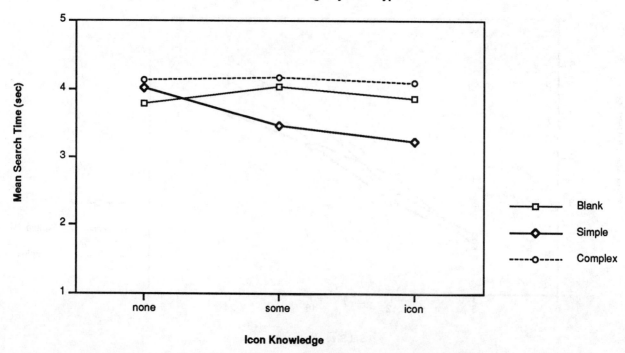

Finally, icon type interacted with match level, $F(4,84) = 8.21$, $p < .001$. Since match level only makes sense for the simple and complex conditions (all icons appear identical in the blank condition), the overall mean for the blank icon condition is presented for comparison in Table 2. This is one of the more interesting effects. If the target icon is unique to the display in the simple icon condition, the advantage of that condition over the others is substantial. However, if the display consists of half targets, this advantage is substantially reduced or even eliminated.

Table 2. Icon Type by Match Level means (in seconds)

	Match Level		
Icon Type	1	2	3
Blank	3.89	3.89	3.89
Simple	3.06	3.46	4.20
Complex	3.87	4.08	4.45

Other results

Besides results involving icon type, there were several other effects of interest. First, a practice effect was observed $F(1,3202) = 5.02$, $p = .025$—subjects got slightly faster over time. However, while this effect is statistically reliable, it is of little practical significance. This regression accounts for less than 0.2% of the variance ($R^2 = .0016$), and has a very shallow slope (a .0057 second improvement per trial).

There was also an effect for the particular icon being searched for. Obviously, with the blank icons, there was no such effect—the means are included merely for comparison. However, there was an effect for the particular icons within the simple icons, $F(4,1062) = 2.96$, $p = .019$, and within the complex icons, $F(4,1062) = 3.51$, $p = .007$. Table 3 presents the means. Not surprisingly, the complex icon that was the most successful was the one that could likely be found on the basis of a single feature (curvature, for example). The "best" icon in the simple group is the only icon with repeating horizontal lines, another unique feature.

Finally, regression analyses were conducted to test the visual search model, $f_m(n) = f_v(n) + f_s(t)$. Due to the fact that there were interactions involving icon type, set size, icon knowledge and file name knowledge, only a portion of the data was used to ensure consistency of process for all comparisons. In the real-world task, there are typically a fixed number of icons available, so a user is most likely to know what the icon is. File names are more variable, so it is assumed that the file name is not exactly known. That is, data in the "icon" condition of icon knowledge and the "no" condition of file name knowledge was selected for regression analysis.

For the blank icons, the linear regression of time on set size was reliable, $F(1,527) = 163.0$, $p < .0001$, and accounted for nearly a quarter of the variability ($R^2 = .24$), which is quite good for non-aggregated data. (If the data is collapsed for each subject, the R^2 rises to near .70.) The regression yields the equation $f_s(n) = .930sec + .235sec*n$. The number of matching icons in each trial (t) was then plugged in to the preceding equation and subtracted from the total time, which is $f_m(n)$, yielding an estimate of $f_v(n)$. Mean $f_v(n)$'s for each set size are presented in Figure 4. Clearly, the $f_v(n)$ for complex icons increases much more with increases in set size than does the $f_v(n)$ for simple icons. In fact, $f_v(n)$ for simple icons seems to follow the predictions made by the model of Cave and Wolfe [3, 13]: an initial increase at small set sizes which flattens out as set size grows.

Table 3. Means for specific icons (in seconds)

	Icon				
Icon Type	1	2	3	4	5
Blank	3.89	3.89	3.89	3.89	3.89
Simple	3.08	3.34	3.65	3.88	3.88
Complex	3.52	4.09	4.14	4.36	4.59

The estimate of visual search time was regressed on set size for each type of icon. Due to the large number of data points and excellent power, accounting for even small amounts of variance yields statistical reliability. The best comparison, then, is in the amount of variability accounted for by the linear effect. For the simple icons, the regression was, of course, reliable, $F(1,176) = 10.0$, $p = .0018$. However, this accounted for only about 5% of the variability ($R^2 = .05$). For complex icons, the regression is again reliable, $F(1,176) = 52.5$, $p < .0001$. In this case, the proportion of variance accounted for is much greater—almost five times as great, in fact ($R^2 = .23$). This suggests that a linearly increasing model is much more appropriate for the visual search with complex icons than for simple icons, which means that simple icons should hold an advantage, particularly at larger set sizes.

Figure 4. Visual Search Time vs. Set Size by Icon Type

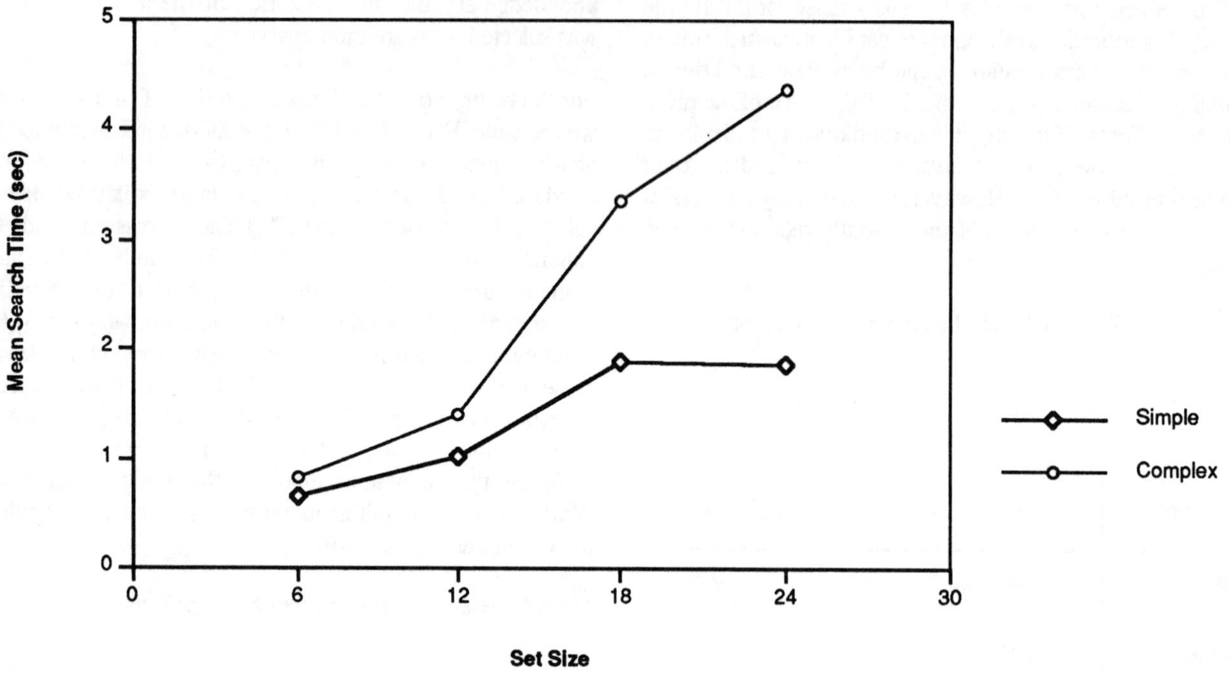

DISCUSSION

Clearly, one of the most important factors in icon search is the type of icon used. Simple icons clearly outperform blank and complex icons, especially with larger set sizes. There is support for the two-pass model, and the slope for the visual search component with simple icons is much flatter than the slope for the purely semantic search or for the visual search with complex icons. The lesson: for icons to be effective aids to visual search, they must be simple and easily discriminable. Simple icons are more effective with larger set sizes, allow effective use of icon knowledge, are less affected by a lack of file name knowledge, and are especially effective when they are unique to the display. With simple icons, there is reason to accept the design assumption that icon pictures make finding files easier.

Complex icons are consistently worse than even blank icons. They seem to clutter the display with information that users are unable to employ to their advantage. Thus, if the icons are complex and difficult to discriminate quickly, the assumption that icon pictures are useful in this task clearly does not hold.

Though the experiment was done in monochrome, one could easily extrapolate the basic guideline to color as well: use only a few, easily discriminable colors. Simply because many computer displays now support some 16 million colors should not be taken as a mandate to use more than a few.

Perhaps counter-intuitively, practice does not seem to help users find documents more quickly. This is one area where it seems that the novice/expert distinction is not meaningful. It does not seem possible to compensate for poor icon design simply with practice.

This research does not address several important issues, such as semantic sorting (e.g. alphabetically by name) or spatial organization (aligned to a grid vs. scattered placement). These factors may play a significant role in finding documents with icons. It is interesting to note that many experienced Macintosh users, for instance, choose to view their files not by icon, but as a list of names sorted by date or alphabetically by file name.

This research also does not address the use of icons in tasks other than visual search. It may be the case that complex icons can usefully serve other functions in which the speed of visual search is not particularly important or in which there are few icons on the display.

ACKNOWLEDGEMENTS

I would like to thank David Cater for his help in running subjects and generating experimental materials. I would also like to thank Susan Bovair and Neff Walker for their comments on earlier drafts of this paper. This research was supported primarily by a graduate fellowship to the author from the National Science Foundation.

REFERENCES

1. Baecker, R., Small, I., & Mander, R. (1991). Bringing icons to life. *Proceedings of CHI'91*, 1-6.

2. Byrne, M. D. (1991). The misunderstood picture: A study of icon recognition. Poster presented at CHI'91.

3. Cave, K. R., & Wolfe, J. M. (1990). Modeling the role of parallel processing in visual search. *Cognitive Psychology, 22*, 225-271.

4. Fisher, D., Coury, B. G., Tengs, T. O., & Duffy, S. A. (1989). Minimizing the time to search visual displays: The role of highlighting. *Human Factors, 31(2)*, 167-182.

5. Fisher, D., & Tan, K. C. (1989). Visual displays: The highlighting paradox. *Human Factors, 31(1)*, 17-30.

6. Fisher, D. L., & Tanner, N. S. (1992). Optimal symbol set selection: A semiautomated procedure. *Human Factors, 34(1)*, 79-95.

7. Hemmenway, K. (1981). Psychological issues in the use of icons in command menus. In *Proceedings of CHI'81*, 20-23.

8. Jones, W. P., and Dumais, S. T. (1986). The spatial metaphor for user interfaces: Experimental tests of reference by location versus name. *ACM Transactions on Office Information Systems, Vol. 4, No. 1*, 42-63.

9. Nolan, P. R. (1989). Designing screen icons: Ranking and matching studies. In *Proceeding of the Human Factors Society 33rd Annual Meeting* (pp. 380-384). Santa Monica, CA: The Human Factors Society.

10. Schneider, W., & Shiffrin, R. M. (1977). Controlled and automatic human information processing: I. Detection, search and attention. *Psychological Review, 84*, 1-66.

11. Shiffrin, R. M., & Schneider, W. (1977). Controlled and automatic human information processing: II. Detection, search, and attention. *Psychological Review, 84*, 127-190.

12. Triesman, A. M., & Gelade, G. (1980). A feature-integration theory of attention. *Cognitive Psychology, 12*, 107-141.

13. Wolfe, J. M., Cave, K. R., & Franzel, S. L. (1989). Guided search: An alternative to the feature integration model for visual search. *Journal of Experimental Psychology: Human Perception and Performance, 15*, 419-433.

Queries-R-Links: Graphical Markup for Text Navigation

Gene Golovchinsky and Mark Chignell

Department of Industrial Engineering
University of Toronto
416-978-8951, mark@vered.rose.utoronto.ca

ABSTRACT

In this paper we introduce a style of interaction (interactive querying) that combines features of hypertext with Boolean querying, using direct markup of text to launch queries. We describe two experiments that compare the relative ease of expressing Boolean queries as text versus a graphical equivalent. The results of these experiments show that the expression of queries in the graphical format is no more difficult than the textual equivalent. We then describe the Queries-R-Links system that we have developed at the University of Toronto. Queries-R-Links uses the graphical markup method to launch Boolean queries interactively using direct markup of text. This work represents significant progress towards information exploration systems that combine the useful features of information retrieval querying and hypertext browsing.

KEYWORDS: Querying; Text Retrieval; Navigation; Hypertext, Pen-Based Interaction

INTRODUCTION

Hypertext and Boolean querying represent alternative styles of navigation in large collections of text. Information exploration is a pervasive activity that subsumes both hypertext and information retrieval [18]. Alternative styles of information exploration appear to be merging as they are integrated into more flexible information exploration systems, by adding querying features to hypertext [14], [4] and by the use of browsing within information retrieval systems [15].

The distinction between information retrieval systems and hypertexts is blurred further when we consider methods for launching queries from within text. With these methods, the words within the text serve as "surrogate anchors" that can be linked together to form queries. However, these surrogate anchors differ somewhat from the embedded menus [9] of hypertext since they are not highlighted. Another difference is that the selected words may be combined into more complex queries using AND and OR

operators. The resulting interactive queries combine features of browsing and Boolean querying.

Interactive querying allows users to launch queries from within text using graphical markup. It avoids the high cost of existing methods of creating large hypertexts, while adding the richer semantics of Boolean expression to the task of traversing links. It should be noted that interactive querying is a style of interaction that can be implemented for any text retrieval system that allows Boolean queries to be launched while text is being viewed. Since interactive querying starts from a particular point in the text, it assumes that the user or information seeker has already found an entry point into the database through other means.

In this paper we describe two experiments that assess the effectiveness of the graphical markup version of Boolean expressions that is used in interactive querying. We also describe the Queries-R-Links system for interactive querying that we have developed.

QUERYING AND TEXT RETRIEVAL

Boolean querying and hypertext represent two contrasting approaches to text browsing and retrieval. Boolean retrieval systems are relatively easy to implement, but they can be difficult to use (e.g., [1]). Hypertexts are generally easier to use (requiring users to choose among available links rather than construct a query), but they are more difficult to implement.

The creation of hypertext documents involves an authoring process that includes the selection of texts and the partitioning of these texts into self contained chunks, or nodes. These nodes are then linked, forming a hypertext document. Manual authoring of hypertext can be time consuming and prone to errors. Methods for automating the creation of hypertext from text have been developed (e.g., [3], [5], [6]), but the usability of the resulting hypertext documents remains open to question. For instance, [12] obtained mixed results in experiments that compared the usability of automatically created and manually authored hypertexts. Other usability problems such as disorientation can be experienced in large hypertext documents, whether created automatically or manually (e.g., [11]).

Usability problems have also been encountered in querying systems. Boolean queries provide a great deal of power, flexibility and context independence at the cost of a variety of usability problems. Boolean queries are difficult to formulate (e.g., [1]) for a number of reasons. These reasons range from the ambiguity of AND and OR operators, to difficulties with NOT, problems with nesting and parentheses, and operator precedence [17]. When expressed textually, Boolean syntax uses the English words AND and OR to represent set union and intersection. This syntax implicitly borrows the English meanings of these words. These meanings are sometimes ambiguous and can be misinterpreted in Boolean expressions. For example, in English the word "and" can correspond either to the Boolean AND operator or to the OR operator. The word "or" in turn, can signify both inclusive and exclusive OR operators. Thus there are difficulties in using both Boolean queries and hypertext. Graphical expression of Boolean queries (e.g., [10]) may offer some advantages over textual queries. The research reported here developed a method of interactive and graphical querying that combined some of the features of Boolean querying and hypertext.

TEXTUAL VS. GRAPHICAL QUERYING

A critical issue in developing a markup based query system is whether or not people are able to express queries graphically. Two experiments were carried out that compared how well people could express Boolean queries as text strings versus graphical queries. Twenty-nine third year University of Toronto industrial engineering students participated in the first experiment. The subjects were asked to convert queries into either textual or graphical form using a questionnaire booklet.

Figure 1 shows an example of a graphical query. The query was composed by drawing bubbles around the terms and connecting ANDed terms with lines. The OR operator was represented by the absence of a line between terms. All of the subjects constructed 32 graphical queries and 32 textual queries. About half the subjects completed the textual exercises first and the rest solved the graphical problems first. After completing the first set, the subjects read the instructions to the second problem set and proceeded to solve 32 more problems. The time to complete each block of 32 problems was also recorded.

Figure 1. Example of a graphical query representing the expression poetry and Milton or poetry and Shakespeare.

The answer to each question was graded in terms of whether or not the syntax (i.e., exact format) or semantics (the idea) were correct. Each category was scored either yes or no. If the subject made small syntactic errors but captured the proper relationship among the keywords, the question was scored no on syntax and yes on semantics.

Experiment 1

There was extremely high variability in subject performance in the experiment (with syntax scores ranging between 0 and 24 out of 32, with the corresponding range for semantics scores being between 10 and 30). Thus a contingency table analysis was used to pool the data across all subjects. Using the semantic measure as the dependent variable, there was a tendency for subjects to perform better when using the graphical notation ($\chi^2(1)=2.967$, $p<0.10$) with 621 of the graphic responses being scored as correct versus 587 of the text responses. There was also a small but statistically reliable difference between the textual and graphical conditions among the syntax scores. Subjects reproduced the graphical syntax more accurately (427 syntactically correct responses versus 385 for textual) than the textual version ($\chi^2(1)=4.113$, $p<0.05$). Thus subjects answered about one more question (out of 32) per subject correctly in the graphical condition for both the syntactic and semantic measures.

The average time for forming the 32 text queries was 15.5 minutes vs. 16.2 minutes for graphics queries. However, this effect (as tested by analysis of variance) was not statistically significant. 19 out of 27 subjects who had an opinion preferred the graphic style. There was no relation between preference and performance. There was no evidence of learning (no order effect) in this experiment, which was not surprising since there was no feedback given.

The results suggest that graphical queries are easier to express. Since the observed effect was relatively small, we replicated the experiment with a second group of subjects. The first group of subjects were industrial engineering students who had been taught about data flow diagrams that resembled the graphical form of the queries. Thus, we were concerned that our results may not generalize to people without data modeling experience. A large number of semantic errors in the graphical condition could be attributed to subjects' attempts to construct a data flow model rather than a Boolean query in solving the exercises.

Table 1. Contingency table for semantics vs. presentation style for Experiment 2.

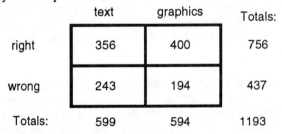

	text	graphics	Totals:
right	356	400	756
wrong	243	194	437
Totals:	599	594	1193

Experiment 2

In the second experiment we recruited 20 participants with relatively low computer experience and little if any data modeling background (as indicated in responses to a questionnaire administered at the beginning of the experimental session). The experimental procedure was similar to the first experiment with the following exceptions. Two questions were deleted because they were poorly worded, leaving 30 questions per condition. Minor wording changes were made to the instructions to clear up some confusions that had occurred in the first experiment (as reported by the subjects).

Table 2. Contingency table for syntax vs. presentation style for Experiment 2

	text	graphics	Totals:
right	200	273	473
wrong	399	321	720
Totals:	599	594	1193

There was a significant difference ($\chi^2(1) = 8.034$, p<0.005) in the semantic measure between conditions. Both conditions produced more right than wrong answers, using the semantic measure. Performance in the textual condition was poorer because subjects tended to translate the words in the question (and, or) to the query verbatim. While in some cases this was the proper answer, in other cases the opposite operator was appropriate. Table 1 shows the contingency table for the semantics data. It can be seen that the ratio of right to wrong answers was considerably higher in the graphical query condition.

There was a strongly significant difference ($\chi^2(1)=19.696$, p<0.0001) between the two conditions on the syntax measure. As shown in Table 2, subjects scored less than half right in both categories, but they did significantly better in the graphics condition.

Discussion

In our experiments we tested a total of forty-nine subjects. In both samples, an advantage was found for the graphical queries, using contingency table analysis. Thus the advantage of graphical queries cannot be attributed to the diagramming and programming experience that the participants in the first experiment had. This suggests that the task of graphically marking up queries on text should not be inherently more difficult (and is most likely easier) than conventional methods of expressing Boolean queries in text.

Relatively naive subjects were used in our experiments, and as a result the performance scores were fairly low across both experiments (averaging 21 out of 32 for semantics and 14 out of 32 for syntax). The relatively poor performance can be attributed to lack of feedback. If subjects began with an inappropriate strategy, they had no feedback to help them correct it during the experiment. However, in an interactive querying system such as the one described below, information seekers receive two types of feedback. First, the interpretation of each graphical query is echoed back as a Boolean textual query. Second, they see the effect of each query as they browse through the resulting postings.

It seems evident that graphical querying was no worse than textual querying in our experiments, but the answer to the question of whether they are better under the experimental conditions used is open to interpretation. Using contingency table analysis we found significant differences in both experiments. Pooling the results of both experiments, scores were better for graphics versus text queries on both the semantic (20.8 versus 19.2) and syntactic (14.3 versus 11.9) measures. However the standard deviations were high (around 6 and 7 for both conditions across both the experiments). Thus analysis of variance did not show a significant effect in either experiment, although the ANOVA results for the data pooled across both experiments approached significance (p<.10) for both the syntax and semantics measures.

QUERIES-R-LINKS

We developed a system called Queries-R-Links to implement interactive querying by combining graphical markup with full text retrieval. This system exploits people's preference for expressing Boolean queries in the graphical form. Queries-R-Links was developed as part of our research into "Flexible Text Visualization" [16]. The basic idea in Queries-R-Links is to mark up queries directly on text and then use a fast full text retrieval engine to almost instantaneously provide a list of hits (postings). These postings can then be selected as if they were links. Thus a full text retrieval system is used to construct queries by graphical markup. This allows information exploration similar to hypertext browsing.

A major difference between hypertext browsing and interactive querying in this case is the need to markup the text before links are displayed. Instead of selecting among pre-authored links, users have to mark up the query themselves. If they are successful, they then have a focused set of links that correspond to the current topic of interest, rather than more generic, pre-authored links. In Queries-R-Links, hits (postings) are shown as single lines with keywords from the query highlighted (this is a feature inherited from the full-text retrieval engine that the system currently uses). This preview capability provides users with feedback about the just-formed query. Based on this information users may reformulate the query to broaden or refine the search before selecting a hit.

Graphical queries are an interesting alternative to the expression of Boolean queries as text strings. It seems natural to mark up interesting words in the current text rather than switch to a command line and start typing keywords and Boolean operators. Expressing graphical queries from within text in conjunction with a fast full text retrieval system creates a dynamic, interactive, immediate and reversible interface to information that encourages a somewhat hypertext-like style of exploration and navigation. Users of Queries-R-Links form queries, examine results, adjust queries to produce new hits, and iterate in this manner as they collect information.

Formally, the graphical markup of a query on the text may be thought of as a one to many hypertext link. The selectable hits then provide a menu of end-point options for the link. Seen from this hypertext perspective, each query defines a set of N+1 text fragments that are mutually interlinked. One of the elements of this set is the text where the query was formed, and the remaining N items are the text fragments that satisfy the query constraints.

Queries are formed using AND clusters. The AND clusters represent queries in non-negated disjunctive normal form. This form is used as a relatively simple but expressive method of querying that avoids the use of negations, parentheses and nested expressions. Expressions in non-negated disjunctive normal form (DNF) do not use the NOT operator, and each expression is a collection of disjoint AND clusters (e.g., [A AND B] OR [C AND D]). Any Boolean query (without negation) can be expressed in non-negated DNF. Words are selected by clicking on them, and dragging between words creates a line representing the AND operator. OR relations are indicated by the absence of connecting lines. Queries-R-Links also allows the user to enter additional keywords in the margin. These words may then be linked in the same manner. Thus queries may include words that do not appear in the text currently being viewed.

Graphical Querying

Several features of querying via graphical markup combine to produce a powerful querying environment. The absence of textual operators eliminates the negative transfer from English phrases. Unlike traditional textual commands, the graphical notation does not depend on a specific order of operators and keywords, thus encouraging a more natural and declarative style of interaction. However, while the words "AND" and "OR" are no longer used, clearly the meaning of the corresponding logical operators must still be understood.

Interactive querying supports an object-based model of the query process. Because all operations are performed on visible objects (words and lines), no syntax or spelling errors are defined in this notation. This eliminates a significant source of frustration among novice and occasional users. Constructing each query from a collection of keyword and operator objects in a two-dimensional space also makes them easier to edit. The user no longer needs to insert or delete text in the middle of a long command line, but points to the desired object to affect the changes. The query is updated automatically as operators and keywords are added, changed or removed. Thus preview and undo capabilities follow naturally from the interface.

Each query may be refined and reformulated until the desired hit set is obtained. Once a hit is selected, the document is scrolled to the appropriate location, and the newly displayed text is marked up with the query that satisfied the search criteria. This query can be edited by the user to reflect the new information. Thus the output of one interaction becomes the input to the following one.

The query formulation, navigation refinement and reformulation can all be performed with mouse clicks without having to home back to the keyboard. Thus normative models of HCI may predict more efficient performance (e.g., the GOMS model, [2]), depending on the additional effect of the tradeoff between recalling keywords (for a command line query) versus scanning the text visually for words to be used in an interactive query.

Query History

The Queries-R-Links interface maintains a history of selected hits. The history is important so that users know where they came from. The importance of history seems to be particularly relevant in hypertext navigation [11]. Each time a hit is selected, the complete state of the system is saved in the history list. This list is visible on the display, and selecting one of the entries will cause the system to be restored to that state. This includes the displayed text, the marked up query and the resulting hits. Once added to the list, an entry does not change. If the user makes a change to a restored query and follows one of the generated links, a new entry is added to the history list.

Localizing Concepts

Queries-R-Links has a number of other features that facilitate text browsing, including a slider that controls the character-based proximity setting used by the AND operator when computing matches. Decreasing the range reduces the number of hits. A set of radio buttons may be used to restrict the scope of the operators to a single sentence, paragraph or chapter. In general, any number of such constructs can be defined for a document or database as dictated by its structure.

Interaction Style

Figure 2 shows a screen shot from Queries-R-Links. A simple interactive query has been constructed using two keywords that were selected by pointing and clicking. The hits window (lower left) shows the corresponding query results. The window on the right shows the history of prior queries. As no operator was specified connecting the two terms, OR is implied. The number of hits increases to reflect the broader query. Figure 3 shows the next modification to the query where the implied OR operator is replaced with an AND operator, thus reducing the size of the hit list. At this point, the slider in the control panel (lower-right corner) can be used to reduce the proximity range (narrowing the scope of the AND operator), thereby further reducing the number of hits.

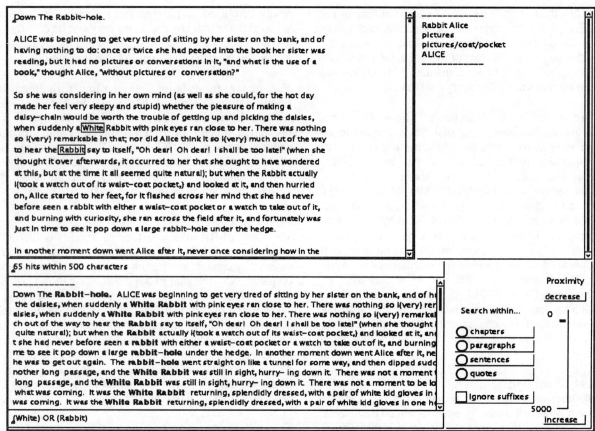

Figure 2. The   initial   query   consists of two terms.

Additional Capabilities

The interactive querying style of interaction is not limited to text-based databases. The notation extends easily to hybrid documents containing both text and graphics. Although not implemented in the current version of Queries-R-Links, a document containing graphical elements can be manipulated with this notation. While the underlying mechanism of representing and searching graphical data depends on the search engine of choice, the interface can remain the same. Thus when graphics or portions thereof are selected by clicking on them, a new object is added to the query (which may be supplemented with keywords that are attached to the selected graphic). This object may now be connected to other text and graphics objects comprising the query.

The important point is that although the underlying search engine may be performing a radically different search, the interface remains consistent and predictable. By combining text and graphics into a common notation, these extensions would make such an interface a useful part of a multimedia interface to multimedia information systems [13].As pen-based technology matures, users will be searching larger and larger databases from their pen-based computers. We believe that the graphical notation developed for Queries-R-Links lends itself naturally to pen-based input.

While the bulk of the interface need not change significantly, certain aspects would be improved by using the pen. For example, a more sophisticated selection technique that involves bracketing the key phrases could be implemented. The application of pen input technology to the interaction style described in this paper should be mutually beneficial for pen-based interfaces and interactive querying.

The current implementation uses `pat` [5] to perform searches. `pat` bases its searches on an inverted index that is compiled for a given document. While this is a useful approach to retrieving information, it is by no means the only one. For example, the system described in [8] was designed around SMART, an information retrieval package that uses relevance feedback to retrieve information. Their interface encapsulated the standard command-driven interface by wrapping it in a GUI. The new interface did a good job of implementing the relevance feedback interface, but the query was still formed by typing Boolean expressions and the standard SMART commands were simply replaced by suitably labeled buttons. This interface could be streamlined by the sort of graphical markup described above. For example, documents selected for browsing could be marked up to adjust the query that was used to retrieve them.

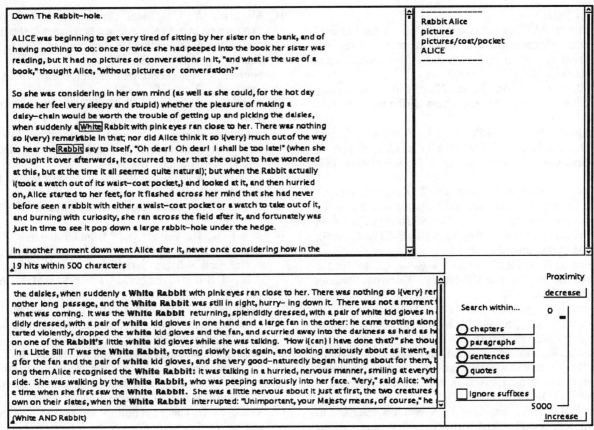

Figure 3. The default OR operator is replaced with the AND operator by connecting the two keywords with a line.

The Queries-R-Links system we developed can be adapted easily to reflect the strengths of an available search engine while retaining the generality of the interaction style. In fact, it should be possible to integrate multiple search engines under one interface, letting the interface determine which search engine should be used depending on the selected data.

CONCLUSIONS

We described a software environment for interactive querying (Queries-R-Links) and reported two experiments that compared the ease of formulation of graphical queries with that of Boolean text queries. In these experiments, graphical queries yielded equivalent or better performance than textual queries for both syntactic and semantic measures, without taking significantly longer to form. In addition, a large proportion of the subjects preferred to use the graphical queries.

Based on our studies and experience with the Queries-R-Links system we believe that interactive querying is a natural and powerful method for text browsing. There are a number of reasons why interactive querying may assist the browsing process: 1) the powerful functionality of a full text retrieval engine, 2) the ability to launch queries from within text, 3) the greater ease of use of graphical queries over textual queries, and 4) the use of a direct manipulation interface for querying.

Recognition of graphical queries is only one aspect of a realistic information retrieval system. While it is heartening that graphical markup appears to help (or at least, doesn't hurt) the user in querying, we expect that direct manipulation and rapid feedback, along with the ability to express queries from within text will enhance the usability of Queries-R-Links in relation to other forms of information retrieval.

The name "Queries-R-Links" reflects our belief that interactive queries can be used as dynamic (user-constructed) links between related fragments of text in large databases. Queries-R-Links is an interesting example of how new kinds of search and browsing functionality can be obtained by using different regions of the information exploration space [18]. The results reported in this paper also provide support for evolving electronic book and text browsing technologies that combine interactive querying with pen-based interfaces.

ACKNOWLEDGEMENTS
This research was supported by the Information Technology Research Center of Excellence of Ontario and by an operating grant (OGP0089710) to the second author from the National Science and Engineering Research Council of Canada. We also thank Alberto Mendelzon, Frank Tompa, and Darrel Raymond for their assistance.

REFERENCES

1. Borgman, C. Why are online catalogs so hard to use? Lessons learned from information-retrieval studies. *Journal of American Society for Information Science* 37 (1986), 387-400.

2. Card, S. K., Moran, T., and Newell, A. *Psychology of Human-Computer Interaction*. Erlbaum, Hillsdale, NJ, (1981).

3. Chignell, M.H., Nordhausen, B., Valdez, J.F., and Waterworth, J. A. The HEFTI model of text to hypertext conversion. *Hypermedia* 3, 3 (1991), 187-205.

4. Egan, D., Remde, J., Landauer, T. K., Lochbaum, C. and Gomez, L. Behavioral evaluation and analysis of a hypertext browser, in *Proc. CHI'89 Human Factors in Computing Systems* (Austin, April 30-May 4, 1989), ACM Press, pp. 205-210.

5. Fawcett, H. J. *PAT: The user's guide*. Centre for the New Oxford English Dictionary, Waterloo, Ontario, Canada (June 1988).

6. Furuta, R., Plaisant, C., and Shneiderman, B. A spectrum of automatic hypertext construction. *Hypermedia* 1, 2 (1989), 179-185.

7. Furuta, R., Plaisant, C., and Shneiderman, B. Automatically transforming regularly structured linear documents into hypertext. *Electronic Publishing* 2, 4 (1989), 211-229.

8. Li, T., Chiu, V., and Gey, F. X-Window interface to SMART, an advanced text retrieval system. *SIGIR FORUM* 26, 1 (Spring 1992), 5-16.

9. Marchionini, G. and Shneiderman, B. Finding facts vs. browsing knowledge in hypertext systems. *IEEE Computer* (January 1988), 70-80.

10. Michard, A. Graphical presentation of Boolean expressions in a database query language: design notes and an ergonomic evaluation. *Behavior and Information Technology* 1, 3 (1982), 279-288.

11. Nielsen, J. *HyperText and HyperMedia*. Academic Press, New York, NY, 1990.

12. Nordhausen, B., Chignell, M. H., and Waterworth, J. The missing link? Comparison of manual and automated linking in hypertext engineering, in *Proc. HFS 35th Annual Meeting* (San Francisco, September 2-6, 1991) HFS, pp. 310-314.

13. Price, R.J. Multimedia Information Systems, In J. A. Waterworth (Ed.), *Multimedia: Technology and Applications*. Ellis Horwood, Chichester, England, 1991. 114-150.

14. Remde, J. R., Gomez, L. M. and Landauer, T. K. SuperBook: an automatic tool for information exploration - hypertext?, in *Proc. Hypertext '87* (Chapel Hill, November 13-15, 1987) ACM Press, 175-188.

15. Thompson, R. H. and Croft, W. B. Support for browsing in an intelligent text retrieval system. *Int. J. Man-Mach. Stud.* 30, (1989). 639-688.

16. Tompa, F., Woods, D., Chignell, M. H., and McLeod, I. Flexible Text Visualization. Project report submitted to the Information Technology Research Centre of Excellence. Waterloo, Ontario, Canada (1991).

17. Vigil, P. J. The psychology of online searching. *Journal of American Society for Information Science* 34, 4 (1983). 281-287.

18. Waterworth, J. A. and Chignell, M. H. A model of infor-mation exploration. *Hypermedia* 3, 1 (1991) 35-58.

The Applied Ergonomics Group at Philips

Ian McClelland

Applied Ergonomics Group, Philips Corporate Design
Building SX, PO Box 218, 5600 MD
Eindhoven, Netherlands
Tel: +31 40 733311
E-Mail: McClell@nlvxe1.ce.Philips.nl

INTRODUCTION

This paper outlines who we are, our perspective on usability, some of the challenges that face us, and gives insight into some of our project work.

WHO ARE WE?

The Applied Ergonomics (AE) group functions as a specialist support group within Corporate Design (CD). In January 1993 the AE group had 10 ergonomists, serving a staff of over 200 in CD. CD has responsibility for the industrial design of all Philips products. Philips has a diverse product portfolio covering consumer and professional applications, and operates in markets worldwide. Almost all the work of the AE group is for products using embedded software, some of which are called 'computers'.

OUR MISSION

In response to Corporate calls for more customer focus, CD is adopting a user centred design strategy with the accent on usability as a key factor. CD interprets usability in a broad perspective by advocating a systematic approach to the treatment of user issues affecting the acceptance and aesthetic aspects of a product. The AE group interprets usability as defined by ISO 9241 Pt11 (see below).

The AE mission is to ensure that high levels of usability are designed into the products to the benefit of the end user. This means establishing usability as a specified design objective. The challenge is to integrate 'users needs', interaction design, and evaluating the usability of solutions into a holistic and iterative design process. Realising the integration of usability into product development requires significant changes to the way we work and the design process in which we work.

Integration into the Design Process

CD operates primarily in the 'design creation' phase of product development, often based on existing concepts and specifications. This results in project objectives being dominated by the technical aspects of design solutions at the expense of usability goals. The AE group continually

argues that more attention needs to be placed on 'user needs analysis' work and using design studies as tools to derive usability requirements for product concepts. Such a shift in focus cannot be achieved without management recognising usability as a specific objective and ensuring that the resources are available to support the work required. Such changes have substantial consequences for the organisation of projects and for resource allocation, see also Gould (1988,b).

Knowing our Users

Knowledge of our users and product usage is often dispersed amongst specialists in product development groups, but not made available in a form and at a level of detail which is directly useful in the design process. This is a particular problem in determining usability and acceptance criteria for the high volume consumer electronics business. We need better methods to articulate user requirements and usability issues so that they can be evaluated against commercial and technical demands.

Integration of Skills

The ergonomists have to integrate their skills with those of the industrial and graphic designer into an effective partnership, especially in relation to developing new product concepts and interaction design. The approach of industrial and graphic design to user issues is typically inspirational and intuitive. The ergonomist relies heavily on more systematic approaches. Achieving an effective partnership requires teamwork to enhance the complementary nature of the skills. Teamwork is a vital skill which CD needs to develop further.

The Skills of the Ergonomist

Ergonomists need to adapt their skills to support the synthesis of appropriate design solutions based on the identification of user needs and through setting realistic usability goals, as advocated by Gould (1988,a), Rubinstein et al (1984), Whiteside et al (1988). We need to avoid the traditional 'remedial' role of the ergonomist. Operationally we must work as 'designers'. Ergonomists who have worked in a traditional academic or scientific context do not always easily adapt to this change in perspective.

SOME RECENT PROJECT WORK

The work of the AE group together with our CD design colleagues is beginning to challenge approaches to user interface design. The few cases below give insights into our work for some products now in the market.

Managing Portable/Mobile Communications

Intense team work between ergonomics, screen graphics design, and software engineering was a major success factor in developing the DS3000 terminal for controlling radio and telephone communications. The terminal was touch screen based. Users were police, fire services etc. Interaction design proposals were based on field studies which identified essential usability, and user acceptance characteristics. The operators' tasks were key in integrating interaction designs, the screen graphic design, prototype development, and the SW specification. The design has positively influenced product sales. A customer based evaluation study is planned.

Scanning Electron Microscope

The first UI design proposals for a new product generation using a mouse driven windowed system replicated existing hardware based operating concepts. A task based conceptual model for the UI was developed by the ergonomist partly through attending a basic operator training course. The task based concept replaced the first proposals. It was selected because of a more logical grouping of functions and more consistent presentation format.

In-Car Entertainment Systems

The basic functions of 5 current car radio-cassettes were evaluated in a usability test. The test used a car equipped with video and logging apparatus to measure subjects' performance. Tasks were carried out under driving and stationary conditions. Recommendations included; direct access controls where possible, rotary controls for audio levels, advice on the functional layout of controls and labelling. (Johnson et al, 1992)

The Philips PCF 20 Fax

Close working between industrial design, graphics design, and ergonomics led to an award winning design. Design goals were to improve on existing designs and to create an error tolerant design. First studies showed weaknesses in the operating procedures originally proposed by engineering. This led to a redesign of the procedures based on examining competitor products and typical use. Time scales precluded full usability testing but less formal walk-throughs with users demonstrated that improvements were achieved.

Electronic Case Handling Office (ECHO)

ECHO is a case handling system for insurance companies and other organisations, and features electronic images of documents in a GUI. Comprehensive usability studies of a pre-release system revealed some procedural and dialogue inefficiencies, but also that the basic conceptual structure and interaction mechanisms (navigation and window operation) were easily learned. Significant improvements to the first commercial release have been made. (ECHO is now a Digital Equipment BV product)

STANDARDISATION

The group actively participates in International Standardisation, including the International Organisation for Standardization (ISO). Contributions have been made to ISO DIS 9241, Part 11, "Usability Specification and Measures" which defines usability as "the effectiveness, efficiency and satisfaction with which specified users can achieve specified goals in particular environments".

Expressing usability in terms of the context of use is a basic principle in our approach to designing usable products.

In addition, the group acts as secretary to IEC (International Electrotechnical Commission) TC3 SC3C "Graphical Symbols for use on Equipment" and the chairman of ETSI (European Telecommunications Standards Institute) STC HF1 "Human Factors: Telecommunications Services".

RESOURCES

The AE group has a usability laboratory. This is now undergoing redevelopment. CD makes use of several proprietary simulation tools for interaction design. We also cooperate extensively with SW engineering departments in the development of UI prototypes.

ACKNOWLEDGEMENTS

The perspective and project work described in this paper reflects the work of all members of the Applied Ergonomics group, past and present. The success of the project work described is also due to close collaboration with many colleagues working in the CD Design Groups.

REFERENCES

1. Gould, J D, 1988 a, How to design usable systems. Handbook of Human-Computer Interaction, Ed. M Helander, North-Holland, Amsterdam.

2. Gould, J D, 1988 b, Designing for usablity: the next iteration is to reduce organisational barriers. Proceedings of the Human Factors Society, 32nd Annual Meeting.

3. Rubinstein, R, Hersh, H M, 1984, The Human Factor. Digital Press, Digital Equipment Corporation.

4. Whiteside, J, Bennett, J, and Holtzblatt, K, 1988, Usability Engineering: our experience and evolution. Handbook of Human-Computer Interaction, Ed. M Helander, North-Holland, Amsterdam.

Selected references from the work of the Group

1. Johnson, G I, Rakers, G, 1990, Ergonomics in the Development of Driver Support Systems. 22nd Symposium on Automotive Technology & Automation.

2. Johnson, G I, v Vianen, E P G, 1992, Comparative evaluation of basic car radio controls. Proceedings of the Ergonomics Society's Annual Conference.

3. McClelland, I L, 1990, Product Assessment and User Trials. Evaluation of Human Work, Ed. J R Wilson, E N Corlett, Taylor and Francis, London.

4. McClelland, I L, Brigham, F R, 1990, Marketing Ergonomics - how should ergonomics be packaged. Ergonomics, 33,5,519-526.

5. Thomas, D B, McClelland, I L, Jones, D J, 1991, Ergonomics and Product Creation at Philips. 11th Congress of the International Ergonomics Association.

Information Design Methods and the Applications of Virtual Worlds Technology at WORLDESIGN, Inc.

Robert Jacobson, Ph.D.
and the WORLDESIGN Team

WORLDESIGN, Inc.
5348-1/2 Ballard Avenue NW
Seattle, WA 98107 USA
+1-206-781-5253, -5254 fax
info@worldesign.com

ABSTRACT

Information design is a new professional practice that systematically applies the lessons of human-computer interaction and human factors studies, communication theory, and information science to the presentation of complex data. WORLDESIGN, Inc., an information design studio, practices information design with an emphasis on virtual worlds technology in the service of its corporate, mostly industrial customers.

KEYWORDS: Information design, virtual worlds technology, information environments, industry, applications, collaborative design, craft guilds.

THE FORMAL PRACTICE OF INFORMATION DESIGN

Today's customers of information systems (especiall those built around computers) live with text, video, multimedia, and hypermedia presentations of information that are as quirky as the individualistic styles of the engineers and graphics artists who created the systems on which these presentations run. Moreover, because most of these presentations must be displayed on a conventional computer terminal, their imagery is confined within a "picture frame," like pieces in a museum, and restricted to two-dimensional pictures with no or point-source sound; or at best, simulated three-dimensional pictures with stereo sound.

Although one can claim that information has been "designed" ever since the first hieroglyphics were devised, this process has been and remains — even today, with all the available HCI research — ad hoc and highly idiosyncratic. Information design is a new profession that attempts to systematize the provision of information, to make information more easily apprehended, understood, and acted upon [1].

WORLDESIGN, Inc., an information design studio in North America, attempts to apply formal information design rules to solve its clients' information-based problems. Where appropriate, it uses virtual worlds technology to liberate information from the computer terminal to produce inclusive, shared three-dimensional "information environments" built around multi-screen projection and 3D sound technology.

OVERVIEW OF WORLDESIGN, INC.

Information design as practiced at WORLDESIGN is a synthesis of lessons from information science, design theory, human factors science, phenomenology and the philosophy of perception, cognitive science, and participatory design. We work with our clients to identify and solve specific information-based problems for which there appear to be technology-supported design solutions. For now, our methods are largely experimental, but we hope over time to build a comprehensive theory of information design.

WORLDESIGN, organized in early 1992, is a "spinoff" of the Human Interface Technology Laboratory (HIT Lab) located on the campus of the University of Washington. WORLDESIGN applies tools developed at the HIT Lab and elsewhere. WORLDESIGN develops essential technology when it is not available elsewhere, but more often it consults with technology managers to specify necessary new design tools that may have commercial potential. A case in point is new 3D visual and aural technology for "realizing" certain types of GIS displays.

SPECIFIC PROJECTS

WORLDESIGN's first client has been Evans & Sutherland, for which WORLDESIGN has consulted about developments in the virtual worlds industry. For a major European auto manufacturer, WORLDESIGN has been commissioned to develop a "corporate visualizer," a device by which the firm's employees (from the CEO to the shopfloor workers) to get the "big picture," how the firm's many projects and organizations interrelate. The firm's intent is to enhance a shared corporate identify and vision, like those inculcated among Japanese workers, without forcing on its own workers impossibly alien cultural behaviors. For the Electric Power Research Institute, WORLDESIGN is designing a "network cockpit" enabling operators at various points in the "power management system" to vigorously interact with the system, always staying on "the edge" (a metaphor that itself requires further definition). WORLDESIGN is investigating the feasibility of a similar cockpit for financial traders. A fourth project involves creating a "virtual design environment" for architects and urban designers employed by an overseas regional authority. Projects are the responsibility of self-managed workteams.

PEOPLE INVOLVED

WORLDESIGN currently employs 16 people, 12 of whom are professional information designers who fall into one of three categories: "information counsellors" (who study situations from the client-side), "world designers," and "worldsmiths" (technologists who integrate actual systems). Consultants provide specialized domain and technology advice. The firm's business managers (who are responsible for marketing, finance, and administration) also have design backgrounds. WORLDESIGN's business plan calls for it to grow in size to 30 professionals over three years The employees' backgrounds are relevant to their individual practices, though none could be described as conventional. The main characteristic they share is a strong spatial sense demonstrated by extensive use of metaphors, style of explanation, media preferences, and so forth.

INDUSTRY SUPPORT

Our startup funding was provided by Evans & Sutherland, the manufacturer of computer image generators. As a showcase for the latest in virtual worlds technology, we have also received support from Sun Microsystems, Sense8, Hewlett Packard, and other suppliers in the field. Also, we invite our suppliers' and clients' employees to participate with our staff on project workteams; several are resident at WORLDESIGN's offices on a temporary basis.

ORGANIZATIONAL STRUCTURE

WORLDESIGN, although a corporation, is organized as a modern crafts guild. In this we have been guided by the renowned British industrial designer (and WORLDESIGN advisor), Dr. Michael Cooley. We work cooperatively toward evolving the practice of information design. In Summer 1993, at the conclusion of our first year of work, we hope to sponsor a small invitational conference on information design at which we will also discuss the appropriateness of craft guild organizations for this type of professional endeavor.

IMPLICATIONS FOR THE HCI FIELD

Information design as practiced at WORLDESIGN is still largely a matter of testing hypotheses against real-world applications. Our hope is to develop a comprehensive theory (comparable to the design theories in more conventional fields) on which information designers can rely in building information environments, including virtual worlds. Our experience also can provide parameters by which technology can be evaluated for its usefulness, guiding the production of better information design tools. The jury is still out. If WORLDESIGN is successful, however, researchers and developers in the human-computer interaction field may find it a valuable source of case studies and an impetus for greater attention to R&D on the part of funding sources and clients.

REFERENCE

1. For example, in our practice we draw upon the work of statistician Edward Tufte, communications theorist Brenda Dervin, psychologist Donald Norman, dramatist Brenda Laurel, landscape architect Lawrence Halprin, designer Richard Saul Wurman, and architect Romedi Passini.

The Silicon Graphics Customer Research and Usability Group

Mike Mohageg

Silicon Graphics Computer Systems, Inc.
2011 N. Shoreline Blvd., P.O. Box 7311
Mountain View, CA 94039–7311 USA
E-mail: michaelm@esd.sgi.com

INTRODUCTION
Description of the Company
Silicon Graphics Computer Systems, Inc. is a leading supplier of visual processing computer systems. Our goal is to pioneer true 3D computing, to define new classes of visual computing, and to provide practical, beneficial, and cost-effective solutions for a variety of industries.

Goals/Mission of Group
The Customer Research and Usability Group provides usability consulting services to improve the competitive value and ease of use of products. We have been in existence since June of 1990.

Range of services/activities. Our group works in an environment with extremely short, intense product development cycles. Depending on the project, we get involved at various stages of the development cycle. We offer a wide range of services: 1) qualitative and quantitative customer research (focus groups, customer panels, conjoint analyses), 2) competitive analyses, 3) usability requirements and full system functional requirements, 4) design consulting, 5) design reviews, 6) heuristic analyses, 7) usability testing, 8) data collection and analysis during alpha and beta phases, 9) ergonomic standards reviews, and 10) in-house ergonomics consulting.

Range of products addressed. The group works on both hardware and software products. Generally, the issues of concern with hardware products are: 1) overall system installation, 2) system upgrades (e.g., adding boards, drives, peripherals), 3) system maintenance (e.g., installing and removing memory, power supplies, CPU modules), 4) usage and comfort of input devices and displays, and 5) usability of system unit components (e.g., symbols, connectors and jacks, control panels). We also work on a variety of software products: 1) the GUI desktop, 2) system management utilities (e.g., printer management), 3) network management utilities, 4) Silicon Graphics software applications that are shipped with every system (e.g., a drawing and presentation

tool, on-line documentation), and 5) selected third-party applications.

Funding model. Funding for the majority of the group's activities is provided by our division; however, we support projects on a company-wide basis. The group manager budgets for equipment, services, software, subjects, and other items necessary for supporting projects on a yearly fiscal basis. We also reserve funds for outside services. These services include hiring contractors for short term projects and using the services of other companies (e.g., market research firms, professional video consulting). In special circumstances, the group may contract services for projects funded by other divisions, but the service provided is managed in our group.

General profile of staff. The Customer Research and Usability group has a manager and 3 permanent employees at the engineering level, who are Members of Technical Staff at Silicon Graphics. Usually there are several contract human factors engineers as well. The staff members have advanced degrees in Computer Science, Industrial and Systems Engineering, and Psychology. This varied background allows us to better address the needs of our clients.

INVOLVEMENT IN THE DESIGN PROCESS
Context for Work
A permanent staff member of the group sits on the product *business team*, which meets once a week. This forum allows group members to participate in developing the product concept and vision and raise usability issues on design problems. Detailed input to the design is made by participating in *design meetings* or having one-to-one discussion sessions with designers. *Informal contacts* are also very useful in influencing the design.

Approach
Generally, we take a *proactive* approach to getting involved in the design process. There is discussion at the management level to determine the needs for each project requiring usability input; this determines the extent and timing of involvement, and participation in the project. Projects are usually scoped and planned well in advance. However, the *reactive* situation is always a reality in industry. At times

product managers or lead engineers request help to solve a usability problem just before release of the product.

Methods

Early in product definition, we collect *focus group* and other market research data to provide engineering with intelligence on customer needs and usability objectives. Where design cycles allow, we use *iterative design and testing methods*. We provide recommendations based on reviews and testing of products.

EVALUATION AND USABILITY TESTING
Resources

Lab Facilities. We maintain a 1200 sq. ft. laboratory with two separate subject–experimenter test suites and a large observation room, where developers can watch their products being tested on video monitors. Stationary and mobile video cameras are used to record events; the video signals are routed into the experimenter and observation rooms. Also, large one–way mirrors between the subject and experimenter rooms allow for close observation of test participants. An intercom system allows communication between these two rooms in each test suite. One suite is used for hardware testing and the other for software testing. Both suites use ergonomic and fully adjustable furniture and lighting. Each room is independently cooled and ventilated.

Tools & equipment.

- Computers. We use 3 IRIS Indigo^{TM} and 2 Personal IRIS^{TM} workstations for both hardware and software testing, data collection and analysis. A Compaq DeskPro 386, and Apple Macintosh II are also available for use in competitive analysis or prototyping.
- Video equipment. The lab offers a wall–mounted, remote controlled camera, and 2 additional tripod–based camcorders. Additionally, we use a Silicon Graphics VideoCreator^{TM} to do high quality real time RGB to NTSC conversion of monitor signals, thereby eliminating the need for an extra camera. Two S–VHS VCRs and a digital A/V mixer allow for manipulating the video signals in a variety of ways for concurrent viewing or presentation at a later time. A fully–featured S–VHS editor is also used.
- On–line data collection. We have developed an on–line data collection tool for our platform. This tool records events of interest (mouse click, window manipulations, task times, etc) across applications. This tool is invaluable for collecting objective performance data.

Approach

Non–testing evaluations. We do *usability reviews* where 2–3 engineers from the group will review the products based on pre–established usability goals/objectives or accepted standards (e.g., ANSI/HFS–100). In *heuristic evaluations* our staff and other internal reviewers load software on

personal machines and try it. We provide these users with a set of "heuristics" to use in judging the usability of the product and they report violations and usability bugs.

Evaluations involving tests. We often *test to a standard* set in usability goals/requirements, or set by a domestic or international standards committee. *Testing design alternatives* against one another (for both performance and preference) is also an important approach. *Competitive tests/reviews* are performed for certain competitive products. *Early concept tests*, where we test the viability of a particular approach or design, are another method of providing valuable information to designers. We may perform a quick test of a UI element/concept to determine its feasibility.

Methods

Controlled lab tests. Lab tests are the most frequent type of testing of pre–released products. The excellent lab facilities allow for collecting useful information for design and evaluation purposes. The level of "control" in the tests ranges from multi–factorial designs (with true manipulation of design features as independent variables) to performing a quick test of a few common/important tasks for a particular product. In these latter situations there is less control over variables; the objective is simply to identify problem areas.

Field studies. The group conducts evaluations of alpha, beta, and released products with the Silicon Graphics installed base. Samples of these evaluations include telephone surveys of overall system usability, surveys of specific hardware components (e.g., the mouse), and customer visits to collect beta feedback on products.

RESULTS/IMPACT
IRIS Indigo^{TM}

Over 200 subjects were tested at various stages of product development. Major impact included alterations to memory sockets and modules, drive sleds, and the inclusion of international symbols. Installation time was reduced to 10 minutes or less.

On–Line Documentation

Members of the group were involved in the design process and conducted both early and summative tests. Our contribution led to a 60% task time improvement over the original design and an 18% increase in accuracy.

KEY PUBLICATIONS

In the 2.5 years of the group's existence we have published roughly 10 journal and conference articles, along with participating in various special interest panels at CHI and the Human Factors Society Annual Meeting. Also, group members serve as referees for conferences and professional journals.

Filtered Suggestions

Joris Verrips

Paramaribostraat 138
1058 VP Amsterdam
The Netherlands
+31-20-6852275

ABSTRACT

MTYP is a program that helps to select texts or macros with very few keystrokes using Filtered Selections. Each newly typed in letter filters suggestions that contain it with a priority for uppercase letters.

Evaluation of TYP, MTYP's predecessor, showed that higher cognitive functions are more important for effectiveness of use than a mere reduction of the number of keystrokes.

This was used as feedback to development and has led to automatical acceptance of unique suggestions accompanied by a beep to limit eye screen contact and to improvements of the filter as well.

These functions can be toggled on and off and it is interesting to experience the final system using a data base that simulates a counter.

With MTYP it is possible to select each out of 700 different product names with an average of 3.27 keystrokes and hardly any memory load. But 700 names seems about the upper limit for effective Filtered Selections to be possible. TYP was designed as a "language sensitive editor" for programming languages and can be demonstrated as well.

MTYP implements a selection mechanism that might also be applied for
- fast interactive file selection (an example of fast interactive list selection).
- fast interactive macro selection and command selection.
- an electronic counter possibly in combination with a chord keyboard.
- poor man's speech recognition: type or speak very few letters to select frequent commands.
- poor man's handwriting recognition (see above).

None of these possibilities has been implemented.

In real life people often prefer to memorize abbreviations or numbers to prevent eye screen contact or a paper search and they may well prefer them over Filtered Suggestions.

It is not clear if further research is indicated as this would be very time consuming and TYP is hardly ever used.

A floppy disc for DOS machines with MTYP and TYP's prototype on it is available.

Literature:
Branching Selection of Suggestions
Verrips, Joris
Interacting With Computers
4, 1 April 1992, pp. 68-82

From Undo to Multi-User Applications — the Demo

Michael Spenke

GMD Gesellschaft für Mathematik und Datenverarbeitung mbH
(German National Research Center for Computer Science)
P.O. Box 1316
W-5205 Sankt Augustin 1
Germany
Email: spenke@gmd.de

ABSTRACT

The object-oriented history mechanism of the GINA application framework and its relevance for multi-user applications are demonstrated. The interaction history of a document is represented as a tree of command objects. Synchronous cooperation is supported by replicating the document state and exchanging command objects. Asynchronous cooperation leads to different branches of the history tree which can later be merged.

KEYWORDS: User Interface Management Systems, CSCW, Command Objects, Undo, Dialog History.

INTRODUCTION

GINA (the Generic INteractive Application) is a class library which allows the implementation of state-of-the-art direct-manipulation user interfaces [7]. Applications are created by defining subclasses of GINA classes and adding and overriding methods. The behaviour of a typical application is inherited in this way. The unlimited history mechanism is generically implemented in GINA and therefore available in all applications. It is based on command objects describing user actions and the resulting state transitions of a graphical-interactive application.

The history mechanism was originally developed to implement a flexible undo/redo facility and to store the complete dialog history together with a document so that all steps necessary to create the document can later be demonstrated in an animated replay ("interaction recorder"). However, it turned out that command objects are also ideally suited to implement multi-user applications with a replicated architecture: After each user action, the resulting command object is broadcast to all other sites to maintain both an identical document state and a common dialog history.

Each command object is marked with a vector timestamp of a virtual time mechanism [3,4], so that conflicts due to concurrently executed commands are detected. In order to resolve such conflicts, undo and redo operations are automatically performed to rearrange the commands into a linear order.

Furthermore, users can easily switch to asynchronous cooperation where exchanging commands is stopped and separate dialog histories are generated. Later on, the histories can be merged using the redo mechanism, leading again to a common document state. Often, this merging can be performed completely automatically, however, sometimes conflicts between commands of different users must be resolved interactively.

The ability to undo arbitrary isolated commands of the dialog history ("selective undo") is especially important for multi-user applications: Normally, the last command submitted by a certain user is to be undone, which is not necessarily the last command in the global history, because other users may have performed further commands in the meantime [6].

The amount of coupling between the interfaces in a distributed session can be varied by specifying which kinds of commands are broadcast to other participants. Users can decide to exchange only state-changing commands or to exchange commands for browsing, scrolling and object selection as well. Finally, in the tightly coupled mode, the feedback during command specification (dragging objects, pulling down menus) is also immediately transmitted.

The interaction recorder, i.e. the ability to perform an animated replay of the past, is also of special importance in distributed sessions, because users can easily miss something happening on their screens when they are absent or distracted for a moment.

GINA has been implemented in Common Lisp/CLOS and is based on OSF/Motif. It is freely distributed, and the currently released version contains the unlimited linear history mechanism. Recent extensions include selective undo, the interaction recorder [1] and support for multi-user applications [2]. This work is part of the development of a distributed shared work environment based on the metaphor of a virtual office building where users can meet, communicate, and cooperate.

DEMO OVERVIEW

First, some of the standard GINA demo applications are shown to illustrate the general concepts of GINA and the unlimited undo/redo mechanism. Next, the interaction recorder is demonstrated in the context of a simple graphical editor. User interactions such as dragging objects, selecting from menus, and operating dialog boxes are recorded and can be replayed and animated.

In the main part of the demo, different forms of cooperation in a multi-user spreadsheet are demonstrated in relatively realistic scenarios. This example was chosen because recent studies [5] have shown that spreadsheet co-development is the rule, not the exception. It is assumed, but not demonstrated, that users can communicate at least over an audio connection during the session.

In the first scenario, members of a group negotiate about the distribution of a budget. The requirements of each participant are entered in separate areas of the sheet. In this phase the user interfaces are loosely coupled, i.e. each participant independently works in a different section of the sheet, but cell entries are kept consistent. Later on, in the negotiation phase, the interfaces are tightly coupled, and modifications are performed in close cooperation of the group.

In the second scenario, it is demonstrated how two users develop a new spreadsheet model in a distributed session, repeatedly switching between synchronous and asynchronous cooperation. The initial layout is designed in a tightly coupled session. Then data are entered into the sheet in parallel. After the data entries have been merged, they are checked for correctness in parallel and again the corrections are merged. Finally, some formulas are entered and the derived values are discussed and analyzed in close cooperation.

In this scenario the cooperation between users with different levels of programming skill is also demonstrated: While entering formulas, the two users ask a remote expert to demonstrate how to replicate formulas by copy and paste operations. Later they replay the demonstrated commands using the interaction recorder to completely understand all details of the solution.

CONCLUSIONS

A general, application-independent history mechanism based on command objects is demonstrated. It has been generically implemented in the GINA application framework and thus been introduced into a number of non-trivial applications with state-of-the-art direct-manipulation user interfaces. The demonstration shows that our object-oriented representation of the dialog history as an integral, persistent part of the document state enables a number of improvements of the user interface for both single and multi-user applications:

- A selective undo/redo of arbitrary, isolated commands is possible, which is especially important for multi-user applications.

- An animated replay of the dialog history can serve as a help facility. In a distributed shared session an expert can demonstrate the necessary interactions to solve a problem, and a novice can later replay and analyze the solution.

- A smooth transition between synchronous and asynchronous cooperation is possible. Separately edited versions of a document can later be merged, because all modifications leading away from the common state are available as different branches of the dialog history.

FUTURE WORK

The benefits of the proposed mechanism have been proven but the optimal user interface is still an open question. Without a better visualization of the history tree end users cannot exploit the full power of the concept. There must be special support for users negotiating which of the asynchronously performed modifications to a document will be retained. Special care has to be taken to visualize and animate the commands performed by other users in order to make them understandable. The different levels of coupling between users will be integrated with the virtual room system. For example, leaving a room carrying a document means to switch the session to decoupled mode.

ACKNOWLEDGEMENTS

The concepts presented here have been developed by the GINA group consisting of Christian Beilken, Thomas Berlage, Andreas Genau, Markus Sohlenkamp and the author.

REFERENCES

1. Berlage, T. and Spenke, M. The GINA Interaction Recorder. In *Proceedings of the IFIP WG2.7 Working Conference on Engineering for Human-Computer Interaction* (Ellivuori, Finland, Aug 10-14, 1992).

2. Berlage, T. From UNDO to Multi-User Applications. To be published, GMD 1992, available from the author.

3. Ellis, C. A. and Gibbs, S. J. Concurrency Control in Groupware Systems. In *Proceedings of the ACM SIGMOD International Conference on the Management of Data* (Portland, OR, May 31-Jun 2, 1989), pp. 399-407.

4. Mattern, F. Virtual Time and Global States of Distributed Systems. In *Proc. Workshop on Parallel and Distributed Algorithms*, Bonas Oct. 1988, North-Holland / Elsevier, pp. 215-226, 1989.

5. Nardi, B. A. and Miller, J. R. An Ethnographic Study of Distributed Problem Solving in Spreadsheet Development. In *Proceedings of the Conference on Computer Supported Cooperative Work (CSCW '90)*, ACM Press, Los Angeles, California, 1990, pp. 197-208.

6. Prakash, A. and Knister, M. J. Undoing Actions in Collaborative Work. In *Proceedings of the Conference on Computer Supported Cooperative Work* (Toronto, Canada, Oct 31-Nov 4, 1992), pp. 273-280.

7. Spenke, M. and Beilken, C. An Overview of GINA — the Generic INteractive Application. In *User Interface Management and Design*, Proceedings of the Workshop on User Interface Management Systems and Environments (Lisbon, Portugal, June 4-6, 1990), D.A. Duce et al., Eds., Springer Verlag, Berlin, pp. 273-293.

Common Elements in Today's Graphical User Interfaces: The Good, the Bad, and the Ugly

Moderator: A. Brady Farrand
Tandem Computers
10300 North Tantau Avenue, Loc 55-54
Cupertino, CA 95014-0725
farrand_brady@tandem.com
(408) 285-2769

Panelists: Marc Rochkind, President, XVT Systems
Jean-Marie Chauvet, General Manager, Neuron Data, Paris
Bruce "Tog" Tognazzini, SunSoft Corporation
David C. Smith, Apple Computers, Inc.

ABSTRACT
This panel will identify some of the similarities amongst the different familiar graphical user interfaces that make them seem so indistinguishable. This panel will then identify some of the similarities that don't belong in any modern user interface.

KEYWORDS: Graphical user interface design, common GUI, design esthetics

INTRODUCTION
Microsoft Windows, Apple Macintosh, UNIX Motif, ...several Graphical User Interfaces continue to compete for the title of "standard" GUI, and the market share that goes with it. Each claims to be a "unique" environment for the user, with its own appearance and its own functionality.

One familiar comment has been voiced many times by folks looking at these GUIs:

"What's the difference? They are all basically the same."

This panel will explore that similarity amongst the most familiar graphical user interfaces. We will first look at the common elements that determine the similarity. We will then look for common elements that should not be in any graphical user interface.

The Familiar GUI- Common Elements Across Platforms
The functionality provided by the different GUIs *is* similar. They present their information in rectangular windows. Commands selected from menus tell the computer what to do with the information. Text is typed into fields, items are chosen from scrolling lists, buttons are clicked, icons are dragged. Are these common elements just surface issues, or is the underlying functionality really similar?

The similarity would be proven if applications written for one GUI could be replicated with few changes in another GUI. This is happening today. Microsoft is releasing "Excel" and "Word" for both Macintosh and Windows machines. FrameMaker has migrated from UNIX to other platforms. Most major graphical software applications are being rewritten, with few changes, for multiple platforms. Even more interesting, some applications are being written in a single language for multiple platforms.

Special tools are needed to write a single program that can be run on a PC with MS Windows, or on a Macintosh, or on a UNIX box with Motif. For students of a single common GUI, programming environments that supply these tools are fascinating. These are the programming languages that define the single common GUI.

The reality of a single "common GUI" is being proved in the marketplace by the recent success of firms that provide these programming environments. What can they tell us? These firms have a unique perspective. Their lifeblood is identifying the common elements. They make their money by providing a programming environment that easily creates these common elements. They:

- identify the common elements by creating a programming environment that features them

- identify the elements that are available on some, but not all, of the environments

- encourage user interface designers to create GUIs that are the same from one platform to the next

The first two members of this panel represent the most successful common GUI development environments. Marc Rochkind from XVT and Jean-Marie Chauvet from Neuron Data will characterize the common GUI that their products support. They will identify the important elements found in all the graphical user interfaces. To better understand what is the same, they will also identify the elements that differ from one GUI to the next.

The Difficult GUI- the Wrong Common Elements

As designers working with the common GUI, or one of its parent user interfaces, it is important to know what elements need to be improved. The common GUI is so familiar that we no longer look at it with a critical eye. But we must not ignore its flaws.

Once identified, these elements should be eliminated. That may not be easy to do. However, knowing them, our user interface designs could avoid the problems, or at least compensate for them.

One reason for the problems is that some familiar elements of many graphical user interfaces may exist only because some predecessor user interface did it that way. Radio buttons are not the only metaphor for mutually exclusive pushbuttons. A clipboard does not have to hold only one item. Menus contain commands for objects because the previous command-line interface used the same commands for the same objects; a direct-manipulation interface may provide a better way to control.

The other members of this panel will criticize the bad and the ugly elements of the common GUI. They are entitled; they originated and promoted many of the now-familiar elements of graphical user interfaces, both good and bad. Bruce "Tog" Tognazzini and David C. Smith have strong views on what is good and bad in current user interface designs.

PANELISTS

Marc Rochkind

Marc Rochkind is President and Founder of XVT Software, the first commercial product for cross-platform GUI design and development. He founded the company in 1987. Before that he was a founding member of Emerging Technology Consultants, which develops and markets text editing and word processing software for PCs and UNIX. Marc also spent twelve years at Bell Laboratories where he was a member of the technical staff and later a technical supervisor. At Bell he invented the Source Code Control System (SCCS). He also made many contributions to the UNIX operating system including writing two books on UNIX programming.

GUI interfaces are new as far as human interfaces to computers go, and brand new to many users, who are themselves new to computers. They are also new to many programmers. As with most new technologies, the focus is not always on what is really important. Two interfaces (e.g., Motif and OPEN LOOK) are perhaps superficially different (witness their scrollers), but they may be pretty much alike underneath.

This talk will explore the fundamental similarities and differences between different user interfaces, and shed light on what is really important (to users and developers) and what is only surface deep.

Jean-Marie Chauvet

Jean-Marie Chauvet manages the Neuron Data office in France; he is a co-founder of Neuron Data and a co-designer of Nextpert Object. Nextpert Object is Neuron Data's development system which works in concert with their Open Interface tools as a common user interface design environment. Previously he was a visiting scientist at The Robotics Institute, Carnegie Mellon University, Pittsburg. There he was involved in research work in the areas of artificial intelligence and machine learning. Mr. Chauvet holds a degree from L'Ecole Polytechnique, Paris.

Tribal Feuds in Flatland: A Brief Incursion into LinGUIstics

Abstract

Rapid development and deployment of mission-critical custom software applications are key to success in the 1990's. The demand for graphical user interfaces (GUIs) has risen sharply, placing greater demands on developers. The various GUIs, however, differ not only in appearance but also have many unique functions. Even operations that look similar are often implemented in very different ways. This places an additional burden on the developers when learning or writing code for different platforms. Instead, software tools can implement a functional <u>superset</u> of all the widget collections. These tools can be not only a superset but also a consolidation in which corresponding widgets are merged into one representation. This involves going beyond the tribal feuds between contenders of different look and feels, and asking what and why should elements be common among environments.

An Incursion Into Linguistics

The GUI is usually divided into three distinct layers: the operating system, the windowing environment, and the so-called toolkit. The operating system, while being responsible for the non-graphic part of the GUI, still supports the GUI with memory, process and communication management services. The windowing system *per se* is responsible for the low-level management of events, for the drawing primitives, and for the windows management. On top of these layers, the toolkit implements standard behaviors in small graphical elements, called widgets or controls, that populate our GUI windows. The application designer usually writes code that uses the widgets to handle the user interface.

Of course, as operating systems differ from one hardware platform to the other, so do windowing environments and toolkits. Even the term "window" has several different exceptions in different programming environments: a window is a rectangular display of a part of a document, but in some systems a window is also a process, and in some others a button is also a window. As vendors, consortia, and software houses battle for market share they crusade for imposing their toolkit, windowing system and operating system to the market. A successful strategy for doing so is to simplify the GUI component relying and capitalizing on elements made popular by precursors. This is what we are witnessing in the industry nowadays. Each toolkit therefore ubiquitously tries to reassure by providing so-called "common" widgets, while still retaining its own set of new pieces to distinguish it from other competitors.

If widgets are words of the language of user interfaces, each toolkit has grown its own vocabulary evolved from a common subset—a least common denominator. However, the vocabulary is not the main source of difficulty, as everyone who learned another language understands. What makes language difficult to learn is grammar. Anyone can learn how to use a pushbutton, a menu, or a text field in a user interface. It is a completely different situation when the window is in context, among other windows, and contains a number of interacting widgets displaying high volumes of data or complex data. The interaction of widgets is where the difficulty lies for the application developer.

A now well-developed angle of attack on the issue of "commonalities" between toolkits is the so-called "virtual toolkit" approach. The virtual toolkit directly targets the vocabulary issue, by providing another software layer on top of the native toolkits with a single application programming interface (API). Since vocabularies are similar, this approach works well for the common elements, but it is restricted to the least common denominator of the various dialects.

A new angle of attack, therefore, is to try solving the grammar issue first, from which the vocabulary solution will be a natural consequence. The idea is to abstract the different interactions rather than the widgets themselves into a toolkit that links directly to the windowing environment rather than the native toolkits. This approach supports true portability without sacrificing extensibility. Not only all widgets of all native toolkits can be implemented and supported by this toolkit, in a platform independent fashion, but the toolkit can be expanded to integrate custom-built widgets or application-specific widgets, which are portable in exactly the same way.

Bruce "Tog" Tognazzini

Bruce Tognazzini, author of "Tog on Interface" and a Distinguished Engineer in the new Human Interface Engineering organization at SunSoft, has been designing human-machine interfaces for better than thirty years. He spent fourteen years at Apple where he led at various times both the Apple II and the Macintosh human interface efforts.

The Macintosh interface was, in many ways, a step backwards from the interfaces found on the Apple Lisa and Xerox Star computers. Because the original Macintosh memory size was tiny—128K—and the computer, by explicit philosophy, lacked any provision for for a hard disk, the Macintosh's designers were forced to abandon many features of the Lisa and the Star.

When the Macintosh became a commercial success, others used it for a model for their own, far more powerful computers. They often faithfully duplicated design decisions forced exclusively by the limitations of the tiny, original Macintosh machine. The reason seems traceable to a firmly-held belief that somehow the folks at Apple hit upon the ideal interface ten years ago and that the best anyone can do now is to duplicate it.

Documents Inside of Tools

We have come to accept that the way to create or edit a document is to open that document inside of an application, or tool. This is equivalent to having to slide your entire house inside a hammer before you can hang a picture on the wall or having to put your teeth inside your toothbrush before you can brush them.

Free from this limitation, we could enter the era of plain-paper documents. Tear off a piece of fresh stationery and do with it as you will. Place a picture here, work out a spreadsheet there, lay some text behind it. Tools—any tools—are brought to bear on a single, final document.

The Apple Lisa and Xerox Star computers were both document-centered machines. Why weren't they copied? Because the Macintosh was the computer all the copiers saw, and they never revisited a single decision.

Explicit Save

Why don't our so-called friendly computers save our work every 30 seconds or so? Because on a 128K machine with a tiny, single disk drive, it is impossible to have both the program disk and the data disk in the computer at the same time. And the program disk has to be there most of the time, because there isn't enough room in memory for all of the program, so it has to be swapped in off the disk all the time. Hence, there is normally no disk in the computer to which the data could be auto-saved. This is another limitation faithfully reproduced in windowing systems designed for multi-megabyte computers with resident hard disks.

Trash Subject to Restrictions

In most cases, it is quite impossible to drag an object from inside an application across the desktop and drop it in the trash. Why? Because that's the way those young geniuses at Apple did it, but only because the original Macintosh was so small that there was not enough room for the application and the desktop (in the form of the Finder) to be inside the computer at the same time. Therefore, there was no possibility of anyone dragging something from the application to the trash because the trash was not there at the time. Yet another limitation being faithfully reproduced.

2nd Generation Interfaces

The Macintosh interface is almost a decade old. The computers of today don't sport 128K of memory, they sport 128 megs of memory. Gigabyte hard disks are all around us and Terabyte optical storage is waiting in the wings. The assumptions that drove the design of the Macintosh have not been valid for at least seven years, and they will not be valid tomorrow. It is time to get on with the task of developing the interfaces that will leave the doddering old Macintosh interface in the dust, even as the Macintosh left the command line interface of old in the dust behind it.

The new interfaces will break down the barriers that plague us today. Applications—tool sets—will be brought to bear on any document the user wishes. Documents will be protected from loss at all times. Users will work in a tightly integrated visual environment that is far more in tune with the task needs of today's (and tomorrow's) users.

The advent of pen-based notebook computers has finally awakened designers to the reality that the Macintosh is not the perfect interface that will live forever. People are no longer doing text editing, they are doing page layout and document processing. People are no longer doing black and white doodles, they are manipulating true-color images and editing video. They are no longer doing simple geometric drawings, they are building 3-D rotational models. These new tasks are bringing the old interfaces to their knees.

The first company to really go back to the drawing board, eliminate all the obsolete assumptions of the past, and build a new interface responsive to the needs and abilities of today's sophisticated users can expect as great a "win" as Apple experienced with the Macintosh.

David C. Smith

Dave Smith is a Senior Research Scientist at Apple, where he is currently investigating educational software. He was one of the chief designers of the Xerox Star graphical user interface. He is the lead author of the two major papers on that user interface design. He is credited with the invention of icons and the desktop metaphor in user interfaces.

Bruce Tognazzini is correct that the Macintosh user interface, and other familiar user interfaces, are less advanced in some ways than those of the Apple Lisa or Xerox Star. His analysis that the reasons for this are largely historical is also correct. Yet what surprises me more is how little any of the "standard GUIs" have advanced the state of the computing art during the past decade. I was one of the designers of the Xerox Star in the late 1970's. We invented icons and the desktop metaphor, but we viewed these ideas as a *starting point* for user interface progress, not as an end. We expected that by the end of the 1980's the industry would have moved well beyond the direct manipulation desktop interface. It has not happened.

What could have happened?

- Proactive vs. reactive. In the standard GUI, nothing happens until the user clicks on something. Then there is a brief flurry of activity while the computer performs the appropriate actions—either selecting something or executing a command. Afterward the computer returns to the idle state. This is a *reactive* interface; the computer reacts to the user's stimuli. There are two things wrong with it. (1) It wastes a lot of computing power. The

computer sits idle most of the time. In fact, the effective utilization of most personal computers over a 24 hour period is *zero*. And this is on a worldwide scale! (2) It forces the user to do everything. How much nicer it would be if a user could delegate tasks to the computer, and the computer would take responsibility for performing them. For example, I'd like to be able to say "watch the news wires, and tell me if anything about Boris Yeltsin comes by." The computer would *proactively* alert the user whenever it had accomplished one of its tasks. This could also be characterized as a *delegation* interface instead of a *direct manipulation* one.

Aside: There is a lot of activity currently on the topic of computer "agents" (persistent proactive processes). Agents may well be the next big advance in human-computer interaction.

- Information access. The volume of information generated continues to grow at an increasing rate. Yet our ability to access and manage it has improved little. We still can't access the contents of the USA's Library of Congress (or any library) from our desks. Even if we could, we have no good ways of finding information in it, short of talking to a human librarian. I don't need folders; I need a librarian agent!

- Human-human communication. Forget the human-computer interface; what about the human-human interface, when the humans are more than a few hundred yards apart? Personal computers still do a remarkably poor job of facilitating person-person communication. Perhaps a virtual reality interface such as Bellcore's "Cruiser" will finally provide some non-trivial assistance.

- End-user programming. Today, fifteen years after the advent of personal computers, the potential power of computers remains largely untapped. People are relegated to using generic applications written by developers who can only guess at their needs. People have no practical way of making *their* computer address *their* jobs. The only way to tap this power is for people to program their computers themselves. The reason that they can't is that the process of programming does not follow good user interface principles, ironically the same principles that all the standard GUIs obey.

- Developer productivity. It takes too long to write applications, and the time is increasing. This is a tremendous barrier to innovation. Suppose it took one tenth as long; imagine the applications we would have in our hands by now! We need to make a concerted effort to improve programming tools.

It is not too late. Starting today, we could obtain all of these advances by the end of the decade. It's just that we in the Star project expected the decade to be the 1980's instead of the 1990's.

Human Performance Using Computer Input Devices in the Preferred and Non-Preferred Hands

Paul Kabbash
Computer Systems Research Institute
University of Toronto
Toronto, Ont. Canada M5S 1A4
416-978-1961, kabbash@dgp.toronto.edu,
buxton@dgp.toronto.edu

I. Scott MacKenzie
Dept. of Computing & Information Science
University of Guelph
Guelph, Ont., Canada N1G 2W1
519-824-4120, mac@snowhite.cis.uoguelph.ca

William Buxton
University of Toronto & Xerox PARC,
c/o Computer Systems Research Institute
University of Toronto
Toronto, Ont. Canada M5S 1A4
416-978-1961, buxton@dgp.toronto.edu

ABSTRACT

Subjects' performance was compared in pointing and dragging tasks using the preferred and non-preferred hands. Tasks were tested using three different input devices: a mouse, a trackball, and a tablet-with-stylus. The trackball had the least degradation across hands in performing the tasks, however it remained inferior to both the mouse and stylus. For small distances and small targets, the preferred hand was superior. However, for larger targets and larger distances, both hands performed about the same. The experiment shows that the non-preferred hand is more than a poor approximation of the preferred hand. The hands are complementary, each having its own strength and weakness. One design implication is that the non-preferred hand is well suited for tasks that do not require precise action, such as scrolling.

KEYWORDS: Hand comparisons, computer input, Fitts' law.

INTRODUCTION

Increasingly, human-computer interaction supplements the familiar QWERTY keyboard with spatial controllers such as the mouse, stylus, or trackball. Nearly all such non-keyboard devices are operated with the preferred, "dominant" hand only. This contrasts with the everyday world, where the non-dominant hand is also used to perform spatial tasks. If one wants to design user interfaces to capture this common skill, there is little in the literature to serve as a guide.

This paper explores the performance of the non-preferred hand when interacting with various computer input devices for pointing, selecting, and dragging tasks. It is a repeat of an earlier experiment [11], that investigated the preferred hand in these same tasks. We compare performance across hands for three input devices: mouse, trackball, and stylus. The metrics for comparison in the present report are movement time and accuracy.

PREVIOUS RESEARCH

This study builds upon previous research in three distinct areas: Fitts' law models for psychomotor behavior, lateral asymmetries, and HCI. On its own, each is represented in the literature; however, only a few studies have attempted to reconcile issues of mutual interest.

Fitts' Law Models

One of the most robust and highly adopted models of human movement is Fitts' law [4,5]. The model is, arguably, the most successful of many efforts to model human behavior as an information processing activity. (For detailed reviews, see [10,12,20].) Fitts was interested in applying information theory to measure the difficulty of movement tasks and the human rate of information processing as tasks are realized. Fitts argued that the amplitude of a move was analogous to electronic signals and that the spatial accuracy was analogous to electronic noise. He proposed that the "index of difficulty" (*ID*) of a movement task could be measured in "bits" as the logarithm of the amplitude moved (*A*) divided by the tolerance or width (*W*) of the region within which the move terminates.

In this paper, we use the Shannon formulation for the index of task difficulty [10]:

$$ID = \log_2(A/W + 1). \tag{1}$$

In calculating *ID*, we adjust target width to reflect the spatial distribution of responses. This is in keeping with the information theoretic premise of the law, in which target width is analogous to a Gaussian distributed "noise" perturbing the intended signal (i.e., amplitude). The normalized target width is usually called the "effective target width," W_e [10].

Lateral Asymmetries

Three theories have been proposed to account for the between-hand performance differences in rapid aimed movements.

The first is that preferred and non-preferred hands differ primarily in their use of sensory feedback control [6,17,21]. In expounding this theory, Flowers [6] contrasted "ballistic" and "controlled" movements. He found that the preferred and non–preferred hands of strongly lateralized subjects achieved equal rates in a rhythmic tapping task, but that in a variation of Fitts' reciprocal tapping task (ranging from *ID*=1 to *ID*=6) the preferred hand outperformed the non–preferred hand by 1.5 - 2.5 bits/s, with differences marked at all but the lowest two *ID*s.

A second theory is that the preferred hand is less "noisy" in its output function. Accordingly, increases in movement amplitude or decreases in movement time require a greater force, which leads to greater output variability and thus more errors [16]. Annett et al. [1] suggested that this theory could be adapted to account for differences between hands in a peg transfer activity in which movement time was a dependent variable.

A third model, which predicts a left-hand advantage for larger target distances, was suggested by Todor and Doane [18]. This model, in a sense, expands on Flowers' notion of feedback control by incorporating both a left-hemisphere/right-hand superiority for sequential processing, and a right-hemisphere/left-hand superiority for non-adaptive parallel processing. The model was based on Welford's proposal that rapid aimed movements are composed of two distinct parts: a "fast distance-covering phase and a slower phase of 'homing' on to the target" [20]. The first phase is similar in speed to ballistic movement, but the second phase requires an additional process of visual control. They hypothesized, assuming contralateral control for the movements, that the right and left hands should exhibit a performance advantage in task conditions favoring the dominant processing mode of the contralateral hemisphere; specifically, that within tasks of equivalent calculated difficulty, movement time in the right hand should increase as the width and amplitude of the target grows larger while it should decrease in the left hand.

Although the association between motor programming and the spatial complexity of a task has been questioned in the literature, particularly by Quinn et al. [19], our interest in the Todor and Doane model is primarily in the practical result. In designing computer interfaces that allow for separate input from the non-preferred hand, it is useful to discern features of the task, aside from difficulty, that give a consistent advantage (or disadvantage) to the non-preferred hand. The issue of program complexity in itself, however, will not be directly addressed.

Human-Computer Interaction

A number of studies have been published which compare the usage of various input devices. This literature is effectively surveyed elsewhere [7,13]. However, we have found few studies that compare performance of the dominant vs. non-dominant hand in spatial tasks. An exception is Boritz, Booth, and Cowan [2] who tested a group of left-handed subjects and a group of right-handed subjects in a simple target selection task. Their study was flawed, however, in that the left-handed group had considerable prior experience using the mouse in the right hand, owing to the forced position of the mice in the computer lab.

Buxton and Myers [3] performed two experiments examining two-handed input. In the first, the non-dominant hand scaled an object while the dominant hand positioned it. In the second, the non-dominant hand navigated (scroll and jump) through a document while the dominant hand selected specified pieces of text. These experiments clearly demonstrated that users could easily use the non-dominant hand in such tasks.

MacKenzie, Sellen, and Buxton [11] showed that Fitts' law was applicable beyond traditional target acquisition tasks to include tasks such as dragging. This experiment provided half of the data for the current study. It tested the mouse, trackball, and tablet-with-stylus and found performance decrements for dragging compared to pointing. This degradation was concluded to be due to interference between the target acquisition task and maintenance of the dragging state (for example, holding down the mouse button while dragging). This degradation was found on each device for the criterion variables movement time and error rate. The amount of degradation was not uniform across devices, however. Significant one-way effects and two-way interactions revealed that the trackball was more prone to errors during dragging. Movement time was significantly longer for the trackball on both tasks; however the degradation during dragging was more pronounced for the mouse than for the trackball or stylus.

The experiment described in the next section emerged from the following hypotheses:

H1   Preferred and non-preferred hands yield the same speed, accuracy, and bandwidth using the mouse, trackball, and stylus in pointing and dragging tasks.

H2   Devices using small muscle groups (e.g., trackball) produce smaller differences between hands than devices using large muscle groups (e.g., mouse & stylus).

Of course, the first hypothesis is a null statement leading to the usual statistical tests. Differences were fully expected. A major motivation in the present study was to determine the extent of such differences.

METHOD

Subjects

In all we tested 24 subjects, comprising two independent groups of 12 (11 male, 1 female in Group 1; 9 male, 3 female in Group 2). The two groups, computer literate staff or students from local universities, served as paid volunteers. All subjects were self-declared right handers; but as an additional criterion for Group 2 we administered the Edinburgh Inventory for handedness [14], requiring a laterality quotient of at least +80.

Apparatus

The two groups were tested at different times, but on identical equipment. Subjects performed the tasks on an Apple *Macintosh II* using three input devices: the standard mouse, a Wacom tablet-with-stylus (model *SD42X*) used in absolute mode with a pressure sensitive stylus, and a Kensington trackball (model *Turbo Mouse ADB Version 3.0*). The equipment was set up with the input device on the right of the keyboard for Group 1 and on the left for Group 2. All devices were adjusted for a control/display ratio of approximately 0.5.

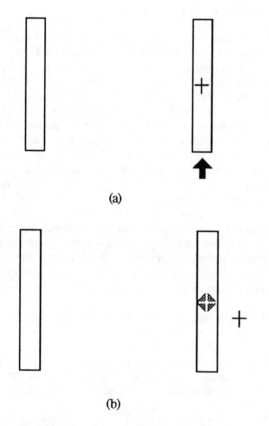

(a)

(b)

Figure 1. Experimental tasks were (a) pointing and (b) dragging.

Procedure

Subjects performed multiple trials on two different tasks with three different devices using their right hand (Group 1) or left hand (Group 2). The operation of the devices and the requirements of the tasks were explained and demonstrated to each subject before beginning. One warm-up block of trials was given prior to data collection.

The two tasks were "point-select" and "drag-select." For the point-select task, shown in Figure 1a, subjects moved the cross-hair cursor (+), back and forth between the targets and selected each target by pressing and releasing a button on the mouse or trackball, or by applying and releasing pressure on the stylus.

The arrow in Figure 1a pointed to the target to be selected. This helped maintain stimulus-response (S-R) compatibility as subjects proceeded. For the dragging task (Figure 1b), subjects acquired the small diamond-shaped object by pressing and holding the device button (on the mouse and trackball) or maintaining pressure on the stylus, and then dragged the object to the other target and deposited the object in the target region by releasing the button or pressure.

Subjects were instructed to balance speed and accuracy for an error rate around 4%. The software generated a beep as feedback for monitoring target misses.

Design

A $2 \times 4 \times 4 \times 3 \times 2$ (hand × amplitude × width × device × task) factorial design with repeated measures was used. Hand was a between-subjects factor, with Group 1 tested on their right (preferred) hand and Group 2 tested on their left (non-preferred) hand.[1] All other factors were within-subjects. The *A-W* conditions were chosen to exactly mimic Fitts' [4] original experiments with a stylus. There were four levels each for *A* (64, 128, 256, or 512 pixels) and *W* (8, 16, 32, or 64 pixels).

The *A-W* conditions were presented in random order with a block of ten trials performed at each condition. A session consisted of a sequence of sixteen blocks covering all *A-W* conditions. Ten sessions were sequenced for each device, alternating between pointing (five sessions) and dragging (five sessions). The initial task was chosen by the toss of a coin. Device ordering was counterbalanced.

The system collected three measurements for each trial: movement time and the *X* and *Y* selection coordinates. Dependent variables were movement time, error rate, variable error, constant error and bandwidth. Each of the accuracy measures describes different response behaviors (see, for example, [12]).

Error rate is simply the percentage of misses in the total number of trials.

---

[1] This was a between-subject factor because we ran the non-preferred hand subjects (Group 2) as a follow-up experiment to [11]. The data for Group 1 are taken from [11].

	Left Hand			Right Hand			Both Hands		
	Point	Drag	Both	Point	Drag	Both	Point	Drag	Both
Mouse	879	1084	982	657	900	779	768	992	880
Stylus	814	1021	917	645	786	716	729	904	817
Trackball	1165	1301	1233	1079	1266	1172	1122	1283	1203
Column means	953	1135	1044	794	984	889	873	1060	967

Table 1. Mean movement time (ms) by device, task, and hand.

Variable error is the standard deviation of movement endpoints along the horizontal axis. This corresponds to effective target width ($W_e = 4.133 \times SD_x$; see [10]). There are important distinctions between variable error and error rate despite their high correlation in Fitts' law tasks when error rates are below about 15% [9]. Error rate is especially relevant in HCI research, in the sense that the human operator is interested only in the success or failure in performing an operation, not in whether the effort was, for example, a near or far miss. Variable error, however, captures endpoint variability over all movements and so describes more completely the behavior.

Constant error is the mean deviation of responses from the target center. Constant error quantifies systematic biases of the responses from the target center; i.e., the tendency to overshoot or undershoot the targets.

Bandwidth, a composite of movement time and variable error, is a dependent variable meriting a separate analysis. Due to space limitations, bandwidth is not discussed further in the present paper.

RESULTS

Adjustment of Data
Newman-Keuls tests were performed on the session means at each hand × device × task condition for the first three dependent variables (36 tests). Overwhelmingly, the first session differed from groupings of sessions 2-5, and sessions 2-5 did not differ among themselves; and so, the data from the first session were discarded.

On the remaining data, using the same decomposition, outlier trials were eliminated where the X coordinate was more than three standard deviations from the mean. We also eliminated trials immediately following deviate trials (see [15]).

Movement Time (MT)
For each dependent variable an analysis of variance was used with repeated measures on device and task. Mean movement times for the two hands are summarized in Table 1, decomposed by device and task. As expected, the right hand outperformed the left hand ($F_{1,22} = 15.5$, $p < .001$) with overall movement times of 889 ms and 1044 ms, respectively.

The main effects of device and task were highly significant ($F_{2,44} = 273$, $p < .001$ & $F_{1,22} = 124$, $p < .001$, respectively). The effect of task was reflected in much slower MT for dragging (1060 ms) than pointing (873 ms). There was, however, no interaction of hand × task ($F_{1,22} = .044$), and performance in both hands degraded equally. For each hand the slowest device by far was the trackball with performance on the other two devices slowing somewhat from stylus to mouse. A significant interaction of hand × device ($F_{2,44} = 10.7$, $p < .001$) can be attributed to the trackball. That is, from preferred to non-preferred hand the degradation in mouse and stylus was large but equal (roughly 27%), whereas there was no difference in MT between hands on the trackball ($F_{1,22} = 1.52$, $p > .05$). There was also a significant three-way interaction of hand × device × task ($F_{2,44} = 4.33$, $p < .05$), one interpretation being that, although left-hand MT degraded equally in mouse and stylus going from the pointing task to dragging, the right hand showed greater degradation in the mouse than either the stylus or the trackball.

The effect of amplitude and width on movement time was investigated at each level of difficulty. As predicted by Todor and Doane [18], there was a tendency for left-hand MT to decrease as A and W increased within each ID level and, conversely, for right-hand MT to increase. The decreases in the left hand were in general larger and more consistent than the increases in the right hand, particularly so for the mouse. The effect, seen in Figure 2, extends Todor and Doane's results to a wide range of task difficulties. Their subjects, tested for two task conditions at $ID = 6$, also failed to show significant MT increases in the right hand. As Todor reasoned, this may be due to differential training.

Comparing performance across index of difficulty in Figure 2, it can also be seen that, in agreement with Flowers' feedback control theory, the right hand gained an advantage as target widths grew narrower (for example, conditions 1-4, 1-3, 1-2, 1-1). However, the L – R differences did not change when target amplitudes increased while target width was held constant (for example, conditions 1-4, 2-4, 3-4, and 4-4). Spatial target conditions, rather than task difficulty per se, therefore appear to have accounted for the between-hand MT differences.

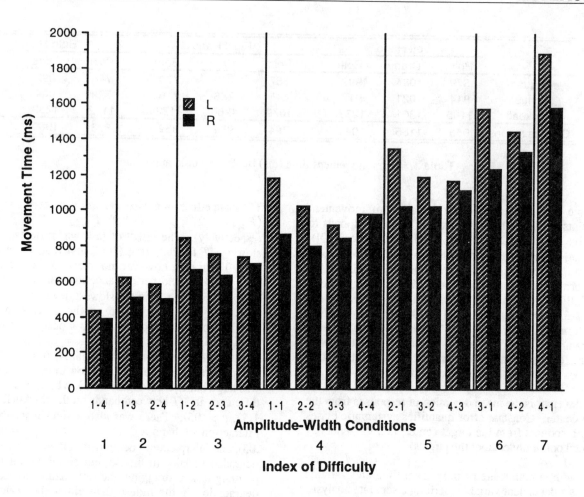

Figure 2. Movement time (ms) by amplitude, width, and hand.
First number of amplitude-width combinations refers to amplitude and second number refers to target width. For amplitude, 1 = 64 pixels, 2 = 128 pixel, 3 = 256 pixels, and 4 = 512 pixels. For target width, 1 = 8 pixels, 2 = 16 pixels, 3 = 32 pixels, and 4 = 64 pixels.

	Left Hand			Right Hand			Both Hands		
	Point	Drag	Both	Point	Drag	Both	Point	Drag	Both
Mouse	3.0	12.0	7.5	2.8	9.8	6.3	2.9	10.9	6.9
Stylus	4.9	12.7	8.8	3.6	12.2	7.9	4.3	12.5	8.4
Trackball	2.8	12.6	7.7	3.3	15.8	9.6	3.0	14.2	8.6
Column means	3.6	12.5	8.0	3.2	12.6	7.9	3.4	12.5	8.0

Table 2. Mean error rates (%) by device, task, and hand.

Accuracy

Error Rate. The two subject groups performed at comparable error rates throughout, except for two device-task combinations (mouse-dragging, where the right hand was superior, and trackball-dragging, where the left hand was superior).

Table 2 summarizes the mean percentage errors by hand, device, and task. In support of **H1**, error rates did not differ between the hands with means of 7.9% for the preferred hand and 8.0% for the non-preferred hand ($F_{1,22}$ = .005). Both hands were far more accurate during pointing than dragging. Error rates during the pointing task were within the desired range of 4% with means of 3.2% in the right hand and 3.6% in the left hand, but were considerably higher for dragging with means of 12.6% and 12. 5% respectively. Although the main effect of task was highly

	$W = 8$	$W = 16$	$W = 32$	$W = 64$	All Widths
Left Hand					
Pointing	9.2	16.1	29.4	56.4	27.7
Dragging	14.2	24.0	43.6	77.5	39.8
Right Hand					
Pointing	9.4	14.8	26.8	49.7	25.2
Dragging	33.7	39.1	54.6	84.2	52.9

Table 3. Mean effective target width (W_e, in pixels) for the trackball by task and W.

significant ($F_{1,22} = 138$, $p < .001$), degradation in the two hands was equal over tasks as evidenced by a lack of hand × task interaction ($F_{1,22} = .102$). In contrast, the two-way interaction of hand × device was significant ($F_{2,44} = 3.93$, $p < .05$) with accuracy from the right to left hand degrading in the mouse and stylus but improving in the trackball. This supports **H2**.

Variable Error / Effective Target Width. Analysis of this dependent variable was directed to the hypothesis of Annett et al. [1] that superior preferred-hand performance for controlled movements is attributable to a greater motor-output variability in the non-preferred hand. Unlike the mouse and the stylus, the trackball showed a significant hand × task interaction (mouse, $F_{1,22} = .565$; stylus, $F_{1,22} = .100$; trackball, $F_{1,22} = 7.04$, $p < .05$). This is shown in Table 3. Whereas results in the right hand for trackball-pointing proved similar to those in mouse and stylus, trackball-dragging yielded a large left-hand advantage, both in mean scores and standard deviations, which was especially apparent at the smallest width. At all target widths in Table 3, the left-hand dragging condition displayed less variable error than the right-hand dragging condition.

The motor-output variability theory predicts that larger target amplitudes should result in either a greater lengthening of movement time in the non-preferred hand or a greater degradation of variable error. Neither result held in the stylus, while only moderate support was found in the mouse. The finding of superior left-hand W_e for the trackball was unexpected and will be discussed below.

Constant Error. Table 4 summarizes constant error by device, task, and hand. Both hands exhibited a small tendency to undershoot the center of the target in all combinations, except for stylus-dragging where the two hands had a similar tendency to overshoot the target. Biases were small, on average falling within one pixel of target center. For all data, the main effect of hand was not significant ($F_{1,22} = .485$). For subsets of the data by device, the effect of hand was significant only for the trackball ($F_{1,22} = 4.49$, $p < .05$). This was again due to the dragging task, where the left hand showed greater accuracy ($CE = -0.143$ pixels vs. -2.38 pixels).

	Mouse	Stylus	Trackball
Left Hand			
Pointing	-1.11	-0.31	-0.98
Dragging	-0.16	+0.75	-0.14
Right Hand			
Pointing	-1.16	-0.42	-0.82
Dragging	+0.49	+1.06	-2.38

Table 4. Constant error (pixels) by device, task, and hand.

DISCUSSION

The most important finding of the study is how the results for movement time essentially extended the findings of Todor and Doane [18]. In tasks of equivalent difficulty, between-hand comparisons showed a right-hand advantage for target width, but a left-hand advantage for amplitude. This held in spite of the traditional Fitts prediction for equal movement time in a given limb system, when the spatial conditions of a task calculate to the same *ID*.

We found nothing in the analysis of accuracy to indicate that this main result was influenced by different speed-accuracy tradeoffs in the two hands. All accuracy measures were in fact largely independent of hand (with some exceptions during mouse-dragging and trackball-dragging). In the case of error rate this is not surprising, since the two subject groups were instructed to monitor performance by error-rate feedback.

Nonetheless, the three accuracy measures used in the experiment clearly captured distinct aspects of subject behavior. Constant error was most sensitive to the mechanical differences between devices. Stylus-pointing yielded smaller constant error than either mouse-pointing or trackball-pointing, presumably because subjects were able to place the stylus on the tablet with pen-point precision as opposed to the trackball technology of the mouse and the trackball; conversely, the mouse and trackball were more accurate than the stylus during dragging (excluding trackball-dragging in the right hand). This was largely due to subjects inadvertently lifting the stylus tip off of the tablet surface while dragging.

Error rate most clearly captured the difficulty of the dragging task. As was seen, both groups settled for much higher error rates during dragging, probably because subjects were unwilling to slow down sufficiently for this task, given their relative success with the pointing task. Only the right-hand group, however, showed unequal degradation between devices.

Going from pointing to dragging in the right hand, error rate for the mouse degraded least of the three devices while movement time degraded most. However, the lack of hand × task interaction on We in the mouse implies that the right-hand group was no less variable during the dragging task, just more careful. The speed-accuracy tradeoff here was most likely an experimental artifact–a side effect of daily work habits–in that all subjects had experience on the mouse but not on the other devices.

Finally, the peculiar results for accuracy during the trackball-dragging condition appear to have captured some underlying asymmetry in the motor function of the two hands. Here all three accuracy measures displayed a large left-hand advantage. Trackball-dragging also showed poor accuracy only in the right hand, in the sense that the left hand was equally accurate across devices when dragging.

Based on earlier results [11], it was speculated that device differences may be attributed to the extent of interference between the muscle groups required to manipulate a device, in particular, that finger-thumb interference would be greater than wrist-finger interference, and that this would contribute to superior performance in the mouse or stylus relative to the trackball. Our results for accuracy in the trackball confirm that finger-thumb independence was a significant requirement for trackball-dragging, but that it primarily affected the right hand. This may be compared to the finding by Kimura [8] that right-handers perform paired finger flexions more easily with their left hand; both results point to superior fine motor control in the left hand. The poor speeds achieved with the trackball in the present experiment, therefore, may simply have been a function of "ceiling effects" for this device. In spite of this, ceiling effects were not found to affect differential accommodations with respect to spatial target conditions on either task. In fact, of the three devices tested, the trackball most clearly supported the Todor and Doane theory.

CONCLUSION

The above provides the foundation on which design decisions can be based. First, for rough pointing or motion, the non-dominant hand is as good as the dominant hand across a large range of task difficulties. Therefore, it is appropriate for tasks that do not require precise action, such as scrolling (for example, as used in [3]). If the non-dominant hand is used for pointing, wide targets should be used.

While there was the least change between hands with the trackball, non-dominant performance with the mouse was still far superior. Readers are cautioned not to draw from this that if one is to use both hands that two mice are the best design choice. The ease of acquiring a fixed position device (such as a trackball, touch pad, or joystick) may more than compensate for slower task performance once acquired. This is something that must be evaluated in context of the specific task.

ACKNOWLEDGMENTS
We would like to thank the members of the Input Research Group at the University of Toronto who provided the forum within which this work was undertaken. We would especially like to acknowledge the contribution of Abigail Sellen a coauthor of [11] which provided half the data for the current paper. Thanks also to Dan Russell for his comments on the manuscript. Primary support for this work has come from Digital Equipment Corp., Xerox PARC, and the Natural Sciences and Engineering Research Council of Canada. Additional support has been provided by Apple Computer Inc., IBM Canada's Laboratory Centre for Advanced Studies, and the Arnott Design Group of Toronto. This support is gratefully acknowledged.

REFERENCES
1. Annett, J., Annett, M., Hudson, P. T. W., & Turner, A. (1979). The control of movement in the preferred and non-preferred hands. *Quarterly Journal of Experimental Psychology, 31*, 641-652.

2. Boritz, J., Booth, K. S., & Cowan, W. B. (1991). Fitts's law studies of directional mouse movement. *Proceedings of Graphics Interface '91* (pp. 216-223). Toronto: Canadian Information Processing Society.

3. Buxton, W., & Myers, B. A. (1986). A study in two-handed input. *Proceedings of the CHI '86 Conference on Human Factors in Computing Systems* (pp. 321-326). New York: ACM.

4. Fitts, P. M. (1954). The information capacity of the human motor system in controlling the amplitude of movement. *Journal of Experimental Psychology, 47*, 381-391.

5. Fitts, P. M., & Peterson, J. R. (1964). Information capacity of discrete motor responses. *Journal of Experimental Psychology, 67*, 103-112.

6. Flowers, K. (1975). Handedness and controlled movement. *British Journal of Psychology, 66*, 39-52.

7. Greenstein, J. S., & Arnaut, L. Y. (1988). Input devices. In M. Helander (Ed.), *Handbook of human-computer interaction* (pp. 495-519). Amsterdam: Elsevier.

8. Kimura, D. & Vanderwolf, C. H. (1970). The relation between hand preference and the performance of individual finger movements by left and right hands. *Brain, 93*, 769-774.

9. MacKenzie, I. S. (1991). *Fitts' law as a performance model in human-computer interaction*. Doctoral dissertation. University of Toronto.

10. MacKenzie, I. S. (1992). Fitts' law as a research and design tool in human-computer interaction. *Human-Computer Interaction, 7*, 91-139.

11. MacKenzie, I. S., Sellen, A., & Buxton, W. (1991). A comparison of input devices in elemental pointing and dragging tasks. *Proceedings of the CHI '91 Conference on Human Factors in Computing Systems* (pp. 161-166). New York: ACM.

12. Meyer, D. E., Smith, J. E. K., Kornblum, S., Abrams, R. A., & Wright, C. E. (1990). Speed-accuracy tradeoffs in aimed movements: Toward a theory of rapid voluntary action. In M. Jeannerod (Ed.), *Attention and Performance XIII* (pp. 173-226). Hillsdale, NJ.: Erlbaum.

13. Milner, N. (1988). A review of human performance and preferences with different input devices to computer systems. In D. Jones & R. Winder (Eds.), *People and Computers IV, Proceedings of the Fourth Conference of the British Computer Society Human-Computer Interaction Specialist Group* (pp. 341-362). Cambridge: Cambridge University Press.

14. Oldfield, R. C. (1971). The assessment and analysis of handedness: The Edinburgh inventory. *Neuropsychologia, 9*, 97-113.

15. Rabbitt, P. M. A. (1968). Errors and error correction in choice-response tasks. *Journal of Experimental Psychology, 71*, 264-272.

16. Schmidt, R. A., Zelaznik, H., Hawkins, B., Frank J. S., & Quinn, J. T. (1979). Motor-output variability: A theory for the accuracy of rapid motor acts. *Psychological Review, 86*, 415-451.

17. Sheridan, M. R. (1973). Effects of S-R compatibility and task difficulty on unimanual movement time. *Journal of Motor Behavior, 5*, 199-205.

18. Todor, J. I., & Doane, T. (1978). Handedness and hemispheric asymmetry in the control of movements. *Journal of Motor Behavior, 10*, 295-300.

19. Quinn, J. T., Zelaznik, H. N., Hawkins, B., & McFarquhar, R. (1980). Target-size influences on reaction time with movement time controlled. *Journal of Motor Behavior, 12*, 239-261.

20. Welford, A. T. (1968). *Fundamentals of skill*. London: Methuen.

21. Woodworth, R. S. (1899). The accuracy of voluntary movements. *Psychological Review* [monograph supplement], *3*(2, Whole No. 13).

The Limits Of Expert Performance Using Hierarchic Marking Menus

Gordon Kurtenbach and William Buxton

Dept. of Computer Science
University of Toronto
Toronto, Ontario Canada, M5S 1A1
Phone: (416) 978-6619, Email: gordo@dgp.toronto.edu, willy@dgp.toronto.edu

ABSTRACT

A marking menu allows a user to perform a menu selection by either popping-up a radial (or pie) menu, or by making a straight mark in the direction of the desired menu item without popping-up the menu. A hierarchic marking menu uses hierarchic radial menus and "zig-zag" marks to select from the hierarchy. This paper experimentally investigates the bounds on how many items can be in each level, and how deep the hierarchy can be, before using a marking to select an item becomes too slow or prone to errors.

KEYWORDS: Marking menus, pie menus, gestures, pen based input, accelerators, input devices

INTRODUCTION

The first couple of times I went into the restaurant I got a menu and surveyed my choices. I generally ordered vermicelli and barbecue pork by saying "dish number 30, please". On my fifth or sixth visit I knew what I wanted and was in a hurry. I didn't wait to see a menu. I looked my waiter in the eye and said, "Lloyd, bring me a number 30". Things happen faster when you know what you want.

This story reveals the philosophy behind an interaction technique we call "marking menus". Marking menus are a type of pop-up menu where, if the user can recall the location of the item in the menu, the item can be selected without having to pop-up the menu. Just like in the story, it's nice not having to wait for Lloyd to bring a menu when you know what you want and how to order it.

Menus are used extensively in human computer interfaces. They provide critical information on what commands are available and a way to invoke commands. Unfortunately, many computer menus do not provide the kind of service that the restaurant in our example does. One cannot order without having to look at the menu and this can be a problem. Some menus require substantial computing before display and this delays the user. Also, menus appearing and disappearing on the screen can be visually disruptive. Finally, a menu may obscure objects on the screen that are the focus of attention.

Some systems do provide methods to by-pass menus but the by-pass mechanism requires an action that is radically different than selecting using the menu. For example, in some systems, a user selects from a menu using the mouse but by-passes the menu using an "accelerator key" on the keyboard. Using our restaurant example again, this would be like changing from ordering verbally, when one has the menu, to ordering with hand signals when one doesn't have the menu. The problem is that one has to learn two different protocols.

Marking menus are designed to overcome this problem. Using a marking menu with a pen based computer works as follows. A novice user presses down on the screen with the pen and waits for a short interval of time (approximately 1/3 second). A radial menu [13] [4] then appears directly under the tip of the pen. A user then highlights an item by keeping the pen pressed and making a stroke towards the desired item. If the item has no sub-menu, the item can be selected by lifting the pen. If the item does have a sub-menu, it is displayed. The user then continues, selecting from the newly displayed sub-menu. Figure 1 (a) shows an example. Lifting the pen will cause the current series of highlighted items to be selected. The menus are then removed from the screen. At any time a user can indicate "no selection" by moving the pen back to the center of the menu before lifting, or change the selection by moving the pen to highlight another item before lifting. Finally a user can "back-up" to a previous menu by pointing to its center.

The other, faster, way to make a selection without popping up the menu is by drawing a mark. A mark can be drawn by pressing the pen down and immediately moving. The shape of the mark dictates the particular series of items selected from the menu hierarchy. Figure 1 (b) shows an example.

The first important point to note is that *the physical movement involved in selecting an item from the menu is identical to the physical movement required to make the mark corresponding to that item.* With marking menus, a user actually *rehearses* the physical movement involved in making the mark every time a selection from the menu is made. We believe that this helps users learn the markings. The second point to note is that *supporting radial menus with markings in this way helps users make an efficient transition from novice to expert.* Novices perform menu selection because they are not familiar with the menu and its layout. As they become experts, they begin to use the

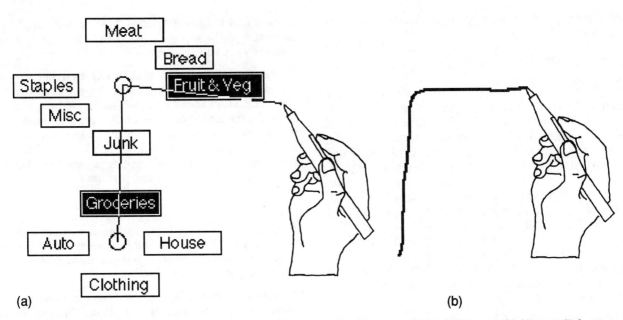

Figure 1. Hierarchic marking menus can be selected from using two different methods. Using method (a), radial menus can be sequentially displayed and selections made. Method (b) uses a marking to make the same selection. Method (a) is good when the user is unfamiliar with the menu. Method (b) is good when the user is familiar with the menu and wants to avoid waiting for the display of each menu.

markings instead. Novices, in effect, "learn on the job" because these two activities are so similar.

Is marking much faster than using the menu? In a study of user behavior with non-hierarchic marking menus in a real application, we found that using a mark was approximately 3.5 times faster than using the menu, even if the 1/3 of second delay to pop-up the menu was subtracted from menu selection time (for example, one user required on average 0.2 seconds to select using a mark and 0.7 seconds to select using the menu) [8]. Displaying the menu actually takes a small amount of time (0.15 seconds in our system). The larger amount of time is consumed waiting for the user to react to the display of the menu, even if the location of the desired menu item is known. While these time savings may seem trivial, one user performed approximately 15,000 selections over 36 hours of work. Using marks helped her complete the task 1.25 hours sooner.

We performed an experiment to address questions one asks when designing an interface that will use hierarchic marking menus.

Q1: Are hierarchic marking menus a feasible idea? Non-hierarchic marking menus have proven to be feasible [9]. Other research has shown that radial menus are faster than linear menus [1]. Thus we can expect marking menus, even without using the faster marking ahead technique, to be faster that traditional linear menus. Nevertheless, the question remains as to whether it is possible to use a marking to select hierarchic menu items.

Q2: How deep can one go using a marking? Just how "expert" could users become? Could an experienced user use a mark to select from a menu which had 3 levels of hierarchy and twelve items at each level? By discovering the limitations of the technique we would be able to predict what menu configurations, with enough practice, will lead to reliable selection using a marking, and which menu configurations, regardless of the amount of practice, will never permit reliable selection using a marking. Also, will some items be easier to select regardless of depth? For example, it seems easier to select items that are on the up, down, left and right axes even if the menus are cluttered and deep.

Q3: Is breadth better than depth? Will wide and shallow menu structures be easier to access with markings than thin and deep ones? Traditional menu designs have breadth/depth trade-offs [5]. What sort of trade off exists for marking menus?

Q4: Will mixing menu breadths result in poorer performance? A previous experiment on non-hierarchic marking menus has shown that the number of items in a menu and the layout of those items in the menu affects selection performance when markings are used [9]. Specifically, menus with 2, 4, 6, 8 and 12 items work quite well for markings. What will be the effect of selecting from menu configurations where the number of items in a menu varies from sub-menu to sub-menu?

Q5: Will the pen be more suitable than the mouse for making marks? The experiment mentioned above also compared making selections from non-hierarchic marking menus using a tablet with a stylus, a trackball and a mouse. The trackball was the worst performer, while the tablet with stylus and mouse performed equally. However, hierarchic marking menus require more complex marks. Will the mouse prove inadequate?

THE EXPERIMENT

Basic Design

In order to determine the limits of performance, we needed to simulate expert behavior. We defined expert behavior as the situation where the user is completely familiar with the contents and layout of the menu and can easily recall the marking needed to select a menu item. To make subjects "completely familiar" with the menu layouts we chose menu items whose layout could be easily memorized. We tested menus with 4, 8 and 12 items. For a menu of 4 items, the labels were laid out like the four points of a compass: "N", "E", "S" and "W". We referred to this type of menu as a compass4. Similarly a "compass8" menu had these four directions plus "NE", "SE", "SW" and "NW". Menus with twelve items, referred to as a "clock" menus, were labeled like the hours on a clock.

Will users of real applications ever be as familiar with menus as they are with a clock or compass? We believe the answer is yes and base this on three pieces of evidence. First, our own behavioral study of users using a marking menu in a real application shows, with practice, markings are used over ninety percent of the time [8]. Other researchers have reported this type of familiarity with pie menus [4]. Second, research has shown that the effects of menu organization disappear with practice [2][10]. In other words, with practice, users memorize menu layouts and navigate directly to the desired menu item. Finally, it must be remembered that a user does not have to memorize the layout of an entire menu. For example, a hierarchic marking

menu could contain 64 items but the user might only memorize the markings needed to select the two most frequently used menu items.

The general design of a trial in our experiment was as follows. The system would ask the subject to select a certain item using a marking (the menu could not be popped up by the subject). The subject would draw the marking and the system would then record the time taken, and whether or not a successful selection was made. We would then vary the menu configuration and input device and see what effect these variables had on selection performance.

Method

Subjects: Twelve right handed subjects were recruited from University of Toronto. All subjects were skilled in using a mouse but had little or no experience using a pen on a pen based computer.

Equipment: A Momenta pen based computer was used. The input devices consisted of a Microsoft mouse for IBM personal computers, and a Momenta pen and digitizer.

Task: A trial occurred as follows. The type of menu configuration currently being tested would appear in the top left corner of the screen. A small circle would appear in the center of the screen. A subject would then press and hold the pen or mouse button over the circle. The system would then display instructions describing the target at the top center of the screen. A subject would then respond by drawing a mark that was hoped to be the correct response. The system would respond by displaying the selection produced by the marking. If the selection did not match the target, the system would beep to indicate an error. The

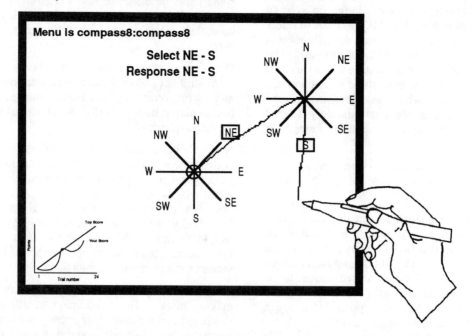

Figure 2: The experiment screen at the end of a trial where the target was "NE-S". After the marking was completed, the system displayed the menus along the marking to indicate to the subject the accuracy of their marking.

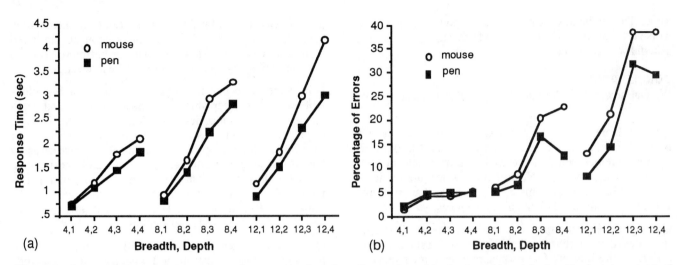

Figure 3: Response time and percentage of errors as a function of menu breadth, depth and input device. Each data point is the average of 288 trials.

system would then display each menu in the current menu configuration at its appropriate location along the marking and indicate the selection from each menu. A subject's score would then be shown in the lower left of the screen. Figure 2 shows the experimental screen at this point. If a selection was incorrect, a subject would lose 100 points and the trial would be recorded as an error. If a selection was correct, the subject would earn points based on how quickly the response was executed. Response time was defined as the time that elapsed between the display of the target and the completion of the marking.

Design: All three factors, device, breadth and depth were within-subject. Trials were blocked by input device with every subject using both the pen and the mouse. One half of the subjects began with the pen first while the other half began with the mouse. For each device, a subject was tested on the 13 menu configurations (breadths 4, 8 and 12 crossed with depths 1 to 4, plus the mixed menu configuration of clock:compass8:clock). Menu configurations were presented in random order. For each menu configuration, a subject performed 24 trials. During the 24 trials, subjects were repeatedly asked to select 1 of 3 different targets. Each target appeared eight times in the 24 trials but the order of appearance was random.

Before starting a block of trials for a particular menu configuration, subjects were allowed 8 seconds to study the menu configuration. Before starting trials with a particular input device, a subject was given ten practice trials using the device on a compass4:compass4:compass4 menu.

Results and Discussion

All three factors, input device, breadth and depth affected response time. Analysis of variance revealed a three way interaction between input device, breadth and depth $(F(6,66)=3.32, p < .05)$ affecting response time. Figure 3 (a) shows these relationships. As one would expect, increasing breadth and depth increases response time, however,

subjects' performance degraded more quickly with the mouse than with the pen.

Subjects responded significantly faster with the pen than with the mouse $(F(1,11)=19.7, p < .001)$. The response time averaged across all subjects, breadths and depths for the pen was 1.69 seconds while the mouse averaged 2.07 seconds. As menu breadth and depth increased subjects' performance with the two devices began to differ. This is shown in figure 3.

Subjects produced significantly more errors with the mouse than with the pen $(F(1,11)=6.41, p < .05)$. Both depth and breadth interacted to affect error rate $(F(6,66)=12.28, p < .001)$. Figure 3 (b) shows that mouse and pen error percentages began to differ once menu breadth reached eight items. For either device, error rates were below 10% for up to menus of breadth 8 and depth 2.

We tested for effects of mixing menu breadths in menu configurations by comparing the performance of a clock:clock:clock menu with a clock:compass8:clock menu. We found no significant performance differences between the two menu configurations.

In order to test the hypothesis that markings which consist of "on axis" items (items on the vertical and horizontal axes) out-perform "off axis" markings, we picked targets for menus of breadth twelve, depths two, three and four such that the experimental data could be divided into 3 groups. With each group we associated an "off axis-level": a1, a2 and a3. Experimental data was placed in group a1 if the target consisted strictly of menu items that were on-axis, such as "12-3-9-3". Group a3 consisted of data on targets that consisted of entirely off-axis targets such as "1-2-1-2". Group a2 consisted of data on targets that were a mixture of on-axis and off-axis menu items, such as "12-7-3-9". Figure 4 shows that axis level had a significant effect on response time $(F(2,22)= 104.84, p < .001)$ and on percentage of errors $(F(2,22)=36.2, p < .001)$. Figure 4 (a) shows how the type of device interacted with off-axis level $(F(2,22)=6.93, p <$

.05). This indicates that subjects' response time on the worse off-axis targets did not degrade as badly with the pen as it did with the mouse.

CONCLUSIONS

We can now revisit the questions posed at the start of this paper.

Q1: Are hierarchic marking menus a feasible idea? Even if using a marking to access an item is too hard to draw or cannot be remembered, a user can perform a selection by displaying the menus. Nevertheless, since the subjects *could* perform the experiment, it is feasible that markings could be used to select hierarchic menu items.

Q2: How deep can one go using a marking? Our data indicates that increasing depth increases response time linearly. The limiting factor appears to be error rate. For menus of four items, even up to four levels deep, the error rate was less than ten percent. This is also true for menus of eight items, up to a depth of two. However, when using markings for menus with eight items or more, at depths greater than two, selection becomes error-prone, even for the expert. However, our "off-axis" analysis indicates that the source of poor performance at higher breadths and depths is due to selecting "off-axis" items. Thus, when designing a wide and deep menu, the frequently used items could be placed at "on-axis" locations. This would allow some items to be accessed quickly and reliably with markings, despite the breadth and depth of the menu.

What is an acceptable error rate? The answer to this question depends on the consequences of an error, the cost of undoing an error or redoing the command, and the attitude of the user. For example, we have data that indicates, in certain situations, experts produce more errors than novices [11]. The experts were skilled at error recovery and thus elected to trade accuracy for fast task performance. Our experiences with marking menus with six items being used in a real application indicates that experts perceived selection to be error-free. Other research reports that menus with up to eight items produce acceptable performance [4]. Marking menus present a classic time versus accuracy trade-off. If the marking error rate is too high, a user can always use the slower but more accurate method of popping up the menus to make a selection.

Q3: Is breadth better than depth? For menu configurations that resulted in acceptable performance, breadth and depth seems to be an even trade-off in terms of response time and errors. For example, accessing 64 items using menus of four items, three deep, is approximately as fast as using menus of eight items, two deep, and both have approximately equivalent error rates. Thus, within this range of menu configurations, a designer can let the semantics of menu items dictate whether menus should be narrow and deep, or wide and shallow.

Q4: Will mixing menu breadths result in poorer performance? The experiment did not show this to be true. This may be due to the fact that our menu labels strongly suggested the correct angle to draw at, and therefore confusion was avoided. A stronger test might be to compare mixing menu breadths using less suggestive labels. However, our results do indicate that, with enough familiarity with the menus, mixing breadths is not a significant problem.

Q5: Will the pen be better than the mouse for making marks? Overall, subjects performed better with the pen than with the mouse. However, for small menu breadths and depths, subjects' performance, with either the mouse or pen, was approximately equivalent. We found this extremely encouraging because it implies that a marking menu is an interaction technique that not only takes advantage of the pen but also remains compatible with the mouse.

FUTURE DIRECTIONS

We are currently experimenting with designing interfaces that use marking menus. When displays become small or very large, marking menus are effective. A mark or selection can be made at a user's current location without a trip to a menu bar or tool pallet. We are currently trying to exploit this advantage on a electronic whiteboard system

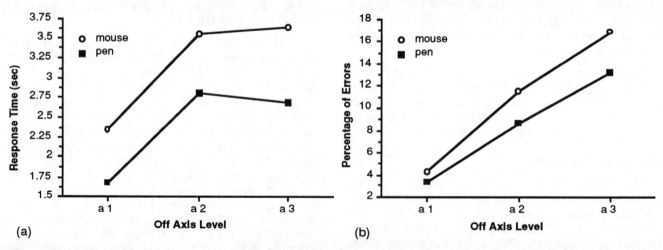

(a) (b)

Figure 4: Average response time and percentage of errors for targets with an increasing number of "off-axis" items.

[3]. We are also using marking menus on small hand-held computers [12]. On small screens, since both the menu and mark "go-away" once performed, no valuable screen space is consumed.

We are continuing to gather both programmer and user feedback on using markings menus in many applications [6].

A marking menu is a specific instance of an interaction technique that supports both the novice and expert user, and trains a novice to become expert. We are investigating how this philosophy can be applied to other types of interaction techniques and markings.

ACKNOWLEDGMENTS

We thank the members of the Input Research Group at the University of Toronto who provided the forum for the design and execution of this project. This work was performed in the Dynamic Graphics Project laboratory at the University of Toronto, to whom we are grateful. We especially thank Scott Mackenzie for his advice on statistical matters and Beverly Harrison for her comments on experimental design. We gratefully acknowledge the financial support of the Natural Sciences and Engineering Research Council of Canada, Digital Equipment Corporation, Xerox PARC and Apple Computer.

REFERENCES

1. Callahan, J., Hopkins, D., Weiser, M. & Shneiderman, B. (1988) An empirical comparison of pie vs. linear menus. Proceedings of CHI '88, 95-100

2. Card S. K. (1982) User perceptual mechanisms in the search of computer command menus. *Proceedings of Human Factors in Computer Systems*. SIGCHI, 190-196

3. Elrod, S., Bruce, R., Gold, R., Goldberg, D., Halasz, F., Janssen, W., Lee, D., McCall, K., Pedersen, E., Pier, K., Tang, J. & Welch, B. (1992) Liveboard: A large interactive display supporting group meetings, presentations and remote collaboration. *Proceedings of CHI '92*, 599-607

4. Hopkins, D. (1991) The Design and Implementation of Pie Menus. *Dr. Dobb's Journal*, December, 1991, 16-26

5. Kiger, J.L. (1984) The depth/breadth trade-off in the design of menu-driven user interfaces. *International Journal of Man Machine Studies*, 20, 210-213

6. Kurtenbach, G. & Baudel, T. (1992) HyperMark: Issuing commands by drawing marks in Hypercard, *Proceedings of CHI '92 poster and short talks*, 64

7. Kurtenbach, G. & Buxton W. (1991) Issues in combining marking and direct manipulation techniques. *Proceedings of UIST '91*, New York: ACM, 137-144

8. Kurtenbach, G. (1992) The evaluation of an interaction technique based on self-revelation, guidance and rehearsal. (in preparation) Ph.D. thesis, University of Toronto

9. Kurtenbach, G., Sellen, A. & Buxton, W. (1993) An empirical evaluation of some articulatory and cognitive aspects of "marking menus". *Journal of Human Computer Interaction*, Volume 8, Number 1

10. McDonald, J. E., Stone, J. D. & Liebelt, L. S. (1983) Searching for items in menus: The effects of organization and type of target. *Proceedings of Human Factors Society 27th Annual Meeting*. Human Factor Society, 834-837

11. Sellen, A.J., Kurtenbach, G. & Buxton, W. (1992) The prevention of mode errors through sensory feedback. *Journal of Human-Computer Interaction*. Vol. 7(2), 141-164

12. Weiser, M. (1991) The computer for the 21st century. Scientific American, September 1991, volume 265, 3, 94-104

13. Wiseman, N.E., Lemke, H.U. & Hiles, J.O. (1969) PIXIE: A New Approach to Graphical Man-machine Communication, *Proceedings of 1969 CAD Conference Southhampton*, IEEE Conference Publication 51, 463

Lag as a Determinant of Human Performance in Interactive Systems

I. Scott MacKenzie

Dept. of Computing & Information Science
University of Guelph
Guelph, Ontario, Canada N1G 2W1
519-824-4120, mac@snowhite.cis.uoguelph.ca

Colin Ware

Faculty of Computer Science
University of New Brunswick
Fredericton, N.B., Canada E3B 5A3
506-453-4566, cware@unb.ca

ABSTRACT

The sources of lag (the delay between input action and output response) and its effects on human performance are discussed. We measured the effects in a study of target acquisition using the classic Fitts' law paradigm with the addition of four lag conditions. At the highest lag tested (225 ms), movement times and error rates increased by 64% and 214% respectively, compared to the zero lag condition. We propose a model according to which lag should have a multiplicative effect on Fitts' index of difficulty. The model accounts for 94% of the variance and is better than alternative models which propose only an additive effect for lag. The implications for the design of virtual reality systems are discussed.

KEYWORDS: Human performance modeling, lag, feedback delay, virtual reality, Fitts' law, speed-accuracy tradeoff

INTRODUCTION

Human interaction with computers is two-way. As participants in a closed-loop system, we issue commands through a computer's input channels and receive results fed back on output channels. Subsequent input depends on the latest output. Not surprisingly, performance is adversely affected when the feedback is subject to delay or lag. Fortunately, lag is negligible in many interactive computing tasks, such as text entry or cursor movement in word processing.

The opposite extreme is remote manipulation systems, where the human operator is physically displaced from the machine under control. The lag may be due to mechanical linkages or to transmission delays in the communications channel. In controlling a space vehicle on a distant moon or planet, for example, transmission delays, or lag, may be on the order of several minutes.

Somewhere in the middle is virtual reality (VR), a genre of interactive system relying heavily on the 3D tracking of hand, head, and/or body motion in a simulated 3D environment. The pretense of reality requires a tight link between the user's view of the environment and the actions – usually hand or head motions – that set the view. When changes in the environment lag behind input motions, the loss of fidelity is dramatic. Although this has been noted in VR research, empirical studies to measure lag and to evaluate its impact on human performance are rare. In this paper, we describe an experiment to measure and model the speed, accuracy, and bandwidth of human motor-sensory performance in interactive tasks subject to lag.

The Source of Lag

Lag is inevitable and can be attributed to properties of input devices, software, and output devices. The sampling rate for input devices and the update rate for output devices are major contributors. Input devices are usually sampled at fixed rates in the range of 10 to 60 samples per second. A 60 Hz rate (every 16.67 ms) is possible when synchronizing with the vertical retrace of many CRT displays. On average, this component of lag is half the retrace period or 8.3 ms. Alone, this is negligible. (8.3 ms is the period of flicker in a fluorescent light fixture driven by a 60 Hz full-wave rectified power source. The flicker is undetectable by the human eye.)

Lag is increased further due to "software overhead" – a loose expression for a variety of system-related factors. Communication modes, network configurations, number crunching, and application software all contribute.

Lag will increase dramatically when output requires substantial computation for graphic rendering. A frame rate of 10 Hz is considered minimal to achieve "real time" animation. Since the construction of the frame only begins when the position is known, the potential for parallel processing is limited. Using standard double buffering (in which the frame is only presented once fully drawn), there is a minimum 100 ms lag to the start of the frame display interval and a lag of 150 ms to the middle of the frame display interval.

In VR, lag is very much present. It is associated mostly with three-dimensional tracking devices attached to the hand or head, as well as the lag caused by the low frame rates. Typical devices include the Polhemus *Isotrak* (used on the VPL *DataGlove*) and the Ascension *Bird*. These devices (i.e., their interfaces) must transmit six degree-of-freedom position and orientation data to the host computer at a high rate while acting in concert with competing processes in the complete VR environment. Maintaining negligible lag is usually not possible.

In one of the few empirical studies on lag, Liang, Shaw, and Green [9] describe an experiment to measure the lag on a Polhemus *Isotrak*. They found lags between 85 ms and 180 ms depending on the sampling rate (60 Hz vs. 20 Hz) and communications mode (networked, polled, continuous output, direct, and client-server). Although the software was highly optimized to avoid other sources of lag, their results are strictly best-case since an "application" was not present. A filtering algorithm was proposed to compensate for lag by anticipating head motion.

The communication link becomes more of a bottleneck as the number of sensors and their resolution increases. The *CyberGlove* by Virtual Technologies provides greater resolution of finger position than many gloves by including more sensors – up to 22 per glove. However, correspondingly more data are required. At the maximum data rate of 38.4 kilobaud, it takes about 5 ms just to relay the data to the host. Although, individual sensors can be disabled to increase throughput for simple motions, a tradeoff is evident between the desire to resolve intricate hand formations and the requisite volume of "immediate" data. If we speculate on future interaction scenarios with full body suits delivering the nuances of complex motions – a common vision in VR – then it is apparent that lag will substantially increase simply due to the quantity of data.

The Effect of Lag

Although lag has been acknowledged and quantified as a compromising parameter in VR systems, and its effect on human performance appears to be considerable, the evidence for this is mostly anecdotal.

In a recent newspaper article touting the promise of VR as a tool for artists [4], lag was cited as a hindrance to user interaction: "The display is low-resolution and cartoonish and because of the enormous computing power needed to generate the environments, there tends to be a brief but noticeable time lag between turning your head and seeing the new point of view" (p. C1). Specific effects on human performance were not cited, however.

On intuitive grounds, Pausch notes that low-latency is significantly more important than high-quality graphics or

stereoscopy [13]. His low-end VR system emphasized presence (i.e., low lag) over output graphics by maintaining seven screen updates per second with wire frame images.

In an experiment with force feedback Brooks, Ouh-Young, Batter, and Kilpatrick [1] concluded that screen updates are needed 15 times per second minimum in maintaining the illusion of continuous change in the force sensed. Even at this rate, subjects objected to the "sponginess" of the feel. Others cite "motion sickness" as a by-product of lag with head-mounted displays [6, 8].

The cognitive co-processor architecture from Xerox PARC [3], in order to maintain the illusion of reality, adopts a "governor" mechanism to ensure the screen is updated every 100 ms – the time for perceptual processing. If loading increases, cooperating rendering processes reduce the quality of the output to maintain the 10 frame per second refresh rate. This is in keeping with Pausch's claim that maintaining low lag is more important than high-resolution graphic output.

Empirical measurements of effect of lag on human performance are rare. There was some research in the 1960s (e.g., [7, 14]) relating to the design of controllers for remote manipulation systems; however the lags tested were extremely long (up to several seconds). In one instance, the apparatus was mechanical [14], and in another lag was programmed as an exponential time constant preventing the cursor from fully reaching a target unless a deliberate overshoot was programmed [7]. In both cases movement time increases due to lag were dramatic – well in excess of the amount of lag. Since lag is on the order of a few hundred milliseconds in VR, its effect on human performance is less apparent.

Lag and the Speed-Accuracy Tradeoff

Certainly, the presence of lag in interactive environments will increase the time to complete motor-sensory tasks; but the extent of the "cost" is uncertain. Error rates may also increase due to lag.

As the difficulty of tasks increases, the degradation in performance may increase non-linearly with lag. To test this, we call on Fitts' law [5], whereby the difficulty of a target acquisition task is rated in "bits" as

$$ID = \log_2\left(\frac{A}{W} + 1\right) \qquad (1)$$

where A is the amplitude or distance to the target and W is the width or size of the target. Equation 1 is a variation known as the Shannon formulation [10].

In repeated trials, if the mean difficulty of a range of tasks (ID, in bits) is divided by the mean movement time to complete the tasks (MT, in seconds), then the dependent variable bandwidth (BW, in bits/s) emerges. (Fitts called this the index of performance, *IP*.) Furthermore, if *ID* is calculated using the effective target width (W_e), adjusted for errors or spatial variability in responses, then bandwidth encompasses speed *and* accuracy.[1] This provocative measure – somewhat analogous to efficiency – holds tremendous promise for measurement and evaluation in human-computer interfaces (e.g., [2]). Adjusting for error rates, the effective index of difficulty is

$$ID_e = \log_2(\frac{A}{W_e} + 1) \tag{2}$$

and

$$BW = \frac{ID_e}{MT}. \tag{3}$$

The prediction model for movement time may be obtained through linear regression as follows:

$$MT = a + b\ ID_e \tag{4}$$

The slope reciprocal, $1/b$, is often interpreted as bandwidth. Provided the intercept is small, $1/b$ in Equation 4 will be very similar to the bandwidth calculated using Equation 3.

It has been suggested that target acquisition may consist of a succession of discrete movements, each subdividing the target space until the probe is within the target, similar to a binary search. The index of difficulty can be interpreted as a measure of the number of movements required (averaged over a number of trials). The effect of lag, therefore, should occur at each of the discrete movement stages. To accommodate lag in our model, we multiply by the index of difficulty. Thus, we replace the conventional single parameter Fitts' law model (Equation 4) with

$$MT = a + (b + c\ LAG)\ ID_e, \tag{5}$$

where the additional coefficient, c, is the weighting for the *lag* ×*ID* interaction. Conveniently, in the absence of lag Equation 5 reduces to Equation 4.

In the next section we describe an experiment using a target acquisition task to measure the effect of lag on the speed, accuracy, and bandwidth of human performance in motor-sensory tasks on interactive systems.

METHOD

Subjects
Eight subjects from the University of British Columbia (where the second author was on sabbatical) served as paid

---

[1]The method for transforming W to W_e was first presented in 1960. See Welford [15, p. 147] or MacKenzie [10] for detailed discussions.

volunteers. All subjects had prior experience using a mouse.

Apparatus
A Silicon Graphics *personal IRIS* with a standard CRT and an optical mouse was used. The C-D gain of the mouse was set to one.

The cursor was a 7×7 pixel green square with a 1 pixel black dot in the centre (1 pixel = 0.035 cm). The goal was to get the central dot within the target boundaries.

The software was optimized to reduce overhead. All mouse samples and screen updates were synchronized to the vertical retrace of the CRT (60 Hz). Lag was introduced by buffering mouse samples and delaying processing by multiples of the screen refresh period (16.67 ms increments). The minimum lag was, on average, half the retrace period, or 8.3 ms.

Procedure
The following discrete target acquisition task was used: At the initiation of a trial the cursor appeared 300 pixels from the left side of the screen, and the target appeared to the right of that position by the appropriate amplitude for that trial. Target width varied but target height was consistently 400 pixels. The subject completed a trial by moving the cursor so that the black dot in the centre of the cursor was somewhere over the target. The target was selected by pressing one of the mouse buttons.

To initiate the next trial, the subject lifted the mouse, moved it to the right of the mouse pad, and swept it across to the left side of the mouse pad. This correctly positioned the mouse to start the next trial, which followed after an interval of 2 seconds.

Subjects were demonstrated the task and allowed warm-up trials prior to each change in experimental condition.

Design
A $4 \times 3 \times 4$ fully within-subjects repeated measures design was used. The factors were lag (8.3, 25, 75, & 225 ms), target amplitude ($A = 96, 192$ & 384 pixels), and target width ($W = 6, 12, 24,$ & 48 pixels). The A-W conditions yielded six levels of task difficulty, ranging from 1.58 bits to 6.02 bits.

A block consisted of 56 trials arranged as follows: For each lag, testing was done for 3 amplitudes and 4 widths yielding 4 groups of 12 trials. However, at the start of each group two practice trails were given to familiarize the subject with that particular lag. Thus we obtain,

> 2+12 trials with lag 1,
> 2+12 trials with lag 2,
> 2+12 trials with lag 3, and
> 2+12 trials with lag 4.

These groups were given in a random order for each trial block.

Measure	Lag (ms)				Performance Degradation at Lag = 225 ms[a]
	8.3	25	75	225	
Movement Time (ms)	911	934	1059	1493	63.9%
Error Rate (%)	3.6	3.6	4.9	11.3	214%
Bandwidth (bits/s)	4.3	4.1	3.5	2.3	46.5%

[a]relative to lag = 8.3 ms

Figure 1. Mean scores and performance degradation in movement time, error rate, and bandwidth over four levels of lag.

Each subject received 24 blocks of 56 trials where the blocks consisted of the 24 possible orders of 4 lags. The 24 blocks were given in a unique random sequence for each subject. Additionally, at the start of each session, the subject received a practice block of trials, selected at random. Subjects completed all blocks in either two or three sessions.

RESULTS AND DISCUSSION

As expected, there were significant main effects for lag on movement time ($F_{3,21}$ = 208.7, $p < .0001$), error rate ($F_{3,21}$ = 4.71, $p < .05$), and bandwidth ($F_{3,21}$ = 227.7, $p < .0001$). Figure 1 gives the mean scores for each level of lag as well as the percentage degradation at 225 ms lag compared to the measures at a negligible lag of 8.3 ms. (Recall that 8.3 ms is as close to zero lag as was possible given the 60 Hz sampling rate for the mouse.)

Error rates were quite reasonable (under 5%) except at the highest lag of 225 ms where they were over 11%. The bandwidth figures of around 4 bits/s for the lags up to 75 ms are similar to those found elsewhere (e.g., [12]).

A lag of 225 ms relative to 8.3 ms increased the mean movement time by 1493 - 911 = 582 ms, or 63.9%. Similarly, error rates increased by 214% and bandwidth dropped by 46.5%. These represent dramatic performance costs. The high error rate at 225 ms lag indicates that the performance degradation is more serious than suggested solely on the basis of the extra time to complete tasks. Subjects natural tendency to anticipate motions was severely compromised by the lag. Adopting an open-loop or "wait-and-see" strategy would solve this (as noted by Sheridan & Ferrell [14]), but would further increase movement times.

Task difficulty (*ID*) also had a significant effect on movement time ($F_{5,35}$ = 116.8, $p < .0001$) and error rates

($F_{5,35}$ = 6.70, $p < .0005$).[2] As well, there was a significant *lag* x*ID* interaction effect on movement time ($F_{15,105}$ = 30.4, $p < .0001$) and error rate ($F_{15,105}$ = 2.42, $p < .005$). The interaction is easily seen in Figures 2 and 3. As tasks get more difficult, performance degradation increases, particularly at 75 ms and 225 ms lag.

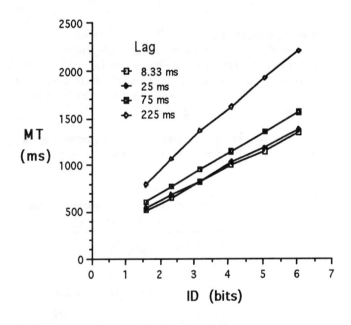

Figure 2. Movement time vs. index of task difficulty over four lag conditions.

---

[2]Note: *ID* rather than *ID$_e$* was used in the ANOVA and in Figures 2 and 3 showing the *lag* x*ID* interaction. This was necessary since effects in an analysis of variance must be nominal variables. After the transformation, *ID$_e$* becomes a random variable. *ID$_e$* was used in calculating *BW* and in building the regression models.

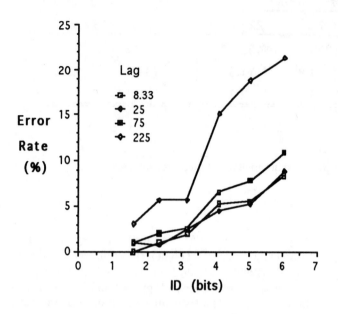

Figure 3. Error rate vs. index of task difficulty over four lag conditions.

A Prediction Model

Rather than present Fitts' law models under each lag condition, we feel it more relevant to integrate lag with Fitts' index of task difficulty in a single prediction model. This idea is developed in the series of models shown in Figure 4.

The first two entries are simple linear regression models, predicting movement time solely on the index of task difficulty (ID_e, adjusted for errors) or lag. The fit is poor in both cases.

The third and fourth models in Figure 4 combine ID_e and lag using multiple regression. The third entry is the traditional multiple regression model with ID_e and lag entered a separate predictors. The fit is very good ($R = .948$) with the model accounting for 89.8% of the variance in the observed movement times. However, the fit is improved ($R = .967$) in the fourth model which accommodates the interaction effect seen in Figures 2 and 3 and discussed earlier. The result is a model which accounts for 93.5% of the variance in observations. Rounding the coefficient 1.03 to 1.00 yields

$$MT = 230 + (169 + LAG)\ ID_e. \tag{6}$$

At lag = 0, this reduces to

$$MT = 230 + 169\ ID_e, \tag{7}$$

which is the same as a model found in a separate study also using a mouse in a discrete target selection task (see [11] Eq. 4). Each millisecond of lag in Equation 6 adds 1 ms/bit to the slope of the prediction line.

Although we must be cautious in extrapolating beyond the 225 ms lag used in the present experiment, it is easy to see that further increases in lag will bear severe costs in performance, particularly with difficult tasks. As a simple example, at lag = 500 ms and $ID = 7$ bits, the predicted time to complete a target selection task using Equation 5 is 5.9 s. The same task in the absence of lag will take about 1.4 s. (Note that the prediction carries a 4% probability of error because the model was adjusted for errors.)

Model for MT (ms)[a]	Fit[b]	Variance Explained
$MT = 435 + 190\ ID_e$	$r = .560$	31.3%
$MT = 894 + 46\ LAG$	$r = .630$	39.8%
$MT = -42 + 246\ ID_e + 3.4\ LAG$	$R = .948$	89.8%
$MT = 230 + (169 + 1.03\ LAG)\ ID_e$	$R = .967$	93.5%

[a]LAG in ms, ID_e in bits

[b]$n = 48$, $p < .0001$ for all models

Figure 4. Prediction models for movement time based on lag and the index of task difficulty.

CONCLUSIONS

Lag has been shown to degrade human performance in motor-sensory tasks on interactive systems. At 75 ms lag, the effect is easily measured, and at 225 ms performance is degraded substantially. A model has been presented showing a strong multiplicative effect between lag and Fitts' index of difficulty. The model explains 93.5% of the variation in observations.

These findings are of particular and immediate value to designers of interactive 3D computing systems, such as virtual reality. The present study is only a first step, however, since we investigated 2D movements only. A 3D exploration of the human performance cost of lag is needed using a task such as grasping for objects in 3-space with an input glove while viewing the scene through a head-mounted display.

Lag must be taken seriously and recognized as a major bottleneck for usability. The current attitude of acknowledging lag but "learning to live with it" will be increasingly unacceptable as VR systems shift from research curiosities to application tools. Whether through additional parallel processors or through higher performance hardware, such systems must deliver a faithful recasting of reality in order to garner user acceptance. A major component of this is the delivery of near-immediate response of graphic output to input stimuli.

ACKNOWLEDGMENT

We gratefully acknowledge the support of the Magic Lab at the University of British Columbia in providing equipment and space for running the experiment. This research was supported by the Natural Sciences and Engineering Research Council of Canada.

REFERENCES

1. Brooks, F. P., Jr., Ouh-Young, M., Butter, J. J., & Kilpatrick, P. J. (1990). Project GROPE: Haptic displays for scientific visualization. *Computer Graphics*, 24(4), 177-185.

2. Card, S. K., Mackinlay, J. D., & Robertson, G. G. (1991). A morphological analysis of the design space of input devices. *ACM Transactions on Office Information Systems, 9*, 99-122.

3. Card, S. K., Robertson, G. G., & Mackinlay, J. D. (1991). The information visualizer, an information workspace. *Proceedings of the CHI '91 Conference on Human Factors in Computing Systems* (pp. 181-188). New York: ACM.

4. Dafoe, C. (1992, September 5). The next best thing to being there. *The Globe and Mail*, pp. C1, C5.

5. Fitts, P. M. (1954). The information capacity of the human motor system in controlling the amplitude of movement. *Journal of Experimental Psychology, 47*, 381-391.

6. Foley, J. D., van Dam, A., Feiner, S. K., & Hughes, J. F. (1990). *Computer graphics: Principles and practices* (2nd ed.). Reading, MA: Addison Wesley.

7. Gibbs, C. B. (1962). Controller design: Interaction of controlling limbs, time-lags, and gains in positional and velocity systems. *Ergonomics, 5*, 385-402.

8. Laurel, B. (1991). *Computers as theatre*. Reading, MA: Addison-Wesley.

9. Liang, J., Shaw, C., & Green, M. (1991). On temporal-spatial realism in the virtual reality environment. *Proceedings of the ACM SIGGRAPH and SIGCHI Symposium on User Interface Software and Technology – UIST '91* (pp. 19-25). New York: ACM.

10. MacKenzie, I. S. (1992). Fitts' law as a research and design tool in human-computer interaction. *Human-Computer Interaction, 7*, 91-139.

11. MacKenzie, I. S., & Buxton, W. (1992). Extending Fitts' law to two-dimensional tasks. *Proceedings of the CHI '92 Conference on Human Factors in Computing Systems* (pp. 219-226). New York: ACM.

12. MacKenzie, I. S., Sellen, A., & Buxton, W. (1991). A comparison of input devices in elemental pointing and dragging tasks. *Proceedings of the CHI '91 Conference on Human Factors in Computing Systems* (pp. 161-167). New York: ACM.

13. Pausch, R. (1991). Virtual reality on five dollars a day. *Proceedings of the CHI '91 Conference on Human Factors in Computing Systems* (pp. 265-269). New York: ACM.

14. Sheridan, T. B., & Ferrell, W. R. (1968). Remote manipulative control with transmission delay. *IEEE Transactions on Human Factors in Electronics, 4*, 25-29.

15. Welford, A. T. (1968). *Fundamentals of skill*. London: Methuen.

COMPUTER IMAGE RETRIEVAL BY FEATURES: SUSPECT IDENTIFICATION

Eric Lee
Management Science
St. Mary's University
Halifax, NS, Canada B3H 3C3
elee@bootless.stmarys.ca
(902) 420-5734

Thom Whalen
Division of Behavioural Research
Communications Research Centre
3701 Carling Avenue, Ottawa, Canada
thom@rick.doc.ca
(902) 990-4683

ABSTRACT

Correct suspect identification of known offenders by witnesses deteriorates rapidly as more are examined in mugshot albums. Feature approaches, where mugshots are displayed in order of similarity to witnesses' descriptions, attempt to increase identification success by reducing this number. A methodology is proposed for system design and evaluation based on experiments, computer simulations, and four classes of system performance measures: identification performance, retrieval rank, tolerance performance, and feature quality. This was used to develop a system for 640 mugshots of known offenders. In three empirical tests, over 90% of witness searches resulted in suspects retrieved in the first eight mugshots.

KEYWORDS: computer image retrieval, information retrieval, feature retrieval.

INTRODUCTION

The identification of suspects by witnesses or victims is frequently of central importance in solving crimes. Three methods are commonly used to identify suspects: verbal descriptions; composite methods such as Photofit or Identikit; and mugshot albums.

Verbal descriptions lack sufficient detail and accuracy to be of much use [2]. Composite procedures are relatively unsuccessful, because they do not generate an accurate, detailed image of the suspect [3]. The mugshot album approach is more successful, because people are good at face recognition [4].

Nevertheless, the album approach suffers fundamental problems. The task is tiring, time-consuming, and confusing as witnesses often examine thousands of photos. The probability of selecting the correct suspect (a hit) decreases

rapidly after the first 100-200 examined, while the probability of selecting the wrong person (a false alarm) increases rapidly [1,4,7,8,9].

In response to such difficulties, researchers have turned to feature approaches to image retrieval [e.g., 4,5,6,9]. A set of features is used for distinguishing among mugshot photos in a database. In our feature retrieval system, users describe a suspect (i.e., whose photo they wish to retrieve) in response to a set of queries (e.g., on a 5-point scale, *Height: How tall was this person?*). The system matches the witness' description with those of mugshots in the database. Mugshots are presented to witnesses in order of similarity to their description.

In a classic paper, Harmon [6] introduced the feature approach to suspect identification. However, Ellis' [4] investigations established its value over the traditional album approach.

The purpose of the present paper is twofold: first, to establish the viability of our feature approach using a mugshot database of known criminals, and second, to discuss methodological and theoretical issues raised by differences among the three feature approaches of Harmon, Ellis, and our own.

SYSTEM DESIGN AND TESTING

Other researchers, such as Ellis, have defined success somewhat restrictively as successful identification (e.g., hits, misses). Such a position can limit the process of design and development. Our approach is predicated on a wider definition of success including identification success, retrieval rank, system tolerance, and feature quality.

Identification performance is the ability of witnesses to identify suspects successfully from their photos and includes such measures as hits, misses, false alarms, and non-retrievals. Retrieval rank is the rank order of a suspect's photo when the database photos are arranged in order of similarity to a witness' description. Tolerance performance measures the ability of a system to tolerate witness errors on some features (error tolerance), and omission of others (omission tolerance), and still perform acceptably (as measured by retrieval rank). The fourth class of measures, which we call uncertainty measures, assess informational properties of the features themselves: informativeness, orthogonality, sufficiency, consistency, and observability.

We argue that system performance is most accurately measured by retrieval rank. Earlier presentation of target photos markedly improves identification performance [1,4,7,8,9]. System and user performance, on the other hand, are confounded in measures of identification success. Therefore, our immediate objective is minimization of retrieval rank.

To achieve this, we follow seven stages in design and development: feature generation, feature selection, database construction, retrieval program design, computer simulations, and empirical testing.

Feature Generation
To generate a large pool of potential features, we sampled 25 photos. Since mugshots were unavailable initially, we used black and white mugshot-like photos of 25 students.

The second step consisted of a pairwise comparison process where each sample photo was compared with the other 24. For each distinct pair of photos a feature was noted which characterized the first individual but not the second.

Feature Selection
We used five criteria for selecting features from this pool: informativeness, orthogonality, sufficiency, observability, and consistency. To optimize system performance, we selected features which were, on the basis of pilot studies, maximally informative; mutually orthogonal; observable and memorable; consistently coded by different people; and the number of system features minimized while still discriminating among mugshots. From the pool we selected 90 facial features (e.g., straight vs. curly hair, bald vs. full head of hair, thin vs. thick neck).

The Mugshot Database
The database consists of 640 official mugshot photos of known offenders. (In contrast, Harmon and Ellis used photos of non-offenders.) Colour photos were taken under standard conditions -- frontal view of face from the shoulder up (90 x 125 mm prints). The suspects are all white males, aged 18-33.

Each mugshot was coded on 90 facial features by one of 12 raters (males and females in their early twenties). The raters received no training or instructions. Raters coded directly from the photo which was always available for inspection, as would be the case if police officers coded the mugshots. Coding time per mugshot was approximately five minutes.

Each feature is coded on a 5-point Likert scale (e.g., narrow nose 1 2 3 4 5 broad nose).

The Feature Retrieval System
Witnesses work directly on the system without an intermediary. Feature queries appear on the screen in succession. They describe suspects using the same 90 5-point scales.

Similarity between witness and database descriptions is measured by a Euclidean metric as Harmon [6] did, that is, we sum the squared deviations between witness and database feature descriptions and take the square root of the sum. In the Ellis system, similarity is measured by the number of feature matches. Preliminary research in our lab suggests the Euclidean metric minimizes retrieval rank relative to other metrics.

EXPERIMENT 1
An empirical test of our prototype was conducted to test its effectiveness in identifying suspects. Subjects entered their descriptions of suspects on our computer system but did not search through the actual mugshots. System performance was measured by retrieval rank of the target rather than identification success. This procedure simplifies the experimental process, reduces time required to conduct the experiment, and reduces the security risk created when subjects view many mugshots.

Method

Subjects. Five subjects, including males and females in their early twenties, were tested.

Procedure. Subjects first searched for a practice mugshot. Then five target mugshots, randomly selected from the database, were presented, one at a time. Order of presentation was counterbalanced. Subjects had 10 sec to examine a mugshot. (Ellis' testing procedure was followed to increase comparability of our two systems.) For each target, subjects answered the 90 feature queries on the computer. They were encouraged to answer all queries, guessing if necessary, though skipping was permitted. No feedback was provided between trials, and subjects were limited to one search per target.

Apparatus. The feature retrieval system, programmed in C, is implemented on a Sun Sparc 1+.

Results
The target was frequently among the most closely matching mugshots. Mean retrieval rank was 17.40 (median = 8.25). The worst performance was 80 (i.e., the 80th mugshot among 640 to be presented for inspection).

Error and omission rates for witnesses were quite low. The

percentage of features omitted by witnesses averaged 11%, varying from 4% - 17%. Mean deviation between witness and database descriptions was .74 and varied between .42 and 1.16. Error and retrieval rank are not perfectly correlated. For example, the greatest error was 1.16, yet the system retrieved the suspect's photo first.

Discussion

System performance was good. Over 80% of the searches resulted in retrieval of the target in the top 5% of the database mugshots (i.e., in the first 32 mugshots). Performance compares favourably with the 321 photos a witness would examine, on average, to find a suspect in an album of 640 mugshots (assuming targets are in the album).

Though performance of our system was good, the instructions encouraged guessing which may impair performance by increasing errors. On the other hand, our procedure, which presents the features in a fixed, predetermined order, may impair witness recall. Recall may improve if witnesses first describe a suspect in their own words. Those hypotheses are tested in the next experiment.

EXPERIMENT 2

The primary objective was to test an alternative procedure for eliciting suspect descriptions from witnesses which would discourage indiscriminate guessing and improve recall. Instructions to subject witnesses were changed in two ways. First, they wrote out a suspect's description by listing clearly recalled characteristics. Then they answered our feature queries on the computer. Second, when using the computer system, subjects were encouraged to skip features which could not be recalled with confidence. They were not limited, however, to describing features written down earlier. We expected performance, with prompting, to be superior to that without.

Method

Subjects. Five subjects, aged 21 to 43, were tested, including both males and females.

Procedure. The Experiment 1 procedure was used. However, guessing was discouraged and subjects wrote out a description of a suspect before using the computer system. No practice was given.

Five mugshots were randomly selected from the database. The five mugshots were presented to each subject in counterbalanced order. Subjects had 10 sec to examine each target.

Results

Retrieval performance was very good. Mean retrieval rank was 4.12 (median = 1.25). The target was ranked in the top eight most similar mugshots to the subject's description in 96% of all searches. Worst performance was a rank of 43.

There was a significant advantage for the Experiment 2 over 1 methods in mean retrieval rank, as hypothesized, between-groups $F(1,8) = 10.87$, $p < .01$. This result must be interpreted with caution since subjects were not randomly assigned.

Unlike actual witnesses, our subjects performed five successive searches for different target individuals. That these results are not an artifact of practice is supported by the complete absence of any order effects ($F < 1$).

The effect of prompting can be assessed by comparing subject performance based on using all features, both written and prompted, with performance based on features derived strictly from the written list (i.e., with and without prompting witnesses with the list of features). On average, subjects used significantly more features with prompting than without, 61.0 versus 35.8 (sign test: 24 of 25 searches, $p < .001$). (Subjects listed on paper an average of 21.4 items but many items translated into responses to several of our features).

Performance without prompting was very good. Mean retrieval rank was 6.34. Performance was better, however, when prompting was permitted, than when retrieval was based strictly on written features (mean retrieval rank = 4.12 versus 6.34, respectively). This difference was not significant by repeated measures analysis ($F < 1$). Since the data were highly skewed, however, a sign test was conducted. The prompting of subjects by listing features on the computer significantly improved performance (sign test: 13 improvements versus 5 declines with 7 ties, $p < .05$).

On average, subjects omitted 29% of the 90 features. The average deviation between witness and database codings was .59. Subjects answered on average significantly fewer feature queries in the second experiment (89% for the first versus 71% for the second), between-groups $F(1,8) = 8.86$, $p < .02$. The average error also fell from .74 to .59, but this difference was not significant, $F(1,8) = 2.30$, $p = .17$.

Discussion

The changes in procedure improved system performance. Searches resulted in the successful retrieval of 96% of target suspects in the first eight mugshots. The new search procedure reduced mean retrieval rank from 17.40 in Experiment 1 to 4.12.

Because we changed two aspects of the search procedure, there are two alternative explanations of the improvement in performance: either the written description facilitated accurate recall, or the instructions minimized inappropriate guessing (or both worked). The written description was effective since performance was good when retrieval was based on written features only (mean rank = 6.34).

On the other hand, if the instructions discouraging guessing had an effect then one would expect subjects in Experiment 2 to have answered fewer of the first 90 feature queries, and to have made fewer errors. This was true for omissions as subjects answered on average significantly fewer feature queries (89% versus 71%) and the error also fell from .74 to .59 (though not significantly).

Thus, both explanations received support. The present experiment cannot be considered definitive, however, because it was not specifically designed to test between the two explanations.

Our approach differs from Ellis' in the use of prompting. In Ellis' approach, an intermediary interprets the witness' verbal description and codes it on the system. Witnesses are not prompted with a list of system features for describing suspects. Ellis argues the advantage of this approach is to reduce inappropriate guessing of forgotten features, "which is inherent in prompting witnesses with the complete list of parameters." The effectiveness of prompting was tested directly, in the present experiment. Contrary to Ellis' expectation, the prompting of subjects by listing features on the computer significantly improved performance.

EXPERIMENT 3

The purpose of this experiment was to eliminate asymmetric transfer and range effects, to increase generalizability by testing more subject witnesses, and to explore the effect of using witness judgments of absolute certainty on some features to eliminate mugshots.

In the first two experiments, subject witnesses searched for several target offenders. Such repeated-measures designs are plagued by practice, order, carry-over, asymmetric transfer, range and context effects [11]. Analysis of the first two experiments showed no effect of practice on performance. However, the effects of asymmetric transfer and range effects cannot be eliminated by randomization, counterbalancing, or taking out order as a factor in the design. To eliminate these potential problems in the present study, subjects searched for a single target offender.

The present study also examines the effect on system performance of witness judgments of absolute certainty. We used these judgments to eliminate retrieval of some database images. In a study on paintings, such judgments significantly improved system performance [10].

Method

Subjects. Ten subjects were tested, five male and five female. Ages ranged from 19 to 30. Subjects included university students and secretaries as well as workers from the local community.

Procedure. The procedure was identical to that for Experiment 1 with four exceptions. First, subject witnesses provided a written description of their suspect. Second, subjects were asked to list those features for which they were absolutely certain of their judgment. Only then did they answer the feature queries on the computer retrieval system. Third, after answering the system queries, subjects searched the database mugshots, one by one, in rank order. They were asked to identify the target suspect. Fourth, only a single target was presented to each subject witness. No practice was given. Guessing was not discouraged. Subjects were randomly assigned one of two targets, randomly selected from the database.

Apparatus. The computer retrieval system was set initially to operate without certainty judgments. After completion of testing, the certainty judgments were used to eliminate any database mugshot differing maximally (i.e., by 4 on the 5-point scales) from the witness's feature description on at least one feature. The remaining database mugshots were ordered as usual from most to least similar to the witness's description.

Results

All 10 subject witnesses correctly identified their target offender. The mean retrieval rank of targets was 9.70 (median = 2.50). The worst performance was a rank of 30.

The effect of absolute certainty was assessed by re-entering subjects' feature descriptions on the system and adding the certainty judgments. Mean retrieval rank was reduced to 4.10 (median = 1.00). Searches with ranks less than eight were increased from 60% to 90%. A mixed ANOVA indicated significant main effects of certainty and mugshot, $F(1,8) = 11.91$ and 5.72, respectively ($p < .05$). Interpretation of the main effects must be qualified because the interaction of mugshot with certainty was also significant, $F(1,8) = 11.92$, $p < .01$. Certainty significantly improved performance for only one mugshot target. For the other target, performance was already optimal for four subjects and close to optimal for the remaining subject. In no case did certainty judgments impair performance. Subjects listed an average of 7.4 characteristics with certainty (corresponding to 12.0 system features).

The average percentage of features omitted was 8.9%. The mean deviation between witness and database codings was 0.78.

Discussion

The design of the present experiment eliminated all possible sequence effects. Since retrieval performance was still very good, it is unlikely that range or asymmetric transfer effects significantly altered performance in Experiments 1 and 2.

The good retrieval performance in the present experiment replicates that found in the first two experiments. Eliciting certainty judgments on system features significantly improved performance. Though the effect was substantial, only 3 of the 10 target searches were actually improved.

Subject witnesses correctly identified all target offenders from their photos. This superior level of identification performance is undoubtedly attributable to the early presentation of target mugshots to witnesses [e.g., 4].

COMPUTER SIMULATIONS

To assess the effect of database size and varying error and omission rates on system performance, we simulated both large mugshot databases and the behaviour of witnesses searching for target suspects. We constructed a simulated database of 10,000 mugshots with descriptions patterned after those of the 640 database mugshots. Witness behaviour is simulated by randomly omitting some features and making errors on a proportion of the remaining ones in a database feature decription. For any given combination of error and omission probability, 200 trial searches for targets were conducted (targets randomly selected). Error rate was varied from 5 to 35% while omission rate varied between 10 and 90%. All errors committed by a simulated witness were made as large as possible (e.g., a 2 in the database is recoded as a 5 for the simulated witness). Empirical rates correspond approximately to 30% omits and 20% errors.

Table 1
Retrieval Rank for Simulated
Searches of 10,000 Mugshots[1]

		P(omission) (%)				
		.10	.30	.50	.70	.90
	.05	1	1	1	2	177
	.15	1	1	26	69	722
P(error)	.25	14	71	119	401	1487
	.35	389	789	1090	1670	2580

[1] Each entry based on 200 searches.

The results indicate that the system has a high degree of tolerance for both witness errors and omissions, and the ability to handle large databases.

DISCUSSION

The system has the properties we want. Retrieval performance is good. In three experimental tests of the system, retrieval rank of target mugshots averaged 17.40, 4.12, and 4.10. For the revised system tested in Experiments 2 and 3, over 90% of all searches resulted in retrieval ranks less than eight. In Experiment 3, all suspects were successfully identified. Unlike Harmon and Ellis, these results were obtained using photos of known offenders.

Computer simulations suggest the current system should perform well even when database size is increased to over 10,000 mugshots. Moreover, the system has a high degree of tolerance both for witness errors and omissions. Performance was good even with error rates as high as 25% and omission rates up to 50%.

The present experiments and simulations cannot be considered definitive. Nevertheless, the results strongly support our contention that feature retrieval systems hold considerable promise for the future.

Performance comparisons between different retrieval systems can be problematic without a direct experimental test between them. However, performance of the present system compares favourably with that reported by Ellis et al. [4]. Ellis reports that 84% of all computer searches resulted in retrieval of the target within the top 24 database mugshots retrieved. Thus, performance of both feature retrieval systems is very good.

This good performance was achieved despite marked differences in the two feature retrieval systems in use of intermediaries, feature measurement, and prompting of witnesses with feature queries. Contrary to Ellis' expectation, the prompting of subjects by listing features on the computer significantly improves system performance.

Our subjective approach to feature measurement may be contrasted with Ellis' physical measurement of features from the photo itself. According to Ellis, the advantages of physical measurement are the potential accuracy with which they can be made and the potential for eventual automatic encoding of facial features. The disadvantages are that people do not encode faces in this way, offenders must be photographed under carefully controlled conditions (e.g., identical facial position and distance from camera), and witness responses on subjective 5-point scales must be translated into codes for comparison with physical measurements of database mugshots.

Ellis has argued that Harmon's procedure, averaging subjective rating of 10 judges to reduce coding error, effectively precludes the practical use of the subjective approach to feature retrieval. The successful performance of our system supports our contention that multiple judges may not be required for subjectively-based systems.

We have argued for the use of several classes of system performance measures in system development: identification, ranking, tolerance, and uncertainty measures of feature quality. The last three classes were instrumental in the successful development of our system. We argue that one need not rely, as Ellis and others have done, strictly on identification performance.

REFERENCES

1. Davies, G.M., Shepherd, J.W. and Ellis, H.D. Effects of interpolated mugshot exposure on accuracy of eyewitness identification. *Journal of Applied Psychology*, 64(1979), 232-237.

2. Ellis, H.D. Practical aspects of facial memory. In *Eyewitness testimony: Psychological perspectives*, G.L. Wells and E.F. Loftus, Eds. Cambridge University Press, New York, 1984.

3. Ellis, H.D., Davies, G.M. and Shepherd, J.W. A critical examination of the Photofit system for recalling faces. *Ergonomics*, 21(1978), 297-307.

4. Ellis, H.D., Shepherd, J.W., Shepherd, J., Klin, R.H. and Davies, G.M. Identification from a computer-driven retrieval system compared with a traditional mug-shot album: A new tool for police investigations, *Ergonomics*, 32(1989), 167-177.

5. Goldstein, A.J., Harmon, L.D. and Lesk, A. Identification of human faces. In *Proceedings of the IEEE*, 59(1971), 748-760.

6. Harmon, L.D. The recognition of faces. *Scientific American*, 229(1973), 70-82.

7. Laughery, K.R., Alexander, J.F. and Lane, A.B. Recognition of human faces: Effects of target exposure time, target position, pose position, and type of photograph. *Journal of Applied Psychology*, 51(1971), 477-483.

8. Laughery, K.R., Fessler, P.K., Lenorovitz, D.R. and Yorlick, D.A. Time delay and similarity effects in facial recognition. *Journal of Applied Psychology*, 59(1974), 490-496.

9. Lenorovitz, D.R. and Laughery, K.R. A witness-computer interactive system for searching mug files. In *Eyewitness testimony*, G.Wells and E. Loftus, Eds. Cambridge University Press, New York, 1984.

10. MacGregor, J.N., Lee, E.S. and Whalen, T. The feature matching approach to the computer retrieval of graphics: An enhancement, *Information Services and Use*, 9(1989), 127-137.

11. Poulton, E. C. Unwanted range effects from using within-subject experimental designs. *Psychological Bulletin*, 80(1973), 113-121.

Empirically-based Re-design of a Hypertext Encyclopedia

Keith Instone, Barbee Mynatt Teasley and Laura Marie Leventhal

Department of Computer Science
Bowling Green State University
Bowling Green, Ohio 43403 USA
+1-419-372-2337   FAX +1-419-372-8061
e-mail: instone@hydra.bgsu.edu

ABSTRACT

This paper reports on the processes used and guidelines discovered in re-designing the user interface of the hypertext encyclopedia, HyperHolmes. The re-design was based on the outcomes of a previous experiment and was evaluated experimentally. Results showed that the new system resulted in superior performance and somewhat different styles of navigation compared to the old system and to paper. The study provides empirical support for design guidelines relating to tiled windows, navigation tools, graphics and hierarchical navigation.

KEYWORDS: hypertext, design, experiment, empirical results, usability, navigation, electronic encyclopedia.

INTRODUCTION

While many of the general design principles for computer user interfaces apply to hypertext, hypertext design offers its own unique problems. Thus, there is a critical need for a more systematic study of usability issues in hypertext, and, more importantly, for the development of design guidelines based on empirical results. In 1989, Nielsen [18] stated that the empirical hypertext literature was "much too sparse" to do a meta-analysis, but he was hopeful that a trend toward more empirical studies would become the norm. Today, three years later, Nielsen notes (private correspondence) that many recent hypertext projects have included some form of usability testing. Nonetheless, he adds, "we still do not have sufficiently many broad empirical studies of the fundamental issues in hypertext."

Several authors have suggested design issues for hypertext which seem worthy of empirical study, including the use of metaphors [14], the structure and contents of nodes and links [1], and standard ergonomic issues [15]. However, such studies, especially as the basis of design principles, have rarely materialized. For example, of the 82 papers presented at the first three ACM conferences on hypertext [8, 9, 10], only 6 of these provide empirical results to substantiate their claims. While descriptions of practice and experience and of prototypes are valuable, the arena of hypertext is mature enough to warrant empirical and theoretical study.

The present paper concerns the evolution and design of a hypertext encyclopedia, based on a series of empirical studies. It describes how it was determined what changes to the interface were needed and how the effects of those changes were measured. In addition, design guidelines based on the results are outlined.

Previous Empirical Results: Hypertext vs. Paper

Prior research comparing the performance and usability of hypertext to paper (e.g., books) has found neither medium to be uniformly superior [5, 4, 16, 23]. For example, in prior studies [17, 13], we compared users' performance on a question-answering task using either a hypertext or paper version of an encyclopedia of Sherlock Holmes information, called HyperHolmes I. (Sherlock Holmes is a fictional detective who is the main character in numerous short stories by Sir Arthur Conan Doyle.) The questions varied in the amount, type and location of the information needed to answer them. The questions were composed to involve combinations of the following three dimensions:

Fact vs. Inference. "Fact" questions could be answered using information from a single entry in the hypertext encyclopedia. (Each entry comprised one node in the hypertext.) "Inference" questions required combining information from two entries.

Text vs. Nontext. "Text" questions were answerable from entries that contained only textual material, whereas "nontext" questions required some information from graphical entries (i.e., maps).

Title vs. Content. "Title" questions had a keyword in the question that also appeared in the title of an entry. "Content" questions could be answered by looking for a keyword from the question in the contents of the entries— merely scanning the titles would not suffice. (Note that nontext entries did not allow this distinction.)

These dimensions were combined into five question types: Fact/Text/Title, Fact/Text/Content, Fact/Nontext, Inference/Text, and Inference/Nontext.

Novice computer users served as subjects. They first received training on using a Macintosh, and then training and exercises using HyperHolmes I. The training took approximately 30 minutes. They then performed the experimental task, answering three sets of questions, where a set was comprised of one question from each of the five types.

Performance on the two media was assessed in terms of accuracy and speed. The results showed that the book users were marginally faster than the hypertext users. However, the hypertext users were marginally more accurate overall. The hypertext version of the encyclopedia was especially superior to paper media for those questions which were best answered through the use of electronic searching (i.e., Fact/Text/Content).

Weaknesses of Hypertext
These results, and the work of others, suggest two potential weaknesses of hypertext:

Extracting information from graphics. In our previous study, hypertext users were less accurate than book users when answering questions based on graphical materials. Similarly, chemists had difficulty extracting information from graphics using two versions of an electronic library system [4].

Using navigational support tools. Our earlier study also found that users often did not use navigational tools that would have made answering certain questions easier. Typically, these tools were those which did *not* mimic an analogous operation that the user already knew from using books. As Wright suggests [27, p. 4], "exploiting the full potential of hypertexts may require an extension of the strategies people already have for dealing with print."

Possible Explanations
There are at least three possible explanations for the deficiencies of hypertext that we and others have found:

Retrieving information from screens. In a review of the literature on reading from paper versus reading from screens, Dillon [3] concludes that "although reading from computer screens may be slower and occasionally less accurate than reading from paper, no one variable is likely to be responsible for this difference." The role of and utilization of graphics in hypertext is also an important issue. For example, it was found that users had a range of strategies for utilizing graphics [28]. Readers would often not access potentially useful diagrams when left to their own strategies. Prompting increased the frequency of looking at diagrams, but did not improve comprehension. Having the users unexpectedly encounter the diagrams was most effective. Other researchers have also noted that graphics are not always the most effective way to present information [e.g., 20, 12].

Learning problem-solving strategies. It has been demonstrated that training is of critical importance in the use of interactive, multi-windowed systems [25]. In previous studies of hypertext versus paper media, the training time has varied from one-hour [5], to thirty-minutes [17], to under ten minutes [16]. In our previous study, the users' level of accuracy remained constant across trials, while their speed became significantly faster. This suggests that practice enhances speed. It also suggests that to improve accuracy, additional training on use of the tools or on how to utilize information from graphics might be necessary.

Providing a quality interface. Wright [27] points out that in assessing hypertext, it is not sufficient to just ask "whether it works." There is an interplay among the design decisions that influence the perceived characteristics of adequacy, acceptability and adaptability. *Adequacy* refers to the goodness of the mapping between the task to be performed and the software. A particular system might work better for some tasks than others. *Acceptability* relates to known and feasible alternatives. If a system is the best available tool to solve a problem, it will be used. If better alternatives are available, it will not. In this case, the product itself does not change, only the user's perception of the product. *Adaptability* relates to the total environment in which the tool is used. Notepaper, pens and highlighters are often utilized along with paper books to adapt books to the task at hand. Hypertext designers need to begin looking beyond the confines of their systems to the environment in which they will be used. Pinpointing exactly which aspects of the user interface relate to these three qualities is not an easy task. However, it is important to keep these goals in mind.

Goals of the Current Study
In this paper we describe the development and assessment of a second version of our hypertext encyclopedia, HyperHolmes II. The goal was to determine which of the factors discussed above affected the performance of HyperHolmes I users. One approach would be to simply revise the training materials and increase the training time. However, this approach is less interesting than seeking to make the system itself easier to learn and easier to use.[1] Thus, while the content and structure of the original document were unchanged, the interface was altered. The two hypertext systems were then compared in an experiment to determine if the changes were an improvement. Those changes which resulted in significant improvement would point to empirically-based guidelines for hypertext designers.

In the following sections HyperHolmes I and HyperHolmes II are described, with emphasis on the specific ways that they are different. Next, the results of an experiment comparing the two systems are presented along with a discussion of the design factors which influenced the results. We conclude with suggestions for the design of hypertext interfaces.

HYPERHOLMES I
HyperHolmes I is a hypertext version of *The Encyclopædia Sherlockiana* [26]. It contains over 3400 entries and 10,000 links. The entries, consisting of text and graphics concerning Sherlock Holmes and various aspects of the Sherlock Holmes stories, are presented in the large window with a dark background, as shown in Figure 1. Capitalized

---

[1]After all, hypertext has been *defined* in terms of the freedom that users feel when moving through the information [19].

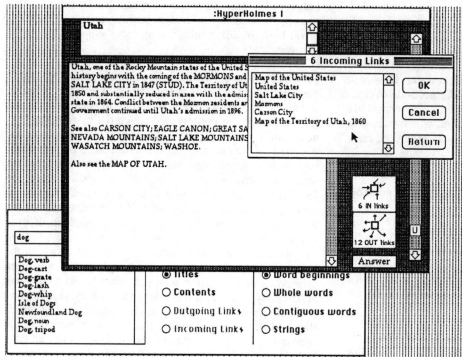

Figure 1: HyperHolmes I has overlapping windows

list and return to the current node. Incoming links approach the functionality of bi-directional links [19].

The Outgoing Links tool provides a list of other nodes in the document that are pointed to by the current node. This is redundant to the standard, in-line, hypertext links (i.e., the capitalized words). However, because the window containing the list of links remains on the screen when the user jumps to a different card, the user can more easily follow a series of jumps from the current card than through use of the standard links.

The Search Tool is the bottom-most window in Figure 1. After the user enters a key and initiates a search, a list of matching entries are listed. The user can go to the nodes listed by clicking on their titles.

words in the entries are hypertext buttons (i.e., clicking on them initiates a jump to the related entry). Several tools aid navigation through the document, including: incoming links, outgoing links, a search mechanism, a back-track arrow, and an alphabetic scroll bar. Many of the tools are accessible through overlapping, multiple windows. (For a more complete description of the HyperHolmes I interface, see [13, 11].)

The Holme card and Overview Menu card are special orienting cards. The Holme card acts as a "home" base and appears when the document is first opened. Users can return to the Holme card at any time by using the Holme button which is present on every screen. (It is obscured in Figure 1 by the Incoming Links window.) The Overview cards are special nodes that summarize and outline a subset of the contents of the encyclopedia, e.g., all of the information about London. One special overview card, the Overviews Menu, lists all of the overviews that are available. The easiest way to get to the Overviews Menu is by using a special button on the Holme card. While the HyperHolmes data do not have a strict hierarchical structure, users can access the data hierarchically by navigating via the Holme and overview cards.

The Incoming Links tool provides a list of the other nodes in the document that have links pointing to the current node. When the user selects the "IN links" icon in the main window, the Incoming Links window pops up with a list of of the incoming links for the current node. For example, there are 6 entries in the stack which contain references to "Utah" (see Figure 1). The Incoming Links window is modal and is not dismissed until the "OK" or "Cancel" button is pressed. This modality provides browsing capabilities, because users can easily jump to nodes in the

HYPERHOLMES II

HyperHolmes II is identical in content to HyperHolmes I. The modifications to the user interface focused on making the navigational support tools (e.g., search engines, incoming links) simpler to use and more salient. Previous research has shown that additional navigational tools can lead to a wider and more efficient coverage of the hypertext document [6]. The following are the most significant support tool changes that were made.

Replacing Overlapping Windows with Tiled Windows

By switching from version 1.2.5 to 2.0 of HyperCard, it was possible to expand the main HyperHolmes window. The HyperHolmes II window is 35% larger, allowing the Incoming Links and Search tools to be constantly available and in fixed locations (see Figure 2), while keeping the Holmesian information on the left unchanged. Research has found that bigger is generally better with regard to display size [22, 21, 7]. In the domain of hypertext, it was found that displaying more lines of the hypertext content led to better performance [22]. Although the re-design does not use the extra display space to show more of the hypertext contents, we still anticipated that the added display space would be beneficial.

The major benefit of the larger main window, however, was expected to be the fact that the tool windows would not overlap the content of the document. The tiled windows would, in theory, be more salient because the tool would be present all of the time, no information would become hidden, and windows would not have to be moved around by the user to reveal covered information. A study of tiled versus overlapping windows [2] found that tiled windows could yield better performance for some tasks and some

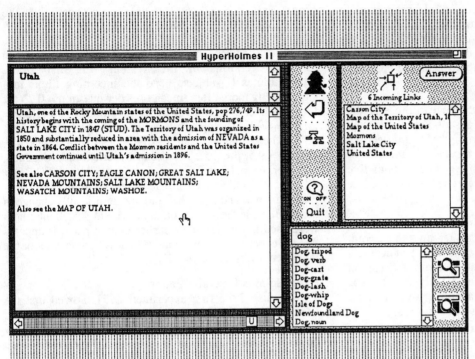

Figure 2: HyperHolmes II has tiled windows

The first simplification of the search tool was to make it a tiled window in the lower right portion of the screen, instead of a separate (non-modal) window that overlapped the main window.

The second simplification was to remove some of the search choices. In HyperHolmes I, users had a choice of the search criteria, as well as the search space. The criteria were "Word beginnings," "Whole words," "Contiguous words" and "Strings." The user could also search in either the title or the contents of each entry. In the earlier study, users typically started with a word beginnings/title search. If they did not get useful results, they then tried some of the other options. This strategy was often not successful.

In HyperHolmes II, "Word beginnings" was the only criterion for the key term. The single decision the user had to make was on the search space: titles or contents. Icons were used to represent the two search options (see the bottom right corner of Figure 2). We expected that with searching always available and easy to do, users would perform more searches, and perform searches more successfully.

Finally, a refinement in the search algorithm, coupled with an improvement in the efficiency of HyperCard's built-in "find" function, led to almost a 20% improvement in raw search speed.

Adding an Overviews Tool

In the earlier study, the Overviews Menu card was a frequently selected card, representing 7% of the total cards visited. The easiest way to get to this card was via the Holme card, which contained a button representing the Overviews Menu. In fact, 68% of the visits to the Holme card were immediately followed by a visit to the Overviews Menu card. Due to the observed high use, a special button was made for the Overviews Menu and added to the set of tools. (It is represented by an inverted tree icon, shown in the middle of Figure 2.) Using this tool, the user could save a step and go directly to the Overviews Menu, resulting in fewer visits to the Holme card and easier access to the Overviews cards. Because the addition of the Overviews button reduces the depth of the hierarchy of non-data cards, we were interested to see how its presence affected navigation patterns.

WAS THE RE-DESIGN A BETTER DESIGN?

To determine whether the new design for HyperHolmes was in fact a better design, the question-answering task from the earlier study was repeated using new subjects. This allowed

users. Because two of our overlapping windows were also modal windows, we expected the tiled, non-modal windows would be an improvement. Another advantage would be that the information is presented without the user being forced to request it.

Removing the Outgoing Links

The purpose of the Outgoing Links tool was to provide a more powerful, browsing-like interface for the outgoing (capitalized words) links. However, users in the earlier study did not often use the Outgoing Links button to navigate. When they did, they did not take advantage of its more powerful browsing capabilities, and it rarely helped them in answering the questions. For HyperHolmes II, the Outgoing Links tool was abandoned altogether.

Simplifying the Incoming Links

The Incoming Links tool provides information about nodes which refer to the current node. This information would otherwise be available only through tedious node-by-node search. In the earlier study, the Incoming Links tool was used much more effectively than the Outgoing Links tool was. Out of 15 subjects, 11 used the Incoming Links tool and all 11 used it to help them find a correct answer. In general, it was not used as a browsing tool. Typically, the tool was used to take a look at the nodes which pointed to the current node and then make a single jump. Thus, we wanted an interface to make these two tasks easier. To this end, the list of incoming nodes was placed in a tiled window, always present on the upper right portion of the screen. (See Figure 2.) The list was put in sorted order to make it easier to scan. Also, the browsing aspect of the tool was eliminated—a click on a name in the list simply took the user to that node without preserving the (old) list window.

a comparison of users' performances with HyperHolmes I and HyperHolmes II to see which interface was better under which conditions. In addition, HyperHolmes II could be contrasted to the paper version of the encyclopedia to see how the re-designed interface compares with the baseline, traditional medium.

The materials and method were identical to those in the HyperHolmes vs. Paper experiment described earlier, except that the tutorials and exercises were updated to reflect the new interface. Again, the subjects received 30 minutes of training and then were asked to answer three sets of five questions. Twelve subjects were recruited from the same pool of novice computer users.

HyperHolmes II versus HyperHolmes I

Performance. The questions were scored on a three-point scale, where 0 indicated an incorrect answer, 1 indicated a partially correct answer, and 2 indicated a completely correct answer. The results are shown in Table 1. HyperHolmes II users were significantly more accurate overall than HyperHolmes I users, with means of 1.73 and 1.38, respectively, $F(1,25) = 12.5$, $p < .05$.

HyperHolmes II users were also significantly faster than HyperHolmes I users overall in total seconds required to answer each question, with means of 178 and 236 seconds, respectively, $F(1,25) = 11.3$, $p < .05$. Of particular interest is the great improvement (nearly 100 seconds) in speed to answer Inference/Nontext questions.

The interaction between question type and system was not significant for either accuracy or speed.

Navigation. The total number of nodes visited serves as an indication of efficiency in answering questions. HyperHolmes II users visited significantly fewer nodes while answering the questions (mean cards per question = 8.3 for HyperHolmes II vs. 14.2 for HyperHolmes I), $F(1,25) = 23.8$ $p < .001$. Looking at the types of cards visited, HyperHolmes II users visited significantly fewer text cards per question (means = 5.7 and 9.0, respectively, $F(1,25) = 11.4$, $p < .05$). Surprisingly, both groups visited the exact same number of nontext (map) cards on average (1.5). Visits to the Holme and Overview Menu cards dropped dramatically. HyperHolmes I users went to the Holme card a mean of 1.3 times per question, compared to a mean of just 0.17 for HyperHolmes II users, $F(1,25) = 21.4$, $p < .001$. For the Overview Menu card, the mean number per question dropped from 1.0 down to 0.25, $F(1,25) = 14.3$, $p < .001$.

The decline in use of the Holme and Overview Menu cards indicates that users were less likely to use a hierarchical navigation approach. We conclude that they were not becoming "lost" as often and were therefore not relying on the hierarchy to re-orient themselves. This conclusion is supported by subjective evidence, as well. In a post-task questionnaire, subjects were asked if they ever became lost while using the system. Two-thirds of the HyperHolmes I group said "Yes," while only one-fourth of the HyperHolmes II users reported becoming lost.

Interface Specifics. A comparison of tool usage between the two versions of the system was also done. HyperHolmes II subjects used the Incoming Links tool significantly more often (mean uses per question = 0.23 for HyperHolmes I versus 1.0 for HyperHolmes II, $F(1,25) = 20.6$, $p < .001$). HyperHolmes II users performed about 50% more searches (mean uses per question of 2.4 vs. 4.0, $F(1,25) = 9.5$, $p < .05$). The use of hypertext links declined, however, from 4.7 to 2.5 mean uses per question, $F(1,25) = 7.8$, $p < .05$. Other interface features, including the back-tracking arrow and scroll bar, did not significantly change in usage. Because the new Incoming Link and Search interfaces were used more than their earlier counterparts, it appears that the enhancements were indeed partly responsible for the improved performance with HyperHolmes II.

HyperHolmes II versus Paper

The results of the first experiment [17] showed that the Paper users performed better than HyperHolmes I users on some tasks. For example, the Paper group did significantly better on Fact/Nontext questions. Also, Paper users were marginally faster overall. The changes to HyperHolmes II seem to have overcome these shortcomings and performance using HyperHolmes II is at least equal to the Paper version in all respects. Like the HyperHolmes I group, the HyperHolmes II group was significantly more accurate overall than the Paper group (mean accuracy per question = 1.73, 1.23 for Paper; $F(1,23) = 62.2$, $p < .001$). HyperHolmes II users were just as fast as Paper users overall, but neither group was significantly faster.

As in the earlier study, HyperHolmes II was particularly useful in providing a speedier and much more accurate way to answer Fact/Text/Content questions than Paper. These questions require page by page searching in Paper, but can be answered using the Search tool (with the Contents option selected) in either version of HyperHolmes.

A disappointing prior result from the HyperHolmes I vs. Paper experiment was that the simple look-up of key terms (i.e., Fact/Text/Title questions) was faster with the book. Although this is how the book was designed to be accessed, and our users were experienced in using books in this manner, we had hoped that hypertext would at least be equivalent to paper in this regard ("simple tasks should remain simple"[2]). It was possible that the presence of the extra support tools in HyperHolmes I was somehow interfering with the task of finding an entry by its title. The re-designed search interface in HyperHolmes II seems to have overcome this problem. HyperHolmes II users were just as fast as Paper users in answering Fact/Text/Title questions, and, furthermore, were more accurate.

Interestingly, both the speed and accuracy performance of HyperHolmes II users equalled Paper users on the two nontext questions while HyperHolmes I users were clearly

---

[2]This is related to the more-famous KISS axiom.

	Accuracy (0 to 2)			Speed (seconds)		
	HH II	HH I	Paper	HH II	HH I	Paper
Fact / Text / Title	1.89	1.51	1.39	120	176	125
Fact / Text / Content	1.61	1.16	0.26	248	223	323
Fact / Nontext	1.89	1.44	1.76	137	222	124
Inference / Text	1.47	1.38	1.27	231	301	242
Inference / Nontext	1.81	1.42	1.46	155	256	189
OVERALL	1.73	1.38	1.23	178	236	201

Table 1: Accuracy and speed results for two hypertext versions (HH II = HyperHolmes II and HHI = HyperHolmes I) and the paper version for five types of questions.

inferior to the Paper group. It appears that by improving the navigation support tools, the hypertext graphics became as accessible and usable as the paper graphics. This suggests that in the earlier study, it was not the process of extracting the information from the graphics that was affecting performance, but the process of locating the graphics. One reason why this issue is particularly relevant to HyperHolmes may be because the maps in HyperHolmes are very tightly linked with the rest of the document. The 42 maps have an average of 14 outgoing links and 7 incoming links. Thus, it is important that the user recognizes these interconnections and is able to navigate readily to the graphics. In a "document browsing" system like SuperBook, where the graphics are not as tightly woven in with the text, other means may be necessary to make the graphical information more accessible [4].

CONCLUSIONS

By empirically studying the use of HyperHolmes I and re-designing the interface based on the results, we were able to significantly improve performance on a question-answering task using HyperHolmes II. In addition, users became lost less often and relied less on the hierarchical overviews, opting instead for freer, more direct, navigation to their destinations. It is important to note that the content of the document did not change in size, structure or appearance; nor was the amount of training increased. The changes were solely in the user interface and dealt mainly with improving the navigation support tools. Interestingly, the difficulties that the HyperHolmes I users had with the graphical material were eased by enhancing the navigation tools.

The results of the two usability studies of HyperHolmes provide empirical bases for design guidelines. These include: the use of tiled windows, information concerning incoming links, access to graphics, and provision of a hierarchical structure. Each of these is discussed in somewhat more detail below.

Our results suggest that tiled windows, as opposed to overlapping windows, are easier to use, leading to increased accuracy and speed for our tasks and our users. This is consistent with [2]. Unfortunately, there is the inevitable problem of screen space. Tiled windows may not be a feasible alternative with smaller screens.

Incoming links are not often implemented in hypertext systems. However, the information provided by knowledge of incoming links can make some tasks easier to perform.

Thus, they appear to be useful as an additional mechanism for navigation.

The usability study of HyperHolmes I and a study by [4] both found that users had some difficulty finding and/or using information from graphics. In the present study, answering questions from graphics proved no more difficult or time-consuming than answering questions from text, compared to both HyperHolmes I and paper. We suggest that navigational access to graphics is an important design consideration for hypertext.

Several prior studies [13, 14, 24], including the earlier study with HyperHolmes I, found evidence that users often employ a hierarchical strategy in navigation, although use of the strategy decreased with practice. In the present study, we found little use of hierarchical navigation. This suggests that while a hierarchical overlay is not necessary when navigation tools are easy to use, it may be prudent to provide one for novices, or when the interface will not be extensively prototyped, tested for usability, and refined.

It should also be noted that one reason we chose *The Encyclopædia Sherlockiana* to implement in hypertext was because it is a carefully-written book with a wealth of cross-references. That is, the material had a good structure, which mapped naturally into hypertext. Materials which have a more linear structure or which are less-carefully structured might present more of a challenge to the interface designer, and might require additional guidelines.

Although the design changes between HyperHolmes I and II resulted in substantial improvements, there are still many avenues for development. One goal would be to add more features, such as a history list and/or a node-marking mechanism, while maintaining an interface that is equally easy to use and to learn. This might be especially difficult given the present amount of display space. Another challenge would be to add the many illustrations which are linked to only one piece of text from *The Encyclopædia Sherlockiana* and to try to make them as accessible as the paper versions. Finally, the interface has only been tested with novice users. A challenge would be to determine what features, if any, need to be added for the more expert user, and to add them in such a way that novice users are unaffected. These features might include additional browsing tools and more sophisticated search criteria (e.g., boolean connectors for key terms).

The introduction proposed that some of the previous usability problems found with hypertext could spring from a variety of sources, including the nature of on-line presentation, insufficient practice or training, and the quality of the interface. It appears from our results that many previously-recorded difficulties were, to a great extent, a function of the interface. While having little impact on the functionality of a hypertext system, strategies such as switching from overlapping windows to tiled windows, or making a tool more visible, can have a profound and significant effect on the usability of the system. Designers should note that comparative studies of hypertext systems can be quite revealing and can lead to better designs. We encourage others to continue the trend toward a more empirically-based study of hypertext systems.

ACKNOWLEDGEMENTS

The authors would like to thank John Farhat, Rod Hughes and Erik Brown for their helpful comments on earlier versions of this paper. This research was supported by an Academic Challenge Grant from the Ohio Board of Regents to the Computer-Human Interface Laboratory at Bowling Green State University.

REFERENCES

1. Begoray, J. A. An introduction to hypermedia issues, systems and application areas. *International Journal of Man-Machine Studies*, 33, 1990, 121-147.

2. Bly, S. A., and Rosenberg, J. K. A comparison of tiled and overlapping windows, *CHI '86 Proceedings*, 1986, 101-106.

3. Dillon, A. Reading from papers versus screens: A critical review of the empirical literature. *Ergonomics*, 35 (10), October 1992, 1297-1326.

4. Egan, D. E., Lesk, M. E., Ketchum, R. D., Lochbaum, C. C., Remde, J. R., Littman, M. and Landauer, T. K. Hypertext for the electronic library?: CORE sample results, *Hypertext '91 Proceedings* (New York: ACM), 1991, 299-312.

5. Egan, D. E., Remde, J. R., Gomez, L. M., Landauer, T. K., Eberhardt, J. and Lochbaum, C. C. Formative design-evaluation of SuperBook, *ACM Transactions on Information Systems*, 7 (1), 1989, 30-57.

6. Hammond, N. and Allinson, L. Extending hypertext for learning: An investigation of access and guidance tools. In Sutcliffe, A. and Macaulay, L. (eds), *People and Computers V*, Cambridge: Cambridge University Press, 1989, 293-304.

7. Hansen, W. J., and Haas, C. Reading and writing with computers: A framework for explaining differences in performance, *Communications of the ACM*, 31 (9), September 1988, 1080-1089.

8. *Hypertext '87 Proceedings*. New York, ACM, 1989.

9. *Hypertext '89 Proceedings*. New York, ACM, 1989.

10. *Hypertext '91 Proceedings*. New York, ACM, 1991.

11. Instone, K., Leventhal, L. M., Teasley, B. M., Farhat, J. and Rohlman, D. S. *What do I want?* and *How do I get there?*: Performance and navigation in information retrieval tasks with hypertext documents, *Proceedings of the East–West International Conference on Human-Computer Interaction* (St. Petersburg, Russia, August 4-8, 1992), 85-95.

12. Joel, W. J., White, R. and Tucker, W. Analysis of the effectiveness of graphics in computer aided instruction. In Salvendy, G. and Smith, M. J. (eds), *Designing and Using Human-Computer Interfaces and Knowledge Based Systems*, Amsterdam: Elsevier Science, 1989, 376-383.

13. Leventhal, L. M., Teasley, B. M., Instone, K., Rohlman, D. S. and Farhat, J. Sleuthing in HyperHolmes: Using hypertext vs. a book to answer questions, to appear in *Behaviour and Information Technology*.

14. Leventhal, L. M., Teasley, B. M., Instone, K. and Farhat, J. Age-related differences in the use of hypertext: Experiment and design guidelines. Bowling Green State University, Computer Science Department Technical Report 92-DEC-01, 1992.

15. Marchionini, G. Hypermedia and learning: Freedom and chaos. *Educational Technology*, 28 (11), November 1988, 8-12.

16. Marchionini, G. and Shneiderman, B. Finding facts vs. browsing knowledge in hypertext systems, *IEEE Computer*, 21 (1), 1988, 70-80.

17. Mynatt, B. T., Leventhal, L. M., Instone, K., Farhat, J. and Rohlman, D. S. Hypertext or book: Which is better for answering questions?, *CHI '92 Proceedings*, 1992, 19-25.

18. Nielsen, J. The matters that really matter for hypertext usability, *Hypertext '89 Proceedings* (New York: ACM), 1989, 239-248.

19. Nielsen, J. *Hypertext and Hypermedia*. New York: Academic Press, 1990.

20. Petre, M. and Green, T. R. G. Where to draw the line with text: Some claims by logic designers about graphics in notation. In D. Diaper, D. Gilmore, G. Cockton and B. Shackel (eds), *Human-Computer Interaction—INTERACT '90,* New York: Elsevier-Science, 1990, 463-468.

21. Reisel, J. F., and Shneiderman, B. Is bigger better? The effects of display size on program reading. In G. Salvendy (ed), *Social, Ergonomic and Stress Aspects of Work with Computers*, (New York: Elsevier Science Publishers), 1987, 113-122.

22. Shneiderman, B. User interface design and evaluation for an electronic encyclopedia. In G. Salvendy (ed), *Cognitive Engineering in the Design of Human-Computer Interaction and Expert Systems*, (New York: Elsevier Science Publishers), 1987, 207-223.

23. Shneiderman, B. User interface design for the Hyperties electronic encyclopedia, *Hypertext '87 Proceedings* (New York: ACM), 1989, 299-312.

24. Simpson, A. and McKnight, C. Navigation in hypertext: Structural cues and mental maps. *Hypertext 2 Conference*, 1989.

25. Tombaugh, J., Lickorish, A. and Wright, P. Multi-window displays for readers of lengthy texts. *International Journal of Man-Machine Studies*, 26 (5), 1987, 597-615.

26. Tracy, J. *The Encyclopædia Sherlockiana*. New York: Avenel, 1987.

27. Wright, P. Cognitive overheads and prostheses: Some issues in evaluating hypertexts. *Hypertext '91*, New York: ACM, 1991, 1-12.

28. Wright, P., Hull, A. and Black, D. Integrating diagrams and text. *The Technical Writing Teacher*, XVII (3), 1990, 244-254.

Bridging the Paper and Electronic Worlds: The Paper User Interface

Walter Johnson[1], Herbert Jellinek[1], Leigh Klotz[2,] Jr. Ramana Rao[1], Stuart Card[1]

[1]Xerox Palo Alto Research Center
[2]Fuji Xerox Corporation
3333 Coyote Hill Road
Palo Alto, CA

ABSTRACT

Since its invention millenia ago, paper has served as one of our primary communications media. Its inherent physical properties make it easy to use, transport, and store, and cheap to manufacture. Despite these advantages, paper remains a second class citizen in the electronic world. In this paper, we present a new technology for bridging the paper and the electronic worlds. In the new technology, the user interface moves beyond the workstation and onto paper itself. We describe paper user interface technology and its implementation in a particular system called XAX.

INTRODUCTION

Since its invention millenia ago, paper has served as one of our primary communications media. Its inherent physical properties make it easy to use, transport, and store, and cheap to manufacture. But paper also has its shortcomings. It is a passive medium, whose contents are not easily manipulated by hand nor processed by machine. It cannot easily take advantage of new methods for manipulating, communicating, filing, and processing information afforded by advances in desktop computer software. In this paper we present a method for bringing together the paper and electronic worlds through a new hybrid *paper user interface* technology. In the new technology, the user interface moves beyond the workstation and onto paper itself. This allows user interfaces to be produced that so blend into the user's world that they seem to disappear.

The properties of paper are so well suited for its uses as a medium for information that predictions of its early demise seem exaggerated. Its ease of use makes it universally accessible. Its low cost allows it to be used in quantity. Its light weight makes it portable. It can be inscribed with writing or drawings by the simplest hand tools, yet it is also easily inscribed with color photographs in mass quantities by machine and serves well as a primary medium of modern commerce and culture. But the properties of paper are also limiting. Inscriptions on it are fixed and cannot be moved

around. It is passive and does not, for instance, automatically rearrange the words in a paragraph when a new one is inserted. Its contents cannot be automatically processed, for example to detect misspelling or to sum columns of numbers. Only slowly can its contents be transmitted over distances.

Electronic media have almost the opposite profile of strengths and weaknesses. Figure 1 shows media divided into three categories: paper, electronic image, and electronic data structure. Many technological inventions can be seen as implementations of transformations between these categories: copying takes paper into more paper. Electronic printing renders data structures into images and prints images onto paper. Scanning takes paper into electronic images. Communications technologies transform these categories over space: fax takes paper into electronic images into electronic images at a distance into paper. Information filing and retrieval transforms these categories over time.

In the 1970's and early 1980's effort was focused on running "downhill" in the diagram, from data structures through to paper (and also on transformation within a category, such as text-editing). Since the late 1980s and surely through the 1990s more effort is being focused on going "uphill" from paper to electronic image to data structure. As this succeeds, we begin to have the possibility of viable processing loops that go through paper, yet have access to the information processes made possible through electronics. The user can potentially interact with such a system either electronically, through a workstation user interface, or, as we shall suggest, via paper, through a paper user interface. The paper user interface we describe in this paper is one of the first attempts to develop user interfaces in this new medium.

PAPER AND THE ELECTRONIC INFRASTRUCTURE

Although an imaging revolution has been predicted for years, scanning systems that can handle volumes of documents are costly and have been limited to use in large routinized environments such as forms processing. Image scanning systems for personal or small workgroup settings have generally been used solely for the purpose of scanning the occasional piece of artwork for desktop publishing.

507

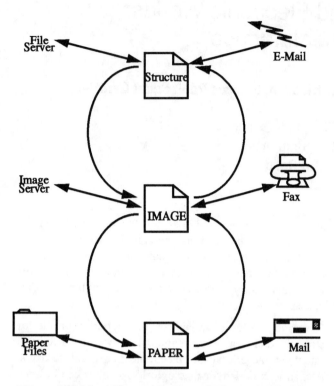

Figure 1: Bridges between Paper and Electronic Worlds

More than the cost and simple lack of desire for imaging systems is responsible for this lack of acceptance. Two other factors have limited the success of this revolution. The first is ease of use: scanners have been available for many years, yet are far less prevalent than fax machines. To use a fax machine, one must know little more than how to make a phone call. To use a scanner, one must know the scanner hardware, the computer's operating system, and a specific scanning software package. The second is functional: even when stored on the computer, image files are notoriously useless to the average user. Most environments provide little support for images, making it difficult to print, fax, display, or integrate them into other documents.

Recently, several technologies have matured to the state where solutions to many of these problems are at hand. Light-lens photocopying is gradually being superseded by digital reprographics, leading to cost reductions in high quality digital document handling systems. Users are beginning to understand and expect advanced image capabilities in reprographic systems. The rapid proliferation of computer fax modems offers a widespread capability to capture image files on personal computers.

This confluence of events in the change of the computational infrastructure removes barriers to the introduction of paper into the electronic document life cycle. The problem that remains is the essential "lifelessness" of paper documents, and the resulting scanned images. Regardless of the structure underlying an electronic document, once it is printed it is just

marks on paper. Thus, paper is a dead end, a by-product of the cycle. Much energy has been spent on character and layout recognition as a means to put electronic life back into paper documents. While difficult at best, the vagaries of document and character recognition are exacerbated by the distortions imposed during the processes of printing, distributing and scanning documents. Characters and fonts that can be recognized in an clean 400 spot-per-inch image become unrecognizable in a skewed and stretched 200x100 spot-per-inch fax-based image.

Recent work at Xerox PARC, led by Dan Bloomberg and David Hecht, has seeded the development of an end-run around these problems in document recognition. The basic technology is a method for embedding digital data in documents as diagonal marks on paper, and reading back this data from images of the documents. These marks, which Bloomberg has labeled simply "glyphs," are robust in the face of the range of distortions introduced in printing, copying, faxing, and scanning. Furthermore, they are scalable, and thus useful for encoding information in documents scanned or printed at very low and very high resolutions. Finally, their simple, regular pattern fails to catch the eye, so they are not visually distracting when embedded in a paper document.

The impact of the embedding of digital data on paper goes beyond that of simple character and layout recognition, for it makes possible the encoding of information not only about the marks that actually exist *on* the paper, but also the *structure* that is behind those marks. Accurately determining the content and structure of a document from its image has thereby enabled us to complete the "document loop," going from structure, to image, to paper, to image, and back to structure

PAPER USER INTERFACE

Robust digital data, together with other image processing techniques, enabled us to create a system in which ordinary paper becomes a computational interface. We call this concept a *paper user interface*. Using the paper itself as the computer interface, as opposed to a screen-based interface that accesses page images, provides substantial benefits to users.

First, people are accustomed to using paper. Not only is it the predominant medium in their daily work lives, but it is intertwined with all aspects of life. This historical reliance on paper means that the infrastructure for its use is common and available: pencils, pens, erasers, typewriters, fax machines, copiers, envelopes, file cabinets surround us in the most mundane of environments.

Second, people know *how* to use paper. This knowledge of "paper's syntax" exists even when the semantic knowledge is lacking: for example, in filling out a form, one can easily determine which boxes to check, and which to write in, on an income tax form, even when one has no idea of what numbers actually go in the box. Thus the learning curve for paper-based computation is minimized.

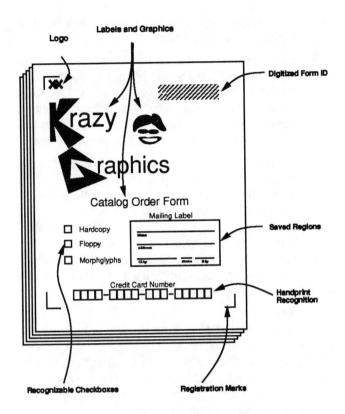

Figure 2: A Paper User Interface

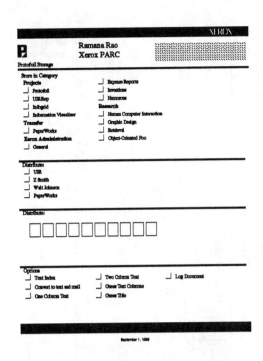

Figure 3: A Protofoil Storage Cover Sheet.

We developed the notion of a *form* as a kind of paper user interface to application programs. A form is a paper interface to a computer application, just as a dialog box is a screen interface to a computer application. Forms combine the simple paper syntax and infrastructure support of paper with the functionality of computer applications.

Figure 2 shows a typical form: it is a piece of paper with machine-readable marks, human-readable marks, and human-markable areas. The logo, form ID, and registration marks are machine-readable marks. These marks are included in every form, and serve to identify it to the machine. The checkboxes, handprint regions, and saved image regions are interface areas for users to give information to the application. Finally, arbitrary text and graphics included on the form allows the application to give information to the user.

Cover Sheets: A Paper User Interface

We explored the use of *cover sheet* forms as a paper user interface to a document services system. A cover sheet is placed in front of a document in a scanner or fax machine connected to a document services system. A cover sheet is a form that allows the user to specify the actions to be taken on the document which follows it.

Figure 4 shows what happens when a person uses a cover sheet to interact with a document services system. In this example, the user uses a cover sheet with document distribution (fax telephone number) options. She marks the intended recipients on the cover sheet, and places it together with a

document in the input feeder of a fax machine. The page images are then sent via to the document services system, where it interprets the form image as a request to fax the document following it to a specified location. The document services system then uses its computer fax modem to send the document to its destinations.

Requirements for Paper User Interface

We have identified several conditions required for paper to be useful as a computational medium. First, processing has to be reliable and rapid. Although PC and workstation users have become accustomed to periodic unexplained breakdowns, users of ordinary paper-handling office equipment have developed an intuitive understanding of the failure modes of these machines: if the paper goes in, it will come out or become jammed in a visible, physical way. This statement is true for copiers, printers, and most easy-to-use fax machines. Speed depends on the application: for example, time-dependent applications such as broadcast distribution of faxes must be initiated in a timely fashion. The system must have a mechanism for prioritizing applications if more than one job can be in progress.

Second, the user's time must be separated from the scanner's time. One of the main benefits of paper is that it enables the user to perform the work anywhere that she might ordinarily use paper---at the office, at home, on an airplane, in the car. The physical interaction with the computer---via a fax machine or a scanner---must not be a bottleneck. Since the paper itself directs the processing, the user need not be present while scanning occurs, since her role in the process is

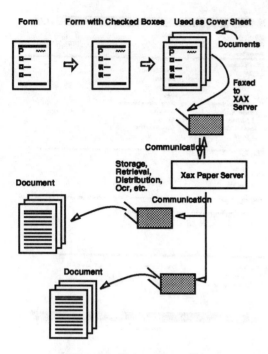

Figure 4: Using Cover Sheets.

over once the paper starts moving. This implies that the system must be capable of batch processing, since the user may want to submit an hour's or day's work at one time.

Finally, since integration with the electronic world was one of our goals, we wanted to provide electronic access to whatever functionality we provided via paper, as well as to the documents stored via paper. An unpublished companion paper [1] describes an electronic filing system that uses paper user interface as well as workstation interface technology.

XAX PAPER SERVER

In order to explore these issues in context, we designed and implemented a prototype "paper server," XAX, which is still in use at PARC. XAX consists of a server, a forms editor, and a client-server interface. XAX provides a framework for supporting applications which use paper interfaces. We describe one such application, Protofoil, and then focus on the components of XAX.

The Protofoil Application

Protofoil is a prototype document management system which provides an electronic filing cabinet that can be accessed by both paper and computer workstation. Protofoil gives users three basic services: document storage, document distribution, and document retrieval. The Protofoil server is built on top of XAX, which provides the paper interface to these documents. (Workstation access comes from a separate client program, not discussed here.)

Users can fax or scan documents into Protofoil, have them indexed by preselected keywords or by the recognized text of the documents, and retrieve the documents based on these features. Indexing, search, and retrieval are all accessable via both paper and computer display [2]. Documents can be distributed by fax or by electronic mail of the recognized text.

The paper interface to Protofoil consists of a set of cover sheets. A Protofoil cover sheet is a configurable paper interface that gives the user access to any pre-selected collection of Protofoil services. Users can create new, personal Protofoil cover sheets using the XAX forms editor. The cover sheet shown in Figure 3 allows the bearer to to store a document in a local Protofoil document database, add any of a list of pre-determined keywords, and distribute a document to any of a set of pre-determined recipients.

The XAX Server

XAX consists of a WYSIWYG form editor, a form description language, an action description language, and a server. The SPARC-based server processes the forms, performing recognition of form type, execution of actions, storage of documents, and (optionally) dynamic creation of new forms resulting from retrieval requests.

The XAX server (Figure 5) is charged with the recognition and interpretation of incoming documents, which arrive via scanner or fax. Independent scanner and fax driver programs, running anywhere on the Xerox Internet computer network, create sequences of page image files in a special spool directory known to the Xax server. When a new image sequence arrives, the server first splits it into one or more runs of pages, each consisting of a form followed by zero or more pages that it pertains to.

Decoding the glyph information, the server determines the identity of the form, locates the appropriate action description file, and processes the page image, looking for the glyphs, clipped regions, and checkboxes it expects to find there. The server passes that information, along with pointers to the individual page images, to the action procedure for the form, which is then free to use this information in any way required.

XAX Form Editor

The form editor, XAXEDIT, assists the user in designing forms to meet new information-processing needs. Superficially similar to structured graphics editors like MacDraw, XAXEDIT presents the user with a palette of elements, such as checkboxes and text strings, with which to draw a new form. Those elements can be broadly lumped into two classes: those with semantics and those without. Examples of the former include checkboxes and clipped regions, and examples of the other class include text, line art, and bitmaps.

XAX Forms

Forms must always bear certain registration marks and glyphs

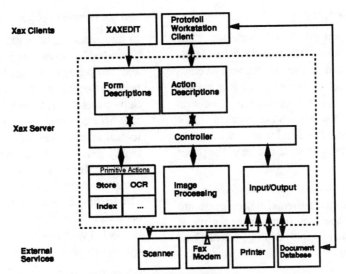

Figure 5: The XAX Server.

in given positions - this is how the system recognizes them as forms. The user is free to add other elements to the form, as determined by the application she is creating. A completed form is thus comprised of three types of information: a form description, which lists all elements of the form in a simple Lisp-based language, and which XAXEDIT can both read and write; Action descriptions, which represent the semantic elements of the form and the actions they perform, and drive the XAX server's image-processing routines; and a description in either Postscript or Xerox Interpress format that encodes how to print the form. (See Figure 3.) A pointer to the files containing this information is encoded in the glyphs on every form.

While forms can be created manually, the system is also required to compute them automatically in response to user queries via another form. For example, upon storing any document in Protofoil, the user needs some way of accessing and interacting with it later. The Protofoil-store action procedure automatically creates a new form that "points at" the document, bearing checkboxes that allow the user to print or delete it. This ability to compute new forms on the fly helps to close the paper--computer loop.

Image processing

In order to recognize forms, several types of image processing operations are performed on every document entering the system. Logo and registration mark detection are performed on every page in order to determine the presence of a form, correct for skew, and enable batch processing of jobs. Glyph recognition enables to server to decode a unique 256 bit ID for each form. Another operation locates each checkbox on a form, and determine its status, checked or unchecked, while others lift and scale hand-printed regions that contain titles, recipient names, and other information a user may handprint on a form. Finally, the system uses the ScanWorx™ system from Xerox Imaging Systems for optical character recogni-

tion.

Document Database

XAX provides a generic interface to a document database. The initial design of the system was based upon a remote database, but was judged by users to be too slow. The current design utilizes a local database provided by a system built on top of XAX, Protofoil. Although storage is local to each user's primary workstation, remote access is enabled both via electronic and fax networks.

EXPERIENCE

In our experience with XAX, we found three classes of user: casual users, who used the system infrequently or for a short time, document storage (Protofoil) users, and document services (mainly OCR) users. The top four document storage users stored over 400 documents, totaling over 1300 pages; the top two OCR users scanned 40 documents, totaling over 140 pages.

All users previously had access to scanners, workstations, document storage systems and OCR software. Our interviews revealed that the primary advantage of paper user interfaces over existing systems was ease of task initiation; the users felt that document entry, retrieval, and OCR were simplified by elimination of cumbersome workstation interfaces.

To compensate for the static nature of their paper forms, our users came to modify and add to their form sets frequently. We observed that the patterns of change were different for the document storage and OCR users.

Document storage users tended to have three phases of form use: introduction, specialization, and separation. In the introductory phase, users experimented with one or two forms created for them, with storage options based on categories they supplied. In the specialization phase, users developed new forms, adding and deleting categories from the initial list. In the separation phase, users grouped related sets of categories and moved them onto separate forms.

OCR users underwent different phases of form use. They tended to do little experimentation, but instead used a simple form for mailing the recognized text to themselves. Eventually, they would request new forms allowing access to parameters of the OCR package, such as specification of column layout or language. Unlike document storage users, OCR application users tended to reuse filled-in forms with complex option selections, exploiting the persistent nature of the paper medium.

Complexity of interaction is a significant barrier to the use of any system. In document service systems, where users are handling large volumes of paper, we found use of a paper interface minimized complexity by keeping interactions within the single paper domain.

CONCLUSION

Pen-based computing, as instantiated in notebook computers, leverages only some of the properties of paper. The same holds true for "paper-like" interfaces [3], which are more appropriately called "stylus-based." The use of paper in the modern world persists *because* of its physical properties, not only despite them. Paper is convenient, requiring no batteries. It is light, readable, and durable. It has a tangible, persistent existence that is valued in legal and business transactions. These properties do not diminish the value of alternative media, such as notebook computers, but they do imply that paper has utility that will not simply disappear with the increasing electronization of the world. And as long as a significant amount of paper exists among us, then pragmatically, one of our main goals should be {\em integrating},

and not *removing* paper from our electronic lives.

In this paper we have argued that the physical and historical properties of paper make it suitable for many kinds of work, and that paper itself can leverage these properties and additionally become a computational interface. The XAX Paper Server was created to demonstrate the infrastructure needed to enable computational paper interfaces. The basic technological advance needed to build a scalable PaperUI processing system was the capability of embedding data on paper, thus enabling us to robustly determine the identity and semantics from paper forms, our basic interface mechanism. The feasibility of XAX is further demonstrated by the existence of a PC software product based on it and its successors, Xerox PaperWorks™.

REFERENCES

[1] R. Rao, W. Johnson, L. Klotz, and S. Card. Bridging the paper and electronic worlds: An electronic file cabinet for the information worker's paper documents. 1993. *Unpublished manuscript.*

[2] *D. R. Cutting, J. Pedersen, and P-K. Halvorsen. In* object-oriented architecture for text retrieval. In Conference Proceedings of RIAO '91, Intelligent Text and Image Handling, Barcelona, Spain, *pp. 285-298, April, 1991.*

[3] *C. G. Wolf, J. R. Rhyne, and H. A. Ellozy. Paper-like user interfaces.* In Designing and Using Human-Computer Interfaces and Knowledge-based Systems: Proceedings of the Third International Conference on Human-Computer Interaction, *pp. 494-501. Elsevier, 1989.*

Integrated CSCW Tools Within a Shared 3D Virtual Environment

Christer Carlsson
Distributed Systems Laboratory
Swedish Institute of Computer Science
Box 1263, S-164 28 Kista, Sweden
tel:+46 8 752 15 60
E-mail: cc@sics.se

Lennart E. Fahlén
Distributed Systems Laboratory
Swedish Institute of Computer Science
Box 1263, S-164 28 Kista, Sweden
tel:+46 8 752 15 39
E-mail: lef@sics.se

ABSTRACT

With the advance of computer graphics hardware and computer communication technology it is now possible to build personal interactive 3D interfaces. Our research goal is to use this technology to create CSCW environments.

There are several problems with existing CSCW applications and environments. We specifically address three intimately connected problem areas:

- awareness (what are other users doing?)
- focus (where is my attention directed?)
- interaction metaphors (how do I do something?)

Our approach is to let each user be represented by a 3D icon ("body icon") and graphically model the user's input devices in 3D space. Users navigate between applications in 3D space and can meet and collaborate in the environment. There is a direct correspondence between a user's body icon, input devices and the actions taken by the user. We claim that this gives users a more detailed and natural understanding of other users activities than in conventional CSCW systems. By using direct (real world) metaphors in the interaction with applications, it is our hope that the cognitive load on the users is reduced and the awareness and focus effects are increased.

To enable us to do experiments with 3D CSCW environments, we have built the Distributed Interactive Virtual Environment[1] (DIVE) software [3]. DIVE is a heterogeneous software framework for creating multi-user, multi-application 3D distributed user environments. Unlike some other multi-user virtual reality systems (e.g. [2, 4]), DIVE is not based on a client-server model, instead all participating nodes are treated as peers with respect to control and data

distribution. This means that DIVE scales to a large number of users running many applications just by adding more workstations to the network. The functionality of DIVE makes it possible to integrate different applications in the same 3D environment.

The main demonstration will consist of software for virtual conferences and remote collaboration written in DIVE. The software supports virtual meetings, collaborative drawing and document distribution.

The metaphors we use in the CSCW applications are "brutally" direct. Users meet at a conference table, draw on the white-board in the room and documents are distributed from hand to hand. The mechanisms for handling user control, awareness and focus are based on the ideas of aura and focus [1, 5].

KEYWORDS

CSCW, Virtual Reality, Interactive 3D Graphics, User Interface.

REFERENCES

1. Benford, S., Bullock, A., Cook, N., Harvey, P., Ingram, R. and Lee, O. K. *From Rooms to Cyberspace: Models of Interaction in Large Virtual Computer Spaces*, The Univ. of Nottingham, UK (to appear in Interacting With Computers in 1993).

2. Blanchard, C., Burgess, S., Harville, Y., Lanier, J., Lasko, A., Oberman, M. and Teitel, M. *Reality Built for Two: A Virtual Reality Tool*, ACM SIGGRAPH Computer Graphics 24:2, pp. 35-36.

3. Carlsson, C. and Hagsand O. *The MultiG Distributed Interactive Virtual Environment*, Proceedings of the 5th MultiG Workshop, Stockholm, December 18, 1992.

4. Codella, C., Jalili, R., Koved, L., Lewis, J. B., Ling, D. T., Lipscomb, J. S., Rabenhorst, D. A., Wang, C. P., Norton, A., Sweeney, P. and Turk, G. *Interactive Simulation in a Multi-Person Virtual World*, Proceedings of CHI'92, Monterey, May 3-7, 1992, pp. 329-334.

5. Fahlén, L. E., Ståhl, O., Brown, C. G. and Carlsson, C. *A Space Based Model for User Interaction in Shared Synthetic Environments*, Proceedings of INTERCHI '93, Amsterdam, April 27 - May 2, 1993.

1.DIVE has been created within the MultiG program, a Swedish national research effort on high speed communication networks and distributed applications.

The paper model for computer-based writing

Ann Fatton, Staffan Romberger and Kerstin Severinson Eklundh

IPLab, Department of Numerical Analysis and Computing Science
Royal Institute of Technology
S-100 44 Stockholm, SWEDEN
E-mail: annfa@nada.kth.se, srom@nada.kth.se, kse@nada.kth.se

INTRODUCTION

When writing or reading on paper, we usually have a robust perception of the text as a spatial object with inherent structure. By a quick visual inspection of a book in our hands, and by flipping the pages for a few seconds, we get a preliminary feel for the size, structure and content of the text material. Not only are we guided by those physical cues in the process of approaching a new text, they also enable us to remember the text by its appearance and spatial arrangement (see e.g. [2]).

In contrast, during on-screen writing and reading with a word processor, users often lack a global perspective of the text. In fact, the use of word processors has been shown to cause problems for writers in reading and evaluating long documents on the screen. The word processor is usually used on a small screen, showing only a very restricted part of the text at a time. Moreover, when the user makes revisions or shifts position in the text, the location of the text relative to the screen window varies. This contributes to writers lacking an adequate "sense of the text" when writing a long document [1].

WRITING ON 'SHEETS OF PAPER'

An experimental writing system, *Paper*, has been constructed on the basis of a metaphor of paper sheets [3]. The goal is to explore the usefulness of such a model for achieving a "physical overview" of a text during writing and reading.

The program is written in the Smalltalk language, and intended to be used on a graphical workstation with a large, high-resolution screen (19" or 21"). The current version runs on Apple Macintosh and has a direct-manipulation interface consistent with the Macintosh interface style.

The basic idea is that the user writes on "sheets of paper" implemented as rectangular windows. All the pages in one document have the same size. When a page is full, a new page automatically appears on which the user can continue writing.

The individual pages of a text can be moved around the screen by pointing at them and dragging them to the desired position. When many pages fill the screen, commands for navigating between pages, spreading out and piling pages can be used.

The following are some of the most important aspects of the paper sheet metaphor:

• **overview** — the possibility to spread out the pages of a document on a desktop, making it possible to see several pages simultaneously. The possibility of stacking pages together helps the writer to organize the desk and get a perspective over a specific part of a text.

• **constant position of the text relative to the page** — the constance of the text position should support the writer's spatial memory, making it possible to remember where on the page a certain part of the text appears.

• **continuity in the writing process** — the user should be able to write a continuous text without interruption when switching to a new page.

• **local/global context** — while a global context is necessary for the writer to get a global sense of the text, a local context of 2 or 3 consecutive pages is also needed to support the writer's current activity.

There are a number of problems in how the paper model should be implemented. For example, it is not evident how the model should support the insertion of new text within previously written text. In the current version of *Paper*, a page is split into two pages when a major insertion is made, whereas minor corrections fit within the blank spaces of the page. Generally, one may have to make priorities between partly conflicting aspects of the model, such as the support for the user's spatial memory on the one hand, and the access to a sufficient local context, on the other. We are currently developing a version of *Paper* which will be the basis for experiments in testing the model.

REFERENCES

1. Hansen, W. J. & Haas, C. (1988) Reading and writing with computers: a framework for explaining differences in performance. *Communications of the ACM*, 31, Sept. 1988, 1080-1089.

2. Lovelace, E.A. & Southall, S.D. Memory for words in prose and their locations on the page. *Memory and Cognition*, 11, 429-434.

3. Severinson Eklundh, K., Romberger, S. & Englund, P. (1992) Writing on sheets of paper: a spatial metaphor for computer-based text handling. *Proc. EP92 (Int. Conf. on Electronic Publishing and Document Manipulation)*, Lausanne, Switzerland.

THE HUMAN GUIDANCE OF AUTOMATED DESIGN

Lynne Colgan

British Aerospace plc
Sowerby Research Centre
(FPC 267) PO Box 5
Bristol BS12 7QW, UK
+44(0)272-366988
colgan@uk.co.bae.src

Robert Spence

Dept. of Electrical Engineering
Imperial College
Exhibition Road
LONDON SW7 2BT, UK
+44 (0)71-225-8505
bobs@uk.ac.ic.ee

Paul Rankin

Philips Research Laboratories
Cross Oak Lane
Redhill
Surrey RH1 5HA, UK
+44(0)293-785544
rankin@prl.philips.co.uk

ABSTRACT
This 5-minute video describes the potential of automated design ('optimisation') and identifies associated difficulties which can be overcome by an interface allowing the designer to guide the automated design process. Within the context of electronic circuit design the video then shows a system, called CoCo, for the control and observation of circuit optimisation. Illustrations focus on graphical interfaces used for (a) describing the circuit, (b) describing the required performance and (c) the human guidance of the automated design of that circuit. Jargon has been suppressed so that workers in related fields can see the implications of the idea.

ENGINEERING DESIGN
Engineers who design artifacts such as electronic circuits choose **parameter** values so that the artifact exhibits acceptable **properties**. Typically, this process is carried out by manual iteration. A hundred or more iterations may be required, and often the complexity of the problem and conflicting objectives mean that the full potential of a design is never realised.

AUTOMATED DESIGN
But algorithms are available which can *automatically* adjust the parameters of an artifact in order to better satisfy the customer's requirements on its properties, a process also called **optimisation**. Paradoxically, such potential can only be realised via a suitable interface with a human designer. The designer needs to be able, in familiar language, to state the problem, to suggest a possible starting solution and then to observe and guide the optimisation. Such guidance allows the expertise and knowledge of the designer to complement the algorithmic power of the optimisation.

THE COCO SYSTEM
The video illustrates the potential of the human guidance of automated design in the context of electronic circuit design, by showing a computer-aided circuit design system [1] called

CoCo (for control and observation of circuit optimisation). It focuses on the use of CoCo's three graphical interfaces.

OPTIMISATION PROFILE
The MINNIE interface allows a circuit diagram to be sketched and the predicted performance viewed. The designer then uses the MOUSE interface to describe performance limits and the relative importance of different performances. The Cockpit then allows the designer to observe the step-by-step progress of an optimisation, and interrupt if appropriate.

THE COCKPIT
To enhance the designer's insight into the circuit, the Cockpit visually encodes, and presents at each iteration, data concerning several circuit attributes. Many are encoded qualitatively by circles whose size indicates the discrepancy between desired and achieved circuit performance. The designer can scan a hierarchy of detail from an overall measure of performance discrepancy down to individual voltages and currents. Also displayed are parameter values and the sensitivity of the overall performance discrepancy to these parameters. A 'video-like' control allows the designer to replay the progress of the optimisation, perhaps to investigate a trade-off indicated by correlated changes in circle sizes.

EXPERT ADVISORY SYSTEMS
The video shows how two expert advisory systems also assist the designer. One facilitates the selection of the optimisation algorithm. The other monitors the electrical condition of the circuit being designed and, like an alarm system, draws the designer's attention to potentially undesirable situations such as the overheating of a transistor.

CONCLUSION
The video highlights the potential for automated design and the need for an effective interface blending the complementary capabilities of the human designer and computer algorithms. A novel system to support this argument is shown in action.

REFERENCE
1. Colgan, L., Rankin, P.R. and Spence, R. Steering Automated Design, in Artificial Intelligence in Design, Oxford, Butterworth-Heinemann, (1991), pp.211-230.

BROWSING GRAPHS USING A FISHEYE VIEW

Marc H. Brown
James R. Meehan

Manojit Sarkar

DEC Systems Research Center
130 Lytton Ave.
Palo Alto, CA 94301
{mhb,meehan}@src.dec.com

Department of Computer Science
Brown University
Providence, RI 02912
ms@cs.brown.edu

The accompanying videotape demonstrates a system for viewing large graphs [2]. It's one of many possible implementations of a general framework for graphical fisheye views that we have developed.

The graph in the video represents direct routes between major cities in the United States. An obvious way to see more detail about an area is to zoom into the graph. However, as the user zooms into an area, less of the graph is visible so the global structure of the graph is lost. This becomes more acute as the user pans the zoomed image.

An alternate way to browse the graph is to use the graphical fisheye view technique. In a fisheye view, the area of interest is shown with detail while the rest of the structure is shown with successively less detail [1]. Notice that the entire structure is always visible. Compare Figs. (a) and (b).

As the user moves the *focus* (the point under the cursor), the graph constantly changes to keep the area near the focus enlarged. Smooth, real-time animation provides the feedback necessary to keep the viewer oriented. Compare Figs. (b) and (c).

Our system allows the user to control various parameters that control the display. For example, the user can control the amount of magnification of the area near the focus and the corresponding demagnification and repositioning of all other vertices.

The user can also make some vertices "more important" than others. For example, in the graph in the videotape, the importance of each city is proportional to the city's population. The size of a vertex is a function of both its importance and also its distance from the focus, and the user can control the

way the two components are combined. Compare Figs. (c) and (d).

The videotape also demonstrate the user setting a threshold so that unimportant vertices are not displayed. By "unimportant", we mean those vertices that either have been assigned a very low importance, or are far away from the focus. Compare Figs. (d) and (e).

In summary, a graphical fisheye view is a useful technique for visualizing information. It shows both local detail of a particular area as well as global context of how that area fits into the entire structure. Our system gives users interactive control over a variety of parameters that govern the display, and it has allowed us to explore some of the many interesting properties of fisheye views.

ACKNOWLEDGMENTS

Manojit Sarkar was supported by summer research internship from DEC's Systems Research Center, and in part by ONR Contract N00014–91–J–4052, ARPA Order 8225.

REFERENCES

[1] George W. Furnas. Generalized Fisheye Views. In proceedings of CHI, 1986 (Boston, MA, April 13–17, 1986), ACM, New York, 1992. pp. 16–23.

[2] Manojit Sarkar and Marc H. Brown. Graphical Fisheye Views of Graphs. In proceedings of CHI, 1992 (Monterey, CA, May 3–7, 1992), ACM, New York, 1992. pp. 83–91.

 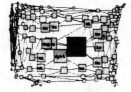 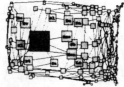 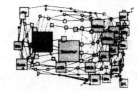 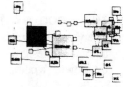

(a) Initial graph *(b) Focus on St. Louis* *(c) Focus on Salt Lake City* *(d) Factoring in vertex importance* *(e) Increased threshold*

High Interaction Data Visualization Using Seesoft™ to Visualize Program Change History

Joseph L. Steffen and Stephen G. Eick

AT&T Bell Laboratories, Room IHC 1P–336
P.O. Box 3013, 1000 E. Warrenville Road
Naperville, IL 60566-7013, USA
Tel: +1 708 713 5378
E-mail: Joseph_L_Steffen@att.com

ABSTRACT
A problem in developing large software systems is understanding the source code. This problem is difficult because of the volume of code. The listing for a moderately sized system with 100,000 lines, printed 50 lines per page, would run 2,000 pages. This video shows a new software tool, Seesoft™, that applies scientific visualization techniques to visualizing code. The visualization approach is to represent files in a directory in columns and the source code lines as rows of colored pixels. The indentation and length of each row of pixels corresponds to the actual code. The color of each row of pixels is determined by a statistic such as the age, programmer, or type of line, that we obtain from the change management system. The visual impression is that of a miniature picture of the source code with the indentation showing the usual C controls structure and the color showing the spatial distribution of the statistic. A user may adjust the display using direct manipulation techniques to discover interesting patterns in the code. Software engineering concepts such as complexity and bug fix on fix density can be visualized.

The main interest of this work to the human factors community is the use of graphical user interface for selecting and combining statistics from a database, the effective use of hundreds of colors to display a mass of data, and the reduction of the point-and-click direct manipulation metaphor to just pointing, e.g. something of interest will occur where ever the mouse points to on the display.

KEYWORDS: Direct manipulation, graphical user interface, scientific visualization.

517

Exploring Remote Images:
A Telepathology Workstation

Catherine Plaisant , David A. Carr and Hiroaki Hasegawa*

Human-Computer Interaction Laboratory
Center for Automation Research

University of Maryland
College Park, MD 20742
Tel. (301) 405-2768
plaisant@cs.umd.edu

Telemedicine is the practice of medicine over communication links. The physician being consulted and the patient are in two different locations. A first telepathology system has been developed by Corabi Telemetrics. It allows a pathologist to render a diagnosis by examining tissue samples or body fluids under a remotely located microscope.

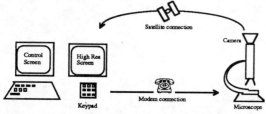

Figure 1: Simplified diagram of a telepathology system.

Of course it would seem natural to digitize the entire specimen at the highest magnification and then leisurely explore the transmitted image. But this is not currently practical because the specimens are very high definition 3D color objects requiring too long to digitize and having impractical storage requirements. Therefore the specimen still needs today to be explored under a microscope.

The consulting pathologist sits at the receiving workstation, remotely manipulates the microscope and looks at the high resolution image of the magnified sample, transmitted via satellite, microwave or cable. A scanned low resolution global view of the whole slide is displayed on the control screen. A red rectangle indicates the position of the microscope stage which can be moved by dragging the rectangle. These actions can be handled with direct manipulation principles. Unfortunately, several limiting factors exists: time delays (about 1.5 seconds for transmission and activation of a command), inadequate position feedback, and increased probability of breakdown. Those factors lead us to the notion of remote direct manipulation [1]. We are exploring various interfaces and conducting experiments to determine which configuration will beneficially replace the existing interface. A satisfactory interface also has to let the pathologist manipulate the main controls while still looking at the high resolution image.

At first two prototypes were built on our simulator. A start-stop interface using a keypad (users specify a start command followed by a stop command), similar to the existing interface, and a proportional commands interface using a trackball (users specify movement commands incremental and directly proportional to the input device movement). We conducted a pilot study to determine the effect of time delays on performance using the two interfaces. The initial results [2] showed the benefits of the direct manipulation of the red rectangle on the global view when the time delays are very long but our trackball interface didn't seem to be helpful. On the other hand users comments suggested that providing more feedback would improve the performance. These improvements were made and the improved interface was tested in the same conditions. With the feedback improvement the trackball interface exhibited the best properties and was significantly faster for expert users.

A second experiment was performed to estimate the benefits of providing an intermediate local map for navigation at high magnification. Our experience shows that an intermediate view should be introduced when the ratio overview-to-detail is above 1:20. Certainly, by the time the ratio reaches 1:40 users have serious difficulties and the global overview is more of a hindrance than a help.

Current references:
1. Keil-Slawik et al. Remote direct manipulation: A case study of a telemedicine workstation. In Bullinger H.-J. (Ed.), *Proc. of the 4th Int. Conf. on HCI*, Stuttgart (Sept. 91). Amsterdam, Elsevier. pp. 1006-1011.
2. Carr, D., Hasegawa, H., Lemmon, D., Plaisant, C. The effects of time delays on a telepathology user interface, in *Proc. of 16th AMIA SCAMC conference*, Baltimore (Nov.92). New York, McGraw-Hill, Health Professions Division, pp. 256-260.

Acknowledgements: We appreciate the support of the State of Maryland MIPS program, Corabi Telemetric and the System Research Center of the University of Maryland.

* on visit from Sony Corp. Japan

QOC IN ACTION:
USING DESIGN RATIONALE TO SUPPORT DESIGN

Diane McKerlie & Allan MacLean

Rank Xerox Cambridge EuroPARC
61 Regent Street, Cambridge, UK., CB2 1AB
mckerlie@europarc.xerox.com & maclean@europarc.xerox.com

Design Rationale emphasises working with explicit representations not only of possible design solutions, but also of the reasons and processes behind them. Although the arguments for using Design Rationale are compelling, there is still very little experience of applying the current approaches in practice. To explore its use in a practical setting we have been collaborating with the Open University[1] using QOC (Questions, Options, Criteria) to design hypermedia interfaces for presenting course material (currently text books, course notes, and videos). This video illustrates some of the ways in which we have used QOC to support our activities.

The QOC perspective on design rationale has evolved over several years (e.g. [2], [3], [4]). QOC represents design reasoning as a network of *Questions* which highlight key design issues, *Options* which represent alternative solutions to these issues and *Criteria* which represent the reasons for or against the various Options. This semi-formal notation effectively represents the design space around the design being produced, thus situating it in a broader context than would otherwise be the case. Much of the work to date has focused on the properties of the approach and the notation, but some has examined how it relates to design practice. For example, the QOC notation has been used to describe the discussions of designers working together [3], [4]. This has demonstrated parallels between the fundamental concepts of QOC and the concepts "naturally" used by designers. It has also helped to highlight a number of areas where QOC might help to improve the effectiveness of the design process – for example, by encouraging an explicit emphasis on important issues and by helping organise, structure, and index the progress of the design process.

The hypermedia interface design project provides an opportunity to explore these possibilities. For the current phase of the project, the main aim is to explore different ways in which QOC might support early design so that we can gain experience of how to make best use of it. The five-person project team is distributed across two geographical locations, about 60 miles apart. The design activities include individuals working on their own, the use of various forms of electronic communication, and face to face meetings of all or part of the project team.

---

[1] The Open University in Milton Keynes, UK offers distance education degree programmes and is a major publisher of educational material.

QOC has supported a range of design activities in a variety of ways. We use QOC diagrams as a resource for *reflecting* on the current state of the design and developing design ideas, either working individually or with other team members. We use QOC to support group work by helping members *communicate* with each other (cf. [1]). QOC diagrams are used as a vehicle to explain, elaborate, compare, and review design ideas and issues. They have also been used as aids to re-assess previously made design "decisions", and as aids for reaching agreement during decision making. As the team has become accustomed to using QOC, we increasingly find it being spontaneously used as a natural form of expression during group meetings. It also serves as a basis for *documenting* records of our design reasoning. Even though the development of a design idea might have been chaotic and opportunistic, QOC provides a basis for *organising* the underlying reasoning and the variety of other design representations we use. For example, we maintain on-line design records which use QOC to structure design artifacts such as notes, sketches, scenario descriptions and prototype screen-shots.

In summary, understanding and preserving reasoning behind our design decisions has made a valuable contribution to our interface design project. It has also resulted in a record which we hope will prove useful in future phases of the project.

REFERENCES

1. Bellotti, V. (1993) Integrating theoreticians' and practitioners' perspectives with design rationale. In Proceedings of INTERCHI'93.

2. MacLean, A., Young, R., & Moran, T. (1989). Design Rationale: The argument behind the artifact. In Proceedings of CHI'89: Human Factors in Computing Systems, April 30 - May 4, Austin, Texas, 247-252. New York: ACM.

3. MacLean, A., Bellotti, V. & Young, R. M. (1990). What rationale is there in design? In Proceedings of the INTERACT '90 Conference on Human-Computer Interaction, 207-212. Amsterdam: North-Holland.

4. MacLean, A., Young, R., Bellotti, V. & Moran, T. (1991). Questions, Options, and Criteria: Elements of Design Space Analysis. Human-Computer Interaction, Vol 6 (3&4). [Special Issue on Design Rationale: John M. Carroll & Thomas P. Moran (Eds.)], 201-250.

Touch-Typing With a Stylus

David Goldberg and Cate Richardson

Xerox Corporation
Palo Alto Research Center
3333 Coyote Hill Rd.
Palo Alto, CA 94304
goldberg@parc.xerox.com
(415)-812-4423

ABSTRACT

Keyboards are a vital part of today's computers. Although keyboards are somewhat bulky, they are well suited to PCs (even portable laptops) and workstations. In the future of Ubiquitous Computing [3], pocket-sized and wall-sized computers will be common. A keyboard is not very suitable for these sizes of computers. Thus many manufacturers are providing electronic pens or styli (we use the two terms interchangeably) as the primary input device for computers. A stylus is attractive because it works very well over the entire range of sizes. However, it is not very convenient for text entry. The state of the art is to print characters, with boxed entry recommended to improve accuracy [1]. This is slow and error prone [2]. This suggests that a major impediment to the widespread use of styli is the problem of finding a convenient way to enter text.

There is an analogy between keyboards and styli. Keyboards can be used with no training: the letters can be tapped out one-by-one using hunt-and-peck. This is similar to what is currently done with styli. No new training is required, and letters are printed one-by-one. However, unlike styli, keyboards have a "growth path." With practice, hunt-and-peck with two fingers can become faster than handwriting. If even higher speeds are desired, then keyboard users can learn touch-typing. Touch-typing not only achieves high speeds, it also enables "eyes-free" operation, that is, the ability to type without having to look at your hands. This suggests that the solution to the problem of stylus text entry requires developing an analogue of touch-typing.

Our approach to developing touch-typing for a stylus is based on introducing a special alphabet of *unistrokes*. Like touch-typing for keyboards, unistrokes have to be learned. Unistrokes have the following advantages over ordinary printing:

- They are designed somewhat like error correcting codes. When written sloppily, they can still be distinguished from one another.

- Each unistroke is a single pen-down/pen-up motion, hence the name *unistroke*. Not only does this mean that recognition cannot have segmentation errors (that is, errors in determining which sets of strokes belong to a single multi-stroke letter), but it means that letters can unambiguously be written one on top of another. Thus unistrokes can be entered in a small box just big enough to hold one letter.

- The unistrokes associated with the most common letters ('e', 'a', 't', 'i', 'r') are all straight lines, and hence are fast to write.

The unistroke design is being evaluated by having users send several e-mail messages per day using a stylus front-end to the Unix mail program. Based on measurements from this program, it appears that unistrokes may be able to support an entry rate as high as 3.5 letters/sec (touch typing is typically 6-7 letters/sec).

The video gives the motivation for unistrokes, briefly shows text entry using a conventional pen-based interface [1], discusses the unistroke alphabet and how it was designed to be easy to learn, and then shows a skilled writer using unistrokes.

REFERENCES

1] Robert Carr and Dan Shafer. *The Power of PenPoint*, Addison-Wesley, 1991.

2] Walter S. Mossberg, "Notepad PCs Struggle With One Small Task: Deciphering Writing.", *Wall Street Journal*, Thursday July 23, 1992.

3] Mark Weiser. "The Computer for the 21st Century," *Scientific American*, 94-104, Sep 1991.

ARGOS: A Display System for Augmenting Reality

David Drascic
Human Engineering Research &
Consulting (HERC)
19 Pleasant Home Blvd
Downsview, Ont., Canada M3M 2B4
e-mail: drascic@ie.utoronto.ca

Julius J. Grodski
Defence & Civil Institute of
Environmental Medicine (DCIEM)
P.O. Box 2000
North York, Ont. Canada M3M 3B9
e-mail: jul@dretor.dciem.dnd.ca

**Paul Milgram, Ken Ruffo,
Peter Wong, Shumin Zhai**
Dept. Industrial Engineering,
University of Toronto
Toronto, Ont. Canada M5S 1A4
e-mail: milgram@gpu.utcs.utoronto.ca

ABSTRACT

This video describes the development of the ARGOS (Augmented Reality through Graphic Overlays on Stereovideo) system, as a tool for enhancing human-telerobot interaction, and as a more general tool with applications in a variety of areas, including image enhancement, simulation, sensor fusion, and virtual reality.

KEYWORDS: stereoscopic displays, 3-D, virtual reality, remote manipulation, teleoperation

NOTE: Portions of this video are in alternating field stereoscopic video format. Appropriate viewing equipment is needed to perceive the stereoscopic effect. [5]

HUMAN-ROBOT INTERACTION

This project began by examining the human-machine interface of a particular telerobot, identifying two key problem areas: information flow from the robot to the operator (feedback), and information flow from the operator to the machine (commands/instructions).

Visual Feedback Interface

Most telerobots use monoscopic video (MV) as the primary feedback link for the operator. MV lacks binocular depth cues, however, hampering the user's perception of locations of objects in the remote world. Using stereoscopic video (SV) for remote manipulation can reduce task execution time, error rates, and training times. [2] Recent studies have shown that operators strongly prefer SV, and rate it more comfortable and usable than MV. [1]

Control Interface

Most telerobots are controlled manually, requiring continuous attention from highly skilled operators. Fully autonomous telerobots are not yet possible in unstructured environments, but it *is* feasible to transfer some of the workload from the operator to the machine [6]. A semi-autonomous robot can carry out simple movement commands if a method of communicating precise three dimensional coordinates to the robot is available. Humans are poor at *absolute* judgement of position, but can make accurate *relative* position judgments using SV displays. [3] If a pointer with an accurately known position is available, operators can use it to specify arbitrary points in the remote world, using their own sense of relative position.

We have created a *virtual pointer* using calibrated stereoscopic computer graphics (SG), and with our ARGOS system combine the SG image with the SV, so that the *virtual pointer* appears within the remote world. The operator can move it around freely and, by aligning it with objects in the remote world, can determine their position. [3] ARGOS combines human abilities of perception and comprehension with computer abilities of precise calculation and graphic displays to create an *augmented* system with greater functionality than either alone.

ARGOS APPLICATIONS

We call our system *ARGOS*, meaning "Augmented Reality through Graphic Overlays on Stereovideo". Rather than trying to create a virtual or artificial reality, ARGOS serves to give operators sufficient and necessary information for carrying out tasks in a natural, spatial manner. By enhancing the reality of the SV displays with our SG images, we *augment* their usability and functionality.

An extension of the *virtual pointer* is the *virtual tape-measure*, which can be used to measure sizes and distances in the remote world. [5] For example, the *virtual tape-measure* can be used to measure the sizes and positions of landmarks on a microscopic scale, such as within cells.

With sufficient graphic and computing power, it is possible to create and animate virtual objects of any complexity and realism desired. Working in structured environments, ARGOS can enhance video images by overlaying wire-frame edges on known objects. [4] In unstructured environments, ARGOS can integrate information from other sensors such as radar and sonar with the SV. Architectural visualisation, training, medical imaging and simulation are some of the fields that we are currently exploring. Machine vision capabilities are expanding the potential of our ARGOS system even further. [6]

ACKNOWLEDGEMENT

This work, and the production of this video, were carried out under contract for, and in cooperation with, the Defence and Civil Institute of Environmental Medicine.

REFERENCES

1. Drascic, D., Grodski, J.J. "Using Stereoscopic Video for Bomb Disposal Teleoperation: A Preliminary Study", *SPIE Vol. 1915 Stereoscopic Displays and Applications IV*, Feb. 1993

2. Drascic, D. "Skill Acquisition and Task Performance in Teleoperation using Monoscopic and Stereoscopic Video Remote Viewing", *Proceedings of the Human Factors Society 35th Annual Meeting*, 1367-71, Sep. 1991

3. Drascic, D., Milgram, P. "Positioning Accuracy of a Virtual Stereographic Pointer in a Real Stereoscopic Video World", *SPIE Vol. 1457 Stereoscopic Displays and Applications II*, March 1991

4. Milgram, P., Drascic, D., Grodski, J.J. "Enhancement of 3-D video displays by means of superimposed stereographics", *Proceedings of the Human Factors Society 35th Annual Meeting*, 1367-71, Sep. 1991

5. Milgram, P., Drascic, D., Grodski, J.J. "A Virtual Stereographic Pointer for a Real Three-Dimensional Video World", *INTERACT '90: Third IFIP Conference on Human-Computer Interaction*, August 1990

6. Zhai, S., Milgram, P. "A telerobotic virtual control system", *SPIE Vol. 1612, Cooperative Intelligent Robotics in Space II*, Nov. 1991

TALKING TO MACHINES

Christopher K. Cowley, writer and director
Dylan M Jones, producer

School of Psychology
University of Wales
PO Box 901
Cardiff CF1 3YG
Wales, UK
Tel. (0222) 874000
E-mail: COWLEY@UK.AC.CARDIFF.TAFF

KEYWORDS

Speech, recognition, interfaces.

ABSTRACT

Despite some extravagant claims made regarding the potential of machines which recognize speech input, it is unlikely that they will ever match the speech processing capabilities of humans. The truly conversational computer is still a long way from being realized, and the performance of many contemporary recognizers leaves much to be desired. A machine that may perform efficiently for the experienced user in a controlled laboratory setting can often present substantial problems for unskilled users when it is finally installed in the workplace. Building reliable and acceptable speech interfaces is a subtle and sophisticated process. There is a common assumption that speech interfaces automatically improve system performance when, in fact, the opposite is often the case, particularly if speech is simply added to an existing system rather than included from the outset of development. However, if human factors issues are addressed at the inception of projects rather than as an afterthought, and the machines capabilities are not overloaded by overambitious design, a great deal can be achieved with devices that can reliably recognize a few selected utterances and take full advantage of the unique properties of spoken dialogue. The user is afforded greater freedom of movements and is thus released from the constraints imposed by conventional keyboard/screen interaction. Furthermore there is the option of multi-tasking using speech and manual interfaces concurrently.

The film shows how dialogue design and error correction strategies, informed by human factors research, can lead to the development of usable and profitable systems. It starts with a simulation of a truly conversational machine to show the level of performance necessary to compete with human recognition. Template matching recognition is clearly explained so that viewers can see how most devices actually work. The film then shows the Digital Equipment Corporation's DECvoice in a number of voice input and output scenarios which highlight typical design problems and solutions. It concludes with a set of guidelines which will help designers make reasoned decisions about when and how to use speech recognition and avoid the typical problems experienced by users. The film ends with an example of a system which, having been designed with the guidelines in mind, is usable, efficient, and practical within the constraints of contemporary technology.

GUIDELINES FOR SYSTEM DESIGNERS

1. Train the machine in the place it will be used.

2. Use speech consistently for one part of a task.

3. Do not use speech too often.

4. Do not use voice input for spatial information.

5. Develop a special command vocabulary.

6. Incorporate clear error-correction strategies.

7. Provide feedback about the recognizer's activities.

8. Use multiple criteria to evaluate the system.

ACKNOWLEDGEMENTS

We would like to extend our thanks to Jon Barrett, John Brooke and Chris Bartlett of Digital's Evolutionary Systems Centre, whose support and encouragement has been vital to the success of our video productions.

The ALFRESCO Interactive System

Oliviero Stock
and the NLP Group

IRST-Istituto per la Ricerca Scientifica e Tecnologica
38050 Povo, Trento - Italy
Ph.: +39-461-814444
stock@irst.it

KEYWORDS

Natural language processing, Artificial Intelligence, Multimediality

ABSTRACT

This work is aimed at building a dialogue system in which natural language is the basic communication channel, but the computer is seen as an active agent that allows a multimedia type interaction. In this way the means of communication are amplified, with the possibility of refering to images and other texts.

ALFRESCO is an interactive system for a user interested in frescoes. It runs on a SUN 4 connected to a videodisc unit and a touchscreen. The particular videodisc in use includes images about Fourteenth Century Italian frescoes and monuments. The system, beside understanding and using language, shows images and combines film sequences. Images are active in that the user may refer to items by combining pointing with the use of linguistic demonstratives; for example, the user can point to a detail of a fresco and say "can I see another painting representing this^ saint ?" Also, the system's linguistic output includes buttons that allow the user to enter in an hypertextual modality. The dialog may cause zooming into details or changing the focus of attention into other frescoes. The overall aim is not only to provide information, but also to promote other masterpieces that may attract the user.

The knowledge of the system is represented as:
• a KB expressed in a KLOne-like language used for defining everything the system can reason about: frescoes, monuments, painters, contents of frescoes, towns etc. and providing the base for ALFRESCO's deductive inference capabilities;
• a NoteCards hypermedia network containing unformalized knowledge such as art critics' opinions on the paintings and their authors.

The system is based on several linguistic modules such as: a) a chart-based parser able to deal with flexible expressions and in particular idiomatic forms and some kinds of ill-formed input; b) a semantic analyzer able to disambiguate the sentence in the given domain through interaction with the parser; c) a component that builds the logical form interacting with the KB; d) a topic component that takes into account also deixis (references to images); e) a pragmatic component, substantially based on a model of the interest of the user; f) a natural language generator that takes into account the user's interest model. The generated output is in the form of an hypertextual card: the text is enriched with dinamically generated buttons that the user can click to get more information and explore "the surroundings".

The interaction of hypermediality with AI and NLP technology opens a wide range of new perspectives for the development of intelligent interfaces, especially in the art and cultural domain: we believe that it will ultimately lead to an innovative paradigm for man-machine interaction.

ACKNOWLEDGMENTS.

The videodisc "Italian Art History" was provided by Rizzoli SpA; we take this occasion to thank them.

REFERENCES

1. Carenini, G., Pianesi F., Ponzi, M., and Stock, O. Natural Language Generation and Hypertext Access. To appear on *Applied Artificial Intelligence, An International Journal*, 7 (2), 1993.

2. Lavelli, A., Magnini, B., and Strapparava, C. An Approach to Multilevel Semantics for Applied Systems, in *Proc. ANLP-92, 3rd Conference on Applied Natural Language Processing*, Trento, 1992, pp. 17-24.

3. Stock, O. Parsing with Flexibility, Dynamic Strategies and Idioms in Mind. *Computational Linguistics*, 15 (2), 1-18, MIT Press, 1989.

4. Stock, O. Natural Language and Exploration of an Information Space: The AlFresco Interactive System, in *Proc. IJCAI-91, 12th Intnl. Joint Conference on Artificial Intelligence*, Sydney, 1991, pp. 972-978, .

Hyperspeech

Barry Arons

Speech Research Group
MIT Media Laboratory
20 Ames Street, Cambridge, MA 02139
+1-617-253-2245, barons@media-lab.mit.edu

ABSTRACT

Hyperspeech is a speech-only hypermedia application that explores issues of speech user interfaces, navigation, and system architecture in a purely audio environment without a visual display. The system uses speech recognition input and synthetic speech feedback to aid in navigating through a database of digitally recorded speech segments.

KEYWORDS

Speech user interfaces, speech applications, hypermedia, speech as data, speech recognition, speech synthesis, conversational interfaces.

OVERVIEW

The hyperspeech system demonstrated in the video is an interface that presents "speech as data," allowing a user to wander through a database of recorded speech without any visual cues [1,3,4]. Navigating in the audio domain is more difficult than in the graphical domain, since the ear cannot browse a set of recordings the way the eye can scan a screen of text and images.

Audio interviews were automatically gathered by telephone, and manually segmented by topic into approximately 80 nodes. Over 700 typed hypertext-style links [2] were created to connect logically related comments and ideas. After listening to a particular node, links can be followed for: exploring comments from a particular speaker, hearing supporting and opposing views, or browsing the database at several levels of detail.

The interface allows the user to actively drive through the database rather than being passively "chauffeured" around by menus and prompts. This ability is based on a common set of navigational commands (i.e., link types that can be followed) that are independent of location in the database.

Every effort has been made to streamline the conversational interaction since time is such a valuable commodity in voice systems. For example, transitions from one interaction modality to another (e.g., from recognizing a word to playing a recorded segment) are designed for low system response time. Secondly, all actions by the system are easily interruptible by the user, and provide immediate

feedback that an interrupt was received. Finally, the speech segments are played back at a faster rate than originally recorded, without a change of pitch. However, if a user asks to repeat a segment, it is replayed at normal speed for maximum intelligibility.

The system currently runs on a Sun SPARCstation; recorded segments are played directly on the workstation. A speaker-dependent isolated word recognizer and text-to-speech synthesizer are used for input and feedback. Note that the entire system (i.e., recognition, synthesis, and time-compression of speech) could be entirely software-based, and run in real-time on a current generation workstation.

The user interface evolved significantly during an iterative design process. Navigation in the initial design was difficult because of too much feedback, changing menus, and lack of stable audio landmarks. The current system, as shown in the video, demonstrates that interacting with a computer by voice can be very powerful, particularly when the same modality is used for both input and output. While the video presents the interface to a particular hypermedia application, the project's goal is to explore more general forms of interaction with speech data.

THINGS TO NOTE IN THE VIDEO

There are several points to listen for in the video:
- The quick transitions and system response time.
- The change in speed when a speech segment is repeated.
- The use of speech as both the primary data of the system, as well as for I/O.
- The difference between navigating and retrieving information in the speech domain and a traditional hypertext system that uses a display and mouse.

REFERENCES

1. Arons, B. Hyperspeech: Navigating in speech-only hypermedia. In *Hypertext '91 Proceedings*, pp. 133-146. ACM, 1991.

2. Conklin, J. Hypertext: An introduction and survey. *IEEE Computer*, 20(9):17-41, Sept. 1987.

3. Muller, M.J. and Daniel, J.E. Toward a definition of voice documents. In *Proceedings of COIS '90*, pp. 174-183. ACM, 1990.

4. Stifelman, L.J., et al. VoiceNotes: A speech interface for a hand-held voice notetaker. In *Proceedings of CHI '93*. ACM, 1993 (this volume).

IMPACT: Interactive Motion Picture Authoring system for Creative Talent

Hirotada Ueda, Takafumi Miyatake, and Satoshi Yoshizawa

Central Research Laboratory, Hitachi, Ltd.
1-280, Higashi-koigakubo, Kokubunji-shi, Tokyo 185, Japan
Tel: +81-423-23-1111, Fax: +81-423-37-7718

E-mail: ueda@crl.hitachi.co.jp, miyatake@crl.hitachi.co.jp, yoshi@crl.hitachi.co.jp

INTRODUCTION

We are developing a multimedia authoring system, called IMPACT [1]. It is not easy for non-professional users to get good quality motion pictures and to edit them, for instance, in order to create multimedia presentations that express their concepts. To make this kind of tasks feasible for everyone, image-recognition technology is applied. Visualization of the structure of motion pictures is also very important [2]. A couple of visualization technique are developed for time axis editing.

FUNCTIONS

The automatic cut-separation function divides a video strip (a natural-motion picture taken by a TV camera) into cuts (the basic chunks of a motion picture) and visualize the structure of the video along the time-axis.

To help the user edit a motion picture, it is important to give him a description of the cut in the editing process. For this purpose, an automatic cut classification function was installed in IMPACT. It detects the characteristics of the movement of the filmed object or the camera work (zooming and panning).

Extraction of certain objects from a picture is used for motion picture synthesis and semi-automatic scene description. Processes of object extraction from a still pictures are shown in the video as an easy-to-understand example of a motion picture presentation, as well as the usage of these functions.

TIME AXIS EDITING

As each cut of a video is divided and iconified, editing along the time axis can be directly manipulated. The editing stage in IMPACT is shown in Figure 1. In the lower window, iconified cuts are arranged in a time sequence order. This is a visualized structure of the motion-picture. Each cut is shown as a box whose thickness is proportional to its time length. Furthermore, colored arrows which indicate the results of cut classification are superimposed on corresponding cut icons. Therefore, the user can intuitively understand the time-space structure of the entire motion picture at a glance. In a previous video editing, a huge number of fast-forward and rewind motions are used until such images settled in the user's mind.

When the user edits this motion picture, he will pick an appropriate cut, drag, and put it in the upper work window in his desired sequence.

CONCLUSION

A new approach to achieving an interactive natural-motion-picture dedicated multi-media authoring system is shown. It indicates the appropriateness of the proposed approach.

Acknowledgment

This work was performed partly under the contract of the FRIEND21 project of the Ministry of International Trade and Industry.

References

[1] Ueda, H. et al.: "IMPACT: An Interactive Natural-Motion-Picture Dedicated Multimedia Authoring System", Proc. CHI'91, ACM, pp.343-350 (1991)

[2] Mackay, E. W. and Davenport, G.: "Virtual Video Editing in Interactive Multimedia Applications", Communications of the ACM, 32(7), pp.802-810 (July 1989)

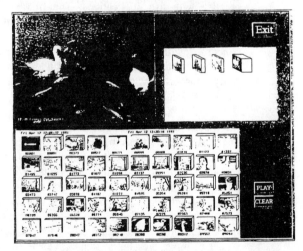

Figure 1. A screen of IMPACT. Thickness of automatically divided cut icon shows its time length. Superimposed color arrows indicate panning, zooming etc.

Microcosm: An open hypermedia system.

Hugh Davis, Wendy Hall, Adrian Pickering and Rob Wilkins.
The University of Southampton
Southampton SO9 5NH, UK
Tel: Hugh Davis 0703 593669
email hcd@uk.ac.soton.ecs

ABSTRACT

Microcosm is an open hypermedia system within which it is possible to make and follow links from one multimedia document to another. The open nature of the system gives rise to a number of difficult user interface issues which are demonstrated in the video.

The system consists of a number of viewers which allow the user to view and interact with many different formats of information. The viewers communicate with Microcosm which then sends messages through a filter chain. Each filter has the opportunity to respond to the messages by processing them, passing them on or blocking them. Important filters are the link databases or linkbases which are able to respond by finding links to other information. In Microcosm documents are not marked up internally: instead the link data is held in these separate linkbases, and the viewers communicate with the linkbases to find what buttons and links exist.

The video shows how Microcosm works in practice with two applications. The first is a package used for teaching cell biology and the second is a set of multimedia documents concerned with Yugoslavia during the second world war, which is used by history students as a study resource. Some features that are emphasised in this video are as follows:

Microcosm allows a spectrum of link types. At one end of this spectrum are specific links or buttons which are manually authored links from a source point to a destination point. Much author effort is required to create such links and then they will tend to impose a particular view point that was intended by the author, but may not be the information required by the reader. Generic links are links that have a fixed destination, but which may be followed from any point in any document where the appropriate object (such as a specific text selection) occurs. These still impose some view intended by the author, but the information tends to be more

general in nature and each link need only be made once, rather than at every occurrence in every source document. As can be seen in the video, one of the key interface issues is whether users require source points for generic links to be highlighted (in the same way as buttons). The procedure required to implement this is very processor intensive and a compromise is currently achieved via a "show link" facility which is invoked at the users request.

At the other end of the spectrum are computed links. These links are generated dynamically at run time using information retrieval techniques, and allow the author or user powerful tools, fully integrated with the hypermedia interface with which to explore a system of text documents that may be otherwise unlinked. Such links require no authoring effort and do not impose any view of the content upon the reader, but may result in a number of links being suggested that are not relevant. To the user, generic links and computed links are currently presented similarly for the sake of consistency. This can however be very confusing to users since the way the two types of links are derived is very different.

Finally, because Microcosm is an open system it is easily possible to make links into and out of applications that are not part of Microcosm. It is possible to program many Windows applications to talk to the Dynamic Data Exchange (DDE) and in this case it is possible to treat such an application as a Microcosm viewer. In the video we see Word for Windows in use as a Microcosm viewer. When it is not possible to use the DDE it is possible to communicate via the clipboard and we show links being followed by simply cutting a selection to the clipboard. This is one of the most powerful features of Microcosm but leads to a number of problems with the design of an interface that is consistent across different applications.

Multimedia Documents as User Interfaces

M. Cecelia Buchanan, Polle T. Zellweger, and Ken Pier

Information Sciences and Technologies Laboratory
Xerox PARC, 3333 Coyote Hill Road, Palo Alto, CA 94304
(415) 812-4000
{buchanan, zellweger, pier}@parc.xerox.com

INTRODUCTION

Previous work has demonstrated the use of documents as user interfaces, in which static document elements, such as words and pictures, become user interface interaction elements, such as menus and buttons [Bier 90]. In this videotape, we demonstrate our extension of this concept to dynamic multimedia documents, allowing user interface designers to create multimedia documents and to specify dynamic interaction elements within them.

This video was taped from the screen of a Sun Microsystems SPARCstation 2. The audio portions of the multimedia documents were recorded and played back using TiogaVoice and the Etherphone voice management system [Zellweger 88].

THE FIREFLY MULTIMEDIA DOCUMENT SYSTEM

The testbed for our experiments is a multimedia document system called Firefly [Buchanan 92b]. We have implemented a prototype of Firefly in the Cedar programming environment [Swinehart 86].

Because Firefly explicitly maintains information about the temporal synchronization constraints among the data in a document, it has several advantages over other systems. First, directly specifying temporal constraints among the data allows the system to provide a more natural, direct manipulation user interface for editing multimedia documents. Second, Firefly can invoke a temporal constraint solver to construct temporal layouts for documents automatically. Finally, because temporal constraints record the author's intentions and because the system automatically creates temporal layouts, the maintenance of documents is simplified.

A Firefly multimedia document consists of three parts: *media items* describing the information to be displayed in the document, *temporal synchronization constraints* specifying the temporal ordering of media items, and *operation lists* for controlling the display behavior of the media items.

Authors construct Firefly documents using a direct-manipulation interface consisting of two parts: a set of *media editors* and a *document editor*.

Firefly uses an open architecture that allows authors to continue to use existing media editors to create and edit media items, and to mark *events* within them. Events specify potential points of synchronization within a media item.

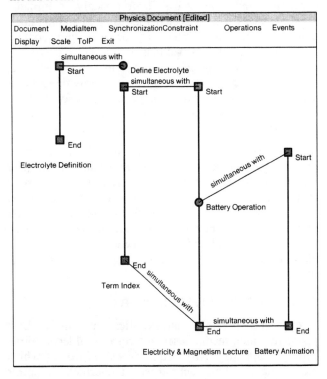

Figure 1: A sample document in the Firefly document editor.

Authors specify the temporal behavior of a multimedia document using the document editor shown in Figure 1. To specify the temporal ordering of events in different media items, authors can place temporal synchronization constraints between those events. To control the display behavior of a media item, authors can associate operation lists with events in that media item. For example, operation lists can be used to increase the volume of an audio recording or to zoom in on a particular portion of an image.

Firefly provides a *Scheduler* component that automatically produces a temporal layout for a document using a temporal constraint solver based upon linear programming [Buchanan 92a]. If a temporal layout cannot be created, the Scheduler can negotiate with the media items to adjust their durations within an allowable range. This ability to stretch or shrink a media item's duration to obtain an optimal temporal layout is conceptually similar to TEX's ability to stretch or shrink the amount of white space (glue) between items to be typeset (boxes) to obtain an optimal spatial document layout [Knuth 81].

MULTIMEDIA USER INTERFACES

Recently, user interfaces have been extended to incorporate dynamic media, such as audio and video. The hope is that multimedia user interfaces will be more expressive and easier to use. Unfortunately, multimedia user interfaces will be even harder to build and maintain than traditional user interfaces, because they contain multiple pieces of data that must be presented according to specific temporal relationships. Therefore, multimedia user interface builders must provide tools for supporting the rapid prototyping and internationalization of multimedia user interfaces as well as powerful tools for constructing and maintaining these interfaces.

Multimedia document authoring systems represent a promising approach to constructing multimedia user interfaces, because they already provide sophisticated tools for managing dynamic media. An additional requirement is that it be easy to connect the user interface to the underlying application. We have used the Firefly multimedia document system to gain experience with multimedia documents as user interfaces.

CONCLUSIONS AND FUTURE WORK

Firefly has several characteristics that make it a powerful multimedia user interface builder. First, Firefly supports *rich media synchronization*, which allows data to be synchronized at intermediate points and provides support for asynchronous behavior, such as programs and user interaction. Second, Firefly provides

a powerful mechanism that allows data to be replaced in a way that maintains the original temporal behavior of the document, even if the new data has a different duration. Finally, the replacement mechanism combined with the ability to automatically produce temporal layouts allows Firefly to support both rapid prototyping and internationalization.

Firefly is still evolving. In the future, we plan to provide support for hierarchical media items, so that entire multimedia documents can themselves be media items in other documents. Further experiments using multimedia documents as user interfaces will be pursued.

ACKNOWLEDGEMENTS

We thank the Xerox PARC Communications Group for their work on shooting and producing this video, the Active Documents group for their comments on the script, and the National Museum, New Delhi for the use of the Gita-Govinda painting image [Vatsyayan 87].

REFERENCES

[Bier 90] Bier, Eric A., and Goodisman, Aaron, "Documents as User Interfaces". In R. Furuta (ed). *EP '90: Proc. of the Intl. Conference on Electronic Publishing, Document Manipulation and Typography*, Cambridge Univ. Press, 1990, pp. 249-262.

[Buchanan 92a] Buchanan, M. Cecelia, and Zellweger, Polle T., "Scheduling Multimedia Documents Using Temporal Constraints", *Proc. Third Intl. Workshop on Network and Operating System Support for Digital Audio and Video*, (San Diego, CA), Nov. 1992.

[Buchanan 92b] Buchanan, M. Cecelia, and Zellweger, Polle T., "Specifying Temporal Behavior in Hypermedia Documents", *Proc. ACM Conference on Hypertext*, (Milan, Italy), December 1992, pp. 262-271.

[Knuth 81] Knuth, Donald E., and Plass, Michael F., "Breaking Paragraphs into Lines", *Software-Practice and Experience*, Vol. 11, pp. 1119-1184.

[Swinehart 86] Swinehart, D., Zellweger, P.T., Beach, R., and Hagmann, R., "A Structural View of the Cedar Programming Environment", *ACM Trans. Prog. Lang. and Syst.*, 8, 4, Oct. 1986, pp. 419-490.

[Vatsyayan 87] Vatsyayan, K., *Mewari Gita-Govinda*, National Museum, New Delhi.

[Zellweger 88] Zellweger, P.T., Terry, D., and Swinehart, D., "An Overview of the Etherphone System and Its Applications", *Proc. Second IEEE Computer Workstations Conference*, (Santa Clara, CA), March 1988, pp. 160-168.

GRAPHICAL EDITING BY EXAMPLE

David Kurlander

Department of Computer Science
Columbia University
New York, NY 10027

E-Mail: djk@microsoft.com

INTRODUCTION

Graphical editing, like many applications facilitated by computers, often involves repetitive tasks. To reduce repetition, programmers can write procedures to automate these tasks, however most users do not know how to program, and the repetitive tasks that they perform are frequently too specialized for the application programmer to anticipate. End users would benefit from the ability to customize and extend their applications for the tasks they usually perform.

Programming by example systems and demonstrational interfaces aim to give end users this capability. Such systems are programmed simply by using the applications, rather than through an ancillary extension language. Innovative systems such as Pygmalion, Tinker, SmallStar, Peridot, Metamouse, and Eager have all explored ways of bringing more power to the non-programming end user [1]. The accompanying videotape demonstrates Chimera, a system built to explore new demonstrational techniques in the domains of graphical editing and interface building.

DESCRIPTION

Chimera employs five novel demonstrational techniques to make such editing easier. While most of these techniques are independently useful, they also work together to make a more powerful system. The five techniques demonstrated in the videotape are summarized below:

Graphical search and replace is the graphical analogue to textual search and replace in text editors, and is useful for making repetitive changes in graphical documents [2]. Search patterns can include graphical attributes such as fill color and line style, and searches can be performed on shape as well, optionally matching objects at arbitrary rotations and scales. Graphical replacements can alter the same or different set of graphical attributes and shape.

Constraint-based search and replace extends graphical search and replace to match on geometric relationships, not just complete shape [5]. Constraints in the search pattern specify relationships to look for, and constraints in the replacement pattern indicate which relationships to change, as well as which to hold constant.

Constraints from multiple snapshots allows constraints to be specified by demonstration [4]. The user provides snapshots of multiple valid configurations of a scene, and the system automatically determines which constraints are valid in all of them. The prior technique can be used to infer

constraints from a *static* scene, however this technique can infer constraints from a *dynamic* scene, which contains more information.

Editable graphical histories follow a comic strip metaphor to display graphical user interface commands in a series of panels [3]. Related operations are coalesced in the same panel, and each panel shows only those scene objects participating in the operation, plus a little scene context. These panels are useful for reviewing the history, undo and redo.

Graphical macros by example allow the user to, at any time, scroll through an editable graphical history, and encapsulate useful sequences of commands into macros [6]. These macros can be parameterized and generalized to work in other contexts. They can use graphical and constraint-based search as flow of control mechanisms.

ACKNOWLEDGMENTS

My advisor, Steven Feiner, helped direct this research. Eric Bier suggested the problem of graphical search and replace, and worked with me on that component.

REFERENCES

1. Cypher, A. *Watch What I Do: Programming by Demonstration.* To appear 1993.

2. Kurlander, D. and Bier, E. A. Graphical Search and Replace. Proceedings of SIGGRAPH '88. In *Computer Graphics 22,* 4 (August 1988). 113-120.

3. Kurlander, D. and Feiner, S. A Visual Language for Browsing, Undoing, and Redoing Graphical Interface Commands. In *Visual Languages and Visual Programming,* S. K. Chang, ed. Plenum Press, NY 1990. 257-275.

4. Kurlander, D. and Feiner, S. Inferring Constraints from Multiple Snapshots. Columbia University Tech. Report CUCS-008-91. May 1991.

5. Kurlander, D. and Feiner, S. Interactive Constraint-Based Search and Replace. In *CHI '92 Proceedings.* May 1992. 609-618.

6. Kurlander D. and Feiner, S. History-Based Macros by Example. To appear in *UIST '92 Proceedings.* November 1992.

*Author's current address: Microsoft Research, One Microsoft Way, Redmond, WA 98052-6399.

GUIDING AUTOMATION WITH PIXELS: A TECHNIQUE FOR PROGRAMMING IN THE USER INTERFACE

Richard Potter

Human-Computer Interaction Laboratory
Center for Automation Research
University of Maryland
College Park, MD 20742
Tel. (301) 405-2725
potter@cs.umd.edu

INTRODUCTION

Accessing data is a critical challenge for users who write programs to process data already stored in the computer. This *data access challenge* is particularly acute for end-user programming because the users' data often exists in applications like word processors, drawing editors, and spreadsheet applications whose internal workings are unknown to the users. Regardless of how easy their programming system is to use or how skilled they are at using it (whether it be C, PASCAL, keyboard macro, or programming by demonstration), the system is of no use if it can not access the data of interest. This challenge will be all the more frustrating to users when the data is clearly represented on the computer display but cannot be accessed.

This research shows how simple pattern matching on the pixel representations in the computer display buffer can significantly enhance a programming system's ability to access data. Because pixel representations are a low-level representation, the algorithms that make use of this representation are different than what one would expect for a given task. The video shows the operation of Triggers, a programming system developed to demonstrate that these algorithms exist, are understandable, accomplish useful tasks, and can be easily implemented.

Pixel-based data access seems to run counter to the widely acknowledged fact that high-level data and constructs improve programming productivity. Unfortunately, this fact has led to wide spread acceptance of a conclusion that, strictly speaking, does not logically follow: that programming with *low-level* data and operators is inherently inefficient. This research shows that the inherent visual nature of pixels, the high degree of regularity of modern graphical user interfaces, and the user's extensive familiarity with the display content make programming at the pixel level appropriate.

© 1993 ACM 0-89791-575-5/93/0004/0530...$1.50

Triggers currently implements only two simple types of pixel-based data access. One is the *specific location match* where Triggers tests for a rectangular pixel pattern at specific location on the computer display. The other is the *pixel pattern search* which locates a rectangular pixel pattern within a rectangular region on the computer display. These two tests are enough to show the usefulness of pixel-based data access for automating meaningful tasks.

THE VIDEO

The video demonstrates how a user can program Triggers to automate the wrapping of a properly sized rounded rectangle around a preexisting text field in an *unmodified copy of MacDraw II*. MacDraw II conveniently places a gray bounding box around a selected field. Pixel pattern searches using pieces of this bounding box as the pattern give enough data access to determine the size and location of the text field. Triggers then simulates a series of keystrokes and mouse actions that create the rounded rectangle. Other examples from graphic and text domains are briefly shown.

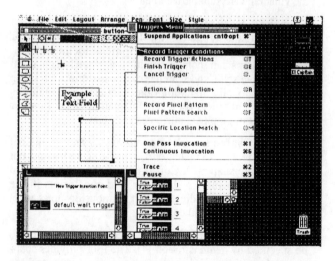

Triggers is part of a larger research effort to create programming systems that allow users to productively weave programming activity into their daily work. Not all data can be easily accessed with such simple pattern matching, but when the opportunity of regularity presents itself, users should be able to take advantage it.

INFERRING GRAPHICAL CONSTRAINTS WITH ROCKIT

Solange Karsenty and Chris Weikart

Digital Equipment Corporation
Paris Research Laboratory
85, Avenue Victor Hugo
92500 Rueil-Malmaison, FRANCE
{karsenty,weikart}@prl.dec.com

James A. Landay

School of Computer Science
Carnegie Mellon University
5000 Forbes Avenue
Pittsburgh, PA 15213, USA
landay@cs.cmu.edu

INTRODUCTION

Graphical constraints define relations among graphical objects that must be maintained by an underlying system. The automatic maintenance of these relations has become important in increasing the functionality of graphical editors and user interface builders. Yet this increase in functionality has also brought the users of these tools the difficult task of specifying the constraints – generally by writing mathematical equations that define the relations which must hold.

The purpose of *Rockit* [2] is to identify the possible graphical constraints between objects in a scene and allow the user to quickly and easily choose and apply the desired constraints. Rockit is embedded in a graphical editor that allows the creation of application objects by direct manipulation. The user creates graphical objects and applies constraints to them. Typical objects include diagrams, circuits, flowcharts, and also standard application widgets. The supported constraints include connectors, aligners, and spacers. In this videotape, we illustrate our system through the construction of a slider.

RULES AND GRAVITY FIELDS

When a user manipulates an object, Rockit infers constraints between that object and other objects in the scene. Rockit uses object-defined *gravity fields* to filter out unlikely constraints. Gravity fields are regions surrounding vertices and midpoints of objects. Rockit only considers constraints with objects whose gravity fields intersect with the position of the dragged object. These remaining constraints are passed on to a rule system which determines the likely constraints to be applied between the dragged object and selected objects in the scene. The rule system encodes knowledge about how objects are related and thus how they can be constrained among one another. For instance, rules can express that a line is more likely to be connected to a box than to a text object.

USER INTERACTION AND FEEDBACK

As the user manipulates an object, it will gravitate towards the most likely constraint: when the dragged object enters gravity fields, it moves as a result of an applied gravity force. For instance, when connecting the line to the box in the videotape, the user drags the line endpoint towards the box and the line moves slightly towards the box's upper midpoint. It is easy to try other scenarios by pressing a key, causing the system to cycle through the most likely possibilities. For example, when we try to place the label at a fixed distance below the box, Rockit first proposes a connector, then an aligner, and finally a spacer – the desired constraint. Rockit gives the user both graphical and sonic feedback [1] to indicate the inferred constraints. Audio conveys information about the constraint type and the intensity of the force applied to the dragged object. It is an essential complement to purely graphical feedback, which can be problematic in a graphical editor: using graphical attributes for feedback may confuse users who wish to use the same styles for creating their own graphical objects.

One unique feature of Rockit is that it usually infers the desired constraint very quickly. By using both graphical and rule-based methods, Rockit is able to vastly reduce the number of possible constraints it considers, and is therefore able to propose constraints quickly. Users do not need to continually answer questions, produce multiple snapshots, or specify constructor objects. In addition, users do not need to specify the constraints explicitly as in many previous systems. The cycling feature combined with appropriate feedback makes the system easy to learn and use. Another unique feature of our system is that it allows the rule system to change dynamically. This allows Rockit to improve the quality of its inference based upon similar actions performed repeatedly.

REFERENCES

[1] Solange Karsenty, James A. Landay, and Chris Weikart. Audio Cues for Graphic Design. In CHI'92 Posters and Short Talks Proceedings, pages 77–78, Monterey, CA, May 1992.

[2] Solange Karsenty, James A. Landay, and Chris Weikart. Inferring Graphical Constraints with Rockit. In People and Computers VII, pages 137–153, September 1992, Proceedings of the HCI '92 Conference.

Tourmaline: Macrostyles by Example

Andrew J. Werth
Bell Communications Research
444 Hoes Lane, Room RRC 4D-516
Piscataway, NJ 08854
Phone: (908) 699-3575
E-mail: ajw1@cc.bellcore.com

Brad A. Myers
School of Computer Science
Carnegie Mellon University
Pittsburgh, PA 15213
Phone: (412) 268-5150
E-mail: bam@cs.cmu.edu

ABSTRACT

Tourmaline is a system that simplifies the formatting of complicated headings and captions in a WYSIWYG word processor. The style systems of typical commercial word processors, although very useful, are too limited when a user needs to format items such as paper headings, which may contain many different styles within a single heading. The style systems of some batch oriented systems give the user more power by providing macro facilities to automatically format text, but these systems are extremely difficult to learn and use. Tourmaline uses demonstrational techniques [2] to combine the ease-of-use of WYSIWYG with the power of batch oriented text formatters. The system allows users to define *macrostyles* by example. A macrostyle is an abstract representation of a text object that allows different parts of the object to have completely different formatting attributes.

In Tourmaline, the user provides an example of a correctly formatted heading using the word processor's WYSIWYG interface. The system then examines the prototype heading and identifies the various text objects that make up the heading. Using attributes of those objects, such as their typographical characteristics and their position within the heading, combined with heuristics about how headings are generally structured, Tourmaline attempts to categorize each of the objects into a logical class (such as *title* or *author name*). Sometimes the system is unsure about how to classify an object so it asks the user for assistance through a simple dialog box. Once all elements of a heading have been classified, Tourmaline infers a generalized description of that particular heading (a *macrostyle*). A macrostyle may then be applied to other headings within the document to ensure a consistent look throughout (see Figure 1). This makes it very easy for users to consistently format composite text objects without having to learn a complicated batch formatting language.

Tourmaline is implemented on top of Microsoft Word for Windows 2.0 ("WinWord") using the built-in programming language WordBasic [1]. It will run on any IBM PC-compatible computer running Microsoft Windows 3.1.

KEYWORDS

Text formatting, Demonstrational Interfaces, Programming by Example, Inferences, Heuristics, Macrostyles.

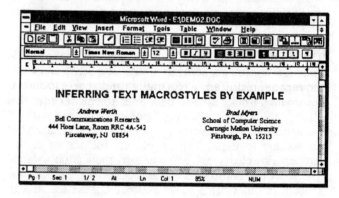

Figure 1: A sample screen from Tourmaline showing a paper title that has been automatically formatted by the system.

REFERENCES

1. Microsoft. *Microsoft WordBasic—Using WordBasic.* WexTech Systems, Inc. and Microsoft Corp., 1991.
2. Myers, B.A. Demonstrational Interfaces: A Step Beyond Direct Manipulation. COMPUTER 25, 8 (Aug. 1992), 61-73.

The Active Badge System

Andy Hopper*[†], Andy Harter[†] and Tom Blackie[†]

*University of Cambridge, Computer Laboratory, New Museums Site, Pembroke St.,
Cambridge, CB2 3QG, United Kingdom,
and
[†]Olivetti Research Ltd, 24a Trumpington St., Cambridge, CB2 1QA, United Kingdom.

ABSTRACT

The Active Badge is used to provide information about where people are [Want et al. 1992, Want and Hopper 1992]. It is battery powered, transmits in the infra-red spectrum and is approximately 60x60x8 millimetres. The transmissions take place every 15 seconds and identify the badge. Receivers are linked by wire to a computer and are placed so as to define cells for the coverage required. Normally they correspond to spaces occupied by one or a number of people. The badge has a light-dependent resistor used to reduce power consumption by decreasing the frequency of transmissions when in the dark. This also means that the user can switch the badge off by placing it in a pocket or face down on the table. Not all badge transmissions are picked up by a receiver, but by using simple algorithms in the receiving software the system can be made sufficiently accurate to be very useful. As well as transmitting the Active Badge can receive which makes possible a more secure system by using a one-way authentication function. Two buttons, two visible LEDs and a tone generator are available for simple interactions. Reciprocity of use is ensured by making badge information available to all computer screens in the organisation.

Many different applications which use the badge sighting information can be devised. One of the first is the provision of location information about individuals. A typical interface is shown in Fig.1. and gives the name of the person, their position and the number of the nearest telephone. The column marked "seen" makes it easy to distinguish between individuals who are static and those who are in the process of moving from one place to another. If the badge has not been sighted for three minutes, this column shows how many minutes ago the badge was last sighted (eg. 35mins), and after an hour changes to a time (eg.12:20). The "status" column gives simple information about the users' (apparent) circumstances. The most important single piece of information is that somebody is not available. A more subtle but equally important observation is that the badges provide a mechanism for people to be less intrusive with respect to others. Our initial thoughts were that the number of phone calls would go up because people could make contact more easily. In fact a self-filtering process takes place where people do not contact others if they see them in circumstances where they may not wish to be disturbed. Various versions of the user interface have been tried including map displays, simple natural text generation systems and others.

The Active Badge is used in a security role to control door locks and to blank a computer screen when the user walks away. It has also been integrated with a multimedia communications system [Hopper 1992]. A video-phone can be routed to a position nearest to a user. Who is calling (not where they are) is indicated to the recipient which makes it easier to decide which response to give. It is also possible for both sides of a conversation to know who else is nearby to prevent confidential discussions taking place when other people are in

	Name	Telephone	Position	Seen	Status
P	Ainsworth	343	Accounts	Static	Alone
M	Chopping	410	R410 MC	Friday	
D	Clarke	316	R316 DC	12:30	
D	Garnett	218	R435 DG	12:20	
T	Glauert	232	R310 TG	35 mins	
S	Gotts	0	Reception	Static	With Jackson
D	Greaves		Floor 3 Corridor	Moving	Alone
A	Hopper	334639	Univ Comp Lab R76	Static	
A	Jackson	0	Reception	Moving	With Gotts
A	Jones	210	Meeting Room	Static	At a gathering
T	King			Yesterday	Away in Italy
J	Martin	310	Machine Room	24 Dec	
O	Mason	210	Meeting Room	Static	At a gathering
D	Milway	BUSY	R211 DM	Static	Alone
J	Porter	398	Library	Static	Alone
C	Turner		Front Door	Yesterday	
R	Want	308	R215 RW	7 mins	
M	Wilkes	210	Meeting Room	Static	At a gathering
S	Wray	204	R212 SW	Static	Alone

14:09 Tuesday 8 January 1991

Fig.1. Active Badge Display

ear shot but out of view. The badge data is also integrated with a video-mail system. Video-mail is most popular in a form where the user does not type anything and there is very little information to help subsequent retrieval. The badge data is used to annotate automatically the video stream. This permits the retrieval of all the video-mail files sent by a particular user, the ones that were recorded with visitors present, or any other category which can be derived from the badge annotations.

A Badge suitable for attaching to equipment has been designed and has similar properties to the Active Badge for personnel. It uses less power by only transmitting every 5 minutes and it can be attached in a way which indicates whether the equipment is switched on. By using the network of receivers, some objects can be located at the same level of granularity as personnel. It is now possible to have an automatic inventory control system which keeps account of what is there and where it is. Tagging in this way will make possible an environment in which the location of all equipment, all I/O devices, all cameras and microphones, is known. With such an active environment it is possible to think of new applications which combine location information of personnel and of equipment.

REFERENCES

[Want,R.,Hopper,A.,Falcao,V.,Gibbons,J. 1992] The Active Badge Location System. *ACM Trans. on Inf. Sys.,* Jan.1992.

[Want,R.,Hopper,A. 1992] Active Badges and Personal Interactive Computing Objects. *IEEE Trans. on Consumer Elect.,* Feb.1992.

[Hopper,A. 1992] Improving Communications at the Desktop. *Rep. of Royal Soc. Discussion Meeting on Communications After 2000 AD,* Chapman and Hall, 1992.

IMAGINE
A Vision of Health Care in 1997

Steve Anderson, Shiz Kobara, Barry Mathis and Ev Shafrir

User Interaction Design
Hewlett-Packard Company
1266 Kifer Road
Sunnyvale, California 94086
408/746-5028
mathis@sde.hp.com

ABSTRACT

IMAGINE is a vision of health care in the year 1997 augmented by a variety of integrated information technologies. The film is not a literal prediction, but rather a projection of where current technologies are headed and what changes they will produce in the fields of medical diagnosis, patient care and hospital administration. Though produced at Hewlett-Packard, IMAGINE represents the capabilities of many companies and is a demonstration of open systems and their integration.

The film's three scenarios highlight a range of situations. All pose problems in patient treatment or cost control, and in each it is information, delivered when and where it's needed, that provides the solutions.

All of the medical proceedures, information presentations, and interaction techniques were reviewed by experts in the fields concerned. Cardiologists, neurologists, pathologists, nurses and administrators provided abundant critical review to ensure accuracy. While this process was time consuming for such a fast paced film, it was felt to be essential for acceptance by the medical community.

TECHNOLOGIES SHOWN

- Continuous speech recognition
- Intelligent agency
- Mobile, pen-based computing
- Advanced diagnostic techniques
- Wireless, non invasive patient monitoring
- High resolution digital video
- Network-enabled integration of patient records
- Collaborative conferencing & communications

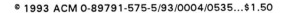

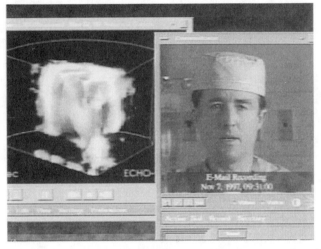

The user is viewing a recorded video message with enclosed action segment of 3D Ultrasound of a patient's heart.

Medical staff using workstations for live video communications including patient records and live vital sign readings.

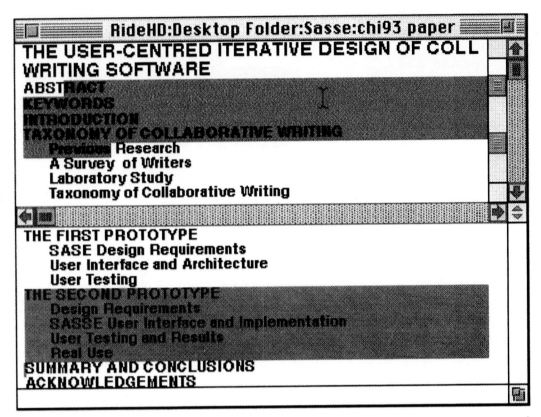

Baecker, et al., Colour Plate 1: SASSE is in outlining mode. The green user is working at the beginning of the document and her view appears in the upper half of the screen. An observation view of the red user appears in the lower half of the screen.

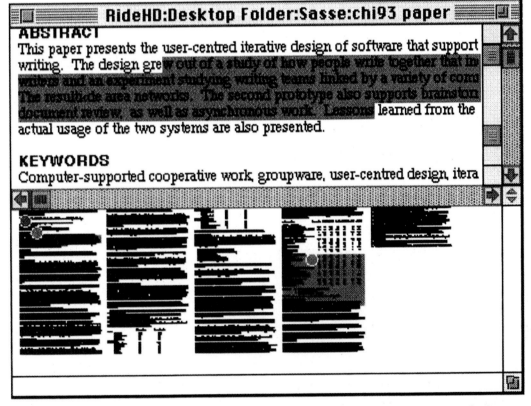

Baecker, et al., Colour Plate 2: SASSE's normal text display for the green user appears in the upper half of the screen. A gestalt view of the entire document appears in the lower half of the screen. There are 3 users (green, gray, and red) working concurrently on the document. The red user is working midway through the document and has selected a large region of text.

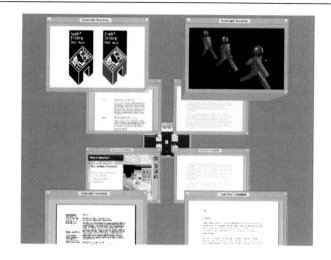

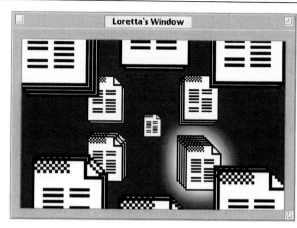

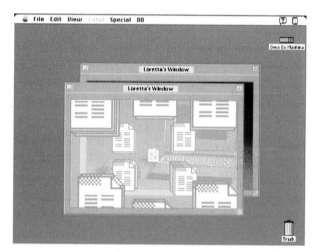

Staples, Color Plate 1, above left: Introduction of varied window thicknesses to augment spatial depth and distinguish between types of window content. Here, a window "box" in the upper right houses a fully rendered model—an object type not based on a paper document metaphor.

Staples, Color Plate 2, above right: Halo amidst consistently illuminated objects.

Staples, Color Plate 3, left: Semi-transparent contents within an opaque window frame overlaying an opaque window.

Staples, Color Plate 4, below: Windows and window boxes organized within a desktop "landscape" utilizing active foreground and passive background areas .

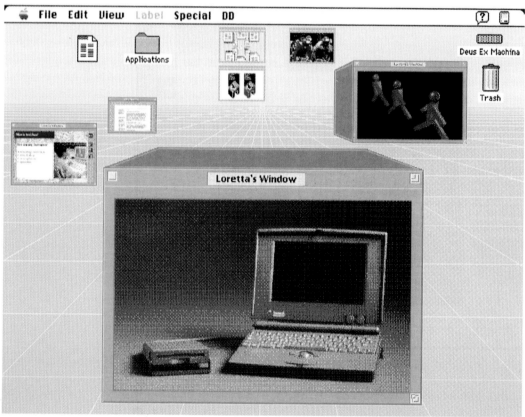

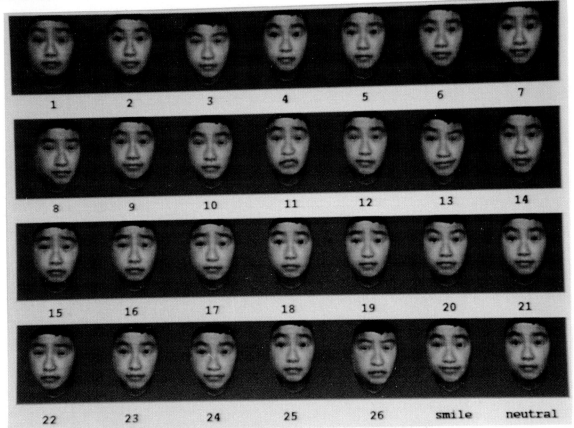

Takeuchi, Nagao, Color Plate 1. Communicative Facial Displays

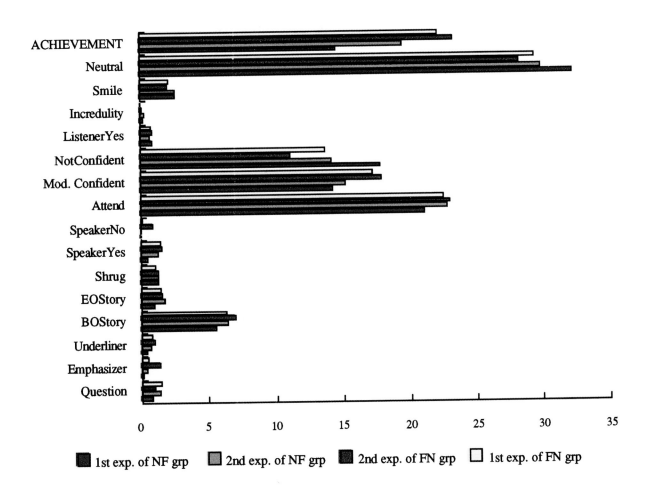

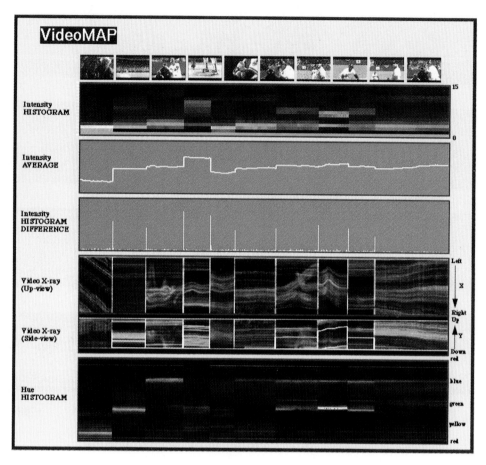

Tonomura, Plate 1   VideoMAP

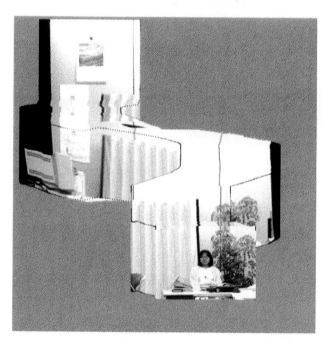

top-front view

front view

Tonomura, Plate 2   VideoSpaceIcon

Ueda, Plate 1. Processing of object presence judgment

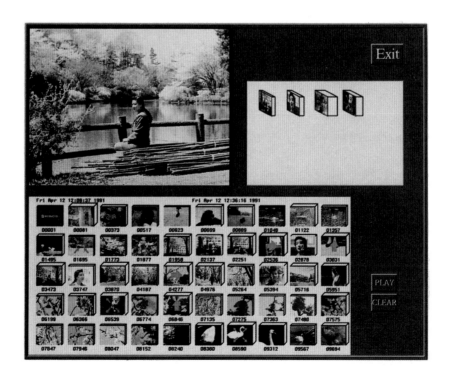

Ueda, Plate 2. A screen of the time axis editing stage

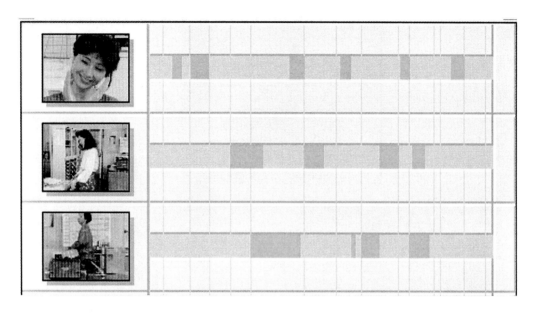

Ueda, Plate 3. A close up of the object index window

(a) Micon representation before search

(b) Micon representation after search

Ueda, Plate 4. A close up of the components window when a certain object is searched
(Arrows of motion analysis results are off)

Venolia, Color Plate 1

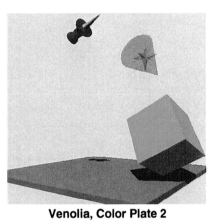

Venolia, Color Plate 2

Venolia, Color Plate 3

Venolia, Color Plate 4

ACM SIGCHI
MEMBERSHIP APPLICATION

Scope:

The scope of SIGCHI consists of the study of the human-computer interaction and includes research and development efforts leading to the design and evaluation of user interfaces. The focus of SIGCHI is on how people communicate and interact with computer systems. SIGCHI serves as a forum for the exchange of ideas among computer scientists, human factors scientists, psychologists, social scientists, systems designers and end users.

Membership Includes:

- Subscription to SIGCHI Bulletin (quarterly)
- CHI Conference Proceedings.

Topics:

Human factors in the interaction process; monitoring and evaluating the computer-human interface; methods, techniques and components of the user interface; cognitive functions involved in the interactive process; interaction between hardware, software, the task and the user; and promoting and understanding of the relationship between studies of user psychology and technology of computing and systems design.

Please check the appropriate membership dues below.

To add SIGCHI to ___ Adding SIGCHI to ACM Membership..$30.00

ACM Membership ___ Adding SIGCHI to ACM Student Membership...$10.00

ACM Membership #_____

Annual subscription cost of $16.02 is included in the member dues of $30.00 (for students, cost included in $10.00)

Membership Note: If you are an ACM Member, send no money now. SIGCHI can be added to your current membership period at no cost. You will be billed when your membership is renewed. You will receive only those issues of the newsletter that are published from the time you join SIGCHI until your membership expires. (Current ACM members need only provide their membership number above)

To Join SIGCHI ___ SIGCHI Membership only (non-ACM) $52.00
___ Subscription to SIGCHI only $50.00

To Join ACM ___ ACM Associate Member Dues $77.00
and/or SIGCHI ___ ACM Associate Dues & SIGCHI Member Dues...$107.00
___ ACM Student Member Dues..$23.00
___ ACM Student Dues & SIGCHI Member Dues $33.00

ACM Associate and Student Member Dues includes a subscription to the monthly *Communications of the ACM*. For Voting Member privileges contact Member Services at address below.

Overseas Air Options ___ Partial Air................. $16.00 ___ Full Air.................... $50.00

Purposes: To advance the sciences and arts of information processing; to promote the free interchange of information processing among computing specialists and the public; and to develop and maintain the integrity and competence of individuals engaged in the practice of information processing.

As an ACM member, I subscribe to the purposes of ACM:_____
Signature

___ *Information about ACM and SIGCHI membership? Please provide your name and address below.*

Name (please print)_____ E-Mail_____

Mailing Address_____ Phone_____

City_____ State or Province_____ Country/Zip Code_____

Form of Payment ___ Check (payable to ACM) ___ Money Order ___ Amex ___ Mastercard ___ Visa

If paying by credit card: Card #_____ Card Expiration Date:_____

Signature_____

If you have any questions about ACM and/or SIG CHI membership contact:

ACM Member Service Department, Phone: (212) 626-0500, E-Mail: ACMHELP@ACMVM.BITNET, Fax: (212) 944-1318
Mail to: Association for Computing Machinery, P.O. Box 12115, Church Street Station, NY, NY 10249